# Encyclopedia of Retirement and Finance

# Encyclopedia of Retirement and Finance

VOLUME I: A–I

Lois A. Vitt, *Editor-in-Chief*

*Consulting Editors*
E. Craig MacBean and Jurg K. Siegenthaler

*Associate Editors*
Jamie Losikoff-Kent, Candace D. Jenkins,
Mary Helen McSweeney, Julie Overton, Sandra L. Reynolds,
M. Shelton Smith, Denise Talbot-White

*Managing Editors*
Ingrid Carlson
Jay Schweig

Foreword by Yung-Ping Chen
Introduction by Dallas L. Salisbury

Published under the Auspices of the Institute for Socio-Financial Studies

GREENWOOD PRESS
Westport, Connecticut • London

**Library of Congress Cataloging-in-Publication Data**

Encyclopedia of retirement and finance / Lois A. Vitt, editor-in-chief ; consulting editors, E. Craig MacBean and Jurg K. Siegenthaler ; associate editors, Jamie Losikoff-Kent . . . [et al.] ; foreword by Yung-Ping Chen ; introduction by Dallas L. Salisbury.
p. cm.
Includes bibliographical references and index.
ISBN 0–313–32495–6 (2 vols. : alk. paper)
1. Old age—Economic aspects—United States—Encyclopedias. 2. Retirement planning—United States—Encyclopedias. 3. Retirement income—United States—Law and legislation—Encyclopedias. 4. Aged—Finance, Personal—Encyclopedias. 5. Retirement—Economic aspects—United States—Encyclopedias. I. Vitt, Lois A. II. MacBean, E. Craig. III. Siegenthaler, Jürg K., 1939– IV. Institute for Socio-Financial Studies. V. Encyclopedia of financial gerontology.
HQ1064.U5E524 2003
305.26'03—dc22 2003058417

British Library Cataloguing in Publication Data is available.



Library of Congress Catalog Card Number: 2003058417
ISBN: 0–313–32495–6

First published in 2003

Greenwood Press, 88 Post Road West, Westport, CT 06881
An imprint of Greenwood Publishing Group, Inc.
www.greenwood.com

Printed in the United States of America

The paper used in this book complies with the Permanent Paper Standard issued by the National Information Standards Organization (Z39.48–1984).

10 9 8 7 6 5 4 3 2 1

# Contents

# The Editors

## EDITOR-IN-CHIEF

LOIS A. VITT, Ph.D., is Chair and Founding Director of the Institute for Socio-Financial Studies (ISFS), Middleburg, Virginia. Dr. Vitt has a background in business and finance for both entrepreneurial companies and investment banking firms, and she is a consultant to financial services companies and community organizations. She has conducted research on consumer decision making, financial literacy education, consumer health finances, the finances of retirement and aging, and financial instruments and organizations. Dr. Vitt has conducted studies for the Employee Benefit Research Institute (EBRI) and the Consumer Health Education Council (CHEC) on Consumer Health Care Financial Education and Consumer Health Values, and she also directed *Personal Finance and the Rush to Competence: Financial Literacy Education in the U.S.* for the Fannie Mae Foundation. She has developed interdisciplinary curricula and taught undergraduate and certificate courses in the social psychology of money and finance and the finances of aging for American University and Catholic University of America. Dr. Vitt pioneered the development of real estate financing vehicles for the capital markets, and her research on the beneficial effects of homeownership has been presented to audiences around the world. She received an Executive M.B.A. from Pace University, New York, and M.A. and Ph.D. degrees in Sociology at the American University in Washington, D.C.

## CONSULTING EDITORS

E. CRAIG MACBEAN is a financial gerontologist with expertise in financial life planning, frailty planning, long-term care insurance, annuities, and life and health insurance. He is skilled in sales management and marketing financial products and is a consultant on long-term care issues. Mr. MacBean has broad knowledge of aging policy and the finances of aging and is a member of the Board of Directors of the National Council on Aging (NCOA). He also serves on the Board of Advisors of the National Institute on Financial Services for Elders (NIFSE). He is an author of *Thriving after 55: Your Guide to Fully Living the Rest of Your Life* (2000) and is an accomplished columnist, speaker, and educator on topics that span the finances and inner-life experiences of aging. Mr. MacBean is a senior fellow of the Institute for Socio-Financial Studies. He is a graduate of Wesleyan University, Middletown, Connecticut, and completed three years of study at Union Theological Seminary, Richmond, Virginia.

JURG K. SIEGENTHALER, Ph.D., is Professor Emeritus of Sociology at American University. His research and teaching earlier—at Cornell, the University of California at Los Angeles (UCLA), and Rutgers—have encompassed the sociology of work and organizations as well as social policy analysis. Interests in work and retirement issues connected his previous specializations with social-gerontological topics. Among his studies in recent years are an international comparison of rights of older adults, a review of innovations in different social security systems in response to population aging and other social changes, an examination of how systems of social protection provide for older single women, and a review of flexible work schedules and older workers. He has been a visiting researcher with the International Social Security Association and the U.S. Social Security Administration. A special interest of his is the relationship between aging research, policy, and professional practice as the field of financial gerontology develops.

## ASSOCIATE EDITORS

JAMIE LOSIKOFF-KENT is a Senior Research Associate and Administrative Officer with the Institute for Socio-Financial Studies. She is a contributing researcher and author of the study *Personal Finance and the Rush to Competence: Financial Literacy Education in the U.S.* (2000), published by the Fannie Mae Foundation, and *Consumer Health Care Finances and Education: Matters of Values* (2000), published by the Employee Benefit Research Institute (EBRI). Ms. Losikoff-Kent has over 20 years of experience in project administration, planning, and resource development with local governments, regional agencies, and nonprofit organizations in the areas of community and economic development. Ms. Losikoff-Kent has a special interest and expertise in community and housing development issues, having worked as Executive Director of Habitat for Humanity in Charleston, South Carolina, and in Virginia and as Senior Project Director for the Christmas in April Program of Northern Virginia. Ms. Losikoff-Kent received her undergraduate degree from Antioch University. She earned her M.A. at the Danish National School of Design in Kolding, Denmark.

CANDACE D. JENKINS is a research associate at the Institute for Socio-Financial Studies. She edits and manages documentation for over 20 Department of Defense (DoD) and Veterans Health Administration (VHA) contracts for the Military Health System at Integic Corporation where she is the Manager and Editor in the Documentation Department. She is accomplished in training, auditing, and writing quality assurance policies and procedures. She graduated summa cum laude with a B.A. in English from Shenandoah University and is pursuing graduate education in English with a concentration in Professional Writing and Editing at George Mason University.

MARY HELEN McSWEENEY, Ph.D., is the Director of the Undergraduate Program in Health Administration and the Undergraduate Concentration in Long-Term Care at the University of Scranton in Scranton, Pennsylvania. Her professional expertise is in the areas of health care finance, long-term care issues, and employee benefits, and prior to her academic career, Dr. McSweeney served as an Economist and Consultant for Equitable Life's benefits division. She has written and researched extensively and is the author of the book *Long-Term Care: An Emerging Employer Benefit* (2002). She was a 1998 International Foundation of Employee Benefit Plans Research Fund recipient for her research on employer-sponsored long-term care insurance. Dr. McSweeney received a B.A. from Wellesley College and an M.I.A. and M.Phil. from Columbia University. She earned her Ph.D. in Economics from the Graduate Center, City University of New York. In addition, she is a Certified Employee Benefits Specialist (CEBS) and Certified Benefits Professional (CBP).

JULIE OVERTON, M.S.G, M.H.A., is the Program Manager of the National Resource Center on Supportive Housing and Home Modification at the University of Southern California (USC) Andrus Gerontology Center. She is a supportive housing and long-term care specialist whose primary expertise is in the area of home modification. Her most recent research has focused on analysis of state home modification efforts, specifically California, and ascertaining the environmental coping strategies of caregivers and care recipients via focus groups. Ms. Overton teaches two online courses—"Home Modification: The Basics and Beyond" and "Building Home Modification Awareness through Community Building"—as part of the Center's Executive Certificate Program in Home Modification. Ms. Overton has been the Program Manager for several Administration on Aging–funded National Resource Centers at the USC Andrus Gerontology Center over the past 14 years. She has published over 20 reports and articles including "The National Directory of Home Modification and Repair Programs" and "Critical Factors Affecting the Growth of Assisted Living" and presented over 50 workshops on home modification and accessibility issues to professionals, consumers, and caregivers. Ms. Overton has organized and led several local home modification coalitions in California, composed of professionals and consumers dedicated to improving the local housing stock. Ms. Overton is a founding member of the National Home Modification Action Coalition, a group of national associations and experts dedicated to increasing the availability and awareness of the importance of supportive home environments. She has a Master of Science in Gerontology and a Master of Health Administration from the University of Southern California.

SANDRA L. REYNOLDS, Ph.D., is Associate Professor of Gerontology at the University of South Florida in Tampa and an expert in banking and the finances of aging. She teaches sociocultural aspects of aging, and business management in an aging society. At the graduate level, she teaches research methods and population aging. Dr. Reynolds is a Fellow of the Gerontological Society of America and serves on the Board of Advisors of the National Institute on Financial Services for Elders (NIFSE). Her research has included disability among older adults, guardianship, advance directives, financial exploitation of older adults, health care trends for older adults, and working life expectancy for today's workforce. As a former Trust Banker, she acted as a guardian of the estate for many clients over the years. Dr. Reynolds received her undergraduate degree in Sociology from the University of Connecticut, a degree in Trust Banking from the New England School of Banking at Williams College, and her Ph.D. in Gerontology from the University of Southern California, Andrus Gerontology Center.

M. SHELTON SMITH, Ph.D., is a Senior Fellow at the Institute for Socio-Financial Studies and an Independent Consultant in Social and Health Psychology research. Dr. Smith has expertise in research design, measurement, and statistical analysis and has had extensive experience coordinating research programs and teams. Prior to starting her consulting practice, Dr. Smith taught Psychology at the University of Northern Iowa from 1992 to 2000, first as an Assistant Professor and then as an Associate Professor. She was the Coordinator of Research at Meharry Medical College's "I Have a Future" project, a longitudinal teenage pregnancy prevention study. Dr. Smith received her Ph.D. in Social Psychology, with an emphasis in Health Psychology, from Vanderbilt University in 1988.

DENISE TALBOT-WHITE, M.A., is the Gerontology Specialist at the Mature Market Institute at MetLife in Westport, Connecticut. The Mature Market Institute is MetLife's information and policy resource center for issues concerning aging, retirement, long-term care, and the mature market. The Institute provides research, training and education, consultation, and information to support MetLife and its business partners. Ms. Talbot-White is the editor of *QuickFacts*, the Institute's monthly newsletter, writes consumer publications that focus on caregiving and long-term care, and serves as a trainer on the mature market. She is currently on the West Hartford, Connecticut, Senior Citizen Advisory Commission and served on the Delegate Council for the National Institute on Financial Issues and Services for Elders (NIFSE), a constituent group of the National Council on the Aging. Ms. Talbot-White has been in the corporate environment for a number of years and prior to joining MetLife in October 1999 was employed as an Advertising Assistant for a major health insurance company, working in the Medicare/Health Maintenance Organization product area. She received her B.S. from Central Connecticut State University, New Britain, Connecticut, and her M.A. in Human Development and Gerontology from Saint Joseph College, West Hartford, Connecticut.

## MANAGING EDITORS

INGRID CARLSON, M.S.F.S., is a Research Fellow, Project Director, and Strategic Development Consultant at the Institute for Socio-Financial Studies. Ms. Carlson has worked in strategic development and as a business planning associate for consulting firms and not-for-profit groups, including a foreign policy media program, a human rights media awareness group, and the United States Equestrian Team. Her expertise includes spearheading new initiatives, developing strategic business plans for organizations, heading project management teams, and streamlining operations. Ms. Carlson received her Master's from Georgetown University's School of Foreign Service, where she studied International Business-Government Relations and Foreign Policy. She received her B.A. in Psychobiology from Mount Holyoke College.

JAY SCHWEIG, formerly a Research Associate and Editor at the Institute for Socio-Financial Studies, is a doctoral student in the Mathematics Department at Cornell University. He was an administrator and assisted in the development of and taught three mathematics enrichment courses at George Mason University (GMU), where he also taught several additional math courses. Mr. Schweig earned his B.S. in Mathematics, summa cum laude, from GMU. He received the Mary K. Cabell Award to the Outstanding Mathematics Student and an Award for Academic Achievement in Mathematics. He was an editor and writer for the *Expulsion* newspaper at GMU.

# The Contributors

The opinions expressed in the articles in this *Encyclopedia* are those of the author(s) and do not necessarily reflect those of the agencies or organizations with which they work or are affiliated.

*W. Andrew Achenbaum, Ph.D.*, Professor of History and Social Work, University of Houston, Houston, TX

*Laura Addington, C.F.M., M.S.F.S.*, Addington Financial Group, Greenville, TX

*Michele C. Adler, M.P.H.*, Social Security Administration, Office of Disability and Income Security Programs, Office of Program Development and Research, Baltimore, MD

*Linda Albert, Ph.D. Candidate*, University of South Florida, Department of Gerontology, Tampa, FL

*John Ameriks, Ph.D.*, TIAA-CREF Institute, New York, NY

*Carol Anderson, M.S.*, President, Money Quotient, Inc., Poulsbo, WA

*James A. Anderson, Ph.D.*, College of Weekend Studies, Jacksonville University, Jacksonville, FL

*Sia Arnason, Ph.D.*, Codirector, Samuel Sadin Institute on Law, Brookdale Center on Aging of Hunter College, City University of New York, New York, NY

*William Arnone*, Partner, Ernst & Young LLP, New York, NY

*Barry K. Baines, M.D.*, Medicare Medical Director, UCare Minnesota; Associate Medical Director, Hospice of the Twin Cities; CEO, The Legacy Center, Minneapolis, MN

*Victor S. Barocas*, Managing Director, Strategic Management Group, LLC, Chicago, IL

*Thomas D. Begley, Jr., J.D.*, Begley & Bookbinder, PC, Morristown, NJ

*Hubert Bermont*, Consultant on Career Consulting, Princess Anne, MD

*Leigh Bernstein, J.D.*, Fleming & Curti, Tucson, AZ

*Robert H. Binstock, Ph.D.*, Professor of Aging, Health, and Society, School of Medicine, Case Western Reserve University, Cleveland, OH

*Karen Brelsford*, Adjunct Faculty, Financial Planning Division, Howard Community College, Columbia, MD

*Kenneth A. Bretthorst*, Chairman, First St. Louis Securities, St. Louis, MO

*Clifton D. Bryant, Ph.D.*, Professor, Department of Sociology, Virginia Tech University, Blacksburg, VA

*Veronica M. Bukowski, C.P.B.A., C.P.V.A.*, Bukowski-Stanton Associates, New Hope, PA

*Jon E. Burkhardt*, Senior Study Director, WESTAT, Rockville, MD

*Cathleen Burnett, Ph.D.*, Department of Sociology/Criminal Justice and Criminology, University of Missouri, Kansas City, MO

*Sean Cahill, Ph.D.*, Director, NGLTF Policy Institute, New York, NY

*John W. Callinan, J.D.*, Attorney-at-Law, Wall, NJ

*W. Donald Campbell, M.B.A.*, Consultant in Finance and Housing, Falls Church, VA

*Kathleen Carlisle*, Vice President of Marketing/Public Relations, Tech Federal Credit Union, Roanoke, VA

*Andrew Carswell, Ph.D. Candidate*, Visiting Assistant Professor, University of Georgia, Department of Housing and Consumer Economics, Athens, GA

*Pinar Cebi, Ph.D.*, Research Associate, American Council for Capital Formation, Washington, DC

*Susan M. Chambré, Ph.D.*, Professor of Sociology, Baruch College, City University of New York, New York, NY

*Hong-Bin Chen, M.D., Ph.D.*, Assistant Director, State Data Center on Aging, Florida Policy Exchange Center on Aging, University of South Florida, Tampa, FL

*Yung-Ping Chen, Ph.D.*, Frank J. Manning Eminent Scholar's Chair, Gerontology Institute, University of Massachusetts, Boston, MA

*Zhan (Sandy) Chen, M.S., Ph.D. Candidate*, Associate Professor, Department of Consumer Sciences and Retailing, Purdue University, West Lafayette, IN

*Alfred J. Chiplin*, Attorney-at-Law, National Senior Citizens Law Center, Washington, DC

*Rachel Christensen, M.P.H.*, Employee Benefit Research Institute, Washington, DC

*David L. Christopherson, Ph.D., C.L.U., G.R.*, St. Cloud State University, St. Cloud, MN

*Elizabeth Clemmer, Ph.D.*, AARP Public Policy Institute, Washington, DC

*Christine Cody, R.N.C., M.S.N.*, Vice President, Professional Education/Innovation, National Hospice and Palliative Care Organization, Alexandria, VA

*John Collins, Ph.D.*, Professor of Religion, Wake Forest University, Winston-Salem, NC

*Francis P. Conner, A.C.S.W., L.M.S.W.*, Department of Sociology, West Georgia College, Carrollton, GA

*Fay Lomax Cook, Ph.D.*, Director, Institute for Policy Research, Professor of Human Development & Social Policy, Northwestern University, Evanston, IL

*Stephanie Cory, M.S.G.*, Research Assistant, University of Southern California, Andrus Gerontology Center, Los Angeles, CA

*Nancy J. Cox, M.S.W.*, Director, Partners in Caregiving, Department of Psychiatry & Behavioral Medicine, Wake Forest University School of Medicine, Winston-Salem, NC

*Stephen Crystal, Ph.D.*, Research Professor and Chair, Division on Aging, Institute for Health, Health Care Policy and Aging Research, Rutgers University, New Brunswick, NJ

*Neal E. Cutler, Ph.D.*, Boettner/Gregg Chair in Financial Gerontology, Widener University, Chester, PA

*Teri Daniel*, President & Owner, InsideOut HR Solutions PLLC, Ashland, KY, and Instructor, College of Business, Marshall University, Huntington, WV

*Michele F. Davis*, Associate Director of Education, TIAA-CREF Institute, New York, NY

*Sharon A. DeVaney, Ph.D.*, Associate Professor, Department of Consumer Sciences and Retailing, Purdue University, West Lafayette, IN

*Tracy Dietz, Ph.D.*, Department of Sociology & Anthropology, University of Central Florida, Orlando, FL

*Patricia E. Dilley*, Professor, University of Florida, Levin College of Law, Gainesville, FL

*C.L. (Tim) Dimos*, Attorney-at-Law, Middleburg, VA

*Andrew Quang Do, Ph.D.*, Professor of Finance, Department of Finance, College of Business Administration, San Diego State University, San Diego, CA

*Kenneth J. Doran*, Attorney-at-Law, Doran Law Offices, Madison, WI

*Karen Duggan, C.A.*, Canadian Institute of Chartered Accountants, Toronto, Ontario, Canada

*Michael E. Edleson, Ph.D.*, Senior Vice President and Chief Economist, NASDAQ, Rockville, MD

*Chip Eubank, C.F.P.*, Eubank Financial Group, Dallas, TX

*Ann E. Fade, R.N., J.D.*, Choice in Dying, Inc., New York, NY

*Mark Fagan, Ph.D.*, Department of Social Work, Jacksonville State University, Jacksonville, AL

*Ronald A. Fatoullah, Esq.*, Ronald Fatoullah & Associates, Great Neck, Forest Hills, and Brooklyn, NY

*Charles H. Fay, Ph.D.*, Professor of Human Resources, Chairman of HRM Department, School of Management and Labor Relations, Rutgers, The State University of New Jersey, Piscataway, NJ

*Lucy Rose Fischer, Ph.D.*, Independent Consultant, St. Louis Park, MN

*Paul Fronstin, Ph.D.*, Employee Benefit Research Institute, Washington, DC

*Heather J. Gibson, Ph.D.*, Associate Professor, Department of Recreation, Parks and Tourism, University of Florida, Gainesville, FL

*Stephen M. Golant, Ph.D.*, Department of Geography, University of Florida, Gainesville, FL

*Jordan E. Goodman*, President, Amherst Enterprises, Ltd., and Proprietor, www.moneyanswers.com, Scarsdale, NY

*Roberta Gosier*, Owner/Director, Help Unlimited, Inc., Silver Spring, MD

*Mathew Greenwald, Ph.D.*, Mathew Greenwald & Associates, Inc., Washington, DC

*Rebecca Gronvold-Hatch, Ph.D.*, Professor of Sociology, Mt. San Antonio College, Walnut, CA

*Sherman D. Hanna, Ph.D.*, Professor, Consumer and Textile Sciences Department, Ohio State University, Columbus, OH

*Sally Hass*, Benefits Education Manager, Weyerhauser, Employee Benefits, Federal Way, WA

*Catherine Hawes, Ph.D.*, Program on Aging and Long-Term Care, Social and Health Policy Research Center, Research Triangle Institute, Research Triangle Park, NC

*Celia Ray Hayhoe, Ph.D., C.F.P.R.*, Family Financial Management, Cooperative Extension Specialist, Virginia Tech, Blacksburg, VA

*Rona S. Henry, M.B.A., M.P.H.*, The Robert Wood Johnson Foundation, Princeton, NJ

*Jean M. Hogarth, Ph.D.*, Consumer & Community Affairs, Federal Reserve Board, Washington, DC

*Karen C. Holden, Ph.D.*, Professor of Public Affairs and Consumer Science, La Follette School of Public Affairs, University of Wisconsin, Madison, WI

*Andrew Holmes, Ph.D.*, Assistant Professor, Business Management Department, Brigham Young University, Provo, UT

*Harriet Howe, Ph.D.*, Visiting Assistant Professor of Sociology, University of North Florida, Jacksonville, FL

*Donald A. Hunsberger, Esq.*, The Law Offices of Donald A. Hunsberger, Orange, CA

*Kennes C. Huntley, C.L.U.*, Department of Finance, Insurance and Real Estate, Mankato State University, Mankato, MN

*Gail A. Jensen, Ph.D.*, Professor, Institute of Gerontology, Wayne State University, Detroit, MI

*David R. Johanson, Esq.*, Johanson Berenson LLP, Attorneys & Counselors at Law, Napa, CA

*Marshall B. Kapp, J.D., M.P.H.*, Office of Geriatric Medicine & Gerontology, Wright State University School of Medicine, Dayton, OH

*Enid Kassner, M.S.W.*, Senior Policy Advisor, AARP Public Policy Institute, Washington, DC

*Mary Anne Keefer, B.A., M.A.*, Adjunct Professor, Lord Fairfax Community College, Middletown, VA

*T. Erle Keefer*, President, Belair Inc., Huntley, VA

*Chris Kelly, Ph.D. Candidate*, University of Southern California, Andrus Gerontology Center, Los Angeles, CA

*Marilyn C. Kennedy, M.P.A.*, Public Administration, University of Arizona, Tucson, AZ

*Eun-Jin Kim, Ph.D. Candidate*, Department of Consumer and Textile Sciences, Ohio State University, Columbus, OH

*Andrew S. Kochera*, Senior Policy Advisor, AARP Public Policy Institute, Washington, DC

*James E. Konlande, D.C.*, Life Chiropractic College West, San Lorenzo, CA

*Janet L. Kuhn, Esq.*, Law Offices of Janet Kuhn, McLean, VA

*Kevin J. Lamiman*, Associate Editor, Better Investing Magazine, National Association of Investors Corporation, Madison Heights, MI

*Thomas P. Langdon, J.D.*, Attorney-at-Law, Southington, CT

*Jinkook Lee, Ph.D.*, Professor, Department of Consumer and Textile Sciences, Ohio State University, Columbus, OH

*Jean D. LeMasurier*, Deputy Director, Health Plan Benefits Group, Center for Beneficiary Services, Centers for Medicare and Medicaid Services, Baltimore, MD

*Walter Leutz, Ph.D.*, Associate Professor, Schneider Institute for Health Policy, Heller School, Brandeis University, Waltham, MA

*Phoebe Liebig, Ph.D.*, Associate Professor, University of Southern California Andrus Gerontology Center, Los Angeles, CA

*Jo Ann Linck*, Accredited Financial Counselor, Russell Resources and Instructor, Financial Planning, Howard Community College, Columbia, MD

*Charles F. Longino, Jr., Ph.D.*, Reynolds Gerontology Program, Wake Forest University, Winston-Salem, NC

*Jamie Losikoff-Kent*, Senior Research Associate, Institute for Socio-Financial Studies, Middleburg, VA

*E. Craig MacBean*, Senior Research Fellow, Institute for Socio-Financial Studies, Middleburg, VA

*Ronald J. Manheimer, Ph.D.*, Executive Director, North Carolina Center for Creative Retirement, and Research Associate, Professor of Philosophy, University of North Carolina, Asheville, NC

*Robert D. Manning, Ph.D.*, Caroline Werner Gannett Professor of the Humanities, Rochester Institute of Technology, College of Liberal Arts, Rochester, NY

*Jerry J. McCoy, LL.B.*, Attorney-at-Law, Law Offices of Jerry J. McCoy, Washington, DC

*Christopher R. McDowell, Esq.*, Dinsmore & Shohl LLP, Cincinnati, OH

*V. Karen McMahon*, President/Owner, Telecommute-Now, Warrenton, VA

*Mary Helen McSweeney, Ph.D.*, University of Scranton, Scranton, PA

*Stacey Meshnick, Esq.*, Ronald Fatoullah & Associates, Great Neck, Forest Hills, and Brooklyn, NY

*John N. Migliaccio, Ph.D.*, President, Maturity Mark Services Co., White Plains, NY, and American Institute of Financial Gerontology, Deerfield Beach, FL

*Steven S. Miner*, Research Director, Ragatz Associates, Eugene, OR

*Scott A. Miskiel, M.S.*, Law Offices of Scott A. Miskiel, Cottonwood, AZ

*Karlyn Mitchell, Ph.D.*, College of Management, North Carolina State University, Raleigh, NC

*Harry R. Moody, Ph.D.*, Senior Associate, International Longevity Center—USA, New York, NY

*Robert J. Morlock, Ph.D.*, Global Outcomes Research, Pfizer Pharmaceuticals Group, Ann Arbor, MI

*Cyril Morong, Ph.D.*, Associate Professor of Economics, San Antonio College, San Antonio, TX

*Nancy Morrow-Howell, Ph.D.*, School of Social Work, Washington University, St. Louis, MO

*Phyllis H. Mutschler, Ph.D.*, Executive Director, National Center on Women and Aging, Heller School for Social Policy and Management, Brandeis University, Waltham, MA

*Robert J. Myers, LL.D.*, International Actuarial Consultant, Silver Spring, MD

*Rajesh Narayanan, M.B.A., Ph.D.*, Assistant Professor and Gardner Fellow of Finance, Department of Finance, Ohio University, Athens, OH

*Robert Newcomer, Ph.D.*, Professor, University of California, San Francisco, CA

*Brenda Watson Newmann, C.R.P.C.*, Financial Author/Writer and Chartered Retirement Planning Counselor, Half Moon Bay, CA

*Christy Nishita, Ph.D. Candidate*, Research Assistant, Andrus Gerontology Center, University of Southern California, Los Angeles, CA

*John R. Nofsinger, Ph.D.*, Assistant Professor of Finance, Department of Finance, Insurance, and Real Estate, College of Business and Economics, Washington State University, Pullman, WA

*Barbara O'Neill, Ph.D.*, Interim Extension Specialist in Financial Resource Management, Rutgers Cooperative Extension, Newton, NJ

*Tonya M. Parrott, Ph.D.*, Professor of Sociology & Gerontology, Quinnipiac University, Hamden, CT

*Mars A. Pertl, Ph.D.*, Fogelman College of Business and Economics, The University of Memphis, Memphis, TN

*Ronald Peterson, M.S.*, President/CEO, Three Arrows Capital Corp., Bethesda, MD

*Diane S. Piktialis, Ph.D.*, Work-Life Product Director, Ceridian, Boston, MA

*Stephen L. Poe, Ph.D.*, Department of Business and Finance Administration, University of North Texas, Denton, TX

*Nancy C. Porter, Ph.D., C.F.C.S.*, Interim Department Chair for Family and Youth Development, Interim State Program Leader for Family and Consumer Sciences, Clemson, SC

*Janice K. Purk, Ph.D.*, State University of West Georgia, Department of Sociology, Anthropology, and Criminology, Carrollton, GA

*Jon Pynoos, Ph.D.*, Andrus Gerontology Center, University of Southern California, Los Angeles, CA

*Patricia Quigley, Ph.D.*, James A. Haley VA Hospital, Patient Safety Center, Tampa, FL

*Ganas K. Rakes, Ph.D.*, Finance Department, Ohio University, Athens, OH

*Sandra L. Reynolds, Ph.D.*, Associate Professor, Department of Gerontology, University of South Florida, College of Arts & Sciences, Tampa, FL

*Suzanne Reynolds-Scanlon, Ph.D. Candidate*, Department of Gerontology, University of South Florida, College of Arts & Sciences, Tampa, FL

*Dorothy P. Rice, Sc.D. (Hon.)*, Professor Emeritus, University of California, San Francisco, CA

*Jihane K. Rohrbacker*, Communications Director, National Association of Professional Geriatric Care Managers, Tucson, AZ

*Jeffrey I. Roth, M.A., J.D.*, Professor of Law, Touro College Law Center, Huntington, NY

*Linda R. Rounds, Ph.D.*, School of Nursing, University of Texas Medical Branch, Galveston, TX

*N. Lee Rucker, M.S.P.H.*, National Council on Patient Information and Education (NCPIE), Bethesda, MD

*Thomas V. Rush, Ph.D.*, Social Security Administration, Office of Disability and Income Security Programs, Office of Program Development and Research, Baltimore, MD

*Debra S. Sacks, R.N., J.D.*, Senior Staff Attorney, Samuel Sadin Institute on Law, Brookdale Center on Aging of Hunter College, City University of New York, New York, NY

*Dallas L. Salisbury, M.P.A., A.B.D.*, Chief Staff Executive, Employee Benefit Research Institute, Washington, DC

*Ann Elizabeth Sammon*, Senior Manager, Membership Section, American Institute of Certified Public Accountants, New York, NY

*Judith A. Sangl, Sc.D.*, Agency for HealthCare Research and Quality, Department of Health and Human Services, Rockville, MD

*Kathleen K. Scholl, Ph.D.*, Consumer Economics, General Accounting Office, Washington, DC

*Dennis G. Shea, Ph.D.*, Professor, Health Policy and Administration, Penn State University, University Park, PA

*Jurg K. Siegenthaler, Ph.D.*, Professor Emeritus, Department of Sociology, American University, Washington, DC

*Linda A. Siegenthaler, M.A.*, Consultant, Silver Spring, MD

*Michael A. Smyer, Ph.D.*, Dean & Associate Vice President for Research, Graduate School of Arts and Sciences, Boston College, Chestnut Hill, MA

*Ben J. Sopranzetti, Ph.D.*, Assistant Professor, Rutgers University, Department of Finance, Piscataway, NJ

*Richard H. Stanton, C.P.B.A., C.P.V.A.*, Bukowski-Stanton Associates, New Hope, PA

*Norman Stein, Ph.D.*, Visiting Professor, University of Maine School of Law, Portland, ME

*Catherine M. Sullivan, M.P.A.*, The Brookings Institution, Washington, DC

*Ralph B. Swisher, Ph.D.*, Department of Homeland Security, Washington, DC

*Kenn Tacchino, J.D., LL.M.*, Professor of Taxation and Financial Planning, Accounting, Law & Taxation Department, Widener University, Chester, PA

*Lynn Q. Taylor*, Senior Policy Analyst, Institute for Health Policy Solutions, Washington, DC

*Margo Thorning, Ph.D.*, Senior Vice President and Chief Economist, American Council for Capital Formation, Washington, DC

*John H. Thornton, Ph.D., C.L.U.*, College of Business Administration, University of Texas, Denton, TX

*Paul Thrasher, C.P.A.*, Halt, Jackson and Thrasher, Alexandria, VA

*Sandra Timmermann, Ed.D.*, Director, Mature Market Institute, MetLife, Westport, CT

*David J. Tolan, J.D., C.L.U.*, Tolan Schueller, Inc., Milwaukee, WI

*Ronald Turner, J.D.*, George Butler Research Professor and Professor of Law, The University of Houston Law Center, Houston, TX

*Peter Uhlenberg, Ph.D.*, Department of Sociology, University of North Carolina, Chapel Hill, NC

*Jack L. VanDerhei, Ph.D.*, Department of Risk, Insurance, and Healthcare Management, The Fox School of Business and Management, Temple University, Philadelphia, PA

*Valentine M. Villa, Ph.D.*, Adjunct Assistant Professor, UCLA Public Health–Community Health Sciences, Los Angeles, CA

*Lois A. Vitt, Ph.D.*, Director and Founder, Institute for Socio-Financial Studies, Middleburg, VA

*Anne S. Welch, M.A.*, Program in Human Development and Social Policy, School of Education and Social Policy, Northwestern University, Evanston, IL

*Paul Westbrook, C.F.P.*, Westbrook Financial Advisers, Westfield, NJ

*Robert Whaples, Ph.D.*, Department of Economics, Wake Forest University, Winston-Salem, NC

*Monika White*, President/CEO, Center for Healthy Aging, Santa Monica, CA

*Joshua M. Wiener, Ph.D.*, The Urban Institute, Washington, DC

*Steven Wilber, Ph.D.*, Research Associate, American Council for Capital Formation, Washington, DC

*Bradley R. Williams, PharmD*, Associate Professor, University of Southern California School of Pharmacy and Andrus Gerontology Center, Los Angeles, CA

*Flora Williams, Ph.D.*, Consumer and Family Sciences, Purdue University, Lafayette, IN

*David P. Willis, M.P.H.*, National Institute on Aging, Bethesda, MD

*Louisa Woodville, M.A., M.B.A.*, Intersections Inc., Chantilly, VA

*David L. Wray*, President, Profit Sharing/401K Council of America, Chicago, IL

*Bernadette Wright, Ph.D.*, Policy Research Analyst, AARP Public Policy Institute, Washington, DC

*James D. Wright, Ph.D.*, Department of Sociology & Anthropology, University of Central Florida, Orlando, FL

*Rui Yao, Ph.D.*, Assistant Professor, South Dakota State University, Brookings, SD

*Sarah Zapolsky, M.S.*, Senior Research Advisor, Knowledge Management/Membership Group, AARP, Washington, DC

# Core Topics

## Advisors, Advice, and Support

Accountants
Agents and Brokers
Asset Allocation after Retirement
Banking Services for the Mature Market
Cash Flow Planning for Retirees
Corporate Eldercare Programs
CPA Eldercare Services
Credit Scores
Estate Planning
Ethics in Financial Planning
Financial Advisors
Financial Counseling for Mid- to Later Life
Financial Education for Seniors
Financial Literacy
Financial Planning Process
Financial Recovery in Later Life
Frailty Planning
Geriatric Care Managers (GCMs)
Gerontological Social Work
Investment Advice
Investment Clubs
Investor Education
Life Planning
Marketing to Mature Adults
Ombudsman
Physician–Older Patient Relationships

Retirement Expense Planning

Retirement Planning

Retirement Planning Software

State and Area Agencies on Aging

## Economic and Income Security

Accelerated Death Benefits

Cost-of-Living Adjustments (COLAs)

Disability Programs, Federal and State

Economic Status of Older Men and Women

Means-Testing in Public Programs

Medicaid

Nutrition Programs

Old-Age Provisions and Economic Status

Social Security Privatization

Social Security Program of the United States

Supplemental Security Income (SSI)

Veterans' Benefits

## Employment, Work, and Retirement

Age Discrimination in Employment Act (ADEA)

Attitudes about Retirement

Business Succession Planning

Cash Balance Pension Plans

Consulting in Retirement

Defined Benefit Pension Plan

Defined Contribution Plan

Early Retirement Incentive Plans (ERIPs)

Economic History of Retirement

Employee Benefits in the Public Sector

Employee Benefits in the United States

Employee Retirement Income Security Act (ERISA)

Employee Stock Ownership Plans (ESOPs)

Employer-Sponsored Long-Term Care Insurance

Entrepreneurship

Flexible Benefit Plans

Individual Retirement Account (IRA)

Job Lock

Keogh Plans

Life Planning in the Workplace

### Family and Intergenerational Issues



### Financial Investments and Insurance

## Health Care and Health Coverage



## Housing and Housing Finance

## Legal Issues



## Quality of Life and Well-Being

# Foreword

During the coming decades, retirement of the 76 million baby boomers—those born from 1946 to 1964—will pose significant challenges for society as well as for boomers themselves. These challenges stem partly from the fact that the younger population cohorts have far fewer people available to work and pay taxes to defray the costs of public and private retirement benefits and health care. At the same time, increasing longevity compounds the problem. In short, lower fertility and greater longevity are making it more difficult for society as well as for individuals to prepare for retirement, both financially and nonfinancially.

In 2012, the oldest boomers will be 66 years old, the age at which Social Security will pay full retirement benefits to those who are eligible. In 2031, the youngest baby boomers will reach age 67, the age at which full Social Security retirement benefits will be due those who qualify. Medicare will cover the oldest boomers beginning in 2011 and the youngest in 2029 if the current eligibility age of 65 remains unchanged.

Financial needs during retirement are provided for privately by individuals and families or collectively by society, or by a combination of both. While individuals and families are responsible for satisfying their individual retirement needs, they need to operate in a basically sound and stable macroenvironment. In policy discussions, it is therefore important to understand the complementary roles of individual and collective responsibilities.

Individuals can and must do their part. Recognizing differences in individual preferences and within limits, one could argue that people can and should try, among other salutary lifestyle behaviors, to stay healthy in order to reduce expenses for themselves and to conserve health care resources for society at large. They should spend their income reasonably, save early and consistently, invest prudently, and diversify their investments. They should plan for the contingency of long-term care needs to avoid impoverishing themselves or their families or becoming a public charge.

Despite these and other like efforts, however, only the wealthiest may succeed, absent an overall social framework that encourages and supports individual efforts. We need a stable government and a well-functioning economy with ethical conduct by business, labor, and government. We need collective measures that are organized or facilitated by government, business, and labor, such as social insurance programs for income security and health care security that are solvent for the long term, work-based pensions that are secure and reliable, and a system of work and retirement that includes arrangements to accommodate those who seek work during older ages. And we need the support and assistance of civic, charitable, and religious organizations. Many such institutions and practices do exist today, but we also need to innovate more, strengthening what we already have and introducing new and better ways.

The challenge of policy development for ensuring greater old-age economic security in the new century lies, in my view, with seeking approaches that balance individual and collective responsibilities. Individual responsibility is expressed by what may be expected realistically of individuals and their families and friends. Collective responsibility is demonstrated by the array of public sector policies (i.e., federal, state, and local governments) and private sector policies (i.e., business, labor, and nonprofits, such as civic, religious, and charitable organizations). To embark on the task of reviewing and modernizing public and private retirement policies for the future, we have as a starting point the *Encyclopedia of Retirement and Finance*. This comprehensive inventory of policies, institutions, practices, and problems is another significant editorial contribution of Lois A. Vitt.

The relative roles of individual and collective responsibilities have undergone significant changes historically. For many decades before the Great Depression starting in 1929, the predominant opinion was that Americans could, by and large, provide for their own old age by individual savings and family assistance and by private philanthropy and public charity if all else failed.

The cataclysmic event of the Great Depression—stock market collapse, bank failures, and mass unemployment—uprooted the social mores of the time, as it exposed, more starkly than in previous business downturns, the hollow protective power of self-reliance, particularly in an industrial society. Mass unemployment for long years stripped many individuals of their ability to earn a living, let alone to save for future needs; a protracted period of financial crises simply swept away much of the life's savings of many people. Those financially catastrophic occurrences, which exacted untold human costs of ruined dreams and shattered lives, made it clear that, as President Franklin D. Roosevelt declared in his June 1934 message to Congress, it was necessary "to employ the active interest of the nation as a whole through government" to provide safeguards "against misfortune which cannot be wholly eliminated in this man-made world of ours."

Thus was ushered in an era of government intervention in the ensuing four decades (from the mid-1930s to the mid-1970s), witnessing passage of various major pieces of social legislation in pensions and health care—Social Security, Medicare, Medicaid, and the Employee Retirement Income Security Act (ERISA), to name the most significant.

Since the mid-1970s, however, political pressures have mounted to provide incentives for individuals to take more responsibility for their own future. By the 1990s, welfare reform, Medicare + Choice, and the continuing debate about Social Security privatization attested tellingly to changing attitudes. Ideology aside or in conjunction, those actual and proposed changes in policy direction reflected a confluence of factors. These factors juxtaposed diminished the fiscal capacity of the government (resulting from slackening productivity and economic growth) against the improved economic status of older people, rendering less compelling the advocacy for age-based social programs on their behalf.

Individuals are increasingly urged by politicians to assume more responsibility for their own retirement. Wittingly or unwittingly, some individuals also declare that they prefer to increase their self-responsibility. However, while individual responsibility is necessary and desirable, it has not proven sufficient. Not everyone has the financial sophistication or good luck to make winning investment choices. Collective responsibility is essential since many conditions in employment, pensions, investments, and health care that adversely affect individuals are occurring at the societal level through no fault of their own.

For example, in recent times, many workers and retirees have fallen victim to the business failures caused by corporate fraud, as illustrated by the notorious cases of Enron, WorldCom, Arthur Andersen, and their ilk. Stock market slumps have substantially shrunk the financial wealth of many individuals; they have also contributed to the large underfunding of many pension plans. Unemployment has sapped the ability of many individuals' ability to earn an income, let alone to save for their future. Bear stock markets have generated skepticism or reluctance about investing in equities among many investors and would-be investors. Medicare cuts to health care providers have put a large number of the program's participants at financial and health risks.

Development of public and private sector policies for the century that is unfolding must recognize that potential problems brought about by new and emerging demographic and economic realities carry with them new opportunities as well. For example, when the number and proportion of older people increase, a society is aging. Although an aging society could result in increasing scarcity of workers in the traditional age groups, it may also hold out the promising prospect that some older people, who would have retired under traditional rules and practices, may choose to work longer if conducive work environments are created. The outcome depends a great deal on whether we choose to live under the institutional arrangements that were once meaningful but have now become constraining or whether we venture to alter these arrangements in favor of new and more flexible work and pension systems in order to better utilize our human resources, including those represented by older people.

The world is what we collectively make of it. In designing and maintaining policies for future retirees, we must underscore the role of the government sector in fostering a supportive environment. We must understand how private sector policies of business, labor, and nonprofits may promote or hinder needed adjustments in our institutions and programs as demographic and economic circumstances change. And we must expect individuals and families to do what they can and should in service to themselves and to society. In short, to ensure greater old-age economic security, we need to balance individual and collective responsibilities, as we marshal our resources, private and public. Serving as a sourcebook, the *Encyclopedia of Retirement and Finance* will be valuable to concerned individuals as well as to specialists and policymakers in both the public and private sectors.

Yung-Ping Chen, Ph.D.
Frank J. Manning Eminent Scholar's Chair
Gerontology Institute
University of Massachusetts at Boston

# Preface

The visibility of mid- to late-life finances as a major personal and national issue has increased significantly since the first edition of this *Encyclopedia* was published in 1996 as the *Encyclopedia of Financial Gerontology*. Whether readers' concerns are for the financial well-being of clients, colleagues, students, older relatives, or themselves, the times are vastly changed from just seven years ago. There is widespread uncertainty due to the changed nature of the country's national security and economic priorities. Employers continue to seek answers to the pressing problem of escalating employee benefits, particularly health benefits. Workplace trends that shift both risks and costs to employees continue as well. There is an anxious new tone audible in the voices of thought leaders, policymakers, employers, and financial advisors, all of whom are calling on Americans to take more responsibility for their future personal finances.

Research suggests that Americans *like* feeling responsible for themselves and their loved ones. After all, about 90% of the nation's infirm are cared for by family members. When they know what is expected of them, and when they are given the tools and the opportunity to become successful at whatever they undertake, Americans accept—and even seek—responsibility. Still, the sheer numbers of baby boomers who are aging into their retirement years is enough to ring alarm bells in every sector of the general economy, and most aging baby boomers today have neither the knowledge nor the savings required for successful retirement.

Americans today face changing trends and financial complexities unknown to their parents or grandparents. There is a bewildering array of decisions, planning goals, and choices to be made concerning work, health care, saving, investing, borrowing, family and intergenerational issues, plans for how to live in retirement, and plans even for approaching frailty and death. In short, Americans, in ever increasing numbers, must address financial issues that grow exponentially as people age in contemporary society. This revised and enlarged edition of the *Encyclopedia* was planned with these financial and social realities in mind.

This *Encyclopedia* is a multidisciplinary, authoritative, comprehensive, and readable mosaic of the financial topics, vehicles, services, advisors, costs, structures, programs, institutions, products, investments, issues, and social policies that impact nearly every aspect of people's everyday lives. One thing is certain: regardless of how much we think we know about the financial details of our approaching retirement and later years, we all could know a lot more. As a financial literacy educator, researcher, and advocate, I've seen the growing—and ubiquitous—hunger that Americans at all ages and life stages have for greater financial knowledge and for the confidence to apply it competently. What I've learned as well is that everyone needs help in finding resources that enhance their comprehension of modern finances—from asset allocation to the U.S. Tax Code to reverse mortgages, from Medicare to health maintenance organizations (HMOs) to caregiving options, from investments to consumer protection to retirement planning, from credit scores to 401(k)s to investor education.

When asked by colleagues, students, friends, and other seekers of information about the finances of aging, I have directed them first to the *Encyclopedia*, which I have often used myself. My experience in consumer financial education during the past several years led to this revised edition, which has been expanded to include many additional topics about preretirement and retirement issues. Included in the new edition are entries that span the array of employer-sponsored health and retirement benefits, which are increasingly central to working Americans and to their partners and family members. There is a great need for this financial knowledge to reach the many professionals who advise, support, sell products to, serve, assist, and teach mid-life and later-life clients. There is also a need for professionals and practitioners to help consumers themselves become educated about these topics.

Entries have been arranged to provide information at any alphabetical point. Readers are directed elsewhere by the references to other topics that appear at the end of each article. For teachers interested in using the *Encyclopedia* as a textbook, or advisors who are interested in specific life areas, a core set of articles under generic headings—e.g., "Advisors, Advice, and Support," "Economic and Income Security," "Employment, Work, and Retirement," "Family and Intergenerational Issues," "Financial Investments and Insurance," "Health Care and Health Coverage," and others—appear under "Core Topics" at the front of the book. Readers are also directed to Appendix C, Organizations and Resources, for the addresses, telephone numbers, and Internet addresses of the organizations referred to in many entries.

The contributions to this *Encyclopedia* have enriched these volumes with a breadth of research, knowledge, information, and perspectives on the finances of retirement and later life that have not before been collected into one reference. My debt to the Consulting Editors and to the Associate Editors who helped to weave the technical and varied language of many disciplines into a cohesive whole is gratefully acknowledged. Achieving this was a special challenge that was met so that professionals across the spectrum of aging and financial services, and consumers as well, could feel comfortable with the array of some otherwise difficult topics. Ingrid Carlson, Managing Editor of the *Encyclopedia*, and Jay Schweig, who managed the details of the contributions before Ingrid, kept the lines of communication open and running smoothly between the authors, editors, and the Greenwood Publishing Group.

Special thanks are due to production manager Karen McMahon, for her dedication and excellent administrative and technical assistance, and to John Donohue and Susan Badger for their superb project editing. We are grateful to Greenwood Publishing Group editors George Butler and Doug Goldenberg-Hart for their vision and Steven Vetrano for his valued assistance. Finally, we commend Greenwood Publishing Group for its commitment to the ideal of a public that is more knowledgeable—and thus less anxious—about the financial issues of later life. We are all in their debt.

Lois A. Vitt
Middleburg, VA

# Introduction

Public and policymaker concern about retirement savings led to passage in 1974 of the Employee Retirement Income Security Act (ERISA) and to the Social Security Act Amendments of 1983. The Arthur Andersen, Enron, and WorldCom debacles of this new century have once again put retirement savings on the front pages of our news magazines and papers and as the headline story on television news. The *Encyclopedia of Retirement and Finance* is being published at a time of great need for basic information. This need encompasses the public, the media, and decision makers.

The *Encyclopedia* makes clear what a complex web of issues reformers must deal with as they seek to follow the lead of ERISA in strengthening retirement opportunity and retirement security. Needed reform once again surrounds Social Security, as projections make clear that the near-solvency crisis of 1983 will repeat itself within 20 years if action is not taken. Again, basic information for understanding is essential.

The first baby boomers will reach the magic Social Security age for full benefits at 66 (yes, 66 for the first wave and 67 for later waves) in 2012, less than a decade ahead. For them, it is time to focus on when and whether they can afford to retire at 66. Too many will not read this *Encyclopedia* and will sign up for Social Security when they reach age 62. They will not have learned that benefits are about 30% less if you take them at 62. Further, they will not have read that for the average earner that means an age 62 income replacement for a single individual at about 25% of final-year earnings (about $600 per month or $7,000 per year). While barely enough to live on, it is not the stuff that cruises and the "good life" are made of.

Too many will not read this *Encyclopedia* and will fail to ever open an Individual Retirement Account (IRA)—only 7% contributed in 2001 according to the Internal Revenue Service. Nor will they contribute to a savings or 401(k) plan at work—of those who could in 2001, the government reports that 24% chose not to do so, and over 80% chose to contribute less than the law allowed. Reading a few select articles within this *Encyclopedia* would give them a clear understanding of why they should open that IRA and contribute to that plan at work: it is tax effective; Social Security alone will not provide livable income; and as an average American, if I do not save, no one will do it for me.

Too many will not read this *Encyclopedia* and will think that "life expectancy" can be counted on to end before the money runs out. They will continue to miss the desired use of *average* in descriptions of life expectancy. They will focus on media reports that the "life expectancy" of a woman born today is 79, or a woman at 65 today is 85, without understanding that they must always assume the word *average* and understand that "*I have a 50% probability of living longer if I make it to that age.*" For myself, my dad turned 89 and my mom 87 in 2002. Both have now lived beyond multiple "average age specific life expectancies" and can now expect, on average, another 5 years. But it keeps rolling forward! The tables suggest that if I make it to 65, I, on average, can expect to live until 80, while my family and personal history suggest a number closer to 100. What if I retired at 62 with only an inadequate Social Security benefit and then lived to 100? A pretty financial picture it would not be. A reading of this *Encyclopedia*, however, would keep people from making that mistake as it guided them to knowledge about living longer and to retirement calculators that would make the numbers and the needs very clear.

Too many will not read this *Encyclopedia* and, as a result, will not have visited the many helpful articles or used the recommended retirement calculators. They will have missed the notations in the calculators and the knowledge offered here about "Health Benefits" and "Long-Term Care" and the savings needs that these represent during long years of retirement.

Too many will not read this *Encyclopedia* and will not have the information to help themselves and to advise and care for family members on issues ranging from accident insurance to accountants to assisted living to cash flow planning for retirees to drugs to reverse mortgages to salary reduction plans to titling assets to wills, and so much more.

Lois Vitt and the Greenwood Press are to be congratulated on this expanded new edition of the *Encyclopedia of Retirement and Finance*. This *Encyclopedia* should become a staple of gift giving as the baby boomers continue to age: from child to aging parent, to help them understand what they should be doing to prepare for the future; from parent to college-bound youth, to help them understand why they should seek to avoid high interest rate credit card debt and start saving early to enjoy the full magic of compound interest; from aged parent to graying adult children, as a means of sharing what they wish they had done to be better prepared for their ever-extending years; from employer to employee; or from financial advisor to client. As a transfer of information or as suggested reading, these volumes can literally help reduce pain and increase future economic security if they are read and absorbed.

Two-thirds of today's retirees live almost entirely on Social Security. The same is going to be true for the baby boom generation unless they begin to take action now. As this *Encyclopedia* documents, Social Security benefits will be paid at later ages and at the same time decline in the percentage of final earnings they pay. Even with that, the program will require either large tax increases or substantial benefit reductions in the decades ahead. Social Security is an antipoverty floor of income that will not be expanded for most Americans in any reform. The aging of the baby boomers will move the proportion of the population over the age of 65 from the current 13% to nearly 23%. This carries changes that are documented in this *Encyclopedia* for every generation alive today and for those yet to be born. The *Encyclopedia of Retirement and Finance* is a public service volume that will enhance economic and income security. The time for reading it and taking action is now!

Dallas L. Salisbury
President and CEO, Employee Benefit Research Institute
Washington, DC

# Encyclopedia of Retirement and Finance

# A

**ACCELERATED DEATH BENEFITS,** payment by an insurance company of part, or all, of a life insurance policy's death benefits before the insured's death in the event of certain qualifying events such as terminal illness. Availability of accelerated death benefits helps people who are facing death, life-threatening medical events, or confinement to a nursing home or extended care facility to access funds that would otherwise only be available to survivors. Familiarity with life insurance basics aids understanding of accelerated death benefits.

## Normal Life Insurance Policy Benefits

An insurance company will pay the "face amount" (death benefit) of an in-force life insurance policy to the beneficiary when the insured dies. This is the case for all forms of life insurance, including term, endowment, whole life, universal life, and variable life. In term life policies, a promise to pay upon death while the policy is in force is the only policy benefit. In an endowment policy, the insurance company pays the face amount if the insured dies during the term of the endowment and also pays the face amount if the insured survives the policy's term. For example, in an Endowment at Age 65 policy, the death benefit is paid if the insured dies before age 65 or when the policy matures as an endowment if the insured lives to age 65. Whole life policies are really endowment at age 100 contracts and will pay the death benefit to the beneficiary if the insured dies before age 100 or to the insured if he or she lives to that age. Universal life and variable life policies may extend death benefit protection beyond age 100.

All forms of life insurance other than term also have a savings, or cash value, element. In whole life or endowment policies, premiums are set so that the cash value equals the face amount of the policy at the end of the policy term. In universal and variable life policies, the cash value is determined by the level of premium payments and the interest or investment results. The policy owner can borrow from this cash value, creating a debt against the policy's death benefit for the loan amount plus interest. Loans against life insurance policies do not have to be paid back but will be subtracted from the death benefit of the policy if not repaid before the insured's death. In universal and variable life policies, the cash value can also be withdrawn. In all cases, the policy can be completely or partially surrendered to get the cash value, but then the accompanying death benefit is also lost. A policy owner who borrows against the cash value or makes a partial withdrawal, or surrenders the policy to get all of the cash value, may use the money for any purpose, including costs associated with poor health. An insured's access to cash value is a "living benefit" available to the policy owner, often without incurring any income tax liability.

### Other Living Benefits

Although funds provided under a life insurance policy's accelerated death benefit (ADB) option are sometimes called "living benefits," this term is also used to describe payments made by viatical settlement firms. A viatical settlement firm provides cash to terminally ill policy owners by purchasing their life insurance policies for some percentage of the death benefit. The less time the insured has to live, the higher the percentage. The firm then names itself as beneficiary, continues paying the policy premiums, and collects the policy proceeds upon the death of the insured. Viatical settlements (sometimes called "living settlements" or "senior settlements") are available to virtually anyone who has owned a life insurance policy for at least two years and is expected to live less than 12 years.

Accelerated death benefit options have been developed by life insurance companies as an alternative to viatical settlements, although they are not mutually exclusive. In many cases, life insurance policies with accelerated death benefit provisions make a viatical settlement unnecessary, although accelerated death benefit provisions of life insurance policies are generally much more restrictive than viatical settlements.

During the late 1980s, Canadian life insurers introduced accelerated death benefit options to help terminally ill AIDS (acquired immunodeficiency syndrome) patients, and they have become an increasingly popular product of U.S. life insurers. Though the original intent was to help AIDS victims, the accelerated death benefit option can be an important living benefit to anyone facing the costs associated with a terminal illness or other debilitating condition.

### The Accelerated Death Benefit Option

There are, generally, four situations in which a life insurance company will advance payment of some of the death benefits of an in-force life insurance policy: (1) diagnosis of a terminal illness where the remaining life expectancy is six months or one or two years; (2) permanent confinement to a nursing care facility; (3) inability to perform activities of daily living; or (4) onset of a dread disease, such as cancer. Virtually all (more than 90%) policies that make provision for accelerated death benefits will accelerate for short life expectancy. At the time of the 1998 American Council of Life Insurance and the Life Insurance Marketing and Research Association (ACLI/LIMRA) *Accelerated Death Benefits* survey, 73% of companies offering ADB for terminal illness set the requirement at an expectation of death within 12 months. Now more use the definition of a terminally ill individual found in the Health Insurance Portability and Accountability Act (HIPAA) of 1996—someone "who has been certified by a physician as having an illness or physical condition that reasonably can be expected to result in death in 24 months or less from the date of certification"—as qualification for the benefit. When exercised due to terminal illness, the ADB payment typically is determined by discounting some or all of the death benefit. In most policies, some type of medical certification that a qualifying event has occurred must be provided to the insurer before the option may be exercised.

The ADB option is becoming an increasingly popular feature of life insurance policies. According to the 1998 survey by ACLI/LIMRA, the number of ADB option policies increased from about 1.13 million to at least 39.9 million from 1991 to 1997, and the number of insurers offering this feature increased from 113 to 245 during this same time period, despite the fact that the number of active life insurance companies dropped by 25% from 1994 to 1997. More employers include the ADB option as part of group life plans, given the low cost of providing this popular benefit to employees.

Terms of ADB options vary from insurer to insurer and can be offered as a feature of a new policy, added as a rider to an existing one, or made available by policy endorsement or administrative practice. Depending on policy terms and state laws, the maximum amount that can be accelerated ranges from 25% to 100% of a policy's face value. Often, minimum policy size and maximum benefit limitations are also imposed by companies. The policy owner may receive an ADB payment as a lump sum or in monthly installments, and no restriction is made on the use of such funds. In some policies, the ADB payment becomes a lien against the policy's death benefit, in which event access to the policy's cash value may be restricted by the amount of the lien.

Costs of ADB options also vary. Although some insurers charge an additional premium for the ADB option, many ADB policies do not carry an additional charge unless the option is exercised. Some insurers charge no additional premium for this feature. When the option is exercised, the insurer may charge a percentage of the policy's face value, an administrative fee, or both. Typically, the fee charged offsets interest lost by the insurer in paying the death benefit earlier than actuarially anticipated.

Prudential Insurance Company of America, in 1990, was the first major U.S. insurer to offer the ADB option and is among the top insurers in the nation in terms of ADB claims paid. From 1990 to 1994, Prudential paid more than $55 million on 680 claims for ADB payments, an average payment of more than $80,000 per claim (Armstrong 1994). About one-half of these payments went to cancer patients, about 27% went to AIDS victims, about 12% went to heart patients, and the remainder went to those diagnosed with other terminal illnesses. Under the Prudential ADB policy, insureds may accelerate up to 90% of the policy's face value if they are diagnosed with a terminal illness, and up to 70% or 80% of the policy's face value if they are confined to a nursing home.

ADB policies have been criticized on the grounds that this feature defeats the purpose of life insurance and usurps funds necessary to provide for family members after the insured's death. Unrestricted access to these funds, it can be argued, may save or prolong the life of the insured, which may not be in the best financial interests of the insured's dependents. As a result, many state laws limit the amount of the death benefit that may be accelerated and paid to the insured. Conversely, acceleration of the entire death benefit permits more of the insured's medical bills and other expenses to be paid prior to death, leaving more of the insured's other assets available to meet the needs of family and dependents.

Prior to January 1, 1997, uncertainty surrounding how accelerated benefit payments should be treated for income tax purposes was a major obstacle to their wider acceptance. Although life insurance proceeds usually are not taxable to the beneficiary, it was unclear whether receipt of an accelerated payment of the death benefit to the policy owner would be subject to income taxation. The Health Insurance Portability and Accountability Act of 1996 answered that question in the negative, effective on the first day of 1997, and both accelerated death benefit payments and viatical settlements are excluded from income for tax purposes if the insured is either a "terminally ill" or "chronically ill" individual. Terminally ill means that the insured can be reasonably expected to die within two years. Chronically ill means that an insured cannot perform at least two out of six activities of daily living without substantial assistance or requires substantial supervision to be protected from threats to health and safety due to severe cognitive impairment. Any policy owner who wishes to exercise the ADB option should consult a tax attorney or financial advisor prior to doing so.

Life insurance policies with the accelerated death benefits option offer a feasible, compassionate response to financial problems brought about by the onset of terminal illness. (See also ACTIVITIES OF DAILY LIVING [ADLs]; DEATH BENEFITS; ELDER LAW PRACTICE; FINANCIAL ADVISORS; LIFE INSURANCE; LONG-TERM CARE INSURANCE, PRIVATE.)

**Organizations**

American Council of Life Insurers
LIMRA International
Viatical Life Settlement Association

**Suggested Readings**

Shilling, Dana. 2000. *Financial Planning for the Older Client.* 5th ed. Erlanger, KY: National Underwriter.

Wolk, Gloria Grening. 1997. *Cash for the Final Days.* Laguna Hills, CA: Bialkin Books.

**References**

American Council of Life Insurance (ACLI). 2002. *Life Insurer's Fact Book 2002.* Washington, DC: Author.

American Council of Life Insurance (ACLI) and LIMRA International. 1998. *Accelerated Death Benefits.* Washington, DC: ACLI.

Armstrong, Sean. 1994. "AIDS and the Trusted Advisor: Accelerated Life Insurance Benefits for the Terminally Ill Patients." Best's *Review—Life Health Insurance Edition.* Oldwick, NJ: A.M. Best.

*Stephen L. Poe, John H. Thornton, and Kennes C. Huntley*
*Updated by E. Craig MacBean*

**ACCIDENT INSURANCE,** a form of insurance that is designed to cover expenses sustained as the result of an accident. This insurance generally applies to personal types of loss such as disability, death, medical expenses, and at times, loss of income. While the inclusion of accidental loss as a cause of loss in disability and Medicare Supplemental Insurance policies is important, the value of insurance policies that only cover losses caused by accidents is questionable.

As with any type of insurance, premiums paid should provide a needed benefit when loss occurs. Most experts question the value of accident insurance, especially if decisions to purchase such coverage are driven, as people age, by fear of increased vulnerability to accidents. The fact is that often an accident policy does not provide benefits beyond a certain age, and exclusions may include chronic conditions or illness that could contribute to or cause the insured to suffer an accident. A careful distinction must be made between an "accident" as a cause of loss and "accident insurance" as a type of protection. Most insurance covers accidents, but accident insurance typically covers only accidental death and dismemberment.

### Accidents Only

An accident-only policy pays a stated benefit if an injury arises from an accident, sometimes under very specific conditions. These benefits may be a specified amount per day for a stated period if one is hospitalized, a death benefit if one dies because of an accident, or a stated benefit if one loses a limb, becomes paralyzed, loses hearing, or loses eyesight because of an accident. One appeal of accident insurance policies is the method of payment, which typically is made directly to the policyholder rather than to the hospital. While some may argue that the proceeds can be used to offset nonmedical expenses, accident policies pay only in the event of death or dismemberment from an accident, and most deaths occur because of illness. Further, since the benefits are payable only when an accident occurs, this type of policy does not provide substantial support for financial planning purposes.

### Accidental Death and Dismemberment (AD&D)

This type of policy, or endorsement to life insurance or disability insurance, typically pays a benefit upon accidental death or loss of a limb, hearing, speech, or eyesight because of an accident. For example, the accidental death benefit may be a specified amount in the event of death by accident (e.g., $100,000). The dismemberment feature will also pay a specified amount upon loss of two limbs (e.g., $100,000) or a lesser amount in the event of the loss of one limb (e.g., $50,000).

The value of this policy, or endorsement, must be assessed relative to the need for such coverage. As people age, it is likely that some wealth has been accumulated, and the AD&D benefit may be a windfall and not needed. If one has not accumulated wealth, then the advisability of incurring costs for this type of insurance is also questionable. Another consideration is the occurrence of natural death or dismemberment caused by sickness. No benefit is provided for this latter case. Further, some AD&D policies provide coverage only until a specified age or under specific conditions.

### Travel Accident

Travel accident policies pay a specified benefit if death occurs while traveling, sometimes on a specific carrier or if payment was made on a specific credit card. They typically cover business-related travel for employees who travel on business. They are also offered through credit card companies. They can be specially purchased for annual travel or bought as trip insurance at an airport or with a travel ticket. Travel accident insurance, when provided through a credit card, may well be sufficient to cover any need. A person should check the benefits provided by the credit card company supplying the card.

Accident insurance, as described in this section, is by itself seldom of substantial value. While accident as a cause of loss is important in health insurance, sickness as a cause of loss occurs with much more frequency. Whether a loss is caused by sickness or an accident, the premium outlay may be better applied toward regular life insurance or regular health insurance. When considering accident insurance alone, one should seriously consider the need for, and thus the value of, such coverage. (See also AGENTS AND BROKERS; LEISURE; LIABILITY INSURANCE; LIFE INSURANCE.)

**References**

Black, Kenneth, Jr., and Harold D. Skipper, Jr. 2000. *Life and Health Insurance*. 13th ed. Upper Saddle River, NJ: Prentice Hall.

Rejda, George E. 2001. *Principles of Risk Management and Insurance*. 7th ed. Boston, MA: Addison-Wesley.

Trieschmann, James S., and Sandra G. Gustavson. 1995. *Risk Management and Insurance*. 9th ed. Mason, OH: South-Western.

Vaughan, Emmett H., and Therese M. Vaughn. 1999. *Fundamentals of Risk and Insurance*. 8th ed. Hoboken, NJ: John Wiley and Sons.

*Mars A. Pertl*

**ACCOUNTANTS,** professionals who are trained for and work in the field of accounting. Accountants generally have extensive academic experience in accounting, but their degrees, including advanced degrees, may be in business administration, finance, or economics. Some accountants choose to work for organizations as employees, while others choose to provide accounting services to clients for a fee. An accountant who provides such services, in most states, must be registered and licensed as a "public accountant." Public accountants are entitled to call themselves certified public accountants (CPAs) when they have passed a rigorous examination, known as the Uniform Certified Public Accountant Examination, administered by the American Institute of Certified Public Accountants (AICPA).

CPAs and other public accountants practice as sole practitioners or affiliate into accounting firms, which range in size from small local firms to large national or international firms. Most organizations require accountants to be qualified as CPAs. Individuals, including seniors, usually are best served by sole practitioners or small- to mid-size firms where accountants specialize in providing personal service. Services usually fall into three areas: (1) accounting and audit, (2) tax planning and preparation of tax documents, and (3) consulting.

*Accounting and auditing services* are more commonly provided to businesses than to individuals, although business financial statements and reports are often utilized by business owners in their personal financial affairs. Services include reviewing books of account, assisting with the recording of transactions, and the preparation of financial statements and/or reporting on financial statements. There are three types of reports that CPAs issue, depending on the level of services that CPAs have performed on financial statements:

*Compilation*. The accountant takes the client's information and puts it in the form of financial statements without auditing, reviewing, or attempting to verify the accuracy or completeness of the information. These statements are usually prepared for a single purpose and may not follow generally accepted accounting principles.

*Review*. The accountant conducts a review of the financial information, using inquiry, analytical procedures, and discussion. The statements must follow generally accepted accounting principles.

*Audit*. This report is the highest form of assurance. The auditor follows generally accepted auditing standards to obtain reasonable assurance that the financial statements are free of material misstatement. Audit procedures include examining, on a test basis, evidence supporting the accounting principles and disclosures in the financial statements and also assessing the accounting principles used and significant estimates made by management as well as evaluating the overall financial statement presentation. The auditor can then give his or her independent opinion that the financial statements present fairly, in all material respects, the financial position of the company and the results of its operations in accordance with generally accepted accounting principles.

Accountants can also follow standards that allow them to provide assurance on certain nonfinancial items, such as whether a contract is being complied with or whether an individual or organization is following established policies and procedures.

*Tax planning and preparing federal and state tax forms* prompt most individuals to seek an accountant. Accountants are also usually well equipped to assist their clients in the event of a federal or state income tax audit. Some accountants are experienced in estate planning, including charitable contribution strategies, estate valuation services, Medicaid planning, preparation of wills, and business succession planning. These services are often provided in tandem with related legal services, and many accountants can recommend attorneys in these areas, if necessary.

*Consulting services* include financial planning, arbitration, eldercare or PrimePlus services, business advisory services, corporate and personal bankruptcy, due diligence and forensic investigation, litigation support, mergers and acquisitions, performance measurement, valuations for individuals and businesses, computer assistance and support, and information technology.

Some qualities to look for in the selection of an accountant are reputation, professional accreditation (academic degrees, certification), and professional affiliations (membership in the AICPA or relevant state societies). Experience is of paramount importance. The body of accounting information is immense; the accountant chosen should have a specialty in the client's area of interest or should be a member of an accounting firm large enough to embody several areas of specialization.

Personal chemistry is most important in establishing a relationship with an accountant where personal finances are discussed. A good rule of thumb is to interview three different accountants before choosing one, and a list of candidates can be developed by asking friends and relatives for suggestions. A personal banker or lawyer may also have suggestions. The local state society of CPAs will provide a list of CPAs in a specific state, and the state board of accountancy will check the licensing status of prospective CPAs. (See also CPA ELDERCARE SERVICES; FINANCIAL ADVISORS; GERIATRIC CARE MANAGERS [GCMs]; TAXPAYER ISSUES OF OLDER ADULTS.)

### Organizations

American Institute of Certified Public Accountants
CPADirectory.com
National Society of Accountants

### References

Bisk, Nathan M. 2002. *Financial Accounting and Reporting*. Tampa, FL: Bisk Publishing Co.

Magill, Harry T., Gary John Previts, and Thomas R. Robinson, 1997. *The CPA Profession: Opportunities, Responsibilities, and Services*. Upper Saddle River, NJ: Pearson Education.

Shim, Jae K., and Joel G. Siegel. 1989. *Encyclopedic Dictionary of Accounting and Finance*. New York: MJF Books.

*Paul Thrasher*
*Updated by Ann Elizabeth Sammon*

**ACTIVITIES OF DAILY LIVING (ADLs),** the core daily personal care activities that are necessary in order for people to be able to live independently. Loss of mental functioning is measured by other standardized tests and referred to as cognitive impairment. ADLs are particularly important because along with cognitive impairment, and in some cases "medical necessity," they are the mechanism used by the insurance industry to determine qualification for long-term care benefits and may also be used to determine qualification for admission to a nursing or assisted living facility. ADL dependence may be temporary, such as a need for assistance in bathing following surgery. When the aging process causes a loss in one or more ADLs, however, the loss is usually permanent and has an emotional impact that accompanies the physical limitation itself. Incomplete recovery from an accident or an acute episode of illness and deterioration of a chronic condition such as arthritis are common causes of the loss of independence.

The Katz Index of Independence in Activities of Daily Living—known as the Katz ADL scale—is the standard general measurement of an individual's ability to function independently in six areas: bathing, continence, dressing, eating, toileting, and transferring. In addition to an assessment of a person's ability to walk and get around (*ambulation*), the following ADLs are used to determine the amount and type of long-term care people may need. Subjects are scored yes or no on these sorts of definitions of independence:

- *Bathing*. Bathes self completely or needs help in bathing only a single part of the body such as the back, genital area, or disabled extremity. Long-term care insurance policies say this somewhat differently, generally referring to an ability to keep clean without assistance, including the ability to take a bath or shower safely. Bathing is usually the first ADL people fail.
- *Continence*. Maintains complete self-control over bowels and bladder.
- *Dressing*. Gets clothes from closets and drawers, puts them on, and fastens all buttons and other fasteners independently. Long-term care policies often specifically add the ability to put on a prosthesis without help as a measure of independence.
- *Eating*. Once prepared, gets food from plate into mouth without assistance. Preparation of food is not part of this measure.
- *Toileting*. Goes to toilet, gets on and off, arranges clothes, cleans genital area without help.
- *Transferring*. Moves in and out of bed or chair unassisted. This does not preclude the use of assistive devices such as handrails and supports.

As a memory aid, the seven ADLs (including ambulation) offer a sort of alphabetical mnemonic device ABCDE-TT when grouped by the first letter of each.

ADLs are not the only way loss of independence is measured and monitored, but because they describe the ability to manage self-care, they are the most basic. More refined ADL sets that are specific to diseases such as Alzheimer's are used by clinicians and caretakers where appropriate.

Other, less debilitating but nonetheless disconcerting losses are measured by instrumental activities of daily living (IADLs). Where ADLs measure the ability to function independently at a basic level, IADLs are used to measure ability to function in the community. What in other circumstances may be thought of as chores are in this setting the standard for whether or not a person needs caregiving assistance. There is not the standard measure of IADLs that the Katz scale provides for ADLs. The Mayo Clinic uses a scale that measures shopping, housework, accounting, food preparation, and transportation and goes by the unfortunate shorthand of SHAFT, based on the first letter of the five instrumental activities. Other lists often also include the ability to do laundry, use a telephone, manage money and medication, and participate in social activities.

People generally need help with IADLs before they need help with ADLs, and generally the loss of independence is not limited to one activity. Because the loss of independence is so frightening, exacerbated by the high value the U.S. culture places on independence, older people with IADL or ADL dependencies may try to hide their infirmity and may neither seek help nor accept it willingly. (See also EMPLOYER-SPONSORED LONG-TERM CARE INSURANCE; FRAILTY PLANNING; GERIATRIC CARE MANAGERS [GCMs]; LONG-TERM CARE INSURANCE, PRIVATE; LONG-TERM CARE INSURANCE: INDIVIDUAL DISABILITY-ESCALATING ANNUITIES [IDEAs]; LONG-TERM CARE INSURANCE [LTCI]—A CONSUMER'S PERSPECTIVE.)

**References**

Abrams, W.B., M.H. Beers, and R. Berkow. 1995. *The Merck Manual of Geriatrics*. White Station, NJ: Merck Research Laboratories.

Katz, S. 1983. "Assessing Self-Maintenance: Activities of Daily Living, Mobility and Instrumental Activities of Daily Living." *Journal of the American Geriatrics Society* 31(12): 721–26.

Katz, S., T.D. Down, H.R. Cash, et al. 1970. "Progress in the Development of the Index of ADL." *Gerontologist* 10: 20–30.

Katz, S., and M.W. Stroud. 1989. "Functional Assessment in Geriatrics: A Review of Progress and Directions." *Journal of the American Geriatrics Society* 37: 267–71.

Lueckenotte, A.G. 1990. *Pocket Guide to Gerontological Assessment*. Philadelphia, PA: C.V. Mosby.

*E. Craig MacBean*

**ADULT DAY CARE.** See Day Programs for Adults.

**ADVANCE CARE PLANNING.** See Accelerated Death Benefits; Advance Directives; Durable Power of Attorney; Living Will; Long-Term Care Insurance, Private.

**ADVANCE DIRECTIVES,** legal documents used to provide instructions about medical care, financial assistance, and organ and tissue donation, in the event of serious illness or incapacity. Advance directives enable a person to maintain control as death approaches; they are designed to relieve family members and loved ones of the burden of having to make difficult medical and financial decisions.

End-of-life medical treatment can be very costly. Approximately 27% of all Medicare expenditures occur in the last year of life (Emanuel 1996), and many fear that assets accumulated over a lifetime could quickly dissipate in unwanted medical treatment. Advance directives ensure that individuals receive their desired end-of-life treatment. While there is yet no evidence that using advance directives lowers health care costs, they can and do save individuals from receiving unwanted medical treatment and indirectly save medical expenses.

### Types of Advance Directives

Types of advance directives include living wills, durable powers of attorney, and organ and tissue donation. There are two types of durable powers of attorney—the durable power of attorney, used for designating a surrogate to make financial decisions, and the durable medical powers of attorney, used to name a surrogate to make medical and health care decisions.

In contrast to the durable powers of attorney, living wills allow individuals to specify their end-of-life treatment wishes in writing. Subject to certain legal limitations, living wills include instructions concerning the use or withdrawal of artificial life support in end-of-life situations. Living will laws often require the attending physician, and sometimes an additional physician, to certify that the patient's condition is not expected to improve before the advance directive can be given effect.

Every state and the District of Columbia have at least one statute addressing advance directives. As of 2001, three states have a living will only (Pennsylvania, Louisiana, and Montana), three states have durable powers of attorney for health care only (Massachusetts, Michigan, and New York), 32 have both living wills and durable powers, and 13 states have a document that combines the living will and durable powers, called an advance health care directive (Gunter-Hunt, Mahoney, and Sieger 2001). The majority of these statutes require the agent to make health care decisions according to the patient's wishes, if known, or in the patient's best interests. The scope of an agent's authority is generally broader than the provisions contained in a living will. An agent is typically not limited to decisions about ending life support. These documents also address matters of health care management and grant the power to procure health care services and personnel. Medical power of attorney laws often set restrictions on who can serve as an agent. Frequently, health care providers and health care institutions are not permitted to act as agents for patients in their care.

Differences between state documents can create confusion for an older adult who may have an advance directive in one state, yet receive medical care in another state. Most states have laws that address the issue of reciprocity between states, but many states honor out-of-state documents only to the extent that they do not conflict with their own laws.

### Historical Development

Advance directives were developed in response to the technological advances of modern medicine. The first living will was drafted at a 1967 meeting of the Society for the Right to Die, but nine years passed before the first living will law was enacted. In 1976, California became the first state to pass legislation that directly addressed the issue of end-of-life decision making. Also in 1976, the *Quinlan* case in New Jersey became the first right-to-die case to reach a state supreme court. Karen Ann Quinlan, a 21-year-old woman, was in a persistent vegetative state as a result of respiratory arrest. Her father sought court approval to remove her from the ventilator that was breathing for her. The court ruled that individuals have a constitutional right to refuse medical treatment and ordered the treatment stopped.

In 1990, the U.S. Supreme Court issued its landmark decision in the *Cruzan* case. In *Cruzan*, the Court recognized that every competent individual has a constitutional interest in being free from unwanted medical treatment. The case involved a young woman who was permanently unconscious after a car accident and whose life was being sustained by artificial tube feedings. The Missouri Supreme Court had ruled that tube feeding could not be stopped unless clear and convincing evidence of Ms. Cruzan's wish to refuse such treatment could be provided. Although the U.S. Supreme Court found a constitutional basis for the right to refuse medical treatment, the Court ruled that Missouri's clear and convincing evidence requirement was appropriate. One implication of the ruling is that verbal expressions of the desire to refuse medical treatment are not sufficient. Another implication is that individual states are free to define their own standards of evidence as they see fit. In general, this lack of specific guidance from the Supreme Court has led to increased impetus toward the allowance of advance directives, as state legislatures prefer to err on the side of caution.

The *Cruzan* decision also addressed the question of one's right to refuse artificial nutrition and hydration. Early right-to-die legislation frequently required that tube feeding be provided even when other types of life-sustaining treatment could be terminated. In the *Cruzan* decision, the Supreme Court explicitly rejected the idea that tube feeding is different from other forms of life support. Newer statutes generally recognize that nutrition and hydration may be refused but require that instructions for such refusal be explicitly set forth in the advance directive.

Responding to the rulings in the *Cruzan* case, in 1991 Congress passed the Patient Self Determination Act (PSDA), which requires federally funded health care institutions to provide patients with information about their rights to make advance directives. Health care facilities that receive Medicare funding must also provide staff and community education on the use of advance directives, although there has been no federal oversight on how well facilities have met such obligations. The PSDA leaves the substance of laws regarding advance directives to states, and it is too early to judge the impact PSDA will have on the use of advance directives.

### Religion and Refusal of Treatment

Most religions do not specifically address the use of advance directives. Instead, they focus on two related issues: (1) when it becomes appropriate to withhold or withdraw medical treatment, and (2) how treatment termination is distinguishable from suicide and assisted suicide. In general, major religious traditions permit limits on medical treatment provided at the end of life.

Roman Catholic doctrine generally permits patients to refuse life-sustaining treatments. In the Church's statement on refusal of life-sustaining treatment, the *Declaration on Euthanasia* (1980), Pope John Paul II announced that medical treatments may be withdrawn if they impose on the patient

> strain or suffering out of proportion with the benefits which he or she may gain from such techniques. . . . [W]hen inevitable death is imminent in spite of the means used, it is permitted in conscience to take the decision to refuse forms of treatment that would only secure a precarious

> and burdensome prolongation of life, so long as the normal care due to the sick person in similar cases is not interrupted.

This position of the Roman Catholic Church has been interpreted differently among individuals, groups, and clergy. The greatest disagreement centers on whether artificially administered nutrition and hydration may be withheld or withdrawn under the *Declaration.* Most mainline Protestant churches have taken positions that are generally consonant with those articulated by the Roman Catholic Church. In the Protestant religious tradition, there is no absolute authority or specific formula to guide end-of-life medical treatment. There is a rich tradition affirming the values of individual autonomy and responsibility toward others, however, that would argue in favor of a person's right to refuse unwanted medical treatment. Reformed and Conservative Judaism does not oppose withholding or withdrawing treatments that prolong the dying process, although there is disagreement among Conservative rabbis about whether artificial nutrition and hydration may be withheld or withdrawn. In Orthodox Judaism, all life-prolonging measures are required to be provided unless a person cannot be kept alive for more than three days.

### Attitudes toward Executing or Implementing Advance Directives

While an overwhelming majority of adults agree that advance directives are important, the percentage of adults who have executed them remains low. For example, although it is estimated that only some 20% to 30% of older adults have advance directives (Greene 2002), a 1991 Gallup poll found that 84% of the public would wish to terminate life support if there was no hope for recovery, while only 9% would wish to continue life support. In the same survey, 75% of respondents said they wanted a written living will at some future time, while only 17% said they would not want one (Gallup and Newport 1991). Interestingly, a more recent study found that 93% of older adults specified no life-sustaining treatment in their treatment preferences, an additional 6% wanted no life-sustaining treatment if they were in an irreversible coma, and only 1% wanted everything possible done to prolong life (Gross 1998).

The portability of advance directives may be the greatest limitation on their use. It is unclear whether an advance directive written in one state must be honored in another. Increasingly, states guarantee reciprocity if out-of-state documents have been executed properly under either state's law, but many states still lack such reciprocity. Moreover, hospitals and nursing homes are risk averse and may be unwilling to honor an out-of-state advance directive even with the legislative authorization to do so.

Another institutional limitation of the recognition of advance directives—specifically the right to refuse unwanted treatment—consists of "conscience exclusions," which allow a health care facility to reject advance directive provisions on principle if honoring them would violate a religious or moral belief. Although facilities are required to give written notice of such a policy at the time of admission, many patients and families fail to read them thoroughly or to understand the importance of the materials they are given. Facilities that will not stop treatment must transfer a patient to one that will. In practice, it is difficult, however, to find facilities willing to admit patients solely for the purpose of terminating treatment so that death can occur.

Even where the law is clear that a competent adult may refuse medical treatment through an advance directive, many health care facilities remain reluctant to stop treatment. Reasons include misunderstanding of the law; conviction that what is medically appropriate is not consistent with personal, moral, or religious beliefs; the presence of family conflict or disagreement about end-of-life issues; and concern about potential liability.

Finally, there are personal barriers to discussions of end-of-life treatment preferences. Some of these barriers include cultural diversity, educational background, lack of familiarity with the health care system, and desire to delegate decisions entirely to family. For instance, discussions of end-of-life treatment options connote disrespect of the older adults in the Chinese American community. There are several studies published on the characteristics of those who execute advance directives but few regarding why individuals choose to do so.

Cultural issues can also strongly affect the end-of-life decision-making process. For example, Hopp and Duffy (2000) found that Whites were more likely than African Americans to execute advance directives. In addition, African Americans are more likely to opt for life-sustaining measures and prefer the involvement of multiple family members in treatment decision making. African Americans may also fear that the real agenda behind advance directives is to deny them needed care. Studies with Hispanic or Latino family caregivers have found that physicians are advised, for example, not to discuss autopsy decisions with families of dementia victims in order to avoid the appearance of giving up on the patient too soon. On the specific issue of end-of-life decision making, Mexican American families have indicated that when the medical establishment is respectful, empathic, and personal with the family, establishing a bond of mutual trust and goodwill, together they may be able to decide to terminate supportive care with *dignidad* (dignity).

### Trends and Alternative Directives

Two new types of law permit end-of-life medical treatment decisions by others in the event of decisional incapacitation. The first involves surrogate decision making and provides that individuals, usually in order of priority, are empowered to make decisions for an incompetent patient who has no living will or durable medical powers of attorney. While these types of laws simply codify health care decisions traditionally made for incompetent patients, increasing medical regulation and oversight and fears of liability have made doctors reluctant to rely any longer on informal decision making without explicit legislative authorization, particularly after the rulings on *Cruzan*. Commonly, the surrogate (typically a family member or close friend) is required to consider the patient's personal, moral, or religious beliefs when making decisions. Surrogate decision making is often included as a provision within a living will statute. Twenty-three states and the District of Columbia currently provide for surrogate decision making (Choice in Dying 1994).

The second type of law is a nonhospital do-not-resuscitate (DNR) order. Emergency medical technicians, feeling trapped by laws that require aggressive treatment for individuals obviously near the end of life, have joined state medical associations and other organizations to develop and lobby for nonhospital DNR orders. DNR orders allow individuals to refuse emergency resuscitation in advance of an emergency. Usually a DNR order must be completed by an individual and his or her doctor. Some nonhospital DNR legislation provides for wallet-size versions of the official form or for identification bracelets or necklaces to indicate that the individual should not be resuscitated. In order to be effective, the individual must keep the form or other official notification on hand at all times so that it is available to emergency personnel. So far, 19 states have statutes authorizing nonhospital DNR orders, but more are likely to be passed (Choice in Dying 1994). Because both DNR laws and local policies are new, the public and many health care professionals remain unaware of them.

Beyond these legal developments, discussion and research focuses on the larger process of communication among patients, their health care providers, families, and others regarding appropriate care when a patient cannot make decisions. The goal of such advance care planning is to shape future clinical care to fit people's preferences and values. (See also DURABLE POWER OF ATTORNEY; ELDER LAW PRACTICE; FRAILTY PLANNING; HOSPICE CARE; LIVING WILL; NURSING HOMES.)

**Organizations**

American Academy of Family Physicians
Choice in Dying, Inc.

**References**

Allen-Burge, R., and W.E. Haley. 1997. "Individual Differences and Surrogate Medical Decisions: Different Preferences for Life-Sustaining Treatments." *Aging & Mental Health* 1: 121–31.

Choice in Dying. 1994. *Right-to-Die Law Digest*. New York: Author.

*Cruzan v. Director, Missouri Department of Health*. 1990. 110 S. Ct. 2841.

*Declaration on Euthanasia*. 1980. Adopted by the Sacred Congregation for the Doctrine of the Faith, approved by Pope John Paul II. Released to the public on June 26.

Emanuel, E. 1996. "Cost Savings at the End of Life." *Journal of the American Medical Association* 275: 1907–14.

Gallup, G., and F. Newport. 1991. "Mirror of America: Fear of Dying." *The Gallup Newservice* 55: 33.

Greene, K. 2002. "Many Consider a Living Will Important, But Wait Too Long." *Wall Street Journal Sunday*, April 21. Available online at http://online.wsj.com/public/us.

Gross, M.D. 1998. "What Do Patients Express as Their Preferences in Advance Directives?" *Archives of Internal Medicine* 158: 363–65.

Gunter-Hunt, G., J.E. Mahoney, and C.E. Sieger. 2001. "A Comparison of State Advance Directive Documents." *The Gerontologist* 42: 51–60.

Hill, T. Patrick, and David Shirley. 1992. *A Good Death*. New York: Addison-Wesley.

Hopp, F.P. 2000. "Preferences for Surrogate Decision Makers, Informal Communication, and Advance Directives among Community-Dwelling Elders." *The Gerontologist* 40: 449–57.

Hopp, F.P., and S.A. Duffy. 2000. "Racial Variations in End-of-Life Care." *Journal of the American Geriatrics Society* 48: 658–63.

*In re Quinlan*. 1976. 70 NJIO.

Sulmasy, D.P., P.B. Terry, C.S. Weisman, D.J. Miller, R.Y. Stallings, and M.A. Vettese. 1998. "The Accuracy of Substituted Judgments in Patients with Terminal Diagnoses." *Annals of Internal Medicine* 128: 621–29.

Teno, Joan M., Hilda Lindermann Nelson, and Joanne Lynn. 1994. "Advance Care Planning: Priorities for Ethical and Empirical Research." *Hastings Center Report*, Special Supplement (November–December).

Vaughn, G., E. Kiyasu, and W.C. McCormick. 2000. "Advance Directive Preferences among Subpopulations of Asian Nursing Home Residents in the Pacific Northwest." *Journal of the American Geriatrics Society* 48: 554–57.

Wilber, K.H., and S.L. Reynolds. 1995. "Rethinking Alternatives to Guardianship." *The Gerontologist* 35: 248–57.

*Ann E. Fade*
*Updated by Sandra L. Reynolds*

**AGE DISCRIMINATION IN EMPLOYMENT ACT (ADEA),** a federal law prohibiting age discrimination in employment and promoting the employment of older persons based on ability rather than age. The ADEA protects working men and women who are at least 40 years of age or older and renders unlawful an employer's, employment agency's, or labor organization's failure or refusal to hire, discharge, or otherwise discriminate against any individual with respect to his or her compensation, terms, conditions, or privileges of employment because of age.

## Enactment of the ADEA

In 1964 the U.S. Congress passed, and President Lyndon B. Johnson signed into law, the Civil Rights Act. Title VII of that law prohibits employment practices that discriminate on the basis of race, color, religion, sex, or national origin. Congress considered but ultimately rejected an amendment that would have added age to the list of protected categories covered by Title VII but did instruct the U.S. secretary of labor to investigate the problem of age discrimination in employment. Complying with that directive, the secretary issued a report that found and concluded, among other things, that many employers practiced age discrimination based on stereotypes about older persons; that age discrimination harmed the national economy by depriving it of productive workers; that this form of discrimination inflicted economic and psychological injury on older persons; and that federal revenues were diverted to the increasing costs of government benefits paid to those adversely affected by age discrimination in the workplace.

In 1967, President Lyndon Johnson submitted a bill to Congress with this message on age discrimination:

> In economic terms, age discrimination is a serious and senseless loss to a nation on the move. But the greater loss is the cruel sacrifice in happiness and well-being, which joblessness imposes on these citizens and their families. Opportunities must be opened up to the many [older] Americans who are qualified and willing to work. We must end arbitrary age limits on hiring.

Congress heeded the president's call, passing the ADEA in 1967 (see 29 U.S.C. Section 621 et seq). As initially enacted, the ADEA prohibited age discrimination only in the private sector and then only against employees ages 40 to 65. Congress subsequently extended protection to most federal and state employees and expanded the class of protected employees by lifting the age ceiling to 70 and then eliminated that ceiling altogether (with certain exceptions). Thus, the ADEA today covers most private sector and public employees who are 40 years of age or older. It exempts, however, small employers with fewer than 20 employees. In a significant decision dealing with the rights of employees to sue their state employers under the ADEA, *Kimel v. Florida Board of Regents* ([2000] 528 U.S. 62), the U.S. Supreme Court held that states enjoy immunity under the Eleventh Amendment to the U.S. Constitution from ADEA suits seeking money damages brought by private individuals. Recent cases have made clear that the states enjoy no such immunity in ADEA suits brought by the Equal Employment Opportunity Commission (EEOC), the federal agency created by Title VII and empowered to enforce that statute as well as the ADEA.

Most states have age discrimination legislation, and some of those laws are more expansive than the ADEA. The important distinction between the ADEA and some state laws is that action can be brought against an employer with less than 20 employees. In addition, the ADEA does not preempt state law.

### Proving Violations of the ADEA

Two categories of claims can be brought under the ADEA: disparate treatment claims and disparate impact claims. Disparate treatment claims are those in which an individual or class of individuals contends that an employer intentionally refused employment, salary, or promotion or terminated an individual's employment or otherwise discriminated against a person or persons because of age. Disparate impact claims arise when an employee challenges an age-neutral employment practice that has a disproportionate impact on older employees, even when there is no proof that the employer had acted according to discriminatory intent or motive.

### Disparate Treatment Claims

In proving a disparate treatment claim of age discrimination, an individual may present direct evidence that an employer refused to hire, retain, or promote that person because he or she was too old for the job. For example, direct evidence of discrimination would be found where an employer openly and unambiguously refused to hire a person on the ground that the company did not hire persons who were over age 40. Direct evidence of discrimination is also of significance in mixed-motive cases involving both legitimate *and* illegitimate factors in an employment decision, as in the Supreme Court's decision in *Price Waterhouse v. Hopkins* ([1989] 490 U.S. 228). Where a plaintiff establishes that his or her age was an unlawful motivating factor in the decision, the burden of persuasion shifts to the employer to show that the decision would have been the same absent consideration of age. Although the *Price Waterhouse* mixed-motive analysis, as applied to Title VII cases, was changed by Congress in the Civil Rights Act of 1991, some courts continue to apply the 1989 approach to cases arising under the ADEA.

Most employers are sufficiently sophisticated to avoid such direct discriminatory action, and when such proof is lacking, employees must prove disparate treatment and ADEA violations through inferential rather than direct evidence. Courts have developed an allocation of burdens scheme applicable to inferential employment discrimination cases. As first set forth in *McDonnell Douglas Corp. v. Green* ([1973] 411 U.S. 792) and other Supreme Court Title VII decisions, an aggrieved individual initially must prove a case of age discrimination that will generally be established if (1) the individual is a member of the class protected by the statute, (2) is qualified for the position in question, (3) was subjected to an adverse action by the employer, and (4) the job or position was given to a person outside the plaintiff's protected group. Applying the *McDonnell Douglas* framework to age discrimination claims, courts generally held that a prima facie case is established where (1) the employee was in the age group protected by the ADEA, (2) the employee was discharged or suffered an adverse job action (demotion, denial of promotion, etc.), (3) at the time of his or her discharge or other adverse employment action, the employee was performing the job at a level that met the employer's legitimate expectations, and (4) the employee was replaced by someone of comparable qualifications outside the protected class. (In its important 1996 decision in *O'Connor v. Consolidated Caterers Corp.* [(1996) 517 U.S. 308] the Supreme Court held that the fourth factor—replacement by someone outside the protected class—is not a required element of the ADEA prima facie case. In so holding, the Court reasoned that the fact that one person in the protected class has lost out to another person in the protected class is irrelevant, so long as he has lost out because of his age.)

If the individual proves a prima facie case, the employer must produce evidence rebutting the inference of discrimination. That burden is met by the employer's articulation of a legitimate, nondiscriminatory reason for its actions. Where the employer meets this burden of production, the burden of persuasion shifts back to the aggrieved individual who must prove that the employer's articulated reasons were pretextual, i.e., were not the true reasons and were unworthy of credence. A showing of pretext, combined with a plaintiff's prima facie case, may permit (but does not compel) a fact finder (a judge or jury) to conclude that an employer has engaged in unlawful discrimination. In other cases, as explained by the Supreme Court in *Reeves v. Sanderson Plumbing Products, Inc.* ([2000] 530 U.S. 133), more evidence may be required to satisfy the plaintiff's burden of establishing that the ADEA was violated.

### Disparate Impact Claims

A different methodology, initially developed in Title VII cases, governs disparate impact cases. A plaintiff must first present a prima facie case of disparate impact and show, generally with statistical data, that an employer's facially neutral employment practices have a significant adverse effect on older employees. If the plaintiff meets his or her burden, the employer must then show that the challenged practice is job related or had a manifest relationship to the employer's business. The plaintiff can rebut the employer's showing by demonstrating either that the employer could have satisfied its legitimate business purposes in a less discriminatory manner or that the employer was using the practice as a pretext for discrimination.

In a 1993 Supreme Court case, *Hazen Paper Co. v. Biggins* ([1993] 507 U.S. 604), the Court declined to consider or answer the question whether the disparate impact theory is available under the ADEA, with three justices noting that there are substantial arguments that it is improper to carry over disparate impact analysis from Title VII to the ADEA. In its 2001–2002 term the Court announced that it would take up that question in a case involving ADEA claims brought by employees terminated by their employer during a series of company reorganizations. The Court later removed that case from its docket, however, leaving for another day a final resolution of this important ADEA issue.

### Employer Defenses to ADEA Claims

The ADEA arms employers with a number of defenses against claims of age discrimination. The most important of these defenses is that age is a bona fide occupational qualification reasonably necessary to the normal operation of the particular business. For example, courts have permitted mandatory retirement ages for certain law enforcement officials. But one court struck down an airline policy of refusing entry-level employment to pilots over 35 years of age, while another court approved a bus company's policy of refusing entry-level employment to drivers over 40 years old. The ADEA also provides defenses for employers who can demonstrate that an employment decision was based on (1) reasonable factors other than age, (2) a bona fide seniority system, or (3) a bona fide employee benefit plan.

It is noteworthy that an employer may not adopt a policy of discharging employees over age 40 involuntarily in a corporate reorganization, nor adopt a seniority system that retires an employee over age 40 involuntarily. Prior to 1989, the EEOC and virtually all federal courts that considered the question took the position that older employees could be treated differently in an employee benefit plan only if the employer could demonstrate a cost justification for the disparate treatment. In a surprising decision, *Public Employees Retirement System v. Betts* ([1989] 492 U.S. 158), the Supreme Court rejected the cost justification approach and held that an employer could discriminate on the basis of age in employee benefits plans unless the employee could show that the plan actually intended to discriminate in some non–fringe benefit aspect of the employment relationship. Congress reacted to and expressly overruled the *Betts* decision with the Older Workers Benefit Protection Act (OWBPA) of 1990. Under that statute, an employee benefit plan is bona fide only where, for each benefit or benefit package, the actual amount of payment made or cost incurred on behalf of an older worker is no less than that made or incurred on behalf of a younger worker.

An employer can also defend against an age discrimination claim by showing that an employee relinquished his or her ADEA rights under a waiver agreement meeting the minimum statutory standards set forth in the OWBPA. The OWBPA provides that a waiver is not knowing and voluntary unless it is written in a manner calculated to be understood by the individual, specifically refers to rights and claims arising under the ADEA, applies only to claims in existence at the date of the execution of the waiver, is given in exchange for consideration in addition to anything of value to which the employee is already entitled, advises the employee to consult with an attorney before executing the agreement, gives the employee at least 21 days to consider the agreement, and provides for at least 7 days after the execution of the agreement for the employee to revoke the waiver. (Other provisions apply where waivers are asked of groups or classes of employees.) A release or waiver not in compliance with the OWBPA's requirements does not bar an ADEA claim. In *Oubre v. Entergy Operations, Inc.* ([1998] 522 U.S. 422) the Supreme Court so held and further held that an age discrimination suit could be pursued even though the employee did not return or offer to return to the employer the monies he or she received for signing the waiver and release.

The Supreme Court has allowed employers to limit their liability in ADEA cases where evidence of employee misconduct is discovered subsequent to the employee's termination. *McKennon v. Nashville Banner Publishing Company* ([1995] 513 U.S. 352) held that such after-acquired evidence of employee wrongdoing does not bar a valid ADEA claim but does bear on the remedy to be ordered. As a general rule, the Court concluded, neither reinstatement nor front pay is an appropriate remedy, and backpay should be calculated from the date of the unlawful discharge to the date of the employer's discovery of wrongdoing of such severity that the employee would have been fired if the employer had known of the misconduct at the time of the discharge.

### Criticism of the ADEA

Some commentators have argued that the ADEA is unwise and inefficient legislation. In his 1992 book *Forbidden Grounds: The Case against Employment Discrimination Laws*, Richard Epstein argued that employment discrimination statutes serve no legitimate purpose and that, in the labor marketplace, employers and employees will agree to contracts where the contracts offer gains to each. Barring structural failures in the marketplace, it is expected that labor will move to jobs where it is most highly valued. For Epstein, the right policy in the labor and employment market is to keep all barriers as low as possible. The ADEA has precisely the opposite effect, in his view, since it raises barriers to entry. Concerns that older workers will face obstacles in the labor market can be addressed by the market itself, he argues, for a firm that passes over superior older workers in favor of inferior younger ones will find itself at a cost disadvantage that it cannot recoup in the market. Another prominent critic of the ADEA, Richard Posner, has argued that the ADEA was sold by means of emotional rhetoric concerning the plight of older workers and is at once inefficient, regressive, and harmful to them. These views ignore the economic and psychological harm inflicted by discriminatory employment practices in which age-based stereotypes are substituted and serve as proxies for relevant abilities and performance. Although the costs of age (and other workplace) discrimination may be hard to quantify, they are real and merit reflection. Any market failure addressed and corrected by the ADEA may have actually increased rather than decreased societal net wealth.

### The Future of the ADEA

Judicial trends have narrowed the scope and efficacy of the ADEA and other civil rights legislation. Courts are increasingly calling on employment discrimination plaintiffs to meet substantial burdens and matters of proof in order to establish discriminatory intent and motive. The Supreme Court has insulated states from ADEA suits brought by private plaintiffs. Congress, which in the past amended the ADEA to make it more hospitable for employees, is less inclined to expand the reach of civil rights laws; as a result, plaintiffs increasingly seek redress under state laws where available.

These judicial and legislative trends come at a significant time. Members of the baby boom generation are now moving into protected status under the ADEA, and a majority of the workforce will soon have ADEA protection. Indeed, persons age 55 and older comprise the fastest-growing segment of the U.S. workforce, and the median age of all workers will be 40.6 years by the year 2010. These older workers may create and benefit from strong political pressures leading to the expansion of ADEA protection against those who would discriminate on the basis of age, while those who are not protected by the statute may resent and counteract such pressures. It is difficult to predict what this will mean in terms of age discrimination law and policy and the political, economic, and social forces that strengthen or weaken legal protections for older workers. (See also OLDER AMERICANS ACT; WORKFORCE PATTERNS, CHANGES IN; WORKING RETIREES.)

**References**

Barrier, Michael. 2002. "An Age-Old Problem." *HR Magazine* 47: 1047–49.

Epstein, Richard. 1992. *Forbidden Grounds: The Case against Employment Discrimination Laws.* Boston, MA: Harvard University Press.

*Hazen Paper Co. v. Biggins.* 1993. 507 U.S. 604.

*Kimel v. Florida Board of Regents.* 2000. 528 U.S. 62.

*McDonnell Douglas Corp. v. Green.* 1973. 411 U.S. 792.

*McKennon v. Nashville Banner Publishing Company.* 1995. 513 U.S. 352.

*O'Connor v. Consolidated Caterers Corp.* 1996. 517 U.S. 308.

*Oubre v. Entergy Operations, Inc.* 1998. 522 U.S. 422.

*Price Waterhouse v. Hopkins.* 1989. 490 U.S. 228.

*Public Employees Retirement System v. Betts.* 1989. 492 U.S. 158.

*Reeves v. Sanderson Plumbing Products, Inc.* 2000. 530 U.S. 133.

Rosen, Benson, and Thomas H. Jerdee. 1976a. "The Influence of Age Stereotypes on Managerial Decisions." *Journal of Applied Psychology* 61: 428–32.

Rosen, Benson, and Thomas H. Jerdee. 1976b. "The Nature of Job-Related Stereotypes." *Journal of Applied Psychology* 61: 180–83.

Rosner, Richard. 1995. *Aging and Old Age.* Chicago: University of Chicago Press.

U.S. Department of Labor. 1965. *The Older American Worker: Age Discrimination in Employment.* Washington, DC: Author.

*Norman Stein and Ronald Turner*
*Updated by Ronald Turner*

**AGENTS AND BROKERS,** persons authorized to represent others or to negotiate on their behalf, usually for compensation. Health and financial concerns of older people and their families bring them into contact with an array of professional agents and others who operate under the laws of agency: accountants, attorneys, financial advisors, attorneys-in-fact, real estate and insurance agents, trustees, and persons who have been authorized to make medical decisions under advance directives. There is little literature that distinguishes between agency and brokerage, and much confusion surrounds the practices and ethics of those who are engaged to act on the older person's behalf, especially those in fiduciary relationships.

An agent is a person or entity authorized by another (the "principal") to represent and to act on the principal's behalf. The agreement of agent and principal constitutes an agency relationship. The agent acts only with the principal's consent and is subject to his or her direction and control. When acting under an agency arrangement, the agent's chief obligations are (1) loyalty to the principal, (2) obedience to the principal's instructions, (3) diligence in the performance of duties, (4) accountability for the principal's funds or property, and (5) full disclosure to the principal of all material facts. Actions taken under an agency relationship bind the principal in third-party transactions. Thus, third parties dealing with agents must bear in mind that the first loyalty of the agent, by law, is owed to the principal. There are many types of agency appointments, but most fall under two broad categories of agency: general and special.

A broker is an agent employed to make bargains and contracts for compensation, according to *Black's Law Dictionary*. When a broker enters into a transaction as a middle person or negotiator to bring buyer and seller together, he or she is acting as a "dual agent." There are many different types of brokers, and the term extends to almost every area of business. The term *broker* is often misused and misunderstood by consumers when referring to real estate, insurance, and other types of persons who actually work in agency relationships under most state laws. Certain industries are often closely regulated—the real estate and legal industries, for example—and their members are required to disclose agency relationships, obligations, and fee arrangements and to avoid conflicts of interest. In other industries—such as insurance and securities and commission-based financial planning—advisors and counselors do not supervise closely the agency and disclosure practices of their representatives. As a result, securities brokers—even those who are well intentioned—often call themselves financial advisors or financial service representatives. The effect of this is to elevate their profession and obscure how they are compensated.

### General and Special Agents

*General agents* have been delegated authority by a principal to handle all matters connected with a particular (personal or business-related) situation, trade, or employment. They may exercise extremely broad authority, without restriction or qualification, for a principal; this includes entering into several types of contracts; making decisions; buying and selling property, goods, and services; and entering into short- or long-term obligations and/or commitments. A *managing agent* may be vested with exclusive and general power to exercise complete judgment and discretion in all management matters for his or her principal (person or organization).

*Special agents* are appointed to act on behalf of their principals in a limited capacity, usually in a single transaction or a series of acts not involving a continuity of service. An example of special agency is a literary agent appointed to enter into publishing negotiations and contracting arrangements on an author's behalf. A purchasing agent is typically a special agent as well, authorized to act on behalf of a company concerning matters of purchasing special materials such as supplies or inventory. A purchasing or literary agent would not be authorized to bind his or her principal in any matter other than the transaction or series of acts explicitly specified in an agency agreement.

Whether dealing with a special or general agent, third parties who have contact with agents should determine the exact scope of authority and range of actual power that have been delegated by the principal to the agent. It is important for anyone who deals with an agent to know directly from the principal, in as clear a manner as possible, what the scope of authority is in order to make informed judgments as to the appropriateness of the transaction under consideration. Without this knowledge, the third party dealing with an agent runs the risk of entering into agreements that go beyond the scope of the agent's authority. When compensation is involved, it is important to become aware of the fees charged or commissions customarily paid in the particular agency arrangement.

### Common Agency Arrangements

*Insurance agents* are agents of insurance companies who have been hired as (1) general agents to manage sales operations on either a local or a regional basis or (2) special agents authorized only to sell insurance. An insurance general agent is authorized to act on behalf of a specific insurance company with respect to nearly every business matter concerning sales operations. They may not make underwriting or premium determinations. Insurance special agents are authorized only to sell insurance and do not have the authority to modify any terms of existing insurance agreements. Insurance agents, who earn commissions based on the insurance they sell, may represent one or many different companies. Since the cost of insurance varies greatly from company to company, it is important to shop for comparable coverage and service. Not surprisingly, high-cost policies usually pay high commissions to agents.

*Real estate agents* usually represent the seller of real estate. If an agent acts as a buyer's agent, they are still compensated from the sales commission paid by the seller unless specific alternative compensation arrangements have been made. The loyalties of real estate agents may seem especially confusing to buyers, since they can be genuinely motivated to bring buyers and sellers into harmonious and satisfactory transactions. Under real estate agency agreements (listings), however, agents are hired to sell real estate, and it is the seller who is the principal in this agency relationship. Buyer brokerage arrangements, however, where agency and compensation are specified, are increasing in real estate transactions.

*Financial advisors* or *managers*, employed as agents to manage assets or purchase investments on behalf of principals, may be acting instead as dual agents or brokers, because they are compensated by commissions based on sales of the financial products sold in addition to fees based on a percentage of assets managed. Increasingly, to avoid such conflicts of interest, financial advisors are charging a fee only for the time spent on a client's behalf. It is always important to understand the exact relationship one has with a financial services professional, his or her motivation for recommending an investment, and the manner in which the financial representative is compensated.

Many uncompensated agency relationships may exist in the lives of older persons as well, but all agency agreements require great care and planning before entering into them. Among the more serious types of agency created are those in which persons are delegated authority under powers of attorney, durable power of attorney, and advance directives for health care in the event of incapacity. (See also ACCOUNTANTS; DURABLE POWER OF ATTORNEY; ETHICS IN FINANCIAL PLANNING; FINANCIAL ADVISORS; LIFE INSURANCE; LONG-TERM CARE INSURANCE [LTCI]—A CONSUMER'S PERSPECTIVE; REAL ESTATE INVESTMENTS.)

### Organizations

Duff & Phelps
Institute of Certified Financial Planners
International Association of Financial Planners
International Board of Standards and Practices for Certified Financial Planners, Inc.
Moody's
National Association of Personal Financial Advisors
Standard & Poor's

### Suggested Readings

Jaffe, Charles A. 2001. *The Right Way to Hire Financial Help: A Complete Guide to Choosing and Managing Brokers, Financial Planners, Insurance Agents, Lawyers, Tax Preparers, Bankers, and Real Estate Agents*. 2nd ed. Cambridge, MA: MIT Press.

Wilson, Ray, and Thomas Early. 1998. *Bought, Not Sold: Single Agency, Buyer's Brokers, Flat Fees, and the Consumer Revolution in Real Estate*. Greenfield, MA: Cogna Books.

**Reference**

Garner, Bryan A., Henry Campbell, and Henry L. Black, eds. 2000. *Black's Law Dictionary*. 7th ed. St. Paul, MN: West Group.

*Donald A. Hunsberger*

**AGING AMERICA,** the changing proportion of older adults in the overall U.S. population. The age structure of any population is affected by the rates of fertility, mortality, and migration. Increased life expectancies (LEs) of infants and children escalated during the first half of the twentieth century, caused principally by the elimination of poor hygiene and sanitation and by decreasing rates of infectious diseases. Throughout the twentieth century, however, reductions in mortality for children reached a floor, and reductions in mortality for older adults began to occur, in large part because of improvements in cardiac and other medical care. This trend resulted in the aging of the U.S. population during the latter half of the twentieth century. This factor was compounded by the declining fertility rate throughout the century, which would further increase the proportion of older people in the U.S. population. In the twenty-first century, the U.S. population will age further, due to the increased birthrate between 1946 and 1964 of the baby boom—the oldest baby boomers will be 65 in 2011.

It was not until the baby boom approached middle age that policymakers and the public took notice of this phenomenon. Population pyramids graphically portray the changing nature of the U.S. population, during 1900, 1970, 2000, and 2030 (Himes 2001). In 1900, the U.S. population can be characterized as a pyramid, with high birthrates and generally increasing mortality rates with increasing age. By 1970, the baby boom had begun to reshape the U.S. population, creating a bulge of people at the youngest ages. In 2000, the baby boom is in middle age, and the "pyramid" now looks more like a rectangle; this process is complete by the time we reach 2030, at which time the baby boomers reach old age. This phenomenon is referred to as the rectangularization of the population.

### Size and Location of the U.S. Population

In 1990, adults aged 65 and older comprised approximately 12.5% of the U.S. population. By 2070, the 65+ group will constitute approximately 21% of the U.S. population (Figure 1). Of increasing interest, particularly to the service sectors of American business, is the explosive growth of those who are 85 and older. In contrast to the 65+ group, the 85+ group is expected to more than triple between 1990 and 2070, constituting approximately 5% of the U.S. population by 2070 (U.S. Census Bureau 1999).

Older adults live in virtually every state in the nation, but there are concentrations in certain areas. Table 1 displays the ten states in which older adults make up the highest proportion of the U.S. population for 1990 and 2000 (Hetzel and Smith 2001). Florida is first in both years (18.3% in 1990; 17.6% in 2000), followed by Pennsylvania. After that the order changes, but the states listed in the top ten are pretty much the same states at both times, with the exception of Missouri in 1990 and Connecticut and Maine in 2000. Table 2, on the other hand, shows the top ten and bottom ten states in terms of older adult growth rate between 1990 and 2000, with Nevada growing 72% over the decade and the District of Columbia losing 10%.

One of the most important components in current and projected growth in the older

**Figure 1**
**Projected Growth of the Older Population: 65+ and 85+ between 1990 and 2070**

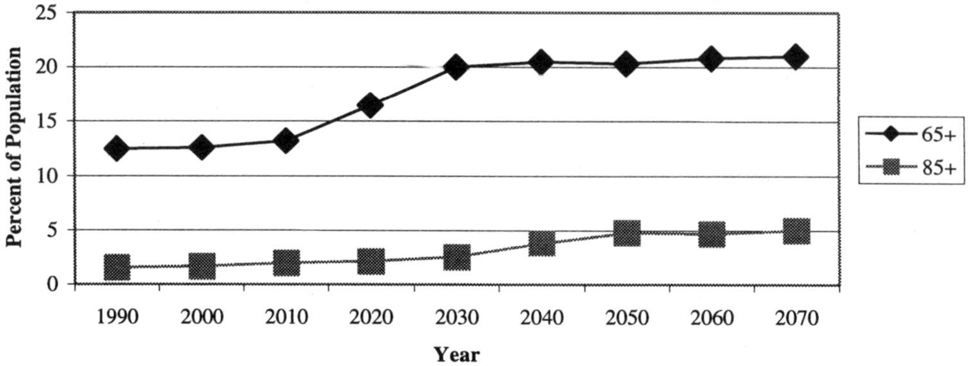


*Source*: U.S. Census Bureau 1999.

**Table 1**
**Change in Oldest States between 1990 and 2000 in Rank Order**

| 1990 | | 2000 | |
|---|---|---|---|
| Florida | 18.3 | Florida | 17.6 |
| Pennsylvania | 15.4 | Pennsylvania | 15.6 |
| Iowa | 15.3 | West Virginia | 15.3 |
| Rhode Island | 15.0 | Iowa | 14.9 |
| West Virginia | 15.0 | North Dakota | 14.7 |
| Arkansas | 14.9 | Rhode Island | 14.5 |
| South Dakota | 14.7 | Maine | 14.4 |
| North Dakota | 14.3 | South Dakota | 14.3 |
| Nebraska | 14.1 | Arkansas | 14.0 |
| Missouri | 14.0 | Connecticut | 13.8 |

*Source*: Hetzel and Smith 2001.

population is increasing life expectancy during the twentieth century. In 1900, for example, the life expectancy for the U.S. population at birth was 47 years. By 1950, that figure had increased to 68, and by the year 2000, to nearly 77.

### Differences in Life Expectancy

While life expectancy has increased for the total population, life expectancy for women has been higher than for men. Table 3 demonstrates that total life expectancy at birth rose from age 47.3 to 76.9 between 1900 and 2000. For men, however, the increase has been slower: in 2000, life expectancy for women is nearly 80, while for men, it is 74. At age 65 women can expect 19 more years of life, and men only 16 more. This differ-

**Table 2**
**Top Ten and Bottom Ten in Growth of the Older Population, 1990 to 2000**

| Fastest Growing | Change 1990–2000 | Slowest Growing | Change 1990–2000 |
|---|---|---|---|
| Nevada | 71.5 | District of Columbia | –10.2 |
| Alabama | 59.6 | Rhode Island | 1.2 |
| Arizona | 39.5 | Iowa | 2.4 |
| New Mexico | 30.1 | West Virginia | 3.0 |
| Hawaii | 28.5 | New York | 3.6 |
| Utah | 26.9 | North Dakota | 3.8 |
| Colorado | 26.3 | Kansas | 4.0 |
| Delaware | 26.0 | Nebraska | 4.1 |
| South Carolina | 22.3 | Illinois | 4.4 |
| Wyoming | 22.2 | Massachusetts | 5.0 |

*Source*: Hetzel and Smith 2001.

**Table 3**
**Life Expectancy at Birth and at Age 65 by Gender, in 1900, 1950, and 2000**

| Year | At Birth | | | At Age 65 | | |
|---|---|---|---|---|---|---|
| | Total | Male | Female | Total | Male | Female |
| 1900 | 47.3 | 46.3 | 48.3 | 11.9 | 11.5 | 11.2 |
| 1950 | 68.2 | 65.6 | 71.1 | 13.9 | 12.8 | 15.0 |
| 2000 | 76.9 | 74.1 | 79.5 | 17.9 | 16.3 | 19.2 |

*Source*: Himes 2001.

ence is reflected in Figure 2, which shows the marital status of men and women age 65 and older. The two groups that most closely reflect the impact of this gender disparity in life expectancy are those who are married and widowed. Nearly 75% of men age 65 and older are married, compared to 44% of older women. Conversely, only 15% of men are widowed, while 45% of older women are widowed (Himes 2001).

Differences in life expectancy are more remarkable between racial/ethnic groups. In Figure 3, we examine data between 1940 and 1992 for Whites and African Americans. While good data were not available for African Americans until the 1970s, certain patterns can be observed. African Americans have lower life expectancy than Whites, but only when broken down by gender. Rates for White females are consistently highest, followed by African American females. African American female rates are similar to,

**Figure 2**
**Marital Status, Ages 65 and Older**

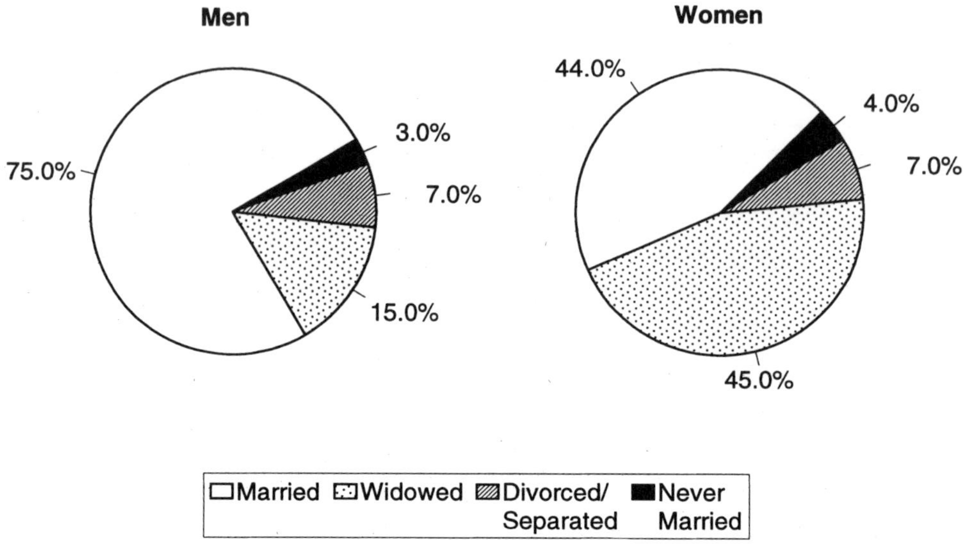


*Source*: Himes 2001.

**Figure 3**
**Changing Life Expectancy for Whites and African Americans, 1940 to 1992**

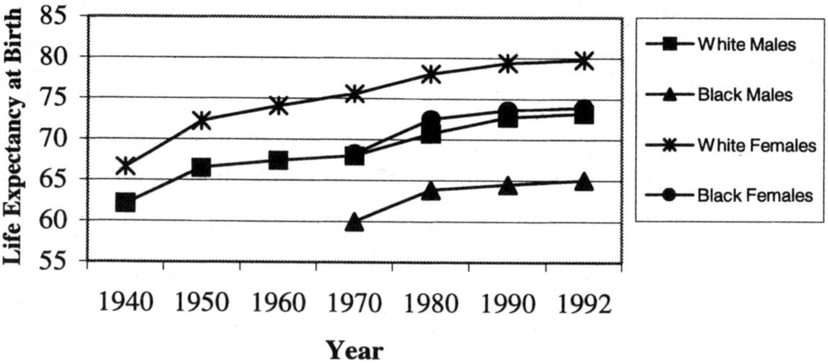


*Source*: Himes 2001.

but slightly higher than, those for White males. The lowest life expectancy rate is for African American males. The intraracial difference between the sexes, however, is approximately the same for African Americans as for Whites.

The impact of these differentials is not directly reflected in the current and projected racial composition of the older U.S. population. In Figure 4, the current proportion of all African Americans, Hispanics, and "other" races represents approximately 18% of the older adult population in the year 2000. By 2050, however, it is projected to represent 36% of the older adult population. This is due to the fact that the racial composition of the U.S. population is made up of other factors in addition to life expectancy. In the case

**Figure 4**
**Older Americans by Race and Ethnicity, 2000 and 2050**

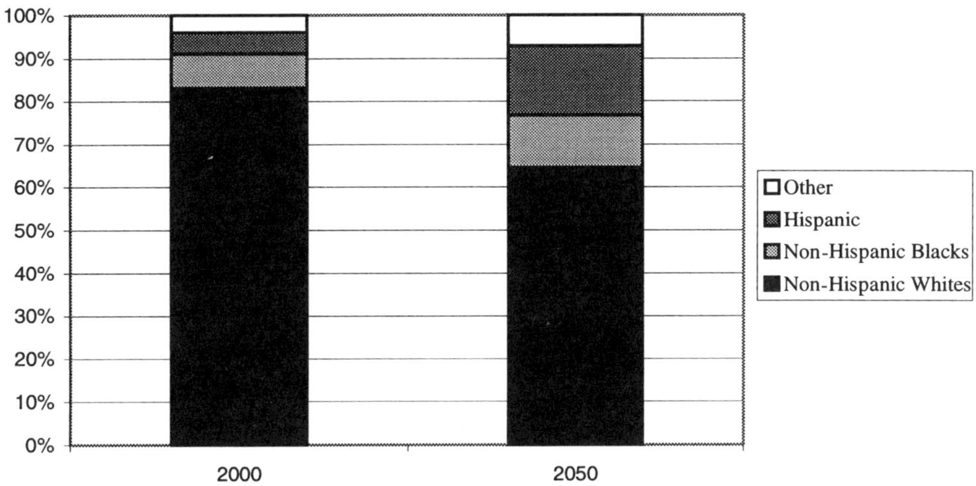


*Source*: Himes 2001.

**Table 4**
**Poverty Rates among Older Men and Women, by Race/Ethnicity, 2000**

| | Percent in Poverty | | | |
|---|---|---|---|---|
| | **Total** | **Non-Hispanic White** | **African American** | **Hispanic** |
| Total, Ages 65+ | 10.2 | 8.3 | 22.3 | 18.8 |
| Men | 7.5 | 5.8 | 17.1 | 17.6 |
| Women | 12.2 | 10.2 | 25.8 | 19.6 |

*Source*: Himes 2001.

of the racial makeup of the U.S. population, non-White residents tend to have higher fertility than White residents. In addition, most migration into the United States is of young non-Whites in good health. These factors will account for the shift in the racial/ethnic proportion of the older adult 50 years from now.

In general, older adults in the United States are no more likely to be poor than the rest of the U.S. population, with approximately 10% living in poverty. Table 4, however, shows gender and racial differences in poverty rates. Rates for older women are 12.2% and 7.5% for older men. African American women have 151% the poverty rate of African American men, while Hispanic women have 11% higher poverty rates than Hispanic men.

### Socioeconomic Status

The major difference is between the races: while Whites have poverty levels less than the average (8.3%), African Americans have 2.7 times and Hispanics have 2.3 times the

**Table 5**
**Sources of Income among Americans Age 65 or Older, in Income Quintiles, 1998**

| | Income Level | | | | |
|---|---|---|---|---|---|
| | **1st Quintile** | **2nd Quintile** | **3rd Quintile** | **4th Quintile** | **5th Quintile** |
| Total | 100 | 100 | 100 | 100 | 100 |
| Social Security | 82 | 80 | 64 | 45 | 18 |
| Asset Income | 2 | 6 | 10 | 14 | 28 |
| Pensions | 3 | 7 | 15 | 24 | 21 |
| Earnings | 1 | 3 | 7 | 13 | 31 |
| Public Assistance | 10 | 2 | 1 | 1 | 1 |
| Other | 2 | 2 | 3 | 3 | 2 |

*Source*: Himes 2001.

poverty rate of Whites. There are also some marked gender differences. Both African American and Hispanic men have poverty rates three times that of White men, while Hispanic women have twice the poverty rate, and African American women have 2.5 times the poverty rate, of White women.

All but the top income quintile of older adults relies heavily on Social Security income (see Table 5 for sources of income for older Americans). For the two bottom quintiles, Social Security makes up 80% or more of total income, compared to 18% for the highest quintile of older citizens. Any new or revised policies regarding the preservation of the U.S. social welfare system for older adults (e.g., Social Security, Medicare, Medicaid) must take into account both the disproportionate number of non-White older Americans in the lower-income quintiles and the potential increase of older adults who will be highly dependent on Social Security for their future income.

### Health Differences

The aging of the U.S. population will also have an impact on the U.S. health care system, particularly with the explosive growth of the 85+ group. Figure 5 presents information on the prevalence of chronic conditions among different age groups, and Figure 6 presents similar information for Whites, African Americans, and Hispanics (Himes 2001).

Figure 5 presents the prevalence of arthritis, hypertension, heart disease, cancer, diabetes, and stroke; in only one case do those who are 85+ have lower rates than those between 70 and 74—diabetes. Rates of hypertension and cancer appear to be relatively stable by age group, while arthritis, heart disease, and stroke are significantly more prevalent in the 85+ group. The reason diabetes goes in the reverse direction is probably one of selection, as people may be dying of diabetes prior to age 85.

For older Whites, African Americans, and Hispanics, prevalence rates also vary (Figure 6). Older African Americans have the highest rates of arthritis, hypertension, diabetes,

**Figure 5**
**Chronic Health Conditions, by Age Group**

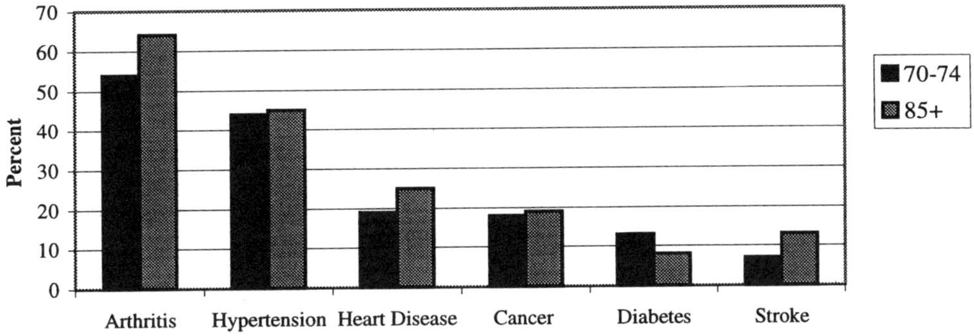


*Source*: Himes 2001.

**Figure 6**
**Chronic Health Conditions, by Race/Ethnicity**

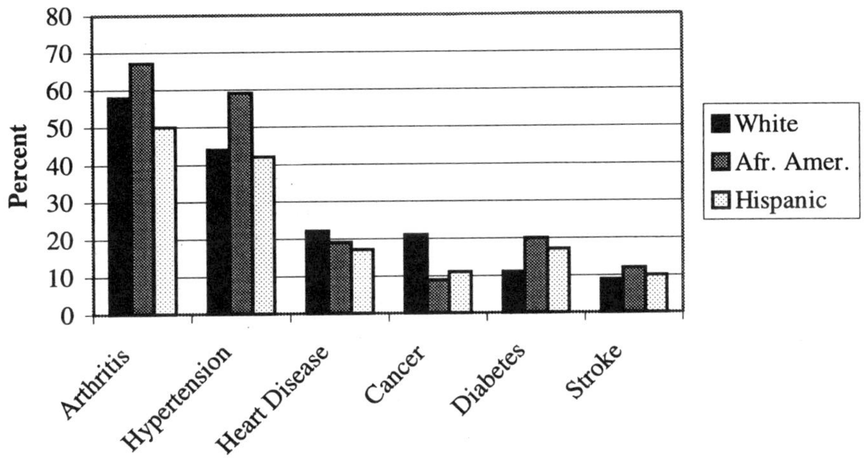


*Source*: Himes 2001.

and stroke, but they have significantly lower rates of cancer than Whites, and the racial differences in heart disease prevalence appear to be minor. Hispanics have the lowest levels of arthritis and hypertension, but differ little from African Americans on the other chronic conditions (Himes 2001). African Americans may have low rates of cancer due to one of two factors: (1) they may not be diagnosed as readily, because of relatively low participation in cancer screenings and preventive tests, or (2) they may not be receiving equally good cancer care, and thus more might be dying of cancer as compared to other groups.

These differences in health can translate into differential rates of functional limitation—basic activities of daily living (e.g., bathing, feeding, dressing, etc.) and instrumental activities of daily living (e.g., managing money, taking medications, preparing meals, etc.). When older adults become too impaired to perform many of these tasks,

**Table 6**
**Percent of 60+ Population in the Oldest and Youngest Countries, 2000 and 2050**

| Oldest Countries | | | | Youngest Countries | | | |
|---|---|---|---|---|---|---|---|
| 2000 | | 2050 | | 2000 | | 2050 | |
| Country | % | Country | % | Country | % | Country | % |
| Italy | 24.1 | Spain | 44.1 | Niger | 3.3 | Niger | 5.0 |
| Greece | 23.4 | Slovenia | 42.4 | Yemen | 3.6 | Angola | 5.2 |
| Germany | 23.2 | Japan | 42.3 | Uganda | 3.8 | Yemen | 5.3 |
| Japan | 23.2 | Italy | 42.3 | Somalia | 3.9 | Somalia | 5.7 |
| Sweden | 22.4 | Austria | 41.0 | Burundi | 4.3 | Uganda | 5.7 |
| Belgium | 22.1 | Greece | 40.7 | Angola | 4.5 | Burkina Faso | 6.5 |
| Spain | 21.8 | Czech Rep. | 40.1 | Congo | 4.5 | Ethiopia | 6.6 |
| Bulgaria | 21.7 | Armenia | 39.5 | Zambia | 4.5 | Liberia | 6.7 |
| Switzerland | 21.3 | Switzerland | 38.9 | Burkina | 4.8 | Burundi | 6.8 |
| Latvia | 20.9 | Bulgaria | 38.6 | Chad | 4.9 | Mali | 7.0 |

*Source*: United Nations Population Division 2002b.

assistance typically comes from a spouse, adult children, other relatives or friends, and paid care. While American long-term care policy has traditionally relied on the institutional solution of hospital, nursing home, or rehabilitation center, the vast majority of care for frail older adults is delivered in the community by family members.

### International Perspective

How does the United States compare to the rest of the world? Life expectancy rates in the United States are similar to but not as strong as other developed nations, and they are clearly stronger than for developing countries. Table 6 displays the percentage of age 60 and older persons in the countries identified as the oldest and youngest for the year 2000 and projected for the year 2050 (U.N. Population Division 2002a). The United States makes neither list; in the year 2000, the 60+ population makes up approximately 14% of the U.S. population and in 2050 is projected to increase to 20%. The oldest countries today range between 21% in Latvia to 24% in Italy. By the year 2050, the oldest countries will range from 39% in Bulgaria to 44% in Spain. The youngest countries also show increases in their older populations, but not enough to approach the old-age proportions in the developed world. In 2000, the youngest countries had older populations ranging between 3% (Niger) and 5% (Chad), and by 2050, the youngest countries will have somewhere between 5% (Niger) and 7% (Mali).

These differences also are reflected in the relative life expectancy rates in the developed and developing world. Table 7 compares the United States to the ten countries with the highest rates—the developed world—and those with the ten lowest rates—the developing world (United Nations Population Division 2002b). In 1995, the United States ranked eleventh in the developed world. In contrast, the United States is clearly ahead of the ten countries with the lowest life expectancy rates in the developing world.

**Table 7**
**Ten Highest and Lowest Countries in Life Expectancy at Birth, Ranked in 1995 and Compared to the United States**

| **Highest LE Countries** | **Life Expectancy 1995–2000** | **Life Expectancy 2045–2050** |
|---|---|---|
| Japan | 80.5 | 88.0 |
| Sweden | 79.3 | 84.6 |
| Iceland | 78.9 | 83.1 |
| Australia | 78.7 | 83.0 |
| Switzerland | 78.6 | 82.9 |
| Canada | 78.5 | 82.8 |
| Israel | 78.3 | 83.5 |
| France | 78.1 | 84.0 |
| Norway | 78.1 | 83.7 |
| Belgium | 77.9 | 83.8 |
| United States | 76.5 | 82.6 |
| **Lowest LE Countries** | | |
| Sierra Leone | 37.3 | 61.5 |
| Rwanda | 39.4 | 64.2 |
| Zambia | 40.5 | 66.0 |
| Burundi | 40.6 | 64.3 |
| Mozambique | 40.6 | 62.8 |
| Malawi | 40.7 | 64.0 |
| Uganda | 41.9 | 67.8 |
| Afghanistan | 42.5 | 62.4 |
| Zimbabwe | 42.9 | 66.3 |
| Guinea-Bissau | 44.1 | 66.0 |

*Source*: United Nations Population Division 2000b.

## Conclusions

The U.S. population is getting older along with much of the rest of the world. This population will increase both in numbers and in diversity as the baby boom generation ages. The proportion of older U.S. adults in the twenty-first century projected to be female, minority, frail, poor, and highly dependent on Social Security for their economic survival is growing. In terms of planning, the nation must preserve and improve Social Security, Medicare, Supplemental Security Income (SSI), and Medicaid in order to maintain the safety and dignity of this population. For financial professionals, preserving and growing the assets of those fortunate enough to have resources and income outside of the social welfare system will become an increasingly critical factor for those numbers of older adults expected in the twenty-first century. (See also ATTITUDES ABOUT

RETIREMENT; ECONOMIC HARDSHIP MEASURES IN THE OLDER POPULATION; ECONOMIC HISTORY OF RETIREMENT; ECONOMIC STATUS OF OLDER MEN AND WOMEN; HISTORY OF RETIREMENT; U.S. PERSONAL SAVING RATE.)

**Organizations**

National Center for Health Statistics
Social Security Administration
U.S. Census Bureau

**References**

Hetzel, L., and A. Smith. 2001. *The 65 Years and Over Population: 2000.* U.S. Bureau of the Census, C2KBR/01-10. Washington, DC: U.S. Census Bureau.

Himes, C.L. 2001. "Elderly Americans." *Population Bulletin 56, No. 4.* Washington, DC: Population Reference Bureau.

United Nations Population Division. 2002a. *World Population Projects: The 2000 Revision.* Available online at http://www.geohive.com/charts/pop_age.php.

United Nations Population Division. 2002b. *World Population Projects: The 2000 Revision.* Available online at http://www.geohive.com/charts/pop_lifespan.php.

U.S. Census Bureau. 1999. *Population Projections Program, Population Division.* Available online at http://www.census.gov/population/www/projections/natsum-T3.html.

*Sandra L. Reynolds*

**AGING INTO DEBT,** the increasing numbers of midlife and older consumers indebted to banks, retailers, and credit card companies for the purchase of goods and services. The most rapid growth of consumer debt has been by Americans who are least able to pay it off, among them older workers and retirees. Between 1977 and 1986, the debt/income ratio rose only modestly for adults aged 35 to 44 (81.4% to 81.5%) and 45 to 54 (58.4% to 62.0%) but climbed dramatically for adults aged 55 to 64 (35.7% to 51.8%) and those aged 65 to 74 (19.4% to 41.2%). According to a recent study of household debt by SRI Consulting Business Intelligence, households under 65 years old reported a 95% increase in debt from 1992 to 2000, whereas households over 65 years old reported a 164% increase. Not surprisingly, the Consumer Bankruptcy Project at Harvard University (Sullivan 2001) found that the fastest growth in consumer bankruptcy in the 1990s was among the oldest households. Between 1991 and 1999, the study reports that bankruptcy filings increased 120% among households aged 55 to 64 years old and 119% among households over 65 years old. In 2001, the authors estimated that nearly 82,000 seniors filed for bankruptcy—up from almost 24,000 in 1991. Although medical expenses and the loss of a spouse are the most common reasons for bankruptcy among U.S. seniors, a growing factor is the rise of consumer loans—especially credit card debts—that are used to provide financial assistance to family members (particularly children and grandchildren).

The societal trend of rising consumer indebtedness is ominous as today's relatively debt-free retirement population is being replaced with more financially insecure segments of the baby boom generation. Indeed, boomers are much more tolerant of credit card debt than Depression Era seniors. This is illustrated by a 1998 U.S. Federal Reserve Board survey (based on respondents' self-reports) that includes questions on credit card payment practices. The following responded that they "Almost Always Pay Off Balance":

under 39 years old (39.0%), 35 to 44 years (46.5%), 45 to 54 years (48.2%), 55 to 64 years (61.0%), 65 to 74 years (74.0%), and over 75 years (86.3%). Significantly, the survey was conducted at the end of the longest economic expansion in U.S. history. This suggests that many members of the boomer groups (35 to 44 and 45 to 54 years old) opted to revolve their high-cost consumer debts even during their prime income-earning years; only 1.7% more older boomers paid off their credit card balances than younger boomers. Overall, this consumer debt pattern reflects greater financial obligations due to life-cycle needs, structural constraints (lower income, higher cost of living, employment disruptions) as well as cultural factors such as a preference for consumption over saving.

Credit card use among seniors is increasing. As younger cohorts of credit-dependent households age, they are replacing older adults without credit cards. As a result, the proportion of seniors with credit cards jumped sharply in the 1990s, from only 45% in 1992 to about 60% in 2000. Three out of every four U.S. households now possess universal credit cards. According to the SRI Consulting Business Intelligence study, the proportion of seniors with some consumer debt rose from 35% in 1992 to nearly 60% in 2000. This is consistent with the sharp escalation of credit card debt during this period and with the growing importance of consumer credit to America's older citizens.

In 2002, three out of five U.S. households revolved charges on their credit card accounts. On average, the cumulative net, outstanding credit card debt per "revolver" household was over $13,000 in 2002. This is instructive since those income groups least able to repay high-interest consumer loans have registered the greatest increase over the last decade. According to data from the Survey of Consumer Finances (SCF), the largest increase was reported by the working poor (annual income less than $10,000), followed by senior citizens (65 years and older). Between 1989 and 1998, average credit card debt among all households with an outstanding balance increased 66%, from $2,482 to $4,120. Among low-income households, it soared from $494 to $2,030 (311%) and it climbed from $1,497 to $3,608 (141%) among the oldest households.

The most striking differences in consumer credit card use among older Americans are associated with age and gender. Seniors in the United States are not a homogenous population as reflected in their different social activities and consumption patterns. The lifestyle of Americans 55 to 70 years old is distinct from those aged 70 to 75. The younger group is much more active, and its middle-class members are more able to enjoy and to afford travel and leisure activities such as entertainment, education programs, and cultural events. According to AARP, over two-thirds of its VISA cardholders are between 50 and 65 years old, and most of their purchases are for hotel accommodations, plane tickets, restaurant meals, and consumer catalog products. In response to the growing demand of its members, AARP offered its first fixed-rate VISA card in 1990 and added four "Classic" VISAs and a VISA Gold Card four years later. AARP's exclusive credit card marketing contract yields millions of dollars in annual royalties to the association. Members should examine the terms of their AARP "affinity" credit cards to determine whether they are receiving the most competitive benefits available.

The analysis of credit card use by the oldest seniors is more complex due to variations in family resources, cultural attitudes, and gender differences. The oldest age groups experience changing familial roles as well as the loss of a spouse, other family members, and friends. These groups are more likely to be composed of single women (especially widows) with fewer financial resources, and less experience and employment outside of the household. In addition, older senior women are more likely to be primarily dependent on the retirement and Social Security benefits of their husbands. They are least likely to have credit cards, since many lose them following the loss of an authorizing spouse, and they may lack an established credit history on their own.

Two other factors characterize the credit usage patterns of America's oldest seniors. First, those older than 70 are most likely to be culturally averse to using consumer credit due to harsh memories of the Great Depression and lack of familiarity with current consumer lending practices. Moreover, older seniors tend to pay for purchases with cash or checks. Lack of experience with revolving credit underlies the skepticism of many seniors to "amazing" credit card offers or fear that banks will charge exorbitant fees and interest rates. In fact, ignorance of these new bank lending practices is responsible for occasional inquiries from older AARP members about whether credit card purchases are free "gifts." In addition, many older seniors are lonely and look forward to the empowerment, entertainment, or companionship of discussing orders with catalog or home shopping salespeople, not to mention the excitement of the anticipated arrival of their purchases. AARP records indicate a high purchase-return cycle among the oldest cardholders, especially after they realize that credit purchases are returnable and refundable.

### Corporate Policies and Consumer Issues

As U.S. longevity increases and health care costs soar, many older Americans face the prospect of outliving their retirement resources. Personal health and maintenance expenses are escalating, and more of America's older adults have little recourse but to use credit for purchasing necessary medicines and even groceries. Moreover, many seniors who had planned on living in a mortgage-free home are finding that rising tax assessments, escalating insurance premiums, and other home maintenance–related costs are claiming a growing portion of their fixed incomes. At the same time, difficult job markets, divorce, and life-cycle crises are leading adult children and grandchildren to seek help with living expenses or even to share the residences of older relatives. More recently, retirees on fixed incomes are encountering greater personal pressure to provide financial assistance to family members by borrowing from costly bank credit cards. This new access to financial resources is not only exacerbating stressful family relations but also leading to new forms of financial elder abuse and fraud. Many low-income seniors are being targeted for fraudulent financial schemes and financial (and physical) abuse because of the availability of bank credit cards. These range from impersonal telemarketing scams to improper "loans" to flagrant theft by nursing staff and even relatives and neighbors.

For most seniors, greater practical knowledge about credit can help ease some of the anxieties and burdens of consumer debt. First, the Equal Credit Opportunity Act (ECOA) of 1975 forbids discrimination in granting access to credit on the basis of race, color, religion, national origin, sex, marital status, or age. While minimum financial standards must be satisfied for credit approval, industry practices still exist that effectively evade antidiscrimination statutes such as credit score procedures that may impact credit applications based on the age, race, or gender of the applicant. Creditors cannot discriminate against persons receiving income from Social Security or public assistance and must establish clear criteria for their credit-scoring systems that evaluate income from annuities and pensions. Even so, creditworthiness standards can include age as a factor as long as the evaluation procedures are statistically defensible.

Various forms of indirect discrimination may be widespread, but they are hard to prove in the consumer credit industry. The reasons are that banks tend to initiate the credit card application process, many people are involved in the final approval, and a variety of formulas are used that are based on different interpretations of personal credit histories and other subjective factors. For example, seniors tend to have low income-to-asset ratios and few consumer debts. The credit-scoring system, however, favors consumers with higher incomes and a current history of repaying installment and revolving loans. As a result, debt-free seniors with low monthly incomes will tend to receive relatively lower, aggregate credit scores from consumer reporting agencies (CRAs). This subtle form of institutional discrimination is significant since consumer credit scores are the primary information used in the process of evaluating consumer loan applications.

Although the ECOA guarantees fair access to consumer credit, its purview does not include other sources of discrimination such as credit limits, interest rates, and financial penalties. Other federal laws such as the Truth in Lending Act (TILA) and the Fair Credit Reporting Act (FCRA) are concerned with the obligation of credit card companies to disclose the financial terms of their lending agreements and to explain the decision to reject an application for a consumer loan.

One problem with consumer credit practices involves the rise of deceptive "bait-and-switch" policies. That is, a favorable contract initially is offered to the consumer and is subsequently amended by fine-print inserts that can impose a higher interest rate and fee structure, force arbitration over disputes, reduce the "grace" period, give fewer membership benefits, and increase annual member fees as well as add other new contractual terms. Many companies will not explain specific reasons for raising an interest rate, which may be based on the payment history or outstanding loans with other financial institutions.

If the interest rate on a credit card has been suddenly increased and/or a consumer loan application has been denied, it is important that the consumer obtain a personal credit report from each of the three credit reporting agencies listed below. Each CRA receives information from different sources, and thus all three should be scrutinized. Under the FCRA, a consumer has the right to a free credit report each time an application for a loan has been rejected; some states require CRAs to offer one free credit report to their residents every 12 months. After examining the credit report(s), the consumer should immediately send a written request (by mail or fax) to change inaccurate information with any substantiating documentation. For example, errors typically encountered include loans that were mistakenly added to the file, old information still on file (negative information should be deleted after seven to ten years), debts from an ex-spouse or family members, and "phantom" loans due to bank mergers where the same debt is reported multiple times under the name of different financial institutions. Under the FCRA, the CRA must respond to the consumer's written request within 60 days.

Consumers must be vigilant in examining their monthly credit card statements for clerical errors and unknown charges so that they can be contested as soon as possible. This is due to the increase in telemarketing campaigns that are designed to confuse seniors while surreptitiously obtaining their permission to join a new or special membership program. In many cases, seniors do not understand that they have given their "oral consent" to a "trial period" since a formal contract was not signed and mailed to the company. Instead, they are shocked to learn that the membership and/or purchase costs are conveniently billed to their credit card accounts. This hard-sell tactic is used most commonly by companies selling magazine subscriptions, credit protection programs, and insurance products. This is the reason that telemarketers request permission to record the conversation with you as proof of a verbal contract.

In order to terminate these programs and rescind their fees, a letter disputing the charges must be written directly to the complaint department of the bank that issues the credit card (different from the address for sending the monthly payment) or directly to the company that provides the product or service. Calling the customer service department of the credit card company will not necessarily initiate the process for canceling past and future charges from the telemarketing company. In fact, a credit card account will continue to be charged at regular intervals—even indefinitely—and the right to dispute such charges, if a letter is not sent to the appropriate complaint department, may be inadvertently waived.

The primary reason for credit reporting agencies and credit card companies to compile detailed personal consumer histories is to assess individual creditworthiness. Unfortunately, these consumer profiles have become valuable resources for other companies to market their products. The result is an intensifying struggle over personal privacy. Indeed, financial institutions not only estimate the probability of expected consumer repayment of installment loans, but they are also interested in what a person is buying and where the products are purchased. Thus, creditors and mass marketers know much more about consumption and living patterns than could have been imagined only a couple of decades ago. This has important implications for future mass-marketing campaigns as well as the fraudulent use of consumer credit accounts.

### Advocacy Groups Unsuccessful

Consumer advocacy groups have not been successful in enacting a federal "opt-in" provision that requires personal authorization for the selling or "sharing" of private consumer information to other commercial interests. As a result, the new financial services "conglomerates" such as Citigroup (merger of Citibank and Traveler's Group) are permitted by federal law to share individual background information with all of their subsidiaries. This explains how obtaining a Citibank credit card can lead to solicitations from its separate insurance and investment divisions. For example, a high savings account balance may produce unwanted solicitations for mutual funds from Citigroup's investment subsidiary (Salomon Smith Barney), while a medical condition may lead to a rejection for a Traveler's insurance policy and the subsequent denial of a Citibank loan application.

At present, the only recourse for consumers is to contact their individual credit card companies and request that they "opt out" from existing corporate marketing programs that share their personal consumer information with other corporations. This lack of protection of personal information has contributed to the unprecedented increase in "identity theft." This is the fraudulent procurement and use of credit by assuming another person's identity. Most people do not know that they have been victims until they are contacted by debt collectors or are rejected for new credit cards or other consumer loans. Further information on this important topic is available from the U.S. Federal Trade

Commission (a complaint can be filed from its Web site), the Consumers Union, and the U.S. Public Interest Research Group.

As the financial pain of consumer debt absorbs a growing proportion of household incomes, the appeal of home equity and debt consolidation loans has soared. The 1986 federal tax reform law phased out the deductibility of interest charges (over five years) on consumer debt such as credit cards and auto loans. As a result, one of the few options for reducing the effective cost of consumer credit is to convert credit card debt into home equity loans with fully deductible interest. Unfortunately, many families have learned the hard lesson that higher mortgage payments together with unforeseen economic crises (medical expenses, job loss, divorce) can result in the loss of their home through bank foreclosure and even bankruptcy. Another costly surprise may occur when consumer debts are purposefully hidden from household members. The unsuspecting spouse is astounded to learn that he or she is obligated to pay for one-half of all the consumer debts incurred during the marriage, regardless of the reasons for the loans and who benefited from them. This is relevant in the case of divorce but not in the case of death, since heirs cannot inherit the personal debts of the deceased unless they have cards issued in their own names. Of course, creditors do have the legal right to file claims on the financial assets of the estate while it is in probate.

### Debt Consolidation Strategies

Increasingly, many financially desperate households have found that the encumbrances of consumer credit have pushed them to the precipice of bankruptcy and into the tangled web of debt consolidation companies. Not all "nonprofit" debt management companies serve the consumers' interest, and many are created merely to benefit the business founders. As a result, these companies must be selected with caution due to the large numbers of "upfront" fees that are required. In addition, most nonprofit enterprises receive a substantial amount of their operating expenses from the financial services industry and actually are created to serve the interest of creditors. These factors should be used as a guide for evaluating potential debt management companies. If a company is not certified by the National Foundation for Consumer Counseling (NFCC), the terms of the contract and its claims for negotiating lower payoff settlements should be examined with greater vigilance. Some reputable nonprofit agencies are listed below.

Lastly, many families have developed mutual aid strategies to help relatives who have found themselves overwhelmed with consumer debt. Some even cut up credit cards or freeze them in a glass of water. Psychologists suggest special care during the holidays and other meaningful social events when many people tend to overuse their credit cards. Suggested remedies range from managing a household fund for gift-giving expenses throughout the year to limiting the number of gifts or total cost of all holiday giving. Such suggested changes in personal behavior may not offer much help to the growing number of people who rely on their credit cards for necessities, although they may provide guidance for those who use them for discretionary purchases. The latter is important to those aging baby boomers who soon will be confronting their retirement with smaller nest eggs and greater personal indebtedness than their parents. Although older Americans have been more successful in resisting credit card debt, tomorrow's senior citizens may find it an unwelcome encumbrance in coping with the financial vagaries of their "golden years." (See also BABY BOOMERS AND RETIREMENT; BANKING

SERVICES FOR THE MATURE MARKET; BANKRUPTCY; CONSUMER CREDIT; CREDIT SCORES; EDUCATION OF OLDER ADULTS; FINANCIAL RECOVERY IN LATER LIFE; LEISURE; MARKETING TO MATURE ADULTS.)

### Organizations

About, Inc.
Bank Rate
Card Rate
Card Web
Credit Card Nation

### Consumer Credit Reporting Agencies

Equifax
Experian
TransUnion

### Nonprofit Consumer Credit Counseling Services

Coalition for Responsible Lending
Consumer Counseling Centers of America, Inc.
Consumer Federation of America
Consumers Union
Council of Better Business Bureau
Debtors Anonymous

### Federal Regulatory Agencies

Green Path Debt Solutions
National Consumer Law Center
National Foundation for Consumer Counseling

### Nonprofit Consumer Action Organizations

Springboard, Consumer Credit Counseling Service
U.S. Federal Reserve System
U.S. Federal Trade Commission
U.S. House of Representatives, Committee on Financial Services
U.S. Public Interest Research Group
U.S. Senate, Committee on Banking, Housing, and Urban Affairs
U.S. Treasury, Office of the Comptroller of the Currency

### Suggested Readings

Daskaloff, Alexander. 1999. *Credit Card Debt: Reduce Your Financial Burden in Three Easy Steps*. New York: William Morrow & Company.

DeGraff, John, David Wann, and Thomas H. Naylor. 2001. *Affluenza: The All-Consuming Epidemic*. Seattle, WA: Berrett-Koehler Publishers.

*Enough!* Center for a New American Dream, 6930 Carroll Avenue, #900, Takoma Park, MD 20912; (877) 683–7326. Available online at http://www.newdream.org/.

Matthews, Arlene Modica. 1993. *Your Money, Your Self: Understanding Your Relationship to Cash and Credit*. New York: Simon & Schuster.

Newtonian Finances Ltd. 2003. *Credit Card Nation*. Education Modules. Available online at www.creditcardnation.com/.

### References

Drentea, Patricia. 2000. "Age, Debt and Anxiety." *Journal of Health and Social Behavior* 41 (December): 437–50.

Kennickell, Arthur B., Martha Starr-McCluer, and Brian J. Surette. 1998. "Summary Descriptions of 1998 Survey Results." *Federal Reserve Bulletin* 86: 1–29.

Mishel, Lawrence, Jared Bernstein, and Heather Boushey. 2003. *The State of Working America 2002–03*. Ithaca, NY: Cornell University Press.

Pollin, Robert. 1990. *Deeper in Debt: The Changing Financial Conditions of U.S. Households*. Washington, DC: Economic Policy Institute.

Seniors USA. 2002. "American Seniors Rack Up Debt Like Never Before." Available online at http://senrs.com.

SRI Consulting Business Intelligence. 2003. "Do You Have Too Much Debt?" Available online at http://www.SmartMoney.com/debt/calculator/index.cfm?story=debt-toomuch.

Sullivan, Teresa A., Deborah Thorne, and Elizabeth Warren. 2001. "Young, Old, and in between: Who Files for Bankruptcy?" *Norton Bankruptcy Law Adviser* 9A (September). Rochester, NY: West Group.

Sullivan, Teresa A., Elizabeth Warren, and Jay L. Westbrook. 2000. *The Fragile Middle Class: Americans in Debt*. New Haven, CT: Yale University Press.

Survey of Consumer Finances. 2000. "Recent Changes in U.S. Family Finances: Results from the 1998 Survey of Consumer Finances." Available online at http://www.hec.ohio-state.edu/scf/.

*Robert D. Manning*

**ANNUITIES,** the right to receive fixed, periodic payments, either for life or for a term of years. Annuity contracts purchased from insurance companies may start the payments right away (immediate annuities) or may start them at some future date (deferred annuities). Annuities can be purchased with either a lump sum of money (single premium annuity) or a series of payments (flexible premium annuity). Any money put into an annuity will earn a return. How it earns the return depends on whether it is a fixed annuity, an equity-indexed annuity, or a variable annuity. The money put into the annuity plus the earnings are the annuity account value. All annuities have both tax advantages and tax disadvantages, depending on perspective and the tax-triggering event. Annuities are the only financial instrument that can shift longevity risk—the risk of outliving assets—from an individual to an insurance company.

An annuity is a contract between the purchaser of the annuity and an insurance company on behalf of an annuitant or annuitants—the person or people who will receive the payments under the terms of the contract. Most commonly, the annuitant and the owner are one and the same person, but they do not have to be. The policyholder may also have a beneficiary to whom ownership of the annuity, or the right to receive payments, will pass in the event of the owner's death. The beneficiary is unlikely to be the same person as the annuitant but may be.

### Fixed Annuities

In fixed annuities, the insurance company guarantees that the money deposited in the annuity will not decline in value. The insurance company will absorb any investment loss and retain any investment gain. The insurance company will also credit interest to the monies deposited in the annuity based on its investment experience and both market and marketing considerations. This has both positive and negative implications. Although insurance companies appear to assume all of the investment risk in fixed-rate fixed annuities, this is only true with regard to the principal investment, not with regard to return on the investment. The common objection to fixed annuities is that the rate of interest credited is variable at the insurance company's discretion, albeit within parameters stated in the policy. Because an insurance company's investment experience may fluctuate, relative to the market, rates of interest credited to a block of in-force policies may be less than competitive from time to time.

### Equity-Indexed Annuities

Equity-indexed annuities (EIAs) were developed to respond to the concerns raised by the negative implications of fixed annuities. EIAs are fixed annuities that share the advantages of other fixed annuities—primarily, that the account value is guaranteed not to decline regardless of what happens in the stock and bond markets and that interest earnings are not subject to current income taxation—but they shift the determination of how much interest to credit to the annuity from the insurance company to an independent equity index such as the Standard & Poor's 500 (S&P 500). For example, if during a given year the S&P 500 index increases by 7.4%, then an EIA linked to it would be credited with 7.4% interest, regardless of how much the company actually earned. Different companies use different indexes, with the S&P 500 the most common, but the NASDAQ, NASDAQ 100, Russell 2000, and Dow Jones Industrial Average are also available. Some EIAs allow a choice as to the percentage of the annuity value to be indexed to each of a number of indexes, or a fixed account. There are also other variables (such as participation rate, cap, and measuring period) in the interest crediting formulas of equity-indexed annuities that differ from company to company and annuity to annuity, which make comparing EIAs more difficult.

### Variable Annuities

Variable annuities represent the opposite end of the risk spectrum from fixed annuities. In variable annuities, the policyholder takes on the risk for both principal and interest by allocating deposits to the annuity among "subaccounts" that are similar to mutual funds and will rise and fall with market conditions. For example, if the underlying subaccounts decline 30% in value, then the policyholder's annuity account also declines 30% in value. Conversely, if the underlying subaccounts increase 20% in value, then the policyholder's account value increases at a like rate. Policyholders have the right to move their underlying investments among subaccounts with reasonable frequency, so that they can allocate their funds to the market sectors with which they feel most comfortable at a point in time. Variable annuities have mortality and expense risk charges and administrative fees on top of the loads and expenses in the subaccounts, so that performance is partially offset by expenses—which can be significant.

### Withdrawals

It is generally not possible for an annuity owner to withdraw *all* of the money placed in an annuity without penalty for some period of time because of surrender charges. Surrender charges are imposed to protect the insurance company against loss of the use of funds paid in, or receipt of expenses and fees, before it has a chance to recuperate the costs it incurs in issuing the annuity. These costs include commissions and, in some cases, bonuses to the policyholder, along with the administrative costs associated with the policy. Surrender charges are usually only imposed during the first 6 to 12 years of a policy's existence. After surrender charges expire and before annuitization, all the monies in the account can be removed without penalty.

In addition, it is common for a policyholder to be able to withdraw some percentage—usually 10%—of either premiums paid or the account value (premiums paid plus interest credited) each year without penalty. Taking periodic payments (annuitizing the contract), even over a very short period of time, will often preempt imposition of surrender charges. Further, some policies waive surrender charges in the event of nursing home admission or similar life situations. Once periodic payments start and the annuity is "annuitized," there is almost no chance of stopping the payments and getting a lump sum instead, although that may be one of the annuity options.

### Annuity Payouts

Subject to the kinds of restrictions or penalties noted, the owner of an annuity can receive money from an annuity in amounts that range from the full amount to whatever the insurance company will pay per period for a given length of time. This ability to convert assets to income is what annuities were designed to do. What sets them apart from other financial instruments are the guarantees available during payout, the most important being the guarantee to pay for the life of an annuitant. A common error in the financial community is to compare guaranteed annuity payouts with nonguaranteed rates of return on investment instruments, discounting the value of annuity guarantees. As the population's life expectancy extends toward age 100 and investment managers continue to experience volatile markets, these guarantees become increasingly valuable.

Whether purchasing an immediate annuity or annuitizing a deferred annuity, an owner has several choices for how frequently he or she wants payments made—monthly, quarterly, semiannually, or annually—and for how long they are to be guaranteed. While the owner makes the choices, it is the annuitant who receives the payments and whose life is used to measure life-term guarantees. The following classifications are the most common terms guaranteed under annuity payment obligations:

*Term certain*, also known as *period certain*, involves the promise of the insurance company to make payments for a specified number of years regardless of the number of years the annuitant survives. For example, with a 20-year period certain annuity, the insurance company commits to payments for 240 months, even if the annuitant dies prior to the end of the 20-year term (the balance of payments would be received by a named beneficiary). It should be noted that the longer the period certain, the lower the amount of money the insurance company guarantees to pay periodically for the term of the annuity payout.

*Life contingencies* are commitments by the insurance company to make payments until the annuitant, or the last survivor of two or more annuitants, dies. Life contingencies guarantee that the annuitant cannot outlive his or her money and thereby shift longevity risk from an individual to the population at large through the medium of the insurance company. There are three general categories of life contingencies: life only, life with minimum guarantees, and joint life (with or without minimum guarantees). *Life-only* annuities guarantee an amount of money will be paid periodically (usually monthly) to the annuitant for as long as the annuitant lives. Of the life contingency payouts, life only has the highest periodic payment and, depending on the age of the annuitant, life only may offer the highest of any annuity payout option.

*Life with minimum guarantees.* Although it is inherent in the nature of risk spreading that some people will appear to "win" by living a long time and others will appear to "lose" by dying relatively soon after payments commence, insurance companies offer optional minimum guarantees for those who are uncomfortable with this reality. The lowest form of guarantee, and therefore the least penalty to the amount of the monthly payout, is the guarantee to make payments for the life of the annuitant or at least until the amount of the premium (in an immediate annuity) or the account value (in a deferred annuity) has been paid out. This is known as *life with installment refund.* A variation is *life with immediate refund*, wherein the promise of the insurance company is to make periodic payments for the life of the annuitant and, should the annuitant die before the premium or account value has been paid out, refund the balance in a lump sum upon proof of death. The monthly payment in a life with installment refund will be slightly lower than the monthly payment in a life-only arrangement, and the monthly payment in a life with immediate refund will be lower than in a life with installment refund arrangement.

The next step away from life only is *life with a minimum period certain*, most commonly life with 10 or 20 years certain but available with a wide variety of minimum guarantee periods. In a life with 10 years certain arrangement ("life and 10"), the insurance company guarantees to make periodic payments for as long as the annuitant lives, but should the annuitant die before 120 monthly payments have been made, payments go to the beneficiary for the balance of the 120 months.

*Joint life* guarantees may be had with or without the kinds of guarantees covered above but primarily exist to make it possible for a couple to have the security of knowing neither partner can outlive their money. *Joint and survivor* (sometimes referred to as "joint and full survivor" or "joint and 100% survivor") refers to an annuity whose payments are based on the life expectancies of two or more individuals, most commonly the lives of a husband and wife. Under the terms of a joint and survivor annuity, the payout period is calculated based on the combined life expectancies of the husband and wife. The death of one spouse does not end the obligation of the insurance company to continue paying benefits to the surviving spouse. In fact, the entire basis of a joint and survivor annuity rests on the principle that payments will continue to be made regardless of which spouse survives the other. Payments under a joint and survivor annuity are lower than payments based on the life of one individual alone. Payments made under a *joint and X% survivor* arrangement would be less severely discounted because the insurance company's guarantee would be smaller than under a straight *joint and full survivor* arrangement. For example, a *joint and 50% survivor* arrangement would guarantee a certain amount to be paid periodically for as long as both of the annuitants are alive, then half that amount to be paid for as long as the survivor of them lives. This is obviously a less expensive guarantee than the promise to pay the same amount as long as either of two annuitants lives.

Annuity payments, regardless of whether from a fixed or variable deferred annuity or the purchase of an immediate annuity, are usually fixed from the point where they commence. Regardless of inflation, changes in bond and money instrument yields, or equity market performance, the amount determined at the point of annuitization is the amount that is paid out for the duration of the annuity, which may stretch into decades. In the late 1990s and early years of the twenty-first century, inflation has been an impediment to wider use of annuities for retirement income.

The insurance industry has begun to respond. It is now possible to link annuity payouts to the same financial indexes as equity-indexed annuities use during the deferral period. On the variable side, it is possible for annuity payouts to be linked to the underlying performance of stock, bond, and money market subaccounts, just as during the deferral period (variable annuitization). These relatively new developments are made possible by availability of options and financial derivatives that can be used to hedge or back up insurance companies' guarantees.

### Tax Treatment of Annuities

The great attraction of deferred annuities, whether fixed or variable, is that all earnings that accrue during the deferral period are free from current income taxation. Depending on the length of a deferral period, and the income tax bracket of the owner, the effect of this tax deferral can double or even triple the value of an account at the point of surrender or annuitization. Advocates of variable annuities, especially, were able to portray this as an ideal solution to the problem of funding retirement income during the bull markets of the 1990s.

The payback is that every dollar of gain withdrawn from an annuity is treated as ordinary income rather than capital gain. While the logic of this is easy to grasp for fixed annuities, since interest is taxed as ordinary income, it can be harder for variable annuity advocates to explain (or to explain away) since it means giving up favorable capital gains treatment. As with every financial decision, the benefits of current income tax deferral must be weighed against the exposure to higher income taxation later.

Annuity payments are treated as partially excluded from income taxation, at least until the total investment in the contract has been recovered. The amount of each payment that can be excluded is determined by dividing the investment in the contract (generally, total premiums paid minus any prior nontaxable distributions) by the "expected return" under the contract and multiplying the payment by that ratio, known as the *exclusion ratio*. The expected return is determined by multiplying the amount of the payment by the remaining number of payments. That, in turn, is determined either by the terms of the contract (in the case of period certain arrangements) or by the use of life expectancy tables provided by the Internal Revenue Service. The effect of this is to spread the income tax burden over a much longer period of time than would be available with a lump-sum distribution.

As with other financial matters, tax considerations do not end with death. The full value of deferred annuities that have not been annuitized are includable in the estate of the owner at the time of the owner's death, and beneficiaries receive no stepped-basis on the gains in the contract. Some variable annuities have death benefits to accomplish the same result, however. In addition, deferral cannot continue unless the beneficiary is the spouse. In general, distributions must begin within one year of the owner's death and must be paid out over the greater of the life expectancy of the beneficiary or five years.

### Private Annuities

By contrast to commercial annuities, private annuities are not paid by insurance companies but rather are arrangements between individuals by which property is exchanged for a series of payments, generally with a life contingency. Private annuities are frequently established where a property that is being exchanged is of importance to the parties (usually a parent and a child), and there is a desire to maintain control over the property at the same time that the property is being removed from the estate of the transferor. In other words, private annuities are often established where a parent removes property from his or her estate and passes it to a child in exchange for a promise to make periodic payments of an agreed amount to the parent. Fair and accurate valuation of the transferred property and amounts of the periodic payments are important to receiving desirable income tax treatment. (See also AGENTS AND BROKERS; ASSET ALLOCATION AFTER RETIREMENT; CASH FLOW PLANNING FOR RETIREES; FINANCIAL PLANNING PROCESS; WEALTH SPAN.)

**Organization**

National Association for Variable Annuities

**References**

Conners, Brian, and James W. Eckel. 1999. *Planning for the Golden Years with Variable Annuities*. Lexington, MA: Lexington House.

Shapiro, David, and J. Streiff. 2001. *Annuities*. Chicago: Dearborn Trade Publishing.

Williamson, Gordon K. 1999. *Getting Started in Annuities*. New York: John Wiley & Sons.

*E. Craig MacBean*

**AREA AGENCIES ON AGING.** See Older Americans Act.

**ASSET ALLOCATION AFTER RETIREMENT,** an approach to investment decision making under age-specific circumstances. During working years, when assets are most likely to be acquired, asset allocation tends to follow traditional views of portfolio structure. After some provision for liquidity or emergency funds, which (for example) could be three to nine months' cash flow needs, other financial assets normally can be considered long term, permitting the investor to take more risk with his or her portfolio. Most financial advisors agree that people in their twenties or thirties should structure their retirement portfolios into various asset classes that are diversified and that are likely over time to provide high returns (albeit with volatility), such as common stocks or equity (stock) mutual funds that do not have a fixed or stated rate of return (fixed income). Securities without fixed incomes have a higher expected rate of return and historically have outperformed fixed income assets (e.g., bonds) by about 5% per year over long periods of time. (In some years these variable return investments earn several times the returns of fixed income assets, and in other years they have negative comparable returns. But over a reasonably long period, these equity securities are expected to outperform fixed return assets.)

Many people feel that it is worth the risk of uncertain return and increased volatility in order to obtain a rate of return that approximates an additional 5% on average per year. Consider a 25-year-old saver deciding between a fixed account with a 7% return and a variable account expected to earn 12%. If this saver invests $100 per month until age 65, the fixed account will be worth $262,481. If the variable return account had been chosen, however, the account may have grown to $1,176,477, a difference of $913,996. Since year-to-year variations in the equities markets have historically averaged a higher return, it is easy to see why young savers are directed into variable return investments and why they are advised to buy and hold them for the longer term. However, there is a built-in fallacy to this kind of thinking. It is linear and assumes that the returns will be the same percentage year in and year out. As investors age, however, their ability to take advantage of the benefits of variable return securities diminishes. The nature of retirement requires liquidation of assets to provide current income, and when assets are sold, a commensurate decline in income based on a decreasing capital account also occurs.

Fear of reduced income prompts many retirees to invest in more predictable fixed return assets, but this investment strategy risks possible loss from inflation. Sixty-five-year-olds, on average, have 17.3 years left to live (15.2 years for men and 19.0 years for women). This means that 65-year-old retirees must plan for at least 20 years of retirement. If they invest only in fixed return assets, they will achieve little real portfolio growth, due to inflation. A $250,000 retirement nest egg, for example, invested in fixed accounts earning 7% will provide an income of approximately $2,000 per month for 20 years. While this may be adequate today, inflation may reduce the purchasing power of this income over time. By the twentieth year, assuming an inflation rate of 3%, the purchasing power of $2,000 will be $1,107. At 5% inflation, this monthly income would be worth only $754. Many retirees face this potential dilemma as they try to allocate their financial assets. Investment only in stocks yields no current fixed income, but investments in fixed income securities may fail to meet their needs for growth to offset the effects of inflation.

### Mixed Allocations of Assets

A mixed allocation approach is called for, with some investments in fixed income assets and some portion invested in variable return assets. The question is, how much should be allocated to each type of investment, and how should this change as retirees grow older? Most retirees tend to worry more about market risk than inflation risk and tend to buy portfolios dominated by fixed return assets. Inflation effects must be considered, however, when the planning horizon is greater than five years. As a retiree ages, inflation risk becomes less important. Proper allocation, then, requires consideration of how time affects both market risk and inflation risk.

One common guideline that some advocate in this situation is to invest a percentage equal to 100 minus the retiree's age in variable return assets: for a 62-year-old, 38% (100 minus 62) of assets; the balance in fixed income assets. By the time one reaches age 75, this percentage will drop down to 25%. As individuals grow older, their expected planning horizon becomes shorter. This reduces the significance of inflation risk, making a more conservative approach appropriate. Healthy 60-year-olds may be justified in keeping more than 40% of their portfolios in variable return assets.

The basic principle underlying all retirement planning strategies regardless of the age of the planner is diversification. Individuals who have decided that they want to put 40% of their portfolio in variable return assets and 60% in fixed income assets still must decide how to invest within these asset classes. The overwhelming majority of people should invest through some type of mutual fund rather than trying to purchase individual securities. Mutual funds provide two essential elements not readily available to the purchasers of individual assets: diversification and low transaction cost. Mutual funds offer professional management for a management fee, which eliminates the need for constant analysis by savers but are generally a bargain for small investors.

With thousands of different mutual funds from which to choose, this can be complex. There are two approaches to this problem. First, savers can narrow the funds down independently. *Fortune* and *Forbes* magazines rank the performance history of many of the top funds on a yearly basis, and the rankings are done by category. As a place to start, investors should look at investment-grade bond funds for the fixed assets and the "growth and income" common stock funds for the variable assets. These rankings are complete with phone numbers that can be called to obtain additional information. A second approach would be to work with a professional financial advisor who can assist with portfolio selection.

Both of these approaches have pitfalls. By investing without an advisor to guide decision making, investors may miss valuable growth, income, and tax information. On the other hand, when professional financial advisors are contacted, advice may be motivated by self-interest rather than what is best for the retiree. Using a "fee-only" planner can mitigate this risk. In either case, it should be remembered that financial planning decisions rarely should be made in haste. One may simply put the money in a money market fund or certificate of deposit for a few weeks or even months during the decision-making period. Taking time to gather information from several sources before funds are invested is wise. If professional help is desired, several advisors may be contacted before making a decision as to who to retain. After the initial setup of the portfolio, changes will need to be made periodically in order to adjust for changes in the expected planning horizon and to rebalance the portfolio. A valuable guideline is to consider making changes at least once a year but not more than twice a year. The annual review is a time to consider changes.

Financial planning becomes more complicated prior to and during retirement. The need for current income invalidates the typical assumptions that long-range planners use. In order to balance the market risk and inflation risk associated with postretirement planning, a mixed approach must be employed. Assets must be allocated over both fixed income assets such as bonds and variable return assets such as common stock. As a retiree grows older, the balance of these two types of assets can change. However, these problems are not insurmountable. The guidelines suggested above provide a framework that will balance portfolios to provide for current income and allow for growth to overcome problems with inflation. (See also BONDS, CASH FLOW PLANNING FOR RETIREES; EQUITY SECURITIES; FINANCIAL ADVISORS; MUTUAL FUNDS; REAL ESTATE INVESTMENTS; RISK TOLERANCE; SAVINGS INVESTMENTS; WEALTH SPAN.)

**References**

Bernstein, William J., and David M. Darst. 2000. *The Intelligent Asset Allocator: How to Build Your Portfolio to Maximize Returns and Minimize Risk.* New York: McGraw-Hill.

Gibson, Roger C. 2000. *Asset Allocation: Balancing Financial Risk.* 3rd ed. New York: McGraw-Hill.

*Andrew Holmes*

**ASSET PROTECTION.** See Asset Allocation after Retirement; Cash Flow Planning for Retirees; Estate Planning; Financial Advisors; Financial Counseling for Mid- to Later Life; Medicaid; Trusts; Wills.

**ASSISTED LIVING,** living arrangements that promote the philosophy of personal control and responsibility for frail older persons within homelike group residences. Assisted living arrangements generally include:

- Group or congregate living situations that provide room and board as well as social and recreational opportunities
- Assistance to residents who need help with personal care needs and supportive services
- Protective oversight or monitoring
- Help available around the clock and on an unscheduled basis.

As of 1998, approximately 521,000 residents lived in 11,500 U.S. facilities that were marketed or described by the administrator as assisted living or that were similar in size and services to self-described assisted living facilities (Hawes, Rose, and Phillips 1999). However, only 4,693 of these facilities provided either or both the level of services or privacy consistent with the assisted living philosophy (Hawes, Phillips, and Rose 2000). These facilities served nearly 200,000 residents. In the assisted living setting, residents remain in charge of their own lives. They exert as much responsibility as their physical and mental capacities permit, including their right to make decisions about their care and safety.

Many facilities and states that do not use the term *assisted living* have programs that meet this definition. Conversely, this definition does not include facilities that offer little personal care assistance or privacy, or nursing homes that offer institutional care, even if they describe themselves as offering assisted living. Usually, residential facilities using the term *assisted living* espouse a philosophy of maximizing resident autonomy, providing a homelike environment, meeting residents' scheduled and unscheduled needs, and minimizing the need to move. However, the degree to which their management practices reflect the philosophy may vary.

### Background

Prior to the growth of assisted living, much of the discussion about reforming long-term care had focused on institutional care and centered on nursing home financing and access—how to provide nursing home care to people without impoverishing them or depleting the public treasury. Since the late 1980s, however, private developers and administrators of state programs led by Oregon have offered assisted living as a way of providing support services in a group residential environment. Assisted living offers many frail older persons appropriate care while preserving their dignity and autonomy, and in many situations, it can do so at lower cost than nursing homes or home care. Frail older persons, fearing the institutional character and loss of independence associated with life in a nursing home, have embraced the arrangements and philosophy of assisted living.

The aim of assisted living is to enable frail older persons to live as independently as possible in a homelike atmosphere. This is accomplished through building design and care practices that facilitate independent functioning and reinforce residents' autonomy, dignity, privacy, and right to make choices. The philosophy of resident independence encompasses the concept of "the dignity of risk," also advocated by members of the disability community. It asserts the rights of residents to make decisions about their care and safety that others may consider risky. It is based on the notion that psychological health and well-being should be considered along with physical safety.

### Living Arrangements and Assistance

In better facilities, the design of the building reflects the philosophy of promoting independence. Residents usually live either in private rooms with baths, individual temperature controls, and doors that lock or in small apartments with kitchenettes. They often bring their own furniture. The decor and scale are homelike throughout the building, often with one or more small sitting rooms that encourage residents to visit with each other and entertain guests. Many assisted living facilities explicitly avoid fluorescent lighting, long corridors, tile floors, and the nursing stations that are associated with nursing homes. The facilities, however, typically provide handrails, wide hallways, some type of emergency call system, and grab bars and other features in bathrooms, all of which help assure physical security and promote independence. The buildings also include a laundry, central kitchen, and other areas to support the delivery of services.

Assisted living buildings vary in size and type. They may be freestanding structures expressly designed to enhance the independence of frail older persons. Many continuing care retirement communities have a campus that includes three levels of housing and services: independent housing with some social and recreational services and perhaps one communal meal, an assisted living building to which residents move when they need personal care assistance or monitoring, and a separate building for nursing care. Other structures, including large private homes, schools, hotels, and nursing homes, have been remodeled to accommodate assisted living programs. The size of the buildings ranges from those in which 15 or fewer residents live (often in remodeled homes) to those with 100 or more residents. In building new structures, many developers choose to accommodate about 30 to 70 residents, which they believe is few enough to retain some residential character but large enough to allow economies of scale in providing services.

The typical program of assistance offers help with at least some activities of daily living (ADLs)—dressing, bathing, using the toilet, transferring to and from a chair, or eating—as well as supervision of medication and protective oversight. Before moving in, the resident or a family member describes the resident's needs and works with the staff to decide what help will be provided, how, and when. Most facilities offer a standard package of services, but they differ in what they "bundle" into these packages. They may also provide additional services "in-house," if needed, but at a higher fee, or help arrange for such services, including nursing care, from a third-party provider. Residents can also obtain assistance around the clock. Other services usually available include help with arranging doctor appointments, transportation for shopping and other excursions, social and recreational activities, housekeeping, nutrition counseling, and provision for special diets. Residents' preferences are taken into account in the scheduling of services, such as help with a bath. Residents often have the option of doing their own laundry, making their beds, cleaning their apartments, and fixing tea and coffee or light meals. Relatives are also encouraged to visit and join in these tasks.

### Assisted Living Compared to Other Living Arrangements

While assisted living is similar to home care, congregate housing, board and care homes, and nursing homes, it differs from those programs in significant ways.

*Home Care.* The minimum time block for which home care usually can be scheduled is two hours. While this is ideal for help with dressing, bathing, housekeeping, and meal preparation, two-hour time blocks are inappropriate when assistance needs to be available throughout the day and evening. Assisted living can take advantage of economies of scale by using a core staff to offer both brief periods of assistance and general oversight to a much larger group of people than can home care. For this reason, assisted living is particularly appropriate for persons without friends or relatives to supplement assistance purchased from home health agencies.

*Congregate Housing.* Congregate housing programs usually offer support services such as a meal a day, transportation, and housekeeping to residents living in private apartment units. Although residents may be able to obtain assistance with some ADLs, even otherwise excellent congregate housing programs may not offer protective oversight and 24-hour assistance.

*Board and Care Homes.* Most board and care homes offer the protective oversight, homelike atmosphere, and some of the ADL assistance available in assisted living. However, board and care homes are generally smaller than assisted living facilities and typically do not provide the level of privacy or services found in assisted living. The board and care industry has been plagued with allegations of abuse and low quality, including putting residents at risk of harm from medications errors. Meager levels of public assistance available for the low-income residents who comprise about one-half of the population in board and care homes across the country exacerbate these problems (Hawes, Wildfire, and Luk 1993). In contrast, developers of assisted living have aimed their programs at moderate- and upper-income groups. However, many quality problems have recently been found in assisted living as well. These problems are most often due to low staffing levels, inadequate staff training, and high staff turnover.

*Nursing Homes.* Nursing homes usually care for persons with complex or unstable medical conditions who need continuing nursing supervision. Standardization of services in nursing homes and the assignment of two or more residents to a room, while encouraging quality care and cost control, have also contributed to nursing homes' institutional and regimented atmosphere. The requirement that a nurse always be on duty enables nursing homes to serve residents with various medical needs but adds a medical orientation to nursing home life and raises costs.

Studies comparing the costs of publicly subsidized nursing homes and assisted living have reached mixed conclusions. Cost data from Oregon, the only state to mandate assisted living to serve nursing home–eligible residents, do indicate some potential for savings. Rates for Oregon's assisted living residents who receive Medicaid, all of whom are nursing home–eligible, are about two-thirds as much as Medicaid rates for Oregon's nursing home residents (Hawes, Wildfire, and Luk 1993). That assisted living is serving persons with somewhat lower levels of service needs is illustrated by the fact that 20% of Oregon's assisted living residents eventually move to nursing homes. That 80% do not need to move to nursing homes, when many are nursing home–eligible, indicates the potential savings to both Medicaid programs and private-pay residents. Some studies, however, suggest that assisted living care does not save money, because many of the individuals served in assisted living would not have entered a nursing home in the absence of Medicaid funds for assisted living because family members would have continued to care for them at home.

### Private Sector Fees and Public Assistance Programs

Developers have built and marketed assisted living primarily for middle- to upper-income older persons—those able to pay $2,000 a month or more—a cost prohibitive for many older persons. According to a survey of 300 assisted living facilities in 1998, only 20% of facilities charged a single rate. The other 80% charged varying rates, depending upon room sizes or apartments or for assistance beyond the facility's standard package of services. Most of the basic monthly rates ranged between $1,100 and $2,900 per month (Hawes, Phillips, and Rose 2000). Only 7% of the residents surveyed by the National Investment Center (NIC) and the Assisted Living Federation of America (ALFA) (1998) received public assistance for services (provided through Medicaid), and only 9% received public assistance for shelter costs (provided through the federal Supplemental Security Income program).

Public assistance for low-income persons is almost always inadequate to cover charges in typical assisted living programs. The federal government provides Supplemental Security Income (SSI) payments to impoverished older and disabled persons, but the federal benefit rate was only $545 a month in 2002. Although most states and some counties provide an additional amount, the total is far short of the typical base cost of $2,000 for assisted living arrangements.

Since it began in 1965, the federal Medicaid program has subsidized care in nursing homes. States pay varying proportions of the Medicaid rate, from 21% to 50%, depending on the cost of nursing home care in the state and the per capita income in the state. States have begun recognizing that assisted living can postpone or substitute for some nursing home admissions, offering states the potential to reduce their Medicaid expenditures. In a National Academy for State Health Policy survey in 2000, Robert Mollica found that 38 states reported having approval for at least one Medicaid-sponsored program to fund services for persons in assisted living or board and care. Usually, these programs serve relatively few people or are otherwise limited in scope, but there are a few exceptions. The percentage of licensed facilities participating in Medicaid varies from a low of 2% in New Mexico to a high of 93% in Oregon (Mollica 2000). Nationwide, only 11% of assisted living administrators report that they would accept Medicaid, if available (Hawes, Phillips, and Rose 2000).

Because the cost of assisted living often exceeds residents' incomes, many residents spend down their assets to pay for assisted living. A 1999 study by the National Investment Center (NIC) found that nearly two-thirds (64%) of assisted living residents reported an annual income of less than $25,000, an amount insufficient to cover a year's stay in most assisted living facilities. Residents who had been in assisted living longer had significantly fewer net assets than newer residents, suggesting that many residents are spending down their assets.

### Financing Assisted Living Construction

Several efforts, both public and private, are helping assisted living become more affordable by lowering the cost of constructing assisted living facilities. The Department of Housing and Urban Development (HUD) has two programs that subsidize developers of affordable assisted living, allowing them to provide assisted living at a lower cost to consumers. Under the first program, the Assisted Living Conversion Program, HUD allocated $50 million per year from fiscal years 2000 to 2002 to provide grants to help owners of nonprofit low-income senior housing apartments to convert dwelling units into assisted living apartments (HUD 2001). The other HUD program, Section 232 of the Federal Housing Administration's (FHA) mortgage insurance program, was extended by the 1992 Housing Act to include assisted living facilities (Section 232 already covered nursing homes and board and care homes).

A private source of financing for the construction of affordable assisted living facilities is the Coming Home Program, a program of the National Cooperative Bank (NCB) Development Corporation in partnership with the Robert Wood Johnson Foundation. The Coming Home Program is providing three-year grants of up to $300,000 to nine states to foster affordable assisted living for low-income older persons. The program focuses on rural areas, where fewer assisted living facilities are available.

A few states have implemented programs that provide funds from the Medicaid program to help nursing home owners convert all or part of a nursing home to assisted living or other supportive service, such as adult day services, or to close the nursing home and construct a new assisted living facility. The first such program was instituted in Nebraska; the program provides grants or loan guarantees to nursing homes to convert wings or entire facilities. The state estimates that the Medicaid program will recover the costs of the program over a 13-year period through reduced Medicaid spending on nursing home care (Mollica 2000).

## Changes around the Corner

Stakeholders, including regulators, providers, and consumers and their advocates, continue to discuss many issues presented by this relatively new combination of housing and supportive services. Some of the issues and questions are frailty level (how much "aging in place" is appropriate for assisted living before a very frail resident needs to move to a nursing home?); living arrangements (should private rooms with baths be mandatory?); risk and autonomy (to what extent can the resident make decisions about lifestyle and care, even if the decision increases the resident's risk of health or safety problems?); flexibility of regulations (how much leeway should providers have to determine procedures in their facility?); and financing (how to make the advantages of assisted living available to persons with low income). (See also BOARD AND CARE HOMES; COMMUNITY-BASED CARE; CONTINUING CARE RETIREMENT COMMUNITIES [CCRCs]; FRAILTY PLANNING; HOME CARE SERVICES FOR OLDER ADULTS; HUD-ASSISTED RENTAL HOUSING; MEDICAID; NURSING HOMES.)

### Organizations

AARP
American Association of Homes and Services for the Aging (AAHSA)
American Senior Housing Association (ASHA)
Assisted Living Federation of America (ALFA)
Consumer Consortium on Assisted Living (CCAL)
National Center of Assisted Living (NCAL)
NCB Coming Home Project

**References**

Hawes, Catherine, Charles D. Phillips, and Miriam Rose. 2000. *High Service or High Privacy Assisted Living Facilities, Their Residents and Staff: Results from a National Survey*. Washington, DC: Department of Health and Human Services.

Hawes, Catherine, Miriam Rose, and Charles D. Phillips. 1999. *A National Study of Assisted Living for the Frail Elderly: Results of a National Survey of Facilities*. Washington, DC: Prepared for U.S. Department of Health and Human Services.

Hawes, Catherine, Judith Wildfire, and Linda Luk. 1993. "The Regulation of Board and Care Homes: Results of a Survey of the 50 States and the District of Columbia." *National Summary, State Summaries*. Washington, DC: AARP.

Lewin-VHI Inc. 1996. *National Study of Assisted Living for the Frail Elderly: Literature Review Update*. Washington, DC: Prepared for the Office of the Assistant Secretary for Planning and Evaluation & Administration on Aging, U.S. Department of Health and Human Services.

Lutzky, Steven, Lisa Maria B. Alecxih, Jennifer Duffy, and Christina Neill. 2000. *Review of the Medicaid 1915(C) Home and Community Based Services Waiver Program Literature and Program Data*. Washington, DC: Prepared for Department of Health and Human Services, Health Care Financing Administration.

Mollica, Robert. 2000. *State Assisted Living Policy: 2000*. Portland, ME: National Academy for State Health Policy.

National Investment Center (NIC). 1999. *Income Confirmation Study of Assisted Living Residents and the Age 75+ Population: A Follow-up to the NIC National Survey of Assisted Living Residents*. Annapolis, MD: Author.

National Investment Center (NIC) and Assisted Living Federation of America (ALFA). 1998. *National Survey of Assisted Living Residents: Who Is the Customer?* Annapolis, MD: Author.

NCB Development Corporation. 2001. *Affordable Assisted Living: Backgrounder*. Available online at http://www.ncbdc.org/.

Redfoot, Donald L. 1994. "Long-Term Care Reform and the Role of Housing Finance." *Housing Policy Debate* 4: 23–25.

Regnier, Victor A. 1994. *Assisted Living Housing for the Elderly: Design Innovations from the United States and Europe*. New York: Von Nostrand Reinhold.

U.S. Department of Housing and Urban Development (HUD). 2001. "Assisted Living Conversion Program (ALCP) for Eligible Multifamily Housing Projects." *Federal Register* 66(38): 12339–60.

U.S. General Accounting Office (GAO). 1999. *Assisted Living: Quality-of-Care and Consumer Protection Issues in Four States*. Washington, DC: GAO, GAO/HEHS-99-27.

*Elizabeth Clemmer*
*Updated by Bernadette Wright*

**ATTITUDES ABOUT RETIREMENT.** Retirement policies and pension systems were initially implemented as a means to move older workers out of the labor force. Retirement has since evolved into a normative, anticipated life stage, one that has become an institutionalized part of most modern societies (Brown 1996). Workers look forward to retirement, actively choose to retire as soon as it is financially feasible, and once retired report high levels of satisfaction with their lives (Schulz 1995).

However, labor force advantages and disadvantages tend to influence individual retirement experiences; thus attitudes toward retirement may vary based on a number of factors. Prospective health status and income are not only identified as concerns of those contemplating retirement, but they also consistently emerge as factors associated with retirement satisfaction. Poor health is often a precursor of early retirement, and individuals with health problems are more likely to report dissatisfaction with retirement. Those with adequate financial resources, obtained through pension benefits (public and private) and savings, and who are in good health, are most likely to express positive perceptions of retirement. These key resources enable retirees to more fully pursue activities associated with the retirement lifestyle—travel and leisure, education, volunteering, and other opportunities—free from the obligations of work life. Individuals with inadequate retirement income sources and/or poor health tend toward a more pessimistic attitude about retirement. Similarly, the state of the economy and its potential impact on retirement wealth can negatively or positively impact attitudes toward retirement.

Disparities in labor force experiences by gender and ethnicity affect attitudes toward retirement. Men are generally more likely to retire due to work circumstances or job characteristics, and women are more likely to retire for personal reasons. Women's experience of work often includes delayed entry into the labor force, interruptions in participation, lower occupational job status, and lower salaries, which result in lower levels of labor force attachment and, more important, decreased income benefits in retirement. As a result, retirement not may be as attractive an option for women. Additionally, the timing of women's retirement is not often actively chosen but rather dictated by the needs or actions of others, that is, assumption of a caregiving role or retirement in conjunction with that of a husband's.

Attitudes toward retirement may also be influenced by proximity to the retirement event; individuals approaching retirement are inclined to spend more time thinking about and planning for retirement. These activities tend to reinforce positive perceptions of a pending retirement experience and are associated with postretirement levels of life satisfaction. Estimates of persons who have not thought about or planned for retirement range from 10% to 40%. Individuals who strongly identify with their occupational status and exhibit high levels of attachment to the workforce are less likely to view retirement as a positive life event and may in fact forego retirement altogether in favor of continued labor force participation. (See also BABY BOOMERS AND RETIREMENT; HISTORY OF RETIREMENT; RETIREMENT PLANNING; RETIREMENT PREPAREDNESS.)

**Organizations**

AARP
Employee Benefit Research Institute

**References**

Brown, Arnold S. 1996. *The Social Processes of Aging and Old Age*. 2nd ed. Upper Saddle River, NJ: Simon & Schuster.

Cavanaugh, John C., and Fredda Blanchard-Fields. 2002. *Adult Development and Aging*. 4th ed. Belmont, CA: Wadsworth Group.

Ekerdt, D.J., J. Hackney, K. Kosloski, and S. DeViney. 2001. "Eddies in the Stream: The Prevalence of Uncertain Plans for Retirement." *Journal of Gerontology: Psychological Sciences* 56B: S162–70.

Morgan, Leslie A., and Suzanne Kunkel. 2001. *Aging: The Social Context*. 2nd ed. Thousand Oaks, CA: Pine Forge Press.

Schulz, James H. 1995. *The Economics of Aging*. 6th ed. Westport, CT: Auburn House.

*Linda Albert*

**ATTORNEYS,** individuals who advocate on behalf of or counsel others or are employed to prepare for trials in courts of law. While elder law practice is growing more important as the population ages, there are many areas or specialties within the practice of law. A specialty involves additional study, training, or experience. A patent attorney, for example, frequently has additional training as an engineer in order to perform within the specialty area of patent law. In seeking an attorney, a client should inquire about the attorney's background to determine the level of his or her expertise in the area of specialized need. Local bar associations can also refer attorneys by specialization.

## Areas of Specialization

*Appellate Law.* Attorneys handling litigation matters that have progressed beyond the trial level are appellate attorneys. Courts of appeal include state and federal courts, as well as the supreme courts of the states and the federal government. Generally, the party who has lost a trial is the person who appeals, although either party may need to seek an attorney who specializes in the appeals process and has taken cases before courts of appeal in the past.

*Bankruptcy Law.* Bankruptcy law involves dealing with the federal bankruptcy statutes, which allow individuals to reorganize and/or terminate indebtedness by declaring bankruptcy. Under this law, the rights of the bankrupt and the creditors (entities owed money by the bankrupt) must be protected. In bankruptcy law, attorneys usually specialize in representing either the bankrupt or the creditors. It is not common practice in larger jurisdictions for attorneys to represent both creditors and bankrupt individuals, although it does happen on occasion. A person seeking a bankruptcy attorney should make an effort to find an attorney who customarily represents individuals in similar situations. When seeking protection against a bankruptcy proceeding by a debtor, one should seek a creditor's bankruptcy attorney.

*Business and Corporate Law.* Attorneys who specialize in the area of business and corporate law practice in a wide range of areas. They typically incorporate businesses; review contracts, leases, and loan documentation; consider matters of securities law; and in general, advise business owners and managers. Because of the broad area of practice within this specialty, practitioners of business law frequently have additional training or education such as a certified public accountant (CPA) or an individual with a Master of Business Administration (M.B.A.). Business and corporate attorneys need knowledge and familiarity in the areas of banking, finance, securities law, corporate law, and general management in order to serve the interests of their business and corporate clients. They usually do not go to trial and more frequently are transactional lawyers.

*Business Litigation.* Attorneys specializing in business and corporate litigation are trial lawyers rather than transactional attorneys in most cases. In this specialization, as with most areas of litigation, the most important asset of a business litigator is his or her litigation experience rather than knowledge of business and corporate law. Business litigators generally sue over matters such as collections, contract law, copyright or trademark infringement, unfair business practices, or other business matters.

*Construction Law.* Certain lawyers specialize in the area of law related to building, renovating, remodeling, and/or demolishing residences and commercial buildings. Lawyers practicing in the area of construction law must be familiar with municipal regulations, building codes, civil engineering, soil engineering, zoning, construction financing, and local building practices. As with many areas of the law, lawyers who practice in this field are important to seek out not just for their knowledge in the legal area but also for their knowledge of how construction practices work in their geographic regions. The problem of working with a general practitioner in matters of construction law arises from the fact that frequently attorneys not familiar with construction practice are similarly unfamiliar with practical problems of dealing with local governments and other bureaucracies in matters of seeking permits, gaining approval of plans, or obtaining other required clearances.

*Copyright Law.* Individuals who seek to publish magazine articles, books, music, poetry, or computer software programs should work with a copyright lawyer. Copyright lawyers protect the rights of their clients who have created any form of written or performed work. Copyright lawyers often also practice trademark and patent law (see below). Copyright law, like patent law, is highly specialized and requires detailed familiarity with pertinent federal statutes.

*Criminal Law.* Attorneys who practice criminal law work either as prosecutors on behalf of a government body or as defense counsel on behalf of individuals accused of criminal acts. When seeking the services of a criminal attorney, it is advisable to find someone who has dealt specifically with the alleged crime. An individual accused of violating a criminal statute against drunk driving, for example, should seek an attorney who regularly defends against drunk driving charges. Lawyers who defend against particular crimes are more familiar with jury responses and more knowledgeable about the particular criminal statute that may have been violated. Criminal lawyers are trial lawyers who should be able to demonstrate prior experience before the courts in question, whether municipal, state, or federal. A lawyer who has not had criminal trial experience in the past is not a good candidate to defend in a criminal law trial.

*Elder Law.* Attorneys who are engaged in elder law practice are experienced in working with state and federal statutes related to Medicaid and Medicare; state and federal social services programs; estate, probate, and trust law; as well as matters related to conservatorship and retirement law. Attorneys who practice in the area of elder law are not necessarily prepared to practice in every area of law in which an older person may require assistance. Rather, this area is specialized in the specific matters referenced above.

*Estate, Probate, and Trust Practice.* Estate planning lawyers (often elder law practitioners) must be experienced in matters of taxation, property law, and to some extent, family law. They assist their clients in drafting wills and trusts, and in other matters related to the ownership of property, in a fashion that will minimize the cost of probate and estate taxes and fees. Attorneys who are not experienced in estate planning should not be called upon to draft complicated testamentary documents, since the area is highly specialized and an inexperienced lawyer in this field can cause unexpected transfer fees to result at the time of death.

*Family Law.* Family attorneys handle adoptions, separations, and divorces and help alter or amend family status. Lawyers who have never tried a divorce case should advise prospective clients that they are unfamiliar with this area of the law. A client who is sued for divorce or who intends to sue for divorce should seek the advice and counsel of a family law attorney. Of all the areas of legal practice, few are more prone to misinformation than the area of family law practice. It is best to seek out the services of a family law attorney as soon as one is needed, rather than relying on the advice of friends. Family law attorneys must also be familiar with the effects of tax law as a result of divorce.

*Immigration Law.* Immigration attorneys assist clients in seeking visas to foreign countries and in seeking "Green Cards" that permit foreigners to reside in the United States. They also help clients from foreign nations obtain citizenship in the United States. Immigration law is largely federal, and it is highly important that an individual wishing to assist friends or family members in obtaining work permits or temporary visas in the United States seek an immigration law attorney. Since violations of immigration law are federal offenses that carry serious penalties, the assistance of an immigration attorney is crucial to assure smooth transition for individuals needing help in these matters.

*Insurance Law.* Lawyers who practice in the area of insurance law specialize in a subspecialty of business and corporate law. They represent two types of clients: (1) insurance companies who wish to protect their interests from claimants and (2) individuals who seek to enforce claims against their own insurance companies or those of individuals who caused them to suffer some loss. In both cases, insurance attorneys usually have a background in both business law and trial law, with the trial experience being the more important of the two areas.

*International Law.* Individuals who wish to conduct business outside the United States, or who seek to transact even a single matter in a foreign country, should seek the services of an international law practitioner. These attorneys, besides having experience in international law, should have experience with the particular foreign nation. International attorneys should be familiar with the legal aspects of international law, as well as cultural and social customs of the particular nations in which business is to be conducted.

*Labor Law.* Labor lawyers practice in two specific areas: They represent employers, and they represent employees. As with bankruptcy law, lawyers seldom practice on both sides of labor law. Someone seeking the services of a labor attorney, therefore, should determine whether the attorney has historically represented employers or employees and be guided accordingly to the type of representation needed. Labor lawyers work both as trial lawyers and as negotiators for their clients. Some labor lawyers also work with employers to create documents such as employee handbooks and employment contracts designed to protect the employer from lawsuits by employees. Labor law involves federal statutes, including the Americans with Disabilities Act (ADA), the Employee Retirement Income Security Act (ERISA), the National Labor Relations Act (NLRA), and state laws related to workers' compensation and unemployment insurance. Labor lawyers should also be familiar with such matters as sexual harassment, age discrimination, and wrongful termination.

*Patent and Trademark Law.* Lawyers who practice in the area of patent and trademark law strive to protect the property rights of their clients regarding new inventions and the business symbols that their clients may develop. Patent and trademark attorneys, like copyright attorneys, frequently conduct searches to determine whether inventions or trademarks have been previously claimed or discovered by other parties. Patent and trademark attorneys may be trained as engineers prior to becoming attorneys, as they are often required to examine blueprints or product designs. An individual who seeks to obtain a patent or trademark should deal only with a specialist in this area.

*Personal Injury/Medical Malpractice.* Attorneys who represent clients in lawsuits concerning accidental injuries or other physical harm, including medical malpractice claims, are referred to as personal injury attorneys. Attorneys defending against personal injury lawsuits are usually defense attorneys or insurance attorneys. Most personal injury attorneys enter into contingent fee agreements, where clients agree to pay a percentage of any judgment awarded in lieu of hourly fees. Lawyers who represent injured parties usually do not work as defense attorneys or insurance attorneys. In medical malpractice litigation, the plaintiff must establish (1) that a physician-patient relationship existed, (2) the applicable standard of care (a national standard), (3) violation of the standard of care, (4) that the injury is compensable, and (5) a causal connection exists between the violation of care and the harm. The plaintiff must produce appropriate expert witnesses to substantiate the claim. Medical malpractice lawyers' charges vary widely. A contingency fee may be based upon an increasing percentage, should a case extend over a long period of time, typically from one-fourth to two-thirds of the award, although some states regulate the amount of this percentage.

*Real Estate Law.* People who buy or sell property may do so without the assistance of an attorney, choosing instead to work with real estate agents and brokers until settlement, which usually involves lawyers skilled in the practice of real estate law. The cost of using an agent or broker, however, ranges from 3% to 6% of the total transaction cost and is primarily justified when the agent or broker finds a buyer for the property. When a buyer is already known to the seller, however, it is generally less expensive to obtain the services of a real estate attorney, who will typically charge by the hour, rather than a percentage of the transaction. People buying property, on the other hand, are well advised to use real estate attorneys who can assist them with both the legal and transactional complexities of contracting, title work, financing, and settlement.

*Tax Law.* One of the most highly specialized areas of legal practice is tax law. Many lawyers in this area have additional training beyond their law degrees, evident by such degrees or designations as CPA, M.B.A., or LL.M. Few lawyers are able to practice in the area of tax law while working in other fields because the tax law is quite complex. Tax attorneys assist clients in matters of personal income tax, estate tax, corporate tax, and real estate tax. Within these and other tax areas, lawyers are more particularly trained and highly specialized in civil or criminal tax court matters.

There are many other areas of specialization in the law besides those listed in this article. Any person seeking the services of an attorney should ask for a referral to an attorney who has performed these services in the past. (See also BANKRUPTCY; BUSINESS SUCCESSION PLANNING; DURABLE POWER OF ATTORNEY; ELDER LAW PRACTICE; ESTATE PLANNING; TRUSTS; WILLS.)

**References**

Jones, Vivian C. 1994. *Legal Research for Non-Lawyers: A Self-Study Manual*. Washington, DC: Special Libraries Association.

Roth, Bette J., Randall W. Wulff, and Charles A. Cooper. 1993. *The Alternative Dispute Resolution Practice Guide*. New York: Lawyers Cooperative Publishing.

*Donald A. Hunsberger*

# B

**BABY BOOMERS AND RETIREMENT,** financial and other later-life issues facing an increasingly large group of future older adults, all born between 1946 and 1964. In developed countries around the world, the demographic balance of generations is shifting from dominance by the young toward hegemony of the mature. In the United States specifically, the top of the population pyramid is losing its members who were raised on thrift, economic depression, and world war; replacing them are those who were raised during times of increasing consumption and deficit spending. This shift has important implications for the future retirements of today's workers.

To project how this shift might shape the retirement landscape of the future, it is important to review a few points. First, the boomers will not change as they get older; the institution of retirement will. According to the General Social Survey opinions, levels of political and social liberality or conservatism and consumer-spending habits depend not so much upon a respondent's age as they do upon a person's cohort, or year of birth. To ask, "At what age will the boomers start behaving like their parents?" is the wrong question. If today one's grandparents are very conservative, it is because they were conservative when they were younger. We now realize that boomers are going to remain consistent with themselves as they age. Those who have always been liberal will remain liberal into their sixties and beyond. In 2003, the oldest boomers will be 57 years old with a life expectancy of about 25 more years (U.S. Bureau of the Census 1999). This implies a potential retirement lasting 15 years or more. A retirement of that length can be an expensive proposition, but how much is needed to finance it is dependent on a multitude of variables.

### Factors Affecting the Retirements of Boomers—Positive

Several factors shape the paths that boomers may take as they age. Below are some of the issues that will strongly affect how successful this generation will be in reaching their retirement goals. Among the many positive factors potentially affecting the boomers' retirement are changing incentives to continue working, longer life with a potentially healthier lifestyle, evidence of increasing desire to continue working, and new career opportunities.

*Removal of Income Limits for Social Security.* Under prior law, beneficiaries of full retirement age but still under age 70 were subject to an annual earnings limit, which was

$17,000 in 2000, beginning with the year in which they attained full retirement age. For those in this age group, the deduction was $1 for every $3 of earnings over the exempt amount. Under new law effective January 1, 2000, these earnings limitations and deductions are eliminated for those of full retirement age, beginning with the month they attain full retirement age. Boomers, therefore, can continue working full-time once they reach full retirement age and start collecting their Social Security retirement benefits at the same time without losing any of their benefit amounts. If a boomer decides to keep working full-time after full retirement age while starting to collect benefits, this effectively is a raise. If a boomer wishes to switch careers, work part-time, work part of the year, or work in some other flexible situation, he or she may do so without a concurrent reduction in total income.

Another potential implication of the removal of earnings limits is that employers may be inclined to allow more schedule flexibility for persons of full retirement age in return for paying boomers somewhat less. Effectively, boomers could be seen as subsidized workers, and as such, they would pose less of a risk to hire than older adults are traditionally, though erroneously, thought to be.

*Longer Life and the Chance for a Longer, Healthy, and Active Lifestyle.* Given advances in medical technology and public health, and hoping that boomers take their health into their own hands through diet modification, better habits, and exercise, this generation may be able to maintain an active lifestyle far longer than most of today's older adults.

*Boomer's Inclination to Continue Working.* A new AARP study (Montenegro, Fisher, and Remez 2002) on multicultural work habits of persons aged 45 plus released in September 2002 shows conclusively that people work for more than just a paycheck. Even those surveyed who initially said they were not very engaged in their work went on to express a sense of purpose, involvement, social connection, and status that was provided by employment. Given this, it is unlikely that these engaged employees will find much to attract them to the traditional retirement paradigm that involves a sudden and complete stoppage of work. It is more likely that they will decrease their hours gradually, work part-time, or retire altogether from their career to volunteer or to work in another field of interest.

*Generational Momentum Might Create New Career Opportunities.* With the inclination to work, with good health, and with flexible work arrangements (if they are to be had), it is likely that boomers will want to redefine what it means to be retired. It is also likely that "retirement" will include more work for pay among older adults than is presently being seen among retirees today.

### Factors Affecting the Retirements of Boomers—Negative

The vision above is a positive one, but boomers face many barriers to creating a new retirement paradigm. These may include unanticipated costs of aging, the economic cost of divorce, unrestrained consumption patterns, and uncertainty surrounding health and health care.

*Unanticipated Costs of Aging.* Given the low level of understanding about what Medicare does and does not cover (i.e., prescription drugs or nursing home care for themselves or their parents), retirement could become very unpleasant for some of the boomers who choose to live "just for today." Whether boomers are planning to fully retire and live on their savings and pensions, or whether they plan to spend more today and extend their working life, the costs of medical care and other personal consequences of illness are greatly underestimated by boomers. Professionals assisting aging baby boomers, as well as newly widowed older adults, would do well to raise this issue when planning for adequate retirement financing.

*Economic Effects of Divorce in Older Age.* In 2001, about 17% of all boomers were divorced or separated, and another 12% were never married (U.S. Bureau of the Census 1999). The financial effects of divorce will weigh heavily on women, especially when there are children in the family. While child support is a part of most divorce settlements involving children, pension benefits and rights to spousal benefits from Social Security are more often forfeited by divorcing women. If a boomer ex-wife has taken time out of the workforce to raise children, her primary insurance amount calculation for Social Security will contain a number of "zero years," or years in which no earnings were recorded by Social Security but which are factored into the average lifetime earnings amount. If pension and Social Security spousal benefits have not been negotiated in the divorce, or if the couple had been married for fewer than ten years, then the woman would get nothing for that period or would get a reduced Social Security benefit when she becomes eligible for retirement (Crittenden 2001).

*Unrestrained Consumption, Debt, and Insufficient Savings.* Baby boomers are enthusiastic consumers but traditionally poor savers, and they are not known for achieving balance between competing short-term wants and long-term goals. This first consumer generation has not been strong in balancing competing needs such as a desire for material goods against longer-term goals such as college tuition for children or retirement for themselves. Dream vacations and indulging in housing and automobile upgrades also detract from the more mundane task of saving for retirement.

Mind-set differences between today's older adults—the depression and World War II generation—and many aging baby boomers can hardly be overemphasized. Boomers carry more debt of all kinds than any other generation before it. Types of debt include relatively high levels of revolving credit, such as credit card debt, as well as large mortgage and home equity loans. This means that baby boomers have relatively less equity in their homes, a major asset for most of today's older adults.

*Lack of Ability to Work or Opportunity to Work.* Personal or family illness and disability may cut short the working or active lives of boomers who experience it. If they are adequately insured and have prepared for later life, chances are they will fare well even if they become disabled. If, however, they did not save for retirement and believed they could work during later life, they may experience disappointment if or when they become physically unable to work or to maintain their former lifestyle. This negative factor falls into a larger shadow falling over boomer retirement prospects—denial.

### Barriers Boomers Face When Planning Ahead

Denial can manifest itself in the form of unwillingness to plan for retirement, ill health, or frailty. It may be a factor when making ill-advised long-term investment decisions or other failures to plan financially. If boomers are suddenly unable to work, or if the economy has not treated their retirement investments as well as hoped, the quality of later life can be severely impacted. The Employee Benefit Research Institute (EBRI) retirement confidence survey has consistently found a disconnect between current retirement reality and worker expectations for future retirement. For example, 57% of workers in the 2002 survey are planning to work to beyond age 65 or "never retire," but the same survey showed that only 24% of current retirees actually worked past age 65. More important, 45% of current retirees said they retired "earlier than planned," and many of them did so because of illness, a layoff, caring for a sick family member, or other reason largely beyond their immediate control. Some boomers may not be planning for retirement because they assume they will be able to keep working, either because they have to or because they want to. This may leave them vulnerable should they find themselves retired at 66 or earlier for unforeseen reasons.

Finally, boomers cannot save what they do not have. Ten percent (10%) of boomers were at or below 125% of the poverty level in 2001. Though official poverty is often a cyclical rather than a long-term state, boomers experiencing hard times are less likely to have pensions, 401(k) plans, or other savings. If they do, they usually have less income that they can feasibly set aside as savings.

### Conclusion

As a large cohort of aging adults, baby boomers have the potential political clout to effect many changes that might enhance their ability to continue working, as well as to retire successfully. Changes to the health care system, particularly in the area of long-term care, will be essential to ensure continuing improvements in health, not only for the most affluent of baby boomers but for all. In addition, the baby boomers need to use their numbers to influence business and community leaders to further understand the creative and cost-effective contributions that retirees can have on the economy. First, however, they will need to understand it themselves. It is becoming increasingly important for the baby boomers to become more fiscally savvy—the comfort of their futures will depend on it. (See also AGING AMERICA; DIVORCE AND OLDER ADULTS; HISTORY OF RETIREMENT; PENSION PLANS; RETIREMENT EXPENSE PLANNING; RETIREMENT PLANNING; U.S. PERSONAL SAVING RATE.)

#### Organizations

AARP
American Savings Education Council (ASEC)
Employee Benefit Research Institute (EBRI)

#### References

Anderson, R.N., and P.B. DeTurk. 2002. *United States Life Tables, 1999. National Vital Statistics Reports*. Vol. 50, No 6. Hyattsville, MD: National Center for Health Statistics.

Crittenden, Ann. 2001. *The Price of Motherhood*. New York: Metropolitan Books.

Davis, James A. 2000. *Testing the Demographic Theory of Attitude Change: Secular Trends in Attitudes among U.S. Householders, 1972–1996*. Chicago: NORC.

Montenegro, Xenia, Linda Fisher, and Shereen Remez. 2002. "Staying ahead of the Curve: The AARP Work and Career Study." Washington, DC: AARP.

U.S. Bureau of the Census. 1999. "Statistical Abstract of the United States." Available online at http://www.census.gov/Press_Release/www/1999/cb99-238.html.

*Sarah Zapolsky*

**BANK ACCOUNTS.** See Banking Services for the Mature Market; Individual Retirement Account (IRA); Medical Savings Accounts (MSAs) and Medical IRAs; Savings Account Trusts; Savings Investments; Wealth Span.

**BANKING SERVICES FOR THE MATURE MARKET.** Banking services and products offered through banks that are of interest to seniors include checking and savings accounts, online banking, travel clubs, trusts, annuities, certificates of deposit, reverse mortgages, safety deposit boxes, money orders, traveler's checks, account information, direct deposit, automated teller machines (ATMs), check balancing, bill payment, and education on estate planning, probate, and financial management. In 2000 there were more than 35 million seniors; by 2030 that number is expected to grow to 70.3 million as baby boomers reach retirement age (Administration on Aging 2002). In a survey by AARP, 37% of boomers say that personal finance tops their list of things they would like to improve. Sixty percent (60%) of the boomers are looking to centralize all their accounts in a local bank rather than a brokerage house (Dullum 2003); however, brokerage firms are leading the way in offering these centralized services.

Most seniors live independently in the community; in 2000 only 4.5% of those over 65 lived in nursing homes (Administration on Aging 2002). This older population regularly conducts banking activities. Of families headed by someone aged 55 to 64, 14.4% owned CDs with a mean value of $12,000; 14.3% owned savings bonds with a mean value of $1,000; 6.1% owned bonds with a mean value of $60,000; 26.7% owned individual stocks with a mean value of $15,000; 21.3% owned mutual funds with a mean value of $60,000; and 59.1% owned retirement accounts with a mean value of $55,000. Of families headed by someone aged 65 to 74, 29.7% owned CDs with a mean value of $20,000; 11.3% owned savings bonds with a mean value of $2,000; 3.9% owned bonds with a mean value of $71,400; 20.5% owned individual stocks with a mean value of $85,000; 19.9% owned mutual funds with a mean value of $70,000; and 44% owned retirement accounts with a mean value of $60,000. Of families headed by someone aged 75 and older, 36.5% owned CDs with a mean value of $25,000; 12.5% owned savings bonds with a mean value of $3,000, 5.7% owned bonds with a mean value of $35,000; 21.8% owned individual stocks with a mean value of $60,000; 19.5% owned mutual funds with a mean value of $70,000; and 25.7% owned retirement accounts with a mean value of $46,000 (Aizcorbe, Kennickell, and Moore 2003). In fact, customers who are 50 years old or older use four times as many retail banking services as younger patrons (Sullivan 1990).

Over 93% of those aged 55 and older own transaction accounts. Those aged 55 to 64 have a mean balance in the account of $5,500; for those aged 65 to 74 the mean is $8,000; and for those aged 75 years and above the mean is $7,300 (Aizcorbe et al. 2003). Checking account customers visit banks about three times a month, while savings account customers visit only three times a year (Massie 1990). Major exceptions to this include minority group members, women, and the oldest old (those aged 85 and older), who often have few assets, little savings, and low security benefits.

### New Trends in Banking Services

Seniors are looking for free services, preferred rates, and bonuses when they choose financial institutions. For example, in November 2002, Bank of America announced a new program with free banking services and preferred rates with no penalty for early withdrawal of up to $2,500 if the senior had laddered CDs. (Laddered CDs are CDs of the same amount that mature at different times [i.e., every six months for 3 years]. Thus you take advantage of interest rate movements if you think interest rates will rise in the near future and still have access to your money. A laddering CD calculator is available at http://bankofamerica.com to show how CD customers can use laddering to increase their earning power.) The program at Bank of America also offers security protection for debit and credit cards, financial education, and special customer service ("Bank of America" 2002).

While online banking is on the rise, many seniors still want personal contact (Dixon 2003). While 85% of those who say they will definitely not go online are seniors, the number of seniors who use the Internet is growing (15% of Internet users). Currently, the wealthier and better educated seniors go online. While 13% of seniors go online at work, most seniors (84%) were encouraged by their families to go online. Forty-four percent (44%) of seniors who use the Internet get financial information and 12% use it to sell stocks. Eight percent (8%) of senior Internet users have used online banking (Fox et al. 2002).

As baby boomers retire, more and more seniors will use the Internet for travel, medical information, games, chatting, e-mail, and banking. As their mobility decreases, seniors find that it is easier to do things on the Internet (Jenkins 2002). Of the seniors aged 50 to 64 who use the Internet, 16% use online banking, 50% get financial information, and 15% sell stocks (Fox et al. 2002). The majority of these cite convenience as the reason they switched to online banking (Fox 2002).

Travel services and investment services are offered by many banks to attract seniors. Those aged 50 and older made up 80% of the luxury travel market (White 2000). Travel services offer fully planned itineraries that are geared toward seniors for day trips as well as longer vacations with people of similar interest. These can range from a visit to a nearby outlet mall to a trip to England or a cruise to Alaska, and usually a travel club representative from the bank accompanies the group. Some banks offer senior VIP customers reduced fees for investment services; some also offer financial education and retirement planning. Seniors need to be aware that investment products bought through a bank are not covered by FDIC insurance. These investments carry the same risk as investments of a similar type bought through a brokerage firm; however, the bank does offer one-stop convenience that many seniors prefer. Banks are also starting to offer branch services at retirement communities to aid seniors.

### High Fees to Receive Electronic Payments

As many low-income seniors are now required to receive Social Security and Supplemental Insurance payments electronically, they are paying high fees to be able to receive checks from payday lenders and other check cashing companies rather than from banks. For example, in 1999, Corus Bank in Chicago received $1.3 million in fees from 60,000 Social Security recipients who were not customers to have checks cut and sent to a check cashing company of their choice (Woker 2000). The bank says that the recipients signed disclosures that they understood the fees involved.

### High Overdraft Fees

Another area of concern to seniors is fees for overdrafts. Many banks are not automatically linking savings and checking accounts to cover insufficient funds; instead they are charging fees of up to $35 to cover these overdrafts. Since a check can be put through several times before the consumer receives notice in the mail, it is easy to accumulate

$70 to $100 in fees with one check. Since the bank takes its fees out of any money in the account, other checks may bounce. Covering overdrafts with a line of credit is also expensive (interest rates can be as high as 20%). Besides a fee for this service, banks charge daily interest until the "loan" for the overdrafts is repaid. With most banks, putting funds in the account does not automatically repay the loan. The person must tell the bank to take funds to repay the overdraft. The least expensive way to have overdraft protection is for people to link a savings and a checking account. There is a fee of $7 to $15 to transfer the funds if there is an overdraft, which is minimal compared to the other ways of handling overdrafts.

### Predatory Lending

Predatory lending is another problem that seniors face. Eighty percent (80%) of seniors own their own homes and have paid off their mortgage or are close to paying off their mortgage. A recent study found that seniors were three times more likely to have subprime mortgages than people under the age of 35 (Calhoun et al. 2001). Lenders that charge high fees, prepayment penalties, balloon payments, and high interest rates fall into the category of predatory lenders. They target low-income seniors with loans for home repairs and improvements or as home equity loans. Loan flipping, another type of predatory lending, is making a home loan that refinances an existing home loan when the new loan does not have a tangible net benefit to the borrower.

Another type of predatory lender is the payday or check cashing company that charges a fee, which is really a disguised interest rate for services. This loan has high fees and is made without regard to the borrower's ability to repay the amount, which can cause the borrower such financial hardship that it can be almost impossible to repay the loan. For example, it may cost $20 to cash a check for $100, so the borrower will receive $80.00. The company then holds the check for up to two weeks and then cashes it. Chances are that the borrower will not have an extra $100, as many people in this situation live from paycheck to paycheck, so the borrower must write a check for $120 to have the $100 to cover the first check, thereby paying another $20 fee. This works out to an annualized interest rate of 590%!

### Banking Safety

Banking safety involves several issues. One is personal security when using an ATM machine. If seniors need to do banking after hours, they need to carefully inspect the area where the ATM is located. Users want to be sure that the area is well lit and that they can be seen easily by others. Other safety issues to consider are ensuring that parking is close to the ATM and that there are no places nearby where a person can hide. Check for security cameras and never go alone. Drive-up machines are the safest, and personal identification (PIN) numbers should always be safeguarded (Mizell 1994).

### Elder Financial Exploitation

Financial abuse includes mishandling, fraud, or theft of a person's income, money, accounts, assets, or property by another person, such as a family member, a friend, a paid caregiver, a neighbor, a repair person, a bogus charity, or a con artist (Virginia Department of Social Services 2002b). It may include forgery, misappropriation of cash withdrawals and other money, abuse of joint bank accounts, abuse of powers of attorney, abuse of ATMs, fraudulent use of credit cards, and illegal transfers of property. According to a 1996 study, the most common types of abuse in order of prevalence are inability to handle finances due to self-neglect, financial abuse by a substance-abusing "roommate" or boarder, someone else living off the income of a frail or confused older person, abuse by a home care worker, misappropriation of cash, and abuse of power of attorney (Sacks 1996). A survey of three banking intuitions in New York found that the types of abuse most encountered by banks were forgery, misappropriation of funds, abuse of joint accounts, and abuse of powers of attorney. Most abusers were immediate family members or other relatives (Sacks 1996).

As cognitive impairment increases with age, the oldest old are the most vulnerable to financial abuse. Many states have added financial exploitation to their legislation on elder abuse. Some states, such as Virginia, while not making it mandatory for bank employees to report a suspicious transaction, free their employees from liability if they do make reports to Adult Protective Services. A bank employee may be the first to recognize unusual activity in a senior's account. Signs of abuse may be unusual activity on a senior's account through use of an ATM, debit, or credit card. Other signs of abuse may include checks for larger-than-usual amounts, several checks written to one person, or checks where the signature or amount may have been altered. New acquaintances who take up residence with the senior may indicate another sign of abuse, especially if the senior appears afraid of the person. Requests to notarize documents to change titles or other documents in favor of a new acquaintance may indicate abuse, especially if the senior cannot articulate why the changes are being made. Eviction notices, unpaid utility bills, or concern or confusion about missing funds may be another sign that seniors do not know where money is going. Missing documents and redirected mail may be another indication of abuse (Virginia Department of Social Services 2002a).

Seniors can protect themselves by taking some of the following steps: staying socially active, documenting their financial arrangements, not giving away property in exchange for promises of lifelong care, getting to know the staff at the financial institutions that they use, being cautious of the use of joint accounts, clearly stating their intentions, including any payment provisions in any power of attorney, never signing anything they do not understand, being aware of door-to-door scams, and planning ahead for the future control of assets. The more contact seniors have with others, the more likely someone will notice a problem before it gets out of hand (Virginia Department of Social Services 2002b).

By documenting the distribution and planning for financial issues in the event of incapacity, seniors can reduce the chance of abuse. However, seniors need to choose carefully and decide whether a family member or a third party may be the best person to handle their finances. Social service agencies in some states have people to assist seniors with financial issues. Many areas have legal services to assist seniors in executing the necessary documents. When these documents are brought to the senior's financial institution, bank employees should be aware of signs of abuse.

### What Banks Can Do for Seniors

Seniors are looking for free services, preferred rates, and bonuses. They are starting to participate in online banking and this participation should grow as the baby boomers retire. However, as services increase to meet these needs, the opportunities to take advantage of seniors increase. Seniors need to watch for hidden fees, and they need to be aware of safety issues at ATMs. The banking industry can assist seniors by being mindful of these issues.

In addition, it is often the banking industry that can best spot financial abuse. Institutions need to train their personnel and their customers to spot abuse. Seniors should not give their PIN number to anyone or use it where others can see it. Banking staff need to watch for strangers who accompany seniors to the bank where withdrawals are made and the money is given to the stranger. Monitoring accounts for unusual activity is another way to stop financial abuse. Having a reputation of being senior friendly should assist the banking industry in participating in this expanding market. (See also ANNUITIES; ESTATE PLANNING; LIVING WILLS; PROBATE; REVERSE MORTGAGES; SAVINGS ACCOUNT TRUSTS; SAVINGS INVESTMENTS.)

### References

Administration on Aging. 2002. "A Profile of Older Americans: 2002." Available online at: http://www.aoa.dhhs.gov/aoa/stats/profile/highlights.html.

Aizcorbe, Ana M., Arthur B. Kennickell, and Kevin B. Moore. 2003. "Recent Changes in U.S. Family Finances: Evidence from the 1998 and 2001 Survey of Consumer Finances." *Federal Reserve Bulletin* (January). Available online at http://www.federalreserve.gov/pubs/bulletin/2003/0103lead.pdf.

"Bank of America Launches 'Advantage to Seniors'." 2002. *PR Newswire*, November 21.

Calhoun, Mike, Margot Saunders, Elizabeth Renauart, Mark Benson, and Sharon Hermanson. 2001. "Home Loan Protection Act: A Model State Statute." AARP Stock Number D17346 (November).

Dixon, Guy. 2003, "Online Banking Is on the Rise, But Many Like the Personal Touch." *Globe and Mail, Metro*, January 23, B5.

Dullum, Justin. 2003. "Which Way to Boom Town." *Northwestern Financial Review* 188(3): 1042–1254.

Fox, Susannah. 2002. "Online Banking." *Pew Internet Project Data Memo. Pew Internet and American Life Project*. Available online at http://www.pewinternet.org.

Fox, Susannah, Lee Raine, Elena Larsen, John Horrigan, Amanda Lenhart, and Tom Spooner. 2002. "Wired Seniors." *Pew Internet and American Life Project*. Available online at http://www.pewinternet.org.

Jenkins, Henry. 2002. "Technology Review—The Aging Net." *MIT Technology Review*, December 11.

Massie, Marcy. 1990. "Package Deal for the Mature Market." *Bottomline* (March): 79–83.

Mizell, Louis R., Jr. 1994. *Street Sense for Seniors*. New York: Berkley Publishing Group.

Sacks, Debra. 1996. "Prevention of Financial Abuse, Focus of New Institute at Brookdale Center on Aging." *Aging Magazine* 367: 86–89.

Sullivan, Michael. 1990. "Seniors Today's Hottest Market." *U.S. Banker* (June): 16–22.

Virginia Department of Social Services. 2002a. *Prevent Financial Exploitation in Virginia: A Guide for Financial Institutions*. Richmond, VA: Author.

Virginia Department of Social Services. 2002b. *Prevent Financial Exploitation in Virginia: A Guide for Seniors and Adults with a Disability*. Richmond, VA: Author.

White, Sarah. 2000. "Why Overlooking Seniors Is Old-Time (& Expensive) Thinking." *Credit Union Journal* 4(26): 12.

Woker, Chris. 2000. "Bank Accused of Flaunting CRA Says It's Giving People What They Want." *American Banker* 165(63) (March 31): 1.

*Celia Ray Hayhoe and Kathleen Carlisle*

**BANKRUPTCY,** a set of legal procedures for dealing with severe debt problems and obtaining a financial fresh start. More than 1 million Americans each year file bankruptcy cases to seek relief from debts. Older persons file for bankruptcy in fewer numbers than younger adults. They tend to be better established financially and are less likely to be involved in aggressive or risky activities. Nevertheless, tens of thousands of older Americans file for bankruptcy every year. Having debt problems and being in poverty are not the same thing, although they can, of course, coincide. A person with substantial assets, income, and a comfortable lifestyle can become financially overextended, from either a precipitous drop in income or a surge in debt. On the other hand, a person with extremely limited means may be financially stable with few or no debts.

Bankruptcy can eliminate or modify debts so as to give the petitioning debtor a financial fresh start. There are two types of bankruptcy cases ordinarily applicable to individuals. They are commonly referred to by the chapters of the U.S. Bankruptcy Code that provide for them. The first is "straight bankruptcy," or "Chapter 7." The formal name is a "liquidation" case, which refers to the possible sale of the petitioning debtor's property to raise money to pay debts. In most cases, however, little or no property is actually sold. The primary effect of nearly all Chapter 7 cases is the discharge or cancellation of some or all debts. The second type is a "debt adjustment," or "Chapter 13," case. Under Chapter 13, a debtor makes at least partial payment on debts through the court, usually over three to five years. Chapter 13 provides a method for dealing with some types of debts that would not be resolved in a Chapter 7 case. Individuals are also eligible, under certain conditions, to file a Chapter 11. This bankruptcy proceeding, a reorganization option designed primarily for corporations and other businesses (also known as Chapter 12), applies only to farmers and is relatively rare.

Bankruptcy cases are governed by federal law (Title 11, U.S. Code) and are handled in a special branch of the federal courts. Each state has one or more federal court districts, and some districts have offices in more than one city or conduct hearings in cities other than where the court offices are located.

### The Bankruptcy Process

A bankruptcy case starts with the filing at an office of the bankruptcy court of a petition, which is a short request for protection under the bankruptcy law. At the same time or soon after, the petitioner also files a prescribed set of disclosure forms. The forms include lists of debts and assets, statements of income and expenses, and certain other financial information. In a Chapter 13 case, the petitioner also files a specific plan for making payments through the court. A husband and wife can file a joint petition under either chapter.

The filing triggers a sweeping court order that protects the debtor from debt collection efforts while the bankruptcy case is pending. This prohibition, known as an "automatic stay," halts legal proceedings such as lawsuits, federal and state tax collections, wage garnishments, and foreclosures. It also stops collection letters and telephone calls. With regard to many creditors, this prohibition eventually becomes permanent through a "discharge of debts" court order at the end of the bankruptcy case. Meanwhile, even creditors who are not subject to permanent discharge are still temporarily restrained by the automatic stay from attempting to collect while the case is before the court. There is one mandatory court appearance, usually about a month after the filing. The hearing is formally called a meeting of creditors, although creditors need not attend and rarely do. At the hearing, a trustee who has been appointed to review the case asks the debtor to verify under oath that the information in the filing is accurate and requests additional information as necessary.

A routine Chapter 7 case may be essentially complete at that point. If no creditor objects and the trustee does not seek to sell any of the debtor's property, the court will issue the order discharging debts and close the case, sometimes fewer than four months from the filing. In a Chapter 13 case, the debt repayment plan is submitted after the meeting of creditors for approval, or "confirmation" by the judge. The trustee makes a recommendation for or against confirmation based on his or her analysis of the legality and financial feasibility of the plan. Creditors may also object, and a hearing is held by the judge, if necessary. If the plan is confirmed, payments are made to the trustee, to be passed on to creditors. If the judge rejects the plan, the petitioner usually has three choices: amend the plan and try again, switch to a Chapter 7, or dismiss the case and deal with the debts outside of bankruptcy law.

### Dischargeable and Nondischargeable Debts

Many types of debts may be discharged and eliminated in a bankruptcy case if the debtor meets the tests and requirements of the law. There are two important groups of exceptions to that rule, however. First, bankruptcy law classifies certain types of debts as not able to be discharged. Second, most liens, including real estate mortgages and automobile purchase loans, remain valid after a bankruptcy, and that often forces the debtor to keep paying that account. Nondischargeable debts include most taxes, although income taxes that have been due for at least three years are usually dischargeable if no fraud has occurred. Alimony and child support payments (past or future) owed by the debtor are not dischargeable. A debt owed by one spouse to another to balance a divorce property settlement, however, may be discharged. Student loans are not dischargeable. This rule is usually interpreted also to apply to parents or others who have cosigned a student loan.

A debt is not discharged if the creditor proves it resulted from the use of a false financial statement by the debtor or from actual fraud. A debt arising from embezzlement, larceny, or deliberate injury to property is not dischargeable, nor are criminal fines and restitution. Claims or court awards for death or personal injury from an auto accident in which the debtor was driving while impaired by alcohol or other drugs is not dischargeable. Other auto accident claims involving property damage only, or based only on ordinary negligence, are dischargeable. The process for determining if a debt is not discharged varies. A creditor seeking to block discharge of a debt on ground of fraud, embezzlement, larceny, and injury to property must object in the bankruptcy court or lose its rights. Other exceptions, including taxes, student loans, and alimony or support, require no particular steps by the creditor. Virtually any other debt or financial obligation not covered by those exceptions can be discharged in bankruptcy.

### Mortgages and Liens

Real estate mortgages, automobile liens, and other liens against property of the debtor are usually not affected by a bankruptcy filing. The creditor usually retains the right to go after the property for at least partial payment of the debt. The debtor can nearly always keep the property by paying the loan as before.

Liens on household goods or similar personal property, however, which have declined in value from the original purchase price of the collateral, usually are canceled outright in the bankruptcy. So are most liens that arise from lawsuits and court judgments. When a lien does survive a bankruptcy, the debtor generally has three choices for dealing with the situation afterward:

1. The debtor can keep the collateral and keep paying the loan; home mortgages and car loans are often handled in this way.
2. The debtor can surrender the collateral and discharge the debt.
3. The debtor can attempt to negotiate new payments based on the value of the collateral. When the amount of the debt exceeds the value of the collateral, creditors are often willing to negotiate a new deal.

### Bankruptcy's Effects on Property

To obtain a discharge of debts in a Chapter 7 bankruptcy case, the petitioning debtor must disclose his or her property. This allows the trustee to review it for possible sale of some items to be applied toward the petitioner's debts. In fact, however, usually little or no property is sold this way. This is because two classes of property are not subject to sale, and these exceptions often cover everything the debtor owns.

The first exception is for property subject to a lien or mortgage. For example, a debtor owning a $100,000 home free of debt would, in most states, be forced to accept a sale of the house, and some or all of the proceeds would go to creditors. If the same home were subject to a $100,000 mortgage, however, the home and mortgage would ordinarily pass through the bankruptcy case unaffected. The mortgage ties up the value of the house for the mortgage holder, leaving no value for other creditors to go after. This principle generally applies as well to automobiles and other collateralized property.

The second exception involves "exempt property" laws. These laws protect some types of property from being seized by creditors, whether in bankruptcy or outside of it. The actual exempt property rules vary greatly from state to state. In bankruptcy, the debtor may keep specific property even while unpaid debts are permanently discharged. All values for such exemption purposes are based on net value, or "equity," above the amount of any liens and are doubled for a joint husband and wife filing.

Property values in the "federal" exemptions that apply in many states provide an illustration of what is protected. The federal exemptions protect $8,700 in homestead equity; $2,775 in a motor vehicle; $9,300 in household furnishings and personal apparel; $9,300 in life insurance cash value; all Social Security benefits and nearly all pension accounts; certain other small amounts or specialized items; and $9,650 in the debtor's choice of any property, including additional amounts of the specific categories just listed.

Exempt property laws in some states are more generous, including homestead exemptions that range up to $100,000, and in a few states have no dollar limit at all. Some states, however, have property exemptions that are more limited than the federal exemptions.

### Causes of Bankruptcy

Every case is different, but some of a few basic themes recur in nearly all bankruptcies. The most frequent cause is unemployment. Illness and injury are often factors as well. A sudden drop in income is the fastest way for a reasonable debt load to become unmanageable, and a significant minority of the population is vulnerable to incurring medical expenses beyond insurance benefits and/or their ability to pay directly. For a person in the workforce, medical problems can also interfere with income. Divorce or separation usually increases expenses without increasing resources. Business failures often leave an owner with substantial debts. Poor planning and irresponsible use of credit are less pervasive causes of bankruptcy than is widely assumed, but they do occur. Regardless of the origin of debt problems, some individuals endure years of collection calls and letters, and even legal proceedings, without filing or even considering bankruptcy. Others realize they are headed for serious trouble and begin to take steps toward filing bankruptcy before they actually miss a payment.

### Chapter 13 Repayment Plan

Many more Chapter 7 bankruptcy cases are filed each year than Chapter 13 debt repayment cases. This is not surprising, as a Chapter 7 bankruptcy produces a prompt discharge of debts, while a Chapter 13 requires a lengthy series of payments through the court, usually over three years. There are several reasons, however, why some people choose Chapter 13.

A debtor whose property would not be fully protected by exemption laws or liens, and so would lose some property in a Chapter 7, may be able to keep that property by filing under Chapter 13. Also, Chapter 13 rules allow a debtor to catch up on and reinstate a home mortgage, even if the lender has started foreclosure and refuses to negotiate. To make this process work, the debtor must be able to make both the required original payments plus catch-up payments. A Chapter 13 filing may be used by a debtor with a recent Chapter 7 discharge. The same debtor cannot receive another Chapter 7 discharge for six years, but it is possible to file again under Chapter 13. Multiple bankruptcy filings, however, often indicate that an individual has serious underlying problems and may be in need of financial or other counseling.

A few kinds of debts that are not dischargeable in a Chapter 7 bankruptcy (including some accident and injury claims) can be discharged in a Chapter 13, even if only a small percentage is paid through the court. A debtor can also sometimes use Chapter 13 to pay a debt while preventing the creditor from going after a cosigner. In practice, however, the same result can usually be achieved with voluntary payments after a Chapter 7 filing.

### Bankruptcy and Credit Ratings

Most people considering bankruptcy are concerned about their credit rating, but this should usually not be a substantial factor in the decision-making process. If debt problems are serious enough to consider bankruptcy, resolving existing debts must be the first concern. A bankruptcy filing may actually improve access to credit. It removes much current debt, which is a key factor in new credit decisions. It also assures that there will be no new Chapter 7 filing for many years. Bankruptcy debtors should bear in mind, however, that if overextended credit was a cause of the problem, taking steps toward future borrowing may be unwise. It is often assumed that a Chapter 13 repayment filing is preferable from a future-credit perspective, but there is no good reason for this belief.

### Hiring a Bankruptcy Attorney

Bankruptcy is a specialized area of law. Persons with debt problems should take care to locate attorneys who are experienced in bankruptcy law. Unless the matter is urgent, comparison shopping for a lawyer is highly recommended. While it is legally possible to file without the assistance of a lawyer, the law is complex enough to make that risky. If the debtor does not have enough property or income to pay the attorney's fees, the stakes may not justify bankruptcy either.

### Changes in the Bankruptcy Laws

Bankruptcy law was rewritten in 1978 and was amended from time to time during the following years. From the late 1990s to 2003, discussions about bankruptcy in the U.S. Congress have been dominated by a series of proposals backed by many large banks and credit companies. These proposals have been designed to make it more difficult for consumers to walk away from their debts. Bankruptcy reform, which has come close to congressional passage only to fail several times during the past six years, may be passed during 2003. Consumer advocates have criticized the current bill for proposing changes that are intended to prevent individuals from filing Chapter 7, force full payment of all debts in Chapter 13, remove discretionary authority from judges and trustees, and empower creditors and their attorneys with many new legal presumptions. These groups charge that the new laws dramatically shift the burden of proof onto debtors seeking debt relief, thus increasing expense and legal difficulty for all filers. They add that it will punish ordinary taxpayers who have lost jobs, health insurance, or both and will be potentially detrimental to small businesses and their ability to reorganize, while producing few benefits. Nevertheless, the controversial H.R. 975, the Abuse Prevention and Consumer Protection Act of 2003, passed the House and was placed on the Senate legislative calendar (Senate Bankruptcy Reform Bill 2003) in March of 2003. Supporters of the reform legislation agree that the window of opportunity to get the bill through the Senate will narrow with the beginning of the 2004 election season. (See also AGING INTO DEBT; ATTORNEYS; CONSUMER CREDIT; ELDER LAW PRACTICE; FINANCIAL RECOVERY IN LATER LIFE.)

#### Suggested Reading

Snyder, Stephen. 2000. *Credit after Bankruptcy: A Step-by-Step Action Plan to Quick and Lasting Recovery after Personal Bankruptcy*. Fishers, IN: Bellwether, Inc.

#### References

Elias, Stephen, Albin Renauer, Robin Leonard, and Kathleen Micho. 2002. *How to File for Chapter 7 Bankruptcy*. 10th ed. Berkeley, CA: Nolo Press.

Epstein, David G. 2002. *Bankruptcy and Related Law in a Nutshell*. 6th ed. Florence, KY: West Wadsworth.

Tabb, Charles Jordan. 1977. *The Laws of Bankruptcy*. New York: Foundation Press.

*Kenneth J. Doran*

**BOARD AND CARE HOMES,** residential settings that provide more support services than boarding or rooming houses and most congregate apartments but less than the level of care that persons receive from many assisted living facilities and nursing homes. They are usually defined as nonmedical, community-based residential settings that house two or more unrelated adults and provide room, meals, protective oversight or supervision, and some type of assistance or personal care, such as medication supervision or reminders, help with bathing, dressing, and other daily activities, organized activities, and transportation to medical appointments. With some exceptions, board and care facilities are typically small and provide residential care in a more homelike environment than nursing homes. Many are actually private homes converted to several single or shared bedrooms, while others are large, multistory buildings.

Both policymakers and older people and their families have sought to expand the range of care alternatives for persons with chronic illnesses or disabilities and those who need assistance with basic activities of daily living. Families remain the major source of such care and assistance to older adults, providing an estimated 80% of long-term care. When more care is needed or no family is available, other supports are available including in-home help, respite care, caregiver services, adult day care programs, home health care, nursing homes, and a variety of residential settings including board and care homes.

### Characteristics of Board and Care

There is considerable variation across the country in the regulation, costs, and types of people who reside in board and care homes. They are known by many different names, including personal care homes, rest homes, domiciliary care homes, residential care homes, adult congregate living facilities, adult foster homes, sheltered care homes, homes for the aged, adult foster care homes, and assisted living facilities. A study by the Research Triangle Institute (RTI), under contract with the U.S. Department of Health and Human Services (DHHS), estimates that about 34,000 licensed board and care facilities house more than 600,000 residents with an equal number of residents served in unlicensed homes (HHS Press Office 1995). Thus, more than 1 million older Americans and disabled and mentally ill individuals may be living in board and care homes. Unlicensed facilities also vary greatly and include personal residences, larger multiunit retirement facilities, and assisted living facilities.

Board and care homes vary greatly in size from 2 beds in private homes to more than 1,400 beds in high-rise buildings. Most are small, with 2 to 10 beds, but the majority of board and care residents live in larger facilities. According to the RTI study, while 67% of licensed homes have 10 or fewer beds, nearly two-thirds of residents are in homes with 11 or more beds (Hawes, Mor, and Brown 1994). Less than 25 residents reside in 87% of this type of facility (Damron-Rodriguez, Harada, and McGuire 2001). One-third reside in facilities with 51 or more beds. More than half reside in unlicensed homes with more than 51 beds. These larger unlicensed homes include assisted living facilities and retirement communities that provide meals, protective oversight, and some services. More than 80% of licensed homes are for-profit facilities. Eighty percent (80%) of unlicensed homes are for-profit facilities and 40% are nonprofit.

In addition to size, board and care homes differ in terms of physical environment, monthly charges, services, and mix of residents. They vary from three to four residents to a room in modest surroundings to private apartments with plush settings. Most have common areas with community or living rooms and outside sitting areas, although only about half allow residents access to a kitchen to fix a snack. Homes also vary in atmosphere, some being more institutional, and others more homelike. Some encourage residents to bring their own furniture, others only a few possessions.

Homes also vary in mix of residents. Some house mainly older residents. Data from the ten-state RTI study found that more than 60% of the 3,200 residents were 75 or older; more than 30% were 85 or older. Other homes, though not specifically licensed as such, mainly house persons with persistent mental illness or developmental disabilities. In states where the use of psychiatric hospitals has been reduced, board and care homes are an important alternative for the mentally ill. Other homes include frail older persons; persons with cognitive impairment; dementia, such as Alzheimer's disease; mental illness; and developmental disabilities.

Board and care homes are also coping with more complex problems. Forty-three percent (43%) report that they care for residents with alcohol abuse problems, and 14% report drug abuse problems. Some states also find that board and care homes are increasingly used to provide shelter for persons who have been homeless (Hawes, Mor, and Brown 1994). The care needs of the residents also vary. A recent study of two California board and care homes found that 75% of the residents required help with their medications, 52% used aids for walking, and 29% needed bathing assistance (Damron-Rodriguez, Harada, and McGuire 2001).

To meet the needs of this mix of residents, board and care homes offer a wide range of services. More than 90% of licensed homes report providing three meals a day, laundry, some personal care such as bathing and dressing, storage, and supervision and assistance with administration of medications. More than 80% of the licensed homes report providing organized activities, recreational trips, and transportation to medical appointments. Only 25% report providing nursing care by a licensed nurse, but half report that outside agencies provide nursing care. Homes vary on whether residents who need nursing care may stay in the home. Some states, such as Florida and Oregon, allow daily nursing care to be provided in some classes of board and care homes, while others limit the services such homes may provide.

One key characteristic of board and care homes is what Damron-Rodriguez and colleagues call "relatively open boundaries" (2001). Compared to nursing home placement, which typically follows hospitalization, residents can move in and out of board and care facilities from their own homes or from health and social services. This is partly due to the fact that reimbursement for this level of care is mostly private.

### Payment and Regulation

Regulation of board and care homes is largely a state responsibility, and each state sets its own standards. Unlike nursing homes, no federal quality of care and life or safety standards exist for board and care homes, nor is there any federal policy on payment. As a result, in most states, care is paid by the residents or their families and, in some cases, the federal Supplemental Security Income (SSI) program. SSI, available to persons who are poor and aged, blind, or disabled, is the main source of public funds for board and care, although some states also use Medicaid funds to pay for some services to residents, usually through waiver programs with strict eligibility criteria.

The RTI study for DHHS found that, in 1993, 81% of the SSI rates with state supplements ranged from $400 per month to $700 per month. These monthly rates generally covered room, board, personal laundry, special diets, and assistance with eating, dressing, and toileting. However, in about one-fifth of the licensed homes, there was an additional charge if the resident needed a special diet or personal assistance with eating, dressing, and toileting, and three-fourths of the homes charged extra for incontinence supplies. Among unlicensed homes, almost half charged extra for special diets, 35% added charges for personal laundry, and 30% charged extra if the resident needed help with personal care. Private pay rates ranged from $600 per month to $4,200 per month; 74% of the rates were between $800 and $4,200 per month (Hawes, Mor, and Brown 1994). According to information on the AARP Web site, rates range from $350 to $3,000 per month (AARP 2003), but costs remain a function of location; for example, a board and care home in Santa Barbara, California, will cost significantly more than one in Lubbock, Texas. In any case, board and care homes cost approximately half of nursing homes and are considered quite cost-effective for those who need 24-hour supervision without skilled care.

Just as there is tremendous variability across homes and across states in terms of payment policies, considerable variation is found across the states in the nature of the regulatory system established to ensure resident safety, quality of care, and quality of life. In California, for example, board and care homes fall under the same regulations as assisted living facilities. There, board and care homes that house older adults (60 and older) are called residential care facilities (RCFs) or residential care facilities for the elderly (RCFEs). Inspection of homes ranges from monthly in one state to every 18 to 24 months in another, although a majority of states inspect homes once a year. Some notify homes in advance of inspection, while others conduct unannounced inspections. Some use nurses or social workers to inspect homes, while others rely on generalists or sanitarians. Fire departments inspect all licensed homes in all states. Since regulations and their enforcements differ so significantly from state to state, it is essential that consumers considering board and care as an option check with their state licensing office for local information.

### Information for Consumers

The variability across homes and states offers many positive possibilities to consumers but also makes gathering and evaluating information prior to selecting a board and care home absolutely essential. Consumers can choose small homes with a more personal environment, large facilities offering a wide range of services, a shared room, or a private apartment. They can seek homes with a relatively homogenous set of residents or homes with a mix of younger and older persons having a range of conditions and needs. They can select homes that provide minimal assistance or a wide range of services that will address changes in the needs of the resident. Choices include homes with protective and specialized environments and homes that offer a less structured environment and greater autonomy.

Consumers and their families should consider what aspects of the environment—physical setting and amenities, services provided, and philosophy about care—are most important. They should also consider how the home will address changing needs over time and what will happen if private funds are exhausted and help from public programs, such as SSI or Medicaid, is needed to pay for care. Thus, the consumer and his or her family may wish to know the following information in advance:

- What range of services does the home offer, and is there an additional charge for any of them?
- What activities are available? Does the home arrange transportation to senior centers, shopping, entertainment, and medical appointments?
- What autonomy and choices are available? Do residents decide about bedtime? Can they fix a meal or eat a snack? Can residents close their door for privacy? Do staff knock on the door before entering the room? Is there assigned seating at meals? Must residents get permission to leave the facility for the day? What are the policies on visiting hours?
- Is there a residents' council that participates in setting policies and addressing problems or complaints? Is there a residents' bill of rights?
- How will a temporary illness or change in condition requiring more assistance or nursing care be handled?
- Does the home have an existing arrangement with a home health agency or temporary nursing service, and if so, what is the reputation of that agency?
- Will the home allow hospice care if the resident has a terminal illness and wishes to remain in the home until death?
- What is the home's policy and practice on the use of physical restraints?
- If the resident needs help taking medications, who in the home provides such assistance or supervision, and what are their qualifications?
- What does the home do to help residents maintain their maximum physical, social, and cognitive functioning?
- What is the resident mix?
- What is the monthly rate? What does it cover? What is extra? What happens if the resident changes from private pay to SSI or some other public payment?
- What is the home's policy on discharging residents?
- Who licenses or regulates the home? Who acts on complaints or helps resolve problems that may arise?

Other important considerations are suggested on the Seniors-site Web site (2003) and include the following:

- Will living in a board and care home provide residents with the independence, privacy, and security wanted?
- How often is housekeeping and laundry done? Does laundry service mean personal laundry as well as linen service?
- Is the home accessible to public transportation, places of worship, and shopping?
- Will the board and care home be able to meet special dietary needs?
- Can residents use their own furnishings?
- Is there a living room, TV room, or room for social activities?
- Are pets permitted?
- Is there just one telephone, or is there an option for a private phone?
- Are bathrooms private or shared?
- Is there a common area or extra bedroom for guests?
- Are there locks on the individual rooms?
- Is it possible to avoid climbing stairs, if difficult for you?

- Is the home in compliance with state and local standards for fire safety and health?
- To what extent does management assume responsibility for the security of personal belongings?

Several agencies or groups help consumers and their families evaluate homes and make choices, and they often have local chapters and guides. Long-term care ombudsmen, well known for their important and positive role in nursing homes, can be accessed through local or area agencies on aging and visit residents in board and care homes to help resolve problems or complaints. The National Citizens' Coalition for Nursing Home Reform (NCCNHR) has become increasingly active in helping consumers and their families with issues related to board and care. Finally, state licensing agencies and national- and state-level associations representing board and care homes can provide information and address complaints filed or problems brought before them.

Consumers can also find help on the Internet. There are numerous Web sites that provide information on varying residential care facilities and guides for older adults and families as they make important care decisions. For example, search for "housing," "residential care facilities," "board and care homes," "senior housing," or any similar term on global search engines such as Yahoo® or Google®. Or go directly to Web sites for organizations such as AARP, Alzheimer's Association, professional associations such as the American Association of Homes and Services for the Aging or the Assisted Living Federation of America, or government agencies such as the Department of Health and Human Services, State Aging Units, or local Area Agencies on Aging. Other organizations that will provide information and assistance include American Health Care Association, Assisted Living Facilities Association of America, National Association of State Long-Term Care Ombudsman Programs, National Citizens' Coalition for Nursing Home Reform, and Older Women's League. (See also ASSISTED LIVING; BABY BOOMERS AND RETIREMENT; COMMUNITY-BASED CARE; FRAILTY PLANNING; HUD-ASSISTED RENTAL HOUSING; NURSING HOMES.)

### Organizations

AARP
Helpguide
Seniors-Site

### References

AARP. 2003. "Housing Options for Older People." Washington, DC: Author. Available online at http://www.aarp.org/confacts/housing/housingoptions.html.

Clark, R.F., J. Turek-Brezina, C. Chu, and C. Hawes. 1994. "Licensed Board and Care Homes: Preliminary Findings from the 1991 National Health Provider Inventory." U.S. Department of Health and Human Services, Office of the Assistant Secretary for Planning and Evaluation, April 11, 1994.

Damron-Rodriguez, J.A., N. Harada, and J. McGuire. 2001. "Residential Care Facilities for the Elderly: Toward Understanding Their Place in Community Based Long–Term Care." *Journal of Housing for the Elderly* 15(1–2): 43–56.

Hawes, C., V. Mor, and F. Brown. 1994. "The Effect of Regulation on Quality of Care in Board and Care Homes: Results from a 10-State Study." Paper presented at the annual meeting of the Gerontological Society of America, Atlanta, GA.

HHS Press Office. 1995. "HHS Releases Report on Board and Care Regulations." Washington, DC: Author.

Seniors-site.com. 2003. "Board and Care Homes for Senior Citizens." Available online at http://seniors-site.com/housingm/boardcar.html.

*Catherine Hawes*
*Updated by Monika White*

**BONDS,** financial contracts between borrowers (issuers) and lenders (bondholders) in which the borrower agrees to repay a loan with interest according to a prearranged timetable. Bonds are medium- to long-term (7 to 30 years) negotiable debt securities. They provide funds to governments, government agencies, government bodies (states and municipalities), supranational organizations such as the World Bank, and corporations. Bonds differ from other loan contracts because they are brought to market by investment banks for issuers and are then traded in the financial markets. Bonds are well suited to retired investors wanting a steady cash income stream over long periods of time.

Until the 1970s, bond investing was uncomplicated, with most investors pursuing simple buy-and-hold strategies. Investors needing to sell their bonds benefited from stable bond prices. Defaults were rare because borrowers were of high-quality credit, and these factors combined to make bonds fairly safe investments. Since the 1970s, however, investing in bonds has become more complex due to greater price volatility, a decline in the credit quality of borrowers, and a spate of bond market innovations. While bonds can still be safe investments, greater care is needed in selecting them.

## The Basic Bond Contract

The most common type of bond is a promise by the issuer to make payments of interest over the term of the bond and to repay the principal (face amount) of the bond when it becomes due. If the bond is purchased at a price below the face value, the yield to maturity (return on investment) is greater than the stated interest rate. If the bond is purchased at a price above the face value, the yield to maturity is less than the stated interest rate.

Additional bond features are provided in the bond indenture, the loan agreement between the issuer and those who buy the bonds. One feature is that a bond issue is secured by specific assets, or that it is unsecured and backed only by the earning power of the borrower. Another feature is seniority, that is, how far up in the queue of claimants the bondholder stands in the event of default. The borrower may have the right to pay off the bond before its maturity date, known as the call feature, or be obliged to repay the bond gradually, according to a timetable, rather than on the maturity date. In addition to these features, the indenture may include any number of protective covenants, which are detailed promises designed to protect lenders. Compliance with all terms of the indenture is monitored by the trustee, usually a bank.

Certain bond features do not typically appear in the indenture: tax treatment, credit quality, and marketability. Tax treatment depends on the characteristics of both the borrower and lender, making generalizations difficult. Interest income is usually taxed as ordinary income in the period received, although interest from bonds issued by some government units and in certain geographic areas may be exempt from taxes. Capital gain is taxed only if realized.

Higher rates of return are required from less creditworthy borrowers as compensation for bearing the risk of default. To aid investors in credit quality judgments, borrowers pay a bond-rating agency to assess the likelihood of default. The leading bond-rating agencies, Moody's and Standard and Poor's (S&P), use similar standards and rating schemes. Both agencies categorize bonds as either "investment grade" or "speculative grade," also known as junk bonds. Default is unlikely on the former, whereas default is more likely, or has already occurred, on the latter. Within these broad categories the agencies assign finer ratings. The agencies continually monitor borrowers for changes in credit quality and may upgrade or downgrade bonds as situations change.

A final bond feature not covered in the indenture is marketability. Although a few bond issues are traded on exchanges such as the New York Stock Exchange, most are traded in over-the-counter markets by bond dealers. A bond dealer stands ready to buy bonds at a price called the "bid price" and to sell bonds at a higher price called the "ask price." The difference, the "bid-ask spread," is the transaction cost a bondholder pays when buying or selling bonds. Whether a bond can be sold quickly at a fair price depends mainly upon the average daily trading volume in the bond issue. Trading volumes range from heavy to thin.

### Bond Prices, Returns, and Risks

An investor who wants to sell a bond prior to maturity must be concerned with bond prices and how they relate to bond returns. Although the price, return, and risk properties of bonds cannot be fully detailed without the use of mathematics, the basics are easily described.

Bonds earn their returns in two ways: interest (the income yield) and value changes (the capital gains yield). Since interest payments are fixed, fluctuations are reflected in the current price an investor is willing to pay for the bond. A simplified illustration is useful. Suppose an investor buys a ten-year, $1,000 par-value bond with a 6% interest rate (coupon). If the market interest has increased from 6% to 8% since the bond was purchased, the bond's value (price) will decrease from $1,000 to $864.10. A decrease in market interest, for example, to 5%, will have the opposite effect. The $1,000 bond will become more valuable and increase to $1,135.90.

To use another example, if the market return of a 20-year, $1,000 bond with a 10% coupon declines from 10% to 8%, the bond's value (price) will rise from $1,000 to $1,197.93. The longer the term of a bond, as the example shows, the more sensitive is its price to changes in required return. Hence, a 2% change in required return produces a larger price change in the 20-year bond than the 10-year bond ($197.93 versus $135.90).

There are several risks of investment in bonds. Interest rate risk is the uncertainty in a bond's return due to uncertainty about future required market returns. An investor who buys a bond knows the interest income from the bond but faces the risk that future market increases could reduce the value of the bond. This is a problem if the investor needs to sell the bond unexpectedly. This form of interest rate risk is called price risk, which increases with a bond's term to maturity (duration). Although an investor can minimize exposure to price risk by investing in bonds with short durations, this strategy exposes the investor to another form of interest rate risk, reinvestment risk.

An investor in short-term bonds must find new bonds when old ones mature. Market changes may force the investor to accept new bonds with lower rates of interest. Unfortunately, an investor can minimize exposure to reinvestment risk only by investing in longer-term bonds and, thereby, increasing exposure to price risk.

Additionally, bonds are prone to inflation risk. Returns earned by bonds with given terms to maturity reflect a consensus forecast of the average annual rate of inflation expected during that term. Actual inflation rates may differ substantially from expectations, however. An unexpected increase in the inflation rate reduces the purchasing power of bond income and, hence, the effective (or real) return from a bond.

Default risk, that is, the risk that the borrower will fail to make a payment of interest or principal, is another type of risk. Borrowers more prone to default must offer bonds with higher coupons. Subsequent changes in the financial condition of the issuer, as tracked by bond rating agencies, may affect the return investors require to hold the bonds and, hence, their market price.

Most bonds are also subject to prepayment risk, the risk that the borrower will repay the loan early. Prepayments occur most often in the wake of a general decline in interest rates, when borrowers can obtain new loans at lower rates. Prepayments force bond investors to seek new investments at a time when bond returns are less favorable. A final form of risk is liquidity risk, the risk that an investor will be unable to sell a bond quickly at a fair price. Liquidity risk is inversely related to the volume of daily trading in the bonds and varies considerably by bond type and by issuer.

### Major Bond Issuers

Major issuers of bonds held by private individuals include the U.S. Treasury, corporations, municipal governments, and specialized mortgage lenders. Bonds of these issuers differ mainly in their credit quality, tax treatment, and marketability.

The U.S. Treasury sells both marketable and nonmarketable bonds. Treasury bonds with terms of between two and ten years are called Treasury notes. The minimum denomination for marketable Treasury bonds is $1,000. Backed by the taxing power of the U.S. government, Treasury bonds are virtually free of default risk. Interest income is subject to federal income tax but not state and local income tax. Marketable Treasury bonds are actively traded in "thick" markets. Nonmarketable Treasury bonds include U.S. Savings Bonds, which are issued in eight denominations from $50 to $10,000 and typically are held by small investors.

Like the U.S. Treasury, corporations sell both marketable and nonmarketable bonds. (Mortgage bonds, debentures, subordinated debentures, and convertible bonds are special types of corporate bonds). In contrast to stockholders, bondholders are not owners, have no voice in corporate governance, and have no claim on corporate income beyond the interest and principal payments stipulated in the bond indenture. Most corporate bonds have $1,000 par values and their interest is subject to income tax. Most marketable corporate bonds trade relatively infrequently, making them less liquid than Treasury bonds.

Until the late 1970s, only large corporations with unblemished credit records could sell bonds, with the result that most corporate bonds were of investment grade. During the 1980s, however, bond investors became willing to accept greater default risk in return for higher coupons. This change in investor sentiment led to bond selling by corporations whose creditworthiness warranted speculative bond grades. The evolution of the so-called junk bond market was arguably the most important bond market innovation of the 1980s.

Until the October 1987 stock market crash, investors holding well-diversified junk bond portfolios enjoyed returns that more than compensated for the default risk of the bonds. Since then, returns have been substantially lower.

Municipal bonds are bonds sold by state and local governments to finance such projects as road building and school construction. Municipal bonds fall into two broad categories: general obligation bonds backed by the taxing powers of the issuing government, and revenue bonds backed by the projects financed. Municipal bonds sell in minimum denominations of $5,000. Interest income is exempt from federal income tax and is usually exempt from state income tax when the bondholder resides in the state of the issue. Municipal bonds are prone to default risk; consequently, municipalities pay to have their bonds rated. Daily trading volumes range from moderately high for recent, large offerings to low for older and smaller offerings.

Bonds backed by mortgages have become increasingly popular since their development in the 1970s. Pass-throughs and collateralized mortgage obligations, or CMOs, are special types of mortgage-backed bonds. Most mortgage-backed bonds are issued by one of three federal agencies: the Government National Mortgage Association, the Federal National Mortgage Association, and the Federal Home Loan Mortgage Corporation. These agencies buy mortgages and sell bonds whose payments are based on the mortgage payments. Thus, mortgage-backed bonds are much like shares in a mutual fund. Minimum denominations are $25,000. Interest income from mortgage-backed bonds is taxed as ordinary income. Because these three federal agencies have the implicit guarantee of the U.S. federal government, mortgage-backed bonds issued by them are virtually free of default risk. Mortgage-backed bonds issued by these agencies are actively traded.

### Investment Strategies

The choice of an investment strategy hinges on the investor's investment objective. Three common investment objectives are income generation, total return maximization, and capital protection. Different objectives involve different trade-offs between the two components of bond return and the five types of risk.

Investors seeking stable incomes are more concerned with the income component of bond returns than with the capital gains component. Investors with this objective should probably favor a buy-and-hold strategy, buying and holding bonds with high coupons, low default risk, and low prepayment risk. In practical terms, this means gravitating toward longer-term, high-grade Treasury, corporate, municipal, and mortgage-backed bonds.

Investors seeking maximum total return give equal weight to the income and capital gains components of bond return. Total return maximization requires the assumption of substantial risks. Maximizing income return probably requires a willingness to consider high-coupon, speculative-grade corporate and municipal bonds, which subject the investor to default risk. Maximizing capital gains return probably requires a willingness to realize capital gains and cut capital losses by selling "winners" and "losers" at appropriate times, transactions that subject the investor to liquidity risk and reinvestment risk. Capital gains returns can sometimes be enhanced by altering the duration of a portfolio to take advantage of changes in investors' required returns on bonds. However, in light of the relatively low historical return on bond portfolios generally, especially in inflation-adjusted terms, investors seeking to maximize total return would do well to consider investing in common stocks instead of bonds.

Investors striving to protect the value of their portfolios are more concerned with the possibility of capital losses than with generating income. Investors with this objective should probably focus on high-quality, shorter-term bonds, thereby minimizing possible losses from default risk and the price component of interest rate risk. In practical terms, this probably means selecting shorter-term Treasury, corporate, municipal, and mortgage-backed bonds.

A relatively recent bond market development is the growth of bond mutual funds. Similar to equity mutual funds, bond mutual funds purchase bonds and sell shares representing proportional ownership in the underlying bonds. Bond funds tend to specialize in a particular type of bond (Treasury, corporate, municipal, or mortgage-backed) and a particular term to maturity (short-term, intermediate-term, or long-term). Bond funds aid in the construction of diversified bond portfolios, since shares in bond funds can be purchased for amounts far smaller than the minimum denominations of most types of bonds. Greater diversity also potentially reduces exposure to interest rate risk, default risk, and prepayment risk. Bond funds also tend to reduce liquidity risk, since shares of bond funds trade more actively than do the underlying bonds. Although bond funds offer investors new opportunities to reduce risk, these funds are by no means free of risk. Investors should select bond funds with investment objectives compatible with their own. (See also ASSET ALLOCATION AFTER RETIREMENT; INVESTOR EDUCATION; MUTUAL FUNDS; RISK TOLERANCE; U.S. SAVINGS BONDS; WEALTH SPAN.)

**References**

Fabozzi, Frank J., ed. 1991. *The Handbook of Fixed Income Securities*. 3rd ed. Homewood, IL: Dow Jones–Irwin.

Logue, Dennis E., ed. 1995. *The WG&L Handbook of Financial Markets*. Cincinnati, OH: South-Western Publishing.

Thau, Annette. 1995. *The Bond Book*. Chicago: Probus Publishing.

*Karlyn Mitchell*

**BROKERS.** See Agents and Brokers.

**BUDGET TECHNIQUES.** See Cash Flow Planning for Retirees; Financial Advisors.

**BUSINESS SUCCESSION PLANNING,** a process by which management and ownership of a business entity are transferred from one person or group to another, thus allowing the business to continue. The process may become complicated when transferors and transferees are members of the same family. Factors such as equality and fairness may prevail over business factors such as experience, technical ability, and accountability. Business succession has a gerontological component since a high percentage of businesses are transferred because the owner would like to retire, is concerned about obtaining funds for retirement, or wishes to transfer the responsibility to the next generation.

Only recently has the emotional aspect of business succession planning been recognized by practitioners. Since many problems in the construction of a successful business plan are legal and financial, successful technicians in this field tend to be attorneys and financial advisors. A client, especially the founder of the enterprise, tends to identify with the company. This strong identification may account for both the reluctance of entrepreneurs to retire and the observed, shortened life expectancy of those who do.

The business succession planning process involves two areas that should be considered separately: (1) family and ownership and (2) issues concerning business management. If ownership of the business will be transferred within the family, issues include stock distribution to children, equal stock rights, selling rights, and rights to employment. None of these, however, relates solely to the efficient, profitable operation of the enterprise. These issues concern continuation of a successful family relationship, but if not addressed as an integral part of the planning, the successful continuation of the business may be impossible.

Ownership succession raises other issues, including control of the business, the protection of nonvoting or minority shareholders, company philosophy regarding income distribution, compensation, and prerequisites for active versus inactive shareholders demanding high dividends. Transfer of ownership may require significant amounts of cash and sophisticated tax planning and other technical assistance. Within a family situation, the parties seeking to justify a low value for tax purposes but fair market value for interfamily transfers complicate the problem. Tax law is designed to frustrate efforts by entrepreneurs selling their businesses to family members for less than fair market value. If the business is to be sold to other than a family member, fair market value is, of course, the appropriate price. In either case, the source of cash and method of payment are critical to the success of a succession plan.

Another consideration in an ownership succession plan is time. Business owners frequently believe they have completed a succession plan when they have instead executed a "buy/sell" agreement. These agreements deal with ownership but in most cases do not address problems incident to the family or to ownership systems. Most important, buy/sell agreements are contingency plans, and they provide for the evolution of stock interests when some event (e.g., death, disability, or retirement) occurs. They do not address the more complex problems of transition necessary for a successful succession plan.

Management succession issues may conflict with family ownership arrangements. Successful management depends on accountability. Few family businesses establish job descriptions for family members or conduct performance evaluations or reviews. In today's competitive environment, management must have the power to establish performance criteria and to enforce these standards. In family businesses, questions arise regarding power to establish criteria and enforce standards. Compensation strategies for successful businesses will be based on accomplishments rather than on family ties.

### Retirement Planning

A critical element in the decision by a business owner to devise a succession plan may be whether he or she has adequate sources of retirement income, independent of the enterprise. The retirement decision involves psychological and economic factors. For many entrepreneurs, their businesses are central to their lives; the mortality component associated with retirement planning may prevent effective business succession planning. Therefore, if the succession plan is designed to become effective when the business owner retires, instead of during working years when the business owner can plan to use the proceeds to acquire a new business or to diversify investments, the development of a retirement strategy may be essential for the succession plan itself.

The psychological component of this strategy must take into account the identification problem through a period of mentoring and task transferal. The time for actual transfer of management responsibilities (not necessarily simultaneous with the transfer of control) should be fixed, and the entrepreneur/founder should thereafter act only as counselor.

When the retiring party fails to create a new focus for the energies that have brought business success, internal conflict and crisis may result. It is recommended that retirees phase into retirement using volunteer work, politics, travel, sports, or education as replacement activities for work. The key is to avoid the shock of a sudden retirement.

## Financial Aspects of Business Succession Plans

If the business is to be sold, a cash purchase presents fewest problems for the entrepreneur when the sum is sufficient to create adequate retirement cash flows. When ownership transfer is to be accomplished through gifts, installment payments, or sophisticated transfer arrangements, certain issues must be addressed. They include the cash flow needs of the entrepreneur, future inflation, and the extent to which other assets, income potential, and qualified plan investments exist.

A strategic plan for business succession overarches considerations of retirement security and psychological adjustment. Here, considerations of wealth transfer, family equity, management ability, accountability, and tax efficiency must be harmonized. The technical assistance of experienced tax and legal advisors is valuable. Where there are competing interests within a family, it may also be prudent to retain the services of a business psychologist to help the parties understand how they may best contribute to the success of the family enterprise.

In summary, addressing tax and technical legal issues is essential to the success of a business succession plan, but the parties must also recognize the emotional component that is frequently present in these transactions. Matters of control, asset balancing, retirement security, and personal identification can become threshold considerations that must be addressed before the process can begin. Beginning the process as early as possible can minimize the emotional concerns and allow development of the planning in a deliberative fashion. (See also ATTORNEYS; ENTREPRENEURSHIP; FINANCIAL ADVISORS; WORKING RETIREES.)

### References

Alcorn, P. 1982. *Success and Survival in the Family-Owned Business.* New York: McGraw-Hill.

Chasman, Herbert D. 1983. *Who Gets the Business?* Rockville Center, NY: Farnsworth Publishing.

Cohn, Mike. 1992. *Passing the Torch.* New York: McGraw-Hill.

Danco, L. 1975. *Beyond Survival.* Cleveland, OH: Center for Family Business.

Drucker, P.F. 1985. *Innovation and Entrepreneurship.* New York: Harper & Row.

Hollander, B.S. 1983. "Family-Owned Business as a System: A Case Study of the Interaction of Family, Task, and Marketplace Components." Ph.D. dissertation, School of Education, University of Pittsburgh.

Lansberg, I. 1985. "The Succession Conspiracy: Mapping Resistances to Succession Planning in First-Generation Family Firms." Unpublished paper, Yale University.

Rosenblatt, P.C., L. de Mik, R.M. Anderson, and P.A. Johnson. 1985. *The Family in Business:*

*Understanding and Dealing with the Challenges Entrepreneurial Families Face*. San Francisco, CA: Jossey-Bass.

Ward, John L. 1987. *Keeping the Family Business Healthy*. San Francisco, CA: Jossey-Bass.

*David J. Tolan*

# C

**CAPITAL GAIN,** positive change in the value of a capital asset over a specified time period. All assets owned, except for a few business assets, are termed capital assets. When an asset is sold and the owner receives income or profit in excess of the purchase price plus costs, capital gain is realized and taxes are paid. Under the most recent tax law, the Taxpayer Relief Act of 1997, the tax rate applied depends upon:

1. *Type of assets sold.* Qualifying for the lowest rates are stocks, bonds, mutual funds, and other securities. Taxed at a slightly higher rate are business or investment real estate, collectibles, and depreciation.
2. *Cost basis.* The original price paid for an investment in the capital asset (including commissions). If realized capital losses exceed realized capital gains, the excess can be offset against other income up to $3,000 per year.
3. *The length of time the assets are held before being sold and income level.* There are three holding periods for capital assets sold: those held for less than a year are considered *short term*, those held for more than a year but less than five years are considered *long term*, and those held for more than five years are considered *super long term*. Short-term capital gains are taxed at ordinary income tax rates, while long- and super-long-term capital gains receive preferential tax treatment. If an individual is in the 15% ordinary income tax bracket, long-term capital gains are taxed at a reduced rate of 10%, while super-long-term capital gains are taxed at an even more reduced rate of 8%. If an income tax bracket greater than 15% applies, then long-term and super-long-term capital gains are taxed at 20% and 18% rates, respectively. For the 18% tax rate to apply on super-long-term capital gains, the assets must have been purchased on or after January 1, 2001. For assets purchased before that date, the 20% tax rate applies.

## Long-Term Capital Gain on Homes

For many people, the single largest capital gain transaction is usually the sale of a principal place of residence. This occurs when the home is sold for more than the original purchase price plus the cost of any improvements. For most homeowners, the Taxpayer Relief Act of 1997 effectively eliminates capital gains taxes on the sale of their homes by exempting from taxation gains of up to $500,000 for couples filing jointly ($250,000 if filing singly). To be eligible for the exemption, the home in question should be the principal place of residence and occupied for at least two years in the five years prior to the sale. This is not a one-time exemption. It is available once every two years. (See also BONDS; EQUITY SECURITIES; ESTATE PLANNING; FINANCIAL ADVISORS; MUTUAL FUNDS; REAL ESTATE INVESTMENT; RELIGIOUS GIVING BY OLDER ADULTS; TAXPAYER ISSUES OF OLDER ADULTS.)

**References**

Gitman, Lawrence J., and Michael D. Joehnk. 2002. *Fundamentals of Investing*. 8th ed. Boston, MA: Addison-Wesley.

Ho, Kwok, Grady Perdue, and Chris Robinson. 1999. *Personal Financial Planning*. North York, Ontario: Captus Press.

Keown, Arthur J. 2001. *Personal Finance*. Upper Saddle River, NJ: Prentice Hall.

*Ganas K. Rakes*

**CASH BALANCE PENSION PLANS,** employer-sponsored defined benefit pension plans in which the benefit is defined by account value rather than monthly lifetime retirement income. Cash balance plans are often referred to as "hybrids" because they have some of the characteristics of traditional "defined benefit" (DB) pension plans and some of the characteristics of "defined contribution" (DC) plans, such as 401(k). In general, traditional defined benefit plans promise qualified employees an income benefit for life (or some other period) starting at "normal retirement age," without regard to how much (or little) the employer must contribute to the plan to fund the benefit. Defined contribution plans, on the other hand, promise only how much the employer will contribute to a qualified employee's account from time to time until the employee retires but they make no promises with regard to investment earnings or results, let alone a monthly income benefit for life.

Cash balance plans have some of the characteristics of both. They promise a defined benefit but define it in terms of a hypothetical account balance rather than an income stream at retirement. As with a 401(k) defined contribution plan, cash balance plan benefits are typically expressed in terms of an individual pension account balance so that an employee can understand exactly what the employer is depositing toward his or her retirement annually and what the account value is after earnings have been credited. Cash balance plans, however, still meet the same Employee Retirement Income Security Act (ERISA) minimum funding, vesting, and participation standards that other defined benefit plans are required to meet. And like other traditional DB plans, they are guaranteed by the Pension Benefit Guaranty Corporation (PBGC), a protection that is generally highly valued by employees.

In addition to expressing benefits in terms of an account value, cash balance plans are like defined contribution plans in that they offer benefit portability through the availability of lump-sum payments or tax-free "roll-overs" to an Individual Retirement Account (IRA) or a subsequent employer's pension plan after changing jobs or retirement.

Two key attributes distinguish a cash balance plan from a defined contribution plan. One is that the investment decisions—and risks—are the responsibility of the employer, not individual employees. The investment earnings allocated each year are based on a formula defined by the plan document. These investment credits are not directly tied to actual investment results with plan assets. So, with respect to this portion of their retirement funds, employees are insulated from any investment gains or losses whatsoever. Employees will receive the stated investment credit each year, regardless of the performance of the market or the employer's actual investment results, whether better or worse than the plan formula.

The other factor that distinguishes cash balance plans from defined contribution plans is the availability of payouts as a series of monthly payments for life. Cash balance plans must offer employees the ability to convert their account balances to lifetime annuities, although nearly all employers offering such programs allow (and speak in terms of) single lump-sum distributions as well. While both defined benefit and cash balance plans are required to offer payment of an employee's benefit in a series of monthly payments for life, the emphasis on account balance as opposed to lifetime income can lead an employee retiring from a cash balance plan to take the lump sum and expose himself or herself to the risk that the money will not last as long as life does.

Since Bank of America pioneered the concept of a cash balance pension plan in 1985, there has been a growing trend toward the adoption of these "hybrid" retirement programs. Employers are continuing to move away from "paternalistic"-type employee benefits in which the ultimate payout takes the form of a life annuity. They are also eliminating historical policies that provide employees with retirement benefits for life.

For corporate-sponsored retirement plans, this has meant an increased emphasis on the payment of benefits in the form of lump-sum distributions (e.g., the payout of the total benefit in one single payment). It has also sparked the rethinking of retirement benefits offered by many employers, some of which have substituted cash balance pension plans for defined benefit plans. More than $330 billion in assets has been transferred from traditional pension programs to these hybrid-type plans over the past two decades (Williamson 1999). In fact, these plans have grown so popular that at least 22 of the Fortune 100 companies have implemented such a program for some or all of their employees (Williamson 1999). Another 300 or more firms are said to be waiting in line for approvals as soon as the Treasury Department issues new regulations and lifts its moratorium on plan approvals, which is scheduled to happen in 2003. That doesn't count those that have made the conversion without waiting for Internal Revenue Service (IRS) approval.

The need for new regulations came in the wake of high-profile corporate plan conversions. In such cases, employees cried "foul" after being informed of cuts in long-term employees' projected pension benefits. Some employees were told they would lose almost two-thirds of what they had been counting on for their retirement planning due to the conversion. This was further aggravated by "wear-away" periods—numbers of years after the conversion during which long-term employees would have to work without any additional contribution to their cash balance plan because their existing benefit, derived from the defined benefit plan in which they had been participating, was greater than what they would have accrued had the cash balance plan been in effect from the beginning of their employment. The ensuing congressional hearings, class action lawsuits (in which the courts ultimately backed employees over employers), and charges of age discrimination led the IRS to declare a moratorium on issuing new approvals of cash balance pension plans.

In December 2002, the U.S. Treasury Department issued some long-awaited guidance to employers about cash balance plans. These proposed regulations, issued under Internal Revenue Code Section 411 (b)(1)(H), prohibit age discrimination in benefit accruals and are fairly comprehensive in nature. Although a public hearing on the regulations was held in April 2003, the rules are not yet final as this article goes to press.

In essence, the regulations generally indicate that a company cannot directly or indirectly affect a participant's benefit accrual based on age. The result is that future conversions to cash balance plans will likely provide transition credits to older and longer-service workers to make up for any "lost" benefits created by the conversion to a cash balance plan. A secondary result is that employers will likely put more emphasis on eliminating the "wear-away" affect that sometimes occurs when the opening balance is calculated at the time of conversion. Not everyone is satisfied with the proposed regulations, however; over 200 members of Congress have signed a letter asking President George Bush to direct the Treasury to scrap them and start over again with more sensitivity to older workers.

The problem is not cash balance plans in and of themselves but rather what happens to employees—and especially middle-age to older employees with long service to an employer—in the event of a conversion from a traditional defined benefit pension plan to a cash balance plan. When a company decides to alter its retirement plan—or even considers doing so—employees can (and do) get nervous. The uncertainties surrounding a major change in company benefits are understandable, and companies themselves often have a lot of questions about the best way to make those changes. Cash balance conversions can be particularly complex and sensitive, especially when it comes to older employees. Changing benefits later in an employee's career can generate mistrust and suspicion. To successfully undertake the move to this new type of plan requires care, planning, and a great deal of communication among all parties concerned. All of that being said, however, there are structural differences between traditional defined benefit plans and cash balance plans that necessarily work against long-service, middle-age to older employees in the event of a conversion.

Given that a typical defined benefit pension formula is some factor times final compensation (or final average compensation) times *number of years of service*, it is apparent why this is so. The biggest variable is the number of years of service. An employee who stays with one employer for an entire career may have a multiplier as large as 25 or 30 or more. Further, an employee who stays with one employer for 25 or 30 years is likely to have received a lot of raises, and so the high multiplier for number of years of service is applied to a high compensation or average compensation number. For this reason, traditional defined benefit pension plans can be seen to favor older, long-term workers, and conversions of traditional plans to cash balance plans will result in real losses to those employees.

On the other hand, an employee who shifts jobs even only every 7 to 10 years or so will not have a very big multiplier in a traditional DB plan. According to statistics published by the Employee Benefit Research Institute, only 12% of employees work a complete career (e.g., 30 years or more) with a single company (EBRI 1999). For the 88% of Americans who do switch jobs, benefits are frozen each time they change jobs, and there are no subsequent increased results from the defined benefit pension formula due to long service or higher pay. As a result, a mobile employee who switches jobs just twice during a career will find that his or her defined benefit pension is significantly lower than that of a similarly situated employee who stays with the same employer for the long haul.

In contrast, a portable cash balance plan can be seen as the best of both worlds for both the mobile employee and his or her employer. The mobile employee gets benefit credits and investment credits every year, can see and identify them clearly, and take them along if (when) he or she changes jobs—all free of investment risk and backed by the Pension Benefit Guaranty Corporation. From the employer's perspective, no more keeping track of ex-employees for 20 or 30 years to pay them a relatively small monthly benefit when they reach normal retirement age. No more uncertainty about how long retired employees will live, which means no more guessing what their pension liability *really* is. Cash balance plans result in greater certainty of cost for employers, although they do not necessarily result in a reduction of real economic cost.

In the near term, many employers may see a temporary decrease in their pension expense as reported on their financial statements. These results are attributable to accounting anomalies affecting how pension expense is recorded for traditional and cash balance plans. This short-term accounting impact sometimes creates an erroneous impression that an apparently more generous plan is somehow less expensive. The reality is this: Better benefits cost more. The long-term economic impact is often an increase in employer costs but more predictable expenses. In summary, recent history indicates that cash balance conversions can be particularly complex and sensitive, especially when it comes to older employees. Changing benefits later in an employee's career can generate mistrust and suspicion. To successfully undertake the move to this new type of plan requires care, planning, and a great deal of communication among all parties concerned. How to take care of older, long-service employees in the wake of a conversion is where the controversy about cash balance pension plans can be found. (See also AGE DISCRIMINATION IN EMPLOYMENT ACT (ADEA), DEFINED BENEFIT PENSION PLAN; DEFINED CONTRIBUTION PLAN; PENSION PLAN; RETIREMENT PLANNING.)

**References**

Campbell, Sharon. 1996. *EBRI Special Report 32/Issue Brief Number 171*. Washington, DC: EBRI, March.

Daniel, Teresa A. 2000. *Cash Balance Pension Plans: A Practical Primer*. Washington, DC: International Foundation of Employee Benefit Plans.

Demby, Elayne Robertson. 1999. "Cash-Balancing Act." *Plan Sponsor* 7(1) (February). Washington, DC: EBRI. Available online at http://www.ebri.org.

Employee Benefit Research Institute. "Retirement Patterns and Bridge Jobs in the 1990s." Available online at http://www.ebri.org/ibex/ib206.htm.

Inglis, R. Evan, and Richard R. Joss. 1999. "Smoothing the Way for Cash Balance Plans." *HR Magazine* (December).

Maury, Mary, and Victoria Shoaf. 2001. "The Effects of Adopting Cash-Balance Pension Plans." *Business Horizons* (March).

McCarthy, E.I. 2000. "Staying Off the Cover of Time." *Journal of Accountancy* (February).

Quick, Carol. 1999. "An Overview of Cash Balance Plans." *EBRI Notes* 20(7) (July).

Williamson, Christine. 1999. "Cash Balance Catches Fire." *Pension & Investments* 27 (May): 11.

*Teri Daniel*

**CASH FLOW PLANNING FOR RETIREES,** the process by which the flow of income necessary to sustain a given standard of living in retirement is identified and financed.

It is perhaps the most critical part of retirement planning. Cash flow planning for retirees depends crucially on two factors: (1) the resource constraints a retiree faces in terms of assets and other sources of income and (2) the desires and needs a retiree has for spending in retirement. Both of these, in turn, depend to a great degree on when the planning is done.

While cash flow planning is of clear importance to retirees, it is of even greater importance to preretirees. By the time a person retires, the resource constraints he or she will face as a retiree are typically firmly in place. Some modification of these financial constraints may be possible in cases where a return to work is possible; however, in many cases this is not feasible. For preretirees, decisions with regard to saving or spending for current consumption will play a critical role in determining the constraints that will be faced later in retirement. Intelligent investing, asset allocation, and luck (good and bad) each have a role in determining financial constraints in retirement, but the determination of how much to save is the most critical variable. It is difficult, if not impossible, for preretirees to make optimal saving decisions without a firm idea of their cash flow needs in retirement. Without paying some attention to cash flow planning in retirement, preretirees may make decisions that result in resource constraints that are much more restrictive than they need to be or end up with constraints that are too slack, resulting in unnecessarily forgone spending when young and a waste of resources when old.

### Identifying a Retirement Standard of Living

There are at least two schools of thought with regard to the basic principles involved in planning for retirement spending. The first, and most common, approach poses the problem as a seemingly simple determination of the income needs of a retiree relative to preretirement income. This is typically expressed as a "replacement rate," in which a retiree targets a given fraction of his or her preretirement income level as an amount adequate to sustain a desired lifestyle without working. Often, a particular level of income is given as a rule of thumb (e.g., 80% of preretirement income). While this rule appears to provide simple and easily communicated guidance, it masks several aspects of the complexity of the problem. At least two questions left unanswered by such rules of thumb are: (1) Why is 80% (or any other figure) the "right" number? and (2) How, exactly, does a dollar of accumulated assets get transformed into a stream of income at the point of retirement?

A second, perhaps preferable, approach to retirement cash flow planning attempts to rectify the first deficiency by being much more careful about the determination of the spending desires of retirees instead of spending being determined by income level. This approach involves a highly detailed determination of the spending needs and desires of the retiree and his or her household. While many financial professionals unfortunately consider such analysis unglamorous and unexciting work, it is perhaps the most basic and critically important form of financial planning. Such a determination of cash flow needs or desires typically includes a detailed estimation of living expenses, including items such as dining and groceries, mortgage or rental payments, health, life, and long-term care insurance premium payments, and predicable one-time expenditures (such as large planned gifts or outlays). Expected annual or lump-sum expenditures on other items, such as travel, clothing, and replacement of large durables, are also tallied and cataloged.

### Additional Considerations

In addition, anticipated future rates of increase or decrease in living expenses (due to inflation or other considerations) must be estimated and described and the projected needed amounts "grossed up" to account for estimated future income tax rates. Sustaining the purchasing power of the income received—accounting for inflation—is the first variable that must be dealt with. Inflation will not be a major issue if death occurs shortly after retirement, but increasing life expectancies suggest this is a significant matter. Inflation can best be built into this projecting needs phase of cash flow planning rather than in the later process of determining sources and amounts of cash flow and an appropriate investment profile. What matters most is that it only be done once—and not accounted for twice.

Grossing up is the process of calculating how much gross income is needed at a projected effective tax rate to arrive at a needed amount of income. For example, it takes $1,250 at a 20% effective tax rate to have $1,000 to pay for living expenses. How one projects and coordinates the inflation and taxation factors is an important but inexact exercise, and often the advice of a financial advisor is especially desirable for this step.

Finally, another category of expense must be included: considerations such as providing a bequest to heirs, making a charitable donation to other beneficiaries, or creating a reserve for emergencies. This step will affect the calculation of assets that are available to supply the necessary income. To make an effective assessment of how to finance cash flow needs in retirement, a detailed description of all of these needs, and other planned expenditures, is critical. These calculations produce a detailed pattern of expected expenditures over the retiree's lifetime and that of his or her spouse and dependents.

### Financing Projected Cash Flow Needs

Once the cash flows to be financed are determined, whether via a detailed version of the determination of planned expenditures or the simpler "rule of thumb approach," the question of how each $1 of assets will be turned into an income flow must be addressed. How much income will each dollar generate, and for how long? This is the basic issue of longevity risk (the risk that a person will live either beyond, or not until, their "life expectancy"). This source of uncertainty presents perhaps the most significant challenge for cash flow planning in retirement.

Fortunately, the most significant source of income for most retirees, Social Security, is structured to overcome both longevity risk and the eroding effects of inflation. Income payments continue as long as retirees or dependents are alive to receive them. In other words, longevity risk is not a factor in Social Security income flows. In addition, Social Security income payments are indexed to price inflation, and thus this income is not subject to erosion by high inflation. The second most common source of cash flow after retirement, traditional company pensions (called "defined benefit" pensions), also enable retirees to receive an income stream that will last at least until their death. In some cases, continuing income payments are made to dependents after the death of the covered worker. In most cases, the income payments available through employer-provided defined benefit pensions are not explicitly tied to inflation.

For some people, Social Security and traditional pension benefits provide the basic foundation from which most retirement expenditures will be funded. For those who are not able to fund their expenditures from these two sources alone, other resources saved for retirement must be tapped. Other assets, accumulated either inside a tax-preferred savings account such as an Individual Retirement Account (IRA) or a 401(k)-type pension plan, are increasingly necessary for financing retirement spending. Efficient use of these assets to fund an income stream is an important issue.

In much of the literature directed at financial planners and their more knowledgeable clients, the only mechanism considered for the liquidation of accumulated balances to finance expenditures is a process of systematic or periodic withdrawals (Bengen 1994; Pye 2000). Researchers have analyzed the sustainability of various patterns of withdrawals over long periods of time, and their results may be seen by many as surprising: while the sustainability of systematic income withdrawals varies with asset type, the rate at which one can safely liquidate such assets over a long period is far below that which is typically assumed by some individuals and even some financial advisors. For example, the study by Pye (2000) finds that a withdrawal rate of 4% over even a ten-year period has only a 92% chance of success.

Basically, these results suggest that if future rates of return on financial assets are similar to past returns, one must spend at low rates and conserve for the possibility of a long expenditure period and even modest rates of inflation in retirement. If a person lives a long time in retirement, the amount of assets left for bequests or other purposes will be substantially reduced.

If, on the other hand, a person does not live a long time in retirement, the consequences of longevity risk are that funds and assets will be left as unspent, unplanned (and in some cases constitute an undesired) bequest. It is important to note that this risk is entirely separate from financial, or market, risk. Choosing a combination of risky or risk-free assets in a portfolio will certainly affect total financial risk and total expected return on the level of assets available to a retiree, but such planning will not necessarily affect longevity risk. Even if a retiree could obtain a very high, guaranteed rate of return on accumulated assets, he or she could still spend too much, or too little, as a result of not knowing how long he or she may need to spend.

More recent research on retirement cash flow focuses on alternatives to systematic withdrawals for financing retirement cash flows and on immediate life annuities in particular. Immediate life annuities are an insurance product through which individuals can convert an asset or lump sum into an income stream that is paid to them (and/or to a spouse partner or other beneficiary) as long as they live. These vehicles enable those with 401(k) or other accumulated assets to obtain a benefit similar to that of a "traditional" company pension.

The basic rationale for the use of life annuities for this purpose is explained in an article that is now over 35 years old (Yaari 1965). This theoretical paper shows that in the absence of an overriding bequest motive, and even reasonable cost assumptions, rational, risk-averse individuals would exclusively use a life-contingent annuity arrangement to fund consumption expenditures. This results because under these assumptions as long as one is alive and continues to enjoy spending, the annuity vehicle effectively provides a higher rate of total return. When a bequest motive is introduced, the result changes, but it is not completely reversed. Because of the desire to leave a bequest, assets also have value when one is no longer alive. It follows that individuals then rationally hold back some assets from the life-contingent "annuity pool" in order to finance their bequests. As a consequence, they only "partially annuitize" a portfolio of assets.

Recent results, in particular those of Ameriks, Veres, and Warshawsky (2001), and more recently, Ibboston (2002), illustrate that given real-world assumptions and costs, the use of immediate life annuities (i.e., partial annuitization) can provide a means for hedging longevity risk, thereby increasing the likelihood and size of funds being left unannuitized while funding a retirement cash flow. Immediate life annuities can therefore provide a means for individuals to plan more effectively for the desired use and disposition of their assets for financing cash flow in retirement. Immediate life annuities can efficiently finance stable periodic income needs, while unannuitized assets can be set aside and managed appropriately for emergency or contingency planning and bequests.

There has as of yet been surprisingly little practical research related to the determination of the optimal level of annuitized and unannuitized assets for the financing of cash flows in retirement and the optimal management of those assets. Part of this is a result of the fact that there are many complex issues surrounding the use of annuities in retirement. These include the critical issue of cost. The cost issues are perhaps most clearly addressed in a recent article by Mitchell et al. (1999).

In addition, there is an issue of timing. Because immediate annuity purchases are irreversible, there may be a value to postponing their use, especially for younger individuals (Milevsky and Young 2002). As self-managed retirement account balances begin to account for more and more of the financial resources dedicated to generating cash flow in retirement, it seems clear that the appropriate use of annuities and other mechanisms of financing retirement will need to receive far greater attention.

Because there are few effective rules of thumb, in general, the cash flow planning for retirees is a challenge that can only be tackled by careful and thorough financial planning, judicious allocation and management of assets, and appropriate use of the vehicles available to hedge longevity risk. (See also ASSET ALLOCATION AFTER RETIREMENT; RETIREMENT EXPENSE PLANNING; RETIREMENT PLANNING; RETIREMENT PLANNING SOFTWARE; WEALTH SPAN.)

**References**

Ameriks, John, Robert Veres, and Mark J. Warshawsky. 2001. "Making Retirement Income Last a Lifetime." *Journal of Financial Planning* 14:60–76.

Bengen, William P. 1994. "Determining Withdrawal Rates Using Historical Data." *Journal of Financial Planning* 14–24.

Ibbotson Inc. 2002. "The Role of Immediate Annuities in Retirement." Available online at http://www.ibbotson.com/default.asp.

Milevsky, Moshe, and Virginia R. Young. 2002. "Optimal Asset Allocation and the Real Option to Delay Annuitization: It's Not Now or Never." Working Paper, York University.

Mitchell, Olivia S., James M. Poterba, Mark J. Warshawsky, and Jeffrey R. Brown. 1999. "New Evidence on the Money's Worth of Individual Annuities." *American Economic Review* 89: 1299–1318.

Pye, Gordon B. 2000. "Sustainable Investment Withdrawals." *Journal of Portfolio Management* (Summer): 73–83.

Yaari, Menahem E. 1965. "Uncertain Lifetime, Life Insurance, and the Theory of the Consumer." *Review of Economic Studies* 32: 137–50.

*John Ameriks*

**CHARITABLE CONTRIBUTIONS,** gifts made to eligible organizations consistent with existing laws and designed to benefit society from an educational, religious, moral, physical, or social standpoint.

One characteristic of American society is its array of nonprofit institutions. Writing nearly 200 years ago in *Democracy in America*, Alexis de Tocqueville observed upon visiting the United States:

> Americans of all ages, all stations in life, and all types of disposition are forever forming associations. . . . [They] combine to give fetes, found seminaries, build churches, distribute books, and send missionaries to the antipodes. Hospitals, prisons, and schools take shape in that way. . . . In every case, at the head of any new undertaking, where in France you would find the government or in England some territorial magistrate, in the United States you are sure to find an association.

Today, U.S. colleges and universities, hospitals, schools, zoos, museums, and other institutions are admired worldwide. One factor that makes these institutions unique is that so many of them are supported primarily by voluntary contributions of cash and property from private citizens. This system of voluntary support for nonprofit institutions is sometimes characterized as a parallel to the private enterprise economic system.

### Why We Give

Contributions are encouraged by such widely varied motivations as the affection one feels for his or her college, the gratitude of a patient treated in a nonprofit hospital, the compassion of a person whose loved one has been lost to a dreaded disease for which a cure is being sought, or the deep feelings a churchgoer holds for his or her religion. While individual motivations differ, one important incentive encouraging charitable giving is the tax treatment of charitable contributions in the United States.

The most fundamental tax incentive is the income tax charitable deduction. Amounts given to qualified charitable organizations can be deducted from the donor's income in computing his or her income tax. There are a number of detailed limitations, but for most donors who itemize their deductions, amounts given to charity are deductible up to one-half of their income. Any excess over the amount deductible in a given year may be carried over and deducted in each of the five subsequent taxable years.

### Contributors Must Have Receipts

All tax deductions must be proven since the Internal Revenue Service is understandably skeptical of the taxpayer who has no evidence to support a claimed deduction. Charitable contributions, however, are subject to even more stringent rules in this regard.

Donors' deductions for contributions of $250 or more may be disallowed unless they have timely receipts from their donees stating the amount contributed (or, in the case of property contributions, a description of the contributed property), plus a description and the estimated value of any goods or services provided to the donee in consideration of his or her contribution. If no goods or services are given to the donor, the receipt must state that fact. This latter rule is designed to prevent donors from claiming deductions for amounts that are really purchases rather than contributions. An example would be a payment of $1,000 to a symphony orchestra organization for a fund-raising event, where the donor received the right to attend a concert and a postconcert dinner; if the value of the concert and dinner totals $250, the donor's deduction is limited to $750, and the receipt must tell him so.

Many individuals give freely of their time, talents, and money. These contributions of services and other volunteer time are not deductible, although volunteers may deduct any out-of-pocket expenses incurred in rendering services to a charitable organization. Blood donors likewise receive no tax benefits.

### Planned Giving: More for the Money

In addition to a straightforward gift of cash or property, there are other ways to structure charitable contributions so as to provide substantial benefits to the donor and the recipient. This approach, often referred to as planned giving, generally involves contributions that produce an income stream to the donor, followed by an eventual transfer to a charitable beneficiary. The term *planned giving* refers to gifts other than simple cash donations and is subject to a number of sophisticated rules. Planned giving transfers can offer particularly attractive benefits to persons who are either retired or planning for their retirement. Several planned giving vehicles are designed specifically for donors who, like retirees or prospective retirees, want to make a charitable gift but are also concerned about their income.

### Charitable Remainder Trusts (CRTs)

These are trusts that make distributions to the donor or another beneficiary for life, or for a term of up to 20 years, then turn the remaining trust property to a charitable beneficiary. There are two types of CRTs. The charitable remainder unitrust pays a stated percentage (at least 5%) of the trust corpus to the donor or other beneficiary each year. Thus, if the value of the trust assets doubles, the current payout will also double, and if the value of the trust declines, the distributions likewise go down. The other type, the charitable remainder annuity trust, pays out a fixed amount to its current beneficiaries each year for as long as the trust continues. Some donors like the certainty of a fixed payout, while others prefer the potentially increasing income provided by the unitrust alternative.

Upon creating a CRT, the donor receives a current income deduction equal to the actuarial value of the charitable remainder interest in the trust. If the trust is funded with appreciated property (i.e., property that would produce a capital gain and hence a capital gain tax if the donor sold it instead of contributing it), an additional benefit is available. Because the CRT is exempt from income tax, this capital gain tax will be avoided if the property is transferred to the trust and then sold by the trustee. Since 1997, a CRT will not qualify for either of these benefits unless the value of the charitable remainder interest in the trust is at least 10% of the total trust assets.

### Pooled Income Funds

The CRT can produce dramatic results but may be impractical for smaller gifts, since donors must create and maintain a trust with the help of attorneys knowledgeable in this area. There is annual upkeep as well, for the trust must file annual income tax returns and perhaps pay trustee's fees and other expenses as well. These expenses may be justified if the donor is contemplating a fairly large gift of $50,000 or more since the donor can customize the trust to fit his or her plans.

This expense is avoided when a donor uses a pooled income fund operated by a charity in lieu of creating a trust. The fund pools together the contributions of many donors into a single investment fund that pays income to the donors for life and at the donor's death distributes the donor's share to the charity that maintains it. As with the CRT, the donor receives a charitable tax deduction for the actuarial value of the charity's interest in the donor's contribution.

The expense of creating and maintaining a pooled income fund is borne by the fund's sponsoring charity. The donor signs a one-page instrument of transfer and sends it back to the charity with a contribution. Most funds have a minimum contribution, usually $5,000. The fund is usually managed by a skilled investment manager at no cost to the donor.

While the pooled income fund resembles a mutual fund, it is actually very different. Many planned giving vehicles resemble investments, but they are not investments, and this is important to remember. All of the tax benefits flow from the pooled fund or trust because the property contributed has been given irrevocably to a charitable organization. This is the opposite of an investment, which the purchaser owns and can sell or leave to children or other private beneficiaries.

### Charitable Gift Annuities

The charitable gift annuity is a different arrangement that produces a result much like the CRT or the pooled income fund. Instead of a trust or fund, the charity and the donor enter into a private annuity arrangement. The donor gives the charity cash or property and receives in exchange the charity's promise to pay to the donor (and/or another beneficiary) a stated amount for life. The actuarial value of the annuity stream is less than the value of the cash or property given to the charity, and the difference is the amount of the donor's income tax charitable deduction.

In times when interest and dividend rates are low, the charitable gift annuity is generally favored over the pooled income fund for smaller gifts because the donor/beneficiary generally receives a larger income amount. In addition, a part of that income is generally tax free under the rules governing annuities.

### Planning for Retirement—A Practical Example

Norris and Martha have some stock they bought ten years ago for $12,000. This stock is now worth $75,000 but pays them only $1,000 per year in dividends. If they sell the stock to reinvest in higher-income investments, they will have only about $52,000 left after capital gains taxes. At a 5% return, that would produce income of $2,600 per year. They would like to provide an eventual bequest to their church, but feel they will need their nest egg for retirement.

If Norris and Martha transfer the stock to a CRT, the trustee can sell the stock and have virtually the entire $75,000 available to reinvest; at 5%, that would produce annual income of $3,750, an increase of more than 40% over the dividends they now receive. The trust will provide Norris and Martha with an income stream that will continue for as long as either of them is alive, and upon the death of the last, the remaining trust property will pass to their church. If they want even more income, they can have their trust drafted with a higher payout, 7% or 8%, for example.

Additionally, Norris and Martha will be entitled to an income tax deduction in the year they create the trust. The amount of that deduction depends upon several variables—their ages, the terms of the trust (primarily its payout rate), and the IRS actuarial interest rate for the month in which they create the trust.

Although this example involved a CRT, Norris and Martha may receive similar benefits using a pooled income fund or a charitable gift annuity. Selecting the best vehicle may require the help of an experienced charitable gift planner. Most universities and larger charities have such planners on staff to help donors make this selection; even though a donor may prefer to have advice from an independent source rather than the potential donee organization, the donee's planned giving officer can still be an important (and free) source of information. Most donees will gladly provide such information but advise the donor to consult his or her own advisors for advice on the tax consequences of a proposed gift.

### Other Charitable Arrangements

There are other ways to structure charitable contributions to cover particular financial circumstances. For example, a person might use a charitable lead trust to generate large estate and gift tax savings on large transfers. Such a trust operates much like the CRT except the positions of the parties are reversed. The charitable lead trust makes distributions to charity for a stipulated number of years, after which the remaining trust property is turned over to the donor's family. Such trusts are often established by means of a decedent's will. Newspaper accounts described the use of such an arrangement under Jacqueline Kennedy Onassis's will to virtually eliminate estate taxes on her large estate.

A bargain sale arrangement may be used to transfer property to charity by means of a sale, but the price is less than the full value of the property. For example, a school may want to acquire land adjacent to its campus; the owner is willing to sell it to the school for $40,000 even though it is worth $100,000. Thus, the "seller" is really a donor and has made a $60,000 charitable contribution. He or she has also made a sale and may have a capital gain tax to pay. On these facts, since the property was sold for only 40% of its full value, only 40% of the tax basis would be used in computing capital gain. Thus, if the donor/seller in this example had paid $40,000 for the land in question, he or she would realize a gain for tax purposes of $24,000 (sales proceeds of $40,000, less 40% of the $40,000 cost basis, or $16,000).

Finally, some donors are reluctant to make a contemplated charitable contribution because they do not want to deny their children or other beneficiaries the property they would be contributing to charity. For this situation, the donor might want to consider a wealth replacement trust. Although not an actual charitable device, such a trust is often used in conjunction with a sizable charitable transfer. For example, if a donor is considering making a contribution of $100,000 to a CRT, some of the distributions from the trust could be used to buy a $100,000 life insurance policy through an irrevocable life insurance trust. Such a trust is called a wealth replacement trust because it allows the donor to replace the wealth being given to charity. The CRT will provide the donor with an income stream for life, and upon the donor's death, the charity receives the property remaining in the CRT, and family beneficiaries receive the policy proceeds, with no estate tax payable on either amount.

A wealth replacement trust requires caution. If a donor has serious reservations about the amount of a proposed charitable contribution, the proposed contribution may be too large. No responsible charity, under normal circumstances, would encourage a donor to give away a major portion of the donor's estate while he or she was still alive and might potentially need the funds. Moreover, the purchase of insurance is entirely separate from the proposed charitable contribution, and the donor must decide whether such insurance is necessary or desirable.

### Family Foundations and Alternatives

A person who is very charitably-minded may wish to consider creating his or her own charity to facilitate ongoing support for causes or organizations deemed important. If the amounts in question are large enough to warrant the cost, a *family foundation* can be created. This is a private charity (either a nonprofit corporation or a trust) that is qualified with the Internal Revenue Service as a charitable organization for tax purposes. Amounts transferred to a foundation are deductible for income tax purposes, and amounts left to it on the death of the donor are also deductible for federal estate tax purposes. The foundation can hold such amounts as an endowment fund to generate investment income that it can devote to its charitable purposes.

A family foundation can serve a number of nontax purposes as well. A donor who contributes funds to a family foundation can maintain ongoing control of the contributions as they are kept in the foundation or passed on to other charities. This provides institutionalized yet flexible giving and allows the donor and his or her family to maintain and endow an ongoing charitable giving program that even lasts past the donor's death. A foundation can offer a donor privacy and insulation from unwelcome charitable solicitations. In addition, the foundation serves as a family institution or memorial and can help with the personal development of younger family members—introducing them to philanthropy and to the basics of investments and money management.

Most family foundations operate primarily by making grants to other charitable organizations, as determined by its trustees or directors, but it may also have active charitable operations of its own. The tax rules governing foundations are quite complex—including limitations on the deductions allowed to donors and a series of operating restrictions. For this reason, a person contemplating creating a foundation should consult an attorney who is familiar with these rules.

Much of the advantage of a foundation can be accomplished without the cost and complication by using a *donor-advised fund*. Such funds are offered by community foundations in virtually every region of the United States and by a number of financial institutions and mutual fund firms—even by some colleges and national charities. A donor-advised fund may be maintained by a charity, or it may be a separate charitable organization in its own right.

The donor's gifts to the fund are charitable contributions, fully deductible for tax purposes. The fund uses those contributions to create an account for the donor from which distributions will be made to other charitable organizations. The donor and his or her family retain the right to make nonbinding recommendations or advice to the sponsoring charity as to what distributions will be made from their account, and the sponsoring charity is free to accept or reject that advice. Although the donor thus has no real legal control over his or her account, as a practical matter, the donor's advice is typically followed. So long as the donor and the family make recommendations for grants to recognized, publicly supported charities, the use of a donor-advised fund enables the donor to achieve almost the same effect as a family foundation but without the accompanying expense and complication. (See also ANNUITIES; ATTORNEYS; ELDER LAW PRACTICE; ESTATE PLANNING; RELIGIOUS GIVING BY OLDER ADULTS; TRUSTS; WILLS.)

**References**

Arthur Andersen and Co. 2003. *The Tax Economics of Charitable Giving*. Chicago: Arthur Andersen.

Bowen, William G. 1994. *The Charitable Non-profits: An Analysis of Institutional Dynamics and Characteristics*. San Francisco, CA: Jossey-Bass.

Colliton, James W. 1993. *Charitable Gifts*. Colorado Springs, CO: Shepard's/McGraw-Hill.

*Internal Revenue Code* (Title 26, U.S. Code). Section 170.

McCoy, Jerry J., and Kathryn W. Miree. 2001. *Family Foundation Handbook*. New York: Aspen Publishers. Available online at http://www.aspenpublishers.com/.

Nagai, Althea K., Robert Lerner, and Stanley Rothman. 1994. *Giving for Social Change: Foundations, Public Policy, and the American Political Agenda*. Westport, CT: Praeger.

Tocqueville, Alexis de. 2001. *Democracy in America*. Ed. Richard D. Heffner. New York: Signet.

U.S. Congress. 1994. Senate Committee on Commerce, Science, and Transportation. Subcommittee on the Consumer. *Charitable Solicitation Fraud: Hearing before the Subcommittee on the Consumer of the Committee on Commerce, Science, and Transportation*. Washington, DC: GPO.

*Jerry J. McCoy*

**COHABITATION,** heterosexual couples living together without legally being married. Although infrequent, cohabitation does occur among couples older than 65. As with marriage after age 65, availability of a partner plays a significant role in cohabitation trends. Since most men ages 65 and older are married, there is a shortage of men 65 and older for cohabitation. More women than men survive to older ages, but even so, older men cohabit at rates two to three times the rates for older women. This percentage varies with race/ethnicity and 5-year age groupings.

The U.S. Census Bureau identified 3.8 million households as unmarried-partner households of which 5.3% were opposite sex unmarried-partner households. The number of people 65 and over who are living together in a cohabiting household increased 7% from 1980 to 1990, and 60% from 1990 to 2000, for an overall increase of 71%. One of the difficulties in measuring the change in cohabitation over time is how this living arrangement is measured. Prior to 1990, the number of cohabiting couples was estimated using indirect methods of inferring cohabitation. When using these methodologies, some households are included that do not meet the Census Bureau's POSSLQ definition (roommates), and some "true" cohabitors in households are not included because of the presence of children aged 15 and over. In 1990, the Census Bureau added the category of unmarried-partner households in the Current Population Survey and the census.

At the present time, most general knowledge about cohabitation is based on data collected about the younger population (35 years old and younger). The availability of data that reflects self-reported cohabitational status in large public samples will make it easier for researchers to conduct studies of older cohabitants, of which there are few. However, cohabiting data taken from the census and Current Population Survey are likely to underrepresent the actual number of cohabiting households due to reluctance of many, especially seniors, to report nontraditional consensual unions. Older adults often are uncomfortable with cohabitation and may be reluctant to disclose their status as cohabitors. The ageism that persists in society, especially as it relates to sexuality in later years, is reflected in the behavior of older adults. While older people may accept children who cohabit, they may avoid cohabitation themselves due to concerns about what peers might say or think.

For many older people to consider cohabitation as an alternative to other living arrangements, they must have strong reasons that transcend their natural unwillingness to go against societal and familial customs. Economic factors may constitute the most important reason seniors have to consider cohabitation. The adage "two can live cheaper than one" is not without some truth, and economic incentives to cohabit may parallel economic theories of marriage. If both partners have resources to contribute to the household, there may be economic gains to cohabitation in retirement. Constraints to marriage for seniors may come in the form of federal taxes and Social Security or death benefits.

A marriage penalty or tax on marriage originates from the "breadwinner system," under which men earned income and women had no market earnings. One-earner couples in this system are equated with two-earner couples. Despite today's workplace realities, the marriage penalty still exists, and retired older persons are not necessarily exempt. Elevated Social Security income is now taxable, and other sources of income in retirement have always been taxable. In addition to potential loss of survivor's benefits under Social Security upon remarriage before age 60 and the lower rate paid for a spouse benefit than a widow benefit, the maximum allowable earned benefits for a two-earner couple are less than they would be if each were collecting benefits as individuals. Private pensions can be at risk upon remarriage as well. Eligibility for Medicaid benefits is another important economic consideration for those older persons who might wish to remarry. When an eligible person marries, Medicaid regulations require that the savings of the new partner must be exhausted before eligibility is reinstated.

Intergenerational inheritance transfers may also be a factor in decisions either to remarry or cohabit. Research indicates that adult children cite inheritance as the biggest concern in their opposition to remarriage of parents. Courts, however, are moving toward recognition of cohabitational relationships, and precohabitation contracts may become necessary to ensure that inheritance will pass directly to children. In addition, trends indicate an increase in bequests to nonfamily members, including cohabitants, which may spur adult children to contest wills that contain such bequests.

In research that focuses on the portion of the population that is 45 years old and older, several economic factors—job income, Social Security and Supplemental Security Income, investment income, and homeownership—have been found to increase the likelihood that an older person will cohabit. The lower the income at advanced ages, the higher the proportion of older people who cohabit. Seniors tend to cohabit if they no longer can work for health reasons or when they are eligible for entitlement income. The effects on cohabitation are not as clear for homeownership. Cohabitors are more likely to be renters than their married counterparts. However, cohabitors are more likely to be homeowners than older single persons who are not cohabiting.

There are several reasons to expect an increase in cohabitation among those 65 and older. First, decreased mortality rates will increase the population aged 65 and older who are available to cohabit. Second, because divorced persons are more likely to cohabit, an increase in divorce is likely to bring about a corresponding increase in cohabitation. Third, the population aged 45 to 64 has a higher propensity to cohabit than those aged 65 and older, and it is likely that as these persons age, they will continue to have higher proportions of persons cohabiting. Finally, those who came of age during the 1960s and later have embraced cohabitation as an acceptable alternative to marriage. They undoubtedly will reflect this acceptance in their own lives as they age into the twenty-first century. (See also ESTATE PLANNING; FINANCES OF AGING IN THE GAY COMMUNITY; MARRIAGE AND OLDER ADULTS; SOCIAL SECURITY PROGRAM OF THE UNITED STATES; TITLING ASSETS.)

**References**

Casper, Lynne M., and Philip N. Cohen. 2000. "How Does POSSLQ Measure Up? National Estimates of Cohabitation." *Demography* 37(2) (May): 237–45.

Eekelaar, John J., and Sanford N. Katz, eds. 1980. *Marriage and Cohabitation in Contemporary Societies: Areas of Legal, Social and Ethical Change.* Toronto: Butterworths.

Fields, Jason, and Lynne M. Casper. 2001. *America's Families and Living Arrangements: March 2000.* Current Population Reports, P20-537. Washington, DC: U.S. Census Bureau.

Gronvold-Hatch, Rebecca. 1995. *Aging and Cohabitation.* New York: Garland Publishing.

Smock, P. 2000. "Cohabitation in the United States: An Appraisal of Research Themes, Findings, and Implications." *Annual Review of Sociology* 26: 1–20.

Spanier, Graham B. 1985. "Cohabitation in the 1980s: Recent Changes in the United States." In *Contemporary Marriages: Comparative Perspectives on a Changing Institution*, ed. K. Davis with A. Grossbard-Schectman. New York: Russell Sage Foundation.

*Rebecca Gronvold-Hatch*

**COMMODITIES,** goods, produce, wares, and in general, all items that are bought and sold in commerce. Out of this large group, only certain items are traded as commodity future contracts, mainly due to their universal acceptance and marketability throughout the world. These include, but are not limited to, raw agricultural goods in the agricultural area, such as corn, wheat, soybeans, sugar, coffee, cocoa, and orange juice. Additional examples include the meat markets of cattle, pork bellies, and other food products; the energy complex of crude oil, heating oil, and unleaded gas; and the precious metals, such as gold and silver. Newer financial instruments traded as commodities are Treasury bonds and Treasury bills, eurodollar bonds, international currencies (the European euro, the Japanese yen, the Korean won), and more recently, stock index futures, weather futures, and electricity futures. Futures are contracts, standardized in quantity and quality, for the purchase or sale of a commodity at a specified future time and place. All transactions are placed through a commodity exchange by a member of the exchange.

Commodities investment is often considered the high-wire act of the investment arena. *Substantial risk* is the first key term associated with commodity trading. In the hands of knowledgeable and sophisticated professionals, commodities can be an investment that provides substantial gain or risk transfer. As a means of enhancing financial security for one's older years, the first rule for the individual investor is to understand thoroughly the investment tool and the risk of capital; the saying that 95% of commodity players lose contains some truth. Once thoroughly understood, however, commodities trading can enhance a diversified portfolio when sufficient risk capital exists to permit it.

Buyers or sellers must post collateral, or margin, which is a promise to perform when trades are made in order to show good faith in fulfilling their future obligations. The value of contracts is determined by the price of entry, or cost per unit, multiplied by the quantity. The transactions are contractual obligations to be satisfied prior to the designated date of delivery, either by taking or making physical delivery of the approved grade and quantity of the commodity.

The majority of commodities transactions are closed out prior to delivery by offsetting sales or purchases of the same commodity on the exchange for an equivalent quantity and delivery date. Contractual obligations of certain futures contracts, for example, a stock index future, are satisfied by offsetting sales or purchases or by cash settlements of the amount on the expiration date of the contract. The investor's profit or loss is the difference between the price at which the person acquired the futures contract and its value on the offsetting trade or, if held until expiration, its value on the expiration/settlement date.

Futures markets are organized by commodity futures exchanges. The exchanges standardize the terms of all contracts, oversee trading, and coordinate all payments. Only members of an exchange are permitted to trade. Historically future orders received by member firms were transmitted to the exchange floor for execution. This is achieved by an open outcry system where bids and offers are presented to all members of the pit or ring present at the time. While this open outcry system is still used, technology in the late 1990s brought the advent of computer screen–trading networks where buyers and sellers are matched electronically within a few seconds.

The two largest exchanges in the United States are the Chicago Board of Trade (CBOT) and the Chicago Mercantile Exchange (CME). Other exchanges include the New York Mercantile Exchange (NYMEX), the Commodity Exchange (COMEX), and the Kansas City Board of Trade (KCBOT). Foreign commodity exchanges include the London International Financial Futures Exchange (LIFFE), the Singapore International Financial Futures Exchange (SIMEX), and the Korean Futures Exchange (KOSPI).

In the United States, legislation by Congress was enacted to regulate trading, the exchanges, the brokers, brokerage houses, advisors, and pool operators. The controlling legislation, known as the Commodity Exchange Act (1974), is designed to promote the orderly and systematic marketing of commodities and commodity futures contracts, while preventing fraud, speculative excess, and price manipulations. The act is implemented by the rules and regulations set by the Commodity Futures Trading Commission (CFTC). The CFTC is the government agency responsible for regulating domestic commodity exchanges and commodity futures trading. The National Futures Association (NFA) is the self-regulatory body of commodity professionals. Any violations of the Commodity Exchange Act are subject to punishment including revocation of registration, civil fines, and imprisonment.

The two basic groups of participants in futures trading are "hedgers" and "speculators." Those individuals or companies directly involved with the production, marketing, or processing of certain commodities (the cash commodity or actuals market), such as farmers or mining companies, utilize futures markets primarily for hedging, a strategy designed to minimize losses from price fluctuations over a period of time. This generally covers the time between which merchandisers or processors contract to sell their raw or processed commodities and the time they must deliver. The objective of hedgers in the futures market is to protect the profit they expect to earn from their farming, merchandizing, or processing operations. Many hedge strategies share the basic concept of minimizing risk exposure to interim price fluctuations. Other examples of hedging include U.S. companies that rely on imported goods or parts for manufacturing. If the company requires 5 million European euros in three months to pay for parts, the company can lock in the exchange rate by using the currency futures market to offset devaluation over that period of time.

Unlike hedgers, speculators generally do not expect either to deliver or receive physical commodities, or to hedge against price volatility, but rather to profit from price fluctuations in the value of commodity futures contracts. Speculators, often derided as gamblers, provide an essential element in futures trading—liquidity. Hedgers tend to be all buyers or all sellers at a given time. Without speculators to sell to or buy from—in other words, to take the opposite side of the risk—futures markets could not function. The efficiency of any free market operation requires a fairly equal number of buyers and sellers, and imbalance of the buyer/seller ratio is similar to an imbalance in demand and supply of a given commodity. When corn crops are destroyed by natural forces, for example, the price of corn rises drastically because demand is greater than supply, not because of speculators in the futures market. Inflation worries may cause a rise in gold prices not due to lack of the supply of gold but rather to individual beliefs (correct or incorrect) that gold is a safer investment when inflation rises. Speculations in the commodity markets are essential to hedging and help achieve a stabilization of price.

Most trading for individual investors is through brokerage houses, whether individuals are making decisions or are part of pools or funds where managers handle trading strategies. Brokerage houses charge commissions for each trade enacted, and all trading transactions are made through members of a commodity exchange. Margin accounts are set up for the trading activities, and margin requirements (basically downpayments) range roughly from 5% to 20% of contract values.

In stock investments, investors are required to place a margin (downpayment) of 50% or more of the stock price, with the remainder amount loaned at a broker loan rate to fulfill 100% of the purchase obligation. Commodity margins are based on fixed minimums per unit or per contract, ranging from 5% to 20% of the actual cost of the futures contracts, and are good-faith performance bonds. There are no loans made to cover the additional costs of the contracts. This creates opportunities to leverage larger positions in commodities than in stocks, but price movements in commodities, relative to margin requirements, can create very large losses or profits, and it is in this area that investors must thoroughly familiarize themselves to fully comprehend the risk. Profits and losses are treated similarly to stocks in tax rules: both are capital items. However, there are no state or federal taxes involved in the purchase or sale of commodity positions.

The leap in volume of commodity trading during the last 30 years has been dramatic. Commodity trading is now global in nature, particularly in financial and stock index futures trading. The different levels of income-producing investments, whether personal or corporate, domestic or international, along with the shifting coalition of interest groups, keeps the financial structure in a constant state of change. Desires to preserve and increase capital motivates financial innovations around tax and regulatory restrictions imposed by government, and reactions can be transitory or lasting. The Eurodollar bond market, for example, was created by reaction to U.S. ceilings on the rate of interest commercial banks could offer on time deposits. With the volatility of interest rates in the 1960s and

1970s, U.S. commercial banks were aware that this restriction did not apply to dollar-denominated time deposits in their overseas branches, particularly in western Europe. Eurodollar financial futures were created and are still traded in the futures market despite subsequent regulation changes and interest rate retraction.

Index contracts, Eurodollar bonds, and financial futures are all part of a complex and creative international investment market so intertwined it appears incomprehensible to the average investor. These complex instruments can be daunting to the uninitiated, but like the challenges of modern medical and tax forms and procedures, choices to further financial gain through commodities can be sorted through with the assistance of knowledgeable specialists and a thorough understanding of risk for investors, whether they are in their middle years planning for retirement or have already retired. (See also AGENTS AND BROKERS; ASSET ALLOCATION AFTER RETIREMENT; EQUITY SECURITIES; FINANCIAL ADVISORS; RISK TOLERANCE.)

### Organization

Commodity Futures Trading Commission (CFTC)

### References

Bernstein, Jacob. 2000. *How the Futures Markets Work*. Upper Saddle River, NJ: Prentice Hall.

Chicago Board of Trade. 1999. *Commodity Trading Manual*. Ed. Frank Rose. New York: AMACOM.

Schwager, Jack D. 1984. *A Complete Guide to the Futures Markets*. New York: John Wiley & Sons.

Waldron, Richard E. 2000. *Futures 101: An Introduction to Commodity Trading*. North Quincy, MA: Squantum Publishing.

*Mary Anne Keefer*

**COMMUNITY-BASED CARE,** senior care services that include case management, home health care, homemaking, adult day care, transportation, home-delivered meals, and other.

Community-based long-term care covers a broad spectrum of services that vary in type, target population, intensity (level of skill, amount of care), duration, and cost. These programs are intended for people with chronic physical or mental disabilities. A defining and unifying characteristic of community-based long-term care is that the objective is to support the ability of the patient/client to remain living in the community rather than an institution.

Community-based services often entail services that take place in a person's home—for example, a visiting nurse, home health aide, homemaker, or various therapies provided at home. However, the service setting might be institutional if the overall purpose is to sustain independent living—for example, adult day care, respite care, or assisted living programs. Care coordination or case management is often an important component of community-based long-term care, especially when the target population is geographically dispersed and there are diverse sources and resources for services.

### The Substitution Hypothesis

Does access to community-based long-term care prevent or postpone nursing home placement for at-risk older people? Research in the 1970s suggested that a substantial number of nursing home residents could be cared for at home if adequate community-based long-term care were available and that a modest amount of formal community-based services might reduce caregiver burden and burnout and thus prevent inappropriate institutionalization (Seidl et al. 1983; Williams et al. 1973).

The expectation that community-based services could substitute for institutional long-term care for disabled persons and frail older persons provided the rationale for a series of demonstration projects. The substitution hypothesis is built on the following premises:

- *Community-based long-term care is desirable.* There is ample evidence that people overwhelmingly prefer to remain in their own homes and avoid nursing home placement (Kane and Kane 1987). Long-term institutionalization tends to be a "last resort."
- *Nursing home placement can be prevented or substantially delayed.* This premise refers particularly to persons with moderate levels of impairment who either lack close relatives or whose care has exhausted their family caregivers. As numerous studies have shown, at-risk older people who lack informal caregivers are much more likely to be institutionalized than older adults who have comparable disabilities but who have spouses or adult children able and willing to care for them (Fischer and Hoffman 1984; Shanas and Maddox 1985). The implication is that, for these persons, nursing home placement may be inappropriate or premature.
- *Community-based long-term care is more cost-effective than institutional care.* This is a corollary to the previous point—that persons with moderate disabilities who do not require full-service facilities can be served instead with relatively inexpensive interventions.
- *Community-based long-term care improves quality of life for disabled persons and their caregivers.* Although the emphasis of the substitution hypothesis is often on the potential for cost savings, the benefit of community care is equally important. A substantial body of research literature, over many years, has documented the human cost for older adults and their caregivers of inadequate access to community-based services (Estes, Swan, and Associates 1993; Fengler and Goodrich 1979; Fischer and Hoffman 1984; Fischer et al. 1998).

### Evaluations of Community Care Demonstration Projects

The substitution hypothesis has been tested in a number of community care demonstration projects, including several federally sponsored projects. Much of the policy interest in these demonstration projects has been on the cost benefits of community-based services compared to institutional care. Overall, however, most evaluations of the demonstrations have not supported the substitution hypothesis in terms of a cost-offset effect. The largest and most elaborate evaluation was the National Long Term Care Demonstration, the Channeling project. The Channeling project, as well as other demonstrations, failed to find a significant difference in nursing home placement or hospital utilization. In their review of community-based long-term care demonstrations, Kemper, Applebaum, and Harrigan (1987) concluded: "The demonstrations have shown that expanding publicly financed community care does not reduce aggregate costs, and it is likely to increase them—at least under the current long-term care service system." But they also reported that the demonstrations were associated with higher life quality, so they added: "It is wrong, therefore, to conclude that expanding public financing for community care is not cost effective. Costs are likely to go up, but so are benefits." Weissert, Cready, and Pawelak (1988) found a few projects saved money—but only those where the cost of the intervention was very modest.

PACE—Program of All-Inclusive Care for the Elderly—is another model for providing services to frail older people. The program began in the early 1970s in San Francisco's Chinatown and now has multiple sites around the United States. Each site serves 120 to 150 participants, most of whom come several times a week to adult day care centers, where they receive services from physicians, nurses, social workers, therapists, and others. Patients that are unable to leave their homes are eligible for home care (Eng et al. 1997; Shannon and Van Reenen 1998). A study of hospitalization rates for PACE participants found that short-term hospital utilization among PACE participants is low compared to hospital use for other older and disabled populations (Wieland et al. 2000).

The Social Health Maintenance Organization (S/HMO) is another federally sponsored demonstration project intended to substitute home and community-based services for more costly institutional care. The S/HMO model creates financing for a community-based long-term care benefit, a care management system that identifies members eligible for that benefit, and coordination mechanisms that integrate the delivery of long-term care within the medical care system. While most other long-term care demonstrations were designed to serve primarily or exclusively frail or disabled populations, the target population in the S/HMO is composed of an approximate cross section of the community-based population, with a subset eligible for long-term care services. The S/HMO concept was to add a "social" component to Medicare HMO services, in order to meet the non-medical/support needs of older enrollees with chronic conditions and disabilities.

A recent study used the closure of an S/HMO in Minnesota as a natural experiment to test the substitution hypothesis. The study followed a cohort of former Minnesota S/HMO enrollees and a cohort of enrollees in a comparable Oregon S/HMO, where the program continued to operate. The researchers compared the probability of long-term institutionalization or death, controlling for site effects, age, gender, and comorbid medical conditions. The research found that the loss of this community-based care program was associated with a 40% increased risk of institutionalization over the next five years (Fischer et al. 2001).

### Community-Based Long-Term Care in Future Public Policy

Over the last 20 years or so, in almost every developed country, rates of institutionalization have dramatically decreased and community-based services have increased (Amaradio 1998; Melzer et al. 1999; Merlis 2000). In part, this has resulted from deliberate policy initiatives to support and facilitate community-based services. Undoubtedly, much of the increase in community-based care also reflects the preferences of frail older persons and their families.

Long-term care has been a particularly thorny issue in public policy in the United States—often not even making it to the table in recent debates on health care reform. Currently, Medicare and most private medical plans in the United States cover acute and postacute care but deny claims for long-term custodial care (Estes, Swan, and Associates 1993; Leutz 1999). Public programs, most notably Medicaid, finance a substantial proportion of long-term care, but these benefits are restricted to persons with very low incomes or assets (Amaradio 1998; Bodenheimer 1999; Feder, Komisar, and Niefield 2000). Thus, the very wealthy, who can afford to pay out of pocket, and the very poor, who are eligible for public benefits, are the most likely to have access to both institutional and community-based long-term care services (Fischer et al. 1998; Merlis 2000; Murtaugh et al. 1997).

The substitution hypothesis is appealing because of its win-win premise: that patients benefit *and* there could be a cost offset in terms of public monies. The lack of dramatic research evidence for a cost offset has disappointed gerontologists and policy planners. A commentary in *Gerontologist* argued that "there is no impact" so that "the original justifications for community based services, including respite care, are no longer valid" (Callahan 1989).

The aging of the baby boom generation portends a sharp increase in the numbers and proportions of people surviving into very old age and, almost inevitably, an increased demand for long-term care. Providing good-quality, cost-effective long-term care, including both community-based and institutional care, will be an ever-more-urgent national priority. (See also DAY PROGRAMS FOR ADULTS; FRAILTY PLANNING; GERIATRIC CARE MANAGERS [GCMs]; HOME CARE SERVICES FOR OLDER ADULTS; HOME MODIFICATIONS FINANCING; REVERSE MORTGAGES.)

**References**

Amaradio, L. 1998. "Financing Long-Term Care for Elderly Persons: What Are the Options?" *Journal of Health Care Finance* 25: 75–84.

Bodenheimer, T. 1999. "Long-Term Care for Frail Elderly People—The On Lok Model." *New England Journal of Medicine* 341: 1324–28.

Callahan, J.J. 1989. "Play It Again Sam—There Is No Impact." *Gerontologist* 29(1): 5–6.

Eng, C., J. Pedulla, G.P. Eleazer, R. McCann, and N. Fox. 1997. "Program of All-Inclusive Care for the Elderly (PACE): An Innovative Model of Integrated Geriatric Care and Financing." *Journal of American Geriatric Society* 45(2): 223–32.

Estes, C.L., J.H. Swan, and Associates. 1993. *The Long Term Care Crisis: Elders Trapped in the No-Care Zone*. Newbury Park, CA: Sage Publications.

Feder, J., H.L. Komisar, and M. Niefeld. 2000. "Long-Term Care in the United States: An Overview." *Health Affairs* 19: 40–56.

Fengier, L.R. et al. 2001. "Community-Based Care and Risk of Nursing Home Placement." Paper presented at the annual meetings of the Gerontological Society of America, Chicago, IL, November.

Fischer L.R. 1990. "Medicare HMOs and Home Health Care." *Journal of Aging Studies* 4(2): 171–93.

Fischer, L.R., C.A. Green, M. Goodman, M. Aickin, K.K. Brod, F. Wei, L.W. Phelps, and W.N. Leutz. 2001. "Community-Based Care and Risk of Nursing Home Placement." Paper presented at the annual meetings of the Gerontological Society of America, Chicago, IL, November.

Fischer, L.R., and C. Hoffman. 1984. "Who Cares for the Elderly: The Dilemma of Family Support." In *Research in Social Problems and Public Policy*, ed. M. Lewis and J. Miller. Vol. 2. Greenwich, CT: JAI Press.

Fischer, L.R., W. Leutz, A. Miller, T.L. von Sternberg, and J.M. Ripley. 1998. "The Closing of a Social HMO: A Case Study." *Journal of Aging and Social Policy* 10: 57–75.

Kane, R.A., and R.L. Kane. 1987. *Long-Term Care: Principles, Programs, and Policies*. New York: Springer Publishing Co.

Kemper, P., R. Applebaum, and M. Harrigan. 1987. "Community Care Demonstrations: What Have We Learned?" *Health Care Finance* 8(1): 87–100.

Leutz, W.N. 1999. "Five Laws for Integrating Medical and Social Services: Lessons from the United States and the United Kingdom." *Milbank Quarterly* 77: 7–110.

Leutz, W., M.R. Greenlick, and J. Capitman. 1994. "Integrating Acute and Long-Term Care." *Health Affairs* 13: 55–74.

Melzer, D., B. McWilliams, C. Brayne, T. Johnson, and J. Bond. 1999. "Profile of Disability in Elderly People: Estimates from a Longitudinal Population Study." *British Journal of Medicine* 318: 1108–11.

Merlis, M. 2000. "Caring for the Frail Elderly: An International Review." *Health Affairs* 19: 141–49.

Murtaugh, C.M., P. Kemper, B.C. Spillman, and B.L. Carlson. 1997. "The Amount, Distribution, and Timing of Lifetime Nursing Home Use." *Medical Care* 35: 204–18.

Seidl, F.W., R. Applebaum, C. Austin, and K. Mahoney. 1983. *Delivering In-Home Services to the Aged and Disabled: The Wisconsin Experiment.* Lexington, MA: Lexington Books.

Shanas, E., and G.L. Maddox. 1985. "Health, Health Resources, and the Utilization of Care." In *Handbook of Aging and the Social Sciences*, ed. R. Binstock and E. Shanas. 2nd ed. New York: Van Nostrand.

Shannon, K., and C. Van Reenen. 1998. "PACE (Program of All-Inclusive Care for the Elderly): Innovative Care for the Frail Elderly: Comprehensive Services Enable Most Participants to Remain at Home." *Health Program* 79(5): 41–45.

Weissert, W.G., C.M. Cready, and J.E. Pawelak. 1988. "The Past and Future of Home- and Community-Based Long-Term Care." *Milbank Quarterly* 66: 309–88.

Wieland, D., V.L. Lamb, S.R. Sutton, R. Boland, M. Clark, S. Friedman, K. Brummel-Smith, and G.P. Eleazer. 2000. "Hospitalization in the Program of All-Inclusive Care for the Elderly (PACE): Rates, Concomitants, and Predictors." *Journal of American Geriatric Society* 48(11): 1373–80.

Williams, T.F., J.G. Hill, M.E. Fairbank, and K.G. Knox. 1973. "Appropriate Placement of the Chronically Ill and Aged: A Successful Approach by Evaluation." *Journal of the American Medical Association* 226: 1332–35.

*Lucy Rose Fischer*

**CONDOMINIUMS,** a form of real estate ownership in which owners have full ownership rights to individual dwelling units consisting of all airspace found within the interior surfaces of walls, ceilings, and floors and an undivided interest in the common areas of the complex. The common areas include the land under the condominium unit, exterior walls, roof, lobbies, hallways, meeting rooms, elevators, and the surrounding areas such as parks, pools, tennis courts, and parking areas. Condominium ownership was legislated in the United States only in the 1960s, but this form of ownership dates back to ancient Rome. Many condominium developments today are located in popular retirement areas, such as California, Arizona, and Florida, appealing to retirees and to older adults seeking warm weather and carefree ownership.

Similar to other forms of ownership, the use of condominium units is privately restricted according to certain covenants, conditions, and regulations. Owners of condominium units inevitably become members of the condominium owner's association, which is usually an unincorporated association that governs the management of the property and its common areas. The purpose of the association is to determine and regulate conditions of ownership and occupancy and to maintain the common areas in the condominium building or complex. The condominium association is run by a board of directors elected by the owners, and the board usually hires a property manager and related staff to administer the complex. Subcommittees composed of residents are often charged with specific administrative responsibilities. A condominium association is responsible for various tasks, including interior and exterior building maintenance and repairs, safety, financial and budgetary topics, rules and regulations, and social functions. It also oversees insurance and tax matters and sets forth policies concerning delinquent fees or assessments from individual owners.

Association fees paid by owners fund routine maintenance of the condominium complex, including interior maintenance such as plumbing or electrical work and exterior maintenance such as roofing or landscaping. The association may also collect assessments to pay the property taxes for the common areas. Some portion of the fee is set aside in a building reserve fund in the event of large unexpected future maintenance expenses. Residents may still be charged one-time assessments to cover larger maintenance demands (e.g., new roof, new plumbing) when the condominium association reserve funds are insufficient. Most important, the condominium association has the responsibility of enforcing rules and regulations established for the complex. Responsibilities can range from handling a complaint from a disgruntled owner to having a lien levied against a unit because an individual owner has not paid the required fees or assessments.

Condominium ownership offers older adults a host of benefits, including a maintenancefree lifestyle, a relatively low-cost form of housing, and the use of common area facilities for social functions—typically holiday parties, swimming, tennis, or golf. Pets may be permitted by the condominium association's regulations in some complexes, and others have gates or employ full-time security guards for added safety. Since most neighbors live close together, theft is discouraged, and aid may be available in case of medical and other emergencies. The satisfaction of occupants will often depend on the regulations established for the complex and how well the management performs. Owners can voice opinions at association meetings, which are held at regular intervals and can cover such topics as association dues or necessary changes in current rules or regulations.

A condominium unit usually costs less than a single-family detached home. Mortgage payments on a condominium unit are typically comparable to rents paid for apartments, yet condominium ownership offers tax benefits, equity buildup, and the possibility of future appreciation in value. Unlike rentals, owners may decorate the interior of their unit as they wish, and they are free from anxieties such as fear of eviction, the need for negotiating lease terms, and future rent increases. Since management is employed and supervised by the condominium association, it is often particularly responsive to the unit owners. Older buyers, therefore, may find living environments that are quieter, more mature, and better suited to their specific needs.

Noticeable disadvantages associated with condominium unit ownership may include overcrowding, an overbearing condominium association, rules and regulations that are too restrictive, and limitations on financing the unit. The high land costs associated with today's real estate markets force many developers to maximize the density of units in condominium complexes in order to achieve a worthwhile profit. Noises from neighbors can become a nuisance, especially for older newcomers who may have lived in single-family detached residences. Dense living environments can limit the amount of privacy enjoyed by owners, and some housing complexes lack adequate visitor parking spaces to host guests.

Requests for needed maintenance may be mishandled or handled slowly by managers of some complexes, and this can be a burden for some older persons who may need expeditious repairs. An interested buyer should become aware of rules and regulations concerning the condominium complex and also seek out the opinions of residents on the efficiency and consideration of management. If there is disagreement between management and owners or among owners on how situations should be implemented or handled, tension may result. Improper or inefficient management, poor market conditions, or poor construction can cause condominium association fee increases.

Prospective owners should also consider pertinent financing and future refinancing of condominium units, since most lenders follow strict guidelines when considering such financing. For example, if the number of owner-absentee (rented) units in the complex reaches a certain percentage (typically 30% to 50%), it may be difficult for a potential buyer to arrange financing. Problems can also arise when the owner of a condominium unit wishes to obtain secondary financing, as some lenders refuse to make home equity loans on condominium units. Further, most lenders prefer to diversify their mortgage portfolio and will usually limit the number of units in any given complex. The financing restrictions on condominium units are not only applied to conventional mortgages but also to government agency mortgages such as Federal Housing Administration (FHA) and Veterans Administration (VA) loans. (See also AGENTS AND BROKERS; ASSET ALLOCATION AFTER RETIREMENT; CORPORATE ELDERCARE PROGRAMS; FINANCIAL ADVISORS; HOME CARE SERVICES FOR OLDER ADULTS; HOMEOWNERSHIP.)

**Suggested Readings**

Irwin, Robert. 1999. *Tips and Traps When Buying a Condo, Co-Op, or Townhouse*. New York: McGraw-Hill.

Shapiro, Sylvia. 1998. *The Co-Op Bible: Everything You Need to Know About Co-Ops and Condos: Getting In, Staying In, Surviving, Thriving*. New York: St. Martin's Griffin.

**References**

Freedman, Warren. 1992. *The Law of Condominia and Property Owners' Associations*. New York: Quorum Books.

Kiplinger's Personal Finance Magazine, eds. 2002. *Kiplinger's Buying & Selling a Home*. 7th ed. Washington, DC: Kiplinger Books.

Shilling, James D. 2002. *Real Estate*. 13th ed. Cincinnati, OH: South-Western/Thomson Learning.

Wiedemer, John P. 1990. *Real Estate Finance*. 6th ed. Englewood Cliffs, NJ: Prentice-Hall.

*Andrew Quang Do*

**CONSERVATORSHIP.** See Attorneys; Durable Power of Attorney; Elder Law Practice; Guardianship.

**CONSULTING IN RETIREMENT,** using expertise gained over a career, or through other life experience, to generate income after retirement. Everyone who has reached the stage of maturity where retirement is possible has acquired expertise of one sort or another, and it is expertise that consultants sell in blocks of time. Indeed, time and expertise are the only two inventories stored by consultants.

In letting government contracts, the U.S. government categorizes consultants as "experts." This is accurate; successful consultants are experts. By last count there were approximately 280 different fields of consulting expertise. So anyone who has retired and who feels that he or she does not wish to spend the rest of his or her life playing golf, gardening, surfing the Internet, or watching television has the potential to become an independent consultant. For some, this is a most productive period of life that permits work on projects that are of interest, and at times that are convenient, for the consultant.

A good current economic environment exists for independent consultants. Not only have the services industries far outstripped manufacturing in the gross national product (GNP), but both private and public organizations are resorting more and more to outsourcing their services requirements in order to keep their staffs to a minimum. Outsourcing, of course, means the retaining of consultants. All independent consultants combined earn as much as do the big international consulting firms such as Booz-Allen and McKinsey and Company—over $35 billion a year.

The life of a successful independent consultant has many advantages. There are no office politics with which to contend, and the consultant is not accountable to a superior. The client is seldom the consultant's "boss"; indeed, it is the client who is in need of assistance or has a problem to be solved, not the consultant. A consultant may have the opportunity to travel extensively at a client's expense. And losing a client seldom involves the financial tragedy of losing a job because there are usually other clients to step in and to pay a consultant's fees. Perhaps best of all, the consultant chooses the number of hours to work and the amount and time of days to take off. The client typically accommodates to the consultant's calendar.

The first issue is to clearly identify the expertise around which the consultancy will be established. For many people, this will be clear from the experience of having been a source of information to colleagues before retirement. For others, it will be a non-work-related field of interest that has always occupied leisure time and attention. For still others, it may be a field that has been a lifelong interest that can now be developed into expertise with the extra time available after retirement. However it has developed, the first step is to clearly identify the area of expertise that will be marketable to and required by a sufficient number of prospective clients. Yet expertise is not all that is required to set up a successful consultancy. Other important factors include a person's own makeup, personality, and character.

It typically takes six months to one year of marketing consulting expertise to make a consulting venture successful. Patience and perseverance are required by an aspiring consultant, or this career path may prove too frustrating to maneuver. Consulting will seldom produce a steady income but rather it typically has drought periods as well as very profitable ones. If an individual (and his or her spouse) cannot get used to going without a steady paycheck, then consulting is not a wise path to pursue. Further, a consultant must be self-motivated and not easily distracted. There will be no one pushing a consultant to accomplish tasks in the same way an employee has a superior directing his or her effort. Also, most consultants work out of their homes, and a disciplined approach to self-appointed tasks is imperative so that family affairs and household chores do not interfere. Finally, even though many potential clients will engage in conversations that do not lead to paying engagements, a beginning consultant cannot take this personally or develop contempt for his or her client universe.

There is a financial benefit to setting up a consultancy in one's home. Most retirees have few tax deductions, and the Internal Revenue Service (IRS) will allow a deduction for mortgage or rent and utilities for whatever percentage of space in one's home is used for an office. Education and training, insurance, health care, automobile, and other expenses in connection with the business may be allowable as well.

Ninety percent (90%) of beginning consultants do not make it past the first 12 months. This is not because they are not experts in their respective fields; most of them are. It is because they do not understand the business of consulting. And although consulting is considered a profession, it is also a business. Doctors, dentists, and accountants are also professionals who must acquaint themselves with good business principles and practices in order to succeed. This statistic is not presented to dissuade or discourage anyone from consulting but to reinforce the requisites of consulting success.

One factor that can lead to lack of success in consulting is the mistaken belief that as a "professional" salesmanship is not a requirement. Nothing could be further from the truth. In point of fact, a beginning consultant must sell the most difficult intangible thing of all: him- or herself.

Finally, some may be discouraged from entering the profession because of negative publicity in today's media about the misdeeds of a few large consulting firms or unflattering jokes about consultants. Some consultants are rethinking the use of the word *consultant* altogether and are calling themselves "counselors" or are changing the names of their businesses from consultancies to "advisories." A final obstacle in today's economic environment is the increasing numbers of middle managers who have been downsized or who have taken early retirement and now have calling cards as "consultants" but may not be taking consulting seriously. Nevertheless, consulting—when practiced by an expert who is honorable, helpful, ethical, and innovative—is a noble profession from which great rewards can be reaped during later life.

The best business practices of successful consultants are not optional and are devoted to the following areas:

- Marketing expertise to gain clients
- Representing oneself as a true professional
- Setting fees knowledgeably for client acceptance
- Writing winning proposals
- Avoiding risk when contracting with a client
- Conforming to the highest ethical standards of the consulting profession

There is no college or university that offers a degree in consulting. While some universities (notably Harvard Business School and the Wharton School) offer courses in consulting as part of their M.B.A. programs, the courses deal essentially with management consulting only. Business courses such as those outlined above are often available at local community colleges or extension programs, as well as on the Internet.

Finally, many independent consultants who have enjoyed a successful, profitable career may do so in a phased manner. The workload is always within the consultant's control, and they may enjoy the wonderful feelings accompanying the successful completion of a project well done for as long as they wish after normal "retirement." (See also BUSINESS SUCCESSION PLANNING; ENTREPRENEURSHIP; KEOGH PLANS; LIFE

PLANNING; PENSION PLANS FOR THE SELF-EMPLOYED; WORKING RETIREES.)

### Reference

Bermont, Hubert. 1997. *How to Become a Successful Consultant in Your Own Field.* 3rd ed. Roseville, CA: Prima Publishing.

*Hubert Bermont*

**CONSUMER CREDIT,** credit extended by banks, credit card companies, other financial institutions, and retailers to older persons for the purchase of goods and services on a flexible payment schedule. Unlike traditional installment borrowing, which features a specified monthly payment over a fixed period of time (such as a traditional auto or home mortgage loan), the desirability of "revolving" consumer credit is its flexible terms of repayment. That is, the payment is interest only until the principal is due in full, such as in a "balloon payment" in some home equity loans, or the consumer can choose the size of the monthly payment (in most credit cards a minimum of 1% to 2% of outstanding principal) and thus the length of the repayment period that determines the total cost of the loan. This is significant since credit cards, in particular, are distinguished by whether they must be paid in full (charge cards) or in part (revolving accounts) at the end of the monthly billing cycle. An example of a charge account is *American Express*, and examples of revolving accounts are *VISA* and *Mastercard* on which an outstanding balance is financed over succeeding months. It is important to note that the *Discover* credit card is issued by a financial services company, while VISA and Mastercard are membership associations. The primary goals of VISA and Mastercard are marketing and improving the transaction processing technology for its member banks. Major financial institutions such as Bank of America issue individual credit card accounts.

Charge accounts typically do not impose interest charges (unless the payment is late), but they often require a membership fee. In comparison, credit cards levy a finance charge on the outstanding balance and on any new purchases during the billing cycle. Some also impose a membership fee and, in addition, charge a growing assortment of fees including those for late payment, exceeding credit limits, cash advances, and overdraft protection on personal checking accounts. With the exception of special reward programs, such as frequent airline travel accounts, annual membership fees may be waived as "a courtesy" to loyal customers simply by calling the customer service department of the credit card company.

Credit cards can be used without incurring finance charges or penalty fees by paying the entire balance in full before the end of the specified "grace" period. Extra fees, however, may be assessed for convenience services, especially when traveling out of state or in other countries. For instance, automated teller machines (ATMs) in shopping malls provide access to different information networks across the country, and a credit card may incur "user" fees if the ATM is not part of the card issuer's bank system.

### Smart Cards

Also, there are new technologically sophisticated "smart" cards that feature computer chip "brains" that can be used in many different financial information networks throughout the United States. They can access a variety of financial services accounts (checking, savings, credit) as well as serve as a repository of purchasing information that can be transferred to different vendor systems for future marketing programs. If, for example, a consumer purchases groceries or medicines at the supermarket, the items purchased will be added to the consumer's credit card information file and will be downloaded to a shopping profile that is stored in the supermarket's computers as well.

There are certain variants of credit cards that offer atypical credit arrangements. People with poor credit histories, for example, may obtain "secured" credit cards that require a bank deposit equal to the extended credit amount. Such cards may also carry membership charges and very high interest rates (19% to 29%). Typically, charges are limited to the amount of the accountholder's deposit, although some companies may increase the credit limit by 50% to 300%, in accordance with the customer's payment record. Other products include check cashing cards from banks (that may include the VISA trademark) and that electronically pay for purchases from checking accounts at the "point of sale" (POS) and debit cards that immediately deduct purchases from a checking or savings account. Annual account and activation fees may be charged, and each POS carries certain transaction costs. Some banks offer their customers "overdraft" protection on check cashing and debit cards. This is essentially a loan or additional line of credit that usually incurs a transaction fee plus finance charges at the standard credit card interest rate.

*Check cashing* and *debit* cards may be used in the same financial transaction systems as bank credit cards, but they do not have the same benefits. For example, they do not include the generous fraud and purchase protection that are provided by bank credit cards. Many consumers learn this expensive lesson only after the theft of their checking, savings, and overdraft lines of credit. In comparison, the major credit card companies offer 100% protection against theft as long as unauthorized activities are reported within a reasonable period of time. This policy is designed to encourage shopping over the Internet without fear of financial liability from the fraudulent use of credit cards (Manning 2001).

### Credit Cards in America: A Brief History

Although bank credit cards are a relatively recent innovation, typically marked by the establishment of the "businessman's *Diner's Club* card" in 1950, U.S. society has historically depended upon the availability of consumer credit. For example, farmers depended on store credit before the harvest of their crops in rural America, whereas industrial workers were issued "script" for purchases in the company store that were later deducted from their wages. Significantly, both forms of consumer credit often produced a form of debt/labor servitude. This common experience was recounted in the famous lyrics of Tennessee Williams, *"I owe my soul to the company store."*

Even in the mid-twentieth century, local merchants frequently extended informal or "open book" credit to their most reliable customers since it fostered customer loyalty and future business sales. Not surprisingly, strong social ties between merchants and consumers in small-town America reinforced the social control functions of debt (stigma and shame) and work discipline (dependence on future credit). Public scorn for failing to repay one's debts was an embarrassment to the debtor as well as to his or her extended family and was avoided whenever possible. As a result, persistent indebtedness often took on moral and religious overtones, and thrift was equated with godliness, self-discipline, and hard work. These social factors encouraged financial responsibility and limited the number of people who failed to repay their debts. When widespread violations of these Puritan-inspired values occurred in the early twentieth century, a calamitous loss of family homesteads and personal property resulted during the Great Depression. Today, these devastating experiences still constitute powerful intergenerational reminders of the social and economic consequences of failing to "save for a rainy day."

After World War II, the rising U.S. standard of living combined with the rapid proliferation of suburban residential communities encouraged new forms of consumer credit that were not based on personal relationships. Furnishings for new homes and the purchase of new automobiles required greater amounts of consumer credit than were traditionally available from local banks. The unprecedented geographic mobility of postwar America undermined informal credit networks, because small businesses were reluctant to offer informal credit to unknown or potentially transient customers. These factors contributed to the profound transformation of Main Street USA, from downtown business districts with primarily small shopkeepers to suburban shopping malls with their corporate retail "anchors." Large retail stores such as Sears, Roebuck and Montgomery Ward included formal consumer charge and proprietary credit card accounts. These credit programs were designed primarily to reinforce customer loyalty since they could not be used in other stores. Even with high annual finance charges, most proprietary credit card programs were not profitable due to high account management expenses.

### U.S. Industrial Restructuring and Banking Deregulation: The Rise of the Universal Bank Credit Card

Only 25 years ago, today's ubiquitous use of "universal" bank credit cards might have seemed a futurist fantasy. Prior to the deregulation of the financial services industry in 1980, banks made consumer loans as "installment" credit. Loan approval was based on an assessment of the applicants' household income, personal assets, credit repayment history, and outstanding debt. Preferred clients had financial collateral and repaid their loans on a fixed time schedule. Similarly, financial companies and banks cautiously issued charge cards and revolving credit cards to low-risk clients, primarily upper- and some middle-income households, who used them for convenience or for business. Although the high inflation rates and stagnant real wages of the late 1970s encouraged greater levels of consumer borrowing, banks were reluctant at first to increase their lines of revolving credit. When they did, outstanding credit card debt increased from nearly $3 billion in 1970 to about $47 billion in 1980.

In the early 1980s, several factors contributed to the emergence of consumer financial services as a highly attractive market for banks: major losses from Third World loan delinquencies, a sharp rise in U.S. commercial real estate foreclosures, escalation of personal and corporate bankruptcies, decline in corporate borrowing, collapse of the junk bond market, and costly deregulation policies. The Reagan administration's deregulation of the banking industry was accompanied by an effective campaign against inflation, which fell from 18% in the late 1970s to 3% in the mid-1980s, but interest rates for consumer financial services remained high. With the restructuring of America's manufacturing industries, and the cost efficiencies of computer information technologies, banks turned to retail merchants and consumers to market their highly profitable consumer credit services.

Banks expanded their credit card portfolios and shifted their marketing focus from affluent "convenience" users to middle-income "revolvers." With interest rates stable at over 20%, banks soon realized that the economically stressed American middle classes were willing to accept increasing balances on their credit cards—even with inflation under 5%. As credit card profits spiraled, banks sought to sustain their growth by marketing to traditionally neglected groups: senior citizens, the working class, and college students. The success of mass-marketing campaigns, which generated billions of dollars in interest and fee revenues, contributed to a dramatic upsurge in credit card users and to the consolidation of the credit card industry.

Between 1980 and 1990, credit card debt jumped from $47 billion to almost $200 billion, and it nearly tripled again to over $570 billion in 2000. Whereas the top 50 banks accounted for about one-half of the consumer credit card market before 1980, today the top 10 banks control about 80% of outstanding credit card debt. Seventy-six million American households possess nearly 1.6 billion credit cards. Outstanding net credit card debt is in excess of $620 billion, while outstanding installment debt has crossed the $1.0 trillion threshold. In addition to retail purchases, credit cards can be used for most small business and consumer transactions, including the payment of taxes and purchases from the U.S. Postal Service and other federal and municipal governments. Credit cards, in fact, are all but required by airlines, hotels, auto rental, and other travel booking companies. They are the financial backbone of television home shopping clubs and Internet commerce. As Americans have struggled with intensifying spending pressures into the twenty-first century, credit cards have been used to launch new households and new businesses, to cushion domestic crises and survive periods of unemployment, to finance college tuition, medical emergencies, and even burial costs. With the innovation of cash advances and credit card checks or vouchers, revolving credit can now be used to buy or pay for anything. In addition, credit cards have created numerous conveniences such as detailed records of all transactions, free purchase protection and insurance benefits, instant access to cash (ATMs), and an immediate line of credit for entertainment, speculative, or investment transactions.

Some "affinity" or sponsored credit card programs enable consumers to accumulate points for a variety of gifts as well as free or discounted air travel, gasoline, long-distance telephone calls, and even the downpayment on an automobile. In sum, the universal credit card has revitalized the financial services industry with its high-cost products and created a plethora of valuable and innovative conveniences for American consumers. While credit cards have become a part of American culture, at issue are the significance and ramifications of their growing use by seniors.

### Demographic and Economic Background

The number of Americans aged 65 years and older was 35.3 million in 2000 (12.8% of the U.S. population). Estimates by the U.S. Census Bureau, based on medium growth assumptions, are that this population will climb to 40.1 million in 2010 (13.1%), to 53.3 million in 2020 (16.4%), and then rise sharply to 70.1 million in 2030 (20.1%) as the baby boomer "bulge" enters retirement. By 2050, an estimated 80 million Americans will be at least 65 years old, and those aged 80-plus will increase significantly as well. American society will be composed of a growing proportion of nonworking seniors whose increased longevity will require greater resources for living and for medical care. As early baby boomers transition into retirement, consumer debt will play an increasingly important role in limiting the size of their financial "nest egg" as well as their ability to finance necessary or discretionary expenditures on high-interest consumer credit cards.

The prosperity of the post–World War II era has provided older adults with an increasing range of financial resources in retirement. Today, Social Security, Medicare, and private pensions supplement income from personal savings, investments, and family support. Compared with other developed nations, Americans have been only moderate savers, except during World War II when the U.S. savings rate exceeded 25%. During the next four decades, the personal savings rate was relatively stable at 8%, peaking at 10% in 1973. Over the last two decades, however, this rate has fallen precipitously—from about 7% in 1980 to zero at the end of 1999.

Some analysts argue that the U.S. personal savings measure substantially understates household wealth due to the appreciation of stock market investments in private pensions and 401(k)s in the 1990s. Although considerable stock market wealth was accumulated in this period, its unequal distribution tends to be overlooked. Between 1983 and 1998, an analysis of the national Consumer Finance Surveys (CFSs) reveals that the net worth of the bottom 40% of U.S. households actually declined (from $4,700 to $1,100), and the middle 20% rose by $5,500 (from $55,500 to $61,000). Even the next 20% of U.S. households, where significant stock gains would be expected, experienced only a moderate increase in net worth, from $133,600 to $161,300. Most stock market wealth is concentrated in the top 1%—especially the top one-tenth. These data, moreover, precede the $7+ trillion of losses in the equity markets over the last two years, which has intensified the pressure on U.S. households to increase personal savings. For many baby boomers, the sharp decline in their stock market investments will require an extension of their working careers or a lower standard of living in retirement, or both. Indeed, employment rates for older adults are rising, as is the proportion of seniors relying on Social Security for their primary income. This situation is exacerbated by the sharp decline in investment returns on low-risk certificate of deposits and public and corporate bonds.

For most Americans, the equity in their homes constitutes the bulk of their retirement assets. Between 1979 and 2001, the Federal Reserve Board reports that mortgage debt as a proportion of disposable household income soared from 46.6% to 73.2%. Families have extended the credit card repayment period and folded other forms of consumer debt into their primary home mortgages. Today, on average, total household debt is over 110% of disposable household income. For seniors with paid-off mortgages, their housing investment provides the potential for accessing home equity with reverse mortgages, but this possibility will not exist for the growing numbers of Americans entering retirement years with substantial outstanding mortgage debt on their homes.

These asset formation patterns are illustrative of a new and disturbing trend among baby boomer American households in the twenty-first century: spending rather than saving home equity for retirement. The Federal Reserve Board does not report any home equity loans in 1979. In 2001, on average, home equity accounts for 9.5% of disposable U.S. household income. Consequently, baby boomers are repaying higher interest credit card debt by obtaining larger home mortgages during the prime of their careers rather than accumulating retirement assets for what may otherwise have been their "golden years." (See also AGING INTO DEBT; BABY BOOMERS AND RETIREMENT; CREDIT SCORES, FINANCIAL COUNSELING FOR MID- TO LATER LIFE; FI-

NANCIAL EDUCATION FOR SENIORS; FINANCIAL RECOVERY IN LATER LIFE.)

**References**

Bilker, Scott. 2002. *How to Be More Credit Card and Debt Smart.* Vol. 1. Barnegat, NJ: Press One Publishers.

Drentea, Patricia. 2000. "Age, Debt and Anxiety." *Journal of Health and Social Behavior* 41 (December): 437–50.

Hall, Margaret. 2001. *Credit Cards and Checks (Earning, Saving, Spending).* New York: Heinemann.

Manning, Robert D. 2001. *Credit Card Nation: The Consequences of America's Addiction to Credit.* New York: Basic Books.

Mishel, Lawrence, Jared Bernstein, and Heather Boushey. 2003. *The State of Working America 2002–03.* Ithaca, NY: Cornell University Press.

Pollin, Robert. 1990. *Deeper in Debt: The Changing Financial Conditions of U.S. Households.* Washington, DC: Economic Policy Institute.

Seniors USA. 2002. "American Seniors Rack Up Debt Like Never Before." Available online at http://www.senrs.com.

Sullivan, Teresa A., Elizabeth Warren, and Jay L. Westbrook. 2000. *The Fragile Middle Class: Americans in Debt.* New Haven, CT: Yale University Press.

*Robert D. Manning*

**CONSUMER PROTECTION FOR OLDER ADULTS,** federal, state, and local statutes enacted to protect older consumers. Legislation that protects older consumers includes the unfair and deceptive acts and practices statutes, the home solicitation sales acts, the Honesty in Sweepstakes Act, the Truth in Lending Act, the Fair Credit Reporting Act, and the Fair Debt Collection Practices Act. Unfair and deceptive acts and practices statutes exist in all 50 states and the District of Columbia. These statutes prohibit unfair, false, misleading, and deceptive acts or practices committed by sellers, not only in the sale of goods and services but also in advertising or soliciting the sale of goods and services. In 2000, the Protecting Seniors from Fraud Act (P.L. 106–534) was enacted, requiring the secretary of Health and Human Services (HHS) to disseminate information designed to educate senior citizens and raise awareness about the dangers of fraud. In addition, the act directs the attorney general to conduct a study that would provide assistance in developing new crime prevention strategies pertaining to crimes against seniors and to include statistics in the National Crime Victimization Survey on crimes that impact seniors.

The federal government's principal consumer protection agency is the Federal Trade Commission (FTC). Under the Federal Trade Commission Act, Congress has directed the commission to prohibit unfair or deceptive acts or practices. The recent FTC law enforcement initiatives that are of particular importance to older consumers include health care initiatives, financial practices initiative sales and promotional practices initiatives, and enforcement initiatives against fraud.

Older consumers are disadvantaged in the market due to their physical, psychological, and social frailty. Many fraudulent business activities are specifically targeting older people; in some scams, 80% or more of the victims are 65 or older. Older adults are often the deliberate targets because many older people have cash reserves or other assets to spend on seemingly attractive offers. However, they are frequently the least able to rebound from being victimized.

The frequency of occurrence and actual monetary loss are expected to be even greater than reported. Consumer abuse tends to be underreported, especially by older adults, because they are afraid of being considered incompetent or unintelligent (Friedman 1992; Lee, Soberon-Ferrer and Lee 1996; McGhee 1983). In addition to monetary loss, psychological costs including the emotional stress of being defrauded are also substantial (Friedman 1992; Lee and Soberon-Ferrer 1997).

### Health Care Initiatives

*Health Claims.* Health care is of particular concern to older consumers, and older consumers may be particularly vulnerable to false or misleading claims about health care products and services because the marketing of such products and services often relates to conditions associated with aging (FTC 2003). Two federal agencies devote substantial resources to preventing the dissemination of unsubstantiated or otherwise deceptive claims about the health benefits of particular products or services. The Food and Drug Administration has a primary responsibility for the safety and labeling of over-the-counter (OTC) drugs, foods, and dietary supplements, and the Federal Trade Commission is responsible for making sure that advertising about the health benefits of OTC drugs, devices, foods, and dietary supplements is truthful, not misleading, and substantiated by solid scientific support. The most dramatic growth in health-related marketing has been in the dietary supplement industry, including vitamins, minerals, herbs, and hormones, with an estimated 100 million U.S. consumers using such supplemental products.

As a part of efforts to protect consumers against false or misleading claims, the FTC launched "Operation Cure.all," a comprehensive law enforcement and consumer education campaign directed at protecting consumers from Internet health fraud. The FTC has also provided continuing effort to ensure that consumers get accurate and reliable information about weight-loss products and programs through "Operation Waistline," a coordinated, long-term consumer education and law enforcement program.

*Medicare Fraud.* Another form of health care fraud is Medicare fraud, which refers to unnecessary service supply or low-quality service that does not satisfy the standard. Medicare fraud tends to accompany billing for services that were never rendered or billing for a service at a higher rate than is actually provided. The U.S. General Accounting Office estimates that $1 out of every $7 spent on Medicare is paid inappropriately due to fraud or abuse. Last year, Medicare lost nearly $13 billion to improper claims.

In 1995, Operation Restore Trust (ORT) was enacted. Through ORT, the Administration on Aging (AoA) joined with an antifraud plan in the Medicare and Medicaid programs. AoA trained approximately 2,500 staff and collected $187 million in fines, recoveries, and settlements. In 1996, Congress enacted the Health Insurance Portability and Accountability Act (HIPAA) to fund protecting Medicare program integrity. This reduced Medicare's payment error rate from 14% to 6.8% during 1990–2000. Health and Human Services and the Department of Justice coordinate federal, state, and local health care law enforcement programs. During the past four years, the federal government has conducted 1,291 criminal prosecutions and recovered a total of $3.4 billion in fines, judgments, and settlements. In addition, individuals and businesses who are convicted of

Medicare fraud may not receive payments from Medicare, Medicaid, and other federal health care programs. During fiscal year 2000, 3,350 individuals and businesses were excluded from doing business with Medicare and Medicaid.

The Office of Inspector General (OIG) monitors the Medicare and Medicaid programs at HHS through evaluating and criminal investigating. These activities help to improve quality of health care and reduce fraud and abuse. Also, OIG maintains an antifraud hotline against Medicare fraud. The hotline received over 500,000 calls in 2001 and has fielded over 1.5 million calls since 1995.

### Sales and Promotional Practices Initiatives

*Telemarketing*. One of the most frequent types of elder consumer abuse occurs through telemarketing. More than a quarter (26%) of telemarketing fraud reports were from older consumers (NCL 2002). The top three telemarketing frauds toward older adults are sweepstakes and prize offers (average loss: $2,752), magazine sales (average loss: $98), and credit card loss protection plans (average loss: $229). Targeting consumers with financial problems, scammers guarantee a credit card regardless of bad credit history. Most credit card issuers do not charge in advance, but the free offers end up with monetary losses.

The Securities and Exchange Commission and the FTC provide protection from deceptive telemarketing through the Federal Securities Laws and Telemarketing Sales Rules (TSR), respectively. The state also may bring a civil action to enforce the rule of the commission and to obtain compensation for its residents. FTC's amended TSR includes a national "do not call" registry to stop unwanted sales calls. This rule also allows consumers to request to be put on the company's own "do not call" list. The law requires telemarketers to search the registry every 90 days and delete phone numbers on the registry from the list. A violation of this rule would fine the telemarketer up to $11,000 for each call.

Amended TSR also restricts unauthorized billing. Before billing, telemarketers should get a customer's consent to be charged. In the case of a "free-to-pay conversion" offer, a telemarketer should have a customer's permission to use a particular account number, confirm the number by repeating the last four digits, and record the entire phone transaction. The new sales rule also requires caller ID (identification) transmission to protect privacy and help in law enforcement efforts. Telemarketers must transmit their telephone numbers to caller ID services. Other continuing telemarketing sales rules are as follows: Calling times are restricted to the hours between 8 A.M. and 9:00 P.M. Telemarketers must make their identities clear before making a sales pitch. Telemarketers must disclose all material information about the goods or services they are offering and the terms of the sale.

*Funeral Services*. A funeral can cost $10,000 or more, and this expensive consumer purchase is often made at an emotionally difficult time, often a first-time purchase (FTC 2003). Under the Funeral Industry Practices Rule (16 CFR Part 453), funeral providers should provide consumers timely and clear information relating to the range of funeral goods and services offered and the prices charged. FTC, state attorneys general, and AARP have collaborated in their enforcement approaches since the rule became effective in 1984, including investigations and test shopping across various geographic areas and, since 1999, test shopping more vigorously.

*Energy and Home Appliances.* Older consumers often try to save on expenses by cutting down on energy use. The Appliance Labeling Rule requires the manufacturers of home appliances to provide consumers accurate information about energy usage levels for home appliances. The rule requires that manufacturers disclose specific energy information at the point of sale in the form of an Energy Guide label that is affixed to the covered product.

*Home Improvement.* Most elder homeowners periodically have repairs or maintenance work. Many home improvements are performed in inadequate or fraudulent home repair work. According to the National Association of Consumer Agency Administrators (NACAA) and the Consumer Federation of America (CFA), home improvement fraud is a highly ranked elder consumer crime. Among the common fraudulent home improvement practices are charging high prices for low-quality materials; misrepresenting the need for repairs, the work to be performed, or the materials to be used; and using deceptive pricing.

State statutes and their enforcement regarding home improvement scams differ among states. Some states have no applicable laws or regulations, while others have specific statutes regarding home improvement contractors. The enforcement of state laws that cover home improvement contractors plays a key role in protecting consumers. The AARP has developed a model statute for regulating home improvement contractors. This requires home improvement contractors to be licensed, to carry certain insurance coverage, and to grant consumers the recovery of damages and costs.

### Enforcement Initiatives against Fraud

At the federal level, there are two important enforcement initiatives to identify fraudulent or deceptive schemes. First, in 1997, the FTC established the *Consumer Sentinel* as a Web-based law enforcement network, which allows law enforcement agencies in the United States, Canada, and Australia an immediate access to consumer complaints. Both public and private consumer organizations, including 64 local offices of the Better Business Bureaus across the nation, the National Consumers League's National Fraud Information Center, Project Phonebusters in Canada, and the U.S. Postal Inspection Services, contribute consumer complaints to the Consumer Sentinel database, from which law enforcement agencies can identity theft, telemarketing scams, and other consumer abuse in a timely manner.

Building on the Consumer Sentinel, the FTC works closely with foreign governments and launched a pilot project called *econosumer.gov*, a joint effort of the commission, agencies from 12 other countries, and the Organization for Economic Cooperation and Development (OECD) to gather and share cross-border e-commerce complaints. This project allows law enforcers from around the world to access a database of consumer complaints specifically about cross-border Internet transactions.

The growth of the Internet and e-commerce has been explosive, and not surprisingly, the boom in e-commerce has been accompanied by online fraud and deception. In 2000, roughly 26% of all fraud complaints reported to the Consumer Sentinel were related to online fraud and deception. The top ten Internet scams identified through an analysis of complaint data in the Consumer Sentinel database were Internet auction fraud, Internet service provider scams, Internet Web site design/promotions (Web cramming), Internet information and adult services, pyramid scams, business opportunities and work-at-home scams, investment schemes and get-rich-quick scams, travel/vacation fraud, telephone/pay-per-call solicitation frauds, and health care frauds.

Finally, identity theft is rapidly growing due to increasing e-commerce transactions, which allow the scammers to easily access personal information. An identity theft victim often realizes that he or she was defrauded after having a problem with using credit. The U.S. General Accounting Office reported a huge increase in identity theft, costing millions of dollars (Stana 2002). The Identity Theft Act (1998) made it a federal crime to misuse identification of another person. The crime is investigated by federal investigative agencies, such as the U.S. Secret Service, the Federal Burea of Investigation (FBI), and the U.S. Postal Inspection Service, and prosecuted by the Department of Justice. Also, privacy principles were set out in the 1980 OECD *Guidelines for the Protection of Privacy and Personal Data*, taking into account the OECD *Ministerial Declaration on the Protection of Privacy*. (See also CPA ELDERCARE SERVICES; CRIME PROTECTION; DISASTER PREPAREDNESS AND OLDER ADULTS; ELDER LAW PRACTICE; FINANCIAL ELDER ABUSE; OMBUDSMAN.)

**References**

AARP. 2002. "Talking to an Old Audience about Fraud: Information for Crime Prevention Officers." Washington, DC: AARP.

Federal Trade Commission (FTC). 2003. "Staff Summary of Federal Trade Commission Activities Affecting Older Consumers." Available online at http://www.ftc.gov/os/2001/10/agingrpt.htm.

Friedman, M. 1992. "Confidence Swindles of Older Consumers." *Journal of Consumer Affairs* 26 (1): 20–46.

Lee, J., and L.V. Geistfeld. 1999. "Elderly Consumers' Receptiveness to Telemarketing Fraud." *Journal of Public Policy & Marketing* 18(2): 208–17.

Lee, J., and H. Soberon-Ferrer. 1997. "Consumer Vulnerability to Fraud: Influencing Factors." *Journal of Consumer Affairs* 31(1): 70–89.

Lee, J., H. Soberon-Ferrer, and G. Lee. 1996. "The Elderly: Vulnerability to Deception and Fraud." *Consumer Interests Annual* 42: 423–28.

McGhee, J.L. 1983. "The Vulnerability of Elderly Consumers." *International Aging and Human Development* 17(3): 223–46.

National Consumer League (NCL). 2002. "One in Four Telemarketing Victims Age 60 and Older." Available online at http://www.natlconsumersleague.org/elderfraudweek.htm.

Stana, R.M. 2002. "Identity Theft: Available Data Indicate the Prevalence and Cost." *Justice Issues*. Washington, DC: GAO.

*Jinkook Lee and Eun-Jin Kim*

**CONTINUING CARE RETIREMENT COMMUNITIES (CCRCs),** residential communities distinguished by the presence of communal dining facilities and a range of nonacute medical care on campus. CCRCs are one of several types of planned residential communities that also include assisted living, congregate housing, and retirement communities/resorts (such as Del Webb's Leisure World). Characteristically CCRCs comprise a campus setting and three levels of care: independent living units, assisted living/personal care units, and a skilled nursing facility (SNF). Because CCRCs offer this continuum of shelter and care, they are considered one type of long-term care option (e.g., adult day care, assisted living, nursing homes). They usually include a service package of meals, activities, and transportation, as well as health care. They also constitute a housing option that, thanks to supportive services, enables residents to age in place within a community defined by the campus setting. Indeed, the median annual residence turnover (18%) for CCRCs is low compared to that for assisted living (60%) and independent living residences (39%) (American Seniors Housing Association [ASHA] 2002b).

### A Brief History

Although CCRCs are regarded as a relatively new approach to caring for older adults, their roots go back to the Middle Ages. In Europe, medieval craft guilds developed housing to provide safe, secure environments for their members when they became old and no longer were able to work. In the latter part of the nineteenth century, some U.S. nonprofit church, fraternal, and community groups ran facilities that provided food, shelter, and health care for their older members for the rest of their lives, even if they were unable to pay. They were called "lifecare" or "total care" communities; an individual's estate was often surrendered in return for perpetual care. As the need for additional facilities emerged, larger pools of capital were required, giving rise to nonrefundable entrance fees that could be used as seed money for other projects.

There were about 25 lifecare communities in the early 1960s; 20 years later, their numbers had grown to about 400 facilities. In the mid-1980s, articles were published about lifecare communities going bankrupt, which gave rise to resident fears, underwriter unwillingness to finance facilities, and some state regulation (Scott and Maziarka 1987). One factor was the inability of communities to get nursing home licenses as states sought to control the number of SNFs, making it difficult for CCRCs to honor their guarantee of lifetime care. Other factors were the lack of access to low-cost capital and the need for more funds (e.g., monthly fees) as residents' longevity increased and their needs grew, as well as for more sophisticated actuarial calculations to project costs appropriately.

Despite these problems, the numbers of CCRCs continued to grow in the 1990s as more older adults sought freedom from the upkeep and maintenance of their single-family homes. They also looked for an option that provided continued care without their being a burden to their families, usually located within 25 miles of where they lived before entering the facility. The failure rate now is very low due to the greater sophistication of the investment community, more educated residents, improved actuarial techniques and better management, and strengthened regulation of the financial aspects of CCRCs. Today, the American Association of Homes and Services for the Aging (AAHSA) estimates slightly more than 2,000 CCRCs serve approximately 625,000 older adults in all 50 states and the District of Columbia and that more than 40% of all CCRCs are found in five states: California, Pennsylvania, Florida, Illinois, and Ohio. The average age of CCRC campuses is 25 years.

One recent trend is the emergence of for-profit CCRCs. Because relatively few communities have been built within the last decade, this has led to pent-up demand and more financing becoming available for for-profits. This group of CCRCs tends to be more upscale than those operated by nonprofits, although the higher-end market is limited.

### Living Arrangements

CCRCs facilitate an independent lifestyle, combined with security. If residents become frail or ill, they know their needs will be met in a familiar environment, rather than having to relocate to a new place, as is true of those who live in their own homes and apartments or in stand-alone assisted living facilities (Golant 1992). However, in some CCRCs residents must move from one level of care to another, which often requires going to live in another wing or floor or perhaps a separate building. Most persons entering a CCRC, whether a single individual or a couple, reside in an apartment or cottage and move to a personal care unit or assisted living when, or if, their health declines. If their health status warrants 24-hour skilled nursing care, residents subsequently move to the SNF.

The average CCRC includes about 200 independent living units that can be studio or efficiency apartments and one-, two-, or three-bedroom apartments or cottages (Golant 1992). The larger units include a living room, a kitchen, and a bath; studios typically include a kitchen alcove and a bath. Apartments are decorated with the resident's own furniture and other belongings. Since the 1980s, two-bedroom units have become more popular; most CCRCs find it difficult to market studios and end up combining them into larger units, entailing substantial remodeling costs.

Residents usually retain use of their automobile, requiring the CCRC to provide adequate parking spaces, and typically eat some meals in their own units. Eating one meal a day in the congregate dining room supports residents' need for community and interaction. They are expected to be able to carry out most instrumental activities of daily living (IADLs) (e.g., shopping, cooking, money management, house cleaning, taking medications without supervision), as well as activities of daily living (ADLs), such as bathing, dressing, eating, toileting, and getting out of their unit without assistance. When a resident is unable to perform one or two ADLs or a combination of ADLs and IADLs, he or she moves to assisted living or a personal care unit, where help with these activities is provided. These units are often clustered together in a separate wing or floor or even a separate building. The likelihood of this kind of move occurring is greater today as the average age of a CCRC resident is 81, compared to age 79 just a decade ago (Golant 1992). These units are typically one room with a bath. Residents eat their meals in a congregate dining room that, in some instances, may be separate from the dining room serving the independent living units. Depending upon contract provisions, personal care is either provided by the CCRC or can be obtained on a fee-for-service (FFS) basis. In some CCRCs, personal care services may be provided in the independent living unit, especially if a spouse also resides there.

Should residents experience greater impairment in ADLs or cognitive function, they may be moved to the skilled nursing level of care. SNFs are usually housed in a separate building on a contiguous part of the CCRC. Sometimes a CCRC may contract with an SNF located next door to its campus. One advantage of the CCRC SNF for couples is that as one spouse needs a higher level of care, they may reside in separate care levels but are able to contact or be with each other with relative ease.

### Services and Amenities

CCCRs offer a variety of services to residents. These include building and grounds maintenance, utilities, activity and recreational programs, light and/or heavy house cleaning, laundry, meals including special diets, transportation and parking, emergency call and security systems, home modifications (e.g., grab bars), and various kinds of exercise and therapy programs. Amenities include libraries, barber and beauty shops, game rooms and auditorium/chapel, private dining rooms (for family celebrations), overnight accommodation facilities for guests, arts and crafts programs, cable television, swimming and therapeutic pools, garden plots, woodworking shops, and small convenience stores. The most typical amenities offered by at least 80% of CCRCs include beauty and barber shops, activities, crafts and multipurpose rooms, laundry facilities, libraries, and private dining rooms (ASHA 2002a). Increasingly, residents are looking for services and amenities related to their interests in health and wellness and in technology. Computer training and hookups, putting greens, yoga and a health office for checkups, and health promotion classes are among the new kinds of activities being offered, especially by larger CCRCs. Some CCRCs also provide services to nonresidents, similar to European "service houses." These can include adult day care, respite care, meal services, and support groups. This is one strategy being used by lower-cost CCRCs that may also admit nonresident patients to the nursing care unit.

## Payment Methods

The continuum of care offered by the CCRC is governed by a contract to which the resident agrees at the time of entry. Residents must abide by a variety of financial and legal obligations that are unique to this housing and care option. The contract governs both the financial and care relationship between the resident and the community. CCRC contracts take several forms. Knowledge of the various options offered under these contracts and how they are financed is important for those contemplating a move into a CCRC, as well as for those with primary responsibility for an older person's well-being and professionals who provide older adults with legal and financial advice or who provide retirement planning services to clients of all ages.

There are three general approaches to financing CCRC residency: entry fee, monthly fee only, and equity. Under an endowment or entry fee plan, the resident pays a lump sum upfront; this can cost from less than $100,000 up to more than $500,000, particularly in California. Such fees are often partially deductible as prepaid health care for income tax purposes. The entry fee is commonly in addition to monthly fees or other periodic fees that are payable during the time the individual or couple resides in the CCRC. These can increase over time.

The entry fee may be partially or totally refundable or nonrefundable to the resident upon leaving, death, or transfer. Under most contracts, the portion that is refundable decreases over time—typically, 2% per month over 50 months. Communities with more liberal refunds usually balance off that policy with higher monthly fees. CCRCs with large entry fees and less liberal refunds are likely to provide strong guarantees of lifetime care, accompanied by limits on how much monthly fees can be raised during the resident's tenure in the community. Communities with small or no entry fees and more generous refund policies are likely to have weaker lifecare guarantees, unless management has a "benevolence" or "endowment" program that helps pick up some of the costs. Entry fees and monthly fees vary greatly from CCRC to CCRC. The amounts depend on the type of unit occupied, the type of health care coverage, and the resident agreement and payment plan offered.

Two other approaches include the monthly fee only and the equity plan. The former is a rental arrangement with a service package and/or health care package, similar to many assisted living arrangements (http://www.aahsa.org/member/backgrd4.as). The latter plan is somewhat rare. It involves the purchase of the living unit as real estate, with the actual ownership of the unit being transferred upon sale to the resident. In equity contracts, the resident (owner) participates in any changes in the value of the unit from purchase. In this kind of contract, health-related service arrangements vary, but usually the resident is required to purchase service and/or health packages.

Within any of these general approaches there are three major types of contracts, primarily focused on health care coverage: extensive, modified, or fee-for-service. The *extensive* or all-inclusive contract includes housing, residential services and amenities, and unlimited long-term nursing care, usually without substantial increases in periodic payments except for normal operating cost and inflation adjustments. This arrangement combines a large health care insurance element with residential living. In essence, a resident shares the cost of SNF and catastrophic health care with all other residents.

*Modified* agreements include housing, residential services and amenities, combined with a substantial—but not unlimited—amount of long-term nursing care at no additional cost. For example, the contract may specify 30, 60, or 90 days, per lifetime or per year. Once the limit is reached, the resident who is availing him- or herself of these services pays a per diem or discounted per diem amount for additional nursing care.

By contrast, less than one-third of CCRCs offer a *fee-for-service* (FFS) contract. This arrangement includes housing, residential services, and amenities but does not cover assisted living or SNF costs. Residents are guaranteed access to health care service, but they must pay prevailing rates. In essence, they pay only for the long-term nursing care services actually used. Entry and monthly fees tend to be lowest under this kind of contract, but total monthly costs may not be; many FFS CCRCs require no advance or a minimal fee.

CCRCs allow older adults to make more efficient use of their financial resources by assuming the financial risk for housing, food, and care needs for the rest of their lives; by providing a form of long-term care insurance; by avoiding the need to pay for two types of housing at the same time (a home or apartment and an SNF); and providing economies of scale in the delivery of services such as home care. However, there are business risks associated with CCRCs. For example, while they function like insurance companies in assuming risk, especially the risk of the cost of providing long-term care, they have far fewer customers on which to base expected cost projections and over which to spread actual costs. CCRCs also may encounter adverse selection and, by providing quality care, may exacerbate their financial exposure by extending the lives of their residents if they do not also adjust for the financial risk of increased resident life spans.

## Regulation

To counter some of these problems, policymakers focus on protecting residents' investments and ensuring that the terms of the contract with the CCRC are upheld. CCRC regulation can take three forms: self-regulation via an accreditation process; regulation via accounting protocols and procedures; and state regulation. AAHSA, through the Continuing Care Accreditation Commission (CCAC) founded in 1985, accredits both nonprofit and for-profit communities. Using a series of standards, the CCAC seeks to assure consumers that a CCAC-accredited provider has met specific predetermined standards of quality in three areas: governance, finance and strategy, and health and wellness. It also seeks to help providers develop, interpret, and evaluate all components of their organizations and to provide the commission with a reliable basis for making accreditation decisions.

Integrated strategic planning and a self-study are crucial aspects of this accreditation process. As of 1997, 246 CCRCs in more than 25 states were accredited by the CCAC (CCAC 2002). However, only three states accept this accreditation in lieu of a state review (ASHA 2002c).

To evaluate financial strengths and weaknesses of CCRCs, three rating agencies are active: Fitch Investors Service, Standard and Poor's, and Moody's Investor Service. Several organizations also provide benchmarking studies based on financial ratios and trends. Other factors such as management and board experience, facility location, and competitive pressures are equally important in evaluating the overall strength of a CCRC. Standards promulgated by the Financial Accounting Standards Board (FASB) also affect nonprofit CCRC financial ratios, including FASB #116, Accounting for Contributions Received and Made, and FASB #117, Financial Statements of Not-for-Profit Organizations. These reports can reassure consumers and their advisors about the viability of a CCRC to make good on its guarantees of lifelong care.

Finally, all states regulate a CCRC's health care unit in accordance with the Centers for Medicare & Medicaid Services (CMS) guidelines. In addition, 39 states regulate CCRCs on financial and other aspects, but with considerable variation. State insurance agencies have primary responsibility for CCRC oversight, followed by health and then aging agencies. Contract forms must be submitted to 30 of the 39 states for review. Not all states require disclosure of a CCRC's financial report to residents. One-third do require such disclosure before a contract is signed, but 17% only require it if the resident requests it. Other states require disclosure based on some combination of before or at signing and some additional time period (e.g., annually, semiannually), or on request. Thirty of the 39 states have some designated period in which residents can rescind their contract, ranging from 7 days to 1 year; the most frequent time periods are 7 days, 10 days, and 30 days (ASHA 2002c).

Given the focus of policymakers on preserving the residents' investment, it is a matter of some concern that not all 39 states with CCRC regulations have explicit requirements for reserves or for the escrow treatment of entry fees. Of a less serious nature, but related to the ability of residents to protect their investment, less than half of these states have enacted legislation enabling residents' rights to organize through an association.

### Consumer Information

*Caveat emptor*—let the buyer beware—is a wise admonition for older adults who are contemplating a move into a CCRC. To determine if a CCRC is the right choice, prospective residents need to learn about the full range of services and amenities offered and to weigh the different senior housing options and the expenses of each. Two basic kinds of consumer information exist to help older consumers make good decisions: directories of different CCRCs (and often other housing options), often grouped by state or by region, and booklets or brochures that provide information and often worksheets to enhance decision making. AAHSA and an organization called Lifestyles provide the first kind of information to help prospective CCRC residents find a community to fit their needs. The AAHSA directory (AARP 2002c) profiles more than 500 CCRCs and also identifies accredited communities, while Lifestyles information focuses on all kinds of housing options in a given region.

Information provided by AARP, and other AASHA information, may be of greater relevance to a consumer trying to decide whether or not to enter a CCRC. The AARP, like one AAHSA brochure (AARP 2002b), features a range of housing options, including CCRCs, to enable consumers to make overall comparisons between CCRCs and other kinds of senior housing and care arrangements. AAHSA's guidebook for consumers (AARP 2002d) provides tips on how to conduct an initial search and emphasizes criteria to be addressed: services and ownership arrangements, location and management; common contract provisions; and specific services and charges, fee increases, and contract termination. Worksheets and consumer checklists are included.

Ultimately, the decision to enter a CCRC or not is likely to be a permanent decision, not only about housing and care but also about lifestyle preferences. Many seniors do not want to live in age-segregated housing or with large groups of other people. Many also want to age in place and, assuming that home care services are available, may just as easily be able to afford the costs of such care as to pay CCRC costs. Purchasing a long-term care insurance policy with an inflation-adjustment factor and with coverage for both home-based and SNF care is another option for those who can afford a CCRC. Additionally, those wishing to bequeath an estate to family members or a favorite charity may be less able to pursue that goal, unless they can find a CCRC with an equity contract or a liberal refund policy. Despite these cautions, the CCRC lifestyle, wide range of services and amenities, and peace of mind for both seniors and their families will continue to make this housing and care option attractive to many older people. (See also CPA ELDERCARE SERVICES; FINANCIAL ADVISORS; FINANCIAL PLANNING PROCESS; FRAILTY PLANNING; HOMEOWNERSHIP.)

### Organizations

AARP
American Association of Homes and Services for the Aging (AAHSA)
American Seniors Housing Association (ASHA)
Continuing Care Accreditation Commission

### Suggested Reading

Simmons, Henry C., and E. Craig MacBean. 2000. *Thriving after 55: Your Guide to Fully Living the Rest of Your Life*. Richmond, VA: Prime Press.

### References

AARP. 2002a. *The Continuing Care Retirement Community: A Guidebook for Consumers*. Washington, DC: American Association of Homes and Services for the Aging.

AARP. 2002b. *The Continuing Care Retirement Community: A Life-Style Offering Security and Independence*. Washington, DC: American Association of Homes and Services for the Aging.

AARP. 2002c. *The Consumers' Directory of Continuing Care Retirement Communities*. Washington, DC: American Association of Homes and Services for the Aging.

AARP. 2002d. *Selecting Retirement Housing*. Washington, DC: American Association of Homes and Services for the Aging.

American Seniors Housing Association (ASHA). 2002a. *Non-profit Housing and Care Options for Elder People*. Washington, DC: Author (in English and Spanish).

American Seniors Housing Association (ASHA). 2002b. *Seniors Housing Statistical Handbook*. 3rd ed. Washington, DC: Author.

American Seniors Housing Association (ASHA). 2002c. *State of Seniors Housing 2001*. Washington, DC: Author.

Continuing Care Accreditation Commission. 2002. *Seniors Housing: State Regulatory Handbook*. Washington, DC: Author.

Golant, Stephen M. 1992. *Housing America's Elderly*. Newbury Park, CA: Sage Publications.

Golant, Stephen M. 2002. *Standards of Excellence*. Washington, DC: Continuing Care Accreditation Commission.

Scott, Terence J., and Robert F. Maziarka. 1987. *Elderly Housing Options*. Chicago: Pluribus Press.

*Phoebe Liebig, Marilyn C. Kennedy, and Stephanie Cory*

**COOPERATIVE OWNERSHIP IN HOUSING,** a form of ownership in which a corporation (or trust or partnership) holds title to a multiunit development and grants occupancy rights in specific units to shareholders under proprietary leases. Individuals do not hold title to their dwelling unit; instead, they own stock in a corporation that owns the building or development. The cooperative buyer becomes a shareholder in the corporation and enters into a "proprietary" lease for a particular dwelling unit. Cooperative owners thus have leasehold rights to their housing units and ownership rights in the cooperative housing corporation. The lease payment covers a pro rata share of the amounts needed to cover operating expenses, taxes, and the mortgage debt of the whole complex. Owners of cooperative housing are eligible for income tax deductions for their shares of the mortgage interest and property taxes paid by the cooperative corporation. This is in contrast to the owners of condominiums, who have ownership of their occupied units plus an ownership interest with all other owners in the common area. Owning a cooperative apartment can be significantly less expensive than renting an apartment because landlord profits are not found in cooperative housing.

Some of the advantages and disadvantages of condominium ownership also apply to cooperative housing. An important distinction is that individuals owning stock in a corporation that owns cooperative housing assume the additional financial responsibility of keeping the corporation solvent. When an owner defaults on payments in cooperative ownership, the remaining share owners are responsible for paying the defaulted portion of the mortgage, real estate taxes, and operating expenses. If there are large enough numbers of defaulted share owners, the financial burden may have a snowball effect, causing other share owners in the cooperative housing complex to default. This snowball phenomenon is less likely to occur in condominiums, since owners obtain their own financing and are responsible for their own mortgage payments and property tax assessments. Individual owners therefore are not liable for the default on any other owner's financing obligations.

Since mortgage lenders cannot take the dwelling unit itself as collateral, and many do not wish to make long-term loans that are collateralized by the shares in the cooperative corporation, obtaining financing or refinancing for a cooperative unit can be difficult. (An exception occurs where cooperatives are a common form of homeownership. In New York, for example, lenders readily make loans to purchasers of cooperatives.) This may be an important factor for prospective owners to consider, especially if the market should sour and shareholders become unable to sell their units. Then the only option is to sublet temporarily, but almost all cooperative apartment complexes impose subleasing restrictions on the owner. Additionally, the managing board of the cooperative can reject a prospective buyer, causing the sale of one's cooperative shares (and the dwelling unit) to take longer.

As rents continue to rise, and as the demographic profile in the United States changes to reflect an increasingly older population, easy-to-maintain homeownership options such as cooperatives are likely to increase in popularity. This trend will be encouraged by the current high costs associated with purchasing raw land and building materials, compelling developers to build more housing complexes with increased numbers of dwelling units per acre than before. The condominium and cooperative forms of ownership offer older buyers more affordable options, as well as an assortment of exterior amenities and opportunities for increased social activities. Efficiently managed cooperative and condominium projects may thus constitute excellent housing options for the U.S. older population. (See also CONDOMINIUMS; FINANCIAL ADVISORS; FRAILTY PLANNING; HOMEOWNERSHIP; HOUSING COUNSELING FOR OLDER AMERICANS.)

**Organization**

National Association of Housing Co-operatives

**Suggested Readings**

Irwin, Robert. 1999. *Tips and Traps When Buying a Condo, Co-op, or Townhouse*. New York: McGraw-Hill.

Kiplinger's Personal Finance Magazine, eds. 2002. *Kiplinger's Buying & Selling a Home*. 7th ed. Washington, DC: Kiplinger Books.

Shapiro, Sylvia. 1998. *The Co-op Bible: Everything You Need to Know about Co-Ops and Condos: Getting In, Staying In, Surviving, Thriving*. New York: St. Martin's Griffin.

**References**

Golant, Stephen M. 1992. *Housing America's Elderly: Many Possibilities/Few Choices*. Newbury Park, CA: Sage Publications.

Shilling, James D. 2002. *Real Estate*. 13th ed. Cincinnati, OH: South-Western/Thomson Learning.

Smith, Halbert C., and John B. Corgel. 1992. *Real Estate Perspectives*. Boston, MA: Irvin.

Taishoff, Lewis C. 1981. *Cooperative Housing Conversions*. New York: Praeger.

*Andrew Quang Do*

**CORPORATE ELDERCARE PROGRAMS,** a form of employee assistance for the benefit of employees' older relatives. Human resource professionals in U.S. companies have extended the meaning of eldercare to include a variety of innovative programs designed to help employees who care for an older member of the family.

Several rapidly converging factors have contributed to the growing numbers of corporate eldercare programs: the aging of America, costs of family caregiving, changes in family structure that have eroded traditional caregiving at home, increased employment of women outside the home, and changing societal values about the balance between work and family life. Because of the demands it places on an employed caregiver, the care of older adults has emerged as a bottom-line issue for leading companies. Caregiving can take a personal toll on a company's employees and impair their productivity on the job. It is estimated that caregiving costs U.S. businesses $11 to $29 billion each year.

Benefits of corporate eldercare programs accrue to several constituencies: employed caregivers, their companies, and older persons who are the indirect beneficiaries of the assistance their younger relatives receive by way of information and resources to help older individuals with their current needs.

### Types of Corporate Eldercare Programs

Company eldercare programs vary widely. Some companies have recast existing benefits—flextime programs, leave benefits, work schedule adjustments, and financial benefits—to encourage their use for the dependent care needs of employees, including care of children, adolescents, and older adults. Others offer initiatives designed specifically for eldercare. A 1994 General Accounting Office survey found that medium and large companies who employ a combined 23 million workers offer at least flexible scheduling options that could be identified and actively supported as usable for eldercare. Of the total, 9 million people work for corporations that also provide assistance specifically designed for eldercare, such as information about long-term care services and support groups for caregivers. More than 8 million people work for companies planning to expand existing eldercare options or to offer new ones.

### Publications

Substantial numbers of companies have published or distributed eldercare information to their workforce. These have ranged from comprehensive handbooks on issues associated with aging and the service system to information about specific topics such as Alzheimer's disease. Other firms have developed work and family resource libraries that include books, videos, and audiocassettes on popular eldercare issues.

Eldercare has also moved to online providers. Some company programs enable employees to download "tip sheets" and resource information and to order larger booklets and books online.

### Fairs and Support Groups

Many companies have supplemented informational materials with workshops, seminars, and support groups for employees who are currently caring for an older relative. Numerous corporations employ outside experts or services to conduct these seminars. Topics can include financial concerns such as estate planning, paying for nursing home care, and understanding the insurance needs of older persons. Some companies have even begun to offer these events virtually through use of phone and computer technology.

### Financial Assistance

Few companies provide direct financial assistance to employees or their relatives, but many offer dependent care assistance plans (DCAPs) under the Internal Revenue Code to employees. This benefit, however, can help only a small proportion of employed caregivers because DCAPs are limited to older adults who are legal dependents of the employee. Several companies offer long-term care insurance to their employees, and the employee can sometimes purchase a policy for a parent as well. In most cases, employees pay the full premium for coverage of a portion of nursing or home care costs for themselves or their older relatives, should long-term care be needed in the future.

## Consultation and Referral Services

The most common response by large employers has been to take a broad approach to the range of eldercare problems employees face by offering them consultation and referral services. These services have been viewed as critical, since employees cannot come to work unless they have made care arrangements for their older relatives. Consultation and referral services have been designed to address specific issues including information, referrals to care providers, and individual counseling.

Eldercare consultation and referral services, when comprehensively delivered, include access to an eldercare professional. This professional provides expert counseling and helps the employee identify concerns and reach informed decisions, based on detailed knowledge of national and local community resources. The services also provide education through counseling and written materials that help employees select appropriate care. They can refer to providers as diverse as home health and transportation programs, elder law attorneys, and bill-paying services. Employees and their families remain responsible for selecting and paying for any services they choose. In 2001, a Hewitt Associates survey found 40% of companies in their sample now offer consultation and referral services.

## Development of Services

Several companies have gone beyond consultation and referral programs to increase the supply and quality of eldercare (and child care) services in communities where employees, retirees, or older relatives live. IBM, in 1989, earmarked a portion of its Fund for Dependent Care Initiatives for eldercare projects such as respite care and development, recruitment, and training of in-home health and social service workers. Later, the American Business Collaboration, which used IBM funds to leverage investment by other companies with similar needs, continued some investment in the eldercare infrastructure. AT&T also announced, in 1989, a significant Family Care Development Fund of $10 million, jointly funded by its unions and management. This fund continues to provide seed money to encourage the development and improve the quality of child and eldercare programs.

## Decision Making

There is no best way to select an eldercare program. Many companies, however, go through a series of steps in examining eldercare options. These include examining existing benefit programs, assessing employees' eldercare responsibilities and needs, examining costs, and selecting an approach to meet the needs of the broadest group of employees.

## Care Management Services

The newest corporate eldercare response extends support to more involved caregivers by paying part of the cost of geriatric care management service, such as in-person assessments and professional evaluations of facilities, such as assisted living and nursing homes.

Improving employee productivity, retaining experienced workers, and responding to employee requests are the primary reasons corporations offer eldercare plans. Reasons given by companies not planning to introduce or expand eldercare benefits include concerns about costs, lack of a needs assessment, or being unaware of the issue (General Accounting Office 1994). However, the needs of employees with eldercare responsibilities are becoming more prevalent. Some of the impacts of caregiving include lost productivity in American corporations, loss of top performers, absenteeism, and tardiness. While corporate eldercare is still in its infancy, innovative programs already in place help companies achieve their business objectives and increase employee productivity, and older persons receive the information and care they need. As the numbers of aging Americans increase even more rapidly in the decades ahead, and as the baby boom generation moves into retirement age, demand for corporate eldercare programs is likely to increase, and even more innovative programs are likely to be developed. (See also CPA ELDERCARE SERVICES; EMPLOYEE BENEFITS IN THE UNITED STATES; GERIATRIC CARE MANAGERS [GCMs]; GERONTOLOGICAL SOCIAL WORK; HOME CARE SERVICES FOR OLDER ADULTS.)

### Organizations

Bureau of National Affairs
Conference Board
National Alliance of Caregiving

### References

General Accounting Office. 1994. *Long-Term Care: Private Sector Elder Care Could Yield Multiple Benefits*. Washington, DC: Author.

Hewitt Associates. 2002. "Spec Summary™: Work/Life Benefits 2001–2002 (U.S.)." Available online at http://was4.hewitt.com/hewitt/.

Neal, Margaret, Neal Chapman, and Berit Ingersoll-Dayton. 1988. *Eldercare, Employees and the Workplace: Findings from a Survey of Employees*. Portland, OR: Research Institute on Aging, Portland State University.

Rodgers, Francene, and Charles Rodgers. 1989. "Business and the Facts of Family Life." *Harvard Business Review* (November–December).

*Diane S. Piktialis*

**COST OF FAMILY CAREGIVING,** the estimated financial impact of caring for older and disabled persons. One out of four families in the United States is caring for an aging relative or other loved one, and as longevity rates increase, this number is likely to grow. Despite the changes in family structure that have seen the nuclear family disperse, a family member still provides an estimated 80% to 90% of all care to the frail older adults in our population. The strain on the family—with fewer siblings to care for aging parents than in previous generations, more women in the workforce, divorce and remarriage, and family members living in different parts of the country—can be great, but family members continue to take responsibility for their loved ones. While they provide care willingly, they also often pay a price emotionally, physically, and financially.

### Financial Impact on Caregivers

Caregiving has a financial impact on caregivers, both in terms of the money they spend on behalf of their loved ones and, if they are employed, in real lost wealth over their lifetime. It is estimated that caregivers spend $95 to $357 per month to assist those they are caring for with groceries, medications, home modifications, and other out-of-pocket expenses; on a national basis this adds up to $1.5 billion per month (National Alliance for Caregiving/AARP 1997).

While these out-of-pocket expenses incurred by caregivers had been documented previously, until recently there were no calculations of the income and savings losses incurred by caregivers who were in the workforce. Employed caregivers, balancing work and caregiving responsibilities, often must pass up promotions or relocation possibilities, go from full-time to part-time work, take leaves of absence, or leave the workforce altogether as a result of the obligations to provide care. As a result, their income may be reduced and retirement savings may suffer as well. The MetLife (1999) Juggling Act Study estimated that the average loss in total wealth as a result of "free" caregiving is $659,139 over a lifetime. This includes lost wages ($566,443), lost Social Security benefits ($25,494) and for those who had them, lost pension benefits ($67,202).

Caregivers might also be called upon to pay for round-the-clock care at home or in a nursing home, resulting in an even greater financial burden for them or their loved ones. Neither Medicare nor private health insurance covers most long-term care costs. Nursing home care in 2002 averaged $61,000 per year, not including the costs of prescription drugs, medical care, and other expenses.

### Financial Impact on Businesses and the Economy

The financial impact of caregiving does not fall solely on the caregiver. It lands heavily on other elements of the economy as well. Although a half a day here and an hour late getting to work there seem insignificant when taken individually, an estimate made in 1999 of the aggregate costs of caregiving in lost productivity to U.S business ranges from $11.4 billion to over $29 billion per year (MetLife 1997). These estimates were based on the costs of employee absenteeism, workday interruptions, supervisors' time, and replacing employees who move from full- to part-time, retire early, or leave the workforce altogether. There is no way to estimate the impact on noncaregiver employees' productivity due to their inability to rely on these employee caregivers.

A more recent report (Alzheimer's Association 2002) on the economic impact of Alzheimer's disease in the United States puts the cost to U.S. business at $61 billion—in 2002 alone. This was approximately equal to the net profits of the top ten Fortune 500 companies. Of the total cost, $24.6 billion is the cost of health care for those employees, spouses, and retirees who have Alzheimer's disease. The other $36.5 billion is the total cost to businesses of workers who are caregivers for people with Alzheimer's disease. This includes (in round numbers): absenteeism, $10 billion; productivity losses, $18 billion; worker replacement cost, $6 billion; continuing insurance for workers on leave and temporary worker replacement fees, $2 billion; and Employee Assistance Program usage, $64 million.

Both studies point to the dramatic real dollar costs of "free" family caregiving, and no one is projecting that these costs will decline.

### Monetary Value of Caregiving

If family members suddenly stopped caring for their loved ones, who would pay for the care they provide? In 1997, the market value of care provided by unpaid family members and friends was estimated at $196 billion (Arno, Levine, Memmott 1999).

Updated figures for the year 2000 indicate that the value of "informal" uncompensated care is somewhere between $140 billion and $389 billion (Arno 2002). While impressive enough on their own, these figures are even more significant when compared to national spending for home health care ($32 billion) and nursing home care ($83 billion) (Arno 2002).

### Public and Private Policy Implications

The financial burden on caregivers has come to the attention of policymakers, thanks to the growing influence of the caregiver advocacy movement and increased coverage of caregiver issues in the media. However, there are few federal or state policies in place to provide assistance to caregivers. The costs for services needed by the care recipient are not tax deductible unless the older person is a legal dependent. In the 107th session of Congress (2001–2002), legislation was introduced with bipartisan support to provide a tax credit for those who take care of a family member, but it was not passed. A few states have initiated programs that provide some financial support for caregivers, but for the most part, families bear the costs of care unaided.

While Medicaid provides a safety net and funds long-term care for individuals who have limited assets or who spend down and can no longer pay privately, governments in all our states are facing a fiscal crisis. The 2001 report on "The Role of Medicaid in State Budgets" by the Kaiser Commission on Medicaid and the Uninsured noted that the increased cost of caring for older and disabled Medicaid beneficiaries was the single largest factor behind the $12.4 billion increase in federal Medicaid spending between 2000 and 2001 (Kaiser Commission on Medicaid and the Uninsured 2001). Its authors also observe that, according to data gathered by the National Conference of State Legislatures, 44 states are reporting that revenues have come in below forecasted levels in fiscal year 2002, and a smaller—but still significant—number of states are reporting that their expenditures are exceeding budgeted levels. In these states, Medicaid is often cited as one of the programs that is growing most rapidly.

With state revenues down and the costs of care spiraling, state budgets are close to the breaking point, and their ability to fund the future long-term care needs of their impoverished citizens is in jeopardy. Public policies that can help caregivers continue to provide care for loved ones at home would have a positive impact on the caregiver, care recipient, and the nation. Programs such as day care for adults, respite care, and caregiver training may provide enough support to keep a loved one at home longer and thus avoid (or delay) placement in assisted living or a nursing home facility. While this will partially alleviate the financial burden on the Medicaid system, its real significance lies in the positive impact on the lives of the caregivers.

Today's caregivers also must plan for their own future long-term care needs and consider financial tools, such as long-term care insurance, to cover the costs of care for themselves, should it become necessary. It is likely that those who have had hands-on experience in providing care and who understand the costs involved will be more likely to plan ahead for themselves, but there can be no guarantees. The trends noted above will not abate any time soon, and neither will the financial impacts on individuals and both state and federal government. (See also COMMUNITY-BASED CARE; CORPORATE ELDERCARE PROGRAMS; CPA ELDERCARE SERVICES; DAY PROGRAMS FOR ADULTS; HOME CARE SERVICES FOR OLDER ADULTS;

LONG-TERM CARE INSURACE, PRIVATE; LONG-TERM CARE INSURANCE [LTCI]—A CONSUMER'S PERSPECTIVE.)

### References

Alzheimer's Association. 2002. *Alzheimer's Disease: The Costs to U.S. Business in 2002*. Chicago: Alzheimer's Association.

Arno, P. 2002. "Economic Value of Informal Caregiving: 2000." Paper presented at the American Association for Geriatric Psychiatry, Orlando, FL, June.

Arno, P., C. Levine, and M. Memmott. 1999. "The Economic Value of Informal Caregiving." *Health Affairs* 18(2): 182–88.

Kaiser Commission on Medicaid and the Uninsured. 2001. "The Role of Medicaid in State Budgets." *The Henry J. Kaiser Family Foundation*, Policy Brief, October.

MetLife. 1997. *The MetLife Study of Employer Costs for Working Caregivers*. Warwick, RI: Author.

MetLife. 1999. *The MetLife Juggling Act Study: Balancing Caregiving with Work and the Costs Involved*. Warwick, RI: Author.

National Alliance for Caregiving/AARP. 1997. *Family Caregiving in the U.S.: Findings for a National Survey*. Bethesda, MD: NAC.

*Sandra Timmermann*

**COST-OF-LIVING ADJUSTMENTS (COLAs),** periodic additions to income payments that enable recipients to purchase the same amount and quality of goods and services over time despite inflation. As experienced by older Americans, COLAs are annual increases to Social Security benefits and other income payments that reflect the previous year's inflation rate in urban areas. Although a common perception is that older persons dependent on Social Security are protected from losing purchasing power, in actuality, after a few years they often cannot maintain the level of living they had upon retirement and experience increases in their cost of living greater than increases in their retirement income.

Understanding the reasons why COLAs fail to keep up with the cost of living as experienced by older Americans can be beneficial for planning a secure retirement. Financial advisors often advise their older clients to earn a return on retirement investments that is greater than the inflation rate, but their clients are often satisfied with conservative investments instead of those that outperform the current rate of inflation. The following provides information that financial advisors can use to explain to their clients why they are jeopardizing their financial future by being content with rates of return that only meet the current rate of inflation.

### Why Do COLAs Fail to Keep Up?

Key points about COLAs that affect older Americans are as follows: (1) COLAs do not adjust for cost of living, (2) COLAs are introduced with a time lag and always reflect what happened in the previous year—not what is currently happening in the U.S. economy, (3) not all sources of retirement income have COLAs, and (4) COLAs are based on an inflation rate that older Americans do not necessarily experience.

*First*, COLAs are calculated with a measure that does not reflect the cost of living. The Consumer Price Index (CPI) is used to determine COLAs, but this index measures changes in prices only and does not incorporate other changes that may occur. Beef prices, for example, may increase more rapidly than other meat prices, and older persons may change their shopping patterns to substitute poultry for beef. Behavior changes that alter the cost of living are not reflected in the CPI and cause the CPI to overstate inflation as experienced by those who purchase lower-priced substitutions. The CPI is based on out-of pocket expenditures. However, it does not include taxes such as income and Social Security tax contributions. Therefore, changes in tax rates are not reflected in the CPI.

*Second*, by the nature of how the calculations are made, COLAs reflect inflation from the previous year. When rapidly rising inflation is experienced, COLAs do not compensate for the large price increases that retired persons see currently when they shop. The reverse is true when inflation occurs at a slower pace than the previous year and the COLA is greater than the rate of change in prices older persons are currently paying.

*Third*, not all retirement income has COLAs. Even benefits with COLAs, such as Social Security and federal Civil Service Retirement, have experienced COLA freezes, cuts, and delays.

*Fourth*, the CPI used to calculate COLAs for older Americans does not necessarily reflect the changes in prices for goods and services they buy. Social Security COLAs are determined by changes in the Consumer Price Index for Urban Wage Earners and Clerical Workers (CPI-W), an inflation index based on the spending patterns of households in which more than one-half of the income comes from clerical or wage occupations. The CPI-W represents about 32% of the total U.S. population, and it excludes retired persons. Another index, the Consumer Price Index for All Urban Consumers (CPI-U) is based on the expenditures reported by almost all urban residents. The CPI-U includes retired persons, professional employees, the self-employed, the poor, the unemployed, wage earners, and clerical workers (who are also in the CPI-W). It represents about 87% of the U.S. population. The CPI-W registered a lower rate of inflation in three of ten years from 1990 to 1999. Older Americans who are dependent on Social Security can lose the ability to maintain their level of living when their COLAs are based on the CPI-W.

Older Americans are thought to experience lower rates of inflation than the younger population, since older people buy different goods and services. This difference is important when the items purchased have different rates of price change. It has been suggested also that the broad use of senior citizen discounts lowers the cost of living for older adults.

### Consumer Price Index for Older Adults

In the late 1980s, the U.S. Department of Labor's Bureau of Labor Statistics (BLS), the government agency that calculates the CPI, was directed by Congress to calculate an experimental Consumer Price Index for the Elderly (CPI-E). This experimental index for Americans 62 years old and older is based on existing data, reweighted to reflect expenditure patterns in the older population. A comparison with published CPIs found that older adults experienced a higher rate of inflation from 1983 through 1999 than the rates reported for either the CPI-W or the CPI-U. However, it is important to remember that the CPI-E is an experimental index and is not regularly published by the BLS.

In order to calculate a nonexperimental Consumer Price Index for the Elderly that could be used to determine COLAs, the measure must be designed to reflect the purchase behaviors of the older adults. The item and outlet samples surveyed for the index must represent the older population as well. Specifically, BLS must identify what should be tracked every month and where to gather prices for these items. The Consumer Expenditure Survey, used to determine the "market basket" of goods and services that consumers buy for the CPI-W and the CPI-U, does not include enough older persons to determine a CPI-E market basket. The Point-of-Purchase Survey is used to learn where consumers shop but does not include enough older adult buyers to determine which outlets should be surveyed each month.

Broadening the surveys to include a larger older adult household population would take years and would be costly and is unlikely under current budgetary constraints. Nonetheless, since an overstatement of the inflation rate could result in an overpayment of billions of dollars each year in Social Security, federal retirement, and military COLAs, the cost of developing a new index may be a good investment. If, however, a CPI-E demonstrates that COLAs understate inflation and Social Security COLAs increase, obviously more federal funds would be paid out in benefits. In the meantime, planning for a solvent retirement becomes a more difficult task. To keep up with the cost of living, retirement funds need to be placed in investments where they increase in value. Doing so, however, is likely to place the funds at a greater risk of loss.

## Planned Changes for the CPI

In 1997, BLS Commissioner Katharine G. Abraham announced that a third CPI will be published in addition to the CPI-U and the CPI-W. Publication of the new index began in mid-2002 and will use a different "superlative" formula to calculate it. The term *superlative* has been associated with it, in part, because the formula is considered to provide a more accurate representation of the cost of living. It will be called "CCPI-U" because the formula "chains" price changes from one month to another in its calculation. In essence, it makes an adjustment for consumers who switch to different items as a result of price changes—those instances, for example, when consumers substitute poultry for more expensive beef products.

The uses of the CCPI-U will most likely be affected by the manner in which BLS will release the data. Critical expenditure information, such as how much more poultry and how much less beef was purchased in a month, is not immediately available to calculate the CCPI-U. Therefore, each month BLS will publish an "initial" CCPI-U index number, which will be revised and later finalized. In February each year, the prior year's initial index numbers will be revised and released as "interim" CCPI-U index numbers. Also, in February, the numbers for two years ago will be revised again before they are published as "final" CCPI-U index numbers. Until the CCPI-U is published and its uses are observed, it is not clear what the value will be, especially to older Americans and their financial advisors, of a more accurate measure of an annual rate of inflation that is two years old when it is published. (See also CASH FLOW PLANNING FOR RETIREES; DAILY MONEY MANAGERS; FINANCIAL ADVISORS; FINANCIAL PLANNING PROCESS; SOCIAL SECURITY PROGRAM OF THE UNITED STATES; WEALTH SPAN.)

### References

Amble, Nathan, and Ken Stewart. 1994. "Experimental Price Index for Elderly Consumers." *Monthly Labor Review* 117 (May): 11–16.

Bureau of Labor Statistics. 1988. *An Analysis of the Rates of Inflation Affecting Older Americans Based on an Experimental Reweighted Consumer Price Index. A Study Prepared for the Senate Select Subcommittee on Aging*. Washington, DC: U.S. Department of Labor.

Bureau of Labor Statistics. 1998. *Understanding the Consumer Price Index: Answers to Some Questions*. Washington, DC: U.S. Department of Labor. Available online at http://www.bls.gov/cpi/cpi1998g.htm.

Bureau of Labor Statistics. 2000. "Experimental Consumer Price Index for Americans 62 Years of Age and Older, 1995–99." *CPI Detailed Report* (February): 5–7.

U.S. Senate. Special Committee on Aging. 1987. *Developing a Consumer Price Index for the Elderly*. Washington, DC: GPO.

*Kathleen K. Scholl*

**CPA ELDERCARE SERVICES,** also called CPA PrimePlus Services[SM], cover a wide range of financial and lifestyle management services that certified public accountants (CPAs) provide to older adults or their families. CPAs who provide these services have training and experience that give them the knowledge and skills necessary to serve the unique concerns and needs of their clients. These services can range from assistance with day-to-day needs, such as assistance with money management, to assistance with evaluating living options and creating plans to fund those lifestyle choices. CPAs can act as the point person for the client or work as one part of a team of professionals, such as lawyers, insurance professionals, social workers, and nurses. Some CPAs have hired these other professionals as part of their firm in order to serve all of their clients' needs.

CPAs who provide CPA eldercare services consider all the needs of the client when providing services to them. They understand the nonfinancial as well as the financial aspects of providing services to mature clients. For example, they understand that the evaluation of future living options involves many issues—Where do you want to live? How do you want to live? How do you feel about the approaching move?—as well as whether different properties meet their needs and desires (criteria) or how the client can fund his or her ideal living option.

CPAs providing these services are bound by their professional ethics to act with objectivity and integrity, and the services they provide are also regulated by State Boards of Accountancy in their respective states.

Here is a list of the financial and nonfinancial services that a CPA can provide directly or with the assistance of other professionals to his or her eldercare clients:

**Financial Services**

- Planning for fiduciary needs
- Evaluation of health care and lifestyle financing options
- Receive, deposit, and account for client receipts
- Ensure expected revenues are received
- Make appropriate disbursements
- Submit claims to insurance companies
- Confirm accuracy of provider bills and appropriate reimbursements
- Protect client from predators by controlling checkbook and other assets
- Estate planning

- Income tax planning and preparation
- Gift tax return preparation
- Estate tax return preparation
- Preparation of employment tax returns for household help
- Read and analyze financial transactions
- Evaluate investments and trust activity
- Portfolio management
- Risk management and insurance planning
- Verify third-party calculations, such as pension payouts, insurance payouts, and annuity payouts
- Read and analyze reports from fiduciaries
- Snowbird issues

**Nonfinancial Services**

- Eldercare planning
- Plan for housing and support service needs
- Plan for declining competency
- Plan for death or disability of one or both spouses
- Evaluate alternative costs of retirement communities and other housing
- Evaluate housing and care alternatives
- Provide inventory of services available in the community
- Lifestyle management services
- Help arrange for transportation, housekeeping, and other services
- Manage real estate and other property
- Snowbird services
- Concierge services
- Coordinate support and health care services
- Needs assessment
- Help family monitor care (act as "eyes and ears" of the family)
- Establish standards of care expected
- Communicate expectations to care providers
- Evaluate and report on the performance of other outside parties, such as caregivers or contractors
- Family facilitation

Many but not all CPAs provide CPA eldercare services. If your CPA does not provide these services, he or she can refer you to a CPA who does.

Chartered accountants (CAs) in Canada also provide eldercare services under the name CA eldercare services (or CA PrimePlus Services™). For clients with assets in both the United States and Canada or who have extended stays in both countries, eldercare services can be provided throughout the year. (See also ACCOUNTANTS; FINANCIAL

ADVISORS; FINANCIAL PLANNING PROCESS; GERIATRIC CARE MANAGERS [GCMs]; GERONTOLOGICAL SOCIAL WORK.)

*Ann Elizabeth Sammon*

**CREDIT SCORES,** a three-digit number usually falling between 300 and 850 that indicates the credit risk posed by a consumer to a lending or other financial organization; the higher the score, the lower the risk. Credit bureau scores are often called "FICO® scores" because most credit bureau scores used in the United States are produced from software developed by Fair, Isaac and Company. FICO scores are provided to lenders by the three major credit reporting agencies: Equifax, Experian, and TransUnion. The score is a snapshot of a consumer's credit risk potential. It is used to make 25 billion credit decisions each year, including over 75% of mortgage loan originations. More than 40 of the nation's 50 largest financial institutions rely on the FICO score to determine an individual's creditworthiness. Although other financial institutions will calculate their own credit score, often they include the FICO score in addition to other information about the consumer.

The company's founders, William Fair, an engineer, and Earl Isaac, a mathematician, generated the first score in 1958, two years after establishing Fair, Isaac and Company. In the 1960s and 1970s, Fair Isaac coupled complex mathematical formulas with low-tech data-gathering methods to create their scoring system. By the mid-1980s, the company was using credit history that Equifax, Experian, and TransUnion gather on millions of people. Together, these three credit bureaus track 90% of the borrowing and payment histories of Americans. In 1989, Fair, Isaac and Company updated its credit scoring formula to predict consumer credit behavior, and the new scores were introduced in partnership with Equifax.

Credit scores today carry more weight than ever. Banks, mortgage companies, credit, and other financial institutions use credit scores to tell whether or not a consumer is a good credit risk. Insurance companies use a customized version of the credit score for underwriting purposes to predict future losses and to determine the level of individual policyholder risk. Many organizations and individuals rely on credit scores, from potential employers screening job applicants to landlords gauging a tenant's ability to meet his or her monthly rental payments.

FICO scores are calculated from mathematical formulas that rely upon four types of information:

1. Payment history accounts for 35% of the score. Timely payments are good; late payments lower the score. A mortgage is the most important bill to pay on time.
2. How much money is owed on all accounts, how much is paid and satisfied, and the percentage of the credit limit that is currently being used adds up 30% of the score. Using the full credit limit also lowers a score.
3. Length of credit history accounts for 15% of the score (long and solid is preferred over short and erratic). Lenders like to see a mix of debt beyond credit cards. Having a mortgage and auto loan, for example, shows that a person can obtain financing and handle money management activities. Borrowing from finance companies lowers the score.
4. The number of recently opened accounts and the mix of credit cards, installment loans, and mortgages are tallied in the score. Customers who shop around in an effort to secure the best

deal used to be penalized after a 7-day window, but today all loan requests within a 14-day period are counted as a single credit inquiry.

The key, however, is not any single piece of data but rather how the variables interact. A missed payment may weaken one score by as much as 100 points but may have a smaller effect on another. The models analyze outstanding debts, then compare credit history against the actual payment performance of Americans in numerous categories, from consumers with a lot of credit experience ("thick" files) and those with relatively little ("thin" files) to consumers with new credit accounts and those with delinquent records (*Consumer Reports* 2001a). In order for a FICO score to be calculated, the report must contain at least one account that has been open for six months or longer. In addition, the report must contain at least one account that has been updated in the past six months. This ensures that there is sufficient information, and enough recent information, on which to base a score.

Credit risk is the single most important factor that lenders look at in the credit process but the least understood by consumers. Many people have turned to third-party credit monitoring services in order to understand the ramifications of credit report blemishes and errors that deleteriously affect their score. It is estimated that revenue from such credit monitoring services will total $420 million in 2002 and will grow to $1 billion by 2007 (Online Banking Report 2003). Analysts claim that consumer sales of credit scores, credit reports, and related products should total roughly $600 million in 2003 and could easily reach $1 billion by 2005. Some suppliers of these products offer educational resources for consumers as well. Credit monitoring companies also help consumers contact credit bureaus to have misinformation in their reports corrected. In cases of potential fraud, consumers are helped to notify police and banking institutions.

### Do Credit Scores Discriminate?

Credit reports, from which scores are calculated, must conform to the 1971 Fair Credit Reporting Act (FCRA) and subsequent 1996 amendments. The law gives consumers certain rights, such as access to their credit files and the right to dispute inaccurate information, which credit bureaus must correct or delete. Credit scores, however, are not subject to the FCRA, which specifically excluded them in the 1996 amendments, and as financial institutions have increased their reliance on the quick assessment these scores afford, they have become mired in controversy.

The FICO formula and scores were kept under wraps until mounting pressure from consumer advocacy groups and legislators forced the company and the credit depositories to rethink their policy to keep consumers in the dark. An upstart Internet lender, E-Loan, first gave consumers access to their scores, and as a result, Fair, Isaac and Company began selling scores through their online site (http://www.myfico.com/). Today, credit scores assess an individual's credit risk without relying on such discriminatory data as skin color, gender, or even income, according to Fair, Isaac.

Others disagree. While credit scoring is an apparently neutral and legal method of screening potential credit applicants, this screening device may encode subtle discriminatory criteria.

Discriminatory or not, use of credit scores is pervasive. Most lenders and brokers nationwide obtain credit risk scores that are calculated using proprietary Fair, Isaac and

Company software installed at each of the three national credit bureaus. FICO scores are generated when electronic credit files are ordered and run through the software. About one in three credit reports contains serious errors. Today's high-speed, automated underwriting environment emphasizes credit scores with little opportunity for review of the underlying files and records that produce the scores (Harney 2002a). Sixty percent (60%) of U.S. consumers have credit scores between 700 and 850, with the median score of 720. Twenty-seven percent (27%) of consumers' scores fall between 600 and 700 points, and inaccuracies in this range can be very costly. For example, a score between 620 and 640 is marginal and can result in a decision to extend a prime mortgage loan versus one that is "subprime." This decision will result in significant differences in interest rate and in the monthly payment a consumer must pay.

Mortgage industry experts estimate that 350,000 to 400,000 applicants are overcharged every year when lenders incorrectly label them high risk or subprime borrowers because of their credit score (Harney 2002b). A nationwide survey drives home the correlation between a good credit score and money saved. If, for example, a consumer is seeking a 30-year, $300,000 mortgage, with a FICO score of 500 to 599, she would qualify for a 10.2% loan, or $2,677.16 a month; at 620 to 674, she would be quoted 8.43%, or $2,291.87 a month; and at 700 to 719, the rate falls to 6.7%, or $1,935.83 a month. The added cost between the two extremes amounts to almost $9,000 annually.

### Dealing with Credit Bureaus

Correcting mistakes in a credit report can be a frustrating process, according to people who have tried. Serious credit report errors can take more than six months to correct—credit bureaus average 23 weeks to correct errors—and in some cases, consumers will be able to obtain no results at all. Inaccuracies are not the only factors that negatively affect a score. It is estimated that 30 million Americans have accurate but blemished credit reports because of late payments, collections, judgments, bankruptcy filings, and the growing problem of identity theft.

Consumers can follow certain steps to improve their score, including:

- Limit shopping for credit to a 14-day window.
- Limit credit to 80% of available credit and pay more than the minimum payment.
- Pay bills on time.
- Apply only for credit that is needed.

### Conclusion

Credit scores can give creditors an instantaneous assessment of a person's risk—an amazing feat when one considers the technological orchestration of the million bits of information that traverse the wires each day. Consumers move every year and three million last names change due to marriage or divorce. Six million or more U.S. consumers own second homes and often use both addresses. Tens of millions of consumers use a business address for at least one credit card. All those changes notwithstanding, the vast majority of information in the consumer reporting system is positive information. Credit scoring today is available to consumers who can have access to their score. Experts agree that consumers should make an effort to learn what is in their credit file and know their credit score. Knowing what's in a credit report and understanding the score is a critical part of financial management, according to Mitch Haws, vice president of public relations at Equifax, one of the big three national credit bureaus. (See also AGING INTO DEBT; CONSUMER CREDIT; FINANCIAL COUNSELING FOR MID- TO LATER LIFE; FINANCIAL RECOVERY IN LATER LIFE; HOMEOWNERSHIP; IDENTITY THEFT.)

### Organizations

Equifax
Experian
FICO
TransUnion

### References

Consumer Reports. 2001a. "New Assault on Your Credit Rating." January.

Consumer Reports. 2001b. "A Breakthrough for Borrowers." June.

Deagan, Brad. 2002. "Getting Your Credit History Doesn't Have to Be a Headache." *Wall Street Journal*, August 6.

Forster, Stacy. 2002. "If Credit Report Firms Can Flag Errors, Why Not Do It for All?" *Wall Street Journal*, July 26.

Harney, Kenneth R. 2002a. "Data Correction Services Help Borrowers Hurt by Wrong Scores." *Washington Post*, June 15.

Harney, Kenneth R. 2002b. "Mortgage Insurance Premiums Rise for Some Borrowers." *Washington Post*, August 17.

*Online Banking Report*. 2003. "Top 10 Industry Developments." January.

*Louisa Woodville*

**CRIME PROTECTION,** recognition of factors that increase vulnerability to crime and measurements and strategies to reduce possible victimization. According to the Bureau of Justice Statistics (2001), persons 65 years old or older are the least likely of all age groups in the United States to become victims of crime. In fact, crime victimization rates among older adults have generally been declining for more than 20 years. Personal safety, however, is a growing concern for older Americans, who as a group express a high fear of crime.

Like the general population, older adults are more likely to experience property crimes such as larceny, burglary, fraud, and vandalism and are least likely to be victimized by violent crimes (Bureau of Justice Statistics 2001). Assault was the most common of the violent crimes experienced by older victims (McCabe and Gregory 1998).

Alston (1986) describes who is likely to become a victim of crime by three characteristics: attractiveness, exposure, and guardianship. Attractiveness is related to "benefit," as some potential victims represent greater opportunity for gain than others. Wearing jewelry or carrying a purse usually can influence attractiveness. Exposure has to do with visibility and proximity. Visibility is a factor when persons are outside on the streets, and proximity suggests that it may be easier to victimize someone close by than having to travel to some distant suburb. Guardianship refers to forms of physical or social protection. Physical protection might involve staying home after dark, whereas social protection would include walking, or living, with a companion.

Purse snatching, like pocket picking, happens on public streets, where exposure and attractiveness combine with lack of guardianship to identify certain individuals as targets. It happens to persons who appear unstable and off guard. Purse snatching and pocket picking are exceptions to the negative relationship between age and victimization, as persons 65 years old and older are about as likely as those younger than 65 to be victims of personal larceny with contact. Home burglary most often victimizes older persons. In burglary, proximity, opportunity, and physical protection are key to selecting targets. Most burglars do not want to meet their victims and usually enter when no one is home. A Kansas City study of older Americans reported that most burglary victims had no outside lights burning, thus lowering their guardianship factor.

Attractiveness, exposure, and lack of guardianship are the characteristics of older persons most likely to become victims. Since older men are more likely to be on the streets, they are more likely to become victims. Blacks are more likely than Whites to be victims, due to their greater likelihood to reside in inner-city areas where crime is generally higher (exposure). Marriage provides guardianship, and married people enjoy the lowest victimization rates. Despite these patterns, there is no convincing evidence that older people are particularly sought out as targets for serious crimes.

### Fear of Crime

Fear of victimization may be unrelated to actual crime rates, and extreme fear can be explained partially by media exaggeration of all violent crimes. A survey of Chicago residents, however, shows that fear of crime is positively correlated to victimization rates once rates are adjusted for exposure to risk. Thus, fear of crime should not be interpreted as irrational or unjustified and, in fact, can be reduced by lowering victimization rates (Stafford and Galle 1984). Fear among older persons is greatest when they lack social integration in the neighborhood and when they see neighborhood compositions changing, abandoned buildings becoming more widespread, and unsupervised teens loitering in their proximity. These community attributes add to a sense of loss of control, a characteristic strongly related to fear of crime (Donnelly 1989).

### Costs of Crime

Personal contact with offenders during the crime is likely to produce greater fear, anxiety, and feelings of vulnerability as a result of the encounter. Those who already feel powerless and alienated find these feelings reinforced. Psychological costs to older victims, however, are not uniform and do not appear to differ from those of younger victims. Although burglary is a property crime, for example, it is perceived by young and old as a personal threat because it violates the idea of home as a safe place. Financially, older persons do not, in an absolute sense, lose more than younger persons, but if they are in a marginal economic position, those losses they do incur pose a greater source of hardship. Further, older persons are more likely to be injured when they are physically attacked (Bachman, Dillaway, and Lachs 1998). Ultimately, all costs of crime depend on the social, economic, and physical resources older persons possess; those of lesser means are more vulnerable to the consequences of criminal acts.

### Reducing Risks of Victimization

Older persons can reduce risks by being alert and by keeping the three characteristics of victims in mind. Staying home, thus avoiding outside activities, tends to increase isolation and may increase suspicion and fear as well. A more effective strategy is to improve individual and community awareness of the risk factors.

In terms of attractiveness, older persons should look more alert and carry a purse tightly, if at all. With regard to exposure, traveling with companions helps substantially. Guardianship support includes locked doors, bright lights, and stronger window frames. Having adequate homeowner's or renter's insurance is important. Resources available in most communities assist individuals in victimization prevention programs. AARP has a wide range of pamphlets and brochures that outline practical strategies for personal safety.

Crime prevention also requires involvement at the community level. Rather than retreating into the home and becoming prisoners of fear, older persons should become involved in neighborhood and community activities. Knowing neighbors and participating in community programs are ways of staying connected. Safety programs include school safety programs, Safe House programs, escort services, Neighborhood Watch, and local dispute resolution. Being involved reintegrates citizens into a changing community and increases commitment to the physical and social environment. Seniors, having time and experience to offer, are invaluable to these efforts. (See also CONSUMER PROTECTION FOR OLDER ADULTS; ELDER LAW PRACTICE; ETHICS IN FINANCIAL PLANNING; FINANCIAL ELDER ABUSE; GUARDIANSHIP; OMBUDSMAN.)

### References

Alston, Letitia. 1986. *Crime and Older Americans*. Springfield, IL: Charles C. Thomas.

Bachman, Ronet, Heather Dillaway, and Mark Lachs. 1998. "Violence against the Elderly." *Research on Aging* 20: 183–98.

Bureau of Justice Statistics. 2001. *Victim Characteristics*. Washington, DC: U.S. Department of Justice.

Donnelly, Patrick. 1989. "Individual and Neighborhood Influences on Fear of Crime." *Sociological Focus* 22: 69–85.

McCabe, Kimberly, and Sharon Gregory. 1998. "Elderly Victimization." *Research on Aging* 20: 363–72.

Stafford, Mark, and Omer Galle. 1984. "Victimization Rates, Exposure to Risk and Fear of Crime." *Criminology* 22: 173–85.

*Cathleen Burnett*

# D

**DAILY MONEY MANAGERS,** a rapidly growing profession whose members provide personal finance and business management services, and some social support assistance, to seniors and to others requiring such services. Daily money managers (DMMs) manage personal monetary affairs, organize financial documents, keep financial records, monitor health insurance claims and payments, and maintain bank accounts. They can be a second pair of eyes and ears for their clients and act as a facilitator or an advocate on specific living and care issues. Daily money management has emerged and grown from both financial services and social services roots.

Daily money managers do not take the place of other professionals, such as attorneys, accountants, and social workers. Rather, their work complements and facilitates the work of other financial professionals. By handling day-to-day financial tasks, the information needed by these other professionals is more available and in good form when they receive it. For example, a DMM, by managing bank accounts and other financial affairs, can provide accurate bank records and other documents that are needed by a tax professional in order to file income taxes. Some DMMs are also qualified to prepare and file state and federal tax forms when they are due.

At this time, daily money management is an unregulated field. Practitioners have a variety of professional and educational backgrounds, including social work, accounting, financial planning, and general business experience. Persons seeking DMM services may contact the American Association of Daily Money Managers, their local Area Agency on Aging, or the Better Business Bureau or seek a referral to a DMM from someone they know and trust. Since involvement of an outsider in personal financial affairs may be a sensitive issue, it is strongly recommended that persons seeking this type of service interview more than one DMM and hire the one who best complements their values and style in the management of their day-to-day finances.

The American Association of Daily Money Managers (AADMM) was formed in 1996. The mission of this organization is to:

- Foster high standards of client services provided by practitioners.
- Support the growth of the profession.

- Provide members with education and support in their efforts to provide quality service.
- Pursue respect and recognition of the field of daily money management.

The AADDM has grown into a network of providers of daily money management services in most states around the country. Most daily money management is performed by sole proprietors of small businesses that serve a specific geographic area. A list of member practitioners and other information on the field is available on the AADMM Web site: http://www.aadmm.com/. (See also ACCOUNTANTS; BANKING SERVICES FOR THE MATURE MARKET; CASH FLOW PLANNING FOR RETIREES; CPA ELDERCARE SERVICES; FINANCIAL ADVISORS; GERIATRIC CARE MANAGERS [GCMs]; GERONTOLOGICAL SOCIAL WORK.)

**Organization**

American Association of Daily Money Managers (AADMM)

**Suggested Reading**

American Association of Daily Money Managers. "Daily Money Management: What Is It and How Can It Help Me?" Available by contacting the Association at (301) 593-5462 or Info@AADMM.com.

*Roberta Gosier*

**DAY PROGRAMS FOR ADULTS** (also known as adult day care; adult day centers; adult day services), community-based, nonresidential group programs designed to meet the needs of functionally and/or cognitively impaired adults through individualized care. Day programs are structured to provide a variety of health, social, and other related support services in a protective setting during any part of a day but less than 24-hour care. Adult day programs are designed to serve adults who need supervision, social interaction, and assistance with more than one activity of daily living (eating, walking, toileting, bathing, dressing). The adult day center environment recognizes and attends to emotional and intellectual needs, as well as to physical needs.

A national study of adult day services found that the majority of adult day centers are open Monday through Friday for eight or more hours a day. Some centers, however, offer extended hours of service during the week, are open on weekends, and provide overnight care. Twenty-one percent (21%) of centers are medical models, 37% are social models with no medical component, and 42% are a combination of the two. Day programs provide a vast array of services such as meals and snacks, therapeutic activities (e.g., exercise programs, art therapy, music therapy, pet therapy), health monitoring, nursing care, medication management, assistance with activities of daily living (e.g., walking, eating, toileting), personal care services (e.g., bathing, hair care, nail care), rehabilitative therapies (e.g., physical therapy, speech therapy, occupational therapy), medical services, social services, counseling, caregiver education and support groups, care management, and transportation.

Although adult day centers serve a population that ranges in age from 18 to over 100, the average age of persons attending them is 72 (Partners in Caregiving [PIC] 2003). The two most prevalent health conditions are 52% dementia (all forms) and 41% frail older persons who have no dementia but are in need of supervision and/or at risk of social isolation. Twenty-four percent (24%) of participants are diagnosed with mental retardation and/or developmental disabilities, and 23% are physically disabled but cognitively intact (e.g., stroke, Parkinson's disease, multiple sclerosis). Other health conditions include chronic mental illness, HIV/AIDS, and traumatic brain injury.

Most people attending an adult day center live with a spouse or an adult child, and the average length of stay is two years. The number one reason for discharge from the center is placement in a residential setting such as a nursing home, and the number two reason is death (PIC 2003). Adult day programs have become a practical and appealing part of the solution to long-term care needs—a viable, cost-effective, community-based service option that helps individuals in need of chronic care remain at home, in the community, and with family and friends for as long as possible.

### Overview/Need

The model for adult day programs in the United States was the psychiatric day hospital started in the Soviet Union in the 1940s. Similar programs began in the 1950s in England. Experience showed that these programs reduced the need for in-patient beds. The first day program in the United States opened in the 1960s at Cherry Hill State Hospital in Goldsboro, North Carolina. Adult day programs subsequently expanded from medical services, transportation, and meals to offer supportive health and social services for marginally impaired and/or socially isolated individuals residing in the community.

Between 1969 and 1973, fewer than 15 adult day centers were in existence in the United States (Webb 1989). By 2002, over 3,400 centers had been established, of which 60% are located east of the Mississippi River (PIC 2003). Of these centers, over half have been operating for more than ten years. While a majority are not-for-profit and operate under the umbrella of a large parent organization (e.g., nursing home, hospital, senior service organization), there has been an increase in the number of for-profit adult day centers from 16% of centers open for ten years or more to 44% of centers opened within the last five years.

A minimum community population base of 20,000 is necessary to support an adult day center. It is estimated that 1% of that number, or about 200 people, are potential candidates for an average daily census of 20 to 30 people per day (Cox and Reifler 1994). Generally, two to three participants must be enrolled to support one daily slot, since many people use day center services on a part-time basis. Although the field is in flux, with centers opening and closing on a regular basis, growth is evident, with 26% of all adult day centers having opened during the past five years (PIC 2003). Growth, however, lags behind the need for adult day centers, with 1,770 of 3,141 counties nationwide currently underserved. With only 39% of requirements for adult day care being met, 5,415 new adult day centers are needed (PIC 2003).

### Regulations/Funding

There are no federal regulations for adult day programs. Funding or other regulatory standards usually exist at the state level, but the type of state agency overseeing adult day programs varies widely. The majority of centers (79%) report being certified or licensed by their state, with only 6% accredited on a voluntary basis by the Commission on Accreditation of Rehabilitation Facilities (CARF), the national accrediting body of adult day programs (PIC 2003).

On average, adult day centers serve 25 people per day at a cost of $56 per day (PIC 2003). The average daily fee, however, is only $46 per day, or less than cost. Cost and daily fees vary by state and by center, depending on the range of services offered. Most centers have a sliding fee scale, offering discounts based on income.

Overall, the largest source of revenue (38%) comes from public third-party reimbursements, which includes federal and state funds coming into a center on a fee-for-service basis (PIC 2003). The number-one reimbursement source in this category is Medicaid Home and Community-Based Waiver dollars, reported by 60% of adult day centers as a source of revenue. In some states, however, this revenue stream is not available. And in some states in which it is, day centers cannot access these funds unless they are a medical model. Also, Medicaid eligibility varies by state, and there are limits on access to those participants meeting income criteria.

Private and out-of-pocket payments comprise 35% of total revenue—the second largest source of income for adult day centers (PIC 2003). Other operating revenue (from managed care contracts, private long-term care insurance, and ancillary services such as bathing) totals 13% of all revenue (PIC 2003). And although private long-term care insurance plays only a small role in financing adult day centers, there is an increasing trend for insurance companies to provide reimbursement for adult day programs in long-term care policies (Henry and Reifler 1997). The remaining income at 14% comes from nonoperating revenue, such as United Way dollars and money from donations/contributions, fund-raising events, and grants. And when looking at revenue compared to expenses, 44% of centers report operating at a deficit (PIC 2003).

### National Initiatives

The financial viability of adult day centers was of primary interest to The Robert Wood Johnson Foundation when, in 1987, it created the first national adult day services demonstration program—the Dementia Care and Respite Services Program (1988–1992). With cofunding from the National Alzheimer's Association and the Federal Administration on Aging, the foundation sought to demonstrate that adult day centers could serve people with dementia and that they could do so in a financially viable manner. A particular emphasis was on fee-for-service payments, as opposed to philanthropy. The success of this program led to another foundation initiative, Partners in Caregiving: The Dementia Services Program (1992–1996), a four-year replication program that continued to demonstrate that adult day centers could effectively care for people with dementia in the community (versus nursing home placement) and could be financially viable at the same time.

Findings from the four-year demonstration program showed that adult day centers can be financially self-sufficient. Four factors proved to be statistically significant predictors of better financial performance (percentage of total expenses covered by net operating revenue): a higher ratio of daily fees to unit cost; staying open a full day (i.e., 7:30 A.M. to 6:00 P.M.); receiving government fee-for-service reimbursement in addition to private pay; and a higher average daily census (Reifler et al. 1997).

However, a higher ratio of daily fees to unit cost means giving consumers and funding sources the opportunity to pay the full cost of service. Because of their nonprofit status, and their mission to serve everyone who needs service, many day center boards and staff are often reluctant to charge the full costs for fear high fees will prevent people from using the service. One way to balance the tension between pursuing their mission while operating in a fiscally sound manner is for day centers to charge full cost but offer discounts on a case-by-case basis, depending upon need. Philanthropy can then be used to fund the discounts.

Increasing the number of people served per day results in economies of scale and lowers unit cost, since some large expenses (e.g., rent, administration) remain fixed regardless of the number of people served. Pursuing government reimbursement gives day centers a way to serve people who might not otherwise be able to afford services and provides another funding stream to help cover operating expenses. Being open a full day allows day centers to serve a wider range of participants, including those whose caregivers work. Being open a longer day also gives nonworking caregivers more choice in using the service.

Overall, the demonstration sites were able to meet 63% of their total expenses with net operating revenue (Reifler et al. 1997). During the four-year replication program, improvements were made, with the replication sites (overall) meeting 83% of their cash expenses through net operating revenue (Reifler et al. 1999). Today, 37% of adult day centers across the country do not track financial performance. The Dementia Care and Respite Services Program and Partners in Caregiving also showed gains that can be made through attention to marketing and other essentials for success (Henry et al. 1997). From a marketing perspective, the most successful adult day centers are those that show a willingness to adapt in order to fit the needs and wants of individual participants and their caregivers and to find creative solutions to problems. Solving the customer's problem helps centers become more competitive and thus more financially viable. Also, from the perspective of the caregiver and participant, the quality of a program can be judged further by the availability of transportation, a full day of engaging activities that offer choices, professional/trained staff, links with other community services, support services for caregivers, and a well-functioning board of directors.

With widespread needs existing in the community and the profile of services and financial support becoming solidified, adult day programs continue to grow in importance and strength as part of the continuum of care. (See also COMMUNITY-BASED CARE; CONTINUING CARE RETIREMENT COMMUNITIES, [CCRCs]; HOME CARE SERVICES FOR OLDER ADULTS; LONG-TERM CARE INSURANCE [LTCI]—A CONSUMER'S PERSPECTIVE; TRANSPORTATION.)

### Organizations

Administration on Aging
Brookdale National Group Respite Program
National Adult Day Services Association
National Alzheimer's Association
National Association of Area Agencies on Aging
National Association of State Units on Aging
Partners in Caregiving: The Dementia Services Program

### References

Cox, N.J., and B.V. Reifler. 1994. "Dementia Care and Respite Services Program." *Alzheimer Disease and Associated Disorders* 8 (Suppl. 3): 113–21.

Henry, R.S., N.J. Cox, B.V. Reifler, and C. Asbury. 2000. "Adult Day Centers." In *To Improve Health and Health Care 2000: The Robert Wood Johnson Foundation Anthology*, ed. S.L. Isaacs and J.R. Knickman. San Francisco: Jossey-Bass.

Henry, R.S., and B.V. Reifler. 1997. "Coverage of Adult Day Services in Long Term Care Insurance Policies." *Journal of Applied Gerontology* 16(2): 221–34.

National Adult Day Services Association. 2002. *Adult Day Services Fact Sheet*. McLean, VA: Author.

Partners in Caregiving (PIC). 1995. "The Dementia Services Program." In *Life after Diagnosis—Adult Day Services in America*. Winston-Salem, NC: Wake Forest University School of Medicine.

Partners in Caregiving (PIC). 2003. "The Adult Day Services Program." *National Study of Adult Day Services*. Winston-Salem, NC: Wake Forest University School of Medicine.

Reifler, B.V., N.J. Cox, B.N. Jones, J. Rushing, and K. Yates. 1999. "Service Use and Financial Performance in a Replication Program on Adult Day Centers." *American Journal of Geriatric Psychiatry* 7(2): 98–107.

Reifler, B.V., R.S. Henry, J. Rushing, K. Yates, N.J. Cox, et al. 1997. "Financial Performance among Adult Day Centers: Results of a National Demonstration Program." *Journal of the American Geriatrics Society* 45: 146–53.

Von Behren, R. 1986. *Adult Day Care in America: Summary of a National Survey*. Washington, DC: National Council on the Aging/National Institute on Adult Daycare.

Webb, L.C., ed. 1989. *Planning and Managing Adult Day Care: Pathways to Success*. Owings Mills, MD: National Health Publishing.

*Nancy J. Cox and Rona S. Henry*

**DEATH BENEFITS,** money and/or in-kind benefits paid to the survivors of the deceased (also called survivor benefits). These benefits are usually provided to eligible survivors of the deceased upon receipt of proof of death, such as a copy of the death certificate. Amounts may be paid in one lump sum, as in life insurance policies and the Social Security lump-sum burial expense payment, or they may be paid over time, as in Social Security survivor benefits.

Historically, death benefits go back at least to biblical times, when a person who killed or injured someone was required by law to pay an indemnity to the kin of the injured or deceased, and the person who killed or disabled a slave was required to reimburse the master. The practice of paying an indemnity in the case of wrongful death expanded over the years to include workers killed on the job and soldiers killed during war. In 1935, the Social Security Act established the practice in America of paying government benefits to dependent survivors of workers who died.

### Public Death Benefits

Publicly paid death benefits come primarily from three programs: Social Security, the Veterans Administration, and Worker's Compensation. Of these, the most common is survivor's insurance under Old-Age, Survivors, and Disability Insurance (OASDI), paid to eligible dependents of deceased workers by the Social Security Administration. Eligible dependents include widows or widowers 60 years old or older, disabled widows or widowers age 50 or older, younger widows or widowers caring for children younger than 16 years old or disabled children, unmarried children younger than 18 years old (or up to 19 if they are attending elementary or secondary school full-time), unmarried children disabled before age 22, or dependent parents age 62 years and older. Survivor benefits under OASDI consist primarily of monthly payments based on earnings of the deceased if he or she was still working when death occurred. If the deceased had already retired or was receiving Social Security Disability payments at the time of death, survivor benefits are tied to the deceased's monthly payments. Under OASDI, survivors—a spouse living with the worker at the time of death, or dependent children—are also eligible for a lump-sum payment of $255.00 toward funeral expenses. (Information can be found at http://www.ssa.gov/).

The Veterans Administration pays two types of survivor benefits: (1) dependency and indemnity compensation (DIC) for dependent survivors of service persons who die of a service-connected injury or illness while on active duty; or (2) death pensions for spouses and children (18 years old or under or 18 to 23 years old and attending school) of veterans who died of non-service-connected illness or injury. Eligibility for death pensions may depend on the income of the dependents.

Dependent survivors of all honorably discharged wartime veterans are eligible for survivors benefits whether the death was service connected or not, while survivors of peacetime veterans are only eligible if death was service connected. "Wartime service" applies to all declared wars and undeclared wars such as the Korean and Vietnam conflicts. Burial allowances of $300 are available for veterans of wartime service and for peacetime veterans whose deaths are service connected. When death occurs while the veteran is in a Veterans Administration (VA) hospital or under contracted nursing home care, some of the costs for transporting the deceased's remains may also be reimbursed. When death is service connected, moreover, survivors may apply for a $2,000 lump-sum payment in lieu of the smaller allowance when they have surviving dependents.

Veterans who are honorably discharged are eligible for burial flags and internment in national cemeteries. Spouses and minor children may also be eligible for burial in national cemeteries. Information is available from funeral directors, local veterans affairs offices, and online at http://www.va.gov/.

Each state and territory pays benefits under Workers' Compensation laws to survivors of workers killed or fatally injured on the job. While state laws are similar, each state controls the manner of determining eligibility, amount of benefits, and length of time survivors receive payments. Under Workers' Compensation, spouses are eligible until remarriage, and dependent children are eligible until a specified age. Most states have Workers' Compensation boards or commissions that hear cases and award compensation; some states allow the court system to make these determinations. Burial allowances vary under Workers' Compensation.

### Private Benefits

Survivor benefits are paid under life insurance policies and through pension plans offered by employers as part of employees' benefits. Life insurance pays a predetermined sum directly to beneficiary(ies) named in the policy or to the estate of the deceased, if so designated. While benefits are usually lump-sum payments, other options are available, such as lifetime income for the spouse or periodic payments for a specific length of time. Benefits may increase in cases of accidental death and may be denied in cases of suicide.

Life insurance held by a creditor to secure payment of a debt is paid directly to the mortgage or lien holder when death of the insured occurs. Most lending institutions require such credit insurance if a loan amount is substantial, and while this requirement protects the bank, it reduces survivors' financial burden as well.

Survivor benefits from pension plans are available under certain circumstances. If an employed spouse is vested in a pension plan but dies before retirement, a death benefit tied to the amount of retirement proceeds may be payable to the widowed spouse or other assigned beneficiary. When someone elects to continue payments to a spouse after death, a reduction in pension payments during lifetime is usually required. Death benefits under employee pension plans may be paid as a percentage of the employee's average pay, expected pension, or accrued pension. Pensions, life insurance, and similar accounts usually provide a death benefit that is not subject to probate.

Other death benefits are paid through fraternal organizations and through special life insurance plans for employees of the federal government. More specific information may be obtained from a local Social Security Administration office, VA office, Employment Security office (Workers' Compensation), or the financial office of an employer. (See also LIFE INSURANCE; PENSION PLANS; SOCIAL SECURITY PROGRAM OF THE UNITED STATES; VETERANS' BENEFITS.)

### Organizations

Department of Veterans Affairs
Office of Worker's Compensation Programs
Social Security Administration

### References

Quadagno, Jill. 1987. *The Transformation of Old Age Security*. Chicago: University of Chicago Press.

Quadagno, Jill. 2002. *Aging and the Life Course*. New York: McGraw-Hill.

Roy, F. Hampton, and Charles Russell, eds. 1992. *The Encyclopedia of Aging and the Elderly*. New York: Hamilton Printing.

Walker, Alexis, Margaret Manoogian-O'Dell, Lori McGraw, and Diana White. 2001. *Families in Later Life*. Thousand Oaks, CA: Pine Forge Press.

*Francis P. Conner*
*Updated by Janice K. Purk*

**DEFINED BENEFIT PENSION PLAN,** an employer-sponsored, formula-driven retirement plan that provides a fixed amount of pension benefit at the employee's normal retirement age (usually age 65). The amount of benefit received typically depends upon whether the benefit is a flat dollar amount or a percentage of pay, as well as the employee's length of service and earnings. For example, an employee might receive 1% of pay or a flat dollar amount for each unit of service provided to the organization. Defined benefit plans are typically noncontributory for employees but require an annual contribution from employers who offer the plan.

If the defined benefit plan provides for a pay-related benefit, the benefit may be calculated according to the total earnings of an employee (a career average approach) or the last few years of an employee's company service, such as three to five years (a final pay approach). The final pay approach benefits the employee by calculating a plan payout at the highest years of individual earnings. The career average approach, in contrast, calculates the mean earnings of the employee over every year of employment and may include years of low earnings. This calculation may produce a benefit that penalizes the employee for long years of service. In addition, the value of benefits under a final pay approach may provide for preretirement inflation protection, where the employer assumes the cost associated with that inflation.

The formula used in a defined benefit plan may provide for a full unit of benefit for each year of service, or there may be a maximum period over which benefits are credited. The design of the formula should reflect the employer's objectives as to income replacement levels (i.e., 50% to 70% of pay). Most defined benefit pay–related plans are integrated with Social Security benefits so that the total payout between the employer-sponsored plan and Social Security is less than 100% of pay. This approach recognizes that Social Security is of greater value to less highly compensated employees and helps the employer design a plan that contributes a reasonable amount toward an employee's retirement.

Any tax-qualified pension plan must provide that employee contributions to the plan are vested at all times and that accrued employer contributions are vested by normal retirement age. Two types of vesting schedules exist: (1) five-year "cliff" vesting, where all benefits vest after five years of service, and (2) graded vesting, where 20% of benefits vest after three years of service, and that percent increases in 20% increments until 100% vesting occurs after seven years. Defined benefit plans also provide that if an employee terminates his or her employment, the vested benefit is payable at retirement. However, many plans have a provision that small benefit amounts (less than $5,000) may be payable at the time of termination of employment.

The most common form of death benefit under a defined benefit pension plan is a joint and survivor benefit where some part of the employee's benefit is payable in periodic installments to the employee's spouse or other survivor. For a spouse, the benefit is payable for life, while for a child, benefits may be payable only until the child reaches a certain age. Defined benefit plans may also provide for disability benefits by treating the disability as a form of early retirement, or the plan may have a separately stated disability benefit with more liberal age and service requirements. Defined benefit plans are subject to the Employee Retirement Income Security Act (ERISA) plan termination requirements, and employers sponsoring these plans are required to pay annual Pension Benefit Guaranty Corporation (PBGC) premiums. If, for any reason, the plan is terminated with insured but unfunded benefits, the employer's net worth may also be exposed to liability.

Since the enactment of ERISA in 1975, the total number of private sector tax-qualified retirement plans more than doubled (from 311,000 to 730,000), but the number of defined benefit plans has decreased from an estimated 170,000 plans in 1985 to 56,000 plans in 1998. Suggested explanations for the decline include: (1) increased government regulation; (2) workplace trends that increasingly favor defined contribution plans; (3) business environment and risk associated with funding and managing pension plans; (4) firm size; (5) global competition faced by employers in recent years, which has increased the need for more flexibility in plan design; and (6) the successful marketing efforts of consultants and defined contribution plan service providers.

With recent changes in business investment conditions, many employers have introduced hybrid pension plan arrangements, that is, those that incorporate characteristics of both defined benefit and defined contribution pension plans. A popular type of defined benefit hybrid plan is the "cash balance plan," where the plan provides a determinable benefit, but the employee's accrued benefit is expressed as an account balance, and the annual "contribution" or credits paid to this account may be expressed as a percentage of the employee's current pay. However, actual employer contributions and return on plan assets may not be the same as the annual addition and increases credited to employee accounts.

There are many arguments for and against defined benefit pension plans. Employers seeking specific income replacement goals for their employees can achieve this through a defined benefit plan. Defined benefit plans favor long-service employees who are in turn protected from the effects of preretirement inflation. They are also a favorite plan choice for union leaders, who can influence an employer's choice of pension plans. Defined benefit plans require employers to commit to pay the cost of promised benefits, including any increases in inflation and despite any adverse investment results. However, during times of a booming stock market, employers may not need to make any annual plan contributions. Until recently, prior contributions plus investment returns alone provided sufficient plan funding for some large employers.

Defined benefit plans also have implications for plan participants. Since these plans are formula driven and noncontributing, employees may be unaware of accumulated earnings that exist within a plan. However, a defined benefit plan offers no direct investment risk to participants, and plan sponsor bankruptcy risk is limited to the risk of losing benefits not guaranteed by the PBGC, should an employer become insolvent. These factors have different meanings for each type of employer who must weigh the needs of employees against the reality of their financial structure and future economic performance. (See also CASH BALANCE PENSION PLANS; EARLY RETIREMENT INCENTIVE PLANS [ERIPs]; EMPLOYEE BENEFITS IN THE PUBLIC SECTOR; EMPLOYEE BENEFITS IN THE UNITED STATES; PENSION PLANS; PENSION PLANS FOR THE SELF-EMPLOYED.)

**References**

Rajnes, David. 2002. "An Evolving Pension System: Trends in Defined Benefit and Defined Contribution Plans." EBRI *Issue Brief*, September.

Rosenbloom, Jerry S. 2001. *The Handbook of Employee Benefits: Design, Funding and Administration*, 5th ed. New York: McGraw-Hill.

*Mary Helen McSweeney*

**DEFINED CONTRIBUTION PLAN,** an employer-sponsored retirement savings program that does not guarantee a fixed pension benefit but promises a specified contribution to an account into which an employee also makes contributions. The employer contribution may be a fixed percent or a flat dollar amount, or it may be related to profits. How much an employee receives in a benefit, therefore, depends upon the level and frequency of contributions, length of plan participation, as well as choices of investment vehicles. Consequently, the responsibility for accumulating a pension benefit under a defined contribution plan rests primarily in the hands of the employee.

There are various types of defined contribution plans. These include (1) money purchase plans, which require a fixed percentage of compensation to be contributed annually to each eligible employee; (2) deferred profit sharing plans, where the employer contribution is discretionary or related to profits; (3) Section 401(k) cash or deferred arrangements, where employees contribute up to legally allowable amounts and employers have the discretion to match these contributions; (4) savings or thrift plans that typically act as a supplement to another defined contribution plan such as a 401(k); and (5) employee stock ownership plans (ESOPs) that are either a qualified stock bonus plan or a stock bonus and money purchase plan qualified under Internal Revenue Code (IRC) Section 401(a). A brief explanation of each plan type will be provided below.

Money purchase plans require a fixed contribution from an employer, but employees may also contribute from after-tax income according to predetermined contribution rates stipulated in the plan and frequently expressed as a percentage of pay. An example of such an arrangement is a 3% employee contribution with an employer match of 50 cents for every dollar contributed.

Profit sharing plans typically have formula-driven contributions made only by an employer (i.e., noncontributory for the employee), which are allocated to employees in proportion to their level of compensation and possibly service with the organization. Employees may also supplement their account balances by making additional contributions on an after-tax basis. However, there is tremendous flexibility within the plan, since contributions need only be made if the level of corporate profits are sufficient, thereby containing plan costs.

Section 401(k) cash or deferred arrangements (CODAs) offer an employee the choice between cash or deferred employer contributions to a qualified retirement plan. In addition, employees can make elective contributions of amounts that could otherwise be received in cash on a pretax basis, which reduces their taxable income and helps to avoid federal income taxes until the point of distribution. CODAs may be part of a profit sharing plan or stock bonus plan (including thrift and savings plans) and may be subject to certain safe harbor contribution requirements. CODAs are subject to limits on elective deferrals ($11,000 maximum in 2002), a limit on compensation applicable for determining contributions and benefits, and IRC Section 415 limits ($25,000 of employee's compensation or $35,000, the latter being indexed to cost-of-living requirements). They are also subject to coverage tests under nondiscrimination requirements. Recent legislative changes created a small employer version of 401(k) plans, or SIMPLE (Savings Incentive Match Plan for Employees) 401(k)s. In these plans, employers are not subject to meeting nondiscrimination requirements in exchange for meeting specific contribution rules (100% of employee contributions equal to 3% of their compensation or nonelective contributions equal to 2% of compensation for each employee making over $5,000 in the year).

Thrift plans (which frequently accompany 401(k) plans) promote employee savings by requiring a minimum employee contribution to be credited with an employer match. Employee participation is voluntary, and the employee can determine his or her level of contributions subject to certain plan minimum and maximum levels. Contributions are generally made to a trust fund, and employees have the option of taking in-service withdrawals of their own monies or all or a part of employer vested contributions. Many employers instituted thrift plans as a vehicle for accumulation of supplemental retirement benefits, as well as meaningful benefits during years of active employment.

Employee stock option plans are similar to profit sharing plans but are different in that distributions are made in company stock. While it is an employee benefit plan, ESOPs are well known as a vehicle for companies to borrow based on their credit to finance purchases of company stock for the firm's employees. An ESOP must meet distribution, put option, nonallocation, and voting requirements.

From 1975 to 1998, the number of qualified private sector–defined contribution plans rose from 208,000 to 673,000, with growth concentrated in smaller firms. While assets in both defined benefit and defined contribution plans increased, defined contribution plan assets grew exponentially, from $74 billion in 1975 to almost $2.1 trillion in 1998 (Rajnes 2002). Although interest in defined benefit plans has been reported recently among employees, more employers prefer defined contribution approaches because of the flexibility of these plans, growing employee job mobility, and a need for employees to learn how to manage their own retirement income. Employers are also seeking new approaches to integrate the best aspects of defined benefit and defined contribution plans, which may be accomplished by offering both plans, or a hybrid such as a cash balance plan. An important factor for future defined contribution plan design is the passage of H.R. 1836, the Economic Growth and Tax Relief Reconciliation Act of 2001 (P.L.107-16), or EGTRRA. Key provisions of EGTRRA include increased limits on contributions to qualified retirement plans, faster vesting of employer matching contributions, and greater flexibility with respect to withdrawals, rollovers, and plan contributions. This legislation provides new incentives to encourage sponsorship of both defined benefit and defined contribution plans and may encourage workers to continue to earn vested rights in plans to protect their retirement income. (See also ANNUITIES; INDIVIDUAL RETIREMENT ACCOUNT [IRA]; PROFIT SHARING PLANS; RETIREMENT PLANS—401(k); RETIREMENT PLANS—403(b).)

**References**

Rajnes, David. 2002. "An Evolving Pension System: Trends in Defined Benefit and Defined Contribution Plans." EBRI *Issue Brief*, September.

Rosenbloom, Jerry S. 2001. *The Handbook of Employee Benefits: Design, Funding and Administration*. 5th ed. New York: McGraw-Hill.

*Mary Helen McSweeney*

**DERIVATIVES** financial instrument contracts having a value that is derived from the value of an underlying financial product. Examples of the underlying product or "basis" are equity securities, commodities, bonds, foreign currency, short-term negotiable debt securities, and money market products. Options and futures traded on exchanges are derivatives contracts, as are over-the-counter options and forwards sold by dealers and bought by investors.

As synthetic investment instruments, derivatives fashioned from currencies, stocks, bonds, commodities, and other underlying financial products are designed to manage the risks of doing business, conserve capital, and enhance earnings. They also provide a source of investment and speculation. Most age groups, including older persons, indirectly experience the effects of derivatives trading. Pension funds utilize them, and many companies in which older investors hold stocks, bonds, or shares in mutual funds use them as well. Some money market accounts allocate part of their funds using interest rate derivatives as yield stabilizers and enhancers. There are derivatives for interest rate risks, currency risks, commodity risks, credit risks, insurance risks, and many other purposes.

For the large majority of individual investors, derivatives are neither a common nor appropriate direct investment vehicle. Only those who are fully acquainted with derivative instruments and investment risks should consider them. Most derivatives require highly technical mathematical software to build, value, and keep fluctuating risk profiles updated. On Wall Street, the design of exotic derivatives has taken on a "rocket science" aura that requires personnel with high-level math skills and access to sophisticated computer technology. Large losses and possible financial market disruptions due to derivatives trading and investment have been widely publicized, such as the multibillion-dollar crisis with Long-Term Capital Management in 1998.

Older persons and their financial advisors should be familiar with the concept of derivatives, because these investments will continue as key financial tools for corporations, government bodies, pension funds, mutual funds, banks, and other institutional investors in the future. Any inducements given older individuals to use derivatives as a speculative investment, however, should be thoroughly investigated and understood, and at least one second opinion should be obtained before any such investment is made.

### Types of Derivatives

Derivatives come in two basic forms: option type and forward type. Both types may be traded on an exchange, such as commodity futures and stock options. They may also be traded privately by an arrangement between interested parties over the counter (OTC). Option-type derivatives give buyers the right, but not the obligation, to buy or sell an asset at a specific price over defined periods of time. The price for this right is usually a small percentage of the underlying asset value. For example, corporate stock options allow employees to profit from a change in the firm's stock price without owning the underlying shares. Forward-type contracts commit buyers and sellers to trade a specific quantity of assets at a set price on a set future date. Forward types include futures, forwards, and swaps. Normally, no money exchanges hands until the delivery date, when the contracts are often settled in cash rather than by exchanging assets. When homeowners apply for a mortgage and lock in an interest rate for a future settlement date, typically 60 days, they have secured a privately traded forward derivative contract (commitment) from the mortgage lender. Like options, a relatively small performance margin deposit is required, which ranges from 1% to 20% of the value of the underlying assets covered by the contract. This is the *leverage effect* in the debate about derivatives.

### Market Size and Leverage

The global derivatives market is estimated to be over $100 trillion, an amount greater than ten times the U.S. gross domestic product (GDP). The estimated market size is a notional value reflecting the full value of the underlying assets, but this overstates the economic value of derivative transactions. Industry estimates indicate that the replacement cost of most derivatives that would be lost upon default by the counterparty to the transaction ranges from 3% to 6% of the notional value. To place notional value in perspective, consider an insurance policy as a form of derivative. For $750 of insurance, the car owner covers the loss of a $25,000 car. The $25,000 car represents the notional value. It would cost $750, not $25,000, to obtain a replacement policy.

The great power of derivative instruments, and most of the controversy, results from this leverage. A $10,000 performance margin deposit might control, for example, $10 million in underlying bonds, and there is real concern that during chaotic trading or a financial crisis such leverage could trigger or accelerate a financial domino effect. Critics worry about a set of outcomes where too many participants could be overleveraged and unable to meet margin and loss calls, which would precipitate mass liquidations of portfolios with few, or no, buyers to cushion the liquidations. The result could trigger financial and stock market collapses.

On the other hand, there are significant members of the global financial community, including central bankers, who believe that the interlocking web of derivatives will act ultimately as a smoothing effect to forestall a domino effect. They believe derivatives can dampen the impact of a financial crisis. Derivatives could allow various entities to hedge in such a manner as to forestall mass liquidations and thereby ride out intermittent financial storms that might randomly erupt. Without derivatives, they would be forced to liquidate and might accelerate financial collapse instead.

## Two Types of Investors

Two classes of derivative users are *hedgers* and *speculators*. Commercial interests are the primary hedgers, because hedging is designed to lock in a price and to minimize losses that can result from price fluctuations between the time contractual obligations are made and the time they are delivered. Business, for example, contracts to deliver a raw or processed material, financing, or a financial instrument at some future time. A firm will hedge by using derivatives to protect its anticipated profit against adverse price fluctuation over the time period from order receipt to final delivery and customer payment, thereby reducing uncertainty. Unlike the hedger, the speculator primarily seeks to profit from price fluctuations in the underlying securities or assets and assumes the risks associated with such fluctuations. For the hedger, the minimum deposit represents a low-cost avenue to insure against the risk of price movement over time. For the speculator, the power of leverage represents an opportunity to multiply a relatively small initial investment into a large profit. For both types of investors, derivatives represent the potential for large losses as well.

Such leverage is at the center of debates about the appropriateness of derivatives use by certain participants. Regulation is under consideration for certain industries, such as banking and pension funds, to prohibit certain types of derivatives as not appropriate while allowing other types of derivatives that are. The challenge facing legislative and regulatory agencies worldwide is to create an environment that would allow the positive effects of derivatives to continue without excessive regulation. To this end, steps are being taken to better display, explain, and account for these complex instruments with greater transparency. In the immediate future, more companies and financial institutions will disclose in annual reports, mutual fund offerings, and other information sources their use and degree of involvement in derivatives. This will better inform older investors, and their advisors, about the holdings and levels of risk within the investment portfolios of the corporations, banks, insurance companies, mutual funds, and other organizations in which they invest.

### Why Derivatives Evolved

During the past 30 and particularly last 15 years, the global financial markets have witnessed an increasing demand for cost-efficient protection against the risks of large and volatile foreign exchange, interest rate movements, and even credit quality risks. Without better protection against future unpredictability, companies could not function, plan, compete, and grow efficiently in global markets. When a U.S. company receives an order from Germany or Japan to be delivered in three months, it needs to hedge in a cost-effective manner against fluctuations in currency exchange rates that could wipe out its profit when paid in Eurodollars or yen.

Derivatives have provided the ability to "unbundle" and transfer certain risks from entities not willing, or unable, to manage the risks to those who desire to do so. U.S. companies, for example, not wanting to bear the risk of foreign exchange are now able to hedge their exposure by purchasing an option that guarantees the future exchange rate price and amount. The counterparty, the seller of the option, is willing to take on the exchange rate risk for a price called the *premium paid.*

The financial shocks in the 1980s and 1990s, such as the 1987 stock market crash, the failures of major banks, hedge funds, insurance companies, and securities firms, and the savings and loan crisis, have continued to reinforce the need for better financial tools to anticipate and prevent future crises. As a result of major advances in finance the evolution of derivatives has accelerated. These advances include the speed and sophistication of information processing and communications technology. Derivatives have allowed the traditional financial risks—market, credit, legal, and operational—to be managed in new, innovative, low-cost ways. In the financial, regulatory, and media arenas since the 1990s, however, negative impressions of derivatives trading remains. But a different viewpoint suggests that derivatives are necessary financial tools to control future price and market volatility for the benefit of all consumers. Mediating these opposite viewpoints and making the disclosure, measurement, control, and use of derivatives more orderly and understandable are the challenges that face the global markets for these exotic investments. (See also AGENTS AND BROKERS; ETHICS IN FINANCIAL PLANNING; FINANCIAL ADVISORS; INVESTOR EDUCATION; RISK TOLERANCE.)

#### References

Crouhy, Michel. 2000. *Risk Management.* New York: McGraw-Hill Trade.

General Accounting Office. 2002. *Financial Derivatives.* Washington, DC: GAO. Available online at http://www.gao.gov/.

Global Derivatives Study Group. "Group of Thirty." Available online at http://www.group30.org/.

Hull, John C. 2000. *Options, Futures, and Other Derivative Security.* 4th ed. Englewood Cliffs, NJ: Prentice Hall.

Schwartz, Robert J. 1997. *Derivatives Handbook: Risk Management and Control.* Wiley Series in Financial Engineering. New York: John Wiley & Sons.

Wilmott, Paul. 1998. *The Theory and Practice of Financial Engineering.* New York: John Wiley & Sons.

*T. Erle Keefer*

**DISABILITY PROGRAMS, FEDERAL AND STATE,** programs that provide cash support, health care coverage, and direct supportive services to eligible people with disabilities. The Americans with Disabilities Act and eight major federal and two major state programs serve sizable proportions of the disabled population aged 50 or over. These programs are typically limited to people under age 65, and the specifics of enrollment vary with the individual agency involved.

## Background

Federal disability programs serve people of all ages, but most disability programs target children or working adults ages 18 through 64. Since disabilities increase with age, many programs include large numbers of people aged 50 through 64 in their later working years. The eight federal programs are (1) Social Security Disability Insurance (SSDI); (2) Supplemental Security Income (SSI); (3) Medicare; (4) Medicaid; (5) Black Lung Program; (6) the Veterans Administration Disability Compensation Program; (7) the Veterans Administration Pension Program; and (8) the Veterans Administration Health Services Program. The two state programs are (1) Workers' Compensation and (2) Temporary Disability Insurance.

People may receive benefits from more than one program if they meet eligibility requirements. Specific eligibility requirements vary, depending on the program purpose, and requirements may change over time as the result of amendments to law, new regulations, or court decisions. Eligibility is determined by factors related to disability as well as to age, income, veteran status, or work experience. Federal and state offices administering specific disability programs should be contacted directly for the current eligibility requirements.

The concept of disability has generally shifted from diseases, conditions, and impairments to a focus on functional deficits caused by these factors. Disability measures used in clinical settings or research often underlie or are incorporated into program eligibility. Disability is defined in research as significant difficulty with or the inability to perform certain daily functions (i.e., working, keeping house, living independently) because of a health condition or medical impairment.

Some commonly used factors in assessing disability are:

- *Sensory Impairments.* Difficulty with or the inability to see, hear, or speak.
- *Cognitive/Mental Impairments.* The presence of or resulting disabilities from cognitive/mental impairments (e.g., Alzheimer's disease, mental illness, mental retardation).
- *Functioning of Specific Body Systems.* Capacity of specific body systems (e.g., climbing stairs, walking three blocks, lifting ten pounds).
- *ADLs/IADLs.* Difficulty with or the inability to perform the activities of daily living (ADLs) without assistance, typically including bathing, dressing, eating, toileting, getting in or out of a bed or chair, and walking; and/or the instrumental activities of daily living (IADLs), which generally include using the telephone, shopping, preparing meals, cleaning house, doing laundry, doing yardwork, managing personal finances, and managing medications.
- *Working.* Inability to work, limitations in the amount or kind of work, and/or ability to work only occasionally, irregularly, or part-time.

### The Americans with Disabilities Act

The intent of the Americans with Disabilities Act (ADA) of 1990 is to protect the civil rights of persons with disabilities. Equal opportunity provisions pertain to employment, public accommodation, transportation, state and local government services, and telecommunications.

For purposes of the ADA, disability is present if an individual meets one of the following three tests: (1) There is a physical or mental impairment that substantially limits one or more major life activities; (2) there is a record of such an impairment; or (3) the individual is regarded as having an impairment. The ADA definition is identical to the one used in Section 504 of the Rehabilitation Act of 1973 and in the Fair Housing Amendments of 1988.

### Major Federal Disability Programs

#### *Social Security Disability Insurance*

Social Security Disability Insurance (SSDI) is the primary social insurance program that protects workers from loss of income due to disability. SSDI provides monthly cash benefits to disabled workers under age 65 and to certain dependents. SSDI is intended for workers who stop working early (before age 65) because of a disability.

*History*. The 1935 Social Security Act established the federal Social Security system to provide old-age benefits for retired workers. The SSDI program was enacted in 1956 to provide benefits to disabled workers aged 50 through 64 years and disabled adult children of deceased or retired workers. Subsequent amendments widened SSDI coverage to include certain dependents and workers younger than age 50 (Social Security Administration [SSA] 2000).

*Administration*. SSDI is federally administered by the Social Security Administration.

*Scope*. In January 2002, 6.9 million persons received SSDI benefits: 5.3 million disabled workers under age 65; 204,100 disabled widows/widowers aged 50 to 59; and 672,100 adults under age 65 who were disabled in childhood. One-half of disabled workers were between the ages of 50 and 64. In January 2002, the average monthly benefit was $815 for disabled workers, $537 for disabled widows/widowers, and $542 for adults disabled in childhood. SSDI benefits end at age 65, when workers who stop working early due to disability are converted to regular retirement benefits (SSA 2002a).

*Funding*. Funding is provided through the Disability Insurance portion of the Social Security payroll tax on earnings. The payroll tax is 7.65% of earnings, of which 5.6% is for the Old-Age and Survivors Insurance (OASI) portion of Social Security, 0.6% for the SSDI portion, and 1.45% for the Hospital Insurance (HI) portion of Medicare. A matching 7.65% tax is borne by employers. For 2002, the OASI and Disability Insurance (DI) parts of the payroll tax are collected only for the first $84,900 of earnings, but there is no earnings limit for the HI payroll tax (SSA 2001).

*Eligibility*. In order to become eligible for SSDI, an individual must have worked the required number of Social Security–covered work quarters and must have a severe impairment that makes him or her unable to perform his or her previous work or any other kind of substantial gainful activity. Insured work quarters are credited annually for those years during which an individual works, is covered by Social Security, and earns a specified amount, which is adjusted upward each year. Only four quarters can be credited each year. In 2002, one quarter of coverage is credited for $870 of earnings (this figure is adjusted annually).

Workers over age 31 must be fully insured and have at least 20 quarters of coverage during the 40-quarter period up to time of disability to receive SSDI. Fully insured status means the person has 1 quarter coverage for every year after he or she attained age 21. Persons who have 40 quarters are fully insured for life. There are special rules for persons under age 32. Workers between the ages of 24 and 31 must be fully insured and have at least 1 quarter of coverage for every 2 quarters up to time of disability to receive SSDI. Persons aged up to 24 years must have at least 6 quarters coverage in the 12 quarters up to and including the quarter the disability began.

For SSDI, disability is defined as the inability to engage in any substantial gainful activity (earn more than $780 per month for disabled and $1,300 for blind persons in 2002) by reason of a medically determinable physical or mental impairment that can be expected to last for a continuous period of at least 12 months or result in death as stated in Social Security Act, Section 223(d) (Committee on Ways and Means 2000; SSA 2002b).

After a claimant is technically qualified, State Disability Determination Services examines medical evidence to determine if the claimant's mental or physical impairment is severe enough to have more than a minimal effect on the claimant's ability to work. If so, the claimant's medical condition is compared to the SSA Listing of Impairments, covering each major body system (SSA 2002a). Claimants whose medical conditions are at least as severe as those in the listing are considered disabled. Claimants who are not found disabled are evaluated at two additional steps. A determination is made regarding whether the claimant can do his or her past work, based on assessments of his or her physical and/or mental abilities.

If it is determined that claimants cannot do their past work, then a determination is made as to whether they can do other work that exists in the national economy. This assessment is based on the individual's residual functional capacity, age, education, and work experience. Jobs are said to exist in the national economy if there are significant numbers with requirements that are within the functional abilities and vocational qualifications of claimants.

Dependent coverage and survivor benefits are offered through SSDI. Disabled individuals can receive SSDI in three ways: on their own as disabled workers (described above), as widows or widowers (who are aged 50 to 59) of insured individuals, and as adults aged 18 to 64 who became disabled in childhood, whose parent(s) either receive SSDI, are Social Security retirees, or are deceased (but had been insured under Social Security).

Disability determination criteria for disabled widows/widowers is identical to those used for disabled workers and adults disabled in childhood. Dependent coverage is also provided to nondisabled family members (spouses who are either aged 60 or older or who care for one or more entitled children younger than 16). Survivor benefits are paid to the widowed aged 60 or older; to the widowed of any age if they are caring for a dependent child who is either younger than 16 or disabled; to unmarried children younger than 18 (or 19 if in elementary or secondary school); or to dependent parents aged 62 or more.

An SSDI beneficiary may, under certain circumstances, also receive SSI payments for their disability.

### *Supplemental Security Income*

The Supplemental Security Income (SSI) program provides monthly cash payments to low-income aged, blind, and disabled persons.

*History.* The SSI program was established by the 1972 amendments to the Social Security Act, which replaced earlier federal grants to the states for old-age assistance and aid to the blind and to the permanently disabled. It began operation in January 1974.

*Administration.* The SSI program is administered by the Social Security Administration.

*Scope.* In January 2002, 5.4 million blind or disabled persons received SSI, with monthly payments averaging about $423. Approximately 39% of those receiving SSI because of blindness or disability are aged 50 or over (SSA 2002b).

*Funding.* Funding comes from federal general revenues. Many states have chosen the option to supplement federal SSI payments with their own funds.

*Eligibility.* Unlike SSDI, people receiving SSI because of blindness or other disability have no prior work requirements but must meet a financial means test. Persons under age 65 must meet disability and financial criteria, whereas those aged 65 or over need only meet the financial means test. SSI payments may be received by individuals or couples. Both members of a couple must be aged, blind, or disabled and must meet the financial means test in order to collect payments. There are no dependent or survivor benefits under SSI. Disability determination is the same as in the SSDI program. Under certain circumstances, an SSI recipient may also receive SSDI benefits because of disability.

### *Medicare*

Medicare, enacted in 1965, provides health insurance coverage to persons 65 or older, certain disabled persons under age 65, and individuals of any age with end-stage renal disease.

*History.* Medicare was established by the Social Security Amendments of 1965 under Title XVIII. As part of the 1972 amendments to the Social Security Act, Medicare was extended, under certain circumstances, to persons receiving SSDI and to those with kidney disease (SSA 2001). Until the passage of the Balanced Budget Act (BBA) of 1997 (P.L. 105–33), Medicare consisted of two parts: Part A, or Hospital Insurance (HI), and Part B, or Supplementary Medical Insurance (SMI). Under the BBA, a new provision, Part C, more commonly known as the Medicare + Choice program, expanded beneficiaries' options for participation in private sector health care plans (SSA 2001). Because HI (Part A) is financed through the Social Security payroll tax, HI is automatically extended to individuals eligible for Social Security. SMI (Part B) is a voluntary program available only by paying monthly premiums (Committee on Ways and Means 2000).

*Administration.* The Medicare program is administered by the Centers for Medicare & Medicaid Services (CMS) in the Department of Health and Human Services. CMS was formerly known as the Health Care Financing Administration (HCFA).

*Scope.* As of July 2000, over 39.6 million persons were enrolled in some part of the Medicare program: 34.3 million were aged 65 or over and 5.3 million were under 65.

Of these, almost 292,000 persons (of all ages) were reported to have end-stage renal disease (ESRD) (CMS 5% Denominator File). There were $236.5 billion in Medicare payments made during fiscal year 2001, of which $31.9 billion were for persons under 65 years of age receiving SSDI. In July 2000, approximately 3.7 million disabled individuals between the ages of 45 and 64 were enrolled in Medicare. During 2001, of the total Medicare beneficiaries (aged and disabled), approximately 15.6% were enrolled in Medicare + Choice and other prepaid health plans (USDHHS 2002).

*Funding.* Funding for Part A of Medicare comes from the HI portion of the Social Security payroll tax and is automatically deposited in the HI Trust Fund. In 2002, the HI payroll tax was 1.45% of earnings for employees and 1.45% for employers. Self-employed persons are taxed 2.9% of earnings for HI. The SMI part of Medicare is financed by a combination of monthly premiums, which generally cover about 25% of program expenditures, and federal general revenues, which cover the remaining 75% (Committee on Ways and Means 2000). In 2002, the monthly SMI premium was $54 (USDHHS 2002). Financing for Medicare + Choice comes from the HI and SMI Trust Funds (SSA 2001).

Medicare beneficiaries are responsible for charges not covered by Medicare. These charges can include noncovered services, deductibles, coinsurance, copayments, limits, premiums for Part B and voluntary Part A, and premiums for supplemental insurance (i.e., Medigap). Payments can be made out of pocket, through a health insurance plan (often referred to as "Medigap" insurance), or through Medicaid.

*Services.* Traditional fee-for-service Medicare coverage has two parts. Part A, or HI, is subject to deductibles, coinsurance, and limits and generally covers all Medicare beneficiaries. Part A covers inpatient hospital care, skilled nursing and/or rehabilitative post-hospital care in a skilled nursing facility (generally only within 30 days of a hospital stay of at least 3 days), home health care (which can also be covered under SMI), and hospice care (for terminally ill persons who are expected to live for less than six months). Part B, or SMI, has deductibles and monthly premiums. Part B covers physicians' and surgeons' services, outpatient services from certain other medical providers, emergency room and outpatient clinic services (including same-day surgery), ambulance services, home health care not covered by Part A, laboratory tests, x-rays, diagnostic radiological services, certain preventive screening services (e.g., tests for breast cancer, cervical cancer, prostate cancer, bone mass, diabetes monitoring, immunizations for influenza, pneumonia, and Hepatitis B), ambulatory surgical center services, certain physical and occupational therapy and speech pathology services, outpatient rehabilitation services, certain mental health care services, radiation therapy, dialysis, certain transplants, approved durable medical equipment and supplies for home use, and drugs that cannot be self-administered (Committee on Ways and Means 2000; SSA 2001; USDHHS 2000a). Medicare + Choice plans provide Part A and B services at a minimum (except for hospice care) and may offer expanded services, such as routine examinations, dental care, and prescription drugs (SSA 2001).

*Eligibility.* Persons aged 65 or over who are entitled to Social Security, federal employees covered under HI, and certain employees of state and local governments and nonprofit organizations are enrolled in Medicare. There are two ways that persons under age 65 can be eligible for Medicare: (1) SSDI beneficiaries are enrolled in Medicare 24 months after receiving SSDI benefits (the 24-month waiting period is waived for persons with amyotrophic lateral sclerosis), and (2) persons in the ESRD program are enrolled in Medicare after three months. Medicare recipients who are eligible because of SSDI are aged 20 to 64. Former SSDI beneficiaries under age 65 who are no longer entitled because they have earnings that exceed the substantial gainful activity amount can exercise the option to purchase Medicare Part A and B premiums (SSA 2001).

A Medicare beneficiary, under certain circumstances, may also be covered by Medicaid.

### *Medicaid*

Medicaid is a joint federal and state program that pays for the health care of low-income and medically indigent individuals.

*History*. Medicaid was established, along with Medicare, by the Social Security Amendments of 1965. Medicaid replaced earlier programs that provided medical payments for needy individuals.

*Administration*. Medicaid is jointly administered by the states and territories and the federal Centers for Medicare & Medicaid Services. CMS was formerly known as the Health Care Financing Administration (HCFA).

*Scope*. During fiscal year 2000, $194.7 billion in Medicaid payments were made for an estimated 41.7 million persons. Nearly 18% of Medicaid recipients who were blind or disabled accounted for 38% of payments. During that time, $39.5 billion of all Medicaid expenditures went for nursing facilities, $9.9 billion for intermediate care facilities for the mentally retarded (ICF-MRs), and $18.3 billion for community-based long-term care. Altogether, 20.3% of all Medicaid expenditures were spent on nursing facilities, 5.1% on ICF-MRs, and 9.4% on community-based long-term care (USDHHS 2002).

*Funding*. Medicaid is funded by the federal and state governments. Federal dollars come from general revenues. The federal-to-state match rate is derived annually by comparing the states' average per capita income to national figures. The federal share of total Medicaid spending was 56.8% in 2000. By law, this share can range from 50% to 83% in these states. During 2000, the federal match rate was 50% for ten states. Mississippi had the highest federal match rate at 76.8% (USDHHS 2002).

*Services*. Medicaid covers required and optional services. Required services include inpatient hospital services, outpatient hospital services, physician services, nursing facility services for those aged 21 or over, rural health clinic services, home health care for those eligible for skilled nursing services, laboratory and x-ray services, federally qualified health center services, and many services for prenatal care and pediatrics. Optional services include diagnostic services, clinic services, intermediate care facilities for the mentally retarded, prescribed drugs and prosthetic devices, optometrist services and eyeglasses, nursing facility services for those under age 21, transportation services, rehabilitation and physical therapy services, and home and community-based care to certain persons with chronic impairments. Additional services provided under the home and community-based care may include personal care services, chore services, respite care services, and adult day care. Three Medicaid services that are important for people with disabilities are (1) nursing facilities, (2) home health services, and (3) personal care services. Nursing facilities are mandatory for people aged 21 or over who receive cash payments from SSI or Temporary Assistance to Needy Families (TANF) but are optional services for others. Home health services are mandatory for the same Medicaid recipients for whom nursing facility services are provided. Personal care services are provided in a person's home by a qualified person under the guidance of a registered nurse (SSA 2001).

*Eligibility.* Medicaid coverage is generally extended to persons receiving cash assistance under TANF and to those who receive SSI. Medicaid coverage is mandatory for many pregnant women and children near the poverty level and persons in specially protected groups, such as persons who lost cash assistance from SSI due to increased earnings or Social Security benefits but who may be covered by Medicaid for a certain time. Medicaid coverage is also mandatory for certain low-income Medicare beneficiaries who receive help from Medicaid in paying their Medicare premiums, deductibles, coinsurance, and other cost-sharing features. Those Medicare beneficiaries under age 65 who no longer receive SSDI due to increased earnings may also be eligible for Medicaid to purchase Medicare premiums for a period of time.

Eligibility for Medicaid is complex and varies from state to state. People with comparable illnesses, disabilities, and incomes may be eligible for Medicaid in one state but not in another.

Many of the disabled who are eligible for Medicaid also receive SSI cash assistance. However, there are a number of optional state programs through which ill or disabled persons who do not receive SSI can receive Medicaid.

Receipt of SSI typically guarantees eligibility for Medicaid in most states. As of December 2000, 11 states had exercised their authority to impose more restrictive eligibility criteria for Medicaid than SSI uses: Connecticut, Hawaii, Illinois, Indiana, Minnesota, Missouri, New Hampshire, North Dakota, Ohio, Oklahoma, and Virginia. These states permit individuals to deduct their medical expenses from their incomes when determining eligibility. Under this system, known as "spend down," if an otherwise eligible applicant's income exceeded the state's income standard for Medicaid eligibility, applicants would become eligible after incurring sufficient medical expenses to reduce their income below the standard. States must extend Medicaid eligibility to certain groups of disabled people who may not receive SSI but who are deemed to meet SSI income and resource standards.

States can elect to establish a medically needy program, under which disabled individuals whose income exceeds SSI standards but who need assistance with medical expenses can obtain eligibility by spending down. The medically needy option is exercised by most states.

The home and community-based care waiver program, elected in every state except Arizona, where the entire Medicaid program operates under a demonstration waiver, will aid in keeping certain disabled persons in the community rather than in institutions.

Under certain circumstances, Medicaid recipients may also be covered by Medicare. Approximately 6 to 7 million persons have some level of coverage in both programs (USDHHS 2002).

### *Black Lung*

Black Lung benefits are paid to coal miners who are totally disabled as a result of pneumoconiosis (i.e., Black Lung disease), to widows of miners who died from Black Lung disease, and to their dependents (SSA 2001). The legal definition of pneumoconiosis is "a chronic dust disease of the lung and its sequelae, including respiratory and pulmonary impairments, arising out of coal mine employment" (USC 902 (b)). Both surface and underground coal miners are covered. Medical expenses for treating pneumoconiosis are also covered.

*History.* The Black Lung Program was established by the Federal Coal Mine Health Safety Act of 1969 (SSA 2001).

*Administration.* The Black Lung Program is administered by the Department of Labor. There are two programs: Part B and Part C. Part B covers miners, widows, and dependents whose payments are based on claims filed before July 1, 1973. Part C covers claims filed after that date (Committee on Ways and Means 2000).

*Scope.* About 70,900 persons were paid Part B benefits in December 2001, of whom only 9,900 were coal miners. The remainder were widows (55,900) or dependents (5,100). During that same time period, approximately 47,500 persons were paid under Part C, of whom 14,500 were coal miners, 31,600 were widows, and 1,400 were dependents. About 92% of people receiving Part B and Part C Black Lung benefits are aged 65 or over. Altogether, in December 2001, $37.7 million was spent for Part B and $26.4 million for Part C beneficiaries. During 2001, approximately $52.4 million was spent on medical care for Black Lung beneficiaries (U.S. Department of Labor 2002).

*Funding.* Part B is funded through federal general revenues, and Part C of the Black Lung Program is funded by an excise tax on coal of $1.10 per ton of coal from underground mines (55 cents from surface mines), with a cap of 4.4% of the coal's selling price.

*Eligibility.* A miner must meet three general conditions: (1) have (if deceased, had) pneumoconiosis; (2) be totally disabled by the disease (or have been totally disabled at the time of death); and (3) the pneumoconiosis must have been caused by coal mine employment.

### *VA Disability Compensation Program*

The VA (Veterans Affairs) Disability Compensation Program provides cash assistance to veterans with service-connected disabilities, that is, illness or injury incurred or aggravated while in military service. Employment is not a factor; veterans can be employed and still receive benefits.

*History.* Veterans' health, disability, and pension programs have grown out of a long history of benefits provided to veterans. Disability pensions were provided to veterans of the Revolutionary War by the Continental Congress. In 1789, Congress enacted a veterans pension program.

*Administration.* The VA Disability Compensation Program is administered by the Department of Veterans Affairs (VA).

*Scope.* In fiscal year 2001, 2.3 million veterans with service-connected disabilities and survivors of 294,000 deceased veterans received $19.7 billion through this program. The largest share of veterans receiving benefits for service-connected disabilities served in the Vietnam era (32.9%). Another 19% served in World War II and 16.9% in the Gulf War. Altogether, approximately 30.3% of veterans with a service-connected disability were aged 70 or over in fiscal year 2001 (U.S. Department of Veterans Affairs 2002b).

*Funding.* Funding is provided from federal general revenues.

*Eligibility.* An individual must have a partial or total impairment by injury or disease incurred or aggravated during military service. A VA Rating Board employs criteria developed by the VA to rate the extent of a disability, and the illness, injury, or disease manifestations must have arisen during service. Dishonorably discharged veterans are not eligible. While the SSDI, SSI, and Black Lung Programs have an "all or nothing" disability determination process, wherein a person either is or is not determined to be eligible to receive benefits, a range or band of eligibility exists in the VA Disability Compensation Program. This range is contained in the disability ratings system, from 0% to 100%, and is based on the presumed reduction in income caused by the disability. Dependent allowances and survivor benefits are paid under certain circumstances.

### *VA Disability Pension Program*

The VA Disability Pension Program pays cash benefits to older, low-income war veterans who have become permanently and totally disabled from non-service-connected causes or who have attained the age of 65. Certain low-income requirements must be met. This program is similar to SSDI because there are employability standards.

*Administration.* The VA Disability Compensation Program is administered by the Department of Veterans Affairs.

*Scope.* In fiscal year 2001, this program served 557,000 pensioners, including surviving spouses, at a cost of $2.3 billion (U.S. Department of Vetrans Affairs 2002b).

*Funding.* Funding is provided from federal general revenues.

*Eligibility.* A veteran must be permanently and totally disabled or must have attained the age of 65. Surviving spouses need not be disabled to qualify; however, they must meet more strenuous income limitations. An individual must have an injury or disease sustained outside of military service rendering a veteran permanently and totally impaired. Impairment is determined based on the veteran's ability to function at work and at home. Persons with dishonorable discharges are not eligible. Low-income criteria are based on income and family size. In 2002, income limits were $9,556 for a veteran living alone and $12,516 for a veteran living with one dependent (U.S. Department of Veterans Affairs 2002b). Benefits are paid to surviving spouses and children if the veteran served in specified wartime periods. Survivors must meet the same conditions as for the VA Disability Compensation Program.

### *Veterans Health Services*

The Veterans Health Administration (VHA) administers a nationwide health care network that provides medical care services to eligible veterans.

*Administration.* The Veterans Health Services programs are administered federally by the Department of Veterans Affairs. (For further details, contact the nearest VA health care facility or call 1-877-222-8387.)

*Scope.* During fiscal year 1999, the Veterans Health Services programs cost $18 billion and were provided to 3.6 million persons. There were approximately 752,000 inpatient episodes and 38 million outpatient visits (Committee on Ways and Means 2000).

*Funding.* Funding is provided from federal general revenues.

*Eligibility.* To receive hospital and outpatient medical care, veterans must generally be enrolled with the VA. They may apply for enrollment at any time. Veterans do not have to be enrolled if they (1) have a "service-connected" disability of 50% or more, (2) want care for a disability that the military determined was incurred or aggravated in the line of duty but that the VA has not rated, during the 12-month period following discharge; or (3) want care for a service-connected disability only.

*Services.* Nursing home care in VA or private nursing homes may be provided for veterans who are not acutely ill and who are not in need of hospital care. Veterans generally must have received care in a VA facility for transfer to a private nursing home. VA will provide nursing home care to veterans whose service-connected disability requires such care and to veterans with a service-connected disability rated at 70% or more who need this type of care. Most other veterans are eligible for nursing home care on a space and resource available basis.

*Hospital Care and Outpatient Medical Services.* Certain non-service-connected and 0% noncompensable service-connected veterans receiving care for non-service-connected conditions must provide income information to establish eligibility for VA health care. Veterans whose income exceeds established thresholds are required to participate in the cost of their care through the medical care copayment program.

*Extended Care Services.* Certain veterans are required to agree to pay a copayment for extended care services. The following veterans are exempt from copayment requirements for extended care services: (1) veterans who were receiving extended care services on or before November 30, 1999, and who have been continuously receiving these services since that date; (2) veterans with a compensable service-connected disability; and (3) veterans whose annual income is less than a single veteran non-service-connected disability pension income amount in effect under title 38 U.S.C. 1521(b).

*Medications.* Certain veterans are required to pay a copayment for each 30-day or less supply of medication provided on an outpatient basis (other than medication administered during treatment) for treatment of a non-service-connected disability. The following veterans are exempt from copayment requirements for outpatient medications: veterans who (1) have a service-connected disability of 50% or more; (2) require outpatient medication for a service-connected disability; (3) have an annual income that does not exceed the maximum annual rate of VA pension that would be payable to them if they were eligible for a VA pension under 38 U.S.C. 1521; (4) require medication necessary to treat conditions related to military service such as exposure to Agent Orange, ionizing radiation, or environmental contaminants; (5) experienced sexual trauma while in the military; or (6) have head and neck cancer resulting from nasopharngyl radium treatment (U.S. Department of Veterans Affairs 2002).

## Major State Disability Programs

### *Workers' Compensation*

Workers' Compensation provides cash payments to workers (or their survivors) and medical and rehabilitation services to workers who have disabilities or who have died because of accidents on the job or occupational diseases.

*History.* The first Workers' Compensation law was enacted in 1908 to cover federal employees in certain hazardous occupations. By 1916, all federal workers were covered, and by 1920, Workers' Compensation programs had been established in all but seven states and the District of Columbia. By 1949, all states had Workers' Compensation programs (SSA 2001).

*Administration.* There are 53 separate Workers' Compensation programs administered by the states, the District of Columbia, the Virgin Islands, and Puerto Rico. The U.S. Department of Labor administers Workers' Compensation programs for federal civil servants, Longshore and Harbor Workers, the Black Lung Program (see above), and programs under the recently enacted Energy Employees Occupational Illness Compensatory Program of 2000. (The Energy Employees Occupational Illness Compensatory Program of 2000 went into effect on July 31, 2001. Persons covered under this program and who are eligible for benefits and medical expenses include Department of Energy employees and contractors and subcontractors (and certain survivors) of the Department of Energy who were exposed to beryllium and who contracted chronic beryllium disease or who have chronic silicosis and worked at least 250 days in mining tunnels for underground nuclear weapons sites in Nevada and Alaska. Benefits are also provided to uranium miners and other individuals covered under the Radiation Exposure Compensation Act. [Committee on Ways and Means 2000; SSA 2001]).

*Scope*. In 2000, $45.9 billion in benefits were paid. Approximately 56% of these benefits were cash payments, and 44% of benefits were for medical and rehabilitation services for these individuals. Workers' Compensation benefits are second only to the SSDI and Medicare programs for providing cash benefits and medical coverage. Weekly cash payments for workers vary by state but are typically limited to no more than two-thirds of a state's average weekly wage. There are no national figures on the number of people receiving Workers' Compensation benefits.

*Funding*. Workers' Compensation benefits are financed almost entirely by employers. Employers' costs averaged 1.25% of payroll in 2000 (Mont et al. 2002). Many employers have private insurance, some large employers are self-insured, and others operate in states that have state funds allotted for Workers' Compensation. Workers' Compensation coverage for most jobs in private industry is compulsory. Nationwide, about 97% of the labor force is covered by Workers' Compensation.

*Eligibility*. Disabilities or death can be caused by work-related injuries or occupational diseases, though the impact of the latter is often difficult to establish. Employer negligence is not an issue. However, Workers' Compensation benefits are generally not paid if the cause of the injury was intoxication of the worker, willful misconduct, or gross negligence. Unlike the SSDI and SSI programs, where eligibility is limited to those with permanent total disabilities, Workers' Compensation can provide for four types of disability: temporary total disability, temporary partial disability, permanent total disability, and permanent partial disability. Most cases involve temporary total disability.

Benefits vary by the type of disability. Temporary total and temporary partial disability benefits are paid to the worker while he or she is recovering (unable to perform regular job). Temporary partial disability benefits are uncommon. Permanent total disability benefits are paid to the worker, with survivor benefits being paid to his or her dependents when the worker dies from an occupational illness or injury. Permanent partial disability benefits are paid to the worker to compensate for his or her permanent loss of earnings (or permanent impairment).

### *Temporary Disability Insurance*

Temporary Disability Insurance (TDI) provides workers with cash benefits for temporary nonoccupational disability or maternity. Five states (California, Hawaii, New Jersey, New York, and Rhode Island), Puerto Rico, and the railroad industry provide these benefits.

*History.* Federal law does not provide for a federal-state system of short-term disability comparable to the federal-state system of unemployment insurance, but in 1946 the Federal Unemployment Tax Act was amended to permit some states to use some of these funds for disability benefits. Railroad workers receive TDI under the Railroad Unemployment Insurance Act, as amended in 1946.

*Administration.* Program administration within the state is mostly done in the same state agency that administers unemployment insurance, but some states have private plan administration.

*Scope.* In general, the benefit amount is intended to be at least one-half of the weekly wage loss; however, minimum and maximum payment amounts are specified. Payment duration ranges from 26 to 52 weeks.

*Funding.* Authority to provide these disability benefits under the Federal Unemployment Tax Act does not provide for payment for administration. Employees may be required to contribute to the cost of TDI, with the exception of the Railroad Program. In most programs employers also are required to contribute. In general, the state government does not contribute.

*Eligibility.* A worker should be unable to perform his or her regular or customary job due to a mental or physical condition, but some states have more strict disability requirements. In all states a pregnant worker receives full benefits. Vesting eligibility for benefits differs, with some plans providing for immediate eligibility and others requiring some probationary work period (SSA 2001). (See also ELDER LAW PRACTICE; MEDICAID; MEDICARE; SOCIAL SECURITY PROGRAM OF THE UNITED STATES; SUPPLEMENTAL SECURITY INCOME [SSI]; VETERANS' BENEFITS.)

### Organizations

Centers for Medicare & Medicaid Services
Social Security Administration

### References

Adler, Michele. 1991. "Programmatic Definitions of Disability: Policy Implications." *Proceedings of the American Statistical Association.* Government Statistics Section. Alexandria, VA: ASA.

Adler, Michele. 1996. "Disability Programs, Federal." In *Encyclopedia of Financial Gerontology,* ed. Lois A. Vitt and Jurg K. Siegenthaler. Westport, CT: Greenwood Press.

Burwell, Brian, Bonnie Preston, and Sarah Bailey. 1990. *Task II: Federal Programs for Persons with Disabilities.* Washington, DC: U.S. Government Printing Office.

Committee on Ways and Means. U.S. House of Representatives. 2000. *2000 Green Book (Background Material and Data on Programs within the Jurisdiction of the Committee on Ways and Means).* Washington, DC: U.S. Government Printing Office.

Mont, Daniel, John F. Burton, Jr., Virginia Reno, and Cecili Thompson, with the advice of the Study Panel on National Data on Workers' Compensation and the Steering Committee on Workers' Compensation. 2002. *Workers' Compensation: Benefits, Coverage and Costs, 2000 New Estimates.* Washington, DC: National Academy of Social Insurance, May.

Social Security Administration. 1995. *Disability Evaluation under Social Security.* Baltimore, MD: Author.

Social Security Administration. 1997. "Social Security Programs in the U.S." Pub. 13-11758.

Social Security Administration. 2000. *A Brief History of Social Security, Issued on Social Security's 65th Anniversary, August 2000*. Baltimore, MD: Author.
Social Security Administration. 2001. *Annual Statistical Supplement to the Social Security Bulletin 2001*. Baltimore, MD: Author.
Social Security Administration. 2002a. *Program Operations Manual System*. Baltimore, MD: Author.
Social Security Administration. 2002b. Unpublished program statistics.
U.S. Department of Health and Human Services. Centers for Medicare & Medicaid Services. 2002. *2002 CMS Statistics*. CMS Pub. No. 03437. April.
U.S. Department of Health and Human Services. Health Care Financing Administration. 2000a. *Medicare and You*. Washington, DC: Author.
U.S. Department of Health and Human Services. Health Care Financing Administration. 2000b. *A Profile of Medicaid, Chartbook 2000*. Washington, DC: Author, September.
U.S. Department of Labor. 2000. *Black Lung Program Regulations, 2000 Amendments: Employment Standards Administration, Regulations Implementing the Federal Coal Mine and Safety Act of 1969, as amended 20 C.F.R. Parts 718, 722, 725, 726, 727, 65 Fed. Reg. 79919*. Washington, DC: Author.
U.S. Department of Labor. Black Lung Program. 2002. Unpublished data.
U.S. Department of Veterans Affairs. 2002a. *Federal Benefits for Veterans and Dependents. 2002 Edition*. Washington, DC: Author.
U.S. Department of Veterans Affairs. 2002b. *Internal Review*. Washington, DC: Author.

*Michele C. Adler and Thomas V. Rush*

**DISASTER PREPAREDNESS AND OLDER ADULTS,** emergency preparedness, disaster response, financial assistance, and social services provided to older adults during a widespread disaster and to assist them in recovery. Typical disasters are earthquakes, hurricanes, riverine floods, flash floods, tornadoes, severe thunderstorms, power failures, residential fires, large-scale industrial accidents, and wildfires. Less typical, but of increasing concern, are terrorist attacks.

Managing the problems posed by disasters can be complex because each hazard—natural, technological, or national security—brings a different combination of effects, and disasters of any kind may range from difficult to catastrophic in intensity and scope. Emergency management is commonly organized into four phases: (1) preparedness; (2) prevention (mitigation); (3) response; and (4) recovery. Assessing the financial implications will be easier after reviewing both the costs that might be incurred and the assistance that may be available for items or actions identified in each phase.

## Preparedness

Preparedness steps can be grouped into four sets: (1) Know the hazards. (2) Develop plans: determine evacuation routes; have the contents of an evacuation kit ready to "grab and go"; have a plan for getting back together with family or caregivers; prepare checklists for emergency stock of personal, medical, and household supplies; list emergency telephone numbers. (3) Obtain emergency supplies, including cash, and make financial provisions for expenses if it is necessary to leave home for a week or more. (4) Rehearse or practice plans. Personal financial planning should provide for any emergency with the recognition that most governmental disaster assistance is for presidentially declared major disasters only. Preparedness measures should include available cash and credit resources, protection of valuable papers, and access to important supplies such as food, water, medications, and prescriptions.

Preparedness steps begin by obtaining information about the hazards that are likely to be in the area and what to expect in the event of a disaster—information that can be obtained from the local office of emergency management or Red Cross chapter. Recent catastrophic events have helped increase the knowledge and awareness of emergency managers and disaster services as to the specific needs of the older adults and the disabled in emergency situations. More attention is now paid to preparedness measures designed to ensure the adequacy, promptness, and effective manner of delivery of financial assistance and social services. Advance arrangements for helping older persons evacuate, get to shelters, and receive the care they need once they are in shelters have become common.

Older persons living independently should know where to go if evacuation is necessary. Planning may include making advance arrangements for transportation to a safe shelter and arranging evacuation assistance for those who need physical help, including immediate assistance in case of fire. Service agencies providing evacuation assistance should know how to locate individuals needing help and have information about where they can go.

The likelihood of disability increases with age, and the need for awareness of the special needs of older adults with disabilities in disaster situations is critical not only to survival but also to their successful recovery. For example, those with impaired mobility should know in advance what help they will need if evacuation should become necessary, including special assistance available in public shelters, and who will provide it. Making necessary arrangements provides assurance that assistance will arrive promptly when needed.

Older adults are more affected by major stress, such as the dislocations caused by disaster, than are younger adults. Evacuation to public shelters is a particularly difficult adjustment for many, especially if they are in a shelter without family or acquaintances. Long-term or permanent relocations actually shorten the remaining life span of some. Staying with friends, family, or other acquaintances is less stressful. If that is not possible and it is financially feasible to make standby arrangements for public lodging, advance arrangements can be made with hotels or motels out of the disaster area (for example, when planning a community evacuation in the event of a hurricane). If such standby arrangements are made, the stress is further reduced if the older person has a chance to visit the lodging at some point in the context of a vacation or recreational visit, so that it is more familiar if they return.

Flood insurance, underwritten by the U.S. government, is available through many insurance carriers and will pay for all covered losses, not just those in areas covered by major disaster declarations. Flood insurance is not covered by general household policies. Some insurance against specific hazards, such as earthquake insurance, is also available.

### Prevention

Mitigation measures, such as strengthening the physical protections provided by a residential, commercial, or public property, and community facilities available where such properties are located, usually require at least a modest investment, but they are the most important means of reducing the total costs of disasters.

Either relocation to a safer area or other physical mitigation measures to avoid disaster impact should be investigated and may be necessary to protect both buildings and occupants against the force and effect of floods, high winds, earthquakes, fires, or other disasters.

### Response

Response steps are those taken at the time a disaster threatens or occurs. Hurricanes and riverine floods afford plenty of warning time. Flash flood and tornado warnings may not be possible until little time remains. While they cannot yet be predicted, when earthquakes do occur, public warnings give instructions from local authorities about aftershocks, fire hazards, and damaged roads, bridges, and water and sewer systems. Individuals should be prepared to follow the instructions of officials and to adapt the actions from their plan to fit the situation. It may be necessary, for instance, to go to the "safe room" in one's home in the event of tornado or hurricane force winds if evacuation is not a feasible option. An unexpected evacuation may be necessary in these or other types of dire emergency.

Immediate emergency needs for shelter, food, clothing, personal items, first aid, medical care, and emergency financial assistance are available from local social service agencies and volunteer and humanitarian organizations such as the American Red Cross, Salvation Army, and a host of other organizations, whether or not the event is a presidentially declared major disaster or a state governor formally declares a disaster.

### Recovery

Recovery begins with returning home to clean up and make repairs. One of the most important objectives of the Federal Emergency Management Agency (FEMA) and state and local governments after any disaster is to inform individuals of the assistance available and to help them with the application and delivery process. Information outlining available aid programs is disseminated by FEMA through radio, television, newspapers, mass distribution of pamphlets, community relations teams, and toll-free telephone help lines. Recovery includes elements of prevention and preparedness against the next disaster. The recovery process may also lead to a decision to relocate, away from hazardous areas such as floodplains, coastlines, or unstable slopes. Individual assistance from Federal Disaster Relief and from state and local assistance is made available at this point. Disaster relief programs are designed to help people get back on their feet and to make recovery possible. They do not restore all losses and are only available in areas identified in formally declared disasters.

Disaster victims can get information and apply for disaster assistance in a number of ways. Toll-free numbers are available for disaster victims to apply for certain types of disaster programs and obtain information about others. Federal, state, and local emergency management agencies and other social service organizations have substantially improved the help they provide for older persons in establishing eligibility for various kinds of assistance.

A presidential declaration of a major disaster can make a broad range of assistance available to victims. This may include the following:

- Disaster housing, until alternative housing is available, for disaster victims whose homes are uninhabitable. Home-repair funds may be given to owner-occupants in lieu of other forms of disaster housing assistance, so that families can quickly return to their damaged homes.
- In areas covered by disaster declarations, FEMA may provide technical assistance and hazard mitigation grants that can provide up to 75% of the cost of FEMA-approved projects to reduce the severity of future disasters.
- Disaster unemployment assistance and job placement assistance for those unemployed as a result of a major disaster.
- Individual and family grants to help meet disaster-related necessary expenses or serious needs when those affected are unable to meet such expenses or needs through other programs or means.
- Legal services to low-income families and individuals.
- Crisis counseling and referrals to appropriate mental health agencies to relieve disaster-caused mental health problems.
- Loans to individuals, businesses, and farmers for repair, rehabilitation, or replacement of damaged real and personal property and some production losses not fully covered by insurance.
- Assistance in handling flood insurance claims.
- Agricultural assistance, including technical assistance; payments covering a major portion of the cost to eligible farmers who perform emergency conservation actions on farmland damaged by the disaster; and provision of federally owned feed grain for livestock and herd preservation.
- Veterans' assistance, such as death benefits, pensions, insurance settlements, and adjustments to home mortgages held by the Department of Veterans Affairs (VA) if a VA–insured home has been damaged.
- Tax relief, including help from the Internal Revenue Service, in claiming casualty losses resulting from the disaster, and state tax assistance.
- Waiver of penalties for early withdrawal of funds from certain time deposits.
- The Cora Brown Fund, to assist victims of natural disasters for those disaster-related needs that have not been or will not be met by government agencies or private organizations that have programs to address such needs.

### Disaster Assistance and Long-term Care Facilities

When considering long-term care facilities, such as nursing homes, independent living, or assisted living facilities for older persons, it is wise to inquire about the type of disaster insurance they carry and the type of disaster arrangements they will provide for the safety of their residents in the event of an actual disaster. The situation of older adults in such settings, both before and after the trauma of disaster, is characterized by general potential vulnerability. Even though the basics of shelter and food are provided, it is more difficult for older adults to recover. Since recovery depends in part on having sufficient financial resources for support and care, and because of the exceptional costs incurred when major disasters do occur, the quality of life for the older adults—and life itself—may be threatened substantially. Institutions must be in a position to evacuate residents to another facility and care for them adequately, should a disaster occur.

### Psychological Consequences

Disasters often leave victims feeling disoriented and helpless. Although this applies to disaster victims of all ages, the severity increases when individuals are physically incapable of rebuilding, especially older and disabled persons. For older persons, damage to their homes or personal property, financial losses, new surroundings, strange faces, and disruptions of daily routine may cause great psychological stress. Some stress can be ameliorated by preparedness measures that instill feelings of confidence and success in coping with disaster. Mental preparedness, therefore, may be as important as financial and property preparedness in preventing feelings of helplessness among older victims. The important point to remember is that all elements of preparedness are mutually supportive and reinforcing, in older victims as with everyone. (See also FINANCIAL ADVISORS; FINANCIAL RECOVERY IN LATER LIFE; FRAILTY PLANNING; HOMELESSNESS AMONG OLDER ADULTS; HOME MODIFICATIONS FINANCING.)

### Organization

Federal Emergency Management Agency.

### Suggested Readings

Federal Emergency Management Agency. 1983. *Tips on Handling Your Insurance Claim*. Washington, DC: U.S. GPO.

Federal Emergency Management Agency. 1991. *Your Family Disaster Plan* (L-191). Washington, DC: Author, September.

Federal Emergency Management Agency. 1992. *Your Family Disaster Supplies Kit* (L-189). Washington, DC: Author, rev. March.

Federal Emergency Management Agency. 1993. *Emergency Preparedness Checklist* (L-154 English and Spanish). Washington, DC: Author, rev. August.

Federal Emergency Management Agency. 1995. *Preparing for Emergencies: A Checklist for People with Mobility Problems* (L-154M). Washington, DC: Author, rev. September.

Federal Emergency Management Agency. 1997a. *Before Disaster Strikes: How to Make Sure You're Financially Prepared to Deal with a Natural Disaster* (FEMA 291). Washington, DC: Author, rev. May.

Federal Emergency Management Agency. 1997b. *A Guide to Federal Aid in Disasters* (FEMA 262). Washington, DC: Author, June.

Federal Emergency Management Agency. 2002. *Are You Ready? A Guide to Citizen Preparedness* (H-34). Washington, DC: Author, rev. June.

Federal Emergency Management Agency. 2003. *Action Guidelines for Senior Citizens (for Hurricanes)*. Washington, DC: Author.

### Reference

American Institute for Certified Public Accountants (AICPA), American Red Cross (ARC), National Endowment for Financial Education (NEFE). 2003. *Disaster Recovery: A Guide to Financial Issues*. Published jointly by AICPA, ARC, and NEFE. Available online at http://www.redcross.org/services/disaster/beprepared/financeprep.html.

*Ralph B. Swisher*

**DIVORCE AND OLDER ADULTS,** dissolving a marriage, or already having dissolved a marriage, after age 65. Early in this century, divorce was uncommon and difficult to obtain. In 1900, only one divorce occurred in 13 marriages, but by the 1990s, divorce was commonplace, with one divorce for every two marriages. The most dramatic increase in divorces occurred between 1965 and 1980, when the divorce rate more than doubled. Since 1980, divorce rates have persisted at high levels, and the increased incidence of divorce over time has important implications for all segments of the U.S. population, including older adults.

Few studies have focused on the significance of divorce for older adults; one reason for this neglect among researchers may be the relatively small proportion of divorces that occur within the older adult population. In 1990, for example, fewer than 2% of the 2.3 million persons becoming divorced were over age 65. (The National Center for Health Statistics [NCHS] has not published detailed divorce data since 1990. The NCHS ceased collecting these data for budgetary reasons and because some states ceased collecting detailed information.) Further, a relatively small number (fewer than 7%) of all older persons currently are divorced. Despite these statistics, a growing proportion of older persons is affected by divorce, and divorce has significant consequences for the older adult population.

### Changes in the Divorce Rate over Time

One way to view the impact of divorce trends on older adults is to observe changes over time in the proportion of ever-married persons who have experienced a divorce before reaching older age. Since the majority of divorces occur in the early years following marriage, the most critical determinant of divorce for people entering later life is the divorce rate that existed 30 or 40 years earlier. The majority of divorces experienced by persons reaching age 65 in 1990, for example, occurred between 1945 and 1960 (when they were between ages 20 and 35). About 20% of persons reaching age 65 in 1960 had divorced, compared to 30% of those reaching age 65 in 1990 and 40% of those reaching age 65 in 2000. For those reaching age 65 in 2020, it is expected that nearly 50% will have divorced. Thus, only in recent years has the upsurge in divorces that occurred after 1965 begun to have an impact on the marital history of older adults. However, rapid changes will occur over the next several decades as those baby boomers, who married after 1965 and experienced high divorce rates over their adult lives, enter later life stages and become an increasingly large proportion of the older population.

### The Currently Divorced

A second perspective on divorce in later life looks at the proportion of people who are currently divorced when reaching later life. Due to remarriages, the proportion who are currently divorced is significantly lower than the proportion who have ever divorced. The percentage of women who were divorced when they reached age 65 more than quadrupled between 1960 and 2000, but this only meant a growth from 2% to 9% of the relevant population. Projections by the Social Security Administration suggest that 20% of women entering later life around 2025 will be divorced. The actual percentage could exceed this projection, however, if divorced persons in the future remarry at lower rates than this projection anticipated. Changing marriage, divorce, and remarriage experiences of the baby boomers will lead to large changes in the marital and family characteristics of future older populations.

### Divorce and Well-Being

The significance of divorce for well-being in later life has been demonstrated in three areas of study—mortality and morbidity, economics, and intergenerational support. A number of studies have examined the relationship between marital status and mortality.

These studies consistently find that both men and women who are married experience lower death rates than their unmarried counterparts. Among the unmarried, the divorced have higher death rates than the widowed or the never-married.

The survival disadvantage of divorced compared to married persons is greater among men than women. Marital status differences in mortality are greater among middle-aged than older persons, but divorced older people still have significantly higher death rates than the married older person. The high death rate of those divorced is especially strong for causes of death related to lifestyle and psychological state—suicide, homicide, accidents, and cirrhosis of the liver. Studies of morbidity also find that divorced persons are the least healthy of any marital status category and are more likely to suffer from both acute illnesses and chronic diseases.

### Financial Consequences of Divorce

Cross-sectional studies of divorced older adults reveal they have the lowest income of any marital status category. Divorced females over age 65 are more than four times as likely to be in poverty than married females (24% versus 5%), and divorced males are about three times as likely to be in poverty than married males (17% versus 5%). The disadvantaged economic status of the divorced persists in multivariate analyses, which control for factors correlated with poverty, such as race and education level. The divorced also are relatively disadvantaged with respect to assets. For example, about 80% of married and widowed older women live in homes they own, compared to 50% of divorced women.

Most older persons who are divorced experienced their divorce earlier in life. Longitudinal analyses shed light on why the negative consequences of divorce tend to persist into their older years, especially for women. At the time of divorce, both partners usually experience a loss of wealth (frequently associated with loss of home equity). Following the divorce, men are often able to recover their former standard of living within a few years. Women, however, tend to have lower earning potential and are much less likely to experience economic recovery. Upon reaching later life, they are less likely to have accumulated significant assets and are less likely to have adequate pension incomes.

The Social Security program, technically sex neutral, also contributes to the lower economic status of older divorced women. At retirement, any worker retains the right to the primary benefit he or she earned as a covered worker. Social Security benefits for most men are unaffected by divorce, but for women who have depended on their husband's income after marriage, divorce can have a significant impact. If the marriage lasted for less than ten years, a divorced spouse is not entitled to any spousal benefit. If the marriage lasted for more than ten years, a divorced spouse (at age 65) is entitled to 50% of her former spouse's primary benefit (or 100% of her own primary benefit if it is greater), while her former spouse receives 100% of the benefit. Thus, a divorced woman who has not had earnings equal to her former spouse's will receive a smaller Social Security benefit. In many cases, there is also an unequal splitting of private pension benefits that were accumulated prior to divorce.

Research documents the important role that adult children play in the lives of most older persons. Those who have a high level of contact and interaction with their adult children receive much of their instrumental assistance and emotional support from their children. Divorced persons do not experience the same quality of intergenerational relationships as the nondivorced. Whether or not they have remarried, older men who are divorced from the biological mother of their children are much less likely to maintain contact with these children. Also, divorced men are less likely to receive help from these children or to view their adult children as a potential source of support in case of need. Further, stepchildren do not fill this vacuum, since divorced men do not have stronger ties with their stepchildren than with their biological children. Divorce also negatively affects mother-child relationships in later life, although the effect is not as striking for mothers as fathers.

The proportion of older persons who are divorced or who have experienced an earlier divorce is increasing and will continue to increase for several decades. Approximately one-half of baby boomers who will enter old age between 2010 and 2030 will have experienced a divorce from their first marriage. As discussed above, evidence suggests that divorce has negative consequences for well-being in later life. Compared to those who are married, those divorced on average experience greater poverty, have higher death rates, and receive less support from adult children. Negative effects of divorce on economic status are greater for women than men, while negative effects on social support networks are greater for men. If the current relationship between divorce and well-being persists, divorce will play an increasingly important role in shaping aging experiences, and a growing number of older people will experience adverse consequences associated with marital instability. (See also CASH FLOW PLANNING FOR RETIREES; ECONOMIC HARDSHIP MEASURES IN THE OLDER POPULATION; ECONOMIC STATUS OF OLDER MEN AND WOMEN; FINANCIAL SECURITY IN RETIREMENT; INTERGENERATIONAL CONFLICT AND FINANCIAL ISSUES; MARRIAGE AND OLDER ADULTS.)

### Suggested Reading

AARP. 1994. *Women, Pensions and Divorce: Small Reforms That Could Make a Big Difference.* Washington, DC: Author.

### References

Butrica, Barbara A., and Howard M. Iams. 2000. "Divorced Women at Retirement: Projections of Economic Well-being in the Near Future." *Social Security Bulletin* 63: 3–12.

Cherlin, Andrew J. 1992. *Marriage, Divorce, Remarriage.* Rev. and enlarged ed. Cambridge, MA: Harvard University Press.

Cooney, Teresa M., and Peter Uhlenberg. 1990. "The Role of Divorce in Men's Relations with Their Adult Children after Mid-Life." *Journal of Marriage and the Family* 52: 677–88.

Fethke, Carol C. 1989. "Life-Cycle Models of Saving and the Effect of the Timing of Divorce on Retirement Economic Well-Being." *Journal of Gerontology* 44: S121–28.

Holden, Karen C., and Hsiang-Hui Daphne Kuo. 1996. "Complex Marital Histories and Economic Well-being: The Continuing Legacy of Divorce and Widowhood as the HRS Cohort Approaches Retirement." *The Gerontologist* 36: 383–90.

Pezzin, Liliana E., and Barbara Steinberg Shone. 1999. "Parental Marital Disruption and Intergenerational Transfers: An Analysis of Lone Elderly Parents and Their Children." *Demography* 36: 287–97.

Uhlenberg, Peter, Teresa Cooney, and Robert Boyd. 1990. "Divorce for Women after Mid-Life." *Journal of Gerontology* 45: S3–S11.

*Peter Uhlenberg*

**DRUGS AND SENIOR CITIZENS,** the utilization of prescription medications by older adults. Persons aged 65 years and older account for 12.0% of the U.S. population (U.S. Census Bureau 2002). In 2000, the mean number of annual prescriptions for this age group was 25.5, versus only 7.1 for persons under 65 (Thomas, Ritter, and Wallack 2001). Of the 35 million older people enrolled in the Medicare program, 83% (29 million) file at least one prescription drug claim. Medicare, however, lacks an outpatient prescription drug benefit (hospital prescription medications are covered).

The utilization of prescription medicines by older adults is driven by many factors, including:

- Changing health status due to natural forces of aging, preventive measures, availability of new medicines
- Market forces such as the restructuring of retiree health benefits
- Expanding sources for health information, particularly the Internet
- Public policy focus on improving patient safety and reducing medication errors

### Changing Health Status

In 2000, persons aged 65 to 74 represented 53% (18.4 million) of the older adult population. Those aged 75 to 84 represented 35% (12.4 million), and those aged 85 and older accounted for 12% (4.2 million). From 1990 to 2000, the fastest growing segment was those aged 85 and older, which increased by 30%. A survey of adults age 65 and older found that 76% take at least three medications, and one-third take eight or more (American Society of Health-System Pharmacists 2001). The National Ambulatory Medical Care Survey (1999 Summary, released July 2001) found that 66% of visits to office-based physicians resulted in at least one prescription being written. Among patients aged 65 to 74, over one-fifth (21.6%) had visits with physicians that resulted in at least four drug "mentions." For patients 75 years and over, nearly one-quarter (24.6%) had office visits with at least four drug mentions (Cherry, Burt, and Woodwell 2001).

Overall, only 4.5% of older adults resided in nursing homes in 2000; of those 85 and over, 18.2% were in nursing homes. However, this is considerably less than the 24.5% of the oldest old in nursing homes during 1990. This may be due in large part to the rapid proliferation of alternate care options, such as assisted living facilities and continuing care retirement communities that offer multitiered levels of care.

Among nursing home residents, there was an average of 6.7 routine medication orders and 2.6 "as-needed" orders (Tobias and Sey 2001). However, among all residents, 27% took nine or more regularly scheduled medications. This is a significantly higher number than the same survey found in 1997.

A study examining drug utilization among assisted living facility (ALF) residents found the mean number of medications to be 6.2 (Armstrong, Rhoads, and Meiling 2002). The similarity to the average number of routine medications in nursing home residents may change with further study of ALF residents (a growing but understudied population) and with medication reviews by specially trained geriatric pharmacists that are becoming more common.

Overall, the utilization of prescription medications by older people is expected to increase due to (1) clinical literature and medical practice guidelines that recommend additional medications for disorders common to older adults, such as heart failure and diabetes; (2) enhanced treatment of previously undertreated conditions, such as depression and pain; and (3) an increased focus on wellness and preventive health, with pharmacologic treatment for conditions such as osteoporosis (Tobias and Sey 2001).

According to the Food and Drug Administration (FDA), most drug-related problems in the older adult population are due to pharmacokinetic differences related to age itself (e.g., drug absorption or excretion) or to age-associated conditions such as renal impairment, congestive heart failure, or multiple drug therapy (FDA 1994). Since 1998, the FDA has required specific labeling for geriatric patients on certain classes of medicines. Priority classes for implementing the geriatric labeling were antidepressants; nonsteroidal anti-inflammatory drugs; digoxin, antiarrhythmics, and calcium channel blockers; oral hypoglycemic agents; anticoagulants; and quinolones.

### Market Forces

Because Medicare does not provide outpatient prescription drug coverage, many seniors incur high out-of-pocket drug costs. In 1999, retail outpatient prescription drug spending increased 18.4%, and in 2000 the rate of growth slowed slightly to 14.5%. Overall health care spending rose 7.2% from 1999 to 2000, the largest jump in a decade (Strunk, Ginsburg, and Gabel 2001). Of the 9,900 prescription drugs on the market, 23 of the 50 top sellers accounted for 50% of the increase in drug spending (Jacob 2001). For older adults, mean total drug spending rose from $827 in 1997 to $1,378 in 2000, an 18.5% annual increase (Thomas, Ritter, and Wallack 2001).

The primary factor in this growth was the number of prescriptions per person. This grew from 20.7 in 1997 to 25.5 in 2000 (or 7.1%) for older adults versus from 6.2 to 7.1 prescriptions (or 4.7%) for younger populations. Historically, "high-cost" seniors (those who incur greater total pharmaceutical expenditures) use more brand-name drugs, treat more conditions, and use more medications overall. To obtain prescription drug coverage, seniors have several options. Many purchase a "Medigap" insurance plan that covers outpatient medicines. Some retirees retain employer-sponsored health insurance that have deductibles and require copayments for drugs. Low-income Medicare beneficiaries with few assets may qualify for state-sponsored pharmaceutical assistance programs. In 2001, 20 states offered such programs (Tilly and Wiener 2001). Further, some older people may enroll in "Medicare + Choice" managed care or fee-for-service plans, if locally available. In 2001, 5.6 million Medicare beneficiaries chose these plans, which represents a 12% decline since 1999 (Centers for Medicare & Medicaid Services 2001). Historically, these plans included outpatient drug coverage, but this is changing. In 1999, 78% of Medicare + Choice enrollees had such coverage; by 2001, only 35% of enrollees were in plans that featured drug coverage.

Insurance coverage for prescription drugs is a significant factor in the access to and appropriate use of medicines by older adults. Researchers who studied a nationally representative sample of Medicare beneficiaries with coronary heart disease found that use of statins—relatively expensive medications that improve survival—ranged from only 4.1% in Medicare patients with no supplemental outpatient drug coverage to 27.4% in those with employer-sponsored coverage. Nitrate use also occurred less frequently in persons with Medicare coverage only (Federman et al. 2001).

### Access to Health Information

Another trend affecting drug utilization by seniors is expanding sources of drug information. First, since 1997, the Food and Drug Administration has permitted the pharmaceutical industry to advertise their products "direct to consumers" (DTC) much more aggressively, particularly on television. The pharmaceutical industry spent over $2 billion on DTC ads in 2000 versus $1.3 billion in 1998—the first full year after the FDA relaxed the guidelines.

Many of these broadcast DTC ads (whose companion pieces usually appear in newspapers and magazines) promote drugs used to treat chronic conditions common in older adults, such as hypertension, cholesterol reduction, diabetes, arthritis, and depression. These ads often feature grandparents playing with their grandchildren, thus reinforcing the pitch to seniors. An AARP study (Foley and Gross 2000) of consumers' familiarity with printed DTC ads found that those age 60 and older appear to obtain less information from the ads, and they are less likely than younger consumers to understand whether the advertised product requires a prescription. Further, AARP found that only 48% of older consumers notice the small print in the ads (containing indication, directions, and risk information) versus 66% of persons aged 18 to 39. Older consumers also tended to talk with their pharmacists and physicians about their medications less than younger consumers. Thus, older consumers "may be more vulnerable than others to the 'medication information gap,' " AARP notes.

One way that older adults are fighting this vulnerability is by turning to the Internet for health and medicine information. (Internet users age 65 and older represent the fastest-growing segment of new users.) Most of the DTC broadcast and print ads have an electronic component—product-specific Web sites developed by pharmaceutical manufacturers to provide more information for consumers and health care professionals. Such Web sites may feature online consumer health newsletters geared to the relevant health conditions as well as coupons or rebates. Still other Web sites allow consumers to conduct an electronic medicine review where they type in the names of their prescription and nonprescription medicines and can receive warnings about possible drug-drug or drug-food interactions.

Unfortunately, the unregulated Internet is also home to unsubstantiated health claims, to online pharmacies that bypass direct health professional evaluation (completing a short questionnaire is all a consumer may need to obtain a prescription medicine via these disreputable Web sites), and to drug information for which risks and benefits may not be presented clearly, if at all. Homebound older adults who surf the Internet for health information, others who do not have regular access to a licensed health care professional, and those without high reading levels may be most at risk (Berland et al. 2001). To encourage safe online shopping for pharmaceuticals, the FDA and the National Council on Patient Information and Education formed the CyberSmart Safety Coalition (see http://www.fda.gov/).

### Patient Safety and Appropriate Use of Medicines

Two reports from the Institute of Medicine (IOM) (Washington, DC), *To Err is Human* (1999) and *Crossing the Quality Chasm* (2001), brought the term *patient safety* into the public health lexicon. The first IOM study found that medication errors were the most common type of medical error. Consequently, there has been a growing research focus on the appropriate use of medicines in the older adult population. (Much of this is driven by the anticipation that a Medicare outpatient prescription drug benefit will be enacted this decade.)

One examination of a Medicare managed care population found that nearly one in four such beneficiaries potentially used medication inappropriately (Fick et al. 2001) This subset had a substantially higher number of providers prescribing their medicines, significantly higher total health care costs, and a higher mean number of inpatient, outpatient, and emergency room visits. The authors judged the "prevention and recognition of drug-related problems" in this population to be the "principal challenge in patient safety in the next decade."

In 2001, the Agency for Healthcare Research and Quality (AHRQ) awarded $50 million worth of grants for patient safety, with over $38 million devoted to promoting safe medicine use (AHRQ 2001). Many of these research projects are specific to improving medicine use and reducing errors in the older adult population. The following organizations develop and maintain timely consumer messages regarding the safe use of medicines:

- National Council on Patient Information and Education (NCPIE) (Bethesda, MD)—http://www.talkaboutrx.org/
- Alliance for Aging Research (Washington, DC)—http://www.agingresearch.org/
- United States Pharmacopeia (Rockville, MD)—http://www.usp.org/
- SMART Coalition (Sacramento, CA)—http://www.smartcoalition.org/

To reduce risk of medication errors, NCPIE recommends that older adults and/or their caregivers:

1. Ask questions of the physician, nurse, and/or pharmacist about what a medicine is for, exactly how to use a new medicine, what side effects to watch for, and when the medicine will no longer be needed.
2. Tell all health care professionals about all other prescribed and over-the-counter medicines being taken, including dietary supplements (keep an updated, written list).
3. Learn what other medicines, drinks, and activities to avoid when taking a new medicine.
4. Ask if any monitoring tests (such as for blood count or liver or kidney function) are required while on a medicine; keep all appointments for such monitoring; and share results with all health care professionals involved in all facets of health care.

Older adults play an important role in managing their own care, particularly when medicines are involved. Incorporating the above points into each health care visit can help ensure safe, appropriate medicine use. (See also MEDICARE + CHOICE; MEDICARE SUPPLEMENTAL INSURANCE; NUTRITION PROGRAMS; PHARMACISTS; PHYSICIAN–OLDER PATIENT RELATIONSHIPS; RETIREMENT PREPAREDNESS.)

**Organization**

CyberSmart Safety Coalition

**References**

AHRQ. 2001. "New Research Projects Awarded to Improve Patient Safety." Available online at http://www.ahrq.gov/qual/newgrants/index.html.

American Society of Health-System Pharmacists. 2001. "New Study Reveals One-Third of Seniors Take Medications Prescribed by Two or More Physicians." August 6. Available online at http://www.ashp.org/.

Armstrong, E.P., M. Rhoads, and F. Meiling. 2002. "Medication Usage Patterns in Assisted Living Facilities." *The Consultant Pharmacist* 16(1): 65–69.

Berland, G.K. et al. 2001. "Health Information on the Internet." *Journal of the American Medical Association* 285(20): 2612–21.

Centers for Medicare & Medicaid Services. 2001. "The Medicare + Choice Program in 2001 and 2002." Fact Sheet, August 29. Available online at http://www.hcfa.gov/facts/fs010829.htm.

Cherry, D.K., C.W. Burt, and D.A. Woodwell. 2001. *National Ambulatory Medical Care Survey: 1999 Summary. Advance Data from Vital and Health Statistics*. No. 322. Hyattsville, MD: National Center for Health Statistics, July 10.

FDA. 1994. "Guideline for Industry Studies in Support of Special Populations: Geriatrics." Available online at http://www.fda.gov/cder/guidance/iche7.pdf.

Federman, A.D., et al. 2001. "Supplemental Insurance and Use of Effective Cardiovascular Drugs among Elderly Medicare Beneficiaries with Coronary Heart Disease." *Journal of the American Medical Association* 286(14): 1732–39.

Fick, D.M., et al. 2001. "Potentially Inappropriate Medication Use in a Medicare Managed Care Population: Association with Higher Costs and Utilization." *Journal of Managed Care Pharmacy* 7(5): 407–13.

Foley, L.A., and D.J. Gross. 2000. "Are Consumers Well-Informed about Prescription Drugs? The Impact of Printed Direct-to-Consumer Advertising." *AARP Public Policy Institute*, April. Available online at http://research.aarp.org/.

Institute of Medicine. 1999. *To Err Is Human*. Washington, DC: Author.

Institute of Medicine. 2001. *Crossing the Quality Chasm*. Washington, DC: Author.

Jacob, Julie A. 2001. "A Few Drugs Spark Rise in Prescription Costs." *American Medical News*, October 1.

National Council on Patient Information and Education. 2000. *Medicine: Before You Take It, Talk About It*. Bethesda, MD: Author.

Strunk, B.C., P.B. Ginsburg, and J.R. Gabel. 2001. "Tracking Health Care Costs." *Health Affairs*. Available online at http://www.healthaffairs.org/.

Thomas, C.P., G. Ritter, and S. Wallack. 2001. "Growth in Prescription Drug Spending among Insured Elders." *Health Affairs* 20(5): 265–77.

Tilly, J., and J.M. Wiener. 2001. "State Pharmaceutical Assistance Programs for Older and Disabled Americans." *Health Affairs* 20(5): 223–32.

Tobias, D.E., and M. Sey. 2001. "General and Psychotherapeutic Medication Use in 328 Nursing Facilities: A Year 2000 National Survey." *The Consultant Pharmacist* 16(1): 54–64.

U.S. Census Bureau. 2002. "March 2002 Current Population Survey." Available online at http://www.census.gov/population/socdemo/age/ppl-167/tab01.pdf.

*N. Lee Rucker*

**DURABLE POWER OF ATTORNEY,** a legal document in which an individual (the "principal") appoints and authorizes another to act as his or her agent ("attorney-in-fact"). The power of attorney is durable because it remains in effect if the principal becomes ill or mentally incapacitated. The power can be general or specific to a certain transaction such as an authorization to sign on another person's behalf in a real estate settlement. A general durable power of attorney (DPOA) is typically very broad, authorizing the attorney-in-fact to make medical decisions if necessary, sign checks, cash in savings or investment accounts, buy or sell a home or other asset, and in general do anything that the principal could do. Other DPOAs are more narrowly drawn, such as a durable power of attorney for health care, a type of advance directive for use in a medical emergency.

As in all powers of attorney, the power is revoked upon the death of the principal. Nondurable powers of attorney automatically become invalid upon the death or incapacity of the principal, but DPOAs remain effective if the principal becomes completely incapacitated. "This power of attorney . . . shall not terminate on disability of the principal" effectively distinguishes a nondurable power of attorney from one that is durable.

Assuming a person is fortunate enough to have a completely trustworthy person to act on his or her behalf, a DPOA is an excellent way to plan for the management of financial, medical, and practical affairs in the event of temporary or permanent disability. It can spare loved ones trauma, expense, and the red tape of a guardianship or conservatorship proceeding. The choice of attorney-in-fact (not necessarily professional attorneys) is typically a spouse, adult child, or close friend. In drafting a DPOA, critical issues arise and must be considered carefully. It may be inappropriate, for example, to grant fiduciary powers to the same person empowered to make medical decisions.

Nondurable powers of attorney did not contemplate the types of functions today's guardianship-avoidance instruments may usefully permit. It took more than three decades for every jurisdiction to enact legislation permitting DPOAs, and until every jurisdiction had taken such action, most nationwide organizations refused to accept them. Today, the DPOA has become an essential part of estate planning, but acceptance of DPOAs by financial institutions and other organizations can still pose practical problems. Some financial institutions will request an affidavit executed by the attorney-in-fact that states the power of attorney has not been revoked and that the principal is still living. In an increasing number of jurisdictions, problems have been resolved by statutes that indemnify against the risks of persons relying in good faith on a DPOA after revocation of the DPOA or after the death of the principal.

Generally, any power of attorney will be construed narrowly and should contain an explicit recitation of the powers granted by the document. Gifts might be designated as "$11,000 per year, per donee 'annual exclusion' " and recipients limited to "children and grandchildren." Or a DPOA may be drafted broadly so that all assets may be given in the sole judgment of the attorney-in-fact to someone else, including the attorney-in-fact. Broad powers are often essential for married couples when planning for the possibility of long-term illness or incapacity. A spouse, acting as attorney-in-fact for an institutionalized spouse, needs a broad power of attorney in order to take advantage of laws permitting the "community spouse" (the non-ill spouse) of an institutionalized Medicaid recipient to preserve assets and protect against impoverishment. Gift-giving power under a DPOA should be carefully considered in light of the specific potential needs of the individual who will grant such power.

Whether estate planning, planning for charitable contributions, or for Medicaid eligibility, careful consideration must be given to defining the extent of the power and the class of donees. DPOAs may be beneficial for estate tax and Medicaid planning purposes. In the case of a wealthy individual, removing assets from the principal's taxable estate while he or she is incapacitated may save otherwise unnecessary estate taxes. If someone is a candidate for care under Medicaid, it is essential to consider whether authorization of asset divestment is appropriate. Anyone considering granting a DPOA must realize, however, that a power of attorney in the wrong hands is an invitation for financial elder abuse.

Depending on who is serving as attorney-in-fact, an individual may wish to include protective language requiring record-keeping and reporting. If one adult sibling is serving as attorney-in-fact, other siblings may wish to require a copy of the DPOA and all copies of financial and other records periodically. When a nonrelative is named as attorney-in-fact, he or she may have to account to the principal's family members. Particularly when asset divestment powers are included, an agent must be trusted to act in the same manner in which the principal himself or herself would act under the circumstances. Keeping everything "out in the open" may help avoid potential abuse and animosity among family members. Finally, even the most beloved adult child may not be a good candidate for attorney-in-fact if he or she has problems such as drug or alcohol abuse or is frequently on the edge of financial problems.

Although most forms of DPOA do not include provisions for compensation, payment may be appropriate in certain cases. Compensation may protect the principal, for example, by providing an incentive to the attorney to handle duties that become burdensome. For principals who are also parties to recoverable trusts, parallel provisions should be included in both the trust document and the DPOA to accomplish the coordination of objectives.

## A Case Illustration

Drafted properly, the DPOA can be the single most important legal instrument anyone can execute. The following example illustrates its usefulness. Mrs. Murphy's husband has been in a nursing home with Alzheimer's disease for four years. Two years ago, Mr. Murphy qualified for Medicaid, after most of their savings had been spent on his care. Mrs. Murphy is now in bad health and wishes to move to a continuing care retirement community. In order to afford her new living arrangement, Mrs. Murphy must sell her house and invest the proceeds from the equity to supplement her income. She and her husband are both owners of the house as "tenants by the entirety," however, so the house cannot be sold without her husband's signature. But he is not competent to sign the required legal papers. If Mrs. Murphy had obtained a broadly drafted DPOA from her husband while he was still capable of executing one, she could proceed with the sale. If she does not have a power of attorney, she must spend thousands of dollars in legal fees obtaining the permission of a court to sell the house. Because her husband has been receiving Medicaid in the nursing home, and depending on the state in which she resides, the court might order that one-half of the proceeds from the sale of the house be turned over to Medicaid and/or the nursing home, leaving her with inadequate resources. The importance of a carefully drafted durable power of attorney simply cannot be overstated. (See also ADVANCE DIRECTIVES; ELDER LAW PRACTICE; FINANCIAL ADVISORS; FRAILTY PLANNING; HEALTH AND LONGEVITY.)

### References

Alexander, George J. 1988. *Writing a Living Will: Using a Durable Power-of-Attorney*. New York: Praeger.

Berg, Adriane G. 1993. *Financial Planning for Couples*. New York: Newmarket Press.

Cohen, Elias. 1984. *Durable Power of Attorney: An Important Alternative to Guardianship, Conservatorship, or Trusteeship*. Washington, DC: U.S. Department of Health and Human Services.

Haman, Edward A. 1994. *The Power of Attorney Handbook: With Forms*. Clearwater, FL: Sphinx Publishers.

Levitin, Nancy. 1994. *Retirement Rights: The Benefits of Growing Older*. New York: Avon Books.

*Janet L. Kuhn*

# E

**EARLY RETIREMENT.** See Corporate Elder Care Programs; Early Retirement Incentive Plans (ERIPs); History of Retirement; Individual Retirement Account (IRA); Keogh Plans; Pension Plans; Working Retirees.

**EARLY RETIREMENT INCENTIVE PLANS (ERIPs),** plans that extend the benefits offered to workers or give additional financial inducements that motivate employees to retire prior to the age or time they otherwise would retire. Early retirement incentive plans first appeared on the employee benefit landscape in the late 1970s and early 1980s. The nation was struggling with "stagflation," and many firms sought to reduce their labor costs without resorting to layoffs. At the same time, the long-term trend toward earlier retirements was proceeding unabated. Many workers expressed a desire to enjoy the "leisure" that could be secured through the early retirement provisions of many companies' defined benefit plans. ERIPs offered enhancements to these benefits, allowing employees to retire earlier than they had planned. They proved popular among salaried and hourly workers alike and were smiled on by unions. No wonder, then, that a study of Fortune 100 firms in 1989 found that eight out of ten had offered such programs (BNA 1989).

When first offered, firms could not reliably predict how many or which workers would accept them. Especially when ERIPs were generous, and their eligibility criteria quite broad, firms lost many workers they would have wished to retain. Sometimes they found they had to hire back these new retirees as consultants or independent contractors. For example, a survey of 232 private and public employers by Mercer Human Resource Consulting found that 35% hired back retirees as consultants or independent contractors, and 37% brought back retirees as temporary or part-time employees. In the past two decades, however, firms have become much more sophisticated in targeting offers to avoid such outcomes.

During the past several years, the popularity of ERIPs has been on the wane. Several factors are involved in their diminished use. First, the ranks of potential retirees have been thinned by two decades of offering such programs. In addition, many employers have faced the need for substantial reductions in their workforce or the need for cutting particular jobs in response to a merger—goals that were unlikely to be achieved with ERIPs alone.

Moreover, while earlier programs had been able to call on the ample funds available in defined benefit plans, newer retirement plans were likely to take the form of defined contribution plans, which are not readily useful in creating ERIPs. Indeed, many firms making layoffs today are in the service industry, where workers may not be covered by *any* retirement plan. And with declining stock values, many defined benefit plans are finding that they now must add funds to pension reserve funds in order to cover their obligations for current and future retirees. Companies must annually report the actual—not just the estimated—value of their pension funds. Under federal law, if a firm's loss exceeds 10% of the greater of a pension's liability or the fair market value of assets, it must by law begin making contributions to the plan (Kerchoff 2002).

Finally, rapidly rising health care costs and the legal issues raised in interpretations of Employee Retirement Income Security Act (ERISA) or the Older Workers Benefit Protection Act (OWBPA) legislation served to dampen the enthusiasm of firms regarding ERIPs. Although retiree health benefits—at least helping to bridge a worker until (s)he was eligible for Medicare—were a standard part of earlier ERIP packages, firms now find the costs of such benefits prohibitive. Without a guarantee of protection from rising health care costs, potential early retirees find ERIPs much less attractive.

Despite these influences, ERIPs continue to exist. In fact, they have been widely adopted within higher education and are being offered by states and local communities to achieve downsizing objectives. A 2001 article by the *Chronicle of Higher Education* reported that since 1994 "nearly half of all colleges have offered financial incentives to encourage faculty members to retire early" (Fogg 2001). Before describing the most recent set of ERIPs offered by corporations, academic institutions, or government, a review of the basic characteristics of such programs is in order.

First, participation in ERIPs is voluntary. Firms are careful to target an entire class of employees, or a particular location; this protects them from charges of age discrimination. Second, these programs are short term. They are often called "open window plans" because offers are made and must be accepted during a limited time period, typically one to two months, though the range may run from one day to one year. Finally, these plans provide *one-time* cash and/or pension plan adjustments. Some also provide continuation of other benefits (e.g., health and life insurance) for a specified period. The range of benefits offered is described below, but, as already noted, firms have gained a good deal of experience in the design of ERIPs and are able to be more selective in setting eligibility requirements. They also have become less generous in the benefits packages being offered.

While firms and employee benefit consultants agree that, to be most effective, an offer should occur only once, many firms do offer such plans periodically—some nearly every year. A Hewitt Associates 1992 survey of nearly 700 companies, for example, found that one-fifth had offered two programs since 1988; 7% had offered three, and 3% had offered four or more (Hewitt Associates 1992). A 1999 report by Watson Wyatt found that 31% of firms had offered more than one window plan. Unfortunately, workers exposed to frequent ERIPs come to believe that they will be able to postpone retirement and still receive an offer "when the right time comes." Indeed, in 1998, 81% of retirements from employers with pension plans took place prior to retirees' sixty-fifth birthdays (*Employee Benefit Plan Review* 1999).

### Prevalence

Because ERIPs are not as widespread as they had been a decade or two ago, there are fewer reports detailing their dimensions. Price Waterhouse Coopers (2001) surveyed 114 firms in 2001 and reported that 12.3% had made such an offer to employees. Watson Wyatt surveyed 75 large companies in 1998–1999, finding that 61% had offered at least one ERIP in the previous ten years. In 2002, however, Watson Wyatt's survey found that only 17% of U.S. firms had offered such plans in the prior three years.

In 1997, Spencer and Associates surveyed 221 private and 68 public/nonprofit employers; 10% of the former and 13% of the latter provided ERIPs for employees. Of those offering ERIPs in 1995, half of the private employers had made prior offers, while only one-third of the public firms had done so. Seventy percent (70%) of the private firms not offering a 1995 ERIP had offered one in the past. In 1998, Spencer and Associates reported:

> A booming economy over the 1994-1998 period creating a tight labor market, witnessed a sharp decline in the proportion of early retirements attributable to early retirement window offers and "sweeteners." In 1992, following two years of ferocious recession-induced downsizing, 37.6% of early retirements that year were the result of such offers. That proportion dropped to 14.5% in 1994, 6.12% in 1996, and 4.89% in 1998. ("Robust Economy" 1999)

In addition to reports from employee benefit consulting firms, there is a national survey that studies retirement decision making, the Health and Retirement Survey. Since 1992, every two years, the federal government has collected information about retirement plans of respondents. In 1992, the sample for the survey ranged from 51 to 61 years of age. In both Wave 1 (1992) and Wave 2 (1994), any of these men and women who had worked in the past 20 years were asked about window plans they had been offered. Nearly 9 % (8.8%) had been offered at least one such plan; three out of ten who received one offer received more than one, usually from the same employer.

### Eligibility

The majority of firms offering ERIPs use a combination of years of age and service to define those eligible for a window plan offer. Or they may have a "magic number" that can be reached by different combinations of age and service. For example, if the number is 75, then a person aged 55 with 20 years of service and another aged 60 with 15 years of service would both be eligible. Eighty-nine percent (89%) of the plans surveyed by Hewitt Associates in 1997 used a combination of age and service criteria to define which workers would be eligible for ERIPs; only 8% used age alone, and only 3% relied solely on service years to define eligibility (Hewitt Associates 1997). Watson Wyatt's 1999 survey also showed age 55 as the minimum age requirement for 20 firms, while 13 companies reported that they required employees to have 10 years' tenure in order to qualify for an ERIP. In 2002, Watson Wyatt reported that 45% of firms surveyed used the criteria defining early retirement in their defined benefit plan, while 41% included younger workers and 12% restricted the offer by job class and another 25% restricted it to workers in certain locations.

### What Is Offered

For ERIPs within a defined pension plan, the most common incentive is the addition of age or service credits in calculating pension benefits. Typically, "5 and 5"—adding five years to age and/or five years to length of service—is offered. Other incentives may reduce or eliminate the penalty for early retirement, provide cash supplements until an employee is eligible for Social Security (in the main, at age 62, though some plans bridge payments to age 65), provision of life insurance, outplacement assistance, and less often, retiree health benefits (Hewitt Associates 1997).

When a defined benefit plan is not extant—if instead a firm has a defined contribution plan, for example—or when an employer wishes to design incentives that would not be permitted under ERISA rules, other incentives are utilized. Watson Wyatt (2002) reports that a cash payment/severance pay was offered to 43% of targeted employees. Cash offers varied; for example, some workers are offered one to two weeks per year of service, while others may be offered an additional 5% of pay. Lump-sum options also are attractive to employees:

> As a special supplement to the retirement benefit, you can give people the option to take the present value of the supplement in lump sum and roll over into an individual retirement account—if the defined benefit plan normally doesn't give a lump sum option—making one available in window is so attractive you may not have to sweeten the pension at all. (Richard Koski, quoted in Brenner 1998)

The economic environment in 1998 appeared much rosier than it did in 2002, however. After several years of recession, potential retirees were far less sanguine about their chances of finding another job if they accepted an employer's ERIP offer.

### Acceptance Rates

It is important to note *when* the window plans are offered in evaluating acceptance rates. Hewitt Associates (1997) reported that participation rates varied from 1% to 79%, while Watson Wyatt (1999) found that rates ranged from 1% at Dow Chemical (in 1995) to 100% at American Home Products (in 1998). Allstate (1994), J.C. Penney (1997), Motorola (1998), Nationwide Insurance (1995), and Texas Utilities (1997) all reported acceptance rates of 80% or higher (Watson Wyatt 1999). Spencer Associates (1998) reported that in 1995, 42.4% of those eligible in private firms accepted these offers; by 1997 that proportion rose to 52.3%.

Price Waterhouse Coopers (2001) reported that of the firms that offered ERIPs in the form of unreduced benefits, over half (57.1%) of employees accepted these offers. Watson Wyatt's 2002 report also shows that 55% of eligible employees accepted ERIPs, noting that acceptance rates were highest when age and service credits *and* cash payments were provided.

In looking at the Health and Retirement Survey sample, Charles Brown (1996) reports that those accepting a window plan were more likely to anticipate that layoffs would occur and that wage growth would slow or halt. Interestingly, they are also less likely to have a spouse who works outside the home and more likely to have a health condition that limits the kind or amount of work they can do. He notes: "A subtler implication is that window offers may be accepted precisely because they are a sign that employer stability and traditional wage increases are less certain if one remains."

In fact, focus groups of state employees in Connecticut—both those who had accepted and those who had rejected an early buyout—showed that most thought the ERIPs and the way they were offered were commendable. However, those who had rejected the offers spoke of the "deterioration in the work environment" because of the increased workload (Rix 1997).

Not everyone observing these plans believes them to be benign. Some worry that the overall reduction in benefits, particularly when one considers the decline in the value of a 401(k) or 403(b) portfolio, may mean that there will not be sufficient assets to provide a reasonable standard of living in retirement. "Other analysts wonder whether . . . [ERIPs] are not just a new way of turning American veteran employees into contingent workers" (Walsh 2001, 1).

## ERIPs in the Halls of Ivy

On January 1, 1994, an amendment to the Age Discrimination in Employment Act (ADEA) became law, ending mandatory retirement at age 70 for tenured faculty. In 1998, Ashenfelter and Card (Clark and Hammond 2000) conducted a study of faculty at 37 institutions and found that the end of mandatory retirement had, indeed, led to marked declines in the proportion retiring. There were no significant differences by gender or race, but faculty with higher salaries as well as those teaching at research universities were much less likely to retire before or at the age of 70. The consequence was that with no, or very small, increases in budgets, colleges and universities found it difficult to hire any of the Ph.D.s who had received their degrees in the prior 10 years. Achieving increased diversity among faculty members was also a challenge.

Universities and colleges scrambled to find ways to induce aging faculty members to retire. A survey in 2000 by the American Association of University Professors (AAUP) Committee on Retirement found that among 608 public and private institutions with 75 or more full-time faculty members, there were widely varying retirement plans, some with structures that contained early retirement incentives (Fogg 2001). A little more than one-third of the institutions offered a buyout, though these were twice as common at private institutions. In about half of the cases in which buyouts were offered, all tenured faculty members were automatically eligible if they met the age and years-of-service requirements. At about 90 of the institutions there was an increase in annual retirement benefits (Fogg 2001). Some institutions also offered phased-retirement programs; they were especially useful for public institutions and community colleges since they are able to keep experienced teachers while allowing them to reduce their workload. Uncertainty regarding the legality of setting an upper age limit for incentives caused institutions to shy away from using ERIPs, but recent cases have allowed their use. And because public sector plans are not subject to ERISA, age-based formulas are available for use in those settings.

### Conclusion

The recent economic downturn, widespread downsizing and restructuring of many firms in corporate America, and the increased use of defined contribution or cash balance pension plans has diminished the use of ERIPs in the late 1990s and the beginning of the twenty-first century. There has also been a change in people's expectation of work. No longer do men and women believe that they will have a lifetime career with one firm. And many firms no longer believe they must play a paternalistic role in their worker's retirement planning. Retirement security has become the individual's responsibility. (See also FINANCIAL PLANNING; HEALTH BENEFITS; JOB LOCK; LIFE PLANNING; RETIREMENT EXPENSE PLANNING.)

#### References

Brenner, Lynn. 1998. "Quitting Time." PLANSPONSOR, May. Available online at http://www.assetpub.com/archive/ps/98-05psmay/may98ps32.html.

Brown, Charles. 1996. "Early Retirement Windows." Presented as part of the Health and Retirement Study for the National Bureau of Economic Research, Cambridge, MA.

Bureau of National Affairs, Inc. (BNA). 1989. "Despite Legislative Encouragement, Workers Reluctant to Stay on the Job." *BNA Pension Reporter* 16 (May 15): 854.

Charles D. Spencer and Associates, Inc. 1998. "Early Retirement Incentives in 1995 and 1997. Fewer Offers, More Takers, in Private Sector." *Spencer's Resource Report* (June 26).

Clark, Robert, and Brett Hammond. 2000. "Implications of Changing Retirement Policies and Patterns in Higher Education." PRC #P2000-6. University of Pennsylvania, Wharton School, Pension Research Council.

Fogg, Piper. 2001. "Early Retirement Offers to Faculty Members Are Common, a Study Finds." *Chronicle of Higher Education* (August 10).

Hewitt Associates. 1992. *Early Retirement Windows, Lump Sum Options, and Postretirement Increases in Pensions*. Lincolnshire, IL: Author.

Hewitt Associates. 1997. *Employer Approaches to Workforce Reduction*. Lincolnshire, IL: Author.

Kerchoff, Sue. 2002. "Pensions Squeeze." *Boston Globe*, October 25.

LaRock, Seymour. 1996. "Early Retirement Incentives in 1995: More Takers for Fewer Offers." *Employee Benefit Plan Review* 3 (September): 54.

Price Waterhouse Coopers. 2001. *Severance and Retention Practices*. New York: Author.

Rix, Sara E. 1997. "Update on the Older Worker: 1997 Participation Rises and Unemployment Falls." *Data Digest* 33 (AARP Public Policy Institute, April 1998): 1–2.

"Robust Economy Sends Early Retirement Soaring to 81% of 1998 Retirements." 1999. *Employee Benefit Plan Review* 54(5) (November): 50–51.

Walsh, Mary Williams. 2001. "No Time to Put Your Feet Up as Retirement Comes in Stages." *New York Times*, Business/Financial Desk Section 1 (April 15), 1.

Watson Wyatt. 1999. *Survey of Early Retirement Windows and Postretirement Benefit Increases Provided by Large U.S. Companies as of January 1, 1999*. Washington, DC: Author.

Watson Wyatt. 2002. "Employers' Report on Early Retirement Windows." *Insider*. Available online at http://www.watsonwyatt.com/us/pubs/insider/.

*Phyllis H. Mutschler*

**ECONOMIC HARDSHIP MEASURES IN THE OLDER POPULATION,** measures used to assess either the lack of basic material necessities or the experience of serious financial difficulties of older adults. Unlike the official poverty threshold, which is based on household income, measures of economic hardship use nonincome items to determine levels of privation. Economic hardship measures probe such things as whether individuals have adequate food, housing, access to medical and dental care, and clothing; whether they can pay for their necessities each month; and how satisfied they are with their financial situation. The study of economic hardship is still fairly new in the United States, and the corresponding body of literature is small and exploratory.

Determining the level of economic hardship among older persons is important because many of the major social welfare programs available provide in-kind benefits rather than income, such as food, medical care, housing, and utilities. Economic hardship measures give a more accurate indication than income of the success with which these public programs provide for persons age 65 and older. As the work of Holden and Smeeding (1990) has shown, there are older persons whose incomes are too high to qualify for public programs but too low to provide security against potentially devastating life events.

Economic hardship measures are a purer measure of the factors associated with standards of living than income-based measures. The amount of food families can buy, the kind of housing they can afford, or the extent to which they can access medical care and transportation can only be approximated from income. With economic hardship measures, however, these capacities can be measured directly.

Reports of income and living standards are particularly disparate among the older population. Comparing reports of hardship in a number of economic areas to official poverty thresholds, Mayer and Jencks (1989) found that a family's official income-to-needs ratio explains less than one-fourth of the variance in material hardship. Similarly, there was little overlap between level of income and level of satisfaction with financial well-being in this population. Income and financial assets explain only about 25% of older adults' reports of financial satisfaction (George 1993). The apparent discrepancies between income and perceptions of financial well-being, and between the poverty line and the consumption patterns of older adults, emphasize the need for alternative measures of economic well-being.

### Economic Hardship Measures versus the Official Poverty Threshold

Economic hardship measures and the official poverty threshold both try to determine what proportion of society is marginalized by a low standard of living. Both attempt to define a minimum standard below which hardship occurs, and both measure resources; however, the similarities end there.

Economic hardship measures typically define *minimum standard* as lacking adequate levels of certain necessities, such as inability to purchase needed food. Minimum standard definitions may vary, however, depending on the survey and the domain studied. Measures of economic hardship use reports of consumption and consumptive capacity to determine *resources*. For example, respondents are asked if there were times they had no food or were unable to pay bills. In contrast, the official poverty threshold is set at a minimum standard, three times the amount of money the U.S. Department of Agriculture (USDA) estimates is required for a family to purchase a minimally nutritious diet. This minimum standard calculation is adjusted for household size and for heads of households age 65 and older. Household income is then compared to the minimum standard, and households with incomes less than the minimum standard are considered to be living below the poverty threshold.

There are several problems with the poverty threshold as a measure of economic well-being among older adults. Originally, adjustments in the official poverty threshold for age of household head were justified on the basis that older persons had fewer dietary requirements, thus lower food costs, and a lower minimum standard. This assumption is problematic for several reasons. Studies of consumption have found that persons age 65 and older spend the same or greater proportions of their income on food than younger households (Cook and Settersten 1995). Additionally, these studies have found that persons over age 64 spend a higher proportion of their income on housing, health care, and utilities than younger households, even when controlling for income levels.

The present poverty measure was criticized in a National Academy of Sciences (NAS) review in 1995 for its noninclusion of in-kind benefits, as well as its failure to take account of the ways in which the cost of various goods, such as food, housing, and medical care, has changed relative to other goods since it was developed in the early 1960s (Citro and Michael 1995). In response, the Census Bureau calculated four experimental alternative measures, one of which generally follows the NAS recommendations (Short et al. 1999). This alternative measure adjusts poverty thresholds by geographical differences in cost of living, counts noncash benefits as income, and subtracts from income some work-related, housing, and child care expenses.

While not proposing measures of self-perceived hardship such as those discussed above, the Census Bureau also calculated three other alternative poverty measures that vary in their treatment of family composition and residence. These included a Different Child Care (DCM) measure that assigns fixed amounts of child care expenses to working families with children, based on number and age of the children; a Difference Equivalence Scale (or DES) measure that uses a new method for adjusting for changes in expenses as family size increases; and a No Geographic Adjustment (or NGA) measure that, unlike the NAS measure, does not adjust thresholds for geographic differences in cost of living. The alternative measures were standardized to the 1997 official poverty lines in such a fashion that each produced the same overall U.S. poverty rate as the official rate and applied to income data for 1999, according to the U.S. Bureau of the Census. Interestingly, the 65+ poverty rate was considerably higher for each of the alternative measures than for the current official measure, while the child poverty rate was lower (there was little change for working-age persons). For example, while the 1999 poverty rate for persons 65 and over was 9.7% by the official measure, it was 13.3%, 13.0%, 13.7%, and 13.6%, respectively, for the four alternative measures. By contrast, information from the U.S. Bureau of the Census states that the poverty rate for persons under 18 years of age was 16.9% under the official measure, but was 14.8%, 15.5%, 14.3%, and 14.6% for the four alternative measures. These results have been taken to support the argument that the official poverty lines underestimate the real prevalence of poverty among older people.

In contrast to both the official and alternative measures of poverty, which are based on income adjusted in various ways for objectively measurable proxies for need, "economic hardship" measures reflect a concept based on consumption—whether individuals have, or think they have, access to adequate levels of goods and services. The poverty threshold measures income, or resources, which is at best only an indirect measure of consumption. Persons may be able to consume beyond their income by borrowing, drawing on savings, or using nonmonetary exchanges. Conversely, those who have adequate income may choose not to spend it on necessities, thereby ending up with inadequate levels of consumption. Finally, households also have different needs, tastes, priorities, and levels of efficiency that may alter the relationship between income and consumption. Since income is only an indirect indicator of consumption, alternative measures of economic well-being that are not income based are needed.

### Measuring Economic Hardship

Although alternative measures have been part of the European statistical literature for almost 30 years, they have only recently been used in the United States, and the empirical literature in the United States is still surprisingly limited. Some studies of economic hardship measure material hardship or lack of needed goods and services. Other studies look at "level of living," which includes nonmaterial components, such as access to education, working conditions, family relations, and measures of material needs. Still other studies focus on subjective financial well-being and measure how satisfied people are with their financial situation. Though the methodology differs, all of these studies have a common goal: to determine levels of hardship and deprivation through the use of nonincome measures.

Finding measures of economic hardship that compare households of different sizes and different needs is difficult. Although it is obvious that people of different ages and health statuses have different needs, it is not obvious what kinds of measures can be used to standardize the ratio of resources to consumption. The first major study to use nonincome measures of economic well-being, the Swedish Level of Living Survey, outlined nine areas of living conditions: (1) health and access to care, (2) employment and working conditions, (3) economic resources, (4) knowledge and educational opportunities, (5) family and social integration, (6) recreation and culture, (7) housing and neighborhood facilities, (8) security of life and property, and (9) political resources. Most work on *material hardship* has concentrated on basic necessities—food, housing, clothing, access to medical and dental care, and transportation—while recognizing that there are other items that contribute to quality of life, the lack of which may also cause considerable hardship.

To determine adequate levels of these factors, *hardship* is defined differently depending on the survey questions asked. Most surveys question whether respondents could afford what they needed. Other surveys ask if there was a time in the past year when respondents had to go without items that they needed, could not afford to buy needed food, or could not afford to pay the rent or mortgage; if they had no access to medical insurance; or if there were times when they had to go without needed medical attention. Some researchers look at housing conditions, such as levels of disrepair, or at the presence of durable goods such as dishwashers, automobiles, and air conditioners, as indicators of well-being. Some studies also use subjective assessments of economic well-being, which generally ask the respondents about their levels of satisfaction with income, financial resources, and current living standards or the extent to which they worry about making ends meet.

### Empirical Data

Studies consistently have found that persons over the age of 64 report fewer material hardships than younger adults. For example, Mayer and Jencks (1989) reported findings from the Chicago Hardship Study showing that, on average, families with heads age 65 and older had 36% as much income as younger families of the same size who reported the same number of hardships.

Also using Chicago Hardship Study data, Cook and Kramek (1986) found that households with heads age 65 and older were the least likely age group to report experiencing one or more hardships in the areas of food, rent, housing conditions, medical, dental, or utilities. Fewer adults age 65 and older said grocery spending was inadequate, and less than one-half as many adults over 65 as those under 65 reported a time when they needed food but could not afford it. Very few age 65 and older reported a time they could not afford to pay the rent, they had been evicted, or had utilities discontinued. The 65 and older sample was less than half as likely as younger age groups to report having two or more physical housing problems.

Lower levels of hardship among older adults, however, do not mean they are universally better off than younger adults. Without controlling for income, Cook and Kramek also found that older adults spent less on groceries than those aged 50 to 64, and a higher percentage of adults over age 65 spent less than the USDA minimum than adults aged 50 to 64. Older persons in the Chicago Hardship Study reported more medical problems than younger adults. They were as likely to say they had been sick and needed help but were less likely than younger adults to say they went without medical care or dental care because of lack of money. The data show that the domains in which persons age 65 and older are most likely to experience hardship are medical care, food, and housing. Similarly, national survey data indicate that the risk of hardship related to medical care is substantial among low-income older adults, with about 40% of beneficiaries with incomes below the poverty level, in fair or poor health, with ADL (activities of daily living) limitations, reporting difficulty paying their medical bills or getting needed health care (Neuman et al. 1999). In a Baltimore survey, 50% of disabled minority women, and 13% of disabled White women, reported financial difficulty acquiring food, and such difficulty was associated with symptoms of depression (Klesges et al. 2001).

Subjective assessments of economic well-being were measured in the Chicago Hardship Study by asking respondents to express feelings about their standard of living and making ends meet. Without controlling for income, those aged 65 and older were less satisfied with their standard of living than those aged 18 to 49, but more satisfied than those aged 50 to 64. Similarly, of persons reporting no hardships, those aged 65 and older were less satisfied with their standard of living than those aged 18 to 49, but slightly more satisfied than those aged 50 to 64. However, persons aged 65 and older who had experienced at least one hardship had the lowest satisfaction with their standard of living of any age group. Members of the oldest group were the least likely to be worried about making ends meet, regardless of whether they had experienced a hardship. Reviewing the literature on subjective assessments of economic well-being, George (1992) found that even though older adults had lower income on average than younger adults, older adults consistently reported higher levels of satisfaction with their income, financial resources, and standard of living than younger adults. Thus, both financial satisfaction measures and material deprivation measures appear to provide quite a different perspective on age differences in economic disadvantage than do the alternative poverty measures discussed above, one that places older people in a relatively more favorable light.

Although the poverty threshold adjusts over time for changes in consumer prices, it does not account for changes in consumption habits and priorities of society. Changing priorities in society are not captured by a poverty threshold based on income alone. In 1963, when the poverty line was being developed, it was considered unnecessary for households to have a telephone, whereas now this need is seen differently. Thus, alternative measures of deprivation that are based directly on consumption are important supplements to the poverty thresholds. Several studies suggest that widely used economic indicators may be misleading in terms of the overall living conditions in society. For example, although conventional wisdom has maintained that the U.S. standard of living declined in the 1970s, measures in four areas (health, housing, transportation, and food) have shown that conditions in these areas actually improved (Jencks 1984).

The relationship between changes in income and objective and subjective measures of economic hardship over the past three decades is less clear. Objective income levels of older persons have increased since 1973, while there has not been a concomitant increase in financial satisfaction. This may reflect differences in expectations between cohorts. For example, recent cohort analyses of financial satisfaction trends from 1972 to 1996, using data from the General Social Survey, indicate that perceived financial satisfaction did increase within cohorts as they aged but that satisfaction was markedly lower in the younger cohorts, leading to an overall reduction in financial satisfaction over time due to cohort succession (Hsieh 2000, 2002).

### Explaining Levels of Economic Hardship in Older Adults

Although age differences in reports of material hardship have been found consistently, little work has attempted to untangle the effects of age and other factors on reports of economic hardship. The factors that put some older adults at risk for economic hardship and those that make others resilient to it have also not been explored in detail. Studies asking individuals to state an amount of money they perceive as a "just sufficient" level of income or "enough income to make ends meet" may provide some clues to the reasons for age differences in reports of economic hardship. These studies have found that older adults have lower expectations of their economic resources, which suggests that they may report fewer economic hardships than younger adults because their idea of a sufficient level of income is lower than younger adults. Perceptions of poverty may change little over a lifetime, and older persons experiencing lower incomes in the 1920s, 1930s, and 1940s may have unchanged criteria for what constitutes an adequate standard of living, consistent with the findings by Hsieh discussed above.

Some researchers suggest that older adults may report fewer hardships because they are more likely to have assets than younger adults. They are more likely to own their homes, and older homeowners are less likely to have mortgages (Keister 2000). Several studies have found that, in general, older adults underreport income and assets, making them seem objectively less well-off than they are (Crystal and Shea 1990, 2002; Smith 2002). Other possible explanations are more speculative. Some suggest that older adults are better managers of money, or that they have different tastes, but these explanations have not been investigated empirically. Others propose that measures of past hardships do not capture the economic worries of the older population, which may have more to do with future ability to pay bills, especially large medical expenses, as their health deteriorates (George 1992; Holden and Smeeding 1990). These worries are shared with those who have not yet reached age 65. For example, in the 2001 Health Confidence Survey sponsored by the Employee Benefit Retirement Institute, 49% of respondents reported lacking confidence that they would be able to afford health care without financial hardship in retirement, and 51% lacked confidence that they would be able to afford prescription drugs that they need without financial hardship (Employee Benefit Research Institute 2002).

Since the study of economic hardship is a new field, there is simply not an adequate amount of research to understand specifically why older persons report different levels of economic hardship from those reported by younger adults. Yet this focus of inquiry has been valuable in bringing to light some of the complexity of the levels of well-being across age categories. (See also ECONOMIC STATUS OF OLDER MEN AND WOMEN; FINANCIAL COUNSELING FOR MID- TO LATER LIFE; FINANCIAL EDUCATION FOR SENIORS; FINANCIAL LITERACY; MEANS-TESTING IN PUBLIC PROGRAMS; MINORITY OLDER ADULTS.)

**References**

Allen, Susan M., and Vincent Mor. 1997. "The Prevalence and Consequences of Unmet Need. Contrasts between Older and Younger Adults with Disability." *Medical Care* 35(11): 1132–48.

Citro, Constance F., and Robert T. Michael, eds. 1995. *Measuring Poverty: A New Approach.* Washington, DC: National Academy Press.

Cook, Fay Lomax, and Lorraine M. Kramek. 1986. "Measuring Economic Hardship among Older Americans." *The Gerontologist* 26: 38–47.

Cook, Fay Lomax, and Richard A. Settersten, Jr. 1995. "Expenditure Patterns by Age and Income among Mature Adults: Does Age Matter?" *The Gerontologist* 35: 10–23.

Crystal, Stephen, and Dennis Shea. 1990. "Cumulative Advantage, Cumulative Disadvantage, and Inequality among Elderly People." *The Gerontologist* 30(4): 437–43.

Crystal, Stephen, and Dennis Shea. 2002. "Cumulative Advantage, Public Policy, and Late-Life Inequality." In *Focus on Economic Outcomes in Later Life*, ed. Stephen Crystal and Dennis Shea. Public Policy, Health, and Cumulative Advantage. Vol. 22 of *Annual Review of Gerontology and Geriatrics*. New York: Springer.

Employee Benefit Retirement Institute. 2002. "Health Confidence Survey, 2001 Results: Confidence in Health Care System." *EBRI.* Available online at http://www.ebri.org/hcs/2001/index.html.

George, Linda K. 1992. "Economic Status and Subjective Well-Being: A Review of the Literature and an Agenda for Future Research." In *Aging, Money and Life Satisfaction: Aspects of Financial Gerontology*, ed. Neal E. Cutler et al. New York: Springer.

George, Linda K. 1993. *Financial Security in Later Life: The Subjective Side*. Philadelphia, PA: Boettner Institute of Financial Gerontology.

Holden, Karen C., and Timothy M. Smeeding. 1990. "The Poor, the Rich, and the Insecure Elderly Caught in Between." *Milbank Quarterly* 68: 191–219.

Hsieh, Chang-ming. 2000. "Trends in Financial Satisfaction among Middle-Age and Old-Age Americans, 1972–1996." *International Journal of Aging and Human Development* 51(2): 105–13.

Hsieh, Chang-ming. 2002. "Trends in Financial Satisfaction: Does Poverty Make a Difference?" *International Journal of Aging and Human Development* 54(1): 15–30.

Jencks, Christopher. 1984. "The Hidden Prosperity of the 1970s." *Public Interest*. 77: 37–61.

Keister, Lisa A. 2000. *Wealth in America: Trends in Wealth Inequality*. New York: Cambridge University Press.

Klesges, L.M., M. Pahor, R.I. Shorr, J.Y. Wan, J.D. Williamson, and J.M. Guralnik. 2001. "Financial Difficulty in Acquiring Food among Elderly Disabled Women: Results from the Women's Health and Aging Study." *American Journal of Public Health* 91(1): 68–75.

Mayer, Susan E., and Christopher Jencks. 1989. "Poverty and the Distribution of Material Hardship." *Journal of Human Resources* 24: 88–114.

Neuman, Patricia, Diane Rowland, Michelle Kitchman, Drew Altman, Catherine Schoen, Karen Davis, and E. Puleo. 1999. "Understanding the Diverse Needs of the Medicare Population: Implications for Medicare Reform." *Journal of Aging and Social Policy* 10(4): 25–50.

Short, Kathleen, Thesia Garner, David Johnson, and Patricia Doyle. 1999. "Experimental Poverty Measures: 1990 to 1997." *Current Population Reports, Consumer Income Series*. No. P60-205. Washington, DC: U.S. Census Bureau.

Smith, James. 2002. "Measurement of Late-Life Income and Wealth." In *Focus on Economic Outcomes in Later Life*, ed. Stephen Crystal and Dennis Shea. Vol. 22 of *Annual Review of Gerontology and Geriatrics*. New York: Springer.

*Fay Lomax Cook and Anne S. Welch*
*Updated by Stephen Crystal and Fay Lomax Cook*

**ECONOMIC HISTORY OF RETIREMENT.** Retirement is often difficult to measure, so economic historians have focused on the labor force participation rate. The current definition of *labor force participation* includes those who are employed and those who are unemployed (actively searching for a job). Before 1940, the census used the concept of gainful employment, which included all those who claimed to have had an occupation in the past year, whether or not they worked. Table 1 gives labor force participation rates from 1850 to 2000 for older men in the United States, using both definitions. (For an international comparison, see Table 2.) The retirement rate can be approximated by subtracting the labor force participation rate from 100%. The data show that retirement was fairly rare in the mid- and late 1800s. After 1880 retirement rates began to climb, generally rising from decade to decade—with a few interruptions.

Why have retirement rates generally risen over time? The earliest theory stressed the effects of the "modernization" of the economy. It argued that the shift from an agricultural economy to an industrial economy between about 1880 and 1930 pushed older men out of the workforce. During this period new production processes increasingly prohibited workers from laboring at their own paces, rapid technological change and shifts in the occupational mix made some older workers' skills obsolete, higher capital-to-labor ratios raised the cost of using less efficient workers, the rationalization of big business and the scientific management movement sought efficiency at every margin and created mandatory retirement schedules and policies against hiring workers over a certain age, and stiff competition came from the young and immigrants who were willing to adopt a relentless work pace. According to this argument, changes such as these worsened the employment prospects of older workers, pushing them onto the "industrial scrap heap." An additional concern was that attitudes about the abilities of older persons changed between the Civil War and the Great Depression, so that they may have been increasingly viewed as peripheral, less capable members of society.

Most economic historians now reject these views, however. Carter and Sutch (1996), for example, show that at the beginning of the twentieth century it was farmers and other self-employed workers who were most likely to retire. They conclude that the shift out of agriculture would tend to *lower* retirement rates, rather than pushing men into early retirement. Costa (1998) concurs, finding that declines in part-time work, nonfarm self-

**Table 1**
**Labor Force Participation Rates of Older Men in the United States, 1850–2000**

| Year | Age 65 and over | | Age 55–64 | |
|---|---|---|---|---|
| | Gainful (%) | Current (%) | Gainful (%) | Current (%) |
| 1850 | 76.6 | | 92.2 | |
| 1860 | 76.0 | | | |
| 1870 | | | | |
| 1880 | 78.0 | | 95.2 | |
| 1890 | 73.8 | | | |
| 1900 | 65.4 | | 91.0 | |
| 1910 | 58.1 | | 91.1 | |
| 1920 | 60.1 | | 89.1 | |
| 1930 | 58.0 | | | |
| 1940 | 43.5 | 41.8 | 82.2 | 86.1 |
| 1950 | 47.0 | 41.4 | 88.1 | 85.8 |
| 1960 | 40.8 | 30.5 | 83.8 | 84.8 |
| 1970 | 35.2 | 24.8 | 86.7 | 81.5 |
| 1980 | 24.7 | 19.9 | 77.4 | 71.9 |
| 1990 | 18.4 | 16.3 | 67.0 | 67.6 |
| 2000 | | 17.5 | | 67.3 |

*Notes*: This table only includes rates for men because the negative relationship between labor force participation and retirement has not existed historically for women. From 1950 to 2000, the participation rate of women below age 65 climbed very strongly, while the rate for older women showed little long-term trend, falling slightly from 1955 to 1985 and then rising slightly. The rates for women 65 to 69, for example, have been 15.5% (1950), 17.8% (1960), 17.3% (1970), 15.1% (1980), 17.0% (1990), and 19.4% (2000) (Gendell and Siegel 1992). The labor force participation rate of Black males over 65 was originally much higher than the overall rate but fell below it after 1950. The Black male rate was 87.3% in 1880, then fell to 84.1% (1900), 76.8% (1920), 54.6% (1940), 37.3% (1960), and 15.7% (1990).

*Source*: Costa 1998.

employment, and farming cannot explain the rise of retirement and showing that about half of older Union Army veterans who had been common laborers in 1900 were able to move upward to jobs as farmers (20%), professionals/proprietors (16%), and artisans (15%) by 1910. Whaples (1991) shows that gainful employment rates of older men were not generally affected by the configuration of occupations in local labor markets, nor by the size and capital intensity of firms. Haber and Gratton (1994) argue that mandatory retirement was adopted jointly with seniority plans (and sometimes pensions) that protected older workers, even as they made it more difficult for some older men to find jobs. In addition, Range and Vinovskis (1981) find little change in the images of older adults in a content analysis of popular magazines and question the claim that ageist attitudes worsened during this period. Rather than being ejected from the labor market, many older industrial workers in the late 1800s and early 1900s seem to have been able to "retire" more gradually. In jobs that required substantial brawn, many retired "on the job" by switching to less physically intense occupations (Ransom and Sutch 1986).

The new consensus is that rising levels of wealth and lifetime income have been the

**Table 2**
**International Comparisons of Labor Force Participation Rates of Men Aged 65 and Over**

| Year | Percentages | | | |
|---|---|---|---|---|
| | United States | Britain | France | Germany |
| c. 1890 | 73.8 | 65.5 | 54.1 | 58.0 |
| c. 1910 | 58.1 | 56.9 | 51.1 | 52.0 |
| c. 1930 | 58.0 | 47.9 | 48.1 | 29.7 |
| c. 1950 | 47.0 | 31.1 | 36.2 | 26.8 |
| c. 1970 | 35.2 | 18.6 | 10.6 | 17.2 |
| c. 1990 | 18.4 | 8.2 | 3.5 | 5.1 |

*Note*: This table compares labor force participation rates of older men in the United States to those in Britain, France, and Germany. It shows that the American experience of a long-term rise in retirement rates has been similar to that in Europe but that the retirement rate in the United States has generally been 10 to 20 percentage points lower.

*Source*: Costa 1998.

driving force behind increasing retirement rates in the United States, particularly before 1940. Costa (1998) shows that the retirement of Union Army veterans in 1900 and 1910 was strongly linked to the size of their pensions. In 1900, for example, 39% of veterans under 70 in good or fair health who received monthly pensions of $15 or more were retired, while only 22% of those with smaller pensions were retired. Likewise, among those in poor health the retirement rates were 54% for those with larger pensions and 36% for those with smaller pensions. Overall, she finds that a 1% increase in pension amount, controlling for health and other factors, increased retirement by 0.73% in 1900 and 0.47% in 1910. Costa then uses the 1910 pension-retirement relationship to project the retirement trend in light of the fact that wealth levels rose considerably during the twentieth century. This procedure implies that about 90% of the rise in retirement rates in the decades before 1930 can be explained by rising wealth and that up to 60% of the retirement rise before 1990 may be similarly explained. These rising wealth levels counteracted the effects of improved health among older adults. Advances in medical technology, lessened occupation hazards, and better early life health and nutrition improved the health of older persons substantially over the course of the twentieth century, which would otherwise have increased older men's labor force participation rates. The rising wealth of older Americans is also reflected in their housing and household arrangements. In 1880, 46% of all retired men age 65 and older were living in a household headed by their children or other relatives. By 1920 this fraction had fallen to 32%, then to 13% in 1960 and 5% in 1990. Costa also argues that the falling price of leisure goods and the increase in the variety of recreational activities (such as television) have made leisure more attractive to older people and played an important role in increasing retirement rates.

Finally, there is the role of government in fostering the increase in retirement rates. In the late 1800s and early 1900s nearly 1 million people (mostly older Americans) received Civil War pensions. They covered over half of older native-born Northern males, made up 42% of the federal budget at their peak, and are probably largely responsible for the large drop in older men's labor force participation rates from 1890 to 1910 and the slight rebound to 1920 as the post–Civil War generation reached retirement age. However, the United States was later than most western European nations in instituting a state-sponsored old-age pension system covering the general population when it passed the Social Security Act in 1935. In its early years, Social Security's welfare component, Old Age Assistance (OAA), dominated the Old Age Insurance (OAI) component, which bases monthly benefits on the amount of taxes workers have paid into the system. Disability Insurance was added to the package in 1956. As the decades have progressed the fraction of older persons receiving Social Security benefits and the level of these benefits have increased. In 1940, only 23% of the population 65 years and older received Social Security benefits. A decade later this rose to 40%, then 73% (1960) and 89% (1970), as coverage was extended to groups initially excluded, including farmers, domestics, professionals, and the self-employed. Meanwhile, the inflation-adjusted average monthly benefits of retired workers more than doubled between 1950 and 1975 (Myers 1981).

Before the long-run historical trend in retirement rates became understood, some observed the post-1940 trend and concluded that Social Security had played the key role in driving the retirement rate upward. However, recent studies emphasize that Social Security's influence on the retirement trend has been "modest." Leonesio (1993) summarizes recent research by saying that while "the social security system has contributed to the popularity of retirement at ages 62 and 65, [it] appears to be a minor force in the long post–World War II trend to retire at earlier ages" Parsons (1991), however, estimates that Old Age Assistance was responsible for the unusual trend in retirement rates between 1930 and 1950, with a huge drop from 1930 to 1940 and a slight rebound from 1940 to 1950. OAA was available only to those who had no regular employment and provided a strong incentive for low-paid and unemployed older workers to retire. Parsons estimates that the new availability of OAA combined with its earnings restrictions increased the retirement rate for men 65 and over by about 6 percentage points in 1940.

While the forces behind the adoption of Social Security are manifold and complex, most historians argue that Social Security was ultimately enacted because of society's desire for economic security. Beginning around 1900, reformers launched a campaign to solve the "problem of old age." They echoed and amplified the fear that old age would inevitably mean dependency, poverty, and worst of all, a trip to the poorhouse. Poorhouses were tax-supported residential institutions to which people were required to go if they could not support themselves in the 1800s and early 1900s (Crannel 2000). Interestingly, much of the reformers' rhetoric (and perhaps public perception) was out of touch with economic reality. For example, Haber and Gratton (1994) estimate that despite the misrepresentation of reformers the proportion of older adults in the poorhouse remained constant at about 2% throughout the late nineteenth and early twentieth centuries. Families adopted many strategies to avoid old-age poverty during this era, including savings, pensions, working, and relying on the wages of children. Average annual household incomes of those 60 and over were only modestly lower than those in their forties and fifties, and Gratton (1996) shows that real wages of older workers rose sharply from 1890 to 1950, with positive age-earnings profiles across the life cycle. However, the Great Depression changed everything. With it the savings and wealth of many older people evaporated and unemployment among this population and those supporting them became a serious problem. "It took the Great Depression to launch social security in the United States" (Achenbaum 1986); without it the country might never have adopted Social Security.

Social Security was designed to solve poverty and dependency by transferring wealth to older adults and to combat unemployment among the young by luring the old out of the labor market. Its goal was to induce retirement. Initially, there was a limit of only $15 per month that retirees could earn in the labor market. If they earned more, they lost their Social Security benefits. This "retirement test," a legacy of the Great Depression, has been gradually eased over time. In 1950, the income threshold was raised to $50, and the retirement test was eliminated for those aged 75 and older. In 1960, for the first time, earnings over the exempt amount did not produce total loss of benefits, instead—for income in a certain range—benefits were reduced $1 for every $2 in earnings. In 1990, this rate was cut to $1 for every $3 in earnings for workers above the normal age of retirement. In 2000, as unemployment reached its lowest rate in over 30 years, both houses of Congress unanimously voted to eliminate the retirement earnings test for workers above Social Security's normal retirement age.

At the same time that Social Security was conceived, established, and expanded, private pensions grew tremendously. American Express adopted the nation's first corporate pension in 1875, and by the early twentieth century pensions had become widespread among railroads. It is estimated that by 1913 about 9% of the non–farm labor force was covered by a pension (Craig and Trawick 1993). This grew to nearly 14% in 1929 but collapsed to 4% during the depression, before rebounding to 25% in 1950. By 1988 about 58% of middle-aged full-time, private sector workers were covered by private pensions.

Before employer-based pensions became widespread, many workers purchased annuities, called tontines, directly from insurance companies.

> However, in 1906, after a public scandal of alleged mismanagement and impropriety in the insurance industry and an extensive investigation which exposed abuses in the handling of tontine insurance funds, the State of New York prohibited any further issue of tontine insurance. Other states quickly followed suit and the individually-purchased pension disappeared. (Ransom, Sutch, and Williamson 1993)

Company pensions arose to fill this void. The use of pensions was also accelerated by the federal government's creation of tax breaks for them, beginning in 1938. Thus, workers who desired to save for retirement found that their best option was a company pension. (See also EMPLOYEE BENEFITS IN THE PUBLIC SECTOR; HEALTH BENEFITS; HISTORY OF RETIREMENT; PENSION PLANS; RETIREMENT MIGRATION; SOCIAL SECURITY PROGRAM OF THE UNITED STATES.)

### References

Achenbaum, W. Andrew. 1986. *Social Security: Visions and Revisions*. New York: Cambridge University Press.

Carter, Susan, and Richard Sutch. 1996. "Myth of the Industrial Scrap Heap: A Revisionist View of Turn-of-the-Century American Retirement." *Journal of Economic History* 56: 5–38.

Costa, Dora. 1998. *The Evolution of Retirement: An American Economic History, 1880–1990.* Chicago: University of Chicago Press.

Craig, Lee, and L. Michelle Trawick. 1993. "Federal Regulation and the Growth of Private-Sector Pensions, 1913–1950." Paper presented at the annual meeting of the Gerontological Society of America, New Orleans.

Crannel, Linda M. 2000. *Poorhouse Story*. Available online at http://www.poorhousestory.com/.

Gendell, Murray, and Jacob S. Siegel. 1992. "Trends in Retirement Age by Sex, 1950–2005." *Monthly Labor Review* 115: 22–29.

Graebner, William. 1980. *A History of Retirement: The Meaning and Function of an American Institution, 1885–1978*. New Haven, CT: Yale University Press.

Gratton, Brian. 1996. "The Poverty of Impoverishment Theory: The Economic Well-Being of the Elderly, 1890–1950." *Journal of Economic History* 56: 39–61.

Haber, Carole, and Brian Gratton. 1994. *Old Age and the Search for Security: An American Social History*. Bloomington: Indiana University Press.

Leonesio, Michael. 1993. "Social Security and Older Workers." In *As the Workforce Ages: Costs, Benefits, and Policy Challenges*, ed. Olivia Mitchell. Ithaca, NY: ILR Press.

Myers, Robert J. 1981. *Social Security*. 2nd ed. Homewood, IL: Irwin.

Parsons, Donald. 1991. "Male Retirement Behavior, 1930–1950." *Journal of Economic History* 51: 657–74.

Range, Jane, and Maris Vinovskis. 1981. "Images of Elderly in Popular Magazines: A Content Analysis of Littell's Living Age, 1845–1882." *Social Science History* 5: 123–69.

Ransom, Roger, and Richard Sutch. 1986. "The Labor of Older Americans: Retirement of Men on and off the Job, 1870–1937." *Journal of Economic History* 46: 1–30.

Ransom, Roger, Richard Sutch, and Samuel Williamson. 1993. "Inventing Pensions: The Origins of the Company-Provided Pension in the United States, 1900–1940." In *Societal Impact on Aging: Historical Perspectives*, ed. K. Warner Schaie and W. Andrew Achenbaum. New York: Springer.

Whaples, Robert. 1991. "The Shortening of the American Work Week: An Economic and Historical Analysis of Its Context, Causes, and Consequences." *Journal of Economic History* 51: 454–57.

*Robert Whaples*

**ECONOMIC SECURITY.** See Pension Plans; Pension Plans for the Self-Employed; Social Security Program of the United States; Supplemental Security Income (SSI); Wealth Span.

**ECONOMIC STATUS OF OLDER MEN AND WOMEN.** Within the last 20 years, the economic status of older adults in the United States has improved, but there are still disadvantaged subgroups among the older population. An excellent source of data on the economic status of Americans is the Survey of Consumer Finances. The surveys are collected every three years under the sponsorship of the Federal Reserve Board of Governors (Kennickell, Starr-McCluer, and Surette 2000). A unique feature of the surveys is that information is collected on the assets and liabilities of a household, and the random sampling design of the surveys allows researchers to generalize the results to all American households.

*Measures of Economic Status.* Income is the most commonly used measure of economic status, but other measures such as net worth and homeownership are also useful. For instance, income is a measure of the amount that a household receives on a regular basis, but income may be insufficient to cope with unexpected expenses. If an emergency occurs, it is important to know the net worth of the household. Furthermore, many older Americans are homeowners, and the home may be their most valuable asset. Unfortunately, it may take several months to sell a home and convert its value to a stream of income. Therefore, three measures of economic status must be evaluated: household income, net worth, and homeownership.

The components of household income include earned income, asset income, government payments, and so forth. Net worth is the value of total assets minus the value of total liabilities. It includes the market value of the home minus the total amount of the mortgage on the home.

Instead of presenting the average values of income and net worth, the median value will be presented. The median represents the midpoint, so 50% of households will be above the median and 50% will be below the median. In 1998, the median value of household income was $33,000, and the median net worth for all American households was $73,800.

*Age and Economic Status*. Examining the Survey of Consumer Finance data for 1998 revealed that the median value of income peaked before retirement and declined as households aged. The relationship between age and income is consistent with life cycle stage theories (Ando and Modigliani 1963; DeVaney and Zhang 2001). Households headed by an individual aged 34 or younger had a median income of $27,000, while those aged 35 to 49, 50 to 64, 65 to 74, and 75+ had a median income of $44,000, $42,000, $24,000, and $17,000, respectively. The Social Security Administration reported that the major sources of income for those 65 and over in 2002 were Social Security (reported by 90% of older persons), income from assets (reported by 59%), public and private pensions (reported by 41%), and earnings (reported by 22%) (Administration on Aging 2003).

The values for median net worth for the same age categories (less than 34, 35 to 49, 50 to 64, 65 to 74, and 75 and older) were $9,300, $73,800, $128,090, $150,900, and $129,100, respectively. The noticeable increase in median value of net worth between the youngest category (less than 34) and the age 35 to 49 category is probably due to the purchase of a home by households age 35 to 49 and increased saving as households become more well established. The decline in net worth for the oldest category (75 and over) suggests that some older households may be spending down their savings in retirement (Ando and Modigliani 1963). Reasons for this could include the older adults' ineligibility for a pension, little or no asset income, or dependence on Social Security (Bieker, DeVaney, and Chen 2001; DeVaney and Zhang 2001). Other reasons might be a lack of knowledge in investing one's pension (DeVaney and Kim 2003), having a low tolerance for risk (DeVaney and Chien 2001), or increased spending on health care costs (Rubin and Nieswiadomy 1997).

*Homeownership and Economic Status*. Examining the amount of household income and net worth by homeownership of households of all ages in 1998 revealed that the median income of homeowners of all ages was twice that of renters ($46,000 compared to $22,000). However, the median value of net worth for homeowners of all ages was 21 times greater than the net worth of renters ($152,170 compared to $7,200).

*Race and Economic Status*. When households were categorized by race, White households had higher income and higher net worth in 1998. Median income for White households was one and one-half times greater than median income for non-White households

**Table 1**
**The Influence of Age and Race on Income and Net Worth**

| Age | Race | Variable | Median |
|---|---|---|---|
| 65 to 74 | White | Income | $ 26,000 |
| | | Net worth | $179,200 |
| | Non-White | Income | $ 11,000 |
| | | Net worth | $ 25,000 |
| 75 and over | White | Income | $ 18,000 |
| | | Net worth | $146,700 |
| | Non-White | Income | $ 8,100 |
| | | Net worth | $ 35,490 |

*Source*: Federal Reserve Board 1998.

($37,000 compared to $23,000). In contrast, median net worth was almost six times greater for White households compared to non-White households ($97,250 compared to $16,600).

Table 1 shows median income and net worth in 1998 for White and non-White households headed by an individual who was age 65 to 74 and for those aged 75 and over. The age group 75 and over non-White households had less income, but they had more net worth.

*Marital Status and Economic Status*. Another perspective considers the amount of income and net worth of those who are married compared to those who are unmarried. The term *married* includes those who cohabit as partners in addition to those who are legally married. The term *unmarried* includes those who have never married and those who are separated, divorced, or widowed. As might be expected, the married couples were more well off than unmarried men, who in turn were more well off than unmarried women. Median income in 1998 for all couples was $50,000, followed by $27,000 for all unmarried men and $17,000 for all unmarried women. Median net worth for couples in 1998 was $124,120, while it was $25,540 for unmarried men and $30,280 for unmarried women.

Table 2 shows median income and net worth in 1998 by marital status and age category. Income declined with age for couples, unmarried men, and unmarried women. There was no consistent pattern for the change in net worth and age. Some households may have encountered large expenses for health care (Rubin and Nieswiadomy 1997), or some other situation may be affecting the amount of net worth.

Several conclusions can be drawn about economic status. When all ages are considered, homeowners were better off than renters, couples were better off than unmarried men, who were better off than unmarried women, and Whites were better off than non-Whites; however, those in the oldest age category were less well off than were those in younger categories and some changes occur. (See also AGING AMERICA; DIVORCE AND OLDER ADULTS; ECONOMIC HARDSHIP MEASURES IN THE OLDER POPULATION; FINANCES OF AGING IN THE GAY COMMUNITY; MARRIAGE AND OLDER ADULTS.)

**Table 2**
**The Influence of Age and Marital Status on Income and Net Worth**

| Age | Marital Status | Variable | Median |
|---|---|---|---|
| 65 to 74 | Couple | Income | $ 37,000 |
| | | Net worth | $226,000 |
| | Unmarried man | Income | $ 22,000 |
| | | Net worth | $ 94,400 |
| | Unmarried woman | Income | $ 15,000 |
| | | Net worth | $ 90,930 |
| 75 and over | Couple | Income | $ 26,000 |
| | | Net worth | $260,400 |
| | Unmarried man | Income | $ 18,000 |
| | | Net worth | $141,000 |
| | Unmarried woman | Income | $ 13,000 |
| | | Net worth | $ 87,420 |

*Source*: Federal Reserve Board 1998.

### References

Administration on Aging. 2003. Washington, DC. Available online at http://www.aoa.gov/aoa/stats/profile/highlights.html.

Ando, A., and F. Modigliani. 1963. "The Life Cycle Hypothesis of Saving: Aggregate Implications and Tests." *American Economic Review* 53(1): 55–84.

Bieker, R., S.A. DeVaney, and Z. Chen. 2001. "Determinants of Employment among Older Americans." *Financial Counseling and Planning* 12(2): 33–42.

DeVaney, S.A., and Y. Chien. 2001. "A Model of Savings Behavior and the Amount Saved in Retirement Accounts." *Journal of Financial Service Professionals* 57 (March): 72–80.

DeVaney, S.A., and H. Kim. 2003. "Women's Knowledge of Their Pension Plans." *Journal of Family and Consumer Sciences* 95(2): 19–25.

DeVaney, S.A., and T.C. Zhang. 2001. "A Cohort Analysis of the Amount in Defined Contribution and Individual Retirement Accounts." *Financial Counseling and Planning* 12(1): 89–104.

Federal Reserve Board. 1998. "Survey of Consumer Finances." Washington, DC: Author. Available online at http://www.federalreserve.gov/pubs/oss/oss2/98/scf98home.html.

Kennickell, A.B., M.S. Starr-McCluer, and B.J. Surette. (2000). "Recent Changes in U.S. Family Finances: Results from the 1998 Survey of Consumer Finances." *Federal Reserve Bulletin* 86 (January): 1–29.

Rubin, Rose M., and Michael L. Nieswiadomy. 1997. *Expenditures of Older Americans*. Westport, CT: Praeger.

*Sharon A. DeVaney and Zhan (Sandy) Chen*

**EDUCATION OF OLDER ADULTS.** In the United States, older adult education is shaped more by consumer demand and the rise of a multitude of nonprofit educational organizations than by state-run institutions or government policies. Fueling the demand is a new generation of retirees who are more affluent, better educated, and healthier than any previous generation in American history. Thirty or 40 years ago, only a tiny fraction of the population, the wealthy and healthy, could really enjoy a robust Third Age. Now leisure time has become democratized, giving millions of ordinary citizens more options than they had ever imagined (Laslett 1991). And since prior education remains a main determinant of demand for education in the later years (Snyder, Hoffman, and Geddes 1997), this combination of factors has generated a growing population of older learners.

Responding to meet this demand, community-based, nonprofit organizations as well as for-profit educators have supplemented traditional providers such as adult education programs at colleges and universities. Some of the new players that have come upon the U.S. scene in the last 20 to 30 years include Elderhostel, a travel-learning program offering those 50 and over one- or two-week-long residencies at educational centers in the United States and abroad and reaching about 300,000 annually; Institutes for Learning in Retirement (ILRs), largely run by participants who help to develop curricula, teach, and govern some 300 programs connected to college and universities, involving about 100,000 annually; a department store–based senior center–type program called OASIS (Older Adult Service and Information Systems) at some 30 shopping center locations across the country and serving approximately 300,000 annually; SeniorNet, a senior-user computer network with over 100 centers where courses on computer use are taught by members to members; and Shepherd's Centers, religious organization–sponsored, volunteer-run community service and education centers located at churches and synagogues (Manheimer, Snodgrass, and Moskow-McKenzie 1995).

In addition, there are 15,000 community-based senior centers supported by local municipalities, usually also receiving some federal and state funds that, in addition to social services and low-cost or free meals, offer a variety of recreational and educational programs. And in addition, there are 1,200 community colleges, many that attract older learners to free or low-fee programs in subjects ranging from crafts to foreign languages. Publicly funded American colleges and universities in many states offer tuition-free enrollment in regular college classes for those 62 or 65 and over on a space-available basis. Educational programs are also offered free or for a fee through college and university alumni organizations, hospitals, banks, investment companies, museums, labor organizations, recreation centers, and the Internet. There has also been a surge of outdoor education programs ranging from inexpensive hiking and biking clubs to businesses offering deluxe adventure trips to exotic places (Manheimer 1998).

Most of the organizations described offer nonformal or noncredit courses, seminars, workshops, and learning tours and depend on user fees to operate. Others, such as colleges and universities, also offer credit and degree-generating courses, though participation rates remain relatively low for people over 55 or 60. Workplace- or workforce-related education and training is offered by many companies and businesses, but, as we shall see, the private sector is slow to see the value of enhancing the skills of older workers. The most recent national survey of how and where senior adults participate in continued learning shows the largest growth in nonformal, community-based programs.

According to the National Household Education Surveys (NHES), during the 1990s, the percentage of people in the United States aged 66 to 74 who took at least one adult education class in the previous year more than doubled—from 8.4% in 1991 to 19.9% in 1999. The biggest growth in participation of individuals aged 55 to 74 was in community-provided, nonformal education. This includes not-for-credit courses, workshops, and seminars offered by churches, libraries, department stores, senior centers, and so on, where the rate went from 4.6% in 1991 to 11.6% in 1999. This compares to rates of 5.5% taking courses in a school or university in 1991 and 8.6% in 1999. The increase among the "young-old" surpassed that of any other age group.

Age-related role expectations still seem to be a defining factor for workplace educational participation. Participation rates for job-related education reveal modest increases compared to younger age groups. For example, between 1991 and 1999, the rate of those ages 48 to 56 participating in educational programs offered by business or industry rose from 12.6% to 19.6%, while for the age group 66 to 74, the rate rose from 2.0% to 4.8%. This reflects a continuing trend as business and industry prefer to invest their training dollars in the younger workforce.

Degree of prior education remains the chief predictor of educational participation for adults of all ages. But greater visibility of educational opportunities and a growing acceptance of the value of lifelong learning were also factors. In all likelihood this trend will continue as an even better educated American baby boom population enters the retirement period and since the average age of retirement in the United States holds fairly steady at about 63. However, another strong trend, a desire to return to the workforce after formal retirement in both full- and part-time second careers, may alter this pattern (AARP 1999). If the high percentage of today's baby boomers actually do seek postretirement careers, there should be a huge increased demand for continuing education.

Unprecedented participation rates of older adults in adult education confirm an overall pattern—emergence of a so-called lifelong learning society. It is estimated that almost half of the entire adult population in the United States participates in organized education in a given year (Belanger 1999; Belanger and Tuijnman 1997). With regard to older adults, the United States is in what might be called a "rehearsal stage." While the United States is certainly an "aging society" with a median age of 36 that will rise to 39 by the year 2010, it is the aging of the huge baby boomer population (born between 1946 and 1964) that will truly challenge cultural and educational institutions. Currently, those 65+ make up 13% of the U.S. population, and those 60+ comprise about 1%. The United States actually saw little growth in the percentage of its 65+ population during the 1990s because of the low birthrate for the cohort born during the era of the Great Depression of the 1930s and into the early part of the 1940s. But by the year 2020, those 65 and over will comprise 18% of the U.S. population, and that percentage will continue to rise until the 2050s (23%). The percentage of college-educated older adults will rise from the current 12% to 20% by 2010 and continue to rise dramatically thereafter (Manheimer 1994). Moreover, this rising percentage applies to a numerically vastly larger cohort.

In the current rehearsal stage, we have seen demand for education growing as education in the later years is viewed as valuable for everything from preparation for second or third careers, personal enrichment and psychological growth, prevention or delay in the onset of cognitive decline, and aiding in adjustment to life beyond or after work. In all likelihood, the demand for educational opportunities will overwhelm current providers in terms of both numbers and range of curricular diversity. People in every industry in the United States have been trying to predict what baby boomers will want in their role as consumers. And this is no less true for providers of lifelong learning opportunities. But thinking only in terms of consumers may be a big mistake. What is called for is new leadership and vision.

Currently, organizational leadership in older adult education is fragmented and decentralized in the United States. There is no organized group lobbying Congress or state governments for increased funding to educational programs primarily serving older adults. There are a number of national associations with subcommittees or affinity groups focused on older learners. For example, the American Society on Aging has its Lifetime Education and Renewal Network (LEARN), which is composed of about 250 individuals whose work (usually only in part) is associated with some form of older adult education. And the American Association of Higher Education has its division of Older Adult Education. The American Association for Gerontology in Higher Education (AGHE) focuses primarily on professional-level teaching of gerontology and only to a slight extent on education for seniors. Most individuals associated with the Institute for Learning in Retirement are also members of a consortium, the Elderhostel Institute Network (EIN), affiliated with the Elderhostel organization. EIN's main activities consist of biennial regional conferences and maintenance of an informative Web site. After 11 years, EIN is still struggling for survival.

Professionally speaking, older adult education has no real independent standing. As a field, it is a subject of peripheral concern to both aging and educational organizations. The field lacks monetary significance since it is not a major revenue source for institutions of higher education. Only a few nonprofit organizations, Elderhostel perhaps the most significant, derive their main income from offering services and programs to seniors. Education for seniors, however, is seen as an important marketing tool for investment companies, banks, hospitals, and cultural organizations, which regard it as a mechanism to attract potential clients, contributors, and members. In the sphere of higher education, affiliated ILR programs have proven to be an entrée to successfully solicit major donors.

Even in the area of research, where millions of dollars are spent on the causes of and potential remedies for cognitive decline as related to aging, hardly any research looks at the potential impact of older adult education on sustaining cognitive functioning. And little research involves applying what has been learned in cognitive science to better ways to educate or foster older adult learning.

Having presented this largely negative view, how can one argue that older adult education has a positive future?

The key lies in understanding the larger framework of an aging society and the growing ranks of members of the so-called Third Age. The modern phenomenon of retirement as an expanding segment of the life course has been shaped by private and public sector policies emerging in the middle to late part of the twentieth century. For the United States, these include government Social Security, private pension plans, public health care insurance, and federal anti-age discrimination laws. Meanwhile, social attitudes toward retirement continue to change. Major national studies show that 75% to 80% of today's baby boomers plan to extend their working years (AARP 2000) by engaging in postretirement employment. The majority of middle-aged adults regard later life not simply as a period for rest and relaxation but as a time for personal growth through acquiring new skills, exploring new leisure activities, and expanding involvement in current ones. Community service among older adults has been rising as seniors view volunteering as both a way to give back to society and as a mechanism for establishing new friendships to offset those lost when exiting the workforce.

The media further reflect these changes. Books about getting the most out of the retirement years are flooding bookstores, and articles on new roles for older adults fill the pages of magazines and newspapers. New books are appearing each year on the progressive role older people will play in improving the quality of life in society. And major popular films keep appearing showing older people as both socially redeemable and redeeming of those of younger generations.

Nor can one underestimate the antiaging, stay-young ethos so prevalent in the United States, where billions of dollars are spent on cosmetic surgery. Critics are probably correct that preoccupation with youthfulness may cloak a denial of the aging process and fear of death. But the quest to extend youthfulness may also involve the desire to stay socially engaged and connected to productive roles that garner social approval and produce self-esteem.

Given the positive respect for education in American society and for the long tradition of education serving as a mechanism for economic advancement, personal growth, and an indicator of social stature, older adult education should fare well in the coming years. However, the question remains: What are the characteristics of future successful programs, and will everyone benefit? Here are my predictions.

A rapidly growing pool of competent, college-educated adults will soon reach their retirement years. Even though many will choose to work part-time, they will also seek out continued learning opportunities. Many of these individuals will be attracted to educational organizations that allow them to play active roles by helping to shape curricula, teach by drawing on both their expertise and life experiences, organize courses, participate in governing the organization, and serve in a multitude of ways that satisfy their desire for a renewed sense of community. They will be prepared to pay sufficient fees and to volunteer their time to make these organizations financially viable.

Those educational organizations that can generate an image of creative or productive aging, either by being associated with institutions primarily serving younger generations such as colleges and universities or by linking to age-neutral organizations such as museums and cultural groups, will attract seniors who seek continued learning but who shun identification with being old, infirm, or needy. Opportunity to learn together with younger people through formal courses and informal exchange will be attractive to a subset of these older learners who prefer intergenerational and age-integrated experience.

Programs that offer hands-on experiences rather than passive, traditional classroom learning will attract the growing legions of experiential learners ranging from those seeking courses in the arts, environmental sciences, fitness, outdoor study, and adventure.

Flexible scheduling of learning opportunities including evening or weekend programs, and intensive short courses will appeal to those continuing to work full- or part-time and to those who want to mix education with myriad other activities such as travel, family involvement, and recreation. Education via the Internet and through computer user groups should continue to grow but will supplement, not replace, face-to-face learning experiences. Older learners will increasingly expect telecommunications to be utilized in their learning experiences.

Given continued rapid technological changes and a highly unstable and unpredictable global political situation, those educational organizations that can help learners assimilate new knowledge will enjoy increased participation rates.

Again, because older adult education does not fall into one academic discipline but overlaps several and is marginal to all, opportunities to prepare for professional careers in the field are lacking. There is a great need for curricula to help prepare planners, administrators, and educational facilitators of older adults that incorporates the latest research findings on cognitive and emotional development in midlife and old age. The pedagogy of older persons, sometimes called andragogy or "gerontagogy," needs to be infused into both adult education degree programs and social gerontology. Ensuring high-quality programs remains limited to counting enrollments rather than utilizing professional assessment techniques.

The downside of this optimistic picture of the future of older adult education is that it will leave many behind. Those privileged by earlier college education who can afford user fees and tuition will discover a wealth of opportunities, while those with lesser levels of prior formal education, who lack skills for accessing educational programs and/or cannot afford to pay for them, will have few resources to draw on. There have been few signs, even during the economically heady years of American affluence of the 1990s, that the federal or state governments plan to become major players in leveling the playing field. The era of government support to bring free or low-cost educational opportunities to working-class and underserved people (including minorities) is long past. Unless large advocacy organizations such as AARP start lobbying for an expanded role for lifelong learning that includes older adults, this situation is unlikely to change. The United States does not enjoy a long tradition of government-sponsored adult education programs such as is found in the Scandinavian countries.

Older adult education in the United States is such that it will take a wide range of private and public organizations to develop innovative programs for older learners and compete for their time, energy, and money. This ensures a wide diversity of programs, curricula, and delivery formats (e.g., in person, via the Internet) and lets participants "vote with their feet" as far as which programs succeed and which fail. Moreover, the American tradition of voluntary service supports an increasing number of senior adults to take leadership roles in older learner programs. In this sense, older adult education can be highly emancipatory and empowering. Too often government-designed and -managed educational programs, even innovative ones, become resistant to change and entrenched in bureaucracies that seek to perpetuate themselves, or funding priorities change and programs disappear overnight.

The negative side is that recruitment and access to these programs are limited to the well educated, well off, and well connected. There are few cultural and educational organizations that have the resources or ability to reach underserved populations. When they do, it is usually episodic and often based on the whims of outside funding sources such as private foundations and government agencies. Perhaps older adults who are themselves leaders and organizers of educational programs will take it upon themselves to develop outreach programs to the underserved. (See also ATTITUDES ABOUT RETIREMENT; FINANCIAL EDUCATION FOR SENIORS; LEISURE; LIFE PLANNING; VOLUNTEERING.)

### References

AARP. 1999. *Baby Boomers Envision Their Retirement.* An AARP Segmentation Analysis. Washington, DC: Author.

AARP. 2000. *A Profile of Older Americans: 2000.* Washington, DC: U.S. Department of Health and Human Services, Administration on Aging.

Belanger, P., ed. 1999. *The Silent Revolution of Adult Learning Societies: Who Participates in Adult Learning?* New York: Elsevier Science, Ltd.

Belanger, P., and Albert Tuijnman, eds. 1997. *New Patterns of Adult Learning: A Six-Country Comparative Study*. New York: Elsevier Science, Ltd.

Laslett, Peter. 1991. *A Fresh Map of Life: The Emergence of the Third Age*. Cambridge, MA: Harvard University Press.

Manheimer, R.J. 1994. "Life Enrichment Opportunities." Unpublished paper.

Manheimer, R.J. 1998. "The Promise and Politics of Older Adult Education." *Research on Aging* 20: 391–414.

Manheimer, Ronald J., Denis D. Snodgrass, and Diane Moskow-McKenzie. 1995. *Older Adult Education: A Guide to Research, Programs, and Policies*. Westport, CT: Greenwood Press.

Snyder, T.D., C.M. Hoffman, and C.M. Geddes. 1997. *Digest of Educational Statistics, 1997*. Washington, DC: U.S. Department of Education, National Center for Educational Statistics.

*Ronald J. Manheimer*

**ELDER LAW PRACTICE,** the legal practice of counseling and representing older persons or their representatives. It is the only area of law that is described by the clientele that is served rather than by the substantive area of law involved. Most clients are aged 55 and older. They range from the worker about to take early retirement to the older persons who are frail. The elder law attorney assists the senior citizen in a wide range of financial concerns, from basic estate planning to asset protection for long-term care.

### Health and Personal Care Planning

Elder law attorneys advise clients about, and help prepare, advance directives for health care. These documents are also known as medical powers of attorney, living wills, or health care declarations. All 50 states and the District of Columbia have laws permitting advance directives, based on the constitutional right to privacy. Through an advance directive a person sets forth his or her intentions regarding medical treatment in the last stages of life. An advance directive is usually accompanied by the appointment of a health care representative to act on behalf of the person. Elder law attorneys also counsel health care representatives and families about medical and life-sustaining choices. It is sometimes necessary to go to court to enforce an advance directive or to obtain an order to terminate life in the absence of an advance directive.

### Premortem Legal Planning and Fiduciary Representation

This area of elder law, commonly called estate planning, includes giving advice and preparing documents concerning wills; trusts; durable, general, or financial powers of attorney; charitable giving; and the financial and tax implications of proposed actions. The attorney's role is to assist in the development of a plan for distribution of a person's assets to plan for avoidance of federal and state taxes upon the transfer of assets, to avoid probate where appropriate, and to provide protective measures for the client that may be triggered upon disability.

Fiduciary representation includes seeking the appointment of, giving advice to, and representing persons serving as executor, personal representative, attorney-in-fact, trustee, guardian, conservator, representative payee, or other formal or informal fiduciary. An elder law attorney gives such legal advice as may be necessary to the fiduciary in performing his or her duties. Advance care planning for the appointment of and instruction to fiduciaries adds to flexibility and reduces costs in carrying out the wishes of the older person who may no longer be able to care for himself or herself. In the absence of a power of attorney, a guardian may have to be appointed to manage the affairs of an incompetent adult.

### Legal Capacity Counseling and Protective Arrangements

Unfortunately, some older persons become incompetent and incapable of understanding the nature and consequences of particular acts or decisions. The medical community has developed client capacity screens that can be helpful in identifying whether a person is competent to act. The legal community also has developed a number of tests or standards to determine what level of capacity is needed for various acts.

On occasion, a person may seek guardianship for a parent or other older person over that person's objection. If the older person is competent, it is inappropriate to appoint a guardian. Another concern is whether the person applying to be appointed guardian is best suited to act as such. A close living relative, for example, is not always the best choice to handle the affairs of the older person. The elder law attorney may be called upon to represent the person who is the subject of the guardianship proceeding or other family member. In the case of guardianship or conservatorship, an elder's financial resources should be protected.

### Public Benefits and Insurance Advice

One of the most dynamic areas of elder law involves devising plans for assisting older people in obtaining or dealing with Medicare, Medicaid, Social Security, Supplemental Security Income (SSI) benefits, veterans benefits, and food stamps. Perhaps the largest single area in public benefits advice for elder law attorneys involves protecting the family's assets in situations requiring long-term care.

The elder law attorney designs a plan that may involve the use of trusts, annuities, or transfers of assets within the framework of the Medicaid law that makes a nursing home patient eligible for benefits. Usually the family depletes some of its own assets prior to Medicaid eligibility, but the spouse remaining at home is able to save some assets, and assets can also be protected for children. Elder law attorneys also advocate for clients in obtaining Medicare benefits or assist in dealing with the administrative apparatus when problems arise.

Older adults have special needs relating to insurance that range from health and life insurance to long-term care, home care, Medicare supplemental insurance (Medigap), and long-term disability insurance. Clients often call upon elder law attorneys to analyze the various types of policies that are available and to make recommendations about what is needed and affordable.

### Resident Rights Advocacy

Patients and residents in hospitals, nursing facilities, continuing care retirement communities, assisted living facilities, adult day care facilities, and those cared for in their homes by others have certain rights. On occasion, the rights of the patient are ignored by the hospital or the nursing home. Problems may involve financial elder abuse, or range from the use of unlawful restraints to sexual abuse by members of a nursing home staff. Older persons entering continuing care retirement communities often require the assistance of an elder law attorney to review the contract and occasionally to resolve disputes that arise between the community and the resident. An elder law attorney may be called upon to interpret the contract and help enforce the rights of the resident.

Nursing homes and other elder facilities may become aggressive in attempting to discharge patients when the insurance available to pay for a patient's care expires. The elder law attorney enforces the rights of the patient to prevent unlawful discharge. The financial issue of who will pay—the patient, a public assistance program, or the institution—is typically the issue to resolve.

### Housing Counseling

Most older persons prefer to live in their own homes. Unfortunately, many do not have sufficient income to pay taxes, insurance, and maintenance and sustain a lifestyle that affords dignity. Elder law attorneys often are able to assist such clients in obtaining reverse annuity mortgages. Under a reverse mortgage, the homeowner receives a monthly check from the lender and can continue to live at home. The amount of the check is based on an appraisal of the property, the prevailing rate of interest, and the life expectancy of the borrower. The mortgage contract calls for repayment of the mortgage only when the borrower moves from the home or upon his or her death. The attorney must review the documents to be sure the homeowner is protected. A reverse mortgage holds the potential for helping the older person be financially independent.

Many communities have loan programs available to older homeowners for purposes of rehabilitating their homes. The programs often provide that after a certain period of years the loan is forgiven. Other programs do not forgive the loan but make funds available at a below-market rate of interest. An attorney can be helpful in assisting a client in obtaining such loans. Many communities have subsidized senior citizen housing available, which an elder law attorney can assist low-income older persons to obtain.

### Employment and Retirement Advice

At the time of retirement, questions arise about options relating to employee benefits, pension funds, retiree health benefits, and unemployment benefits. There are often substantial tax consequences and significant financial considerations involving the retiree and the retiree's spouse. An elder law attorney is in a position to advise retirees on the options available and how they will financially impact the retiree and spouse.

### Income, Estate, and Gift Tax Advice

A substantial amount of advice that elder law attorneys give their clients relates to passing assets from one generation to another. Federal estate tax, inheritance tax, and gift tax affect these transfers. Elder law attorneys develop plans for transferring assets in such a manner as to minimize or, if possible, eliminate transfer taxes. Proper income, estate, and gift tax advice can enable older persons to stretch their dollars to remain independent and pass assets on to future generations.

### Tort Claims against Nursing Homes

On occasion, patients in nursing homes are illegally restrained or neglected, or they fall or are injured in some other way. They may be subjected to mental, physical, sexual, or financial abuse by nursing home staff. These cases are difficult because often the only witness is the older person, and in some cases the capacity of the older person is diminished and his or her testimony may be suspect. Litigation can be successful in protecting the rights of nursing home patients and in gaining compensation for physical and mental injuries suffered. An elder law attorney is often able to represent the nursing home patient or family members in this regard. Tort claims against nursing homes may result in compensation or even punitive damages.

### Advocacy

Elder law attorneys advocate for their clients not only in the traditional judicial forums but also in the halls of state and federal legislatures and before state and federal regulatory agencies. As public entitlement programs are squeezed, the older and disabled are often affected adversely. Elder law attorneys and their allies in the aging community are often effective voices on behalf of those unable to help themselves.

### Discrimination in Employment and Housing

As American businesses downsize and restructure, the victims are often aging workers. In many cases early retirement programs are structured in such a way as to compensate older workers for the rights they are relinquishing. Those who accept early retirement packages usually sign a written waiver of any rights they have based on age. However, older persons may be discriminated against through early termination or failure to hire, based solely on age. There are a number of elder law attorneys who specialize in age discrimination cases.

Elder law is a relatively new area of law, and most people are not aware of it. The National Academy of Elder Law Attorneys was established in 1988. The organizations listed below can provide help in learning about and obtaining an elder law attorney. (See also ADVANCE DIRECTIVES; DURABLE POWER OF ATTORNEY; LIVING WILL; TITLING ASSETS; TRUSTS; WILLS.)

#### Organizations

AARP Legal Counsel for the Elderly
Commission on Legal Problems of the Elderly
National Academy of Elder Law Attorneys
National Senior Citizens Law Center

#### Suggested Reading

Regan, John J. 1989. *Your Legal Rights in Later Life*. Washington, DC: AARP.

#### References

Margolis, Harry S. 1995. *The Elder Law Portfolio Series*. Boston, MA: Little, Brown.

Mezzullo, Louis A., and Mark W. Wolpert. 1992. *Advising the Elderly Client*. New York: Clark, Boardman and Calaghan.

Regan, John J. 1982. *Tax, Estate and Financial Planning for the Elderly*. New York: Matthew Bender.

*Thomas D. Begley, Jr.*

**EMPLOYEE BENEFITS IN THE PUBLIC SECTOR,** benefits available to federal, state, and local government employees. In 2001, there were about 19 million government employees in all three groups. While these government workers have much in common

**Table 1**
**Numbers and Union Representation of Private and Public Sector Unions, 2001**

| | Total Employed | Represented by Unions |
|---|---|---|
| Private Wage and Salary Workers | 101,605,000 | 9.7% |
| Government Workers | 19,155,000 | 41.8% |
| Federal | 3,284,000 | 36.6% |
| State | 5,677,000 | 34.5% |
| Local | 10,195,000 | 47.5% |

*Source*: U.S. Bureau of Labor Statistics (BLS) 2002.

with private sector workers, there is one key characteristic in which they are very different: the degree of unionization. Higher union membership among federal employees has a pronounced effect on both traditional and nontraditional benefits. Table 1 shows the number of workers in the public and private sectors and the degree of unionization in each sector.

Because of the heavy degree of unionization, government employers are less able to reduce or drop current benefits and are reluctant to introduce new benefits programs. Thus, government benefits programs look much more like earlier private sector programs. A second general factor impacting public sector employee benefits is the degree of political activity by employee unions and individual employees. Legislators and officials depending on the votes of public sector employees for winning margins are reluctant to cut benefits levels for fear of being targeted by unions or other public activists.

The following description of public sector benefits is of necessity broad; exceptions will occur in many public jurisdictions. Five different benefit areas are considered: retirement and capital accumulation programs, income protection plans, medical and other health benefits, paid time off, and services and miscellaneous benefits.

## Retirement and Capital Accumulation Programs

There are three basic types of these programs, all designed to allow an employee and his or her spouse to live in relative comfort after they reach some retirement age. Mandated programs include Social Security. The second type of capital accumulation program includes organization-supported individual accumulation programs. The third program type is the company pension plan, whether a defined benefit plan (the traditional pension), a defined contribution plan such as a 401(k) or the equivalent public sector 403(b), or a hybrid plan such as a cash balance plan.

Social Security did not apply to federal employees until P.L. 98-21 was passed in 1983. This placed all federal employees hired after January 1, 1994, under the provisions of the Social Security Act and also prevented states from terminating Social Security coverage for state and local government employees if they were already covered. About one-fourth of state and local workers are still not covered by Social Security in the sample studied by Rajnes (2001). Thus, some state and local pension programs are the sole source (aside from personal savings) of retirement income for many public sector em-

**Table 2**
**Incidence of Income Protection Plans in Medium and Large Private Establishments, in State and Local Governments, and in the Federal Government**

| | Medium and Large Private Establishments | State and Local Governments | Federal (Civilian Workforce) |
|---|---|---|---|
| Life Insurance | 87% | 89% | 100% |
| Multiple of Earnings | 1.5 | 1.6 | ~ 1 |
| Flat Dollar Amount | $16,947 | $18,922 | Pay (rounded up to nearest $000) + $2,000 |
| Accidental Death and Dismemberment | 68% | 58% | 100% |
| Long-Term Disability Insurance | 43% | 34% | 100% |
| Survivor Income Coverage | 5% | 1% | Annuitant option |

*Sources*: BLS 1998; OPM 1997, 1998 data.

ployees, and this has had the effect of an upward bias on pension levels. Many provisions of the Employee Retirement Income Security Act (ERISA) do not apply to public sector retirement programs.

State and local government workers generally receive retirement benefits as well; 98% get retirement of one kind or another, with 90% getting defined benefit pensions and 14% participating in defined contribution plans. About 22% of all plans require no employee contribution. Using a much larger sample than Rajnes, the Bureau of Labor Statistics (BLS) found only 10% of employees are not covered by Social Security, and an additional 82% of employees have plans that are not integrated with Social Security.

### Income Protection Plans

Income protection programs are designed to protect the employee and his or her family in the event the employee becomes unable to work. They are typically mandated at some base level (if they exist at all), but organizations often supplement one or more of these programs. Typical income protection plans include workers' compensation, unemployment insurance, disability coverage, and life insurance. Table 2 shows the incidence of various income protection plans in the private sector, state and local governments, and the federal government. Data series are available online from the Bureau of Labor Statistics, and the data are from that source. Private sector data are from 1997; public sector data are from 1998. Federal civilian workforce data are from the Congressional Budget Office (1998) and the Office of Personnel Management's (OPM) Web site.

### Medical and Other Health Benefits

These programs cover the range of health care requirements of workers. Hospitalization and surgery/major medical are the two largest (and most expensive) categories of health

**Table 3**
**Incidence of Medical and Other Health Benefits in Medium and Large Private Establishments, in State and Local Governments, and in the Federal Government**

| | Medium and Large Private Establishments | State and Local Governments | Federal (Civilian Workforce) |
|---|---|---|---|
| Medical Care Benefits | 76% | 86% | 100% |
| Employee Premium Contribution Required | 80% | 75% | 100% |
| % in HMOs | 33% | 39% | n.a. |
| % in PPOs | 40% | 35% | n.a |
| Prescription Drug Coverage | 100% | 100% | 100% |
| Dental Care | 59% | 60% | 100% |
| Vision Care | 26% | 43% | Through HMO/PPO |
| Sickness/Accident Insurance | 55% | 20% | 100% |
| Drug Treatment | 97% | 99% | 100% |
| Alcohol Treatment | 96% | 99% | 100% |
| Wellness Programs | 36% | 35% | % unknown |

*Sources*: BLS; OPM; Congressional Budget Office (CBO) 1997, 1998 data.

benefits, although health maintenance organizations (HMOs), preferred provider organizations (PPOs), and other managed care solutions have been substituted for them. Other benefits in this category include long-term care insurance, prescription drug plans, and coverage for vision and hearing care.

Analyzing actuarially adjusted data from a sample of public and private sector employers, Long and Marquis (1999) concluded that public sector employees are more likely to be covered than private sector workers (79% to 60%), although this difference largely disappears for private sector employers of 500 or fewer employees. State and local government employers pay the highest share of premiums for single coverage, followed by private sector employers; the lowest share is paid by federal employers. Family coverage is just the opposite, with federal employers paying a higher share for dependent coverage than either private sector employers or state and local government employers, who pay about the same share.

A comparison of specific health benefits offered by private sector employers, state and local government employers, and the federal government is shown in Table 3.

Paid time-off programs vary widely across sectors. Traditionally, the largest paid time-off programs are vacation and holidays. Other categories are personal days, special-purpose days (jury duty, bereavement, military service, etc.), family leave, sabbaticals, rest and meal times, and community service leave. The value of paid time off is frequently ignored, since there are no out-of-pocket costs involved. However, if the average paid time off in an organization includes 3 weeks of vacation and 11 holidays, 10% of payroll (52 weeks × 5 days = 260 days work per year/26 paid days off) is devoted to

**Table 4**
**Incidence of Paid Time Off in Medium and Large Private Establishments, in State and Local Governments, and in the Federal Government**

| | Medium and Large Private Establishments | State and Local Governments | Federal (Civilian Workforce) |
|---|---|---|---|
| Vacation | 95% | 67% | 100% |
| Vacation days at 1 year | 9.6 | 12.6 | 13 |
| Vacation days at 5 years | 13.8 | 15.6 | n.a. |
| Vacation days at 10 years | 16.9 | 18.6 | n.a. |
| Vacation days at 20 years | 20.3 | 22.3 | 26 |
| Holidays | 89% | 73% | 100% |
| Number of paid holidays | 9.3 | 11.4 | 10 |
| Personal days | 20% | 38% | n.a. |
| Sick leave | 56% | 96% | 100% |
| Military leave | 47% | 76% | 100% |
| Jury duty | 87% | 95% | 100% |
| Funeral leave | 81% | 65% | 100% |

*Sources*: BLS; OPM 1997, 1998 data.

paid time off. Private sector data are from 1997; public sector data are from 1998. Federal civilian workforce data are from OPM's Web site.

### Paid Time Off

A comparison of paid time off as shown in Table 4 provides a mixed picture. Vacation and holiday time is more generous in the public sector when it is offered. Sick leave has a much higher incidence in the public sector. Other paid time off is generally more prevalent in the public sector but not for every type of leave. Federal paid time off is the most generous except for number of paid holidays.

### Services and Other Miscellaneous Benefits

A variety of miscellaneous benefits are given by organizations. These include Christmas and related bonuses, dependent care (both child and elder care), family leave programs, employee assistance programs, legal services, financial planning, property and liability insurance, paid or subsidized meals, discounts on products and services, parking, and gym and other health/recreation services.

Table 5 shows the incidence of selected miscellaneous benefits in the private sector, state and local governments, and the federal government. Data series are available online from the Bureau of Labor Statistics, and the data are from that source. Private sector

**Table 5**
**Incidence of Miscellaneous Benefits in Medium and Large Private Establishments, in State and Local Governments, and in the Federal Government**

| | Medium and Large Private Establishments | State and Local Governments | Federal (Civilian Workforce) |
|---|---|---|---|
| Child Care | 7% | 8% | Agencies may use appropriated funds to support childcare for low-income federal workers. |
| Job-Related Education | 67% | 63% | Agencies may support. |
| Non-Job-Related Education | 20% | 22% | No support, but agencies may make accommodating work schedule adjustments. |
| Employee Assistance Programs | 63% (1992) | 95% | 100% |

*Sources*: BLS; OPM 1997, 1998 data.

data are from 1997; public sector data are from 1998. Federal civilian workforce data are from OPM's Web site.

## Summary

The Congressional Budget Office (1998) estimates that the overall value of federal government employee benefits is well above that of typical private sector employees, and in selected age/service categories may be as high as 7.2%. Online data from the Bureau of Labor Statistics (Employer Cost for Employee Compensation) shows that state and local governments paid an average of $8.73 per employee per hour for benefits, compared to the private sector's cost of $5.63 per employee per hour. While some of this difference may be due to different demographic profiles in the two groups, it appears that public sector employees receive a higher level of benefits overall than do private sector employees. (See also ANNUITIES; EMPLOYEE BENEFITS IN THE UNITED STATES; RETIREMENT PLANS—403(b), SOCIAL SECURITY PROGRAM OF THE UNITED STATES; VETERANS' BENEFITS.)

## Organizations

American Federation of Government Employees
American Federation of State, County, and Municipal Employees
Council of State Governments
Employee Benefit Research Institute
Government Finance Officers Association
International Personnel Management Association
U.S Bureau of Labor Statistics
U.S. Office of Personnel Management

### Suggested Reading

Mitchell, Olivia, and Michael Hustead, eds. 2001. *Pensions in the Public Sector*. Philadelphia: University of Pennsylvania Press.

### References

Bureau of Labor Statistics. 1998. "National Compensation Survey—Benefits." Available online at http://www.bls.gov/ncs/ebs/home.htm.

Bureau of Labor Statistics. 2000. *Employee Benefits in State and Local Governments, 1998*. Washington, DC: Government Printing Office.

Bureau of Labor Statistics. 2002. "Union Members in 2002." Washington, DC. ftp://146.142.4.23/pub/news.release/union2.txt.

Congressional Budget Office. 1998. *CBO Memorandum: Comparing Federal Employee Benefits with Those in the Private Sector*. Washington, DC: Author.

Long, Stephen S., and M. Susan Marquis. 1999. "Comparing Employee Health Benefits in the Public and Private Sector, 1997." *Health Affairs* November–December: 183–93.

Office of Personnel Management (OPM). n.d. "Information for Federal Benefits Officers." Available online at http://www.opm.gov/asd/.

Rajnes, David. 2001. *State and Local Retirement Plans: Innovation and Renovation*. EBRI Issue Brief Number 235. Washington, DC: Employee Benefit Research Institute.

*Charles H. Fay*

**EMPLOYEE BENEFITS IN THE UNITED STATES,** benefits intended to promote financial security of employees by insuring against uncertain events and to raise living standards by providing targeted services. Employee benefit programs also add to economic stability by helping to secure the income and welfare of American families, which helps the economy as a whole.

The U.S. employee benefit system is a partnership among businesses, individuals, and the government. Most employment-based benefits, such as pensions and health insurance, are provided voluntarily by businesses. The government supports these voluntary employment-based benefits by granting them favorable tax treatment. Other benefits, including Social Security, unemployment insurance, workers' compensation, and family and medical leave, are mandatory. The government also supports individual financial security programs through individual retirement accounts, favorable taxation of life insurance contracts, and tax-free death benefits.

### A Brief History

Employee benefit programs have existed in the United States since colonial times. Early programs include the Plymouth Colony settlers' military retirement program in 1636; Gallatin Glassworks' profit sharing plan in 1797; American Express Company's private employer pension plan in 1875; Montgomery Ward's group health, life, and accident insurance program in 1910; and Baylor University Hospital's formalized prepaid group hospitalization plan in 1929. The federal government's involvement in the provision of such benefits further expanded coverage. In 1935, Congress mandated basic retirement income protection under the Social Security program; in 1956, it added income protection for disabled workers and their dependents; and in 1965, it added health insurance for older and disabled Americans under the Medicare program. Moreover, voluntary employment-based benefit programs became more prevalent as federal tax preferences for employee benefits coincided with rising tax rates, strengthening incentives to provide private benefits.

### The Role of Employee Benefits

Today's employment-based benefit programs represent a national commitment to provide some measure of income security and access to certain services (especially medical care) to active workers, displaced and disabled workers, retirees, and their families.

*Income Security.* A family's income security can be threatened if a wage earner dies or becomes disabled. Group life insurance and long-term disability insurance, often provided voluntarily by employers, can help to alleviate such unexpected financial losses. Employment-based pension and savings plans can also help to provide economic security for workers who look forward to a period of voluntary retirement in old age. Mandatory government programs also address the need for income security. The Social Security Old-Age, Survivors, and Disability Insurance (OASDI) program provides an income base, in the form of a lifetime annuity, to nearly all retired and disabled workers and their surviving spouses. Workers who become unemployed or disabled may qualify for temporary unemployment insurance or workers' compensation payments, respectively.

Nearly all Americans will benefit from one or more private and public income security programs during their lifetime. In February 2001, 74.3 million workers (67.8% of wage and salary workers) worked for an employer that sponsored a retirement plan. Of these 74.3 million workers, 90.7% participated in an employment-based retirement plan (Copeland 2001). In 2001, 34.9% of all older adult (age 65 and over) married couples and 34.8% of all unmarried older individuals had income from employment-based pensions according to Employee Benefit Research Institute (EBRI) estimates from the March 2002 Current Population Survey (Fronstin 2002).

Mandatory government programs provide nearly universal coverage. In 1999, the Social Security system covered 151.8 million employees and self-employed persons, and 44.6 million persons, including the older disabled and their dependents and survivors, were receiving benefits. An estimated 92.9% of older married couples and 93.0% of older unmarried individuals received income from Social Security in 2001 according to EBRI estimates of data from the March 2002 Current Population Survey (Fronstin 2002).

*Access to Important Services.* The U.S. employee benefit system also seeks to provide American workers and their families with access to certain vital services, especially medical care. Many American workers participate in group health insurance programs sponsored voluntarily by their employers or negotiated by employers and unions. Coverage may be limited to acute hospital care or may include such routine services as dental exams and physician visits. Often, an employee's dependents are covered. Of the civilian population under age 65, 65.6%, or 162.3 million persons, were covered by employment-based health insurance in 2001 (Fronstin 2002). Among workers age 18 to 64, 73.7% had employment-based coverage.

Some employers and unions make health insurance benefits available to retired employees. The Agency for Health Care Quality and Research reports that 12% of employing establishments in the United States provide access pre-65 and 11% access post-65 for retirees. The 44% of the workforce with employers of 500 or more employees are more likely to have access than those working for small firms. In 2001, 96.1% of the older population received health insurance coverage through the Medicare program. However, Medicare does not cover all medical services; for example, it does not cover maintenance prescription drugs.

Employee benefit programs are not limited to income security and health insurance. Specialized benefit programs help provide access to a wide range of important services, including ongoing education and training, child care, long-term care, and legal assistance. Other employee benefits, such as subsidized parking, product discounts, and relocation expense reimbursement, can provide convenience and cost savings for employees. Employee benefits also include paid sick leave, holidays, vacations, and maternity or paternity leave.

### Tax Treatment

The Federal Internal Revenue Code has provided tax incentives since 1921 for employment-based pension plans, since 1939 for compensation received for injuries or sickness, and since 1942 for health plans. The Social Security program, as initially enacted in 1935, provided retirement income to workers and their spouses; in 1956, the program was extended to provide income to disabled workers (their dependents were included in the program in 1958); and in 1965, the program was extended again to provide health insurance coverage to the older, disabled, and low-income individuals as Medicare and Medicaid.

The general tax treatment of employee benefit programs has remained relatively consistent over the years. Employer contributions to health insurance remain tax exempt to employees and tax deductible to employers; in addition, the benefits received under employment-based health plans are not treated as taxable income. Taxes on most retirement programs are deferred until benefit receipt. Other benefits, such as life insurance, dependent care, and educational assistance, are tax exempt up to specified dollar limits. Vacations and other time-off benefits, bonuses and awards, and severance pay are fully taxable.

### Meeting Changing Needs

Given such a wide range of options, compensation packages can be tailored to achieve employer and employee goals and can change in response to workers' needs and preferences. Demographic changes in the American workforce and general population have influenced, and are likely to continue influencing, the provision and design of employee benefit programs.

*An Aging Population.* One change in progress is the shift in the U.S. population's age distribution. Members of the large baby boom cohort (individuals born between 1946 and 1964) currently compose a disproportionately large part of the overall workforce, especially in new and fast-growing industries. As this cohort ages, and the smaller baby bust cohort (individuals born between 1965 and 1975) enters the labor force, the age distribution of the workforce will shift toward older workers, whose needs and preferences may differ from those of younger workers. As the baby boom cohort begins to retire, an increasing proportion of Americans will be older and living longer and will depend on sources other than employment for income and vital services. These forces will affect both income security and health care insurance programs.

Developments in the retirement plan market may in part represent a response to workforce changes. It has been well documented that, in the private sector, participation in defined contribution plans (which promise a specified contribution to an employee's account) is growing faster than participation in traditional defined benefit pension plans (which promise a specified benefit at retirement). The number of active participants in a defined benefit plan where the defined benefit plan was the primary plan declined slightly between 1975 and 1998 (from 27 million to 23 million), while the number of active participants in a defined contribution plan where the defined contribution plan was the primary plan grew during those years (from 4 million to 29 million) (U.S. Department of Labor 2002).

Defined contribution plans historically have offered faster vesting than defined benefit plans, and defined contribution lump-sum benefits are more portable than defined benefit plan deferred annuities. Thus, younger workers may anticipate future job changes and therefore place a higher value on faster vesting and benefit portability common to defined contribution plans. In addition, young families may be attracted to defined contribution plan provisions that allow access to money in the account prior to retirement in cases of financial hardship and on termination of employment (although preretirement and hardship withdrawals are generally subject to a 10% excise tax and regular income tax). However, as the baby boom cohort ages and the workforce becomes weighted more toward older workers, preferences may shift again toward defined benefit plans, which are generally characterized as providing more secure retirement protection than defined contribution plans for long-tenure employees working at the same company until retirement. Also, it is possible to save more money in the last several years before retirement in a defined benefit plan than in a defined contribution plan.

The effects of the aging population on retirement programs can already be seen in the Social Security Old-Age and Survivors Insurance (OASI) program. Partly as a result of increased life expectancies, past population shifts are reflected in a decrease in the ratio of OASI-covered workers to OASI beneficiaries from 16.5 in 1950 to 3.7 in 1970 to 3.9 in 2001. Under intermediate assumptions, the ratio of OASI workers to beneficiaries is expected to decrease to 2.5 in 2030 and to 2.1 in 2080 (U.S. Department of Social Security 2002). In response, taxes imposed on employers and employees to finance the pay-as-you-go OASI system were raised from 1.5% in 1950 to roughly 4.8% in 1983. The rates were revised again under the Social Security Amendments of 1983 and increased incrementally to 5.3% in 2002. Moreover, in anticipation of the baby boom's retirement, the retirement age will rise incrementally to age 67 for people born in 1960 or later.

Health care benefit programs are also affected by the aging of the population. The older generally require more health care than the working-age population. The effects of this trend on medical expenditures are exacerbated by the rapid pace of health care price inflation. Between 1982 and 2000, the price level of medical services and commodities rose 169.0%, compared with a 78.4% increase in consumer prices overall. Propelled by these factors, national health expenditures reached 13.2% of the U.S. gross domestic product in 2000, up from 5.1% in 1960. Between 1960 and 2001, employer spending for health insurance (excluding Medicare) increased an average of 11.8% per year, to $327.4 billion. In response to these developments, employers are taking steps to slow the growth of their health care costs. Increasingly, employers are requiring employees to share the cost of health insurance premiums and/or pay a larger portion of health costs out of pocket. It is hoped that cost sharing and other cost management measures will discourage unnecessary utilization of health care services.

The Medicare program, like OASI, has already been affected by demographic shifts and rapid health care inflation. The employer/employee tax rate for Medicare Hospital Insurance (HI) increased from 0.6% in 1970 on a maximum taxable amount of $7,800 of annual earnings to 1.45% in 2002, with no cap on the maximum amount of annual earnings subject to the tax. In anticipation of further cost increases, Congress changed Medicare's reimbursement system in 1983 to the prospective payment system (PPS) for inpatient hospital care and in 1989 to the resource-based relative value system (RBRVS) for outpatient physician services.

As the population ages, the proportion requiring nursing home care or other long-term care will increase. Currently, private insurance for such health care needs is not widely available, and federal financing for nursing home care is generally available only under the Medicaid program, with eligibility subject to stringent means tests. Many find this situation unacceptable, and pressure is building to make other provisions for financing long-term care, either through expanded provision of voluntary private insurance (perhaps through employers), through a mandatory government program, or both.

*Balancing Work and Family.* Family structure has changed radically from the days when it typically consisted of a father who was the sole wage earner, a mother who stayed at home, and two children. Today, both husband and wife often work, children are in day care, and there are many single-parent families. The increase in labor force participation by women, especially those with young children, has implications for employee benefits that cannot be overlooked. In 1980, 44.1% of married women with children under age 6 were in the labor force, compared with 70.5% in 2001 (U.S. Department of Commerce 2002). In 1998, out of a total of 68.4 million children, 29.0 million (42.3%) lived in a two-parent family in which both parents worked; 11.7 million (17.2%) lived in a two-parent family where one parent worked; 13.5 million (18.8%) lived in a one-parent family in which the parent worked; and 3.1 million (4.5%) lived in a one- or two-parent family in which the parent or parents were unemployed (U.S. Department of Commerce 2000).

These trends have led to public and private responses that attempt to help workers better balance work and family needs. Legislation has been enacted at the federal and state levels that requires employers to provide a minimum period of parental leave and promotes federal and more state involvement in child care access, affordability, and quality.

*Flexibility.* Another response to a changing workforce is the growing use of flexible benefit plans. Within such arrangements, employees are permitted choices among benefits and/or benefit levels. Employees thus may exchange benefits that they consider less valuable for others better suited to their needs. Employee benefit programs, whether public or private, that address these and other needs can enhance the economic security of individual workers and their families. The provision of benefits such as child care and parental leave can help smooth career progress, to the overall advantage of labor markets. Thus, these and other benefits can help families and employers reconcile the personal needs of the home with the economic needs of the workplace.

### Conclusion

Social Security provides a floor on income protection for those over the age of 62 who choose to retire. The average income replacement rate, however, is near 40%, with the rate being no more than 27% for the 12% of the workforce that earns over $89,000 per year. Unions and employers have sponsored voluntary retirement plans to aid individuals in supplementing Social Security. About 42% of retired Americans report such supplemental income today. Medicare pays for an average of half of health expenses for retirees. Those who have retired from large public and private employers have access to cost-effective supplemental health insurance, and others have access to Medigap policies to purchase. Active workers are most likely to have health insurance from their employer or union, and most workers lucky enough to have short-term disability protection and life insurance have it through employment. Many workers have a wide range of employee-pay-all benefits available to them at work. In short, mandatory programs provide a floor of protection, employment-based voluntary employee benefits add levels of protection, and individual savings and purchased insurance secure a level above what employers and unions provide. (See also DEFINED BENEFIT PENSION PLAN; DEFINED CONTRIBUTION PLAN; EMPLOYEE STOCK OWNERSHIP PLANS [ESOPs]; HEALTH BENEFITS; PENSION PLANS; RETIREMENT PLANS—401(k).)

#### References

Copeland, Craig. 2001. "Pension Participation: February 2001." *EBRI Notes* 22 (December): 12.

Employee Benefit Research Institute. 1994. *Retirement in the 21st Century . . . Ready or Not. . . .* Washington, DC: Author.

Employee Benefit Research Institute. 1997. *EBRI Databook on Employee Benefits.* 4th ed. Washington, DC: Author.

Fronstin, Paul. 2002. "Sources of Health Insurance and Characteristics of the Uninsured: Analysis of the March 2002 Current Population Survey." *EBRI Issue Brief,* no. 252 (December).

Rosenbloom, Jerry S., ed. 2001. *The Handbook of Employee Benefits: Design, Funding, and Administration.* 5th ed. New York: McGraw-Hill.

U.S. Department of Commerce. Bureau of the Census. 2000. *Statistical Abstract of the United States, 2000.* Washington, DC: GPO.

U.S. Department of Commerce. Bureau of the Census. 2002. *Statistical Abstract of the United States, 2001.* Washington, DC: GPO.

U.S. Department of Labor. 1996. *Employee Benefits in Small Private Establishments.* Washington, DC: GPO.

U.S. Department of Labor. 2000. *Employee Benefits in State and Local Governments, 1998.* Washington, DC: GPO.

U.S. Department of Labor. Bureau of Labor Statistics. 1999. *Employee Benefits in Medium and Large Private Establishments, 1997.* Washington, DC: GPO.

U.S. Department of Labor. Pension and Welfare Benefits Administration. 2002. *Private Pension Plan Bulletin. Abstract of 1998 Form 5500 Annual Reports.* Washington, DC: GPO.

U.S. Department of Social Security. 2002. *Annual Report of the Board of Trustees of the Federal Old-Age and Survivors Insurance and Disability Insurance Trust Funds.* Washington, DC: GPO.

Yakoboski, Paul, and Celia Silverman. 1994. "Baby Boomers in Retirement: What Are Their Prospects?" *EBRI Special Report SR-23/Issue Brief,* no. 151 (July).

*Dallas L. Salisbury*

**EMPLOYEE RETIREMENT INCOME SECURITY ACT (ERISA),** statute that federalized the law of employee benefits in the private sector. ERISA substantially modified the federal tax treatment of pension plans, introduced a federal fiduciary law of employee benefit plans, created federal jurisdiction for most employee benefits litigation, expanded disclosure and reporting requirements for employee benefit plans, preempted most state laws relating to employee benefits, vastly extended the scope of Department of Labor regulation of employee benefit plans, and created the Pension Benefit Guaranty Corporation, which insures pension benefits in most defined benefit pension plans.

Congress enacted ERISA in 1974 primarily as a response to grassroots pressure to provide greater federal protection of pension benefits. The statute covers not only pensions but all employee benefit plans. While the statute enhanced federal protection for pensions, it also pushed aside state law protection of employee benefit rights and (as interpreted by the federal courts) extended only limited remedial measures to aggrieved employees, leaving some employees with reduced, rather than increased, rights.

### Structure of ERISA

ERISA has four titles. Title I amended the labor laws of the United States. The title includes seven parts: (1) reporting and disclosure, (2) participation and vesting, (3) funding, (4) fiduciary responsibility, (5) administration and enforcement, (6) continuation of health coverage (often referred to as "COBRA," the name of the legislative act (Consolidated Omnibus Budget Reconciliation Act) adding these provisions to Title I); and (7) limitations on preexisting conditions in health plans for employees changing jobs (often referred to as "HIPPA," after the title's name, the "Health Insurance Portability and Accountability Act"). COBRA and HIPPA were added to ERISA by amendment in 1986 and 1996, respectively.

Title II of ERISA amended the Internal Revenue Code (IRC). Certain amendments to ERISA parallel provisions in Title I. For example, Title I and Title II include identical vesting requirements. But other provisions of Title II have no analogue in Title I. These latter requirements reflect tax policy goals rather than employee protection goals. Among these provisions are the rules in IRC Section 415, which restrict the size of contributions to defined contribution plans and benefits from defined benefit plans. The policy basis for this rule is that the tax benefits enjoyed by participants in pension plans should be limited to the creation of reasonable levels of retirement savings. The IRC and regulations also include complex rules requiring tax-qualified pension plans to cover reasonable levels of rank-and-file employees and prohibiting discrimination in favor of highly compensated employees. In addition, some provisions in the Internal Revenue Code provide penalty taxes for violations of provisions that are primarily enforced by the Department of Labor under Title I of ERISA.

There are important differences between Titles I and II. A participant in a pension plan may bring a civil action to enforce any of the rules in Title I of ERISA; actions to enforce Title II generally must be initiated by the Internal Revenue Service (IRS). A plan's failure to follow rules in Title II can lead to the plan's loss of tax benefits, imposition of penalty taxes, or both, depending on the particular rule and its sanctions; no such penalties generally attach to a plan's failure to comply with rules in Title I, although there are certain civil penalties in Title I, especially for certain violations of its fiduciary provisions.

Title III of ERISA includes miscellaneous provisions, statements of primary jurisdictional authority between the IRS and the Department of Labor, and the creation of a certification process for pension actuaries.

Title IV of ERISA establishes the Pension Benefit Guaranty Corporation and the defined benefit plan termination insurance program. There is a separate insurance program for single-employer and multiemployer defined benefit plans. Additionally, Title IV governs other aspects of defined benefit plan termination and, in 1980, was amended to impose "withdrawal liability" on employers who withdraw from underfunded multiemployer pension plans.

### ERISA's Vesting and Participation Rules

ERISA's most notable contribution to employee benefit protection was its establishment of minimum vesting standards for retirement benefits. It requires most plans to provide that employees obtain a nonforfeitable right to their benefit at least as quickly as would occur in either of two statutory standards. The first standard provides that employees must have a nonforfeitable right to 100% of their benefits after 5 years of service. The second standard provides that employees must have a nonforfeitable right to 20% of their benefits after 3 years, and then increasing by 20% per year, so that after the seventh year, employees will have a 100% interest in their benefits. The first standard is commonly referred to as "cliff vesting," the latter standard as "graded vesting." (Congress had originally included three alternative vesting standards in ERISA, including a 10-year cliff vesting standard and a 15-year graded vesting standard. In 1986, Congress eliminated another type of vesting, based on the sum of years, service, and age, and which was known as Rule of 45 Vesting. It also reduced the time periods for graded and cliff vesting.)

ERISA also has rules to prevent evasion of the vesting standards. Rules defining service and the accrued benefit to which the vesting rules apply are most important. ERISA also prohibits a plan from conditioning participation on more than one year of service or attaining an age greater than 21.

Title I of ERISA also includes a special rule that prohibits employers from discharging, disciplining, or discriminating against employees for exercising rights under the plan or the statute, or for the purpose of interfering with the attainment of any right to which such participant may become entitled under the plan. An employer violates the statute if it fires employees for the purpose of preventing them from vesting in their benefits. The vesting and participation rules appear in both Title I and Title II of ERISA.

### Fiduciary Standards

Title I of ERISA creates an elaborate set of fiduciary rules for most employee benefit plans. ERISA's legislative history indicates that Congress intended to adopt "principles of fiduciary conduct . . . from existing trust law, but with modifications appropriate for employee benefit plans." At the plan level, ERISA Section 403(a) requires that employee benefit plan assets be held in trust, with certain limited exceptions. Moreover, ERISA's substantive fiduciary provisions apply to all plans, even those not structured in trust form.

At the individual level, ERISA defines fiduciaries broadly as persons or entities who exercise discretionary authority or discretionary control over the management, administration, or disposition of plan assets, or render investment advice for a fee. The definition of fiduciary is broadly encompassing, and the courts and the Department of Labor have interpreted the term liberally. As noted, ERISA's legislative history indicates that its fiduciary section "in essence, codifies and makes applicable to . . . fiduciaries certain principles developed in the evolution of the law of trusts." ERISA effects this codification with two related sets of fiduciary standards, the first a series of general trust principles, the second a list of specifically proscribed activities.

The general trust principles provide that plan fiduciaries must discharge their duties solely in the interests of the plan's participants, act prudently, diversify plan investments, and act in accordance with plan instruments. The statute's legislative history indicates an expectation "that courts will interpret the prudent man rule and other fiduciary standards bearing in mind the special nature and purposes of employee benefit plans intended to be effectuated by the Act."

The second set of standards is a more particularized set of prohibitions against fiduciaries causing the plan to enter transactions with parties already related to the plan ("transactional prohibitions"), using plan assets for the fiduciary's own account, or acting on behalf of a party with respect to a transaction involving the plan. The transactional prohibitions are broad and explicit, proscribing dealings with "parties in interest," a term encompassing most individuals and entities with preexisting relations with the plan. ERISA includes statutory exemptions from the prohibited transaction rules and establishes a procedure in which the Department of Labor can create further exemptions administratively.

The Department of Labor, a plan fiduciary, or the participant may bring an action on behalf of a plan against a fiduciary who breaches its obligations under the statute. Moreover, the IRC imposes a tax on a party who has engaged in a prohibited transaction with a plan.

The federal courts, and to a lesser extent the Department of Labor, have been called on to interpret many aspects of ERISA's fiduciary laws. Three judicially developed areas are significant and warrant attention: the recognition of a settlor/fiduciary distinction; the applicability of ERISA fiduciary law to misrepresentations; and limitations on remedies for fiduciary violations.

*Settlor/Fiduciary Distinction.* ERISA's fiduciary law requires fiduciaries to act solely in the interest of the plan's participants. Many fiduciaries, however, are also the plan sponsor, who are responsible for amending, and terminating, the plan. This raises the question of whether an employer/fiduciary will violate ERISA's fiduciary rules by terminating a plan or amending its provisions in a way that advances the employer's own interests. Courts have resolved this question by recognizing that the fiduciary requirements apply only to employers when they are acting in a fiduciary, as opposed to a settlor, capacity. Decisions to amend a plan or terminate a plan are considered fiduciary functions. Thus, the Supreme Court, for example, held in *Hughes Aircraft Co. v. Jacobson*, 525 U.S. 432 (1999), that an employer's decision to amend a plan could not be attacked in litigation by plan participants as violating the fiduciary rules, even though the amendment advanced the employer's interests over the employees who had been contributing a portion of their compensation to the plan.

*Misrepresentations.* The Supreme Court, in *Varity Corp. v. Howe*, 516 U.S. 489 (1996), resolved an open question: whether a fiduciary's misrepresentations to a participant in an employee benefit plan violate ERISA. The fiduciary, who was also an employer, argued that making misrepresentations to an employee was not actionable because ERISA's fiduciary provisions were concerned only with actions that harm the plan itself—such as misuse of plan assets—and not with actions that harm individual participants. The fiduciary also argued that its misrepresentations were made in its capacity as employer and not as a fiduciary and thus not actionable for reasons analogous to the justification for the settlor/fiduciary doctrine (see above). The Supreme Court rejected both arguments and held that fiduciary misrepresentations could be actionable under ERISA, at least in certain circumstances.

*Remedies.* The Supreme Court has held that participants who sue fiduciaries for causing them individual harm (as opposed to harm to the plan itself) may obtain equitable but not legal relief. Because money damages is generally a form of legal rather than equitable relief, this holding has limited the ability of participants to fully remedy some breaches of fiduciary harm.

The basis for the Supreme Court's holding is that the section of ERISA authorizing a participant to bring a civil action to remedy individual harm limits relief to injunctive or other equitable relief. In the most recent of the cases on this subject, *Great-West Life and Annuity Co. v. Knudson*, 534 U.S. 204 (2002), the Supreme Court ruled that money damages would generally be considered "equitable relief" only if it involved the right to a specific item of identified property. In that case, the Supreme Court also reviews the history of its jurisprudence on this subject.

### Employee Civil Actions for Benefits and Other Relief

ERISA has by and large federalized jurisdiction over employee benefit claims. Section 502(a)(1) provides that a participant may bring action in federal court to recover benefits under the plan, to enforce rights under the plan, or to clarify future rights to benefits under the terms of the plan. Thus, a participant may bring an action to recover benefits under the plan. Courts, however, have generally refused to award punitive damages or damages to compensate employees for other injuries. Courts have also held that a plan's decision to deny benefits generally is entitled to deference from the courts (if the plan includes language indicating that such deference was intended by the plan's drafters), making it more difficult for employees to recover benefits arguably due them under plan language. A good discussion of this area of law can be found in Kathryn J. Kennedy's "Judicial Standard of Review in ERISA Benefit Claims Cases" (1991).

In addition to providing jurisdiction for benefit claims, ERISA also authorizes participants to bring civil actions against certain parties in other circumstances. Section 502(a)(2) of ERISA, for example, authorizes participants to bring civil actions against fiduciaries whose breaches cause damage to an employee benefit plan. Under this section, a court may order a fiduciary to pay a plan for losses that it suffered, to restore profits earned by the fiduciary using plan assets, and to provide other equitable and remedial relief. The Supreme Court has held that under this section relief must flow directly to the injured employee benefit plan; thus, individuals personally harmed by a fiduciary's behavior may not sue for relief under the section. The Supreme Court has also held that this section applies only to fiduciaries (as defined by ERISA) but does not apply to nonfiduciaries who assist a fiduciary in violating the statute.

Another section of ERISA, Section 502(a)(3), provides for equitable relief when any individual—including someone who is not a fiduciary—violates duties under ERISA. As already noted in this article, however, "equitable relief" includes monetary payments in only limited circumstances.

### ERISA Preemption

ERISA preempts state laws that relate, directly or indirectly, to employee benefit plans, with only a few exceptions. The scope of ERISA preemption is broad; courts have held that state law rights to punitive and extra-contractual damages are preempted; that state wrongful discharge law is preempted to the extent the discharge related to an employee benefit plan; that state law actions for misrepresentation are preempted when the misrepresentation involved a plan; that state law garnishment exemptions for employee plan benefits are preempted; and that a state law prohibiting a pension plan from offsetting benefits by a worker's compensation award is preempted.

There are exceptions to ERISA preemption, most notably state insurance law. Thus, a health benefit plan funded through an insurance policy is subject to state insurance law. ERISA has thereby encouraged employers to self-fund health plans in order to escape state regulation. In the area of health care plans, ERISA preemption has been especially problematic, since it has prevented states from attempting to enact health care reforms if they impose conditions or require certain conduct of private sector plans.

It should be said that the judicial approach to preemption has been undergoing an important transition. In the first two decades following ERISA's enactment, courts tended to interpret ERISA preemption literally and thus quite broadly. But a 1995 Supreme Court case signaled a possible change in future preemption cases. The case, *New York State Conference of Blue Cross and Blue Shield Plans v. Travelers Insurance Co.*, 514 U.S. 645 (1995), involved a New York State law that imposed a surcharge on hospital reimbursement served by commercial insurers. The plaintiffs in the case argued that this law imposed an indirect economic cost on employee health care plans, since it skewed the economics of choosing between Blue Cross or a commercial insurer. The Supreme Court, however, held that Congress almost certainly did not intend to invalidate most laws imposing indirect burdens on plans, even though it might be possible to construe the ERISA preemption broadly enough to catch such laws. The case has been regarded by some commentators as taking a more limited and commonsense approach to preemption than it had taken in earlier cases.

### Funding and Protection of Defined Benefits

ERISA has attempted to protect employee interests in defined benefit pension plans in two distinct ways. First, ERISA imposes minimum funding rules for pension plans. Employers who fail to fund in accordance with the rules are subject to excise taxes. The minimum funding rules, however, have been criticized as too lenient, particularly in allowing plans to base benefits on past service and then amortizing those liabilities over relatively lengthy periods of time.

Second, Title IV of ERISA established the Pension Benefit Guaranty Corporation (PBGC) to strengthen retirement security by guaranteeing some benefits for defined benefit plan participants. The PBGC insures that payment of a specified portion of promised benefits from private defined benefit plans will be paid to the participants regardless of the status of the sponsor or the level of funds in the pension plan. The PBGC is funded by premiums paid by private sponsors of defined benefit plans, but the agency has been the focus of attention because of potential program deficits and the exposure faced by the PBGC in underfunded plans. Other critics of the PBGC program have contended that the effect of requiring all sponsors to pay premiums, even those whose plans are adequately funded, has the effect of shifting wealth from healthy to unhealthy sectors of the economy. Since ERISA's enactment, the PBGC premium structure has been reformulated to add a component that varied with the amount of plan underfunding and is now partly based on the risk of termination with insufficient assets.

Title IV provides a special program for multiemployer plans that become insolvent. The multiemployer premiums are set lower than the premiums for other plans; the PBGC benefit guarantees are also generally lower than those applicable to other plans. In 1980, Title IV was amended to impose withdrawal liability on employers that cease contributing to an underfunded multiemployer plan. The withdrawal liability equals the withdrawing employer's share of the plan's unfunded vested benefit obligations.

### Reporting and Disclosure

Title I of ERISA imposes reporting requirements on employee benefit plans. In addition, Title II imposes reporting requirements on employee benefit plans, and Title IV imposes reporting requirements on defined benefit plans subject to the PBGC plan termination rules. Generally, a plan may satisfy the primary reporting requirements with a single form developed by the Department of Labor, the IRS, and the PBGC. Plans are generally required to prepare a summary annual report. There are also numerous specific reporting obligations imposed by the different ERISA titles.

Plan administrators and sponsors must make disclosure to participants in employee benefit plans. The most important disclosure requirement is that the plan sponsor or plan administrator must prepare a summary plan description and distribute it to plan participants. The summary plan description must be written in a manner that is comprehensible by a participant. On request, the plan must also provide participants with a benefits statement and certain other information. Failure to comply with a request for information within 30 days can lead to a penalty of up to $100 per day.

### Spousal Protections

Title I and Title II of ERISA require in certain retirement plans that married pension participants be paid their benefits in the form of a joint and survivor annuity, unless the participant's spouse consents to a different form of distribution. Additionally, retirement plans must provide a preretirement survivor annuity in most cases.

### COBRA

In 1985, Congress amended ERISA to provide that sponsors of employee health benefit plans must give former participants and their beneficiaries an opportunity to purchase continued coverage from the plan at the time their coverage under the plan would otherwise end because of death, divorce, termination of employment, loss of dependency status, or reduction of hours. The period of continuation is 36 months, except on termination of employment or reduction of hours, in which case the coverage period is 18 months.

### HIPPA

In 1996, Congress enacted the Health Insurance Portability and Accountability Act, which amended ERISA to provide new protections for participants in group health plans. The most important of HIPPA's provisions limits a group plan's ability to impose preexisting limitation conditions on a new enrollee. HIPPA defines preexisting condition as one to which medical advice, diagnosis, care, or treatment was recommended or received during the 6-month period prior to the individual's enrollment. A limitation on preexisting conditions may not generally last for more than 12 months after an individual's enrollment date (18 months for late enrollees), and even that period is generally reduced by the number of days of an individual's prior coverage under a group health plan in which he or she participated within 63 days of the new employment.

### Special Tax Provisions

The IRC includes a number of rules that reflect tax rather than employee protection concerns and thus have no analogue in Title I of ERISA. Among these provisions are limitations on benefits from defined benefit plans and on contributions to defined contribution plans; rules requiring that plans cover at least a minimum number of nonhighly compensated employees; rules that prohibit plans from discriminating against non–highly compensated employees; rules imposing excise taxes on certain preretirement distributions from retirement plans or excessive distributions from retirement plans; and rules that require pension plans to begin paying out benefits after employees attain age 70½.

### ERISA and Its Critics

Consumer groups have criticized ERISA as not adequately living up to its promise to enhance protection of employee benefits. Such groups argue that a hostile federal judiciary has distorted the statute to dilute employee protections intended by Congress. Among the specific complaints is the deferential standard courts generally use to review plan denials of employee benefits, the restrictive reading of ERISA's remedial provisions, and the broad reading of ERISA's preemption provisions to deprive employees of state law rights they enjoyed before passage in ERISA. In the area of health benefits, where the statute creates few federal rights but preempts most state law rights, employees often find themselves stripped of most rights. In one case, *McGann v. H and H Music Co.*, 946 F.2d 401, 408 (CAS 1991), an employer amended a health plan to cap benefits for AIDS at $5,000. ERISA preempted state law that would have made the cap illegal but provided no federal remedy for the employee.

The business community also is critical of ERISA, whose complexity and compliance costs dampen employer enthusiasm toward sponsorship of employee benefit plans. This is especially the case with ERISA's tax provisions, which have spawned hundreds of pages of detailed regulation that is often unfathomable except to highly trained experts.

ERISA's tax side has also spawned considerable debate. The Joint Committee on Taxation of Congress estimates that the government loses approximately $100 billion in tax revenue each year because of the favorable tax treatment of pension and profit sharing plans. The orthodox explanation for this tax expenditure—the largest in the federal budget—is that it will produce significant retirement savings for individuals who would not otherwise save adequately for retirement. The tax nondiscrimination rules, which require minimum levels of coverage for rank-and-file employees and benefits roughly proportional to pay, is the statutory vehicle to achieve this end. Yet critics have argued that the nondiscrimination rules are too malleable by plan sponsors who wish to skew benefits to affluent employees and do not result in satisfactory levels of coverage for other employees. Others, however, argue that the nondiscrimination rules are too complex as they now stand and thus discourage sponsors from adopting plans at all (see, e.g., Orszag and Stein 2001).

These disparate lines of criticism reflect a fundamental tension in ERISA: Government regulation is necessary to ensure that private law adequately delivers benefits, but too much regulation diminishes the willingness of employers to sponsor plans at all. If this tension is intractable, the next decades may find the nation moving toward either direct government provision of health and retirement benefits or, alternatively, the abandonment of the notion of providing benefits through regulated, tax-subsidized private plans. (See also DEFINED BENEFIT PENSION PLAN; DEFINED CONTRIBUTION PLAN; EARLY RETIREMENT INCENTIVE PLANS [ERIPs]; EMPLOYEE BENEFITS IN THE UNITED STATES; EMPLOYEE STOCK OWNERSHIP PLANS [ESOPs]; PENSION PLANS.)

### Organizations

Employee Benefit Research Institute
Pension Rights Center

### References

American Bar Association, Section of Business Law. 1994. *ERISA Basics: A Two-Part Primer on ERISA Issues: An ABA Satellite Seminar*. Chicago: American Bar Association.

Kennedy, Kathryn J. 1991. "Judicial Standard of Review in ERISA Benefit Claims Cases." *American University Law Review* 50: 1083.

Orszag, Peter, and Norman Stein. 2001. "Cross-Tested Defined Contribution Plans: A Response to Professor Zelinsky." *Buffalo Law Review* 49: 629.

Salisbury, Dallas L., and Nora Super Jones, eds. 1994. *Pension Funding and Taxation: Implications for Tomorrow*. Washington, DC: Employee Benefit Research Institute.

Stein, Norman. 1993. "ERISA and the Limits of Equity." *Law & Contemporary Problems* 56: 71.

U.S. Congress. Senate Committee on Labor and Human Resources. 1994. *Recent Court Decisions Affecting ERISA and Executive Annuities*. Washington, DC: GPO.

*Norman Stein*

**EMPLOYEE STOCK OWNERSHIP PLANS (ESOPs),** an employee benefit plan that is qualified for tax-favored treatment under Section 401(a) of the Internal Revenue Code of 1986, as amended (the "Code"). A plan is qualified under Section 401(a) of the Code if it complies with various participation, vesting, distribution, and other rules established by the Code to protect the interests of employees. An ESOP is a type of deferred compensation plan that invests primarily in stock of the corporation that sponsors the ESOP, as further described in Section 4975(e)(7) of the Code and the applicable regulations thereunder. An ESOP also must comply with various reporting and disclosure requirements and fiduciary responsibility rules of the Employee Retirement Income Security Act (ERISA) of 1974, as amended.

An ESOP is a "defined contribution plan" because the employer's contribution is defined and the employee's benefit is variable. Each participating employee's account is credited with a certain number of shares of company stock and/or cash or other assets over the period of his or her employment. Upon retirement, death, disability, or other termination of service (after partial or full vesting), the employee's account is distributed to him or her (or to his or her beneficiary) in shares of company stock, in cash or a combination of both. The actual dollar amount of the vested benefit to be distributed to the employee is determined by applying the current fair market value of the company stock in his or her account to the number of shares of company stock in such account. The employer also may distribute the employee's account balance in six substantially equal annual installments of company stock and/or cash, or a combination of both, over a five-year period, in which case the actual dollar amount of the vested benefit to be distributed to the employee will vary from year to year based upon the fair market value of company stock. Furthermore, the employer may decide to distribute an employee's vested account balance in one lump sum in the form of company stock, and then the employer or the ESOP trust may repurchase the company stock with a secured promissory note that is adequately secured, bears a reasonable rate of interest, and is payable over a five-year period of time. An employee's benefit, thus, is not defined—as with a defined benefit pension plan—but is dependent upon the fair market value of his company stock.

### What Do Employees Receive from an ESOP?

All assets (company stock and other investments) held by an ESOP trust are allocated each plan year to the accounts of all employee participants in the ESOP by a formula usually based on the proportion of an employee's salary to total covered payroll. The ESOP trust's assets are held in an ESOP trust established under a written trust agreement between the employer and the trustee(s) and administered by a board of trustees and/or administrative committee (consisting of employees and/or other individuals) responsible for protecting the interests of employees and their beneficiaries. The ESOP trust sometimes is administered by an institutional trustee.

An employee is not taxed on contributions to his or her ESOP account (or income earned in that account) until the employee's benefits are actually received. Even then, "rollovers" (into an individual retirement account [IRA], for example) or special averaging methods can defer or reduce the income tax consequences of distributions.

An ESOP, like most employee benefit plans, is generally designed to benefit employees who remain with the employer the longest and contribute most to the employer's success. Therefore, an employee's ownership interest in company stock and other assets held in the ESOP trust usually is based on the number of years of employment and amount of compensation. The employee's ownership interest in the ESOP is called his or her "vested benefit," and the provisions that determine the employee's vested benefit are called the "vesting schedule." Although there are various vesting schedules that may be used (extending for periods up to seven years), most are designed so that the longer the employee stays with the employer, the greater his or her vested benefit becomes.

If an employee terminates employment for any reason other than retirement, death, or disability, his or her vested benefit under the ESOP will be determined by referring to the vesting schedule. All company stock (and other assets) in which the employee does not have a vested benefit (because he or she has not worked long enough) will be treated as a forfeiture, which is allocated among the ESOP accounts of the remaining ESOP participants on the same basis as employer contributions. If an employee retires (e.g., at age 65), dies, or becomes totally and permanently disabled, he or she usually will be 100% vested in his or her entire ESOP account balances.

After an employee's participation in the ESOP ends, the employee (or beneficiary) is eligible to receive a distribution of the vested benefit. There are many permissible times and methods for making this distribution. For example, it may be made as soon as possible after an employee's termination of employment, or it may be deferred for a period of up to six years following the plan year in which the employee's employment terminates. Distribution of a former employee's vested benefit must, however, start in the plan year following retirement, total and permanent disability, or death. Distribution may be made in a lump sum or in installments over a period of up to five years (six installments). In a closely held company, distributions are usually made in the form of cash or in shares of company stock that may be sold back to the employer.

### How Does an ESOP Benefit Employers?

As a technique of corporate finance, the ESOP can be used to raise new equity capital, to refinance outstanding debt, or to acquire productive assets through leverage with third-party lenders. Because contributions to an ESOP trust are fully tax deductible (within certain limits), an employer can fund both the principal and the interest payments on an ESOP trust's debt service obligations with pretax dollars. Furthermore, an employer that implements an ESOP and combines the ESOP with a broad-based employee ownership culture will likely experience productivity and profitability improvements relative to similarly situated employers that do not do the same. Empirical evidence strongly supports this conclusion.

### Federal Income Tax Consequences of an ESOP for the Employer

Employer contributions to an ESOP trust are tax deductible within the limitations of the Code. An employer may contribute to an ESOP trust and deduct up to 25% of covered payroll for each taxable year (provided, however, that such contributions may be allocated to ESOP participants' accounts for the ESOP's corresponding plan year). If the ESOP trust has borrowed and is leveraged, the employer may increase contributions beyond the 25% level to the extent that the excess is used to pay the ESOP trust's interest expense (and the employer is a C corporation). Furthermore, reasonable cash dividends paid on company stock held by an ESOP trust are deductible if applied to the repayment of the ESOP trust's debt or if currently distributed in cash to ESOP participants. Under Section 415 of the Code, the annual additions that may be allocated to the account of an individual ESOP participant each plan year normally may not exceed the lesser of 100% of his or her covered compensation or $40,000 (for plan years beginning on or after January 1, 2002). The annual additions include employer contributions, any employee contributions, and certain forfeitures that are allocated to the employee's account, although contributions used to pay loan interest will usually not be considered annual additions (for C corporations and provided that not more than one-third of employer contributions are allocated to the accounts of highly compensated employees [as defined in Section 414(q) of the Code]).

In a C corporation ESOP, contributions to the ESOP that are used to pay the interest on the ESOP trust's loan from the corporation are fully tax deductible, and they are not included in the 25% contribution limit so long as not more than one-third of the contributions are allocated to the accounts of "highly compensated employees." In a C corporation, reasonable cash dividends on ESOP trust-held company stock also are deductible and not included in the 25% contribution limit if they are passed through directly to ESOP participants, are used to repay a leveraged ESOP trust's loan within the plan/fiscal year of deduction, or are reinvested in company stock at the direction of participants instead of being passed through to them.

In S corporations, distributions on ESOP trust-held company stock are not deductible and may be used to repay an ESOP trust's loan if they are paid on shares of company stock that have not been allocated to ESOP participants' accounts—provided, however, that there is an exception to this rule with respect to distributions of earnings from the company's accumulated adjustments account or accumulated earnings and profits. In no event, however, may distributions of earnings to an S corporation ESOP be passed through to ESOP participants. To the extent that such distributions of earnings are not or may not be used to repay an ESOP trust's loan, they may be used for ESOP distribution purposes.

Under current law, as enacted in 1997 for years beginning on or after January 1, 1998, S corporation ESOPs are exempt from the unrelated business income tax (UBIT); thus, if an ESOP trust owns all of an S corporation, no current tax is imposed on the corporation's income. (That income is eventually taxed because ESOP participants in S corporations are taxed on ESOP trust distributions, as are C corporation ESOP participants.) The Economic Growth and Tax Relief Reconciliation Act of 2001 (the "2001 Act"), which President George Bush signed into law on June 7, 2001, restricts the abuse of this provision by plans designed to benefit only a small number of employees, whether in a very small company or where a small number of employees try to set up an S corporation ESOP just for their own benefit while operating a larger company whose employees are not participants in the ESOP.

The ESOP community of not-for-profit organizations, companies, professionals, and consultants strongly supported the antiabuse S corporation restriction in the Act. In fact, the 2001 Act, which includes H.R. 10 and S. 742, the Portman-Cardin and Grassley-Baucus bills, is landmark legislation for ESOPs, and no prior legislation in U.S. history has been as positive for retirement plans governed by ERISA, including ESOPs. The 1984 and 1986 tax bills, under the guidance of former Senator Russell Long (the first and possibly the strongest-ever ESOP advocate in Congress) and the National Center for Employee Ownership's executive director Corey Rosen, among many others, included the most advantageous specific ESOP legislation ever passed. Those bills, however, included many cutbacks in retirement plan incentives for defined contribution plans in general.

The 2001 Act also includes the first expansion of an ESOP tax incentive for a C corporation (expansion of the deduction for reinvested dividends paid on company stock held by an ESOP trust) enacted by Congress in 15 years. The 2001 Act solidifies the legislative environment for S corporation ESOPs, will help ensure this significant tax incentive for ESOPs, and will make them attractive to a growing number of corporations. This legislation also makes funding defined contribution plans more flexible and attractive to employers and permits substantially more dollars to be added to rank-and-file employees' retirement plan accounts.

### Tax Benefits to Selling Shareholders

ESOPs provide a significant tax incentive for a shareholder of a closely held C corporation who plans to sell his or her company and retire. An ESOP trust provides a market for the stock of such a closely held company. Section 1042 of the Code provides a special tax incentive for certain sales of company stock to an ESOP trust, subject to satisfying a number of specific rules. Thus, a shareholder of a closely held C corporation may be able to sell company stock to an ESOP trust, reinvest the proceeds in other debt or equity securities of publicly traded or closely held domestic operating corporations, and defer taxation of any capital gain resulting from the sale. As a result, the retiring shareholder can derive substantial financial security and liquidity for purposes of retirement. Because the tax liability from the sale is merely deferred, however, the shareholder's subsequent sale of the securities purchased with the proceeds from the sale to the ESOP trust will trigger a recapture of the deferred tax. If such securities flow through an estate, the step-up in basis that occurs will help the shareholder and his or her heirs avoid the tax permanently.

The tax deferral has one downside that many selling shareholders focus on in that a subsequent sale of the replacement debt or equity securities will trigger the tax that had been deferred by the sale to the ESOP trust. To address this problem, an investment alternative has been developed and carefully refined in recent years—an innovative security known as an "ESOP Note."

ESOP Notes are publicly registered securities, issued by highly rated companies such as United Parcel Service, AIG, DuPont, and General Electric Capital Corporation. Morgan Stanley Dean Witter, PaineWebber, Merrill Lynch, Wachovia Securities, and other investment advisory firms have helped bring to market a number of similar securities in recent years. These ESOP Notes often have a maturity of 40 to 60 or more years and bear a floating-rate coupon indexed to 30-day commercial paper, LIBOR, or some other floating-rate index. These securities also normally have call protection for 30 to 50 years. ESOP Notes can be margined (without recourse) up to 90% or more of their market value, if properly structured, allowing investors access to a substantial portion of their initial sale proceeds to create an actively managed portfolio without triggering any tax liability on the part of the selling shareholder. The borrowing cost is usually the broker call loan rate (or, in recent years, a much better negotiated rate with institutional lenders such as Bankers Trust) plus a spread (in larger transactions, 50 basis points or lower), which is greatly offset by the income earned on the ESOP Notes. There are a number of traps for selling shareholders who do not properly structure their reinvestments in these securities, so caution and due diligence are warranted.

### Voting Rights

In a closely held corporation, unless otherwise determined by the board of directors, employees have voting rights on allocated shares of company stock only with respect to certain major corporate issues, such as merger, certain sales or liquidation of the corporation, and recapitalizations that require the vote of the corporation's shareholders. On other matters, shares of company stock held by the ESOP trust are usually voted in the best interests of the ESOP's participants by the ESOP's board of trustees or administrative committee that has been appointed by the corporation's board of directors to administer the ESOP. Furthermore, unallocated shares of company stock and uninstructed shares of company stock (allocated shares for which the board of trustees or administrative committee do not receive instructions) are normally voted by the ESOP's board of trustees or administrative committee.

### Diversification

Unlike other qualified retirement plans, which typically diversify their holdings by investing in various assets, an ESOP trust, by law, must invest primarily in the company stock of the corporation that sponsors the ESOP. Because ESOP trusts must invest in the company stock of such a corporation, there is a higher risk for the employee. Nonetheless, employees approaching retirement age qualify for a limited exception, which permits diversification of their ESOP accounts. Participants who are at least age 55 and have completed at least 10 years of participation in the ESOP (in which they have received allocations in each of 10 plan years) are eligible to make annual elections over a period of 5 years to diversify 25% of their ESOP stock account balance (on an aggregate basis) and at the end of the sixth year to make a final election to diversify up to 50% (again, on an aggregate basis). This does not apply, however, to certain "de minimis" amounts in participants' ESOP accounts.

To meet the diversification requirement, the ESOP must offer at least three investment options other than company stock. Alternatively, the ESOP may satisfy the diversification requirement by distributing to the participant the portion of the account balance that the participant elected to diversify or by allowing a transfer to another plan.

The diversification rules are applicable only with respect to stock acquired by the ESOP trust after December 31, 1986. The ESOP may permit diversification of company stock acquired before that date and may permit diversification of a greater percentage of the participant's ESOP account balance.

### Intangible Benefits of an ESOP

For the retiring employee or the selling shareholder, the financial and tax benefits may not be the only important aspects of an ESOP. The retiring employee may derive great satisfaction from receiving evidence (in the form of monetary rewards) of ownership in a company that he or she helped build. The selling shareholder may feel more at ease by placing company stock in the "friendlier" and certainly more familiar hands of the employees. These intangible elements may prove to be as rewarding to the retiring employee and/or selling shareholder as the financial security ESOPs may provide. (See also ASSET ALLOCATION AFTER RETIREMENT; EMPLOYEE RETIREMENT INCOME SECURITY ACT [ERISA]; EQUITY SECURITIES; INFLUENCES ON RETIREMENT INVESTMENT DECISIONS; PROFIT SHARING PLANS.)

#### Organizations

ESOP Association
National Center for Employee Ownership

#### References

Howitt, Idelle A. 2001. *Employee Stock Ownership Plan Answer Book.* New York: Aspen Publishers.

Little, Kenneth E. 2000. *Ten Minute Guide: Employee Stock Option Purchase Plans (10 Minute Guides)*. Indianapolis, IN: Macmillan USA.

National Center for Employee Ownership. 1993. *How Small Is Too Small for an ESOP?* Oakland, CA: Author.

National Center for Employee Ownership. 1994. *Employee Ownership Fact Sheet*. Oakland, CA: Author.

Rodrick, Scott, ed. 1999. *Employee Stock Ownership Plans: A Practical Guide to ESOPs and Other Broad Ownership Programs: 2000 Edition*. Orlando, FL: Harcourt Brace.

Rosen, Corey, and Michael Quarrey. 1987. "How Well Is Employee Ownership Working?" *Harvard Business Review* (September–October).

*David R. Johanson*

**EMPLOYER-SPONSORED LONG-TERM CARE INSURANCE,** insurance provided as an employee benefit to cover the potentially catastrophic financial impact of an illness or period of frailty where long-term care is required. The market for long-term care insurance exploded during the 1990s and has continued to grow throughout the early portion of the twenty-first century. This market has two key segments: one for individual policies and the other for employer-sponsored and other group products. Sales of employer-sponsored long-term care policies generated premiums of nearly $55 million in the year 2001 according to LIMRA International, while in-force premiums collected posted an increase of 16% (LIMRA International 2002). The number of new employer-sponsored groups grew 10% in the same year, while the average size of these groups declined from 168 participants in 2000 to 147 in 2001, indicating a move toward offering long-term care insurance in the small employer market.

What factors account for growing interest in the employer-sponsored long-term care insurance market? Legislative changes such as the passage of the Health Insurance Portability and Accountability Act (HIPAA) of 1996, which defined tax-qualified long-term care policies, and the Federal Long-Term Care Security Act of 2000, which initiated the sponsorship of long-term care benefits for federal employees, the military, and their families, created market opportunities for employer-sponsored products. Growing awareness of the aging of the U.S. population, as well as increasing numbers of employees with eldercare responsibilities, has also elevated awareness, understanding, and interest in insurance products that could alleviate their financial pressures and facilitate payment for quality long-term care services. A MetLife study found that caregiving by employees impacts employers' bottom line: Informal caregiving costs U.S. employers between $11.4 billion and $29 billion a year due to lowered productivity (MetLife 2001).

Group long-term care insurance has evolved from its early form as nursing home insurance into current policies capable of meeting a variety of consumers' needs. Policies can be explained in terms of eligibility, plan design, and administrative components. Active employees and their spouses, parents and parents-in-law, and retirees and their spouses typically are eligible for coverage; some groups like the federal government plan extend benefits to adult children of employees. Most group long-term care insurance is offered on a voluntary, employee-pay-all basis and is fully portable, and the majority of policies are HIPAA tax qualified, paid through payroll deduction. A key aspect of today's product is that in most plans actively-at-work employees can enroll without medical underwriting, that is, on a guaranteed issue basis, during their initial eligibility period (either when the plan is first offered or as they are newly hired). Family members may be subject to medical exams, although spouses of active employees may go through a simple interview to determine that they have no immediate long-term care needs. Waiting periods for benefits, or an elimination period, are typical and can range from 30 to 180 days.

An employee is typically presented with one of two types of long-term care policies by their employer: one that is a reimbursement model (pays for services covered in the policy after they are delivered) or an integrated policy with "pooled benefits" (policyholders can use the dollars paid for any type of long-term care service that they feel is appropriate). Policies are subject to satisfaction of benefit triggers, which are usually two or three out of five limitations in "activities of daily living" (limits in ability to bathe, dress, transfer, toilet, and eat) or the presence of cognitive deficits such as Alzheimer's or related dementia. Today's policies offer a rich array of benefits coverage for nursing home services, home care (both skilled and custodial), and nursing home alternatives such as assisted living, board and care homes, and adult day care centers. Some plans cover respite and hospice care, and many offer an alternate care benefit, which is designed to provide reimbursement for services of providers not covered by the policy when it may be required by the consumer. Other common benefits are case management services, homemaker or chore services, bed reservation reimbursements, durable medical equipment coverage, home-delivered meals, spousal discounts, survivorship benefits, restoration of benefits, and caregiver training. The range of benefits offered depends on the plan desired by the employer, as well as the needs of the employee population (McSweeney 2002). Benefits may also be supplemented by certain consumer protection benefits, such as inflation protection (adjusts benefits by a fixed percentage in any given year) or nonforfeiture options (employees receive a certain portion of premiums back if they decide to terminate the policy). Other policy models coordinate long-term care insurance with other benefits, such as life insurance or long-term disability coverage. Premium or rate guarantees to protect employees from future increases may also be negotiated by employers for these policies (McSweeney 2002).

Who purchases employer-sponsored long-term care insurance? According to surveys by the Health Insurance Association of America, the average purchaser is age 43, well educated, has more income, plans for the future, and chose to participate in the plan because of employer sponsorship. A survey of 93 large employers conducted by the Lewin Group found that employees enroll in long-term care plans when education and communication about the benefit is clear and when senior management is actively involved in the process (Lutzky, Corea, and Alecxih 2000).

What is the future outlook for employer-sponsored long-term care insurance? According to the 2001 *MetLife Study of Employee Benefit Trends*, 90% of employers surveyed will be introducing a wide array of new work/life benefits, and long-term care insurance is the fastest growing offering in the near term, with 12% of employers expected to add this option within the next 18 months (MetLife 2001). Senior management "championship" of the benefit and comprehensive preenrollment education campaign on the value of long-term care insurance are also key indicators for a successful plan enrollment. While long-term care insurance cannot be offered as part of a flexible benefits program in the workplace, passage of pending legislation in Washington as well as state initiatives to offer tax credits and ultimately full deductibility of long-term care premiums for the consumer will open the market considerably for this employer benefit. (See also EMPLOYEE BENEFITS IN THE UNITED STATES; FRAILTY PLANNING; HEALTH BENEFITS; LIFE PLANNING; LONG-TERM CARE INSURANCE: INDIVIDUAL DISABILITY-ESCALATING ANNUITIES [IDEAs]; LONG-TERM CARE INSURANCE, PRIVATE.)

#### Suggested Reading

Gajda, Anthony, and Morris Snow. 2001. "Long-Term Care." In *Handbook of Employee Benefits*, ed. Jerry S. Rosenbloom. 5th ed. New York: McGraw-Hill.

#### References

Coronel, Susan. 2001. "LTC Insurance in the Workplace: A Study of Why Employers Choose to Enroll or Not to Enroll in Long-Term Care Plans." Presentation at the 15th Private LTCI Conference, Miami, FL, August.

LIMRA International. 2002. "U.S. Group Long-Term Care Insurance: 2001 Sales and In-Force." Windsor, CT: LIMRA International, June.

Lutzky, Steven, John Corea, and Lisa Alecxih. 2000. *A Survey of Employers Offering Group Long-Term Care Insurance to Their Employees*. Falls Church, VA: Lewin Group.

McSweeney, Mary Helen. 2002. *Long-Term Care: An Emerging Employer Benefit*. Scottsdale, AZ: WorldatWork.

MetLife. 2001. *2001 MetLife Study of Employee Benefit Trends*. New York: MetLife.

Stucki, Barbara. 2001. "LTC Insurance at Work: The Role of Retirement Planning." Presentation at the 15th Private LTCI Conference, Miami, FL, August.

*Mary Helen McSweeney*

**ENTREPRENEURSHIP,** the initiation and assumption of the financial risks of a business and its management. The decision to start a business is often complex. Many factors, including the need for achievement, the need for control over one's destiny, the willingness to take risks, the loss of one's job, and other forms of displacement may prompt a person to start his or her own business. While some writers see no link between age and the decision to start a new business, others have found close links. When age is a significant factor, it is often for psychological reasons.

Entrepreneurial opportunities are most likely to be pursued by people with a college education who are in their late thirties and have established careers. Age is relevant to entrepreneurship, and entrepreneurship is important for the aged. Of those who are employed at age 65 or older, 27% are self-employed (Maddox et al. 1985). It is useful to examine the relationship between entrepreneurship and aging through the internal or psychological aspects of a person's decision to become an entrepreneur.

### The Entrepreneur and Hero Compared

Joseph Campbell believed that the entrepreneur was the real hero in our society. Although he never systematically compared the entrepreneur and the hero, it is interesting to do so. Heroes and entrepreneurs are called to take part in an adventure that is a simultaneous journey of self-discovery, spiritual growth, and the personal creativity they make possible. An entrepreneur's journey closely resembles the journey of the hero in mythology as outlined in Campbell's book *The Hero with a Thousand Faces* (1968). There is a strong similarity between the journey that entrepreneurs take and the adventure of heroes. Entrepreneurs and heroes also have similar personality traits. Myths describe the universal human desires and conflicts we see played out in the lives of entrepreneurs. Ian MacMillan and Rita Gunther McGrath (*Wall Street Journal* 1992) of the Wharton School's entrepreneurial center found that entrepreneurs, no matter what country they call home, think alike. Campbell found that the basic pattern in the hero's journey is the same in every culture.

Heroes bring change. Campbell (1968) refers to the constant change in the universe as "The Cosmogonic Cycle" that "unrolls the great vision of the creation and destruction of the world which is vouchsafed as revelation to the successful hero." This recalls Joseph Schumpeter's theory of entrepreneurship as creative destruction. A successful entrepreneur simultaneously destroys and creates a new world, a new way of life. Henry Ford destroyed the horse and buggy age while creating the world of the automobile. Campbell's hero finds that the world "suffers from a symbolical deficiency" and "appears on the scene in various forms according to the changing needs of the race." Changing needs and deficiencies correspond to the changing market conditions or the changing desires for products. The entrepreneur is the first person to perceive changing needs. Campbell believed that people become creative when they engage in an activity, pursue a career or entrepreneurial venture, because it is what one loves to do and because it bestows on one a sense of personal importance and fulfillment. It is not the social system that dictates that it be done; rather, the drive comes from within. It is this courageous action that opens up doors and creative possibilities that did not previously exist.

### Relationship of the Hero's Journey to Aging

The hero's goal is now to find a purpose in life. Campbell's and Erik Erikson's (1963) heroes are similar, because the hero's journey is a quest for personal identity that can be found in service to others or to society, or in finding and delivering a boon. During the generativity versus stagnation stage, which comes in the second half of life, in Erikson's eight ages of man, people become willing to take risks in order to be creative or make their mark upon society. Generativity involves establishing and guiding the next generation, but it also includes productivity and creativity, which, along with the willingness to take risks, are essential to entrepreneurship. For Campbell, the act of creating involves the willingness to take a risk and cross a boundary into a new domain of ideas. To be unwilling or afraid to do so is to be controlled by what he calls "the elder psychology" or the unwillingness to strike out on one's own and take risks.

The paradox, then, is that although entrepreneurship may be an important path for people to discover themselves and "do something meaningful for society" as they become older, they must resist this "elder psychology," which Campbell believes blocks risk taking, creativity, and entrepreneurship. When a person is able to champion things becoming, he or she can achieve generativity by making a significant and unique contribution to society. If one is able only to maintain the status quo, he or she will stagnate and will remain self-centered and unable to contribute to society. Almost by definition, entrepreneurs are champions of things becoming.

In counseling and advising older adults in the area of entrepreneurial activity, it is useful to keep these insights from mythology and psychology in mind. They deal with the deepest of needs and forces in the human psyche. For an older person contemplating a new business venture, it will be helpful to recognize that it is not just the potential financial gains or losses involved that are important. The entrepreneurial act may be a life-defining and self-defining act, one with deep personal and perhaps even spiritual implications for the individual and his or her relationship with society. Entrepreneurs are often seen as having different attitudes toward risk: What a nonentrepreneur might view as a great financial risk the entrepreneur may see as a cost of learning and adventuring. The venture is an end in itself, more than the profit. People who start new businesses in the second half of life may view risk in this way, because they feel such a strong need to define themselves and contribute to society. The formation of a viable new business may be one of the finest legacies that anyone can create.

The American growth miracle of the 1990s was largely propelled by entrepreneurs and small business. Even with record growth and stock markets, Fortune 500 companies were largely laying off workers during this time, with small business employment needs sharply surpassing the layoffs. Countries around the world such as Germany and Korea went scrambling for ways to emulate this growth and to find fertile ways to foster entrepreneurship for their own economies. Often, this required a radical change from a dependency on industry and its supporting banks, tax structure, and university education to a concerted search by these institutions to find new ways to nurture young businesses and the technologies upon which they seemed to thrive.

In addition to impressive resources in business and entrepreneurship in printed form at your library or from resources such as common-line bookstores, the Internet has become an impressive resource for starting and building a business. Local community colleges and economic development agencies also will often provide free or low-cost courses on forming a business. (See also BABY BOOMERS AND RETIREMENT; BUSINESS SUCCESSION PLANNING; CONSULTING IN RETIREMENT; GROWTH CAPITAL FOR OLDER ENTREPRENEURS; RISK TOLERANCE; WORKING RETIREES.)

### References

Campbell, Joseph. 1968. *The Hero with a Thousand Faces*. Princeton, NJ: Princeton University Press.

Erikson, Erik H. 1963. *Childhood and Society*. New York: W.W. Norton.

Ettenberg, Elliott. 2002. *The Next Economy*. New York: McGraw-Hill.

Jung, Carl G. 1956. *Symbols of Transformation*. New York: Harper Torchbooks/Bollingen Library.

Maddox, George L. et al. 1985. *The Encyclopedia of Aging*. New York: Springer.

Nesheim, John L. 2000. *New High Tech Companies*. New York: Free Press.

Rae, David. 2000. *The Entrepreneurial Spirit: Learning to Unlock Value*. New York: Silver Lake Publishing.

Ries, Al. 1996. *Focus*. New York: Harper Business.

Slywotzky, Adrian J. 1996. *Value Migration*. Boston, MA: Harvard Business School Press.

Smith, Richard L., and Janet Kiholm Smith. 2000. *Entrepreneurial Finance*. New York: John Wiley and Sons.

Vinturella, John B. 1998. *Entrepreneur's Fieldbook*. New York: Prentice Hall.

*Wall Street Journal*. 1992. February 6, A1.

*Cyril Morong*
*Updated by Ronald Peterson*

**EQUITY SECURITIES** represent shares (stock ownership) in a corporation or in certain designated assets of a corporation or other entity. Shares in investment companies (mutual fund shares) are also broadly referred to as equity securities or equity funds when the investment objectives are to own and hold stocks. Two types of equity securities represent ownership in corporations: preferred stock and common stock. The key distinction between these types of stock ownership is the manner and form in which each class of shareholder participates in corporate earnings.

One advantage of these corporate forms of ownership is that shareholders have limited liability from transactions gone wrong in a corporation. Unlike other forms of business ownership such as sole proprietorships or general partnerships, corporate shareholders are shielded from exposure to loss in the event that firms cannot meet financial or other obligations. In unincorporated businesses, owners may be held personally responsible for payment of unsatisfied claims, for example, and creditors may file claims against owners' personal assets: houses, cars, bank accounts. This is not the case for corporate shareholders. While they can experience a complete loss of their investment, corporate shareholders are protected from further personal liability beyond the value of their investment in the stock.

## Common Stock

Unlike general partners in a partnership or an owner in a sole proprietorship, stockholders have little or no control over management decisions affecting the corporation or whether and when they will be paid a return on their investment in the company. Shareholders, in sufficient numbers, elect a board of directors to manage the company for them and through the exercise of voting rights affect management's policy decisions. Elections for board of director positions and amendments to corporate charters are typically done at annual shareholders meetings. Although some shareholders choose to vote in person, most shareholders prefer to vote by proxy. A proxy is a power of attorney appointing a specific agent for the specific purpose of voting at the annual meeting.

Shareholders have a preemptive right to purchase new shares of company stock before they are offered for sale to the general public. If a shareholder currently owns 5% of the outstanding stock of a firm, the preemptive right entitles the shareholder to purchase 5% of the new stock issue. This preemptive right allows shareholders to maintain a fixed percentage of ownership in firms if they wish. If not, their ownership in the firm declines, or is "diluted."

Investors in common stock have a residual claim on earnings distributions and receive their income only after all other claims have been satisfied. Income is either paid out in the form of dividend payments or is reinvested in the business as retained earnings. The immediate cash benefit to dividend payouts is obvious; however, shareholders also benefit when firms retain earnings and reinvest them. By reinvesting earnings, research and new projects can be funded, production capacity increased, facilities built or renovated, and other activities undertaken to increase future value of the stock. These investments in the firm can then result directly in new cash dividends or indirectly in future stock value and increased stock prices.

Additionally, by having residual claims on a firm's income, stockholders have residual claims on the firm's assets in the event of liquidation. This means that if a firm goes into bankruptcy and the courts decree that its assets must be liquidated in order to satisfy outstanding claims, then stockholders end up with whatever is left over after all other claims have been satisfied. The residual value is often only a small fraction of the shareholders' initial investment. One of the benefits of stock ownership is that when the market is doing well the potential returns can be large. However, a disadvantage is that when the market is doing poorly, stock returns can be meager (or even negative if the stock price drops significantly).

The return on an investment in common stock can be broken down into two components: dividend yield and capital gain. The dividend yield is calculated by dividing the dividend paid at the end of the period by the stock's price at the beginning of the period. Although firms do not have to pay dividends, the historical trend has been that once a firm sets a level of dividends, then only in cases of extreme financial distress will it reduce the dividend level. Thus firms where a large percentage of the stock return comes from dividend payments (utilities, for example) can be attractive investments for individuals who rely on investment income for their livelihood.

Capital gain is the other component in the return on a stock investment. Capital gain reflects the appreciation in the firm's stock price: If stock is sold for a price that is higher than the purchase price, sellers realize a capital gain on the investment.

Much has been written about whether shareholders prefer to receive their income from dividends or capital gains. One classic theory is the bird-in-hand theory of dividend payments, which stems from the old adage, "A bird in hand is worth two in the bush." This theory states that shareholders prefer firms to pay out their earnings as dividends rather than retain them, because dividends represent income that is paid out as cash now, whereas capital gains (the result of plowing the income back into the firm) may take a long time, if ever, to be realized. Thus, with dividends there is no risk of the shareholders not realizing their income, while with capital gains there is the risk that the stock price will not appreciate once the money has been plowed back into the firm.

## Preferred Stock

Like common stockholders, preferred stockholders receive dividends. However, preferred dividends act like rates of interest. They are set at a specific percentage called the dividend rate, and this rate may be fixed or may float with the market.

It is crucial that before making investment decisions, investors carefully gauge what their time horizon is, how much risk they are willing to take, and whether they need the investment income to finance their daily activities. Investors must also be aware that stocks are risky investments and that they may not be an appropriate investment choice for everyone. As discussed above, when firms go bankrupt, a substantial portion of stockholders' initial investments may be lost. It would therefore be advisable for novice investors to seek the advice of certified financial planners before investing a sizable proportion of their wealth in equity securities. (See also AGENTS AND BROKERS; INVESTMENT CLUBS; INVESTOR EDUCATION; MUTUAL FUNDS; REAL ESTATE INVESTMENTS.)

### References

Brigham, Eugene F., and Joel F. Houston. 2000. *Fundamentals of Financial Management*. 9th ed. Mason, OH: South-Western.

Haugen, Robert A. 2000. *Modern Investment Theory*. 5th ed. Englewood Cliffs, NJ: Prentice Hall.

Reilly, Frank K. 2002. *Investment Analysis and Portfolio Management*. 7th ed. Mason, OH: South-Western.

*Ben J. Sopranzetti*

**ESTATE PLANNING,** the process of accumulating, preserving, protecting, and transferring wealth from one person or generation to another. The estate planning process begins with a review of an individual's short-range and long-range goals and objectives. These goals are synthesized into a lifetime accumulation and transfer plan that sets forth the steps necessary to accomplish those things that are important to the individual.

Every person's goals are different. Some individuals may not be concerned with transferring large amounts of wealth to family members at death, while others may view this as one of their more important objectives. As the income and standard of living for Americans has risen, a new concern has arisen in the estate planning arena—the possibility of leaving too much to one's heirs. Warren Buffet has been credited with a succinct expression of this goal: "I want to leave enough to my children so that they can do anything, but not so much that they can do nothing." For individuals who have accumulated large amounts of wealth, this may be a very real concern that has to be taken into consideration in developing an estate plan.

A common misconception about estate planning is that estate planning is only important for the wealthy. While it is true that wealthy individuals typically have to pay estate taxes to both the state and federal governments, the estate planning process involves much more than tax planning. At its core, estate planning is the process of achieving one's long-range goals by following an action plan designed to get you where you want to be. No matter what your level of net worth, developing an estate plan is important if you have transfer objectives that you wish to achieve, regardless of the presence or absence of an estate tax impact.

Another misconception about estate planning is that the plan only springs into action when someone dies. Every estate plan will have provisions to deal with what should happen upon an individual's death. Well-designed estate plans, however, include lifetime planning options that will help achieve an individual's goals during life while at the same time minimizing adverse consequences at death. Individuals who do not take advantage of lifetime planning opportunities often find that they cannot easily achieve their transfer goals and objectives.

### Basic Planning

In its simplest form, an estate plan is an expression of an individual's goals and objectives concerning property.

Some individuals may decide that the best estate plan is to spend (or give away) everything before they die. This is often expressed in common jokes about estate planning, such as, "My estate plan is to have the check to the undertaker bounce" or "I want to spend my last dime on my last day." Using this approach, there is no need to worry about taxes or fighting heirs. This could be dangerous, though, because if the individual lives longer than expected, he or she may run out of money. Alternatively, if the individual dies before he or she intended, excess assets will have to be dealt with. Even when there is no intent to leave assets to others, it is wise to engage in estate planning to ensure that there will be sufficient assets during one's own lifetime and that anything left after death is dealt with appropriately.

When an individual wishes to leave some property to others, estate planning is even more important. How the property is transferred, as well as how much is transferred to each beneficiary, can become important. A basic understanding of these issues is key to participating in the planning process.

### Transfer of Property during Lifetime

Property transfers during lifetime can take two primary forms: the transfer can be a gift or it can be a sale.

If property is transferred by gift, the new owner's basis in the property for purposes of calculating gain or loss at the time of subsequent sale is carried over from the donor. An adjustment can be made if gift taxes were paid on the transfer. Each year, up to a certain amount ($11,000 in 2003) of property can be transferred to each of any number of recipients without triggering gift tax liability. One of the best ways to help reduce the size of an individual's estate is to make regular annual exclusion gifts of surplus property to the intended recipients.

In some circumstances, a sale of the property may be a more appropriate planning technique. If the property is sold to a family member, payments can be deferred under an installment note. Unlike the situation with gifts, a sale of the property allows the purchaser to have a basis equal to what he or she paid for the property (which is usually greater than the seller's basis).

### Transfer of Property at Death

Property can be transferred in three ways upon an individual's death: (1) through the probate process, (2) by operation of law, or (3) by contract.

The probate process is a court-supervised procedure whereby ownership of property is transferred from the decedent to his or her heirs. Probate is the "catch all" process, since it governs the disposition of all property that does not pass by operation of law or by contract. Typically, the probate process begins shortly after an individual's death when a petition for probate is submitted to the probate court (called surrogate or orphan's court in some states). Once the petition is filed, the opening of the estate is advertised so that creditors can make claims against the estate. The decedent's property is gathered and recorded and, after the payment of debts, final medical expenses, and funeral expenses, distributed to the heirs. If an individual had drafted a will during his or her lifetime, the will governs the distribution of the property. If no will was drafted or no will could be found, default rules found in the state statutes (called the intestacy laws) take over to determine who will receive the property. Generally, the intestacy laws transfer the property to close relatives of the decedent. In the event that there are no close relatives living at the time the individual dies (no family members closer than the cousins of first cousins under the Uniform Probate Code), the property "escheats," or is transferred, to the state in which the decedent was domiciled at death.

The advantages of probate include court supervision of the disposition of property and the ability to settle all debts of the decedent and extinguish debts that were not submitted to the court in a timely manner. Probate can be costly, however. In some states, the court costs, coupled with executor, attorney, and accountant fees, can be as high as 6% of the value of the probate estate. One way to help avoid probate in high-cost states is to use a revocable trust arrangement (see below) in conjunction with a will. Be aware, though, that while use of a revocable trust will avoid probate, it will not exempt property from federal or state estate or inheritance taxes.

Jointly held assets are the classic examples of property that passes by operation of law. Usually, this form of ownership is associated with real estate. For example, a husband and wife may own their residence as joint tenants with right of survivorship, meaning that, upon the death of the first cotenant, the property passes automatically by operation of law to the surviving cotenant. Any two or more people can own property as joint tenants with rights of survivorship, but in some states, a special form of property ownership is available for spouses only—tenants by the entirety. Tenants by the entirety is simply a joint tenancy with right of survivorship that cannot be severed without the consent of both parties. Property that passes by operation of law does so automatically and is not considered to be part of the probate estate.

The last form of property transfer at death is transfer by contract. Property is transferred by contract in arrangements where beneficiary designations are allowed. Classic examples include death benefits on life insurance policies, pension plan accumulations, and Individual Retirement Accounts (IRAs). These assets will pass directly to the named beneficiary and will not be part of the probate estate. An important reason for frequently reviewing your estate plan is to assure that beneficiary designations are still appropriate.

### Common Estate Planning Documents

Estate planning documents include all of the arrangements made to manage property during lifetime or at death. A *will* changes the state default rules (intestacy laws) by directing the distribution of the decedent's property to the individuals or institutions named under the terms specified in the will and appoints the person who will manage the estate (the "executor" or "executrix"). It also allows the appointment of a guardian for minor children, which is perhaps one of the most important issues for young families. Due to the changing nature of client goals and objectives, as well as the levels of wealth achieved or remaining, the provisions contained in a will should be reviewed frequently.

*Powers of attorney* can be created to allow for the management of property or to provide for medical care when an individual is unable to take care of these items himself or herself. *Premarital (prenuptial) agreements* may have the effect of changing state default rules concerning the disposition of property at death and are often used for estate planning purposes in conjunction with other documents.

A *trust* is a contract between a person (the "grantor") and another person or an institution (the "trustee") to hold and manage property for the benefit of one or more beneficiaries. Trusts are characterized by two sets of adjectives: one that describes when the trust is created and another that describes whether the terms of the trust can be changed. First, a trust can be characterized as a "living" ("inter-vivos") trust or a "testamentary" trust. Living or inter-vivos trusts are created during the grantor's lifetime; testamentary trusts are created at the grantor's death. As used here, "created" refers to when the trust becomes effective, not when it was written. Second, a trust is described as revocable if its terms can be changed during the life of the grantor, and irrevocable if they cannot. Revocable living trusts are often used to avoid probate and to provide for asset management in the event of the grantor's disability but are not effective for avoiding death taxes.

Irrevocable living trusts, often funded only with life insurance policies, may trigger gift taxation upon creation but generally will not be included in the estate of the grantor. Testamentary trusts are often used to help manage the federal estate tax liability that will be faced by a married couple.

### Federal Gift, Estate, and Generation Skipping Transfer Taxes

When property is transferred during lifetime, gift taxes generally apply. There are several ways to avoid paying gift taxes, however. The first technique involves the direct transfer (i.e., a transfer that does not involve a trust) of property with a value less than the gift tax annual exclusion ($11,000 for 2003). As long as the total amount of direct gifts made to an individual during a year does not exceed the gift tax annual exclusion, no gift tax will be due. In addition to the annual exclusion amount, an individual can pay educational and medical expenses directly to the provider of the services on behalf of another without triggering gift tax liability. Any gifts made in excess of these amounts, or gifts made through trusts that will not qualify for the annual exclusion, will trigger a gift tax liability. That liability is first offset by the gift tax applicable credit amount (the tax calculated on a value of $1 million for gift tax purposes), and any tax due in excess of the credit will need to be paid by the donor.

Estate taxes apply to property transferred at death. Every individual, however, can leave the applicable estate tax credit amount to his or her heirs without triggering federal estate tax. The first $1 million (in 2003) of taxable transfers during lifetime or at death is shielded by the applicable credit amount. In 2003, the applicable credit for gift and estate tax purposes is the same, and the highest marginal estate tax rate is 49%. If property with a greater value is transferred at death, it will be subject to estate tax. Pursuant to the 2001 Tax Act (Economic Growth and Tax Relict Reconciliation Act [EGTRRA] 2001), beginning in 2004 an individual can leave up to $1.5 million estate tax free at death. Note that this differs (by $500,000) from the amount that can be transferred during lifetime under the applicable gift tax credit.

Any amount that is given to a spouse or to a qualified charity during lifetime or at death will not be subject to either gift tax or estate tax. These are referred to as the Marital and Charitable Deductions for Gift and Estate Tax purposes. Charitable giving is often an important estate planning tool and should not be overlooked in planning the estate. Caution should be exercised in giving too much to a spouse, however. Recall that every person can leave the applicable estate tax credit amount to his or her heirs without triggering a federal estate tax. For example, in a typical situation where a married couple has "I love you wills" (i.e., a will that leaves everything to the surviving spouse), the benefit of the applicable credit of the first spouse to die will be lost. If, instead, the first spouse to die created a trust (called a credit shelter trust) funded with their remaining applicable estate tax credit amount, the assets in the trust will not be included later in the surviving spouse's estate for tax purposes even if the surviving spouse is a beneficiary of the trust. The remainder beneficiaries (usually children) would receive the amounts in the credit shelter trust, plus the surviving spouse's applicable estate tax credit amount, estate tax free at the death of the surviving spouse.

The generation skipping transfer tax applies whenever property is transferred to a "skip person." A skip person is someone more than one generation below the transferor. There are many issues that need to be considered for generation skipping transfer tax planning, and a full discussion is beyond the scope of this entry. Some basic rules regarding the generation skipping tax are important to know, however. Gifts that qualify for the gift tax annual exclusion are exempt from the generation skipping transfer tax. In addition, any payments for medical and educational expenses of another person made directly to the provider of those services will not trigger the generation skipping transfer tax. Finally, each individual has a lifetime exemption ($1.12 million in 2003) that is sometimes automatically allocated to generation skipping transfers. If the exemption is not automatically allocated pursuant to the code, the transferor can allocate a portion of the exemption by filing a notice of allocation with his or her gift tax return. The exemption amount for generation skipping transfer tax purposes will equal the applicable estate tax credit amount beginning in 2004 ($1.5 million).

### Asset Protection

Even if taxes are not an issue, a good estate plan will take steps to protect an individual's assets from the claims of judgment creditors and outside parties. While a full discussion of this topic is beyond the scope of this entry, it is important to note that the purpose of asset protection is not to defraud legitimate creditors but rather to protect assets against future claims. If Congress permanently repeals the estate tax (the current repeal sunsets, or disappears, on January 1, 2011), asset protection planning as part of the estate planning process will be even more important.

Asset protection is especially important if assets are being left to a child who may be subject to malpractice claims (physicians, attorneys, accountants, etc.). If an outright bequest is made to the child, those assets are available to a judgment creditor. If, however, the assets are left in a trust that benefits the child and has a strong spendthrift provision, it is unlikely that the child's creditors will be able to access the funds.

At a sophisticated planning level, asset protection techniques can be employed to protect property (and future family members who benefit from that property) from additional transfer taxes. In the normal course of events, an individual will die, leaving assets to the children. If the children haven't spent or consumed the assets prior to their deaths, the assets will be taxed again when they are transferred to the grandchildren. Using this approach, transfer taxes are due at the death of each generation of family members. Use of a so-called Dynasty Trust (a perpetual trust that allows beneficiaries to use assets but not own them) can prevent successive transfer taxes from continuously eroding the value of family assets. Dynasty Trusts must be set up in states that have abolished the rule against perpetuities and require special planning and expert advice.

### Cash Needs at Death

When an individual dies, death taxes are due, debts must be paid, medical expenses and funeral expenses must be paid, and there must be some money for the surviving family members to continue to make ends meet. As a result, liquidity planning is very important and should always be considered in estate planning. This is particularly true if an individual holds illiquid assets, such as real estate or business interests. These types of assets are often difficult to liquidate and can cause a liquidity crisis for the estate.

One of the best ways to fund cash needs at death is through the use of life insurance. The proceeds become available at the time when they are needed and can prevent the need to sell illiquid assets to cover estate costs and taxes. There are many types of life insurance, and the best product to use is often determined by the circumstances facing the individual. As a rule of thumb, however, if the life insurance is intended to be in force for ten years or more, it is better to use permanent life insurance contracts (whole life, universal life, variable life, or variable universal life) than term insurance policies.

### Charitable Estate Planning

During lifetime and at death, charitable planning is a powerful estate planning tool. Gifts to charities do not result in the imposition of any transfer tax (gift, estate, or generation skipping). Furthermore, giving to charities can help an individual perpetuate those activities he or she feels are important, even after death.

In some circumstances, a gift to charity can be made that benefits the donor. For example, a gift of a remainder interest in a personal residence or farm will generate an immediate income tax deduction for the donor and relieve his or her estate of the costs associated with disposing of the property after death, although it will deny surviving family members enjoyment of the property. Another example would be the contribution of appreciated property to a charitable remainder trust where the donor receives an income stream for a period of time, followed by a transfer of the remainder interest to a charity. *Charitable lead trusts* can be used to reduce estate tax liability as long as an individual is willing to defer the heirs' receipt of the property. At death, a charitable lead trust could be created that would pay an income stream to a charity for a period of years, following which the remainder interest reverts to family members. Only the value of the remainder interest would be taxed for estate tax purposes. This is the technique that Jacqueline Kennedy Onasis planned to use in her estate, which would have removed 98.6% of the value of her estate from estate taxation. Her children, however, decided to forgo the use of the charitable lead trust and take the property directly from the estate, resulting in a large estate tax liability—and illustrating the point that estate planning is about much more than tax savings.

### Summary

Everyone should consider estate planning and review estate plans frequently. Estates big and small can benefit from the process. The currently scheduled elimination of the estate tax does not eliminate the need for estate planning but rather emphasizes it. Estate planning is an individually tailored process that looks at the long-term goals of an individual and creates an action plan that can be followed to achieve those goals. Taxes are important to consider but should not be the tail that wags the dog. Considering the tax impact of various estate planning options in conjunction with the long-range goals of an individual may, however, make attainment of the individual's goals more likely.

In developing an estate plan, a team approach works best. Involving the financial planner, attorney, accountant, insurance agent, trust officers, investment advisors, and any other individuals regularly involved in managing the financial affairs of the client often leads to a more attainable, well-rounded estate plan than a plan developed by any one advisor. (See also CHARITABLE CONTRIBUTIONS; ELDER LAW PRACTICE; INHERITANCE; INTERGENERATIONAL CONFLICT AND FINANCIAL ISSUES; TRUSTS; WILLS.)

### References

Fontaine, Constance J., ed. 2002. *Fundamentals of Estate Planning*. 6th ed. Bryn Mawr, PA: American College.

Leimberg, Stephan R., Jerry A. Kasner, Stephen N. Kandell, Ralph Gano Miller, et al. 2002. *Tools and Techniques of Estate Planning*. 12th ed. Upper Saddle River, NJ: Prentice Hall.

*Thomas P. Langdon*

**ESTATE TAXES.** See Capital Gain; Charitable Contributions; Elder Law Practice; Estate Planning; Inheritance; Wealth Span.

**ETHICAL WILL,** a method for recording and sharing values, hopes, life lessons, and other personal messages with family and community members.

It is estimated that over the next 20 years more than $6 trillion will pass from one generation to another. This enormous transfer of wealth is likely to occur with little regard for how, and for what purpose, these assets were accumulated or the meaning they represent. Sixty percent (60%) of individuals engage in charitable giving during their lives, yet only 6% bequeath assets to charitable causes after death. How might these assets be leveraged to perpetuate the values of the giver(s) and to improve society?

An ethical will helps answer this question by clarifying one's values and communicating one's life's purpose and meaning to those who survive us. It is both a practical and spiritual tool to use at any stage of life with particular relevance to anyone interested in creating an estate plan or financial plan that perpetuates ideals for generations to come.

### What Is an Ethical Will?

People typically write a last will and testament to provide for the distribution of their material assets. Others write living wills, or advance directives, to provide instructions for end-of-life medical treatment in the event of incapacity. Today, an increasing number of people are exploring ways to preserve a different type of legacy, their personal values, for future generations. Ethical wills are a way to share values, hopes, desires, and life lessons with loved ones. An ethical will can also incorporate meaning into a financial or estate plan for the writer.

### Historical Context

The tradition of ethical wills is not new. The Hebrew Bible first described ethical wills, and the last testament of Jacob, Genesis, chapter 49, is generally regarded as the first ethical will. They were originally associated with a person's final days of life and were transmitted orally on subjects that included blessings, instructions, advice, and funeral arrangements. There are many examples of this tradition in the Hebrew and Christian Bibles (Deuteronomy, chapters 32–33, and John, chapters 15–18, as additional examples). Over the centuries they became written documents and often were attached to or placed with legal wills (even though they were not considered a legal document).

Classifying these documents as "ethical literature" is reasonable based on their contents and subject matter. However, there is a sharp distinction between ethical wills, which are much more practical in tone, and other modern ethical writings that tend to be more theoretical in nature.

During the past five to ten years, the tradition of creating ethical wills has been experiencing a period of rediscovery and revival. This seems likely to be due to the combination of large numbers of baby boomers entering middle age, the aging of their parents, and a realization that there is more to life than just accumulated assets. At present, ethical wills are more likely to be written at transitional life stages and are usually shared with loved ones while the author is still alive. They are also being written to be used as a foundation for estate planning. Ethical wills can be valuable in articulating the most appropriate financial planning options that leverage the writer's philosophical and spiritual legacy.

### Why Write an Ethical Will?

Everyone discovers his or her own motivations for creating an ethical will. This is a partial list of reasons shared by those who have written ethical wills:

- To be remembered for what the person believes and stands for
- To try to insure the continuation of one's values for future generations
- To leave a legacy that is more than material goods or money
- To provide a sense of completion and closure

### When to Write an Ethical Will

People will most often be attracted to this idea at turning points and transitions in their lives such as a significant illness, the loss of a loved one, the birth of a child or grandchild, marriage, financial and estate planning, approaching the end of life.

### Relevance to Estate Planning

The complexity of estate planning, charitable giving options, and estate tax laws requires a better understanding of one's values in order to consider the most appropriate investment alternatives and strategies. For individuals, and the estate planning professionals with whom they work in collaboration, there will be many opportunities to consider the role of ethical wills in their estate planning. The following are two examples that illustrate the complementary nature of estate planning and ethical wills.

*Example 1.* A childless couple, both of whom received their Ph.D.s, wanted to bequeath equal portions of their estate to their nieces and nephews. Their planner introduced the concept of ethical wills and encouraged them to complete one before finalizing their plans.

The couple identified the importance of education as a driving value in their lives and quickly agreed on the importance of education for future generations of their families. Consequently, they set up a "memorial trust fund" that would allow current and future family members to apply for and obtain funds to support higher educational pursuits. They did this in addition to leaving individual bequests. They felt they did something very meaningful and significant for themselves and "made an important statement about what they stood for."

*Example 2.* An attorney encouraged a successful businessman and his spouse to create an ethical will as a means of discovering the couple's important values and to assist the attorney in identifying appropriate estate planning alternatives. Charitable giving and the importance of the family emerged as two high-priority areas. A charitable family foundation was established whereby family members were named as board members of the foundation. Yearly meetings of "the Board" were held at which time family members selected recipients of the charitable gifts from the foundation. This yearly philanthropic activity was designed to convey the importance and responsibility of this family to support institutions that strove to make the world a better place. "The Board" also had the opportunity to get together at least once a year as a family in a setting that allowed for both work and relaxation. (See also ESTATE PLANNING; FINANCIAL PLANNING PROCESS; HEALTH AND LONGEVITY; INHERITANCE; LIFE PLANNING; WILLS.)

### Organization

The Legacy Center

### Suggested Readings

Albom, Mitch. 1997. *Tuesdays with Morrie.* New York: Doubleday.

Ethical Wills. Available online at http://www.ethicalwill.com. More than 20 modern ethical wills are posted on the only Web site dedicated to the topic of ethical wills.

Remen, Rachel Naomi. 1996. *Kitchen Table Wisdom.* New York: Riverhead Books.

Riemer, Jack, and Nathaniel Stampfer. 1991. *So That Your Values Live On: Ethical Wills and How to Prepare Them.* Woodstock, VT: Jewish Lights Publishing.

Schacther-Shalomi, Zalman, and Ronald Miller. 1997. *From Age-ing to Sage-ing.* Victoria, Australia: Warner Books.

### References

Baines, Barry K. 1999. "A Biblical Concept in Estate Planning." *Journal of Retirement Planning* (May–June): 44–49.

Baines, Barry K. 2002. *Ethical Wills: Putting Your Values on Paper.* Cambridge, MA: Perseus Publishing.

Gambone, James V. 2001. *Retirement: A Boomer's Guide to Life after 50.* Minneapolis, MN: Kirk House Publishers.

*Barry K. Baines*

**ETHICS IN FINANCIAL PLANNING,** standards or imperatives in dealing with finances in the lives of older adults. Ethical dilemmas range from questions of professional practice to issues of social responsibility and public policy. The published ethical standards of the financial planning industry provide the groundwork for an analysis of principles and rules to help clarify and distinguish acceptable from unacceptable conduct. Many issues remain to be addressed, however, as the field of financial gerontology emerges and matures, and all professionals or entities acting as financial advisors to older persons must grapple with these principles and issues.

### Professional Financial Planning

The Financial Planning Association (FPA) and the American Institute of Certified Public Accountants (AICPA) have ethical standards, which are codified. Several of the canons of the FPA are quite straightforward, such as the injunction to put public interest above private gain or the imperative to improve professional skills and knowledge. Other imperatives in the canon seem more obscure; for example, the provision encouraging obedience to the law in order to "avoid conduct or activity which would cause unjust harm" to those relying on financial planners.

Unfortunately, the canons of some associations avoid the most serious dilemmas of financial planning: the need to avoid conflict of interest in giving advice; the requirement for truth-telling and disclosure of options and the level of risk; or the balance between paternalism and autonomy in financial decision making. On the other hand, the ethical standards of the AICPA require that certified public accountants (CPAs) not engage in activities that result in a conflict of interest, "in fact or in appearance." Yet in the majority of states CPAs can legally (and ethically) accept commissions for selling or providing financial products and services to older clients in many situations. The disclosure requirements vary from state to state based upon the laws in effect in each state. However, generally speaking, licensed CPAs must adhere to a policy of full disclosure with respect to fees and conflicts of interest.

### Financial Advising

All financial advisors find themselves in a position where advice to an older client could put the client's assets at risk, as financial decisions often do. The risks can be market risks or they can be inflation risk. Regardless of intention, a financial advisor is regarded as an expert. Vulnerable older adults, both those with substantial means and those with modest means, will put their trust in a financial expert. Accordingly, regardless of ethics, codes, or laws, the advisor should assume that the older client believes that the advice being provided is in the client's best interest and unbiased. In light of that trust, what advice is appropriate? Is the idea of a "risk-averse" older adult simply a stereotype to be set aside in favor of customized advice to an individual? It is appropriate to educate clients about all elements of risk. It is also appropriate for advisors to explain risk in a way so that the older client understands the issues that must be considered.

These issues invoke the classic dilemmas of autonomy and paternalism in professional ethics. The pure paternalist position will compel the planner to safeguard the welfare of the older client and to tailor recommendations offered to consider the risk to capital as the primary risk. By contrast, a pure libertarian position will emphasize the complete autonomy of the client and favor complete fact-telling with the ultimate decision left up to the client alone.

Both extreme positions have ethical arguments in their favor. But where a financial advisor has a bias toward one or the other side, it seems imperative to reveal that bias before entering into a contractual relationship to provide financial planning or financial advice.

### Social Ethics

Financial advising on behalf of older clients takes place in a public context and therefore requires the vantage point of social ethics. A serious ethical issue for financial advisors concerns the public status and definition of the finance profession itself. Just who qualifies as a "financial advisor" or "financial planner"? In most states, the professional designation is quite loose and ill defined, unlike that for physicians, lawyers, or architects. As a result, financial advisors with very different levels of competence, including those with serious conflicts of interest (e.g., stock brokers), may present themselves as financial planners to a poorly informed public.

Another ethical dilemma in financial planning arises from the interpersonal and multigenerational structure of the family. The financial planner typically encounters older individuals for whom asset protection and estate planning are major issues. The problem arises in Medicaid planning, where financial planners, as well as attorneys in elder law practice, must take account of the need to plan for long-term care expenditures. There has been strong criticism of middle-class seniors who take advantage of spend-down "loopholes" to qualify for Medicaid and safeguard an inheritance for their children. To what extent should a financial advisor take account of such criticism or ethical concerns? There are clearly situations that warrant such planning—particularly when the concern is that the long-term care costs of one spouse could impoverish the other spouse. The ethical concerns could also be difficult to gauge if there is a spouse or offspring with special needs that are to be provided for by the individual seeking this type of planning.

Another area of intersection between individual ethics and social ethics is the realm of financial elder abuse. Does a financial planner have an obligation to protect an older client when the planner sees evidence of exploitation such as occurs when a frail or cognitively impaired older person gives large amounts of money to a younger caregiver or to an affectionate companion? Does it matter if mental competency is in question, or is there a "right to folly?" Guardianship statutes and programs in many states today are wrestling with this dilemma. However, there is an inexorable movement by statute and regulation to stop such abuse of older persons.

With increasing numbers of "oldest old," including many with significant financial assets, the ethical dilemmas of financial planning, financial advising, and aging will surely loom larger. Instead of relying on abstract codes of ethics, it may be more helpful to follow the example of medical ethics in confronting problems of clinical care: namely, to recognize that ambiguity and uncertainty, including ethical dilemmas, are inherent in planning for all stages of life, including old age, and must rigorously and continuously be addressed. (See also CPA ELDERCARE SERVICES; FINANCIAL ADVISORS; FINANCIAL EDUCATION FOR SERVICES; FINANCIAL ELDER ABUSE; FINANCIAL PLANNING PROCESS; MEDICAID PLANNING.)

**References**

DeGeorge, Richard T. 1990. *Business Ethics*. New York: Collier Macmillan.

Kapoor, Jack R., Les R. Dlabay, and Robert J. Hughes. 2001. *Personal Finance*. 6th ed. Homewood, IL: McGraw-Hill/Irwin.

"Zero in on the Right Financial Adviser." 2003. *Kiplinger's Retirement Report* 10 (February): 2.

*Harry R. Moody*

# F

**FEDERAL AGENCY SECURITIES,** bonds, debentures, notes, and other securities issued to raise funds in support of public functions. As people approach retirement age, they restructure their investment portfolio. Equity securities tend to become less important and fixed income investments more important. As older persons become less willing to take risks, they try to find investments that provide a satisfactory rate of return and reduce the possibility of principal loss.

The Federal Financing Bank and the Government National Mortgage Association (GNMA) are federal agencies that issue securities backed by the full faith and credit of the U.S. government. Most agencies considered here, however, are government-sponsored enterprises (GSEs); the securities they issue are not guaranteed by the U.S. government but involve federal sponsorship. Government-sponsored enterprises are the largest issuers of agency securities and include the Federal Home Loan Bank (FHLB), Federal National Mortgage Association (FNMA), Farm Credit System (FCS), Student Loan Marketing Association (SLMA), and the Federal Home Loan Mortgage Corporation (FHLMC). SLMA and FNMA are also publicly owned and have stock that trades on the national exchanges.

Agencies were created by Congress to meet the special needs of specific segments of the general economy. They can be divided into three broad categories: (1) agencies supporting the mortgage market—FHLB, FHLMC, FNMA, GNMA; (2) agencies supporting agriculture—FCS; and (3) agencies supporting student loans—SLMA. Several other small agencies sell debt securities for specialized purposes. It is useful to analyze agencies by the type of securities they issue. There are two broad categories: (1) agencies that issue notes, debentures, bonds, or discount notes (FCB, FHLB, FNMA, SLMA) and (2) those that issue mortgage-backed securities, primarily "pass-through" securities (FNMA, FHLMC, GNMA). FNMA issues both types, depending on the financial purpose of the funds being raised. Each of these agencies sells securities to the public through a nationwide group of dealers and dealer banks or through individually negotiated or competitive bid transactions.

Over the years, agency securities have become very popular with older investors. Two reasons for this acceptance are their perceived high quality, which assures investors that their principal is relatively safe, and an active secondary market that allows investors to sell their securities quickly when necessary. The majority of agency issues are debentures or short-term discount notes with set maturity dates from 30 days to 20 years and a set coupon rate, which pay interest every six months. Newer issues have some additional features, such as call options and floating rates, but they are not as popular with individuals since they often require a minimum purchase of $100,000. Typically, agencies issue their debentures in denominations of $5,000 to $10,000.

The fastest-growing segment of the agencies market is for mortgage-backed securities, primarily pass-through securities issued by FNMA, FHLMC, and GNMA. Of these agencies, only GNMA carries the guarantee of the full faith and credit of the U.S. Treasury, and because of this guarantee, GNMA securities are among the most popular fixed income investments in the world.

### Government National Mortgage Association

The Government National Mortgage Association was created in 1968 when FNMA was rechartered as a private corporation (privatized). GNMA securities today are the most widely held and actively traded mortgage-backed securities. Through its Mortgage-Backed Securities (MBS) Program, GNMA guarantees securities backed by pools of mortgages, "passing through" the principal and interest payments to the security holder monthly. Since GNMA guarantees the timely payment of principal and interest, the investor takes no risk that the underlying mortgages will become delinquent. Interest paid on mortgage-backed securities is subject to state and local taxes, so investors need to consider this before purchasing them.

### Federal Home Loan Bank (FHLB) System

The FHLB was created by an act of Congress in 1932 and amended by the Financial Institutions Reform, Recovery, and Enforcement Act (FIRREA) of 1989. There are 12 district banks comprising the system. These banks operate as a reserve system for the savings and loan and banking industries to stabilize the flow of mortgage credit. They provide a ready, low-cost source of funds to member institutions, which are then made available to the public. Unlike FNMA and FHLMC, which purchase and then pool mortgages, the FHLB makes advances to its members on the security of their mortgages. Since enactment of the FIRREA, the supervisory and regulatory functions of member institutions reside in the Office of Thrift Supervisor within the Department of the Treasury. Owned by member institutions, the FHLBs do not take deposits. Funds are raised by selling FHLB Consolidated Discount Notes and Consolidated Bank Notes. More than $135 billion of consolidated obligations were outstanding at the end of 1993.

### Federal Home Loan Mortgage Corporation

The FHLMC was chartered in 1970 as a government-sponsored enterprise. It was established to increase the funds available for residential housing by providing a national secondary market in conventional residential mortgages. The FHLMC accomplishes this by purchasing from bankers mortgages that are not guaranteed by any government agency, putting these mortgages into pools, and selling them as pass-through securities backed by such mortgages. Along with FNMA, FHLMC is responsible for maintaining an active secondary market for home sales. Besides the pass-through securities, FHLMC also issues discount notes and short-term debentures, but pass-through securities constitute the vast majority of outstanding debt. Like GNMA securities, FHLMC securities are not exempt from state and local taxes.

### Federal National Mortgage Association

The Federal National Mortgage Association is one of the largest corporations in the United States, based on asset size, and is the largest supplier of funds for home mortgages. It was incorporated in 1938 as a corporation owned by the government. In 1954, it became a mixed public-private corporation, and finally, in 1968, the U.S. Congress split FNMA into two separate corporations, the GNMA, a government agency, and the FNMA, a federally chartered corporation owned by stockholders.

The FNMA supports savings and loan associations, mortgage bankers, commercial banks, and other banks primarily by buying mortgages from them. This availability of funds allows an active secondary market and enables capital to flow to those areas of the country that may need funds. FNMA offers debentures and short-term discount notes and, since 1981, has supported the housing market by purchasing mortgages from originators and generating mortgage-backed securities, which it sells in the capital market. The FNMA has more than $700 billion of outstanding mortgage debt. Income from FNMA securities is subject to state and local tax.

### Farm Credit System

The Farm Credit System is a cooperatively owned system of banks and associations that provide both short- and long-term credit to farmers, ranchers, rural homeowners, and agricultural and rural cooperatives. Twelve federal land banks and associations provide the funding for making long-term loans on secured first mortgages by selling debentures and short-term notes in the money and credit markets. The banks are not depository institutions and rely on the Federal Farm Credit Bank Funding Corporation to raise funds for them. The Funding Corporation issues Farm Credit Consolidated Systemwide Discount Notes, Bonds, and Medium-Term Notes. The income derived from these securities is exempt from state and local taxes, which makes them especially attractive to investors on fixed incomes.

### Student Loan Marketing Association

The Student Loan Marketing Association, like FNMA, is a government-chartered, publicly held corporation that owns one-third of all U.S. student loans. Chartered in 1972, the SLMA was developed in response to problems in the Guaranteed Student Loan Program of 1965. Originally only educational or student loan institutions were allowed to own stock. This was later changed so that anyone could buy nonvoting stock. As a secondary market for student loans, SLMA lends funds for student loans to qualified institutions. The obligations of SLMA are exempt from state and local taxes and from Securities and Exchange Commission (SEC) regulations. Obligations include discount notes, debentures, and floating rate bonds. Investments in SLMA's securities are without much risk because state and federal authorities bear the brunt of the defaults.

A potential investor in federal agency securities should always talk to a financial advisor before committing funds to this large and complex segment of the financial market. There are numerous types of federal agency securities with varying issuers, terms, liquidity, and tax treatments. Only by closely scrutinizing and understanding both the market and one's particular investment needs can investors navigate toward the retirement years with confidence. (See also ASSET ALOCATION AFTER RETIREMENT; BONDS; MORTGAGE INSTRUMENTS; MUTUAL FUNDS; RISK TOLERANCE.)

### References

Bretthorst, Kenneth A. 1988. "Instruments and Markets for Federal Agency Securities." In *The Bankers' Handbook*, ed. William H. Baugh, Thomas I. Storrs, and Charles E. Walker. Homewood, IL: Dow Jones–Irwin.

Rose, Peter S. 1999. *Money and Capital Markets*. New York: McGraw-Hill.

Stuhldreher, Donald J. 1988. "Instruments and Markets for Government Securities." In *The Bankers' Handbook*, ed. William H. Baugh, Thomas I. Storrs, and Charles E. Walker. Home wood, IL: Dow Jones–Irwin.

*Kenneth A. Bretthorst*

**FINANCES OF AGING IN THE GAY COMMUNITY,** the perspectives in a wide range of policy debates that affect aging policies and the financial well-being of the gay, lesbian, bisexual, and transgender (GLBT) community in retirement.

Notable improvements have been seen in public opinion toward gay issues, including support for equal treatment of same-sex couples under Social Security benefits (Yang 1999). There has been a dramatic growth in local and state nondiscrimination laws, such that today more than one in three Americans live in a municipality or state with a sexual orientation nondiscrimination law. Increasingly, corporate America is adopting sexual orientation nondiscrimination policies and offering domestic partner benefits to same-sex partners of employees. Same-sex couples, however, are treated unequally under many aging policies, including income support programs. Also, homophobia is a problem in senior services, and gay elders may have particular caregiving needs and experiences that require special attention.

### The Particular Barriers Gay Seniors Face

The older GLBT population, currently estimated at 1 to 3 million people, will increase to 4 to 6 million by 2030 (Cahill, South, and Spade 2000). Although gay elders share many of the same human needs and concerns as their heterosexual peers, gay and lesbian seniors often experience particular barriers as well, including discrimination; unequal treatment under Social Security, pensions, 401(k)s, and IRAs (Individual Retirement Accounts); and concerns related to housing, health care, and long-term care. Federal programs designed to assist older Americans can be ineffective or even irrelevant for GLBT elders. Several studies—of both nursing home administrators and directors of Area Agencies on Aging—document widespread homophobia among those entrusted with the care of America's seniors (Fairchild, Carrino, and Ramirez 1996). Even senior centers can be hostile places for gay elders. Many gay elders do not avail themselves of services on which other seniors thrive. Some retreat back into the closet, reinforcing isolation and undermining the possibility of a successful experience of aging. GLBT baby boomers—"out" for most of their lives—are increasingly unwilling to retreat to the closet when they encounter homophobia in aging services.

### Long-Term Care Issues

Heterosexism and homophobia are widespread in nursing homes and are symptomatic of a larger sexphobia often associated with those providing services to seniors. In a mid-1990s survey of nursing home social workers, more than half said their coworkers were intolerant or condemning of homosexuality among residents, while most other respondents avoided answering the question. The staff in one nursing home refused to bathe a resident because they did not want to touch "the lesbian," and a home care assistant threatened to "out" a gay client if he reported her negligent care (Cook-Daniels 1997). Many gay elders experience abuse from care providers. Few service providers have instituted policies to address this homophobic behavior, leaving some GLBT elders in hostile and dangerous environments (Parsons 1995).

Gay elders entering assisted living facilities and other institutions are often presumed to be heterosexual and may feel compelled to hide their sexual identity. Long-term relationships may be devalued and unrecognized. Assisted living centers, congregate housing, and home health care services can take proactive steps to minimize discrimination, abuse, and neglect directed at GLBT elders. Caregivers can be trained to be competent in issues of sexuality and gender variance. Nursing homes can include detailed sexuality policies within residents' rights policies and can accommodate the appropriate, private expression of the sexual needs of residents—be they homosexual, bisexual, or heterosexual.

### Particular Caregiving Needs

Gay elders may also have particular care and caregiving needs. Since most caregiving in the United States is provided by biological children, and since gays and lesbians are less likely to have children and appear more likely to live alone in old age than heterosexual elders, an urgent question presents itself: Who will care for GLBT elders? In general, the state fails to recognize same-sex relationships. Some studies indicate that GLBT elders may be more likely to live alone, making innovative support networks critical. Often, gay seniors are estranged from their families of origin due to homophobia and/or fear of rejection. Consequently, they may not be able to rely upon traditional caregiving support networks.

GLBT elders are often perceived to be "single" and without family attachments (even though they may have life partners and even children and grandchildren through those relationships) and are disproportionately relied upon by heterosexual siblings to take care of parents, aunts, uncles, and other aging family members (Shippy and Cahill 2002). Despite attempts by some conservatives to construct "family" and "gay" as mutually exclusive categories, one in three gay men and lesbians provides some kind of caregiving assistance—either to children or to adults with an illness or disability (Fredriksen 1999).

### Unequal Treatment under Retirement Income Support Programs

In a free market system, income is a critical determinant in the quality of life one enjoys in retirement, including quality of care for those elders in need of caregiving. Those serving GLBT elders need to take into account the impact of the unequal treatment same-sex couples experience under policies regulating retirement income. For example:

- Social Security pays survivor benefits to widows and widowers but not to the surviving same-sex life partner of someone who dies. This may cost GLBT elders $124 million a year in benefits that would otherwise be available (Cahill, South, and Spade 2000).
- Married spouses are eligible for Social Security spousal benefits, which can allow them to receive half their spouse's Social Security benefit if it is larger than their own Social Security benefit. Unmarried partners in lifelong relationships are not eligible for spousal benefits. It is unknown how many millions of dollars a year this costs GLBT elders.
- Medicaid regulations protect the assets and homes of married spouses when the other spouse enters a nursing home or long-term care facility; no such protections are offered to same-sex partners.
- Tax laws and other regulations of 401(k)s and pensions discriminate against same-sex partners, forcing the surviving partner in a same-sex relationship into financially undesirable circumstances and subjecting retirement savings assets to distribution and taxation much earlier than makes sense.

Each of these issues is explored further below.

### Social Security

Lesbian, gay, and bisexual people in same-sex partnerships are not eligible for the Social Security spousal benefit or the survivor benefit. This lack of eligibility costs gay elders hundreds of millions of dollars in income per year. The September 11th terrorist attacks illustrated the unfairness of this policy, as same-sex survivors of victims were denied Social Security survivor benefits as well as funds from the victims' compensation fund administered by the U.S. Justice Department.

Social Security survivor benefits allow widows, widowers, and dependent children to put food on the table and provide a sense of fairness when an employee pays into the system his or her whole life but dies before being able to enjoy the retirement benefits. But gay and lesbian survivors are not even eligible for these benefits. In 1998, 781,000 widows and widowers received an average of $442 a month in survivor benefits, a total of $4.1 billion that year. If only 3% of the total population of seniors who survived their life partner are gay, lesbian, or bisexual individuals in same-sex relationships, the failure to pay survivor benefits costs gay seniors about $124 million a year.

The spousal benefit allows husbands and wives to receive an amount equal to 50% of their spouse's monthly Social Security check if that amount is higher than what their own earnings would make them eligible for each month. In marriages where one spouse earns significantly more than the other and/or has a longer work history, taking the spousal benefit instead of the individual's own payment makes sense. However, same-sex partners are not eligible for the spousal benefit.

### Unequal Treatment under Pension Regulations

Because GLBT people can still be legally discriminated against in employment in most of the country, and because gay couples are not treated equally under Social Security, pension income is an important policy issue affecting gay elders. Contrary to a widely held stereotype of gay affluence, gay men and lesbians earn no more than heterosexual men and women. In fact, gay men earn about 15% to 20% less than heterosexual men. Lesbians earn the same as heterosexual women, but because women on average earn less than men, lesbian couple households earn significantly less than heterosexual couple households (Klawitter and Flatt 1998). Many transgender people suffer from significant economic hardship.

Same-sex spouses do not receive the legal protections provided married spouses under the Retirement Equality Act of 1984, which prohibits a married worker from taking a life-only pension benefit without his or her spouse's written consent. The design and administration of pension plans vary greatly from employer to employer. Unfortunately, for same-sex couples in retirement, the one aspect most plans have in common is that very few automatically pay benefits to anyone but a legal spouse following the death of a participant. In addition, if a person dies after becoming vested in a pension plan, but before reaching the age of retirement, a legal spouse may be entitled to a cash benefit beginning in the year that the deceased would have started receiving the pension. The surviving spouse receives this benefit until death, but surviving same-sex partners are usually not eligible for this benefit. However, where a pension death benefit requires a beneficiary designation, there is no discrimination.

### Unequal Treatment under 401(k) Regulations

If a person with a 401(k) plan dies, the tax implications for the beneficiary depend on whether or not the beneficiary is a legal spouse. If the beneficiary is a legally married spouse, then he or she may roll over the total amount of the decedent's account into an IRA with no tax implications except applicable estate taxes. No distribution must occur; the surviving spouse can maintain the funds in an IRA until April of the year following the year in which he or she turns 70½—the age at which withdrawals from retirement accounts become mandatory. However, if the beneficiary is a same-sex partner who is unable to legally marry, then he or she must begin taking distributions right away, which not only generates current income tax liabilities but also defeats the purpose of the retirement savings.

### The Medicaid Spend-Down Provision and Same-Sex Couples

Similar to many heterosexual elders, the lack of coverage for long-term care for most GLBT elders constitutes a crisis in their care as well as personal finances. Often, seniors who enter nursing homes spend all of their assets on their care, then simply apply for Medicaid when they have next to nothing left, a phenomenon known as the "Medicaid spend-down." Medicaid regulations allow one member of a married heterosexual couple to remain in the couple's home for the rest of his or her life without jeopardizing his or her spouse's right to Medicaid coverage. Upon the survivor's death, the state may then take the home to recoup the costs of terminal care. However, since same-sex couples cannot marry, Medicaid regulations do not offer the same protection for same-sex partners, even if they have spent their entire adult lives together. This unequal treatment can force same-sex couples into a Hobson's choice ("an apparently free choice when there is no real alternative"—Merriam-Webster 2003) between getting the medical coverage to meet a partner's health care needs or foregoing medical care in order to avoid giving up the couple's home and life savings. A change in Medicaid regulations to treat same-sex couples equally as married heterosexual couples would be less discriminatory. Same-sex partners should be able to remain in their home without jeopardizing their partners' right to Medicaid coverage (Dean et al. 2000).

### Senior Housing Issues

There are now several gay senior housing projects in various stages of development in Seattle, Boston, and Florida. While such developments are welcome, most units will only be accessible to upper-income people. The housing needs of rural, poor and middle-income GLBT elders can best be addressed by making senior housing gay-friendly and either adding sexual orientation and gender identity to the Fair Housing Act of 1968 or passing a federal nondiscrimination law that covers housing as well as employment.

### Health Care

GLBT seniors may experience physician bias and often lack access to health coverage from a partner's work benefits. Antigay bias in health care is widespread. A 1994 study by the Gay & Lesbian Medical Association found that two-thirds of doctors and medical students reported knowing of biased caregiving by medical professionals; half reported witnessing it; and nearly 90% reported hearing disparaging remarks about gay, lesbian, or bisexual patients (Schatz and O'Hanlan 1994).

Assuming GLBT seniors can find appropriate care, they must then face the problem of paying for it. For many, Medicare plays a vital role in covering medical expenses and is especially vital for GLBT old people, as lifelong incomes may be lower than similar heterosexual-headed households. One shortcoming of Medicare is that it does not pay for prescription medications. This is especially harmful for the larger proportion of older gay and bisexual men who are living with HIV/AIDS (human immunodeficiency virus/acquired immunodeficiency syndrome) and who need expensive antiretroviral medications. While married spouses often take employer-provided health coverage for granted, most private and public sector employers do not provide such coverage to same-sex partners. These two factors—health care provider bias and lack of access to a partner's benefits—mean many gay people may enter retirement without having accessed health care on a regular basis during their lives. When domestic partner health insurance is available, it is taxed, while heterosexual spouse's health benefits are not. Also, the federal Family and Medical Leave Act does not cover same-sex partners.

### Health Care Decision Making

Married heterosexual couples automatically have a right to visit their loved ones in the hospital and to supervise their spouse's funeral arrangements after their death. Additionally, they are commonly, if informally, given deference in terms of their spouse's medical care. These rights and privileges are not automatically granted to same-sex partners.

For example, when a gay man or lesbian is hospitalized, their partner might not be allowed to visit them unless they can present a hospital visitation authorization—a document completed by the hospitalized person specifying who may visit him. Unfortunately, hospital administrators do not always respect these documents, and not all states require hospitals to use these forms. This causes tremendous pain and hardship to members of GLBT families, as it did for Bill Flanigan and Robert Daniel in a Baltimore hospital in October 2000. When Daniel was admitted to the hospital, hospital personnel refused to let Flanigan see his dying partner on the grounds that he was not a family member. They disregarded both Flanigan's durable power of attorney for health care decisions and the fact that he had been recognized as a family member during Daniel's previous hospital stays. Flanigan was not allowed to confer with Daniel's doctors or to let them know that Daniel did not want life-prolonging measures, such as insertion of a breathing tube. Flanigan was finally allowed to see Daniel four hours later—when Daniel's mother and sister arrived. Daniel had already received a breathing tube, contrary to his wishes, and had lost consciousness. Flanigan never had a chance to say good-bye to him (Lambda 2002).

Furthermore, if a gay man or lesbian is incapacitated in the hospital, then his or her closest blood relative will automatically be deferred to for decisions about care unless a medical power of attorney form has been completed empowering the patient's partner to make medical decisions. If this form exists, then the specified health care proxy may act on behalf of the incapacitated person and make decisions as his or her agent. If the incapacitated gay man or lesbian has also completed financial power of attorney forms, then the partner may also act as his or her financial proxy and pay bills or sell assets on behalf of his or her loved one. While completing these forms provides some security to same-sex partners, the cost of writing up legal documents and the requirement that one essentially "out" oneself work to inhibit many gay seniors from taking advantage of this option. State recognition of same-sex couple relationships would provide greater equity in this area.

### End-of-Life Issues

Lesbian and gay families are particularly vulnerable when one member of a couple dies. The rituals that inevitably follow death are more challenging for gay families. In order for same-sex couples to ensure that their remains will be disposed of in an appropriate manner, they may need to complete a "consent to autopsy and disposition of remains" form, because some medical power of attorney forms do not cover this subject. This form enables lesbians and gay men to appoint their partners as agents to carry out their final wishes. However, not all states have this form, and the same issues around cost and privacy apply.

When one member of a heterosexual married couple dies without a will, the other member of the couple automatically inherits any property or assets belonging to his or her spouse. However, the same standards do not apply to same-sex couples. An unmarried couple that purchases a house together without putting both partners on the title has no protections if one of them dies. In fact, if a lesbian or gay man dies without a will, then the partner faces the possibility of losing all objects that can be shown to have belonged to the deceased to a biological family member. Wills are the best insurance against a homophobic family member's challenge to a life partner's desire to stay in a house that was not jointly owned and access to other items left by the deceased.

Another way in which surviving same-sex partners are treated unfairly concerns inheritance taxes. When married couples leave property to a surviving spouse, they enjoy an unlimited marital deduction. One hundred percent (100%) of an estate of any size can be left to a legal spouse without diminution by death taxes, and until 2010 at least, assets will be revalued as of the date of death so that the surviving spouse can sell them without income tax consequences. In contrast, when same-sex partners leave property to each other, the value of the estate being bequeathed beyond $1 million is subject to death taxes. Furthermore, married couples are exempt from property tax reassessment upon death of one spouse. An unmarried partner, in contrast, will be subject to a property tax reassessment, even if the property was owned jointly or willed properly. The tax can be so significant that the survivor might be unable to afford to keep the home (Cahill, Ellen, and Tobias 2002).

### Conclusion

The documented persistence of homophobia in long-term care environments and senior centers presents barriers to care for GLBT elders and challenges for elder service providers. Elder service and health care professionals can address these barriers by mandating training in the particular issues affecting GLBT elders for all those entrusted with their care. Longer-term, professional development institutions such as schools of social work, health professional training programs, and gerontology programs can incorporate competency in serving GLBT populations into their educational programs. More research is needed to understand the particular caregiving needs and practices of GLBT elders. Unequal treatment of same-sex couples under income support programs should be addressed in the political arena. The Democratic National Committee took an important step in this direction by issuing a resolution supporting equal treatment of lesbian and gay couples under Social Security in January 2002. Such a move also enjoys widespread support among the U.S. public (Yang 1999).

The principle of equal treatment regardless of sexual orientation already enjoys widespread support in the United States. Significant majorities support hospital visitation rights, inheritance rights, and Social Security survivor benefits for same-sex couples (Cahill, Ellen, and Tobias 2002). As America ages and a sizable cohort of gay baby boomers enters retirement, GLBT activists are working with elder service professionals and elder activists to ensure that this principle of equality is realized for elder GLBT people as well. (See also COST OF FAMILY CAREGIVING; LONG-TERM CARE INSURANCE [LTCI]—A CONSUMER'S PERSPECTIVE; MEDICAID; MEDICAID PLANNING; PENSION PLANS; RETIREMENT PLANS—401(k)s.)

### References

Cahill, S., M. Ellen, and S. Tobias. 2002. *Family Policy: Issues Affecting Gay, Lesbian, Bisexual, and Transgender Families*. New York: Policy Institute of the National Gay and Lesbian Task Force.

Cahill, S., K. South, and J. Spade. 2000. *Outing Age: Public Policy Issues Affecting Gay, Lesbian, Bisexual, and Transgender Elders*. New York: Policy Institute of the National Gay and Lesbian Task Force.

Cook-Daniels, L. 1997. "Lesbian, Gay Male, Bisexual and Transgendered Elders: Elder Abuse and Neglect Issues." *Journal of Elder Abuse and Neglect* 9(2): 35–49.

Dean, L., I. Meyer, K. Robinson, R. Sell, R. Sember, V. Silenzio, et al. 2000. *Lesbian, Gay, Bisexual, and Transgender Health: Findings and Concerns*. New York: Gay and Lesbian Medical Association and the Center for LGBT Health, Columbia University School of Public Health.

Fairchild, S.K., G.E. Carrino, and M. Ramirez. 1996. "Social Workers' Perceptions of Staff Attitudes toward Resident Sexuality in a Random Sample of New York State Nursing Homes: A Pilot Study." *Journal of Gerontological Social Work* 26(1–2): 153–70.

Fredriksen, K.I. 1999. "Family Caregiving Responsibilities among Lesbians and Gay Men." *Social Work* 44(2): 142–55.

Klawitter, M., and V. Flatt. 1998. "The Effects of State and Local Antidiscrimination Policies on Earnings for Gays and Lesbians." *Journal of Policy Analysis and Management* 17(4): 658–87.

Lambda Legal Defense and Education Fund. 2002. "University of Maryland Medical System to Be Sued Wednesday by Gay Man Prevented from Visiting His Dying Partner at Shock Trauma Center in Baltimore." News Release. Available online at http://www.lambdalegal.org/cgi-bin/iowa/documents/record?record=1011.

Merriam-Webster. 2003. *Merriam-Webster's Collegiate Dictionary*. 11th ed. Springfield, MA: Author.

Parsons, Y. 1995. "Private Acts, Public Places." *Contemporary Long Term Care* 3: 48–52.

Schatz, B., and K. O'Hanlan. 1994. *Anti-Gay Discrimination in Medicine: Results of a National Survey of Lesbian, Gay and Bisexual Physicians*. San Francisco, CA: American Association of Physicians for Human Rights.

Shippy, A., and S. Cahill. 2002. "Family Caregiving among Lesbian, Gay, Bisexual and Transgender Elders in New York City." Paper presented at Third International Family Care Conference, Washington, DC, October 13.

Yang, A. 1999. *From Wrongs to Rights, 1973–1999: Public Opinion on Gay and Lesbian Americans Moves toward Equality*. New York: Policy Institute of the National Gay and Lesbian Task Force.

*Sean Cahill*

**FINANCIAL ADVISORS,** a term applied to a wide variety of professional individuals who provide an even wider variety of financial services and products. Among those who may be referred to as financial advisors are financial planners, stockbrokers, life and health insurance agents, bankers, attorneys, daily money managers, and accountants. While each of these categories represents a field of legitimate financial advice, and may involve licensure and regulation, the scope of services offered by any advisor must be measured against his or her particular training and experience, the emphasis of the advisor's practice, and the personal comfort and rapport between the client and advisor. Choosing a financial advisor is similar to choosing any professional in whom a great amount of trust must be placed. Knowing the array of financial advisors and their area of expertise is key, followed by an individual's understanding of his or her own financial needs and knowledge of sources for personal and organizational referrals. Surrendering total responsibility for one's financial affairs to advisors is always unwise. It is especially important for older individuals to learn and to participate actively in as many details of their own financial management as possible, since doing so can improve one's sense of autonomy and increase feelings of personal accomplishment, security, and well-being.

*Financial planners* constitute a huge and growing population of persons from many different backgrounds with widely varying abilities. Use of the designation "financial planner" requires no specialized license or credential and has been assumed by many stockbrokers, accountants, and insurance salespeople (Savage 1994). However, financial planners who have earned the Certified Financial Planner™ (CFP®) designation are among the most respected in the financial services business. All CFPs have completed a degree course offered at more than 40 colleges and universities around the country or through home study courses. Six core categories comprise rigorous training in subjects ranging from investment advice to tax and estate planning. In addition, to earn the CFP® designation, a ten-hour examination given by the Certified Financial Planner Board of

Standards, Inc., must be passed to demonstrate proof of financial planning–related knowledge.

Creating a financial plan takes both effort and knowledge, and those holding themselves out as financial planners should be compensated for planning. Financial planners are compensated in one of four ways, and persons seeking planning and investment advice should know in advance how they are being charged. Fee-only planners accept no commissions for sales of insurance, annuity, or investment products and are compensated solely by fees charged to their clients for the establishment, implementation, and maintenance of a financial plan, ad hoc advice, and other work performed on either an hourly or fixed-fee basis. Fee-based planners earn most of their income from fees charged to their clients but also earn commissions on sales of insurance and investment products that are recommended to implement the plan. Fee-offset planners also earn commissions but credit them against fees charged to the same client. Commission-based planners charge no fees for their planning work but are instead paid by the companies for which they place, or sell, products. None of these structures *necessarily* poses a conflict of interest, but it is important to take into account a financial advisor's motivation for whatever recommendations are made.

*Stockbrokers and commodities brokers* are registered representatives or principals of National Association of Securities Dealers (NASD) member firms and are licensed by the NASD after passing the examinations for the particular type of license they wish to hold. Different licenses enable an advisor to sell different types of products or to supervise others who do. In addition, they must pass state examinations and be licensed by the state or states in which they sell securities. The examinations are independent of any specified academic background, so it is not necessary for securities brokers to have any special training beyond what is required to pass the tests. Although some brokers do have advanced academic or other training in financial areas, many do not, and great knowledge of the securities industry is not the same as good financial advice.

Securities—stocks (equity securities), bonds, commodities, mutual funds, and variable annuities—are purchased customarily through brokers who are paid a commission based on the dollar amount of each transaction and the number of securities involved. Brokers should be selected based on their honesty, efficiency, accessibility, and ability to provide clients with information about the investments that are being considered for purchase or for sale, the appropriateness of the investment to the client's situation, and the cost of the transaction.

*Insurance agents* are licensed to offer life insurance, health insurance (including Medicare Supplement policies), long-term care insurance, and fixed annuity products to their customers on behalf of the insurance companies they represent. Many life insurance companies (but not all) offer extensive training to their agents, and it is not unusual for an insurance agent to also be licensed to sell mutual funds, variable annuities, and securities. Well-trained insurance agents often act as commission-based financial planners and give a broad base of recommendations to their clients. Many insurance agents have obtained additional designations—CFP®, Chartered Life Underwriter (CLU), or Chartered Financial Consultant (ChFC) are three prominent examples—and have taken advanced training that enables them to provide expert advice to their clients. Financial advisors who are also insurance agents may be "career" agents of a particular company, such as the Northwestern Mutual Financial Network or the Mass Mutual Financial Group, and represent only, or at least primarily, that company's products, or they may be independent brokers who offer products from a variety of companies. The extensive support and training provided to a "career agent" must be weighed against access to the great variety of products available in the marketplace.

*Attorneys* in most states must first obtain a law degree from a law school and then become licensed, after passing the state bar exam, to practice law. Some attorneys have highly specialized backgrounds in taxation and financial consulting, but it is important before engaging the services of an attorney to determine his or her specialized training and area of expertise. No other type of advisor is permitted (by law) to draw some of the instruments that are often a key part of implementing financial advice, such as wills, trusts, and durable powers of attorney. Some attorneys, such as those with an elder law practice, are able to offer very expert advice on the legal issues and instruments most often required in aging, such as advance directives, durable powers of attorney, and wills and trusts, but are inexperienced in investments, pensions, business succession planning, and other areas that impact sound personal financial planning. Even an attorney specializing in the practice of tax law, for example, is likely to have further specialized training within the field of taxation—civil and criminal, personal or corporate—so vast are these and other specialized areas of law. It is the responsibility of a prospective client to ascertain the areas and level of experience that attorneys have, and it is also the duty of an attorney to disclose this information to the client, although many will not volunteer their credentials unless asked.

*Accountants* and *certified public accountants* (CPAs) have backgrounds in dealing with money and, frequently, in income taxation. This experience often affords them a good basis for advising clients on financial matters, although it does not always extend into every area of financial consulting, such as insurance or investments. The services that accountants are best trained to render as financial advisors are those of tax planning, tax projections, tax return preparation, business valuations, and cash flow projections, although the American Institute of Certified Public Accountants (AICPA) has developed specialized training for CPAs in personal financial planning and eldercare and is even offering a professional designation of Personal Financial Specialist (CPA/PFS) available only to CPAs.

*Money managers* typically charge a fee to manage large blocks of funds inside investment portfolios. These individuals have credentials and investment experience that vary, and it is always advisable to obtain an investment history for the firms they represent in order to determine their success track record. However, even successful money managers may not be appropriate for some clients, since the minimum amounts they typically accept for investment management are frequently much higher than most individual investors have available.

Areas of knowledge that individuals should seek in their financial advisors include knowledge of people and how they relate to money; how to handle credit, budgeting, and long-range planning; relevant law, estate, and income taxation; life, health, and long-term care insurance; investment management; Social Security, Medicare, and Medicaid; as well as sensitivity to the needs of older persons in general. Two certification programs designed to educate financial advisors and others broadly about issues in the field of aging as well as individual aging have gained many adherents in the last few years, and people with these designations may be better able to serve a retired client than those without them.

The Certified Senior Advisor (CSA) program was founded by the Society of Certified Senior Advisors in 1997 and consists of a national educational program that trains professionals to better understand the health, social, and financial implications of the aging process. More than 9,000 CSAs, many of them financial professionals, are active members of the society. The Certified Financial Gerontologist (CFG) program is new as we go to press, but it is intended to be an academically rigorous program that certifies financial professionals in aging studies. The CFG program was established by the American Institute of Financial Gerontology in partnership with Widener University and the American Society on Aging. Because these matters are diverse and complicated, it is rare that any one individual can satisfy all areas of need for financial expertise, although most people look to one individual as their key advisor.

Perhaps the most common error made by an individual seeking to implement personal financial objectives is to rely on a specialist in one area to provide services, products, or advice outside the specialist's field of expertise. As examples, most attorneys do not prepare tax returns, CPAs are neither trained nor licensed to prepare trust documents or other legal instruments, and investment advisors may not understand estate planning, goals, or techniques. None of these professional experts may be well grounded in Life Planning, which is an essential part of putting financial matters in perspective. Despite these limitations, individuals seeking financial advice should be aware that there is a significant population of financial advisors who do have backgrounds, training, and experience in specialized areas. Once financial objectives are identified, one should seek assistance from more than one professional in order to obtain the range of help needed for financial planning needs.

### Financial Advisors Designations

*CLU (Chartered Life Underwriter).* This designation is awarded by the American College of Bryn Mawr, Pennsylvania, and requires successful completion of ten courses in such areas as law, finance, estate and income taxation, life insurance, and investments. It requires continuing education to maintain the credential.

*ChFC (Chartered Financial Consultant).* This designation is also given by the American College (see CLU, above) and requires additional, advanced courses in taxation, finance, and investment topics beyond those included in the CLU. The American College primarily trains insurance professionals. It requires continuing education to maintain the credential.

*CFP® (Certified Financial Planner).* This designation signifies a broad amount of training in financial planning, as discussed above. Financial planners who have the CFP designation must earn continuing education credits in order to maintain the credential.

*CPA (Certified Public Accountant).* CPAs have significant academic and on-the-job training and must qualify for the designation by passing rigorous examinations. In order to maintain the designation of CPA, a number of continuing education classes must be completed each year.

*J.D. (Juris Doctor).* The degree conferred by law schools after a three-year academic program. The law school curriculum, at schools jointly accredited by the American Bar Association and the Association of American Law Schools, requires a bachelor's degree from an accredited university and covers the wide range of legal subjects necessary to prepare for the general practice of law.

*LL.M.* An LL.M. is the Master of Laws, a degree that allows a law school graduate to study areas of specialty within the law, such as taxation, labor law, or patent law. (See also AGENTS AND BROKERS; ATTORNEYS; CPA ELDERCARE SERVICES; DAILY MONEY MANAGERS; ELDER LAW PRACTICE; FINANCIAL COUNSELING FOR MID- TO LATER LIFE; FINANCIAL PLANNING PROCESS; LIFE PLANNING.)

### Organizations

AICPA (American Institute of Certified Public Accountants)
American Institute of Financial Gerontology
CFP Board (Certified Financial Planner Board of Standards)
National Association of Financial and Estate Planning (NAFEP)
National Association of Insurance and Financial Advisors (NAIFA)
National Association of Personal Financial Advisors (NAPFA)
Society of Certified Senior Advisors
Society of Financial Services Professionals

### References

Jaffe, Charles A. 2001. *The Right Way to Hire Financial Help*. 2nd ed. Cambridge, MA: MIT Press.

Johnson, Dale S. 1988. *Financial Services: Environment and Professions*. Bryn Mawr, PA: American College.

Savage, Terry. 1994. *New Money Strategies for the '90s*. New York: HarperCollins.

Shim, Jae K., and Joel G. Siegal. In press. *Handbook of Financial Planning: An Expert's Guide for Advisors and Their Clients*. Cincinnati, OH: South-Western.

*Donald A. Hunsberger*
*Updated by E. Craig MacBean*

**FINANCIAL COUNSELING FOR MID- TO LATER LIFE,** performed by financial counseling professionals, often employees of a nonprofit organization organized to assist clients in financial difficulty on a one-to-one basis. Clients are helped to resolve problems that impact their financial well-being, to make decisions that have financial implications for life now and in the future, to improve their financial management, to handle difficult transitions, and to improve functioning in the consumer market and/or legal systems by handling financial or consumer collections and other dilemmas. Financial counseling utilizes information and skills to assist clients in changing behaviors in resource management, consumption, lifestyle, and communication in order to obtain and maintain increased financial security. Problems and barriers to change are identified that interfere with meeting unique objectives for various stages of family life. Steps to resolving problems or implementing decisions are individualized and realistic for the particular client's personality, resource limitations, and needs.

### Need for Financial Counseling

Reasons that clients seek advice or assistance vary greatly. Some perceive seeking assistance as a weakness, while others perceive it as a sign of strength. Clients may be experiencing financial difficulty such as the possibility of foreclosure, recent unemployment, garnishment of wages, the chronic overuse of credit, or facing some critical life event such as divorce, insufficient funds for retirement, gambling, or other spending addiction.

Psychological reasons may include feeling out of control, being unable "to make ends meet," the inability to say no to a spouse or to children, insufficient income for a chosen lifestyle, continuously paying late fees, lack of confidence to reduce expenses, family fights over finances, or anxiety for the future or some other personal emergency. Some clients simply want assistance with decisions, information, or clarification about the confusing mechanics and financial instruments available to them. Some are in a stage of transition and want to improve their economic security, enhance their wealth, reduce risks, or optimize their resources. Some clients are overly optimistic and set unrealistic goals that are impossible to achieve at their particular education or income level. A common problem is overestimating income and underestimating expenses. Lack of experience, not keeping records, or refusal to face reality may cause this problem.

The need for financial counseling is not always due to mismanagement or lack of information about alternative behavior patterns but may occur because of external events or situations beyond the client's control. An unexpected illness, change in family composition, job loss, car or appliance breakdown, legal problems, business failure, and downturn in the economy are a few examples of circumstances that can precipitate a personal financial crisis and the need for counseling.

### Decisions

Decisions in the complex financial arena are difficult: Facing and making decisions is often stressful. Too much information and too many companies, some reputable and others not, cause confusion. Too little information gathered by comparison shopping and experience causes errors and overspending. When people are emotionally disturbed or anxious, they often go in circles and need financial counseling to sort out the priorities, decision-making steps, and the information needed to make good decisions.

Sufficient information is needed for each decision in order to minimize risk or error. The financial counselor can point out the alternatives, the consequences, and steps, but the decision has to belong to the client, who follows through with it. Others in the family who have to implement the decision need to be involved in the decision. Time frames for experimentation or living with a decision and then evaluating can reduce reluctance to try something new.

### Process of Financial Counseling

Financial counseling is assisting clients in the development and creative use of all their resources to achieve economic security or well-being by generating alternatives from which the client chooses. Ultimately the client is assisted to improve quality of life with less wasteful resources. The processes are:

1. *Increasing income through exploration of possible sources based on the premise that income, in the economic sense, is a flow of goods and services and not money alone.* Advice and information are presented to mobilize resources through different employment, business expansion, liquidation of assets, government entitlements, rentals, community resources, early inheritance, and exchange in-kind with others.

2. *Reducing some expenses (or wants), maximizing use of money, avoiding additional*

*financial burdens, or increasing other expenses after analysis of family needs and recording current spending or observing patterns of various family members.* Clients are asked to check a list of alternative ways to reduce expenses, spend less, or practice saying "no" to family members.

3. *Adjusting debts and managing credit and other financial obligations either with a self-administered plan as an assertive consumer or utilizing credit counseling services.* Negotiation theories and skills are applied. Debts are analyzed by how they would hurt the client if not paid: harassment, loss of goods or services, garnishment or court action, and increased costs. Interest rates and legal consequences are noted. Clients are shown the advantages and disadvantages of credit counseling, loan consolidation, bankruptcy, and borrowing from relatives. Forms and addresses are provided for clients to check the accuracy of their credit reports.

4. *Clarifying and prioritizing wants and goals, then planning to meet them sequentially.* This step is listed purposefully after the first three possibilities are explored. Clients are helped to understand the influences and pressures upon them to consume in various ways. They are helped to reconcile wants among family members, to reconcile expenses with income, and to fulfill their wants in less expensive ways; wants are prioritized.

5. *Making decisions after listing them in order of urgency and with time frames for implementation.* Information is given for making the required decisions. Specific steps with time frames and person responsible are written, and clients are asked to clarify what they have heard. In subsequent meetings, clients are asked, "What problems did you have in implementing your decisions (or plans)?" Clients are provided with possible legal consequences of their decisions, financial facts or tax implications, which might be from a referral source or reading material.

6. *Establishing or reorganizing a system of household and financial management.* Appropriate techniques are shown such as necessary record keeping, bill paying on time, tax management, controlling impulsive spending, and communicating effectively with businesses and other family members.

7. *Budgeting or setting up a spending plan with appropriate categories based on individualized needs, personality constructs, and behavior patterns.* The financial counselor provides telescopic vision of possible changes of income from all sources, expenses, and decisions at different stages of the family life. Techniques of "time value of money," cash flow analysis, and net worth analysis are used with some clients in financial counseling but with all in financial planning.

8. *Acting effectively to realize consumer rights, to know the steps for recourse when these rights have been violated, and to effectively resolve a consumer complaint.* The client/consumer can be shown a sample letter for writing an effective complaint letter. The client is motivated and has sufficient confidence to do the research, gather important documents, and communicate effectively to those in authority.

9. *Evaluating programs for meeting past, current, and future needs and protection against risks (insurance).* Areas examined and assessed are housing, transportation, life insurance, health insurance, marital disruption, children's education, investments, and retirement planning. Sources of income and investments can be diversified to increase security. Skills for employment can be enhanced and diversified for transferability and promotion. Drastic changes such as in housing may need to be made for resolving a crisis.

10. *Planning for retirement by reducing current consumption to have income accumulate and generate income for the future.* This acknowledges that the value of money decreases over time, and there is risk in giving up control of current income. The greater the risk, the greater the possibility of income generated. Planning now often includes the necessity of employment after retirement. With a fixed income in retirement, clients have to plan on how they will reduce expenses or be more efficient. The retirement budget plan can include these categories: Years projected, his and her income, fixed expenses, flexible expenses, Social Security, pension, inheritance, sale of property, and liquidation of assets. Some expenses increase, while others decrease. Clients and their children can be creative in sharing housing arrangements. Social Security pamphlets on vital concerns to clients are available. Statements of earnings are checked for accuracy. The temptation for early retirement must be checked with realities, requirements for benefits, and information about pension plans. Changes in other aspects of life to facilitate continued employment can be considered.

11. *Championing change and handling adjustments/crises in lifestyle or family life.*

(See also AGING INTO DEBT; BABY BOOMERS AND RETIREMENT; CONSUMER CREDIT; CONSUMER PROTECTION FOR OLDER ADULTS; CREDIT SCORES; FINANCIAL RECOVERY IN LATER LIFE; PREDATORY LENDING.)

**Organizations**

AARP
Association for Financial Counseling and Planning Education
Attorney General's Office, U.S.
Consumer Information Center
National Foundation for Credit

*Flora Williams*

**FINANCIAL EDUCATION FOR SENIORS.** The baby boom generation (approximately 76 million people born between the years of 1946 and 1964) continues to present challenges for educators striving to provide financial education that meets the learning needs of this audience and results in positive behavior changes and increased financial security. Even greater challenges exist in education for the growing cohort of older seniors. In 2000, the number of persons age 65 and older numbered 35 million and represented 12.4% of the U.S. population. The cohort that is 85 or older is growing the most rapidly of all age groups. If mortality rates continue to improve, this group is expected to double in size between 1999 and 2025 and to increase five times by 2050, when the last of the baby boomers enter this age group (Rogers 1999).

## The Need for Lifelong Financial Education

The body of evidence documenting the need for lifelong financial education for the senior population of this country is growing. According to the AARP *Beyond 50* report (AARP 2002), there is good news and bad news about the financial situation older generations are presently experiencing. On the positive side, the inflation-adjusted income for Americans over 50 is higher (by 17%) than in 1980, and their wealth has increased even faster than their income (36%). More retirees have pensions, and their pension incomes are up by 35%. There have been marked improvements in the level of education in all age groups in the past two decades, and poverty has dropped to an all-time low for persons 65 and older (9.7%).

On the negative side, income growth has been fairly weak (less than 1% per year after inflation) for this segment of the population, and wealth increases (more than 2% per year after inflation) have been distributed unevenly. "And while poverty in old age at a given point in time is at an all-time low, poverty at some point after age 60 is still a fairly high probability event, as well as a pervasive problem for certain vulnerable groups" (AARP 2002).

The experiences of these vulnerable groups in the nation's older population portray a bleak financial picture. According to the National Association of Consumer Bankruptcy Attorneys (NACBA), more than a quarter of a million Americans aged 55 and older filed for bankruptcy in 2001. Further, the number of Americans 65 and older filing for bankruptcy has tripled in the last ten years, making older Americans the fastest-growing age group in bankruptcy.

> The bankruptcy data suggest that, as the population ages, each new wave of older Americans faces more financial risk than its predecessors. The data reveal substantial economic vulnerability among older Americans, and they indicate this trend is getting worse. (National Association of Consumer Bankruptcy Attorneys 2002)

The 1999 Consumer Bankruptcy Project's nationwide survey of families filing bankruptcy reveals that the financial risk exposure for older Americans stems from a variety of reasons including the following: job loss, large medical expenses, credit card debt, death of a family member, and other financial concerns such as providing financial support for other family members. Job loss was the most frequently listed reason (62.1%) for filing bankruptcy for all debtors aged 50 and older, followed by medical expenses (53.0%).

The study reports that older Americans often used credit cards to supplement their income and that they often charge prescriptions and other medical supplies. "Of those aged 50 and over, 45.5% explain that by the time they file bankruptcy, their credit card debts are completely unmanageable" (National Association of Consumer Bankruptcy Attorneys 2002).

The need for lifelong financial education is great regardless of an older person's place on the "have" or "have-not" wealth continuum. The "haves" need continuing education on how to manage their wealth to ensure financial security throughout their lifetimes, and the "have-nots" need programs tailored to avoiding disastrous results from financial risks they encounter and to ensure financial stability. The complexity of financial products and services, along with rapid changes in technology, information availability, public policy, and increasing cases of consumer fraud, demand a financially literate consumer, regardless of age and economic status.

## Education and Successful Aging

Richard Adler (2002), author of "The Age Wave Meets the Technology Wave: Broadband and Older Americans," suggests that in order to age successfully, older adults need to remain engaged in learning throughout later life. He believes lifelong learning is an area of rapidly growing interest among adults and reports that more than 33 million adults over age 45, over one-third of this age cohort, are currently engaged in some form of adult education.

The demand for lifelong learning is currently being addressed by colleges, public schools, Cooperative Extension, and community groups through a variety of formats. Opportunities exist on site at schools and colleges, libraries, museums, public meeting facilities, senior centers, and nursing homes. Alternative media such as newspapers, cable and public television, and educational radio are also utilized. Methodologies include traditional educator-led programs, peer teaching/learning designs, and even instruction provided by regular matriculated students at colleges and universities for an older, non-traditional audience. One example is the "Joining Wisdom with Youth Through Bits and Bytes: Computer Skills Development Through Intergenerational Service Learning" at Clemson University. Residents of a local retirement community are transported to campus where Clemson students teach them how to surf the Internet, scan photos, take digital photographs, and use word processing programs.

One popular lifelong learning environment has been the Elderhostel model. Begun in 1974 at the University of New Hampshire, the Elderhostel concept has expanded to over 1,500 colleges. Once only offered in the summer as one-week programs, Elderhostels are now available all year and may even be international in scope. Seniors typically live on campus, but programs vary and even include 4-H camp environments. The goal is to present older adults with courses that are relevant to their everyday lives and that are enjoyable.

### Lifelong Financial Education Programs for Seniors: A Selected Example of a Traditional Format

When following a more traditional education program design, there are special considerations for older adults concerning physical conditions, methodology, and topics presented in these programs. As adults age, they may have special education needs resulting from changing physical status such as impaired vision or hearing and they often develop chronic medical conditions and become increasingly frail. It is suggested that seniors learn best when the material is relevant and interesting to them and programs are structured so that seniors are allowed to learn at their own pace. "To assure that the audience is motivated, planners should make efforts to develop educational sessions stemming from the issues and problems the elderly identify as concerns" (Penn State University 1990).

Clearly, the financial arena contains issues and problems identified as concerns by seniors. Educational programs designed specifically for this audience should be well received. One example of a financial education program for seniors following a more traditional format is the BE SMART program currently being offered in South Carolina. BE SMART is an acronym for Basic Education for Senior Medicare Awareness to Restore Trust, and it is delivered as a cooperative effort of the South Carolina Department of Health and Human Services (SCDHHS), South Carolina Council of Governments (Administration on Aging), South Carolina Department of Consumer Affairs (SCDCA), and Clemson University Cooperative Extension (CES).

The BE SMART program provides information on topics including the SCDHHS's guarding against Medicare fraud, the SCDCA alert on consumer fraud, and CES's update on maintaining organized financial files, medical records, and important documents. The program is delivered by personnel from each of these collaborating partners, and the Council of Governments assists with marketing and arranges physical facilities for the program, usually senior meal sites.

Senior citizens are often thought of as easy prey for a variety of fraudulent activities. Education is the key to insure the financial security of senior citizens and protect them from the dangers of telemarketers and con artists. BE SMART program presentations made to senior audiences empower them to take control of their financial future.

### Lifelong Financial Education Programs for Seniors: Utilizing Technology

More and more consumer education, protection, and advocacy groups are utilizing nontraditional, nonformal formats to provide financial education and information. The newest format and one that is expanding exponentially uses personal computers and information posted on the Internet to educate consumers. However, there are limiting factors for seniors in accessing this information. The current "generational digital divide" is documented by statistics that show after age 55 the use of computers declines steadily and falls below 20% among persons age 75 and older (Adler 2002).

Subsequently, the appropriate role of technology in conducting educational programs for the aging population is receiving a great deal of attention. Richard Adler states,

> When a solution is proposed to address a problem of aging that involves the use of technology, the objection is often raised that seniors are "technophobic" and are resistant to adopting any new technology. It is true that older adults do not tend to be "innovators" or the "early adopters" of new technologies—that is, they rarely rush in to be "the first on their block" to try out the latest gadget. But once a technology reaches maturity and its benefits are well understood, seniors are as likely to use it as younger people. The key to the successful introduction of a technology for older adults is to make sure it is affordable, easy to use and delivers significant benefits. (Adler 2002)

Until this technology reaches maturity and seniors adopt it on a large scale, a combination of traditional and nontraditional formats will have to be utilized. Seniors who are early adopters of the technology but do not have access to it within their homes have other opportunities to access this information. It is recommended that they visit local senior centers, libraries, or public schools where librarians or media persons are available to provide aid in searching the Internet and providing alternative ways of obtaining information. The Internet provides a wealth of sites dedicated to a wide variety of benefits for seniors, that is, Medicare, Social Security, prescription drug assistance programs, fraud protection, investment information, public benefits, health, and financial advance planning, to name a few. The time spent to overcome "technophobia" can be very rewarding to seniors seeking information to increase their financial knowledge and skills.

Access to lifelong learning opportunities can be difficult for seniors with limited mobility and stamina. Adler identified several projects designed to deliver educational programs directly to seniors at home. The University without Walls (UWW) project was launched in 1989 in New York City.

It has provided in-home education to students ranging in age up to 100 and living in places like Florida, Maryland, Utah and Israel. UWW's hour-long classes are delivered by telephone. When a class begins, each student is called and included on a conference line with the instructor and other students. The program now offers a catalog of dozens of courses in the arts and humanities, legal and financial topics, and health. (Adler 2002)

Membership-based organizations are also providing lifelong learning programs for their members. AARP piloted online courses in the summer of 2001. The courses were developed by college and university faculty in the United States and Britain and focused on the following four areas: technology and science, arts and humanities, history and perspectives, and personal management.

## Lifelong Financial Education Programs for Seniors: A Selected Example of a Combination Approach

The Cooperative Extension System has launched a national initiative entitled Financial Security in Later Life that utilizes both traditional and technological approaches in the design and delivery of financial education. Curricula, program materials, and resources for Financial Security in Later Life educational efforts are primarily available to educators on the Web site located at http://www.reeusda.gov/financialsecurity. However, this Web site also has pages designed to provide information directly to consumers including the following: online Extension programs, online financial management tools, links to Extension programs across the United States, and educational resources. This format provides the best of both the traditional and technological educational designs. The program impacts will be tracked as the Financial Security in Later Life Initiative continues. The feasibility and usefulness of this design will be assessed along with evaluations by end users to determine the success of this financial education approach.

## Conclusions

The need for lifelong financial education programs targeted toward seniors is well documented, the methodologies are varied, and the appeal to this target audience is growing. However, the humble beginning efforts need an influx of creativity and resources. The result will be a generation of older adults who are financially literate and empowered with the knowledge, attitudes, skills, and confidence to practice effective and successful financial management strategies that ensure financial security and stability throughout their lifetimes. (See also EDUCATION OF OLDER ADULTS; FINANCIAL LITERACY; INVESTOR EDUCATION; LIFE PLANNING IN THE WORKPLACE; WORKPLACE FINANCIAL EDUCATION.)

### References

AARP. 2002. *Beyond 50: A Report to the Nation on Economic Security*. Washington, DC: Author.

Adler, Richard. 2002. "The Age Wave Meets the Technology Wave: Broadband and Older Americans." SeniorNet. Available online at http://www.seniornet.org/.

Kausler, Donald H., and Barry C. Kausler. 1996. *The Graying of America: An Encyclopedia of Aging, Health, Mind, and Behavior*. Urbana: University of Illinois Press.

National Association of Consumer Bankruptcy Attorneys. 2002. "Bankruptcy and Older Americans." Available online at http://www.nacba.com/older_Americans.html.

Penn State University. 1990. "Planning Education Classes for Older Adults." Available online at http://agexted.cas.psu.edu/docs/21600640.html.

Rogers, C.C. 1999. *Changes in the Older Population and Implications for Rural Areas: Rural Development Research Report.* Washington, DC: Economic Research Service.

*Nancy C. Porter*

**FINANCIAL ELDER ABUSE,** improper or illegal use of an elder's assets, property, or income. Policymakers, public and private agencies, law enforcement agencies, and the public at large have become increasingly aware of the phenomenon of elder abuse during the past decade. As awareness has increased, the definitions of abuse have been refined, laws to prevent or address abuse have been introduced, many more stakeholders have been identified, elder abuse prevention programs have been initiated in all states and in many localities, and more rigorous research has been conducted.

Notwithstanding all of these efforts, the available data on the incidence of elder abuse remain highly unreliable because only about 21% of abuse is reported to law enforcement agencies or adult protective services programs. The so-called iceberg theory of abuse postulates that only a small percentage of domestic elder abuse is "visible above the waterline." According to this theory, four out of five incidents of elder abuse remain unreported, have not been noticed by others, and remain unidentified and inestimable at this time (Administration on Aging 1996).

## Definitions of Elder Abuse

Definitions of elder abuse vary from state to state, but several broad categories of abuse can be identified, depending on where the abuse takes place or who the abuser is. Domestic elder abuse is abuse that occurs in the elder's home or the home of a caregiver and is perpetrated by someone known to the victim of abuse. Institutional elder abuse occurs in a residential facility and/or was perpetrated by persons that have a legal or contractual obligation to the victim for care and protection. Self-neglect or self-abuse is usually also included in any definition of elder abuse, although this type of abuse is clearly distinctly different from abuse that has been perpetrated by another person. Within these broad parameters, subcategories of abuse can be identified—financial elder abuse being one of seven such subcategories. Financial elder abuse is defined by the Administration on Aging's National Center on Elder Abuse "as the illegal or improper use of an elder's funds, property, or assets."

## The Characteristics of Victims and Perpetrators of Financial Elder Abuse

The National Elder Abuse Incidence Study conducted in 1996 by the National Center on Elder Abuse found that 551,000 older adults in domestic settings experienced elder abuse or self-neglect (these data did not include institutionalized persons). The investigators found that among the victims of elder abuse, women are abused at higher rates than men and that the oldest elders, over the age of 80, are abused or neglected at two to three times their proportion of the older population in general. Slightly over 30% of all elder abuse victims experience financial abuse or material exploitation, and most of them (83%) are White, with another 15.5% being African American. Forty-five percent (45%) of all perpetrators of financial elder abuse were under the age of 40, with another

39.5% being between the ages of 41 and 59. Two-thirds (67%) of the abusers were children of the victim, with other relatives and grandchildren constituting 9.7% and 9.2%, respectively. In general, the victims are not the wealthiest among older adults. Based on substantiated incidents of reported financial elder abuse, close to four in five victims had incomes below $15,000 per year. The most prevalent reporters of financial abuse or material exploitation included friends or neighbors of the victim (15%), hospitals (14.2%), and family members (14%).

In recent years, additional types of financial elder abuse have emerged. For instance, in New York State in 2001, investigative reporters for the *New York Daily News* uncovered egregious incidents of financial abuse by guardians of incapacitated persons—people who had been appointed by the courts to manage the financial affairs or the personal well-being of the incapacitated person. Following these exposures, New York State's chief judge appointed two investigative bodies to determine the extent of abuse by duly appointed fiduciaries (the Commission on Fiduciary Appointments and a special inspector general). As a result of the recommendations submitted by these two investigative bodies, the New York State Office of Guardianship Services was established in 2002 within the Unified Court System to offer guidance to guardians and other fiduciaries and to monitor the quality of care given to incapacitated persons.

A study, "Abuse of Powers of Attorney," conducted by the Albany Law School Government Law Center in New York State in 1994 uncovered substantial problems with abuse of powers of attorney; while the Brookdale Center on Aging also noted abuse of joint bank accounts and other surrogate devices.

Other types of financial abuse now reported in the media include credit card fraud, confidence schemes, mail fraud, and telemarketing fraud. Although all Americans are potential victims of these types of abuse, in 2001 the National Fraud Information Center (NFIC) of the National Consumers League found that over 25% of the victims were people over the age of 60.

### Factors That Contribute to Financial Abuse

The risk factors that contribute to the potential for financial elder abuse include: advanced age; being a woman; living alone in relative social isolation; having some physical or cognitive impairment; and being dependent on others for care and protection. In addition, financial dependence by the abuser on the victim, substance abuse by the abuser, mental health problems of the abuser, and a history of family dysfunction all contribute to the incidence of financial elder abuse.

### Barriers to Addressing Financial Elder Abuse

A major issue in addressing financial elder abuse is the decisional capacity of the victim. Although advanced age cannot be equated with mental impairment, members of the group referred to as the "oldest old" (individuals 85 years or older) are more likely to have some physical or cognitive impairment that manifests in an inability to pay bills or purchase the necessities of daily living. The making of uncharacteristically large gifts may be voluntary and informed but may also be coerced. The belief that it is necessary to hoard or preserve assets to the detriment of personal health and safety may or may not be based on rational concerns or financial obligations. Furthermore, questionable mental capacity of the victim may impede the ability of the criminal justice system to prosecute cases of financial elder abuse because of the victim's inability to testify effectively. Health care facilities, social services providers, and the banking industry complain that the confidential nature of their relationship with the suspected victims of financial elder abuse impedes their ability to report many incidents of abuse to the authorities in the absence of the victim's consent. The banking industry is reluctant to report suspected cases of financial elder abuse when the alleged abuser has a duly executed durable power of attorney or other surrogate authority.

Finally, even when a victim's decisional mental capacity is not in question, it may be impossible to formally address the abuse because victims are often unwilling to report incidents of family dysfunction to law enforcement agencies. Victims of abuse may be dependent on the abuser or be fearful of reprisal. Most are embarrassed, ashamed, and unwilling to admit they were victimized.

### Future Directions

Many jurisdictions are in the process of evaluating the use of mandatory reporting requirements. Some states are revising criminal or civil remedies available to the victims of financial abuse; others are in the process of revising power of attorney statutes to build in safeguards and amending guardianship statutes to enable the courts to order limited or onetime interventions so that immediate action is possible pending a full proceeding.

In addition to statutory revisions, there is increased recognition that training programs on elder abuse must be developed and offered to law enforcement agencies, offices of district attorneys, banking institutions, health care facilities, Adult Protective Services, and the aging network. Finally, corporations, human services programs, self-help groups, and attorneys who specialize in elder law practice are increasingly providing preretirement seminars and counseling to middle-aged persons who are looking forward to their own retirement or who are caregivers for their parents or friends. Such consumer education models include information on the positive and negative aspects of various financial surrogate management devices and health care advance directives, in an effort to encourage the public to "plan ahead for incapacity." (See also CONSUMER PROTECTION FOR OLDER ADULTS; CRIME PROTECTION; ETHICS IN FINANCIAL PLANNING; INTERGENERATIONAL CONFLICT AND FINANCIAL ISSUES; PREDATORY LENDING.)

#### References

Administration on Aging. National Center on Elder Abuse. 1996. "The National Elder Abuse Incidence Study." Available online at http://www.aoa.gov/abuse/report.

Albany Law School. Government Law Center. 1994. "Abuse and the Durable Power-of-Attorney: Options for Reform." New York: Albany Law School.

Brookdale Center on Aging of Hunter College. Jacob Reingold Institute. 1994. "Survey of Financial Institutions." Unpublished manuscript.

National Consumers League. 2002. "National Fraud Information Center, Telemarketing Fraud Statistics." Available online at http://www.fraud.org/02telestats.htm.

*New York Daily News*. 2001. "Senior Taken for Millions, Lawyers Rack Up Fat Fees as Guardians to the Helpless." May 20.

New York State Commission on Fiduciary Appointments. 2001. Report to the Chief Judge.

Office of the Special Inspector General for Fiduciary Appointments. 2001. "A Report to Chief Judge Judith S. Kaye and Chief Administrative Judge Jonathan Lippman."

*Sia Arnason and Debra S. Sacks*

**FINANCIAL GERONTOLOGY, HISTORY OF,** an academic field that embraces multiple perspectives on aging, including population aging, individual aging, and family aging, and focuses on the complexity of relationships among demographic trends, individual attitudes, financial security, and life satisfaction across the life cycle and across generations. An important first definitional concept is to emphasize that *gerontology is not the study of "old people" but is the study of the multiple processes of aging*—including *middle aging*. Consequently, *financial gerontology* focuses not on "old people" but on the financial dimensions of the multiple processes of aging and middle aging. The field pays special attention to how the demographic and financial characteristics of those born from 1946 to 1964 (i.e., the baby boomers) is shaping the social, health, and financial attitudes, hopes, worries, and social policy of the United States in the twenty-first century. The first-born baby boomer will celebrate his or her sixtieth birthday in 2006.

## The Origins of Financial Gerontology: The Boettner Research Institute

The origins of financial gerontology are rooted in the vision of two farsighted, charitable men, Joseph Emery Boettner, a successful businessman, and Davis Weinert Gregg, a successful educator. Born in 1903, Joe Boettner entered the insurance business almost accidentally. A star high school athlete, he was recruited to play in the semipro intramural teams of Philadelphia's booming insurance industry. After successful years in insurance sales and education, he and a few friends purchased the failing Philadelphia Life Insurance Company for $1 per share and built it into a successful company. His post–high school education was at the American College of Life Underwriters, the applied life insurance training division of the University of Pennsylvania Wharton School. The college became independent of the university in 1927, and Mr. Boettner earned his Chartered Life Underwriter (CLU) designation in 1934.

Born in 1918, Davis Gregg graduated from the University of Texas and earned his doctorate from the University of Pennsylvania in 1947, where he studied under the legendary Wharton professor of insurance Solomon Huebner, founder of the American College of Life Underwriters. Gregg was on the faculty of Stanford University when Professor Huebner asked him to come back to the insurance college for a short time. Gregg's "short time" spanned four decades, including 1954 to 1983 as the president of the college.

During these years the high school athlete from West Philadelphia and the Wharton Ph.D. from Texas developed a lifelong relationship built on mutual personal affection and professional respect. Boettner began using his wealth to support higher education, endowing professorships at Penn State University, Temple University, and the American College of Life Underwriters, which was moved from the University of Pennsylvania to its own campus in Bryn Mawr, Pennsylvania, in 1961. Although the focus of these gifts was insurance education, as he grew older Boettner's views of the educational needs of the life insurance industry changed. He often reflected on the fact that he was outliving his accountant, his lawyer, his dentist, his doctor, and other important professionals in his life. While his own financial resources allowed him to deal with these changes successfully, he became concerned about how the average older person faces these kinds of challenges and how financial education could be channeled to meet such challenges.

Davis Gregg's intellectual and administrative leadership transformed the nature of the American College of Life Underwriters. Although its professional designation, the Chartered Life Underwriter, focused on life insurance, more elaborate insurance products such as whole life and universal life insurance served a broader insurance-with-investment function. Consequently, under his leadership the college created a second professional designation, the Chartered Financial Consultant (ChFC), in recognition of the need to train students beyond traditional life insurance practices.

By the 1980s Boettner's concerns about old age and consumer education began to merge with Gregg's views on the need for more comprehensive professional education in life insurance and financial services. From these joint concerns came the idea of a new research institute that would focus on the linkages between personal finance and social gerontology.

With a gift from Boettner, Gregg established a Study Committee of nationally known gerontologists to explore the issues. The committee agreed on four organizing principles: (1) that there was indeed a need for a specialized research program combining gerontology with financial planning; (2) that a social gerontology research center could succeed at a small specialized business school; (3) that the permanent director of the institute should be an experienced gerontologist; and (4) that the goal of the new institute would be both to communicate gerontological concerns to insurance and financial professionals and to communicate financial issues to gerontologists.

In 1986 the American College officially established the Boettner Research Institute and in 1989 renamed it the Boettner Institute of Financial Gerontology to more descriptively reflect its focus and recruited Dr. Neal E. Cutler, professor of political science and gerontology at the University of Southern California's (USC) Andrus Gerontology Center, as the director.

From 1989 to 1991 Gregg, Boettner, and Cutler developed a framework for applied research in financial gerontology. As the initial professional and public recognition of the importance of financial gerontology exceeded the expectations of the institute's founders, a broader set of academic skills and interests than originally envisioned was seen as necessary to meet the challenge of this new field. Consequently, in 1992 the Boettner Institute became chartered as a nonprofit charitable educational corporation with an independently appointed board of trustees of prominent business and gerontology academics and practitioners. The trustees then voted to move the Boettner Institute from the American College to the University of Pennsylvania.

Sadly, within a year, on October 27, 1993, Davis Gregg passed away. In the months following the unexpected death, Boettner developed plans for a permanent educational memorial to his lifelong friend: He endowed the Joseph E. Boettner/Davis W. Gregg Chair in Financial Gerontology at Widener University in Chester, Pennsylvania, the university where Boettner was serving as a lifetime member of the board of trustees. Literally one year later, on October 27, 1994, Joseph Boettner also passed away. In keeping with his wishes, Widener University appointed Dr. Cutler in 1994 to be the first holder of the Boettner/Gregg Chair.

At the University of Pennsylvania, the Boettner Institute became the Boettner Center of Financial Gerontology, and in 2003 it was merged into the Wharton School as the

Boettner Center for Pensions and Retirement Security. The Boettner/Gregg Chair in Financial Gerontology at Widener University continues to emphasize interdisciplinary teaching and applied research; Dr. Cutler teaches in both the School of Human Service Professions (e.g., clinical psychology and social work) and the School of Business Administration. In these ways, the vision of applied research and education of two lifelong friends, a businessman and an academic, comes full circle in an institutionalized way that links their insights as well as their names.

### The Emerging Literature of Financial Gerontology

One measure of the development of a new field of study is the extent of its professional communication or, in academic parlance, its *literature*. By this measure financial gerontology is indeed becoming a well-established field of study. For example, during its Bryn Mawr years, the Boettner Institute organized a series of annual, published lectures that alternated between nationally prominent gerontology and finance leaders. The inaugural Boettner Lecture was given by Dr. George L. Maddox, director of the Duke University Center on Aging; later lectures were given by sociologist Dr. Matilda White Riley, senior behavioral scientist at the National Institute on Aging, and psychologist Dr. James E. Birren, founding director of the USC Andrus Gerontology Center. Maddox, Riley, and Birren are all former presidents of the Gerontological Society of America. Lectures were also given by Dr. William C. Greenough, chairman and chief executive officer (CEO) of TIAA-CREF; Dallas L. Salisbury, president and CEO of the Employee Benefit Research Institute; and Davis Gregg.

Of greater impact was the development of a regular column on financial gerontology written by Dr. Cutler for the *Journal of the American Society of CLU and ChFC*. Because the journal is received by more than 25,000 financial professionals, the column helps to implement one of Joseph Boettner's central goals: the communication of gerontological insights and research findings to the financial services profession. Beginning in 1990, the subjects of these bimonthly written "minilectures" have ranged from the implications of baby boom demographics for retirement to understanding Alzheimer's disease and the costs of long-term care. This series has featured several guest columnists and from time to time presents serious topics using such less serious titles as "Sex, Asset Allocation, and Rock-n-Roll" (introducing financial planning to younger adults) and "Successful Aging, Willard Scott, and Dental Floss" (the health dynamics of individual longevity). The column continues in the renamed *Journal of Financial Service Professionals* written alternatively by Cutler and Dr. Sandra Timmerman, director of the Mature Market Institute at MetLife.

A hallmark event in the development of financial gerontology "as a field" was the publication in 1996 of the *Encyclopedia of Financial Gerontology*, edited by Dr. Lois A. Vitt and Dr. Jurg K. Siegenthaler. Including over 125 authors and articles, the *Encyclopedia*—the predecessor of the present two-volume edition—both symbolizes and defines the growing scope of the field's research and practice. The editors' list of "Core Topics" into which the articles can be "rearranged" for educational purposes identifies the growing expansiveness of financial gerontology: Income Security, Employment and Retirement, Family and Intergenerational Issues, Consumer Services, Health Care and Insurance, Housing and Housing Finance, Legal Issues and Services, Quality of Life and Well-Being.

Finally, the publication of two "traditional" books also marks the evolution of financial gerontology as an identifiable field of study. In 1992 Springer published *Aging, Money, and Life Satisfaction: Aspects of Financial Gerontology*, edited by Cutler, Gregg, and Dr. M. Powell Lawton, an internationally known psychologist and member of the Boettner Institute Advisory Board. This volume identified a conceptual framework for studying aging in a social, economic, and health context, all directed to the role of financial planning in maintaining economic security and life satisfaction in later life. The book included an early statement of Davis Gregg's model of the "human wealth span."

In 2002 Wiley published *Advising Mature Clients: The New Science of Wealth Span Planning*, written by Dr. Cutler. The book builds on a decade of teaching and applied research suggested by Gregg's model and discusses the wealth span model in terms of such subjects as the changing nature of retirement, the financial psychology of middle age, aging children of older parents, the continuum of long-term care and related decisions, and government health and social service programs relevant to the financial questions typically asked by older and middle-aged clients. The book was published in Wiley's "J.K. Lasser Pro" series that is directed toward financial professionals.

### The Future

Over the past decade the phrase *financial gerontology* has become *less unusual* than it was at the beginning. Annual meetings of both practitioners and academics are more likely to see panels and workshops on topics that link aging and money, finance and gerontology. A substantial extension of this bridge-building activity is the recent development of an educational program whose primary goal is to teach a range of gerontological concepts, issues, and data to financial services professionals, the outcome of which is a new professional designation known as the Certified Financial Gerontologist (CFG).

The program is being developed by the American Institute of Financial Gerontology (AIFG) in partnership with the American Society on Aging—a membership organization of 6,000 educators, practitioners, businesspersons, researchers, administrators, and policymakers—and the Widener University School of Business Administration. In keeping with the original vision of a new field of financial gerontology, the goal of the AIFG is to bring gerontology to professionals who are already trained, credentialed, or licensed in their financial profession. Thus, the curriculum leading to the CFG designation emphasizes such subjects as the wealth span model of aging and financial planning; understanding the biology, psychology, and sociology of aging; recognizing and working with the ethical and legal challenges of aging clients and their families; and connecting the variety of age-related health, finance, and social services programs so as to promote financial security and well-being in later life. Thus like the bimonthly columns, the designation reflects the view of financial gerontology as a field that serves as a bridge between gerontological and financial professionals.

In these ways, financial gerontology is moving in the directions that its founders imagined. Starting with the view that researchers should pursue gerontological topics that are of interest and of value to financial practitioners, the field has developed an increasingly important applied research agenda alongside a growing "literature" that reflects and communicates that agenda. Through the meetings and workshops, the articles and the books, and more recently through the establishment of a specialized professional designation, "financial gerontology"—both the phrase and the content—has become increasingly familiar as a central component of both gerontological and financial practice. (See also CPA ELDERCARE SERVICES; FINANCIAL ADVISORS; FINANCIAL LITERACY; FINANCIAL PLANNING PROCESS; RETIREMENT PLANNING; WEALTH SPAN.)

### References

Cutler, N.E. 2002. *Advising Mature Clients: The New Science of Wealth Span Planning*. New York: John Wiley & Sons.

Cutler, N.E., D.W. Gregg, and M.P. Lawton, eds. 1992. *Aging, Money, and Life Satisfaction Aspects of Financial Gerontology*. New York: Springer Publishing.

Vitt, L.A., and J.K. Siegenthaler. 1996. *Encyclopedia of Financial Gerontology*. Westport, CT: Greenwood Press.

*Neal E. Cutler*

**FINANCIAL LITERACY,** an understanding of a broad range of financial topics, from basic money management—budgeting, saving, insuring, and investing—to economics and how households make decisions within a set of economic conditions and circumstances. The consistent themes running through most discussions of financial literacy include:

1. Being knowledgeable, educated, and informed on the issues of managing money and assets, banking, investments, credit, insurance, and taxes in a given economic environment;
2. Understanding the basic concepts underlying the management of money and assets (e.g., the time value of money in investments and the pooling of risks in insurance); and
3. Using that knowledge and understanding to plan and implement personal financial decisions.

### Why Is Financial Literacy Important?

People today are more responsible for their own retirement income security. Over the past 15 to 20 years there has been a shift in responsibility for long-term well-being away from institutions (employers, the government) to individuals. For example, in 1980, 70% of pension plans were defined contribution (DC, as opposed to defined benefit plans; DC plans shift more of the responsibility for the growth of retirement funds to the consumer); by 1997, 92% of plans were defined contribution (Conte 1998). In 1988, one-fourth (25%) of workers were covered primarily by DC plans; in 1998, over three-fifths (63%) were covered by such plans (Copeland 2002). According to Mitchell and Dykes (2001), "[F]uture pension growth will be concentrated in the DC arena, with increasing participant control being exerted over all aspects of the plans—including contributions, investment mix, and payouts."

If families are to make decisions and successfully manage their contributions, investment mix, and payouts, they need to be financially literate. Yet, in one survey, 35% of respondents could not even guess at how much they needed. Of those that did try to provide a savings estimate, on average the number they posed was 44% below their expected needs (Dolliver 2001). In its 2001 Retirement Confidence Survey, the Employee Benefit Research Institute found that only 39% had tried to calculate how much money they will need to save (this was down from 51% in 2000 but up from 32% in 1993) (EBRI 2001).

Using data from the 1998 Survey of Consumer Finances, Montalto (2000) showed that

56% of nonretired U.S. households had fewer assets than they would need to supplement Social Security and pension income throughout their retirement if they planned to maintain their level of living. Level of income, development of a financial plan, and participation in employer-related retirement programs were the most significant factors in determining whether households had saved enough for retirement.

Another possible reason households may be undersaving for retirement could be the complexity of choices offered by employers. In 1994, participants in employers' 401(k) plans had an average of 4.6 investment choices for their funds; by 1998, this had risen to an average of 8.4 (Kochard and Gaumnitz 2000). As the number of choices rise, participants can become frustrated and confused. Madrian and Shea (2000) indicate that employee inertia and procrastination in retirement planning and participation in 401(k) plans may be due to the complexity of choices as well as the lack of information.

Even among households that save, job changes can mean that workers need to move funds from one retirement plan to another. While 60% of payouts made to people changing jobs were rolled over into IRA (Individual Retirement Account)-type accounts, two out of five payouts were spent on consumption. Nearly all payouts over $100,000 were rolled over, while nearly all smaller payouts (under $4,000) were taken as cash (Yakoboski 1997). Small amounts may never have the chance to grow into larger amounts if families don't keep their money invested.

### Credit Literacy

As of May 2002, consumers had about $712.2 billion outstanding in revolving credit, up about 6.8% from the previous year. Some of this credit is paid off each month; however, about 60% of U.S. households revolve some portion of their credit card balances. For those that revolve, the Federal Reserve Board reported that their balances were $4,100 in 1998. Other estimates show credit card balances as high as $8,000 in 2000 (McGinn et al. 2001). One out of five families with incomes under $50,000 spend at least 40% of after-tax income on debt servicing (Kennickell, Starr-McCluer, and Surette 2000). Needless to say, money spent on credit card debt is money that cannot go toward retirement savings.

Bankruptcy has also risen over recent years, from 1.27 million households in 1999–2000 to 1.38 million in 2000–2001. Preliminary data for 2002 period show projections of 1.4 to 1.5 million bankruptcies (ABI World 2002).

Another concern among financial planners is the amount of debt held in home equity loans and lines of credit. Housing equity is the major asset in most households' portfolio, but the growth in both the proportion of households with home equity loans and the value of those loans has implications for the use of housing wealth as an asset in retirement. The proportion of households with home equity loans doubled between 1983 and 1997, from 7% to 13% (Canner, Durkin, and Luckett 1998), and the dollar value of home equity loans nearly tripled from $256.4 billion to $725.6 billion between 1991 and 2002 (Federal Reserve Board 2002). Furthermore, roughly one-third of households who refinance their mortgages "cash out" some of the equity in their homes; in 1998–1999, the average amount of this "cash-out" was about $18,000 (Brady, Canner, and Maki 2000).

Beyond these statistics, there is evidence that financially unsavvy consumers are having problems in the marketplace. For example, there is substantial anecdotal evidence of predatory lending that strips home equity from homeowners. Predatory lending has not been explicitly defined, but it can involve loans that carry high costs—either in terms of interest rates or fees—or practices such as "packing" (adding unnecessary insurance coverage) or "flipping" (frequent refinancing of the loan, usually with fees and charges rolled into the refinanced amount), and features such as prepayment penalties, balloon payments, and mandatory arbitration clauses. While most of the focus on predatory lending has been on home-secured loans, there are other high-cost loans in the market, including high-cost auto loans with interest rates ranging from 15% to 25%, credit cards with interest rates ranging from 20% to 40%, payday loans that can carry annual percentage rates of 300% or more, and rent-to-own transactions with implicit interest rates over 100%.

### What Financial Literacy Initiatives Are Underway?

There seems to be an abundance of activity on the financial literacy front. Vitt et al. (2000) identify 91 programs offered by schools, Cooperative Extension, colleges (including community colleges), the military, faith-based organizations, community groups, employers, and others. The National Endowment for Financial Education lists over 150 educational resources from a wide range of agencies, organizations, and firms in its Economic Independence Clearinghouse database; many of these materials are available in multiple languages.

Just as there are numerous initiatives, so too are there numerous target audiences. Preretirees, youth, military personnel, low-income families, first-time homebuyers, employees, church members, and women are all targets of one program or another. There are programs targeted to various ethnic groups (e.g., Native Americans or immigrants), various situational groups (including prerelease prisoners), and various demographic groups (such as new parents or preretirees). In essence, it would be difficult for a U.S. consumer not to be part of a target audience for at least one financial literacy initiative.

Adult audiences often connect with financial literacy programs through the workplace. However, they are just as likely to find financial literacy programs via community groups, social service agencies, faith-based organizations, or special interest or affinity groups such as the Parent-Teacher Association (PTA) or AARP.

One task facing human resource professionals, counselors, and educators is finding meaningful learning experiences for audiences. In a recent survey, consumers were more likely to say they learned from the "school of hard knocks" than from formal—or even informal—educational experiences (Perry and Ards 2001). A study of low-income consumers revealed a preference for learning from friends and peers who are successful money managers (Hogarth and Swanson 1993). Thus, traditional "classroom" and lecture-format programs may not succeed with some audiences. Toussaint-Comeau and Rhine (2000) discuss the pros and cons of a variety of delivery strategies, including information seminars, pamphlets and brochures, mass media (newspaper, radio, television), individualized learning (video or DVD), and Web-based delivery. They note that delivery strategy, audience, and topic need to be considered holistically when designing financial education initiatives.

As families become more pressed for time and grapple with increased information loads, educators will need to use alternative strategies—Web or computer based, video/DVD, or audiotapes—to deliver financial education programs. However, the efficacy of these delivery methods has yet to be shown.

Legislative and public policy initiatives are also driving and developing financial literacy efforts. In February 2002, the U.S. Senate Banking, Housing and Urban Affairs committee held two days of hearings on financial literacy with testimony from the Federal Reserve, the U.S. Treasury, and the Securities and Exchange Commission as well as other not-for-profit and private sector participants (see http://banking.senate.gov/02_02hrg/020502/index.htm for an example). In April 2002, the U.S. Department of the Treasury announced a new Office of Financial Education to improve financial education for all Americans by developing and implementing financial education policy initiatives and coordinating Treasury's outreach efforts.

**Are Financial Literacy Initiatives Working?**

A number of groups (the Consumer Federation of America, the Jump$tart Coalition for Personal Financial Literacy, Americans for Consumer Education and Competition, the American Savings Education Council) have conducted financial literacy quizzes with different audiences. Most of these show that literacy levels are low.

Researchers have just begun to address the question of how literacy and financial behaviors relate. Perhaps the greatest challenge in financial literacy is measuring the efficacy of any program. Getting one's financial house in order can take time, and longitudinal studies to prove that a particular program is effective are costly to conduct. However, there have been some longer-term impact and evaluation studies that show that financial education can make a difference.

Bernheim, Garrett, and Maki (2001) studied the relationship between high school financial curriculum mandates and adult savings patterns and net worth. The study concluded that mandates increase exposure to financial education, and financial education is associated with higher savings rates and higher net worth. They conclude that "education may be a powerful tool for stimulating personal saving".

Money 2000, a Cooperative Extension System program that focuses on participant debt reduction and/or savings accumulation, includes an extended-period behavioral monitoring program. As of the end of 2000, over 13,000 participants in 22 states reported cumulative increased savings of $10,618,271 and cumulative decreased consumer debts of $8,247,219 (a total effect of $18,865,490 (*Money2000* 2000).

Individual development accounts (IDAs) are a relatively new policy initiative designed to help low-income families build wealth. IDAs are meant to improve access to savings institutions for the poor by providing matching funds for savings toward homeownership, higher education, and microenterprise. Financial education is part of the IDA initiative. An evaluation of 2,378 IDA participants showed that average monthly net deposits "increased sharply as hours of general financial [education] attendance increased from zero to 12, after which it leveled off" (Schreiner et al. 2001). This finding seems to confirm Berhneim and colleagues that education is a powerful tool for stimulating savings.

Hirad and Zorn (2001) examined the effectiveness of prepurchase homeownership counseling on reducing 90-day delinquency rates. "Counseling" was defined as "specific and tailored to the particular needs of the individual, while education typically is administered in a generic program". Borrowers receiving counseling had a 19% lower 90-day delinquency rate than those without counseling and lower delinquency rates than those receiving classroom counseling and home study counseling.

The implication for retirement planning education may be to include one-to-one counseling sessions as part of the educational program. In any case, it is important to recognize that information is not the same as education. Benefits counselors, financial counselors, and community educators can help make sure that information leads to education—and the resultant change in behavior that improves the economic security and stability of the family.

These examples provide some concrete evidence that financial education—in various forms—can work to improve the economic status of families. However, it is important to remind ourselves that at the same time these programs are showing positive impacts at the microlevel, we still see evidence of problems with credit and bankruptcy and with a lack of planning and participation in retirement savings at the macrolevel. There is still much room for improvement in the financial literacy levels of U.S. households. (See also AGING INTO DEBT; FINANCIAL EDUCATION FOR SENIORS; INVESTOR EDUCATION; KING LEAR SYNDROME; RETIREMENT PREPAREDNESS; U.S. PERSONAL SAVING RATE.)

### References

ABI World. 2002. "U.S. Bankruptcy Filing Statistics." Available online at http://www.abiworld.org/stats/newstatsfront.html.

Bernheim, B. Douglas, D.M. Garrett, and Dean M. Maki. 2001. "Education and Saving: The Long-Term Effects of High School Financial Curriculum Mandates." *Journal of Public Economics* 80: 435–65.

Brady, Peter J., Glenn B. Canner, and Dean M. Maki. 2000. "The Effects of Recent Mortgage Refinancing." *Federal Reserve Bulletin* 86: 441–50.

Canner, Glenn B., Thomas A. Durkin, and Charles A. Luckett. 1998. "Recent Developments in Home Equity Lending." *Federal Reserve Bulletin* 84: 241–51.

Conte, C. 1998. *The National Summit on Retirement Savings: Agenda Background Materials*. Washington, DC: U.S. Department of Labor.

Copeland, Craig. 2002. "An Analysis of the Retirement and Pension Plan Coverage Topical Module of SIPP." *EBRI Issue Brief* 245 (Employee Benefit Research Institute).

Dolliver, M. 2001. "Just Blame It on Ignorance, If Not on Improvidence." *Adweek* 42(11): 45.

Employee Benefit Research Institute (EBRI). 2001. "The 2001 Retirement Confidence Survey Summary of Findings." Available online at http://www.asec.org/2001rcs/01rcses.pdf.

Federal Reserve Board. 2002. "Flow of Funds Accounts of the United States." Table L.218. Available online at http://www.federalreserve.gov/releases/Z1/Current/z1r-4.pdf.

Hirad, A., and Peter M. Zorn. 2001. "A Little Knowledge Is a Good Thing: Empirical Evidence of the Effectiveness of Pre-purchase Homeownership Counseling." Working Paper. McLean, VA: Freddie Mac.

Hogarth, Jeanne M., and Josephine A. Swanson. 1993. "Voices of Experience: Limited Resource Families and Financial Management." American Home Economics Association, *Family Economics & Management Conference Proceedings*, 13–28.

Kennickell, Arthur B., Martha Starr-McCluer, and Brian Surette. 2000. "Recent Changes in U.S. Family Finances: Results from the 1998 Survey of Consumer Finances." *Federal Reserve Bulletin* 86: 1–29.

Kochard, Lawrence E., and Jack Gaumnitz. 2000. "The Transition from Defined Benefit to Defined Contribution Pension Plans in the Public Sector." Kansas Public Policy Institute. Available online at http://www.flinthills.org/Publications/General%20Policy/transition.htm.

Madrian, Brigitte C., and Dennis F. Shea. 2000. "The Power of Suggestion: Inertia in 401(k)

Participation and Savings Behavior." NBER Working Paper. Available online at http://www.nber.org/papers/w7682.

McGinn, Daniel, Adam Bryant, Keith Naughton, Kevin Peraino, Erika Check, Joan Raymond, Ellise Pierce, Jane Spencer, Dori Perrucci, Brian Braiker, and Andrea Cooper. 2001. "Maxed Out." *Newsweek*, August 27, 34–41.

Mitchell, Olivia S., and Erica L. Dykes. 2001. "New Trends in U.S. Pensions." Pension Research Council, Wharton School of Business, University of Pennsylvania. Available online at http://prc.wharton.upenn.edu/prc/PRC/WP/wp2000-1rev.pdf.

*Money2000*. 2000. "Impact Data and Research Results." Available online at http://www.money2000.org/prac/impact.htm.

Montalto, Catherine. 2000. "New Study: More, than Half of Americans Behind in Saving for Retirement." Press release from Consumer Federation of America, April 20. Available online at http://www.consumerfed.org/nrl5.pdf.

Perry, Vanessa G., and S. Ards. 2001. "The Freddie Mac Consumer Credit Initiative: How Consumers Learn about Credit and Implications for Consumer Education and Policy." Working Paper. McLean, VA: Freddie Mac, April.

Schreiner, Mark, Michael Sherraden, Margaret Clancy, Lissa Johnson, Jami Curley, Michal Grinstein-Weiss, Min Zhan, and Sondra Beverly. 2001. *Savings and Asset Accumulation in Individual Development Accounts*. St. Louis, MO: Center for Social Development, Washington University.

Toussaint-Comeau, Maude, and Sherrie L.W. Rhine. 2000. "Delivery of Financial Literacy Programs." Federal Reserve Bank of Chicago Policy Studies #2000-7/. Available online at http://www.chicagofed.org/publications/publicpolicystudies/ccapolicystudy/pdf/cca-2000-7.pdf.

Vitt, Lois A., Carol Anderson, Jamie Kent, Deanna M. Lyter, Jurg K. Siegenthaler, and Jeremy W. Kent. 2000. *Personal Finance and the Rush to Competence: Financial Literacy Education in the U.S.* Middleburg, VA: Institute for Socio-Financial Studies.

Yakoboski, Paul. 1997. "Large Pan Lump-sum Rollovers and Cashouts." *EBRI Issue Brief* 188 (Employee Benefit Research Institute).

*Jeanne M. Hogarth*

**FINANCIAL PLANNING PROCESS,** the process of meeting life goals through the proper management of finances. Financial planning is distinguished from financial counseling by a relative absence of crisis orientation and a relatively higher degree of client affluence. Both involve efforts to increase clients' financial literacy. Financial planning proceeds, generally, along a six-step path: (1) establishing and defining the client-planner relationship; (2) gathering client data, including goals; (3) analyzing and evaluating financial status; (4) developing and presenting financial planning recommendations or alternatives; (5) implementing agreed-upon recommendations; and (6) monitoring the plan and keeping it current.

The professionals who prepare financial plans for clients are known as financial planners and can work in several settings including small financial planning practices, large financial services firms, credit unions, banks, and other financial institutions. The setting, however, is not as important as the match between the client and financial advisor, including how well they are able to communicate and the strength of the personal rapport that is developed between them. Financial planners are compensated in different ways for the services they provide. Some earn commissions on the sale of financial products, and others earn fees only for consulting services. Still others earn a combination of both commissions and fees. It is important for prospective clients to understand the system of payment for financial planners, as the form of payment may constitute a conflict of interest or otherwise color the advice being given. Whether a financial planner is paid by fees or by commissions, particularly if commissions are received per transaction, at least part of the underlying incentive is to earn as much as possible. This can mean trading investments more often than is necessary. While no ethical financial planner would do this consciously, a prospective client should be aware of the possibility of investment churning in light of the system of compensation used by the professional.

While all financial planners are trained to provide comprehensive financial planning services, some specialize in one or more areas or work with specific types of clients. Some are specifically interested in and trained to advise future retirees and older adults. Other specialties include planning for long-term care expenses, including advice on regulations concerning Medicaid eligibility, asset management, or business succession planning. Several candidates should always be interviewed until a prospective client is satisfied that his or her financial planning and investment approach and philosophy and that of the financial planner match.

The financial planning process itself begins with an initial meeting, usually in the financial planner's office. The initial meeting is generally held at no charge and is meant to be an introductory meeting at which the client should be concerned with determining the level of rapport possible with the planner and the extent to which the planner seems capable of doing what the client wants done. The first meeting is the time to get a feel for the communication style of the planner and potential compatibility to the client's own style, as well as the planner's skills and expertise.

In addition, the first meeting should initiate the process of establishing and defining the client's life situation and goals. Financial planners should also be able to explain and document the services that they provide and should give the client an understanding of what is expected from them; the client should obtain the same understanding of the planner. The planner should also fully explain how he or she will be compensated and by whom. Finally, planner and client should agree on how long the professional relationship should last and on how decisions will be made regarding implementation of the financial plan.

Subsequent meetings will begin delving into the facts of the client's situation. The planner will ask the client for all information relevant to the client's current financial situation, as well as any foreseeable financial realities such as inheritance or parental (or sibling) dependency. In addition, the planner will ask more questions about the client's aims and goals and clarify expectations for what the financial advisor will do how to judge whether his or her mutually agreed-upon financial plan is working. Establishing these parameters at this point will forestall potential problems in expectations or communication for both parties and establish a foundation upon which the relationship can work. In terms of a client's financial goals, the more the financial planner can know about what the client wants to happen for himself or herself and family, if applicable, the better both will be able to plan for both short- and long-term concerns. Some planners will use these early meetings to delve into the client's psychological relationship to money and family money history for added insight into the client's life situation.

The advisor will need to gather data such as tax returns, mortgage information, investment assets, company benefit information, insurance documents, wills, trusts, and advance directives to get a better understanding of where the client stands financially and legally. Although this can occur in the first meeting, it is more often a two-step process, with the first meeting promoting understanding of the working relationship and then a second (or even third) meeting to go through the data required to develop the plan. At this point the advisor will begin to analyze and evaluate the client's financial status. The planner will develop an analysis that covers all identified areas of concern, as well as any others the planner identifies while doing the analysis. These could include retirement planning projections, income tax analysis, estate planning issues, investment strategies, protection planning, or financial position planning. All the above may be appropriate, or only one or two areas may need to be covered based on what the client and financial advisor have discussed.

Next, the planner will develop and present the financial planning recommendations and/or alternatives and model the results for the client if the recommendations are implemented. The plan itself should provide specific recommendations that address the client's goals. To the extent that the client's goals have been understood by both the client and the planner, the financial plan is likely to be a success. Once the client and the advisor have reviewed the analysis and the recommendations and agree on the plan, the next step, of course, is to implement the recommendations. The planner will either take responsibility for implementing the plan or instruct the client on how to carry out the recommendations, depending on the terms agreed to in the first meeting.

The final step in the financial planning process is monitoring the financial plan. Once the plan is implemented, life happens, and both situations and objectives are dynamic. A financial plan must be reviewed on a periodic basis, generally at least once a year, to make sure it is on track to achieving the client's goals. (See also BABY BOOMERS AND RETIREMENT; CPA ELDERCARE SERVICES; FINANCIAL ADVISORS; LIFE PLANNING; RETIREMENT PLANNING; RETIREMENT PREPAREDNESS.)

**Organization**

CFP Board

**References**

Financial Executives Research Foundation. 2003. *Benchmarking the Planning Process*. Florham, NJ: Financial Executive Research.

Shilling, Dana. 2002. *Financial Planning for the Older Client*. 5th ed. Cincinnati, OH: National Underwriter.

*Chip Eubank*

**FINANCIAL RECOVERY IN LATER LIFE,** the process of overcoming a financial setback such as an investment loss or loss of a job. It is often more difficult to recover from financial setbacks as one gets older. There is less time available to invest for retirement, to recoup money lost in the stock market, or to receive "payback" (with a higher salary) from investments in human capital (e.g., college degree). Therefore, it is wise to begin financial planning in early adulthood, in case something goes awry and to increase one's financial resilience.

Financial resilience is the ability to withstand life events, both negative (e.g., loss of a job) and positive (e.g., birth of a child), that impact one's income and/or assets at any age. Some financially stressful events, such as increased family size, unemployment, divorce, widowhood, disability, and health problems, affect people individually. Others, such as layoffs, plant closings, corporate scandals (e.g., Enron), recessions, stock market downturns, and acts of terrorism, affect large groups of people or society as a whole.

### Later Life Financial Challenges

#### *Unemployment*

Losing a job—at any age—is traumatic, even when a worker receives some severance pay. In addition to loss of income and/or employee benefits, there is a feeling of insecurity as one's way of life is disrupted. Workers faced with involuntary retirement in later life must take stock of their financial resources, marketable job skills, and emotional readiness—or not—for retirement.

The federal COBRA (Consolidated Omnibus Budget Reconciliation Act) law provides an opportunity for continuation of health insurance for up to 18 months, at group rates plus a 2% administrative fee, until an individual policy (or new group coverage) is obtained or a worker is eligible for Medicare. Thus, those who leave a job at age 63½ can use COBRA benefits to tide them over until they are eligible for Medicare at age 65. However, only workers covered by employers with 20 or more employees are eligible for COBRA benefits, and the cost is expensive for someone out of work, often over $600 per month for a family (Von Bergen 2002).

Eight of ten laid-off workers receive severance pay, typically a week of pay per year of service, often with continuation of health insurance benefits while severance pay is received (Siskos 2002). Sometimes it is possible to negotiate for additional perks such as outplacement support, continued benefits, or a larger severance. Another important resource is state unemployment benefits, available to workers who lose a job through no fault of their own. Unemployed workers should file a claim as soon as possible to collect what they are due.

#### *Early Retirement Incentive Offers*

Most workers assume they will decide when to retire. Sometimes, however, an employer suggests it in the form of an early retirement (a.k.a. "buyout") offer. An early retirement offer may or may not be voluntary. If it seems likely that employees will lose their jobs anyway with less generous terms (e.g., a specific department is being targeted), taking a buyout is typically advised (Wollan 2002). Buyout offers often include enhanced pension benefits, lump-sum cash payments, and/or continued group health insurance coverage. A typical offer adds two to five years of age and service credit to pension benefit formulas so that workers receive about the same amount they would have received at the employer's normal retirement age.

Employers offer early retirement incentives to save money, usually during economic recessions. They also want to be good to employees and to minimize damage to morale, which is why they provide buyout benefits instead of a pink slip. Many employers require employees who accept a buyout to sign a release saying that they accept the package in exchange for agreeing not to file an age discrimination lawsuit (Mendels 2001). Usually workers have only 45 to 90 days in which to decide to accept a buyout offer. Key factors to consider include attractiveness of a buyout offer, financial stability of the employer, other employment options, access to health insurance, job enjoyment and stresses, emotional readiness for retirement, and payment methods.

### *Poor or Uncertain Health Prognosis*

A life-threatening disease or chronic, debilitating illness prior to or during retirement is a financial wake-up call. Some people accelerate their retirement date to enjoy unstructured time while they can. Others reduce their work hours because they want to or have to (e.g., fatigue). A revised retirement savings analysis that incorporates the health prognosis is in order. Life expectancy estimates and retirement savings plan contributions may need to be adjusted. A poor or uncertain health prognosis may also prompt the drafting of estate planning documents that, ideally, should be in place regardless of health status. These include a will, living will, and durable power of attorney.

Adequate provisions should be made for an ill person's spouse. This includes life and health insurance, pension benefit distributions, IRA (Individual Retirement Account) withdrawals, and/or trust arrangements. Beneficiary designations on insurance policies and tax-deferred retirement savings plans should also be checked to make sure that they are current and don't conflict with the ill spouse's will.

### *Disability*

Three out of ten workers between ages 35 and 65 are disabled, due to accident or illness, for 90 days or longer, and almost one in five will become disabled for 5 years or more (College for Financial Planning 2002). The financial consequences of losing income for many months can be devastating. Not only do many disabled workers not receive a paycheck, but expenses associated with a disability, such as medical bills, create additional financial pressure.

The best defense against potential loss of earning power is disability insurance that replaces lost income. Unfortunately, many workers have minimal, if any, disability coverage. Some mistakenly believe that Social Security or their employer will cover them. In fact, Social Security uses a strict definition of eligibility that disqualifies many workers, and employer group policies are generally short term (e.g., six months). The best individual disability insurance policies have the following features: a liberal definition of disability as the inability to perform the duties of one's current occupation, coverage to age 65, a noncancellable policy form, and monthly benefits equal to about two-thirds of gross income.

### *Death of a Spouse*

Few events can turn a person's financial life upside down as the death of a spouse. In addition to shock, grief, and loss of a spouse's companionship, there is often less household income than before. There are also many decisions to be made (e.g., investing life insurance proceeds), forms to be completed, and suggestions from "helpful" family members and/or financial salespeople. For some survivors, the pressure to do something—anything—becomes unbearable. Decisions are made quickly, much like a "hot potato" that must be tossed away.

Most experts advise surviving spouses to take their time and not make any major financial decisions immediately. Survivors who receive an insurance settlement or other payment can place the funds in a certificate of deposit (CD) or money market mutual fund until they have time to explore longer-term investment alternatives and/or educate themselves about personal finance. Another important step is to identify and secure available resources. Examples include life insurance policy proceeds, employee benefits, and Veteran's benefits.

### *Divorce*

During the process of divorce, two people are expected to make rational and far-reaching decisions at a time of emotional turmoil. This may also be their first experience with the court system and hiring an attorney. Expenses often increase when one spouse moves out and sets up a separate household. Couples must estimate the dollar value of their household property and divide their debts. If either party doesn't pay a jointly held debt, however, creditors may collect from either spouse. Divorce is particularly devastating, financially, for displaced homemakers that lack current employment skills.

If a marriage lasts ten years or longer, divorced spouses can receive Social Security benefits based on the higher of their ex-spouse's earnings or their own. Divorced persons may be entitled to continuing group health insurance for up to 36 months under the federal COBRA law if they lose their status as a dependent spouse. Asset divisions at divorce are not always equal. For example, if one spouse takes sole possession of the family home, he or she also shoulders the burden of future property taxes, repairs, and possible capital gains taxes. If the other spouse receives the same dollar value in a pension, she or he has an asset that will continue to grow tax-deferred: an apparently equal distribution of property is not. Most states apply equitable distribution statutes to divide marital property.

### *Investment Losses*

Prolonged market slumps, such as from 2000 to the present, significantly erode gains made during previous bull markets. Many investment portfolios in early 2003 are a small fraction of their former value. The last time that investors experienced three consecutive years of stock market declines was 1939–1941 (Stewart 2002). Not surprisingly, many investors have discovered that their risk tolerance isn't as aggressive as they thought it was. Some have sold stock at a loss and fled to cash and bonds paying historically low interest rates.

Investment experts preach patience and a long-term perspective. Investors who try to "time the market" often miss the best trading days that inevitably follow days with large losses. History tells us that after a bear market stocks rise quickly. Since 1926, the S&P 500 index has risen an average of 32% in the first six months after a bear market ("Don't Wait" 2002). Bear markets are particularly traumatic for those approaching or in retirement, who may not have the luxury of time to "ride it out." Limiting withdrawals from investment accounts is often required to reduce the risk of outliving one's income.

## Financial Recovery Strategies

These strategies can help recover lost income and/or assets following one or more of the life events described above. These strategies can also be used by late savers to make up for lost time and to prepare for a comfortable retirement.

*Increase Contributions to Tax-Deferred Retirement Savings Plans.* The 2001 tax law increased annual contribution limits for IRAs and employer 401(k), 403(b), and Section

457 plans, at least through 2010. Just a 1% increase in the amount of pay diverted to savings can result in thousands of additional dollars at retirement. Americans contributed an average of $3,514 to 401(k) plans in 2001 (Opdyke and Higgins 2002). The maximum plan contribution limits are $12,000 in 2003, $13,000 in 2004, $14,000 in 2005, $15,000 in 2006, and higher amounts adjusted for inflation thereafter.

*Take Advantage of Catch-Up Provisions.* Tax law changes also provide workers age 50 and older the opportunity to make additional "catch-up" contributions, above the maximum amounts listed above, to Roth and Traditional IRAs and to employer salary deferral plans. IRA catch-up contributions are $500 for 2003–2005 and $1,000 for 2006 and after. Catch-up contributions for employer plans are $2,000 in 2003, $3,000 in 2004, $4,000 in 2005, and $5,000 in 2006, with amounts adjusted for inflation in 2007 and after. Older workers who take full advantage of the increased contribution limits *and* catch-up contributions will save significantly more than those who invest in taxable accounts or limit their contributions to pre-2002 tax law limits.

*Fund Multiple Salary Deferral Plans.* If eligible to participate, workers can contribute to more than one type of salary reduction plan. For example, the annual maximum for a Section 457 plan is not reduced by amounts contributed to 403(b), 401(k), SEP (Simplified Employee Pension), or SIMPLE (Savings Incentive Match Plan for Employees) plans. Combined salary reduction contributions cannot exceed $24,000 (2 × $12,000) in 2003.

*Accelerate Debt Repayment.* Debt payments can be reallocated to retirement savings once creditors are repaid. Specific strategies include paying more than the minimum amount due, requesting a lower interest rate from existing creditors, and transferring balances to lower rate credit cards or loans. Another time- and money-saving strategy is adding the monthly payment from a paid-off debt to remaining debts, in descending order by interest rate.

*"Moonlight" for Additional Income.* A second job or self-employment, in addition to one's "day job," provides additional income to invest for retirement and access to tax-deferred plans (e.g., SEPs, Keoghs) and tax-deductible business expenses for self-employed persons. It can also serve as a "bridge job" to work following retirement and to provide an opportunity to develop new career skills.

*Invest Aggressively.* The S&P 500 stock index has averaged about 10% since 1926, compared to under 4% for Treasury bills. The more stock in an investor's portfolio, the higher the average annual return over time periods of ten years or more. The trade-off for aggressive investing is increased short-term volatility. Investment risk is reduced over long holding periods, however, based on a principle called "time diversification." A later life investor's investment time horizon can be reset to their entire life expectancy, not just their retirement date, to take advantage of this principle.

*Invest Strategically.* Sector investing involves purchasing investments in companies or industry sectors (e.g., health care) that one believes will do exceptionally well and produce superior performance. An example is identifying companies that make products or services of interest to aging baby boomers. There is more risk, however, due to reduced diversification and the potential for poor timing of sector investments.

*Maximize Tax Advantages.* In addition to making tax-deferred contributions to employer retirement plans, other tax-saving strategies include investing in tax-exempt securities (e.g., municipal bonds) and holding investments for more than a year to take advantage of long-term capital gains rates. Another is investing in tax-deferred annuities with after-tax dollars after maximum contributions are made to an IRA and employer salary reduction plan.

*Spend Less in Retirement.* If you spend less in retirement, you'll need less of a nest egg. The best way to plan ahead is to track current living costs and to project expenses that will end or decrease and those that will get larger or begin for the first time (e.g., Medigap health insurance premiums). For each $50 that projected monthly spending in retirement can be reduced, the amount of savings needed to fund retirement is reduced by about $10,000, assuming you'll need income for about 30 years (Kristof 2002).

*Trade Down.* One way to reduce retirement living expenses is to trade down to a smaller home. Proceeds from the sale, minus the cost of new housing, are available to invest. In addition, maintenance, utilities, and property taxes are often lower on a smaller residence. Up to $250,000 of capital gain for singles ($500,000 for couples filing jointly) is exempt from income taxation.

*Move to a Less Expensive Location.* Taking advantage of differences in housing and other living costs (e.g., property taxes) in different geographic regions is another way to make ends meet. This strategy obviously works only for persons currently living in a high-cost area who can move to an area with lower expenses without other, offsetting negative effects (such as poor access to health care or inability to visit grandchildren).

*Delay Retirement Date.* Remaining on the job a few more years than originally planned provides additional income to invest and postpones withdrawals from invested assets. Working longer also shortens the time that savings must last and can result in higher pension and/or Social Security benefits than what would be available at an earlier age.

*Work After Retirement.* Working after retirement stretches retirement assets by providing income that reduces the amount that must be withdrawn. For example, with $200,000 of savings earning 8%, someone could withdraw 5% ($10,000) annually without touching principal and still have a cushion for inflation (ignoring taxation). Viewed another way, however, for every $10,000 of post-retirement earnings, $200,000 of income-providing assets are not required.

*Obtain a Reverse Mortgage.* Reverse mortgages allow homeowners age 62 and older to borrow against accumulated home equity and receive either a lump sum, monthly payments, or a line of credit. Factors that affect the amount received are the age of the youngest homeowner, the amount of home equity, and current interest rates. The loan is repaid with borrower's equity after the home is sold or the homeowner(s) move or die.

*Consider a Sale-Leaseback.* Another option to tap home equity for retirement living expenses is to sell a house, typically to a family member, and lease it back. This strategy provides income and tax advantages to the new owner and allows the original owner to remain in the home at a reasonable cost.

*Make Tax-Efficient Asset Withdrawals.* Retirement savings last longer when invested assets are withdrawn tax-efficiently. Generally, this means tapping taxable accounts or tax-exempt investments first, followed by retirement accounts made with after-tax dollars, and then accounts funded with before-tax dollars. Withdrawals from Roth IRAs should be made last because they have no minimum withdrawal age and earnings grow tax-free.

*Rethink the Word "Retirement".* The concept of retirement as a prolonged period of total leisure is changing as Americans live longer and healthier lives (Anthony 2001). Studies indicate that a majority of baby boomers plan to work at least part-time when they leave their present job. Many want greater flexibility and stress in the work they perform but desire to remain employed for income, socialization opportunities, and/or daily structure. (See also AGING INTO DEBT; BABY BOOMERS AND RETIREMENT; CONSUMER CREDIT; FINANCIAL COUNSELING FOR MID- TO LATER LIFE; RETIREMENT PREPAREDNESS; U.S. PERSONAL SAVING RATES.)

### References

Anthony, M. 2001. *The New Retirementality*. Chicago: Dearborn Financial Publishing.

College for Financial Planning. *Chartered Retirement Planning Counselor Professional Education Program*. 2002. Denver, CO: Author.

"Don't Wait." 2002. *Kiplinger's Personal Finance* (December).

Kristof, K. 2002. "Is It Time for You to Give Up on the Stock Market?" *The Star-Ledger* (Newark, NJ), October [n.d.].

Mendels, P. 2001. "Pay and Perks." *Business Week Online*, February 26. Available online at http://www.businessweek.com/careers/content/feb2001/ca20010226_383.htm.

O'Neill, Barbara. 2002. "Estimates and Tradeoffs: Planning Strategies for Retirement." *Proceedings of the Association for Financial Counseling and Planning Education.*

Opdyke, J.D., and M. Higgins. 2002. "Repairing the Damage to Your Nest Egg." *Wall Street Journal*, October 1, D1–D2.

Siskos, C. 2002. "No Long Goodbyes." *Kiplinger's Personal Finance* (August).

Stewart, J.B. 2002. "Apocalypse Now?" *Smart Money* (September): 43–44.

Von Bergen, J. 2002. "Health Coverage Adds to Unemployed's Peril." *The Star-Ledger* (Newark, NJ), January [n.d.].

Wollan, B. 2002. *Early Retirement Website*. Iowa State University Extension. Available online at http://www.extension.iastate.edu/financial/earlyret/.

*Barbara O'Neill*

**FINANCIAL SECURITY IN RETIREMENT,** freedom from fear and anxiety about having sufficient financial resources in later life. Whether considered from an individual perspective or from a societal view, the attainment of financial security in retirement may hold challenges.

From an individual perspective, financial security is subjective, grounded in psychological and spiritual considerations. Many people with adequate, even abundant, wealth may worry about running out of money and experience low levels of well-being. Others, who have little in the way of assets and/or material possessions, may experience a sense of security that includes feelings of material sufficiency.

In the macroview, during the twentieth century important progress was made in the United States toward eliminating poverty for people age 65 and older. Averages, however, can be deceiving, and the twenty-first century presents many unresolved questions. Social Security, Medicare, Medicaid, and employment-based retirement programs all face structural challenges, and few baby boomers can look forward to retirement either with pensions they will not outlive or savings and investments sufficient to finance their current lifestyles.

The financial elements of security in retirement may be addressed as four questions:

1. What sources of income will replace earnings from working?
2. How will the costs of acute medical care and chronic drug therapies be paid?

3. How will the costs for care be covered during periods of frailty?
4. What arrangements have been made for personal or charitable survivors?

Answers to these questions involve the following:

1. Adequate retirement income planning;
2. Medicare and Medicare Supplemental insurance (Medigap);
3. Frailty planning (Simmons and MacBean 2000); and
4. Estate (or legacy) planning.

These elements of financial security, of course, are interrelated, and a response to one is likely to impact the others. A strategy, for example, to maximize retirement income by taking a "life only" pension annuity option has obvious and significant implications for estate planning—especially from a spouse's perspective if the only life for which income is guaranteed is the worker's. A frailty planning strategy that relies on impoverishment (Medicaid) is likely to negatively impact both a retirement income plan and an estate plan. Although it may help to pay for chronic drug therapies, it could also leave a bitter legacy. No choice, however, is free of consequences, and financial security depends primarily upon having made adequate preparation for all four elements.

### Retirement Income

Issues around retirement income planning are the most obvious. The traditional "three-legged stool" of retirement income planning—Social Security, pension income benefit, and income from personal savings and investments—is increasingly unsteady. Social Security faces a funding crisis in the first half of the twenty-first century because soon there may not be enough workers paying into the system to support those receiving its benefits. Social Security income lifts more than one in three older persons out of poverty—more than 60% of them women. It is by far the single most important contributor to financial security in old age in America (Porter, Larin, and Primus 1999).

Social Security replaces, on average, almost half of a worker's preretirement income (EPI 2003), or nearly two-thirds of the generally accepted income target for financial security. The prospect of higher income taxes or lower Social Security benefits, however, grows with every year of extended life expectancy and as baby boomers age toward retirement.

In addition, fewer Americans are beneficiaries of pension plans that they cannot outlive. The percentage of workers covered by defined benefit plans (having clearly identifiable monthly benefits upon retirement) has dropped to less than half of those covered in the early 1980s (EPI 2003). For older recipients of proposed cash balance pension plans, this gap is likely to grow.

Beyond these pension benefit trends, "retirement plans," such as 401(k)s and 403(b)s, are really tax-sheltered asset accumulation plans and are largely funded by employees themselves even though they are sponsored by employers. Since both the investment and longevity risks of these plans are borne by individual participants, their future viability for older persons is uncertain. IRAs (Individual Retirement Accounts), whether Roth or regular, present the same investment and longevity challenges. Worse, less than half of all workers participate in any sort of pension (EBRI 2002).

Retirees may be forced to shift their orientation from living on an income they can count on to selling off assets without using them up. Even when retirement planning results in some projected fixed percentage of preretirement income, the difference, psychologically, is between receiving an identifiable amount periodically and confronting the need to harvest assets while preserving the nest egg over a long life—or else run out of money. Analysis has shown that a liquidation rate of 4.5% of assets is sustainable for 20 or more years with better than 95% confidence regardless of investment mix. However, five or ten additional years of life drops that confidence rate to as little as 33% with a conservative portfolio mix of 20% stocks, 50% bonds, and 30% cash (Ameriks, Veres, and Warshawsky 2001). Investment management, then, is becoming a survival skill for some retirees. And those who have the least to manage may have both the greatest need and the poorest prospect of getting expert help.

For those retirees who are likely to need the security of regular monthly income, fixed annuities, including equity-indexed annuities, should be considered. These are financial vehicles that can alleviate fears concerning investment loss and the anxiety of outliving one's money. The popularity of annuities suffered in comparison to the exuberance of the late 1990s when the stock market was considered a much better bet. While sales of annuities are up from $98.5 billion in 1995 to $185.3 billion in 2001, the percentage of investors taking advantage of the guarantees available in these products has nonetheless dropped from 50% to 40%.

### Health Care Expenses

The Medicare program still pays for acute health care for all older Americans, although it faces the same structural shifts as Social Security and, therefore, faces the same threats to programmatic stability. Attempts to incentivize health maintenance organizations (HMOs) to expand the traditional Medicare benefits package by providing dental, chronic prescription drug, and other therapies not otherwise included in original Medicare have not worked well and are declining. The expense of most acute care provided to retirees by their own physicians, in hospitals of their own choosing, is still covered by Medicare at rates for which providers are still willing to work.

However, the "gaps" in Medicare coverage can leave unwary older adults unprotected. The Part A deductible of $840 (in 2003) is not wealth threatening for most Americans, but an extended hospitalization with personal liability for deductibles and copays can create medical debts of over $36,000. Medicare Supplement Insurance (Medigap), standardized into ten plans ("Plan A" through "Plan J"), makes it possible for most retirees to obtain insurance that will cover these and other expenses, including limited prescription drug coverage. Still, extended drug therapies such as for arthritis or high blood pressure are not well covered either in Medicare or Medigap policies, and the costs of prescription drugs threaten financial security.

In addition, Medigap itself is expensive and incomplete. By one analysis, an individual may need to have saved between $116,000 and almost $1.5 million *over and above assets needed to generate retirement income* to pay out-of-pocket health care expenses from age 65 to age 100, and twice that for a couple (EBRI 2003).

### Frailty Care

The financial aspects of frailty are similar. While the preponderance of long-term care is provided by family members, this shifts the costs from the cared-for to the caregiver. The 1999 *MetLife Juggling Act Study* (MetLife 1999) put the extent of this shift at up to $650,000 for some families. The alternative direct cost is often measured by the cost of moving into a nursing home, which is currently just over $5,000 per month per person on a national average. Full-time care at home, however, may be as expensive as institutional care, depending upon the level of care required.

Taxpayer-funded programs to provide security in the event of frailty are scarce, other than Medicaid, which is designed for the impoverished. Either long-term care insurance or extraordinary wealth are necessary to handle the care that extended frailty requires, so that friends, family, and other members of the community of support remain free to bolster the emotional and spiritual well-being of the frail older person.

### Estate Planning

Sense of security in retirement will elude anyone who worries about what will happen to them when someone else dies. Whether the risk is loss of investment expertise, the absolute loss of income (e.g., because a pension benefit has no survivor benefit), the loss of assets to probate and estate taxes, or other circumstance of financial loss, providing for survivors is an element of financial security in retirement.

While money alone cannot provide security, the lack of money can generate insecurity. The key word is *security*, defined in Webster's *Third New International Dictionary of the English Language* as freedom from danger, fear, anxiety, or care. Real security, however, is not measured in currency. It is instead a feeling state: the internal, deep conviction that challenges can be handled as they arise. Information, attention, and intention, along with appropriate answers to the four financial questions, are the foundation of financial security in retirement. The required information is knowledge—and acknowledgment—of the challenges that might lie ahead and of the various tools and techniques to prepare for any that may arise. Information is widely available from employers and from financial services providers, on the Internet, in books and magazines, in financial education classes, and from professional advisors.

Paying attention to the financial details of future living is required over the long term, both before and after retirement. While denial is usually a problem, in retirement, denial is more likely to lead to disaster than to any sense of security. Unwillingness to be proactive about the possibility of frailty is an obvious example. Failure to be mindful creates financial risk, and worse, and the resulting financial problems may be compounded by the human costs of confusion, fear, anxiety, and even shame. Ultimately, financial security in retirement is an individual issue, because security is an individual experience. Government, employer, commercial, and community-sponsored programs and products will support each individual's sense of security to a greater or lesser extent depending upon their relevance and the individual's level of seeking. Collectively, these programs and products have done much to increase the possibility of Americans' financial security in retirement since the days of the Great Depression. (See also FINANCIAL PLANNING PROCESS; LIFE PLANNING; RETIREMENT PLANNING; RETIREMENT PREPAREDNESS; RISK TOLERANCE.)

### Suggested Readings

Cutler, Neal E. 2002. *Advising Mature Clients: The New Science of Wealth Span Planning*. New York: John Wiley and Sons.

Needleman, Jacob. 1991. *Money and the Meaning of Life*. New York: Currency Doubleday.

### References

Ameriks, John, Robert Veres, and Mark J. Warshawsky. 2001. "Making Retirement Income Last a Lifetime." *Journal of Financial Planning* (December).

Economic Policy Institute (EPI). 2003. *Issue Guide on Retirement Security. DOL Private Pension Plan Bulletin: Abstract of 1998*. Number 11, Winter 2001–2002. Washington, DC: U.S. Department of Labor, Pension and Welfare Benefits Administration. Available online at http://www.epinet.org/.

Employee Benefit Research Institute (EBRI). 2002. "An Analysis of the Retirement and Pension Plan Coverage Topical Module of SIPP." *EBRI Issue Brief* 245 (May).

Employee Benefit Research Institute (EBRI). 2003. "Retiree Health Benefits: Savings Needed to Fund Health Care in Retirement." *EBRI Issue Brief* 254 (February).

MetLife. 1999. *MetLife Juggling Act Study: Balancing Caregiving with Work and the Costs Involved*. New York: MetLife Mature Market Institute.

Porter, Kathryn H., Kathy Larin, and Wendell Primus. 1999. "Social Security and Poverty Among the Elderly: A National and State Perspective." Washington, DC: Center on Budget and Policy Priorities.

Simmons, Henry C., and E. Craig MacBean. 2000. *Thriving after 55: Your Guide to Fully Living the Rest of Your Life*, Richmond, VA: Prime Press.

*E. Craig MacBean*

**FLEXIBLE BENEFIT PLANS,** a form of employer-provided fringe benefit that permits employees to pay their share of benefit costs with pretax income and may permit them to choose from among a variety of benefits.

### Tax Treatment of Fringe Benefits Led to Flexible Benefit Plans

As a general rule, fringe benefits (such as health insurance) are a form of compensation that is not subject to income tax, Social Security, or Medicare taxes. This is appealing to employers and employees because more of the employer's outlay accrues to the employee than it does when compensation takes the form of wages and is subject to these taxes. If the employee received the money necessary to buy the benefit, say health insurance, in the form of wages, he or she would have to spend more of his/her earnings because it would be "posttax."

The Internal Revenue Service (IRS) lays out specific rules that need to be followed in order for a fringe benefit to be treated as untaxed compensation to the employee. The following benefits are *tax exempt* to the employee if the IRS rules are followed:

- Health coverage (medical, dental, vision, prescription drug)
- Employee life insurance up to $50,000
- Accidental death and dismemberment benefits
- Pretax disability
- Paid time off
- Adoption expenses

The following benefits are always considered *taxable compensation* to the employee:

- Cash
- Employee life insurance greater than $50,000
- Dependent life insurance
- After-tax disability

If the employer offers a benefit package that allows the employee to choose from among different tax exempt benefits—for example, health insurance or life insurance—the plan as a whole is tax exempt because each included benefit is tax exempt. In 1978, the IRS issued new rules that permitted employers to offer a benefit package that offered a choice between taxable and nontaxable benefits without losing the tax exempt status of the former. It is this statute that governs flexible benefit plans.

### Types of Flexible Benefit Plans

Several types of benefits fall under the heading of flexible benefit plans. Premium conversion plans, flexible spending accounts, and cafeteria plans all fall into this category of benefit. Identifying these plans can be confusing because they often are known by more than one name.

*Premium Conversion Plan.* This is the most common type of flexible benefit plan. Also known as a *premium only plan*, this plan option allows employees to make their contributions to group health and/or group term life insurance with pretax dollars. This means that the wages used to pay the employee's share of the premium will not be subject to federal or state income tax, nor is it subject to Social Security and Medicare taxes. Participation in these plans is voluntary but it is usually in the employee's best interest to participate because it can produce significant savings for most people.

*Flexible Spending Accounts.* The flexible spending account (FSA) allows employees to pay certain medical or dependent care expenses with pretax dollars. The employer may offer a *health care reimbursement account* (HCRA, for medical expenses) or *dependent care reimbursement account* (DCRA, for day care expenses) or may offer both. On an annual basis, the employee elects to have a predetermined amount of salary set aside in these specially designated accounts. Funds from the health care reimbursement account are used to "reimburse" the employee for medical expenses that they have incurred that were not reimbursed by insurance. Likewise, the dependent care reimbursement account would be used to reimburse the employee for day care expenses incurred so that the parent could work.

The amounts contributed to these accounts are not considered taxable income to the employee if certain rules are followed. The most important rule is that any amounts that are unclaimed at the end of the plan year are forfeited—these amounts become the property of the employer. (Typically there is a one- to three-month grace period after the end of the year during which an employee can still file for reimbursement.) This provision is often called the "use it or lose it" provision. There are rules governing what is a permissible expense. For example, day camp for children up to age 13 is a reimbursable expense but sleep-away camp is not. Additionally, the expense needs to be incurred during the year in which the employee is enrolled in the account. Also, these two types of accounts must be kept separate—money cannot be transferred between them. Participation is voluntary, and employees do not need to enroll in both to participate in one.

There are two significant differences between health care and dependent care reimbursement accounts. First, the health care reimbursement account has *no statutory dollar limits* on the amount an employee can contribute. In contrast, in 2002, dependent care reimbursement accounts are limited to the *lowest* of the following:

- The employee's earned income for the plan year
- The spouse's earned income for the plan year (if disabled or a full-time student, income is deemed to be $2,400 if the family has one dependent qualifying for dependent care and $4,800 if the family has two or more qualifying dependents)
- $5,000 (or $2,500 for married employees who file separate tax returns)

A second difference between health care and dependent care reimbursement accounts is that a *uniform reimbursement requirement* applies to health care accounts. This means that the balance that would have been in the account had the full year's contributions been made is available to the employee at any time during the year. Thus, the employee can submit claims at a faster rate than contributions are being collected (although they cannot exceed the total expected contribution for the year). The uniform reimbursement requirement does not apply to dependent care accounts. Unlike health care accounts, employees cannot claim reimbursement from dependent care accounts at a faster rate than they are making contributions.

*Cafeteria Plan*. Reflecting the original intent of the IRS statute, this type of plan offers an employee a choice between tax-exempt benefits and taxable benefits. For example, within a cafeteria plan, an employer might offer a cash rebate for employees who choose not to take health insurance. The health insurance is not a taxable benefit, but the cash is. Other benefits that might be offered as part of the cafeteria plan include any of those from the tax-exempt and taxable lists above. Some employers will also include things like long-term care and group and homeowners insurance as taxable benefit options. Furthermore, a premium conversion plan or flexible spending accounts can also be offered within a cafeteria plan.

Understanding these flexible benefit plan options can be confusing because an employer could offer any of these plans as a stand-alone plan or a combination of any two or all three. When companies offer both a premium conversion plan and flexible spending accounts, this is sometimes referred to as a *flex plan*. When combined with a cafeteria plan, this is sometimes called a *full flex plan*. In addition, there are closely related plans that are not technically flexible benefit plans—*health reimbursement arrangements*, for example.

One or more of these flexible benefit options is increasingly common among employers. In the 2001 *Hay Benefits Report* (Hay Group 2001) of medium and large employers, 84% of employers surveyed offered a premium conversion plan. The same report found that 78% of employers surveyed offer health care reimbursement accounts, and 83%

**Figure 1**
**Example of Potential Tax Savings**

| | | | |
|---|---|---|---|
| Employee's Annual Contribution to Flexible Spending Account and Premium Conversion Plan | | | $3,000 |
| Federal Income Tax Savings | | (28.0%) | 840 |
| FICA Savings | | (7.7%) | 230 |
| | *State Income Tax Savings* | (5.0%) | 150 |
| Total Tax Savings | | | $1,220 |

offer dependent day care reimbursement accounts. In contrast, only 22% of employers surveyed offered full flexible benefit plans.

## Advantages

It is generally an advantage to employees to have access to these types of plans. As illustrated in Figure 1, the tax savings from employee contributions to premium conversion and flexible spending accounts can be substantial. As a rule of thumb, the higher the employee's marginal tax bracket—shown as 28% in Figure 1—the more valuable the exemption.

In the case of dependent care benefits, however, income tax law permits those below a certain income level to take a tax *credit* for dependent care independent of any employer offering. An employee evaluating whether or not to enroll in their employer's dependent care reimbursement account will have to compare these two options to see which gives them the most tax benefit. A given dependent care expenditure cannot be used for both tax vehicles. Generally, participation in a dependent care reimbursement account reduces your dependent care tax credit dollar for dollar.

An additional advantage of the health care reimbursement account is that the expenses that qualify for reimbursement include several that would not typically be covered by a health insurance plan. In addition to the deductibles, cost share amounts, and copays for medical, dental, or prescription drugs, the following expenses qualify for reimbursement:

- Eyeglasses, contacts, and contact lens supplies
- Orthodontia services (must be able to prove medical necessity)
- Radial keratotomy surgery (laser eye surgery)
- Smoking cessation programs
- Hearing devices and batteries
- Acupuncture
- Buying or renting crutches

In the case of a cafeteria plan, the benefit does not take the form of tax savings but rather the ability to customize the benefit package to suit the employee. A flexible benefit plan allows the employee to direct his or her benefit dollars to the options that he or she values most highly. For example, an employee with health coverage through a spouse might want to forego the health insurance and instead direct those dollars to other benefits that might include additional vacation or cash. A single employee might prefer to purchase the health insurance and forego a different benefit.

### Disadvantages

Additional choices also mean more responsibility on the part of the employee. Communications from the employer's human resource department must be studied carefully. Because of the "use it or lose it" rule, particular care must be taken in allocating money to flexible spending accounts. Employees considering this option should know which expenses qualify for reimbursement, and they should understand the procedures that they need to follow to claim reimbursement since documentation of expenses will be required. Finally, they should carefully and conservatively assess their expected expenses.

It is important to remember that, as a general rule, flex plan elections cannot be changed during the plan year unless there is a change in family status such as the birth of a child, marriage, divorce, or death. Of special importance to those considering retirement is the fact that flexible spending accounts are not portable. If an employee terminates or retires before the end of the plan year, he or she will have limited options.

Under COBRA (Consolidated Omnibus Budget Reconciliation Act) provisions, if the employee has not claimed his or her health care reimbursement account balance at the time of retirement or termination, he or she may continue to pay contributions on an after-tax basis for the remainder of the calendar year. This allows the individual to remain eligible to file claims against the account and potentially recover the contributions already made. This would include services received after the date of separation but before the end of the plan year. If the employee chooses *not* to make after-tax contributions, he or she may only seek reimbursement for services received prior to the date of separation. This may be appealing if the employee has already received more health care expense reimbursements than he or she has contributed. In such a case, the employer must absorb the loss.

A *plan year* is any 12-month period of time as determined in the plan's documents. Most often it corresponds with the company's fiscal year. Individuals participating in a dependent care reimbursement account may only seek reimbursement for eligible dependent care expenses incurred during the period of employment. COBRA continuation provisions do not apply to the dependent care account. Since premium contribution plans and flexible spending accounts reduce the salary subject to taxes, they also affect benefits that are based on salary. As a general rule, the advantages of these flexible benefit plans outweigh any effects that might occur for other, salary-based benefits. However, it is wise to review the treatment of these benefits:

*Pension.* Whether or not pension benefits are affected by these salary reductions will vary from company to company. In those companies where there is an effect, employees close to termination of employment or retirement will be impacted most severely because pension benefits are often based on average salary for the last several years of employment.

*Life Insurance/Disability.* Life insurance and disability benefit amounts are also typically based on the salary of the employee. The employer has the discretion to determine whether the full or reduced salary is used to compute these benefits. However, because flexible spending accounts are also advantageous to employers, they are usually willing to base these benefit amounts on the full salary to encourage participation.

*Workers' Compensation/Unemployment.* Workers' compensation and unemployment benefits are based on the average monthly wage. For those who earn above the maximum monthly wage, benefits would not be reduced. However, for lower-income employees, the reduction in potential benefits could be substantial. State law may dictate whether or not these benefits can be based on full salary.

*Social Security.* Because Social Security benefits are based on salary throughout an employee's career, retirement benefits should not be significantly reduced, particularly if the FSA reduction does not occur over the employee's entire career. However, a young employee who has elected a large reduction and becomes disabled could receive a significantly lower Social Security disability benefit. Likewise, the survivor benefits could be significantly lower.

There is very little in the way of organizations or literature that looks at flexible benefit plans from the viewpoint of the employee. Almost all of it adopts the viewpoint of the employer. Because participation in these plans is voluntary, however, employees should be able to enjoy the maximum benefit and avoid the pitfalls with careful planning. (See also HEALTH BENEFITS; PENSION PLANS; POSTRETIREMENT HEALTH COVERAGE [PRHC]; RETIREMENT PREPAREDNESS; WORKFORCE PATTERNS, CHANGES IN; WORKPLACE FINANCIAL EDUCATION.)

**References**

Hay Group. 2001. *Hay Benefits Report.* Philadelphia, PA: Author.

Johnson, Richard E., and Sidney Weintraub. 2002. *Flexible Benefits: A How-to Guide.* 6th ed. Brookfield, WI: International Foundation of Employee Benefit Plans.

Morris, Robin C., Mark Manin, Linda Frayling, and Francesca G. Sclandra. 1999. *Flexible Benefits Answer Book.* New York: Aspen Publishers.

*Lynn Q. Taylor*

**FOOD STAMPS.** See Elder Law Practice; Gerontological Social Work; Minority Older Adults; Nutrition Programs.

**FRAILTY PLANNING,** the practice of preparing for all the implications and aspects of frailty before the onset of significant decline. Frailty defies precise definition but encompasses a spectrum of functional limitations of varying severity and has a broad set of implications. It is best defined as the inability to function with complete independence due to either physical or cognitive limitations or a combination of both. Being frail has interconnected consequences and implications in the domains of personal finance, housing, law, health, psychology, spirituality, and medicine. Such a complex problem calls for a complete response. Planning for the possibility of frailty creates a posture of preparedness, which, in turn, enables individuals and those who love and support them to minimize the experience of fear and suffering and to maximize the quality of life—no matter how long frailty may persist—for both the frail and those in their communities of love and support.

Many people resist the notion of frailty planning on the grounds that "it won't happen to me." Certainly, not everyone will live through a period of frailty. Depending on how you define it, statistics are available stating that between one-third and two-thirds of the population—perhaps even more—will experience a period of frailty that may last as long as 10 or 20 years (especially in the event of Alzheimer's or similar dementia). Instead of analyzing the statistics, consider that none of them suggest that frailty is a chance event that will only happen to a few unlucky individuals. Rather, all the statistics tell us that enough of us will live through a period of frailty that to not prepare for it is unwise.

### Distinguish from Other Planning Disciplines

Frailty planning is related to but is neither the same as nor a subset of retirement planning, financial planning, or estate planning. *Retirement planning* is the practice of preparing for the financial implications of not working. This is normally focused on generating adequate income for routine living expenses and for supporting lifestyle choices—such as extensive travel—at retirement. Because the pre–baby boomers and the baby boomers are more comfortable with psychological and spiritual issues than were their parents, this field is currently undergoing a transformation that is likely to broaden its scope of inquiry to take in issues of meaning and purpose and to deal with more values-related questions as part of the context for its traditional focus on the financial implications of not working. However, some practitioners, reacting to this trend toward a broader focus, will expand by dealing not with more types of issues related to retirement but rather with more financial issues than just retirement. Those who make this choice will likely deal with some elements of frailty planning (such as long-term care insurance) but may not engage the broader issues and implications.

*Financial planning* is defined by the Certified Financial Planner™ (CFP®) Board of Standards as "the process of meeting [one's] life goals through the proper management of [one's] finances. Life goals can include buying a home, saving for [a] child's education or planning for retirement" (http://www.cfp.net/learn/knowledgebase,asp?id=1). While it is general in scope, and is often thought to be synonymous with *retirement* planning, in practice financial planning focuses on asset accumulation and investment allocation and is much more attentive to managing investments than the other related planning disciplines. Since being frail is not generally considered a life goal, financial planners are unlikely to deal with frailty planning, although that should not be said of those practicing Financial Life Planning™ or other more holistic approaches to financial planning.

*Estate planning* is the practice of preparing for the financial implications of dying. That often means minimizing the costs of estate taxes and probate as well as determining who gets what assets or income streams when, how dependents might subsist after the caregiver's death, and how other individuals or institutions that will carry on work or ideas that are important to the decedent will be supported as an aspect of legacy. Because estate planning almost inevitably involves the creation of legal documents (wills and trusts, for example) and frailty planning also involves the creation of legal documents (such as powers of attorney), elder law attorneys are a group of practitioners likely to become involved in frailty planning.

Frailty planning also needs to be distinguished from health care. While not generally considered a planning discipline in the sense of financial, retirement, or estate planning, and while health care is certainly an element of frailty care, one must be careful to avoid the trap of seeing frailty as a purely medical issue. Frailty planning involves health care treatment planning to the extent that it can be predicted prior to the onset of specific conditions, but it also encompasses other disciplines in support of and parallel to health care management issues. Because they may be involved in the sale of health insurance, Medicare Supplement ("Medigap") policies, critical illness coverage or long-term care insurance, life and health insurance agents are another group likely to become involved in frailty planning.

Frailty planning is not yet recognized as a specialty or even a focus area among financial advisors, professional geriatric care managers, ministers, rabbis, imams, or other religious or social services advisors, so getting competent advice can be challenging. However, as the baby boom generation gets older, expect such a focus area to emerge in some service sector. For reasons of expected professional behavior, it appears most likely to come from the financial services arena, although other sectors may prove to be more motivated to serve this population in a proactive, holistic manner.

### The Frailty Planning Process

The frailty planning process is neither long nor especially complex, but it requires care. It is multidisciplinary in that it invites input from real estate professionals, lawyers, financial advisors, and medical professionals as well as social workers, life coaches or guides, and religious professionals. Although there are a variety of approaches to frailty planning, those that take pains to assist the client in clarifying her or his values and those of other affected friends or family members (spouse, children) obviously give better results than those that do not. Frailty planning consists of five steps:

1. *Identifying strategic housing choices, clarifying pros and cons and issues around each, and choosing a strategy.* The biggest issue in frailty care is answering the question, "Where will you live when (if) you become frail?" This is the key issue because it may determine treatment and drive decisions that are otherwise undesirable. For example, an individual who has had a stroke but is mobile with the aid of a walker may not be released from the hospital to home if home means living alone with a second-floor bedroom and a basement laundry. Unfortunately, absent frailty planning, this question must be asked reactively in an emotionally charged environment and often leaves both the frail and their families and friends with unsatisfactory choices, guilt, and resentment. Only a proactive, frailty planning approach can provide for a desirable care setting at the appropriate time, support a sense of security, and prevent feelings of guilt and resentment.

2. *Identifying options for support at various levels of frailty and resources available in the community to address them, coordinating resources with strategic housing choices, and projecting costs.* Regardless of one's strategic choice of housing in the event of frailty, there will be identifiable resources to facilitate a plan of frailty care that meets his or her needs. These may be resources such as nonmedical companion and support services or full- or part-time aides to provide in-home intermittent medical care to support the choice to stay there or to move in with a sibling or a child. Others will want to consider moving into a continuing care retirement community (CCRC) with its continuum of independent living activities and care facilities. In the event that one adopts a strategy of moving from care option to care option as the ability to function independently deteriorates, an investigation of adult day care services, assisted living facilities, or nursing homes (among others) would be called for. In almost all cases the opportunity to meet and to get to know a professional geriatric care manager—and to have the care manager

get to know the individual as a fully functional adult prior to the onset of functional decline—is extremely desirable. Identifying these resources proactively not only allows planning for financing frailty care but also facilitates choice and, in some instances, enables a quality of care that is simply unavailable reactively.

3. *Identifying all financial impacts of possible frailty and choosing a financial approach to provide security; coordinating with other financial matters and planning disciplines.* There are only three sources of funds to pay for frailty care: taxpayer dollars (Medicare and Medicaid), personal dollars, and long-term care insurance. Taxpayer dollars are scarce and, except in the case of the impoverished, not designed to provide the breadth of services (medical, social, legal, spiritual) that is required. Even where the government does provide such services, however, resource constraints are such that adequacy of service must be called into question. Personal dollars are usually allocated on a priority basis to generate retirement income and to be held as reserves to provide a sense of financial security, so they are most often either unavailable or inadequate to satisfy the heavy cash demands of frailty care. Some contingency plans are available on a "just in case" basis, such as contemplating the use of a reverse mortgage to free up home equity without the need to move. However, except for those few cases where acquiring long-term care insurance is either not advisable or not available, it is almost always the most satisfactory response to financial aspects of frailty planning.

4. *Identifying desires for treatment options in acute stages of frailty and creating appropriate legal documents; obtaining consent of others to make health care decisions and financial and other life management decisions in the event one is unable to make those decisions oneself and communicating one's desires to his or her community of support and care.* Just as it is necessary to obtain the consent of named guardians for minor children in the event of the untimely death of their parents (an element of estate planning), so it is necessary to obtain the consent of others—family, friends, trusted advisors—to act on one's behalf in making health care decisions and managing one's worldly affairs in the event of acute frailty. However, neither living wills, durable powers of attorney, nor health care powers of attorney are effective if those who will be affected are not aware of their existence or clear about your desires. Organizations such as Last Acts (http://www.lastacts.org/) offer additional information and support for this part of the process.

5. *Identifying strengths and weaknesses in spiritual life and practice as well as community involvement and support; making and implementing plans to build on strengths and minimize weaknesses.* While many of the issues in frailty planning are legal or financial, the greatest impacts of frailty are emotional and spiritual. The proactive approach outlined in the first four steps of frailty planning is important to minimize the practical problems associated with being frail. An equally proactive approach to enhancing emotional and spiritual skills, and to developing appropriate supportive practices, is essential to well-being through the period of frailty, quality of life, and quality of death.

### Summary

Frailty planning is a responsible and intelligent response to the increased life expectancies we are all experiencing. It has a place in the same pantheon of planning disciplines as financial planning, retirement planning, and estate planning. It does not fit neatly into any one professional discipline, but rather it requires practitioners with the skills and experience to cut across professional disciplines to create dedicated business entities or professional working alliances. The process is simple but perhaps not easy as it requires enough maturity to be able to tackle issues that carry a significant emotional charge. (See also ACTIVITIES OF DAILY LIVING [ADLs]; CASH FLOW PLANNING FOR RETIREES; CONTINUING CARE RETIREMENT COMMUNITIES [CCRCs]; COSTS OF FAMILY CAREGIVING; LONG-TERM CARE INSURANCE, PRIVATE; REVERSE MORTGAGES.)

**Reference**

Simmons, Henry C., and E. Craig MacBean. 2002. *Thriving after 55: Your Guide to Fully Living the Rest of Your Life*. Richmond, VA: Prime Press.

*E. Craig MacBean*

**FUNERALS AND FUNERAL FINANCES.** Since prehistoric times, people have confronted and transcended death through collective means, including group rituals, collective belief systems, and a variety of aggregated death-related customs and behavior. The funeral, and the more extended process of "funeralization," has always occupied a position of centrality in death-related behavior. The funeral acknowledges death, provides a mechanism for the social transition from life to death, offers a venue for saying goodbye to the deceased, and facilitates group reintegration and community reequilibrium (Hayslip, Sewells, and Riddle 2003).

## The American Funeral

During the several centuries of American history, the funeral ritual evolved from a spartan Puritan burial with simple prayers and modest mention of the death at a subsequent church service in the 1600s to a more structured, but still unpretentious, religious service with song, prayer, and sermon in the 1700s. By the 1800s, the funeral service had grown into a lengthy emotional, heavily religious, and complex ceremony involving multiple prayers, numerous songs, strident sermon, and the participation of a large congregation.

By the twentieth century, the United States had become a death-denying society, and the main effort was to avoid confronting death (Stephenson 1985). The deceased was embalmed with the aim of making the body look alive but asleep and peaceful. Bodies were laid out in "slumber" rooms in funeral homes to extend the original aim. Funerals were fashioned so as to aid in insulating the living from the confrontation with death. Funerals became

> increasingly secular, commercial in nature, and seemingly intended to create an aura of an avoidance of death. Funerals are currently shorter than in the past and appear somewhat routine and perfunctory even to the point of being scripted and superficial in manner. (Bryant et al. 2003)

Some services are held in funeral home chapels rather than churches. Many have secular elements mixed with the sacred. Sermons may be brief and quasi-religious, and friends and family members deliver eulogies rather than clergy.

The funeral of the late 1800s, especially the rural funeral, was well integrated into the fabric of community life, and much of the expense of the funeral was borne by com-

**Table 1**
**Funeral Costs**

| Item | Cost |
|---|---|
| Casket | $2,330 |
| Embalming | 420 |
| Other Preparations (Cosmetology, etc.) | 150 |
| Visitation/Viewing | 275 |
| Funeral at Funeral Home | 350 |
| Transfer of Remains to Funeral Home | 154 |
| Hearse (Local) | 185 |
| Service Car/Van | 85 |
| Professional Service | 1,213 |
| Acknowledgment Cards | 18 |
| **Total** | **$5,180** |

*Source*: National Funeral Directors Association, 2001.

munity institutions, especially the church and extended family. Today's funeral, and especially the urban service, is almost exclusively a commercial enterprise with professionals and other outsiders providing a wide array of services with attendant financial costs. Because of the commercial nature of funerals today, the financial burden to the family is not insignificant.

## The Economics of the Funeral

The contemporary funeral is one of the more significant expenditures made by American families, generally exceeded only by major economic outlays such as the home, automobile purchases, and college education for the children. The cost of a funeral can range from $1,500 up to levels of $100,000 or more, depending on the economic resources of the family and/or the idiosyncratic inclinations of the deceased individual or the person selecting the funeral.

The vast majority of American families choose a simple, but dignified, funeral of modest cost that involves the full array of services offered by the funeral home. According to the National Funeral Directors Association, the average cost of an adult funeral in 2001 was $5,180. This figure includes the items and services shown in Table 1.

Several of these items and services could be omitted, such as the visitation/viewing, holding the funeral at the funeral home (using a church instead), and the acknowledgment cards, for a savings of $643. A less expensive casket could be selected for a savings of up to another $1,000, and in most instances, the embalming could also be omitted for a total saving of approximately $2,100. By eschewing these items and services, the total cost of the funeral could be lowered to about $3,000.

The average funeral cost of $5,180 does not include the price of a vault (at approximately $950), which is optional but may be required for interment in some cemeteries. This could raise the average funeral price to $6,130. Other costs not included are those for a cemetery plot or space in a crypt/mausoleum, opening or closing the grave, and monument or marker. These considerations may raise the total cost of funeralization by several thousand dollars, depending on choice.

There seems to be only modest variation in the cost of an average adult funeral from state to state. The average cost generally varies by less than 10% between and among the states. Funeral costs in the United States have risen over the years. In 1957, the average cost of an adult funeral (not including vault, cemetery, or grave marker) was $646. By 1977, it was $1,412. By 1985 it was $2,737, and in 1991, it was $3,742. The cost had risen to $4,782 by 1996. It would appear that the cost of an average funeral has only risen annually at about the same rate as that of inflation. Whether or not the average cost of a funeral will rise significantly in the future will likely be a function of both contemporary and future trends in funerals and the funeral industry.

### Preneed Funerals

Because of the significant and unexpected economic cost of funerals, financial advisors and funeral directors encourage the public to make provision for preneed funerals. The term *preneed* is a generic term that encompasses both *prearranging* and *prefunding*. Basically this process includes selecting merchandise, planning the service, determining the method of viewing and final disposition of the remains, and selecting persons to be involved in the funeral. In short, an individual can now plan his or her own funeral as he or she wishes it to be. This is said to be desirable from the standpoint of removing the burden from surviving loved ones (Aarons 1999), being able to express and implement one's personal (and even idiosyncratic) preferences in regard to one's own funeral, and making appropriate financial arrangements. Normally, *prefunding* attends *prearranging*. Once personalized funeral plans have been made, they are ideally paid for. This is consistent with good financial planning, and at time of death, funeral costs do not invade the principal assets of the estate. Prefunding can be accomplished after making appropriate arrangements with a funeral director, through the establishment of a trust with the funds put into escrow, the designation of a certain portion of life insurance, or through the purchase of burial insurance. AARP conducted a survey in 1995 and discovered that 7 million people had prearranged their funerals (Leming and Dickinson 2002).

There are, of course, disadvantages to preneed funerals. An individual who made specific funeral arrangements at one point in life may have different preferences later but neglect to change the prearrangement agreement, just as some individuals neglect to alter their living wills as their preferences change. Preneed funerals, in effect, preempt the prerogatives of family members who may have strong emotional concerns about the funeral arrangements that are at variance with the preferences of the deceased.

Preneed funerals have another disadvantage, however. They provide a robust opportunity for consumer fraud (Leming and Dickinson 2002). Now that preneed arrangements have become relatively widespread, instances of abuse and fraud are not uncommon (Geller 2001; Lucia 2001; Stepzinski 2002). In this regard, many states are now moving to regulate preneed funeral arrangements (Alabama, for example) and a few states, such as New York, do not permit preneed funeral insurance but insist that funeral expenses be held in trust (Editors of The Times Union 2001). "Burial" insurance, however, has long been popular with less affluent segments of the population, and some insurance industry representatives have attacked bans on funeral insurance as unfair to poorer consumers (Kryshak 2001). While preneed funerals are not without controversy, such arrangements will no doubt continue to grow in use in the future.

### The American Funeral Industry

In 2001, there were 21,757 funeral homes in the United States. The number of funeral homes has remained relatively stable over the past decade or so, although the total number in 2001 is actually down a bit from the 22,153 total in 1996. A total of 34,588 licensed funeral directors operated or worked in these funeral homes in 2001. When embalmers are added, the number of death care professionals rises to approximately 45,000 individuals. There is a curious distribution of funeral homes per state, however. Some sparsely populated states such as Alaska (19) and Nevada (38) have a very small number of funeral homes. Some of the rural states with smaller populations have a disproportionately high number of funeral homes compared to states with much larger populations. Examples here include Alabama with a population in 2000 of 4.4 million and 45,075 deaths and 407 funeral homes, as compared to California with a population in 2000 of 33.9 million and 229,535 deaths and 742 funeral homes, or Mississippi with a population of 2.8 million and 28,671 deaths and 275 funeral homes, as opposed to Texas with a population of 20.9 million and 148,994 deaths but only 1,174 funeral homes (National Funeral Directors Association 2001). This anomaly is likely the result of the fact that the public prefers to patronize a funeral home that is located in their own community, even if quite small. Thus, in rural states like Mississippi, with the population spread about in small communities, there are opportunities for funeral homes to locate in each of these small communities as a matter of convenience. In some of the states with larger populations, the population may tend to be more centralized in a few large urban areas, and a fewer number of large-capacity funeral homes can more readily serve the public's need by virtue of being more centrally located. If the public would be willing to patronize funeral homes that were more centrally located at a greater distance from their home, a significantly fewer number of funeral homes could adequately handle the country's funeral needs.

The funeral industry is economically large. A decade ago in 1993, Americans spent between $9.7 billion and $17.1 billion on funeral, cremation, and cemetery services. According to the National Funeral Directors Association, in 1997 there were 16,031 funeral homes with payroll total receipts of $9,503,010,000. In the same year there were 6,677 cemeteries and crematories with payroll that had receipts of $2,987,878,000. There were also 59,458 cemetery and crematory employees who earned a total of $1,075,090,000 (or an average of $18,082 per employee) (http://www.nfda.org/). Thus, it would appear that the funeral industry generated approximately $13.5 billion. This figure does not include the revenues of other logistical industries that support the funeral industry, such as casket manufacturers, hearse makers, and florists, to mention but some. The figure is higher today and will grow significantly as the number of deaths that occur in the United States rises over time.

### Current Trends

Although not widely known, profits on funerals have been declining over the past two decades. Over a 20-year period, the profit on a funeral decreased from 13.73% in 1980 to 8.64% in 2000 (*American Blue Book of Funeral Directors* 2002). This represents a 63% decline in profits and is viewed as a matter of concern by those in the funeral industry. It is believed that this decline in profitability is primarily the result of rising operating expenses for funeral homes, when the cost of funerals has only approximately risen at the annual rate of inflation. Accordingly, the funeral industry has engaged in several efforts at restructuring in an attempt to restore profitability, and "funeral home owners are searching for economies and additional services to provide their clients which might offset these recent declines" (Salomone 2003).

According to one author, these restructuring efforts have included such measures as:

*Consolidation*. Small, locally owned ("Mom and Pop") funeral homes are increasingly being bought and absorbed into large national funeral corporations that seek to bring an economy of scale to these small mortuaries through improved business practices. Such corporations are also acquiring other types of death-related businesses such as crematoria and cemeteries (Salomone 2003). An example of this practice is Service Corporation International, the largest funeral corporation in the world. Its holdings include 3,611 funeral homes, 193 cemeteries, 55 flower shops, and a number of crematoria (Service Corporation International 2001). This consolidation trend has resulted in four corporations owning approximately 10% of the funeral homes in the United States (Salomone 2003).

*Clustering*. Funeral homes may acquire and integrate various death-related enterprises such as funeral homes, cemeteries, crematoria, floral shops, tombstone businesses, insurance businesses, and so on, into a unified business entity that can "pool resources, assets, personnel and services in the interest of higher profits" (Salomone 2003).

*Preplanning*. This practice allows for an individual to design his or her own funeral in advance, choosing the type of funeral service, details such as a particular variety of casket, and method of body disposition, among other concerns. The cost of the funeral is paid in advance, and the money is put into escrow until the death of the client. This represents a profitable arrangement for the funeral home because "preplanning serves the same purpose as burial insurance; it locks in a customer base so as to insure subsequent business eventually" (Salomone 2003).

### Other Funeral Practice Trends

*Alternative arrangements* are another recent trend in funeralization today. Included here are such accommodations as discount or economy funeral homes that provide a minimalist service. Some such funeral homes are now operating in low-rent structures in less desirable locations. They may utilize less expensive makes or used hearses and essentially offer pick-up, embalming, moderately priced caskets, and delivery service to a home and/or cemetery. They frequently do not have space in their facilities for visitation or funeral services. Such businesses can offer relatively inexpensive "essential service" funerals only for families desiring such arrangements (Smith 2002).

Other alternative arrangements include the *memorial service*. Here the body is initially buried, possibly without being embalmed, or cremated without ceremony, and at a subsequent date, family and friends gather in a home or in some larger facility such as a church or lodge hall for a memorial service, without the body of the deceased. Various individuals may present eulogies to the deceased, and clergy may or may not be present. Services may be either religious or secular or a combination. The service may often be followed by a reception or meal. The relevant factor here is the fact that the funeral home is essentially bypassed, other than picking up and delivering the body to the cemetery or crematoria. Some funeral directors now specialize in providing such minimal arrangements.

A related arrangement involves various "do-it-yourself" measures, such as the family purchasing the casket through a discount casket retailer or online and having it delivered to the funeral home. Funeral homes naturally discourage such a practice but, in some instances, are legally required to permit such an arrangement. In such an eventuality, the funeral home may charge a handling and processing fee. Occasionally, especially in the instance of a small casket, such as that used for a child, the family may even request that they transport the body to the cemetery, thereby saving the cost of the hearse.

Because of scattered families living at some distance from each other, and the expense of traveling to a funeral, the use of electronic arrangements, such as closed-circuit television, videotapes, and virtual funerals, are becoming possible and will increase in the future. Rather than the entire family traveling to the funeral, the funeral can take place with only a few of the members (or none) present, and the service can be videotaped for later viewing, or conceivably broadcast on closed-circuit television to other locations where family members are located. The economic benefits and convenience of virtual funerals are such that an increasing number of families may seek such arrangements in the future.

### Selling New Services

The funeral industry is actively searching for new services to offer as a means of increasing the profitability of funerals. Among the initiatives in this regard is *aftercare*, which might include memorial services for special dates such as birthdays, weddings, or death anniversaries. Aftercare may also include follow-up services for clients needing support, emotional affirmation, or temporary assistance with the practical necessities of life while they are working through their grief. Funeral homes might ultimately provide licensed staff psychologists or social workers as professional grief counselors.

It has also been suggested that funeral homes could offer *DNA coding*. Here the funeral home might "package and preserve blood and hair samples from a corpse for possible use by consanguineal (blood) relatives of the deceased who might want to know the probably genetic links to certain diseases" (Salomone 2003). Finally, the strategy of using the *Internet* as a digital merchandising system for funeral homes is being tried. The funeral home, its products, facilities, equipment, and services can effectively be shown over the Internet. In effect, funerals can be sold in the home via the computer.

### Long-Term Trends in the Funeral Industry

Over the next 75 years the demographics of death in the United States are going to change dramatically, and there are a number of trends and projections that are likely to impact the process of funeralization, the cost of funerals, and the parameters of the American funeral industry.

The current death rate of approximately 8.7 per 1,000 population is projected to rise to 10.9 by 2040 and 13.17 in 2060. It will remain at approximately that level through 2070 and 2080 (Bryant et al. 2003). The rise to 13.17 per 1,000 population from today's 8.7 rate represents an increase of *more than 51.4%*. This is a significant increase in the death rate, which will be the result of increasing life expectancy and a much larger number of persons over 65 years old in the population. This much larger proportion of older adults will, of course, die at some point, pushing the death rate up.

Over the same time period, the overall population of the United States will also increase. This fact, coupled with the much higher death rate, will produce a total annual death figure of 6.5 million persons in 2080, as opposed to only 2.5 million annual deaths, or three times as many deaths as today (Bryant et al. 2003). An annual death total this large would be more than today's 22,000 funeral homes could accommodate. This would suggest that the number of funeral homes in the United States will have to grow at an accelerated pace in order to be able to process that many deaths. Inasmuch as the number of annual deaths may grow at a rate faster than funeral homes can increase, funeral prices may, accordingly, rise in a disproportionate fashion. This cost tendency may be offset to some degree, however, by other long-term trends.

### Cremation

For more than two centuries in the United States, burial (or vault interment) was essentially the exclusive mode of body disposition. In the late nineteenth century, however, cremation emerged as a new mode of body disposition. For many years, cremation enjoyed only limited acceptance in the United States, although in Great Britain and Europe, it achieved a much greater degree of acceptance by the mid-twentieth century. From 1876–1884 until the 1934–1938 period, cremation had only achieved a 2.56% of death usage. By 1981, cremation as a choice of body disposition had risen to 11.01% and subsequently to 25.48% in 2000. Cremation has been projected further to rise to 48.65% of body disposition in 2025 (*CANA Report* 2001) and could become even more widespread over the subsequent 50 years, perhaps ultimately reaching a 75% rate or so. Although funeral homes do presently handle arrangements for cremation, there is significantly less profit here than in burials. In time, the funeral home may be bypassed altogether with a delivery service that takes the dead body directly to the crematoria for a minimal fee. In spite of the very large increase in deaths over the next 75 years, the rising trend of cremation utilization, plus other consumer cost-saving behavior trends, may well offset the higher death rate and impact the funeral industry both in terms of funeral profitability and even the viability of the funeral industry itself. (See also ESTATE PLANNING; ETHICAL WILL; FINANCIAL SECURITY IN RETIREMENT; FRAILTY PLANNING, HOME CARE SERVICES FOR OLDER ADULTS; LIVING WILLS.)

#### References

Aarons, A. 1999. "Prearranging a Funeral Prevents Many Burdens." *Daily News* (New York), June 8.

*American Blue Book of Funeral Directors*. 2002. 38th ed. Iselin, NJ: Kates-Boylson Publications, Inc.

Associated Press. 2002. "Legislature Passes Bill Regulating Pre-Need Funeral Arrangements." 2002. *Dateline* (Montgomery, AL), January 31.

Banks, Dwayne A. 2003. "On the Economics of Death in the United States." In *Handbook of Death and Dying*, ed. Clifton D. Bryant. Thousand Oaks, CA: Sage Publications.

Bern-Klug, Mercedes, Stanley Deviney, and David J. Ekerdt. 2000. "Variations in Funeral-Related Costs of Older Adults and the Role of Preneed Funeral Contracts and Type of Disposition." *Omega: The Journal of Death and Dying* 41: 1.

Bryant, Clifton E., Charles K. Edgley, Dennis L. Peck, and Kent L. Sandstrom. 2003. "Death in the Future: Prospects and Prognosis." In *Handbook of Death and Dying*, ed. Clifton D. Bryant. Thousand Oaks, CA: Sage Publications.

*CANA Report 2001*. 2001. Cremation Associates of North America. Available online at http://www.cremationassociation.org/.

Editors of The Times Union. 2001. "Merchants of Grief: New York State Should Maintain Its Ban on Prearrangement Insurance." *The Times Union* (Albany, NY), October 29.

Geller, Adam. 2001. "Pre-Need Funeral Deals Grow . . . So Does Fraud." *Dayton Daily News*, April 29.

Hayslip, Bert, Jr., Kenneth W. Sewells, and Russell B. Riddle. 2003. "The American Funeral." In *Handbook of Death and Dying*, ed. Clifton D. Bryant. Thousand Oaks, CA: Sage Publications.

Kryshak, Terry J. 2001. "Ban on Funeral Insurance a Denial of Choice." *The Times Union* (Albany, NY), November 11.

Leming, Michael R., and George E. Dickinson. 2002. *Understanding Dying, Death, and Bereavement*. Fort Worth, TX: Harcourt College Publishers.

Lucia, Tony. 2001. "Planning a Funeral without Getting Killed." *The Eagle/Times* (Reading, PA), June 17.

Mclachlin, Mary. 2002. "The Big Business of Death." *The Palm Beach Post* (Palm Beach, FL), February 24.

National Funeral Directors Association. 2001. *NFDA 2001 General Price List Survey*. Brookfield, WI: NFDA Research & Information Department.

Salomone, Jerome J. 2003. "The Evolution of the Funeral Home and the Occupation of Funeral Director." In *Handbook of Death and Dying*, ed. Clifton D. Bryant. Thousand Oaks, CA: Sage Publications.

Service Corporation International. 2001. *2000 Annual Report*. Houston, TX: Author.

Smith, Hilary Groutage. 2002. "The Business of Death: A Look Inside the Funeral Industry." *The Salt Lake Tribune* (Salt Lake City, UT), October 27.

Stephenson, J.S. 1985. *Death, Grief, and Mourning: Individual and Social Realities*. New York: Free Press.

Stepzinski, Teresa. 2002. "Former Coroner Sentenced in Fraud: He Gets 13 Months in Funeral Scam." *The Florida Times Union*, June 1.

*Clifton D. Bryant*

# G

**GENERATION X.** See Retirement Preparedness.

**GERIATRIC CARE MANAGERS (GCMs),** practitioners with a graduate degree in a field of human services (social work, psychology, gerontology) or a substantial equivalent (e.g., a registered nurse [RN]). who specialize in assisting older people and their families with long-term care arrangements. Geriatric care managers may be certified by any one of a number of organizations but are not currently licensed by most states.

Increasingly, individuals and families are turning to geriatric care managers to obtain assistance in caring for frail older relatives. If an older person is experiencing difficulty in taking care of daily needs, is isolated from family, neighbors, and friends, is having difficulty knowing where to turn and what services can help, or wants to do preventive planning, the family may want to consider using the services of a geriatric care manager (Polich et al. 1993).

When an older person becomes frail and in need of assistance, families often face the difficult and time-consuming task of negotiating a complex array of public and nonprofit social service agencies, many of which have waiting lists. Other problems may arise in finding a social or medical service, uncertainty about what a service offers, the need to coordinate services for needs unmet even after receiving support from several agencies, refusal of services or claims, considerations of nursing homes versus alternatives, or help with locating a good facility (Polich et al. 1993).

Attempting to understand complicated eligibility requirements and locating the most suitable services for an older family member can create stress and conflict within families. Relevant questions include whether the older family member has trouble making formerly routine decisions or conducting routine financial affairs and whether guardianship or conservatorship should be considered. Adult children or grandchildren faced with career and other responsibilities in addition to their caregiving concerns can seek the assistance of qualified professional care managers.

Possible sources of referral for geriatric care managers are the National Association of Professional Geriatric Care Managers (http://www.caremanager.org/), Area Agencies on Aging, physicians, or home care agencies. Since most family members want to remain involved in a caregiving role, they can use GCMs for initial assessment and periodic consultation. Others, especially those who live far from their aging parent or relative, might retain GCMs to oversee the long-term care plan that has been arranged and to serve as a liaison between the older person and the family members.

When choosing a professional geriatric care manager, a number of points merit consideration. Care managers should have training and experience, usually a nursing or social work background. Knowledge of long-term care services, financing mechanisms, and local community resources should be evident. Good communication skills are important, as is a manageable caseload (probably no more than 50 to 75 clients). References should be requested from the care manager and investigated (AARP 1989).

The process of obtaining GCM services begins with an assessment of the client's situation, needs, and resources. Next, a service plan is designed and implemented. Either services are provided directly by the care manager, the client is referred to another service provider, or the plan is coordinated with other professional resources, such as the family's attorney, investment counselors, insurance specialists, accountants, physicians, and hospital staff. During this period, results are monitored to ensure that the client's needs are met, that services are delivered, and that modifications are made as the client's status changes.

Services provided by GCMs include:

- Conducting care plan assessments to identify problems, eligibility for assistance, and need for services
- Screening, arranging, and monitoring in-home assistance or other services
- Reviewing financial, legal, or medical issues and offering referrals to geriatric specialists to avoid future problems and conserve assets
- Providing crisis intervention
- Acting as a liaison to families, especially families at a distance, making sure things are going well and alerting families to problems
- Assisting with moving an older person to or from a retirement complex, care home, or nursing home
- Providing consumer education and advocacy
- Offering counseling and support

The cost of geriatric care management can be substantial in the initial evaluation stage. Generally, services fall in the range of $60 to $200 an hour—costs vary depending on geographic location and scope of services offered. Once the plan of care is designed, costs recede as the care manager monitors and maintains the services. Payment can be per hour or on a package basis for an assessment, in conjunction with a sliding-fee scale. Most payment for private care management is made directly by the client, family, or caregiver (Parker 1992).

GCMs have joined efforts with the National Academy of Certified Care Managers and the Case Management Institute to establish a credential in geriatric care management, which will ensure to consumers or purchasers a standard of quality, as well as provide care managers greater access to liability insurance. (See also CPA ELDERCARE SERVICES; FRAILTY PLANNING; GERONTOLOGICAL SOCIAL WORK; GUARDIANSHIP; HOME CARE SERVICES FOR OLDER ADULTS; LONG-TERM CARE INSURANCE [LTCI]—A CONSUMER'S PERSPECTIVE.)

### Organizations

AARP
Children of Aging Parents
National Aging Information Center
National Association of Professional Geriatric Care Managers
National Family Caregivers Association
National Institute on Aging

### Suggested Readings

AARP. 1994. *A Checklist of Concerns: Resources for Caregivers.* Washington, DC: Author.

Amarnick, Claude. 1996. *"Don't Put Me in a Nursing Home!"* Deerfield Beach, FL: Garrett Publishing.

Marcell, Jacqueline. 2001. *Elder Rage, or Take My Father . . . Please! How to Survive Caring for Aging Parents.* Irvine, CA: Impressive Press.

Morris, Virginia, and Robert Butler. 1996. *How to Care for Aging Parents.* New York: Workman Publishing Company.

Rhodes, Linda Colvin. 2000. *Complete Idiot's Guide to Caring for Aging Parents.* New York: Penguin Group.

Wilkinson, James. 1999. *A Family Caregiver's Guide to Planning and Decision Making for the Elderly.* Minneapolis, MN: Fairview Press.

### References

AARP. 1989. *Care Management: Arranging for Long Term Care.* Washington, DC: Author.

Cress, Cathy. 2001. *Handbook of Geriatric Care Management.* New York: Aspen Publishers.

Cutler, Neal E. 1994. "Caring for Elderly Parents: Where Do You Look for Help?" *Journal of the American Society of CLU & ChFC* 48: 38–41.

Gray-Davidson, Frena. 2001. *The Caregiver's Sourcebook.* New York: McGraw-Hill.

Parker, Marcie. 1992. "Private Geriatric Care Management: How Families Are Served." *Journal of Case Management* 1: 108–12.

Polich, Cynthia, Marcie Parker, Deborah Chase, and Margaret Hottinger. 1993. *Managing Health Care for the Elderly.* New York: John Wiley & Sons.

*Jihane K. Rohrbacker*

**GERIATRIC REHABILITATION,** the process of maintaining function, restoring abilities, and preventing complications, along with administration of palliative care (care designed to relieve symptoms but not to cure), for older adults diagnosed with progressive debilitating diseases.

Functional abilities and capacities vary greatly among adults aged 65 and older. Generally, as age increases, the likelihood of disease, comorbidity (additional, accompanying diseases or conditions), and disability will increase. At the same time, normal effects of aging can confound or complicate existing health problems in older adults. Consequently, older adults are more likely to require the assistance of a variety of caretakers. For most older adults, mild levels of assistance are provided by family and friends, but the onset of debilitating conditions may result in deficits that require anywhere from minimum to maximum levels of assistance. Common problems such as osteoarthritis can negatively affect an older person's function due to pain and joint deformities. According to Resnick and Fleishell (2002), the decline in function among older adults in long-term care settings can range 8% to 32% over a six-month period. Impaired function is particularly prevalent among adults over the age of 85.

Orthopedic and medical disorders that necessitate rehabilitation intervention include diabetes, cancer, and fractures. Diabetes can result in peripheral vascular disease and possible future amputations, necessitating significant rehabilitation. Treatment of cancer also can result in compromised use of limbs, possible amputation, and neurological defects requiring rehabilitation. With an orthopedic fracture, the primary problem is hip fracture, a common result (and cause) of falls. As age increases, the risk for falls increases, as does the risk for hip fracture. Falls are the leading cause of death in the home, taking the lives of 10,700 people in 1998, a 9% increase from 9,200 in 1996. While older adults represent 13% of the population, more than 86% of fatal falls are in people 65 years old or older (National Safety Council 1999). Adverse outcomes go well beyond the injuries sustained as a result of a fall. An injurious fall increases estimated medical costs (relative to nonfallers, in 1996 dollars) by $11,042 in hospitals, $5,325 in nursing homes, $253 in the emergency room, and $2,820 in a home health setting (Rizzo et al. 1996). Therefore, the major focus of rehabilitation efforts should be on patient safety, and of course, all rehabilitation efforts must involve the family and support systems.

### Rehabilitation

Rehabilitation is the process of maintaining function, restoring abilities, and preventing complications, along with palliative care for those diagnosed with progressive deteriorating diseases. Rehabilitation in older populations presents particular challenges. The general idea is that older people with functional deficits will be able to increase their ability to perform self-care, and in fact, most research indicates that there are significant rates of recovery among older adults with functional disability. Geriatric rehabilitation, however, is a specialty area that requires that rehabilitation occur across the care continuum, from critical care to community care, and thus occurs within hospitals, nursing homes, community centers, day care centers, and homes.

### Rehabilitation Principles

Rehabilitation principles focus on the individual, his or her interaction with the environment, and reintegration into society. Rehabilitation focuses on promoting positive outcomes and independence for older adults. When applied to the individual, rehabilitation programs are designed based on an interdisciplinary assessment of an individual's need. These needs are related to cognitive capacities, physical skills and abilities, and social integration.

Cognitive capacities include a person's ability to receive and to process information, to accurately perceive his/her environment, and to correctly judge and to compensate for problem solving. With aging, these processes can be impacted due to normal visual changes, sensory deficits, and the onset of dementia, among other things.

Physical skills and abilities are focused on a person's ability to bathe, dress, toilet, transfer, and walk. These skills are considered "basic" activities of daily living (ADLs). The first step in rehabilitation is assessment of the person's self-care abilities and needs for personal care assistance. In addition to functioning, rehabilitation focuses on energy conservation, teaching older adults how to redesign activities in order to conserve energy and how to maximize performance. This emphasis can also promote safety, as fatigue can influence a person's ability to complete normal activities and endure the time required to perform them.

Social integration refers to the ability of the older adult to maintain normal social interaction once faced with the changed circumstances brought about by the need for geriatric rehabilitation. Social interaction skills are examined to help the patient maintain or increase his/her ability to be socially appropriate and/or deal with social isolation and to watch for signs of depression.

### Primary Care Interventions

Primary care interventions focus on sustaining wellness through a variety of interventions. Education and counseling are primary care interventions that teach patients the facts about aging, along with information and techniques to practice safe behaviors in all settings. Tinetti and colleagues (Tinetti and Powell 1993; Tinetti et al. 1994) and Tennstedt et al. (1998) found that the most effective way to help patients to be safe, prevent falls, and increase confidence in their ability to prevent a fall is through health education and counseling.

As with all primary care, avoidance or delay of disease or debilitating conditions is the primary focus. As a person ages, visual and perceptual changes impact his/her safety. Therefore, rehabilitation efforts should also focus on safety assessment, compensation, and retraining. The most effective intervention for successful aging is exercise. Exercise increases muscle tone, strength, and range of motion, while increasing coordination, balance, and confidence. Designing appropriate exercise interventions that progressively increase a person's strength and endurance, while ultimately increasing one's function, is a prominent intervention in rehabilitation. Yet exercise should be an integral component of all levels of care and all interventions, as older adults have been shown to benefit by even small amounts of regular exercise.

In addition, all primary care practitioners should emphasize primary health behaviors and prevention of disease and disability. For example, assessing a patient's exercise level related to fall occurrence should be as common as assessing one's diet in relation to preventing diabetes and atherosclerosis. Primary prevention strategies include increasing a patient's knowledge of fall risk factors by providing factual information, suggesting ways for the patient to improve his/her level of safety and wellness, and promoting physical activity and exercises.

### Secondary Care Interventions

Secondary care has to do with early detection of disease and prevention or slowing of the progression of disease states and disability, once diagnoses have been made. Such prevention programs could include balance training in those with gait irregularities, and strengthening exercises for those who have debilitating diseases with weakness. In older adults, education about diagnoses that place them at risk for further disease or, for example, falls is a major priority for secondary prevention. In addition, patient education about common fall-related home injuries is critical to preventing a fall. Along with the medical information, education on how to modify the home to make it fall-safe is also important. Unfortunately, practitioners often utilize secondary prevention strategies only *after* a fall occurs.

When secondary disease prevention programs are integrated, they focus on disease management. For older adults, the primary diseases necessitating rehabilitation are cardiovascular (carotid artery disease, hypertension), neurological (stroke, transient ischem attack [TIA], Parkinson's disease), or of orthopedic etiology (arthritis, cancer). These diseases require medical management that often involves medication, diet management, and general strengthening exercises.

### Tertiary Care Interventions

Tertiary care involves convalescence, rehabilitation, and minimization of the effects of a disabling condition, such as recovery after a stroke, while maximizing the patient's functioning. For example, while primary and secondary care interventions aim to educate older adults on the risks of high blood pressure, benefits of proper diet and exercise (primary), and proper compliance with hypertensive medications (secondary), the tertiary level of treatment is targeted at maximizing the resumption and maintenance of physical and mental functions lost from the stroke. Tertiary prevention in the form of behavioral and environmental modification is very important for the disabled and frail older persons of all kinds. Assisting patients and families in reducing environmental demands and increasing their functional safety are also goals for tertiary care programs.

Tertiary care is needed when persons have actual loss of functions. Usually, disorders necessitating tertiary care are due to neurological diseases necessitating rehabilitation and include stroke and Parkinson's disease. With these diseases, rehabilitation efforts focus on medical management and restoration of functions. With stroke rehabilitation, the efforts focus on restoration of function and prevention of complications. With progressive muscular disorders, geronotological rehabilitation focuses on energy conservation and exercise strategies that increase balance and coordination while titrating and monitoring medication management. Tertiary care can involve a variety of types of therapy, including physical, occupational, social behavioral, and psychological.

### Adaptive/Assistive Technology

Rehabilitation needs that are specific to the interface between the person and the environment address the need for technology integration. Technology measures include those that support or substitute for losses or declines in function. These technologies can include *orthotic devices*—those that *support body* functions, such as eyeglasses, hearing aides, braces, and slings. The technology and adaptive equipment used to *substitute* for loss of function are *prosthetic devices*. Prosthetic devices include replacement devices such as artificial limbs (prostheses) and dentures. This aspect of rehabilitation that focuses on modification of the environment is adaptive and supportive in nature. The adaptive strategies enable rehabilitation specialists to redesign the environment by providing older persons with grab bars, shower chairs, raised toilet seats, proper lighting, large print telephones, and more. The older adult uses these devices to increase both independence and safety. Adaptive equipment is needed to accommodate for both normal aging and disability-specific functional loss(es).

### Organization of Rehabilitation

Rehabilitation is often provided in acute care hospitals but only on a very short-term basis, as the average length of stay is 72 hours; thus, rehabilitation is generally a secondary intervention following medical stability. Persons are generally transferred to subacute medical units, where the full rehabilitation program can be initiated. Persons may also be referred to acute inpatient rehabilitation programs from either of these settings. Rarely are patients referred to inpatient rehabilitation from progressive cardiac care, but depending on the primary reason for acute hospitalization, or the complications that arise during hospitalization, a person with severe coronary disease will need inpatient comprehensive rehabilitation. The average length of stay in a subacute medical unit is 7 to 14 days, after which a patient will be sent to a nursing home if (s)he is unable to return home. Such referrals are reserved for those individuals who have compromised medical stability and ability to tolerate a comprehensive, intensive exercise program.

Long-term care interventions can extend from one month to six months. For the aging population, these persons are referred to rehabilitation in the skilled care nursing unit, subacute care, a nursing home, or a home health service. Unfortunately, home care is limited to those who are home bound, with limited transportation and social support systems available.

### Clinical Pathways/Guidelines

Irrespective of the practice setting, clinicians from a variety of professions and specialty areas have been developing and utilizing clinical guidelines to promote continuity of care, reduce variations in practice, and ensure that practice is evidence based. As a result, more rehabilitation programs are implementing care programs that are based on clinical pathways and guidelines. These strategies maximize outcomes while increasing efficiency and decreasing cost. While these guidelines continue to be developed, clinical practices continue to be evaluated in relation to program effectiveness.

For example, with the Veterans Health Administration, clinical pathways for falls have been developed based on cause of the fall and level of risk. These pathways include (1) initial assessment of level of risk by the Fall Risk Assessment Tools for inpatients and long-term care facility residents; (2) in-depth assessment of risk factors by the Fall Screening clinics for patients scoring in the moderate- to high-risk levels or outpatients having experienced a fall with injury; and (3) standardized interventions based on particular risk factors. Interventions include (1) education to reduce environmental hazards for patients and caregivers; (2) rehabilitative therapy including individualized rehabilitative therapy for patients unable to participate in group therapies, wellness programs for higher-functioning patients or patients who have transitioned from individualized therapy, and referral to Gait/Balance Biomechanics Laboratories when appropriate; (3) medical interventions including reduction in medications, neurological imaging, improvement in vision/hearing, balance testing; and (4) psychosocial interventions including interventions for depression and environmental hazards. These assessment and intervention guidelines increase outcomes of care while decreasing variations and costs.

### Summary

Successful aging depends on our society's commitment to and relationship with our elders to promote their independence and confidence in their abilities and to compensate for functional declines. We can demonstrate this commitment and relationship through interdisciplinary interventions that address both the unique intrinsic characteristics of patients and populations as well as through interventions that target extrinsic or environmental factors that impact patient safety. Successful aging is dependent on shared accountability and efforts that involve the patient, family, and care providers, appropriately addressing the unique needs of individual patients along the continuum of care (inpatient, outpatient, home health, long-term care). (See also COMMUNITY-BASED CARE; COST OF FAMILY CAREGIVING; DISABILITY PROGRAMS, FEDERAL AND STATE; HEALTH MAINTENANCE ORGANIZATIONS AND MANAGED HEALTH CARE FOR OLDER ADULTS; LONG-TERM CARE INSURANCE, PRIVATE; OLDER AMERICANS ACT.)

**References**

Crimmins, E.M., M.H. Hayward, and Y. Saito. 1994. "Changing Mortality and Morbidity Rates and the Health Status and Life Expectancy of the Older Population." *Demography* 31: 159–75.

Dersteine, J.B., and S.D. Hargrove. 2001. *Comprehensive Rehabilitation Nursing*. St. Louis, MO: W.B. Saunders.

National Safety Council. 1999. *Report on Injuries in America*. Itasca, IL: Author.

Quigley, P., ed. 2003. "Program Guide: The Prevention and Management of Patient Falls. A Program Resource Book." In *Veterans Health Administration: VISN 8: Patient Safety Center*. Tampa, FL.

Quigley, P., S. Smith, and J. Strugar. 1998. "Successful Experiences with Clinical Pathways in Rehabilitation." *Journal of Rehabilitation* 64(2): 29–32.

Resnick, B., and A. Fleishell. 2002. "Developing a Restorative Care Program. A Five-Step Approach That Involves the Resident." *American Journal of Nursing* 102(7).

Rizzo, J.A., D.I. Baker, G. McAvay, and M.E. Tinetti. 1996. "The Cost-Effectiveness of a Multifactorial Targeted Prevention Program for Falls among Community Elderly Persons." *Medical Care* 34: 954–69.

Tennstedt, S., J. Howland, M. Lachman, E. Peterson, L. Kasten, and A. Jette. 1998. "A Randomized, Controlled Trial of a Group Intervention to Reduce Fear of Falling and Associated Activity Restriction in Older Adults." *Journal of Gerontology: Psychological Sciences* 53B: 84–92.

Tinetti, M.E., C.F. Mendes de Leon, J.T. Doucette, and D.I. Baker. 1994. "Fear of Falling and Fall-Related Efficacy in Relationship to Functioning among Community-Living Elders." *Journal of Gerontology: Medical Sciences* 49: M140–47.

Tinneti, M.E., and L. Powell. 1993. "Fear of Falling and Low Self-Efficacy: A Cause of Dependence in Elderly Persons." *Journal of Gerontology* 48 (Special Issue): 35–38.

*Patricia Quigley*

**GERONTOLOGICAL NURSE PRACTITIONERS (GNPs),** advanced practice nurses who assess health status and functional abilities; diagnose and manage common acute and chronic illnesses; perform and interpret selected laboratory tests; develop and implement treatment plans to promote, maintain, and restore health and maximize functional abilities; promote death with dignity; educate and counsel patients and families; act as advocates for older adults; and collaborate with other members of the health care team. GNPs base decisions on scientific data and interpret and use research as a basis for practice. The unifying theme in all of these functions is a focus on health rather than disease and an emphasis on holistic care to meet the medical, psychosocial, and functional needs of older persons.

Gerontological nurse practitioners, as advanced practice nurses, are licensed and registered nurses who have a graduate degree in a nursing specialty and are certified through a recognized certification program. This training prepares them to provide a full range of health services to older adults and their families. The current expectation is that educational programs for GNPs are at the master's degree level and include academic and clinical practice requirements. Upon completion of an approved educational program, GNPs are eligible to apply for national certification and formal recognition of the nurse practitioner role by state licensing agencies.

According to the government report *The Registered Nurse Population* (Spratley et al. 2002), of the 2.2 million nurses employed in 2000, it was estimated that 196,000 or 7.3% of all registered nurses were advanced practice nurses (APNs). Of that total, an estimated 102,829 were nurse practitioners, but only 58,512, or 64%, functioned under this job title. About 74% had national certification, and 62% had a master's degree. Approximately 10% of APNs came from a racial or ethnic minority background. The minority APNs "were more likely to be found among nurse practitioners than among other APNs" (Spratley et al. 2002). As a subcategory, certified gerontological nurse practitioners numbered 3,390, according to the American Nurses Credentialing Center (personal communication, July 9, 2002).

### History, Scope, and Practice Settings

Loretta Ford and Henry Silver at the University of Colorado initially developed the nurse practitioner model in 1965. At first, it was limited to pediatrics but quickly expanded to include other specialties, necessitated by population shifts and health care needs. Likewise, the initial development of the GNP role was intended for primary care settings. However, its expansion and the needs of select populations among older adults have changed this exclusive focus. Gerontological nurse practitioners now practice in long-term care and traditional primary care settings, in community-based clinics, rehabilitation facilities, retirement communities, specialty care clinics, health maintenance organizations (HMOs), or home health care agencies. In 1981, the American Nurses Association established certification for GNPs.

Gerontological nurse practitioners implement practice arrangements in a variety of ways, including collaborative practice with physicians, as a member of a geriatric consult team, through home health agencies, as an employee of a long-term care facility, in an assistive care facility, in an HMO, and in independent nursing practice. In these practice arrangements, GNPs may provide direct care to patients, work with families to improve care or resolve problems, serve as case managers to coordinate a variety of services, consult with or refer to other nurses, physicians, and a variety of health care providers or community agencies, develop or participate in research, or teach students in the health professions. Practice is governed by the laws of the state, by the standards and ethics of the nursing profession, and by standards specifically relating to gerontology and the role of the nurse practitioner.

With the continuing health care crisis and the focus on health care reform at the state level, cost and quality of care have been major issues for many health care providers. Repeatedly, studies have shown that nurse practitioners provide quality health care and perform successfully within an expanded scope of practice. As early as 1986, the Office of Technology Assessment, after analyzing numerous studies of nurse practitioners and other providers, concluded that "within their areas of competence nurse practitioners . . .

provide care whose quality is equivalent to that of care provided by physicians." Further, the study stated that "nurse practitioners . . . are more adept than physicians at providing services that depend on communication with patients and preventive services" (Office of Technology Assessment 1986.) A recent study comparing practice outcomes of nurse practitioners and physicians supported the findings of earlier studies. Mundinger et al. (2000) compared the outcomes for patients in a primary care setting using a large sample size and randomized trial design. The results supported the hypothesis that, using the traditional medical model, outcomes for nurse practitioner and physician care in a primary care setting do not differ.

### Barriers to Practice

Barriers to practice have changed little over the years since the inception of the nurse practitioner role. Among the most commonly reported barriers are lack of knowledge about nurse practitioners among the public and other health care professionals, resistance from physicians, reduced or denied reimbursement, limited hospital privileges, inconsistency in legal authority and scope of practice, resistance to practice autonomy, and lack of full prescribing authority. Certain legal restrictions to practice also exist, many of which have direct economic consequences. Professional licensing boards in each state regulate nurse practitioners; consequently, practice restrictions vary greatly. The most common restrictions to practice are in the area of prescriptive authority and third-party reimbursement. Both of these can have significant impact on access to care.

Prescriptive authority for nurse practitioners varies greatly in the type of drugs that may be prescribed and the degree of independence of the nurse practitioner. Twelve states permit prescribing a full range of drugs without physician involvement, while other states permit prescribing with some degree of physician involvement or delegation using protocols or limit the selection of drugs that may be prescribed. All 50 states and the District of Columbia permit some degree of prescribing authority for nurse practitioners (Pearson 2002). These restrictions are considered by some to have detrimental consequences to the advanced practice nurse's professional stature and to the public's access to health care. The need to continually consult with a physician or to seek a physician's signature limits access to care and increases the cost of health care for the public. In one of the largest studies of APN prescribing practices, Hamric et al. (1998) reviewed advanced practice nurses' prescribing practices. They analyzed data from 32 providers that encompassed 1,708 patients. The researchers evaluated the effectiveness of the prescribing practices using patient outcome, patient assessment of outcome, and physician assessment of the APN practice. "By all three of these measures, APN prescribing practices were safe and effective."

Additionally, third-party reimbursement has direct financial consequences that affect the nurse practitioner and the consumer. The federal government, through the Medicaid and Medicare programs, sets standards for reimbursement that are followed by the states and private insurers. Many nurse practitioners are eligible for Medicaid reimbursement. Still, there are common restrictions, such as reimbursement at a discounted percentage of the rate that is paid for the same service by a physician, or the federal rule that permits individual states to determine whether to reimburse services to specialties other than pediatric and family nurse practitioners—that is, GNPs.

The Medicare program also has permitted reimbursement for services performed by gerontological and other nurse practitioners. Nurse practitioners applying for Medicare billing must be certified to receive direct reimbursement from Medicare. Under the Balanced Budget Act of 1997, qualified nurse practitioners may receive direct reimbursement for Medicare Part B services they provide that would normally be provided by a physician. The services are not restricted by site, geographic location, or presence of the physician on site but only by restrictions of state licensing laws. Medicare reimbursement occurs at a percentage of the fee paid to physicians.

### Outlook

Given the demographic imperative and the importance of deterring institutionalization and improving the effectiveness of nursing home and community-based care, there is a great need for gerontological nurse practitioners. "Advanced practice nurses are proven providers, and removing the many barriers to their practice will . . . increase their ability to respond to the pressing need for basic health care" (Safriet 1992).

Their role is also an active concern of future research, since HMOs and other managed care settings use GNPs to facilitate effective nursing home and home health care continuity, reduce emergency hospitalization, and monitor medication use. Finally, there is substantial promise in collaborative practice arrangements in which physicians and GNPs no longer relate hierarchically, which allows independent practice for the GNP and permits full reimbursement. A move toward such formalized, customary collaboration is also serving the primacy of patients' needs. As Richard Cooper (2001), a health care policy analyst, states, "Ultimately, the success of each discipline will be judged by how effectively it participates in a continuum of care that meets the needs of patients and of the health care system overall." (See also ASSISTED LIVING; COMMUNITY-BASED CARE; HEALTH MAINTENANCE ORGANIZATIONS AND MANAGED HEALTH CARE FOR OLDER ADULTS; MEDICARE.)

#### Organizations

American Academy of Nurse Practitioners
American College of Nurse Practitioners
American Nurses Association
National Conference of Gerontological Nurse Practitioners
National Organization of Nurse Practitioner Faculties

#### References

American Academy of Nurse Practitioners. n.d. "Medicare Regulations." Available online at http://www.acnp.org/medicare.htm.

American College of Nurse Practitioners. n.d. "Medicare & Medicaid Reimbursement for NPs." Available online at http://www.nurse.org/acnp/facts/reimb.shtml.

American College of Nurse Practitioners. n.d. "What Is a Nurse Practitioner?" Available online at http://www.nurse.org/acnp/facts/whatis.shtml.

American Nurses' Credentialing Center. 2002. "Computer-Based Testing for ANCC Certification." Available online at http://nursingworld.org/ancc/certify/cert/catalogs/cbt.pdf.

Cooper, Richard. 2001. "Health Care Workforce for the Twenty-first Century: The Impact of Nonphysician Clinicians." [Electronic Version]. *Annual Reviews of Medicine* 52: 51–61.

Hamric, Ann, Dana Worley, Sharon Lindebak, and Steve Jaubert. 1998. "Outcomes Associated with Advanced Nursing Practice Prescriptive Authority." *Journal of the American Academy of Nurse Practitioners* 10(2): 113–18.

Mundinger, Mary, Robert Kane, Elizabeth Lenz, Annette Totten, Wei-Yann Tsai, Paul Cleary, William Friedewald, Albert Siu, and Michael Shelanski. 2000. "Primary Care Outcomes in Patients Treated by Nurse Practitioners or Physicians: A Randomized Trial." [Electronic Version]. *Journal of the American Medical Association* 283(1): 59–68.

National Conference of Gerontological Nurse Practitioners. n.d. "About NCGNP—What Is a GNP?" Available online at http://www.ncgnp.org/displaycommon.cfm?an=17.

Office of Technology Assessment. 1986. *Nurse Practitioners, Physicians Assistants, and Certified Nurse Midwives: A Policy Analysis*. Washington, DC: GPO.

Pearson, Linda. 2002. "Fourteenth Annual Legislative Update: How Each State Stands on Legislative Issues Affecting Advanced Nursing Practice." *The Nurse Practitioner* 27: 10.

Safriet, Barbara. 1992. "Health Care Dollars and Regulatory Sense: The Role of Advanced Practice Nursing." *Yale Journal on Regulation* 9: 417–87.

Spratley, Ernell, Ayah Johnson, Julie Sochalski, Marshall Fritz, and William Spencer. 2002. *The Registered Nurse Population*. Rockville, MD: U.S. Department of Health & Human Services, Health Resources & Services Administration, Bureau of Health Professions, Division of Nursing.

*Linda R. Rounds*

**GERONTOLOGICAL SOCIAL WORK,** a specialty within the profession of social work in response to the increasing health and social service demands of our aging society. Over the last 25 years, social workers in health, mental health, and community development have reshaped their expertise for older adults whose numbers are increasing. It was once uncommon to work with an 80-year-old client at a mental health clinic; now mental health agencies have social workers whose specific jobs are to serve older clients and their families. In the past, nursing homes were the only option when a dependent older person needed more care than the family could provide; now there are many in-home care possibilities and residential options. Thus, a specialized body of social work knowledge and skills in gerontology has emerged, and the demand for gerontological social workers will continue to increase. Gerontological social workers provide clinical services to elders and their families, develop programs to serve older adults and reshape current programs where consumers are aging, administer social and health care facilities, advocate on behalf of older citizens, and participate in the development of social policies. Gerontological social workers are found in health care (health care clinics, hospitals, home health agencies, hospices); residential care (assisted living facilities, nursing homes); mental health services (geropsychiatric units of acute care hospitals, mental health clinics); specialty nonprofit organizations and community development organizations (the Alzheimer's Association; Housing Options Provided for the Elderly, Inc.); and public agencies (State Units on Aging, Area Agencies on Aging).

Social workers are distinguished from other professionals in gerontology by their knowledge of community resources and the range of options available to ameliorate problems; their psychosocial perspective and multidimensional assessment skills; and their skills in engaging the older person, family, and community in aspects of problem solving. In fact, so many elders and their families request help finding solutions to problems associated with aging that many gerontological social workers are opening private practices. These clinicians often help families understand the situation, access in-home services, or make decisions about residential care. Social workers are standard members of interdisciplinary teams working with older adults in clinical settings.

Social work interventions with older adults usually begin with a psychosocial assessment. Due to the close interconnections of the biological, psychological, and social aspects of aging, assessment can be complicated. For example, an older person may lose the ability to drive because of sensory loss; this person may then become socially isolated and eventually depressed; this depression can lead to problems with confusion. If not assessed thoroughly, it could be concluded that this person has an irreversible dementia, when the confusion is a result of other emotional and psychosocial problems that can be addressed. An assessment completed by a gerontological social worker will often be multidimensional and cover physical functioning, health conditions, mental status, emotional health, social resources, physical environment, service use, and financial resources. In order to maximize self-determination and choice, values and preferences of the older adult, especially for care arrangements, need to be determined. Other professionals are involved as needed or permitted by a client. For example, a neurologist should provide the diagnosis of dementia of the Alzheimer's type. A geropsychiatrist or geriatrician should provide the diagnosis of depression. A medical doctor or pharmacist should do the formal review of the medications. However, the social worker often is the professional with the broadest knowledge of the client. Social workers most frequently work with family or friends of the older client.

Financial resources are often an important part of a complete psychosocial assessment. Sometimes this is a sensitive area of questioning, but a good social worker will allay the client's fear regarding misuse of information. The development of service arrangements depends on a client's resources and entitlements, which must be accurately understood. The assessment must also reveal what informal (family and friends) and formal (paid or from an agency) services are already in place for a client. It is often difficult to get a clear picture of what agencies are involved and who is paying, given the various funding sources currently patchworked together to provide assistance to older persons in need. Providers and funding streams are largely invisible in some cases. The client may know that someone comes three times a week to help, but it is difficult to ascertain, for example, that the local Area Agency on Aging is supplying a person to help with personal care through monies from the Older Americans Act. Some older adults and families still mistakenly believe that Medicare is paying for such services. This mistake is being made less frequently, given an increased knowledge about long-term care. A thorough assessment of financial resources is also needed to ensure that older adults are taking advantage of resources available to them. Surprisingly, only 50% of poor older adults who are eligible for Supplementary Security Income (SSI) actually receive those benefits (Hooyman and Kiyak 2002).

Based on information gained from a psychosocial assessment, social workers can choose from a variety of interventions. Clinical case management is often the treatment of choice. Case management is an intervention aimed at organizing an effective and efficient package of long-term care services to a client. Case management functions include case finding (conducting outreach, determining eligibility, and administering the intake process), assessment (identifying current status and problem), care planning (developing a plan based on needs), coordination (arranging delivery of services), follow-up (monitoring client and services), and reassessment (reevaluating). The term *clinical case management* is used because counseling is important in this process; it is more than just arranging services. Some clients present complex psychosocial situations, and some clients are reluctant to accept services. There is also the need to balance family care and assistance from formal sources. Sometimes clients are in degenerative situations, so service needs are continually changing. Thus, social workers' clinical skills are needed to provide effective case management to older clients.

Case management can also have a financial function. There are service models in which social workers authorize funding. Sometimes, these workers must contain the cost of a service package to a predetermined amount of money (which will assure that in-home care is less than nursing home care). There are models in which case managers approve the expenditure of money for a package of client services and monitor this package but have little direct client contact. Different models of case management call for different amounts of client contact and different degrees of authority to purchase and allocate resources. Social workers are most likely to perform case management roles where there is maximum client contact, given their professional expertise in clinical and family work.

The assessment and care arrangement functions are also the key components of discharge planning, and many social workers provide discharge planning services to patients in nursing homes, day treatment programs, and hospitals. Workers assist older adults and families in identifying care needs and options, in making decisions about informal and formal care arrangements, and in establishing such arrangements. Social workers thus play a role in ensuring continuity of care between acute and extended care facilities and home.

Gerontological social workers provide a range of clinical interventions with older adults and their families. They organize and lead therapeutic groups that address all types of challenges posed in later life, such as widowhood, caregiving, or recovering from and adjusting to a stroke or Parkinson's disease. Often membership to these groups is offered free of charge through nonprofit associations such as the Alzheimer's or Parkinson's Association. Social workers also counsel clients individually and assist with problems of depression or adjustment to multiple late-life losses. Families often need assistance in dealing with an aging relative's increasing dependence, and family counseling around issues of aging is a growing demand. Social workers can bill Medicare for psychotherapy services in response to a diagnosed mental disorder (although current reimbursement rates are low and the bureaucratic process very labor-intensive). Many agencies and private clinicians have sliding scale fee schedules.

Understanding who pays for which services is critical and difficult in gerontological social work. There are 50 major public programs that address the needs of the older population through cash assistance, in-kind transfer, and provision of goods and services (Hooyman and Kiyak 2002). Social workers must know the programs that affect their clients. The core policies that affect gerontological social work practice are Social Security, Medicare, Medicaid, SSI, Older Americans Act services, food stamps, and housing subsidies. Medicare is intended to pay for acute care; social workers often help clients understand coverage and work with the bureaucracy to organize bills. Medicaid, the federal-state program that covers medical care for the poor, covers long-term care in nursing homes, in day care centers, and in the home in some states. Social workers assist clients in obtaining Medicaid coverage and using these benefits to meet their care needs. Block grant money and Older Americans Act funds are used at the local level to provide in-home and meal services to elders in need.

Social workers play key roles in accessing these subsidized services on behalf of their clients. Yet most of the money spent on services by elders and their families comes from private funds. Thus, social workers must educate clients and help make decisions about using money to meet care needs. To help them achieve this expertise, the Boettner Center at the University of Pennsylvania, affiliated with the School of Social Work, plans to offer coursework in Financial Gerontology for Social Workers. (See also DAILY MONEY MANAGERS; FINANCIAL GERONTOLOGY, HISTORY OF; GERIATRIC CARE MANAGERS [GCMs]; MEDICARE; MENTAL HEALTH AMONG OLDER ADULTS; WIDOWHOOD.)

**References**

Barusch, A. 2002. *Foundations of Social Policy*. Itasca, IL: F.E. Peacock.

Butler, R., M. Lewis, and T. Sunderland. 1998. *Aging and Mental Health: Positive Psychosocial and Biomedical Approaches*. Boston, MA: Allyn and Bacon.

Gallo, J., T. Fulmer, G. Paveza, and W. Reichel. 2000. *Handbook of Geriatric Assessment*. New York: Aspen Publishers.

Hooyman, N., and H. Kiyak. 2002. *Social Gerontology: A Multidisciplinary Perspective*. Boston, MA: Allyn and Bacon.

Kane, R.L., and R.A. Kane. 2000. *Assessing Older Persons: Measures, Meaning, and Practical Applications*. New York: Oxford University Press.

McInnis-Dittrich, K. 2002. *Social Work with Elders*. Boston, MA: Allyn and Bacon.

Schneider, R., N. Kropf, and A. Kisor. 2000. *Gerontological Social Work: Knowledge, Service Settings, and Special Presentations*. Belmont, CA: Wadsworth.

Toseland, R., and C. Rossiter. 1996. "Social Work Practice with Family Caregivers of Frail Older Persons." In *Social Work Practice with the Elderly*, ed. M.J. Holosko and M.D. Feit. Toronto: Canadian Scholars Press.

*Nancy Morrow-Howell*

**GOVERNMENT PROGRAMS.** See Age Discrimination in Employment Act (ADEA); Disability Programs, Federal and State; Disaster Preparedness and Older Adults; HUD-Assisted Rental Housing; Medicaid; Medicare; Nutrition Programs; Older Americans Act; Social Security Program of the United States; Supplemental Security Income (SSI); Veterans' Benefits.

**GROWTH CAPITAL FOR OLDER ENTREPRENEURS,** financing available for new enterprises from savings or other funds of the entrepreneur, his or her family, and friends or from a vast number of outside resources. The term *serial entrepreneur* has surfaced to characterize the individuals who are more interested in starting new companies than managing old ones. Simply, there are many people who enjoy the process of developing new companies and expect to stay busy with this very creative process throughout their working lives. While most sources of funds are similar regardless of age, older entrepreneurs may have access to alumni groups, larger networks of friends, established clubs, and so on, that are generally not available to the young. Also, many veterans will have the advantage of career paths that give them impressive credentials to grow new companies.

Sources may include outright grants that may occasionally be obtained from state, local, and federal agencies; bank loans guaranteed by the Small Business Administration or bank equity investments; customer financing; "business angels" (individuals who regularly invest $50,000 to $1 million in speculative new ventures); ethnic groups; social funds; corporate strategic partners; and venture capital. More than 80 different types of capital are available and literally thousands of funding and helping organizations exist, so it pays to do your research. Obtaining such funds often reflects more upon business experience and contacts than it does on the power of an idea, but huge variations in funding criteria exist. Also, in many instances of financing a new company, the entrepreneur may have to give up ownership or otherwise lessen primary control of the business.

A well-thought-out plan is critical to the search for investment funds. The plan will be necessary to detail the purpose and function of the business, as well as to do an examination of such things as competition, markets, risks, personnel, facilities, and the particular niche of the business. Some form of business plan is required for all sources of outside capital today, but the most important single element of planning for a company and being able to convince investors of the merit of investing is a comprehensive and very well thought out marketing plan. A number of templates for writing a business plan can be found on the Internet or in books on just that subject, but the most important thing to remember about a plan is to write down your whole course of action, with some contingencies if critical elements in the plan go awry. You may find that original ideas deviate or that new avenues open up once the business is started.

Once a business plan has been developed and capital sources have been identified, it is important to involve as many people as possible, including business and personal contacts. Involving the local newspaper may be a good place to get the word out to a local community. Finding money is often the most difficult step for any entrepreneur, however, and far too many good business ideas never see the light of day because of failure here. It is important to expect disappointment and that it will be necessary to speak with more potential sponsors than originally thought.

While each of the sources of capital is unique, a perspective on venture capital can be used as a guide for any and all sources of money. If a plan is developed in a form that could be accepted by highly demanding and sophisticated venture capitalists, it should serve well for other sources of capital as well.

### Venture Capital

While venture capital funds came into being just before and after World War II, venture capital now exists in all developed countries and takes on a variety of forms. A few funds invest in startups, but most are looking for companies that fit into certain development stages, industry sectors, geographic regions, or size of financing. A very small portion of all new companies actually receive venture capital financing early on. Instead, these are usually financed by friends and family or business angels. Companies have formed their own venture investment funds as well and routinely finance new firms that fit into their own business interests.

It may be difficult for a new business to have success by soliciting large venture capital firms. A big fund may only invest in 5 or 6 proposals each year out of the 15,000 to 20,000 received. In cases where funding is obtained, the venture capitalist will want a professional business plan and may want the entrepreneur to sign a term sheet, an agreement that protects their interests and gives them priority on assets if the new company doesn't make it.

In addition to the traditional business plan, the entrepreneur will need to answer the following questions:

1. What is the market opportunity in this particular niche, and why does it exist? How will this business meet a market need? Just how big is the opportunity and in what direction is it heading?
2. What is the economic model—including revenues and profits? What is necessary to realize a profit, and when can one be expected?
3. What is the market outreach plan? Marketing plan?
4. What and who is the competition? How will it change? What is the company's comparative advantage—what are the competitors' weaknesses and this business's strengths? How will this company differentiate itself from others, and how will it maintain those differences?
5. Who comprises your management team, board of directors, board of advisors, and why should the background of those individuals convey enough confidence that they can do the job? Do they have experience in developing a company and being responsible for investors' money?
6. Can you provide a set of milestones that indicate just what you're going to do, when you're going to do it, what obstacles must be overcome, and when funds are going to be needed? Can you list the risks to your business model and indicate how you intend to overcome them? Can you give investors a feeling that they can monitor your progress and be in control of their money?
7. Have you provided an exit plan to suggest how your investors are going to make money and when? Are there other businesses that are somewhat comparable that you can use as a model for appreciation?

(See also ATTITUDES ABOUT RETIREMENT; BABY BOOMERS AND RETIREMENT; BUSINESS SUCCESSION PLANNING; CONSULTING IN RETIREMENT; ENTREPRENEURSHIP; WORKING RETIREES.)

**Suggested Resource**

Some sources of venture capital are listed on the Internet and can also be found in pricey annual compilations such as the 2002 *Directory of Venture Capital Firms* (Grey House Publishing, Millerton, NY; http://www.greyhouse.com/).

**References**

Fichera, Dante, and David Richardson. 2001. *Insider's Guide to Venture Capital, 2002*. Sacramento, CA: Prima Publishing.

Gladstone, David, and Laura Gladstone. 2001. *Venture Capital Handbook: An Entrepreneur's Guide to Raising Venture Capital*. New York: Prentice Hall.

Hill, Brian E., et al. 2002. *Attracting Capital from Angels: How Their Money and Their Experience Can Help You Build a Successful Company*. New York: John Wiley.

Peterson, Ronald. 2003. *When Venture Capitalists Say "No"—Creative Financing Strategies & Resources*. Glen Echo, MD: Comanche Press.

Robinson, Robert J., and Mark Van Osnabrugge. 2000. *Angel Investing: Matching Startup Companies*. Boston, MA: Jossey-Bass.

*Ronald Peterson*

**GUARDIANSHIP,** the legal relationship between a ward and a guardian; usually authorized by the probate or equity divisions of a state court. Wards are persons who have been declared by the courts to be incompetent to make particular decisions on their own behalf. Court-appointed guardians act as surrogate decision makers for the ward.

The underlying rationale for guardianship is the legal doctrine of *parens patriae* (literally, "father of the land"), the inherent authority and responsibility of a benevolent society to intervene, even over objection, to protect people who cannot protect themselves. Thus, instead of abandoning cognitively incapacitated individuals to a superficial autonomy to make self-harmful decisions or neglect their own basic needs, the state may exercise its authority to protect even unwilling disabled individuals from their own folly or intellectual deficits.

Every adult is presumed to be legally competent to make individual choices. This presumption may be declared invalid and a substitute decision maker appointed only upon a sufficient showing that the individual is mentally unable to take part in a rational decision-making process. A legal ruling of incompetence signifies that a person, because of a lack of capacity to contemplate and weigh choices rationally, cannot care adequately for his or her own person or property.

Guardianship historically has been a matter of state jurisdiction. Every state has enacted statutes that empower the courts to appoint guardians for decisionally incapacitated persons. Most state guardianship statutes are similar in content because they are based on the Uniform Probate Code (UPC), Article 5, although certain variations in the law and its application exist in the United States, and therefore one's own state statute always must be consulted.

Since the late 1980s, there has been substantial reexamination and revision of existing state guardianship statutes on the part of many state legislatures. Several states have made substantive changes in their guardianship laws by substituting more objective standards for traditional definitions of incompetence that rely heavily on diagnostic labels (e.g., the person is "depressed" or "demented"). These more objective standards are designed to focus on the individual's functional ability to manage personal care or finances on a daily basis. In other words, there is now more focus on the person's ability to meet basic needs rather than just on his or her clinical "condition."

State guardianship statutes today typically contain a two-step definition of competence. First, the individual must fall within a specific category, such as old age, mental illness, or developmental disability. Second, the individual must be found to be impaired functionally—that is, unable to care appropriately for his or her own person or property—as a result of being within that category. Incompetence cannot be equated with a categorical condition (such as advanced years) alone, so the determination of functional, behavioral, or adaptive disability is essential.

A variety of procedural reforms concerning guardianship have been enacted by the states. They are aimed at assuring potential wards greater due process protections against the unnecessary, premature, or improper loss of decisional rights. These procedural reforms deal with such matters as who should perform assessments of capacity, with a marked preference for the multidisciplinary and interdisciplinary perspective; the content of the assessor's report to the court; the appointment of outside visitors to supplement the formal assessment; the right to counsel as advocate; the ward's presence at the hearing; more rigorous requirements with regard to petitions; enhanced notice requirements; formalized hearing procedures and rules; and more specificity in the court's findings and in the order appointing the guardian. Reforms have been passed in the spheres of limited and temporary guardianship as well.

States continue to move away from referring to the legal status of the ward as "incompetent" and toward the language of "decisional capacity," which reflects movement away from emphasis on diagnostic category or label toward more emphasis on an individual's current functional abilities and deficits.

Terminology regarding the judicially created relationship between a decisionally incapacitated person and a surrogate decision maker, however, still varies somewhat among jurisdictions. Although the most common general designation for the court-appointed surrogate is "guardian," some states refer to this entity as a "conservator" (e.g., California). In a majority of states, a court-appointed surrogate with total authority over the ward's personal and financial affairs is called a "plenary" guardian. A surrogate with power over solely financial issues—the disposition of the ward's income and assets—usually is termed a "guardian of the estate" or "conservator." A surrogate decision maker concerning personal (such as medical, residential, and matrimonial) questions only is referred to in most states as a "guardian of the person."

Judicial appointment of a guardian to make decisions on behalf of a person who has been judged incompetent or incapacitated means that the ward no longer retains the legal power to exercise those decisional rights. The legal system historically has treated guardianship as an all-or-nothing proposition, with global findings of incompetence accompanied by virtually complete disenfranchisement of the ward. Plenary guardians ordinarily are awarded total power to control all of the ward's financial and personal matters.

The modern trend, however, has been toward statutory recognition of the concept of limited or partial guardianship and toward the encouragement of judicial deference to this concept. Limited or partial guardianship accounts for the decision-specific, waxing and waning nature of mental capacity for many persons and the ability of some people to make certain kinds of choices rationally but not others. State statutes also have been widely amended recently to permit judges to grant guardianship on a temporary, time-limited basis, rather than the formerly prevalent indefinite orders that shift the burden of proof regarding regained capacity and termination of the guardianship to the ward.

These trends reflect legislative deference to the least-restrictive alternative (LRA) (sometimes called the least-*intrusive* alternative) principle concerning state impingement of an individual's rights to personal autonomy. Under limited, partial, or temporary guardianships, courts fashion their orders to delineate explicitly the particular and exclusive types of decisions that the ward is incapable of making and over which the guardian may exercise proxy authority, with the remaining powers residing with the ward. Limited, partial, or temporary guardianship statutes may be permissive, allowing but not requiring courts to carefully tailor the guardian's power to the ward's needs, or they may mandate that the powers of the guardian be drawn as narrowly as possible. Even in the absence of legislation, state courts have general equity jurisdiction to create limited, partial, or temporary guardianships *sua sponte* (on their own initiative).

A number of policy considerations argue against overuse of the formal legal mechanism of guardianship. Guardianships frequently are expensive, time-consuming, and emotionally draining and result in unnecessary deprivation of basic civil liberties. In many cases, guardianships provide the ward with little meaningful protection against abuse and exploitation. Much attention has been devoted to exploring and developing viable alternatives to guardianship that strike an acceptable accommodation between protection and independence. There has been a significant movement toward greater reliance on these less restrictive and intrusive alternatives to guardianship for older individuals with compromised cognitive and emotional abilities.

Mechanisms that may delay or obviate the need for guardianship to manage one's financial affairs include, but are not limited to, joint bank and other financial accounts, case management, daily money management programs, living or *inter vivos* trusts, durable powers of attorney, and representative payee designations for government benefit checks. (See also ADVANCE DIRECTIVES; ELDER LAW PRACTICE; ETHICS IN FINANCIAL PLANNING; FINANCIAL ELDER ABUSE; FRAILTY PLANNING; TRUSTS.)

### Organizations

American Bar Association, Commission on Legal Problems of the Elderly
Center for Social Gerontology
National Academy of Elder Law Attorneys
National Guardianship Association

### References


Maddox, George L., ed. 2001. *The Encyclopedia of Aging*. 3rd ed. New York: Springer Publishing Company.

Schmidt, Winsor C., Jr. 1995. *Guardianship: The Court of Last Resort for the Elderly and Disabled*. Durham, NC: Carolina Academic Press.

Symposium on Guardianship Law. 2002. *Stetson Law Review* 31(3) (Spring).

Zimny, George H., and George T. Grossberg. 1998. *Guardianship of the Elderly*. New York: Springer Publishing Company.


*Marshall B. Kapp*

# H

**HEALTH AND LONGEVITY,** population characteristics with significant social and economic implications as a result of medical advances and improved living conditions and lifestyles.

### Life Expectancy and Mortality Patterns

The U.S. population aged 65 and older has grown rapidly, which is attributable to declining mortality rates across the entire life span, improved life expectancy, and improved health care. In 1900, a 65-year-old person could expect to live 11.9 additional years to age 77; by 1999, life expectancy at age 65 increased 17.7 years to almost age 83. Life expectancy at age 65 has increased for all people. Whites have shown the most rapid gains in life expectancy. Between 1950 and 1999, Blacks at age 65 gained 2.1 years compared with 3.9 years for Whites; life expectancy at age 65 for Blacks is 16.0 years compared to 17.8 years for Whites. Comparison of life expectancy at age 65 with other industrialized nations shows that the United States ranked tenth for men and twelfth for women in 1996, suggesting room for even more improvement (National Center for Health Statistics [NCHS] 2001).

In 1998, deaths of persons aged 65 and older totaled 1.7 million, or 75% of all deaths. The leading causes of deaths in older adults are heart diseases, malignant neoplasms, cerebrovascular diseases, chronic obstructive pulmonary diseases, and accidents (NCHS 2000). Death rates for all causes have been declining. Factors responsible for the substantial declines in mortality from heart disease and stroke during the past three decades include improved medical care and interventions, greater availability of coronary care units, advanced surgical and medical treatment of coronary heart disease, improved control of high blood pressure, decreased smoking, modified eating habits, increased exercise, and healthier lifestyles.

### Health Status

The health status of older adults can be measured by their own perception of their health, limitations in their usual activities, and restricted-activity and bed-disability days. In 1998, 13% of the noninstitutionalized population reported limitations of activity due to chronic diseases. The rate of activity limitation increases with age, from 6% for those under age 18 to 47% for persons 75 years and over. Among persons aged 75 and older,

30% reported fair or poor health compared with others their age. Almost one out of ten in that age group reported limitations in activities of daily living (ADLs), defined as needing help in bathing or showering, dressing, getting in and out of bed or a chair, using the toilet, and eating; one out of five reported limitations in instrumental activities of daily living (IADLs), defined as needing help in preparing meals, managing money, shopping for groceries or personal items, performing light or heavy housework, and using a telephone (NCHS 2001).

The prevalence of specific, chronic conditions causing limitations of activity among the noninstitutionalized older adults is high. In 1996, 48% of those aged 65 years and over had arthritis, 41% had hypertension, and 24% had heart conditions. Many older adults suffered from impairments: 30% had hearing impairments, 16% had orthopedic impairments, and 17% had cataracts (NCHS 1999). Many suffer from multiple chronic conditions and disabilities. These activity-limiting conditions increase with age. About 27% of persons aged 65 and over have one condition, and 61% have two or more conditions. The United States is estimated to have spent over $500 billion in 2000 (in 1990 dollars) on direct medical care costs for persons with chronic conditions; by the year 2050 the amount is projected to rise to over $900 billion (Institute for Health & Aging 1996).

The numbers of restricted-activity and bed-disability days are significantly affected by the number of conditions. Persons aged 75 years and over with one chronic condition causing activity limitation report 55 restricted-activity days and 26 bed days per person per year. Those with two or more conditions report about twice that amount.

### Medical Care Use

Use of health services increases with age, and older adults consume health services in amounts disproportionate to their numbers in the population. They visit physicians and are hospitalized more frequently than younger people. In 1999, persons aged 65 and older comprised 12.7% of the population, but they had 23.3% of almost 1 billion ambulatory visits, 16.3% of 32 million short-stay hospital discharges, 38.5% of 161 million hospital days, and 68.7% of 1.9 million home health patients. About 6% of the population was 75 years and older in 1999, yet this group accounted for 9.9% of all physician visits, 13.9% of hospital discharges, and 20.2% of the hospital days (NCHS 2001).

Older persons who suffer from chronic and disabling conditions heavily utilize medical resources. Noninstitutionalized people aged 75 and over with chronic conditions causing activity limitation saw physicians on average 16.5 times a year, in contrast to 9.6 times for persons under age 18. Multiple chronic conditions for those aged 75 and over cause the number of physician visits to almost double, from 11.3 visits for those reporting one condition causing activity limitation to 21.6 visits for those with two or more conditions.

The number of hospital days also varies with the number of conditions. The older adults aged 75 years and over with two or more chronic conditions causing activity limitation had 47.7 hospitalizations per 100 persons per year, in contrast to 35.9 for those with one condition. Combinations of these use patterns support the hypothesis that multiple chronic conditions create a significantly greater burden than one condition and that the burden increases with age.

According to the 1999 National Nursing Home Survey, about 4.3% of the persons aged 65 and older and 18.2% of persons aged 85 years and older are in nursing homes.

Other chronically ill older adults were in psychiatric or other chronic disease hospitals, Veterans Administration hospitals, and other long-term care facilities. Generally, older residents of nursing homes suffer from multiple chronic conditions and functional impairments.

### Long-Term Care Needs

Most older persons who have lost some capacity for self-care require a wide range of social, personal, and supportive services. Long-term care (LTC) is defined as physical care over a prolonged period for those persons incapable of sustaining themselves without such care. Long-term care includes a spectrum of services responding to different needs across a range of chronic illness and disability. To address the multiple and varied LTC needs of the aged population, services must cross the boundaries between income maintenance and health, social, and housing programs. A wide range of organizations, professionals, and paraprofessionals are involved in the delivery of LTC. Long-term care services can be delivered in a variety of settings: a client's own home, community foster homes, multipurpose senior centers, day hospitals, day programs, and residential settings, including sheltered housing, board and care homes, residential hotels, old-age homes, nursing homes, rehabilitation centers, and mental hospitals.

Nearly 80% of older adults requiring assistance with ADLs or IADLs live at home or in community-based settings, while more than 20% live in nursing homes or other institutions. The majority of long-term care is provided by unpaid caregivers to older individuals living either in their own homes or with their families. The availability of home care services often plays a significant role in sustaining the capacity of older and disabled persons to maintain their personal independence and often determines admission into institutions. Caregiving is presumed to be the responsibility of women, because the home has traditionally been considered women's domain and caregiving a natural female characteristic. Women represent seven of ten unpaid caregivers, three-quarters of nursing home residents 65 years and older, and two-thirds of home health care users.

With growing numbers of chronically ill older and disabled adults, increased consideration is being given to alternatives in providing LTC services and preventing the need for high-cost institutionalization. Research and demonstrations in the United States have focused on LTC needs, service systems, and financing for older adults. Recent years have seen the development of a variety of community services such as day care, home health, meals-on-wheels, and respite care. Most of these services are aimed at maintaining the independence of the aged or disabled person at home to avoid institutional placement, often viewed as a measure of last resort.

According to the Agency for Health Care Research and Quality, spending for long-term care (home health, nursing home, and Medicaid spending for home and community-based services) amounted to $134 billion, about 11.4% of the $1 trillion national personal health care expenditures in 1999 (Heffler et al. 2001). Individuals needing care and their families paid for almost one-quarter of these expenditures out of pocket, public programs (predominantly Medicaid and Medicare) funded 61%, private insurance accounted for 10%, and other private sources paid the remaining 5%. These amounts, however, do not include the many hidden costs of long-term care. For example, they do not include wages lost when an unpaid family caregiver takes time off from work to provide assistance.

### Financing Medical Care of the Aged

Almost 13% of the noninstitutionalized population was aged 65 and older in 1996, but this group accounted for 33% of all personal health care expenditures. Children and youth under age 18 comprised 27% of the population and accounted for 11% of total spending; adults aged 18 to 64 comprised 59% of the population and accounted for 56% of total spending. For older adults, out-of-pocket funds paid 15%, private health insurance paid 19%, Medicare paid 56%, Medicaid paid 4%, 3% came from other public funds, and the remaining 2% came from other sources (Cohen et al. 2000).

The idea that medical care is a basic right, along with food, clothing, and shelter, was greatly enhanced by the enactment of Medicare and Medicaid in 1965. Medicare is a national health insurance program for the aged and disabled that is administered by the federal government. It is the single largest health insurer in the country, covering virtually all persons aged 65 years and older and certain persons with disabilities or kidney failure. Medicare outlays in 1999 amounted to $214 billion. Over 34 million older persons and 5.3 million persons with disabilities were enrolled in the Medicare program in 1999.

Despite significant protections offered by Medicare, there are gaps in the Medicare benefits package and relatively high deductibles and cost-sharing requirements. To pay for medical deductibles, coinsurance, and uncovered benefits such as prescription drugs and dental care, most Medicare beneficiaries carry some type of supplemental coverage, often at additional cost, to fill the gaps in the Medicare benefit package. In 1999, out-of-pocket spending for health care goods and services and for premium payments by Medicare beneficiaries age 65 and older amounted to $2,430, or 19% of income. These estimates do not include the costs of home care and long-term nursing home care (Gross and Brangan 1999). Older adults experienced higher rates of chronic disease than the younger population and use on average almost four times the number of prescription drugs on average per person. Their prescription drug costs are almost four times that of persons under age 65, $1,378 versus $358, respectively.

Medicaid covers low-income aged, blind, disabled, pregnant, and dependent children and is jointly financed by federal and state governments. Of the 40.6 million Medicaid recipients in 1998, 10% were age 65 and older, accounting for 29% of the $142.3 billion spent under the program (NCHS 2001).

### Expenditures in the Last Year of Life

Various studies have shown that older adults approaching death or institutionalization have high expenditures for medical care. About 5% of Medicare beneficiaries die each year, but they account for more than one-fourth of program expenditures. During the period 1993–1998, program outlays for decedents were about six times the amount reimbursed for services provided to survivors. About 38% of beneficiaries had some nursing home stay in the year of death. Hospice was used by half of cancer decedents and by 19% of all Medicare decedents (Hogan et al. 2001). The high medical costs preceding death are not a new phenomenon, and available data do not support the assumption that high medical expenses preceding death are due largely to aggressive, intensive treatment of patients who are moribund. The data suggest that most sick people who die are given the medical care generally provided to persons with severe illness and functional impairment, and sick care is expensive.

### Future Morbidity Patterns

Changing morbidity and mortality play an important part in estimating future illness patterns and in developing population projections. Considerable conjecture has arisen about future morbidity patterns and their impact on future Medicare costs. A recent study indicates that the prevalence of chronic disability in older adults declined from 26.2% in 1982 to 19.7% in 1999, or 1.7% per year, more than the 1.5% required to preserve Medicare solvency (Manton and Gu 2001). How closely these observed trends in chronic disability among the older population will correspond to future illness patterns is uncertain. The interaction of future demographic changes and changing disability prevalence is unclear. Whatever else happens, however, the projected growth in the number of very old persons would have a significant impact on the need, demand, and costs of medical and long-term care services. (See also ADVANCE DIRECTIVES; ELDER LAW PRACTICE; ETHICS IN FINANCIAL PLANNING; FRAILTY PLANNING; TRUSTS.)

#### References

Cohen, Joel W., Steven R. Machlin, Samuel H. Zuvekas, Marie N. Stagnitti, and Joshua M. Thorpe. 2000. *Health Care Expenses in the United States, 1996*. MEPS Research Findings 12. AHRQ Pub. No. 01-0009. Rockville, MD: Agency for Healthcare Research and Quality.

General Accounting Office. 2001. *Long-Term Care: Baby Boom Generation Increases Challenges of Financing Needed Services*. Washington, DC: Author.

Gross, David, and Normandy Brangan. 1999. *Out-of-Pocket Spending on Health Care by Medicare Beneficiaries Age 65 and Older: 1999 Projections*. Washington, DC: Public Policy Institute, Research Group, AARP.

Heffler, Stephen, Katharine Levit, Sheila Smith, Cynthia Smith, Cathy Cowan, Helen Lazenby, and Mark Frieland. 2001. "Health Spending Growth Up in 1999; Faster Growth Expected in the Future." *Health Affairs* 20(2): 193–203.

Hogan, Christopher, June Lunney, Jon Gabel, and Joanne Lynn. 2001. "Medicare Beneficiaries' Costs of Care in the Last Year of Life." *Health Affairs* 20(4): 188–95.

Institute for Health & Aging. 1996. *Chronic Care in America: A 21st Century Challenge*. Princeton, NJ: Robert Wood Johnson Foundation.

Manton, Kenneth G., and XiLiang Gu. 2001. "Changes in the Prevalence of Chronic Disability in the United States Black and Nonblack Population above 65 from 1982 to 1999." *Proceedings of the National Academy of Sciences USA* 98(11): 6354–659.

National Center for Health Statistics (NCHS). 1999. "Current Estimates from the National Health Interview Survey by P.F. Adams, G.E. Hendershot, M.A. Marano." *Vital and Health Statistics* 19(200). Hyattsville, MD: Centers for Disease Control and Prevention.

National Center for Health Statistics (NCHS). 2000. "Deaths: Final Data for 1998 by S.L. Murphy." *National Vital Statistics Reports* 48(11): 1–51. Hyattsville, MD: Centers for Disease Control and Prevention.

National Center for Health Statistics (NCHS). 2001. *Health, United States, 2001*. DHHS Pub. No. 01-1232. Hyattsville, MD: Public Health Service.

*Dorothy P. Rice*

**HEALTH BENEFITS,** offered by employers in order to provide workers and their families with protection from financial losses that can accompany unexpected serious illness or injury. They also offer the benefits to promote health, to increase worker productivity, and to provide a form of compensation to recruit and retain qualified workers. Health insurance is the benefit most valued by workers and their families. In a 2001 survey, 60% of workers ranked health insurance as the most important employee benefit (Christensen 2002).

Research illustrates the advantages to consumers of having health insurance and the benefits to employers of offering it. In general, the availability of health insurance allows consumers to avoid unnecessary pain and suffering and to improve their quality of life, and employers offering benefits report that it has a positive impact on worker recruitment, retention, health status, and productivity (Fronstin and Helman 2000).

Employment-based health benefit programs have existed in the United States for more than 130 years. In the 1870s, for example, railroad, mining, and other industries began to provide the services of company doctors to workers. In 1910, Montgomery Ward entered into one of the earliest group insurance contracts for its employees.

Prior to World War II, few Americans had health insurance, and most policies covered only hospital room, board, and ancillary services. During World War II, the number of persons with employment-based health insurance coverage started to increase. When the National War Labor Board froze wages and a shortage of workers occurred, employers sought ways to get around the wage controls in order to attract scarce workers, and health insurance often was used in this way. Health insurance was an attractive means to recruit and retain workers during a labor shortage for two reasons: unions supported employment-based health insurance and workers' health benefits were not subject to income tax or Social Security payroll taxes as were cash wages.

Currently, employment-based health insurance is the most common form of health insurance coverage in the United States. In 2001, 104.4 million workers ages 18 to 64 were covered by employment-based health benefits (Fronstin 2002c). Seventy-seven percent (77%) of these workers had coverage through their own employer, while the remainder had coverage through a family member's employer. The employment-based health benefits system also covers 13.7 million nonworking adults, ages 18 to 64, and 44.2 million children under age 18. In 2002, virtually all employers with 200 or more employees offered health benefits to their workers, while 61% of employers with 3 to 199 employees made the same offering (Kaiser Family Foundation and Health Research and Educational Trust 2002).

### Health Insurance Premiums

Under the current tax code, health insurance premiums paid by employers are deductible as a business expense—see Internal Revenue Code (IRC) Section 162(a)—and generally are excluded, without limit, from workers' taxable income.

Employers may choose to pay for the entire health insurance premium, a portion of the premium, or none of the premium, offering the plan but not contributing to its cost. The employee shares of the premiums for both themselves and their dependents generally are paid through payroll deduction and may be paid with pretax dollars under IRC Section 125(a). In 2002, employees paid an average of $38 per month for employee-only coverage (16% of the premium), while they paid an average of $174 per month for family coverage (27% of the premium) (Kaiser Family Foundation and Health Research and Educational Trust 2002).

### Benefit Plan Types

According to a 2002 Kaiser Family Foundation study (http://www.kff.org/), 95% of Americans with employment-based health insurance coverage were enrolled in some kind of managed care plan. Health maintenance organizations (HMOs) and preferred provider organizations (PPOs) accounted for 78% of that enrollment. A managed care system typically provides, arranges for, and finances medical services using provider payment methods that encourage cost containment by contracting with select networks of providers.

Before the spread of managed care in the 1990s, insurance coverage was mostly based on a fee-for-service (FFS) system. Beneficiaries in the plan picked their doctors and hospitals at will. Payment was made by the beneficiary when a service was rendered, or the health care provider accepted assignment of the claim from the beneficiary, and afterward claim forms were submitted to the insurance company (or self-insured plan sponsor) for reimbursement. Under managed care, enrollees are often required to follow utilization review and disease management procedures in order to secure coverage for services received.

Other types of employment-based health benefits include different types of accounts through which workers can pay for health care services. Flexible spending accounts (FSAs) allow employees to pay for noncovered or nonreimbursed health care expenses with pretax dollars; they are not taxed on the amount of money that is put into the FSA (see IRC Sections 105(h)(6) and 125(a)). Medical savings accounts (MSAs) allow small employers (with up to 50 employees) and the self-employed to contribute pretax dollars to accounts used to pay for medical expenses, which are coupled with a high-deductible health insurance plan. There are limits on the number of these plans that may be established, and the legislation authorizing MSAs is set to expire in December 2003, unless renewed by Congress. MSAs were instituted originally in the Health Insurance Portability and Accountability Act (HIPAA) of 1996 and have since been reauthorized.

Some employers are considering ways in which they can restructure health benefits. A few employers have turned to, and many others are considering, a trend that started in the 1980s to give employees more choice among different types of benefit arrangements, while at the same time exposing employees more directly to the cost of providing health benefits and health care services. The terms *defined contribution* and *consumer-driven* have been used to describe a wide range of possible approaches to giving employees more incentive to control the cost of either their health benefits or health care and to reduce the size and volatility of employer spending. Many of these plans include tax-advantaged accounts, called *health reimbursement accounts*, *personal care accounts*, and other names, out of which employees pay for their health care needs (Fronstin 2002b).

### Employee Cost Sharing

Virtually all covered services in health care plans are subject to payment limitations and require the employee to share in the costs of coverage. These cost-sharing features generally include premium contributions, deductibles, copayments, coinsurance, and maximum caps on benefits. These plan features are intended to reduce plan costs, encourage employee cost consciousness, and lower administrative expenses.

A *deductible* is a specified amount of initial medical costs that would otherwise be treated as covered expenses under the plan, which each beneficiary must pay before any expenses are reimbursed by the plan. Deductibles typically range from $100 to $500 per year per person, although they can be higher.

*Copayments* are set dollar amounts that a plan participant pays when he or she seeks medical services, such as a $10 payment for seeing their primary care physician or a $20 payment for seeing a specialist. The most common copayment amount for a doctor visit in all types of plans is $10; however, copayment amounts appear to be increasing (Kaiser Family Foundation and Health Research and Educational Trust 2002).

*Coinsurance* provisions require the plan participant to pay a portion of recognized medical expenses; the plan pays the remaining portion. Commonly, the employee pays 20%, with the plan paying the remaining 80% of recognized charges. Most major medical plans include both deductibles and coinsurance provisions. Thus, once the plan participant pays the deductible (e.g., the first $200 in medical expenses), the plan pays 80% of all other covered charges. Most plans limit beneficiaries' out-of-pocket expenditures for covered services; once a beneficiary has reached the out-of-pocket maximum, covered expenses are reimbursed in full for the remainder of the year.

Most medical plans also impose a *maximum annual* or *lifetime dollar limit* on the amount of health insurance coverage provided. Individual lifetime maximums are usually set at very high levels, such as $1 million or more. Although less common, plans that impose limits may do so on an episodic (or per episode) basis, such as per hospital admission or per disability.

### Services Covered

The term *health insurance* refers to a wide variety of insurance policies. These range from policies that cover the costs of doctors and hospitals for general medical and health care services to those that meet a specific need, such as paying for dental or vision care. In the past, health insurance that covered medical bills, surgery, and hospital expenses was typically referred to as a *comprehensive* or *major medical* policy. Today, when individuals talk about an insurance program, instead of using the term *major medical*, they are more likely to refer to FFS (e.g., indemnity), PPO, POS (point of service), HMO, or some other type of insurance program.

Most insurance programs cover medical expenses for hospital and physician fees, surgical expenses, anesthesia, x-rays, laboratory fees, emergency care, and maternity care. Some programs cover physical exams, preventive care (e.g., vaccinations), health screenings (e.g., mammographies), chemical dependency treatment, prescription drugs, dental, vision, mental health or other psychiatric care, and home health, nursing home, and hospice care. For certain services, there may be limits on how much is covered or how many visits are covered annually.

Most health insurance programs do not cover treatment that is experimental or investigational. Insurance programs typically cover only medically necessary care. A typical definition of *appropriate and medically necessary care* is the standard for health care services as determined by physicians and health care providers in accordance with prevailing practices and standards of the medical profession and community.

Medical plans generally exclude services that are not considered medically necessary, including most types of dental, vision, and hearing care. As a result, stand-alone plans providing these benefits are growing in popularity. Because of their highly elective nature, various limits are placed on the benefits provided. When these benefits are offered by or through a vendor other than the health insurer, they are referred to as being "carved out."

### Federal Protections, Laws, and Regulations

The Employee Benefits Security Administration (EBSA), formerly the Pension and Welfare Benefits Administration (PWBA), an agency within the Department of Labor (DoL), is responsible for protecting the integrity of pensions, health plans, and other employee benefits for more than 150 million people. The agency assists workers in getting the information they need to protect their benefit rights, assists plan officials to understand the requirements of the relevant statutes in order to meet their legal responsibilities, develops policies and regulations that encourage the growth of employment-based benefits, and deters and corrects violations of the relevant statutes.

Several federal laws affect how workers and their families receive health benefits from employment. Two of the major laws are ERISA and COBRA:

*Employee Retirement Income Security Act (ERISA) of 1974.* Offers protections for individuals enrolled in health benefit plans sponsored by private sector employers, provides rights to information, and outlines a grievance and appeals process for participants to get benefits from their plans.

*Consolidated Omnibus Budget Reconciliation Act (COBRA) of 1985.* Contains provisions giving certain former employees, retirees, spouses, and dependent children the right to purchase temporary continuation of group health plan coverage at group rates in specific instances. An employer may charge the departing employee the full cost of the coverage plus 2% to cover administrative costs. In 2002, about 16% of beneficiaries eligible for COBRA benefits actually elected to take the coverage, and claims costs for COBRA were about 150% of active employee claims costs (Charles D. Spencer & Associates 2002).

Both of these laws are administered/enforced by the DoL. Other federal agencies with responsibility for health benefits laws include the Internal Revenue Service, the Department of Justice, and others. Additional laws pertaining to health insurance include the Family and Medical Leave Act (FMLA) of 1993, the Health Insurance Portability and Accountability Act (HIPAA) of 1996, the Newborns' and Mothers' Health Protection Act (NMHPA) of 1996, and the Women's Health and Cancer Rights Act (WHCRA) of 1998. In addition, the Equal Employment Opportunity Commission (EEOC) administers several laws that pertain to employment-based health benefits.

### Trends in Health Care Benefits Coverage

In February 2001, 77.4% of workers ages 18 to 64 were offered health insurance by their employer, up from 73.8% in 1993. However, in 2001, 82% of those workers who were offered it took the insurance, down from 85.2% in 1993. As a result, the percentage of workers covered by their own employer remained largely constant from 1993 (62.9%) to 2001 (63.5%) (Fronstin 2002a).

In 2001, rising health benefit costs coupled with the weak economy began to have an effect on health insurance coverage. According to one survey, health benefits costs increased 11% overall in 2001 (Kaiser Family Foundation and Health Research and Educational Trust 2002). As a result of these cost increases, between 2000 and 2001, the percentage of nonelderly Americans with employment-based health benefits declined from 67.1% to 65.6%, the first decline since the early 1990s (Fronstin 2002c). The Kaiser survey found that costs rose even faster in 2002, at a rate of 12.7% overall. This could lead to even further decreases in coverage rates for employment-based health benefits.

### Retiree Health Benefits

In addition to health benefits for current workers, some employers offer health benefits to retirees. Retiree health benefits originally were offered on a very limited basis in the late 1940s and 1950s. The number of employers offering these benefits expanded in the late 1960s in conjunction with the creation of the Medicare program. The benefits were provided as part of the health plan for active workers, generally without a separate premium structure or separate accounting. In subsequent years, the changing demographics of the workforce, coupled with increasing life spans and rising health care costs, left many employers with higher retiree-to-active-worker ratios, increasing the costs and liabilities of retiree medical benefits.

In 1989, the Financial Accounting Standards Board (FASB) issued Statement No. 106 (FAS 106), "Employers' Accounting for Postretirement Benefits Other Than Pensions," which required companies to account for these benefits and report liabilities for the future value of all promised benefits on their corporate balance sheets, beginning with fiscal years after December 15, 1992. For the first time, the true cost of the benefits was understood (Employee Benefit Research Institute 1988, 1989). Prior to FAS 106, companies were required to disclose information only on the existence of plans and amounts of benefit outflows.

As a result of FAS 106, and the increasing cost of providing retiree health benefits in general, many employers began a major overhaul of their retiree health benefit programs. Some employers placed caps on what they were willing to spend on retiree health benefits. Some added age and service requirements, while others moved to some type of "defined contribution" health benefit. Some completely dropped retiree health benefits for future retirees, while others dropped benefits for current retirees, although this happened less frequently than other changes. While these changes do not appear to be having much impact on current retirees, they are likely to be felt most by future retirees who are not yet or may never become eligible for retiree health benefits.

### Retiree Health Benefits Design and Coverage

There are two basic designs for retiree health benefit plans: one for plans covering retirees under age 65 (early retirees) and one covering retirees age 65 and over. Because of the limited tax preferences of the available funding vehicles, employers are looking to reduce their FAS 106 liability by redesigning their retiree health benefit plans. In general, the percentage of employers offering health benefits to future retirees seems to be declining. An annual survey of employers with 500 or more workers shows that the percentage that currently expect to continue offering health benefits to future early retirees declined from 46% in 1993 to 29% in 2000 (William M. Mercer 2001). The percentage of employers offering health benefits to Medicare-eligible retirees today and planning to offer them to future Medicare-eligible retirees is also declining. A survey that followed a constant sample of employers shows a less dramatic drop of 7% in the likelihood that employers offered retiree health benefits to early retirees and a 9% drop for Medicare-eligible retirees (McArdle et al. 1999).

Most employers continuing to offer retiree health benefits have made changes in the benefit package. Many employers have made modifications to cost-sharing provisions, with employers asking retirees to pick up a greater share of the cost of coverage. Others have tightened eligibility requirements by requiring workers to attain a certain age and/or tenure with the company before they can receive any retiree health benefits. Others have reduced or eliminated the benefits for workers hired (or retiring) after a specific date. Employers have also instituted caps on the total amount of money they are willing to spend on retiree health benefits, either per retiree or on a total aggregate spending basis. In addition to those that have already made changes, more employers also are continuing to consider making changes to retiree health benefits.

It will be a few more years before sufficient data are available to explain how workers and retirees will be affected by cutbacks in retiree health benefits. The accounting requirements of FAS 106 triggered substantial changes to retiree health benefits. However, the changes that employers have made to retiree health benefits do not appear to be having much impact on current retirees. Between 1994 and 2000, the percentage of retirees ages 55 to 64 with retiree health benefits was unchanged at roughly 37%, although it is likely that many current retirees are paying more to maintain retiree health benefits.

The changes that employers have made to retiree health benefits will likely have a greater impact on future retirees. These changes may not have noticeable effects on trends in insurance coverage until a few years after the baby boom generation starts to retire. Retirement behavior patterns may also change as employees nearing retirement age postpone their decision to retire upon learning that, without a job, they may not be able to obtain health insurance coverage. By law, employers are under no obligation to provide retiree health benefits, except to current retirees who can prove that they were promised a specific benefit. In the meantime, it is likely that employers will continue to make changes to retiree health benefits in response to future predicted health care costs and potential federal legislative initiatives.

## Conclusion

For many decades, health care benefit plans have played a significant role in employee benefits planning. Modern technology, increased longevity, and a growing emphasis on good physical and mental health make these plans even more important today. The development of managed care plans and dental, prescription drug, vision, and hearing care plans attests to the dynamic nature of this employee benefit area, as does the development of wellness and employee assistance programs. Future innovative efforts in plan design will be influenced strongly by the continuing need for health care cost management, ever-changing medical technology, and constantly changing government regulations.

While an increasing percentage of Americans was being covered by employment-based health plans between 1994 and 2000, this trend has not continued because of the combination of a weak economy and rising health benefit costs. If health care and health benefit costs continue to increase, a greater proportion of the costs may become the responsibility of the employee as employers seek ways to control their spending on health benefits, both for current employees and for retirees. As a result, fewer workers and retirees may become covered by health care benefits through their employers. (See also EARLY RETIREMENT INCENTIVE PLANS [ERIPs]; EMPLOYEE BENEFITS IN THE UNITED STATES; HEALTH AND LONGEVITY; HEALTH MAINTENANCE ORGANIZATIONS AND MANAGED HEALTH CARE FOR OLDER ADULTS; POSTRETIREMENT HEALTH COVERAGE [PRHC].)

**Organizations**

American Association of Health Plans
American Benefits Council
Blue Cross Blue Shield Association
ERISA Industry Committee
Health Insurance Association of America
Society for Human Resource Management

**References**

Charles D. Spencer & Associates. 2002. "2002 COBRA Survey: More Were Eligible, Fewer Elected, Cost Was 150% of Active Employee Cost." In *Spencer's Research Reports on Employee Benefits*, no. 329.04. Chicago: Aspen Publishers, October.

Christensen, Rachel. 2002. "Value of Benefits Constant in a Changing World: Findings from the 2001 EBRI/MGA Value of Benefits Survey." *EBRI Notes* 3 (Employee Benefit Research Institute) (March): 1–3.

Employee Benefit Research Institute. 1988. *Measuring and Funding Corporate Liabilities for Retiree Health Benefits: An EBRI-ERF Policy Study*. Washington, DC: Author.

Employee Benefit Research Institute. 1989. *Retiree Health Benefits: What Is the Promise? An EBRI-ERF Policy Forum*. Washington, DC: Author.

Fronstin, Paul. 2000a. "Trends in Health Insurance Coverage: A Look at Early 2001 Data." *Health Affairs* 21(1).

Fronstin, Paul. 2000b. "Can 'Consumerism' Slow the Rate of Health Benefit Cost Increases?" *EBRI Issue Brief* 247 (Employee Benefit Research Institute) (July).

Fronstin, Paul. 2000c. "Sources of Health Insurance and Characteristics of the Uninsured: Analysis of the March 2002 Current Population Survey." *EBRI Issue Brief* 252 (Employee Benefit Research Institute) (December).

Fronstin, Paul, and Ruth Helman. 2000. "Small Employers and Health Benefits: Findings from the 2000 Small Employer Health Benefits Survey." *EBRI Issue Brief* 226 (Employee Benefit Research Institute) (October).

Kaiser Family Foundation and Health Research and Educational Trust. 2002. *Employer Health Benefits: 2002 Annual Survey*. Menlo Park, CA: Henry J. Kaiser Family Foundation.

McArdle, Frank, et al. 1999. "Retiree Health Coverage: Recent Trends and Employer Perspectives on Future Benefits." Report published by The Henry J. Kaiser Family Foundation, Menlo Park, CA, October.

William M. Mercer. 2001. *Mercer/Foster Higgins National Survey of Employer-Sponsored Health Plans 2001*. New York: William M. Mercer, Inc.

*Rachel Christensen and Paul Fronstin*

**HEALTH CARE.** See Board and Care Homes; Day Programs for Adults; Drugs and Senior Citizens; Geriatric Care Managers [GCMs]; Gerontological Nurse Practitioners [GNPs], Gerontological Social Work; Home Care Services for Older Adults; Hospice Care; Mental Health among Older Adults; Nursing Homes; Nutrition Programs; Pharmacists; Physician–Older Patient Relationships.

**HEALTH INSURANCE.** See Health Maintenance Organizations and Managed Health Care for Older Adults; Long-Term Care Insurance, Private; Medicaid; Medicare; Medicare Supplemental Insurance; Postretirement Health Coverage (PRHC).

**HEALTH MAINTENANCE ORGANIZATIONS AND MANAGED HEALTH CARE FOR OLDER ADULTS.** Managed care has been an option within the Medicare program for almost 20 years. This approach was initiated because of assumptions about the cost savings and care coordination efficiencies associated with this form of service delivery. Opponents of managed care systems for older Americans believe that these plans have often cost the Medicare program more money per beneficiary than if these individuals had been in fee-for-service care. Additionally, they voice concern that there may be unnecessary restrictions on the frequency and length of physician office visits and on the access to tests, procedures, and specialty care. To place these concerns in perspective, this entry reviews studies that have examined the effectiveness and quality of care with managed care systems. Also discussed are two approaches developed within specialty managed care plans that expressly attempt to integrate the care planning and delivery for persons considered at risk for disability or expensive care.

## Defining Managed Care

Managed care has many meanings within health care. The most fundamental feature is the management of physician practice. This occurs in various ways: the selection of physicians into provider networks, utilization monitoring and feedback, provider reimbursement and financial risk-sharing incentives, and practice guidelines. Combinations of these procedures are used within any one managed care plan.

Managed care plans include health maintenance organizations (HMOs), preferred provider organizations (PPOs), and point of service (POS) plans. HMOs include arrangements where one or more medical groups may have an exclusive contract with the plan (e.g., Kaiser Foundation Health Plan and the Permanente Medical Group) or the more common network HMOs in which the medical group's relationship is not exclusive. There are some plans where the physicians are employees of the health plan (e.g., Group Health Cooperative).

Providers in PPOs are reimbursed on a fee-for-service basis but at a discounted rate for enrolled members. PPO enrollees come from employer groups, unions, and other groups with which the PPO has negotiated the opportunity to recruit such members. Providers participating in PPOs usually have nonexclusive relationships with each other. Providers participate in PPOs to gain ready access to patients.

POS, or point of service, plans are variations on the provider "lock-in" provisions of both HMO and PPO coverage. The distinguishing feature of a POS is that enrollees can be covered for services outside the HMO or PPO network. When outside providers are used, service copayments and deductibles are usually higher than they would be from a network provider. Managed care in the form of prepaid health plans has existed for decades, but they began to become widespread in the 1980s as employers reacted to high rates of increase in health insurance premiums. By the mid-1990s about 60% of employees covered by health insurance were enrolled in some form of managed care plan. This rate varied greatly by region of the country and even community. Enrollment continued to increase, with more than 80 million workers covered by these programs in

1999, although shifts in the economy during the early 2000s has reduced access to employer-based coverage for many. Within the Medicare program, the development of managed care has been both less extensive and less rapid. The high point of enrollment occurred between 1998 and 2000 when 16% of beneficiaries were enrolled in managed care. That proportion declined to 12% by 2002.

Among the incentives for enrolling in a managed care plan throughout the 1990s was that basic Medicare benefits of hospital, physician, limited skilled nursing facility use, skilled home health, and durable medical equipment were covered with lower monthly premiums and lower copayments and deductibles than Medicare supplemental insurance policies. Additionally, many health plans also offered outpatient prescription drug coverage. Many also offered expanded benefits like routine physical examinations and immunizations, within the basic benefits, and vision, hearing, and dental exams, at discounted prices.

Enrollment in Medicare managed care has declined for a variety of reasons. The most important is that there are fewer providers willing to accept Medicare contracts, with the direct consequence that members must return to fee for service if there is no managed care provider available. Several factors contribute to this. One is that Medicare prepaid payments for enrollees have not kept pace with what providers see as appropriate rates of reimbursement. Another is a continuing uncertainty associated with changes in Medicare reimbursement formulas for health plans. By 2004, these begin phasing in. A third factor is negative media coverage about managed care. Not infrequently these stories are about denials or other restrictions on service or treatment.

### Managed Care Practices and Performance

One of the principal ways managed care providers have historically reduced their costs relative to fee-for-service systems is by controlling hospital admissions and lengths of stay. In the mid-1980s before there was preset diagnosis-related hospital reimbursement in fee for service, studies found that managed care hospital days were 10% to 40% lower than fee-for-service reimbursed care. By the early 1990s this difference had reduced, with several studies failing to find differences, even among Medicare beneficiaries.

Findings with respect to physician use are inconsistent. One might expect physician use to be higher if it were preventive or in some manner substituting for hospital use. Staff and group model HMOs tend to have higher physician visit rates, while independent practice plans tend to have similar use as fee for service.

Another means of managed care savings is the possible use of fewer or less costly services. Access to appropriate tests and procedures is both an example of possible cost controls and a presumed indicator of the quality of care within health plans. There is evidence that managed care plans are economical in the use of tests and procedures, while still being attentive to prevention and health promotion. Among Medicare plan members, studies have generally shown equivalent access to routine and preventive care (cancer and hypertension screening tests; breast, pelvic, rectal, and general physical examinations; treatment for congestive heart failure, colorectal cancer, diabetes). The potential for managed care organizations to achieve physician compliance with treatment guidelines and other professionally established standards of care is high. These organizations usually have record systems, which permit them to monitor physician behavior and to know the health conditions affecting members.

While there are likely to have been many occasions when managed care plans and providers have failed to offer or delay tests and procedures, the adverse consequences of this are not reflected in most of the analyses of managed care outcomes: Hospital days are the same or lower in managed care; physician use is the same or higher in managed care. Even studies of health plan satisfaction tend to show that 80% to 95% of members report high satisfaction with their plans, a rate only a few percentage points below the average satisfaction levels of those in fee for service.

## Emerging Directions: Chronic Illness Care and Service Integration

A variety of industry and public policy trends are evident in response to the perceived needs and shortcomings of prior efforts to achieve efficient and equitable care within managed care systems. On the policy side are efforts to strengthen quality assurance and performance monitoring and refinement of the reimbursement formula to assure equitable payment for both the plans and Medicare. There are also changes in clinical practice to embrace geriatric care and chronic illness care and interest in exploring and refining approaches to the integration of acute and chronic care.

Two particular approaches to integration deserve special note: The Program of All-Inclusive Care for the Elderly (PACE) and the Social HMO. Both began operating integrated systems of acute and long-term care (LTC) in the mid-1980s as Medicare/Medicaid demonstrations. In 1990 Congress mandated a test of a geriatric model of Social HMOs, and in 1997 Congress made PACE a permanent Medicare program and expressed intention to do the same for Social HMOs. As of February 2003, there were four Social HMO sites serving 110,000 members and 40 PACE sites serving about 8,000 members.

Both Social HMOs and PACE share four features:

1. *Organizational integration.* A sponsor assembles acute care and LTC services into a contracted service network. Sponsors have included HMOs, hospitals, LTC organizations, and joint ventures.
2. *Capitated finance.* Sponsors operate under full-risk, prepaid, limited financing from Medicare and Medicaid.
3. *Voluntary enrollment with lock-in.* Programs must convince beneficiaries to join, and once they join, they agree to obtain all their acute care and covered LTC through the program's managed system of contracted providers.
4. *Service integration.* The full range of acute and LTC services (e.g., personal care and home-making, adult day health center, nursing facilities) are included in the benefit package, and management systems coordinate service provision.

Social HMOs and PACE differ on five features:

1. *Disabled-only versus broad membership.* PACE services only those who are frail enough to be "nursing home certifiable" (NHC) by state preadmission screening criteria, while Social HMOs serve a broad cross section of the older adults population, including beneficiaries who are frail.
2. *Team versus administrative integration.* PACE sites integrate acute and LTC through a multi-disciplinary team based in an adult day health center, which almost all members regularly attend. Most Social HMOs integrate administratively: acute and LTC managers and providers in remote settings work together through communication and coordination protocols. A "second-

generation" Social HMO site begun in 1996 also uses geriatric teams (medically trained persons who specialize in treatment of older persons) to integrate administratively.

3. *Small versus large scale*: PACE sites are designed to serve about 200 members, which is the limit that can be managed in the day health setting. In 2002 the four Social HMOs were serving between 4,400 and 52,000 members and could grow much larger.
4. *Full versus limited LTC benefits*: PACE covers all community and institutional LTC costs for members, while Social HMOs limit community LTC coverage by either dollar limits ($7,500 to $12,000 per year) or time-limited authorizations. If a Social HMO member is permanently institutionalized, he or she can remain in the Social HMO, but LTC coverage ends after several weeks.
5. *Medicaid versus private supplement to Medicare*: PACE premiums for LTC and other supplemental benefits are paid by Medicaid. These averaged $2,422 per month in 2000 (twice the plans' average monthly Medicare premiums). Few individuals can afford this supplemental premium, so almost all PACE members are persons eligible for both Medicare and Medicaid. In contrast, in 2000 Social HMOs' monthly member premiums ranged from no cost to $190, and only 1% to 6% of Social HMO members were Medicaid eligible. Medicare premiums of $560 to $925 per month provided the bulk of Social HMO funding.

One key challenge for Social HMOs and PACE has been marketing/enrollment. PACE sites rely on referrals rather than mass marketing for new members, and their "competition" is the care options available to Medicare/Medicaid eligibles. Despite extensive recruitment, most PACE sites have lagged well behind enrollment targets due to their small market niche and the requirements to switch to the PACE physician and attend day care. Additionally, the PACE providers screen applicants for both program eligibility and the provider's perception of the appropriateness for enrolling them. More than a third of applicants are not accepted. Social HMOs rely on both internal referrals (in HMO-based models) and mass marketing. Their main competition is other private Medicare supplemental plans. Social HMO sites that have sought to grow large have been periodically stopped by federal enrollment caps; but as small plans, they have also faced challenges creating provider networks.

Another challenge faced by both models is changing the system of care for geriatric patients. PACE's integrated service delivery team has achieved dramatic reductions in hospital and nursing home utilization, while increasing the use of ambulatory, preventive, and therapy services. Changes at Social HMO sites have been more difficult to detect, in part due to the lack of reliable comparison groups but also due to the fact that administrative integration is not as strong an intervention as the PACE team. There is some evidence that the team model in the second-generation geriatric Social HMO has reduced acute care utilization. Reductions in institutionalization have also been more difficult to prove in Social HMOs, in part because formal evaluations did not assess this outcome. There is some evidence from nonrandomized studies of reductions in institutionalization. There is substantial variation among both PACE and Social HMO sites in all these utilization areas.

An ongoing policy challenge for both Medicare and Medicaid has been developing prospective payment formulas for health plans like PACE and Social HMOs that enroll disproportionate shares of members with disabilities. Research shows that disability status is an additional risk/cost factor beyond the demographic and diagnostic data that Medicare and Medicaid include in formulas to pay other health plans. Not accounting for disability levels of enrollees would lead to substantial underpayment for PACE (100% NHC) and at least some Social HMOs (which are 20% to 30% NHC). Several generations of formulas that include disability factors have been developed, but research continues.

Formal evaluations of both Social HMOs and PACE have been inconclusive regarding effects on member health status and mortality or Medicare and Medicaid spending. Neither Social HMOs nor PACE have been evaluated with a randomized comparison design, the two Social HMO models were evaluated only in their early operational phases, and evaluation methodologies have been disputed. The comparability of PACE intervention and comparison groups has also been questioned, in part due to PACE sites' rejection of many referrals/applicants.

### Conclusions

Managed care raises opportunities for both enhanced coordination and more effective care for the older adults. The experience of Medicare managed care and the Social HMO and PACE programs all show evidence of care outcomes at least comparable to those of fee-for-service delivery. Certainly incentives exist with managed care reimbursement for a balance between the service rationing needed to control costs and the proactive care needed to assure desirable quality of care outcomes. Consolidation of managed care plans, and among medical groups and hospitals, and even the withdrawal of managed care programs from many communities reflect the continuing flux associated with this approach to health care delivery and some of the problems it poses for beneficiary participation. (See also COMMUNITY-BASED CARE; MEDICAID; MEDICARE; MEDICARE + CHOICE; MEDICARE SUPPLEMENTAL INSURANCE; PHYSICIAN–OLDER PATIENT RELATIONSHIPS.)

#### References

Newcomer, Robert, Charlene Harrington, and Robert Kane. 1999. "Implications of Managed Care for Older Persons." In *Emerging Systems in Long Term Care*, ed. P. Katz, R. Kane, and M. Mezey. New York: Springer Publishing Company.

Williams, Claudia, Justin Treloar, Janet Lundy, Larry Levitt, and Jain Wang. 2002. *Trends and Indicators in the Changing Health Care Marketplace, 2002*. Menlo Park, CA: Henry J. Kaiser Family Foundation.

*Robert Newcomer and Walter Leutz*

**HISTORY OF RETIREMENT,** late-twentieth-century, middle-class conventions color images of retirement in the United States. Most of us have attended a party that celebrates an older employee's transition to a new stage of life. Colleagues and supervisors offer kind words about that person's dedicated service. The guest of honor receives a watch, a bowl, or some other token to remember the occasion. The newly retired also fills out the paperwork necessary to obtain a monthly Social Security check and to begin to draw on prior investments to the company's pension plan. Those who were forward looking and/or lucky enough can also count on private savings or support from their children to supplement their retirement income. Ideally, as long as the retiree stays healthy, there should be money sufficient to approximate the standard of living enjoyed in that person's peak earning years. Accentuating the positive, I (like most Americans) look forward to "retirement" as a time for leisure, according us in our golden years the freedom to pursue hobbies and to travel, to volunteer, or just to take it easy.

Such images, accurate as far as they go, tell only a small part of the story—and they are becoming anachronistic. Images of Snowbirds vigorously exercising on the beach and playing their cards shrewdly do not convey many other faces of retirement. For openers, "retirement" only lately has become something older workers of moderate means could hope to attain, much less afford to enjoy. Men and women throughout most of recorded history were expected to work as long as they were physically able to do so, lest they become burdens on their families or their community. In any event, most people born before 1900 died before they reached the age of 60 or 70, so demographic realities in the past did not prompt the easy connection we now make between "retirement" and "old age." Exceptions to these three generalizations are few and far between. There is evidence that Chinese bureaucrats as early as the fourteenth century and certain categories of senior military personnel in Britain and France beginning in the seventeenth century were permitted to quit their posts and to collect a pension drawn from the royal coffers. And of course the very rich could always elect to spend their twilight years as part of the leisure class. The paucity of exceptions underscores the point that "retirement" was not perceived as a social norm until quite recently in world history.

Economic and social trends in the early decades of the American Republic are consistent with patterns elsewhere in the world at the time. "Retirement" prior to the Civil War defined several conditions occurring over the life course, not just events in the latter stages. "The morals of young men, as well as their application to science," wrote Noah Webster in 1790, "depend much on retirement" (Webster, 1828). In addition to students, some classes of middle-aged workers were said to retire under certain circumstances. Almanacs, for instance, noted that farmers "retired" from winter's storms to their family circles. In the first edition of *An American Dictionary* (1828), Webster defined retirement as "1. The act of withdrawing from company or from public notice or station. 2. The state of being withdrawn. 3. Private abode; habitation secluded from much society, or from public life. 4. Private way of life." Each of these definitions might pertain to a senior citizen, but none is exclusively age specific. The only mandatory retirements in early U.S. history are to be found in seven states that imposed upper age limits on holding judicial office. No firms or other government agencies before 1865, however, discharged workers because they had reached a certain age. No public or private institution provided an old-age pension, though a prudent person here and in Europe could purchase an annuity (the word entered the English language in the fifteenth century) as a hedge against the possibility that they might outlive their productive years.

*Superannuation* was the term that Americans used when they wanted to describe conditions known "to impair or disqualify by old age and infirmity" workers from gainful employment. Advanced age reduced Daniel Boone and Natty Bumppo from hunters to guides. An old horse that trotted was respectable, Hugh Henry Brackenridge reminded readers in *Modern Chivalry* (1804), but one that tried to speed was contemptible. Yet quitting work on account of disability usually was hazardous: Without an ongoing source of livelihood, many aged men and their dependents were reduced to poverty. The older adult poor had to rely on family, friends, and neighbors for essentials. Some took refuge in the county almshouse—a habitat that hardly jibed with Currier and Ives's romantic depiction of "Old Folks at Home."

Transportation businesses inaugurated the first U.S. corporate retirement plans—several decades after banks had established them in England. In 1875, the American Express Company permitted workers past 60 to receive some compensation upon leaving their posts. The retirement program established in 1884 by the Baltimore and Ohio Railroad, which stipulated minimum age (65) and service (10 years) requirements, became the prototype emulated by other firms. But retirement schemes were not as quickly and effectively institutionalized on this side of the Atlantic as in Europe. Of the 150 plans launched in the United States, only 60 of the several hundred thousand corporations offered employee retirement plans by World War I. A few unions and philanthropies as well as municipal, county, and state entities developed pension schemes, but they covered smaller segments of the labor market. Probably less than 2% of the U.S. workforce was potentially eligible for company-sponsored retirement benefits in 1900.

The rationale for late-nineteenth-century pension programs, moreover, did not give priority to the interests of aging workers. Corporate executives generally viewed pensions as an efficient way to weed out inefficient workers. Pensions were not considered part of employee/employer contracts. As a result, not everybody who thought that they qualified for industrial pensions actually got money upon retirement. Treated as gratuities, incentives for productive service, pensions could be withheld and terminated in economic downturns or at management's discretion. Nonetheless, pensions were becoming engrained in American culture. The 1880 edition of Webster's *American Dictionary* helps us to date a key shift in the meaning of *superannuate*—"to give pension to, on account of old age, or other infirmity." Notice the animus against senescence: Old age, like retirement, was deemed a period of obsolescence.

Corporate pensions surely represent an innovation, but it was the federal government that provided the most extensive and generous measure of old-age security through pensions to military veterans and their dependents. In 1818, Congress granted money and/or land to citizens who had served at least nine months in the Continental Army and were "in need of assistance." (By that time, the youngest Revolutionary soldiers were over 55; most veterans already had died.) Similar means-tested provisions were made belatedly for veterans of the War of 1812 and the Mexican-American War. Pension rolls increased dramatically as the Grand Army of the Republic successfully lobbied for assistance for Union soldiers. (Confederate veterans had to turn to their impoverished state officials for relief.) By 1929, more than four-fifths of all beneficiaries of any private or public plan were recipients of war-related pensions; roughly 80% of all money distributed through pensions came from this single source. Congress viewed the military pension system as a reward for risking one's life for the nation; lawmakers steadfastly rejected attempts to draw analogies between compensation for military service and concern for the plight of veterans of productivity. Some reformers drew attention to the growing incidence of old-age dependency, but most Americans were unmoved by the evidence. Few thought that the financial plight of the older adults was a major problem that required a significant public intervention beyond piecemeal efforts.

The Great Depression changed public attitudes. The catastrophe ushered in a new era in the history of retirement in the United States. Older workers were more likely than young men to be discharged from their jobs, to have lost their life savings, and to have anticipated pensions evaporate in corporate bankruptcies. Hard times, not to mention pressure from the Townsendites (a coalition of older Americans demanding generous stipends that would be spent by beneficiaries each month in return for not working) forced Washington to respond to the needs of senior citizens.

The Social Security Act of 1935 was not the New Dealers' first order of business. Nevertheless, the measure became the cornerstone of the U.S. welfare state. Franklin Delano Roosevelt and his advisors designed Social Security to address the unexpectedly widespread predicament of those who were poor and old and to enable future generations of workers to make provisions for their later years. Title I provided a matching federal-state old-age assistance plan, which offered most citizens over 65 in participating jurisdictions to receive on average a dollar a day in support. Title II initially required 60% of the workforce (mainly white-collar employees) to contribute a percentage of their wages, to be matched by their employers, in return for a guarantee of old-age insurance upon their retirement at age 65. The scope of Title II was radically broadened in 1939: The government promised benefits to the dependents of covered employees.

During the 1950s and 1960s compulsory coverage under Social Security was extended to military personnel, agricultural and domestic workers, and the self-employed. A disability program was grafted onto the system; all Title II beneficiaries became entitled to hospital benefits under Medicare (1965). By the nation's bicentennial virtually every U.S. worker was contributing to the Social Security program. Its monthly checks remain the foundation of the average worker's retirement income. Without Social Security, the incomes of roughly two-thirds of all older Americans would fall below the official poverty line.

As anticipated, Social Security made the nation more security conscious in financial matters related to retirement. Unions advocated the establishment of pension funds for their members as a bread-and-butter issue. Human resource managers resisted at first but then realized that they could reduce corporate taxes by liberalizing their firms' pension plans. A 1948 National Labor Relations Board ruling subjected pension plans to collective bargaining. By 1970, more than a third of the civilian labor force could count on corporate plans to supplement Social Security. In 1962 Congress made it possible for the self-employed to set aside funds for their later years through Keogh plans. The Employee Retirement Income Security Act (1974) systematized and liberalized various individual and corporate plans in the private sector, establishing minimum vesting and funding requirements as well as increasing tax incentives for participating. Within three years Americans had created 649,000 Keogh plans, then with assets worth $6.5 billion. No wonder Peter Drucker called workers' concentration of wealth in pension funds *The Unseen Revolution* (1976).

Over the past quarter-century the expansion of pension plans in the public and private sectors has added new wrinkles to the faces of retirement. Age 65 remains the baseline for calculating a contributor's retirement benefits under Social Security, but many workers take advantage of amendments that make it possible to retire at 60 or 62 and receive an actuarially adjusted check. Private funds are free to establish their own age criteria, though they typically are linked to prevailing Social Security triggers. Corporations and universities periodically entice employees to take early retirement with incentives too generous to forego. But many senior citizens prefer not to stop working entirely. Some work part-time; others work part of the year; still others move in and out of the labor force. Voluntary associations, which Alexis de Tocqueville considered the touchstone of *Democracy in America* (1835), nowadays depend on the talents of older men and women to mentor and tutor, to get out the vote, to fill gaps in the social network in their local community.

Despite all of the progress made in shoring up the safety net, retirement in America remains a risky business. Women tend to be more vulnerable financially on average than men, because of their comparative longer life expectancies, interruptions in work histories, and lower aggregate earnings. Minorities and recent immigrants on average qualify for lower monthly benefits than their native-born, White counterparts who remain on the jobs long enough to become vested in pension plans. Prolonged disabilities or the misfortune of mounting prescription bills or doctors' expenses not covered by a health plan can quickly wipe out a person's retirement resources. And while nearly every worker expects to have the option to retire, recent events have shaken virtually all Americans' confidence in existing pension programs. Conservatives have been trying to privatize Social Security for two decades, arguing that workers would do better investing on their own. The political rancor has made Title II an issue on which candidates can sink their campaigns; liberals are chary to recommend any expansion of existing provisions. Nor are people sanguine about recent developments in the private sector. The anguish of middle-class men and women, who lost their retirement funds through the well-publicized bankruptcy of companies such as Enron, has eroded all other workers' sense of security in a roller-coaster stock market. Given the concatenation of historical factors that affect the meanings and experiences of old age in America and the institutionalization of retirement financing, it is safe to predict that more changes are imminent. (See also PENSION PLANS; SOCIAL SECURITY PROGRAM OF THE UNITED STATES.)

#### References

Achenbaum, W. Andrew. 1978. *Old Age in the New Land*. Baltimore, MD: Johns Hopkins University Press.

Achenbaum, W. Andrew. 1983. *Shades of Gray*. Boston, MA: Little, Brown.

Achenbaum, W. Andrew. 1986. *Social Security*. New York: Cambridge University Press.

Drucker, Peter. 1976. *The Unseen Revolution*. New York: Harper & Row.

Webster, Daniel. 1828. *An American Dictionary of the English Language*. New York: William Collins.

*W. Andrew Achenbaum*

**HOME CARE SERVICES FOR OLDER ADULTS,** services provided in the home to promote, maintain, and restore health or to minimize the effects of illness and disability. Home care encompasses a broad continuum of medical, therapy, and social services, ranging from high-technology medical services, such as intravenous therapy and other skilled medical and therapy services, to low-technology, nonmedical services, such as homemaker services and personal care. Home care can be for short-term purposes, such as postacute or rehabilitative care after a hospital discharge or care for the terminally ill, or for long-term purposes, such as assistance with activities of daily living (ADLs) for persons with chronic disabilities.

### The Home Care Market

The home care market can be divided into two parts: medically oriented and nonmedically oriented. Medically oriented services are more likely to be covered by insurance, and much of the existing information focuses on this market segment; less information is available concerning nonmedical home care. In the nonmedical service arena, there has been growth in consumer-directed care, where consumers have the opportunity to decide when and where services will be provided and how and by whom the tasks will be performed (http://www.consumerdirection.org/). A number of publicly funded programs, either through Medicaid waivers or state-funded programs, have begun to offer consumer-directed services over the past decade (Benjamin 2001). To provide this wide range of services, there are various types of home care personnel, such as registered nurses, home health aides, social workers, physical, occupational, and speech therapists, personal assistance attendants, and homemaker and chore workers.

A total of $32.4 billion was spent in 2000 on home health care (Heffler et al. 2002), as reflected in the national health expenditures maintained by the Office of the Actuary at the Centers for Medicare & Medicaid Services (CMS), formerly known as the Health Care Financing Administration, or HCFA (Cowan et al. 2001). This expenditure amount includes only freestanding home health agencies (HHAs) and excludes hospital-based HHAs. This amount does not include payments by consumers for nonmedical home care services such as homemaker, daily money management, or social services, nor does it include nursing services from nurse registries that are part of temporary help agencies.

Although home health care accounts for only a small portion of national health expenditures (less than 3%), it was one of the fastest growing categories of personal health care expenditures, averaging 20% growth during the 1993–1996 period (Cowan et al. 2001). The passage of the Balanced Budget Act (BBA) of 1997 resulted in a major transformation of the home health care market due to changes in Medicare reimbursement as well as reinterpretations and changes in benefits. The BBA mandated a new reimbursement system called the Interim Payment System (IPS) until a prospective payment system (PPS) was implemented for Medicare home health in October 2000. The IPS paid the lower of an agency's actual cost, an aggregate cost per visit limit, or an aggregate per beneficiary cost limit. The IPS created incentives to reduce unnecessary expenditures and operate as efficiently as possible. The incentive in the prior reimbursement system was for agencies to keep their costs below national limits but provide more visits since there was no aggregate per beneficiary cost limit. The BBA also reinterpreted intermittent and part-time requirements for the Medicare benefit and specifically excluded patients whose only need for skilled care was for venipuncture. Around the time of the BBA implementation, the government increased its oversight of fraud and abuse activities for the home health benefit and intensified medical review of claims. These expanded oversight initiatives also likely contributed to slowing the growth of Medicare home health (McCall et al. 2001).

As a result of all these changes, there was a sizable contraction in the Medicare home health market between 1997 and 2000, with a 50% decline in expenditures and a one-third reduction in number of providers. The changes in Medicare even spilled over into other payers, with Medicaid home health growth slowing from 8.8% to 7.1% (Cowan et al. 2001).

Under the Medicare home health PPS, begun in late 2000, an agency is paid a fixed amount for each patient for each 60-day episode of care, with adjustment for severity of patient's condition and geographical differences in wages. Since there is no limit to the number of episodes as long as they continue to be authorized by a supervising physician, agencies will not have an incentive to avoid longer-stay patients but might avoid shorter-stay patients with higher costs. The impact of this new PPS on the home health market is still unknown.

### Financing

There are several ways for persons to pay for home care: public programs such as Medicare, Medicaid, veterans benefits, private insurance, or out of pocket.

According to data from the National Health Expenditures accounts, which include only medically oriented home care, Medicare and Medicaid and other public sources accounted for 53% of all home health expenditures in 2000 in contrast with 62% of expenditures in 1996, prior to enactment of the BBA (CMS 2002b). During this time period, Medicare declined from 43% in 1996 to 28.4% in 2000, while Medicaid (both federal and state payments) increased from 19% to 24%. Similarly, out-of-pocket spending increased from 15% to 20%. Payment from all private health insurance changed very little, accounting for 26% to 28% of all expenditures.

*Medicare.* A major public payer of home health services for older adults is Medicare. Its coverage is designed for treatment of acute care conditions and for postacute care and is medically oriented. The main requirements are that the person must be certified by a physician to need skilled nursing services, or skilled therapy (physical, speech/language, or occupational) on an "intermittent" basis, and he or she must be "homebound." In 2000, Medicare home health expenditures were only $9.2 billion, as compared to $14.5 billion in 1996. This decline was in response to several actions taken by the Centers for Medicare & Medicaid Services (CMS) described above (CMS 2002a; Cowan et al. 2001).

*Medicaid.* Medicaid is also a major public funding source for home care for persons who meet the strict income and asset financial criteria as well as medical/functional requirements. Medicaid spent $22.2 billion in fiscal year 2001 for home care services for all eligible persons, not just for older adults (Burwell, Eiken, and Sredl 2002). There are three main ways in which Medicaid may provide coverage for home care. First, state Medicaid plans must include home health services (i.e., part-time or intermittent nursing services, home health aide services, and medical supplies, equipment, and appliances suitable for use in the home) to Medicaid eligibles entitled to nursing facility services under the state's plan. Second, states can opt to provide other home health services, such as physical therapy, occupational therapy, or speech pathology and audiology services. As of March 2002, states elected to cover the following optional home health services and/or home health–related services under their plans: physical therapy (50 states), speech, language, and occupational therapy (49 states), and personal care services (36 states) (personal communication with K. Blume, CMS, October 2002). In fiscal year 2001, Medicaid spent $2.6 billion for home health care services, $5.3 billion for personal care services, and $8.5 billion for optional other home health services (Burwell, Eiken, and Sredl 2002; K. Blume, CMS, October 2002).

The third Medicaid mechanism is home- and community-based service (HCBS) waiver program authority, which allows states to provide a mix of medical and nonmedical services to help Medicaid recipients stay in the community when they are in need of Medicaid services in an institution. Examples of the types of services provided under these waiver programs are adult daycare, homemaker and chore services, environmental modifications, and respite care. Some of these services like homemaker and chore services can only be provided under waiver programs. The waiver program has permitted states flexibility to cover a broader number of nonmedically oriented services and to extend the benefit package for waiver participants compared to those under the regular state plan. In 2001, all states had one or more waiver programs with $14.4 billion spent on home and community-based waiver services (Burwell, Eiken, and Sredl 2002; K. Blume, CMS, October 2002). It is estimated that three-fourths of these expenditures were allocated to persons with mental retardation and other developmental disabilities. Only 2.4% of HCBS expenditures was specifically targeted for the aged, and another 19% was spent on aged and disabled combined (Eiken and Burwell 2002). The waiver program has doubled between 1990 and 2001 (13% to 29%) as a percentage of all Medicaid long-term care spending, with less emphasis on institutional care at nursing homes or intermediate care facilities for the mentally retarded (ICF-MRs) (Burwell, Eiken, and Sredl 2002). This shift in Medicaid long-term care expenditures is in accord with the recent Supreme Court decision *Olmstead v. L.C.* (June 22, 1999) that unnecessary institutionalization could be a form of discrimination.

*The Department of Veterans Affairs (VA).* This health system provides noninstitutional long-term care services as part of an extensive continuum of veterans' benefits. The VA's home- and community-based services include the Home-Based Primary Care (HBPC) program, outpatient geriatric care evaluation, home health/homemaker care, home medical equipment, hospice/palliative care, and adult day health care. The HBPC program provides hospital discharge planning and comprehensive primary health care to homebound veterans delivered by a hospital-based interdisciplinary team led by a physician. The HBPC was available at 75 of the 163 Veterans Administration Medical Centers in 2001. Eligible veterans for the HBPC program must be homebound, living within the program service area of the VA medical center, living with a caregiver, have multiple diseases or terminal illness, or be short-term patients needing postacute rehabilitation care. There are no financial eligibility criteria or cost sharing (Department of Veterans Affairs 2002).

*Social Services Block Grant (SSBG) or Title XX Program.* States may also fund home care services through this program. In 1997, 39 states and the District of Columbia used it to partially finance a variety of home services as well as other services. Appropriations for SSBG have steadily declined, from $2.8 billion in 1993, $2.3 billion in 1996, and $1.7 billion in 2002 (U.S. House of Representatives 2000).

*Title III of the Older Americans Act (OAA).* This is another funding source for home care, albeit limited. Any person aged 60 and older is eligible for services, but the program targets funds to the most vulnerable older adults. A 1987 amendment to the act authorized in-home services specifically for frail older individuals. Supportive services (in-home services such as homemakers and home health aides, transportation, home-delivered meals, health education and screening, transportation, and information and referral) accounted for one-third of expenditures in fiscal year 1997, or $210 million, for 1.5 million persons served. Spending was greater for congregate meals ($244 million) and served 2.1 million individuals (Kassner 2001). These services are administered through Area Agencies on Aging (AAA) as part of the Administration on Aging (AoA). AoA also supports a nationwide, toll-free information and assistance directory called the Eldercare Locator (1-800-677-1116). The Locator helps individuals to find the appropriate AAA seeking home care and other assistance for older adults. The reauthorization of the Older Americans Act in 2000 appropriated $113 million to create the National Family Caregiver Support Program. This national program provides information, counseling, training, and outreach to caregivers about available services (AoA 2001).

*State-Only Long-Term Care Programs.* States also devote their own funds to support long-term care services, by allocating funds required by Medicaid and OAA federal matching rules and by subsidizing optional Medicaid services and supplemental services by their own choice. A recent national survey found all but two states provided multi-service home- and community-based programs to older adults. Total expenditures from these state-source programs were more than $1.2 billion in 1996; however, there is substantial variation from state to state (Kassner and Williams 1997). Nearly all these programs cover individuals not meeting the restrictive financial eligibility for Medicaid, and many also serve persons not meeting the Medicaid health and functional eligibility criteria. In addition, some programs supplement services for persons receiving Medicaid services. Nearly all programs cover four core in-home services: personal, homemaker, chore, and respite care. Three-quarters of the programs use cost sharing. Existing state-only programs may decline due to state budget pressures.

*Publicly Funded Consumer-Directed Home Care Projects.* Public programs have traditionally followed a vendor payment model (i.e., an agency-driven model). They have not permitted direct cash payments to clients, nor have they permitted payment to family members for home care services. With the trend toward consumer or self-directed approaches to the delivery of home care, consumers may receive cash payments or vouchers for authorized services, and family members and friends can be hired as providers. There are a variety of selfdirected approaches ranging from a professional monitoring approach to cash and counseling, where individuals receive the cash equivalent of their benefits through direct payments or vouchers. Several public funding sources (e.g., Medicaid waiver, Medicaid state plan, state funds, OAA, Title XX) finance these projects, usually requiring a Medicaid waiver. Consumer direction models approved by Medicaid are available in over half of the states and in a number of state-only programs. Research challenges and questions remain with respect to appropriateness, cost, quality, and accountability of consumer direction.

*Private Sources.* Private funding sources for home care include out-of-pocket payments of either the home care recipient and/or family members, private health insurance, long-term care insurance, and Medicare supplemental insurance. Out-of-pocket costs are not an insignificant component of home care expenditures. Based on the national health expenditure data, out-of-pocket expenditures have increased from 15% to almost 20% between 1993 and 2000 (CMS 2002b).

Employer-sponsored postretirement health insurance often provides home health benefits. Long-term care insurance may provide home care benefits in addition to nursing home coverage. The number of persons buying long-term care insurance has grown in recent years. Between 1993 and 1999, the number of policies sold doubled from about 3.4 million in 1993 to almost 7 million in 1999 (HIAA 2002). In addition, four of the ten standard Medicare supplemental insurance plans offer an at-home recovery benefit linked to the Medicare home health benefit. However, a very small percentage of persons purchased policies with this at-home benefit.

### Home Care Providers

Providers of home care services can be classified into the following categories: (1) agencies certified by the federal government; (2) uncertified agencies, which may or may not be licensed; (3) home care workers from employment or temporary personnel agencies or nurse registries; and (4) independent providers, either through a formal contract or an informal arrangement. These provider types have differing regulatory requirements, payment arrangements, and service levels. For example, only agencies certified by the federal government can receive Medicare reimbursement. These agencies must provide skilled nursing services and at least one therapy service and meet other conditions of participation. Home health agencies are the market segment typically licensed by states, even if they are not federally certified. Many agencies that are licensed are also certified, but not all; one study estimated that about 59% of licensed home health agencies in 1998 were also certified. Certified agencies may have higher charges than noncertified agencies due to more stringent training and supervision requirements.

Statistics on the first two categories (agency providers) exist but vary depending on the criteria used to define home care; statistics on the other categories, specific to home care, are nonexistent. Using a broad definition to include both medical and nonmedical providers, the National Association of Home Care (NAHC) identified 19,690 home care agencies in the United States in 2000, of which 7,152 were Medicare-certified home health agencies, another 2,273 were Medicare-certified hospices, and the remaining 10,265 were home care providers and hospices not participating in the Medicare program (NAHC 2001). Thus, Medicare-certified agencies account for only 48% of the official home care agency providers using NAHC's definition. Using a stricter definition, the 2000 National Home and Hospice Survey indicates that Medicare-certified agencies are a greater proportion of all home health agencies, accounting for 83% (NCHS 2002a).

In addition to Medicare patients, certified agencies serve Medicaid and private-pay clients, which can account for a sizable percentage of their total patient load. The numbers of Medicare-certified agencies increased from 2,924 in 1980 to a peak of 10,444 in 1997, then dropped to 7,152 partly due to changes in Medicare home health care reimbursement with the passage of the 1997 BBA (NAHC 2001). The IPS may have spurred mergers between old and new agencies since agencies that were in existence prior to 1994 were allowed higher cost limits (Van der Walde 2002).

There are several reasons why an agency may not be certified. It may not provide all or any of the services that Medicare requires. Even if certification requirements are met, noncertified home care agencies may simply choose to serve private-pay, Medicaid, or other public program clients instead of Medicare clients. State programs may reimburse uncertified agencies and independent providers as well as certified providers for home health and personal care services. A recent study of noncertified home health care providers in Ohio found that only 10% of providers were noncertified. Noncertified agencies are smaller and focus more on personal care, home health aide, homemaker services, and companion service. Some of these findings are reiterated in the National Home and Hospice Survey, where noncertified agencies were found more likely to offer companion services and less likely to provide skilled nursing services than agencies certified for either Medicare or Medicaid (NCHS 2002b).

Apart from these agencies, persons may also procure home care workers from employment or temporary help agencies, nurse registries, as individual independent contractors, or through private, informal arrangements. It is not known what proportion of the home care market these sources represent. The informal arrangement is an acknowledged "gray" market, similar to that for child care.

### Client Characteristics

The 1998 National Home and Hospice Care Survey (NHHCS) estimated that 7.6 million individuals, or 2.8% of the noninstitutionalized population, receive some type of formal home care service, either medical, nonmedical, or both. Of this number, 69% were aged 65 or older, with the likelihood of use increasing with age. Women, unmarried persons, and persons living alone were more likely to use home health care than men, married persons, and those living with someone. These client characteristics are similar in the 2000 NCHS National Home and Hospice Care Survey. Looking at data only for older adults home health patients, 67% of them received help with either an ADL or IADL, (instrumental activity of daily living) and 59% received help with at least one ADL. Older adult home health clients received the following types of services: skilled nursing services (74%), personal care services (40%), therapy services (29%), and homemaker or companion services (28%) (NCHS 2002a).

### Quality Monitoring and Consumer Involvement

There has been a trend for greater accountability in home care, as in other areas of health care. This includes efforts for standardized data collection for monitoring process or outcomes of patients, development of performance measures, and collection of information about patient perspectives on quality of care received. There is also increased emphasis on dissemination of this information to the public as well as to providers for targeting their quality improvement efforts.

The Omnibus Reconciliation Act of 1989 mandated development of client outcome measures for home health care (Hughes 2001). The result was the Outcome and Assessment Information Set (OASIS), which is a uniform set of patient assessment items developed for monitoring and measuring outcomes of care, adjusted for patient factors that might affect those outcomes. Since 1999, all Medicare-certified home health agencies have been required to use OASIS as a part of a comprehensive assessment of most patients at initiation of care and other specific time points during their care; certain patients are exempt from data collection (e.g., pediatric and maternity patients). The primary goal of OASIS is to improve patient care, but it also contains data items that are essential for case mix adjustment for the Medicare home health prospective payment.

The OASIS data collected by the agencies are transmitted to a central source, then outcome, case mix, and adverse event reports are returned to each agency on an annual basis (since February 2002) for targeting their quality improvement activities. With clinical input, 41 measures were derived from OASIS data for an outcomes-based quality improvement program in Medicare. These measures cover (1) functional outcomes, (2) physiologic outcomes, (3) emotional/behavioral/cognitive outcomes, and (4) utilization outcomes. An additional 13 low-frequency adverse patient outcomes were identified and are reported to the HHAs.

The Centers for Medicare & Medicaid Services plans to use a selected subset of the 41 home health quality measures derived from OASIS as part of its public reporting initiative on quality. It is expected that this information will be available in late 2003 to assist consumers, their families, and other intermediaries (e.g., discharge planners) in selecting home health agencies.

There is interest in obtaining patient perspectives on home care services for quality monitoring. CMS has developed a Consumer Experience Survey for voluntary use by state Medicaid programs for the home- and community-based waiver programs. The survey solicits waiver participants' feedback on four aspects of quality: access to care, respect and dignity, community integration/inclusion, and choice/empowerment. There are two survey versions: one for the disabled older adults population and one for persons with developmental disabilities. The survey and user's guide are expected to be issued in 2003 (Bosstick 2002). Outcome measures for quality are not available to individuals and families who directly hire home care workers rather than contracting with a home care agency.

### Steps in Choosing and Managing Home Care Services

There are several steps that consumers and their family members should follow to obtain home care services:

*Step 1. Assess the Need and Financing for Home Care Services.* A consumer and his or her family should first obtain an assessment of:

- The various types, amount, and duration of home care services they will require from formal home care sources;
- The informal assistance available from family members and friends that would complement formal services to provide the appropriate level of care needed; and
- Whether any of the needed home care services can be paid by federal, state, or other programs or insurance, or if one must pay for any or all of the care out of pocket.

To obtain information on and get an assessment, do the following:

- Contact the local Area Agency on Aging (AAA) or the Eldercare Locator for general information on assessments and services available.
- If one is living at home, contact his or her physician, other health care personnel, and social service and home care agencies.
- If one is being discharged from a hospital, patients and family members should contact the discharge planner and receive a written plan of care from their physician for posthospital home care.

*Step 2. Finding and Selecting Home Care Providers.* For agency providers, lists are available by location from:

- The Eldercare Locator (1-800-677-1116)
- The local Area Agency on Aging.

Additional information sources include hospital discharge planners, other health care and social service professionals, state health departments, as well as telephone directories and the Internet. If one is enrolled in managed care, your primary care physician or care coordinator will be the main gatekeeper for access to formal home care providers.

For independent home care workers not associated with a home health agency, one may check:

- Nurse registries or general employment agencies
- The local newspapers
- Referrals from family or friends
- Posted advertisements for home care assistance

In selecting a particular home care provider, one should consider service reputation and quality. Information on quality of an agency may be obtained through state survey, licensure, and accreditation organizations. The National Association for Home Care's "Consumer's Guide to Home Care" offers a list of questions for help in selecting the right home care provider. For Medicare-certified agencies, one may contact the state health insurance counseling program, the state home health hotline, and the state health department. For privately hired independent home care workers, one needs to interview the prospective care worker, check on references and training, and have a trial work period. With a private arrangement, it is important to have a clear understanding through a signed contract with a home care worker about the work requirements and schedule, taxes, payment, and insurance coverage, expectations about worker performance, and quality of services delivered.

*Step 3. Dealing with Service Problems.* If there are problems or dissatisfaction with the home care nurse or health care worker, contact the home care supervisor, physician, or the State Department of Health, the Area Agency on Aging, the Long Term Care Ombudsman, or the Home Health hotline in the state or county. If the service is provided under the Medicare benefit, one can contact the state Quality Improvement Organization (QIO) to file a complaint.

If denied care by Medicare-certified home health agencies, a written notice from the agency that the services are not covered, are being reduced, or are being terminated is required. If you believe you are eligible for Medicare coverage, you can ask Medicare for an official decision ("demand bill") and ask the agency to send your claim to Medicare. While Medicare decides if you are covered, you agree to pay the agency privately. If Medicare decides you are covered, the agency must reimburse you. If Medicare denies the claim, you have the right to appeal. However, if you lose the appeal, you are liable for payment. (See also COMMUNITY-BASED CARE; HEALTH MAINTENANCE ORGANIZATIONS AND MANAGED CARE FOR OLDER ADULTS; MEANS-TESTING IN PUBLIC PROGRAMS; MEDICAID; MEDICARE; VETERANS' BENEFITS.)

### Organizations

Administration on Aging
Centers for Medicare & Medicaid Services
Consumer Direction, sponsored by National Council on Aging and the National Association of State Units on Aging
Eldercare Locator

Medicare Rights Center: Home Care Channel
National Association for Home Care
Outcome and Assessment Information Set (OASIS)

### Suggested Readings

Centers for Medicare & Medicaid Services. 2002. *Medicare and Home Health Care*. Publication #10969. Baltimore, MD: Author. (Call 1-800-633-4227 [available 24 hours a day] for copy of publication.)

Medicare Rights Center, Home Care Channel. Available online at http://www.medicarerights.org/homecare.html.

National Association for Home Care. 1999. *How to Choose a Home Care Provider: A Consumers Guide*. Washington, DC: Author. (Single copies are free by writing to Attn: Publications, 228 7th Street SE, Washington, DC 20003.)

### References

Administration on Aging (AoA). 2001. *Family Caregiving Fact Sheet*. Washington, DC: GPO.

Benjamin, A.E. 2001. "Consumer-Directed Services at Home: A New Model for Persons with Disabilities." *Health Affairs* 20: 80–95.

Blume, K. 2002. CMS. Personal communication. October.

Bosstick, S. 2002. CMS. Personal communication. December.

Burwell, B., S. Eiken, and K. Sredl. 2002. "Medicaid Long Term Care Expenditures in FY2001." May 10 Memorandum. MEDSTAT Group, Inc., Cambridge, MA.

Centers for Medicare & Medicaid Services (CMS). 2002a. *Medicare and Home Health Care*. Publication #10969. Baltimore, MD: Author.

Centers for Medicare & Medicaid Services (CMS). Office of the Actuary. National Health Statistics Group. 2002b. Available online at http://www.cms.gov/statistics/nhe/.

Cowan, Cathy, et al. 2001. "National Health Expenditures, 1999." *Health Care Financing Review* 22: 77–111.

Department of Veterans Affairs. Office of Congressional and Legislative Affairs. U.S. Committee on Veterans Affairs. 2002. *Testimony by Robert Roswell*, April 26.

Eiken, S., and B. Burwell. 2002. "Medicaid HCBS Waiver Expenditures, FY1995 through FY2001." May 13 Memorandum. MEDSTAT Group, Inc., Cambridge, MA.

Gwyther, Lisa, Edna Ballard, et al. 2002. *Steps to Success: Decisions about Help at Home for Alzheimer's Caregivers*. Washington, DC: AARP.

Harrington, Charlene, Peter Summers, and Valerie Wellin. 2000. "State Medicaid Home Health Licensing and Certification." *Home Health Care Services Quarterly* 18: 77–104.

Health Insurance Association of America (HIAA). 2002. "Long Term Care Insurance in 1998–1999: Summary of Study Findings." Available online at http://www.hiaa.org/research/research_studies.cfm.

Heffler, Stephen, et al. 2002. "Health Spending Projections for 2001–2011: The Latest Outlook." *Health Affairs* 21: 207–18.

Hughes, S. 2001. "Home Health." In *The Continuum of Long Term Care*, ed. C. Evashwick. 2nd ed. Albany, NY: Delmar Thomson Learning.

Kassner, Enid. 2001. *The Role of the Older Americans Act in Providing Long Term Care*. Washington, DC: AARP Public Policy Institute.

Kassner, Enid, and Loretta Williams. 1997. *Taking Care of Their Own: State-Funded Home and Community-Based Care Programs for Older Persons*. Washington, DC: AARP Public Policy Institute.

McCall, Nelda, H. Komisar, A. Petersons, and S. Moore. 2001. "Medicare Home Health before and after the BBA." *Health Affairs* 20(1): 189–98.

National Association for Home Care (NAHC). 2001. *Basic Statistics about Home Care, 2000.* Washington, DC: Author.

National Center for Health Statistics (NCHS). 2002a. "National Home and Hospice Care Survey, 2000." Unpublished estimates.

National Center for Health Statistics (NCHS). 2002b. "National Home and Hospice Care Survey, 1998 and 2000." Unpublished estimates.

Straker, Jane, and Robert Applebaum. 1999. *A Survey of Non-Certified and Non-Licensed Home Health Agencies in Ohio.* Oxford, OH: Scripps Gerontology Center, Miami University of Ohio.

Super, N. 2002. "Medigap: Prevalence, Premiums and Opportunities for Reform." *NHPF Issue Brief,* 782.

United States General Accounting Office. 2001. *Long Term Care: Implications of Supreme Court*'s Olmstead *Decision Are Still Unfolding.* Testimony before the U.S. Senate Special Committee on Aging, September 24.

U.S. House of Representatives. Committee on Ways and Means. 2000. *Overview of Entitlement Programs. 2000 Greenbook.* Washington, DC: GPO.

Van der Walde, L. 2002. *Health Care Industry Market Update: Home Health.* Baltimore, MD: CMS.

*Judith A. Sangl and Linda A. Siegenthaler*

**HOME MODIFICATIONS FINANCING,** mechanisms designed to maximize the safety of disabled and older adults in their own homes through environmental improvements to the residence.

The overwhelming preference of older adults is to age in place in their homes and communities. Modifications to the home can support this preference by helping older adults and their caregivers to perform daily tasks. Home modifications are adaptations to the physical environment that can range from inexpensive railings, rearranged furniture, or extra lighting to more costly ramps, powerlifts, and fully remodeled bathrooms and kitchens. These adaptations address problems such as accessing a home, bathing, and cooking.

Most persons pay for the modifications themselves using savings, assets, or income. According to the 1990 National Health Interview Survey, more than 75% of persons of all ages with home accessibility features paid for these features out of pocket (La Plante, Hendershot, and Moss 1997). However, more extensive and comprehensive modifications, such as elevators and stair lifts, can cost several thousands of dollars. For some people, such changes may be unaffordable, and assistance from outside financing sources may be needed.

## Sources of Financing for Older Adults

There is no federal law or program that solely supports or finances home modifications. What exists, however, is a range of public and private financing sources available to both individuals and home modification programs. However, these sources are far from comprehensive, and eligibility requirements are often confusing, which limits the availability of home modifications to those with unmet needs.

## Home Equity Financing

Home equity loans or second mortgages are common mechanisms to finance changes to the home. A home equity loan is a line of credit that can be accessed over several years for the purpose of home improvements. In contrast, a second mortgage is a separate loan that can be used for home improvements and must be repaid in addition to the existing mortgage. Alternatively, homeowners may benefit from loans that are given directly to remodeling contractors or suppliers. Many remodelers work directly with finance agencies that specialize in remodeling projects. These loans are available only through remodelers or dealers, but they are more convenient and offer lower closing costs to the consumer.

Different departments within the federal government offer financing programs that can be used to improve home accessibility. The Federal Housing Administration operates two loan guarantee programs: Title 1, which can be used to rehabilitate existing homes; and the 203K program, which can be used for purchasing or rehabilitating a home. For rural or suburban homeowners over age 65, low-interest loans and grants for home adaptations are available through Rural Community Development (formerly Farmers Home Administration). In particular, there is a 504 loan program for very low-income homeowners with disabilities and a 504 grant program for persons with very low incomes over the age of 62.

Disabled veterans can benefit from grant programs administered by the Department of Veterans Affairs. The Home Improvement Structural Alterations program provides grants for home modifications that improve the accessibility of the home as well as electrical and plumbing improvements made necessary due to the installation of medical equipment. This onetime monetary award is available to those who were disabled while in the service and those who have become disabled in their older years. However, persons who were not service disabled receive a smaller award. The Special Housing Adaptation Benefit program provides home adaptations such as special lighting and handrails to those who have lost the use of eyes or hands. The Specially Adapted Housing program benefits those who have experienced significant loss, such as the use of legs or upper extremity. These veterans may qualify for a grant to build an accessible home or remodel an existing home. Eligibility for the latter two programs requires that the veteran must have been disabled while in the service.

Some states operate loan programs to help low- and moderate-income persons pay for home modifications. In particular, state housing finance agencies issue bonds for housing construction and other housing-related projects. These agencies are in an ideal position to create revolving, low-interest loan funds for home repair and adaptation. For example, the Minnesota Housing Finance Agency's (MHFA) Fix Up Fund uses housing revenue bonds to help homeowners increase the livability, accessibility, and energy efficiency of their homes. The low-interest loans are made to homeowners by locally participating banks, credit unions, and housing agencies. The MHFA also has a separate Accessibility Loan program funded by state appropriations targeted at households with one or more persons with a long-term physical disability.

Reverse mortgages help older persons remain in their own homes by allowing them to draw down the cash value through a monthly stipend, a lump-sum payment, or a line of credit. Many of these householders could use reverse mortgages to pay for the long-term care they might need over their lifetimes, home modifications or repair, and other needs. The Home Equity Conversion Mortgage Program and Fannie Mae's Home Keeper Program are examples of programs operated by the U.S. Department of Housing and Urban Development (HUD). However, the acceptance and use of the reverse mortgage have been modest, partially due to its complicated nature, the reluctance of many older persons to tamper with a major asset, and the high closing costs associated with the initiation of the mortgage.

### Non–Home Equity Financing

The Fair Housing Amendments Act of 1988 enables renters to request "reasonable" accommodations and modifications that change the physical structure of the individual unit or common areas. However, "reasonable" is a vague term that leaves room for interpretation. Often, "reasonable" depends on whether the changes would present a significant fiscal or administrative burden on the housing provider. In public and federally subsidized housing, the landlord pays for reasonable modifications both to the individual unit and common areas. In the private market, the landlord may or may not be willing to pay for modifications in the common areas and within the individual unit. In such cases, tax credits and tax deductions are available for the expenses incurred for accessibility modifications. However, the landlord is not required by law to pay for changes, and as a result, the tenant may need to assume the cost of the modifications, especially those in individual apartment units. The tenant also has the responsibility of restoring the interior premises to its original condition upon vacating the unit, if such steps can be reasonably performed.

There is anecdotal evidence that some private medical insurers and HMOs (health maintenance organizations) pay for home modifications as a way to reduce the cost of institutional care. While availability is limited, reimbursing for home modifications is consistent with the managed care philosophies of cost-effectiveness and preventative care. Long-term care insurance policies may also provide payouts for home modifications. However, these insurance options are expensive and may not be a viable option for lower-income persons. Unfortunately, Medicare and Medicaid do not reimburse for home modifications. Both programs pay for only medically necessary durable medical equipment and supplies such as hospital beds, crutches, ventilators, and wheelchairs but not for changes to the environment, even those that facilitate the use of such equipment.

### Other Financing Mechanisms

Persons receiving Supplemental Security Income (SSI) or Social Security Disability Insurance (SSDI) benefits can take advantage of several options. For SSI beneficiaries, the Plan for Achieving Self-Support program is a savings plan that allows recipients to set aside income for home modifications without jeopardizing benefits. SSDI beneficiaries and, in certain cases, persons who receive SSI benefits can deduct the cost of home modifications from earnings.

Income tax deductions may also help to compensate for the cost of home modifications. The capital expenses incurred in making the modifications can be treated as a medical deduction, provided that a physician certifies the changes as medically necessary. This option pertains only to persons who itemize expenses and pay more than 7% of their income on medical expenses. Examples of deductible expenses include constructing ramps, widening doors, modifying hardware on doors, and modifying electrical outlets and fixtures. In addition, long-term care tax credits are available in certain states to families caring for older adults and persons with disabled adults at home.

Locally, various organizations can provide small grants, loan equipment, and devices or donate their time and manpower. Local chapters of the Multiple Sclerosis Society,

United Cerebral Palsy, and the National Easter Seal Society are possible options to explore. Persons can also contact local chapters of Habitat for Humanity or Rebuilding Together, which build or rehabilitate homes that include accessibility features. Local civic organizations can also provide aid in the form of money, equipment, or time. For example, the Knights of Columbus is particularly interested in helping children with disabilities (Duncan 1998).

### The Role of Home Modification Programs

Beyond coordinating the financing of home modifications, persons may need help with assessment of the home environment and installation of the needed modifications. For simple home adaptations, persons with disabilities and their families often self-assess their problems, pay for the home modifications, and carry out the necessary labor on their own. However, more complex changes may require the use of various providers such as occupational therapists, remodelers, contractors, tradesmen, handymen, medical supply companies, and social service agencies.

In an effort to provide home modifications, a number of programs have developed across the country to meet the needs of older adults and persons with disabilities of all ages. These programs can assess the environment, obtain materials and products, and make the adaptations. Such programs can be nonprofit or for-profit. In many nonprofit and governmental programs, these services are provided to low-income older adults at little or no cost. However, nonprofits and governmental programs usually have waiting lists, as the need exceeds their capacity. Budget limitations and a lack of stable sources of funding highly restrict the types of changes programs can make and the amount that can be spent on any individual client. Further, significant gaps exist in the geographical coverage of programs, with rural areas particularly underserved.

Most home modification programs piece together funding from several sources. Funding options, especially from governmental sources, are not stable or guaranteed. Programs continually reapply for funding, and the receipt of funding is not assured. Eligibility requirements for these funding sources can vary by locality. Unfortunately, there are no state or federal entitlement programs dedicated to home modification. Home repair is usually the main mission of housing-related programs, and home modification is a lower priority.

### Funding Options for Home Modification Programs

Many programs use Community Development Block Grants (CDBGs) or HOME Block Grants administered by HUD. These funds are passed down from the federal level to states and localities where they can be used for such purposes as community rebuilding, affordable housing, community services, and home repair. Home modifications may be included as part of a home repair initiative. Use of CDBG or HOME funds often requires that homes be brought up to code before a home modification can be installed. For example, broken steps may need to be fixed before special railings can be installed. Such situations represent a significant expense that may raise the costs. In addition, home modification programs are only one of many competing needs that require funding. The primary purpose of CDBG funds is to reverse urban decay and maintain the housing stock in disadvantaged neighborhoods. Nevertheless, CDBG funds are an important source of funds for home modification programs. For example, almost 70% of nonprofit home modification programs in California rely on either city or county CDBG money.

Programs serving older adults, including those with disabilities, may benefit from Title III Older Americans Act funds. These funds are passed down from the federal Administration on Aging to the State Units on Aging and then to local Area Agencies on Aging (AAA). AAAs may have their own home modification program or provide funds to local agencies that provide home modification services. However, home modification is but one of many needs of older adults and may not be of high priority to AAAs. In general, AAAs tend to focus on low-cost items such as grab bars and hand-held showers or more costly but needed items such as ramps.

Medicaid home- and community-based service (HCBS) waivers enable states to "waive" certain federal requirements and develop innovative alternatives to placing Medicaid-eligible persons in hospitals and institutionalized settings. Each state has the flexibility to design a HCBS waiver program that provides services such as case management, home health, respite care, and even environmental modification. Currently, 47 states have in place a Medicaid waiver program that includes environmental modifications. State Medicaid agencies must assure the Centers for Medicare and Medicaid Services that the average per capita cost of providing home- and community-based services will not exceed the cost of institutional care. Furthermore, eligibility is restricted to those who would qualify for Medicaid in an institutional setting, and states can choose to serve all ages or target certain age groups. Medicaid Waiver programs are generally limited to certain geographic areas within states. Those that offer environmental modifications have caps on the amount that can be spent per client.

Home modification programs, particularly nonprofits, also rely on other private funding sources. Many nonprofit programs solicit corporate donations or fund-raising to supplement their budgets. Certain nonprofit programs may require clients to pay a portion of the service cost. Private foundations and voluntary groups such as United Way and Rotary Clubs also provide financial support to home modification programs. Voluntary organizations such as Habitat for Humanity and Rebuilding Together, which build or rehabilitate homes that incorporate basic accessible design features, rely heavily on contributions of supplies and volunteer labor to perform the work.

### Conclusion

Despite the range of financing options available, older adults must be diligent because each financing option has different eligibility requirements and other restrictions. Often agencies administering these sources are unaware of other options if an older adult is not eligible for a certain program. Home modifications programs may be helpful because they are able to coordinate assessment and installation while providing these services at low or no cost to low-income older adults. However, these programs are also limited in the number of persons served, the types of persons targeted, and the kind of modifications provided. While older adults prefer to age in place, they face many difficulties in securing the financing needed to make their home environment safer and more supportive. (See also FRAILTY PLANNING; HOME CARE SERVICES FOR OLDER ADULTS; HOMEOWNERSHIP; HOUSING COUNSELING FOR OLDER AMERICANS; MORTGAGE INSTRUMENTS; REVERSE MORTGAGES.)

### Organizations

Administration on Aging
Centers for Medicare & Medicaid Services
Habitat for Humanity International
Rebuilding Together
Social Security Administration
U.S. Department of Agriculture
U.S. Department of Housing and Urban Development
U.S. Department of Veterans Affairs

### References

Duncan, R. 1998. "Funding, Financing, and Other Resources for Home Modifications." *Technology and Disability* 8: 37–50.

Hyde, J., R. Talbert, and P.J. Grayson. 1997. "Fostering Adaptive Housing: An Overview of Funding Sources, Laws, and Policies." In *Staying Put: Adapting the Places Instead of the People*, ed. S. Lanspery and J. Hyde. Amityville, NY: Baywood Publishing.

La Plante, M.P., G.E. Hendershot, and A.J. Moss. 1997. "The Prevalence of Need for Assistive Technology Devices and Home Accessibility Features." *Technology and Disability* 6: 17–28.

Pynoos, J., P.S. Liebig, J. Overton, and E. Calvert. 1997. "The Delivery of Home Modification and Repair Services." In *Staying Put: Adapting the Places Instead of the People*, ed. S. Lanspery and J. Hyde. Amityville, NY: Baywood Publishing.

Pynoos, J., and C. Matsuoka. 2001. "Housing and the Continuum of Care." In *The Long-Term Continuum of Care*, ed. C. Evashwick. Albany, NY: Delmar Thomson Learning.

Pynoos, J., M. Tabbarah, J. Angelelli, and M. Demiere. 1998. "Improving the Delivery of Home Modifications." *Technology and Disability* 8: 3–14.

Scholen, K. 2000. *Home-made Money: Consumer's Guide to Home Equity Conversion*. Washington, DC: AARP.

*Jon Pynoos and Christy Nishita*

**HOMELESSNESS AMONG OLDER ADULTS.** Reforms of the Social Security system undertaken in conjunction with the War on Poverty of the mid-1960s reduced the poverty rate among older Americans to a level somewhat below that of the nation at large. At one time, older adults suffered the highest rate of poverty of any age group; today they have one of the lowest (Wright and Devine 1994). These facts have lulled many commentators into thinking that poverty and poverty-related conditions such as hunger and homelessness have all but disappeared among America's older population. This is not so.

In any given week, there are very roughly a million homeless people in the United States, although the uncertainties around any such estimate are quite large (Burt et al. 2001). Of these, roughly 2% will be over the age of 65, and an additional 6% will be ages 55 to 64. Thus, the older homeless comprise about 8% of the total homeless population. Compared to the percentage of older persons among the larger poverty population (10% ages 55 to 64 and another 16% ages 65 and up), older Americans are severely underrepresented among the homeless, a demographic oddity that has been noted since the 1980s (Burt et al. 2001; Wright 1989). Contrary to a common stereotype, the homeless are relatively young, with an average age in the mid- to late thirties in most studies, a substantial decline from two decades ago when the average age of the homeless was perhaps 20 years higher (Kutza and Keigher 1991).

At the same time, it is likely that the number of homeless older adults will increase in the coming decades as the general population ages and as the demand for affordable housing increases faster than the supply. It is also possible that there are more older homeless right now than studies suggest because they are less likely than the younger homeless to congregate in particular places and are, therefore, less likely to be counted. Thus, attempting to estimate the prevalence of homelessness among older adults is perhaps even more difficult than estimating the precise number of homeless in general.

What accounts for the apparent "deficit" of older adult persons among the homeless? Two hypotheses have been offered. First, a range of benefit programs become available to people once they turn 65 (among which Social Security, Medicare, and various housing subsidies are the most important); these programs may be sufficient in many instances to get otherwise homeless people off the streets (or to allow aging poor people to avoid homelessness). On the other hand, people with sporadic work histories and less access to resources (e.g., women and ethnic minorities) may find that they are not eligible for these programs or that the benefits provided by them are not adequate to keep them housed. Second and more troubling, homeless people may rarely survive to old age. Some half-dozen studies have now reported that the average age of death for various samples of the homeless men is somewhere in the early fifties (e.g., Hibbs et al. 1994; Wright and Weber 1987).

Older homeless were far more prominent in the Skid Row studies of the 1960s and 1970s (Bahr and Caplow 1973; Bogue 1963) than they are today. Wright et al. (1987) reviewed medical charts for homeless men receiving health services at the New York City Men's Shelter, in the very heart of the Bowery, from 1969 to 1984. Among men seen in the early years of this period, the average age was 44; among those seen in the later years, only 36—an 8-year drop in the average age of homeless men in a 15-year period. The average age has apparently stabilized in the mid-thirties in the years since.

People become older *homeless* through two entirely distinct processes. Some homeless people age into this category, and some older persons lose their housing and become homeless. No study of which we are aware has reported evidence on the relative proportions. Either way, the older homeless face all the problems that homeless people face (regardless of age) and many problems that older people face (regardless of their housing situations). There are also significant interactions that make the situation of the older homeless uniquely problematic, for example, an evident need for the vigor and alertness that are important survival skills for all homeless people, coupled with the limited physical capacity and mental acuity that may accompany aging.

What are the living circumstances of the older homeless in America today? The survey by Rich, Rich, and Mullins (1995) in Tampa showed that the single largest group (46%) lived, literally, on the streets, in parks, abandoned buildings, vehicles, or in other outdoor locations. Fewer than a third (30%) lived in homeless shelters, about a tenth (10%) lived in transitional housing, and the rest in rooms or with family and friends. Many older homeless say they avoid the large overnight shelters because the shelters are unsafe (Cohen and Sullivan 1990), as indeed they are, most of all for older homeless people with compromised mental or physical health (who are much more likely to be victimized or injured than other homeless people) or those dealing with other issues of aging such as deteriorating eyesight, hearing, and mobility.

Issues relevant to the homeless in general are also relevant to the older homeless: mental health, alcohol and drug abuse, physical well-being, outreach, access to community resources, and certainly housing. In addition, a range of other factors complicates the situation of the older homeless. One is the intricate patchwork of age restrictions on various service programs. Homeless people, for obvious reasons, tend to age more rapidly than domiciled people. Some programs for older adults become available at age 55, some at age 60, some at age 62, and some at age 65. Even professional caregivers often have trouble keeping all the restrictions and eligibility criteria straight, and so do the older homeless themselves. Program participation is further compromised when they are not aware of services that are available to them or when they are frustrated or dissuaded by the complexities of the application process.

Concerning mental health, older homeless people evidently suffer from the same emotional and psychological problems that younger adults experience, including depression, anxiety, and schizophrenia. Even otherwise stable and well-balanced persons often develop psychological problems once they are without a home and living on the streets. There is a tendency to minimize mental health among older adults in general as the inevitable consequence of aging. The problem is exacerbated by prejudice toward the aged and, even more, against the aged homeless. The use of psychotropic or neuroleptic medication to manage mental illness among the older homeless is also complicated by the material conditions of their existence. The sedative effects of many of these drugs reduce attentiveness and thus increase the already extreme vulnerability of the older adult homeless to robbery or assault. Many psychiatric medications are strongly contraindicated in the presence of alcohol; as among the homeless generally, alcohol and drug abuse is widespread. Some of these drugs increase photosensitivity, which is a much more serious issue for homeless people than for people who have a roof between them and the sun. Other drugs impair thermoregulation (also uniquely problematic for the homeless), increase the probability of hypotensive episodes, disrupt the normal sleep cycle, and have other side effects that interact in uniquely deleterious ways with the conditions of homelessness.

Owing in part to the relative deficit of older persons among the homeless as well as to methods that may inadvertently exclude them, few surveys of homeless people contain enough homeless among older adults to sustain detailed analyses. One important exception is the study by Rich, Rich, and Mullins (1995). In general, this survey of older homeless in Tampa Bay confirms that what is true of homeless people in general is also true of the older homeless. Other details are instructive. For example, nearly 90% of the older adult homeless report having received assistance with their meals, but only 1% say they have received assistance finding permanent housing, as though nutritional issues are relevant to the older homeless but housing issues are not. Even so, three-quarters of the older homeless report eating fewer than three meals a day. Most say they have no close associates (62%), no health insurance (82%), and no income (67%). When asked about the advantages of being a homeless person, nearly 80% saw none. Data such as these should cause us to abandon the hopeful thought that existing programs of assistance to the aged adequately ameliorate the more degrading aspects of a homeless existence.

Why do older people become homeless in the first place? Several researchers have

**Table 1**
**Reasons for Homelessness Cited by a Sample of Older Adults Homeless in Tampa Bay**

| Reason | Percentage Mentioning Each Reason |
|---|---|
| Cannot afford rent | 76 |
| Cannot afford security deposit | 68 |
| Alcohol abuse | 38 |
| Lost job | 35 |
| Sick, unable to work | 28 |
| Left adult family | 15 |
| Newly released from jail/other legal reasons | 9 |
| Newly released from hospital | 8 |
| Divorce | 8 |
| Abandoned by spouse/family | 7 |
| Asked by family or friends to leave | 7 |
| Mental illness | 5 |
| Drug abuse | 4 |
| Prefers street life | 4 |
| Home foreclosed | 3 |
| Home condemned | 4 |
| Spouse abuse | 2 |
| Other | 16 |

*Source*: Rich, Rich, and Mullins 1995, 121.

attempted to answer this question, including Rich and colleagues (1995) who posed exactly this question to their aged homeless respondents. Results are summarized in Table 1; most other studies have reported similar results. Inability to pay rent or to pay the security deposit necessary to rent a unit were the most commonly mentioned factors by a wide margin and the only factors cited by an outright majority. About two-fifths said their homelessness resulted from alcohol abuse. Other fairly commonly mentioned factors include job loss (35%), physical illness (28%), and familial estrangement (15%). A few were evidently fleeing abusive home situations. Factors such as mental illness or drug abuse (other than alcohol) were mentioned by only about 5%. Similarly, Tully and Jacobson (1994) reported that the three most important factors contributing to homelessness among older adults were poverty, lack of affordable housing, and deinstitutionalization.

Many older adults become homeless for the first time after the death of a spouse or caregiver who formerly provided instrumental or financial support (Rosenheck, Bassuk, and Salomo 2002). Factors such as inadequate income, substance abuse, or mental or physical health problems may become precursors to homelessness only after the loss of a caregiver. Older women and minorities with less experience obtaining formal support as well as older adults who suffer from mental or physical impairment not only may be more vulnerable to homelessness because they have fewer resources. They may also be unable or unwilling to secure appropriate formal support services that would enable them to avoid homelessness.

Recent policy discussions of older Americans have been driven by the image of the "greedy geezer," an image whose inaccuracy is obvious from the very existence of homelessness among older adults. It is, of course, true that the poverty rate among older adults has declined considerably over the past 30 years. Still, there are vast disparities in income among the aged, and their aggregate poverty rate is only very slightly beneath the national rate. Older people become and remain homeless for the same essential reasons that other people do, because they lack the financial resources to live in some other way. From the viewpoint of social policy, the concern is that the declining median age of the homeless population, the relatively lower rate of poverty among older adults, and the widespread but incorrect belief that assistance programs have effectively eliminated poverty among older adults will remove the obvious needs and issues of the older adults homeless from public purview and policy discussion.

A few older homeless report that they actually like being on the streets, but the vast majority in practically every study "express a preference for stable housing and better care settings than they presently experience" (Rich, Rich, and Mullins 1995). It is also apparent that the older homeless are a heterogeneous group. While the group as a whole may be described as being in "double jeopardy," each subcategory has its own resources, problems, and needs. Homeless people do not fit into any single stereotype; nor do the older adults; nor do the older homeless adults. Thus, addressing the problem and providing stable housing and care will remain a challenge. (See also DISABILITY PROGRAMS, FEDERAL AND STATE; MEDICAID; MENTAL HEALTH AMONG OLDER ADULTS; MENTAL HEALTH CARE FINANCING; NUTRITION PROGRAMS; VETERANS' BENEFITS.)

### References

Bahr, Howard, and Ted Caplow. 1973. *Old Men, Drunk and Sober*. New York: New York University Press.

Bogue, Donald J. 1963. *Skid Row in American Cities*. Chicago: University of Chicago, Community and Family Studies Center.

Burt, Martha, Y. Laudan, Edgar Lee Aron, and Jesse Valente, eds. 2001. *Helping America's Homeless: Emergency Shelter or Affordable Housing?* Washington, DC: Urban Institute Press.

Cohen, Carl I., Mildred Ramirez, Jeanne Teresi, Margaret Gallagher, and Jay Sokolovsky. 1997. "Predictors of Becoming Redomiciled among Older Homeless Women." *The Gerontologist* 37(1): 67–74.

Cohen, Carl I., Jeanne Teresi, Douglas Holmes, and Eric Roth. 1988. "Survival Strategies of Older Homeless Men." *The Gerontologist* 28(1): 58–65.

Cohen, Neil L., and A.M. Sullivan. 1990. "Strategies of Intervention and Service Coordination by Mobile Outreach Teams." In *Psychiatry Hits the Streets: Outreach and Crisis Intervention for the Mentally Ill*, ed. N.L. Cohen. New York: Guilford Press.

Gilderbloom, John I., and R.L. Mullins. 1995. "Older Adults Housing Needs: An Examination of the American Housing Survey." *International Journal of Aging and Human Development* 40(1): 57–72.

Hibbs, J.R., L. Benner, L. Klugman, R. Spencer, I. Macchia, A.K. Mellinger, and D. Fife. 1994. "Mortality in a Cohort of Homeless Adults in Philadelphia." *New England Journal of Medicine* 331: 304–9.

Kutza, Elizabeth A., and Sharon M. Keigher. 1991. "The Older Adults 'New Homeless': An Emerging Population at Risk." *Social Work* 36(4): 288–93.

Rich, Diane Watt, Thomas A. Rich, and Larry C. Mullins. 1995. *Old and Homeless—Double Jeopardy*. Westport, CT: Auburn House.

Rosenheck, Robert, Ellen Bassuk, and Amy Salomon. 2002. "Special Populations of Homeless Americans." Available online at http://aspe/hhs.gov/progsys/homeless/symposium/2-Spclpop.html.

Tully, Carol T., and Sharon Jacobson. 1994. "The Homeless Older Adults: America's Forgotten Population." *Journal of Gerontological Social Work* 22(3–4): 61–80.

Wright, James D. 1989. *Address Unknown: The Homeless in America*. Hawthorne, NY: Aldine de Gruyter.

Wright, James D., and Joel Devine. 1994. "Poverty among the Older Adults." *Pride Institute Journal of Long Term Home Health Care* 13(1): 5–16.

Wright, James D., Peter H. Rossi, Janet Knight, Eleanor Weber, Richard C. Tessler, Christine Stewart, Marianne Geronimo, and Julie Lam. 1987. "Homelessness and Health: Effects of Life Style on Physical Well Being among Homeless People in New York City." In *Research on Social Problems and Public Policy*, ed. M. Lewis and J. Miller. Vol. 4. Greenwich, CT: JAI Press.

Wright, James D., and Eleanor Weber. 1987. *Homelessness and Health*. New York: McGraw-Hill.

*James D. Wright and Tracy Dietz*

**HOMEOWNERSHIP.** Currently, over 84% of older persons live in conventional households, while about 9% live in planned supportive group senior housing facilities, such as congregate living facilities, assisted living, continuing care retirement communities, or nursing homes. Another 7% also live in conventional households, but in dwellings that were owned or rented in the names of younger (under age 65) persons. This entry focuses on the older households (householders or heads of households) who owned their dwelling in their names. Most occupy 1-unit attached or detached structures (86%), but significant proportions occupy 2- to 49 unit (5%), and 50+-unit structures (2%). About 7% are owners of manufactured homes (U.S. Census Bureau 2000).

In the year 2000, over 18.2 million out of 22.8 million older households (80%) owned their dwellings. This rate of homeownership is at a historical high, up from 70% in 1973, 75% in 1983, and 77% in 1990. The rate of older adults' homeownership is projected to increase to 84% by 2020 (Joint Center for Housing Studies of Harvard University 2001).

Selling the home is still the exception rather than the rule, although it is more likely following the death of a spouse or the move to a nursing home. Venti and Wise (2001) offer an economic interpretation of the attraction of homeownership. They argue that most older homeowners are unlikely to draw down their housing equity to obtain greater liquid consumer income. Rather, they contend that most older persons think of their home's equity as touchable only in catastrophic circumstances, for "a rainy day," seek to leave this asset to their heirs, and do not intend to finance their retirement consumption patterns through the sale of their house. Thus, they question the validity of the life-cycle hypothesis of consumption. This predicts that individuals accumulate assets in their middle adult years when their earning capacities are highest, savings are increasing, and housing, family, and other consumer costs are declining, and after retirement, they begin to gradually consume their wealth or dissave.

A psychological explanation of older persons' strong preference to stay put emphasizes their strong emotional and sentimental attachment to their current dwellings that contributes to their social status and positive self-image.

Several government programs that offer cash and in-kind income to poor older Americans also discourage moves by older homeowners. In most states, for example, the Medicaid program's eligibility requirements of having almost nonexistent assets do not include the owned home in their computations. This is similarly true for the eligibility provisions of the Supplemental Security Income and Food Stamp program. Thus, means tests for eligibility for social welfare benefits in the United States infrequently require older people to divest themselves of their homes. A possible, but unestablished, counteracting influence on the residential inertia of older homeowners is their ability to benefit from the capital gains tax exclusion ($250,000 for single and $500,000 for joint tax returns) when they sell their personal residences.

Selling the home is also discouraged because of its increased importance as a setting where a growing population of frail older persons can receive personal assistance and health care services. Because older homeowners live in larger dwellings and are less likely to face occupancy restrictions, they can more easily accommodate a family member, housemate, or live-in who will provide caregiving or home upkeep assistance. There is also a greater prevalence of older adult homeowners who are providing temporary shelter to their unemployed or divorced adult children or who are assuming new and demanding grandparent roles by raising their grandchildren.

### Homeowners: A Demographic and Economic Profile

Certain subgroups of older households are more likely than others to own their dwellings (U.S. Census Bureau 2000). The homeownership rate among young-old (age 65 to 74) households is 83%, compared to 77% among old-old households. About 92% of married households compared with 69% of older persons living alone own their homes. African Americans (68%) Asian Americans (53%), and Hispanics (65%) are less likely to own their homes compared with non-Hispanic White older households (83%). Older adults homeowners are also not equally found in all locations. Over 47% of this group is found in the suburbs of metropolitan areas, while 29% is found in nonmetropolitan places, and 24% is located in central cities (U.S. Census Bureau 2000). Older homeowners present a distinctly different demographic profile than older renters. They are more likely to be members of the young-old, married (as opposed to living alone), White, and have a high school education and higher incomes.

About 16% of older homeowners had incomes that placed them below the 100% poverty threshold level; but 30% were below the 150% threshold level. A more complete portrayal emerges when the household incomes of older homeowners are compared with their metropolitan area or nonmetropolitan county's median income and thus reflect cost-of-living differences. About 22% of older households have incomes that are 30% and under of their area's median (extremely low-income group), 44% have incomes that are 50% and under of their area's median (very low-income group), and 66% have incomes that are 80% and under of their area's median (low-income group) (U.S. Census Bureau 2000). Among the group of older homeowners with very low incomes, 41% report no savings, while 26% report savings of less than $25,000. Low incomes are also more prevalent among older households who can be considered "overhoused." An overhoused household has less than 0.5 persons per bedroom (e.g., an older man living alone in a three bedroom dwelling), and over 22% of older households are in this category. About 56% of this group have very low incomes. These households are at greater risk of living in unaffordable housing and to have difficulties paying for their out-of-pocket medical and home care costs, because they are burdened with the upkeep and maintenance of unused dwelling space.

Income differences offer only a partial portrayal of the older homeowner's economic status. Most older homeowners own their homes free and clear (82%). In 1995, of the total home equity wealth ($6.4 trillion) in the United States, 31% (almost $2 trillion) was owned by older households, even as they occupied about 26% of all the owned dwellings (Davern and Fisher 1995). The median equity value of older householders' dwellings (net of mortgage obligations) was $70,000. Including home equity, age 65 and over households had a median net worth of just over $92,000; without it, $24,047. Median net worth, however, declines sharply with age: The median net worth of age 65 to 69 households is $106,408 but only $81,600 for age 75 and over households (Davern and Fisher 1995). These breakdowns still offer an incomplete portrayal of the varied economic circumstances of older homeowners. A substantial share of older homeowners occupy relatively low-valued dwellings. About 13% of older homeowners occupy dwellings valued under $40,000, while about 49% occupy dwellings valued under $100,000 (U.S. Census Bureau 2000). The result is that a significant share of this group is both cash poor and house poor. That is, they have low incomes (80% and under of area median), and they cannot rely on their low-valued houses (less than $100,000) as a financial cushion.

### The Affordability of Dwellings Owned by Older Adults

Overall, in 1999 about 27% of older homeowners were paying 30% or more of their monthly incomes on their housing costs, while 13% had 50% or more housing expense burdens. These costs include payments for mortgages or installment loans or contracts, real estate taxes, property insurance, homeowner association fees, cooperative or condominium fees, and utilities. They do not include either the scheduled or unscheduled costs for maintenance and repairs. The prevalence of a higher housing expense burden is far greater among lower-income homeowners. Among very low-income homeowners, 47% were paying 30% or more and 26% were paying 50% or more of their incomes on their housing costs (U.S. Census Bureau 2000).

Even as many older homeowners have very low incomes (cash-poor) and are confronting burdensome property taxes, insurance, and upkeep expenses, they are reluctant to sell their dwellings. Two important types of government programs have helped to alleviate the financial plight of this group: the federally insured Home Equity Conversion Program (HECP) and state-administered tax relief programs.

The Home Equity Conversion Mortgage (HECM) insurance program was created by the 1987 National Housing Act and made it possible for older households (age 62 and over) to obtain a federally insured reverse mortgage. This is a financial instrument designed to allow older homeowners with lower incomes (cash-poor), but who occupy relatively high-valued homes (house-rich), to borrow against the equity in their dwelling and receive tax-free cash payments, either advanced in one or more lump sums, in a steady stream of monthly income payments, in the form of a purchased annuity, or some combination of these payment types. HECM loans are available to all homeowners age 62 and over who have low outstanding mortgage balances or own their home free and clear. The interest on this loan is not tax-deductible until the debt is repaid. This group would otherwise have difficulty obtaining conventional forward mortgages or home equity lines of credit because of their low incomes. Older households can use these funds for any purpose, whether for a vacation or to pay for health care costs. Borrowers do not have to pay back their loans (and the imputed interest) until they die, sell, or permanently move out of their homes.

While the growth of mortgages processed by HECM has steadily grown, nonetheless, through 2001, only 50,000 reverse mortgages had been insured under this program, along with another 10,000 mortgages produced by the private sector. Moreover, the annual number of originating mortgages has never exceeded 14,000. Thus, this program has addressed the needs of an extraordinarily small percentage of older homeowners to date (Eschtruth and Tran 2001).

Experts explain this low demand by emphasizing that most consumers are reluctant to draw down their housing equity to obtain greater liquid consumer income, emphasizing that even when homeowners move, a large share do not reduce their home equity values. Along with the same factors discouraging moves in general, their staying put may be linked to their desire to leave their wealth to their children and their reluctance to take on any forms of new debt. They may also perceive these instruments as too complex or believe up-front loan costs are too high (these can easily represent as high as 15% to 20% of the loan's principal). Moreover, because those older homeowners who most need financial assistance often live in very low-valued homes, most lenders consider them to be unattractive candidates for a reverse mortgage loan.

After mortgage debt service, property taxes are usually the largest dwelling expenditure of older homeowners, and these taxes may be especially burdensome to the poor. Property taxes are often unpopular with seniors because they can increase more quickly than inflation, they can threaten their ability to afford their homes, and they view them as funding projects (e.g., schools) from which they derive few benefits. Older homeowners have higher property tax burdens than younger homeowners, because on average they live in higher-valued homes.

State governments have attempted to reduce the property tax burden of older homeowners (and renters) in several ways. *Homestead exemptions* lower the assessed value of the property subject to taxation for homeowners. *Homestead credit programs* typically offer direct rebates either as a percentage of taxes or as a fixed credit to qualifying owners such as older homeowners. *Circuit breaker programs* provide a direct tax credit on the property tax bill that is typically larger for lower-income households. A fourth approach, *property tax deferral programs*, allows older homeowners to defer payment of property taxes until they sell the home or die. Deferred property taxes become a lien against the value of the taxpayer's home and have similar financial properties as reverse mortgages.

Every state provides some type of property tax relief program, but the benefits vary greatly. Most states favor targeting relief to low-income older adults households, and 44 states and the District of Columbia have at least one property tax relief program that treats older homeowners more generously than younger homeowners. An AARP investigation found that older homeowners were more aware of, and were more likely to apply for, homestead exemption programs (Baer 1998). In contrast, seniors were less likely to be aware of or to use circuit breaker and homestead credit programs. They most infrequently used property tax deferral programs. Significant percentages of the older respondents reported that they did not apply for these programs because they were unaware of these options or needed more information or help filling out the applications. The report concluded that further outreach efforts would be effective.

Despite these programs, property tax burdens remain high for many low-income older adult homeowners, because eligibility is often restricted to homeowners who have very low levels of income or assets and because the participation rate by older homeowners in these relief programs is often low (Reschovsky 1994).

## The Physical Condition of the Dwellings Occupied by Older Homeowners

In 1999, less than 5% of older homeowners occupied dwellings that had severe or moderate physical deficiencies in their plumbing, heating, or electrical systems, in their common areas, or in their maintenance or upkeep (U.S. Census Bureau 2000). These physically deficient dwellings were more likely to be found in the central cities of metropolitan areas and in rural or nonmetropolitan areas, especially in the southern United States. Older homeowners who occupied very old dwellings, built 1949 or earlier (29%), were especially likely to have these physical deficiencies (10% of group). Only a small percentage of the older occupants in physically run-down dwellings were found to make improvements and repairs (in a previous two-year period), and they were less likely to engage in these upgrading activities than younger homeowners. Older occupants were also more likely to rely on paid help (U.S. Census Bureau 2001).

The living conditions in these older settings contribute to the poorer economic, physical, and mental health of their occupants. Older homes, for example are often less energy efficient and more expensive to heat than newer homes and result in relatively large home heating costs. Older homeowners may also experience lower psychological well-being and, in the extreme, a sense of helplessness and despair because they cannot change the undesirable features of their dwellings. Older persons who lack the health or energy to maintain their homes may perceive such failings as an unequivocal sign of their inability to live independently. In contrast, renters may delay or avoid such harsh self-assessments, not only because they have fewer or less demanding upkeep burdens but also because when these tasks are necessary, they can often be assumed by a landlord. The property values of undermaintained dwellings may also be depressed. Moreover, when these properties are concentrated in the same location, entire neighborhoods may become physically distressed, resulting in higher rates of property depreciation and lower property tax revenues. Community efforts to revitalize these neighborhoods may be difficult to achieve.

Even homes in good physical condition may prove hazardous to older adult occupants if they have architectural design features that create more difficult to use or unsafe environments, especially when their occupants also suffer from physical limitations. These older adult occupants are at increased risk of having dwelling-based accidents (e.g., falls on stairways, floors, and bathtubs; burns or scalds from fires, hot liquids, and hot surfaces, such as heaters).

Most professionals argue that the home can be physically modified in ways that not only reduce accidents but also enhance the independence of older Americans (Pynoos et al. 1997). Estimates as to what percentage of older homeowners have modified their dwellings to accommodate their frailties vary greatly. The most recent and optimistic analysis found that in 1995 only 42% of older adult homeowners in need of home modifications had actually made some adjustments. The most common modifications included handrails or grab bars by about 27.6% of this group. The next most frequent modifications were specially equipped telephones (7.2%), easy-access bathrooms (7.1%), widened doors or hallways (5.9%), easy-access kitchens (5.0%), and door handles instead of knobs (3.8%) (U.S. Census Bureau 2001). Older persons with more severe disabilities and health problems were more likely to make home modifications (Mutschler 1997).

Older persons report that their most needed home modifications include handrails or grab bars, ramps, easy-access bathrooms, specially equipped telephones, easy-access kitchens, elevators or stair lifts, widened doors or hallways, and modified sink faucets or cabinets. Although relatively small percentages of older persons express these needs, many more are probably unaware of their home's hazards and how modifications would be beneficial. Others are discouraged from making home modifications because of the many obstacles linked with implementation. This is especially true for less educated seniors who find it difficult to apply for financial resources to carry out such work. Home modifications are also less likely by households with incomes below the poverty level, who own low-valued homes, and are Hispanic or African American. Seniors generally fear dealing with contractors or home repair personnel because they often overcharge or do shoddy work. Both consumers and professionals, including home builders, remodelers, and human service professionals, sometimes have inadequate knowledge of the physical attributes of the home that would benefit from modification. The older dwellings occupied by today's older adults only compound an already difficult situation. While they may attend to their most serious maintenance needs, older homeowners may overlook the less visible hazards found in their dwellings (U.S. Census Bureau 2001).

Most studies conclude that older persons would be more likely to modify their dwellings if government programs were more available and effective (Pynoos et al. 1997). The most important federal programs that now fund home modification and repair services are the block grant programs sponsored by the U.S. Department of Housing and Urban Development (Community Development Block Grant) and the Department of Health and Human Services' Social Services Block Grants and Title III of the Older Americans Act. The Rural Housing Services, Section 504 home repair loan and grant program, and the Section 533 Housing Preservation Grant (HPG) program also provide grants to nonprofit organizations for the rehabilitation of homes. Weatherization adaptations are funded under the Department of Energy's Low-Income Home Energy Assistance Program (LIHEAP) and the Weatherization Assistance Program. State-sponsored programs are also increasingly important funding sources. Outside of the government, foundations and charitable organizations are also key sources of funds, but their budgets are small. Advocates argue that these programs are underfunded and are poorly coordinated with the other homemaker and personal care services needed by frail older homeowners.

### Future Issues

Traditional assessments of the owned home that are limited to its physical condition and affordability will become increasingly inadequate. Increasing numbers and percentages of older people are opting to age in place in their long-occupied and familiar dwellings. Thus, the dwelling has become not just a source of shelter but also an environment in which older occupants are seeking to cope with physical frailties. The conventional home is increasingly compared with supportive group housing alternatives, such as congregate living, assisted living, continuing care retirement communities, and nursing homes. A central research and public policy issue is the cost-effectiveness of physically and mentally frail older persons receiving shelter and care in their own homes as opposed to relocating to these other settings. (See also CONDOMINIUMS; CONTINUING CARE RETIREMENT COMMUNITIES [CCRCs]; COOPERATIVE OWNERSHIP IN HOUSING; HOME MODIFICATIONS FINANCING; MORTGAGE INSTRUMENTS; REVERSE MORTGAGES.)

#### References

Baer, David. 1998. *Awareness and Popularity of Property Tax Relief Programs.* Washington, DC: AARP.

Davern, Michael E., and Patricia J. Fisher. 2001. *U.S. Census Bureau, Current Population Reports, Household Economic Studies, Series P70-71, Household Net Worth and Asset Ownership, 1995.* Washington, DC: GPO.

Eschtruth, Andrew D., and Long C. Tran. 2001. "A Primer on Reverse Mortgages." *Just the Facts on Retirement Issues* (October): 1–4.

Joint Center for Housing Studies of Harvard University. 2001. *The State of the Nation's Housing, 2001.* Cambridge, MA: The Joint Center for Housing Studies of Harvard University.

Mackey, Scott, and Karen Carter. 1994. *State Tax Policy and Senior Citizens.* Washington, DC: National Conference of State Legislatures.

Mutschler, Phyllis H. 1997. "The Effects of Income on Home Modification: Can They Afford to Stay Put?" In *Staying Put: Adapting the Places Instead of the People*, ed. Susan Lanspery and Joan Hyde. Amityville, NY: Baywood Publishing.

Pynoos, Jon, Phoebe Liebig, Julie Overton, and Emily Calvert. 1997. "The Delivery of Home Modification and Repair Services." In *Staying Put: Adapting the Places Instead of the People*, ed. Susan Lanspery and Joan Hyde. Amityville, NY: Baywood Publishing.

Reschovsky, Andrew. 1994. *Do the Older Adults Face High Property Tax Burdens?* Washington, DC: AARP.

U.S. Census Bureau. 2000. *Current Housing Reports, Series H150/99, American Housing Survey for the United States: 1999.* Washington, DC: GPO.

U.S. Census Bureau. 2001. *Current Housing Reports, Series H151/95-1, Supplement to the American Housing Survey for the United States in 1995.* Washington, DC: GPO.

Venti, Steven F., and David A. Wise. 2001. *Aging and Housing Equity: Another Look.* Working Paper 8608. Cambridge, MA: National Bureau of Economic Research.

*Stephen M. Golant*

**HOSPICE CARE,** specialized care for people during the last phases of illness so that they may live as fully and comfortably as possible. Hospices provide palliative care (pain relief and symptom management) to terminally ill patients and supportive services to patients, their families, and significant others in home- and facility-based settings. Hospice services focus on physical, social, spiritual, and emotional care during the final stages of illness and during bereavement by a clinically directed interdisciplinary team consisting of patients, their families, professionals, and volunteers.

The National Hospice and Palliative Care Organization (NHPCO) estimates there are over 3,100 operational hospice programs (including some with multiple locations) in the United States, including the District of Columbia, the Commonwealth of Puerto Rico, and the territory of Guam. Hospices admitted approximately 700,000 patients in 2000. In 2000, 55% of hospice patients were female and 45% were male; approximately 81% were aged 65 or older. Of all hospice patients, 57% were diagnosed with cancer, 10% had heart-related diagnoses, 6% had dementia, 3% had end-stage kidney disease, 2% had end-stage liver disease, and 16% had other diagnoses. The average length of time a patient received hospice services in 2000 was 48 days (NHPCO 2001).

Hospice provides a coordinated program of services in a variety of home- and facility-based settings. The primary setting for hospice care is the patient's home. The Medicare Hospice Benefit includes a comprehensive set of services in all settings. Covered services include nursing care, which may be continuous during periods of crisis to maintain a patient at home; medical social service; physician service; counseling service; pastoral care; short-term inpatient and respite care; medical appliances and supplies; drugs for symptom management and pain control; home health aide and homemaker services; physical, speech, and occupational therapies; and bereavement counseling. These services are coordinated by an interdisciplinary team of professionals and delivered according to the patient's individualized plan of care. Volunteers are also fundamental to the hospice philosophy and play an integral role in providing care. In a requirement unique to hospice programs, Medicare asks hospices to use volunteers in administrative or direct patient care roles equal to 5% of the total patient care hours of all paid hospice employees.

Hospice care is financed through a number of sources, including Medicare, Medicaid, private insurance plans, patients, and charity funds. In 2000, Medicare and Medicaid accounted for approximately two-thirds of hospice revenues. Medicare reimbursement for hospices is on a prospective, per diem basis, at four different rates relating to the level of home or inpatient care provided. Medicare also imposes an annual aggregate cap on hospice care; for the fiscal year ending October 31, 2001, it was calculated on a per patient basis of $16,650.85.

Medicare covers hospice services when the beneficiary elects the Medicare Hospice Benefit, where the patient is certified by two physicians as terminally ill with a life expectancy of six months or less, and when care is provided by a Medicare-certified hospice program. Once hospice is elected, the beneficiary waives traditional Medicare coverage for the terminal illness, and the hospice benefit covers the four levels of care routine: home care, continuous home care, respite, and general inpatient care. All services are covered with the exception of the patient's attending physician, who bills directly to Medicare Part B. Hospices may require coinsurance from Medicare beneficiaries only for drugs and inpatient respite care. Coinsurance may not exceed 5% of the cost of a prescription (up to a $5 maximum) or 5% of the payment made by Medicare for an inpatient respite day (Lewin-VHI, Inc. 1995).

Interest in hospice care has grown because of its cost-effectiveness relative to conventional care. As has been widely publicized, 28% of all Medicare expenditures (more than $40 billion in 1992) are for people in their last year of life, and almost 50% of these costs are expended in the last two months of life. The federally sponsored evaluation of the first three years of the Medicare Hospice Benefit (Kidder, Merrell, and Dohan 1989) found significant savings for hospice care compared with conventional care. For example, for every dollar spent on hospice care, Medicare saved $1.26. During the last month of life, hospice care averages $3,069, while conventional care costs $4,071 (Lewin-VHI, Inc. 1994). A 1995 Lewin-VHI study, commissioned by NHPCO, showed that for every dollar Medicare spent on hospice, it saved $1.52 in Medicare Part A and Part B expenditures. The 1995 study also showed that in the last year of life, hospice patients incurred $2,737 less in costs than those not enrolled under the Medicare Hospice Benefit. These savings totaled $3,192 in the last month of life, as hospice home care days often substituted for expensive hospitalizations. Other data indicate that hospice patients paid significantly fewer out-of-pocket costs than conventional care patients. According to the National Hospice Study, hospice patients receiving waived medical services under the hospice demonstration project paid about $6 per day in out-of-pocket costs, while hospice patients not receiving waived services under the demonstration project paid $23 per day, and conventional care patients spent $46 per day (Mor, Green, and Kastenbaum 1988).

A recent NHPCO study indicates that the cost to provide aggressive, comprehensive end-of-life care is outpacing Medicare's payments to the hospices that provide the care. The study reveals an average 10% to 20% shortfall between the costs of delivering hospice care and Medicare's reimbursement for the nation's hospice care providers. Particularly striking are the rising costs for prescription medications and outpatient therapies (NHPCO and Milliman 2001).

Research on hospice care also has focused on quality. There is reasonably strong evidence that hospice care provides better quality of life for patients and caregivers. Although it is difficult to evaluate quality of life scientifically, based on available data, significant differences were found in five quality-of-life measures for hospice and conventional care patients. These include measures of pain, satisfaction with interpersonal care, satisfaction with involvement with care, quality of care, and patient's social involvement with the support system. Significant differences were also found to favor hospice in four measures used to evaluate the quality of life of the primary caregiver. Hospice primary caregivers were less anxious and were more satisfied with their involvement in care than the conventional caregivers.

Hospice has been successful in today's health care environment because it addresses people's fears about dying in pain, alone, and without personal dignity. Hospice is particularly important because of its strong emphasis on coordination of services, patient participation in care planning, and patient choice. While the growth of hospice care has been steady over the last decade, its value is becoming more widely known and will undoubtedly increase as the population ages. A recent Gallup Poll suggested that almost 90% of Americans would prefer to use the services commonly associated with hospice care if they were terminally ill rather than undergo multiple hospitalizations, nursing home placements, or disorganized home care treatment. Hospice provides a choice to the terminally ill patient for whom a traditional medical model, with its technological imperative, may no longer be appropriate. (See also ADVANCE DIRECTIVES; HEALTH MAINTENANCE ORGANIZATIONS AND MANAGED HEALTH CARE FOR

OLDER ADULTS; HOME CARE SERVICES FOR OLDER ADULTS; LIVING WILL; MEDICAID; MEDICARE.)

### Organizations

Hospice Association of America
National Hospice and Palliative Care Organization
National Hospice Foundation

### Suggested Readings

Health Care Financing Administration. 2000. *Medicare: Hospice Benefits*. Publication No. HCFA 02154. Baltimore, MD: Author.

National Hospice Foundation. *Hospice Care: A Consumer's Guide to Selecting a Hospice Program; Communicating Your End-of-Life Wishes; The Medicare Hospice Benefit*. Available online at http://www.hospiceinfo.org/.

### References

Gallup Organization. 1996. "Knowledge and Attitudes to Hospice Care." Alexandria, VA: National Hospice Organization.

Kidder, D., K. Merrell, and D. Dohan. 1989. *Medicare Hospice Benefit Program Evaluation: Final Summary Report*. Cambridge, MA: Abt Associates, Inc.

Lewin-VHI, Inc. 1994. *Hospice Care: An Introduction and Review of the Evidence*. Arlington, VA: National Hospice Organization.

Lewin-VHI, Inc. 1995. *An Analysis of the Cost Savings of the Medicare Hospice Benefit*. Arlington, VA: National Hospice Organization.

Mor, V., D.S. Greer, and R. Kastenbaum. 1988. *The Hospice Experiment*. National Hospice Study. Baltimore, MD: Johns Hopkins University Press.

National Hospice and Palliative Care Organization (NHPCO). 2000. *NHPCO Standards of Practice for Hospice Programs*. Alexandria, VA: Author.

National Hospice and Palliative Care Organization (NHPCO). 2001. "NHPCO Facts and Figures." Available online at http://www.nhpco.org/.

National Hospice and Palliative Care Organization and Milliman USA. 2001. *The Costs of Hospice Care: An Actuarial Evaluation of the Medicare Hospice Benefit*. Alexandria, VA: Author.

*Christine Cody*

**HOUSING COUNSELING FOR OLDER AMERICANS,** educational and counseling services for seniors who are experiencing changes or problems with their present housing situation. While housing counseling is offered to the entire population, there are many types of counseling that address the problems that are specific to the older population. The following sections will explore the background of housing counseling; the present status of the industry; the basic elements of the housing counseling process; and the types of counseling services specifically offered to seniors.

### Background of Housing Counseling

The housing counseling industry came into existence through the passage of the 1968 Housing and Urban Development (HUD) Act. Under this legislation, HUD could authorize public and private organizations to provide counseling to mortgagors under its basic single-family mortgage insurance program. Other legislative milestones continued to shape the industry in later years. A 1969 amendment to the original legislation allowed HUD to authorize additional entities to provide counseling and even expanded counseling to include topics such as money management and child care. In 1971, HUD set up a system to approve housing counseling agencies that could serve low- and moderate-income home buyers. The following year, HUD required approved counselors to help implement the assignment program, largely due to an epidemic of defaults that had begun to occur on FHA (Federal Housing Administration)-insured mortgages. In 1972, Congress appropriated $2.5 million to fund the housing counseling work of 31 private agencies in 19 cities nationwide (Feins et al. 1980).

Also during 1972, HUD initiated a two-year demonstration program to assist mortgagors who were delinquent under its Section 235 and Section 237 programs (U.S. Department of Housing and Urban Development 1983). It was only in 1974 that legislation authorized HUD to fund counseling efforts. Section 801 of the 1974 Housing and Community Development Act authorized HUD to grant funding for housing counseling agencies. Funding for HUD's Housing Counseling Program (HCP) has been a source of controversy since its inception, however. Over a period of several years covering many administrations, both HUD and Congress have exhibited alternating strategies for funding the HCP. While Congress agreed philosophically with the notion that counseling prior to homeownership would assist marginally creditworthy, lower-income families in developing the skills to become a successful homeowner, funds were not appropriated continuously for housing counseling until 1977 (U.S. Department of Housing and Urban Development 1983). It was even suggested during the mid-1970s that some housing counseling programs shifted roles from educating the housing consumer to consumer advocacy in light of documented abuses by the housing industry and HUD in its housing counseling programs (Organization for Social and Technical Innovation 1974). During the 1977 fiscal year, funding for counseling efforts began to be appropriated regularly, and the funds set aside for counseling efforts grew from $3 million in 1977 to $12 million in 1993. In 1977 and 1987, HUD legislation broadened counseling to include all of its various single-family homeowner programs, emergency homeownership situations, and home equity conversion programs (Quercia and Wachter 1996). From 1968 to 1982, the percentage of agencies that participated in the HCP and were funded by HUD fluctuated but averaged roughly 16% per year. Nevertheless, funding through HCP was never a consistent or substantial source of funding for most counseling agencies. Other sources of funding included dollars from Community Development Block Grant programs and those from various other federal state and local service delivery programs, which appear to have been utilized to a far greater extent (U.S. Department of Housing and Urban Development 1983). In the spring of 1983, Congress called upon HUD to document "reasonable" housing counseling practices as well as counselor training procedures.

By 1983, of the approximately 600 certified agencies nationwide, approximately 240 received HUD grants in that year (Heintz, Schare, and Turner 1984). After the mild recession and credit crunch of 1989–1991, the industry began to grow precipitously. It was during this period that the industry began to see a large number of housing counseling providers being established. By the end of 1993, it is estimated that over 1,000 counseling agencies and organizations were receiving some form of financial support from both states and the Fannie Mae Foundation (Quercia and Wachter 1996). Perhaps the most significant change within the industry that occurred during the late 1980s and early 1990s is that there was a marked change in the industry's orientation, shifting from primarily a postpurchase default prevention to a prepurchase homeownership program (McCarthy and Quercia 2000).

### Present Status of the Housing Counseling Industry

Despite the fact that the housing counseling industry has been around for decades, the industry has not received much attention until recently. Affordable homeownership programs are expanding across the country, however, and they include homeownership education and counseling as a fundamental component of their strategies. As a result, there are literally thousands of organizations and entities that provide housing counseling services to low- and moderate-income borrowers.

To some in the housing field, counseling is seen as a wasteful, time-consuming, or unnecessary exercise. Rather than embracing the housing counseling concept, some realtors and mortgage bankers have tried to avoid dealing with potential borrowers who state that they are interested in participating in some of the homeownership programs that require a borrower to undertake housing counseling. Furthermore, the fragmented and diverse nature of counseling across agencies, along with the lack of regulation, has many within the housing industry worried about the quality of services delivered by housing counseling and education agencies. This question of quality has become even more important to the banking community in recent years, as the number of commercial banks shrinks through mergers and acquisitions and the local community bank becomes less common in today's society. Slowly, however, the attitudes and feelings toward housing counseling have begun to change, thanks to a proliferation of first-time homebuyer programs and various other initiatives by federal and local governments to help spur participation in the industry by those living in underserved markets. For example, HUD decided in 1996 to reduce user costs of the FHA single-family mortgage insurance program for those home buyers who undergo homeownership counseling. In this arrangement, HUD would cut the up-front mortgage insurance premium from 2.25% to 1.75% of the mortgage amount for home buyers who successfully completed the counseling programs *before* settlement on their home (McCarthy and Quercia 2000). HUD does not, however, require a minimum amount of counseling, nor does it specify a particular type of course curriculum for counselors and educators to follow. The training may be received in either a classroom or in a one-on-one setting.

Today, HUD's Housing Counseling Program has three strategic goals: (1) to improve the quality of renter and homeowner education; (2) to develop a reliable stream of funding and resources for homeownership counseling agencies; and (3) to enhance coordination among local housing providers. In its capacity, HCP funds HUD-approved local housing counseling agencies; national, regional, or multistate intermediaries; and state housing finance agencies that provide counseling and education services. Aside from providing basic counseling services, HUD-approved housing counseling agencies are permitted and even encouraged to conduct community outreach activities with the objective of increasing awareness of homeownership opportunities and improving low- and moderate-income households' access to sources of mortgage credit.

There have even been some social and professional changes related to the industry occurring during the past few years that are worth noting. There has been tremendous growth of personal financial literacy programs in the United States since the mid-1990s. For those populations in which the home-buying process is seen as unfamiliar, formidable, and unattainable, financial literacy programs may be the only remedy available to the underserved market (Vitt et al. 2000). Encouraging steps have been taken by public policy practitioners to help improve the general financial knowledge of people young and old.

### Basic Elements of the Housing Counseling Process

Although housing counseling organizations differ greatly in their structure and function, there are roughly four essential elements of the housing counseling process that most agencies seek to follow. These elements are described in more detail below.

First, counselors seek to establish a working relationship with the housing client in need. It is important that the counselor conveys the message to the client that the counseling experience is essentially a partnership in which both parties understand each other's objectives clearly. The housing counselor must also be supportive of the client's efforts to realize his or her objectives. A standard of confidentiality is therefore crucial in cementing this partnership relationship. Above all, it is imperative that clients who seek counseling, especially those who are experiencing trouble in meeting their bills on time, do not feel as if they are being judged by counselors. Judgmental and subjective behavior on the part of the housing counselor could stigmatize these people from receiving help by a housing counselor in the future, which in the long run could worsen the delinquency problem. In immigrant populations, the housing counselor can also play a vital role by providing low-cost information and consumer outreach in nontraditional markets. This allows counselors to cross cultural and linguistic barriers and helps build community trust in local lending institutions and in the mortgage marketplace.

The second element of the counseling experience is the ability to successfully analyze the problem. A client's problems may be myriad, such as a borrower's lack of familiarity with the housing market; lack of a preplanned budget; lack of understanding of what kinds of features should be available in a standard single-family home; inability to recognize potential hazards such as lead-based paint; overcoming a bad credit rating; familiarity with rights of renters; and a lack of understanding of one's own fair housing rights. Of course, in delinquency counseling, the problems become a little more obvious as people enter the counseling relationship after realizing that they need to improve their personal budgeting habits, especially after a personal financial crisis.

The third part of the housing counseling process involves setting goals for the client. After analyzing the problem, it only makes logical sense that the counselor be involved in the client's setting reasonable, actionable, specific, and tangible goals for the client to reach with the hopes of eradicating the existing or potential delinquency problem. By working together to set and establish these goals, this phase allows the client to further realize that the counselor's relationship with him or her is indeed a partnership, while still realizing that the eradication of the problem in its most fundamental forms still must come from within the person seeking help. The culmination of this particular phase will involve the implementation of a corrective action plan to which the client must adhere.

The final phase of the counseling experience involves the evaluation of the client's results. This process should be a continuous one for the counselor and the client and really just encompasses a follow-up of the client's progress. In order to be effective in this phase, the counselor should be open to reevaluating the goals of the client and his or her corrective action plan as the situation changes. If the client is having troubles in meeting his or her goals, then a new corrective action plan may be formulated.

While the elements of the housing counseling and education intervention are roughly the same for all housing counseling agencies, the program content may in fact vary across agencies. With limited funding available to counseling agencies and local housing issues dominating the efforts of counseling providers, a wide variety of counseling approaches have emerged. Many counseling providers develop their own curriculum and educational materials, yet programs differ according to the topics covered, the breadth and depth of instruction, and the specific goals of the counseling agencies.

### Types of Counseling Services Offered to Seniors

Much of the recent attention on housing counseling services has been focused on counseling efforts tied toward first-time homebuyers. While this is not likely to be an area that seniors utilize often, there are still a wide variety of situations in which seniors feel it is wise to seek the services of a housing counseling agency or provider.

*Reverse Mortgage Counseling*. By far the most common situation in which homeowners seek out the services of a housing counselor is when they are interested in making a reverse mortgage transaction or a Home Equity Conversion Mortgage (HECM). While reverse mortgage counseling services are offered in many areas nationwide, this type of counseling service is perhaps most commonly utilized in areas that serve older neighborhoods containing predominantly "house-rich but cash-poor" older residents with homes of moderate to high value. Many times, counselors will meet with such clients to discuss the advantages and disadvantages of taking on a reverse mortgage. Effective counseling measures on this topic will usually advise the client on (1) the realistic payment streams, tax consequences, and overall financial implications that he or she can expect to receive from entering into a reverse mortgage transaction; (2) other types of financial options that might be available to the homeowner, other than the reverse mortgage; (3) the most reputable lenders of the reverse mortgage product in the area; and (4) possibly even detailed suggestions for legal assistance to ensure favorable contract terms for the client. Currently, FHA and Fannie Mae require reverse mortgage counselors to be certified before offering counseling services on their respective products. FHA goes even further by requiring seniors to receive counseling, in order to be eligible for a federally insured HECM. In many cases, counseling providers are also given educational materials developed in the 1990s by the AARP. Because of the growing popularity of the reverse mortgage and the increasing rise in age of the population, one can expect that reverse mortgage counseling services will grow in magnitude and importance in the future.

*Predatory Lending*. Because older adults are often targets for fraud and abuse (along with low-income and minority populations) by financial services companies, many counseling entities are devoting more attention to the topic of predatory lending. In low-income communities, seniors are especially at risk for becoming victims of predatory lenders, because of the lack of available mainstream banking options available to them. As a result, "subprime" lenders have proliferated throughout these communities, all the while operating under a largely unregulated environment. Although predatory lending has been hard to define in specific terms, housing specialists and public policy officials usually define predatory lending activities as including such practices as (1) steering to high-rate lenders, (2) lending to people who cannot afford the loan, (3) offering exceedingly high interest rates and/or points, (4) inflating appraisal costs, and (5) requiring excessive prepayment penalties, just to name a few. Aside from these situations, seniors may find themselves particularly at risk from predatory lenders in situations involving unnecessary refinancings and unscrupulous reverse mortgage lenders. Housing counselors provide information and education that many mainstream banks and financial service centers can and will provide mortgage services to borrowers at more favorable terms than subprime lenders, regardless of where one is located.

*Fair Housing/Tenant Counseling.* This type of counseling service is offered in many counseling agencies nationwide. Because of the myriad issues that renters face both during their search for housing and after they have moved in, many counseling agencies classify types of tenant counseling into pre- and postoccupancy counseling services. Among other things, tenant counseling helps to (1) explain tenant and landlord legal rights, as well as rights under the Fair Housing Laws; (2) make suggestions about disputes; (3) advise renters on how to handle potential situations involving housing discrimination by age and race; and (4) inform counselees on how to deal with federal and local government assistance programs. Many housing counselors even go so far as to intercede on behalf of the client if he or she is in default on rent payment and is in danger of being evicted from his or her property.

*Other Types of Counseling.* Because there are many things that occur during one's housing situation, it is understandable that a variety of other housing counseling services are available to older clients who have special needs. Seniors are as much in need of default counseling as other members of the general population. Default counseling involves intervening on behalf of a homeowner client who is in arrears on his or her mortgage payments and who may be later thrust into a foreclosure situation as a result. Similarly, a wide array of counselors also provide homelessness prevention counseling. Because homelessness is a growing problem in many areas where housing is unaffordable, counselors can work with older clients to determine how best to avoid homelessness. In heavily populated older immigrant communities, counselors also provide many valuable services. These agencies cater specifically to immigrant populations by providing language services and advice on neighborhoods in which the new immigrants can live. In some situations, older immigrants get caught up in experiencing the "American Dream" of homeownership and decide to purchase a home for the first time—a goal that might have been impractical in their birth nation. Prepurchase housing counselors can certainly help older immigrants navigate the complicated and cumbersome process of applying for a mortgage. Also, there are housing counselors in progressive seniors communities that provide relocation services for older Americans. These specialty counselors provide information on assisted living options and facilities available to seniors as well as information on rental communities for seniors who are interested in downsizing living conditions for their retirement years. Finally, as the older population becomes increasingly more active over time, housing counseling agencies may offer an abundance of home improvement workshops that are led by local area experts. (See also CONTINUING CARE RETIREMENT COMMUNITIES [CCRCs]; GERIATRIC CARE MANAGERS [GCMs]; GERONTOLOGICAL SOCIAL WORK; HOME MODIFICATIONS FINANCING; HOMEOWNERSHIP; REVERSE MORTGAGES.)

**References**

Feins, Judith, D. Bain, Jr., L. Dixon, and John A. Kirlin. 1980. *Results of the Prepurchase Homeownership Counseling Demonstration*. Cambridge, MA: Abt Associates, Inc.

Heintz, Kathleen G., Ann B. Schnare, and Margery A. Turner. 1984. *Report on Housing Counseling Agencies*. Washington, DC: Urban Institute.

McCarthy, George W., and Roberto G. Quercia. 2000. *Bridging the Gap between Supply and Demand: The Evolution of the Homeownership Education and Counseling Industry*. Washington, DC: Research Institute for Housing America.

Organization for Social and Technical Innovation. 1974. *An Evaluation of the HUD Concentrated Default Counseling Program*. Newton, MA: Author.

Quercia, Roberto G., and Susan M. Wachter. 1996. "Homeownership Counseling Performance: How Can It Be Measured?" *Housing Policy Debate* 7(1): 175–201.

U.S. Department of Housing and Urban Development. 1983. *Report to Congress on Housing Counseling*. Washington, DC: Author.

Vitt, Lois A., C. Anderson, J. Kent, Deanna M. Lyter, Jurg K. Siegenthaler, and J. Ward. 2000. *Personal Finance and the Rush to Competence: Financial Literacy Education in the U.S.* Middleburg, VA: Institute for Socio-Financial Studies.

*Andrew Carswell*

**HUD-ASSISTED RENTAL HOUSING,** programs enacted under the National Housing Act (NHA) of 1937, as amended, and administered by the U.S. Department of Housing and Urban Development (HUD). Financial help is provided for older Americans through a variety of public, private, and nonprofit sponsorships where rent is based on a rent-to-income ratio for eligible tenants. Three HUD programs have provided the rent-subsidized housing units that serve the U.S. older population (aged 62 and older): Conventional Low-Rent Public Housing, Section 202 Program, and the Section 8 Program.

Shelter is a basic need that can consume the major portion of a monthly budget. For older people on fixed incomes, housing costs can be overwhelming. Although regulations, requirements, and financing arrangements concerning housing development and tenant subsidies vary, the financial impact on older persons who participate in these rental assistance programs is essentially the same. It is this impact, rather than the subtle differences between programs, that is valuable to understand.

Approximately 1.5 million older families are helped through various HUD-assisted housing programs. According to HUD's 1998 *Picture of Subsidized Households*, HUD housing programs served approximately 37% of older American households with some form of their housing assistance. The Section 8 New Construction and Substantial Rehabilitation program, where most of the property is owned and operated by nonprofit sponsors, provides the bulk of assisted housing to seniors. The Public and Indian Housing Authorities provide the second largest number of apartments to the senior group.

Of major interest to the financial issues of our current and future seniors is their income distribution. This information was developed for the Commission on Affordable Housing and Health Facility Needs for Seniors in the 21st Century, published in 2002. See Figure 1.

Income distribution is an important factor in determining eligibility for assistance in HUD-assisted housing programs. In some instances, those with incomes of less than 80% of their area's median income are eligible for housing assistance. Those seniors with incomes of 50% or less of area median income (AMI) are more likely to apply for such

**Figure 1**
**Income Distribution of 65+ Population, by Area Median Income, 2000**

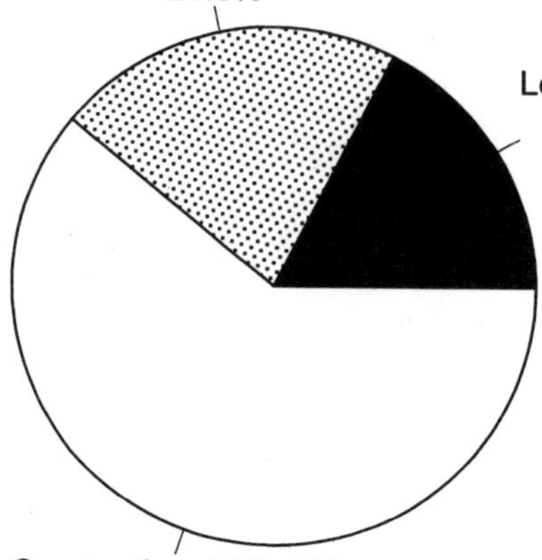


*Source*: Commission on Affordable Housing and Health Facility Needs for Seniors in the 21st Century 2002.

assistance. According to the commission's study, the Current Population Survey classifies 39% of current seniors falling into this "less than 50% category of area median income" and being eligible for HUD-assisted rental programs.

Conventional public housing projects for older adults in most communities are high-rise or garden complexes that are owned, operated, and maintained by local public housing agencies. There are about 3,000 agencies in various U.S. communities, not including American Indian housing authorities. These agencies may acquire, construct, modernize, or lease low-income housing for older individuals and husband-wife couples. Local agency-owners strive to make their developments appear no different from those offered by private owners at market rates. Financial assistance to subsidize operations and maintenance of these properties is funded by HUD to the local agency. In some areas (often large cities) housing supported under these programs is poorly regarded. It sometimes is badly managed and has received negative press. In other areas, particularly small- and medium-sized communities, local agencies provide quality programs, and the housing developments they manage are favorably regarded.

The Section 202 Program, enacted under the NHA in 1959, finances construction by nonprofit sponsors of low-rent apartment developments for older persons and the non-older disabled populations. Originally intended to serve older persons with incomes somewhat higher than Public Housing tenants, 202-funded apartment projects were combined with the Section 8 housing assistance program in 1974, making the units available to lower-income older adults. Tenants spend 30% of their incomes on rent and utilities. Operating deficits are covered by monthly subsidies from HUD. Many of the developments built under Section 202 contain community rooms and recreational services and are outfitted with ramped entries, grab bars, and other design features necessary for older adults residents.

Under the Section 8 Certificate Program, an older adult person or family is issued a certificate attesting to their qualification for rental assistance. An eligible older adult person or family finds suitable housing in the private marketplace and can choose either 202-funded housing run by nonprofit sponsors for older adult persons or privately owned and operated houses or apartments. The Section 8 Certificate represents a commitment to the landlord in either case to pay the difference between what the individual or family can afford to pay and the market rent. Market rents are determined and approved for housing unit types located within particular geographic areas or regions. They represent the maximum rent that would be charged for an apartment by a private landlord. The local housing authority maintains a schedule of approved fair market rents.

The Section 8 Program also includes nonprofit or limited profit, privately owned, and managed housing for older adult residents. The difference from the Certificate approach is that the subsidy is allocated to the individual units, and if a family qualifies, application is made directly to the owner or manager of the privately sponsored, assisted housing development. Services geared to the needs and concerns of an older community may also be provided. They may include free, on-site medical screening, transportation services, meals-on-wheels, and recreation activities at low or no additional cost to residents.

### A Case Illustration

John and Mary Jones are former homeowners now in their late sixties. When their children were grown and gone, they sold their home and rented a two-bedroom apartment for $650, plus utilities that averaged $100 per month. A working-class family, home equity was their only asset, and the amount cleared from the sale of their home was $95,000. They gave their son $15,000 toward a downpayment on his own house and saved $75,000, which now earns interest in a combination of certificates of deposit and passbook savings rates of 3%. Their second-story, walk-up apartment consumes approximately 50% of their monthly income, and their health costs are rising. Mary's arthritis is making it difficult for her to climb stairs. Rents, however, are increasing in the community, and John and Mary can find no affordable ground-level alternative—even a smaller apartment.

To learn whether John and Mary are eligible for federal assistance, their total annual income must be calculated. From combined Social Security and pension payments, they receive income of $15,096 plus $2,350 in interest income, for a total of $17,446. Although the Jones's own a car, jewelry, and other personal effects, these are not counted within the asset definitions, which include only the $75,000 in savings.

Income is the major criterion that qualifies older persons for rental assistance. Amounts are based on the median income for the standard metropolitan statistical area in which the housing is located. Therefore, differences exist in income eligibility criteria throughout the United States. Eligibility income for New York City, for example, would be considerably higher than for Brownsville, Texas. Eligibility is based on personal income in relation to others' personal incomes in their geographic location. Conventional Public Housing apartments allow a family to earn as much as 80% of median income for their area and remain eligible. The Section 8 Housing Assistance Program limits eligibility to 50% of median income for the area.

In almost all geographic areas, John and Mary Jones would qualify under the Conventional Public Housing Program. In many areas, they also would qualify for the lower-income eligibility requirements of the Section 8 Program. John and Mary would be eligible, under federal rules, for a one-bedroom apartment, and a rent-to-income formula would be used to determine the rent they must pay. Rent is based on a family's total annual income, less deductions for individual circumstances. Since most older people do not have children and are not working, two types of deductions are most applicable. The first is an Older Adults Family deduction of $400 for a family head or spouse over age 62. The second is for excessive medical costs. Medical expenses must be substantiated and not reimbursed by medical insurance or other sources.

Mary's arthritic condition is likely to satisfy the excessive medical cost requirement, since she incurs out-of-pocket, nonreimbursed expenses of $750 a year for medical insurance, doctor visits, physical therapy, prescription, and over-the-counter drug purchases connected to her arthritis. After the medical deduction allowance is calculated, the Jones's may deduct $227 for allowable medical expenses plus the $400 allowance for older adult families. Their adjusted income is $16,319.

The formula that must now be applied to determine whether the family's rent is the greater of 30% of monthly adjusted income ($436) or 10% of monthly annual income ($145). In a federally assisted apartment, John and Mary would be expected to pay $436 a month as rent. Since both the Conventional Public Housing and Section 8 Programs, under statute, must provide both shelter and utilities in the total tenant payment, this would reduce the Jones's housing and utility cost by approximately 40% per month.

The Joneses could explore the availability of housing under the Conventional Public Housing, Section 8 Program or private, nonprofit-sponsored housing program using Section 8 federal assistance. In the case of Conventional Public Housing, the Joneses would submit their application to the local housing authority in their community.

Under the Section 8 Certificate Program, the housing authority or agency administering the Section 8/Voucher program establishes the maximum local rent (market rent) for a one-bedroom apartment. Apartments owned by private landlords who meet the Housing Quality Standards set by HUD, who are willing to accept the established market rent established for the local area, would be another option for the Joneses. Private nonprofit organizations who have developed Section 8 New Construction are also another option for John and Mary.

Conventional Public Housing developed and managed by local agencies, together with Section 202 and Section 8 New Construction developed and managed by local nonprofit groups, provide a wide range of ancillary support services to their older adult residents. Common services could include a Senior Center where lunch is available at minimal cost, as well as blood pressure checks and other health screening services. They also may organize social events, trips, and transportation services.

In March 2002, HUD competitive funding became available for the Assisted Living Conversion Program for Eligible Multifamily Developments. This Notice of Funds Availability and the Commission on Affordable Housing and Health Facility Needs for Seniors in the 21st Century are clear indicators that current levels of assistance will not support the needs of the future. In the year 2020, the number of senior households is expected to grow by nearly 53%. The number of seniors in need of affordable housing will also increase at a steady pace. The Seniors Commission Report projects that in 2020, 730,000 additional rent-assisted units will be needed to accommodate the senior households age 65 and older who are likely to have housing problems at the same 5.8 to 1 ratio at which they are accommodated today (Commission on Affordable Housing and Health Facility Needs for Seniors in the 21st Century 2002).

Further information on available federally assisted public housing in a particular locality can be obtained from the local housing authority, the municipal government, or the local HUD field office. (See also FINANCIAL COUNSELING FOR MID- TO LATER LIFE; HOMEOWNERSHIP; HOUSING COUNSELING FOR OLDER AMERICANS; MEANS-TESTING IN PUBLIC PROGRAMS; OLDEST OLD.)

### References

Commission on Affordable Housing and Health Facility Needs for Seniors in the 21st Century. 2002. *A Quiet Crisis in America: A Report to Congress*. Washington, DC: Author.

Foulest, E., and D. Yeas. 1994. *Housing the Aging Population*. New York: Garland Publishing.

Gloat, Stephen M. 1992. *Housing America's Older Adults*. Newbury Park, CA: Sage Publications.

National Association of Housing and Redevelopment Officials. 1981. *Public Housing Management Resource Manual*. Washington, DC: Author.

U.S. Department of Housing and Urban Development. 1989. *Programs of HUD, 1989–1990*. Publication 214-PA(17). Washington, DC: Author.

U.S. Department of Housing and Urban Development. 1994. *Report to the Congress on Older Adults Families, Families with Children, and Disabled Families Served by Federal Housing Programs*. Washington, DC: Author.

U.S. Department of Housing and Urban Development. 1998. *A Picture of Subsidized Households in 1998: United States Summaries*. Washington, DC: Author.

U.S. Senate. Special Committee on Aging. 1993. *Developments in Aging: 1993*. Publication 103-403. Washington, DC: GPO.

*Veronica M. Bukowski and Richard H. Stanton*

# I

**IDENTITY THEFT,** occurs when the identifying information of a person—name, Social Security number, mother's maiden name, or other personal information—is used to commit fraud or to engage in other unlawful activities. It is a silent, invisible crime.

Identity theft headed the top ten consumer fraud complaints in 2001, according to the Federal Trade Commission. This type of theft can be used for a myriad of illegal activities. According to Norman A. Willox, Jr. and Thomas M. Regan of NFC, Inc. (2001):

> Identity fraud is a drug trafficking problem. It is also a cyber crime problem as Eastern European criminals assume or make up passwords and user IDs to steal sensitive consumer data in order to extort unsuspecting companies. It is an alien smuggling problem, a gun-running problem and money-laundering problem. It is, as law enforcement officials have confirmed, a problem at the core of many different types of organized crime, committed locally, nationally and globally.

In the course of setting up bogus accounts, identity thieves typically provide banks and creditors with a false name and address to which bills are then routed. Victims are usually unaware that someone is exploiting their credit until months later when creditors call, demanding payment on fraudulent accounts. Though not responsible for the actual charges a thief runs up, victims must contend with harassing creditors and closed doors as they watch expenses accumulate in their name. In the end, it is consumers who absorb the considerable expense and damage wrought to the merchants, credit issuers, and the financial industry—as much as $11.9 billion a year, but they could actually be greater when law enforcement, criminal justice, attorney time, and merchant losses are tallied.

This is also a costly crime for its scope and breadth. Thefts average $17,000 per victim, with multiple victims exploited simultaneously. According to the Federal Trade Commission, identity theft topped the list of consumer fraud complaints in 2001. That year catalogued between 500,000 and 1.1 million victims. It is also growing at an alarming rate, making it the fastest-growing and most expensive consumer fraud in the country (Gregoire 2002). This explosive growth is catalogued daily; in November 2002, ringleaders of one of the largest identity theft rings victimized more than 30,000 people. Identity theft may also be used in conjunction with other criminal activity such as prostitution, drugs, and terrorism. According to Willox and Regan (2001), identity theft is an integral and indigenous part of most criminal attacks. It is suspected that the terrorist attacks of September 11, 2001, were orchestrated by a well-financed, highly motivated, and resourceful terrorist group who may have taken advantage of ineffective, or non-existent, identification systems.

The emotional cost to victims is considerable as well. Financial loss, even when temporary, can result in wage garnishment, tax refund withholding, or property liens. Furthermore, there can be problems finding employment, renting or purchasing a home, obtaining credit, or drawing from government benefits (Beales 2002). Everyone is vulnerable, as identity thieves may be in positions to have access to highly personal information. In May 2002, Ford Motor Credit Co. notified 13,000 people that their credit reports had been obtained through unauthorized inquiries by thieves who had gained access to Experian credit files. In many cases, an employee who has access to this sensitive information will steal and distribute thousands of consumers' personal files. In March 2002 a former employee of the Prudential Insurance Co. was arrested for selling names he extracted from a database of more than 60,000 policyholders (Fries 2002). In November 2002, a Teledata Communications Inc. employee was arrested for downloading and exploiting the personal identification records of more than 30,000 people (Masters 2002).

A study undertaken by Gartner, Inc. and the National Fraud Center found that 11.6% of consumers who earn $100,000 or more annually had their identities stolen, and 37.5% were victims of credit card fraud. Online shoppers are also vulnerable, according to another Gartner study, which reported that 5.2% of respondents were credit card victims in 2001, and 1.9% were identity theft victims. Gartner further reported that 1 in 12 online consumers has experienced identity theft. Holidays are a prime time for identity thieves. As Americans become more comfortable making purchases online, especially during holiday shopping seasons, they must be aware of the potential dangers on the other side of the modem.

State governments, through their Computer Crimes Units, are becoming increasingly aware of and attuned to this problem. Repercussions can include draining an entire bank account with just a few mouse clicks in the course of a few minutes. There are several problems with tracking and prosecuting identity theft crimes. It is often difficult for law enforcement agents to prosecute identity thieves. Agencies have difficulty exchanging information across state lines because of the ease, fluidity, and legality of selling and trading identification numbers. It is legal, for instance, for Internet companies to sell Social Security numbers and other personal identifying information to a third party. Despite proposed legislation to make this practice illegal, it is still commonly practiced.

### Identity Theft Detection

Evidence of identity theft will often first appear in a person's credit report. Three major companies maintain credit records and issue credit reports: Equifax, Experian, and TransUnion. The information tracked by these companies is a combination of data from banks, brokerage firms, insurance companies, debt collection agencies, courts, and local/regional credit bureaus. Not all companies collect the same information on each person; therefore, a person's credit information may vary from company to company. Approximately 4.5 billion individual bits of data are processed each month to create these individual credit histories (Forster 2002). These reports are then sold to organizations such as banks, brokerages, employers, landlords, utilities, hospitals, doctors, dentists, insurance companies, credit unions, finance companies, retailers, department stores, credit card companies, car dealers, mortgagors, investigators, lawyers, and courts. It is this massive exchange of information, which is easily bought and accessed, that in part has led to the rise in occurrences of identity theft.

### Protective Measures Against Identity Theft

Given that almost anyone who can offer a credit bureau a valid reason can order a person's credit history, financial experts urge consumers to regularly check their credit reports to ensure that no one's tampering with their files. They also recommend enrolling in a monitoring service that alerts them to any updated information. These services let customers know when any credit or identification activity occurs, when a new account is opened, or an inquiry is made into their credit file. By routinely monitoring their credit reports, or having an organization do it for them, consumers can become aware of possible problems before the problem is unmanageable.

There are also other measures consumers can take to protect themselves. Common preventative measures include shredding all documents that have personal identification information on them, limiting the use and disclosure of Social Security numbers, destroying credit offers, avoiding Web sites that ask for too much credit data, and reporting missing bills. Most experts, legislators, and industry leaders agree that there's no easy answer to the problem of identity theft. However, processes are being implemented that will make it more difficult to obtain a person's identification information.

Some proposed ideas include biometrically based "signatures" (verification of identity such as those based on hand or fingerprints) and authentication (use of uniquely identifying information). The private sector has also been enlisted in helping to prevent identity theft. Merchants have access to a wide range of tools, including address verification systems, fraud detection systems, and more consistent identity verification on check and credit card transactions. Overall, the best system will be one with several levels of identity verification. Yet the difficulty in this is that it is often easier and less costly for a merchant to write off a theft than it is for them to implement any of these systems.

### Contact Information

Credit reports are available directly from the credit bureaus: Equifax Inc., 1-800-685-1111; Experian (formerly TRW), 1-800-682-7654; and TransUnion, LLC, 1-800-916-8800. Some companies market three-in-one credit reports: Intersections, Inc., based in Chantilly, Virginia. (1-800-777-9700; http://www.intersections.com/), also offers a monitoring service that lets people know when information on their credit report changes. The better services offer live support that can help consumers differentiate errors from misunderstandings and out-and-out fraud.

### Actions to Take if a Victim of Identity Theft

1. Consumers should contact the three credit bureaus' fraud units, report the theft, and ask that a "fraud alert" be placed on their file and that no new credit be granted without their approval. Consumers should also keep a record of all communications. If enrolled in a monitoring program, contact its Fraud Protection Unit.

2. Consumers should notify all creditors and financial institutions, in writing and by phone, that their name and accounts have been used without permission. Accounts that

are thought to be the objects of theft should be closed, and new credit cards, checks, and account numbers should be issued. Any questionable or fraudulent activity should be reported to the issuing company immediately.

3. Consumers should file a police report with either local police or with the police in the community where the identity theft took place. Consumers should have a copy of this report in hand, as it may be necessary to send a copy to credit card companies, banks, and credit bureaus.

4. Crimes should also be reported to the Federal Trade Commission's ID Theft Clearinghouse toll-free at 1-877-IDTHEFT. The Identity Theft Hotline and the ID Theft Web site (http://www.consumer.gov/idtheft) also provide information and guidelines for those who are victims of identity theft. (See also CONSUMER CREDIT; CONSUMER PROTECTION FOR OLDER ADULTS; CRIME PROTECTION; FINANCIAL ELDER ABUSE; INTERNET USE BY SENIORS.)

### Organizations

Federal Trade Commission Response Center
Identity Theft Resource Center (ITRC)
Intersections, Inc.

### References

Beales, J. Howard. 2002. Senate Committee Hearing, March 20.

Bernstein, Jodie. 1999. "Financial Identity Theft." Prepared Statement for Presentation to the Subcommittee on Telecommunications, Trade and Consumer Protection and Subcommittee on Finance and Hazardous Materials of the House Committee on Commerce, April 22.

Forster, Stacy. 2002. "If Credit Report Firms Can Flag Errors, Why Not Do It for All?" *Wall Street Journal*, July 26.

Fries, Jacob H. 2002. "Worker Accused of Selling Colleagues' IDs Online." *New York Times*, March 2.

Gregoire, Christine O. 2002. *Identity Theft: Restoring Your Good Name*. Testimony to the U.S. Senate Committee on the Judiciary, March 20.

Masters, Brooke A. 2002. "Arrest Made in Identity Thefts." *Washington Post*, November 26.

Willox, Norman A., Jr., and Thomas M. Regan. 2001. "White Paper on Identity Theft." National Fraud Center, October 17.

*Louisa Woodville*

**INDIVIDUAL RETIREMENT ACCOUNT (IRA),** a personal retirement savings plan providing tax benefits and available to anyone regardless of age who receives taxable compensation during the year. For IRA contribution purposes, compensation includes wages, salaries, fees, tips, bonuses, commissions, taxable alimony, and separate maintenance payments. There are no minimum or required IRA contributions. Withdrawals at retirement may be in one lump sum, in the form of an annuity in installments over remaining life expectancy, or as a series of periodic withdrawals. Husbands and wives may each have an IRA, even if one person in that marriage is not working.

## Traditional IRA

A traditional IRA is an IRA available to those under age 70½ who have earned income (i.e., job compensation). Earnings within the traditional IRA are tax-deferred until withdrawal. Contributions to a traditional IRA may or may not be deductible in the tax year

**Table 1**
**Traditional and Roth IRA Annual Contribution Limits**

| Year | Normal Contribution | Catch-up Contribution |
|---|---|---|
| 2002 | $3,000 | $500 |
| 2003 | $3,000 | $500 |
| 2004 | $3,000 | $500 |
| 2005 | $4,000 | $500 |
| 2006 | $4,000 | $1,000 |
| 2007 | $4,000 | $1,000 |
| 2008 | $5,000 | $1,000 |
| 2009+ | Indexed* | $1,000 |

*Normal contribution limits are indexed in $500 increments.

made, depending on the owner's income tax filing status, adjusted gross income (AGI), and eligibility to participate in a tax-qualified retirement plan through employment. A person's annual contribution, whether made to just one or to multiple IRAs, is limited to the lesser of total taxable compensation or to the normal yearly amount shown in Table 1. Individuals over the age of 50 may make an additional catch-up contribution in the amount indicated for the year concerned.

If the traditional IRA owner participates in an employer's qualified retirement plan on any day in the tax year, the deductibility of contributions declines to zero between certain AGI ranges as shown in Table 2.

A working spouse not covered by a retirement plan through employment may make a tax-deductible contribution to a traditional IRA of up to the applicable annual limit shown in the contribution limits table despite the other spouse's coverage under an employer-provided retirement plan. When the couple's AGI reaches $150,000, deductibility for such contributions begins to decline, and it reaches zero at a joint AGI of $160,000.

Money may be withdrawn from an IRA at any time, but on withdrawal it may be taxed and/or penalized. Withdrawals from a traditional IRA will always be taxed, either in whole or in part, at ordinary income tax rates, except for the nondeductible part of contributions. Withdrawals from a traditional IRA prior to age 59½ will result in a 10% excise tax as well as an ordinary income tax. Mandatory distributions for traditional IRAs must begin no later than April 1 of the year after the IRA owner reaches age 70½. Failure to take required minimum distributions at that age results in a 50% excise tax on the amounts not distributed.

### Roth IRA

In contrast to the traditional IRA, a Roth IRA is one in which contributions to the account are not deductible for tax purposes, but contributions and earnings on contributions grow tax free, and "qualified" distributions (i.e., withdrawals) from the account

**Table 2**
**AGI Phaseout Limits for Deductible Traditional IRA**

| Year | Single Filer | Joint Filer |
|---|---|---|
| 2002 | \$34,000–\$44,000 | \$54,000–\$64,000 |
| 2003 | \$40,000–\$50,000 | \$60,000–\$70,000 |
| 2004 | \$45,000–\$55,000 | \$65,000–\$75,000 |
| 2005 | \$50,000–\$60,000 | \$70,000–\$80,000 |
| 2006 | \$50,000–\$60,000 | \$75,000–\$85,000 |
| 2007+ | \$50,000–\$60,000 | \$80,000–\$100,000 |

are not taxable. A "qualified" distribution from a Roth IRA is a withdrawal that meets one or more of the following:

1. Made after the taxpayer attains age 59½
2. Made to a beneficiary after the taxpayer's death
3. Made because the taxpayer is disabled
4. Made by a first-time homebuyer to acquire a principal residence.

Earnings on the account are taxable and subject to an early withdrawal penalty only when a withdrawal is not a "qualified" distribution.

Annual contributions to a Roth IRA are subject to the same contribution limits as a traditional IRA (shown in the contribution limits table), as reduced by any contribution made to a traditional IRA. Contributions to a Roth IRA may be made even after the owner reaches age 70½. The annual contribution limit is phased out as AGI increases from \$150,000 to \$160,000 (married filing jointly) or \$95,000 to \$110,000 (single filer).

Amounts in traditional IRAs may be transferred to Roth IRAs provided the taxpayer's AGI (married or single) for the transfer year is \$100,000 or less. Transferred amounts must be included in that year's income, but the money transferred will be exempt from the 10% excise tax for a withdrawal prior to age 59½. No withdrawal allocable to earnings on the transferred amounts is considered to be a qualified distribution unless it is made more than five tax years after the transfer.

### Education IRA (EIRA)

An Education IRA, also called the Coverdell Education Savings Account (ESA), is an account established to provide funds that will allow a beneficiary to attend a program of higher education. There is no tax deduction allowed for the contribution, but all deposits and earnings may be withdrawn free of tax and penalties if used to pay for the costs of higher education. Beginning in 2002, allowable contributions are \$2,000 per year with phaseouts beginning at \$150,000 for joint filers and \$95,000 for single filers. Contributions may be made regardless of the beneficiary's income but cannot be made on or after the beneficiary's eighteenth birthday. Plan proceeds may also be used free of tax and penalty to pay for the qualified expenses for kindergarten through twelfth grade education in public, private, and/or religious schools. If distributions exceed the education expenses, the earnings must be included in gross income and are subject to the 10% excise tax to the extent of the excess. The EIRA, if unused on or before age 30, may be transferred to another qualifying family member as the new beneficiary for educational use. Such transfers must occur before the beneficiary reaches age 30.

### Rollover (Conduit) IRA

A rollover IRA is a traditional IRA set up by an individual to receive a distribution from a qualified retirement plan. Distributions transferred to a rollover IRA are not subject to any contribution limits. Additionally, the distribution may be eligible for subsequent transfer into a qualified retirement plan available through a new employer. (See also CASH FLOW PLANNING FOR RETIREES; EARLY RETIREMENT INCENTIVE PlANS [ERIPs]; ESTATE PLANNING; FINANCIAL ADVISORS; KEOGH PLANS; MEDICAL SAVINGS ACCOUNTS (MSAs) AND MEDICAL IRAs; PENSION PLANS FOR THE SELF-EMPLOYED; RETIREMENT PLANNING; RETIREMENT PREPAREDNESS; WEALTH SPAN.)

#### References

Gitman, Lawrence J., and Michael D. Joehnk. 2002. *Personal Financial Planning*. 9th ed. Mason, OH: South-Western/Thomson Learning.

Keown, Arthur J. 2001. *Personal Finance*. Upper Saddle River, NJ: Prentice-Hall

The Motley Fool: Personal Finance Web site. Available online at http://www.fool.com/.

*Ganas K. Rakes and Rajesh Narayanan*

**INFLATION.** See Asset Allocation after Retirement; Bonds; Cash Flow Planning for Retirees; Cost-of-Living Adjustments (COLAs); Economic Hardship Measures in the Older Population; Equity Securities; Homeownership; Savings Investments.

**INFLUENCES ON RETIREMENT INVESTMENT DECISIONS** can be grouped into four categories: (1) retirement plan characteristics, (2) employee demographic characteristics, (3) psychological biases, and (4) social effects. Understanding this view of retirement investment influences may benefit plan sponsors, employees, researchers, and others interested in retirement investment behavior.

Increasingly, people are being asked to manage their own retirement savings. Over the past two decades, employee retirement plans have largely shifted from defined benefit plans predominantly managed by professionals to defined contribution plans (such as 401(k) plans) predominantly managed by employees. Yet most employees have difficulty reaping the benefits of managing their own retirement savings and, on average, do not make optimum investment decisions.

### Retirement Plan Characteristics

The more successful defined contribution benefit packages have several characteristics in common, all designed to encourage employee participation and build employee loyalty. These include a substantial contribution match, a greater number of investment options available to employees, the ability to make changes to the plan as often as the employee wishes, and access to targeted investment education programs and/or financial planning services (Hansen 1999).

Employee participation levels for 401(k) plans with employer matching contributions are 18% higher than for plans with no match (Hansen 1999). Most employers do offer some level of matching contributions; 69% of employers that offered 401(k) plans had a contribution match of at least 50%, according to KPMG's *Retirement Benefits in the 1990s: 1998 Survey Data* (1998).

However, while there may be greater participation levels when there is some level of employer match, the *amount* employees contribute decreases slightly when employers make matching contributions (Holden and VanDerhei 2001a). Nevertheless, the total contributions (employer and employee combined) are higher for employees who have employer contributions. It is therefore beneficial to the employee, and to the employer in terms of employee loyalty, for a company to offer some level of matching contribution, especially if it is equal to or greater than 50 cents to the dollar.

In addition, choice in investment options is important to employee participation in benefit plans. Fund types may include international funds, income (bond) funds, money market funds, growth funds, value funds, large cap funds, and mid/small cap funds. This range of choices is especially important to companies who have a heterogeneous and diverse workforce, as there are more options to accommodate the retirement needs of a greater range of employees. There are several reasons why companies may not offer a broad range of investment options. Of increasing importance is the unwillingness of companies to open themselves up to potential legal action by employees who have lost significant amounts of their retirement benefits due to unwise or uninformed asset allocation decisions. Companies may feel that their workforce is not substantially informed on how to invest wisely, and offering more options (especially higher-risk, higher-yield options) has the potential to be more damaging than beneficial over a given time period. Furthermore, a large number of investment choices may serve more to confuse employees than to assist them.

The ability for employees to make changes and adjustments to their retirement plans provides another way for employers to add value to their benefits packages. While it is mandated by law that there must be an "appropriate" number of periods during the year in which an employee is permitted to change his/her retirement plan's asset allocation, recent technological advances now enable many employers to offer employees daily access (and with it the ability to make daily changes) to their account. Interestingly, employees who have access to this type of system tend to take a fairly conservative view of their investments, preferring to take a longer-term view and not engage in daily trading (Hansen 1999).

Finally, educational programs for employees are also seen as a factor for increased employee participation in their company's retirement benefit plan. According to the 1998 KPMG study, participation rates in 401(k) plans are 5 percentage points higher (71% compared to 66%) when employers offer investment education programs than when they don't. Companies have become quite innovative in the programs offered to their employees. Examples include offering intra- and extra-net computer programs, models, and simulations by which employees can see "firsthand" the projected consequences of investment decisions, toll-free telephone investing for employees that spend a majority of their time on the road, and culturally sensitive, targeted programs for diverse work groups. When companies make employee participation in their benefit plans easy, accessible, and personal, employees are more willing to take advantage of benefit plans—thereby helping to build a strong, mutually reinforcing employer-employee relationship.

### *Other Factors Affecting Retirement Plan Participation*

Retirement plans that are structured with automatic enrollment have higher levels of participation than plans requiring employees to opt in (Madrian and Shea 2000, 2001). Other characteristics of the automatic enrollment plan, namely, the rate of contribution and fund allocation, can also influence investment behavior because there is a strong tendency by employees to maintain rates and allocations set as the plan's default options.

Although employees often use the default rates instead of actively choosing contribution amounts and allocations, many prefer *flexibility* in their retirement accounts. They fully expect to work for several different organizations during their working careers. As such, they desire the ability to control their retirement accounts through portability features (Dulebohn, Murray, and Sun 2000). A second flexibility characteristic is the option to borrow from one's 401(k) account. Holden and VanDerhei (2001a) find that participant contribution rates increase in plans that give employees the option to borrow from their accounts. There is a hidden danger, however, in this option. In the event of termination, downsizing, or leaving a position, the borrower may be required to pay back immediately the loan from his or her retirement account. If unable to do so, and if the holder is under 59½ years of age, he or she may be subject to a tax liability for the withdrawn amount, plus a 10% penalty. According to David Wray, president of the Profit Sharing Council, "[Someone] might be obligating [himself] to pay back that loan at one of life's worst times" (Smartmoney.com 2003).

## Employee Demographic Characteristics

Employee demographic characteristics (such as age, income, and job tenure) influence 401(k) participation rates, contribution rates, and allocation preferences. An employee's *age* is associated with several 401(k) plan investment decisions. First, participation rates increase with age. Second, participants who are older tend to contribute more. However, the relationship between employee asset allocation decisions and age appear to be more complicated. Financial advisors usually recommend that the portion of investments allocated to equities decline as the employee's investment horizon declines. A common rule of thumb is that the portion of a portfolio allocated to equities be 100 minus their age. Accordingly, the 30-year-old employee "should" have 70% in equities, and the 60-year-old "should" have 40% in equities. Indeed, younger employees tend to allocate larger portions of their accounts and contributions to equity funds, and older employees tend to allocate more to fixed income securities and bonds. This is somewhat complicated by the fact that employees rarely change their asset allocation after making the initial decisions. Therefore, the realized allocation to equities is mostly a function of the initial decision and the realized returns over time of each asset class.

The most important determinant of participation in an employer-sponsored 401(k) plan may be the employee's *income*. Participation rates are about 35% for employees with an income of less than $15,000, and over 80% for employees with an income of at least $75,000. Also, employees with higher income levels allocate larger portions of their accounts to equity funds (Holden and VanDerhei 2001b). Employees with greater *job tenure* participate more than employees with less job tenure. Likewise, contribution rates tend to increase as job tenure increases.

### Psychological Biases

The human brain is constantly being stimulated with information. To decrease the amount of information received, the brain filters out some information and uses shortcuts to decrease the complexity of other information. These shortcuts allow the brain to make judgments and decisions before fully digesting all the available information. This process causes several psychological biases for the investor.

People often prefer the familiar, and because of this, investors tend to believe that the stock of familiar companies is less risky than that of unfamiliar companies. This misconception is referred to as the *familiarity bias*. The company most people are most familiar with is the company for which they work. In large firms, about 32% of plan assets are invested in the sponsoring companies' stock (Benartzi 2001). The familiarity bias contributes to employees' desire to own the company stock.

Another psychological bias that can affect some investors is the *representativeness bias*. The brain makes the assumption that things sharing similar qualities are alike. The representativeness bias causes investors to buy stocks that represent desirable qualities. That is, they mistakenly believe that a good company is a good investment. Good companies are ones that have a good workforce, or have good management, or have high sales growth. Good investments are stocks that increase in value. The former does not always imply the latter.

Investors also make this error when examining past stock returns. A common misconception is that past returns are representative of what can be expected in the future. This causes investors to chase the winners and buy funds or asset classes that have trended upwards in price. Employees often compound the familiarity bias error described earlier by succumbing to the representativeness bias. That is, they buy more of their company's stock after its price increases.

People have a tendency to do nothing when faced with many choices. *Status quo bias* involves preferring the default choice, which is often the do-nothing option. Indeed, when an employee is participating (or not) in a retirement savings plan, there appears to be an inertia effect such that the participation remains at that given level (Madrian and Shea 2001). Put another way, many employees do not take an ongoing active role concerning their retirement savings. Rather, once a contribution level and fund allocation have been set, it is easiest to put aside further analysis and decision making in favor of maintaining the status quo.

### Social Effects

The effects of social interactions on individual behavior have been modeled, tested, and applied to a wide variety of events. Acknowledging that social interaction may affect financial decisions simply recognizes that people receive and process information through interaction with others. Peer effects influence retirement savings decisions because many people have not thought carefully through the advantages and disadvantages of their plan strategy and may lack their own reasoned information for making retirement investment decisions.

Investing conversations are an important part of gathering information and becoming comfortable with decisions. Because information is obtained and decisions formed through talking with others, sociable people may learn more about investing than less sociable people. As a consequence, highly sociable people are more likely to invest in the stock market or participate in their 401(k) plan (Hong, Kubik, and Stein 2001).

The participation rate of an employee's peers has a large impact on whether he or she decides to participate. The social norms of each peer group develop over time. Some social norms develop to value retirement plans, while others do not. The likelihood that an employee will decide to contribute to a retirement plan is low if his or her peers do not contribute.

### Conclusions

There are many influences on employee retirement investment decisions. This entry summarized some of the research investigating the influences of plan characteristics, employee demographic characteristics, social influences, and psychological biases. Increased understanding of the broader view of retirement investment influences should benefit plan sponsors, employees, researchers, and others interested in retirement investment behavior. (See also BABY BOOMERS AND RETIREMENT; FINANCIAL ADVISORS; FINANCIAL EDUCATION FOR SENIORS; INVESTMENT ADVICE; INVESTOR EDUCATION; RISK TOLERANCE.)

#### References

Benartzi, S. 2001. "Excessive Extrapolation and the Allocation of 401(k) Accounts to Company Stock." *Journal of Finance* 56: 1747–64.

Dulebohn, J.H., B. Murray, and M. Sun. 2000. "Selection among Employer-Sponsored Pension Plans: The Role of Individual Differences." *Personnel Psychology* 53: 405–32.

Hansen, F. 1999. "401(k)—How Good Is Yours?" *Management Review* 88: 55–60.

Holden, S., and J. VanDerhei. 2001a. "Contribution Behavior of 401(k) Plan Participants." *ICI Perspective* 7: 1–19.

Holden, S., and J. VanDerhei. 2001b. "401(k) Plan Asset Allocation, Account Balances, and Loan Activity in 2000." *ICI Perspective* 7: 1–27.

Hong, H., J.D. Kubik, and J.C. Stein. 2001. "Social Interaction and Stock-Market Participation." *Journal of Finance*.

KPMG. 1998. *Retirement Benefits in the 1990s: 1998 Survey Data*. Washington, DC: Author.

Madrian, B.C., and D. Shea. 2000. "Peer Effects and Savings Behavior in Employer-Sponsored Savings Plans." Working Paper, University of Chicago.

Madrian, B.C., and D. Shea. 2001. "The Power of Suggestion: Inertia in 401(k) Participation and Savings Behavior." *Quarterly Journal of Economics* 116: 1149–87.

SmartMoney.com. 2003. "5 Things You Should Know about Your 401(k)." Available online at http://www.smartmoney.com/retirement/401k/index.cfm?story=5things.

*John R. Nofsinger*

**INHERITANCE,** the disposition of one's property upon death. Historically, inheritance was the passing of one's estate to his or her heirs. Who would inherit was strictly predetermined by established law, usually designating the decedent's eldest son. Today, there is a wide degree of latitude in one's options for disposing of property after death. Although most states guarantee a share to a surviving spouse, a person is otherwise free to dispose of his or her property as he or she chooses. Inheritance now applies to any disposition of property after death, whether by will, trust, or operation of law. There are a number of tools available to control who will inherit one's estate. They vary in complexity, cost, and the degree of control the deceased can exercise from the grave.

### The History of Inheritance

Records of inheritance date back as far back as the Book of Genesis. Consider the account of Esau selling his birthright (inheritance) for a bowl of lentil stew. Records of inheritance in the Roman Empire also exist. Seeking a source of revenue for a permanent military, Caesar Augustus imposed what may have been the first "estate tax." The tax was imposed only on assets valued at around 50 pieces of gold or more and was only imposed on inheritances from distant relations.

The modern inheritance system emerged from feudalism, in the early stages of which the strong man extorted or confiscated the land of the weak in return for protection. The lord then "lent" it back to his vassal as long as certain obligations were faithfully performed. After the Norman Conquest of 1066, William the Conqueror confiscated all land owned by the Saxons, redistributing it to his own barons. The king remained the true owner, and the barons held the land as "tenants in chief" as long as they remained obedient. These feudal tenures originally terminated upon death, but it soon became customary to regrant the land to the decedent's eldest son, although, of course, a fee was required. The system provided stability and predictability and by the end of the twelfth century had "crystallized into a 'common law right of inheritance' " (Cribbet et al. 1996). The system was so stable and predictable, however, that the wishes of the deceased were unable to alter the scheme.

In England, where American law originated, the transfer of land (real property) by will was not allowed until 1540, although transfer of personal property by will was more or less unrestricted. In fact, the ecclesiastical courts had jurisdiction over the probate of wills for personal property, and by convincing the flock of believers that a will was necessary for salvation, the Church guaranteed itself substantial fees. Though lawyers have replaced priests, remnants of the Church's probate scheme remain today.

### The Social Merits of Inheritance

The social merits of inheritance have long been debated. Thomas Jefferson, in a letter to James Madison, said "that portion occupied by an individual ceases to be, and reverts to the society" (1789). The Soviet Union went so far as to ban inheritance, but the policy was abandoned as a failure after only four years because it was felt that inheritance encouraged savings and incentives to work and relieved the state of providing for dependents (Dukeminier and Johanson 2000). While a ban on inheritance has proven to be counterproductive, it is not unreasonable to expect a decedent to "pay his tab to society." The nation's estate tax policy is an attempt to balance these competing factors.

While defending the vast wealth he and other industrialists had accumulated, Andrew Carnegie was equally adamant that disparities in wealth should not be perpetuated through inheritance. The industrialists had earned their wealth, after all, but the social utility of leaving great wealth to family members who made no significant contributions to its accumulation was questionable. Does inheritance of wealth encourage the hard work, thrift, and initiative that helped to create it in the first place, or does it perpetuate a class of unproductive ingrates? Carnegie encouraged the altruistic use of one's excess wealth, funding projects that would benefit the public generally. To encourage such altruism, the government should impose severe estate taxes, said Carnegie. While people may argue, "My family is my preferred charity," if asked whether higher taxes on income today or higher taxes after death is preferable, who doubts the likely response?

### Intestacy

A person dying without a will or other estate plan leaves the state to determine who will inherit and prompts the involvement of a probate court, with its attendant costs and delays. Although "intestate succession" laws vary from state to state, they generally distribute specified shares to the spouse and children if they survive the decedent or to other designated relatives if they do not. These laws entail a series of presumptions about how the decedent wanted his or her estate to be distributed—presumptions that may be entirely inconsistent with a person's wishes. After the estate is reduced by probate costs, attorney's fees, and estate taxes, the residue is distributed with no regard to what the decedent really wanted.

For all but the most meager estates, some form of estate planning is needed to ensure that the estate passes according to the decedent's wishes, that estate taxes are minimized, and that probate may be avoided. Traditional estate planning tools include wills and inter vivos ("living") trusts.

### Wills

The will is the backbone of traditional, conservative estate plans. Through a will, one leaves his or her instructions for the distribution of his or her estate. While it does provide a means for expressing one's wishes, those wishes can only be executed by authority of the probate court. Being a judicial proceeding, probate is lengthy, costly, and intrusive. The costs of a simple probate vary, but the AARP found that they can deplete the average middle-class estate by as much as 10%, and costs can skyrocket if the will is challenged.

### Living Trusts

For many people, an inter vivos trust (living trust) is a better option: trusts offer something for everyone. A primary benefit of a living trust is probate avoidance. Because the title to property is transferred into the trust *during the life* of the decedent, court involvement is usually not required. Living trusts have been used for centuries but have only become popular as will substitutes since the middle of last century. The up-front costs of a trust are greater than for a will, since the trust is a more complex document than a will, and title to assets must be transferred. However, the costs of settling a trust estate are generally much less than the costs of probate. Generally, trusts are cost-effective for estates of about $100,000 or more (Wasik 1993). Provisions can be included in a trust that can reduce the impact of estate taxes, though similar provisions can also be added to a will. While probate of a will is a matter of public record, a trust estate can generally be settled privately.

There has been a concern in recent years over the "selling" of living trusts by non-lawyers, and several states have taken measures to curb this "unauthorized practice of law" (Wasik 1993). In his 1993 *Consumer's Digest* article, John Wasik also cautioned that "most of the fraudulent products were being sold by agents or financial planners, not lawyers." People should exercise care when preparing legal documents or taking advice from nonlawyers. A telephone call or letter to the state bar association is a good referral source for qualified estate planning attorneys.

Most people prefer to leave some sort of legacy to those they love: an inheritance. At the personal level, inheritance law offers the tools for a well-informed transfer. At the societal level, the magnitude of inheritance is growing rapidly. The $84 billion of wealth transferred per year at present will increase to $336 billion in the year 2015 and will have a significant impact on the American economy.

### Estate Taxes

Between now and the year 2040, baby boomers will inherit some $10 trillion: an average of roughly $90,000 (Stern 1993). This staggering sum will reshape the nation's social and business fabric and may even become a potential source of revenue for politicians seeking solutions to the budget deficit. Legislators may look increasingly to estate taxes for a solution to counter the mounting deficit, since raising rates on income taxes is an increasingly unpopular move, and budget cuts seem even more elusive. As the debate over deficit reduction continues, society may ask, "Why not let parents and grandparents pay the deficit by increasing estate taxes?" Inheritance, after all, has always been subject to the debts of the decedent.

### Current Law

The government has not, however, exacted an onerous burden on estates. The estate tax has recently undergone extensive changes, which will be phased in over the first decade of the twenty-first century. Under the current system, between now and 2009, the estate tax rate will decline from 50% to 45%, and the amount of one's estate that is effectively exempt from taxation will rise from $1 million to $3 million. In 2010, the estate tax will be repealed altogether, so even Bill Gates's estate would pay no estate tax if he dies in 2010; however, in 2011 the estate tax is revived, with only $1 million being effectively exempt. This may all change, however, depending on politics. A married couple who plans properly may continue to double the estate tax exemption.

While the federal government theoretically will take a substantial share of the nation's largest estates, the vast majority of estates are passed estate tax free to heirs. Current capital gains tax is also structured to favor heirs. If an exempt $1 million inheritance is composed of real estate purchased many years earlier for $100,000, and sold immediately by the heirs, the capital gains tax that would otherwise be owed on the $900,000 appreciated value would be avoided by the heirs. This too will change in the year 2010.

There are several types of mechanisms available to reduce the size of one's estate, but only qualified attorneys and accountants should be consulted for such planning.

### Charities

When considering the sale of a highly appreciated property where capital gains taxes are daunting, people consider giving it away. By using a Charitable Remainder Trust, the appreciated property may be sold now, free of capital gains, and a guaranteed income for life retained from the proceeds. In addition, a current tax deduction is available for gifting the remainder to charity. These tax breaks, coupled with income from the untaxed proceeds of the sale, could pay for or exceed the actual gift to charity. Although the gift must go to the charity at death rather than to one's heirs, the overall tax consequences may dramatically improve the amount of one's net estate.

### Life Insurance

Finally, life insurance is a tool many people use to provide an estate for their family or to fund the ultimate estate tax bill. It is important to realize, however, that insurance proceeds may dramatically increase your estate tax bill if not handled properly. Insurance proceeds can be sheltered from estate taxes through use of an irrevocable life insurance trust.

### Estate Tax Planning

If an estate is large enough that estate taxes could be a potential problem, it is imperative to consult an attorney who specializes in estate planning. Shop carefully, however, because it has been estimated that only 1% of all attorneys can properly draft a living trust (Faltermayer 1991). And even fewer are capable of drafting the more advanced estate planning tools. Spending a little extra now for an attorney who is an expert on estate planning can save a family thousands of dollars later. (See also BUSINESS SUCCESSION PLANNING; CAPITAL GAIN; CHARITABLE CONTRIBUTIONS; ELDER LAW PRACTICE; ESTATE PLANNING; FINANCIAL LITERACY; HEALTH AND LONGEVITY; INTERGENERATIONAL CONFLICT AND FINANCIAL ISSUES; TRUSTS; WILLS; WEALTH SPAN).

#### References

Cribbet, John E., Corwin W. Johnson, Roger W. Findley, and Ernest E. Smith. 1996. *Cases and Materials on Property*. 7th ed. Westbury, NY: Foundation Press.

Dukeminier, Jesse, and Stanley M. Johanson. 2000. *Wills, Trusts and Estates*. 6th ed. Boston, MA: Little, Brown.

Esperti, Robert A., and Renno L. Peterson. 1999. *Protect Your Estate: Definitive Strategies for Estate and Wealth Planning from Leading Experts*. New York: McGraw-Hill.

Faltermayer, Edmund. 1991. "The Financially Perfect Death: Adroit Moves While You're Still Around Can Shrink Estate Taxes and Spare Your Heirs the Long Wait of Probate." *Fortune*, February 25.

Gibbon, Edward. 1988. *The Decline and Fall of the Roman Empire*. Vol. 1. Chicago: Encyclopedia Britannica.

Jefferson, Thomas. 1789. "Letter to James Madison, Paris, September 6, 1789." In *Social and Political Philosophy*, ed. John Somerville and Ronald E. Santoni. Garden City, NY: Doubleday.

Stern, Linda. 1993. "Inheritances: Next Boom for Boomers." *Seattle Post-Intelligencer*, December 28.

Wasik, John F. 1993. "Living Trusts vs. Wills: Estate Planning Guide." *Consumer's Digest* (September–October).

*Scott A. Miskiel*

**INSURANCE.** See Accident Insurance; Liability Insurance; Long-Term Care Insurance (LTCI)—A Consumer's Perspective; Long-Term Care Insurance: Individual Disability Escalating Annuities (IDEAs); Long-Term Care Insurance, Private; Medicaid; Medicare; Medicare Supplemental Insurance; Postretirement Health Coverage (PRHC).

**INTERGENERATIONAL CONFLICT AND FINANCIAL ISSUES,** tensions and disagreements between family members over financial matters, including the distribution of financial assistance between aging parents and adult children. Family and gerontology researchers have only recently turned their attention to the issue of intergenerational conflict, and the subject of how family conflicts impact financial matters has rarely been explored.

### What Is Intergenerational Conflict?

In the contemporary literature on family relations, moderate family conflict is often viewed as a normative aspect of family relationships and has been discussed as a functional and even necessary element for maintaining family harmony (Clarke et al. 1999). It is unclear how much conflict exists between aging parents and adult children. Some studies conducted using quantitative measures reported fairly low levels of intergenerational conflict (Suitor and Pillemer 1988), but Clarke et al. (1999) report a surprisingly high level of intergenerational conflict when examining open-ended qualitative responses. About two-thirds of their sample of aging parents and adult children reported conflicts, tensions, or disagreements. While conflict is typically thought to be highest between parents and their children during adolescence, it is now clear that these earlier conflicts may resurface at later stages in the life course. The literature is mixed regarding whether aging mothers or fathers experience more frequent conflicts with adult children.

How parents and adult children "fight" has also been of research interest. In a study examining the relationship between aging mothers and adult daughters, Fingerman (1995) found that mothers and daughters equally used "constructive" techniques to try to resolve conflicts that arose. However, Fingerman also cited research showing that older individuals have fewer overt conflicts with others, and she suggested that as parents age and adult children mature, they may practice avoidance tactics to prevent conflict over issues that they know will generate tensions. While the most extreme and violent way to resolve conflicts with aging parents may take the form of elder abuse, for the purposes of this discussion the focus is on milder and more constructive forms of conflict and tensions that do not involve physical aggression toward another person.

### What Are the Topics of Intergenerational Conflict?

Very little research has identified the focus of intergenerational conflicts. A qualitative study of conflict and tensions between adult children and their aging parents identified six types of issues that generate conflicts in families (Clarke et al. 1999):

1. Communication and interaction style
2. Personal habits and lifestyle choices
3. Child-rearing practices and values
4. Politics, religion, and ideology
5. Work orientation
6. Household maintenance

The type of conflicts mentioned most by both parents and adult children were the first three. Concerns and conflicts over the allocation of financial resources were included in the "habits and lifestyles" type, and these centered on adult children not saving their money, having spending patterns and priorities that differed from the parents' expectations, and concern over "continued dependency" either because the adult child had not become financially self-supporting or because the aging parent was relying on the adult child for financial assistance.

### How Do Intergenerational Conflicts Impact Exchanges of Financial Support?

Research findings indicate that a strong sense of duty can override other intergenerational relationship qualities, such as low affection or past conflicts, and lead to the exchange of help and support between the generations (Parrott and Bengtson 1999; Whitbeck, Hoyt, and Huck 1994). Retrospective accounts of the quality of intergenerational relationships in the past (both as adolescents and younger-aged adults) can influence the propensity of adult children to give help and support to aging parents (Whitbeck, Hoyt, and Huck 1994). However, this finding varied based on type of help and support given and the level of intergenerational affection and sense of obligation felt. Some studies show no relationship between recent or past conflicts and the exchange of financial support between parents and adult children. Using prospective accounts of family relationships, Parrott and Bengtson (1999) found that earlier conflict in parent–adult child relationships did not interfere with contemporary exchanges of help and support, including financial support to/from a parent/adult child.

Silverstein, Parrott, and Bengtson (1995) identified gender differences in what motivates the supportive behaviors of adult children toward their aging parents, including whether or not financial assistance is given. Intergenerational affection most motivated adult daughters to provide support to parents, while adult sons were motivated by filial obligation, expectation of an inheritance, and frequency of contact with parents. They noted that the anticipation of a financial reward (i.e., an inheritance) could be an incentive to an adult child to provide help and support to aging parents.

However, Parrott and Bengtson (1999) found that levels of financial exchanges between parents and adult children were relatively low, occurring infrequently compared with other types of instrumental support, and the predictors of financial support were related to the need and age of the adult child. In this study, affectionate bonds were not necessary for parents to aid their adult children. On the other hand, affectionate bonds increased the likelihood of financial assistance being given to aging mothers.

The "intergenerational stake hypothesis" also sheds some light on the mixed findings regarding the impact of conflict on financial exchanges of intergenerational support. This theory holds that the older generation perceives more similarity and closeness to the younger generation than the younger generation perceives and reports. Said differently, parents report "less distance" or gaps in their relationships with adult children (Lynott and Roberts 1997). From this interpretation, parents would also be expected to report fewer conflicts and disagreements with their adult children than the adult children report because the parents have more of an investment or "stake" in the relationship over time. This means that adult children may be more affected by the conflicts and differences between the generations than are parents who have a tendency to "view things through rose-colored glasses." Some research backs this up, suggesting that parents perceive relationship characteristics and the meaning of them differently than do their adult children.

Fingerman (1995) found that "older mothers underestimate daughters' negative behaviors and feelings in conflict situations."

### Do Financial Issues Cause Intergenerational Conflict?

For decades, research has shown that financial matters are consistently a source of marital disagreement and conflicts. Thus, it is not surprising that financial issues can also generate conflicts in intergenerational relationships. For example, in families with more than one child it is not uncommon for one child to receive more assistance than another. Those children who need the most (due to divorce, for example) typically get more compared with children who are doing well and do not require financial assistance from parents. This financial dependency tends to create tension between the giver and the receiver. Moreover, sibling conflicts may also arise due to differential financial support from parents to the adult children and perceived inequalities in parental treatment of siblings. It has been shown that perceived feelings of preference for one sibling over another can impact later exchanges of help and support with aging parents (Whitbeck, Hoyt, and Huck 1994).

Financial planners find that adult children often second-guess the investment decisions of their parents. Further, adult children who expect an inheritance may feel angry over spending decisions their aging parents make, such as opting to spend their savings while they are alive versus leaving an inheritance. As Clarke et al. (1999) demonstrated, financial issues can be the object of conflict and tension between parents and adult children when one generation does not approve of how the other is spending their money. Disapproving adult children may take measures to protect their inheritance, including obtaining decision-making authority for the estate of an aging parent or encouraging estate planning practices that ensure savings are not spent down to cover the costs of long-term care for the aging parents. All of these tactics can undermine the autonomy and decision-making ability of the parent and can generate additional intergenerational conflicts.

The financial drain of caring for an aging parent—due to purchasing in-home community-based care or taking time off from work—can lead to conflicts and tensions in the intergenerational relationship as well. This is particularly true if the caregiving costs are competing with the cost of college for a child or the adult child's own retirement plans. In such situations, the dependency of the parent on the adult child may play a role in the level of conflict the adult child experiences, partly because the adult child may feel uncomfortable with the change in parent-child roles or because the adult child may resent the drain of caregiving on financial and emotional family resources.

### How Can Social Exchange Theory Explain Conflict and Financial Support in Families?

A number of studies have focused on the causes of intergenerational conflict and the determinative effect of financial support. Economists would suggest that parents strategically make "investments" in children in anticipation of needed support in old age. They can, for example, withhold or extend financial resources to ensure greater interaction or future assistance (Silverstein et al. 2002). Sociologists tend to point to social exchange theory and reciprocity norms to explain supportive behaviors in families. They suggest that "delayed" or "lagged" reciprocity norms account for the behaviors observed, even in the face of poor-quality relationships. From a life course perspective, it is clear that there is a typical flow of exchanges of support over the life course of individuals in families as their roles, life stages, needs, and resources change. The middle generation typically gives the most to the younger and older generations, while the younger and older generations are net recipients of assistance (Morgan and Kunkel 2001). Why families help each other in this patterned way has been examined in the empirical literature.

Silverstein et al. (2002) "defined lagged reciprocity as the circumstance when the provision of support to older parents was the fulfillment of an obligation to repay a social debt based on that parent's earlier transfers to the child." Looking over a 26-year time period and using six data points, they found that financial transfers were similar to an insurance model, where investments in adolescent and young adult children had a return in the future when the aging parent exhibited a need (defined as a functional impairment) for assistance. Silverstein and colleagues described this as one example of an implied social contract between family members that works to ensure reciprocity in the long term when an aging parent has a need for help. This study found that even when there had been very little or no financial support received from parents at an earlier age, there was still increasing support given to parents as they got older. Thus, some level of altruism was also at work.

Given that there may be a link between income and levels of family violence, it may also be true that the likelihood of nonaggressive conflicts arising in families is higher when an adult child or older parent has limited resources because he/she would have fewer resources to bring to an exchange and reciprocate. This can lead to dependency and may create feelings of tension. Conversely, having few resources may make individuals less likely to generate conflicts because they are dependent on the other for assistance. The same self-interested motivation may be true for individuals in poor health. For example, an aging parent needing assistance due to health problems may be willing to overlook things an adult child does or says that they disagree with because they need the adult child to provide assistance. In situations where the assistance is duty driven, we might expect more expressions of conflict as well, because the behavior is motivated by obligation rather than affection.

### What Impact Will Family Diversity Have on Family Conflict and Financial Issues?

Divorce, step-parent relationships, grandparents raising grandchildren, childlessness, and other family diversity issues further complicate attempts to understand the relationship between intergenerational conflict and financial matters. When there are adult stepchildren and biological children, who receives more financial assistance? How does divorce relate to the amount of conflict between the generations in later life? Does it alter financial assistance between the generations? Do childless individuals have conflicts with other family members who they treat "like a child," and do these have the same impact on financial assistance, or is financial assistance given in these cases based solely on reciprocity rather than obligation? Since research on grandparent-grandchild relations has not focused to date on intergenerational conflicts, it is unclear what impact such conflict might have on financial assistance between the generations. These are questions that must be addressed in future research to better appreciate the complex nature of intergenerational conflict and the implications for financial issues. (See also ELDER

LAW PRACTICE; ESTATE PLANNING; FRAILTY PLANNING; GUARDIANSHIP; KING LEAR SYNDROME; LIFE PLANNING.)

**References**

Clarke, Edward J., Mar Preston, Jo Raksin, and Vern L. Bengtson. 1999. "Types of Conflicts and Tensions between Older Parents and Adult Children." *The Gerontologist* 39(3): 261–70.

Fingerman, Karen L. 1995. "Aging Mothers' and Their Adult Daughters' Perceptions of Conflict Behaviors." *Psychology and Aging* 10(4): 639–49.

Lynott, Patricia Passuth, and Robert E.L. Roberts. 1997. "The Developmental Stake Hypothesis and Changing Perceptions of Intergenerational Relations 1971–1985." *The Gerontologist* 37(3): 394–405.

Morgan, Leslie, and Suzanne Kunkel. 2001. *Aging: The Social Context*. 2nd ed. Thousand Oaks, CA: Pine Forge Press.

Parrott, Tonya M., and Vern L. Bengtson. 1999. "The Effects of Earlier Intergenerational Affection, Normative Expectations, and Family Conflict on Contemporary Exchanges of Help and Support." *Research on Aging* 21(1): 73–105.

Silverstein, Merril, Stephen J. Conroy, Haitao Wang, Roseann Giarrusso, and Vern L. Bengtson. 2002. "Reciprocity in Parent-Child Relations over the Adult Life Course." *Journal of Gerontology: Social Sciences* 57B(1): S3–S13.

Silverstein, Merril, Tonya M. Parrott, and Vern L. Bengtson. 1995. "Factors That Predispose Middle-Aged Sons and Daughters to Provide Social Support to Older Persons." *Journal of Marriage and the Family* 57: 465–75.

Suitor, Jill, and Karl Pillemer. 1988. "Explaining Generational Conflict When Adult Children and Elderly Parents Live Together." *Journal of Marriage and the Family* 50: 1037–47.

Whitbeck, Les B., Danny R. Hoyt, and Shirley M. Huck. 1994. "Early Family Relationships, Intergenerational Solidarity, and Support Provided to Parents by the Adult Children." *Journal of Gerontology: Social Sciences* 49B(2): S85–S94.

*Tonya M. Parrott*

**INTERNET USE BY SENIORS.** Seniors make up roughly 13% of the U.S. population but in 2001 comprised just 4% of the U.S. Internet population. According to the National Telecommunications and Information Administration (U.S. Department of Commerce 2000), Internet use by individuals in the 50+ age group from December 1998 to August 2000 experienced the highest rate of growth (53% compared to a nationwide Internet use growth rate of 35% for the same period). Despite this increase in use, seniors are among the least likely to be Internet users—and those seniors who do go online are less likely than Internet users in other age groups to explore many of the uses of the Internet.

Fifty-six percent (56%) of all Americans go online. Fifty-one percent (51%) of Americans 50 to 64 have access to the Internet and are active Internet users, while only 15% of Americans over the age of 65 have access to the Internet. One factor in this use pattern is that few individuals now over age 65 were in the workforce or attending classes in the 1990s, so their exposure to the World Wide Web and other Internet-based pursuits is limited. Those seniors who were in the labor force are almost three times as likely to be Internet users than those who were not (U.S. Department of Commerce 2000).

Although women outnumber men among senior citizens, senior men outnumber senior women online. The gender ratio of today's online senior population is about 60% male and 40% female. Thirty-two percent (32%) of those senior men who are online have had three or more years of experience with Internet use compared to only 14% of similar senior women. However, seniors (especially senior women) are coming online at faster rates, and the gender gap in Internet use is disappearing (Fox et al. 2001).

Online seniors are more likely to be male, married, highly educated, and enjoying relatively high retirement incomes. Eighteen percent (18%) are widows or widowers (compared to 39% of all seniors). Eighty-one percent (81%) of the Internet senior users only have access at home, in contrast to the 50 to 64-year-old group who are more likely to have access both at work and at home (Fox et al. 2001).

### Barriers to Internet Use

Overall, persons with disabilities are only half as likely to have access to the Internet as those without. Over one-half (52.1%) of the population age 65 and older has a disability (U.S. Department of Commerce 2000). Individuals in this age group account for only 15.6% of the population as a whole but over one-third (37.4%) of the total number of people with a disability. Disabilities common among seniors such as impaired vision (11.4%) and problems with manual dexterity (9.4%) further reduce the likelihood of computer use (U.S. Department of Commerce 2000).

Income is a barrier to Internet use for people in all age groups. Many seniors are on fixed or limited incomes and cannot afford a computer or the monthly fees associated with Internet access. According to U.S. Census information, the median income of older persons in 2001 was $19,688 for males and $11,313 for females. Households containing families headed by persons 65+ reported a median income in 2001 of $33,938 ($34,661 for Whites, $26,610 for African Americans, and $24,287 for Hispanics). For all older persons reporting income in 2001 (32.9 million), 31.8% reported less than $10,000. Only 31.2% reported $25,000 or more. The median income reported was $14,152.

Although education level, specifically literacy, can be a limiting factor in computer and especially Internet use, surveys show a 93% rate of growth in Internet use by individuals age 50 and over who were in the labor force with only an elementary level education and a 53% increase in use among those who did not graduate high school (U.S. Bureau of the Census 2000).

### Most Frequently Used Internet Applications

Although seniors are the least likely group to use the Internet—and those seniors who do go online are much less likely to have sampled all that the Web has to offer—recent studies have identified the Internet applications that are used by the majority of online seniors.

E-mail for communication with friends and relatives is the most heavily used application (92.6%) by online seniors. On a typical day, seniors are more likely to send e-mail than the average Internet user. Many seniors now online were encouraged to go online by family members. Nearly three in five online seniors say that the Internet has improved their connections with family (Fox et al. 2001).

The next highest Internet use among seniors is for research. Research topics include information concerning hobbies and pastimes (most frequent), health and financial information, and current news and events. Senior Internet use, however, differs from that of the average Internet user. While many wired seniors (44%) search for financial news online and seem to enjoy managing online portfolios, few seniors do their banking on the Internet (8%) (Fox et al. 2001).

As a group, online seniors seem to be as engaged as the general Internet population in researching medical information and advice online. Although studies show that senior women are more likely to seek health information online than men, neither education nor income level seem to make much difference in whether or not seniors seek out health information.

### Future Senior Internet Use

According to recent studies, most of the strongest Internet holdouts are older Americans. They are ambivalent about the Internet or distrust it and often do not feel there are any benefits to be had from its use. They are more wary of possible privacy invasions and online tracking of their activities and are more concerned than the average American about businesses and people they do not know getting personal information about them or their families.

Despite these attitudes, the future of Internet use by seniors is changing. There is some evidence that the hesitant senior who may currently just dabble in e-mail will eventually become confident enough to begin exploring more activities online. The more experience a wired senior has, the more likely he or she is to begin to fit the pattern of use seen in the general online population. Internet users with several years' experience typically spend more time in an online session and tend to explore new applications (Fox et al. 2001).

Another factor changing senior Internet use is the "silver wave" of individuals in the 50 to 64 age group who are mostly Internet users now and are likely to keep their Internet access after retirement. An American between the ages of 50 and 64 is three times more likely to have Internet access than someone over the age of 65.

### Sites for Older Americans

In February 1995, in "Internet and E-mail Resources on Aging," the U.S. Administration on Aging (AoA) listed two sites in the field of aging. In the next two years, that grew to approximately 2,500 sites (Post 1997). Today, the "Internet and E-mail Resources on Aging" Web page is no longer maintained. There are currently so many sites related to aging that the AoA, in attempting to keep up with the rapid growth of these sites, has developed a directory of aging-related links in key areas to major Web resources on selected topics and issues from Alzheimer's disease to workforce and aging. There are also links on the AoA Web site to state and area agencies on aging, federal agency consumer Web sites of interest to older adults, metasites (sites with links to many aging sites), and related resources within the AoA Web site. (See also AGING AMERICA; ATTITUDES ABOUT RETIREMENT; BABY BOOMERS AND RETIREMENT; BANKING SERVICES FOR THE MATURE MARKET; INVESTOR EDUCATION; LEISURE.)

#### References

Fox, S., et al. 2001. "Wired Seniors: A Fervent Few, Inspired by Family Ties." *Pew Internet & American Life Project*. Washington, DC. Available online at http://pewinternet.org/.

Post, J.A. 1997. "Internet Resources on Aging: Sites to Start With." *The Gerontologist* 37(6).

U.S. Administration on Aging. 2003. "Internet and E-mail Resources on Aging." Available online at http://www.aoa.gov/.

U.S. Bureau of the Census. 1998. *Current Population Surveys*. Washington, DC: GPO.

U.S. Bureau of the Census. 2000. *Current Population Surveys*. Washington, DC: GPO.

U.S. Bureau of the Census. 2001. *Annual Supplement to the Social Security Bulletin*. Washington, DC: GPO.

U.S. Bureau of the Census. 2002. *Money Income in the United States: 2001. Current Population Reports P60–218*. Washington, DC: GPO.

U.S. Department of Commerce. Economics and Statistics Administration. National Telecommunications and Information Administration. 2000. *Falling Through the Net: Toward Digital Inclusion*. Washington, DC: GPO.

*Jamie Losikoff-Kent*

**INVESTMENT ADVICE,** recommendations about how to invest savings taking into account an individual's financial goals, tolerance for *investment risk* (change in the value of the investment), and *time horizon* (length of time until the money is needed).

Only the very wealthy used to need—or were able to afford—investment advice and other financial planning services. Most workers expected to spend their careers with one company and retire with a gold watch and a guaranteed pension, which, in addition to Social Security payments, would give them a secure retirement income. No longer. Social Security payments alone can't provide a standard of living equal to that during one's working life, and the future of Social Security is less than certain. What's more, fewer and fewer workers have guaranteed pension plans.

Individuals increasingly have been forced to take on responsibility for managing their own retirement savings, whether through employer-sponsored plans such as 401(k)s or through Individual Retirement Accounts (IRAs). Yet the average worker may lack the necessary expertise and time to make informed investment decisions. This has become apparent since 2000, as the declining market has destroyed the savings of many individuals who hadn't followed accepted investing principles such as diversification (dividing money among different kinds of investments) and rebalancing (ensuring that the mix of investments remains appropriate). Having available and affordable investment advice has become essential to the future retirement security of the general population, and making this information available to a wider audience has become a key market niche for many investment firms.

## Why Advice Is Necessary

Defined contribution employer-sponsored plans such as the 401(k) were introduced in the 1980s and became increasingly popular in the 1990s. Before then, most companies that offered retirement plans offered "defined benefit" plans, which are managed by employers and provide a regular pension check to retired employees who qualify based on length of employment. By contrast, "defined contribution" plans, including 401(k) plans (and their equivalents, 403(b) and 457(b) plans, for employees of nonprofit and governmental entities, respectively), require the *employee* to decide how much to contribute and how to invest it. The benefit paid out at retirement depends on employee savings, matching employer contributions (if any), and investment performance. Defined contribution plans have overtaken defined-benefit plans. As of 1998, 58 million private-sector workers participated in defined contribution plans compared with 42 million in defined benefit plans (EBRI 2002d). Forty-two million households had IRAs as of May

2002 (Investment Company Institute 2002). Individuals may have IRAs in addition to either a defined contribution or defined benefit plan.

Employees don't forfeit defined contribution plans and IRAs when they change jobs (except, in some cases, unvested employer matching contributions). This is an advantage over defined benefit plans for an increasingly mobile workforce. However, defined contribution plans present a major challenge by putting the burden of saving and investing on workers rather than employers. Many workers don't save as much as they should for retirement, either through ignorance or because they can't afford to. On limited incomes, many workers may have to make income appropriations decisions, and the short-term expenses, including college expenses and mortgage payments, are very often addressed before saving for retirement.

Misperceptions about retirement and investments may be contributing to the low savings rates. Common mistakes include overestimating investment returns, and consequently over-withdrawing funds in retirement; underestimating the needed income to preserve an active lifestyle; expecting too much from Social Security; depending on an inheritance or a spouse's pension; and underestimating longevity. ("The 2002 National Summit on Retirement Savings" 2000)

Women are particularly at risk of not saving and investing properly for retirement. On average, women live longer than men but earn lower wages. Consequently, they receive lower Social Security payments and lower pension benefits (if they even qualify), and they save less in their retirement accounts. Women also tend to put family financial needs before their own retirement saving, which can hurt them financially in the long run, although it is not clear that they do so to any greater degree than men at comparable income levels.

When people *do* save for retirement, they often don't invest the money appropriately. During the bull market of the 1990s, many individuals with little or no investing experience thought investing was easy. All they had to do was put money in a stock and watch it grow. However, once stock values began to tumble in 2000, individuals who hadn't followed accepted investing principles watched their account balances dwindle and realized they needed help. The 2002 Merrill Lynch "Retirement Survey" found that only 25% of Americans are confident in their investment skills, and over 44% of Americans said they were more likely to seek professional help with their retirement portfolios *after* the economic downturn began. Unfortunately, this realization comes too late.

In addition to the stock market tumble, two other factors created a need for widely available investment advice. First, retirement plan account balances have grown substantially over the last two decades. A five- or six-figure account balance demands more attention than a smaller one. Second, the number of investment choices available in defined contribution plans has increased. When these plans were first introduced in the early 1980s, they generally offered only three investment options. Now, most companies offer at least ten (Cerulli Associates 2002). Some plans offer a "brokerage window" that lets investors choose from the entire universe of mutual funds, and in some cases even individual stocks and bonds. This is quite a large choice, even for experienced investors. With IRAs, the investment choice depends on what is offered by the financial institution housing the account and is generally quite broad.

### Why Employers Hesitate

Many individuals hope to receive investment advice through their employer. In a 2002 study by CIGNA Retirement & Investment Services, 89% of employees said they would "welcome personalized financial-planning advice from their employers." However, only 22% of 401(k) plans surveyed in 2001 by PSCA (Profit-Sharing/401[k] Council of America) offered investment advice.

Why do employers hesitate? The employer is a plan fiduciary, which means it is responsible for ensuring that the plan is administered in the best interests of the participants. This includes selecting reasonable plan investments and performing due diligence on any third party involved with the plan, including an investment advisor. The Employee Retirement Income Security Act (ERISA) of 1974 imposes certain requirements on employers that sponsor retirement plans for their employees. For example, plan sponsors themselves are not allowed to give investment advice to employees, nor are financial companies that sell investment products (such as mutual funds) that are offered by the retirement plan, because of the potential conflict of interest. However, employers are allowed to hire an independent company to provide investment advice. In the PSCA study, employers said they hesitated to make such advice available to their employees because they feared they would be held liable if the advice resulted in an investment loss. They also expressed concern about their ability both to select and to monitor a competent provider in accordance with ERISA.

ERISA also requires retirement plan sponsors to provide employees with enough information about the plan investment options and the plan rules, as well as general investment principles, to enable them to make reasonable investing decisions. Most employers fulfill this obligation through newsletters, company-sponsored investment seminars, or access to investment materials on the Internet. Employers may also offer investment "guidance," which gives individuals an asset allocation recommendation based on their financial goals, time horizon, and risk tolerance. (An asset allocation recommendation details how much to invest in different asset classes—for example, 60% stocks, 30% bonds, and 10% cash—but doesn't recommend specific investment products within those asset classes.)

Investment *advice* goes a step further than guidance and recommends a mix of specific investment products (such as particular mutual funds) in which to invest money. The Department of Labor ruled in 2001 that employers may hire an independent company to provide advice to employees, and even manage their accounts, as long as the advice provider/manager is selected using due diligence and prudence. Some experts even argue that providing independent advice is in the employees' best interests and that *not* doing so increases employers' liability exposure. At the time of writing, Congress was considering proposals to address employers' concerns about liability, but it was not clear what action, if any, would be taken.

### Who Gives Advice?

Many financial institutions offer some form of investment advice or guidance to their clients. Some have developed asset allocation software internally, while others have partnered with independent advice providers such as Financial Engines, Morningstar, or mPower (which was acquired by Morningstar in July 2003) to provide advice on retirement plans. When an individual logs on to an advice Web site through his or her financial institution or employer, information such as the retirement account balance generally is already entered. This data integration makes the process less time-consuming for the individual, meaning that he or she may be more likely to take advantage of the service. Data integration likely will become more prevalent in years to come (Punishill 2003).

A fairly small number of participants with access to purely online advice are actually using it—generally fewer than 25% (Deloitte and Touche 2002). They may be hesitant to put sensitive financial information on the Internet or be confused about the process and not know where to seek help. Increasingly, financial institutions are offering Internet advice combined with human advisors whom employees can phone or meet in person to further discuss their financial plans (Cerulli Associates 2002).

Another option that should be mentioned is that an individual may choose to consult a financial planner on his or her own. Financial planners generally look at the entire household financial situation and determine whether the client is saving enough in the right types of accounts to have a good chance to meet his or her financial goals. If not, the financial planner advises the client on how to save more. After reviewing the client's financial situation and goals, the planner will generally recommend specific investments. Individuals should choose a financial planner carefully, as some receive commissions for selling certain investment products. The Certified Financial Planner Board of Standards publishes a helpful guide to choosing a financial planner, titled "10 Questions to Ask When Choosing a Financial Planner."

### How Good Is Advice?

To paraphrase an old saying, what you get out of advice depends on what you put into it. Advice can only be as good as the assumptions it is based on. These include such things as projected length of life, projected investment performance and interest rates, projected rates of inflation and taxation, salary, and so on. A surefire way to know exactly how much money an individual will have at retirement simply does not exist. Results from any planner online or human will provide an indication, not a guarantee.

The more personal and financial information an individual provides to the advisor, the more the investment advice can be tailored to the individual's situation. This is true whether the advisor is an online program or a live person. Investment advice should, at a minimum, be based on the individual's time horizon until retirement, tolerance for investment risk, and retirement income goals.

Sophisticated advice tools use a technique called Monte Carlo simulation to forecast returns and future values of investments. This computerized technique runs hundreds of scenarios to arrive at a likely result for a mix of investments over a certain period of time. Monte Carlo simulation has been criticized for providing unrealistic results (Harris 2002). However, it also is defended by those who argue that it can give a realistic picture if the right assumptions are used—those that take into account the unpredictable nature of investment returns (Goerz 2002). It has also been suggested that guaranteed return investments should be introduced for retirement accounts to take away the uncertainty of volatile investments such as stocks and high-risk bonds (Bodie 2003).

Many sources of investment advice and guidance available to the mass market via the Internet focus on the accumulation stage—in other words, how to invest money while one is working and accumulating savings. Less attention has been paid to advising people on how to manage their money once they retire and no longer receive a salary. This phase requires a "drawdown" or "retirement income" strategy, with considerations different from the accumulation phase. These include health issues and long-term care insurance and an emphasis on investments that preserve capital and generate income (Cerulli Associates 2002). Advice programs designed for the accumulation phase aren't appropriate for the drawdown phase. Even programs designed specifically for the drawdown phase may have their limitations. The Society of Actuaries studied a number of such software programs. It concluded that, in general,

> their value is in helping people estimate income, retirement needs, and spending . . . [but] the programs are generally not developed to address retirement risks. Instead, the tools mainly mask risk by using averages. This means their results [advice] may not be appropriate for an individual's own situation. (Society of Actuaries 2003)

For example, the effect of a bear market on a retirement account depends in part on its timing. If the market slumps just when retirement is beginning, the effect may be harsher than if it hits later in retirement. This risk, along with many others, must be managed (EBRI 2002b). As baby boomers approach retirement, they will most likely demand this type of planning.

## Conclusion

Individuals are increasingly responsible for saving and investing their retirement nest eggs, and they need help from professionals in the form of advice and/or investment management. This is true both for workers accumulating savings and those near retirement. Each group, and each individual, has different needs that must be addressed if they are to successfully endure stock and bond market fluctuations. The situation is becoming more urgent as the U.S. retirement system increasingly shifts toward accounts that are managed by individuals (who are not necessarily equipped to properly manage investments) and as the baby boom generation approaches retirement. (See also FINANCIAL ADVISORS; FINANCIAL EDUCATION FOR SENIORS; INFLUENCES ON RETIREMENT INVESTMENT DECISIONS; INVESTOR EDUCATION; RETIREMENT PLANNING; RETIREMENT PLANS—401(k).)

### Organizations

Employee Benefit Research Institute (EBRI)
Financial Engines, Inc.
Financial Planning Association (FPA)
Investment Company Institute
Morningstar, Inc.
National Association of Personal Financial Advisors (NAPFA)
Women's Institute for a Secure Retirement (WISER)

### Suggested Readings

Benna, Ted, and Brenda Watson Newmann. 2003. *401(k)s for Dummies*. New York: Wiley Publishing, Inc.

Women's Institute for a Secure Retirement (WISER). 2002. *Your Future Paycheck®: What Women*

*Need to Know About Pay, Social Security, Pensions, Savings and Investments.* Washington, DC. Available online at http://www.wiser.heinz.org.

**References**

Bodie, Zvi. 2003. "An Analysis of Investment Advice to Retirement Plan Participants." In *The Pension Challenge: Risk Transfers and Retirement Income Security*, ed. Olivia S. Mitchell and Kent Smetters. New York: Oxford University Press.

Certified Financial Planner Board of Standards. n.d. "10 Questions to Ask When Choosing a Financial Planner." Available online at http://www.cfp-board.org/cons_10qs.html.

Cerulli Associates. 2002. "Demographics Portend Change." In *The Cerulli Edge U.S. Edition.* Profit-Sharing/401(k) Council of America (PSCA) 45th Annual Survey of Profit-Sharing and 401(k) Plans. Boston, MA: Author.

Deloitte and Touche, LLP. 2002. *Annual 401(k) Benchmarking Survey.*

Employee Benefit Research Institute (EBRI). 2002a. "An Evolving Pension System: Trends in Defined Benefit and Defined Contribution Plans." *Issue Brief* 249 (September).

Employee Benefit Research Institute (EBRI). 2002b. "Can 401(k) Accumulations Generate Significant Income for Future Retirees?" *Issue Brief* 251 (November). Available online at http://www.ebri.org/ibex/ib251.htm.

Goerz, David. 2002. "Crystal Balls and Forecasting the Future with Monte Carlo." *mPower Café.* Available online at http://www.mpowercafe.com/investing/analysis/analysis.3.3.3_12182002.html

Harris, Elizabeth. 2002. "In Search of Better Odds in Retirement Planning." *New York Times*, October 8.

Investment Company Institute. 2002. *Investment Company Institute Fundamentals* 11(3) (September).

Merrill Lynch. 2002. "Retirement Survey." Press release January 2002. Available online at http://www.ml.com/about/press_release/10092002-1_retirement_plans_pr.htm.

Punishill, Jaime. 2003 "Wealth Management 2003: Five Predictions." Forester Research Brief. Available online at http://www.forrester.com/ER/Research/Brief/0,1317,16282,FF.html.

Society of Actuaries. 2003. "Retirement Planning Software." Available online at http://www.soa.org/library/monographs/retirement_systems/m-rs03-1/m-rs03-1_tableofcontents.html.

"The 2002 National Summit on Retirement Savings." 2002. Delegate Resources, Washington, DC. International Foundation of Employee Benefit Plans, Inc. Available online at http://www.ifebp.org/PDF/SummitBackFinal.pdf.

*Brenda Watson Newmann*

**INVESTMENT CLUBS,** small groups of individuals who pool their efforts and resources to invest in the common stocks of publicly traded corporations. Investment club members meet regularly to learn about investing, study publicly traded companies, and reach consensus decisions about the merits of particular stocks. Although investment club structure can vary, participants typically pay a small, set amount each month into a joint account for purchasing stocks. The membership of an investment club generally consists of acquaintances, friends, neighbors, relatives, coworkers, fellow church members, or other like-minded individuals. Investment clubs can provide opportunities to socialize, and members often enjoy a strong sense of camaraderie as they work together on the club's portfolio.

For many Americans, purchasing shares in publicly traded corporations has proven to be the best way to meet long-term goals such as buying a home, paying for education, and funding retirement. During the second half of the twentieth century, the Standard & Poor's 500 stock index increased at an average annual rate of 12.8%. In contrast, long-term corporate bonds had annualized average returns of 6.2%, and U.S. 30-day Treasury bills averaged only 5.2%. The percentages may be somewhat different depending on which periods and indexes are compared, but throughout the past century, the pattern remained the same—stocks delivered higher average returns than other varieties of financial assets.

No guarantee exists that these patterns will continue, of course. But given the historical record, people who include common stocks in their investment programs may have more success increasing the total value of their assets throughout their lives. That will be required to cope with the rising cost of living. Some degree of growth is especially important in retirement when inflation can erode the purchasing power of a fixed income. For example, concern is widespread over evidence that increases in the cost of health care—especially for prescription drugs—may continue to exceed the rate of inflation. And retirees typically are the biggest consumers of medical products and services. In addition, Americans are retiring earlier and living longer on average, so many retirees may have to depend on their nest eggs for longer periods than was true of their parents' generation.

Everyone is aware that stock values rise and fall—sometimes at an alarming pace. Over sufficiently long periods, however, the peaks and valleys cancel each other out, and historically the trend in prices has been upward. The most successful investors tend to be those who invest in high-quality, profitable, growth-oriented companies that they identify through dogged research and purchase when attractively priced. They don't "invest in the market" or view stock shares as commodities they can trade to get rich quickly. They ignore media coverage of the stock market that dwells on the concerns of short-term traders rather than addressing the information needs of long-term investors.

Regardless of how people structure their investments, one key to achieving their goals is to harness the power of compounding. Over long periods, even small investments can grow into substantial sums. Therefore, the younger the investor, the more benefit from compounding. Suppose someone starts investing $2,000 a year at age 19 and stops after 8 years. At a 9% average rate of return, the portfolio would grow to $692,796 by the time the investor reaches age 65. (For the sake of simplicity, this example does not factor in taxes or transaction costs.) The amount invested would total $16,000. To achieve a comparable amount at the same rate of return, another investor who begins contributing $2,000 a year at age 27 would need to continue for 39 years until age 65. The late starter would have invested a total of $78,000—almost five times more—but accumulated only $673,765.

Choosing individual stocks has several advantages over one popular alternative—mutual funds. Deregulation and the resulting competition have helped lower brokerage commissions for stock trades, for example, and many companies now sell shares directly to individual investors at minimal cost. In contrast, mutual funds—particularly those funds that are actively managed—charge a variety of fees and commissions that in recent years have been rising. Fund managers may engage in relatively frequent trading, raising costs, increasing tax liabilities, and eroding the ultimate return to shareholders. Those costs help account for the fact that most actively managed funds fail to generate rates of return that even match the growth rates of major stock indexes.

Mutual funds remain attractive partly because investors can simply pay a fee to have their portfolios managed professionally. But individuals who invest in stocks exclusively through mutual funds miss out on the opportunity to learn how to make their own investment decisions. That's especially true when investors choose index funds—"baskets" of stocks that closely match those constituting indexes such as the Standard & Poor's 500 index, the Dow Jones industrial average, and the NASDAQ composite index. A fund's rate of return therefore will closely follow movements of its index, minus the impact of fees, of course. Index fund investors benefit from the relentless upward movement of the market long term, but they miss the opportunity to become more knowledgeable and informed investors that can come with investment club membership.

Investment club advocates maintain that investors who choose individual stocks through diligent research often can exceed the average returns offered by index funds, especially when they buy shares in quality growing companies at attractive prices and hold them over long periods. Achieving results that are even slightly higher than the market averages can produce much larger portfolios over time, given the mathematics of compounding. For example, over 30 years an initial investment of $10,000 that produces a 12% average annual rate of return—just under the recent 50-year record of the S&P 500—would grow to $299,597. But with an average annual return of 15%, the same $10,000 would produce more than double the result, as it grows to $662,118.

For many people, joining a club is one of the most efficient ways to invest in individual stocks. By pooling their money, members have more to invest. That makes it easier for them to diversify, that is, reduce risk by holding shares in a variety of companies. Participating in a group effort and receiving moral support makes it easier for the average person to stick with a program of disciplined, long-term investing through the ups and downs of the broader market. Also, members can divide up the work of researching companies, which makes stock picking more practical for those who are short of time. And members benefit from sharing their investment knowledge and experience as they develop a disciplined approach to studying stocks and investment.

Small groups of investors had banded together previously, but the second half of the last century saw the investment club movement blossom. The National Association of Investors Corporation (NAIC), a nonprofit membership organization, was founded in 1951 to provide educational services and promote the growth of investment clubs. As of mid-2002, 30,349 investment clubs belonged to the association. The average club membership was 11. A total of 389,174 people belonged to the educational organization, including individual members with no investment club affiliation.

The late George A. Nicholson, Jr., father of the investment club movement, believed in "people's capitalism"—the economic freedom and opportunity that flows when a large portion of the population owns common stocks. He believed that investment clubs were the best means to provide three necessary ingredients for people's capitalism. To foster individual stock ownership—and thereby support modern capitalism and free enterprise—Nicholson and other pioneers of the movement founded NAIC to spread their message and provide members with ways to become educated investors. They taught that investors can stay motivated by establishing clear long-term financial goals, and they developed a set of simple guiding principles.

NAIC advocates a disciplined approach to investing. The nonprofit corporation recommends investing in growth stocks—stocks of companies whose sales and earnings are growing at rates that are consistently higher than the growth rates of their industries or the overall economy. One of the chief characteristics of such a company often is a management team that values growth very highly and makes it a guiding principle for the business.

Another principle that the NAIC teaches is to invest regularly and to reinvest dividends and any capital gains from the sale of shares. Investors are encouraged to seek out corporations that display signs of quality such as consistent growth in sales and profitability. Another principle is to diversify—to build portfolios that include corporations from different size categories, economic sectors, and industries. Investors also are encouraged to remember the "rule of five"—on average, long-term investors can expect three of every five carefully selected holdings to perform as expected or close to expectations, one to prove a major disappointment, and one to exceed original projections by a significant margin.

A club membership of around 16 is considered ideal: with more members, finding a large enough meeting place may prove difficult; with fewer, each member has to take on a larger workload. The members of a new club need to appoint officers, agree upon a structure—a partnership, usually—and file the necessary paperwork. They also must agree upon an investment approach such as the long-term growth strategy the NAIC recommends. They must select a brokerage service to handle their portfolio transactions. The members decide where and how often to meet—monthly meetings are typical—and establish how much each member will contribute regularly to the portfolio.

In some clubs, however, members only consult about stocks—they don't pool their money. While they may reach a consensus about a particular stock, individual members decide whether to buy or sell shares for their own portfolios. This approach is found among "virtual" clubs whose members often live in different areas and confer online.

Each member is responsible for tracking the progress of a few businesses. At meetings they take turns profiling individual corporations. Following such presentations, they vote on whether to purchase or sell some of those companies' shares. Members also give educational presentations, and they may invite outside speakers such as local stockbrokers or financial planners. Discussions of portfolio accounting and other club business are part of most meetings.

Club members in many parts of the country can attend educational seminars and investment fairs sponsored by volunteers in NAIC's 115 regional chapters. NAIC also holds nationwide conferences such as its annual congress, where attendees can go to seminars, meet representatives of publicly traded companies, and talk shop with other investors. (See also EQUITY SECURITIES; FINANCIAL EDUCATION FOR SENIORS; INFLUENCES ON RETIREMENT INVESTMENT DECISIONS; INVESTMENT ADVICE; INVESTOR EDUCATION; MUTUAL FUNDS.)

**Organizations**

American Association of Individual Investors
FoolMart
National Association of Investors Corporation

**Suggested Readings**

Maranjian, Selena. 1998. *Investment Clubs: How to Start and Run One the Motley Fool Way.* Alexandria, VA: Motley Fool Books.

O'Hara, Thomas E., and Kenneth S. Janke, Sr. 1998. *Starting and Running a Profitable Investment Club: The Official Guide of the National Association of Investors Corporation.* Royal Oak, MI: NAIC.

**References**

National Association of Investors Corporation. 2002. *Introducing Teenagers to . . . Investing the NAIC Way!* Royal Oak, MI: Author.

T. Rowe Price Investment Services, Inc. 2001. "Historical Returns for Different Investments." Available online at http://www.troweprice.com/retirement/historical.html.

*Kevin J. Lamiman*

**INVESTMENTS.** See Annuities; Bonds; Commodities; Derivatives; Equity Securities; Mutual Funds; Savings Account Trusts; Savings Investments.

**INVESTOR EDUCATION,** knowledge designed for individuals preparing to invest or already having holdings in the capital markets to help them make informed investment decisions. A generation ago, retirees who had worked for a company that provided a retirement benefit could look forward to receiving a pension check every month for the rest of their lives. Workers who are retiring currently are less likely to have a traditional pension plan, and they must be aware that Social Security benefits will typically fall far short of meeting all their retirement needs. Income to supplement Social Security increasingly comes from periodic distributions from a defined contribution plan, IRA (Individual Retirement Account), or another type of planned retirement savings where workers must make their own investment decisions. Unlike a traditional pension plan, the ultimate payout value of these retirement plans will fluctuate, depending upon the investment choices made, and they may or may not provide adequate income for retirement. Even if a worker uses a financial advisor or other investment expert, he or she must take ultimate responsibility for the investing choices that are made, both before and after retirement.

The dramatic growth of 401(k)-type retirement plans that pay retirement benefits in lump-sum distributions rather than annuities, and the increasing payment of lump sums from defined benefit pension plans, means that individuals are increasingly responsible for decisions that will determine their future retirement. According to Dallas Salisbury, president and chief executive officer of the Employee Benefit Research Institute (EBRI), workers who change jobs or otherwise trigger the distribution of retiree savings must decide whether to spend it immediately, whether to save the lump sum and roll it over, how to invest it, and how fast they can spend it in retirement and not outlive the money (seniorjournal.com 2003).

Investing for retirement requires many assumptions, such as the annual rate of inflation, the after-tax return investments will earn, estimated life expectancy, and expected retirement expenses. Faced with more complex decisions about retirement—from choosing long-term care insurance to asset allocations, from taking distributions from IRAs to selecting stocks, bonds, or mutual funds, from charitable giving to estate planning—today's retirees must learn to make financial decisions that will have long-lasting effects. To make those decisions, workers must become educated even though they may choose to work with a financial planner or other expert. "Don't assume that retirement is a stage of life that will simply take care of itself," say Robert J. Garner and Robert Coplan, authors of the *Ernst & Young's Personal Financial Planning Guide* (1995).

There are several sources of reliable, up-to-date investor information. Local libraries carry traditional print resources—magazines, books, and computers for searching Internet resources. A local senior citizen center may offer classes on Internet use. Senior centers may also offer seminars and workshops on investing, estate planning, and making the most of financial resources. If they do not, individuals may organize programs and invite guest speakers from the community who are qualified to address such topics as the financial markets, diversification, risk management, estate planning, charitable giving, and investing after retirement. Community colleges or universities are good resources for speakers, classes in investing, or financial planning courses. Many offer discounts for seniors who want to take classes, and many others permit seniors to audit courses at reduced tuition rates. (See also DEFINED CONTRIBUTION PLAN; EDUCATION OF OLDER ADULTS; FINANCIAL ADVISORS; FINANCIAL EDUCATION FOR SENIORS; RETIREMENT PLANS—401(k); RETIREMENT PLANS—403(b); RETIREMENT PREPAREDNESS; RISK TOLERANCE.)

### Organizations

American Association of Individual Investors
Bond Market Association
CNN Money
Dow Jones & Co. Online Investing
FinanCenter, Inc.
International Association of Financial Planners
Intuit
Investment FAC
Investors Guide
Mutual Fund Education Alliance
National Association of Investors Corporation
Office of Investor Education and Assistance
Senior Journal
Smart Money University

### References

Gard, Jim. 1996. *The Small Investor*. Berkeley, CA: Ten Speed Press.

Garner, Robert J., and Robert Coplan. 1995. *Ernst & Young's Personal Financial Planning Guide*. New York: John Wiley & Sons.

Lynch, Peter. 1989. *One Up on Wall Street*. New York: Simon and Schuster.

O'Hara, Thomas E., and Kenneth S. Janke, Sr. 1995. *Taking Control of Your Financial Life*. Burr Ridge, IL: Irwin Press.

Seniorjournal.com. 2003. "Baby Boomers to Face Financial Challenges in Retirement." July 25. Available online at http://www.seniorjournal.com/NEWS/Retirement/04-30-01BoomRetirmntThreat.htm.

Tobias, Andrew. 2002. *The Only Investment Guide You'll Ever Need*. San Diego, CA: Harcourt Brace & Company.

*Jo Ann Linck and Karen Brelsford*

# Encyclopedia of Retirement and Finance

# Encyclopedia of Retirement and Finance

VOLUME II: J–Z

Lois A. Vitt, *Editor-in-Chief*

*Consulting Editors*
E. Craig MacBean and Jurg K. Siegenthaler

*Associate Editors*
Jamie Losikoff-Kent, Candace D. Jenkins,
Mary Helen McSweeney, Julie Overton, Sandra L. Reynolds,
M. Shelton Smith, Denise Talbot-White

*Managing Editors*
Ingrid Carlson
Jay Schweig

Foreword by Yung-Ping Chen
Introduction by Dallas L. Salisbury

Published under the Auspices of the Institute for
Socio-Financial Studies

GREENWOOD PRESS
Westport, Connecticut • London

**Library of Congress Cataloging-in-Publication Data**

Encyclopedia of retirement and finance / Lois A. Vitt, editor-in-chief ; consulting editors, E. Craig MacBean and Jurg K. Siegenthaler ; associate editors, Jamie Losikoff-Kent . . . [et al.] ; foreword by Yung-Ping Chen ; introduction by Dallas L. Salisbury.
p. cm.
Includes bibliographical references and index.
ISBN 0–313–32495–6 (2 vols. : alk. paper)
1. Old age—Economic aspects—United States—Encyclopedias. 2. Retirement planning—United States—Encyclopedias. 3. Retirement income—United States—Law and legislation—Encyclopedias. 4. Aged—Finance, Personal—Encyclopedias. 5. Retirement—Economic aspects—United States—Encyclopedias. I. Vitt, Lois A. II. MacBean, E. Craig. III. Siegenthaler, Jürg K., 1939– IV. Institute for Socio-Financial Studies. V. Encyclopedia of financial gerontology.
HQ1064.U5E524 2003
305.26'03—dc22 2003058417

British Library Cataloguing in Publication Data is available.



Library of Congress Catalog Card Number: 2003058417
ISBN: 0–313–32495–6

First published in 2003

Greenwood Press, 88 Post Road West, Westport, CT 06881
An imprint of Greenwood Publishing Group, Inc.
www.greenwood.com

Printed in the United States of America

The paper used in this book complies with the Permanent Paper Standard issued by the National Information Standards Organization (Z39.48–1984).

10 9 8 7 6 5 4 3 2 1

# Contents

# Core Topics

## Advisors, Advice, and Support

Accountants

Agents and Brokers

Asset Allocation after Retirement

Banking Services for the Mature Market

Cash Flow Planning for Retirees

Corporate Eldercare Programs

CPA Eldercare Services

Credit Scores

Estate Planning

Ethics in Financial Planning

Financial Advisors

Financial Counseling for Mid- to Later Life

Financial Education for Seniors

Financial Literacy

Financial Planning Process

Financial Recovery in Later Life

Frailty Planning

Geriatric Care Managers (GCMs)

Gerontological Social Work

Investment Advice

Investment Clubs

Investor Education

Life Planning

Marketing to Mature Adults

Ombudsman

Physician–Older Patient Relationships

### Economic and Income Security



### Employment, Work, and Retirement

## Family and Intergenerational Issues



## Financial Investments and Insurance

Long-Term Care Insurance, Private

Long-Term Care Insurance: Individual Disability-Escalating Annuities (IDEAs)

Long-Term Care Insurance (LTCI)—A Consumer's Perspective

Medicare Supplemental Insurance

Mutual Funds

Predatory Lending

Real Estate Investments

Risk Tolerance

Savings Account Trusts

Savings Investments

Taxpayer Issues of Older Adults

U.S. Personal Saving Rates

U.S. Savings Bonds

## Health Care and Health Coverage

Activities of Daily Living (ADLs)

Advance Directives

Assisted Living

Community-Based Care

Cost of Family Caregiving

Day Programs for Adults

Drugs and Senior Citizens

Geriatric Rehabilitation

Gerontological Nurse Practitioners (GNPs)

Health and Longevity

Health Benefits

Health Maintenance Organizations and Management Health Care for Older Adults

Home Care Services for Older Adults

Hospice Care

Medicaid Planning

Medical Savings Accounts (MSAs) and Medical IRAs

Medicare

Medicare + Choice

Mental Health among Older Adults

Mental Health Care Financing

Nursing Homes

Pharmacists

## Housing and Housing Finance

Board and Care Homes

Condominiums

## Legal Issues



## Quality of Life and Well-Being

Internet Use by Seniors

Leisure

Minority Older Adults

Older Americans Act

Oldest Old

Religious Giving by Older Adults

Retirement Preparedness

Senior Discounts

Snowbird Checklist and Transborder Issues

Transportation

Vacation Homes and Recreational Property

Volunteering

Wealth Span

# J

**JOB LOCK,** usually defined as "a reduction in workers' willingness to quit their jobs arising from the risk of losing health coverage" (Federal Reserve 1998). Employment-related health insurance is a central component of employee compensation—it is no longer a "fringe benefit." As the cost of health care continues to rise, there is both anecdotal and scientific evidence that employee decisions to change employment, including the change from work to retirement, are as much (if not more) influenced by health insurance benefits as by such traditional employment factors as salary, pension, location, and job content.

As the cost of both health care and health insurance increases, workers are increasingly worried about the possibility of losing their health insurance and so may not seriously think about job changes in their financial and personal planning. In 1998, the Employee Benefit Research Institute concluded that "job lock is a growing problem with 27% of Americans age 20 and older reporting that they or an immediate family member had experienced some form of job lock, up from just 13% in 1991" (Employee Benefit Research Institute 1998).

## Job Lock and Retirement Planning

The decision to retire, like the decision to change jobs, is similarly linked to the loss of employer-based health insurance—but with four important differences (and complications).

1. As a kind of "job change," retirement is a more or less permanent move out of the labor force and not simply a change from one employer and "fringe benefit" package to another.
2. From both the maturational aging and the generational cohort perspectives, retiree health insurance (and therefore the retirement decision) is inextricably intertwined with Medicare. Consider the "cohort psychology" of today's preretirees. Those who are 55 to 60 years old in 2003 (born 1943 to 1948) were 17 to 22 years old when Medicare became law in 1965. Thus these middle-agers have spent their entire adult work lives anticipating the availability of a national program of health insurance benefits upon their retirement.
3. Medicare eligibility was set at age 65 at a time when the "official" retirement age, that is the Social Security full-benefits retirement age, was also 65. Although nowadays more people retire early—at age 62 with reduced Social Security benefits, or even younger because withdrawals

from most defined contribution accounts can be made without penalty as early as age 59½—eligibility for Medicare health insurance remains at age 65.

4. Previously, many employers provided paid or subsidized retiree health insurance. In response to Financial Accounting Standards Board (FASB) standards implemented in 1990, however, many of these retiree health insurance benefits have been scaled back or eliminated (Cutler 2002b).

A consequence of these several personal and policy trends is that job lock related to health insurance is a real and complex factor in the retirement decision process for middle-aged and older workers: "There is clear and unambiguous evidence that health insurance is a central determinant of retirement decisions" (Gruber and Madrian 2002).

### New Evidence

In 2002, the Health Confidence Survey (HCS)—a continuing survey of Americans of all ages toward health care issues—included several questions probing the connection between health insurance coverage and the retirement decision (Employee Benefit Research Institute 2002). Because a fifth of the national sample of 1,000 adults said they are retired, the survey asked both projective and retrospective questions about the retirement planning process. We start with the basic question: "When determining what age to retire, how much did [do] you think about access to health insurance benefits?"

| | Not Retired | Retired |
|---|---|---|
| A lot | 54% | 48% |
| A little | 25% | 26% |
| None | 20% | 15% |

Although those already retired thought about health insurance a bit more than do future retirees, the magnitude of concern is parallel. Access to health insurance benefits was and is an important element of the retirement decision.

Because both retirement behavior (early versus age 65) and employer health insurance practices are changing, respondents were asked if they expect to receive health insurance from or through their employer before their Medicare benefits become available. Future retirees who said they plan to retire earlier than age 65 were asked: "How do you expect to get health insurance between [retirement age given] and when you are eligible to receive Medicare?" The parallel question was asked of retirees who retired before age 65.

| | Retired Early | Not Retired |
|---|---|---|
| Employer | 65% | 43% |
| Personal Money | 8% | 37% |
| Go Uninsured | 11% | 1% |
| Other | 14% | 19% |

There is clearly a shift in the role of the employer. Fewer than half (43%) of those who currently plan to retire early see employer-provided health insurance as their "bridge" to Medicare, compared to two-thirds (65%) of current retirees who retired before age 65. Even these 43% may find their optimistic expectations blunted when they begin to engage the "fine print" of the retirement process. What is more clear, however, is that compared to current retirees these future early retirees do not intend to be uninsured (1% versus 11%). Four times as many preretirees intend or hope to be able to purchase health insurance from personal funds.

Alternatively, a more direct response to the declining role of an employer-provided (or -subsidized) insurance bridge to Medicare would be a postponement of retirement until Medicare eligibility arrives; in other words, health insurance job lock. To assess this directly, the Health Confidence Survey asked the following question of respondents who said that their employer offers pre-Medicare health insurance *and* who currently plan to retire early (about 25% of the sample of those not retired): "Would you retire before you are eligible for Medicare if a former employer or union did not provide health insurance benefits for retirees?"

| | |
|---|---|
| No | 60% |
| Yes | 31% |
| Don't Know | 10% |

The implications of this pattern of expectations for job lock are fairly clear: twice as many people would change their current plans and would not retire early.

### Additional Job Lock Complexity

Finally, from the perspective of financial gerontology there are at least three additional health insurance job lock complexities that are central components of retirement planning.

First, employment-connected health insurance is typically health insurance for the whole family. Consequently, the worker's *own* age, retirement, and Medicare eligibility are not the only variables in the equation. Continued health insurance for a spouse and young-adult children are also part of retirement planning and thus become critical elements of the job lock situation.

Second, declines in health insurance benefits and declines in pension benefits do not have equal impact. Families can respond to a decline retirement income in several ways: discretionary purchases can be postponed, permanent or temporary changes can be made in residence or lifestyle, and larger withdrawals can be made from some retirement accounts. Not so for health insurance. People cannot simply decide to not be sick next month. Consequently, job lock is more likely to be a response to the risk of losing health insurance than to losing retirement income opportunities.

Third is financial literacy. The Financial Literacy 2000 survey (Cutler 1997) documented a frighteningly low level of knowledge in this context: substantial proportions of the public (1) thought they almost automatically would receive employer-provided health insurance alongside receiving a company pension and (2) also did not know that Medicare does not begin until age 65. This Medicare illiteracy was more recently reconfirmed by the 2001 Health Confidence Survey. Only 38% of respondents knew that Medicare eligibility begins at age 65; 18% cited ages younger than 65, 4% said "when eligible for Social Security," and 32% said "don't know" (Employee Benefit Research

Institute 2001). (See also EMPLOYEE BENEFITS IN THE UNITED STATES; HEALTH AND LONGEVITY; HEALTH BENEFITS; MEDICARE; POSTRETIREMENT HEALTH COVERAGE [PRHC]; RETIREMENT PLANNING; WORKFORCE PATTERNS, CHANGES IN.)

### References

Cutler, Neal E. 1997. "The False Alarms and Blaring Sirens of Financial Literacy: Middle-Agers' Knowledge of Retirement Income, Health Finance, and Long-Term Care." *Generations* 21 (Summer): 34–40.

Cutler, Neal E. 2002a. *Advising Mature Clients: The New Science of Wealth Span Planning*. New York: John Wiley & Sons.

Cutler, Neal E. 2002b. "Job Lock and Financial Planning: The Impact of Health Insurance on the Retirement Decision." *Journal of Financial Service Professionals* (November): 29–32.

Employee Benefit Research Institute. 1998. EBRI News Release, August 7.

Employee Benefit Research Institute. 2001. "Medicare: Awareness, Confidence, Satisfaction, and Reform." *Facts from EBRI*. October. Available online at http://www.ebri.org/facts/0701fact.pdf.

Employee Benefit Research Institute. 2002. "2002 Health Confidence Survey: Summary of Findings." Fifth in Continuing Series. September. Available online at http://www.ebri.org/hcs/2002/hcs02sof.pdf.

Federal Reserve Bank of San Francisco. 1998. "Health Insurance and the U.S. Labor Market." News Release, April 13.

Gruber, Jonathan, and Brigitte C. Madrian. 2002. "Health Insurance, Labor Supply, and Job Mobility: A Critical Review of the Literature." NBER Working Paper No. W8817. Cambridge, MA: National Bureau of Economic Research, February.

*Neal E. Cutler*

# K

**KEOGH PLANS,** qualified retirement plans for self-employed individuals and their employees. Keogh plans were established by the Self Employed Individuals Tax Retirement Act of 1962, otherwise known as the Keogh Act or H.R. 10. When designed and operated in compliance with Internal Revenue Code (IRC) and Employee Retirement Income Security Act (ERISA) of 1974 guidelines, such qualified plans are afforded special tax treatment: contributions plus earnings on contributions enjoy tax deferral until benefits are received. Self-employed persons, partnerships, and owners of unincorporated businesses can set up a Keogh plan at a financial institution such as a bank or mutual fund, as either a defined benefit or defined contribution plan.

## Defined Benefit Plan

A defined benefit plan is so called because the ultimate retirement benefit is definite and determinable as a dollar amount or as a percentage of wages. To determine these amounts, defined benefit plans usually base the benefit calculation on a combination of years of employment, wages, and/or age. These plans are funded entirely by the employer, and the responsibility for the payment of the benefit and all risk on monies invested to fund that benefit rests with the employer. Benefits typically are not payable until normal retirement age and usually are paid in the form of a lifetime annuity. Monies received as a lifetime annuity will be taxed at ordinary income tax rates and are ineligible for rollover to an Individual Retirement Account (IRA). Lump-sum payments may be transferred to an IRA to defer immediate taxation. On transfer to an IRA, the proceeds are subject to IRA rules and regulations. Early withdrawals (prior to age 59½) are assessed an additional excise tax of 10%.

## Defined Contribution Plan

A defined contribution plan is so called because the contribution is defined, but the ultimate benefit to be paid is not. In such plans, each participant has an individual account. The benefit at retirement depends upon the amounts contributed and on the investment performance of that account through the years. In such plans, the investment risk may rest solely with the employee because of the opportunity to choose from a number of investment options. These plans take many forms and are known by various names such as money purchase, profit sharing, 401(k), or 403(b) plans.

**Table 1**
**Allowable Contributions, 2002–2006**

| Year | 2002 | 2003 | 2004 | 2005 | 2006 |
|---|---|---|---|---|---|
| Amount of allowable contribution | $11,000 | $12,000 | $13,000 | $14,000 | $15,000 |

In 2002, the maximum contribution to a defined contribution plan increased to the lesser of 100% of compensation or $40,000. The maximum dollar amount will be adjusted upward for inflation in later years by $1,000 increments whenever cumulative inflation causes the limit to exceed the next higher $1,000. At retirement, defined contribution plan benefits are typically paid in installments or as a lump sum; however, they may also be paid as an annuity. Income tax ramifications and rollover options are the same as those described above for defined benefit plans. Installment payments for a period of fewer than ten years are eligible for transfer to an IRA, while those lasting for a period of ten years or more are not. In 2002 and later, increased portability will exist between various types of contributory plans, due to transfer allowances among IRAs, 401(k)s, 403(b)s, and 457 plans.

As defined contribution plans, Keogh plans may be structured as a profit sharing, money purchase, combined profit sharing/money purchase, 401(k), or 403(b) plan, the most popular being the latter two.

### 401(k) Plan

Taking its name from the section of the Internal Revenue Code that prescribes the rules under which it operates, the 401(k) retirement plan is one in which an employer permits an employee to defer receipt of part of his or her compensation by contributing that part to his or her account in the 401(k) plan. Deferred contributions are made on a pretax basis, and those contributions and all earnings remain untaxed until withdrawn from the plan. The 401(k) may permit voluntary, after-tax contributions by employees. Earnings on after-tax contributions accumulate tax free until withdrawn. Many 401(k) plans include a matching contribution from the employer according to a set formula (e.g., 50% of the employee's contribution up to a maximum of 6% of compensation). Employers may also make contributions to an employee's account independent of the employee's contribution, and these contributions may be tied to a firm's profits as part of a profit sharing plan.

In 2002, a plan participant may contribute up to the lesser of 100% of pay or the annual dollar limit shown for each year in Table 1. In 2007 and thereafter, the $15,000 limit will increase in $500 increments whenever the cumulative effects of inflation indicate such a rise is needed.

In addition to the normal contribution limits outlined above, starting in 2002 those over the age of 50 may make an additional "catch-up" contribution in the amounts shown in Table 2. In 2007 and thereafter, the $5,000 "catch-up" limit will increase in $500 increments whenever the cumulative effects of inflation indicate such a rise is needed.

**Table 2**
**Allowable "Catch-Up" Contributions, 2002–2006**

| Year | 2002 | 2003 | 2004 | 2005 | 2006 |
|---|---|---|---|---|---|
| Allowable catch-up contribution | $1,000 | $2,000 | $3,000 | $4,000 | $5,000 |

Beginning in 2006, 401(k) plans may allow participants to make contributions through those plans to a Roth-401(k) account. The decision to offer this option is entirely up to the employer. Under this new arrangement, contributions to the Roth-401(k) account will be taxed in the year made, but future qualified distributions from that account will not be taxed. Contributions to a Roth-401(k) account may be made up to the $15,000 maximum yearly limit.

A 401(k) plan generally offers participants an opportunity to direct their account contributions to a broad range of investment options from conservative risk to aggressive risk. These options may include institutional or mutual funds investing in the money market, bond market, or stock market; annuities; guaranteed investment contracts (GICs); company stock; and self-directed brokerage accounts. A typical plan will offer a selection of a money market fund, a bond fund, and a stock fund.

In general, a 401(k) plan limits withdrawals of assets to five occasions: termination from employment, disability, reaching the age of 59½, retirement, and death. Additionally, the plan may optionally include provisions for loans and/or hardship withdrawals.

### 403(b) Plan

Taking its name from the section of the Internal Revenue Code that establishes the rules under which it operates, the 403(b) plan is also known as and sometimes called a tax-sheltered or a tax-deferred annuity program. This plan is for educational, religious, and charitable (i.e., 501(c)(3)) organization employees. It operates under similar maximum contribution rules, catch-up provisions, and withdrawal privileges as a 401(k) plan. Like the 401(k), pretax contributions and all earnings remain tax free until withdrawn. The principal differences between a 401(k) and 403(b) plan is that unlike the 401(k) plan investment options in the 403(b) plan are limited to annuities and mutual funds only. (See also HEALTH AND LONGEVITY; INDIVIDUAL RETIREMENT ACCOUNT (IRAs); INFLUENCES ON RETIREMENT INVESTMENT DECISIONS; INVESTOR EDUCATION; MEDICAL SAVINGS ACCOUNTS (MSAs) AND MEDICAL IRAs; PENSION PLANS FOR THE SELF-EMPLOYED.)

### Organization

Equity Analytics, Ltd.

### References

Adelman, Philip J., and Alan M. Marks. 2001. *Entrepreneurial Finance: Finance for Small Business*. Upper Saddle River, NJ: Prentice Hall.

Gitman, Lawrence J., and Michael D. Joehnk. 2002. Personal Financial Planning. 9th ed. Mason, OH: South-Western.

Keown, Arthur J. 2001. *Personal Finance*. Upper Saddle River, NJ: Prentice Hall.

*Ganas K. Rakes and Rajesh Narayanan*

**KING LEAR SYNDROME,** a predicament illustrated in Shakespeare's play *King Lear* and used as a teaching tool for financial educators, financial advisors, and planners. Nearly 500 years after it was first created, Shakespeare's *King Lear* holds relevant estate planning lessons for preretirees today. According to this teaching viewpoint, King Lear has little right to consider himself "a man more sinned against than sinning," when considering the manner in which he planned and executed the disposition of his estate. Although Lear is in his senior years, he has neither ill health nor failing mental powers to excuse the way he chose to distribute his worldly goods among his three children. His estate planning errors included falling prey to manipulative declarations of love from his children and planning more for his physical comfort than his financial security.

Familiarity with the King Lear syndrome can help seniors preserve both their financial and personal integrity in planning for their later years. Some practical suggestions to be gleaned from *King Lear* include how financial provisions for children can be made while providing for one's own financial security—particularly payment for long-term residential health care, should the need arise.

### Lear's Errors

As a father who relied on the compassion of his children, King Lear would have been better off relying on the kindness of strangers, since with only one exception those who came to the older king's aid were not related by blood. Lear's mistakes included pride and the refusal to look beyond the appearance of things to their substance.

Lear wanted to divide his wealth and lands among his three heirs to avoid the responsibilities of managing his kingdom in his later years. At the same time, he desired to provide for himself. As Lear puts it in the beginning of the play:

> Know that we have divided in three our kingdom; and 'tis our fast intent to shake all cares and business from our age, conferring them on younger strengths while we unburdened crawl toward death.

Lear's motives were clearly reasonable, but the manner in which he planned to divide his estate was unreasonable. Although the king had a court of advisors, none were consulted about the crucial issue of how and among whom his wealth was to be divided. Lear relied instead on his childrens' verbal professions of love for him to measure how significant a child's inheritance should be:

> Tell me, my daughters—
> Since now we will divest us both of rule,
> Interest of territory, cares of state—
> Which of you shall we say doth love us most,
> That we our largest bounty may extend,
> Where nature doth with merit challenge.

In response to their father's request, both of Lear's older daughters are eloquent in their verbal expression of love for their father, one of them claiming to love Lear more than her own husband. In his pride and vanity, Lear eagerly accepts the accolades and professions of love from his two elder children. He does not consider whether their past actions actually reflect this love or whether their future actions are likely to match their flowery words. Thus, Lear's two elder children secure their inheritance. Turning to his youngest and favorite daughter, he bids her to speak:

> Now, our joy,
> Although our last and least,
> To whose young love
> The vines of France and milk of Burgundy
> Strive to be interessed,
> What can you say to draw
> A third more opulent than your sisters?
> Speak.

Lear's third daughter finds she cannot "heave her heart up into her throat" to flatter her father with empty words of love and praise. She tells her father merely that she loves him "according to her bond." The king becomes enraged when she remains adamant in her refusal to flatter him. He thus disinherits the only child who really loves him, banishing her and dividing her portion of the kingdom between her two unworthy sisters. Further, he expels the court advisors who try to dissuade him from his foolish course of action.

Lear has been prideful, refused wise counsel, and made rash judgments. He is soon made to pay, for in their greed his elder daughters deny him the luxuries to which he has become accustomed. He eventually is denied even a roof over his head and ultimately pays for his follies with his life. Even the court fool realizes that the king himself has acted foolishly and tells him so:

> If thou wert my fool, nuncle,
> I'd have thee beaten
> For being old before thy time.
> How's that?
> Thou shouldst not have been old till
> thou hadst been wise.

## Lear's Lessons

The lessons from *King Lear* are harsh. Many who read and study this play and see it performed believe the punishments meted out to Lear are disproportionate to the poor property decisions he has made. While such a reaction may be based on the certainty that one's own children would not behave in a similar manner, wise counsel and proper estate planning should still be employed. Gifting estates to children to avoid taxation, for example, might backfire as it did for Lear. In an emergency, medical or otherwise, one may need to access that money, and children to whom it has been given may not be able to give it back. The desire to make gifts to children is shared by many Americans. Preliminary results of a nationwide survey conducted by the National Institute on Aging

(NIA) illustrate this. More than 12,000 adults aged 51 to 61 were surveyed in this study, and more than one-third expressed a desire to be generous to their families, all having given at least $500 to a child in 1992 (AARP 1993). This kind of gift giving reflects the generosity Americans feel for their offspring.

Such generosity, however, must be tempered with common financial sense under the guidance of professionals in order not to fall prey to the second major error made by Lear. He failed to understand the relationship between money and power, believing he could give away his property and money to his three daughters and still wield the power and command the respect to which he was accustomed. Gerontologist Robert Atchley (1997) comments on the relationship between money and power, using the example of a modern head of state:

> Former President Eisenhower had a great deal of prestige and influence in old age, not because he was old but because he had been both a president and a military chief. A great many of the richest and most influential Americans are old, but their age is not the reason why they are rich or influential. In fact, their wealth and influence discounts their age, in that rich and powerful people are much less likely than others to be disqualified from participation purely on account of age. Age discrimination happens mainly to people who are already disadvantaged.

Lear found that his money and lands were his power base, and when gone, he no longer was respected by others. Thus, protected assets may help insulate an aging person from age prejudice. Like racism and sexism, ageism is an opinion that stereotypes elders as unproductive, old-fashioned in their ways, and outdated in their perspectives (Pai 1990).

Lear's third error was his failure to consult advisors when planning to distribute his wealth. The services of an objective, knowledgeable estate planner can help guide one to a middle course between giving away assets to protect them from taxes or a health care agency and turning over these assets prematurely to well-intentioned children or others. Even if adopting a more optimistic view, the King Lear example can point the way to a proactive stance. According to the King Lear syndrome, assets can help protect against ageism in one's later years. Today's seniors have the opportunity to discover that power lies not so much in the ability to control others but in the ability to control one's own destiny. Approaching financial planning in an analytical and objective way can be of great benefit in later life for everyone involved. (See also FINANCIAL EDUCATION FOR SENIORS; FINANCIAL LITERACY; INTERGENERATIONAL CONFLICT AND FINANCIAL ISSUES; LIFE PLANNING; PLANNING FOR SURVIVING SPECIAL NEEDS CHILDREN.)

**References**

AARP. 1993. "Middle Americans Glum About Prospects." *AARP Bulletin*, September 15.

Atchley, Robert C. 1997. *Social Forces and Aging*. 8th ed. Belmont, CA: Wadsworth.

Garner, Robert J., Robert B. Coplan, Martin Nissenbaum, Barbara J. Raasch, and Charles L. Ratner. 2000. *Ernst & Young's Personal Financial Planning Guide*. 3rd ed. New York: John Wiley & Sons.

Pai, Young. 1990. *Cultural Foundations of Education*. New York: Merrill.

Shakespeare, William. 1980. *King Lear*. New York: Bantam Books.

*James A. Anderson*

# L

**LEGAL ISSUES.** See Advance Directives; Attorneys; Bankruptcy; Divorce and Older Adults; Elder Law Practice; Ethics in Financial Planning; Taxpayer Issues of Older Adults.

**LEISURE.** *Free time*, *nonwork activities*, *hobbies*, *travel*, and *recreation* are all terms associated with leisure. Through the centuries, leisure has been defined in many different ways. For Aristotle and Plato, leisure referred to contemplation and was regarded as "the good life." Likewise, de Grazia (1964) conceptualized leisure as "a state of being," and Pieper (1963) referred to leisure as "a mental and spiritual attitude." The idea that leisure is a state of mind is still present in definitions today and is often articulated as the meanings associated with a particular experience. Inherent in this thinking is the idea that leisure experiences are intrinsically motivated, that is, chosen for noninstrumental reasons (Neulinger 1974).

In his 1899 book, *The Theory of the Leisure Class*, Veblen defined leisure as the "non-productive consumption of time." Instead of being valued as the highest form of living, as in Ancient Greece, leisure was viewed as nonproductive, idle time. This devaluation of leisure was based on the principles associated with the Protestant Work Ethic whereby work is valued and leisure devalued or relegated to conceptions such as residual time, that is, time that is left over once the important tasks in life have been completed.

Defining leisure as nonwork time has proved problematic for many segments of the population who may not be currently employed in paid work such as the retired, the unemployed, and homemakers whose work is unpaid, takes place in the home, and as such, is often not considered "real work." Moreover, homemakers frequently report that their work never ends as the needs of their families are constant—and thus, if leisure is defined as nonwork time, this would imply that they never experience it.

Another way of defining leisure is activity. Dumazedier (1974) suggested that leisure can be defined as activity that is freely chosen and provides opportunities for self-expression and satisfaction. However, this alone might not be a good determinant of leisure, as activities often are not freely chosen, and it is possible that the same activity may be experienced as leisure for an individual in one situation and not in another. For example, playing basketball after school with friends would be leisure; however, playing basketball with the same friends as part of a physical education class in school may not be experienced in the same way, as participation is obligatory rather than freely chosen. As a social being, individual human behavior is influenced by societal values and other factors in one's life, and therefore choices are always relative to these variable factors (Kelly 1982). Because of the changes in lifestyle patterns in the twenty-first century—including the blurring of the lines between work and nonwork time (e.g., people working from home or in constant communication with the office via e-mail or cell phone even when on vacation; the fluid nature of participation in the paid workforce by many individuals including retirees, students, and the unemployed; and the fact that for some leisure is experienced at work)—it has been suggested that leisure be defined as an experience that is intertwined with all components of life. Thus, the meaning an individual assigns to an experience becomes more important in differentiating between leisure and nonleisure than a definition based on activity or time. Current definitions of leisure, therefore, regard it as existential, meaningful action that is characterized by freedom more than by necessity and is embedded in a social and cultural context.

### Leisure and Later Life

In studies of leisure in the lives of retirement-aged women, leisure takes many forms—from being a highly valued part of their lives around which they construct much of their daily lives playing golf, tennis, cards, reading, gardening, socializing, and traveling to a view of leisure as "time left over" when everything else is done (Gibson et al. 2001). These women tend to structure their days around service to others such as volunteer work or family-centered activities that they find meaningful. The idea of meaningful, high-investment activities has been consistently identified as contributing to the life satisfaction of older adults over the years. In retirement, meaningful activities frequently fall into the realm of leisure. These activities, in addition to social engagement, were found to be the strongest predictors of life satisfaction and successful aging among older adults. In studies of widowhood, leisure and social interaction have been identified as important components of widows' adjustment to spousal bereavement (Ashton-Shaeffer 1995).

### Leisure Travel in Later Life

Tourism is a special form of leisure that involves voluntarily traveling outside of an individual's home community, usually for a period of 24 hours or more in pursuit of pleasure. People who take day trips are called excursionists. People in later life enjoy both day trips and longer vacations and use their retirement to do those things, like travel, which were put off during their working careers. Vacation travel can take two forms—one is the annual break in the yearly cycle, and the other is travel as a rite of passage. In Western cultures, travel has long been used as a rite of passage, primarily by young adults transitioning from adolescence into adulthood. Since World War II, with the growth in mass tourism, retirement has often marked the chance for many to take those long-awaited trips that they have postponed because of job and family responsibilities. Javalgi, Thomas, and Rao (1992) found that individuals aged 55 and over account for 80% of all money spent on vacations in the United States, and Smith and Jenner (1997) found that this same age group holds 44% of U.S. adult passports.

In line with the philosophy that meaningful activities contribute to satisfaction in later life, studies have provided some insights into the patterns and meanings associated with leisure travel. The stereotypes of the older traveler on a bus tour of Europe or sitting at the beach watching the world go by may be a reality for some; however, in common with the rest of the population, a range of travel preferences exists. Traits of leisure travelers can be categorized into three types: novelty seekers who travel for new experiences, often viewed as "learning experiences"; active enthusiasts who are attracted to physically active pursuits; and the reluctant travelers, including those who prefer familiarity in their vacation destinations. The educational element of travel is an important motivator for older adults, and educational vacations such as Elderhostel are becoming increasingly popular, due in part to the intellectual stimulation and social interaction found in these types of vacations.

Another common reason for travel among older adults is visiting family and friends. Older adults in the United States may frequently combine vacations with spending time with family, especially with adult children and grandchildren. In line with this, multigenerational travel, particularly travel with grandchildren, may become increasingly popular. Recent marketing campaigns by specialist companies such as Grandtravel and Walt Disney World, showing grandparents and grandchildren enjoying the theme parks together, seem to support this trend.

Some individuals continue to travel well into their eighties because they view it as an important component of their lives. In fact, it has been found that adults aged 76 and 85 who live in continuing care retirement communities rank travel as their favorite activity second only to reading (Brewer, Poffley, and Pederson 1995). For others, interest in travel wanes after the first five years of retirement, to be replaced by home- and community-based activities. Four trends related to travel among individuals aged 65 and over have been identified: as age increases, so does the tendency not to travel; more highly educated individuals tend to travel more; individuals with more mobility problems tend to travel less; and as health deteriorates, so does the tendency to travel. Lack of money, poor health, lack of a traveling companion (particularly for older women), preferring not to drive at night, and disability were the most often cited barriers to travel among older adults; however, perception of health and other personal attributes may be equally important in shaping an individual's desire to travel.

Thus, in common with leisure choices in general, while health and financial restrictions may certainly constrain travel choices, the variety of activities, countries, and prices available is extensive, and the old adage "Where there is a will, there is a way" applies to people's willingness to travel in later life. Cultural self-confidence, that is, an awareness of the world and a level of curiosity to travel outside of the familiar, is probably more influential in determining who will travel than income alone (Graburn 1983). Fully escorted tours are still popular among some older travelers because of the peace of mind of having both a guide and a built-in friendship group. However, in the post–World War II era as more people travel, they have become increasingly experienced and sophisticated and more often prefer to explore the world on their own terms. With the freedom to travel during the less-crowded and cheaper off-peak seasons, leisure travel is an important part of life for many retirees.

### Leisure Education

Years of work, the cultural pervasiveness of the Protestant Work Ethic in shaping conceptions of leisure, and an education system that prepares people for a life of work leave most adults unprepared for the transition to a leisure-oriented life in retirement.

People, then, especially those who devalue leisure, may tend to construct their postretirement lives around service-oriented activities

While life on the golf course or traveling the world is not for everyone, the ability to choose how to structure a satisfying life in retirement is important. Studies consistently find that while health and finances are precursors to a fulfilling retirement, perfect health and abundant financial resources by themselves will not result in a satisfying later life (Wilhite, Sheldon, and Jekubovic-Fenton 1994). Meaningful activity and social interactions are the keys. Thus, while financial planning is an important part of preparation for retirement, that leisure education should also be an essential part of preretirement programs.

Leisure education programs generally consist of some of the following content areas:

- *Leisure awareness*. Identification of the individual's leisure interests and community resources to facilitate these interests.
- *Leisure values*. An examination of an individual's leisure ethic and an understanding of the value of leisure in life.
- *Identification of leisure constraints*. What barriers might prevent individuals from taking part in their chosen activities and how these barriers might be overcome.

The purpose of such programs is to enable individuals to make informed decisions about how to shape their lives, whether it is playing golf or volunteering, or both. Some studies have shown that retirees who expressed dissatisfaction with later life were those who devalued leisure.

Ekerdt (1986) suggests that life in retirement is frequently influenced by what he calls the busy ethic. Retirees are expected to keep busy, and many retirees themselves expect to stay busy. Searle and Iso-Ahola (1988) found that leisure attitude influences leisure choices in retirement with those holding a more positive attitude exhibiting higher life satisfaction. Thus, a leisure education program in preretirement planning might be valuable in helping individuals who have centered their lives around work to identify activities and opportunities in their retirement years around which they can construct a satisfying life. (See also EDUCATION OF OLDER ADULTS; RETIREMENT MIGRATION; RETIREMENT PLANNING; RETIREMENT PREPAREDNESS; SENIOR DISCOUNTS; SNOWBIRD CHECKLIST AND TRANSBORDER ISSUES; VACATION HOMES AND RECREATIONAL PROPERTY; VOLUNTEERING.)

**References**

Ashton-Shaeffer, C. 1995. "The Role of Leisure in the Bereavement Process of Later-Life Widows." Ph.D. dissertation, University of Illinois.

Blazey, M. 1987. "The Differences between Participants and Non-Participants in a Senior Travel Program." *Journal of Travel Research* 26: 7–12.

Brewer, K., J. Poffley, and E. Pederson. 1995. "Travel Interests among Special Seniors: Continuing Care Retirement Community Residents." *Journal of Travel and Tourism Marketing* 4: 93–98.

de Grazia, S. 1964. *Of Time, Work, and Leisure*. Garden City, NJ: Doubleday.

Dumazedier, J. 1974. *Sociology of Leisure*. New York: North-Holland.

Ekerdt, D. 1986. "The Busy Ethic: Moral Continuity between Work and Retirement." *The Gerontologist* 26: 239–44.
Gibson, H., C. Ashton-Shaeffer, J. Green, and C. Autry. 2001. "Leisure in the Lives of Retirement-Aged Women: Conversations about Leisure and Life." *Leisure/Loisir* (August).
Graburn, N. 1983. "Americans' Vacations: Further Comments on Class and Lifestyle." *Annals of Tourism Research* 10: 270–73.
Havighurst, R. 1961. "The Nature and Values of Meaningful Free-Time Activity." In *Aging and Leisure*, ed. R. Kleemeier. New York: Oxford University Press.
Hawkins, B. 1990–1991. "Challenges for Leisure Services in a Graying America." *Leisure Information Quarterly* 17(3): 1–5.
Javalgi, R., E. Thomas, and S. Rao. 1992. "Consumer Behavior in the U.S. Pleasure Travel Marketplace: An Analysis of Senior and Non-Senior Travelers." *Journal of Travel Research* 31: 14–19.
Kelly, J. 1982. *Leisure*. Englewood Cliffs, NJ: Prentice-Hall.
Neulinger, J. 1974. *The Psychology of Leisure*. Springfield, IL: Charles C. Thomas.
Pieper, J. 1963. *Leisure: The Basis of Culture*. New York: Random House.
*Proceedings of the Fourth Meeting of National Leaders in Women's Health Research*. 2001. Gainesville, FL, March.
Smith, C., and P. Jenner. 1997. "The Seniors Travel Market." *Travel and Tourism Analyst* 5: 43–62.
Teaff, J. 1991. "Leisure and Life Satisfaction of Older Catholic Religious Women." *World Leisure and Recreation* 33: 27–29.
Veblen, T. [1899] 1953. *The Theory of the Leisure Class*. New York: New American Library.
Wilhite, B., K. Sheldon, and N. Jekubovich-Fenton. 1994. "Leisure in Daily Life: Older Widows Living Alone." *Journal of Parks and Recreation Administration* 12: 44–78.
Zimmer, Z., R. Brayley, and M. Searle. 1995. "Whether to Go and Where to Go: Identification of Important Influences on Senior's Decisions to Travel." *Journal of Travel Research* 33: 3–10.

*Heather J. Gibson*

**LIABILITY INSURANCE,** a contract that insures a person against losses or from being held legally responsible for injury or damage to another. It also covers defense of lawsuits arising from claims of negligence. Liability coverage specifies the insured person(s), types of insurance provided, limits of coverage, source of liability, and costs of legal defense. The policies provide coverage for a specified type of loss (such as bodily injury and/or property damage) for which the person insured is legally liable. Liability insurance also contains provisions that require reporting the occurrence of a loss or the filing of a lawsuit to the insurer in a timely manner. Companies that insure against liability losses employ the law of averages to spread their risks among many individual policy owners.

### Liability Coverage in General

Liability coverage may constitute the entire policy, such as malpractice insurance, or comprise one element of insurance in a package policy that insures against other types of loss such as automobile or homeowner's insurance.

The average individual is exposed to sources of liability such as motor vehicle use; property; daily activities including employment, professional, and business activities; occupancy of premises; and use of watercraft, aircraft, or other special possessions. Common sources of liability are automobile accidents that might cause personal injuries or property damage. While most people do not face all of these potential sources of liability, a part of personal financial management is assessing whatever risks may be present at any given time. Risk control ranges from not engaging in risky activities to simply exercising great care and loss prevention. Risk financing through the purchase of liability insurance transfers to the insurance company the potential burden of loss and/or damage.

Coverage should include protection against damages because of bodily injury, defined in one personal auto policy as "bodily harm, sickness, or disease, including death that results." Property damage is defined in the same policy as "physical injury to, destruction of, or loss of use of tangible property." Personal injury, which may include libel, slander, defamation of character, invasion of privacy, or assault and battery, is also an important exposure to consider. Because definitions in policy forms may vary, it is important to determine exactly what coverage is provided under each policy purchased.

Limits of coverage specify how much a policy will pay if an individual is found legally obligated to pay. Limits can be stated as "combined single limits" or "split limits." The limits can apply to single coverages or to multiple coverages. Combined single limits typically refer to a specified maximum amount of coverage (e.g., $300,000) for bodily injury and property damage combined. Split limits typically refer to a maximum amount per person for bodily injury, a maximum amount per occurrence for bodily injury, and a maximum amount per occurrence for property damage. For example, a policy designating limits of $100,000/300,000/50,000 would pay a maximum of $100,000 to any one individual, a maximum of $300,000 to all individuals sustaining bodily injury, and a maximum of $50,000 for property damage arising from a single occurrence.

Insurance coverage of defense costs is an important element in a liability insurance policy. If wrongdoing is alleged against an individual and a lawsuit is filed, potentially high costs of defense will be incurred, whatever the outcome of the lawsuit. While most personal liability insurance covers defense costs, all policies should be checked for special requirements or limitations of this type of coverage.

The designation of the person(s) insured in a liability contract is also important. A husband and wife who are residents of the same household may both be insured under personal liability policies, and resident children of the household may also be named as persons insured. In any liability policy, it is important to know exactly who is insured, for failure to do so could result in an uninsured loss. If the policy is available to review, check the definition of "insured" or "covered persons." An individual's insurance agent or broker should also be able to confirm which family members are covered under the liability policy.

The insurance company's reporting requirements are also specified under the terms of a legal liability contract. If an individual is in an accident, the loss must be reported to the insurer promptly. The time specified may be 30 days, immediately, or "as soon as practicable." Any notice of a lawsuit should also be delivered to the insurer promptly. Liability insurance companies have promised to pay those amounts you are legally obligated to pay and to provide defense. Notification of losses, therefore, is especially important, and failure to report a loss could leave one uninsured.

### Specific Liability Insurance

Types of liability insurance most often carried are included in automobile insurance, homeowner's insurance, and the personal umbrella policy. While the following descriptions may not fit all policies, the forms chosen were published by the Insurance Services Office (ISO) and are used by many companies. The elements contained in these descriptions should be used as guidelines only.

Automobile insurance contains a liability insurance component and typically provides protection against liability resulting from bodily injury and/or property damage that may occur in an accident or other mishap. The source of liability for the person named on the policy (declarations), and if residents of the household, the spouse and family members, is "any auto." The "covered auto" is also a source of liability for other persons using it with permission or other organizations who incur liability because of its use by a person insured. "Covered auto" will be defined in the policy. A "covered auto" is typically defined as the auto named in the declarations, a trailer owned by the insured, an additionally acquired automobile, or a temporary, substitute auto. As with all liability insurance, both the insured and the source of liability should be carefully reviewed.

Generally excluded sources of liability are intentional acts; use of automobiles owned but not listed in the policy; vehicles used in the automobile business; use of an auto as a public or livery conveyance; motorized vehicles with fewer than four wheels; and automobiles available for regular or frequent use. Share-the-expense car pools are *not* typically excluded.

Driving without automobile insurance may lead to a violation of state financial responsibility laws and may result in suspension of driving and registration privileges. These financial responsibility laws require that an insured carry a minimum amount of liability insurance, post a bond, or be a recognized self-insurer.

Most drivers purchase complete automobile insurance that includes coverage against bodily liability, property damage liability, medical payments, uninsured motorists, collision, and comprehensive physical damage. Of these types of coverage, bodily injury, property damage liability, and uninsured motorist are most important. Uninsured motorist coverage protects the insured against loss for which an uninsured motorist is responsible. In effect, it pays the amounts that an uninsured motorist is legally obligated to pay the policyholder or person injured.

Some states have enacted "no-fault" laws to counter the expense and time-consuming process of determining who is legally liable for damages suffered in automobile accidents. No-fault insurance, where available, requires that costs of bodily injury and property damage losses be paid by the injured person's insurance company, regardless of who is at fault for an accident. Theoretically, the need for long and expensive court proceedings should be eliminated in no-fault states, but in practice, injured persons are able to pursue recovery of damages in court that exceed no-fault insurance payment limitations.

Homeowner's and renter's insurance protects owners and renters from bodily injury and property damage liability arising from the occupancy of the premises and everyday activities. The dwelling and any other buildings on the property—garages, tool sheds, or other structures—are covered under the property insurance section of homeowner's insurance. The liability section covers loss arising from or on the property itself and activities on properties away from home. Sources of liability include negligent acts or omissions, such as failure to maintain a property or carelessness that results in injury or damage to another (for instance, an individual's dog or cat is typically a covered source of liability). Certain perils may be specifically excluded, and as with all insurance, it is important to understand what risks are and are not covered.

Persons covered by an insurance policy are referred to as "insureds" in most forms. Insureds include the person named in the declarations, the spouse of that person (if they are a resident of the household), and members of the household who are either relatives or persons younger than 21 who are in the owner's care. Exclusions are used to remove some sources of liability. The exclusions include motor vehicle liability; aircraft liability; business and professional liability; intentional acts; some watercraft; liability under workers' compensation laws; owned or rented locations not included as insured locations; or any loss charged as an assessment by an association, corporation, or community of property owners.

As with automobile insurance, a homeowner's policy also provides broad coverage of other perils such as other property coverage and additional living expense coverage. As a package, the cost of comprehensive coverage is usually less expensive than buying the coverages individually.

### Personal Umbrella Policy

A personal umbrella liability policy features two distinct provisions. First, it offers bodily injury and property damage coverage beyond the underlying limits on other specified policies and also covers some exposures not otherwise insured. An individual purchasing a personal umbrella will be required to carry a certain dollar amount of liability insurance in areas such as automobile liability, homeowner's liability, or boat owner's liability. The umbrella applies in excess of these underlying limits. For example, if an individual has $300,000 in automobile liability insurance, $300,000 in homeowner's liability insurance, and a $1 million personal umbrella policy, the resulting combined limits of coverage become $1 million for automobile liability, and $1.3 million for homeowner's liability. Also, by example, when coverage is provided by the umbrella policy, but no underlying limits are required, the insured will have a "self-insured retention" of a specific dollar amount (as specified by the insurance contract). The umbrella would apply in excess of this retention. Second, the umbrella often provides coverage for personal injury such as libel, slander, and defamation of character exposure that is not covered in most underlying policies.

Exclusions include obligations under workers' compensation, disability benefits, or benefits under similar laws; autos owned by other family members or furnished for regular, frequent use; intentional acts; aircraft; some boats; and an act or failure to act as an officer of a corporation or association. This latter exclusion does not usually apply to officers or directors of nonprofit corporations or associations.

The personal umbrella policy is an effective and economical way to increase liability insurance coverage. Other sources of liability requiring coverage not included in the policies discussed here are liability arising from investment property, watercraft, aircraft, workers' compensation for household workers, business, and professional liability.

### Other Potential Sources of Liability

The preceding discussion has focused principally on an individual's personal liability exposures arising from normal everyday activities. However, if one is still working, engaged in a profession, or is an employer, additional exposures must be considered. For example, certain states may require workers' compensation coverage for employees. This might apply to all of an employer's workers, no matter what their job level or responsibilities. Workers' compensation laws vary from state to state and should be checked to determine whether this coverage is required.

Additionally, if an individual is operating a business, then he or she is also subject to liabilities associated with the conduct of the business. This could include liability arising from premises, operations, products, advertising, personal injury, or commercial motor vehicle exposures. If an occupation is categorized as "professional," that is, a physician, lawyer, or similar occupation rendering services or advice, then liability exposures exist arising from the conduct of such profession.

A complete discussion of business and professional liability exposures is beyond the scope of this writing. Due to the complexity of business liability insurance, a professional in the area of business liability insurance should be consulted.

### Importance of Liability Insurance

As society becomes more litigious, the likelihood of a liability claim against an individual increases, and the cost of defending the claim alone may justify liability insurance. Certainly the potential size of a liability settlement or judgment requires serious consideration of liability insurance.

Planning for liability coverage by older persons, however, must be balanced against the income and assets the individual possesses and stands to lose. For many older persons, lifestyle choices may be increasingly risk-averse. However, motor vehicle operation in advanced old age actually may have the opposite effect, increasing the chance of accidents. Although liability insurance is an important protection to consider, the decision of what coverage to buy must be weighed carefully within the overall framework of an older person's lifestyle and his or her financial needs and resources. Perhaps most important to consider, however, is the possibility that an older person's total wealth could be lost or impaired. The liability judgment and defense costs will need to be paid whether or not one has insurance.

Information is available on the Internet for people who want to do additional research on their own. Try searching for the key words *personal liability insurance*, *homeowners*, and *automobile insurance* in any of the search engines available on the Web, including Google®, Lycos®, Alta Vista®, or MSN® Search. Professional organizations such as the Insurance Information Institute and the American Institute for Chartered Property Casualty Underwriters (AICPCU) will also provide information. (See also AGENTS AND BROKERS; ATTORNEYS; FINANCIAL ADVISORS; FINANCIAL COUNSELING FOR MID- TO LATER LIFE; FINANCIAL SECURITY IN RETIREMENT; LIFE PLANNING; RISK TOLERANCE.)

#### Organizations

American Institute for Chartered Property Casualty Underwriters (AICPCU)
Insurance Information Institute

#### References

Green, Mark R., James S. Trieschmann, and Sandra G. Gustavson. 1995. *Risk and Insurance*. 8th ed. Cincinnati, OH: South-Western.

"Insurance Professionals Policy Kit 2002 Edition." Alliance of American Insurers.

Rejda, George E. 2001. *Principles of Risk Management and Insurance*. 7th ed. Boston, MA: Addison Wesley Longman.

Vaughn, Emmett J., and Therese Vaughan. 1999. *Fundamentals of Risk and Insurance*. 8th ed. New York: John Wiley & Sons.

Willams, C. Arthur, Michael L. Smith, and Peter C. Young. 1995. *Risk Management and Insurance*. 8th ed. New York: McGraw-Hill Companies.

*Mars A. Pertl*

**LIFE ESTATES,** land estates whose duration is measured or limited by the life of an individual. A life estate is a legal arrangement whereby the beneficiary, that is, the life tenant, is entitled to the income from, or the possession of, property for his or her lifetime. Upon the death of the life tenant, the property goes to the holder of the remainder interest or to the grantee by reversion.

The law of land estates differs by state. The general legal concepts were introduced into America by English settlers. Some states chose to adopt certain concepts, while others did not. Since the creation of life estates is complex, it is recommended it be done under the direction of licensed attorneys in the state where the real property is located. Familiarity with the law regarding life estates can help preserve seniors' rights, avoid liability for damage to estates, ensure harmony between the parties involved with the land's ownership, and help seniors make educated decisions on whether to create or accept a life estate.

Life estates may be created expressly, implicitly, or by operation of law. Express life estates may only be created by will or deed. Because a life estate is an interest in land, it must be documented in writing. There are two recognized express life estates: those for the life of the grantee and those for the life of another. Express life estates for the life of the grantee include conveyances such as: By and from Albert "to Betty for her life." In this example, Betty will have an estate in land for her own life. When Betty dies, the land will revert back to Albert. Thus, Albert is said to have a reversionary interest in the land.

Another example of an express life estate would be: By and from Albert "to Betty for her life, then to Charles." Betty will have an estate in land for her life, but when she dies, the property will go to Charles, not Albert. Upon Betty's death, Charles may do with the land as he pleases, and there are no restrictions on his ownership. The law recognizes Charles as a "remainderman," which means that Charles is not entitled to the land until the death of the measuring life. Thus, remainder interests, like reversionary interests, are a future estate in land and are known in the law as "future interests." The law considers remainder and reversionary interests as present legal rights that are entitled to protection.

The second type of express life estates are life estates for the life of another. These are called "estates pur autre vie" and are created in the following manner: By and from Albert "to Betty for the life of Debbie." In this example, Betty will have an estate in land only so long as Debbie lives. When Debbie dies, the land will revert to Albert.

Life estates also may be created by implication. In this category, the interest will be created in wills or deeds using language such as: By and from Albert "to Betty after the life of Charles." In this example, a life estate will be implied in Albert until the death of Charles. At Charles's death, the land will go to Betty. Another example would be if Albert wills his land "to Betty from and after the death of Betty's brother, Charles." Here, the life estate cannot be with Albert because he is dead, nor with Betty because

Charles is alive; therefore, the law implies a life estate to Charles and a remainder interest to Betty. Implied life estates are rare and occur mainly as a result of poorly drafted wills and deeds.

The third and last category of life estates are those that occur by operation of law. Legal life estates are created out of the marital relationship. There are two types of legal life estates: "curtsy" and "dower." These are recognized only in a minority of states and the District of Columbia and can be an unexpected trap for the uninformed. Only dower has any significance today. Although a common law dower only applied to the wife and curtsy to the husband, some states have eliminated the distinction between the two and collapsed them into one concept, called "dower." At common law, upon the death of her husband, a widow was entitled to receive a life estate in one-third of the lands owned by her husband during the marriage. Before her husband's death, the wife had only an expectancy of dower, because if she died before her husband, her potential or inchoate dower interest was eliminated.

An example of when dower operates is where Albert buys a tract of land, then marries Betty, and several years later sells the tract to Charles without getting Betty's signature on the deed. If Albert dies before Betty, Betty will be entitled to a one-third life estate in the land currently owned by Charles or his successors. If, however, Betty consented to the sale and signed the deed, she would not be entitled to dower because by signing the deed she waived her dower rights. Dower also operates in the situation where Albert buys a tract of land while married and does not sell it but, upon his death, wills the land to Charles, leaving his wife, Betty, nothing. In such a case, Betty would be entitled to a one-third life estate in the land despite being intentionally left out of the will.

Seniors in states that recognize dower should be aware that if their spouse cuts them out of a will, they may still be entitled to a one-third life estate in real estate their spouse owned at death or sold without permission. If dower has been abolished in the state, "elective share" statutes have generally replaced it to protect the widow or widower from being totally disinherited. If dower exists in a state, buyers should be careful to get the signature of both spouses when buying land from a couple. Otherwise, there may be an unexpected visitor demanding a one-third life estate in the land years later.

Before seniors create life estates, they need to be aware of the rights, duties, and obligations attached. Also, seniors who have acquired life estates should be aware of the legal implications that accompany the acquisition. Those who have remainder or reversion interests in life estates should also be aware of their rights. Generally, life tenants are entitled to all the ordinary uses and profits of the land; however, they cannot lawfully do any act that will injure the interests of the person who owns a remainder or reversion interest in the land. A life tenant is analogous to a trustee of the land because he or she owes certain duties to preserve it for the remainderman (the person entitled to the assets of a trust upon the death of a life tenant). If life tenants injure the land, future interest holders may sue for damages or enjoin the life tenant's actions. Damage to life estates by life tenants falls into one of three categories: (1) affirmative (voluntary) waste; (2) permissive waste; or (3) ameliorative waste.

Affirmative waste applies to structures and natural resources on the land. As a general rule, life tenants may not consume or exploit natural resources on the property, such as timber, coal, oil, and gas. For example, if Albert deeds his land, Blackacre, "to Betty for life, then to Charles," and it turns out that there is a valuable coal deposit under the property, Betty may not open a mine and extract the coal. If she does, Charles, the remainderman, may bring a suit to enjoin the activity and receive damages for the coal removed. In other words, Betty can use the estate but cannot consume the estate. Life tenants, however, are allowed to utilize the natural resources for repair and maintenance of the land. They may cut trees for fences, or mine coal for heating a house on the land, but may not cut trees or mine coal to sell, unless given an express right to exploit these resources.

Permissive waste occurs when the life tenants allow the land to fall into disrepair or fail to take reasonable measures to protect the land. This concept imposes several affirmative obligations on life tenants. First, life tenants have an obligation to preserve the land and structures in a reasonable state of repair, to the extent of the income or profits derived from the land or, if the life tenants are living on the land themselves, to the extent of the reasonable rental value of the land.

The next obligation is to pay interest on encumbrances to the land to the extent of income or profits produced by the land. Life tenants must pay all ordinary taxes on the land to the extent the income or profits from the land permit. If, however, the tax is for a public improvement such as a new curb, sewer, or sidewalk that will last longer than the life estate, the tax or assessment is apportioned equitably between the life tenant and the future holder of the land. There is generally no obligation on life tenants to insure the premises for the benefit of the remaindermen. Both the life tenants and the remaindermen, however, have an insurable interest in the land.

The final category of damages is ameliorative waste, which is counterintuitive and thus a trap for the uninformed. Ameliorative waste occurs when the use of the property is substantially changed, but the change increases the value of the property. At common law, any change to existing buildings or other improvements was always actionable, even if it improved the value of the property. Because of the unexpected harshness of this rule, modern courts have modified it in the following instances. First, if the market value of the remainder interest is not diminished and the remainderman does not object, the use of the property may be changed. Second, if a substantial and permanent change in neighborhood conditions has deprived the property in its current form of reasonable productivity or usefulness, the use may be changed without the remainderman's permission. The classic example of this is where the life estate consists of a single house that is on a piece of prime real estate in Manhattan, New York. If this should occur, the life tenant may be allowed to tear down the old house and build a skyscraper.

Life estates normally terminate upon the death of the measuring life; however, in certain instances, a life estate may terminate earlier. Life estates may be sold by the life tenant. Such a sale, however, does not lengthen the duration of the life estate but merely creates an estate pur autre vie. For example, if Betty has a life estate and sells it to David, David will have a life estate for the life of Betty. Because of the uncertainty of such an estate, David will probably not pay top dollar for the land.

The doctrine of merger is one way that life estates may terminate earlier than the death of the measuring life. This doctrine applies where life tenants sell their interest to the remainderman. For instance, if Albert grants Blackacre "to Betty for life, then to Charles," Betty will have a life estate and Charles will have a remainder interest. Thus, if Betty sells her life estate to Charles, Charles will hold the land in fee simple (own all the rights) because Betty's life estate and Charles's remainder interest will merge, and

Charles will hold all the interest in the land. A person who buys the land from Charles would therefore be willing to pay full price.

Awareness of the rights, duties, and obligations imposed upon life tenants and remaindermen can help seniors plan for their future or take care of their current obligations. Therefore, seniors who are not already aware of the legal implications of this unique form of landownership should consult an attorney in the state where the land is located before creating a life estate or before proceeding with any improvements or other changes to the life estate. (See also ATTORNEYS; CONDOMINIUMS; CONTINUING CARE RETIREMENT COMMUNITIES [CCRCs]; COOPERATIVE OWNERSHIP IN HOUSING; ESTATE PLANNING; HOMEOWNERSHIP; INHERITANCE; REVERSE MORTGAGES; TITLING ASSETS.)

**References**

Lawler, John J., and Gail Gates Lawler. 1940. *A Short Historical Introduction to the Law of Real Property*. Chicago: Foundation Press.

Moynihan, Cornelius J. 1962a. *Introduction to the Law of Real Property*. St. Paul, MN: West.

Moynihan, Cornelius J. 1962b. *A Preliminary Survey of the Law of Real Property*. St. Paul, MN: West.

Powell, Richard R. 1993. *Powell on Real Property*. New York: Matthew Bender.

Thompson, George W. 1979. *Commentaries on the Modern Law of Real Property*. New York: Bobbs-Merrill Co.

*Christopher R. McDowell*

**LIFE INSURANCE,** a contractual relationship under which an insurance company promises to pay a specified sum of money upon the death of the insured to the person or persons designated as the beneficiary(ies). Life insurance contracts represent a fairly simple legal relationship among the insured, the insurance company, and the beneficiaries. However, the purchase and maintenance of, and claims made under, life insurance policies comprise a complex area within law, finance, and consumer decision making.

Life insurance contracts are written by insurance companies for simple and complex situations. Millions of parents insure their lives to protect against their untimely deaths for the benefit of young children. Older parents maintain life insurance to provide financial security for their families. Businesses and governments rely on life insurance contracts to protect against the loss of key executives and officials, and banks often require insurance on the lives of borrowers to assure repayment of loans.

Careful attention is required by anyone purchasing a new life insurance contract or before amending or liquidating an existing policy. As one ages, life insurance becomes more expensive to acquire, and any changes to an existing life insurance contract must be made carefully. Life insurance can be a key tool in financial planning. Insurance proceeds may provide retirement income, accumulated savings, or the payment of estate and death taxes or may be used to make charitable bequests after death.

## Life Insurance Terminology

*Actuarial cost* is based on the scientifically calculated probability that an individual of a certain age will die within any given year. Life insurance premiums are based on actuarial cost, and the method for calculating actuarial cost is determined by mortality tables derived from the statistical experience of thousands of individuals over time. Mortality tables tell insurance underwriters the number of years that an individual of any age can expect to live and enable insurance companies to price the required insurance.

A *life insurance application* begins the process of entering into a life insurance contract and becomes part of the physical life insurance contract. Usually, it will be affixed to the life insurance contract issued to the insured. Information entered into the agreement must be accurate and complete, or it may provide the life insurance company with an excuse to terminate the agreement. The application includes information about the proposed insured's date and place of birth, his or her marital status, profession or occupation, health history, and sometimes the reason for purchasing the life insurance policy—referred to by individuals in the insurance industry as the "insurable interest."

*Cash surrender value* is the account value of permanent life insurance and is the guaranteed cash value of the policy plus premium dividends, if any, paid by the life insurance company. Cash surrender value in a life insurance policy is similar to equity in one's home. To realize the equity, a policyholder may surrender the life insurance policy to obtain the cash value. Both a life insurance policy and a home offer collateral value against which the owner may borrow. For both, value is likely to continue to increase even though the asset has been pledged as collateral.

*Endowment* occurs when a life insurance contract fully matures, and the cash surrender value equals the death benefit. Originally, endowment occurred at age 100, but it occurs at earlier ages under modern policies.

*Insurable interest* is the policy owner's reason for buying life insurance. The financial loss that would be suffered upon the death of one spouse constitutes the other spouse's insurable interest. Similarly, financial loss that might occur when a partner dies constitutes the insurable interest for the partnership. Employers insure key employees based on their insurable interest in the employee. If an insurable interest is absent at the time of issuance, the life insurance company is not legally able to issue a policy.

The Medical Information Bureau (MIB) is a nonprofit trade association composed of member life insurance underwriters. It maintains a large database that gathers and distributes information on the health histories of individuals. The purpose of the MIB is to protect the insurance consumer and insurance company against applicants who shop for favorable coverage without disclosing their medical histories. In most states, if a life insurance company refuses to issue a life insurance policy on an individual's life, it must disclose its reason for denying coverage.

The *medical questionnaire*, sometimes referred to as "Part 2" of the application, is often the most important part of the life insurance application procedure. Life insurance underwriters use this information to determine whether a life insurance policy will be issued. Often the medical questionnaire will prompt an underwriter to require additional information from doctors and hospitals, or from the MIB.

*Policy dividends* represent the return of unused premiums by mutual life insurance companies. Dividends are not guaranteed but are merely projections of anticipated payments. Thus, if interest rates vary from the projections of the insurance company, or if mortality costs are higher than expected, the rate of return for the life insurance policy may be lower than projected at the time of the proposal.

*Premiums* are payments by the policy owner to the insurance company to issue the life insurance contract and keep it in force. Premiums are determined using the actuarial cost of the life insurance contract. Life insurance premiums can vary even with a fixed death benefit for individuals of the same age, depending on the type of life insurance contract.

*Mutual* or *stock companies* are terms that refer to stock life insurance companies owned by shareholders and mutual life insurance companies owned by their policyholders. About 94% of U.S. life insurance companies are stock companies, and about 6% are mutual companies. Mutual companies sell participating policies, for which individuals pay a somewhat higher premium, but overpayments are returned to policyholders in the form of policy dividends. Profits of the stock life insurance companies go to shareholders, while the "profits" of mutual companies go to the policyholders. In the United States, the largest life insurance companies are mutual companies, and frequently, but not always, the word "mutual" appears in the company name.

*Term insurance* is designed to protect dependents and others with an insurable interest against lost income. It is most affordable for the young and becomes increasingly expensive as the insured ages. After age 65, the cost of term insurance may be prohibitive, especially when health problems exist. With ordinary term insurance, premiums increase each year as the likelihood of dying increases. Term insurance builds no cash surrender value, and wide variations in periodic premiums can occur, depending on the insured's health habits and history, age, sex, and the pricing policies of the insurance company. Premiums are paid periodically, and the insurance stays in force for the time the premium covers. When the premiums stop, the policy is canceled. Term insurance can remain in force for many years or for the duration of a trip or vacation.

There are many types of term insurance, and choices must be made at the time of purchase about level versus increasing premiums, payment, renewal and conversion options, and age of expiration. A term rider can be added as a benefit to permanent life insurance. *Periodic term* is a type of term life insurance that is written for a fixed period of time, such as 5, 10, or 20 years. The periodic term is the time an insurance company guarantees to insure an individual, after which the company often will require a physical reexamination or medical questionnaire. *Convertible term* refers to a term life insurance policy that provides for conversion to permanent or cash value life insurance without any proof from the insured that he or she is still healthy enough to purchase the permanent life insurance.

*Permanent life insurance* refers to life insurance policies that have the following characteristics: (1) premiums are calculated based on keeping the policy in force for the life expectancy of the insured; (2) contracts are written and premiums are calculated based on creating cash surrender values; and (3) premiums are calculated so the policy will endow at a specific age.

Permanent life insurance policies offer several options to policyholders. Permanent life insurance provides a way for policyholders to ensure that life insurance benefits will not terminate before life expectancy. For permanent life insurance policies, cash surrender values accumulate on a tax-deferred basis and enable policyholders to gain access to cash surrender value by borrowing against it. While some question the value of being able to "borrow" one's own money, this may be a significant advantage to others who regard the accumulating cash value in life insurance as "forced savings."

Permanent life insurance policies offer the option of terminating life insurance premiums after a given number of years, at which time policy dividends (defined previously) will take over the payment of premiums. This concept affords policyholders a potentially valuable planning tool. Types of permanent life insurance include universal life, whole life or ordinary life insurance, and endowment and variable life insurance contracts. All permanent life insurance contracts offer cash value, loan provisions, and a guarantee to insure until the end of the insured's life.

*Rating systems* analyze the financial status of life insurance companies and offer a basis for comparing the financial stability of companies. Most rating systems examine the investments of insurance companies, their capital reserves, and their ability to pay outstanding liabilities for potential death claims. Insurance rating systems use A+, AAA, superior, or other valuative terminology.

The analysis of ratings is only one variable, however, in choosing a life insurance company and the agent that represents it. Other considerations include the honesty, efficiency, and responsiveness of the agent; the quality of service by local or regional offices of the insurance company; and most important, the appropriateness of the insurance policy under consideration. (See also ACCELERATED DEATH BENEFITS; ACCIDENT INSURANCE; AGENTS AND BROKERS; ANNUITIES; DEATH BENEFITS; ESTATE PLANNING; FINANCIAL ADVISORS; HEALTH AND LONGEVITY.)

**Organizations**

American Council of Life Insurance (ACLI)
Consumer Federation of America (CFA)
National Association of Insurance Commissions

**Suggested Readings**

American Council of Life Insurance. 1994. *A Consumer's Guide to Life Insurance*. Washington, DC: Author.

Davis, Kristin. 1994. "Buying Life Insurance: What the Numbers Don't Show." *Kiplingers Personal Finance Magazine* 48(6): 49–52.

Travis, Dale. 1994. "How Much Life Insurance Do You Really Need?" *Real Estate Today* 27(7): 35–37.

**References**

Black, Kenneth, Jr., and Harold D. Skipper, Jr. 1994. *Life Insurance*. Englewood Cliffs, NJ: Prentice-Hall.

Budin, Beverly R. 1994. *Life Insurance*. Washington, DC: Tax Management.

Crawford, Michael L., and William T. Beadles. 1989. *Law and the Life Insurance Contract*. Homewood, IL: Irwin.

*Donald A. Hunsberger*

**LIFE PLANNING,** the process of (1) helping people focus on the true values and motivations in their lives; (2) determining the goals and objectives as they see their lives develop; and (3) using these values, motivations, goals, and objectives to guide the planning process and provide a framework for making choices and decisions in life that have financial and nonfinancial implications or consequences ("Practical Applications" 2000).

The concept of life planning, as it specifically relates to financial and retirement planning, emerged in the mid-1980s and achieved both growing acknowledgment and notoriety throughout the 1990s. During this period, the validity of life planning was frequently debated among professionals who advocated for this approach versus those who opposed the inclusion of qualitative or subjective factors with traditional quantitative planning and analysis. However, by the year 2000, the term *life planning* not only had become well recognized but had also achieved the status of a "movement," with implications relevant to both practitioners and educators in the field of financial and retirement planning.

### Elements, Scope, and Outcomes of Life Planning

In November 2000, the National Endowment for Financial Education (NEFE) convened a daylong meeting of professionals to discuss the significance of the life planning movement and the corresponding "shift from financial planning to a more personal and holistic focus on [consumer's] financial *and* non-financial needs" ("Practical Applications" 2000). Invited participants were pioneers and proponents of life planning and represented a diversity of professional disciplines and backgrounds. In addition, most of the participants were affiliated with one of two groups: the Nazrudin Project and the International Society of Life and Retirement Planning. The president of the International Society for Retirement Planning, Steven Shagrin, gave the opening presentation and laid the foundation for the intensive dialogue sessions that were to follow. His task was to provide "a definition of life planning as a holistic model that embraces retirement and financial planning and how this model serves clients."

Life planning is the process of (1) helping people focus on the true values and motivations in their lives; (2) determining the goals and objectives as they see their lives develop; and (3) using these values, motivations, goals, and objectives to guide the planning process and provide a framework for making choices and decisions in life that have financial and nonfinancial implications or consequences. The participants accepted this definition and throughout the day worked together to clarify the elements, scope, and practical applications of life planning. One example of this process was the identification and selection of ten meaningful terms that the participants mutually agreed reflected the life planning philosophy:

- Choice
- Consequences of options
- Self-direction
- Intentional
- Empowering
- Holistic
- Integrity
- Personal
- Comprehensive and specialized
- Increased self-efficacy

To summarize and clarify the discussion of these terms, Helen Dennis (Andrus Gerontology Center, University of Southern California) developed the following descriptions as appropriate to the financial and retirement planning context ("Practical Applications" 2000):

1. *Choice.* Life planning implies choice. It focuses on identifying the choices an individual has in mid-life and beyond. Having choices is a goal for individual planning for his or her future. These choices are expressed in financial strategies, retirement decisions, and quality-of-life choices such as careers, relocation, meaningful use of time, and personal and professional growth.
2. *Consequences of Options.* Part of life planning is to address not only the choices but also the consequences of those choices. It requires a "thinking through" of decisions. In fact, if the consequences are not considered, exercising a choice may be ineffective, inappropriate, or even useless.
3. *Self-Direction.* Self-direction implies that individuals are responsible for themselves; they may not be able to control their future, but they can influence it. Self-reliance and personal responsibility are two overriding themes in life planning.
4. *Intentional.* Life planning is not an accidental occurrence. It is a process of intention. At times, this intent needs definition, direction, and clarification. Professionals in life planning can facilitate this process.
5. *Empowering.* The life planning process is designed to empower individuals to make good decisions for themselves and their loved ones. At times, individuals need to recognize that they have the power to design their own future. This is closely aligned to being self-directed and intentional in one's efforts.
6. *Holistic.* Life planning is holistic. *Webster's Dictionary* defines holistic as "an emphasis on the functional relationship between the parts and the whole." Life planning exemplifies the relationship between financial security (an extremely significant part) and the whole—the values, visions, and aspirations of individuals as they see themselves in the present and in the future. The relationship between finances and how individuals plan to live their lives is an irrefutable connection. A holistic approach will strongly increase the probability for individuals to successfully plan and implement their retirement strategies and affect every aspect of their lives.
7. *Integrity.* Integrity suggests honesty. The intention of life planning is one of candor. Individuals make an attempt to be honest with themselves in designing their lives. Professionals are honest in their analysis, presentation of options, and counsel. The professionals involved in life planning consistently keep the welfare of the client as a top priority.
8. *Personal.* Life planning is focused on the individual. Therefore, it is highly personal. No two individuals are the same. The uniqueness of each individual is valued.
9. *Comprehensive and Specialized.* Those involved in life planning cannot be experts in every area, but they should have knowledge and understanding of the total planning challenge. Financial experts should be knowledgeable about nonfinancial issues. Equally important, those dealing with nonfinancial issues should have some understanding of the financial issues. Ideally, life planning will be approached as a team endeavor for the benefit of the adult planning his or her future.
10. *Increased Self-Efficacy.* Self-efficacy implies self-reliance and growth or, using Maslow's approach, self-actualization. One of the values of life planning is to enhance opportunities for growth, self-reliance, and self-satisfaction. These values crosscut the financial and nonfinancial arenas.

Nonetheless, the participants agreed that life planning is more than a philosophy. In order for life planning to be valuable, it must facilitate specific outcomes that represent its philosophy. Such outcomes or characteristics in the lives of individuals should include:

- Being motivated to make wise choices
- Being educated about life choices
- Living purposefully
- Being prepared to meet challenges and opportunities
- Providing structure *and* flexibility
- Making informed decisions and taking action to improve total well-being
- Growing self-awareness
- Being personally fulfilled
- Using and replenishing resources (i.e., stewardship of resources and sustainability)
- Giving back to the community, in all ways

### Implications for Financial and Retirement Planning Professionals

Many financial professionals view the life planning movement as natural evolution of the financial planning profession.

> Thirty years after its birth, financial planning continues to evolve. What began as more or less a better sales tool for financial services product providers is today recognized as a profession in its own right. . . . As the planning profession matures, there is as at least anecdotal evidence that its emphasis may be starting to shift from financial planning to a more personal and holistic focus on their financial *and* non-financial needs. ("Practical Applications" 2000)

Others view the growing interest in life planning as a response to trends within the industry and to consumer demand. In his article "A Look at the Financial Services Revolution," Lewis J. Walker wrote to his colleagues, "If there is any trend firmly in place that will govern our future, it is the revolutionary shift from *product* to *process*." He further explains that this revolution has taken financial service through three phases—from "the order taker" to "the problem solver" to "the problem identifier." Walker identifies the fourth and emerging phase as "the coach: the future of financial advice, a holistic process aimed at the completion of life goals, our own and that of the client(s)" (Walker 2001). Similarly, Tracy Herman, a reporter for *Registered Representative*, describes the role of the contemporary financial advisor as a "life planning concierge with a wealth of resources" (Herman 1999).

Much of this change within the financial services industry is the result of consumer demand. In an article published on the Financial Planning Interactive Web site, Helene Stein and Marcia Brier wrote that the concept of client service has undergone profound, client-driven changes. Therefore, "a full-service or holistic approach to client services is rapidly becoming the strategy of choice for many financial planners" (Stein and Brier 2001). In addition, Mitch Anthony, communications and client relationship-building expert, explained that "today's client is looking for an advisor with interpersonal skills as well as market insight and strategic intellect." In other words, the advisor must possess "equal parts emotional intelligence (EQ) and an intellect (IQ)—a merging of insight and information" (Anthony 2002).

### Implications for Financial and Retirement Education Programming

Life planning is also gaining recognition as an effective approach to financial and retirement planning education programming. In October of 2002, NEFE convened a symposium called "The State of Financial Literacy in America—Evolutions and Revolutions." This was a landmark gathering of professionals, representing the nation's leading thinkers and achievers in the field of financial education. In the closing session of the symposium, participants were asked to record their opinions of various recurring themes and proposed initiatives. When polled electronically, the highest percentage of agreement (96%) was registered for the statement that "financial education should be delivered in a life planning context."

The conclusions and recommendations of researchers also support this trend. The Institute for Socio-Financial Studies (ISFS) conducted a study for the Fannie Mae Foundation to explore the current state of financial education in the United States. In conjunction with this research, focus groups were conducted with employees at Weyerhaeuser and at United Parcel Service. Overwhelmingly, the participants reported that they placed high value on broad-based financial education programs. One of the main reasons the employees appreciated the education they received was because it not only targeted 401(k) investment decisions but also focused on all areas of their financial lives.

In the ISFS/Fannie Mae Foundation report, *Personal Finance and the Rush to Competence*, the authors noted that employees want and need financial education that is communicated in understandable terms (Vitt et al. 2002). In addition, they emphasized that this information is more effective and engaging when delivered in a context that is personally meaningful. Therefore, the ISFS researchers recommended that "life planning approaches to personal financial education should increasingly be built into curricula to help pre-retirees learn proactive ways to think about the future." They observed that the transition from work to retirement is "fraught with a complex set of human and financial concerns" and that traditional programming should be expanded to include lifestyle choices and other nonfinancial topics.

Similarly, research conducted by Carol Anderson supports the conjecture that a life planning perspective increases the effectiveness of financial and retirement education programming (Anderson 1999). She found that the degree or extent of "thinking about retirement" was by far the most powerful predictor of retirement planning action steps than other well-accepted predictors such as age, proximity to retirement, income, education, marital status, and occupation. Therefore, Anderson concluded,

> These results give a strong indication that education that engages pre-retirees in reflective and productive thinking about retirement can stimulate financial planning for retirement, and can help to counteract the negative influences of such factors as lower income, lower occupational status, and lower educational levels.

She recommended that educational materials and programs be designed with these results in mind because traditional programming is "unlikely to stimulate the type of reflective and productive thinking that will result in proactive retirement preparation." (See also FINANCIAL PLANNING; FINANCIAL SECURITY IN RETIREMENT; FRAILTY

PLANNING; LIFE PLANNING IN THE WORKPLACE; RETIREMENT EXPENSE PLANNING; RETIREMENT PREPAREDNESS.)

### References

Anderson, Carol. 1999. " 'Thinking' about Retirement: Research and Implications for Financial Planning Education." *Personal Finances and Worker Productivity* 3(1): 127–37.

Anthony, Mitch. 2002. *Your Clients for Life: The Definitive Guide to Becoming a Successful Financial Life Planner.* Chicago: Dearborn Trade.

Herman, Tracy. 1999. "Retirement Concierge." *Supplement to Registered Representative* (October).

"Practical Applications of Life and Retirement Planning to Financial Planning." 2000. *NEFE White Paper.* National Endowment for Financial Education." Available online at http://www.nefe.org/.

Stein, Helene, and Marcia Brier. 2001. "More Than a Feeling. Financial Planning." August 1. Available online at http://www.financial-planning.com/.

Vitt, Lois, Carol Anderson, Jamie Kent, Deanna M. Lyter, Jurg K. Siegenthaler, and Jeremy Ward. 2002. *Personal Finance and the Rush to Competence: Financial Literacy Education in the U.S.* Middleburg, VA: Institute for Socio-Financial Studies.

Walker, Lewis J. 2001. "A Look at the Financial Services Revolution." *Journal of Financial Planning* 14(10): 60–62.

*Carol Anderson*

**LIFE PLANNING IN THE WORKPLACE,** the array of education, resources, and considerations employers are uniquely qualified to deliver to employees, with significant payoffs to both.

Life planning in the workplace is a human capital initiative that creates the frequently discussed—but rarely realized—employer-employee partnership. In contrast to traditional financial planning and retirement education programs, life planning presents a focused, business-oriented initiative. By ensuring employees' personal visions/goals align with the organization vision, life planning initiatives retain a strategic orientation that can leverage employee contributions.

### Background

Life planning is still a new field. Its advocates argue that it is the natural next step in the evolution of financial planning, although some financial planners think of it as nothing more than a way to distinguish themselves for marketing purposes (Rowland 2002). What is clear is that life planning practitioners go well beyond financial issues in order to help their clients use the financial resources to make a life, rather than spending their life making money. Since the workplace is where most people do that most of the time, it is also the natural setting for life planning. The fundamental goals of life planning include:

- Ensuring that individual employees develop a personal vision for themselves and their families.
- Facilitating the horizontal and vertical alignment of personal, team, department, and divisional visions with the organization's vision.
- Realizing the frequently discussed adult-adult relationships, organizationwide.
- Creating successes based on a company's intellectual capital and organization learning. Concurrently, employees realize their personal and professional goals.

During the latter part of the 1990s many human resource managers realized that the traditional, corporate-sponsored preretirement training program, while well intentioned, proved ineffective. Critics argue that preretirement training offered to employees during the last one to five years of work generally provided "too little, too late." Essentially, any impact beyond the immediate or short term, for many participating preretirees, was minimal. And some corporate observers suggested that these programs proved counterproductive to their organizations' workplace efforts when retirees realized that retirement was not a financially viable option.

The underlying drivers reflect a complex reality. Numerous influences, many interacting and reflecting the contradictory interests of employees, retirees, line managers, senior executives, public policy/political groups, and unions, have created a "Retirement Catch-22." Some of the most evident forces include:

- Increased longevity, which is creating retirement careers that are, in some cases, longer than an individual's total preretirement employment history;
- The transition from defined benefit pension plans to defined contribution and/or hybrid retirement plans, which has shifted the risk from employers to employees/retirees;
- Shifts in public policy—especially Medicare—that are resulting in retirees paying an ever-increasing percentage of their health care;
- Health care cost inflation, which along with changes in FASB (Financial Accounting Standards Board) accounting requirements has reduced the number of company-sponsored retirement health care plans;
- Increased merger and acquisition activity, which together with reengineering and downsizing has produced a significant number of early retirees;
- The increased diversity of family units—domestic partners, single parents, two wage earner families, late career employees starting new families, employees assuming legal/financial responsibilities for parents, grandparents, and grandchildren—which is creating unexpected workforce demographics and benefit liabilities;
- Significant drops in interest rates, along with a volatile stock market, which has made investing for the long term ever more difficult.

Many human resource managers have introduced financial planning initiatives in response to financial planning, as generally offered, as a voluntary benefit, and all employees may elect to attend sessions. Depending upon the organization, participation may be at no cost to the employee. With a singular focus upon finances, and at best a recognition that personal and family goals shape employee decision making, program designs include a variety of components ranging from software programs to group seminars to individual counseling. In retrospect, the hoped-for "silver bullet" evolved into another reactive, short-term solution, and employee participation was low even when the employer's assistance is generous (i.e., no charge to the employees).

Almost every financial planning program kept to a fairly standard script or goal: participating employees will become aware of their financial health and understand the ramifications of various financial decisions. Numerous human resource managers likened financial planning to corporate-sponsored wellness initiatives: as wellness improved one's physical health, financial planning provided opportunities to enhance employees' financial well-being.

These corporate-sponsored initiatives effectively broadened employees' knowledge and the long-short-term ramifications of various decisions (e.g., how to best utilize dollars or invest wisely). However, they presented several limitations. The most commonly cited include:

- *Employers' and vendors' focus was overly parochial or narrow.* Financial planning initiatives proved most effective when the planning process included employer-sponsored benefits and/or vendor products/services. However, most employees do not limit their purchases to their employer's offerings. And when such "external" products/services were part of the analysis, recommendations proved less insightful and accurate.
- *A disconnect between a rapidly changing labor force and available program products/services.* Programs that emanated from the "old" preretirement training model rarely understood the impact and ramifications of demographic and labor force shifts. And among those programs that recognized the potential impact, only the most sophisticated, savvy, and proactive advisors could create practical and meaningful recommendations.
- *Conflicts of interest.* The three most frequently cited complaints can be deemed actual or perceived conflicts of interest. They are: (1) when financial planners did not provide independent recommendations; (2) when financial planners were rewarded for selling preferred products or services; and (3) when quality of service became secondary to the number (i.e., volume/quantity) of employees receiving assistance.

## Life Planning: What It Is, What It Achieves

Life planning redefines personal financial planning; it effects a fundamental reorientation in the employer-employee relationship. At the core is a transition from traditional human resource approaches, where employees are viewed as depreciable commodities, into a human capital model. The fundamental characteristics/outcomes of a life planning/human capital approach include:

*The employer-employee relationship is articulated fully and clearly.* Even when not fully achieved, it provides an ever-present mission: organizations and employees working as strategic partners creating synergies resulting in success for both groups.

*Employees, as human capital, increase in value.* Human capital, like financial capital, becomes value-added with appropriate investment. Succession planning and professional development (e.g., training, skill enhancement, lateral promotions) cascade throughout the organization. As an integrated package, they represent planned investments in employees and the organization.

In contrast, the traditional parental-style organization depreciates employees, like equipment, over time. The defined benefit (DB) pension plan best epitomizes the depreciation strategy: employees' contributions are viewed as value-added for a period of time or until a predefined specified age, such as normal retirement, after which those contributions are viewed as marginal or negligible.

*Human capital's 4 Rs support corporate strategic business goals.* All people processes can be reduced to four essential functions: recruit, retain, retrain, and retire/separate. And with employees established as one of the requisite forces behind organization success, life planning and 4-R analyses become integrated into the corporate culture and planning, both long and short term. In addition, many traditional transactional activities of human resources (HR) or personnel become either outsourced or line management functions and, in some ways, forces the former HR manager to become a human capital champion who partners with the line but also drives requisite organization evolution.

*Intellectual capital is recognized, acknowledged, and leveraged by both company and employee.* Depending upon variables such as organization size, location(s), structure (i.e., centralized, decentralized), ownership (e.g., private, family, public), culture, and industry, employees' life planning efforts represent personalized strategic plans aligning with the corporate plan. Other companies, in contrast, may view individual plans as elements of a jigsaw puzzle that provide the company's competitive advantage. Either way, intellectual capital is recognized and leveraged.

### Making the Shift: From Theory to Action

The shift from concept to practice begins with three elements: reconfiguring the value-added equation, creating and aligning personal vision with organizational vision, and reconfiguring HR into human capital (i.e., moving from a depreciation model to an appreciation model). The first two elements present the greatest organization challenge, while the last is a more mechanical or formulaic issue. Most companies could readily create a template to repackage existing human resource programs and relanguage programs to reflect appreciation rather than depreciation. Redefining personal accountabilities and effecting culture shifts that are both meaningful and sustainable are at least a significantly greater challenge.

### Reconfiguring the "Value-Added" Equation

To realize the potential offered by life planning, each department—from mailrooms through boardrooms—recognizes *what* and *how* their work creates or contributes to business success. In addition, the organization—through its culture—realizes that "value-added" is not a static measurement; it requires mutually recognized accountabilities and/or outcomes that are bidirectional, changing over time. For example:

- The company adds value/invests in the employee, and the employee's job performance adds value to the company. Each has a vision and goals that must support the other.
- What defines satisfactory, above average, or superior performance evolves as both the organization's needs and employees' capacities expand. Those definitions are also contextual; they must be considered in relation to other organizations competing for success in a dynamic global economy.
- Leadership, management, production, organization structures, and communications are all dynamic; they reflect the business at one point in time. Also, position title or rank do not necessarily constitute or predict effective communication, management, or leadership skills. And the skills that produce success in one business (e.g., start-up) may not be good predictors in mature or sunset industries.

### Creating and Aligning Personal with Organizational Visions

All employees have or can develop a vision. Their success at the subsequent tasks—articulating it clearly, aligning it with the organization's vision, mustering the requisite resources to realize it, and lastly, assessing success, including why/why not—is generally contingent upon other forces/factors.

When the employee and company culture just don't fit, the goal will never be met; frequently, however, success occurs when:

- *The company clearly articulates an organization mission.* Companies define their goals; they are communicated to *and* understood throughout the organization. Managers, having created their own vision, serve as role models to other employees, irrespective of company variables.
- *Company communications are open and nonevasive.* Employees adapt to (and demonstrate) company communications patterns as they are experienced. Companies that demonstrate greater openness and honesty will tend to elicit greater openness and honesty from their employees. In contrast, organizations that share little information find employees also offer little beyond the mandatory specifics.
- *Different personal visions and diversity are valued.* All companies tolerate differences. When companies recognize, leverage, and/or find opportunities for those differences, they enhance their competitive advantage, creating value. Essentially, when different visions fuel synergies, win-win scenarios emerge.

In contrast, when differences are devalued (i.e., the differences themselves or degree of differences are perceived or judged to be too great), individuals become stereotyped or characterized as not fitting or nonteam players. Any potential synergies and/or competitive advantages are lost when an employee's vision is either not tolerated or cannot be aligned with that of his or her peers, managers, and the organization.

### Implementing a Life Planning Initiative

In some specific situations, a companywide life planning initiative may provide a greater return on investment (ROI) concurrent with reducing the employer's legal/fiduciary liabilities. Examples include the termination of a traditional DB pension concurrent with or without the introduction of a hybrid (e.g., cash balance) plan.

Generally, the rollout should be planned and aligned with the company's strategic business and human resource plan. Prior to the actual rollout, upside and downside analyses that combine "What if" scenarios with the previously described 4-R scan preclude unanticipated problems. Two different scenarios demonstrate the power of a focused and managed rollout:

*Companies needing to reduce headcount.* During economic downturns, reorganizations, and/or changes in a company's product/service offerings, employers introduce workforce reductions (e.g., layoffs, early retirement windows, voluntary severance). Concurrently, they are also conducting searches for needed skills. One potential alternative to the usual layoffs is in-sourcing (i.e., retrain current employees to meet emerging and/or newly identified skill requirements).

Life planning offers the opportunity to educate workforce segments. More specifically, specific life planning products (e.g., employee's personal vision, assessment of their financial safety net, blueprint to realize their vision) facilitates informed decisions and planned transitions either within the company or from the company.

*Companies competing for scarce skills and/or trying to reduce turnover.* Life planning, by emphasizing the employee/employer partnership, can effect a change in the major reasons that most employees change jobs: a poor manager and belief of no or limited career opportunities. For example, succession plans, training, and other career options articulated in the vision phase can be readily explored, precluding the desire for changing jobs/employer.

### Summary

As organizations search for ways to attract and retain the best possible employees, they will, with increasing frequency, move from the traditional parental organization to a strategic partnership model. As with other strategic partnerships, there will be an ever-increasing emphasis on creating synergies resulting in a win for all groups. Life planning, as a distinct partnership model, begins with the assumption that aligning visions and honest adult-adult communications can leverage talent and create the requisite synergies. (See FINANCIAL SECURITY IN RETIREMENT; FRAILTY PLANNING; LIFE PLANNING; RETIREMENT EXPENSE PLANNING; RETIREMENT PLANS—401(k); RETIREMENT PLANS—403(b); RETIREMENT PREPAREDNESS.)

#### Suggested Reading

Kinder, George. 2000. *Seven Stages of Money Maturity: Understanding the Spirit and Value of Money in Your Life*. New York: Dell Trade.

#### References

Edwards, Paul, and Sarah Edwards. 2001. *Changing Directions without Losing Your Way: Managing the Six Stages of Change at Work and in Life*. New York: J.P. Tarcher.

Moses, Barbara. 1998. *Career Intelligence: The 12 New Rules for Work and Life Success*. San Francisco, CA: Berrett-Koehler.

Reinhold, Barbara B. 2001. *Free to Succeed: Designing the Life You Want in the New Free Agent Economy*. New York: Plume.

Rowland, M. 2002. "Life Crafters." *Bloomberg Wealth Manager* (July–August). Available online at http://www.bloomberg.com/.

*Victor S. Barocas*

**LIVING WILL,** a type of advance directive used to give instructions about future medical care in the event of serious illness or injury. A living will allows an individual to document his or her wishes about future medical care, thereby maintaining some control at the end of life.

### How Living Wills Work

A living will, also sometimes called a "directive to physicians," "health care declaration," or "medical directive," is used to guide physicians and family members in deciding how aggressively to use medical treatments to delay a person's death. Every state except Massachusetts, Michigan, and New York has passed legislation regulating the use of living wills; all have statutes addressing advance directives (Gunter-Hunt, Mahoney, and Sieger 2001). Even in states without living will statutes, living wills are valid following the 1980 U.S. Court *Cruzan* decision that competent adults have a constitutional right to make medical treatment wishes known and have them honored. State law and rules governing the use and implementation of living wills vary. A living will usually goes into effect only when the person who signed it becomes incompetent. Frequently, a law requires that a second doctor confirm the person's condition before a living will can honored.

A legally valid living will must be signed by its originator in the presence of witnesses who indicate that they believe the person signing the document is of sound mind and acting under no duress. Restrictions requiring that witnesses have no interest in the estate of the person making a living will frequently apply, and some states require the attestation of a notary public. Witnessing requirements must be followed exactly, or the validity of the living will can be challenged.

Most states have a standard living will form that is available from health care facilities, state departments of health, or organizations concerned with issues affecting the aging. There are also generic (non-state-specific) living wills, but state-authorized forms help ensure that state requirements are met and that health care providers will honor the document. Since most living wills contain relatively simple checklists or fill-in-the-blanks to indicate one's medical treatment preferences, a lawyer may not be needed.

## Historic Development

Living wills were developed because modern medicine's ability to sustain life, in some cases, has exceeded its ability to cure. As chronic and degenerative diseases became a more common cause of death, and as more people began dying in hospitals rather than in home settings (President's Commission 1983), people looked for ways to regain control of the dying process. At a meeting of the Society for the Right to Die in 1967, the first living will was drafted as a way for people to indicate a wish to avoid life-prolonging treatment in the event there was no hope for recovery. Living wills can also ensure desired care at the end of life, but this aspect is often ignored in the discussion. While a property will becomes effective upon the death of the person making it, a living will becomes effective while its originator is alive and is used solely for making decisions about medical care and treatment.

In 1976, California became the first state to pass legislation that directly addressed the issue of end-of-life decision making, allowing individuals to plan in advance for the treatment they would receive at the end of life. Other states followed with living will statutes; however, early statutes tended to be limited. Under California law, for example, a person had to be diagnosed as terminally ill and expected to die within six months before a legally valid living will could be made.

## Current Legal Issues

New laws and revisions of older laws currently allow individuals more freedom to specify medical treatment through living wills. A competent adult in any state may complete a legally valid living will, but some restrictions still exist, and the most troublesome is the definition of "terminal condition." When narrowly defined by state law, the applicability of a living will is limited. Many living will statutes, for example, define terminal condition such that persons permanently unconscious, or who could be maintained for a substantial period of time on life support without hope for improvement, could be unprotected from unwanted treatment. In states that allow it, the patient should also have a durable power of attorney for health care, allowing a surrogate to direct treatment for a "nonterminal" patient.

Artificial nutrition and hydration (tube feeding) present another problem. Although the

U.S. Supreme Court's *Cruzan* decision determined that artificial nutrition and hydration is a medical treatment that may be refused, many states require specific wording in a living will if tube feeding is not desired. Often all that is required is the additional statement: "I do not want tube feeding." The discontinuation of artificial nutrition and hydration has been the focal point of most major right-to-die court cases. Since terminal patients can frequently be maintained for long periods of time on tube feeding, any instructions accompanying the living will form should be reviewed to see if there are special provisions regarding tube feeding.

As referenced previously, most states allow competent adults to appoint a health care agent who is authorized to make medical decisions in the event of incompetence. Some states allow such an agent to be appointed within the living will form, while others require a separate form, called a durable power of attorney, for health care. Where the option is available, experts advise executing both a living will and a durable power of attorney, since both forms work together. The living will can guide the agent in the decision-making process, and if the agent is unavailable or unable to make decisions when the time comes, the living will can stand on its own. (See also ADVANCE DIRECTIVES; ATTORNEYS; DURABLE POWER OF ATTORNEY; FINANCIAL ADVISORS; FINANCES OF AGING IN THE GAY COMMUNITY; INTERGENERATIONAL CONFLICT AND FINANCIAL ISSUES; KING LEAR SYNDROME; TRUSTS; WILLS.)

**Organizations**

Hemlock Society
Partnership for Caring

**References**

Brown, Carolyn. 1992. *Decide for Yourself—Life Support, Living Will, Power of Attorney for Health Care*. Atlanta, GA: Pritchett and Hull.

Gunter-Hunt, G., J.E. Mahoney, and C.E. Sieger. 2001. "A Comparison of State Advance Directive Documents." *The Gerontologist* 42: 51–60.

President's Commission for the Study of Ethical Problems in Medicine and Biomedical and Behavioral Research. 1983. *Deciding to Forego Life-Sustaining Treatment*. Washington, DC: GPO.

U.S. Senate. Subcommittee on Medicare and Long-Term Care. 1990. *Living Wills Hearing*. Washington, DC: GPO.

*Ann E. Fade*
*Updated by Sandra L. Reynolds*

**LOANS.** See Banking Services for the Mature Market; Bonds; Credit Scores; Home Modifications Financing; Homeownership; Mortgage Instruments; Reverse Mortgages; Seniors Housing Finance.

**LONG-TERM CARE INSURANCE (LTCI)—A CONSUMER'S PERSPECTIVE,** the insurance mechanism by which the risk of the potentially catastrophic financial impact of a significant period of frailty is shifted from a single individual to a large group of people. Long-term care insurance pays for many of the medical, nonmedical, and social support services that are required when an individual becomes frail enough to qualify for a claim.

Long-term care insurance is not health insurance. Stated generally, health insurance (such as Medicare) pays for medical care of acute illness or injury but not for frailty care. It pays for doctors and hospitals that take care of people when they are ill or injured—and recovering—but it does not pay for custodial or supportive care of people who have persistent conditions (such as Alzheimer's) that render them unable to function independently. Long-term care insurance rarely pays for doctors or hospitals. Rather, it pays for professional care such as nursing and physical and occupational therapy and for nonmedical living support services such as home health aides and companions. It also pays for facilities such as adult day care centers, assisted living, and nursing homes that provide a safe and supportive environment for people with chronic conditions that leave them unable to function independently.

Neither is long-term care insurance Medicare supplement ("Medigap") insurance. Medigap insurance covers the holes (deductibles and copays) that exist in both Part A and Part B of Medicare and as such is a form of health insurance. Even though Medicare, Medigap, and long-term care insurance are all usually associated with older people, they each have a distinct purpose.

### Key Considerations for LTCI

The first is that all consumers should seriously consider acquiring long-term care insurance. The appropriate question is not "Who should buy it?" but rather "Who should *not* buy it?" Statistics cannot predict which of us will need long-term care services, but they do demonstrate that so many of us will need them that not to prepare to live through a period of frailty with its attendant costs—now over $60,000 per year on average and only getting worse (MetLife 2002)—is dangerous. There are two exceptions to this rule: (1) those who are already qualified for Medicaid benefits or almost qualified and (2) those who already live in a continuing care retirement community (CCRC) *with an extensive* or "life care" contract, where prefunded long-term care is part of the lifestyle choice of moving to a CCRC in the first place.

Another key consideration for consumers is the life situation of the insured at long-term care insurance claim time. At that point, the dignity and well-being of a person who can no longer function independently due to either physical or cognitive (mental) limitation or deterioration is at stake. Physical limitations that are generally used to determine claim eligibility in long-term care insurance are the inability to bathe safely without help, to maintain control of bowel or bladder, to use the toilet without assistance, to dress oneself or eat unaided, to get in and out of bed, or to move from a chair to a bed independently. Recognized cognitive impairments are generally those that make it unsafe for a person to live without someone to guide or cue their behavior or prevent wandering. When life has gotten to that point, by whatever route, help and assistance are required—and it is expensive. Recent estimates put the cost of frailty care above $5,000 per month, and more than twice that in some urban areas (MetLife 2002). Such situations may persist for years, maybe even decades, without relief.

There is no free frailty care. The traditional alternative to long-term care insurance is referred to as "informal caregiving": direct caregiving by a spouse, sibling, or child (usually female). While some see this as free, such a view overlooks two very important points. First, as demonstrated in *The MetLife Juggling Act Study* (MetLife 1999), the cost to so-called informal caregivers in real lost wealth (wages lost while providing care; lost opportunities for advancement or promotion because of unreliability from the employer's perspective while caregiving; and pension, 401(k), and Social Security benefits generated by those wages over the caregiver's lifetime) is over $659,000. Critics have claimed that this study is flawed because it uses a small data set, but even if it overstates the cost by 100%, it is obvious that this care is not free. Shifting the dollar and cents cost from a frail elder to a hale and hearty family member does not make it disappear.

Second, relying on informal caregiving ignores the cost to the caregiver in other, more profoundly human currencies such as sleep, emotional balance and calm, spiritual peace, physical vitality, and internal satisfaction and well-being. While it is inappropriate to discount the rewards some people experience from caring for another when they are too frail to care for themselves, it is also inappropriate to romanticize the caregiver role. Long-term care insurance will not "pay" these costs, but it will generate the financial resources to pay for professional care so that friends and family can be free (1) to relate to the frail elder out of love and relationship rather than duty and task orientation and (2) to take good care of themselves during an emotionally and spiritually challenging period.

### Alternative Financial Resources

Before committing to premium payments for long-term care insurance, an informed consumer will want to consider alternative sources of funding for long-term or frailty care. There are only two: government programs and personal wealth (Simmons and MacBean 2000). The government programs most often thought of as resources are Medicare and Medicaid, but neither is a viable solution. Medicare is designed for acute care only, and most recent changes to the program only serve to reinforce that focus and move it away from paying for care for chronic conditions. Medicaid, which is essentially a welfare program, does make provision for long-term care for the impoverished among us—but only for the impoverished. While it is possible to "artificially impoverish" oneself for the purpose of taking advantage of Medicaid, a consumer contemplating such a strategy might want to consider both the displacement of the truly impoverished such an approach will create and the probable surroundings and quality of care a chronically underfunded program for the impoverished might provide.

For most consumers, personal wealth is not a resource available to pay for frailty care. Assets are either committed to:

1. Generating income for self or others to live on; and/or
2. Providing a legacy for family members or other causes.

Accessing cash values or death benefits of life insurance may be a way to provide funds for frailty care, but this has obvious implications for the beneficiaries of those policies. Converting home equity through a reverse mortgage or private annuity is another potential source of funds to pay for frailty care, but again, only with implications for survivors that may not be entirely desirable. Some argue that wealthier consumers do not need long-term care insurance because they can self-insure the cost of frailty care, but the truth is that wealthy people do not self-insure foreseeable risks. They want to *use* an insurance company to share the risk, not to *be* an insurance company and take on the risk individually.

There are relatively rare circumstances where buying long-term care insurance is not financially advisable, but that can only be determined with the assistance of a financial advisor who is fully apprised of the facts of the situation and the consumer's attitudes and values relative to living this part of life.

In short, buying long-term care insurance is the responsible, mature choice for almost all those who can qualify for it and afford it.

### Variables

Long-term care insurance is often perceived as overwhelmingly complex, but there are really only eight variables a consumer will want to consider. The first—selecting a responsible, knowledgeable agent—will largely determine how well the consumer is able to deal with the other seven. They are:

1. Choosing *how* the consumer wants the insurance company to pay at claim time.
2. Determining whether or not the insured wants the insurance company to provide his or her care planner.
3. Selecting *what* the insured wants the insurance company to pay for.
4. Deciding *how soon* the insured wants the insurance company to start paying.
5. Choosing *how much* the consumer wants the insurance company to pay.
6. Picking a reliable insurance company.
7. Determining whether the consumer can afford her or his choices or needs to make different ones.

### Choosing an Agent

Long-term care insurance only emerged as a mature form of coverage providing real benefits and value in the mid-1990s. Agent training has been slow to follow suit. There are many committed, highly knowledgeable long-term care agents operating in the United States—and it is important to find one of them. Long-term care insurance is different from all other forms of insurance because claims are so poignant—remember, at the point of claim the insured is no longer able to function independently—and because the services available to respond to a claim are both not widely known and rapidly evolving. It takes someone committed to serving her or his clients to understand the field well enough to be considered an advisor and to stay current. The challenge is to identify such an agent.

Certification is one thing that helps a consumer to meet the challenge. Any agent can invest the time and money to become certified as knowledgeable by applying for one or more of these programs:

*Certified Senior Advisor (CSA).* This designation is sponsored by the privately owned Society of Certified Senior Advisors and educates candidates on the entire spectrum of issues related to aging in the United States. As such, it is not specifically focused on long-term care insurance but rather provides an advisor with a broad background of relevant knowledge. CSAs have to stay current by meeting ongoing continuing education requirements.

*Certified in Long-Term Care (CLTC).* This designation is sponsored by the privately owned Corporation for Long-Term Care Certification and educates candidates in issues around the costs of long-term care and structuring long-term care insurance coverages. The founders of the Corporation for Long-Term Care Certification have close ties to the National Academy of Elder Law Attorneys (NAELA).

*Long-Term Care Professional (LTCP).* This designation is sponsored by the Health Insurance Association of America (HIAA), a well-regarded health insurance industry association, and has stringent continuing education requirements. The LTCP requires successful completion of a four-part curriculum: Long-Term Care: Understanding Needs and Options; Financing Long-Term Care Needs; The Long-Term Care Product: Policy Design, Pricing, and Regulation; and Long-Term Care Insurance Administration.

Certification is not, by itself, a guarantee that an advisor is fully qualified to provide advice and counsel about long-term care insurance, but it is a positive indicator. Two other indicators are the breadth of the agent's product offering (and his or her rationale for which companies are included or excluded) and knowledge of contract terms.

A consumer will be well advised to work with a long-term care insurance agent who represents several companies, or at least several different approaches to policy design and coverage. When asked the question, "What companies do you represent, and why?" an agent should be able to identify resources for both indemnity- and reimbursement-style coverages and a variety of benefit, underwriting, and premium management approaches. Advisors whose product offerings are limited to one company with which they do the bulk of their non–long-term care business, or who are associated with a number of companies but cannot articulate why she or he would use one or the other, may not be well enough versed in issues around frailty and frailty care to render the kind of advice one should have, given what is at stake at claim time.

A simple test that a consumer can use to get an indication of whether an agent understands long-term care insurance is to ask about the details of the grace period in the policy the agent sells most frequently and how and why it differs from others. The grace period is a provision of every insurance policy (not just long-term care insurance) that keeps the coverage in force for a period of time—usually 30 days—after the premium is due if the premium has not been received by the company on time. In LTCI a longer period is very valuable because as people age, they often become forgetful. A lapse for nonpayment of premium just as the policy may be about to mature into a claim is not a desirable outcome, so better LTCI polices do not lapse at that point. Rather, if a premium has still not been received 30 days after a premium due date, the company will send out a second premium notice to the policyholder along with a notice to a third party (such as a child or advisor) selected in advance by the policyholder. If no premium has been received after *another* 30 days, plus time for the mail to get to the policyholder, the policy will lapse. A grace period that is explicitly 65 days is most desirable; one that is effectively that long is the next best thing. In all events, a well-qualified long-term care insurance agent will know and be able to explain the differences.

### Choose How You Want the Insurance Company to Pay You at Claim Time

There are two styles of long-term care insurance: indemnity and reimbursement. In an indemnity-style policy, generally speaking, once the insured has qualified to receive benefits the insurance company sends the insured a check for a set amount per period (usually a month), regardless of the actual cost of services provided during that period. The advantage of this style policy is the flexibility it gives to pay for care that is uniquely suited to the insured (although there may be income tax consequences if funds are not spent on "qualified long-term care services" as defined in the Health Insurance Portability and Accountability Act (HIPAA) of 1996. Such flexibility becomes more and more valuable the further in the future a claim occurs, since best practices of care are a constantly evolving standard. The disadvantages are that (1) the duration of benefit payments becomes a much more critical decision when structuring a policy and (2) this style of benefit is the most expensive.

Reimbursement-style LTCI policies reimburse the policyholder for covered claims incurred up to the lesser of actual cost or the limits of the policy. There are two subcategories of reimbursement-style policies available that can determine how benefits qualified for, but not utilized, are processed. For example, assume a daily benefit of $200 and an incurred covered cost of $140; what happens to the $60? In policies in the "reimbursement—use it or lose it" subcategory, the $60 is retained by the insurance company. In the "reimbursement—benefit bank account" subcategory the $60 is retained in the policy to extend the benefit period. The advantages of reimbursement-style policies are that they are less expensive than indemnity-style policies, and because the insurance company is in the position of approving claims for reimbursement, their vast knowledge of costs and practices may serve to detect or prevent claims abuse or fraud. The disadvantages are (1) the relative lack of self-determination as to how benefits are spent and (2) concern as to whether the benefits specified in the policy will still represent "best practices" or even adequate care practices if the insured does not qualify for claim for 15 or 20 years. This can be mitigated with a strong "Alternate Plan of Care Provision" but is nonetheless more of a concern with reimbursement-style policies than it is with indemnity-style LTCI. "Reimbursement—use or lose it" style policies are the least expensive; reimbursement, "benefit bank account" style polices are the overwhelming majority of new policies sold.

### Determine Whether You Want the Company to Provide Your Care Planner

At the point of claim, when the insured can no longer function independently, the issue that arises is "Who will design the plan of care and who will pay them to do so?" The people who are best at doing this are geriatric care managers, sometimes referred to as care coordinators: skilled and caring people, often from nursing or social work backgrounds whose role it is to develop, implement, and monitor plans of care. The presumption is that all care coordinators have expert knowledge of the local market and can provide informed opinions as to appropriate providers of service. Anyone, whether insured or not, who becomes unable to function independently will want to work with a care manager or care coordinator—even if care is being provided by an "informal caregiver."

The arguments *for* having the insurance company provide your care manager are availability, policy knowledge (presumably, a care manager or care coordinator who often works with any given long-term care insurance company will be familiar with both its policies and practices, thereby arriving at a more practical plan of care more quickly), and the availability of an alternate care manager. If, for some reason, there is a clash between the insured and the care manager appointed by the company, or if there is an emergency and the care manager is unavailable to respond, the insurance company will likely have another care manager available to substitute. Some policies require the use of the company's appointed care manager to receive the full benefit of the policy. In these cases, some people wonder about the independence and autonomy of the care manager.

The arguments *against* having the insurance company provide the care manager have to do with concerns about advocacy and attitudes toward insurance companies. Nobody can insure everything, and to the extent that people are distrustful of insurance companies, it might be desirable to have long-term care insurance that does not provide for or require the use of a care manager of the company's choosing to determine the plan of care. Some insureds prefer to hire and pay for their own care coordinator to act as their advocate with the insurance company and service providers.

### Select What You Want the Insurance Company to Pay For

The choices here fall into two questions: "What care do you want covered?" and "In what setting?" The latter is easier to answer.

The choices are facility-based care, home- and community-based care, or both. Facility-based care is care provided in nursing homes, assisted living facilities, and Alzheimer's and hospice facilities. Definitions of what qualifies as a nursing facility or an assisted living facility are important because the definition in the policy controls whether a benefit will be paid, not how the facility markets itself. A knowledgeable agent will likely know the facilities in the area and whether they meet the definitions in the policies he or she represents most often.

The bigger issue is whether to buy a long-term care insurance policy that only covers facility-based care, or only covers home- and community-based care, or whether to buy an "integrated" policy that will cover services rendered in either setting. An integrated policy will be more expensive than a policy that covers either facility-based or home- and community-based care. However, very few people like the idea of having their insurance policy dictate their plan of care. Long-term care coverage that favors one setting over another either by definition or limitation, or by amount of benefit, will almost inevitably bias the plan of care.

What services are covered in which setting is the other question, although policies vary little in what services are covered in a facility-based setting. Again, a knowledgeable agent should be able to outline them. Differences in coverage are more dramatic for home- and community-based settings than for facility-based skilled care. Almost all policies that cover home- and community-based care cover all skilled home care (such as nurses, physical therapists, occupational therapists, and pulmonary therapists) in those settings. And almost all cover licensed or registered home health aides. Coverage for personal care attendants, chore services, and homemaker services vary much more widely.

### Decide How Soon You Want the Insurance Company to Start Paying

Sooner is always better than later at the point of claim. There are two variables in this category: benefit triggers and waiting periods. Benefit triggers are the terms by which a person qualifies for benefits. All LTCI policies consider the inability to perform some of the activities of daily living (ADLs) and/or cognitive impairment to be triggers.

The most commonly used ADLs are:

1. Bathing (safely)
2. Continence (control of bladder and bowels)
3. Dressing (unassisted)
4. Eating (but does not include preparing food)
5. Toileting (use the toilet and rearrange clothing afterward)
6. Transferring (get in and out of and move between chairs, bed, etc.)

Some policies add mobility as a seventh ADL; some do not include bathing. Inability to perform two out of the six ADLs listed above is the standard benefit trigger for physical limitations. Policies that require an inability to perform three out of six ADLs to trigger benefits are much less desirable, and those that require two out of five and do not include bathing as an ADL effectively require three out of six, because bathing is so often the first ADL that a frail person cannot perform. On the cognitive side, the benefit period begins if the insured requires some form of supervision to be protected from threats to their health and safety.

So-called tax-qualified (TQ) policies, which were defined in the Health Insurance Portability and Accountability Act (HIPAA) of 1996 and given certain income tax advantages, use only these triggers. Non-tax-qualified (NTQ) policies often add a third benefit trigger: "medical necessity." It is unclear whether this trigger, which is a holdover from an earlier generation of nursing home insurance, adds any real benefit, although it certainly calls into question the tax status of any benefits that might be paid regardless of how they are triggered.

Inability to perform activities of daily living, or the point at which a person needs supervision lest he or she be a threat to his or her own health and safety, is not always clear-cut. Unlike a life insurance death claim, the point at which a person with long-term care insurance becomes eligible for claim is very much a judgment call, which raises the matter of waiting periods.

A waiting period is the time between when a person is eligible to go on claim (has tripped a benefit trigger) and when benefits begin to be paid. Waiting periods can range from very short (0 or 7 days) to moderate (20 to 30 days) to long (90 or 100 days) or very long (six months or more). The longer the waiting period, the lower the premium. Keep in mind, however, that there is also a silent waiting period for a lot of frail elders: a period of decline during which pride or routine or busyness masks qualification for benefits before anyone considers filing a claim. Someone is providing care during that period, and often an informal caregiver is already exhausted from doing so. When the claim is approved and the waiting period begins, a longer waiting period often aggravates the situation rather than relieving it.

### Choose How Much You Want the Insurance Company to Pay

Once again, there are two variables: the daily benefit limit and the duration of benefits. In indemnity-style policies, and reimbursement—use it or lose it style policies, the duration is just that. If the policy has a three-year benefit period, and the insured lives for more than three years after qualifying for a claim, the benefits stop after 36 months. In reimbursement—benefit bank account style policies, the duration is just a multiplier to arrive at the initial size of the account. For example, a policy with a five-year benefit period (365 days per year × 5 years = 1,825 days) and a $200 per day benefit has an initial benefit bank account of $365,000 (1,825 days × $200), which can be utilized to pay for covered benefits over whatever period of time it takes, subject to the daily limit of $200. Benefit periods range from one year to lifetime, with two, three, four, and five years commonly available. Daily benefit limits vary from less than $100 to more than $500.

An additional consideration is whether to structure a policy with a flat benefit amount or to structure it to increase over time to keep up with inflation. In most policies there are three choices: no inflation protection, benefits increase at (usually) 5% simple interest, or benefits increase at (usually) 5% compound interest. As a general rule, anyone under 70 at the time of purchase will want to buy the compound interest inflation protection; people buying long-term care insurance in their mid-seventies may decide to choose simple interest instead; and people who defer buying into their eighties may not want any. Additional purchase options (the right to buy a minimal additional amount in the future without evidence of insurability) are another way to try to keep policy benefits in line with future costs. Many advisors recommend them in addition to inflation protection benefits, not as alternatives.

### Pick a Reliable Insurance Company

There is simply no way to determine with certainty whether an insurance company that is currently well managed, offering good products at fair prices, paying claims reasonably and promptly, and generally operating as though they understand that the only reason for their existence is to pay claims will continue to do so. A deregulated financial services sector has and will continue to wreak havoc with standards and norms of operations for insurance companies as well as banks and securities brokerages. Ratings services help; any agent can provide an insurance company's ratings from A.M. Best, Standard & Poor's, Moody's, and Weiss; a good agent can explain them.

Whether a company has been in the long-term care insurance business for a long time is a consideration but not necessarily important. If a company has been in the business for a long time, however, it will be easier to determine whether it knows how to price its products. Have their policyholders been subjected to rate increases? How often? How big? How recent? Has the company learned its lesson? Companies that offer relatively cheap premiums for relatively rich benefit packages are not a bargain, because there is a reduced probability that they will be in business when the insured needs a claim paid.

### Determine Whether You Can Afford Your Choices or Need to Make Different Ones

The final step is pricing your choices: determining how much the premium will be for a given set of choices. Generally speaking, the premium you are quoted will stay level for life, although that is not guaranteed. Again, a knowledgeable agent can provide information on company practices.

The premium is "too much" if paying it would affect your lifestyle. Beyond that, if the insured lives through a period of frailty, someone will need to pay for their care. The only questions are, "Who?" "How much?" and "In what currencies—financial, physical, emotional, or spiritual?" (See also ACTIVITIES OF DAILY LIVING [ADLs]; AGENTS AND BROKERS; ASSISTED LIVING; CONTINUING CARE RETIREMENT COMMUNITIES [CCRCs]; COST OF FAMILY CAREGIVING; DAY PROGRAMS FOR ADULTS; EMPLOYER-SPONSORED LONG-TERM CARE INSURANCE; FINANCIAL SECURITY IN RETIREMENT; FRAILTY PLANNING; GERIATRIC CARE MANAGERS [GCMs]; HOME CARE SERVICES FOR OLDER ADULTS; LONG-TERM CARE INSURANCE: INDIVIDUAL DISABILITY-ESCALATING ANNUITIES [IDEAs]; LONG-TERM CARE INSURANCE, PRIVATE; MEDICAID; NURSING HOMES.)

### Suggested Readings

Driscoll, Marilee, and Kimberly Lankford. 2002. *The Complete Idiot's Guide to Long-Term Care Planning*. New York: Alpha Books.

Shelton, Phyllis. 2001. *Long Term Care: Your Financial Planning Guide*. New York: Kensington Books.

United Seniors Health Council. 2002. *Planning for Long-Term Care*. New York: McGraw-Hill.

### References

MetLife. 1999. *The MetLife Juggling Act Study: Balancing Caregiving with Work and the Costs Involved*. Westport, CT: MetLife Mature Market Institute.

MetLife. 2002. *MetLife Market Survey on Nursing Home and Home Care Costs 2002*. Westport, CT: MetLife Mature Market Institute.

Simmons, Henry C., and E. Craig MacBean. 2000. *Thriving after 55: Your Guide to Fully Living the Rest of Your Life*. Richmond, VA: Prime Press.

*E. Craig MacBean*

**LONG-TERM CARE INSURANCE: INDIVIDUAL DISABILITY-ESCALATING ANNUITIES (IDEAs),** a financing alternative for long-term care, based on the principle that the financial risk of becoming functionally impaired during retirement may be reduced by spreading it three ways simultaneously:

1. Over people, through insurance contracts;
2. Over time, through sales to those under age 60; and
3. Against the inversely related risk of extended longevity (the peril covered by annuities and pension plans).

### Overview

Demand for long-term care services will rise dramatically in the decades ahead. The supply of public funds is inadequate to meet even today's long-term care needs. Yet traditional long-term care insurance product offerings in the private sector today cover only 7% of today's retirees (Blankenheim 2000).

Unlike acute care Medicare supplemental insurance, long-term care insurance policies provide nursing home and/or at-home benefits for those suffering from chronic disabilities during their retirement. Since Mark Meiners (1983) first introduced the prototype long-term care insurance policy, hundreds of insurers and their agents hoped to meet the demand for coverage with such traditional, stand-alone contracts that covered only one risk.

Yet, for a variety of reasons, the growth of sales to retirees has been disappointing over the past two decades. In interviews with 119 financiers, providers, and insurers, the Center for Long-Term Care Financing (Moses and Rosenfeld 2000) found several factors that have contributed to the slow growth of the market among retirees. They include consumer denial, misperceptions about state governments' spend-down requirements under Medicaid, misinformation about Medicare, consumer ignorance, a lack of stronger tax incentives to purchase long-term care insurance, the bad reputation of earlier policies, consumers' fears about rate stability, an inefficient distribution system, poorly focused marketing plans, and competition with prescription drug coverage for greater public awareness.

Ideally, however, long-term care contracts should be purchased by individuals well before they retire since time can enhance the cost-effectiveness of any insurance plan that spreads risk-financing responsibilities over a large number of people.

### New IDEAs

Becoming functionally dependent during retirement is a risk that can be reduced by spreading it, not just over people and time but also against an opposing or inversely related risk. The premise underlying individual disability-escalating annuities (IDEAs) is that disability among older adults tends to be life shortening; that is, that the risks of functional dependence and extended longevity are inversely related. The central hedging principle that underlies the IDEA concept is that for both men and women over 65 as levels of impairment increase, life expectancies decrease.

Since the primary purpose of annuities is to protect against the peril of outliving one's income, the risk of becoming functionally dependent can be cut by packaging disability insurance coverage *with* annuity protection. A single insurance policy can then cover the joint peril of "superannuated-disability." Under such a contract that covers two opposing risks simultaneously, the more disabled that annuitants become, the more monthly cash they can receive to help them pay for long-term care services of their choice since, on average, they have a shorter remaining survival time.

Disability-escalating retirement annuities call not only for monthly annuity payments to continue to retirees as long as they live but also for benefit levels to escalate as the disability status of annuitants worsens. Cash benefits for older people with a disability, unlike those meant to indemnify insureds for lost income or for specific service expenses, are ones of status, like those paid out under annuities.

### Research Findings

Selected for analysis by Christopherson (1992) was the longitudinal *Aging in Manitoba* study (Manitoba Department of Health & Social Development 1973). The government of Manitoba conducted the study to assess the needs of older people and the resources available to meet those needs. Follow-up interviews of original respondents still living were completed during the summer of 1983. Dates of death were recorded for those who died during the intervening 12 years. The principal research findings and conclusions from Christopherson's (1992) analysis of the Manitoba survey data include the following:

1. Each of the nine activities of daily living (ADLs) physical dependency indicators is a more powerful predictor of mortality than virtually any health status or history question.
2. For both men and women aged 65 or over, as levels of functional impairment increase, life expectancy decreases.
3. The nine ADLs studied can be most closely grouped into three disjoint "factors" that largely reflect dependencies within three distinct ADL activity clusters (related to arms, legs, and the body).

Providing actuarially equivalent, disability-escalating, extra cash benefits to disabled insureds starts with a definition of the help they need in performing basic self-care activities at two different levels:

*Level 1.* Needing help with at least two of the nine activities of daily living, so long as those activities are from at least two different clusters.

*Level 2.* Needing help with at least five of the nine ADLs, so long as those activities are from all three clusters.

Supplemental cash benefits payable to functionally dependent annuitants are expressed as percentages of the basic monthly benefits they receive under their annuities. Christopherson (1992) recommends a unisex schedule of extra benefits that escalate not only with the level of impairment but also with the original age of transition to that functionally impaired state, from 20% for those under age 75 at Level 1 to 70% at age 85 or over at Level 2.

Several IDEA pricing assumptions are intentionally conservative. Yet the maximum probable "net cost" of providing this unisex schedule of extra disability benefits is extremely low. Depending on the assumed interest rate used to price an annuity, it may cost as little as a 2% reduction in basic benefits for men and less than a 4% reduction for women to pay for these supplemental disability benefits. For example, a man may choose to finance a $1,000 monthly retirement income under a traditional annuity. For the same total premium contributions during his working years, he could fund an IDEA basic benefit of 2% less than that amount, or $980. But that monthly annuity would escalate, should he become disabled during retirement. The total net cost to annuitants might be reduced further, or even eliminated, by increasing charges payable by those who surrender their deferred annuities prior to retirement.

### Policies for the Future

There are concerns about pricing assumptions in the development of any new insurance product. But a significant degree of security has been introduced into the calculation of the levels and costs of the disability benefits suggested here. Spreading against each other, two inversely related risks (disability and superannuation) lowers the overall variability around survival projections. Eventually, new research data about ADLs and their effects on longevity will likely become available. Until then, it seems safest to use conservative assumptions when generalizing from the Manitoba study findings about impairments and their effects on survival times to current annuitant mortality projections.

The IDEA concept offers real advantages to both consumers and insurers. First, the product protects against the economic consequences of extended longevity by providing monthly benefits guaranteed for life. Second, disability-escalating contracts should be viewed as much more than traditional annuities. Historically, private disability insurance products have been designed to replace a percentage of an individual's working income lost due to accident or sickness prior to retirement. By contrast, IDEAs protect against the peril of disability after retirement by paying escalated cash benefits, not only unrelated to lost income but also regardless of the incurrence of any specific expenses caused by the disability.

By introducing waiting periods before considering claims for escalated benefits, insurers can minimize both their adverse selection risks and policy costs. With a maximum issue age of 60, the joint peril of superannuated disability could be effectively spread over time as well as over insureds. Insurers' verifications of the impairment status of claimants can be combined with active case management assistance to disabled annuitants in finding cost-effective rehabilitation possibilities or in otherwise optimizing their escalated benefits.

By attracting attention to the real retirement planning and estate preservation needs addressed by individual disability-escalating annuities, insurance companies should realize better persistency for their annuity line than they currently do when speaking to those obsessed with merely finding the highest current and tax-deferred interest rate haven for their money. By advocating a comprehensive estate preservation planning program, including the need to protect against the peril of needing long-term care, agents should also realize increasing levels of collateral life policy sales. Furthermore, by bundling together protection against two risks in one product, insurers can overcome the stigma and the psychological barriers of trying to sell stand-alone "nursing home" or even "long-term care" policies. In one recent study Christopherson (2002) examines how fear, love, duty, self-interest, and the quest to leave a legacy interact in complex ways when consumers are confronted with the decision to purchase traditional long-term care insurance.

In the last decade, the first versions of individual disability-escalating annuities (IDEAs) have been developed and introduced into the American and Canadian markets. Interested consumers who are approaching retirement age should ask their independent agents if the insurers they represent are offering protection against the joint peril of superannuated disability. When reviewing competing disability-escalating annuity alternatives, prospective policy purchasers should compare not only current interest rates and length of guarantee differentials but also contract deferral periods, maximum issue ages, underwriting restrictions, waiting periods, surrender charge levels and durations, settlement rate guarantees and options, impairment group definitions, and related benefit-multiplier schedules. (See also ANNUITIES; LONG-TERM CARE INSURANCE, PRIVATE; MEDICARE SUPPLEMENTAL INSURANCE; NURSING HOMES.)

### Suggested Readings

Kumar, Nanda, Mark A. Cohen, Christine E. Bishop, and Stanley S. Wallack. 1995. "Understanding the Factors behind the Decision to Purchase Varying Coverage Amounts of Long-Term Care Insurance." *Health Services Research* 29 (February): 653.

LifePlans, Inc. 2000. *Who Buys Long-Term Care Insurance in 2000? A Decade of Study of Buyers and Nonbuyers*. Washington, DC: Health Insurance Association of America.

Mischke, Gerald A., and Conrad S. Ciccotello. 2000. "Long-Term Care Trends and Demographics: Implications for Financial Planning." *Journal of Financial Service Professionals* 54(5): 54–59.

Mulvey, Janemarie, and Barbara Stucki. 1999. "Retirement Planning for Baby Boomers: The Role of Long-Term Care Insurance." *Journal of Financial Service Professionals* 53(5): 52–60.

Weiner, Joshua M., and David G. Stevenson. 1998. *Long-Term Care for the Elderly: Profile of Thirteen States*. Washington, DC: Urban Institute. Available online at http://www.newfederalism.urban.org/html/occa12.html.

### References

Blankenheim, Tracy A. 2000. "Number of Insurance Policies Double in Less Than a Decade." *McKnight's Long-Term Care News* 21 (May): 3.

Christopherson, David L. 1992. "New IDEAs for Insuring Long-Term Care." *Journal of the American Society of CLU & ChFC* 46(2): 42–53.

Christopherson, David L. 2002. "Predictors of Readiness to Buy Long-Term Care Insurance among Seminar Participants." *Journal of Financial Service Professionals* 56(1): 57–68.

Manitoba Department of Health & Social Development. 1973. *Aging in Manitoba: Needs and Resources*. Winnipeg: Division of Research, Planning and Program Development.

Meiners, Mark R. 1983. "The Case for Long-Term Care Insurance." *Health Affairs* 2: 55–79.

Moses, Stephen A., and David M. Rosenfeld. 2000. *The LTC Triathlon: Long-Term Care's Race for Survival*. Bellevue, WA: Center for Long-Term Care Financing. Available online at http://www.centerltc.com/pubs/triathlon.pdf.

*David L. Christopherson*

**LONG-TERM CARE INSURANCE, PRIVATE,** financial protection against medical and personal care expenses associated with chronic disability that are not covered by the Medicare program. Most policies cover both nursing home and home care services. For long-term care insurance (LTCI), an age-related level premium is the norm—the older one is, the more a policy costs.

Private LTCI policies were first offered in the mid-1980s. Increasing wealth among older adults, greater longevity, changing family structures, and lack of public financing have all contributed to an expanding and rapidly changing market for LTCI. The Health Insurance Association of America (HIAA) reports that the number of companies selling long-term care insurance increased from 75 in 1987 to 124 in 1993, while the number of policies ever sold increased from 815,000 in December 1987 to more than 6.8 million in December 1999 (HIAA 1995, 2002). Because of lapses, there were an estimated 3.5 and 4.0 million policies in force in 2000 (Cohen, Weinrobe, and Miller 2002). Despite this growth, only 11% of all nursing home and home care expenditures in 2001 were paid by private insurance, much of which was coinsurance for the Medicare skilled nursing facility benefit (Levit et al. 2003).

The LTCI market has three components: the individual market, the employer-sponsored market, and the life insurance rider market. At present, the individual market, where policies are sold on a one-on-one basis, overwhelmingly dominates private LTCI, although much smaller sales through employer-sponsored and life insurance markets are increasing and some believe represent the greatest potential sources of future growth.

### Demand and Supply Barriers

Despite promising growth, the market for private LTCI exhibits both demand- and supply-side barriers. On the demand side, there are at least three major obstacles: affordability, lack of knowledge about the risks of long-term care, and misinformation about current coverage.

Historically, older Americans have been disproportionately poor and unable to afford significant premium payments. Although income among older people has risen substantially in the last 20 years, in part due to improvements in public and private pensions, LTCI remains expensive for most older people. The average annual premium for high-quality individual LTCI offered by the leading sellers in 1997 was $2,305 at age 65 and climbed rapidly to $7,022 at age 79 (HIAA 2002). Most studies of LTCI demand find that only a relatively small minority of older people, 10% to 20%, can afford private LTCI (Families USA Foundation 1993; Rivlin and Wiener 1988; Wiener, Illston, and Hanley 1994).

By modeling the market for private and group LTCI under differing affordability assumptions, Wiener and colleagues (1994) found that the employer-based market of younger purchasers has the greatest potential for expansion. Using the Brookings-ICF Long-Term Care Financing Model to simulate the market for long-term care insurance through the year 2018, they found that while only 20% of older persons might purchase long-term care insurance under existing market conditions (assuming premiums are no more than 5% of annual income), up to 76% of the older people could afford coverage if the market were expanded to include substantial numbers of nonolder purchasers.

Encouraging younger individuals to purchase insurance through employers would significantly reduce the price of premiums, but there may be barriers preventing expansion of the employer market. Many employers already face large, unfunded liabilities for retiree acute health care and are not eager to commit to additional costs for long-term care. Challenges arise in stimulating demand among the nonolder who face competing and more immediate financial needs—child care, mortgage payments, children's college education, and their own retirement. Although affordability estimates of LTCI are subject to somewhat arbitrary assumptions regarding an individual's willingness to pay, the number of policies sold remains far below even conservative gauges.

Misinformation about the need for long-term care insurance may help explain why relatively few older individuals purchase LTCI. Many older people believe that Medicare or Medicare Supplemental Insurance covers extensive nursing home and home health services, when they do not. Medicaid is the payer of last resort and will cover nursing home care only after an individual is impoverished. The risks associated with long-term care appear to be largely unrecognized by older adults, yet research suggests that 44% of those turning age 65 in 2000 will spend some time in a nursing home before they die (Spillman and Lubitz 2002).

Insurers of long-term care confront three barriers in bringing their product to market. First, most disabled persons receive no paid services, and how much demand would increase if services—especially home care—were covered by insurance is unknown. Second, a disproportionate number of high-risk individuals may purchase policies, pushing premiums ever higher and causing low-risk policyholders to drop their coverage as prices rise. To protect against adverse selection, insurers usually screen out people with health problems and exclude coverage for preexisting conditions. A third barrier is the lack of claims experience for long-term care, since LTCI is relatively new and use patterns are still developing. This problem is compounded by the length of time between policy purchase and the filing of claims. Even when the purchaser is older, that individual may not need care for 20 years or more. Moreover, changes in disability or mortality rates, utilization patterns, or the rate of return on financial services can dramatically change a profitable insurance product into an unprofitable one.

### Consumer Protection Issues

Long-term care policies have changed dramatically in a short period. Faced with great uncertainty, companies initially tried to anticipate and protect against financial loss by imposing restrictions and limitations on services covered and eligibility for reimbursement. The net effect was to lessen substantially the probability that an insured person who used a nursing home or home care would actually receive insurance benefits.

Over time, policies have improved substantially. While the average policy in force still has restrictions, newer policies provide significantly better coverage. In newer policies, prior hospitalization requirements have been eliminated, policies are guaranteed renewable, Alzheimer's disease is explicitly covered, all levels of nursing home care and more home care are covered, indemnity levels are sometimes indexed for inflation, and a few policies provide some residual benefits to people who discontinue their policies.

Although the quality of policies has improved greatly, problems remain. Consumer protection issues include the absence of adequate inflation protection, the cumulative effect of lapse rates, lack of nonforfeiture benefits, rate increases, and agent and marketing abuses. While high-quality policies are available, current regulations also permit lower-quality policies to be sold as well.

Features such as inflation protection and nonforfeiture benefits are particularly important to look for in a policy, although these features will raise its price. Given the rising costs of long-term care, adequate inflation protection is essential to assure that benefit levels will keep pace with rising prices for long-term care services. Also, most insurance underwriters assume that a majority of policyholders will drop their policies within five years of the initial purchase. Thus, nonforfeiture benefits enable individuals who allow their policies to lapse to recoup some of their investment.

The National Association of Insurance Commissioners (NAIC) has developed model standards requiring insurers to offer their customers the option to purchase policies with inflation protection. However, this model regulation does not prohibit the sale of policies that do not provide adequate inflation adjustments.

### The Future of Long-Term Care Insurance

Private long-term care insurance offers the possibility of prefunding the inevitable societal burden that will occur when the aging baby boom generation needs long-term care. The classic virtue of the competitive market model is that it has the flexibility to adapt to individual needs and wants and to local conditions. Moreover, resistance to new, large government social programs has made large-scale expansion in almost any public program difficult to enact. The marked improvement in the financial position of older adults over the past 20 years has also made it more plausible to argue that private LTCI might be more widely affordable in the future. Likewise, increased awareness of financing long-term care is likely to reduce misinformation among older people about the need to reduce their risk exposure.

Despite recent growth in the market for private insurance, a number of formidable barriers to expansion remain. Good-quality private LTCI is too expensive for most older people. Although the employer-based market exhibits the greatest potential for providing widespread affordable premiums, many employers are likely to resist adding long-term care benefits to employee compensation packages in the near future. Although reforms have helped to improve the quality of long-term care policies, it is unlikely that these reforms will rid the market of policies that exclude individuals with preexisting conditions. Finally, when long-term care coverage is funded privately through the market, rather than through a public program, individuals who can afford higher premiums and better-quality policies will purchase policies, while those with more modest means may be priced out of the market. This scenario raises questions of equity that are not addressed by market-based approaches. (See also HEALTH AND LONGEVITY; HOME CARE SERVICES FOR OLDER ADULTS; LONG-TERM CARE INSURANCE—A CONSUMER'S PERSPECTIVE; MEDICAID; MEDICARE; MEDICARE SUPPLEMENTAL INSURANCE; NURSING HOMES; POSTRETIREMENT HEALTH COVERAGE [PRHC].)

### Suggested Readings

National Association of Insurance Commissioners. 1999. *A Shopper's Guide to Long-Term Care Insurance*. NAIC: LTC-1059. Kansas City, MO: Authors.

Shelton, Phyllis. 2001. *Long-Term Care: Your Financial Planning Guide*. New York: Kensington Publishing Corporation.

### References

Cohen, Marc A., Maurice A. Weinrobe, and Jessica Miller. 2002. *Inflation Protection and Long-Term Care Insurance*. Public Policy Institute #2002-09. Washington, DC: AARP.

Families USA Foundation. 1993. *Nursing Home Insurance: Who Can Afford It?* Washington, DC: Families USA.

Health Insurance Association of America (HIAA). 1995. *Long-Term Care Insurance in 1993*. Washington, DC: Author.

Health Insurance Association of America (HIAA). 2002. *Long-Term Care Insurance in 1998–1999*. Washington, DC: Author.

Levit, Katharine, Cynthia Smith, Cathy Cowan, Helen Lazenby, Art Sensenig, and Aaron Catlin. 2003. "Trends in U.S. Health Care Spending 2001." *Health Affairs* 22(1): 154–63.

Rivlin, Alice M., and Joshua M. Wiener. 1988. *Caring for the Disabled Elderly: Who Will Pay?* Washington, DC: Brookings Institution.

Spillman, Brenda C., and James Lubitz. 2002. "New Estimates of Lifetime Nursing Home Use: Have Patterns of Use Changed?" *Medical Care* 40: 965–75.

Wiener, Joshua M., Laural Hixon Illston, and Raymond H. Hanley. 1994. *Sharing the Burden: Strategies for Public and Private Long-Term Care Insurance*. Washington, DC: Brookings Institution.

*Joshua M. Wiener and Catherine M. Sullivan*
*Updated by Joshua M. Wiener*

# M

**MARKETING TO MATURE ADULTS.** Marketing to the 50+-age marketplace requires the same attention to the basic principles of the "Four Ps of Marketing," product, price, place, and promotion, as selling a product or service to any other market segment. The key, however, is the successful application of these basic principles to the unique "mature markets."

## Defining the Market and the Customer

A good beginning strategy in approaching these markets is to discard unproductive myths about the makeup of the 50+ market itself. It includes "leading-edge" baby boomers, the oldest of whom are turning 57 years old in 2003; the 57- to 64-year-old "Silent Generation"; 65- to 75-year-old active retirees; and 75+ year-old members of the "Greatest Generation," most of whom are female, owing to the greater longevity of women. The 50+ market, therefore, is actually a cluster of markets having a variety of demographic, psychographic, and sociological attributes that combine to identify product needs and desires, marketing approaches, and responses.

The same can be said for the approximately 78 million baby boomers, who have all been lumped into a single market. Suppose, for example, that an early female boomer, born in 1946, married at age 18 and gave birth to her first child, a male, in December 1964. By 2003, the "baby boomer" demographic includes both the 57-year-old mother—perhaps now a grandmother—and her 39-year-old son as the same "market," since by demographic definition they are both "baby boomers." While they might be attracted to the same products in some categories, they are more likely to have divergent needs and tastes in other categories. This is likely to include, moreover, their financial and retirement outlooks and needs. It is also likely that the 57-year-old mother has at least one parent still alive, probably her mother, who is also part of the larger "50+ market."

There are times, of course, when age is a defining characteristic for a financial product such as medical supplemental insurance, or "Medigap" coverage, where the market is composed of individuals age 65 and older. Nevertheless, having a clear idea of various market segments, and their similarities and differences, is one key to successful marketing to mature adults. At the very least, demographic segmentation is essential, including age, gender, socioeconomic status, geographic location, marital status, and education. In some circumstances, religion, health status, race, sexual orientation, and other personal characteristics may be important, depending on the product or market niche on which the marketer decides to focus. Often, age is the *least* productive characteristic on which to base marketing decisions. Author and consultant David Wolfe (1990) characterizes this enormous consumer group as "the ageless market," which has a unique set of attributes that can render traditional marketing techniques all but useless.

In recent years, researchers have begun to segment markets based on generational events and enduring cohort values rather than age, since this holds the potential for identifying lifestyle similarities that can narrow the large and diverse set of mature consumers. These approaches typically start with grouping mature individuals, with as many as four cohorts including 50-year-olds through those in their nineties. Other market researchers assess mature market generations using somewhat different approaches, but all provide an analysis of how shared social and historical experiences and values can be invaluable in helping marketers understand their mature markets customers. Such a perspective allows a product to remain constant, while the marketing message can vary according to the characteristics of the target market. In this way the same product—in the financial services industry this could be annuities, banking services for mature clients, insurance, or brokerage services—may be marketed to both older and younger segments of the market.

Life events, such as the birth of a grandchild, severe illness, death of a spouse or close friend, or retirement, may create reevaluation and change in a consumer's lifestyle and personal life perspective. These shifts in lifestyle and perspective may create opportunities for marketing products associated with these events. For example, caregiving is a major concern of both older and younger mature consumers. Almost 25% of middle-aged households are providing care for an older relative. In a survey of the "average caregiver"—a 46-year-old working female—by the National Alliance for Caregiving (1998), these "informal" family care providers were also found to be much more proactive in planning for their own future care needs, with over one-third either increasing their investments or purchasing long-term care insurance. Awareness of these life events, in conjunction with the other important demographic information, can provide a more focused and successful definition of a product's target market. The decade from age 50 to 60 is particularly ready for this, since the growing numbers of boomer "fifty-somethings" will experience more life-changing events in this 10-year span than in any other decade of their life.

Knowledge of generational and cohort differences also has practical marketing value. Researcher George Moschis (Moschis et al. 2000) of the Center for Mature Consumer Studies has described the buying patterns and preferences of mature markets, including important differences and a surprising number of similarities between the financial product, financial services, and financial marketing and advertising preferences of baby boomers and seniors (i.e., 65+ years old). As marketers make decisions about media, promotion, and collateral marketing materials, understanding these generational preferences can assist in selecting the most appropriate and effective strategies. For example, Moschis found that almost 36% of consumers age 55+ preferred to receive information about new financial services in the mail, almost twice as many as TV/print advertising, the next most preferred source. While 44% of baby boomers and almost as many seniors (36%) prefer information by mail, almost twice as many seniors (18%) compared to boomers (9.5%) prefer to learn the information through group meetings or seminars.

Some financial organizations have also developed psychographic descriptions of mature consumers. Using sophisticated statistical techniques, psychographic segmentation clusters similar individuals within a segment and at the same time differentiates each segment on key differences with other segments. There are many psychographic segments attainable, depending on the target market, product, and so on. Psychographic techniques are most productive when applied to a specific product, service, and consumer target. Moschis (1996) applied such techniques to the 55+ mature market specifically and developed four "gerontographic" segments: Healthy Indulgers (18%), Healthy Hermits (36%), Ailing Outgoers (29%), and Frail Recluses (29%). The advantage of psychographics is that it allows for refined product development and advertising messages. The downside is that there is really no way to identify or contact these consumer segments. There are often demographic correlates within each segment, however, which can help in determining appropriate targeting strategies and distribution channels.

Whatever the most productive approach might be, the most successful financial marketers have used all available resources to understand the mature market customer.

### Reaching the Market and Customer

There is no "formula" for marketing to mature consumers. A strategy or campaign that works with one part of the market can fail miserably when applied to a different segment or even the same target market in a different geographic area. Despite this, experience has allowed marketers to define certain aspects of successful marketing as generally applicable "guidelines" (Medina and Migliaccio 2000).

At face value, many of these seem self-apparent. Yet many marketers consistently ignore some basic tenets of successful campaigns and the physiological, psychological, cohort, and demographic characteristics of their market. Part of the reason may lie in the fact that older consumers are less valued than younger consumers in general, despite their ample buying power, discretionary income, assets, and needs. Television programmers and advertisers tend to focus on the 18- to 49-year-old consumer that as if by magic stops buying on their fiftieth birthday. Marketing to the mature consumer is the consistent and constant application of some sensible marketing insights.

### Advertising

As the body and mind age, various physiological changes occur that mandate some simple, basic responses by marketers. Type size should be larger, preferably 12 point, and font styles should be readable—preferably with a serif font. Dropout type formats, especially if combined with light italic fonts and graphically intense backgrounds, make print ads impenetrable to the boomer and older consumer. Frenetic, loud television ads also miss the mark with older consumers. Direct response and inbound telephone techniques should include full numeric phone numbers and the ability to talk to a "live person" as an option among automatic response menus.

The most important attributes should be a creative approach and respect for the consumer. Older consumers also appreciate wit and humor in advertising, as long as it's "laughing with" rather than "laughing at" them. Poking fun at an older consumer may make points with a younger crowd, but getting that type-marketing message across is very risky. One example of a successful past print and television campaign emphasized that the financial services company made wise investment decisions for its clients and made their money "the old-fashioned way: they earn it." This very effective campaign attracted seniors with money to invest through its use of a very recognizable (at least to the target market) older spokesman and clear connection to the cohort values of hard work, conservative financial strategy, and personal attention important to the affluent senior consumer of the time. The message was simple, direct, and complimentary to the target consumer.

Internet-based marketing is becoming more commonplace and is certainly appropriate for the boomer segment—the first "Internet generation." Older consumers (65+), while the fastest-growing segment of Internet users, are still more prone to respond to traditional print and direct-mail solicitations. Both will use the Internet for information gathering about financial products and services, however, and Web sites providing investing, estate planning, and insurance information, retirement and financial "calculators," and other financial planning tools will find an audience among mature consumers.

### Three Keys to Successful Marketing

Despite the ubiquitous "senior discount," older consumers are more oriented to value than price for most products and services. The oldest mature market segments certainly remember the era of personal attention and service and still value the personal touch. They are generally willing to pay for it, too, although pricing must at least be competitive with other providers of similar products and services. For the mature consumer, the three key marketing tools used by successful marketers are service, patience, and relationship.

#### *Service*

Marketers willing to commit to the mature markets must also commit to a dedication to service. This is often easier said than done, with a great deal of lip service rather than real service. A company or financial professional can demonstrate a service orientation through attention to such issues as convenience, personalized attention to needs, easy access to financial planning tools, and recognition of their business patronage, among other things. The oldest of the mature market remember when stopping for gasoline also included an offer to check the oil and clean the windshield and bank tellers who remembered their name. Attention to service is often more cost-efficient and cost-effective than discounts as a way to attract mature consumers. The older a consumer is, the more they have been marketed to, and the more discerning they are about true service. They also "vote with their feet"—they simply do not return to organizations from which they do not get the level of personal service they expect. On the other hand, they are very vocal and can be a great source of business referrals. The onus is on the marketer to deliver what is promised in advertising and promotion.

Service baby boomers are somewhat different. They have been described as the "do-it-yourself generation," with the leading-edge boomers expressing a consistent skepticism about marketing claims. They expect less handholding but more in the way of helpful tools and access to professional help in executing their plans. The necessity of meeting, or exceeding, client service claims is paramount to successful marketing. One example of this is a very extensive information service, the "Life Advice" series of pamphlets provided by Metropolitan Life Insurance Co., which covers a lifetime of financial, family, and retirement decision making and has given the company high visibility among maturing boomers.

### *Patience*

For the mature markets, patience is more than a virtue; it is an expectation—one that is often frustrating to both marketers and salespeople. The "quick close" on important life and financial issues is better abandoned than pursued as a rule when dealing with older clients. Marketing strategy, however, can be very helpful in setting the stage for product or service purchases. Positioning the financial professional or company more as a trusted advisor who will take the time to understand the client's needs, aspirations, and goals in many areas of their life, and then applying this at the retail level, has been the hallmark of successfully capturing the mature market over the long term. Carefully crafted and long-term communications programs such as newsletters and informational Web sites with clear brand definition are an essential part of a long-term approach to the markets.

### *Relationship*

There are several strategies for relationship building that marketers can take advantage of when reaching out to the mature consumer. The first is creating and maintaining a customer relationship. Building on the foundation of a demonstrated service orientation and patient approach to the consumer, organizations can use traditional and emerging communications to get and hold the attention of their target market and build relationship and trust. Branding is an important component of this. "Loyalty" marketing (i.e., rewarding long-term, consistent clients) is also a successful strategy and retail-level tactic as well. Mature consumers want information, choice, and involvement, so marketing communications must be more than "one-way" presentations of the glories of products or services. Giving feedback, sharing opinions and having them acknowledged, and asking questions and getting a personal reply are all components of the mature consumer's expectation of a relationship with a financial services provider. In the 1980s, banks created a plethora of special "clubs" and accompanying product and service components to attract older consumers, who keep higher-than-average assets in bank accounts and certificates of deposit, and there is evidence of a resurgence of this approach to target the baby boomer cohort.

Another relationship framework that has been used successfully recently has involved capitalizing on the mature consumer's existing relationships with other organizations such as associations, voluntary membership organizations, and other affinity groups. Personal and health insurance, preneed funeral products and services, long-term care insurance, investment services, and legal services have all been effectively marketed and sold through such affinity relationships. The marketer gains the advantage of having the existing relationship between the consumer and the affinity organization provide a level of trust and direct access to target consumers.

Good relationship building with an entire market must be translated to good relationship building with individual consumers. With estimates as high as $136 trillion in intergenerational wealth transfer between today's oldest consumers, their baby boomer children, and "Generation X" and baby boomlet grandchildren, financial marketers have many opportunities as well as challenges in reaching the mature markets. (See also AGING AMERICA; BABY BOOMERS AND RETIREMENT; BANKING SERVICES FOR THE MATURE MARKET; FUNERALS AND FUNERAL FINANCES; HEALTH

AND LONGEVITY; INTERNET USE BY SENIORS; LEISURE; VACATION HOMES AND RECREATIONAL PROPERTY.)

**References**

Medina, Kurt, and John Migliaccio. 2000. *77 Truths about Marketing to the 50+ Consumer*. White Plains, NY: Maturity Mark Services Co.; Philadelphia, PA: Medina Associates.

Meredith, Geoffrey, and Charles Schewe. 2002. *Defining Markets—Defining Moments*. New York: Hungry Minds, Inc.

Moschis, George. 1996. *Gerontographics*. Westport, CT: Quorum Books.

Moschis, George, et al. 2000. *The Maturing Marketplace—Buying Habits of Baby Boomers and Their Parents*. Westport, CT: Quorum Books.

National Alliance for Caregiving. 1998. The *Caregiving Boom: Baby Boomer Women Giving Care*. Bethesda, MD: National Alliance for Caregiving.

Smith, J. Walker, and Ann Clurman. 2000. *Rocking the Ages*. New York: HarperBusiness.

Strauss, William, and Neil Howe. 1991. *Generations*. New York: William Morrow and Co.

Wolfe, David. 1990. *Serving the Ageless Market*. New York: McGraw-Hill Publishers.

*John N. Migliaccio*

**MARRIAGE AND OLDER ADULTS,** marriages occurring after the age of 65. More than half (57%) of the population over age 65 is married. But this general statistic does not reveal important information about marital status in old age, such as marital status differences across age and sex categories, the change in marital status of the older population over time, and differences between married and unmarried groups.

The effects of gender and age on marital status in later life are shown in Table 1. The majority (80%) of men aged 65 to 74 are married, compared to 56% of women. Only about 4% (men and women) never married. More women than men have been widowed, as death rates are higher for men. Fewer women have remarried after divorce. Among the oldest old (those age 85+), the gender gap is even greater. It is nearly four times more likely that a man over age 85 is currently married than a woman.

Marriage after age 65 is uncommon. Only about 2% of all marriages in the 1990s were to persons over age 65. While remarrying after age 60 does not reduce any Social Security benefit to an entitled widowed person, a divorced person who remarries does lose any Social Security benefit that she (he) may have been entitled to, based on an ex-spouse's work history. Tax policies may create a tax penalty for some older people who marry or remarry.

There is evidence that adult children often oppose the potential remarriage of their aging parents since a remarriage could reduce or eliminate their expected inheritance. The odds of an unmarried person marrying after age 65 are six times higher for men than women. This reflects both the large gender imbalance in the older unmarried population and the propensity of older men to marry younger women.

Given historical change in patterns of marriage, divorce, remarriage, cohabitation, and mortality, change over time in the marital status distribution of the older population is expected. Data in Table 2, showing marital status of the older population in 1970 and 2000, and projecting marital status to 2030, confirm this expectation. Consider, for example, changes among women aged 65 to 75. The large decline in death rates produces an expected 50% decline in proportion of widowed women between 1970 and 2030. The increase in divorce rates is even more marked, leading to a 300% increase in the pro-

**Table 1**
**Marital Status of the Older Population, by Age and Sex, 2000**

| Marital Status | 65+ | | 65–74 | | 75–84 | | 85+ | |
|---|---|---|---|---|---|---|---|---|
| | M | F | M | F | M | F | M | F |
| Married | 75.3 | 43.9 | 79.6 | 55.6 | 72.2 | 36.3 | 55.7 | 14.4 |
| Widowed | 14.4 | 45.3 | 8.3 | 31.3 | 19.5 | 54.7 | 37.5 | 79.4 |
| Divorced | 6.1 | 7.2 | 7.8 | 9.3 | 4.1 | 5.4 | 2.8 | 3.0 |
| Never Married | 4.2 | 3.6 | 4.3 | 3.7 | 4.2 | 3.6 | 3.9 | 3.2 |

*Source*: U.S. Bureau of the Census 2001.

**Table 2**
**Marital Status of the Older Population, by Age and Sex, 1970, 2000, 2030**

| Age and Marital Status | 1970 | | 2000 | | 2030 | |
|---|---|---|---|---|---|---|
| | M | F | M | F | M | F |
| **65–74** | | | | | | |
| Married | 78.5 | 46.6 | 79.6 | 55.6 | 71.3 | 56.5 |
| Widowed | 10.9 | 42.0 | 8.3 | 31.3 | 7.3 | 20.4 |
| Divorced | 3.3 | 3.8 | 7.8 | 9.3 | 10.4 | 15.9 |
| Never Married | 7.2 | 7.5 | 4.3 | 3.7 | 11.0 | 7.2 |
| **75+** | | | | | | |
| Married | 61.1 | 21.1 | 69.2 | 31.1 | 65.3 | 31.5 |
| Widowed | 28.3 | 67.6 | 22.7 | 60.5 | 21.4 | 49.8 |
| Divorced | 2.5 | 2.3 | 3.8 | 4.9 | 8.2 | 13.8 |
| Never Married | 8.0 | 8.9 | 4.1 | 3.5 | 5.1 | 4.9 |

*Source*: Bell 1997.

portion of women who are divorced over this time period. The net effect of these trends results in a moderate increase (from 47% to 57%) over this time period in the proportion of older women who are married. For men, the projected increase in the proportion divorced and never married exceeds the decrease in proportion widowed, so it is expected that the percentage of married people will decrease somewhat by 2030.

Later-life marriage has financial implications. As shown by data in Table 3, older unmarried persons are more likely to be living in poverty than married persons. Widowed and divorced men over age 65 are two to three times as likely as their married counterparts to be impoverished, while for women the economic disadvantages of being un-

**Table 3**
**Poverty Rates by Age, Sex, and Marital Status, 1998**

| Sex and Marital Status | Age | | | |
|---|---|---|---|---|
| | 65+ | 65–74 | 75–84 | 85+ |
| **Male** | | | | |
| Total | 7.3 | 7.0 | 7.6 | 7.6 |
| Married | 5.0 | 4.5 | 5.7 | 6.0 |
| Widowed | 10.3 | 11.1 | 10.7 | 8.2 |
| Divorced and Never Married | 17.2 | 18.3 | 15.9 | 12.5 |
| **Female** | | | | |
| Total | 12.7 | 10.6 | 14.4 | 17.4 |
| Married | 4.7 | 4.1 | 5.7 | 8.0 |
| Widowed | 16.9 | 15.6 | 17.7 | 17.3 |
| Divorced and Never Married | 24.0 | 22.4 | 25.8 | 28.3 |

*Source*: Social Security Administration 2000.

married are even greater. Higher poverty rates among elderly widows suggest that women are especially vulnerable to economic losses associated with losing a spouse.

Being married in later life provides an informal (i.e., unpaid) caregiver in case of disability. Research on caregiving indicates that spouses are the preferred and most common caregivers for dependent elderly persons. Those who do not have a spouse often deplete their assets paying for home health care and are more vulnerable to institutionalization. There are more never-married than married persons living in nursing homes, while among the non-institutionalized population married persons outnumber never-marrieds by a ratio of 12:1. The economic and caregiving advantages of older married persons help explain why the married have lower death rates than the unmarried.

Entering later life with a spouse also has an impact on retirement. Studies find that the work histories of married women affect couples' retirement incomes. Over the past several decades, an increasing proportion of married women have participated in the labor force, and a growing proportion of working women hold jobs with pension coverage. These trends suggest future growth in the proportion of retired couples with multiple pension incomes. Couples that approach old age with both spouses in the labor force also face unique issues related to retirement planning. Research indicates that decision making on simultaneous retirement or sequential retirement of husband and wife is complex. This decision depends on later-life family and health events as well as the earnings and pension eligibilities of husband and wife.

Both men and women who are married in later life tend to be economically advantaged, compared with those who are unmarried. Since fewer women than men are married in later life, and since unmarried women suffer greater economic problems than unmarried men, there is a significant gender gap in economic status within the elderly population. This gap leads to discussions of how social policy might be employed to reduce gender inequality in old age. The 1983 Retirement Equity Act, requiring workers to get spousal approval before selecting a pension option not providing for survivor's benefits, is an example of efforts to obtain greater protection for older women. Increasing consideration is being given to the treatment of married and unmarried persons by the Social Security program. The program, enacted in 1935, assumed stable marriages with a working husband and a homemaker spouse. Given the current reality of high rates of divorce and increased female labor force participation, the benefit formula may require revision. (See also AGING AMERICA; COHABITATION; DIVORCE AND OLDER ADULTS; ECONOMIC STATUS OF OLDER MEN AND WOMEN; FINANCIAL SECURITY IN RETIREMENT; SOCIAL SECURITY PROGRAM OF THE UNITED STATES; WIDOWHOOD.)

**References**

Bell, Felicitie C. 1997. "Social Security Area Population Projections: 1997." *Actuarial Study No. 112*. Washington, DC: Social Security Administration.

Burkhauser, Richard V., and Greg J. Duncan. 1991. "United States Public Policy and the Elderly: The Disproportionate Risk to the Well-Being of Women." *Journal of Population Economics* 4: 217–31.

Kaufman, Gayle, and Peter Uhlenberg. 1998. "Effects of Life Course Transitions on the Quality of Relationships between Adult Children and Their Parents." *Journal of Marriage and the Family* 60: 924–38.

Meyer, Madonna Harrington. 1990. "Family Status and Poverty among Older Women: The Gendered Distribution of Retirement Income in the United States." *Social Problems* 37: 551–63.

Social Security Administration. 2000. *Income of the Population 55 or Older, 1998*. Washington, DC: GPO.

Szinovacz, Maximiliane E., and Stanley DeViney. 2000. "Marital Characteristics and Retirement Decisions." *Research on Aging* 22: 470–98.

U.S. Bureau of the Census. 2001. *Current Population Reports*. Series P-20, No. 537. Washington, DC: GPO.

*Peter Uhlenberg*

**MEANS-TESTING IN PUBLIC PROGRAMS,** publicly funded welfare programs that have been designed to assist persons of very low income. Advanced age may be one eligibility criterion for assistance under these programs (Hudson 1995). Means-tested programs place strict limits on monthly income and assets (e.g., bank accounts, stocks, and bonds). They differ from income-tested programs (e.g., some housing programs, veterans' health care) that measure only income and from universal program benefits (e.g., Social Security, Medicare) that are based on a required period of labor force participation, without regard to other sources of income or assets. Means-tested programs are financed via general revenues, thus competing for funding with other public programs. Many are coadministered/cofunded by the federal and state governments. Under federalism, states have a fair amount of flexibility; thus, these programs are highly variable. The major means-tested programs benefiting persons aged 65 and older are Supplemental Security Income (SSI), Medicaid, and food stamps, often "packaged" together, as well as the Low-Income Home Energy Assistance Program (LIHEAP). "Young" retirees ages 51 to 59 (especially those who were "forced" to retire) also receive important support from these programs (National Academy on an Aging Society [NAAS] 2001).

### Supplemental Security Income (SSI)

SSI is a federal income support program, with nationally uniform standards and payments for persons aged 65+ and blind or disabled adults and children. As of 1974, it replaced the former federal-state adult assistance programs in the 50 states and the District of Columbia. Since 1975, SSI monthly cash payments have been increased by the same percentage as the cost-of-living adjustments (COLAs) in Social Security (SS) benefits. About 60% of SSI-aged recipients receive both SSI and SS (Social Security Administration [SSA] 2000). In 1999, 6.64 million persons received SSI at a total cost of nearly $31 million (SSA 2000).

States have the option to supplement the federal program for all or selected categories of persons, and 30 states do so. While the Social Security Administration runs SSI, a few states providing supplements choose to administer the program. Federal benefits alone do not bring recipients up to the poverty level. This is true even for persons who live in states that augment federal payments.

The federal payment is based on an individual's countable income; the first $20 monthly in SS benefits or other earned or unearned income is not counted. Also excluded is $65 monthly of earnings, plus one-half of earnings above that amount. Individuals generally are not eligible for SSI if they have assets greater than $2,000 ($3,000 for couples). Some assets are excluded: a car used for essential transportation, a home, household goods and personal insurance of reasonable value, burial plots and spaces, and life insurance. The value of food stamps, shelter provided by private nonprofits, and most home energy aid is also excluded. Because monthly income is a major determinant of SSI eligibility, even minor fluctuations can cause eligibility problems. The benefits of individuals or couples who live in another's household (e.g., their children's) and receive food and shelter from that source are reduced by one-third. Overpayments of SSI benefits can be recovered.

To receive SSI, one must be a U.S. citizen or national; a lawful permanent resident with 40 work credits; certain noncitizens lawfully residing in the United States who were receiving SSI on August 22, 1996; and certain immigrants and refugees. With some exceptions, people who live in city or county rest homes, halfway houses, or other public institutions are not eligible for SSI. Exceptions include those residing in publicly operated community residences with fewer than 16 persons (e.g., board and care homes) and those living in a public emergency shelter for the homeless or in an institution where Medicaid is paying more than half the cost of the person's care.

Thirty-one percent (31%) of SSI recipients are age 65 and over. Two-thirds of the 2.052 million aged SSI recipients are women (SSA 2000). About 10% of young retirees (ages 51 to 59) participate in the SSI program. Eight percent (8%) of nonworking persons age 60+ also receive SSI (NAAS 2001). The federal payment for older individuals living independently (1999) was $512 (SSA 2000). Illustrating the importance of state supplements, combined federal and state payments in California in 2001were $712 for individuals and $1,265 for couples living independently, and $872 and $1,744, respectively, for those living in nonmedical board and care facilities (SSA 2001).

Older consumers and their families needing information about SSI should contact their local Social Security office. Any of the nearly 670 Area Agencies on Aging (AoAs) nationwide that provide information and assistance to older adults aged 60+ are another source, as are case managers who work with the AoA, and the local or state department of social services/welfare.

### Medicaid

Medicaid, a federal-state medical assistance program for certain individuals and families with low income and assets, was enacted as Title XIX of the Social Security Act in 1965, the same year as Medicare. A cooperative venture jointly funded by the 50 states, the District of Columbia, and the territories and by the federal government, it is the largest source of funding for medical and health-related services for America's poorest people. The states operate the Medicaid program within a framework of federal policies and regulations guided by the Centers for Medicare & Medicaid Services (CMS), formerly the Health Care Financing Administration (HCFA). Each state creates its own eligibility standards; determines the type, amount, duration, and scope of services; sets payment rates; and administers its own program. No two Medicaid programs are exactly alike.

Not all poor persons are covered by Medicaid. To receive federal funds, states must serve specific groups of people who receive federal income maintenance payments: SSI recipients, certain Medicare beneficiaries, recipients of Temporary Aid to Needy Families, and pregnant women and children under the age of six whose family income is below 133% of poverty. However, some states use more restrictive Medicaid eligibility requirements that predate SSI.

States generally have broad discretion in determining which specific groups their Medicaid programs cover. Most have additional "state-only" programs of medical assistance for specified poor persons who do not qualify for federal Medicaid; federal funds are not provided for these programs. States also have the option of providing Medicaid for other "categorically needy" groups: institutionalized individuals below a special income level (up to 300% of the SSI federal benefit rate), recipients of state supplementary income payments, and the "medically needy." The latter includes persons whose income and/or assets are above their state eligibility level. They may qualify immediately or "spend down" via medical expenses that reduce their income to/below their state's income requirement. Federal matching funds also are available for these programs.

Federal policies allow considerable flexibility in the types of services covered by state Medicaid plans; however, some federal requirements are mandatory. Of particular importance to elders are the following required basic services: inpatient/outpatient hospital and physician services, skilled nursing facility (SNF) services for persons aged 21 or older, rural health clinics, home health services for those eligible for SNFs, and laboratory and x-ray services.

States may also receive federal matching funds for a wide range of optional services. The most common are diagnostic and clinical services; prescription drugs, prosthetic devices, and eyeglasses; and optometrist, transportation, and rehabilitation services. States can apply for waivers that allow them to divert Medicaid funds from institutional care settings to home- and community-based care for the chronically impaired, as long as the services are cost-effective. Under the Balanced Budget Act of 1997, states also can opt for the Program of All-Inclusive Care for the Elderly (PACE) as an alternative to institutional care for persons aged 55+ who require SNF levels of care. Using Medicare resources as well, PACE offers and manages all health, medical, and social services to provide care in day health centers, homes, hospitals, and nursing homes.

States may pay health care providers directly on a fee-for-service basis or through managed care mechanisms, such as health maintenance organizations (HMOs). Payment rates must be sufficient to ensure that covered services are available within a geographic area. Providers participating in Medicaid must accept program rates as payment in full; however, states must make additional payments to hospitals with a disproportionately high number of Medicaid and other low-income patients. States may also require nominal deductibles, coinsurance, or copayments by some Medicaid recipients for certain services. Nursing home patients who are expected to contribute most of their income for their care are exempt from this provision.

Medicaid also assists Medicare beneficiaries with low income and few assets by supplementing/filling the gaps in Medicare coverage. Thus Medicaid can act as an equivalent to the "Medigap insurance" purchased by middle- and upper-income seniors. Very low-income Medicare enrollees may also get help from their state Medicaid program in paying Medicare premiums, copayments, and deductibles.

More than 41 million persons received Medicaid in 1999 at a total cost of $180.9 billion (administrative expenditures omitted) (SSA 2000). Costs rose by 17.6% in fiscal year 2002 (HCFA 2002). Four million elders (or 11% of all beneficiaries) receive Medicaid. Payments average about $9,700 per senior (SSA 2000). Ten percent (10%) of young retirees ages 51 to 59 and 10% of nonworkers age 60+ also receive Medicaid services (NAAS 2001).

The program pays for about 45% of long-term care costs for SNF and home health; payments totaled $41.3 billion in 1998 for 3.3 million persons of all ages, at an average cost of $12,375 per recipient (SSA 2000). With legal assistance, some middle-class persons have undertaken "Medicaid estate planning" whereby they divest themselves of assets to become eligible for SNF care. Regulators have cracked down on this practice; states are required to pursue inappropriate payments via estate recovery procedures.

Medicaid is a very complex program, partly because of its relationship to other programs (e.g., SSI, Medicare). It varies markedly from state to state, as well as within each state over time. Consumers and their families may, therefore, require assistance in accessing up-to-date, accurate information about their particular state program. Sources include CMS (via the HCFA Web site: http://www.hcfa.gov/), the health department, and the Health Insurance and Counseling Assistance Program (HICAP) in each state, Area Agencies on Aging (AAAs) and their case management programs, and county health departments. Because SSI, Medicaid, and food stamps are now often "packaged," the local Social Security Administration office is also a valuable resource.

### Food Stamps

The food stamp program was established in 1964 in 22 states to provide the means for low-income persons to obtain a nutritionally adequate diet. In 1977, the program was extended to all 50 states, the District of Columbia, Guam, and the Virgin Islands. It is administered nationally by the Food and Nutrition Service of the Department of Agriculture and operates through local welfare offices. Since 1980, persons with SSI have been allowed to apply for food stamps through local Social Security offices. The program benefits are financed by federal general revenues; however, federal and state agencies share administrative costs. Benefits are in the form of coupons or Electronic Benefit Transfer (EBT) payments, accepted at most retail food stores. States were required to make their EBT systems operable across state lines by fiscal year 2002 (SSA 2000).

The value of the monthly benefit is determined by household size, income, and deductible expenses; every year the amount is updated to account for food price increases. To qualify, a household must have less than $2,000 in disposable assets ($3,000, if one member is age 60+); gross income below 130% of the poverty guidelines for household size; and net income after subtracting six deductions of less than 100% of poverty. Deductions from gross monthly income include: 20% of earned income; a standard deduction ($134 for the year 2000); any amount paid for dependent care and child support; any out-of-pocket medical expense greater than a $35 deductible for persons aged 60+/disabled; and an excess shelter deduction—the limit of $300 does not apply to those age 60+ (SSA 2000). Income limits may change annually.

The minimum benefit for one- and two-person households (the typical elder household) is at least $10 per month, with an average benefit of $127 and $234, respectively (SSA 2000). Eligibility is nearly identical to SSI requirements, and recertification of eligibility is required at least annually; those age 60 or older may do so via a telephone interview or home visit. In addition to purchases at retail food stores, seniors can use their coupons for meals prepared at a nonprofit facility or to purchase concession-priced meals from authorized restaurants.

An estimated 18.2 million persons participated in the food stamp program monthly during fiscal year 1999. The average per capita monthly value of food stamps was about $72. Benefits totaled $15.8 billion, with federal costs of $17.7 billion (SSA 2000). Annual national age breakdowns are not readily available. Eleven percent (11%) of younger retirees (ages 51 to 59) receive food stamps, as do 7% of nonworking persons and 3% of workers age 60 and older (NAAS 2001).

The food stamp program, compared to SSI and Medicaid, is a relatively minor means-tested benefit for seniors but of value to very low-income older persons. The best sources of information are district Social Security and local welfare offices and AoAs.

### Low-Income Home Energy Assistance Program (LIHEAP)

Since 1981, block grants have been awarded to the 50 states, the District of Columbia, and other jurisdictions (e.g., Indian tribes), as well as nonprofit organizations, to assist eligible households to meet home energy costs. These grantees, in turn, make payments directly to an eligible low-income household, or on behalf of such a household, to an energy supplier. Up to 10% of federal funds can be used for state and local planning and administration. Up to 15% can be used for residential weatherization or other energy-related home repairs; waivers can increase that amount to 25%. States and other eligible grantees must apply annually.

Administered by the Department of Health and Human Services, the program allows maximum policy discretion to the states. Typical of block grants, reporting requirements are relatively minimal; annual information about the number of households of seniors, the disabled, or young children served is required. Grantees are not required to provide matching funds for federal funds.

LIHEAP payments are limited to households with incomes under the greater of either 150% of poverty or 60% of the state's median income. Eligibility across the states ranges from 110%, the minimum permitted, to 207% of poverty level. Unlike the other means-tested programs, receipt of SSI is not required. Renters and owners are to be treated equitably. Payments take the form of cash, fuel, prepaid utility bills, or other mechanisms, such as vouchers, stamps, or coupons. The highest level of assistance must be furnished to households with the lowest income and highest energy costs relative to income and family size. Up to 4.1 million households were served during fiscal years 2000 and 2001. A total of $1.7 billion was appropriated for 2002. Pennsylvania and New York received the largest amounts, Hawaii the least, with tribal set-asides provided in 26 states (U.S. Department of Health and Human Services [DHHS] 2002). Statistics on specific numbers of older persons receiving LIHEAP assistance are not readily available.

Older consumers and their families can find LIHEAP information through their local Area Agency on Aging, tribal government, or the governor's office. The DHHS Web site also is a source of information (http://www.acf.dhhs.gov/programs/liheap/).

## Conclusion

Means-tested programs for the elderly are characterized by different eligibility requirements, the involvement of federal, state, and local governments, and diverse payment mechanisms, primarily monthly cash payments or in-kind benefits. Due to the high levels of flexibility and discretion accorded the states, programs vary greatly from one state to another. This geographic diversity means that beneficiaries in one state can differ from those in another; an individual or family who is eligible in one state may not be in another. States also can change their eligibility requirements over time.

This often renders the task of finding information about these "safety net" programs time-consuming and difficult to track. SSI, Medicaid, food stamps, and LIHEAP are vital programs for low- and very low-income seniors, especially older women, and for "young" retirees, 12% of whose income comes from public assistance (NAAS 2001). (See also HUD-ASSISTED RENTAL HOUSING; MEDICAID; MEDICAID PLANNING; OLD AGE PROVISIONS AND ECONOMIC STATUS; SOCIAL SECURITY PROGRAM OF THE UNITED STATES; SUPPLEMENTAL SECURITY INCOME [SSI].)

### Organizations

Area Agencies on Aging
Social Security Administration

### References

Hudson, R.B. 1995. "The History and Place of Age-Based Public Policy." *Generations* 19(3): 5–10.

National Academy on an Aging Society (NAAS). 2001. *What Benefits Do Young Retirees and Older Workers Receive?* Washington, DC: Author.

U.S. Department of Health and Human Services (DHHS). 2002. *Low-Income Home Energy Assistance.* Available online at http://www.acf.dhhs.gov/programs/liheap/.

U.S. Health Care Finance Administration (HCFA). 2002. *Overview of the Medicaid Program.* Available online at http://www.hcfa.gov/medicaid.

U.S. Social Security Administration (SSA). 2000. *Annual Statistical Supplement, 2000.* Washington, DC: Author.

U.S. Social Security Administration (SSA). 2001. *Supplemental Security Income*. Washington, DC: Author.

*Phoebe Liebig*

**MEDICAID,** Title XIX of the Social Security Act of 1965, as amended—a federal/state partnership that is jointly funded by the federal government and the 50 states, the District of Columbia, and the territories. The federal share varies from state to state but comes to 57% overall, ranging from 50% to 77% (Kaiser 2003). Medicaid provides health and long-term care benefits to qualifying low-income and needy people. Created at the same time as Medicare, Medicaid pays doctor and hospital bills, prescription drug costs, and other health care costs for low-income mothers and children, frail elders, and people with disabilities. It is the largest source of funding for medical and health-related services for America's poorest people and pays for long-term care for indigent elderly. In 2002, total costs of the Medicaid program came to $258 billion—not quite $1,000 for every resident of the United States.

States administer the program under federal rules but have, and exercise, wide latitude in designing the program. State participation in Medicaid is not mandatory, but if a state chooses to participate—and all now do—it is required to cover certain groups of people (mandatory eligibles) and may cover other populations (optional eligibles) and receive federal financial support. The mandatory eligibles include people who receive federal income maintenance payments, such as elderly and disabled Supplemental Security Income (SSI) beneficiaries, and pregnant women with incomes less than 133% of the federal poverty line. The optionally eligible "categorically needy" groups include institutionalized individuals with incomes less than three times the federal SSI benefit, people who receive supplementary income payments from the state, and the "medically needy." Medically needy participants have significant medical problems but also too much money to be eligible. They may qualify immediately in some cases but more often must "spend down" by paying for their own care until their income or assets are reduced to below their state's eligibility requirement. Federal matching funds also are available for these programs. Elderly residents of nursing homes are an optional population.

For a state to receive federal matching funds, it must provide some benefits to those it covers but may provide more. Among the mandatory federal requirements are inpatient and outpatient hospital and physician services, nursing home services, home health services for those otherwise eligible for skilled nursing facilities, rural health clinics, and laboratory and x-ray services. Outpatient prescription drug coverage is an optional benefit that all Medicaid programs currently provide. Other optional benefits for which states may get federal matching funds include diagnostic and clinical services, prosthetic devices, eye care (optometrist and glasses), transportation, and rehabilitation services.

States may also apply for waivers from federal Medicaid rules. For example, prior to 1981, in order to receive federal matching funds, Medicaid programs were required to provide long-term care benefits in institutional settings (nursing homes, hospitals, and intermediate care facilities for the mentally retarded). With the passage of the Section 1915(c) Home and Community-Based Services (HCBS) waiver program, states were free to apply for these rules to be waived so that they could develop programs to serve people in their own homes and communities and still receive federal reimbursement. As long as the services could be shown to be cost-effective, these waivers would allow the states to divert Medicaid funds from institutional settings to home- and community-based care for the chronically impaired. There is still an institutional bias in Medicaid programs, but there are now over 260 HCBS programs in the United States, and at least one in every state except Arizona (CMS 2003). The Arizona Health Care Cost Containment System (AHCCCS, pronounced "access") program is essentially a statewide Section 1115 demonstration waiver.

To further complicate matters, under the Balanced Budget Act (BBA) of 1997, states can choose to integrate Medicaid and Medicare for people 55 and older who would otherwise require nursing home care in a skilled nursing facility. This is the PACE program: the Program of All-Inclusive Care for the Elderly, which takes all health, medical, and social services into one program to provide integrated care delivery in a variety of settings ranging from hospitals to home. For most participants, the comprehensive service delivery package enables them to stay at home. PACE also consolidates the funding of patient care for plan participants not only between the Medicaid and Medicare programs but also among service providers. The BBA authorization limited implementation of this idea to 60 programs in the first year and to no more than 20 more each succeeding year.

Beyond all that, a state is always free either to cover other populations or to offer additional benefits but will have to do so at its own expense. So, it is difficult, perhaps even inaccurate, to speak of *the* Medicaid program. There is not one but rather one for every state, the District of Columbia, and the protected territories—over 50 in all. Within broad guidelines, each state creates its own eligibility standards. Each state administers its own program and is monitored by CMS for compliance with federal rules where they apply and must be met to authorize reimbursement. Within the described limits, each state determines how much of what services it will provide to whom for how long and determines how much it will pay a provider to do that. No two Medicaid programs are exactly the same. Not only do eligibility and benefits vary from state to state, but they all also interact with other federal programs, such as Medicare and SSI, and other state programs to make Medicaid very complex.

In all events, Medicaid was designed and intended to be the benefit program for the impoverished of the nation. That has not changed, even though Medicaid's responsibilities have gradually expanded and become more complex since its beginnings as a health care financing program mainly for welfare recipients. In a nation of 281 million people, 44 million, or 15.7%, were enrolled in Medicaid for some or all of 2000 (Guyer 2001). In 2002, 24 million children—more than 1 out of 4 in the United States—were enrolled in Medicaid. They represented 51% of Medicaid enrollees but accounted for only 17% of expenditures. Another 10 million enrollees, 22%, were adults who don't fit into the other two categories and are primarily low-income working parents. They accounted for only 12% of expenditures. Between them, these two categories held 73% of all Medicaid enrollees but accounted for less than 30% of all expenditures. On the other hand, the 8 million blind and disabled, who constituted only 17% of enrollees, accounted for 44% of expenditures, and the 5 million elderly enrollees—only 10%—accounted for 27% of expenditures. Approximately three-quarters of the $258 billion cost of Medicaid between state and federal governments were spent to take care of one-quarter of the beneficiaries (Kaiser 2003).

Approximately one-third of Medicaid spending is for mandatory services, primarily for children. The other two-thirds is for care for the disabled and elderly optional enrollees. For nearly 6.2 million who are both old and disabled (the "dual eligibles"), Medicaid makes Medicare work either by providing full Medicaid and Medicare benefits (90%) or by covering the cost of Medicare's Part B premiums and all cost sharing (6%) or just the Part B premium (3%).

All this care is not without cost, and average annual growth rates of Medicaid spending are a substantial concern, especially to the states. After the unsustainable 27.1% rate of growth experienced in 1990 to 1992, the rate of growth moderated to 9.7% from 1992 to 1995 and 3.2% from 1995 to 1997. That represents the bottom. From 1997 to 1999 the rate of growth in Medicaid spending crept back up to 5.4% but then accelerated further at the turn of the century to 9.0% from 1999 to 2001. In 2002, it climbed 12.8% (Kaiser 2003). Medicaid's share of state spending has grown from 10.5% in 1991 to 14.7% in 2001, and in 2003 Medicare spending by states is expected to grow more than three and a half times faster than state revenues (Guyer 2001). The National Governors Association's assessment is:

> States are in the worst fiscal condition since World War II, and soaring healthcare costs are deepening the crisis. . . . Relief will not come easily. Governors must make difficult decisions as they consider methods to control healthcare spending while preserving healthcare access.

Medicaid expenditures for 2003 are budgeted at $159 billion from the federal government and $121 billion from the states (*President*'s *2003 Budget Proposal* 2002).

Curtailing the increase in cost is a daunting task. Two major policy areas are getting the most attention, although neither holds promises of great savings. The first is further restraining payments to providers. Cuts in payments to hospitals, physicians, and nursing homes were under widespread consideration in 2002 (Alliance 2003). The offsetting concern is that beneficiaries' access to services could be disrupted if too many providers drop out of Medicaid. The program is already seen as paying less than adequate rates, and balance billing is hardly an option with the served population. On the other hand, many of the managed care techniques that have helped to restrain costs for pharmaceuticals have yet to be fully applied to Medicaid programs, so that more use of generic drugs, use of Pharmacy Benefit Managers, adjustments in the dispensing fee paid to pharmacists to actually fill the prescription, and modified formularies may provide some relief.

The other policy area that is getting attention is modifying eligibility. Almost two-thirds of Medicaid expenditures are for optional populations or benefits. According to the Alliance for Health Reform, headed by Senator Bill Frist, Senate Majority Leader, and Senator Jay Rockefeller, D–West Virginia, "Many states are considering cutting back on categories of people eligible for Medicaid, reducing income limits, or postponing planned expansion" (Alliance 2003).

In each state, Medicaid determines the payment rate for services and contracts with providers willing to accept established rates, because providers must accept Medicaid rates as payment in full. States may also require nominal deductibles, coinsurance, or copayments by some Medicaid recipients for certain services. States may either pay health care providers directly on a fee-for-service basis or through managed care mechanisms such as health maintenance organizations (HMOs). These rates do not always cover the cost of providing care. However, Medicaid recipients can obtain health care only from these providers. Beyond that, some variability results from major congressional amendments, which sometimes revamp substantial parts of the system or work themselves through to operational levels over time. Still, Medicaid is a major payor in the health care system. The programs funded half of all nursing home costs and paid for approximately 17% of all hospital and 17% of all prescription drug spending in the United States in 2000 (Mann 2002).

Individuals seeking Medicaid benefits must apply either in person or through an agent or representative. The application requires disclosure of complete financial information for the applicant and spouse, including asset transfers made in the previous five years. Such transfers can disqualify an applicant even if they are currently destitute. Generally speaking, an applicant must have less than $2,000 of assets (not including a house, a car, and miscellaneous other assets) to qualify, but that varies from state to state. Some states use an income ceiling rather than an asset test to determine financial eligibility. A medical report is required from the applicant's physician and nursing home. The completed Medicaid application is the starting point from which a technician will make an initial determination of eligibility. Federal law requires that in most cases decisions be made within 45 days; some states have shortened (but cannot lengthen) that time period.

If benefits are denied, the state must provide a detailed explanation for the adverse decision and the procedure for appeal. The state is then required to hold a hearing before an impartial administrative judge. These hearings are informal, although "on the record" with a tape recording, but strict rules of evidence do not apply. If this decision is adverse, further appeals may be pursued administratively, and when they are exhausted, an applicant may seek review in state or federal court.

Given the complexity of the system, it is perhaps remarkable that Medicaid functions at all. Consumers and their families may require a lot of assistance in getting accurate information about their particular state program. CMS (http://www.cms.hhs.gov/), the local health department, the Health Insurance and Counseling Assistance Program (HICAP) in each state, and the Area Agency on Aging are all resources. Under the waiver programs, Medicaid is doing some innovative work (such as the PACE program) to deliver superior care at manageable costs to the nation's poor. There is great pressure to do even better. (See also COMMUNITY-BASED CARE; MEDICAID PLANNING; NURSING HOMES; OLDER AMERICANS ACT; STATE AND AREA AGENCIES ON AGING; SUPPLEMENTAL SECURITY INCOME [SSI].)

**References**

Alliance for Health Reform. 2003. *Covering Health Issues: A Sourcebook for Journalists 2003*. Washington, DC: Author.

Centers for Medicare & Medicaid Services (CMS). 2003. *Medicaid Information*. Available online at http://cms.hhs.gov/medicaid/.

Guyer, J. 2001. *The Role of Medicaid in State Budgets*. Policy Brief No. 4024. Washington, DC: Kaiser Commission on Medicaid and the Uninsured.

Kaiser Commission on Medicaid and the Uninsured Fact Sheet. 2003. "The Medicaid Program at a Glance." February. Available online at http://www.kff.org/content/2003/200403/.

Mann, C. 2002. "Issues Facing Medicaid and CHIP." In *The Health Care Crisis of the Uninsured: What Are the Solutions?* Testimony presented to the Subcommittee on Public Health from the U.S. Senate, Washington, DC.

*President's 2003 Budget Proposal for the Department of Health and Human Services.* 2002. Available online at http://www.whitehouse.gov/omb/budget/fy2003/bud15.html.

*E. Craig MacBean*

**MEDICAID PLANNING,** the process of spending or otherwise distributing assets and self-impoverishment in order to qualify for Medicaid long-term care benefits. There are currently only four options available to cover the cost of long-term care: private payment, long-term care insurance, Medicare, and Medicaid. Privately paying for the cost of long-term care is only an option for the wealthiest segments of our population, as the cost of long-term care can quickly deplete the life savings of the average American. Long-term care insurance presents a similar problem as the annual cost is prohibitive for many seniors. Finally, Medicare only provides limited coverage for long-term health care costs. Medicaid, therefore, remains the only viable option to cover the cost for long-term care for most Americans—but only if the appropriate planning has been carried out in advance.

### Medicaid: An Overview

Medicaid is a "means-tested" program enacted by Congress in 1964 by Title XIX of the Social Security Act to address the health care needs of individuals who are unable to afford such care. This law is found at Title 42, Section 1396, of the United States Code. The program is jointly funded by the federal and state governments. In order to qualify for Medicaid coverage, an individual must qualify under one of the following criteria: be under 21 years of age or over 65 years of age or disabled, blind, eligible for public assistance, or a recipient of Supplemental Security Income (SSI).

From its inception, states have had the option of participating in the Medicaid program. Once a state opted into the program, it chose from a variety of medical services that it would provide and customized the program within predetermined federal guidelines. Every state also has its own method of issuing guidelines for the administration of the program. In New York, for example, the Department of Health has assumed this responsibility. On the federal level, the Centers for Medicare & Medicaid Services (CMS, formerly the Health Care Financing Administration [HCFA]) promulgates the federal guidelines and oversees state compliance.

In addition to the aforementioned categories of eligible individuals, some states expand coverage for the medically needy. Medically needy individuals have higher income and resource levels but must spend down income and/or resources in order to qualify.

### Income and Resource Eligibility

If an individual's income exceeds Medicaid's allowable income level, he or she can "spend down" the income on medical expenses. However, some states are "income cap" states that do not use the spend-down method. In such states nursing home coverage is limited to individuals whose income does not exceed a certain percentage of the SSI benefit.

Planners in income cap states must deal with the client's income to avoid having excess income that would disqualify the client for Medicaid. One of the most common techniques is the use of a Miller Trust, which diverts income in excess of the income cap amount into a trust, enabling the applicant to become eligible for Medicaid benefits despite his/her excess income. The income limit for individuals who are medically needy may not be in excess of 133⅓% of the highest Aid to Families with Dependent Children (AFDC) payment in the state. For example, the income cap amount in Florida for 2002 was $1,635.

When determining financial eligibility, Medicaid will examine an individual's resources, which must be within allowable levels. If an individual is receiving SSI, it is likely that he or she is also eligible for Medicaid. The resource limit for an SSI applicant was $2,000 in 2002.

Note that the Medicaid agency will take a "snapshot" of the couple's resources upon application. Some resources are "exempt" and do not count, such as a homestead or personal items.

When planning for the individual age 65 or older, one must consider the family structure. If the Medicaid applicant is married, his or her spouse is considered to be a "legally responsible relative" whose income will be considered in determining eligibility. This is called "deeming." In New York, the nonapplying spouse has the right to refuse to contribute to the cost of care for the applicant spouse. This "spousal refusal" is submitted with the Medicaid application. With a spousal refusal, the Medicaid applicant must assign to the state any right of support to which he or she is entitled. The right to exercise the doctrine of spousal refusal is rooted in federal law, but only a few states have sanctioned it with regard to Medicaid.

### Spousal Antiimpoverishment

In 1988, Congress enacted the Medicare Catastrophic Coverage Act (MCCA). MCCA was created to remedy impoverishment of community spouses who were left without the means to support themselves upon institutionalization of their ill spouses. The federal government permitted the states to establish income and resource levels for the community spouse, with a maximum level. New York State has adopted the federal maximums.

Once a Medicaid recipient is institutionalized, he or she is permitted to retain a personal needs allowance and to provide income to a needy community spouse. Community spouses must be permitted to retain a minimum monthly maintenance needs allowance (MMMNA; of up to $2,232 as well as a community spouse resource allowance (CSRA); with a federal minimum level of $17,856 and a maximum of $89,280). The MMMNA is a sufficient amount of income to raise the community spouse's income to 150% of the poverty level of a two-person household. In New York State, community spouses may retain up to the maximum amount. Hence, if a community spouse does not receive enough income to bring her up to the MMMNA, she may keep enough of the institutionalized spouse's income to do so.

The MMMNA may be increased if it is established that, due to exceptional circumstances, the community spouse needs income in excess of the MMMNA. State courts differ in their interpretation of "exceptional circumstances." In New York, see *Gomprecht v. Gomprecht* (629 N.Y.S.2d 190; 1995), where a community spouse was denied an order of support to increase the MMMNA.

Rather than allocate the institutionalized spouse's income, it is often beneficial for a community spouse to retain assets in excess of the community spouse resource allowance in order to generate enough income to meet the MMMNA. For example, consider an institutionalized spouse with Social Security of \$1,200 and a pension of \$300, while the community spouse has Social Security of \$600 and resources of \$475,000. Calculated at 4% interest, the community spouse's interest on her resources would be \$1,583.33 per month (\$475,000 × 4% ÷ by 12). Added to her Social Security, her income totals \$2,183.33. Rather than allocating the institutionalized spouse's income, the community spouse should be entitled to retain her assets, which are in excess of the allowable CSRA, in order to increase her monthly income. This approach is known as the "resource-first rule." Some states, however, use the "income-first rule," first allocating the institutionalized spouse's income. In *Wisconsin Department of Health and Family Services v. Irene Blumer* (122 S.Ct. 962; 2002), the Supreme Court upheld the income-first method, thus giving all states the option to use it.

Attorneys in New York have addressed a related issue in the case of *Robbins v. DeBuono* (7/3/2000 N.Y.L.J. 1 [col. 3]; 1999), New York State's highest court ruled that allocating the institutionalized spouse's Social Security benefits to the community spouse is in violation of the Social Security Act. This is because Social Security income may not be "alienated" or assigned pursuant to federal law. Thus, the institutionalized spouse's Social Security benefits may not first be used to increase the community spouse's income, allowing for allocation of the couple's resources to the community spouse. There is no such rule against alienation of pension benefits.

### Look-Back Period and Asset Transfer Rules

The agency to which the institutional application is made will generally "look back" at an individual's financial records for a period of 36 months prior to the requested "pick-up date" (the date on which the applicant requires Medicaid to begin providing benefits). Under the Omnibus Budget Reconciliation Act of 1993 (OBRA-93), the look-back period in the case of payments to or from certain trusts was increased to 60 months. The "look-back" period is to determine whether income or resources have been transferred by the applicant (or spouse) for less than fair market value (i.e., gifted).

When a gift has occurred within the look-back period, Medicaid will impose a period of ineligibility, or "penalty period," on the applicant. The applicant will then be required to pay privately for his or her care during that period. New York calculates the penalty period as commencing on the first day of the month following the month in which the transfer was made. Some states calculate the penalty starting on the first day of the same month in which the transfer was made.

The penalty period is calculated by dividing the total cumulative, uncompensated value of all assets transferred during the look-back for less than fair market value (i.e., gifts) by the current average monthly cost to a private-pay patient in a nursing facility within the state. New York State has exercised the federally granted option to apply community-based private-pay averages, which differentiate between the various counties. The resulting number is equal to the number of months for which the applicant will be ineligible for institutional Medicaid benefits.

To apply these regulations, consider a New York City resident who has gifted the sum of \$100,000 to his daughter on January 1, 2001. To calculate the penalty period for Medicaid nursing home benefits, divide the \$100,000 gift by \$7,894 (the figure applicable for New York City applicants). The resulting penalty period is 12.66 months commencing on February 1, 2001, and ending on January 31, 2002. Thus, the individual may apply for, and be eligible for, institutional Medicaid benefits as of February 1, 2002, provided his or her resources do not exceed Medicaid eligibility levels at that time.

It is important to note that the OBRA-93 has eliminated the "cap" on penalty periods, which may be a trap for the unwary. For example, suppose that a New York City resident transferred $400,000 to his son on January 25, 2000. If he applies for institutional Medicaid benefits after the 36-month look-back period has elapsed (i.e., February 1, 2003, or thereafter), he would be eligible for institutional Medicaid benefits. However, if that same individual applied for Medicaid only 35 months after the transfer (December 2002), then the Department of Social Services (DSS) would impose a 50-month penalty period ($400,000 divided by $7,894 = $50.67) beginning on February 1, 2000, the month following the transfer. By failing to wait the additional 2 months to apply for Medicaid, this individual would have to pay privately for nursing home care for over an additional year, unless other measures are taken.

Transfers made by a community spouse to any individual or entity other than the Medicaid recipient *after* acceptance has been determined are irrelevant for the purposes of the institutional spouse's Medicaid eligibility. Hence, any postacceptance transfers by a community spouse will not result in a penalty period for the institutionalized spouse.

Federal law exempts certain transfers from the transfer penalty rules. The following list represents the major transfers that are exempt from such rules:

1. The assets were transferred to the individual's spouse or to another for the sole benefit of the individual's spouse.
2. Outright transfers of assets to an applicant/recipient's blind or disabled child or to a trust established solely for the benefit of such child.
3. Transfers for fair market value or for others for valuable consideration.
4. Transfers to a trust established solely for the benefit of an individual under sixty-five years of age who is disabled.
5. Transfer of a homestead to a spouse; a child under the age of 21, or a blind or disabled child; a sibling of the applicant/recipient who has an equity interest in the home and who was residing in the home for a period of at least one year immediately before the date the applicant/recipient became institutionalized; or an adult child who resided in the home for a period of at least two years before the date the applicant/recipient became institutionalized and who "provided care" to such individual that permitted such individual to reside at home rather than in an institution.
6. Transfers of assets exclusively for a purpose other than to qualify for medical assistance.
7. Transfers for less than fair market value that have been returned to the Medicaid applicant/recipient and/or spouse.

### Home Care

Most states have limited home care programs. OBRA-93 gave the states the option of imposing penalty periods for applicants of Medicaid home care benefits. New York State has not done so yet. Therefore, a New York State resident can transfer assets in the month prior to the date in which he or she seeks Medicaid home care benefits, and such benefits will be provided as long as the remaining assets are below Medicaid's resource levels and, further, the need for care is medically established.

### Life Estates

A life estate is an interest in real property not amounting to ownership and limited by a term of life. In 1994, the Health Care Financing Administration of the U.S. Department of Health and Human Services (HCFA, now CMS) established tables valuing life estates based on the life expectancy of life tenants. As an example, the HCFA tables indicate that the life estate of an 80-year-old is valued at .43659. Thus, if an 80-year-old transfers a home valued at $300,000, retaining a life estate, he or she has retained $130,977 of the home's total value, reducing the transfer to $169,023. Therefore the transfer penalty is substantially reduced.

Of course, if the house is sold while the life tenant is alive, a portion of the proceeds belongs to the life tenant. This will affect eligibility if the life tenant is receiving Medicaid benefits.

Further, retaining a life estate results in the reduction of capital gains tax (due to receiving a stepped-up cost basis) if the remainder persons do not sell the property until after the death of the life estate holder. In other words, if an individual inherits property, the value on the date of death of the life tenant is the "cost basis." If the remainder person who inherits the property later sells it, the only gain on which capital gains tax will be paid is the difference between the date of death value and the sale price.

There are other techniques used by the elder law attorney to protect assets, within the framework of the regulations applicable to the state in which the attorney practices. Transferring assets to an irrevocable trust, for example, allows an individual to retain income from his or her assets while rendering the asset unavailable after the applicable penalty period has expired.

Only *gifts* create Medicaid transfer penalties. Therefore, if an individual uses assets to purchase a stream of income, which cannot be revoked or modified, no gift has been made. Rather, existing assets were converted into an income stream. Based upon life expectancy tables issued by HCFA in 1994, if an individual purchases an immediate and irrevocable annuity that is actuarially sound (that is, for a period of time not exceeding the individual's life expectancy), such purchase will not result in a period of Medicaid ineligibility, as such purchase will be considered a *compensated* transfer of assets (HCFA Transmittal No. 64 at 3258.9(B), November, 1994). HCFA defines "actuarially sound" as meaning that "the expected return on the annuity is commensurate with a reasonable estimate of the life expectancy of the beneficiary." In other words, if the annuity provides that payments to the annuitant terminate at the end of or prior to his or her reasonable life expectancy (pursuant to life expectancy charts set forth in HCFA Transmittal No. 64), the annuity is actuarially sound. To the contrary, if the term exceeds the individual's life expectancy, the annuity will not be considered actuarially sound, thus creating a transfer of assets *without* consideration, resulting in a period of ineligibility for Medicaid. As such, the annuity will be considered as a trust-related transfer for less than fair market value, and trusts are subject to a 60-month look-back period. HCFA also provides that the total amount of payments received by the annuitant must be equal to or exceed the initial investment in the annuity.

The annuitant contributes funds and receives in return payments for a period of time based upon his/her life expectancy. With a life annuity, if the individual dies early, the funds may be lost. A way to prevent such loss is to choose an annuity with a term certain. As long as the term does not exceed the annuitant's reasonable life expectancy per the life expectancy charts set forth by HCFA, the annuity will be a transfer for consideration and will not result in a period of Medicaid ineligibility. For example, if a 78-year-old male purchases an annuity for $100,000 to be paid over 16 years, and the table indicates a life expectancy of approximately 8 years, the remaining 8 years of payout will be considered a transfer of $50,000 for Medicaid purposes.

An annuity can be purchased from an insurance company, or a private annuity arrangement can be entered into. A private annuity must be actuarially sound and should use a rate that is 120% of the federal midterm rate for the month the annuity contract begins. See Internal Revenue Code (IRC) §7520(a)(2) and Treas. Reg. Sec. 25.7520-1.

For Medicaid purposes, the annuity must be irrevocable. Neither the owner, annuitant, payee, beneficiary, nor the payment may be changed. In addition, the annuity must contain language that provides that the owner cannot assign the annuity contract benefits to anyone. Since it is not assignable, the annuity does not have any value on the market and is deemed valuable only to the annuitant, payee, and beneficiary. Finally, the annuity must contain language that the contract has no cash value, so that Medicaid will not consider the annuity as an available resource of the annuitant/Medicaid applicant.

For Internal Revenue Service (IRS) purposes, life expectancy tables may not be used when it is expected that there is more than a 50% chance that the annuitant will die within 12 months (Treas. Reg. Sec. 1.7520-3(b)(3)). For Medicaid purposes, states differ on this issue. For example, the New York State Department of Health determines life expectancy solely on age without regard to other factors such as medical condition.

Following are situations in which the purchase of an annuity may be useful:

#### *Use of an Annuity by a Single Institutionalized Individual*

One situation is that of a single individual with no family who is in a nursing home for a relatively short period of time. If the individual purchases an annuity for a term of years based upon his life expectancy, he will receive a stream of income that he will utilize upon returning home.

#### *Use of an Annuity by a Community Spouse*

If a husband and wife have combined assets in excess of the CSRA and an ill husband makes an exempt transfer of assets to his wife in the community, there will be no Medicaid eligibility in most states. Even in New York, which recognizes the federal doctrine of spousal refusal, Medicaid will have the right to recover from the wife to the extent of her excess over the CSRA. In such a circumstance, the wife can purchase an annuity prior to applying for Medicaid for the husband with her assets in excess of the CSRA (for a term of years not in excess of her life expectancy).

### Estate Recovery

The estate lien is the most common form of recovery for benefits paid by Medicaid. Prior to OBRA-93, Medicaid was entitled to recover from the estates of individuals 65 and older for benefits paid. OBRA-93 extended the right of recovery to the estates of individuals who are 55 and older. Recovery may not be made if there is a surviving spouse or a surviving child who is either under 20 years old, blind, or totally disabled.

OBRA-93 defines the term "estate" to include all real and personal property and other assets included within an individual's estate, as defined for purposes of the respective state's *probate* law. However, OBRA-93 permits the optional expansion of the definition of "estate" for recovery purposes to include

> any other real and personal property and any other assets in which the individual had any legal title or interest at the time of death (to the extent of such interest), including such assets conveyed to a survivor, heir or assign of the deceased individual through joint tenancy, tenancy in common, survivorship, life estate, living trust or other arrangement.

California has expanded the definition of "estate" for Medicaid recovery purposes. However, as of the present date, the definition of "estate" has not been expanded in New York State. Thus, in New York, Medicaid may only recover from the probate estate for benefits received after age 55.

The subjects covered here serve only as a general overview of Medicaid planning. We do not recommend reliance upon general information when giving advice. Rather, an attorney practicing elder law in the state of domicile should be consulted prior to effectuating any Medicaid plan. (See also ELDER LAW PRACTICE; ESTATE PLANNING; ETHICS IN FINANCIAL PLANNING; FINANCIAL SECURITY IN RETIREMENT; FRAILTY PLANNING; MEDICARE.)

**Organizations**

Center for Long-Term Care Financing (CLTCF)
National Academy of Elder Law Attorneys (NAELA)

**References**

Bove, Alexander A., Jr. 1996. *The Medicaid Planning Handbook*. 2nd ed. Boston, MA and New York: Little, Brown.

Lieberman, Trudy, ed. 2000. *Consumer Reports Complete Guide to Health Services for Seniors: What Your Family Needs to Know about Finding and Financing, Medicare, Assisted Living, Nursing Homes, Home Care, Adult Day Care*. New York: Three Rivers Press.

*Ronald A. Fatoullah and Stacey Meshnick*

**MEDICAL DIRECTIVES.** See Advance Directives; Durable Power of Attorney; Elder Law Practice; Living Will.

**MEDICAL SAVINGS ACCOUNTS (MSAs) AND MEDICAL IRAs,** two recent innovations in health care financing that combine a high-deductible health insurance policy with an individual savings account. The savings account or IRA (Individual Retirement Account) portion of the plan is designed as a source of self-insurance to cover small medical expenses. The insurance policy portion of the plan provides protection against large medical expenses. By reducing the frequency of insurance claims while providing major medical coverage, MSAs and Medical IRAs are expected to reduce an individual's health care expenses, provide for future medical needs, reduce periods of noncoverage, and create an incentive to wellness.

MSAs and Medical IRAs are similar. Regular payments are made into either account by an employer and participants. With an MSA, funds in the savings account can be used for medical expenses without a tax penalty. With a Medical IRA, at 65 years old, funds can be used for medical or nonmedical expenses, just as in a conventional IRA.

Current tax laws discourage MSAs and Medical IRAs. With the exception of a small pilot program, no federal tax exemptions are granted for deposits into the savings account portion or on the interest earnings of an MSA. The only federal tax exemptions granted for deposits into the retirement account portion of a Medical IRA are exemptions covering regular IRAs, making account holders subject to taxes and penalties for withdrawing funds, even to pay medical expenses. The insurance policy coupled with the account, on the other hand, receives the same tax treatment as other types of health insurance. If paid by an employer, the insurance premium portion of the MSA or Medical IRA is not considered taxable compensation for the worker. Employer contributions toward the savings plan portion of an MSA are also taxable. For an employee, federal, state, and local taxes are paid on deposits in addition to taxes on interest earnings from the account.

Despite these tax disadvantages relative to conventional health insurance plans, some companies have still opted to offer Medical IRA and MSA plans—Golden Rule Insurance Co., Dominion Resources, Inc., and Forbes, Inc., are three. Although experience with these plans has been limited, corporations report advantages over their previous insurance arrangements, including health expenses falling well below the national average, significant premium savings, and a high percentage of employee participation in such plans.

In 1996, the Kassebaum-Kennedy bill (H.R. 3103), which became the Health Insurance Portability and Accountability Act (HIPAA), created a pilot MSA program that would allow no more than 750,000 policies limited to a pool of individuals employed at firms with 50 or fewer employees and those who are self-employed. Congress is now considering expanding this program, allowing all employers and employees to make tax-free contributions into the accounts. In the HIPAA pilot program, funds not spent from a given year's contributions to the savings account portion of the plan become the individual's to use for medical expenses or to purchase health insurance during any period of unemployment. Account balances are the sole property of the account holder, and any money that is left in the MSA can be rolled over to the next year for future health care treatment. Distributions that are not for medical expenses are counted as income. Such distributions are also subject to an additional 15% tax unless made after age 65, death, or disability.

An example of how these plans would work shows the potential for such accounts to provide health insurance benefits today, while controlling costs and providing for health care expenses tomorrow. Currently, the average employer spends about $5,300 annually to provide family health insurance coverage to an employee. To establish a Medical IRA or MSA with similar expenditures, the employer could spend about one-third of that amount for a high-deductible insurance policy (e.g., a $2,500 deductible). Although the premium for a family policy with this deductible would vary with the particular demographics of the insured, in most areas the cost would be between $1,200 and $2,100. At the end of the year, any unspent balance in the MSA/Medical IRA would carry over and accumulate interest the next year. This "use-it-or-keep-it" feature would give many individuals a strong incentive to purchase health care services wisely.

Medical IRAs and MSAs provide several advantages over conventional insurance products. First, by empowering the consumer to decide whether and how much to pay for medical services, the accounts have the potential to foster healthy competition among health care providers, keeping medical expenses at a competitive level. Over the last two decades, health care expenses have grown about twice as fast as the gross national product (Goodman and Musgrave 1993). MSAs and Medical IRAs empower patients to become prudent consumers.

Second, Medical IRAs provide another way to save for retirement, and both plans provide a way to save for future medical needs. In any given year, many Americans incur few or no medical expenses, and many go for several years without significant medical costs.

Assuming an 8% annual interest rate, a $3,500 yearly deposit, and no withdrawals for medical expenses, a Medical IRA would grow to more than $500,000 after 35 years. With yearly withdrawals of $2,500 to pay medical expenses, the account would grow to more than $170,000 in the same period. The potential for long-term savings is the strongest advantage of MSAs and Medical IRAs compared to conventional insurance arrangements (Jensen and Morlock 1994).

Third, MSAs and Medical IRAs provide a source of insurance protection during periods of unemployment. Many periods without health insurance are precipitated by a loss of employment. During periods of unemployment, income typically decreases dramatically, making it difficult for a family to replace lost coverage. With an MSA/Medical IRA plan, however, it often takes only a short time to create a healthy balance in the savings account portion of the plan, and the funds could be used to purchase insurance in the insured's own name or purchase COBRA (Consolidated Omnibus Budget Reconciliation Act) continuation coverage through the previous employer. If they were common, MSAs and Medical IRAs would provide a source of bridge insurance during periods when coverage would otherwise be unaffordable.

The key advantage of Medical IRAs and MSAs, for many individuals, is that these plans guarantee as much financial protection as conventional insurance plans and potentially provide retirement income and funds to pay future medical expenses. The funds accumulated in these accounts could be used in addition to, or in place of, Medigap coverage, that is, to pay for services not covered by Medicare. Potential concerns about MSA plans include the effects of tax exclusions on government revenues, risk selection effects if only healthier employees choose MSAs, and whether MSAs reduce health care costs (Polzer 1995). (See also HEALTH AND LONGEVITY; MEDICARE; MEDICARE + CHOICE; MEDICARE SUPPLEMENTAL INSURANCE; MENTAL HEALTH CARE FINANCING; SAVINGS INVESTMENTS.)

### References

Craig, V. 1993. *Medical Savings Accounts: Questions and Answers.* Alexandria, VA: Council for Affordable Health Insurance.

Gabel, J., D. Liston, G. Jensen, and J. Marsteller. 1994. "The Health Insurance Picture, 1993: Some Rare Good News." *Health Affairs* 13(1).

Goodman, J., and G. Musgrave. 1993. "Personal Medical Retirement Accounts (Medical IRAs): An Idea Whose Time Has Come." *NCPA Media Backgrounder No. 128.* Washington, DC: National Center for Policy Analysis.

Jensen, G., and R. Morlock. 1994. "Why Medical Savings Accounts Deserve a Closer Look." *Journal of American Health Policy* 4(3): 14–23.

Monheit, A., and C. Schur. 1988. "The Dynamics of Health Insurance Loss: A Tale of Two Cohorts." *Inquiry* 25: 315–27.

Polzer, Karl. 1995. "Medical Savings Accounts: Analyzing Potential Impacts." National Health Policy Forum Issue Brief No. 669. Washington, DC: George Washington University.

*Robert J. Morlock*

**MEDICARE.** Title XVIII of the Social Security Act of 1965, as amended, is a nationwide federal health insurance program for people 65 and over, certain disabled persons under 65, and persons of any age with permanent end-stage renal disease. The Medicare program is a social insurance program that provides access to acute medical care and financial protection for Medicare beneficiaries. The original Medicare program consists of two parts: Part A for hospital insurance and Part B for physician and other provider services. Although there were significant changes to the program in 1972, passage of the Balanced Budget Act (BBA) in 1997 resulted in the greatest changes in the Medicare program since its inception. Among the many cost efficiencies enacted, the BBA created the Medicare + Choice Program, also referred to as Medicare Part C, to expand the choice of health plans in Medicare beyond fee for service. Medicare + Choice now includes Medicare managed care plans, preferred provider organizations (PPOs), provider-sponsored organizations (PSOs), private fee-for-service (PFFS) plans, and Medical Savings Accounts (MSAs), although there has been virtually no implementation of the latter three options. Medicare health maintenance organizations (HMOs) are the primary alternative choice to original fee-for-service Medicare. The BBA also mandated that Medicare plans provide improved consumer and quality information to assist Medicare beneficiaries in decision making.

### Eligibility and Premiums

Most Americans aged 65 or older who are citizens or who have been legal residents for 5 years are automatically entitled to protection under Part A of Medicare if they worked for 40 quarters under Social Security. Most individuals establish entitlement to Part A on the basis of work in employment covered by either the Social Security or railroad retirement systems and pay no premiums for Part A. Persons aged 65 or older who are not "fully insured" (i.e., not eligible for monthly Social Security or railroad retirement cash benefits) may obtain Part A coverage, providing they pay the full actuarial cost of such coverage ($316 per month in 2003).

Disabled people under age 65 who have been receiving monthly Social Security benefits for 2 years and disabled railroad retirement system annuitants are also eligible for Part A. In addition, Medicare covers individuals who have end-stage renal disease if they are (1) fully insured for old-age and survivor insurance benefits, (2) entitled to monthly Social Security benefits, or (3) are spouses or dependents of individuals described in (1) and (2).

Medicare Part B is voluntary. All persons aged 65 or older may elect to enroll in the supplementary medical insurance program by paying the monthly premium, which in 2003 is $58.70. The deductible is $100 per year, with a copayment of 20%. Low-income Medicare beneficiaries may be eligible for Medicare savings programs or Medicaid or state assistance programs to help with the Part B premium (see Medicaid).

### Original Medicare Benefits and Costs

*Part A.* After deductibles are met and subject to copays, or coinsurance, Part A of Medicare will pay for medically necessary care in hospitals, skilled nursing facility care (assuming certain other conditions are met), hospice, and some home health care. The measuring unit for Part A benefits is a "benefit period," which is a period of care starting with a covered event, such as a hospitalization, and ending when 60 days have elapsed without care. Deductibles are charged per benefit period.

*Inpatient Hospital Care.* Medicare pays all reasonable expenses for the first 60 days minus a deductible of $840 (in 2003) in each benefit period. For days 61 to 90, a daily coinsurance amount of $210 is deducted. When more than 90 days are required in a benefit period, a patient may elect to draw upon a 60-day lifetime reserve. A coinsurance amount of $420 is also deducted for each reserve day. Inpatient psychiatric care is covered up to 190 days during a Medicare beneficiary's lifetime.

*Skilled Nursing Facility Care.* Coverage includes up to 100 days in a skilled nursing facility for persons in need of continued skilled nursing care and/or skilled rehabilitation services on a daily basis. The admission must follow hospitalization of at least 3 days, not including date of discharge, for the same condition. After the first 20 days, a daily coinsurance amount of $105 is deducted for days 21 to 100.

*Home Health Care.* Medicare covers unlimited home health visits provided to homebound persons who need skilled nursing care, physical therapy, or speech therapy on a part-time or intermittent basis. The patient must be under the care of a physician who establishes and reviews the home health plan of services. Home health coverage is designed for treatment of acute care conditions and for postacute care and is medically oriented. The home health services must be delivered by an agency meeting Medicare conditions for certification.

*Hospice Care.* Medicare will pay for hospice care services provided to terminally ill Medicare beneficiaries with a life expectancy of six months or less, up to a 210-day lifetime limit. A subsequent period of hospice coverage is allowed beyond the 210-day limit if the beneficiary is recertified as terminally ill.

*Part B* of Medicare covers most physician services and outpatient health services, durable medical equipment, home health care beyond the first 100 days, and preventive care. Part B generally pays 80% of the approved amount (fee schedule, reasonable charges, or reasonable cost for covered services) after an annual deductible of $100. Medicare pays only 50% of the Medicare-approved amount for health professional and outpatient services for mental health services.

Medicare now provides services for individuals with Alzheimer's disease who can benefit from physical therapy or occupational, speech, and other therapies that are medically necessary (CMS 2001).

Medicare-participating providers must agree to accept assignment of Medicare claims and not to charge more than the Medicare-approved amount for services and supplies covered under Part B. Medicare beneficiaries pay the 20% coinsurance and deductible. There is a limit on the amount that physicians and other health care providers who do not accept assignment can charge for Part B services. That limit is set at 115% over Medicare's approved amount. The limiting charge does not apply to supplies or equipment.

Services covered by Part B include the following:

*Doctor's Services.* This includes surgery, consultation, and home, office, and institutional visits. Limited coverage exists for services rendered by dentists, podiatrists, and chiropractors. Coverage also includes Medicare-approved health providers who are not physicians such as advanced practice nurses and physician assistants.

*Other Medical and Health Services.* Coverage includes laboratory and other diagnostic tests, x-ray and other radiation therapy, outpatient services at the hospital, rural health clinic services, home dialysis supplies and equipment, artificial devices (other than dental), mental health care, physical, occupational, and speech therapy, and ambulance services.

*Home Health Services.* This includes an unlimited number of medically necessary home health visits for persons not covered under Part A, and home health care beyond 100 days for those who are. No deductibles or coinsurance apply to home health care. Under the Medicare Home Health Prospective Payment System, a home care agency receives a fixed amount for each patient for a 60-day episode of care with adjustment for client condition and location. There is no limit on the number of home care episodes as long as they are approved by the physician.

*Preventive Services.* Coverage expanded with the passage of the Balanced Budget Act of 1997. Coverage now includes bone mass measurement; colorectal cancer screening; diabetes services and supplies; glaucoma screening; women's health services including mammograms, Pap test, and pelvic exams; prostate cancer screening; and vaccinations for flu, pneumococcal pneumonia, and hepatitis B. Further details are available in the *Medicare and You* handbook or from 1-800-MEDICARE (CMS 2002b).

The original Medicare program has substantial cost sharing, no limit on out-of-pocket spending, and virtually no outpatient prescription drug coverage. Mental health benefits are more restrictive than those for physical care. Medicare is primarily an acute care program with expanded coverage for preventive services, although it does not cover routine examinations. Hearing aids and most eyeglasses, most dental care, routine foot care, and long-term care are also excluded. Medicare's coverage limitations, combined with substantial deductibles and out-of-pocket costs, leave Medicare beneficiaries facing substantial expenses (see Financial Security in Retirement).

Beneficiaries can supplement the original Medicare fee-for-service benefits package by choosing a Medicare managed care plan, enrolling in an employer-provided retiree health insurance plan, becoming eligible for Medicaid and Medicare Savings Programs, or purchasing long-term care insurance or a Medicare supplemental insurance plan (Medigap). About 90% of Medicare beneficiaries have supplemental coverage to cover Medicare coinsurance deductibles and noncovered services (MedPAC 2002). Additional sources of medical services are the Department of Veterans Affairs for eligible veterans and TRICARE for Life. TRICARE for Life and the TRICARE Senior Pharmacy Program, established in 2001, supplement Medicare coverage for military retirees and their dependents. TRICARE requires that enrollees be enrolled in Medicare Part B and pay the premium. TRICARE includes prescription drug coverage and also includes wrap-around benefits to cover Medicare's cost-sharing requirements.

### Medicare + Choice

The 1997 Balanced Budget Act established the Medicare + Choice (M+C) program. The objectives of the M+C program were to modernize Medicare benefits, expand consumer choice and information, and reduce out-of-pocket expenses for Medicare beneficiaries. Extensive comparative plan information is available from the Medicare personal plan finder on the CMS Web site, (http://www.medicare.gov/) and from the toll-free Medicare 800 number (1-800-MEDICARE). In 2003, plans can offer reduced Part B premiums as a benefit. Individuals enrolling in an M+C plan may wish to keep their Medigap policy until they decide they are comfortable with the plan. All M+C plans must provide at least the same level of benefits included in original Medicare Plan A and Plan B. Most M+C plans provide basic original Medicare benefits with no additional charges. During the 1990s, enrollment in M+C plans grew as the M+C plans offered additional benefits such as prescription drug coverage, preventive care, hearing and vision coverage, and zero premiums.

Following an early surge, today enrollment is decreasing due to plan withdrawals, provider turnover, benefit reductions for prescription drugs and other ancillary services, and rapid growth in premium charges and out-of-pocket costs. These changes have a particularly adverse effect on low-income Medicare enrollees in poor health and beneficiary satisfaction. Medicare pays the plans a fixed monthly fee, adjusted by location, for each Medicare beneficiary who enrolls. The payment mechanism under M+C does not adjust adequately for health status with the result that chronically ill beneficiaries face large out-of-pocket expenses. Geographic access to M+C plans is very uneven (Gold and Achman 2002; Hash 1997).

In 2003, the Medicare + Choice program will expand to include a preferred provider option (PPO), available in 23 states. This PPO demonstration program, lasting three years, may offer Medicare beneficiaries more comprehensive coverage than the original fee-for-service Medicare or Medicare HMOs. Premiums are expected to be higher than Medicare HMOs; some prescription drug coverage may be available (HHS 2002).

### Financing and Administration

Medicare payments account for 13% of the federal budget and are expected to increase in the future. Medicare covers 34 million Americans age 65 and older and nearly 6 million disabled individuals. Forty percent (40%) of Medicare beneficiaries are low income; these recipients are more likely to have poor health status and no supplemental insurance to cover Medicare cost sharing and uncovered services. Low-income Medicare recipients may be eligible for Medicaid and Medicare Savings Programs.

Eighty-seven percent (87%) of Medicare beneficiaries are in the original Medicare fee-for-service program, and 5 million, or 13%, are in Medicare + Choice plans or Medicare HMOs. Enrollment in Medicare HMOs fell in the late 1990s when the number and choice of Medicare HMO plans available to beneficiaries declined. Beneficiaries can disenroll in these plans at any time of the year and return to original Medicare (KFF 2002; MedPAC 2002).

Medicare is financed by a combination of payroll taxes (FICA, Federal Insurance Contributions Act), premiums, and general revenue. The Medicare Part A Hospital Insurance (HI) Trust Fund finances inpatient hospital, skilled nursing facility, the first 100 days of home health, and other institutional services. The Part B Supplementary Medical Insurance (SMI) Trust Fund finances principally physician and hospital outpatient services. The HI Trust Fund is financed primarily through Social Security payroll tax contributions paid by employers, employees, and the self-employed. Part B is financed from premiums paid by the elderly, disabled, and chronic renal disease enrollees (about 25%) and from general revenue (about 75%).

In the 2002 report by the Board of the Medicare Trust Funds, the trustees reported that the near-term condition of Medicare improved. However, Medicare faces serious financial challenges for the longterm future as Medicare spending increases, the baby boom generation ages, prescription benefits are considered as part of Medicare coverage, and the worker-to-beneficiary ratio continues to deteriorate. Greater program efficiencies, benefit reductions, or increases in the payroll tax may be needed in the future (U.S. GAO 2000b).

### Administration and Procedures

Responsibility for administration of the Medicare program has been delegated by the secretary of the Department of Health and Human Services to the administrator of the Centers for Medicare & Medicaid Services (CMS). The CMS was formerly known as the Health Care Financing Administration (HCFA). CMS provides 24-hour assistance, seven days a week, through the 1-800-MEDICARE assistance center and also through its Web site, http://www.medicare.gov/. The Social Security Administration (SSA) is responsible for determining Medicare eligibility and enrollment. SSA also provides general information on Medicare through its offices, publications, Web site, and information telephone number. Medicare's administrative costs are about 2% of expenditures, compared to about 10% for private health insurance.

Much daily operational work of the Medicare program is performed by "fiscal intermediaries" and "carriers," which have responsibility for reviewing claims for fee-for-service coverage determinations and for making payments. Intermediaries are fiscal contractors for Part A services. The intermediaries determine reasonable costs for covered items and services, make payments, and guard against unnecessary use of covered services. Carriers handle administrative duties under Part B of Medicare, determine charges, make payments, and deal with claims for services provided by physicians and other suppliers under Part B. Medicare beneficiaries receive a Medicare Summary Notice (MSN) that summarizes all the services received that providers bill to Medicare on a monthly basis (CMS 2002a).

### Consumer Issues

A number of issues and problems arise in the Medicare program because of program design and complex billing and administration issues. The increasing burden of costs for services not covered by Medicare is of increasing concern. Beneficiaries have been experiencing a higher burden of out-of-pocket costs, partly because they do not have limits on catastrophic expenses as the under-65 population does. Older Americans' out-of-pocket health costs include cost sharing for Medicare-covered services, outpatient prescription drugs, noncovered services and products, private health insurance premiums, M+C premiums, and the Medicare Part B premium. A recent General Accounting Office study found that 45% of Medicare beneficiaries' health care costs are not covered by Medicare (U.S. GAO 2002a). Elderly Medicare recipients spent an average of $3,757 or 22% of their income out-of-pocket on Medicare and health care expenses in 2002 (Maxwell, Storeygard, and Moon 2002). These costs are distributed unevenly throughout the population. The burden is especially serious for the oldest old, whose use of prescription drugs is highest when their incomes decrease.

CMS introduced the National Medicare Education Project, created by BBA, in the fall of 2002 to inform Medicare beneficiaries and their families about Medicare benefits, new health insurance choices, Medicare rights, costs, and quality of care. The program includes the *Medicare & You, 2003* handbook, a 24/7 helpline at 1-800-633-4227, and the consumer Web site: http://www.medicare.gov/. The Personal Plan Finder available on the Web site provides quality and cost information for use in choice of health plans. This information is also available from the helpline.

Medicare offers beneficiaries who disagree with coverage decisions the right to appeal under Parts A and B and Medicare + Choice plans. The State Health Insurance Assistance Program (SHIP) in each state can be contacted for assistance and resolution prior to pursuing the appeal process. Medicare beneficiaries under Part A can first appeal early hospital discharges to the quality improvement organizations. Appeals can be for denial, reduced payment, coverage, or termination of health services. The initial review level differs whether the appeal is for Part A, B, or M+C plans. Appeals filed under Parts A and B must be filed within 120 days of the denial notice.

Lack of consistency occurs in the application of Medicare coverage rules and in the Centers for Medicare & Medicaid Services policies throughout the country, mainly because of the diversity among carriers making coverage decisions. New CMS rules under review will allow individuals with Medicare to challenge Medicare coverage guidelines through the appeals process. CMS also plans to allow reconsideration of local medical review policy (Chiplin 2002; CMS 2003).

### Quality Issues

CMS works with Quality Improvements Organizations (QIOs) to monitor and improve the quality of care received by Medicare beneficiaries in original Medicare and Medicare + Choice plans. Each state has a QIO that contracts with Medicare. QIOs also review complaints by Medicare recipients about the quality of care received in inpatient and outpatient settings. They also provide information, outreach to beneficiaries, and advice on appeals. Recent budget restrictions have reduced outreach efforts (Pear 2003).

The Medicare program has a Medicare Personal Plan Finder that provides information to consumers about the quality of care Medicare beneficiaries receive in Medicare health plans. This data, available at 1-800-633-4227 or the Medicare Web site at http://www.medicare.gov/, can be used for comparisons of quality of care of health plans in an area. CMS is developing additional measures to rate the satisfaction levels of Medicare beneficiaries in original fee-for-service Medicare.

### Future Issues

The strengths of the Medicare program are reflected in its high satisfaction levels, low administrative costs, along with its stress on the quality of care. The Medicare program needs modernization to reduce the burden of out-of-pocket costs on beneficiaries and broader coverage of preventive services. Both political parties agree that the coverage of prescription drugs needs to be strengthened along with the Medicare + Choice program.

The redesign of Medicare is yet again under policy consideration. The addition of a prescription drug benefit to Medicare raises major design and cost issues in a period of increasing budget deficits (CBO 2002). There is considerable debate on a stand-alone prescription benefit or whether structural changes to Medicare should be included to make Medicare more competitive.

The reform and strengthening of the Medicare + Choice program is another issue awaiting a policy decision. (See also DRUGS AND SENIOR CITIZENS; HEALTH

BENEFITS; MEDICARE + CHOICE; MEDICARE SUPPLEMENTAL INSURANCE; PHYSICIAN–OLDER PATIENT RELATIONSHIPS; SOCIAL SECURITY PROGRAM OF THE UNITED STATES.)

### Organizations

AARP
BenefitsCheckUp
Centers for Medicare & Medicaid Services
Medicare Rights Center
Social Security Administration
State Health Insurance Assistance Programs

### Suggested Readings

Center for Medicare Education. 2002. *Prescription Drug Coverage for People with Medicare*. Issue Brief Vol. 3, No. 9. Washington, DC: Author. Available online at http://www.MedicareEd.org/.

Centers for Medicare & Medicaid Services (CMS). 2002. *Choosing a Medicare Health Plan—Guide for People with Medicare*. Baltimore, MD: Author.

### References

Berenson, Robert, and Bryan Dowd. 2002. *The Future of Private Plan Contracting in Medicare*. Washington, DC: AARP Public Policy Institute.

Centers for Medicare & Medicaid Services (CMS). 2001. *Medical Review of Services for Patients with Dementia*. Available online at http://www.medicare.gov/.

Centers for Medicare & Medicaid Services (CMS). 2002a. *Don't Miss Out on Your Turn for Medicare Savings. What Are Medicare Savings Programs?* #10126A. Baltimore, MD: Author.

Centers for Medicare & Medicaid Services (CMS). 2002b. *Medicare and You, 2003*. Baltimore, MD: Author.

Centers for Medicare & Medicaid Services (CMS). 2003. *New Appeals Process for Medicare*. Available online at http://www.cms.hhs.gov/coverage/8a1.asp.

Chiplin, Alfred. 2002. *The Medicare Appeals Process*. Issue Brief Vol. 3, no. 4 Washington, DC: Center for Medicare Education. Available online at http://www.MedicareEd.org/.

Congressional Budget Office (CBO). 2002. *Issues in Designing a Prescription Benefit for Medicare*. Washington, DC: GPO.

Department of Health and Human Services (HHS). 2002. "HHS Expands Health Plan Options in Medicare + Choice." Available online at http://www.hhs.gov/news/press/2002pres/20020827att.html.

Gold, Marsha, and Lori Achman. 2002. *Average Out-of-Pocket Health Care Costs for Medicare-Choice Enrollees Increase Substantially in 2002*. Issue Brief. New York: The Commonwealth Foundation. Available online at http://www.Cmwf.org/.

Hash, Michael. 1997. *Expanding Private Options in Medicare: Implications for Beneficiaries, Health Plans, and the Program*. Menlo Park, CA: Henry J. Kaiser Family Foundation. Available online at http://www.kff.org/content.

Kaiser Family Foundation (KFF). 2002. "The Medicare Program Fact Sheet." Available online at http://www.kff.org/medicare.

Maxwell, Stephanie, Matthew Storeygard, and Marilyn Moon. 2002. *Modernizing Medicare Cost-Sharing: Policy Options and Impacts on Beneficiary and Program Expenditures*. New York: Commonwealth Foundation.

McCall, Nelda, H. Komisar, A. Petersons, and S. Moore. 2001. "Medicare Home Health before and after the BBA." *Health Affairs* 20(1): 89–198.

Medicare Payment Advisory Commission (MedPAC). 2002. *Report to the Congress: Assessing Medicare's Benefits*. Washington, DC: Author.

Pear, Robert. 2003. "Medicare Officials Order End to Instructive Services." *New York Times*, January 25.

Politi, E. 2002. *Medicare and TRICARE, Center for Medicare Education Brief*. Washington, DC: Center for Medicare Education.

Summer, Laura, and Robert Friedland. 2002. *The Role of the Asset Test in Targeting Benefits for Medicare Savings Programs*. New York: The Commonwealth Foundation.

U.S. General Accounting Office (GAO). 2002a. *Medigap: Current Policies Contain Coverage Gaps, Undermine Cost Control Incentives*. Testimony by William Scanlon before the U.S. House of Representatives Committee on Ways and Means, March 14.

U.S. General Accounting Office (GAO). 2000b. *Financial Outlook Poses Challenges for Sustaining Program and Adding Drug Coverage*. Testimony by David Walker before the Committee on Ways and Means, U.S. House of Representatives, April 17.

*Linda A. Siegenthaler*

**MEDICARE + CHOICE.** Making a good health care coverage choice is one of the most important decisions faced by Medicare-eligible retirees. Most retirees assume that Medicare will cover most of their health care costs. This is not accurate. There are many benefits that Medicare does not cover, including most outpatient prescription drugs, most nursing home, assisted living, and other long-term care, eyeglasses, hearing aids, and disease management for chronic conditions. Even when Medicare does cover a service, for example, physician office visits, there are significant out-of-pocket costs like deductibles, coinsurance, and balance billing amounts (amounts billed to the patient over and above what Medicare allows). Medicare managed health care plans (usually called Medicare + Choice plans) can offer an attractive option to aged and disabled beneficiaries. Beneficiaries who have end-stage renal disease can enroll in a Medicare + Choice health plan if they were already a member before they became eligible for Medicare. While the managed care program has been troubled in recent years, Medicare health plans may still provide the most comprehensive and affordable health option. Consumers should carefully consider their health care status and the benefits and costs of the options available in their county.

## 1994–1997: Medicare Managed Care Is a Very Good Deal

Despite the fact that a private health plan option was available under the Medicare program beginning in 1985, it was not until 1994 that the program began to serve large numbers of beneficiaries. By 1995, 3 million beneficiaries (aged and disabled) had voluntarily enrolled in health plans, most of which were health maintenance organizations (HMOs). Beneficiaries were attracted to the health plans for several reasons. The primary reason was lower costs—health plans were significantly cheaper than private Medigap supplemental policies. In many cases the health plans did not charge a premium at all (compared to a Medigap policy that could cost over $2,000 a year). Plans generally charged only nominal copays, for example, $5 for a physician office visit, and did not impose deductibles and coinsurance. In addition, many health plans offered benefits that Medicare and Medigap policies did not cover such as eyeglasses, hearing aids, and preventive services. Finally, important benefits like prescription drugs were available at low cost.

Initially, Medicare managed care contracts were signed by well-established HMOs in highly penetrated markets, like the West Coast and Minneapolis. These organizations wanted an option to retain their enrollees when they became eligible for Medicare. By 1995, a larger number of health plans began serving the Medicare market throughout the country. In many cases, employers asked health plans to enter a Medicare contract to provide more affordable retiree coverage. Other plans were persuaded that the high-risk Medicare population could be successfully served based on the financial and enrollment experience of Medicare managed care contractors in southern California and Florida.

As Medicare managed care options grew, more physicians signed up with networks, thus attracting their patients to the previously unfamiliar option. The growth of Medicare managed care contractors also meant greater competition. As a result, health plans began increasing benefits to attract more enrollment. Between 1994 and 1997 prescription drug coverage grew dramatically, with most plans covering unlimited brand-name prescription drugs.

### 1998–2002: Fewer Benefits and Fewer Plans

By 1998, there were over 300 health plans serving almost 6 million beneficiaries. Many people expected the Medicare managed care option to continue to grow rapidly, similar to trends in the commercial and Medicaid markets. Medicare enrollment had already reached very high levels in certain markets, for example 60% in Oregon and Arizona. When Congress enacted new legislation in 1997 to expand the private health plan options under Medicare, policy officials estimated that one-third of Medicare beneficiaries nationwide would be enrolled in a health plan by 2002. It was also expected that managed care plans would move to rural areas and offer different models than HMOs, for example, the more open-access preferred provider organization (PPO) model. None of these expectations were met.

Little discussed at the time was the impact of 1997 congressional provisions intended to "balance the budget." Under the government contract, Medicare paid the managed care plan a monthly premium to cover the costs of all Medicare-covered services and required the health plans to assume all financial risk in the event that expenditures exceeded revenues. The health plan payment was based on underlying expenditures in the Medicare fee-for-service program in a county, which had few incentives for efficiency. As a result, in most areas, the Medicare payment exceeded the costs that the health plan incurred for providing Medicare-covered services. Medicare premiums also rose at double-digit rate increases each year during the early 1990s. Coupled with low health care costs during the time, health plans were enjoying record incomes.

The Balanced Budget Act of 1997 changed the payment formula to separate it from the fee-for-service base and guaranteed only a 2% increase in most counties. The timing of the budgetary changes could not have been worse. Health care inflation overall and particularly for prescription drugs had started to rise. Employers and other payers had already extracted discounts from the health plans and were unwilling to pay more. Providers began to "push back" and demand higher payments from the health plans.

The only recourse was for the health plans to raise Medicare beneficiary premiums and scale back supplemental benefits. By 2002, Medicare managed care benefits packages were more complicated and varied; premiums had risen to an average of $40 with some over $100 per month; $0 premium plans were less common; cost sharing for Medicare-covered services had risen; and the availability of drug coverage had decreased (less generous with generics more common than brand drug coverage).

Health plans that were unable to offer a competitive product (which many defined as a low premium and prescription drugs) were forced to cancel their Medicare contract. Between 1998 and 2002, approximately 2.2 million Medicare beneficiaries lost their Medicare managed care plan. The only good news was that 61% of all Medicare beneficiaries retained access to at least one health plan. Some 300,000 beneficiaries were left with no managed care option.

### 2003—Still an Attractive Option for Many

The reality of the Medicare managed care program is that each market is different. Local factors and unique health plan circumstances will dictate how the program evolves. While additional plans are expected to drop out of the Medicare program in 2003, there are still many plans that are committed to offering a Medicare product (generally non-profit plans that are locally controlled). Other plans are located in areas with relatively high payment rates and can be expected to offer a viable product. Researchers have predicted that Medicare managed care plans will continue to serve current enrollees for two to five years without major changes. Congress is considering additional funding, and the Medicare program is seeking to make it easier for plans to stay in the market.

While the costs and benefits may not be as good as the mid-1990s, most current enrollees and potential new enrollees may still find a Medicare managed care contract more affordable with better health care coverage than other health care options. Recent studies by Ken Thorpe and Adam Atherly (Thorpe and Atherly 2002; Thorpe, Atherly, and Howell 2002) found that Medicare + Choice managed care plans are most attractive to Medicare beneficiaries who do not have supplemental coverage through an employer or Medicaid. Beneficiaries with lower income are disproportionately likely to enroll, with 55% of enrollees living in households with incomes below $20,000. The researchers found that 78% of low-income beneficiaries enroll in a health plan in southern California, 67% in Philadelphia, and 51% in Florida. Nationally 40% of African-American and 52% of Hispanic beneficiaries enroll in Medicare + Choice plans. They also found that managed care plans provide an average of $750 in supplemental benefits per enrollee, although this amount will vary by plan. It is estimated that at least one-third of the current enrollees would not be able to afford any supplemental or drug coverage without a managed care option.

Beneficiaries should be cautioned to carefully examine cost-sharing changes for 2003. Plan renewal information and benefits/costs for 2003 are on the CMS Web site, http://www.medicare.gov/. It is expected that costs will increase at the point of service, and benefits will be reduced because health care cost trends are significantly higher than the 2% Medicare payment increase. Some plans may include additional cost sharing on hospital stays (e.g., per diem amounts), and drug coverage is expected to be restructured if not reduced to a discount drug card. Some plans may begin adding coinsurance and deductibles. Some plans are including a cap on cost sharing so that the sickest beneficiaries can predict maximum out-of-pocket costs. It will be important for consumers to understand which specific benefits are included in the cap.

In some states disabled beneficiaries may not be able to buy a Medigap supplemental policy. These beneficiaries may be particularly interested in a Medicare + Choice plan. Managed care plans must be open every year in November and accept applications from any aged or disabled beneficiary who has both Part A and Part B coverage.

CMS just recently expanded its tools to help beneficiaries to understand their health care choices. The Medicare Personal Plan Finder (MPPF) now includes out-of-pocket cost estimates for Medicare + Choice managed care plans, Medigap plans, and original Medicare. These costs are estimated by age and several health status categories. The Internet site is http://cms.hhs.gov/healthplans/.

Although not widely advertised, Medicare managed care plans provide important, extra benefits to beneficiaries with serious and chronic conditions. Many managed care plans offer disease management programs that provide education programs in self-care, nurse case managers, and special tracking systems for patients with diabetes, congestive heart failure, and other chronic conditions. Managed care plans are required to report HEDIS (Health Plan Employer Data and Information Set) data that track important health care indicators. These data generally indicate high access and quality care. For example, Medicare health plans report breast cancer screening for 75% of their eligible enrollees; 93% for beta blocker after a heart attack; 85% testing of hemoglobin A1 for diabetes patients; and 93% for access to adult services. In addition, Medicare managed care plans conduct quality improvement projects that focus on improving processes of care and health outcomes. Recent areas have focused on diabetes, pneumonia/flu vaccines, congestive heart failure, and breast cancer screening. Two-thirds of Medicare managed care plans qualified for a quality bonus payment for achieving high scores in appropriately prescribing ACE (angiotesin converting enzyme) inhibitors for certain patients with congestive heart failure. In 2003, health plans will focus on culturally and linguistically appropriate services. (See also COMMUNITY-BASED CARE; DRUGS AND SENIOR CITIZENS HEALTH AND LONGEVITY; HEALTH MAINTENANCE ORGANIZATIONS AND MANAGED HEALTH CARE FOR OLDER ADULTS; MEDICARE; POSTRETIREMENT HEALTH COVERAGE [PRHC].)

### Organizations

Center for Studying Health System Change (HSC)
Centers for Medicare & Medicaid Services

### References

Achman, Lori, and Marsha Gold. 2002a. "Medicare + Choice: Beneficiaries Will Face Higher Cost Sharing in 2002." Publication Number 533, March. The Commonwealth Fund, Mathematica Policy Research, Inc. Available online at http://www.cmwf.org/.

Achman, Lori, and Marsha Gold. 2002b. "Out of Pocket Health Care Expenses for Medicare HMO Beneficiaries: Estimates by Health Status, 1999–2001." Publication Number 494, February. The Commonwealth Fund, Mathematica Policy Research, Inc. Available online at http://www.cmwf.org/.

Gold, Marsha. 2001. "Medicare + Choice: An Interim Report Card." *Health Affairs* 20: 4.

Kongstvedt, Peter. 2001. "Essentials of Managed Care." In *Medicare and Managed Care*, ed. Carlos Zarabozo and Jean D. LeMasurier. 4th ed. New York: Aspen Publishers.

Thorpe, Kenneth E., and Adam Atherly, 2002. "The Current Role of Medicare + Choice and Its

Near Term Prospects." *Health Affairs*, July 17. Available online at http://www.healthaffairs.org/.

Thorpe, Kenneth E., Adam Atherly, and Kelly Howell. 2002. "Medicare + Choice: Who Enrolls?" A Study Commissioned by the Blue Cross and Blue Shield Association, Emory University, April 25.

Zarabozo, Carlos, and Jean D. LeMasurier. 2001. "Medicare and Managed Care." In *Essentials of Managed Care*, ed. Peter Kongstvedt. New York: Aspen Publishers.

*Jean D. LeMasurier*

**MEDICARE SUPPLEMENTAL INSURANCE,** health insurance with benefits designed to coordinate with Medicare (also known as "Medigap"). Generically, this refers to any type of health insurance that supplements Medicare benefits, including employer-sponsored postretirement group health plans that supplement Medicare coverage for retirees, hospital indemnity insurance, and specified disease policies. For purposes of federal insurance regulation, the term applies to a specific type of Medicare supplemental insurance, that is, an individual or association group policy purchased in the private market.

The Medicare program was designed to provide baseline coverage for acute care services and was never envisioned to cover all the medical care costs of the elderly. It is estimated that, in 1997, Medicare covered about 55% of personal health care expenditures of the elderly (Goody, Mentnech, and Riley 2002). However, there are several types of exclusions or limitations to Medicare coverage. First, some health care expenses such as custodial long-term care, outpatient prescription drugs, and dental care are not covered at all. Second, there are cost-sharing features such as deductibles and coinsurance for covered benefits. Third, there is no out-of-pocket limit on cost sharing, either annual or lifetime, which can result in substantial costs for individuals in poor health. Finally, the Part B premium, which must be paid for enrollment, may also be considered as a gap. Hence, Medicare's "gaps" have prompted the term "Medigap" to describe supplemental Medicare benefits.

The distribution of Medicare supplemental health insurance for the elderly in 1999 was as follows: approximately 60% of the elderly had private Medicare supplemental insurance, either individually purchased or provided through employer-sponsored insurance (Murray and Eppig 2002). Of these, 40% had individually purchased policies, and 60% had employer-sponsored coverage through a previous employer. Approximately 11% of all Medicare beneficiaries can be considered to have public supplemental coverage through Medicaid. Only about 11% had original Medicare fee for service as their sole source of health care coverage, while 18% were enrolled in a Medicare + Choice plan (HMO—health maintenance organization). A small percentage of beneficiaries have more than one source of supplemental coverage (Gold and Mittler 2001).

During the 1990s, the largest change in supplemental insurance was that as managed care membership increased among the elderly, they decreased their ownership of private individual Medicare supplement plans—particularly as premiums rose. However, with the decline in the number of managed care plans participating in the Medicare + Choice program, at least 25% of persons in those plans have reported purchasing Medigap policies, so the number of beneficiaries purchasing Medigap may be on the rise again (Gold and Mittler 2001).

### Characteristics Associated with Supplemental Insurance Status

The 1999 Medicare Current Beneficiary Survey (MCBS) shows that the type of supplemental insurance coverage varies by age, sex, race, income, and health status of Medicare beneficiaries. The proportion of elderly persons with individual Medicare supplemental insurance increased with age. However, only 1% of beneficiaries under age 65 had individual Medigap coverage, although they constitute 13% of all beneficiaries. Beneficiaries aged 65 to 74 had private employer-sponsored insurance as their most common type of supplemental coverage (36%), but this type of insurance covered only 29% of persons aged 85 and older and 21% of beneficiaries under age 65. The oldest old (85+) are more likely than other elderly beneficiaries to have Medicaid coverage, as are almost one-third of beneficiaries under age 65. Persons under age 65 were also the most likely of all age groups to have no supplemental insurance, or fee-for-service Medicare only (Laschober et al. 2002).

Men were much more likely than women to have employer-sponsored coverage; the reverse was true for private individual coverage, where women were more likely than men to have it. The proportion of women with Medicaid was larger than that of men; men were more likely to have Medicare only (Laschober et al. 2002).

Whites were much more likely than Blacks or other races to have both employer-sponsored and private individual supplemental insurance. Black Medicare beneficiaries were more likely than Whites or other races to have only Medicare coverage. Whites were least likely to have Medicaid, Blacks had triple the proportion, and other races had the highest proportion, more than four times that of Whites (Laschober et al. 2002).

More than a quarter of all beneficiaries with income above $10,000 purchase Medigap insurance, while only 17% of persons with income less than $10,000 buy it. As income increases, the percentage of elderly with employer-sponsored supplemental coverage climbs to 51% for those earning more than $30,000, compared to only 11% of persons earning $10,000 or less. As expected, the percentage of persons with Medicaid coverage is greater at lower incomes—37% for those with $10,000 or less income compared to 1% with those over $20,000 income (Laschober et al. 2002).

Persons who report poor or fair health status are more likely to need supplemental health insurance but are less likely to have private individual or employer-sponsored insurance than persons reporting themselves in excellent or very good health (46% versus 63%). Persons in poorer health are more likely than persons in excellent or very good health to have Medicaid coverage (20% versus 5%) or Medicare only (17% versus 10%) (Laschober et al. 2002).

### Regulatory History

In the late 1970s, various studies cited problems in the Medicare supplemental insurance marketplace related either to the policies or to the manner in which they were sold. The most common problems identified were (1) marketing abuses, (2) inadequate information to permit informed choice, and (3) inadequate policy benefits, especially with respect to premiums paid. In response to these problems, Congress enacted the first federal legislation (P.L. 96-265) addressing Medicare supplemental insurance by establishing a "Voluntary Certification of Medicare Supplement Health Insurance Policies"

(June 1980), also known as the "Baucus Amendment" after its chief sponsor, Senator Max Baucus.

The certification program encouraged states to adopt the 1979 National Association of Insurance Commissioners (NAIC) minimum benefit and performance standards. It allowed states to have their own regulatory programs certified by a Supplemental Health Insurance Panel, consisting of state insurance commissioners and the secretary of the Department of Health and Human Services (DHHS). Only four states (Massachusetts, New York, Rhode Island, and Wyoming) did not have certified programs, but they operated under their own, different standards. If states did not become certified, companies could seek certification of their policies by the Secretary of DHHS; however, no companies applied for federal certification.

The 1979 standards included minimum benefit requirements; "expected" minimum loss ratio (total benefit payments divided by total premiums) requirements of 60% for individual and 75% for certain group policies; limits in the duration of preexisting condition clauses; various information and disclosure provisions, such as a buyer's guide and a 30-day "free look" period; and some provisions against duplicative coverage. These (and subsequent) standards are not applicable to group policies established by employers or labor organizations for active or former employees or members, or to plans administered by HMOs or other direct service organizations. HMO supplemental products, however, are subject to the standards. Additionally, policies sponsored by association groups, such as AARP, are subject to the standards.

During the 1980s, further regulatory changes occurred as the NAIC updated its model regulations, which were incorporated into the federal voluntary standards. In 1987, the NAIC enhanced its model regulation to require compliance with actual loss ratios and provided for enforcement mechanisms. Also, there were two main provisions of the Medicare Catastrophic Coverage Act (MCCA) of 1988 affecting Medicare supplement insurance:

1. All companies must submit information on actual loss ratios on standard forms to the NAIC; and
2. Companies are required to file all Medicare supplement advertisements with the state insurance departments.

Even though MCCA was repealed in 1989, the Medigap provisions remained in effect. MCCA was expected to reduce the need for Medigap coverage since there would be an annual cap on Medicare cost sharing and some coverage for prescription drugs.

However, with the repeal of MCCA the Medigap industry got new life, and concern was raised again about the need for additional regulation. The NAIC incorporated many consumer protection provisions into its 1989 Model Regulation, many of which were later codified in federal legislation in the Omnibus Budget Reconciliation Act of 1990 (OBRA-90).

Three aspects of OBRA-90 are significant: (1) federal, rather than state, government has the ultimate responsibility for overseeing the regulation of the Medigap market; (2) the provisions of this legislation are now mandatory rather than voluntary; and (3) ten standard Medigap policies (with a few exceptions) are permitted to be sold. Standardization was adopted to facilitate comparison shopping for Medigap policies. The NAIC designed ten standard Medigap policies—a basic plan that must be offered by all companies selling Medigap products and nine additional standard plans that offer other features. After July 30, 1992; these ten policies are the only ones that can be sold, although previously purchased policies that do not conform to one of these ten standard plans generally can continue to be renewed. Three states (Massachusetts, Minnesota, and Wisconsin) that had standardization programs in effect prior to the enactment of the program were permitted to continue under a waiver.

There are several other provisions affecting Medigap policies sold to the elderly contained in either OBRA-90, the Social Security amendments of 1994, the Balanced Budget Act (BBA) of 1997, or subsequent laws. These provisions are:

- *Renewability.* Policies must be guaranteed renewable.
- *Preexisting Conditions Limitations.* Preexisting conditions period cannot exceed six months, and there is a waiver of waiting period for preexisting conditions in a replacement policy, to the extent of the time the insured had owned the original policy.
- *Minimum Loss Ratio.* The loss ratio requirements increased from 60% to 65% for individual policies, although it remains at 75% for group policies. Insurers must provide for premium rebates or credits in any given year that a group or individual policy does not meet the minimum loss ratio on a cumulative basis.
- *Agent Commission Limitations.* Agent commissions are limited in the initial year of coverage of a new policy.
- *Open Enrollment Guarantees.* Insurers must offer a six-month open enrollment period without any medical underwriting to beneficiaries who are age 65 or older after they first enroll in Medicare Part B. Although this open enrollment is not extended to persons under age 65 who are eligible for Medicare due to disability or end-stage renal disease, they are given a six-month open enrollment period when they become age 65.
- *Guaranteed Issue Protections.* There are additional federal protections regarding a person's right to purchase a Medigap policy in the following specified situations:
  —An individual whose employer terminates retiree benefits;
  —An individual moves out of a plan's service area;
  —An individual whose Medicare + Choice plan leaves the program or leaves the service area where the individual resides;
  —An individual loses coverage because the Medigap insurance company goes bankrupt;
  —An individual leaves a Medigap insurer or Medicare + Choice plan because the entity committed fraud or otherwise failed to fulfill its contractual obligations;
  —An individual who terminates his or her Medigap policy to join a Medicare + Choice plan can return to his or her previous policy; if the original policy from the same company is not available, the individual is guaranteed access to Plans A, B, or C; or
  —An individual who enrolls in a Medicare + Choice plan when first becoming eligible for Medicare at age 65 and leaves the plan within one year is guaranteed access to any Medigap policy.
  —Generally, in these circumstances individuals are guaranteed access to four out of the ten standard plans (Plans A, B, C, or F) but have broader access in the last two situations. Individuals usually have 63 days from the event to obtain such Medigap coverage.
- *Duplicative Coverage Limitations.* Medigap policies are prohibited from duplicating any Medi-

care benefits. Duplication of Medicare coverage is allowed, however, if a non-Medigap health insurance policy (e.g., a hospital indemnity policy) pays benefits directly without regard to other coverage, and if there is disclosure of the duplication on the application. The sale of duplicate Medigap policies is prohibited, but not the sale of Medigap with some other form of health insurance, including employer retiree health coverage. The prohibition of Medigap sales to anyone receiving Medicaid benefits continues, but the law allows three exceptions: (1) the state pays the Medigap premium; (2) the sale is to a Qualified Medicare Beneficiary (QMB) if the policy has prescription drug benefits; and (3) the sale is to a Specified Low-Income Medicare Beneficiary (SLMB), since SLMBs only receive assistance with the Medicare Part B premium and not with coinsurance and deductible amounts. A purchaser of a Medigap policy must state in writing that he or she has no other Medigap policy (or is replacing a current policy) and is not entitled to Medicaid. Policyholders are permitted to suspend their Medigap policies during a period of Medicaid eligibility of two years or less.

A number of states provided additional Medigap protections beyond these federal protections (Scanlon 2002). For example, some states permit longer time periods for the guaranteed issue protections, restrict certain types of premium ratings, or have special open enrollment periods for persons with Medicare under age 65.

Another provision of OBRA-90—Section 4360—authorized federal grants to states for health insurance advisory services for persons with Medicare. The State Health Insurance Assistance Program, or SHIP, is a national program that offers free counseling and assistance via telephone and face-to-face counseling, public education presentations and programs, and media activities. SHIPs must offer services to all eligible persons requesting assistance. Individuals can find their state's SHIP by contacting 1-800-MEDICARE and asking for health insurance counseling. Federal funding from the Centers for Medicare & Medicaid Services (CMS) for the SHIPs is approximately $12 million annually, with many states contributing additional funding and in-kind services.

### The Ten Standard Medigap Policies

Table 1 shows what features are in each of the ten standard plans. The basic benefits included in every plan are:

- Part A coinsurance
- Coverage for 365 additional hospital days after Medicare benefits end
- Part B coinsurance
- The first three pints of blood each year

Each of the plans has a letter designation ranging from "A" through "J," ranging from the most basic to the most comprehensive. Insurers are not permitted to change these designations or to substitute other names, but they may add names or titles to these designations.

Insurers are not required to offer all of the plans; however, they must offer Plan A if they offer any of the other nine plans in a state. As of July 30, 1992, these ten policies are the only ones that can be sold (previously purchased policies that do not conform to one of these ten standard plans generally can continue to be renewed. The 1997 BBA permitted high-deductible versions of the existing F and J Plans. In 2003, the deductible

**Table 1**
**Medigap Plans A through J**

| Covered Benefits | A | B | C | D | E | F* | G | H | I | J* |
|---|---|---|---|---|---|---|---|---|---|---|
| Core Benefits | √ | √ | √ | √ | √ | √ | √ | √ | √ | √ |
| Part A Deductible | | √ | √ | √ | √ | √ | √ | √ | √ | √ |
| SNF Coinsurance | | | √ | √ | √ | √ | √ | √ | √ | √ |
| Foreign Travel Emergency | | | √ | √ | √ | √ | √ | √ | √ | √ |
| At-Home Recovery | | | | √ | | | √ | | √ | √ |
| Part B Deductible | | | √ | | | √ | | | | √ |
| Part B Excess Charges | | | | | | √ | a | | √ | √ |
| Prescription Drugs | | | | | | | | b | b | c |
| Preventive Medical Care | | | | | | | | | | |

*Notes*: SNF = Skilled Nursing Facility.
Plan types A–J represent the ten uniform benefit packages mandated by OBRA 1990. Plan A represents the least comprehensive package; Plan J represents the most comprehensive.
*Plan F and J also have a high-deductible option under which covered individuals must pay a deductible ($1,620 in 2003) before the plan pays anything.
[a]Plan G pays 80 percent of the difference between the physician's charge and the Medicare allowable rate; Plans F, I, and J pay 100 percent.
[b]After $250 deductible, the policy covers 50 percent of prescription drug costs to a maximum of $1,250.
[c]After $250 deductible, the policy covers 50 percent of prescription drug costs to a maximum of $3,000.
This table does not apply for individuals living in Massachusetts, Minnesota, or Wisconsin.

*Source*: Centers for Medicare and Medicaid Services 2003.

was $1,620 for these plans, with a separate deductible ($250) in both for foreign travel emergency and another deductible of $250 for prescriptions in Plan J.

In addition, insurers may offer any of the ten policies as a Medicare Select product. The only difference between Medicare Select and a standard Medigap policy is that the former pays full supplemental benefits only if covered services are obtained from a selected group of health care providers; otherwise, the Select policy may deny payment or pay less than full supplemental benefits. Because of this restriction to certain providers, premiums for these policies are generally lower than for standard Medigap policies. This option was designed as an intermediate choice between a Medicare HMO and a traditional combination of Medicare fee-for-service and a standard Medicare supplemental policy. However, there appears to be little consumer interest in this product.

In 1999, the average annual Medigap premium was more than $1,300 (Scanlon 2002). The most popular standardized plans are C and F, covering almost 40% of the market with an average premium of $1,200. The most comprehensive plans with prescription drug coverage (I and J) had average premiums of $1,700. Since insurers were permitted to renew policies issued prior to standardization without converting them, approximately one-third of policyholders still have nonstandard policies (Gold and Mittler 2001), with average premiums of $1,400 (Scanlon 2002). Policy standardization is viewed as having a major effect on the market, with the range of premiums narrowing between 1991 and 1994 (Super 2002).

### Comparing Private Medicare Supplemental Insurance with Other Health Coverage and Insurance Options

Before making a decision on purchasing a private Medicare supplemental policy, it is a good idea to review other possible health care coverage you have or for which you can qualify. These choices may include help from your state through the Medicare Savings program, employer or union coverage, veterans' benefits, or military retiree coverage. A variety of written, Internet Web sites, telephone, and in-person counseling resources are available to explore these options. Many of these resources are available from or supported by the Centers for Medicare & Medicaid Services. The federal publication *Medicare & You* (CMS Pub. No. 10050) provides a brief overview of possible options, and *Medicare and Other Health Benefits: Your Guide to Who Pays First* (CMS Pub. No. 02179) gives more details. CMS also provides an interactive Internet search tool called Medicare Personal Plan Finder, found at http://www.medicare.gov/, which (1) helps one learn about possible health plan choices, (2) asks a series of questions to help clarify preferences for what is most important (e.g., out-of-pocket costs, extra benefits, access to a particular physician) in order to narrow down these choices, and (3) provides a personalized summary sheet with detailed information about the options in which you have most interest. One also can call the toll-free information hotline 24 hours a day at 1-800-MEDICARE (1-800-633-4227) to get help from a customer service representative. If one wants to obtain in-person assistance, one may call or go to the SHIP program in the state. To find the SHIP locations, call 1-800-MEDICARE or go to the http://www.medicare.gov/ on the Web and select "Helpful Contacts" to find a phone number for the SHIPs.

An important consideration is whether purchase of private supplemental insurance is necessary. If one has difficulty in affording a private Medicare supplemental policy, one should determine if one is eligible for the state medical assistance program for Medicare beneficiaries, sometimes called the Medicare Savings Program. A person may be eligible for one of three Medicaid programs: regular Medicaid, the Qualified Medicare Beneficiary (QMB) program, or the Special Low-Income Medicare Beneficiary (SLMB) program. If one has low income, limited assets, and meets other criteria, one may be eligible for the regular Medicaid program. In some states, one may also be eligible if high medical bills bring one's income and assets down to the same level. The QMB program is for Medicare beneficiaries who are not eligible for the regular Medicaid program but whose income is at or below the national poverty level, and they receive assistance with coinsurance and deductible amounts. The SLMB program is for those with incomes somewhat above the poverty level and they receive assistance with the Medicare Part B premium. Both programs require persons to have assets at or below the same level as regular Medicaid. The Medicaid and QMB programs can function to fill all or part of the Medicare "gaps," and purchase of private supplemental insurance would generally be unnecessary. Applications for Medicaid, QMB, or SLMB programs must be filed at state, county, or local medical assistance offices. Call the 1-800-MEDICARE phone number to find the nearest medical assistance office.

Two other major options to explore are employer group coverage and a Medicare managed care plan. If available, continuing health insurance coverage through a former employer upon retirement may offer several advantages. The employer may pay all or part of the premiums, or the group rates may be lower than those for individual Medigap policies. There is also usually no waiting period for preexisting conditions, and benefits are often more generous than those offered under one of the ten standard Medigap plans, especially when it comes to outpatient prescription drugs. For more information on employer group insurance, you should consult the benefits administrator at a former employer, or a spouse's former employer. Joining a managed care plan (Medicare + Choice) is another alternative to consider, if there is one available in the area. In 2002, about 61% of beneficiaries had access to a plan in their area (Super 2002). The plan will provide for all of Medicare Part A and Part B services (if covered for both), and many plans may also provide benefits beyond what Medicare pays, in exchange for some limits on choice of doctors. For the most up-to-date information on these health plans in your area, look at http://www.medicare.gov/ on the Web and select the "Medicare Personal Plan Finder." One may also contact the state's SHIP program.

### Considerations in Purchasing Private Medicare Supplemental Insurance

Comparing private Medicare supplement policies is simpler now that there are only ten standard Medicare supplement plans in almost all states. A careful examination of the ten plans shown in Table 1, ranging from basic to comprehensive and/or specialized benefits, will help determine which plan would best meet one's needs. Comparison shopping is important, particularly outside of open enrollment, because policy premiums and terms (e.g., medical underwriting, waiting periods) can vary, even within the same plan type. For example, the premium range for a 65-year-old woman in Texas for Plan F ranged from $887 to $2,487 (Super 2002). The best time to buy a Medigap policy is during your six-month Medigap open enrollment period. After this period, a Medigap insurer is permitted to do underwriting (health screening), and you may be rejected for coverage.

Understanding how the policy premium is calculated is also important. A company may base its premium on (1) issue age; (2) attained age; or (3) no age rating. A policy premium based on issue age will continue to base its premium on one's age when bought, whereas a policy premium based on attained age will increase as one grows older. Some companies may also vary premiums by sex or geographic location. The potential for cost increases should also be examined, especially since premiums usually are increased each year as the Medicare coinsurance and deductibles are changed. In addition to premiums, the company's reputation for service and its financial rating should be considered. Financial ratings may be obtained from sources such as A.M. Best and Weiss Rating, Inc., at your public library. Call the State Insurance Department to ask about the company's complaint record.

The primary Medigap publication is *Guide to Health Insurance for People with Medicare: Choosing a Medigap Policy* (CMS Pub. No. 02110). A free copy can be obtained by calling 1-800-MEDICARE. This government publication outlines steps to buying a Medigap policy and provides useful advice on the selection process. These steps include:

- Thinking about how much you are currently spending on health care and thinking about your future health care needs in terms of what benefits you want or need in a Medigap policy; the publication provides a Yearly Health Care Cost Worksheet for estimating.
- Finding out which insurance companies sell Medigap policies in your state.
- Calling the insurance companies and comparing costs—a sample Medigap Policy Comparison Worksheet is provided.
- Choosing the best Medigap policy for you and buying the policy.

Medigap Compare, which is part of the http://www.Medicare.gov/ Web site, is an important Internet resource. It is designed to help find the insurance companies selling Medigap policies in a particular state and provides contact information for the companies. This Web site contains information by company on which plans they offer in particular areas (it can be searched by state, county, or zip code), what rating methods they use to price their plans, whether membership in a particular organization is required to buy one. The Web site also provides general information about Medigap insurance. The Web site was constructed from information received by the companies on policy details or from either the State Insurance Department or SHIPs, which only provided the names and phone numbers of companies selling Medigap plans in the state. One may also contact the state's SHIP program to obtain in-person assistance for Medigap policy information. Many states have published their own Medigap information guides as well.

### Medigap Reform Issues

When the Medicare program was created in the mid-1960s, it was modeled after the private health insurance in effect at the time. Medicare's benefit design and cost-sharing structure have been criticized as not evolving with changes in the medical care and insurance sectors, which include a large growth in use of prescription drugs for treatment, with expanded coverage in insurance, and a cap on catastrophic expenses (Atherly 2001). Medigap, in turn, has been criticized for undermining cost control incentives of Medicare cost sharing by offering first-dollar coverage. Two of the most recent proposals would add two additional Medigap plans to include prescription drug coverage and provide protection against catastrophic expenses in exchange for higher cost sharing (Scanlon 2002; Super 2002). Based on what Medigap policies consumers are currently buying, it is believed that consumer interest in policies with drug coverage and a catastrophic cap but higher cost sharing would be limited (Super 2002). (See also COMMUNITY-BASED CARE; DRUGS AND SENIOR CITIZENS; FINANCIAL SECURITY IN RETIREMENT; FRAILTY PLANNING; MEDICAL SAVINGS ACCOUNTS (MSAs) AND MEDICAL IRAs; MEDICARE.)

### Organizations

Centers for Medicare & Medicaid Services (CMS)
Medicare Personal Plan Finder
Medigap Compare
National Council on Aging (NCOA)
State Health Insurance Assistance Programs (SHIPs)

### Suggested Readings

Centers for Medicare & Medicaid Services (CMS). 2000. *Don't Miss Your Turn for Medicare Savings!* CMS Pub. No. 10126-A. Baltimore, MD: Author, October.

Centers for Medicare & Medicaid Services (CMS). 2000. *Medicare and Other Health Benefits: Your Guide to Who Pays First.* CMS Pub. No. 02179. Baltimore, MD: Author, May.

Centers for Medicare & Medicaid Services (CMS). 2002. *Medicare & You.* CMS Pub. No. 10050. Baltimore, MD: Author, January.

Centers for Medicare & Medicaid Services (CMS). 2003. *Guide to Health Insurance for People with Medicare: Choosing a Medigap Policy.* CMS Pub. No. 02110 Baltimore, MD: Author, March.

### References

Atherly, Adam. 2001. "Supplemental Insurance: Medicare's Accidental Stepchild." *Medical Care Research and Review* 58(2): 131–61.

Centers for Medicare & Medicaid Services (CMS). 2003. "Medigap Compare: Ten Standardized Medigap Plans." Available online at http://www.medicare.gov/mgcompare/search/StandardizedPlans/tenStandardPlans.asp.

Gold, M., and J. Mittler. 2001. "The Structure of Supplemental Insurance for Medicare Beneficiaries." Number 3. Mathematica Policy Research Operational Insights, June.

Goody, Brigid, Renee Mentnech, and Gerald Riley. 2002. "Changing Nature of Public and Private Health Insurance." *Health Care Financing Review* 23(3): 1–7.

Laschober, M., et al. 2002. "Trends in Medicare Supplemental Insurance and Prescription Drug Coverage, 1996–1999." *Health Affairs* 21(2).

Murray, Lauren, and Franklin Eppig. 2002. "Insurance Trends for the Medicare Population, 1991–1999." *Health Care Financing Review* 23(3): 9–15.

Scanlon, W. 2002. *Medigap: Current Policies Contain Coverage Gaps, Undermine Cost Control Incentives.* Testimony before the Subcommittee on Health, Committee on Ways and Means, House of Representatives, March 14 (GAO-02-533T).

Super, Nora. 2002. "Medigap: Prevalence, Premiums and Opportunities for Reform." *National Health Policy Forum Brief No. 782*, September 9.

*Judith A. Sangl*

**MEDIGAP.** See Medicare Supplemental Insurance.

**MENTAL HEALTH AMONG OLDER ADULTS,** the measure of individuals' mental capacities in later life to understand and function in society. Mental health can be conceptualized along a continuum, with mental illness on one end and mental wellness on the other. Mental wellness refers to the individual's mental ability to function fully. This is an active process characterized by the individual's openness to experience, his or her ability to focus attention in the present moment, and confidence in his or her ability to satisfy personal needs.

Definitions of mental illness most frequently used in clinical and research settings often follow the guidelines established by the American Psychiatric Association (APA) in the fourth edition of its *Diagnostic and Statistical Manual of Mental Disorders* (DSM-IV), which was recently updated. Payment and financing data sources, however, often rely on version 9 (adapted for the United States) or version 10 (in other nations) of the World Health Organization's (WHO) International Classification of Diseases (WHO 1975, 1992). The APA, WHO, and a number of other organizations continue to work toward a "comprehensive, reliable, and valid psychiatric diagnostic system" (Regier et al. 2002). From an operational perspective, mental illness in older adults is characterized by patterns of disorders.

## Patterns of Mental Disorders in Later Life

Despite its age the Epidemiologic Catchment Area (ECA) study from the early 1980s provides the most comprehensive description of older adults' patterns of mental disorders. Five important themes emerge from the ECA and other data. First, mental illness is not a part of normal aging. A recent reevaluation of ECA data suggests that the one-year prevalence rate for any diagnosable mental disorder among community-dwelling persons over age 55 is approximately 13% (Narrow et al. 2002). However, concerns about underdiagnosis remain, with some research suggesting the prevalence is twice that level (Jeste et al. 1999).

Three disorders are most frequent for older adults who are mentally ill: anxiety disorders; depression; and cognitive impairment, including the dementias. Anxiety disorders affect approximately 10% of older adults. At least 4% of community-dwelling elderly have serious symptoms of depression. A third category of mental disorders among older adults highlighted by the ECA data is cognitive impairment, including the dementias. The prevalence rate among the oldest age groups follows a now-familiar pattern: increasing prevalence with increasing age, from 2.9% for those 65 to 74; 6.8% for those 75 to 84; and 15.8% for those 85 and older (Narrow et al. 2002). More than four million Americans currently have Alzheimer's disease, and more than 350,000 new cases are expected each year (Brookmeyer, Gray, and Kawas 1998). For all three disorders, less restrictive definitions of disorders can significantly increase estimated prevalence rates.

Rates of disorders vary by setting. For example, older adults in institutional settings present a different picture. Studies show that as many as one-third to two-fifths of older adults who are hospitalized have significant symptoms of depression (Covinsky et al. 1997; Koenig et al. 1997). Approximately one-quarter of elderly emergency department patients have cognitive impairments (Hustey and Meldon 2002). Similarly, between 65% and 90% of nursing home residents have a diagnosable mental disorder, depending upon the methods used to assess and diagnose residents (Burns et al. 1993; Smyer, Shea, and Streit 1994), with 20% to 25% of cognitively intact residents having major depression (Streim et al. 2000). Nearly one-half of new nursing home residents have dementia (Magaziner et al. 2000). Recent data suggest rates of mental illness in nursing homes may be increasing (Office of the Inspector General 2001).

These substantial rates of mental illness in institutional settings remind us of the third important issue. Older adults and health care providers face issues of comorbidity—challenging combinations of more than one mental illness, physical illness, or combinations of both. Depression has been associated with heart disease, diabetes, and cancer, with questions remaining about the causal relationships between the physical and mental conditions (Krishnan et al. 2002). Comorbidity is also often the case with the three most common mental disorders. Nearly one-quarter of older persons with depression have a co-occuring anxiety disorder (Lenze et al. 2002), and comorbid depression and cognitive disorders are also common (Krishnan et al. 2002).

Mental illness among older adults has substantial health consequences for individuals, their families, and society in general. Depression in older adults is closely linked to suicide (Conwell 1994). The suicide rate among persons over age 65 (21 suicide deaths per 100,000 persons) is almost twice as high as the overall national average and higher than among any other age groups (U.S. DHHS 1999). Approximately 60% to 75% of older persons who commit suicide have a diagnosable depression (Conwell et al. 1996). Sadly, the majority of suicide victims had seen their primary care physician within the month prior to suicide (Luoma, Martin, and Pearson 2002).

Depression is also associated with increased risk of mortality for nursing home residents (Rovner et al. 1993) and increased mortality from heart disease (Frasure-Smith, Lesperance, and Talajic 1995). Late-life schizophrenia, while not as common as other mental disorders among the elderly, results in significant functional impairment and reduced quality of life. Behavioral symptoms of dementia (delusions, hallucinations, depression, aggression) result in significant patient and caregiver distress, premature institutionalization, and reduced quality of life.

Many of these consequences are avoidable because effective treatments for many mental illnesses have been developed over the course of the last two decades. Psychopharmacologic and psychotherapeutic interventions are well established for the successful treatment of geriatric depression. Appropriate treatment for anxiety disorders among older persons also typically involves the combination of psychotherapy (cognitive behavioral) and pharmacotherapy. Effective behavioral and pharmaceutical interventions are even being developed for dementia (Doody et al. 2001).

Mental illness and aging represent a huge challenge for the future of the U.S. health care system. The number of older adults with major psychiatric illnesses is expected to double in the next 30 years (Jeste et al. 1999), and the current system fails to diagnose and treat many of the persons who currently suffer from a mental disorder (U.S. DHHS 1999). Without significant changes in medical education, financing methods, and delivery systems, the gap between treatment and need is likely to expand. (See also ECONOMIC HARDSHIP MEASURES IN THE OLDER POPULATION; ECONOMIC STATUS OF OLDER MEN AND WOMEN; LONG-TERM CARE INSURANCE—A CONSUMER'S PERSPECTIVE; MEDICARE SUPPLEMENTAL INSURANCE; MENTAL HEALTH CARE FINANCING; POSTRETIREMENT HEALTH COVERAGE [PRHC].)

### Organizations

Center for Mental Health Services, U.S. Department of Health and Human Services
Mental Health Policy Resource Center
National Alliance for the Mentally Ill
National Citizens' Coalition for Nursing Home Reform
National Institute on Aging—Alzheimer's Disease Education and Referral Center (ADEAR)
National Institute on Aging—NIA Information
National Institute of Mental Health—Mental Disorders of the Aging Branch
National Institute of Mental Health—Public Inquiries Office

### Suggested Reading

Administration on Aging. 2001. *Older Adults and Mental Health: Issues and Opportunities*. Rockville, MD: U.S. Department of Health and Human Services.

Smyer, Michael A., and Sarah Qualls. 1999. *Aging and Mental Health*. Oxford, United Kingdom: Blackwell.

U.S. Department of Health and Human Services. 1999. *Mental Health: A Report of the Surgeon General*. Rockville, MD: U.S. Department of Health and Human Services, Substance Abuse and Mental Health Services Administration, Center for Mental Health Services, National Institutes of Health, National Institute of Mental Health.

### References

Brookmeyer, R., S. Gray, and C. Kawas. 1998. "Projections of Alzheimer's Disease in the United States and the Public Health Impact of Delaying Disease Onset." *American Journal of Public Health* 88: 1337–42.

Burns, B.J., H.R. Wagner, J.E. Taube, and J. Magaziner. 1993. "Mental Health Service Use by the Elderly in Nursing Homes." *American Journal of Public Health* 83(3): 331–33.

Conwell, Y. 1994. "Suicide in Elderly Patients." In *Diagnosis and Treatment of Depression in Late Life: Results of the NIH Consensus Development Conference*, ed. L.S. Schneider et al. Washington, DC: American Psychiatric Press.

Conwell Y., P.R. Duberstein, C. Cox, J.H. Herrmann, N.T. Forbes, and E.D. Caine. 1996. "Relationships of Age and Axis I Diagnoses in Victims of Completed Suicide: A Psychological Autopsy Study." *American Journal of Psychiatry* 153: 1001–8.

Covinsky, K.E., R.H. Fortinsky, R.M. Palmer, D.M. Kresevic, and C.S. Landefeld. 1997. "Relation between Symptoms of Depression and Health Status Outcomes in Acutely Ill Hospitalized Older Patients." *Annals of Internal Medicine* 126: 417–25.

Doody, R.S., J.C. Stevens, C. Beck, R.M. Dubinsky, J.A. Kaye, L. Gwyther, R.C. Mohs, L.J. Thal, P.J. Whitehouse, S.T. DeKosky, and J.L. Cummings. 2001. "Practice Parameter: Management of Dementia (An Evidence-Based Review). Report of the Quality Standards Subcommittee of the American Academy of Neurology." *Neurology* 56: 1154–66.

Frasure-Smith, N., F. Lesperance, and M. Talajic. 1995. "Depression and 18-Month Prognosis after Myocardial Infarction." *Circulation* 91: 999–1005.

Hustey, F.M., and S.W. Meldon. 2002. "The Prevalence and Documentation of Impaired Mental Status in Elderly Emergency Department Patients." *Annals of Emergency Medicine* 39: 338–41.

Jeste, D.V., G.S. Alexopoulos, S.J. Bartels, J.L. Cummings, J.J. Gallo, G.L. Gottlieb, M.C. Halpain, B.W. Palmer, T.L. Patterson, C.F. Reynolds III, and B.D. Lebowitz. 1999. "Consensus Statement on the Upcoming Crisis in Geriatric Mental Health Research Agenda for the Next 2 Decades." *Archives of General Psychiatry* 56: 848–53.

Koenig, H.G., J. Evans, T.L. Patterson, R.K. Heaton, W.L. Koch, and D.V. Jeste. 1997. "Direct

Assessment of Functional Status in Older Patients with Schizophrenia." *American Journal of Psychiatry* 154: 1022–24.

Krishnan, K.R.R., et al. 2002. "Comorbidity of Depression with Other Medical Diseases in the Elderly." *Biological Psychiatry* 52: 559–88.

Lenze, E.J., B.H. Mulsant, M.K. Shear, P. Houck, and C.F. Reynolds III. 2002. "Anxiety Symptoms in Elderly Patients with Depression: What Is the Best Approach to Treatment?" *Drugs and Aging* 19: 753–60.

Luoma, J.B., C.E. Martin, and J.L. Pearson. 2002. "Contact with Mental Health and Primary Care Providers before Suicide: A Review of the Evidence." *American Journal of Psychiatry* 159: 909–16.

Magaziner, J., P. German, S.I. Zimmerman, J.R. Hebel, L. Burton, A.L. Gruber-Baldini, C. May, and S. Kittner. 2000. "The Prevalence of Dementia in a Statewide Sample of New Nursing Home Admissions Aged 65 and Older: Diagnosis by Expert Panel. Epidemiology of Dementia in Nursing Homes Research Group." *Gerontologist* 40: 663–72.

Narrow, W.E., D.S. Rae, L.N. Robins, and D.A. Regier. 2002. "Revised Prevalence Estimates of Mental Disorders in the United States." *Archives of General Psychiatry* 59: 115–23.

Office of the Inspector General. 2001. *Psychotropic Drug Use in Nursing Homes* (OEI-02-00-00490). Rockville, MD: U.S. Department of Health and Human Services.

Regier, D.A., W.E. Narrow, M.B. First, and T. Marshall. 2002. "The APA Classification of Mental Disorders: Future Perspectives." *Psychopathology* 35: 166–69.

Rovner, B.W. 1993. "Depression and Increased Risk of Mortality in the Nursing Home Patient." *American Journal of Medicine* 94: 19S–22S.

Smyer, M., D. Shea, and A. Streit. 1994. "The Provision and Use of Mental Health Services in Nursing Homes: Findings from the National Medical Expenditure Survey." *American Journal of Public Health* 84: 284–87.

Streim, J.E., D.W. Oslin, I.R. Katz, B.D. Smith, S. DiFilippo, T.B. Cooper, and T. Ten Have. 2000. "Drug Treatment of Depression in Frail Elderly Nursing Home Residents." *American Journal of Geriatric Psychiatry* 8: 150–59.

U.S. Department of Health and Human Services (DHHS). 1999. *Mental Health: A Report of the Surgeon General*. Rockville, MD: U.S. Department of Health and Human Services, Substance Abuse and Mental Health Services Administration, Center for Mental Health Services, National Institutes of Health, National Institute of Mental Health.

*Michael A. Smyer and Dennis G. Shea*

**MENTAL HEALTH CARE FINANCING,** sources of funds for care of mental health. The financial aspects of mental illness for older adults reflect the general patterns of treatment and funding for mental health care in America. Inpatient and outpatient care for persons with a mental illness diagnosis are often excluded from coverage by insurers. When covered, such care may be subject to incomplete coinsurance, higher deductible payments, stricter utilization review, and tighter limits on lifetime or annual maximum expenditures. Additionally, as the public system of mental health care was dismantled, patients have had to rely more and more on a system of care that requires payment from private sources.

In fact, recent developments may lead to the conclusion that insurance coverage for older persons with a mental illness is falling increasingly short of what younger persons have (Shea 2003). More than 30 states have passed laws that require insurance to provide mental health benefits comparable to coverage for other services. In addition, Congress passed the Mental Health Parity Act in 1996, which required that almost all plans offer similar lifetime or annual limits on mental and physical health care, and has renewed it annually since. Most of these "mental health parity" laws still leave substantial room for insurers to discriminate against mental health care, and their effectiveness appears to be limited (Sturm and Pacula 1999). Medicare also continues to discriminate in outpatient and inpatient coverage against mental health care (Shea 2003). In addition, while most younger persons with health insurance have relatively generous coverage of prescription drugs, Medicare offers no basic drug benefit. As a result, approximately half of older adults lack stable drug coverage (Stuart, Shea, and Briesacher 2001).

To understand the financial aspects of mental health and aging more completely, it is necessary to examine the insurance coverage options offered to older adults.

*Medicare.* Medicare coverage of mental illness was expanded in the late 1980s by eliminating the dollar limits on outpatient mental health spending, allowing services to be provided by psychologists and social workers, and improving reimbursement for partial hospitalization, among other changes (Bartels and Colenda 1998). Still, access to mental health care is restrictive. While general acute inpatient care for mental illness diagnoses are covered under Medicare Part A (Hospital Insurance), Medicare will pay for no more than 190 days of inpatient psychiatric care in freestanding public or private psychiatric hospitals during a person's lifetime. Medicare's coverage for care in skilled nursing facilities primarily targets posthospital subacute care and is not a program of long-term care for physically or mentally impaired older adults. Medicare also provides a partial hospitalization benefit in community mental health centers and hospital outpatient departments for persons in acute psychiatric distress who are certified by physicians. This benefit is not limited in the number of days like the inpatient psychiatric hospitalization benefit but does require a 20% coinsurance.

Outpatient care for mental illness diagnoses are covered in Medicare Part B (Supplemental Medical Insurance). This includes care that is given while in and out of psychiatric and general hospitals. Under Part B, the services of physicians, psychiatrists, clinical psychologists, and other mental health professionals (e.g., clinical social workers) supervised by a physician or psychologist are covered. For care given by these persons in an inpatient setting, Medicare will pay 80% of the allowed charge; for mental health care in an outpatient setting, however, Medicare pays only 50% of the allowed charge, except for medical management, diagnostic services, and professional services for evaluation, which require only a 20% coinsurance. Medicare does not provide any outpatient prescription drug coverage, including psychotropic drugs.

*Medicaid.* While the state mental health system is the safety net for younger persons with mental disorders, Medicaid offers some limited security for mentally ill older adults. While Medicaid coverage of mental health care varies by state, all state Medicaid programs are required to pay for inpatient and outpatient hospital services, physician services, and skilled nursing facility care for persons over age 21. These programs pay for services regardless of diagnosis, including coverage of mental illnesses. In addition, more than 30 states cover hospital and nursing facility services for persons over age 65 in institutions for mental disorders, and all states provide some prescription drug coverage. Thus, the poorest elderly are offered some coverage of inpatient and outpatient mental health care through Medicaid. However, many states can and do place limits on the numbers and types of drugs that can be used, the number of psychiatric visits or hospital days, or require prior authorization for services.

In both Medicare and Medicaid, however, low reimbursement levels for mental health care providers have for a long time limited access to care. More recent changes under the Balanced Budget Act of 1997 permit Medicaid programs to further reduce outpatient payment for mental health care. Furthermore, in Medicaid programs, strict income and asset limits mean that few older adults can qualify for the program. Fewer than one in nine of the elderly had coverage through Medicaid in 1999 (Murray and Eppig 2002).

*Private Insurance.* Because of the gaps in Medicare coverage, many elderly persons who do not qualify for Medicaid seek out additional sources of insurance coverage. Supplemental insurance coverage for the elderly mainly comes from privately purchased Medicare supplemental insurance (Medigap) policies, postretirement health insurance provided through former employers, or a Medicare health maintenance organization (HMO).

Twenty-four percent (24%) of Medicare beneficiaries have an individually purchased private insurance plan (Murray and Eppig 2002). According to the U.S. Government Accounting Office (GAO), as of 2001, only three of the ten standardized Medigap plans offer coverage of outpatient prescription drugs, and these plans represent only 8% of overall Medigap enrollment; none of the plans offers extra coverage extending beyond the limits on psychiatric hospitalization.

More than one-third of the elderly now have supplemental insurance coverage through a former employer (Murray and Eppig 2002). While no detailed data on mental health benefits in these retiree plans exist, the policies typically mirror those of the younger employed population. Nearly all employer plans cover prescription drugs and inpatient and outpatient mental health in some form; however, these benefits have been changing rapidly in recent years. As prescription drug costs have risen dramatically, employers have turned to tiered coinsurance (different levels of consumer cost sharing for generic and brand-name drugs) and formularies (lists that restrict which drugs can be paid for through insurance) to control costs. In 2002, 57% of covered workers faced a three-tiered cost-sharing arrangement, and 69% were in a plan with a formulary, up from 29% and 43% in 2000, respectively. Nearly one-third of covered workers in these plans have outpatient mental health visits restricted to fewer than 20 visits per year.

Access to these retiree health plans, however, is diminishing. In a recent survey of large employers, 13% indicated that they had eliminated the benefit for future retirees, and another 22% say they are very or somewhat likely to eliminate these benefits for future retirees (Kaiser Family Foundation and Hewitt Associates 2002).

Medicare HMOs were another option available to older persons seeking better mental health coverage. Prior to 1997, Medicare HMOs were paid a fixed amount per person enrolled based on their county of residence, age, gender, and a few other factors. By reducing the use of hospital services through managed care and recruiting a relatively healthy group of Medicare beneficiaries, these Medicare HMOs were often able to keep their costs below the Medicare payment. To meet regulatory requirements and to support marketing efforts, the HMOs often offered enrollees benefits beyond what was traditionally found in Medicare. While few offered improved inpatient or outpatient mental health care, 96% of beneficiaries in Medicare HMOs reported having prescription drug coverage in 1997 (Murray and Eppig 2002).

These added benefits and the rising costs of health care attracted many Medicare beneficiaries to HMOs, with enrollments rising from 3% of the Medicare population in 1991 to 18.4% in 1998 (Murray and Eppig 2002). Only 8% of the Medicare HMO enrollees had a history of a psychiatric disorder (Colenda, Banazak, and Mickus 1998).

However, the rising costs of prescription drugs and changes in the methods of paying HMOs in 1997 began to reduce benefits and, eventually, enrollments. Before the payment changes began to take effect, the generosity of prescription drug coverage fell, with consumer cost sharing rising from 30% to 40% of the total cost from 1993 to 1998 (Briesacher, Stuart, and Shea 2002). Total enrollments in what are now called Medicare + Choice plans have dropped by over 1 million persons (Gold 2001).

In summary, older Americans have even less insurance coverage for mental health treatments than do younger persons. Medicare's coverage falls far short of what most employer plans provide, and only postretirement health insurance offers a reasonable supplement for mental health care. Recent reductions in access to all forms of supplemental insurance suggest older Americans will face even more difficult times in trying to get mental health care. While several recent proposals have been made to add a prescription drug benefit to Medicare and to create mental health parity within the Medicare program, little progress toward passage has been achieved (Shea 2003).

### Costs and Service Use

Although there have been a number of recent studies of the costs to society of certain individual mental illnesses (Greenberg et al. 1999; Pincus and Pettit 2001), there are no recent studies that specifically address total social costs of mental illnesses among older adults. The most complete study indicated that direct health care costs of mental illness in 1985 were \$42.5 billion, including \$12.8 billion in specialty institutions, \$10.6 billion in nursing homes, \$8.8 billion in general acute care hospitals, and \$10.3 billion in physician and other professional services, drugs, and support costs (Rice, Kellman, and Miller 1992). Another \$61.2 billion in indirect and related costs in 1985 were traced to mental illness. Rice, Kellman, and Miller (1992) calculated only the core costs (direct costs plus indirect mortality and morbidity costs) by age and gender. Their results indicate that in 1985, \$17.3 billion of core costs were for persons 65 and older, with more than two-thirds of this amount for women older than 65. For older adults, care in nursing homes constitutes the largest element of mental health care costs, since 90% of the older mentally ill population are in nursing homes (Lair and Lefkowitz 1990). In contrast, adults over the age of 65 represent only 11% of the population receiving inpatient care in specialty institutions and general hospitals. They represent less than 8% of the population receiving outpatient or partial care (Burns and Taube 1990).

Mark et al. (2000) estimate direct health care spending on mental illness (excluding Alzheimer's disease, some dementias, and a few other diagnoses) for 1987 and 1997. They find that spending on mental health rose from \$37.1 billion to \$73.4 billion during that time period, with 69% of spending in the specialty mental health sector. Mental health spending rose at an average of 7.1% per year, below the overall growth in health care spending of 8.2% per year (Mark et al. 2000).

Hospitals (29.5%) and independent practitioners (28.4%) represent the largest share of mental health spending by provider type, while home health (21.5% average annual growth rate [AAGR]) and prescription drugs (12.5% AAGR) were the fastest-growing components. Fifty-five percent (55%) of mental health spending was from public sources, approximately equally divided between federal and state/local governments. Medicare paid for about one-eighth of all mental health spending, while Medicaid and other state/local sources each paid for nearly one-fifth. Private insurance paid for 24% of total mental health spending, while consumer payments were 18%. Medicare and Medicaid spending are the fastest-growing payment sources, growing at 11.8% and 9.7% per year, respectively (Mark et al. 2000).

With the lack of comprehensive prescription drug coverage and the coverage restrictions on inpatient and outpatient mental health care in Medicare, it is not surprising that the estimates of spending on mental health care by older persons that are available suggest that such spending is small. As of 1999, the U.S. Surgeon General's Office reported that only about 5% of total Medicare spending is for care where the primary diagnosis is a mental disorder, and a significant portion of that is on behalf of younger individuals disabled by mental illness. However, this low level of spending understates the importance of mental illness for the cost of health care among older persons in several ways. Certainly, the structure of Medicare's benefits reduces access, and this reduces Medicare spending on mental health care. Furthermore, research clearly indicates that mental comorbidity has a significant impact on total spending and service use by older adults (Callahan, Kesteron, and Tierney 1997; Druss, Rohrbaugh, and Rosenheck 1999; Luber et al. 2001).

Most Medicare spending on mental health care is for inpatient services. In 1995 Medicare spent almost $3.5 billion in total on inpatient psychiatric care, with 53% of that total, or $1.85 billion, on behalf of Medicare beneficiaries age 65 and older. This is equal to approximately $5,600 per discharge for the 328,548 discharges that year (Cano et al. 1997). In 1999 inpatient services accounted for almost half of all Medicare mental health expenditures.

In 1992, Medicare Part B charges for mental health services totaled just $661 million, with $367 million of that total made on behalf of the slightly more than 800,000 persons over age 65 who used services. This represents just over $450 per service user over age 65 (Rosenbach and Ammering 1997). Several studies in the 1990s suggest that more older persons received outpatient mental health services. Demmler (1998) finds that outpatient ambulatory care services increased 15% among people over age 65, while overall psychiatric hospitalizations were declining. Olfson et al. (2002a) find that outpatient treatment rates for depression rose threefold among persons over age 65 from 1987 to 1997, and significant increases in outpatient psychotherapy were seen among adults age 55 to 64 (Olfson et al. 2002b). The U.S. Department of Health and Human Services reports that by 1998, Medicare Part B charges for mental health care were $1.2 billion, yet only $700 million of this was for outpatient services. Furthermore, in outpatient settings, older adults are still largely treated in the primary care sector, rather than in the specialty mental health sector; fewer than 3% of older adults report seeing a mental health professional (Lebowitz et al. 1997). Services for rural elderly are particularly lacking (Lambert and Agger 1995).

A significant amount of mental health costs for older people, however, occurs in nursing homes. The prevalence data on dementia and other mental disorders in nursing homes would suggest that at least half of the $92 billion spent on nursing home care in 2000 (Levit et al. 2002) is attributable to mental disorders, dwarfing spending in other areas. This amount would have to be adjusted even higher if mental comorbidity of nursing home residents is taken into account.

Although a majority of nursing home residents have a primary or secondary diagnosis of a mental disorder, there is substantial unmet need for mental health care in nursing homes. More than half of nursing homes lack access to psychiatric consulting services (Reichman et al. 1998). Data from the 1987 National Medical Expenditure Survey showed that fewer than one-fifth of nursing home residents with a mental disorder had received any treatment from a mental health specialist during their stay. Rates of treatment dropped significantly with increasing age (Shea, Streit, and Smyer 1994).

Under the Nursing Home Reform Act of 1987, nursing homes were required to screen persons seeking admission and residents for mental health needs and provide or direct persons to appropriate mental health services. According to the Center for Mental Health Services (Linkins et al. 2001), there appear to be significant shortcomings in state efforts to implement the Preadmission Screening and Annual Resident Review (PASARR), perhaps because of the costs of meeting the mandate (Shea, Smyer, and Streit 1993). Initial estimates suggest that while service use was beginning to increase in the 1990s, only a little more than one-third of nursing home residents with a mental illness had even a single mental health visit, with older residents and those in rural areas very unlikely to receive services (Shea, Smyer, and Russo 2000).

The bulk of spending for persons in nursing homes is borne by the Medicaid program, which pays for 48% of nursing home costs (Levit et al. 2002). Low Medicaid payment rates and the gaps in Medicare coverage mean that while payers provide funds for the institutionalization of older persons with a mental illness, they often fail to provide adequate funds for mental health services in nursing homes. Most Medicaid nursing home payment systems use a case mix adjustment based on resource utilization groups (RUGs). These systems adjust payments based on hours of nursing care, often failing to capture mental health therapy and pharmaceutical costs needed by persons with a mental illness (Fries et al. 1993).

Much of the recent growth in mental health spending overall has been in the area of prescription drugs. Prescription drug spending by Medicare beneficiaries has been rising rapidly at a rate of 10% to 20% per year (Briesacher, Stuart, and Shea 2002). Community dwelling Medicare beneficiaries with a self-reported mental illness spent $1,081 on prescription drugs in 1997, with 34% of that out of pocket. Medicaid was the largest third-party payer for these persons, paying for 28% of their prescription drugs. Prescription drug spending by these persons rose more than 40% from 1993 to 1997. Persons with Alzheimer's disease living in the community pay out of pocket for almost half of their prescription drug costs, which totaled $953 in 1997. The average Medicare beneficiary with a mental illness filled 32 prescriptions in 1997, while the average beneficiary with Alzheimer's disease filled 30 prescriptions (unpublished data from the Medicare Current Beneficiary Survey available from the authors).

While Medicare and Medicaid both pay for prescription drug costs for inpatients, there is substantial evidence that pharmaceutical treatment of older persons in nursing homes and hospitals is not optimal. Over half of all nursing facility residents are receiving a psychoactive drug, including 35% who are receiving an antidepressant, 21% receiving an antipsychotic, and 15% receiving an antianxiety drug (American Society of Consultant Pharmacists 2001). Koenig et al. (1997) find that only a low proportion of depressed elderly hospital patients are treated appropriately with antidepressants, and a similar finding occurs in nursing homes (Datto et al. 2002; Rovner 1993). Data from the 1980s suggested that nursing homes overmedicated some residents with antipsychotic medications (Avorn et al. 1989). Regulations from the 1987 Nursing Home Reform Act appear to have substantially reduced this practice (McKenzie et al. 1999).

An area of increased concern for mental health and aging is the growing number of older persons residing in assisted living facilities (ALFs). While nursing homes are required to have resident drug regimens reviewed monthly, assisted living facilities, which have a similar resident population, face no federal regulation. Becker, Stiles, and Schonfeld (2002) document that the proportion of ALF residents self-reporting anxiety and depression was more than twice the rate estimated by staff members.

Despite the fact that mental disorders are underdiagnosed and undertreated among the elderly, recent regulatory policy has focused primarily on suspected fraud and abuse in mental health services provided in partial hospitalization, nursing facilities, and the community. A series of reports by the Office of Inspector General (OIG), Department of Health and Human Services, determined that 32% of mental health services provided in nursing homes and 31% of mental health services provided in the community were medically unnecessary. The definition of medical necessity used by the OIG, however, conflicted with practice recommendations from medical professionals (Bartels, Dums, and Shea 2003).

Another important policy development is the growth of integrated delivery systems that incorporate mental health care for older adults. State and federal agencies are interested in how managed mental health care might work for older adults (Robinson, Crow, and Scallet 1998). Medicaid and private insurers have experimented with systems of "carving-out" or "carving-in" mental health benefits, often with significant cost savings but questionable impacts on quality of care (Bartels, Dums, and Shea 2003; Robinson, Crow, and Scallet 1998). Other approaches, such as Social/Health Maintenance Organizations and the Program for All-Inclusive Care for the Elderly (PACE), focus on a comprehensive array of services based on a long-term care model. Some researchers believe that integrated approaches like these could both improve care and save funds (Olfson, Sing, and Schlesin 1999).

Finally, mental health for older adults may be dramatically changed by a recent Supreme Court ruling. The *Olmstead* decision will require states to reevaluate many persons residing in institutions to identify whether they can be served in a less restrictive outpatient setting and revamp their mental health systems to accommodate these changes (Bartels, Dums, and Shea 2003).

### Summary

In summary, the current structure of public and private insurance for mental health care of older adults, with strict limits on use of outpatient care, high coinsurance, and low reimbursement levels, limits the use of outpatient services and prescription drugs. More complete coverage of some inpatient care is available, but limitations on acute care hospitalization generally encourage largely custodial care in long-term care settings. This care, primarily for meeting daily living or personal needs, is delivered by personnel without professional mental health skills or training. Since payers do not explicitly target payments for mental health care in the nursing home, little quality mental health care is given in the setting where many older persons with a mental illness reside. Furthermore, the costs of nursing home care and the costs of mental health services in the community fall heavily on patients and their families. (See also ECONOMIC HARDSHIP MEA-

SURES IN THE OLDER POPULATION; ECONOMIC STATUS OF OLDER MEN AND WOMEN; FRAILTY PLANNING; GUARDIANSHIP; HOMELESSNESS AMONG OLDER ADULTS; MENTAL HEALTH AMONG OLDER ADULTS.)

### Organizations

Center for Mental Health Services, U.S. Department of Health and Human Services
Mental Health Policy Resource Center
National Citizens' Coalition for Nursing Home Reform
National Institute of Mental Health—Mental Disorders of the Aging Branch
National Institute of Mental Health—Public Inquiries Office
National Institute on Aging—Alzheimer's Disease Education and Referral Center (ADEAR)
National Institute on Aging—NIA Information

### Suggested Reading

McGuire, Thomas, and Richard Frank. 1999. "Economics and Mental Health." National Bureau of Economic Research Working Paper #7052. Cambridge, MA: NBER.

### References

American Society of Consultant Pharmacists. 2001. *Nursing Facility Resident Use of Psychoactive Medications Fact Sheet.* Alexandria, VA: Author.

Avorn J., P. Dreyer, K. Connelly, and S.B. Soumerai. 1989. "Use of Psychoactive Medication and the Quality of Care in Rest Homes. Findings and Policy Implications of a Statewide Study." *New England Journal of Medicine* 320: 227–32.

Bartels, S.J., and C.C. Colenda. 1998. "Mental Health Services for Alzheimer's Disease: Current Trends in Reimbursement and Public Policy, and the Future under Managed Care." *American Journal of Geriatric Psychiatry* 6: S85–S100.

Bartels, Stephen J., Arrica R. Dums, and Dennis G. Shea. 2003. "Mental Health Policy and Aging." In *Mental Health Services: A Public Health Perspective*, ed. Bruce Lubotsky Levin and John Petrila. New York: Oxford University Press.

Becker, M., P. Stiles, and L. Schonfeld. 2002. "Assisted Living: The New Frontier for Mental Health Care?" *Generations* 26: 72–77.

Briesacher, B., B. Stuart, and D. Shea. 2002. "Drug Coverage for Medicare Beneficiaries: Why Protection May Be in Jeopardy." Issue Brief 505. New York: The Commonwealth Fund.

Burns, B.J., and C.A. Taube. 1990. "Mental Health Services in General Medical Care and Nursing Homes." In *Mental Health Policy for Older Americans: Protecting Minds at Risk*, ed. B. Fogel, A. Furino, and G. Gottlieb. Washington, DC: American Psychiatric Press.

Callahan, C., J. Kesteron, and W. Tierney. 1997. "Association of Symptoms of Depression with Diagnostic Test Charges among Older Adults." *Annals of Internal Medicine* 126: 426–32.

Cano, C., K. Hennessy, J. Warren, and J. Lubitz. 1997. "Medicare Part A Utilization and Expenditures for Psychiatric Services: 1995." *Health Care Financing Review* 18: 177–93.

Colenda, C.C., D. Banazak, and M. Mickus. 1998. "Mental Health Services in Managed Care: Quality Questions Remain." *Geriatrics* 53: 49–64.

Datto, C.J., D.W. Oslin, J.E. Streim, S.M. Scheinthal, S. Di Filippo, and I.R. Katz. 2002. "Pharmacology of Treatment of Depression in Nursing Home Residents: A Mental Health Services Perspective." *Journal of Geriatric Psychiatry and Neurology* 15(3).

Demmler, J. 1998. *Utilization of Specialty Mental Health Services by Older Adults: National and State Profiles.* Alexandria, VA: National Technical Assistance Center for State Mental Health Planning.

Druss, B.G., R.M. Rohrbaugh, and R.A. Rosenheck. 1999. "Depressive Symptoms and Health Costs in Older Medical Patients." *American Journal of Psychiatry* 156: 477–79.

Fries, B.E., D.R. Mehr, D. Schneider, W.J. Foley, and R. Burke. 1993. "Mental Dysfunction and Resource Use in Nursing Homes." *Medical Care* 31: 898–920.

Gold, M. 2001. "Medicare + Choice: An Interim Report Card." *Health Affairs* 20: 120–38.

Greenberg, P.E., T. Sisitsky, R. Kessler, S.N. Finkelstein, E.R. Berndt, J.R. Davidson, J.C. Ballenger, and A.J. Fyer. 1999. "The Economic Burden of Anxiety Disorders in the 1990s." *Journal of Clinical Psychiatry* 60: 427–35.

HCFA. 2000. *Medicare 2000: 35 Years of Improving Americans' Health and Security*. Washington, DC: Health Care Financing Administration, Department of Health and Human Services.

Kaiser Family Foundation and Hewitt Associates. 2002. *The Current State of Retiree Health Benefits*. Menlo Park, CA: Henry J. Kaiser Family Foundation.

Koenig, H.G., L.K. George, B.L. Peterson, and C.F. Piepff. 1997. "Depression in Medically Ill Hospitalized Older Adults: Prevalence, Correlates, and Course of Symptoms Based on Six Diagnostic Schemes." *American Journal of Psychiatry* 154: 1376–83.

Lair, T., and D. Lefkowitz. 1990. "Mental Health and Functional Status of Residents of Nursing and Personal Care Homes." In *National Medical Expenditure Survey Research Findings* 7. Rockville, MD: Agency for Health Care Policy and Research.

Lambert, D., and M. Agger. 1995. "Access of Rural AFDC Medicaid Beneficiaries to Mental Health Services." *Health Care Financing Review* 17: 133–45.

Lebowitz, B.D., J.L. Pearson, L.S. Schneider, C.F. Reynolds III, G.S. Alexopoulos, M.L. Bruce, Y. Conwell, I.R. Katz, B.S. Meyers, M.F. Morrison, J. Mossey, G. Niederehe, and P. Parmelee. 1997. "Diagnosis and Treatment of Depression in Late Life." Consensus Statement Update. *Journal of the American Medical Association* 278(14): 1186–90.

Levit, K., C. Smith, C. Cowan, H. Lazenby, and A. Martin. 2002. "Inflation Spurs Health Spending." *Health Affairs* 21: 172–81.

Linkins, K., G. Robinson, J. Karp, S. Cooper, J. Liu, and S. Bush. 2001. *Screening for Mental Illness in Nursing Facility Applicants: Understanding Federal Requirements*. SAMHSA Publication No. (SMA) 01-3543. Rockville, MD: Center for Mental Health Services, Substance Abuse and Mental Health Services Administration.

Luber, M.P., et al. 2001. "Depression and Service Utilization in Elderly Primary Care Patients." *American Journal of Geriatric Psychiatry* 9(2): 169–76.

Mark, T., R. Coffey, E. King, H. Harwood, D. McKusick, J. Genuardi, J. Dilonardo, and J. Buck. 2000. "Spending on Mental Health and Substance Abuse Treatment, 1987–1997." *Health Affairs* 19: 108–20.

McKenzie, D., J. Mullooly, B. McFarland, J. Semradek, and L. McCamant. 1999. "Changes in Antipsychotic Drug Use Following Shifts in Policy." *Research on Aging* 21: 304–37.

Murray, L.A., and F.J. Eppig. 2002. "Insurance Trends for the Medicare Population, 1991–1999." *Health Care Financing Review* 23: 9–15.

Office of the Inspector General (OIG). 1996. *Mental Health Services in Nursing Facilities* (OIG-02-91-00860). Rockville, MD: OIG, Department of Health and Human Services.

Olfson, M., S. Marcus, B. Druss, L. Elinson, T. Tanielian, and H. Pincus. 2002a. "National Trends in the Outpatient Treatment of Depression." *Journal of the American Medical Association* 287: 203–9.

Olfson, M., S. Marcus, B. Druss, and H. Pincus. 2002b. "National Trends in the Use of Outpatient Psychotherapy." *American Journal of Psychiatry* 159: 1914–20.

Olfson, M., M. Sing, and H. Schlesinger. 1999. "Mental Health/Medical Care Offsets: Opportunities for Managed Care." *Health Affairs* 18: 79–90.

Pincus, H.A., and A.R. Pettit. 2001. "The Societal Costs of Chronic Major Depression." *Journal of Clinical Psychiatry* 62 (Suppl. 6): 5–9.

Reichman, W.E., A.C. Coyne, S. Borson, A.E. Negron, B.W. Rovner, R.J. Pelchat, K.M. Sakauye,

P. Katz, M. Cantillon, and R.M. Hamer. 1998. "Psychiatric Consultation in the Nursing Home." *American Journal of Geriatric Psychiatry* 6: 320–27.

Rice, D.P., S. Kellman, and L. Miller 1992. "The Economic Losts of Mental Illness." *Hospital and Community Psychiatry* 43(12).

Rice, D.P., and L.S. Miller. 1995. "The Economic Burden of Affective Disorders." *British Journal of Psychiatry* 27: 34–42.

Robinson, G., S. Crow, and L. Scallet. 1998. "Managed Care Policy: Meeting the Mental Health Needs of the Aged?" *Generations* 22: 58–62.

Rosenbach, M., and C. Ammering. 1997. "Trends in Medicare Part B Mental Health Utilization and Expenditures: 1987–92." *Health Care Financing Review* 18: 19–42.

Rovener, B.W. 1993. "Depression and Increased Risk of Mortality in the Nursing Home Patient." *American Journal of Medicine* 94.

Shea, D. 2003. "Parity and Prescriptions: Policy Developments and Their Implications for Mental Health in Later Life." *Generations* 26: 83–89.

Shea, D., M. Smyer, and P. Russo. 2000. "Use of Mental Health Services by Persons with a Mental Illness in Nursing Facilities: Initial Impacts of OBRA 87." *Journal of Aging and Health* 12(4): 589–607.

Shea, D., M. Smyer, and A. Strait: 1993. "Mental Health Services for Nursing Home Residents: What Will It Cost?" *Journal of Mental Health Administration* 28(3).

Shea, D., A. Streit, and M. Smyer. 1994. "Use of Specialist Mental Health Services by Nursing Home Residents." *Health Services Research* 29(2): 169–85.

Stuart, B., D. Shea, and B. Briesacher. 2001. "Dynamics in Drug Coverage of Medicare Beneficiaries: Finders, Losers, Switchers." *Health Affairs* 20: 86–99.

Sturm, R., and R.L. Pacula. 1999. "State Mental Health Parity Laws: Cause or Consequence of Differences in Use." *Health Affairs* 18: 182–92.

*Michael A. Smyer and Dennis G. Shea*

**MINORITY OLDER ADULTS,** persons age 65 and older who belong to ethnic groups regarded as social and cultural minorities. Minorities have often experienced differential and unequal treatment. Members of ethnic groups share a distinct sense of history and bonds of attachment. Minorities frequently regard themselves as objects of collective discrimination by reason of their identifiable cultural distinctions or race (Markides, Liang, and Jackson 1990).

What makes the difference in being considered a minority therefore is not solely numerical but rather a group's sense of lack of power and dominance. As applied to aging, minority status influences an individual's position in the social structure and therefore impacts his or her experiences over the life course. Currently in U.S. society, African Americans, Asian Americans and Pacific Islanders (Asian/Pacific Islanders), Hispanics, and Native Americans are considered minority populations. The importance of making the distinction between minority elderly populations and the majority elderly population (non-Hispanic Whites) is evident when examining the disparities in health and income that exist across our older adult population. While the elderly population as a whole has experienced improvements in health, mortality, and socioeconomic status, disproportionate levels of poor health, chronic illness, functional difficulties, marginal incomes, and poverty persist among minority populations. Accordingly, Hooyman and Kiyak (1999) argue that minority status is associated with a differential experience across the life span, including greater risk of economic insecurity, poor health, and social isolation in old age.

Currently, approximately 13% of older persons are members of a minority population.

By 2050 it is estimated that 35% of the older adult population will be members of a minority group (U.S. Bureau of the Census 1992). With the increasing awareness of the growing diversity among the age 65 and older population has come an increased interest in the experience of minority populations and the importance of policy and program interventions that will improve their health and socioeconomic status. The health and economic status of minority populations is important to consider not only because minority older persons will be more represented among the ranks of the elderly but also because of the impact that these two domains can have on the experience of later life.

### Demographics: The Graying of Minority Populations

The aging of the U.S. population has been well documented. Over the next five decades the population of individuals age 65 and older is expected to double from its current size of nearly 35 million individuals to 70 million individuals (U.S. Bureau of the Census 1996a). Somewhat less well known is the increasing racial/ethnic diversity that will accompany the aging of the population. While the non-Hispanic White population represents a larger proportion of the population age 65 and older, they are growing more slowly than other groups. For example, between 1990 and 1997 the proportion of the population age 65 and older grew more than five times as fast among Hispanics as among non-Hispanic Whites (National Center for Health Statistics [NCHS] 1999). Looking at individual ethnic minority groups that comprise the elderly population between 2000 and 2050, the African American elderly population is expected to increase 200%; the Hispanic population will increase 635%; the Asian/Pacific Islander population will increase 537%; and the Native American population will increase 260%. In comparison, the non-Hispanic White population will increase 80%. Results from the 2000 census show that there are currently a little over 29 million non-Hispanic Whites age 65+, 1.7 million Hispanics, 2.8 million African Americans, 800,000 Asian/Pacific Islanders, and 140,000 Native Americans age 65 and older (U.S. Bureau of the Census 2001). Between 2000 and 2050 the proportion of African Americans among the older adult population will increase from 8% to 10%. The proportion of Asian/Pacific Islanders age 65+ will increase from 2% to 8%. And the proportion of Hispanics in the elderly population will increase from 4% to 16%.

Not only will the proportion of minority group members among the population 65+ increase, but the proportion of elderly within each minority population will also increase. For example, currently persons age 65 and older constitute 8% of the African American population. By 2030 it is expected they will represent 17% of the African American population. The same is true for Asian/Pacific Islander and Hispanic populations. Asian Pacific/Islander elders currently comprise 7% of the Asian population but will represent 16% of the population by 2030. Hispanic older persons, who now represent 6% of the total Hispanic population, will represent 14% of the Hispanic population by 2030 (U.S. Bureau of the Census 1996b). Therefore, over the next several decades we will witness not only an increase in the diversity of the total U.S. elderly population but also the aging of minority populations.

### Health Status of Minority Populations

The bulk of the literature on health disparities has focused on the experience of African American elderly. Studies on Black/White comparisons in health date back to the 1960s.

For the most part they have focused on mortality and morbidity, although more recently studies include self-rated health and functioning. The mortality disparity between African Americans and non-Hispanic Whites continue to persist, except at the oldest ages, that is 85 and older, there appears to be a racial crossover and an African American advantage (Markides and Black 1996). Death rates for all causes of death are higher among African Americans at all ages except those over age 85 and older, where death rates for all causes are lower among African Americans when compared to non-Hispanic Whites (NCHS 1999).

Studies focusing on morbidity and prevalence of disease find that the African American elderly population has high prevalence rates for arthritis, diabetes, and heart disease as well as a high occurrence of disability and difficulty in functioning. The impact of disease is also greater for African Americans; for example, those members of the African American population with high blood pressure are more likely to have greater cardiovascular and renal damage than non-Hispanic Whites (Clark and Gibson 1997). In addition, African American older persons report higher levels of disability and are 1.3 times more likely than older non-Hispanic Whites to be unable to do certain activities, and 1.5 times more likely to be unable to perform one or more activities of daily living (ADLs) (NCHS 1999). National data also find that African American elderly are more likely to rate their health status as poor compared to non-Hispanic White older people (NCHS 1999).

Like older African Americans, elderly Hispanics experience health disadvantages relative to non-Hispanic Whites. A consistent finding in the literature is the high prevalence of diabetes found among the population. Hispanics are two to five times more likely to have diabetes than the general population. The high prevalence of diabetes is of particular concern because of diabetes-related complications that often impact functioning and lead to disability including lower extremity amputations, vascular disease, blindness, and stroke (Hazuda and Espino 1997). In fact, the proportion of Hispanics with major activity limitation and lower body disability is higher than that reported for non-Hispanic Whites nationally. Eighty-five percent (85%) of elderly Hispanics report having at least one chronic condition, and 45% of the population report having some ADL limitation (Espino 1993). Accordingly, Hooyman and Kiyak (1999) argue that, among Hispanics, physiological aging tends to precede chronological aging, with Hispanics in their late forties having health profiles similar to non-Hispanic Whites who are age 65.

While there is a tradition of research on African Americans and Hispanics, the same cannot be said for Asian/Pacific Islanders. Inclusion of Asian/Pacific Islanders in the literature on health disparities did not occur until fairly recently, around the mid-1980s. The available data find that the Asian/Pacific Islander population has a relatively high prevalence of heart disease, hypertension, certain cancers, anemia, and diabetes (Wykle and Kaskel 1994). While the bulk of the research in this area does not disaggregate the Asian/Pacific Islander population but rather "lumps" all Asian groups together, there is some evidence of within-group differences. Japanese older persons are disadvantaged relative to other groups for heart disease, while older Koreans appear to be disadvantaged for diabetes and chronic kidney disease (Kagawa-Singer, Hikoyeda, and Tanjasiri 1997).

As with Asian/Pacific Islanders, the data on Native Americans are also limited. The available data reveal high rates of heart disease, hypertension, rheumatoid disease, and cancer among Native American populations. Older Native Americans have higher incidence than their non-Hispanic White counterparts of accidents, tuberculosis, liver and kidney disease, influenza, and pneumonia (Hooyman and Kiyak 1999). Additionally, as with other minority populations, Native Americans are disadvantaged for diabetes and diabetes-related complications relative to non-Hispanic Whites. Nearly 20% of Native Americans are estimated to have diabetes, and there is evidence that the incidence of diabetic lower-extremity amputation increases with age among Native Americans. It is estimated that nearly 75% of the Native American elderly population have ADL limitations (Kramer 1997).

### Economic Status of Older Minority Populations

One of the primary explanations for the disparities in health experienced by minority elderly populations is the disproportionate levels of poverty and low incomes found among them. While poverty rates have declined among the older population over the last few decades, pockets of poverty and near poverty still exist among minority populations (U.S. Bureau of the Census 2001). Currently, while the overall poverty rate of the older population is 10.5%, the rate across the elderly population varies greatly. Census data find that among the population age 65 and over in 2000, 8.3% of non-Hispanic Whites were living below the poverty level, compared to 22.3% of African Americans, 18.8% of Hispanics, and 10.3% of Asian/Pacific Islanders (U.S. Bureau of the Census 2001). Near-poverty levels are equally compelling. The near-poverty level, that is, 125% of poverty, among the total population age 65 and older is 16.9%. While the near-poverty rate for non-Hispanic White elderly is 14.4%, near-poverty levels for African American older persons is 31.4%, 30.3% for Hispanic elderly, and 18.9% for Asian/Pacific Islanders in 2000, according to the U.S. Census Bureau (2000).

As with poverty, median income also varies greatly across the elderly population by ethnic minority status and gender. The median income for elderly non-Hispanic White males is $18,980, and for non-Hispanic White females, $10,904. Hispanic males age 65 and older have a median income of $11,509, and older Hispanic women, $6,877. Older African American males' median income is $11,331, and older African American women, $7,798 (U.S. Bureau of the Census 1998). Tied to disparities in income are disparities in sources of income. Examination of sources of income across the population find that minority elderly populations are more reliant on Social Security and less likely than non-Hispanic Whites to have income from assets and private pensions. It is estimated that while 43% of non-Hispanic Whites have pensions, only 32% of African Americans and 20% of Hispanics do (Social Security Administration 1998). Minority elders' higher rates of poverty and greater reliance on Social Security for income in old age are linked to their overrepresentation in service industry jobs and labor-intensive occupations that often do not offer pensions or other retiree benefits across their life course. In addition, many members of the current cohort of older persons have experienced segregation in education and employment, institutional racism, and glass ceilings that have precluded economic advancement (Villa 1998).

### Implications for the Retirement Experience of Elderly Minority Populations

What are the implications of poor health and economic vulnerability for the retirement experience of minority populations? According to Hudson (2002), elderly minority individuals, in particular women, "find their work/retirement experience painfully and often diametrically opposite those of many Whites, especially White men" (1). Hudson's observations are based on the experience of minority workers, who, he maintains, are more likely than non-Hispanic Whites to be forced out of the labor market due to their inability to secure or maintain employment but at the same time are less able to retire because of inadequate savings and pension benefits. In their study of pathways to retirement, utilizing the Health and Retirement Survey (HRS), Flippen and Tienda (2002) find that Hispanic and African Americans are more vulnerable to involuntary job loss in their preretirement years and once unemployed are more likely than non-Hispanic Whites to experience protracted unemployment. They hold that this is at least partially attributable to life course inequalities experienced by minority populations.

Because minority populations during their prime-age working years are more likely to be employed in low-skill occupations and in small firms and industries that are vulnerable to downsizing, they are vulnerable to job dislocation and involuntary pathways out of the labor market when they approach preretirement age. Taken together, these findings highlight the importance of rethinking further increases in the age of eligibility for Social Security. Minority elderly populations are highly reliant upon Social Security, largely because of involuntary job loss, labor market difficulties experiences throughout their life course, and lack of private pension coverage. Therefore, Social Security remains an important safety net for ensuring that the inequality in income experienced by older ethnic minorities is not further exacerbated. (See also AGING AMERICA; ECONOMIC STATUS OF OLDER MEN AND WOMEN; HEALTH AND LONGEVITY; MARKETING TO MATURE ADULTS; OLD-AGE PROVISIONS AND ECONOMIC STATUS; OLDER AMERICANS ACT.)

### References

Clark, D.O., and R.C. Gibson. 1997. "Race, Age, Chronic Disease, and Disability." In *Minorities, Aging and Health*, ed. K.S. Markides and M.R. Miranda. Thousand Oaks, CA: Sage.

Espino, D. 1993. "Hispanic Elderly and Long-Term Care: Implications for Ethnically Sensitive Services." In *Ethnic Elderly and Long Term Care*, ed. C. Barresi and D. Stull. New York: Springer.

Flippen, C., and M. Tienda. 2002. "Workers of Color and Pathways to Retirement." *Public Policy and Aging Report* 12(3): 9–12.

Hazuda, H.P., and D.V. Espino. 1997. "Aging, Chronic Disease, and Physical Disability in Hispanic Elderly." In *Minorities, Aging and Health*, ed. K.S. Markides and M.R. Miranda. Thousand Oaks, CA: Sage.

Hooyman, N., and H.A. Kiyak. 1999. *Social Gerontology: Multidisciplinary Perspective*. Boston, MA: Allyn and Bacon.

Hudson, R. 2002. "Getting Ready and Getting Credit." *Public Policy and Aging Report* 12(3): 1–2.

Kagawa-Singer, M., N. Hikoyeda, and S.P. Tanjasiri. 1997. "Aging, Chronic Conditions, and Physical Disabilities in Asian and Pacific Islander Americans." In *Minorities, Aging and Health*, ed. K.S. Markides and M.R. Miranda. Thousand Oaks, CA: Sage.

Kramer, J. 1997. "Chronic Disease in American Indian Populations." In *Minorities, Aging and Health*, ed. K.S. Markides and M.R. Miranda. Thousand Oaks, CA: Sage.

Markides, K., and S.A. Black. 1996. "Race, Ethnicity, and Aging: The Impact of Inequality." In *Handbook of Aging and the Social Sciences*, ed. R.H. Binstock and L.K. George. 4th ed. San Diego, CA: Academic Press.

Markides, K., J. Liang, and J. Jackson. 1990. "Race, Ethnicity, and Aging: Conceptual and Methodological Issues." In *Handbook of Aging and the Social Sciences*, ed. R.H. Binstock and L.K. George. 3rd ed. New York: Academic Press.

Markides, K., and C. Mindel. 1987. *Aging and Ethnicity*. Newbury Park, CA: Sage.

National Center for Health Statistics (NCHS). 1999. *Health, United States. 1999*. Hyattsville, MD: U.S. Department of Health and Human Services.

Social Security Administration (SSA). 1998. *Income of the Population 55 or Older*. Washington, DC: GPO.

U.S. Bureau of the Census. 1992. *Population Projections of the United States, by Age, Sex, Race, and Hispanic Origin: 1992 to 2050*. Washington, DC: GPO.

U.S. Bureau of the Census. 1996a. *Population Projections of the United States by Age, Sex, Race, and Hispanic Origin: 1995–2050*. Washington, DC: GPO.

U.S. Bureau of the Census. 1996b. "65+ in the United States." *Current Population Reports, Special Studies*. P23–190. Washington, DC: GPO.

U.S. Bureau of the Census. 1998. *Money Income in the United States*. Washington, DC: GPO.

U.S. Bureau of the Census. 2001. *Poverty in the United States: 2000*. Washington, DC: GPO.

Villa, V.M. 1998. "Aging Policy and the Experience of Older Minorities." In *New Directions in Old Age Policies*, ed. J. Steckenride and T. Parrott. Albany, NY: SUNY Press.

Wykle, M., and B. Kaskel. 1994. "Increasing the Longevity of Minority Older Adults through Improved Health Status." In *Minority Elders: Five Goals toward Building a Public Policy Base*, ed. J.S. Jackson. Washington, DC: Gerontological Society of America.

*Valentine M. Villa*

**MORTGAGE INSTRUMENTS,** written, publicly recorded documents that provide the terms for financing real estate interests and secure payment of the mortgage debt incurred. Because real estate is a high-priced commodity, buyers often must use borrowed funds in addition to their equity to finance the transaction. In order to borrow, the borrowers must give the lender a mortgage and a promissory note. A promissory note is a security for the loan in which the borrower makes a personal promise to repay the loans. The mortgage is a legal instrument giving the lender a contingent claim against the real property in case of default. Mortgages are recorded following the closing of escrow and are part of a public record. For most people, the purchase of a home is their largest single investment, and home purchases usually require a mortgage. The type of mortgage selected is an important financing decision in the home purchasing (or refinancing) process.

Decisions regarding financing require an understanding of the types of mortgages that are available, and decisions made in later life especially impact retirement, financial planning issues, and future health care concerns.

### Fixed Rate Mortgages

The most common financing used by residential borrowers is a *fixed rate mortgage*. The interest rate is fixed, a repayment period is specified, and the monthly payments are equal over the life of the loan. Unless otherwise specified, the fixed rate mortgage allows the borrower to prepay the outstanding principal before the maturity date. The constant monthly payments of a fixed rate mortgage make it an ideal instrument in periods when interest rate inflation is expected, as the borrower will actually repay the loan in cheaper dollars than borrowed. Its chief disadvantage is that fixed mortgage payments generally limit the amount that can be borrowed because they are calculated as a percentage of income today, rather than accounting for a presumption of increasing income (although the opposite can be true after retirement). Thus, people can generally qualify for a larger loan if the initial mortgage payments are smaller, and a number of different mortgages have been introduced as alternatives to fixed rate mortgages. The most popular of these alternative mortgages is the *adjustable rate mortgage* (ARM).

### Adjustable Rate Mortgages

Unlike fixed rate loans, flexible rate mortgages have variable interest rates that fluctuate according to the movement of some predetermined index. The index, to a large extent, represents the actual cost of funds to lenders. Widely used indices include the Federal Home Loan Bank Board Eleventh District cost of funds index, which includes the average mortgage rates for major lenders on existing homes. The Federal Home Loan Bank Board cost of funds is based on interest and dividends paid or accrued on the thrift institutions' liabilities. These indices are usually less volatile than the Treasury indices, which may be for six-month, one-year, or three-year Treasury notes.

In addition to indexing, a typical ARM also contains other features, such as margin, adjustment periods, and interest rate caps. A margin is a fixed percentage of interest that is added to the index to determine the interest rate on the ARM: margin + index rate = ARM interest rate. For example, given a 2.5% margin and an index rate of 3.5%, the interest rate on the loan would be 6%. If the index rate increased to 6% at the next scheduled adjustment, the new rate on the ARM would be 8.5%. The margin could be considered a risk premium required to compensate the lender for uncertainty in the market. Although margins vary among lenders, borrowers should avoid loans with margins greater than 3%.

Adjustment periods, the period between interest rate corrections for an ARM, usually range from 1 to 36 months. There is no pure ARM in which rates are continuously adjusted; the closest is the monthly adjusted loan. Another feature of the ARM is the interest rate cap, which limits the maximum amount of adjustment and includes periodic and life-of-the-loan caps. These caps provide the borrower with an added incentive to choose an ARM by protecting the borrower from excessive volatility in interest rates. The caps offered by savings and loan institutions or commercial banks vary from 1% to 3%, with a high of 6% for a life-of-the-loan cap.

*Teasers* are a feature to which borrowers should pay attention. A teaser is the initial discount rate offered on all ARMs and represents the spread between a fixed rate mortgage and the initial rate on an ARM. Teasers are primarily used to entice borrowers to select ARMs instead of fixed rate mortgages. Borrowers must evaluate the teaser and margin together, since lenders are likely to use margins to compensate for the teaser rate offered to borrowers. A lower teaser rate can cost the borrower more in the future if the loan carries a high margin, because the rate will be higher on future adjustments. It is normal to observe discounts on ARMs between 1.5% and 2% below the fixed rate market, and some mortgage lenders offer ARMs at even lower rates.

A *step loan* is an adjustable rate mortgage that adjusts only once during its term. Because rates on step loan mortgages are generally higher than the rates on standard adjustable rate mortgages, they are probably not appropriate for older consumers or anyone with a fixed income.

*Convertible adjustable rate mortgages* (CARMs) offer the ability to refinance with a fixed rate mortgage without the cost of refinancing. This loan begins as an adjustable rate mortgage and may be converted to a fixed rate mortgage during a designated period after the first year. The cost of conversion is a nominal fee, and the converted loan has a new term and a rate comparable to that of other current fixed rate loans. ARMs, as indicated, have lower initial rates than fixed rate mortgages, which allow the borrower to qualify for larger loans. The existence of the caps also provides the borrower some protection against excessive increases in interest rates. Borrowers should, however, be concerned about the negative amortization aspects of ARMs. Negative amortization is the result of insufficient monthly payments, in the presence of payment caps, to cover the accrued interest on the loan. These payment shortages may eventually cause the unpaid balance to be greater than the original loan amount. Given the complexity of ARMs, it is particularly important that prospective older borrowers understand all aspects of ARMs before choosing them.

### Graduated Payment Mortgages

*Graduated payment mortgages* (GPMs) are generally not appropriate for older persons, since GPMs equate the expected increase in an individual's income with gradual increases in mortgage payments. Renegotiable rate mortgages (RRMs), or rollover mortgages, have characteristics similar to a fixed rate, level payment mortgage. These mortgages are usually amortized over 30 years, but there is a "balloon payment" due every 3 to 5 years. This means that the outstanding principal balance is due at that point, although the borrower does not have to come with cash to pay it. The amount of the balloon payment is refinanced by the lender. The originator of RRMs on single-family homes must comply with a number of regulations, including automatic renewal, which requires the lender to "roll over" this debt into a new loan at the current market rate of interest. This rate of interest is negotiable and must be agreed upon by both the borrower and lender. The borrower is also free to have another lender refinance the balloon amount if its rate is more competitive. In addition, no discount points or fees are allowed when refinancing the balloon payment with the original lender and prepayment is available without penalty at the time of, or after, the first adjustment. This mortgage is a good option for the short-term, elderly borrower who is averse to risk. It allows a borrower to "lock in" a rate of interest for a considerable period of time, while not initially paying as high a rate as that being charged on traditional fixed rate mortgages.

*Price level adjusted mortgages* (PLAMs) are the most recent innovation in alternative mortgage instruments. PLAMs are especially useful in high inflationary periods. These mortgages guarantee the real return to lenders and borrowers and are beneficial to both parties by keeping real payments constant over the term of the loan. The mechanics of adjustment are quite simple. PLAMs base the initial mortgage payments on a real interest rate. The monthly payments and the unpaid balance on principal are periodically adjusted to the current inflation rate as determined by the consumer price index. Since the payments and outstanding balance are adjusted, the borrower is only charged the current market rate. The lender, on the other hand, is also guaranteed to receive the real return above inflation. PLAMs, because of their inflation adjustments, do not require an accurate forecasting of future inflation.

Furthermore, PLAMs may help ease housing affordability problems. Because of the difficulty in predicting expected inflation forces, mortgage lenders charge higher initial rates to compensate for market uncertainty. The lower payments allow for a larger amount to be borrowed than would otherwise be affordable to the borrower. However, numerous problems plague the PLAM. Since the loan balance is adjusted for inflation, the related increase in payments may become a serious burden if income does not also adjust for inflation. Also, if the value of the property under the mortgage fails to increase at the rate of inflation, the borrower's likelihood of default increases. With a PLAM, equity accumulates more slowly than with most other mortgage instruments. Finally, the total cost of the loan at the beginning of the term is unknown to the borrower since it is based on forecasts.

### Reverse Annuity Mortgages

For retired persons, especially for individuals with large home equity and few (if any) cash assets, reverse annuity mortgages (RAMs) are attractive financing alternatives. In fact, RAMs are designed primarily for retired homeowners. Under this plan, the owner can free up the home equity without having to dispose of the property. The loan is ultimately repaid from the sale of the borrower's residence. The inflows and outflows for a RAM are in reverse of a traditional mortgage loan—its debt is rising and the equity is falling. The reverse annuity borrower basically receives either a series of monthly payments over the term of the loan or a lump sum at settlement, which will be repaid with a large cash repayment upon the sale of the residence, or at a specific date, or the death of the owner-borrower. Payments received are generally not taxable, and interest charged on RAMs is not taxable until it is actually paid. To reduce the risk in a reverse annuity mortgage, the lending institution usually limits the loan to a certain percentage of the owner's equity in the residence. There are several different types of RAMs, including a credit account from which the borrower can withdraw on a needed basis, a lump-sum cash advance, or a monthly cash payment. In essence, reverse annuity mortgages are a financing alternative by which retired homeowners can take equity out of their homes. (See also BANKING SERVICES FOR THE MATURE MARKET; CONDOMINIUMS; COOPERATIVE OWNERSHIP IN HOUSING; HOMEOWNERSHIP; PREDATORY LENDING; REVERSE MORTGAGES.)

#### Suggested Readings

Elred, Gary W. 2003. *106 Mortgage Secrets All Borrowers Must Know—But Lenders Won't Tell.* New York: John Wiley & Sons.

Garton-Good, Julie. 1999. *All about Mortgages: Insider Tips for Financing and Refinancing Your Home.* 2nd ed. Chicago: Dearborn Publishing.

Scholen, Ken. 1998. *Reverse Mortgages for Beginners: A Consumer Guide to Every Homeowner's Retirement Nest Egg.* St. Paul, MN: NCHEC.

#### References

Phillips, Richard A., and James H. VanderHoff. 1994. "Alternative Mortgage Instruments, Qualification Constraints and the Demand for Housing: An Empirical Analysis." *Journal of the American Real Estate & Urban Economics Association* (Fall): 453–77.

Shilling, James D. 2002. *Real Estate.* 13th ed. Cincinnati, OH: South-Western/Thomson Learning.

*Andrew Quang Do*

**Table 1**
**Net Assets of Mutual Funds as of January 2003 (billions of dollars)**

| | |
|---|---|
| Stock Funds | 2,597.4 |
| Hybrid Funds | 324.4 |
| Taxable Bond Funds | 811.5 |
| Municipal Bond Funds | 326.7 |
| Taxable Money Market Funds | 1,991.0 |
| Tax-Free Money Market Funds | 285.5 |
| **Total** | **6,336.5** |

*Source*: Investment Company Institute 2003.

MUTUAL FUNDS, investment companies that raise money by selling shares to the public and investing the proceeds in other securities. The value of mutual fund shares fluctuates with the value of the securities in its portfolio. Professional managers select, purchase, trade, and manage diversified portfolios of stocks, bonds, money market funds, and/or other securities to achieve the financial objectives promised to the shareholders.

Each mutual fund is a separate company, and its investors are the shareholders or owners of the company. They are represented by an elected board of directors, which is legally responsible for fund management. A management company and investment advisor will organize and administer the fund and make investment decisions for a fee, in accordance with the fund's objectives. Notwithstanding the legal structure of the investment company, the management company effectively controls the fund.

There are approximately 8,300 mutual funds in the United States, holding over $6.3 trillion in assets (see Table 1). Although the first mutual funds began in 1924, they did not become popular until the early 1980s. All mutual funds are regulated by the Investment Company Act of 1940 and are registered and overseen by the Securities and Exchange Commission (SEC).

The U.S. mutual fund industry serves the retirement savings and other long-term financial needs of millions of individuals (see Figure 1). An estimated 94.9 million individuals in 54.2 million households, or nearly half of all U.S. households, owned mutual funds as of May 2002, according to a survey by the Investment Company Institute. Fund ownership among U.S. households increased steadily throughout the 1990s, before declining slightly from a high of 56 million households in 2001.

Mutual funds function as an important investment medium for employer-sponsored retirement programs, including section 401(k) plans, 403(b) plans, and SIMPLE (Savings Incentive Match Plan for Employees) plans used by small employers, as well as for individual savings vehicles such as the traditional and Roth Individual Retirement Accounts (IRAs). Mutual funds have become more popular with investors of all ages in the workforce, as the major shift to defined contribution plans (such as the 401(k) in the 1980s and 1990s) made many millions of workers responsible for investing their own

**Figure 1**
**U.S. Household Ownership of Mutual Funds (in millions)**

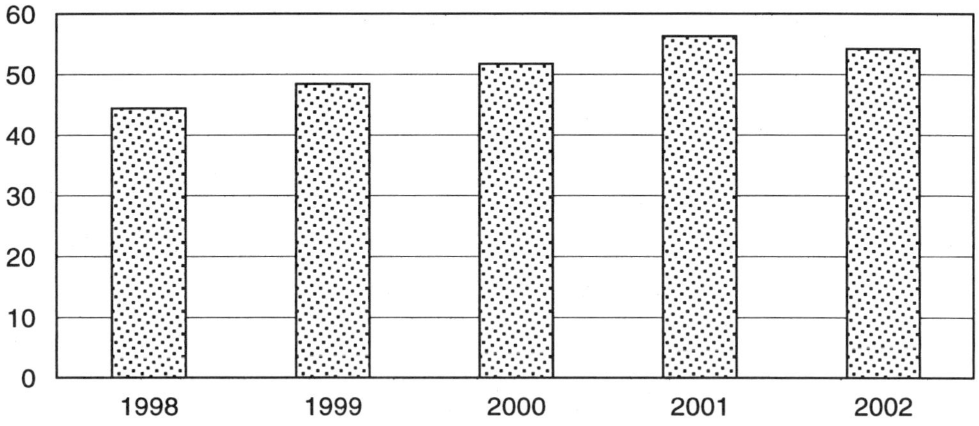


*Source*: Investment Company Institute 2002.

pension accounts. The most popular means of accomplishing this has been through mutual funds, resulting in a natural surge. However, mutual funds remain important to investors in their retirement years, particularly as they consider the investment of a lump-sum retirement or other distribution.

Sixty-two percent (62%) of mutual fund shareholders own funds through defined contribution retirement plans: 31% own funds *both inside* and *outside* of retirement plans, and 31% own funds *solely inside* such plans. Thirty-eight percent (38%) own funds only outside defined contribution plans (see Figure 2).

The primary purpose of mutual funds is diversification. Investors seek high returns but dislike high risk. Holding a single, typical stock implies two to five times the risk of investing in many stocks. By pooling funds to invest in a diversified portfolio of securities, mutual funds can produce investment returns at risk levels resembling the lower risks of the market overall. Small investors would be unable to achieve such diversification on their own.

Convenience, service, and liquidity are other reasons for the popularity of mutual fund investing. The management and administration of the fund reduce an individual's burden. Year-end statements summarize activity, making taxes easier to track. Funds will automatically reinvest dividends and other distributions if desired, and most have convenient retirement plans (such as IRAs) and systematic withdrawal plans. Many fixed income and most money market funds have check-writing privileges. Other popular services are automatic investment plans and telephone switching between funds. Large investment amounts can be purchased or sold without affecting the price (and without commission, for many funds).

Finally, there are benefits of having professional managers pursue and meet fund objectives. Superior performance is the most highly promoted, and most controversial, of these benefits. Cost savings result from high volume, superior information, and professional management. To pursue a specific investment objective and risk level without complicated research is another attractive quality of mutual funds.

**Figure 2**
**Fund Ownership Inside and Outside Defined Contribution Plans, 2001**

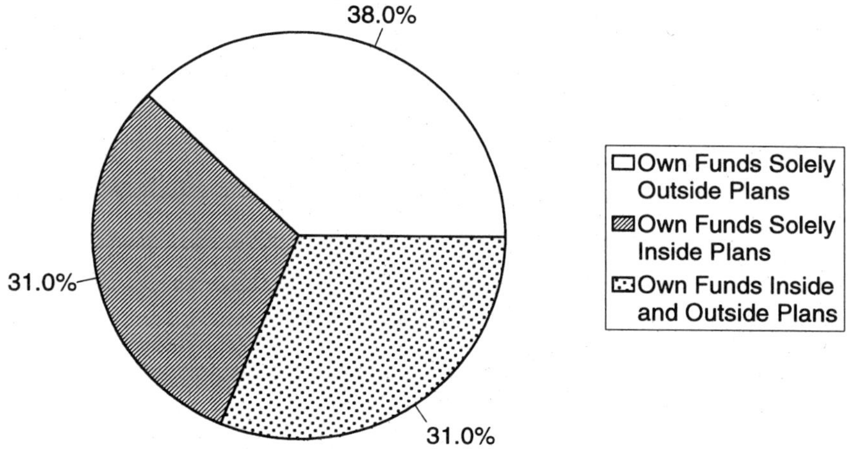


*Source*: Investment Company Institute 2002.

## Types of Mutual Funds

Most mutual funds are *open-ended* investment companies. Investors may buy new shares, increasing the size of the fund; likewise, the size of the fund is reduced when shares are sold. Shares are purchased at net asset value (NAV) plus any sales load; they are sold at the NAV, less any redemption fee or "back-end load." The NAV is simply each share's portion of the net value of the fund's assets: the total assets owned, less any accumulated expenses (liabilities), divided by the number of shares the mutual fund has outstanding. Some funds, called *closed-end* funds, have a fixed number of shares. These publicly traded investment companies' shares are bought and sold like regular stocks, usually on a major stock exchange. Their share prices are not necessarily close to the fund's NAV, as shares sometimes sell at deep discounts or steep premiums.

There are six general categories of mutual funds, differing primarily by underlying asset type. *Money market* mutual funds invest in very short-term securities such as Treasury bills, large bank certificates of deposit (CDs), and commercial paper of large corporations. They aim for constant price stability ($1.00 per share), so their interest rate varies, and they compete with banks for short-term funds. Like other mutual funds, money market funds are not guaranteed, so asset quality is a key concern.

*Fixed income* funds invest in government bonds, corporate bonds, mortgages, and sometimes preferred stock, in order to provide a good return and the safety of a diversified portfolio. *Equity funds* aim for capital growth by holding a diversified portfolio of common stocks. *Balanced funds* hold a mix of stock and bond investments, aiming for both income and growth with broader diversification. Other types of funds include *international funds*, which invest in the stocks and bonds of companies and governments outside the United States. If they hold significant U.S. assets as well, these funds are usually termed *global funds*. Finally, there are a wide array of *special-purpose funds*, which offer a more focused portfolio (such as gold or technology stocks), at the expense of diversification.

The Investment Company Institute identifies at least 22 different categories of mutual funds, based on general type and investment objectives. Money market and fixed income mutual funds, for example, have taxable and nontaxable (municipal) versions. Bond funds may focus on government, high-grade, or high-yield corporate mortgages, or another category of fixed income investment. Equity funds may range from medium-risk growth and income funds to high-risk aggressive growth funds. Index funds, which try to match closely the returns of one of many published investment indices, are also popular. These categories and investment objectives provide some information concerning the risk level of the fund, as well as its overall investment style. The categorizations reflect conscious choices of where the manager wants to position the fund along several investment dimensions, such as asset class, tax status, maturity, diversification, domestic versus international, income versus growth, turnover, and risk.

### Mutual Fund Costs and Operations

The fund's prospectus is an important legal document that provides information concerning investment risks, objectives, fees, loads, and expenses; how to buy and sell shares; services and distributions provided; and many other facts. It is often written in such complex language that the SEC intervened to simplify prospectus texts that now offer investors a one-page summary.

The convenience of professional management and service is costly. Costs of mutual fund investing are direct, indirect, and hidden. A direct cost is a front-end sales load to purchase fund shares, a one-time commission, or a redemption fee when selling and primarily compensates the broker or salesperson. Front-end loads are typically 4% to 5%, but can be as high as 8.5%. If $10,000 is invested with a 5% load, only $9,500 goes to the fund; $500 is a sales charge. Some funds have back-end loads, many of which decline and even disappear as the fund is held for longer periods. There are many no-load funds directly marketed by the fund with no need for a sales load. No-load funds provide the most liquidity. They can be purchased and sold at their NAV.

The majority of mutual funds have 12b-1 fees, which are sales loads in disguise. Named for SEC Rule 12b-1, they allow funds to levy an annual amount (up to 1% of assets) to cover advertising and distribution. Like a one-time load, the 12b-1 fee is often used as compensation for the advice or service of the selling broker, but as an annual charge, it becomes a direct cost.

Indirect costs are paid from assets on an ongoing basis, and the major component of these ongoing expenses is the management fee, a part of every fund's cost structure. Whether a fund is a load fund or a no-load fund, its advisor or portfolio manager charges a fee as an annual percentage of assets on a continual basis. Most management fees range from .5% to 1%. Other expenses paid on an ongoing basis include shareholder services and reporting; custodial, legal, and auditing fees; and directors' fees.

These costs comprise the fund's operating expenses. Stated as a percentage of the fund's NAV, these costs compromise the fund's expense ratio. The median expense ratio for bond funds is 0.85%; for equity funds it is 1.33%; for international funds it is 1.75%; money market fund expenses are considerably lower. The expense ratio is an important number, as the fund's gross investment gains are reduced by this amount before arriving at the fund's actual return to the investor. All prospectuses include a detailed section and table covering the fund's direct and indirect costs and their effect on a hypothetical investment. Some mutual fund costs are hidden, since they show up as neither a one-time load nor as a component of the expense ratio. Brokerage commissions and other transaction costs fall into this category, and these costs can be significant for funds that have a high turnover ratio (lots of trading activity). This multitude of fees, expenses, and other costs can be sizable and may do little to help the fund investor achieve high returns. Funds with higher cost structures must produce higher gross returns to stay even with lower-cost funds, but in practice, this has proven extremely difficult for fund managers to do.

### Mutual Fund Performance

Fund performance is measured in terms of total return—the increase in fund price, plus any dividends or distributions paid out by the fund. If funds receive income, or realize capital gains by selling positions at a profit, they must pass the bulk of the net gains through to the shareholders. When dividends or distributions are paid, the NAV of the fund falls by the amount of the payout. These distributions are taxed at the personal level, not at the fund level. Investors must thus be cautious of profitable, high-turnover funds that are about to make a large distribution, as often happens at year's end. An unwitting buyer may purchase $10,000 of a fund in December only to have a $1,000 taxable distribution on December 31, paid from gains made earlier in the year. The investor could then be left with $9,000 of the fund, $1,000 in cash, and a large tax bill on the entire $1,000 distribution, despite making no profit.

Other key tax issues arise when mutual fund shares are sold. Investors may use several techniques to determine the tax basis (purchase price) of fund shares in order to calculate the profit on the sale. When selling shares, it is prudent to consult with a tax or financial advisor. The reinvestment of dividends or distributions may present an even more difficult problem, since many investors forget to increase the tax basis of shares when reinvesting in new shares with already-taxed distributions. When shares are sold later, they pay taxes on the same money a second time. This is a costly mistake and highlights the importance of keeping good records when dealing with mutual funds and other investments.

Mutual fund returns vary significantly by fund and by period. Long-term average returns are most comparable within fund categories and tend to vary with the risk profile of the fund. During long periods, higher-risk investments are expected to produce higher returns. According to Donald L. Cassidy, senior analyst of Lipper, Inc., in the ten years ended December 2002 domestic equity funds returned an average of 7.67% to 9.41%, domestic and global bond funds returned an average of 5.98% to 6.48%, and international equity funds provided an average 4.42% to 7.82% return. Money market fund returns were somewhat lower, about 3.25% to 4.05% (Cassidy 2003). Fund returns shown represent both simple averages and dollar-weighted averages for the past ten years. Fund performance in the future is unpredictable, and these ten-year figures include both periods of very high returns as well as periods of losses. Several ranking services calculate risk-adjusted returns or otherwise factor risk into their performance evaluations.

Attention paid to past returns may be of limited value, according to consistent findings of academic studies over the past 25 years. Two empirical facts generally issue from serious research: (1) many mutual fund managers fail to outperform comparable market averages, and (2) there is little consistency in the funds showing above-market performance. In an early study (Jensen 1969), and several later studies on mutual fund performance, researchers have found no evidence that fund managers have beaten the market on a risk-adjusted basis. The number of funds with above-average performance five years in a row is basically no higher than the laws of probability would determine. Several implications follow these findings. Investors wanting high returns must accept high levels of risk. Consistent above-average performance may be due to luck or skill. Another important implication is that past returns will tell little about future results.

A look at the cost structure of mutual funds provides information regarding returns. Several analyses have found that funds with higher expense ratios and higher turnover produce, on average, lower net investment results. This is not surprising, since it reflects the dual realities that costs reduce returns unless they are outweighed by additional gains and that it is difficult to produce investment gains consistently. One industry development stemming from this research is the remarkable growth of *index funds*. Instead of trying to "beat thc market," index fund managers attempt to closely match an index, such as the S&P 500. Most make an effort to keep expenses and turnover costs very low, thus surpassing the majority of other funds but not achieving top performance. While a fairly new development, there are now almost 100 index funds tied to a wide variety of market indices.

In addition to the vast amount of information that can be found via the Internet and in current financial periodicals, there are two general types of mutual fund information sources, both of which can be found at most libraries. Most financial periodicals have quarterly or annual mutual fund surveys with a wealth of information on fund performance and fund categories. The second source is a mutual fund update service, guidebook, or directory, providing varying degrees of information and ratings on many popular mutual funds. (See also BONDS; EQUITY SECURITIES; FEDERAL AGENCY SECURITIES; INFLUENCES ON RETIREMENT INVESTMENT DECISIONS; INVESTMENT ADVICE; INVESTOR EDUCATION; RISK TOLERANCE.)

**References**

American Association of Individual Investors. 1995. *The Individual Investor's Guide to Low-Load Mutual Funds*. Chicago: Author.

Cassidy, Donald L. 2003. Of Lipper, Inc., Denver, CO. Telephone conversation with author on April 20.

CDA Investment Technologies. 1995. *Wiesenberger Investment Companies Service*. Rockville, MD: Author.

Fredman, Albert J., and Russ Wiles. 1993. *How Mutual Funds Work*. New York: NYIF.

Investment Company Institute. 2002. *Directory of Mutual Funds*. Washington, DC: Author.

Investment Company Institute 2003. Statistics, January. Available online at http://www.ici.org/.

Jensen, Michael. 1969. "Risks, the Pricing of Capital Assets, and the Evaluation of Investment Performance." *Journal of Business* 42 (April): 2.

*Morningstar Mutual Funds*. Updated twice yearly. Chicago: Morningstar.

Posen, Robert C. 1998. *The Mutual Fund Business*. Cambridge, MA: MIT Press.

Vujovich, Dian. 1992. *Straight Talk about Mutual Funds*. New York: McGraw-Hill.

*Michael E. Edleson*
*Updated by Lois A. Vitt*

# N

**NURSING HOMES,** facilities with three or more beds that routinely provide nursing care services, are the foundation of long-term care (LTC) in the United States. They may be freestanding or a separate unit of a larger entity, such as a hospital or a continuing care retirement community. Today, more than 18,000 nursing homes provide services for more than 1.6 million residents, with an average of 105 beds per facility. The average annual cost for care in a nursing home (NH) is $52,195 per year in a semiprivate room; the range is from $30,660 to $117,165. For a private room, the annual cost ranges from $32,120 to $126,655, with an average of $61,320 (MetLife 2002). The nation spends more than $99 billion a year on nursing home care; 60% of this cost is met by the Medicare and Medicaid programs (U.S. Department of Health and Human Services 2002).

The federal government and the states share responsibility for funding and regulating nursing homes. The national Centers for Medicare & Medicaid Services (CMS), formerly known as the Health Care Financing Administration (HCFA), administers both Medicare and Medicaid and certifies NHs for participation in these programs. The states ensure that federal standards are followed by conducting annual inspections of NHs.

## History of Nursing Homes

The modern NH is a product of age-based programs. The Social Security Act, passed in 1935, improved the economic security of older Americans, reducing their reliance on public almshouses. Private board and care homes helped fill the demand for housing linked with services that were available for frail elders. During the 1940s and 1950s, these small "mom-and-pop" operations developed into larger institutions along the hospital model. National laws, such as the Hill-Burton Act of 1955, established building standards for nursing homes.

The passage of Medicare and Medicaid in 1965 was the next major step in the growth of the NH industry. Medicare was established to pay for acute health care for the aged, but coverage was primarily limited to physician and hospital services. Medicaid, established to provide means-tested health care, contained a provision permitting states to enroll persons who became medically needy by virtue of high medical costs, such as long-term custodial care in a nursing home. Partly as a consequence of an influx of Medicaid-eligible patients, the NH population soared. The number of NHs tripled between 1960 and 1980, and the NH population increased to over 1.6 million during this period.

As the NH industry expanded during the 1970s and 1980s, NH care evolved, becoming more diversified, specialized, and medicalized (Redfoot 2003). One example of this trend is the development of special care units (SCUs), now located in approximately 20% of all nursing homes. They are more common in nonprofit NHs and in larger facilities run by nationwide chains. The majority are devoted to the care of Alzheimer's patients, but they also serve persons with other problems requiring special care (e.g., AIDS [acquired immunodeficiency syndrome], traumatic brain injury). SCUs have specific admission and discharge criteria, specially trained staff and personalized care strategies, and a secured area such as a dedicated floor or wing of a building.

Despite innovations such as SCUs, NH growth slowed during the 1980s, and utilization rates have declined over the past two decades. Some possible reasons for this decline include the development of assisted living, a gradual increase in Medicaid reimbursement for home- and community-based services, and expanded long-term care insurance (LTCI) coverage for non-institutional care. In addition, many states have passed Certificate of Need (CON) laws designed to control the supply of NH beds.

Today, the NH industry is dominated by large corporations. Nearly two-thirds of facilities are in the for-profit sector, with 56% owned or operated by NH chains. Voluntary and nonprofit organizations and federal and state governments operate the remainder (U.S. Department of Health and Human Services 2002).

### Who Lives in a Nursing Home?

Today, 1.6 million people live in NHs. According to the most recent national survey, 90% of current residents are age 65 years or over, with 46% among the oldest old (age 85 years or over). Roughly 10% of the NH population is younger than age 65; these are persons who primarily suffer from mental illness or other central nervous system problems.

The majority of NH residents are White (88.7%); 8.9% are African Americans (Bishop 1999). The latter are underrepresented in NHs, for reasons ranging from poverty and geography to cultural preference; for many, the only financial option is homes exclusively treating Medicaid patients. In addition, few NHs serve groups such as Asians and Native Americans. Older minorities face barriers to NH care due to economics, language differences, NH location within communities, traditions, and both overt and indirect acts of discrimination from NH personnel and White residents (Aeschleman 2000).

Almost three-quarters of residents are female, reflecting higher rates of chronic illness, longer life expectancy, lower marital rates, and lower income among older women. More than half of residents are widowed (Harrington Meyer 2001; U.S. Department of Health and Human Services 2002). Three-quarters of current residents require assistance with three or more activities of daily living (ADLs), particularly bathing (94%) and dressing (87%). More than half of all NH residents receive assistance using the bathroom and nearly half with eating (U.S. Department of Health and Human Services 2002).

### Who Works in Nursing Homes?

There are 1.5 million full-time employees providing care to NH residents. Almost two-thirds of these employees are nursing staff who provide direct services, such as personal care, to residents—registered nurses (RNs), licensed practical nurses (LPNs), certified nursing assistants (CNAs), and orderlies. CNAs and orderlies account for 64% of all nursing staff. A much smaller percentage of employees (6%) provide medical and therapeutic services to residents; this category includes dentists, physical therapists, speech pathologists, dieticians, podiatrists, and social workers (U.S. Department of Health and Human Services 2002). Physicians have a limited role in daily NH care.

### Financing Nursing Home Care

*Medicare.* Medicare funds 14% of NH care in the country. It pays for up to 100 days of postacute care in a NH following an inpatient hospital stay of three days or more. Prior to 1999, NHs billed Medicare retrospectively for every service they provided to residents, creating an incentive for them to provide as much care as possible. However, under the Balanced Budget Act (BBA) of 1997, NHs assign a fixed daily rate prospectively for every incoming Medicare patient, based on a new payment system utilizing the resource utilization group (RUG). The RUG is based on anticipated patient costs, similar to the diagnosis related group (DRG) Medicare uses for hospital care, providing an incentive for NHs to contain costs. The BBA was modified under the Balanced Budget Refinement Act (BBRA) of 1999 to allow a gradual phase-in of the RUG.

*Medicaid.* The largest public payer for NH care is the Medicaid program. Medicaid expenditures for NH care were $39.6 billion in 2000. The program pays for 46% of all NH care in the country (Centers for Medicare & Medicaid Services [CMS] 2000).

Medicaid is not the same in every state. Different payment policies exist; some states include services such as physical therapy and prescription drugs in daily rates; others do not. Medicaid per diem rates for NHs vary; in some states, Medicaid NH rates are only 70% to 80% of private pay rates. This may create an incentive for NHs to admit private pay patients rather than Medicaid patients. Minnesota's equalization law makes such discrimination illegal, and other states are exploring similar laws of their own (Harrington Meyer 2001).

States vary in their use of managed care for the Medicaid population at all ages. Managed care has not had a large impact on Medicaid spending, although Arizona's entire LTC system is capitated, and Texas and Minnesota have recently implemented managed care LTC programs (Burwell 2001).

*Private Spending.* The remaining 40% of NH care is paid through private sources. Almost all of private spending is paid out of pocket by patients and their families. For patients who require around-the-clock skilled nursing care, but neither meet Medicare eligibility requirements nor qualify for the means-tested Medicaid program, private pay is the only option. One source of funds for private pay is long-term care insurance (LTCI). In 1985, LTCI barely existed, but by 1999, more than 6 million policies had been sold. LTCI is expected to expand, due to the increase of the numbers of employers and insurers entering the market and the growing interest in these policies among aging baby boomers.

### Regulation of Nursing Homes

The states once had total responsibility for NH regulation. However, a federal role emerged in the Nixon administration's NH reforms of 1971 and 1972 when federal inspectors began to "validate" state inspections. HCFA, now CMS, assumed this oversight after its reorganization in 1977.

Following an Institute of Medicine report on NH quality in 1986, Congress introduced sweeping changes to NH regulation under the Omnibus Budget Reconciliation Act of 1987 (OBRA-87). The act required NHs to provide comprehensive assessments of residents at admission, and periodically thereafter, to ensure residents receive an appropriate level of care. It also clarified the role of the states and the federal government in NH regulation. Under OBRA-87, state survey agencies inspect every NH in a state every 9 to 15 months and investigate quality-of-care complaints. CMS surveyors determine whether state surveyors follow federal guidelines.

In 1995, Congress enacted current federal standards. Federal and state surveyors are required to specify the scope and severity of NH deficiencies, with sanctions ranging from a directed plan of correction to termination of the nursing home's certification and/or monetary penalties (U.S. General Accounting Office 1999). The CMS has made federal and state inspection results of every Medicare- and Medicaid-certified NH in the country available to the public on its Web site (http://www.medicare.gov/NHCompare). State and local LTC ombudsmen are also excellent resources for NH inspection information and can be contacted using the U.S. Administration on Aging's online Eldercare Locator (http://www.eldercare.gov/).

### Quality of Life/Lifestyle Innovations

Most NH regulation addresses safety and abuse concerns, rather than lifestyle and quality of life. Because elders see NHs as uncaring, they prefer not to live in these institutions, which has led to "humanitarian" reforms. Examples include the Eden Alternative, which focuses on resident lifestyle, and the Wellspring Alliance, which focuses on quality of care. The Eden Alternative provides a human habitat model for NH residents. The core concept is to see long-term care environments as habitats for human beings rather than facilities for older and frail persons, drawing heavily from what Mother Nature has to teach about the creation of vibrant, vigorous habitats.

The Eden Alternative (EA) uses "companion animals, the opportunity to give meaningful care to other living creatures, and the variety and spontaneity that mark an enlivened environment [to] succeed where pills and therapies fail." While an EA evaluation found no beneficial effects in terms of such factors as functional status, survival, or cost of care, qualitative observations suggested a positive change for residents and staff (Coleman et al. 2002).

The Wellspring Alternative consists of 11 facilities in eastern Wisconsin and has been set up to make NHs a better place to live by improving clinical care and creating a better work environment by empowering employees. Key components include clinical consultation and education by a geriatric nurse practitioner, a shared program of staff training, and a multidisciplinary care resource team. A recent evaluation indicates lower staff turnover, higher performance on federal surveys, lower costs than a comparison group, and greater staff vigilance in assessing problems (Stone et al. 2002).

### The Future of Nursing Homes

Predictions of the demise of nursing homes are greatly exaggerated. Acute care patients, especially those with very high levels of disability, will need to be placed in facilities providing skilled nursing services. Continued longevity, even among those with AIDS and dementia, and growing proportions of future elders mean NHs will continue to play an important role in LTC throughout the twenty-first century.

However, patient and facility characteristics may change, largely due to demographics. The percentage of older minorities, particularly Hispanics, is growing nationwide and specifically in states such as California and Texas. As a consequence, NH usage may grow among minority elder populations. A greater number of NHs that serve specific ethnic and racial groups is one potential response to cultural preferences.

Facilities also are likely to change in other ways. Innovations from abroad, reforms of the sort described above, and a thrust toward consumer-driven care options, in keeping with baby boomers' preferences, are likely to change nursing homes, as well. Special care units are likely to continue, partly as a marketing tool but also to accommodate a population that is considerably more frail due to longer life expectancy and more severe chronic health conditions. Finally, it will be important to reduce NH staff turnover and eliminate its negative impact on quality of care. Changes in management philosophy and improved front-line staffing arrangements that are associated with higher quality of care are likely to be adopted.

Nursing homes will likely continue to be a part of the continuum of long-term care settings well into the future, but many are likely to be quite different from those available today. (See also ASSISTED LIVING; COMMUNITY-BASED CARE; CONTINUING CARE RETIREMENT COMMUNITIES [CCRCs]; HOME CARE SERVICES FOR OLDER ADULTS; MEDICAID; MEDICARE.)

### References

AARP. 2002. "Your Health. Checklist: What to Look for in a Nursing Home." Available online at http://www.aarp.org/bulletin/departments/2002/health/0410_health_1.html.

Aeschleman, Heather K. 2000. "White World of Nursing Homes: The Myriad Barriers to Access Facing Today's Elderly Minorities." *Elder Law Journal* 8(2): 367–91.

Bishop, C.E. 1999. "Where Are the Missing Elders? The Decline in Nursing Home Use, 1985 and 1995." *Health Affairs* 18: 146–55.

Burwell, Brian. 2001. "Medicaid Long-Term Care Expenditures in Fiscal Year 2000." *The Gerontologist* 40(5): 687–91.

Centers for Medicare & Medicaid Services (CMS). 2000. *National Health Expenditures: 1996–1998*. Washington, DC: Author.

Centers for Medicare & Medicaid Services (CMS). 2003. "Nursing Home Compare." Available online at http://www.medicare.gov/NHCompare/home.asp.

Coleman, Mary T., et al. 2002. "Eden Alternative: Findings after One Year of Implementation." *Journals of Gerontology, Series A: Biological Sciences and Medical Sciences* 57A: M422–27.

Harrington Meyer, Madonna. 2001. "Medicaid Reimbursement Rates and Access to Nursing Homes: Implications for Gender, Race, and Marital Status." *Research on Aging* 23(5): 532–51.

Kane, Rosalie A. 2001. "Long-Term Care and Good Quality of Life: Bringing Them Closer Together." *The Gerontologist* 41(3): 293–304.

MetLife Mature Market Institute. 2002. *MetLife Market Survey on Nursing Home and Home Care Costs*. Westport, CT: Author.

Redfoot, Donald C. 2003. *Before the Boom: Trends in Long-Term Supportive Services for Older Americans with Disabilities*. Washington, DC: AARP Public Policy Institute.

Stone, Robyn I. 2001. "Providing Long-Term Benefits in Cash: Moving to a Disability Model." *Health Affairs* 20(6): 96–108.

Stone, Robyn I., et al. 2002. *Evaluation of the Wellspring Model for Improving Nursing Home Quality*. Washington, DC: American Association of Homes and Services for the Aged, Institute for the Future of Aging Services.

U.S. Department of Health and Human Services, Center for Disease Control, Vital and Health Statistics. 2002. *The National Nursing Home Survey: 1999 Summary*. Hyattsville, MD: Author.

U.S. General Accounting Office. 1999. *Nursing Home Care: Enhanced HCFA Oversight of State Programs Would Better Ensure Quality*. Report to the Special Committee on Aging, U.S. Senate. GAO/HEHS-00-6. Washington, DC: Author.

Vladeck, Bruce. 1980. *Unloving Care: The Nursing Home Tragedy*. New York: Basic Books.

*Phoebe Liebig and Chris Kelly*

**NUTRITION PROGRAMS,** federally funded programs intended to increase the food-buying power of low-income people or to provide food directly to older people in the form of nutritionally sound meals.

### Food Stamp Program

This program provides low-income households with coupons that can be used like cash at most grocery stores to ensure access to a healthful diet. The U.S. Department of Agriculture (USDA) administers the program at the federal level through its Food and Nutrition Service (FNS). As with many federally funded programs, access to food stamps has been declining over the past decade. For example, the Food Stamp Program served an average of almost 27 million people each month in 1993; by the year 2000, that number was down to 17 million people each month and has been declining since 1984. State welfare agencies administer the program at the state and local levels. One recent development is the Electronic Benefit Transfer (EBT) system, in which a qualified food stamp recipient can arrange to have their benefit transferred directly to a retailer to pay for products received. Nearly 85% of food stamps are currently being handled through EBT.

*Eligibility Requirements.* Of those receiving food stamps in 2000, approximately 10% were age 60 and older, while 51% were children under the age of 19. The rules for the participation of aged (if at least one member of the household is age 60 or older) and disabled households are somewhat more liberal than those for younger and able-bodied households. The restriction on assets (such as automobiles, property other than a personal home and lot, and savings) for food stamp recipients is $2,000 for young and able-bodied households and $3,000 for older persons and the disabled. At the same time, there is a net income limit for participation by older persons and the disabled, while young and able-bodied recipients are subject to both a gross and net income test. The value of the stamps received increases with the number of eligible people in the household and decreases with the net monthly income.

*Items That Can Be Purchased.* Food stamps can be used to buy any food or food product for human consumption as well as seeds and plants for use in home gardens to produce foods.

*Items That Cannot Be Purchased.* Households cannot use food stamps to buy alcoholic beverages and tobacco, hot foods ready to eat and food intended to be heated in the store, vitamins or medicines, pet foods, or any nonfood items (except seeds and plants). However, restaurants can be authorized to accept food stamps in exchange for low-cost meals from qualified homeless, older, or disabled people. Food stamps can never be exchanged for cash.

### Nutrition Services Incentive Program (NSIP)

This program, formerly the Nutrition Program for the Elderly (NPE), helps provide older persons with nutritionally sound meals in community senior citizen centers (congregate dining) or through local meals-on-wheels programs. The NSIP is administered by the U.S. Department of Health and Human Services (DHHS) but receives commodity foods and financial support from the USDA. Under provisions of the Older Americans Act of 1965, the USDA contributes commodity foods and/or cash to DHHS programs for older Americans. The USDA provided reimbursement for an average of more than 2 million meals a month in 1999. Congress appropriated $140 million for 1999, the same as for 1998 and 1997; this represents a major decrease from funding levels of $470 million for NPE for 1994 (AARP 1994).

*Eligibility Requirements.* Age is the only factor in determining eligibility for NPE. People 60 years or older and their spouses, regardless of age, are eligible. Indian tribal organizations may select an age below 60 for defining "older" persons for their tribes. There is no income requirement to receive meals under NPE. Each recipient can contribute as much as he or she wishes toward the cost of the meal, but meals are free to those unable to make any contribution.

*Requirements for USDA Contributions to Local Programs.* In order to qualify for cash or commodity assistance, meals served must meet a specified percentage of the nutritional recommended daily allowance (RDA). States can take part or all of their subsidies in cash, rather than commodities. NSIP has evolved from a program to distribute USDA commodities to senior citizen meal sites to primarily a cash subsidy program in which approximately 94% of program resources are distributed to meal providers in cash.

Many older people require diets and nutritional supplements that are tailored to meet specific needs, based on state of health, level of activity, and medical histories. Researchers who have conducted studies on the nutrient intakes and nutritional status of older participants in NSIP programs have found that participants were more likely to have consumed two-thirds of the RDAs for calcium, vitamin A, and vitamin C than nonparticipants and that men and women aged 75 years and older who were regular participants had more favorable blood levels of hemoglobin, vitamin A, and proteins than nonparticipants or infrequent participants (Splett 1994).

### Other Food Programs for Older Adults

In addition to these major programs designed to ensure the proper nutrition for older adults, those who are 60 and older also have access to other federal food programs. For example, The Emergency Food Assistance Program (TEFAP) is a federal program that helps to supplement the diets of low-income needy persons, including older people, in the event of a disaster. Another example of federal support for older adults is the Commodity Supplemental Food Program (CSFP), under which the USDA buys food and makes it available to state agencies and Indian Tribal Organizations (ITOs), along with funds for administrative costs. State agencies that disperse this food are likely to be Departments of Health, social services agencies, or educational or agricultural programs. (See also DAY PROGRAMS FOR ADULTS; ECONOMIC HARDSHIP MEASURES IN THE OLDER POPULATION; ECONOMIC STATUS OF OLDER MEN AND WOMEN; HOMELESSNESS AMONG OLDER ADULTS; MEANS-TESTING IN PUBLIC PROGRAMS; OLD-AGE PROVISIONS AND ECONOMIC STATUS; OLDER AMERICANS ACT; SUPPLEMENTAL SECURITY INCOME [SSI].)

### References

AARP. 1994. *Nutrition Assistance for Older Americans*. Washington, DC: Public Policy Institute.

Splett, P.L. 1994. "Federal Food Assistance Programs: A Step to Food Security for Many." *Nutrition Today* 29(2): 6–13.

U.S. Department of Agriculture. n.d. "Food & Nutrition Service: Food Stamp Program." Available online at http://www.fns.usda.gov/fsp/faqs.htm.

U.S. Department of Agriculture. n.d. "Food & Nutrition Service: Nutrition Services Incentive Program (NSIP)." Available online at http://www.fns.usda.gov/fdd/programs/nsip/nsip-faqs.htm.

*James E. Konlande*
*Updated by Sandra L. Reynolds*

# O

**OLD-AGE PROVISIONS AND ECONOMIC STATUS,** the trend through which economic status is used increasingly to determine benefits and burdens in U.S. policies toward older persons. Some welfare programs such as Medicaid and Supplemental Security Income (SSI) have long targeted benefits to poor older persons as well as to other impoverished populations. For many years the formula for determining old-age retirement benefits under Social Security has been somewhat more generous to low-wage earners. Since the early 1980s, however, incremental policy changes have eroded the traditional principle that older Americans should all be treated the same, without regard to economic status—a principle that had been regarded as important for maintaining broad political support for such old-age policies.

Some of these policy reforms have targeted program benefits to relatively poor older people. Others have asked wealthier older persons to pay greater taxes or otherwise share more heavily in financing benefits and services, than those older people with less income and wealth. One factor generating these changes has been concerns for the plight of relatively poor older people, but a major additional factor has been efforts to shore up contemporary and future financing of old-age policies.

### The Specter of Unsustainable Old-Age Benefits

Concerns about the costs of programs for older Americans first surfaced in the late 1970s. Academicians and journalists identified a trend through which the proportion of federal expenditures devoted to benefits to older persons had risen to 26%, roughly equivalent to the proportion spent on defense. During the 1980s and 1990s, doubts about the future economic and political viability of old-age benefits were frequently expressed by public policy analysts, political figures, and the media.

Through what Robertson (1991) termed "apocalyptic demography," foreboding scenarios for the decades ahead were generated by plugging into existing policies and institutional arrangements the familiar projections regarding greater numbers and proportions of older Americans in the first half of the twenty-first century. For instance, some health policy experts and biomedical ethicists asserted that health care expenditures on older people—already one-third of the national total—would become a great fiscal "black hole" that will consume an unlimited amount of our national resources (Callahan 1987). Schneider and Guralnik (1990) projected that Medicare costs for persons aged 85 and older would increase sixfold from 1990 to 2040 as estimated in constant, inflation-adjusted dollars. Peter Peterson (1999), former U.S. secretary of commerce, warned that a substantial decline in the ratio of workers to retirees would make it impossible to maintain Social Security when the baby boom cohort reaches old age, and one in five Americans will be aged 65 and older in 2030. Anxieties such as these reached a crescendo by 2001 when expenditures on aging had increased to over 40% of the federal budget and defense spending had fallen to about 16%. The constructs that generate concerns about the future impacts of population aging are usually flawed. For example, the ratio of workers to retirees (or children, or other categories of "dependents") has little to do with the capacity of an economy to transfer resources for their support through such mechanisms as Social Security. Far more important for the requisite national prosperity will be such factors as technological development, natural resources, capital investment, and balance of trade. Further, there is no inherent reason why Social Security must be financed by a payroll tax levied on a worker-by-worker basis. Many nations draw on other sources of revenue to help finance the equivalent of Social Security payments. Similarly, cross-national comparisons of industrialized countries with respect to their proportions of older people and the amount of national wealth spent on health care suggest that population aging, in itself, does not cause health care expenditures to be high or out of control (Binstock 1999; Reinhardt 1999). Much more important in determining costs are the structural features of health care systems and behavioral responses to them by citizens and health care providers.

### The Trend Based on Economic Status

The most important flaw in dire predictions regarding the impact of population aging is that they rely on extrapolations from existing policies. In fact, old-age policies (as well as policies in other arenas) change continuously, and there is every reason to believe that they will keep changing. A prime example of such changes is the trend of incremental reforms in policies on aging to reflect the diverse economic situations of older persons.

A policy to improve the long-run financial viability of Social Security began this trend. The Social Security Reform Act of 1983 provided for the taxation of Social Security benefits and earmarked the revenue from those taxes to be used for financing Social Security itself. For individuals with incomes exceeding $25,000 and married couples with incomes over $32,000, 50% of Social Security benefits were made subject to taxation. Ten years later, the Omnibus Budget Reconciliation Act (OBRA) of 1993 followed this up by subjecting 85% of Social Security benefits to taxation for individuals earning over $34,000 and couples earning over $44,000.

Once the 1983 taxation provision broke the traditional barrier against treating older persons differently in nonwelfare policies, further reforms began to distribute benefits according to economic status. The Tax Reform Act of 1986, even as it eliminated the extra personal exemption that had been available to all persons aged 65 and older when filing their federal income tax returns, provided new tax credits to low-income older persons on a sliding scale. The Older Americans Act (OAA) programs of supportive and nutrition services, for which all persons aged 60 and older are eligible, was gradually targeted to low-income older persons through a series of congressional amendments. In addition, policy changes have permitted OAA programs to charge for supportive services (through "cost sharing"), based on the income level of clients, and to accept "donations" from participants in congregate meal programs. Both charges and donations can now be used to expand supportive services or to facilitate access of older persons to meal sites.

This kind of sensitivity to the economic status of older persons was also applied to the health arena beginning in 1988 through a provision of the Medicare Catastrophic Coverage Act (MCCA). The MCCA established a Qualified Medicare Beneficiary (QMB) program that requires the federal/state Medicaid program to pay Part B premiums, deductibles, and coinsurance payments for Medicare enrollees who have incomes and assets that are below specific federal guidelines for classifying individuals as poor. The income test level is the federal poverty line (FLP); the asset test ceiling is $2,000 for individuals and $3,000 for couples. Then OBRA 1990 created a new eligibility group—Specified Low-Income Medicare Beneficiaries (SLMBs)—for which Medicaid pays Part B premiums (but not deductibles or coinsurance). The asset test for SLMB eligibility is the same as for QMBs, but the income test level is 120% of the FPL. The Balanced Budget Act (BBA) of 1997 further expanded Medicaid coverage of Medicare cost sharing for two groups of qualifying individuals (QIs). QI-1s are individuals who would be eligible as QMBs or SLMBs except that their income is in the range of 120% to 135% of the FLP; their sole Medicaid benefit is payment of the Medicare Part B premium. QI-2s are individuals with incomes between 135% and 175% of the FLP who meet all other QMB eligibility requirements; their Medicaid benefit consists only of the portion of the Part B premium that is attributable to another provision of BBA that shifted the cost of Medicare home health benefits from Part A into Part B.

These various policy reforms have firmly established the principle that it is politically feasible for nonwelfare policies on aging to treat older people differently based upon their economic status. Consequently, this trend has established a workable framework for maintaining government benefits to those older persons who truly need help through public programs, both in the near term and in years when baby boomers will be older adults. And it has managed to do so without stigmatizing the policies that it has affected as "welfare programs." (See also DEFINED CONTRIBUTION PLAN; ECONOMIC STATUS OF OLDER MEN AND WOMEN; HEALTH BENEFITS; MEDICAID; MEDICARE; NUTRITION PROGRAMS; OLDER AMERICANS ACT; SOCIAL SECURITY PROGRAM OF THE UNITED STATES; SUPPLEMENTAL SECURITY INCOME [SSI].)

### References

Binstock, Robert H. 1999. "Older Persons and Health Care Costs." In *Life in an Older America*, ed. Robert N. Butler, Lawrence K. Grossman, and Mia R. Oberlink. New York: Century Foundation Press.

Callahan, Daniel. 1987. *Setting Limits: Medical Goals in an Aging Society*. New York: Simon and Schuster.

Peterson, Peter G. 1999. *Gray Dawn: How the Coming Age Wave Will Transform America—and the World*. New York: Times Books.

Reinhardt, Uwe. 1999. "The Political Economy of Health Care for the Elderly Population." In *Healthy Aging: Challenges and Solutions*, ed. Ken Dychtwald. Gaithersburg, MD: Aspen Publishers.

Robertson, Ann. 1991. "The Politics of Alzheimer's Disease: A Case Study in Apocalyptic Demography." In *Critical Perspectives on Aging: The Political and Moral Economy of Growing Old*, ed. Meredith Minkler and Carroll L. Estes. Amityville, NY: Baywood.

Schneider, Edward L., and Jack M. Guralnik. 1990. "The Aging of America: Impact on Health Care Costs." *Journal of the American Medical Association* 262: 2335–40.

*Robert H. Binstock*

**OLDER AMERICANS ACT,** originally signed into law by President Lyndon Baines Johnson on July 14, 1965, established the Administration on Aging (AoA) within the Department of Health, Education and Welfare (now the Department of Health and Human Services). It was most recently amended and reauthorized in 2000 for a period of five years.

The broad objectives of the Older Americans Act (OAA) are designed to maximize the ability of older persons to age with dignity and independence. The centerpiece of this legislation is a system of social and community services intended to address the multifaceted needs of our nation's elders. Enacted in 1965, the OAA has evolved over time, responding to demographic and societal changes. Reauthorized by Congress in 2000, the act includes:

1. *Title II.* Administrative functions and funding for the Eldercare Locator and pension counseling and information programs.
2. *Title III.* State and Community Programs on Aging. Primarily for persons age 60 and older, these programs include social services and senior centers; congregate and home-delivered meal programs; health promotion and disease prevention; and the Family Caregiver Support Program.
3. *Title IV.* Training, Research, and Discretionary Programs. This portion of the act addresses societal needs for aging-related research, demonstration projects to enhance knowledge in the area of aging services, and training of individuals in the field of aging.
4. *Title V.* Senior Community Service Employment Program. Funds states and private organizations to develop community service employment opportunities for low-income individuals age 55 and older.
5. *Title VI.* Grants for Native Americans. Funding under this title goes to Native American tribal organizations as well as organizations representing Alaskan Natives and Native Hawaiians to provide nutritional and social services for their elder populations.
6. *Title VII.* Vulnerable Elder Rights Protection Activities. Programs funded by this title include state long-term care ombudsmen, elder abuse prevention activities, and systems to provide affordable legal assistance for older persons.

Table 1 provides data on federal funding for OAA programs in 2002. Major provisions of the OAA are described in more detail below.

## Title III Programs

Federal funds for the meals and services authorized by Title III of the OAA are distributed to the 50 states, the District of Columbia, and the U.S. territories based on each state's share of the total U.S. population age 60 and older. Each state has a State Unit on Aging charged with administering these programs. The state must prepare a plan, subject to approval by the federal Administration on Aging. The plan illustrates how the state plans to spend its funds. In addition, the state must submit for approval an intrastate funding formula, indicating how funds will be apportioned throughout the state. All but

**Table 1**
**Fiscal Year 2003 Funding Levels of the AoA**

| Program | Dollars in Millions |
|---|---|
| Supportive Services | $357 |
| Home-Delivered Meals | $225 |
| Congregate Meals | $492 |
| National Family Caregiver Support | $141 |
| Preventive Health | $21 |
| Aging Research | $28 |
| Grants to Indian Tribes | $28 |
| Protection of Vulnerable Older Americans | $18 |

*Source*: U.S. Department of Health and Human Services 2003a.

the smallest states are subdivided into Area Agencies on Aging, which are responsible for contracting with providers who deliver the meals and services.

By law, all persons age 60 and older, and their spouses of any age, are eligible for Title III supportive services and congregate meals. Home-delivered meals are provided only to individuals who are homebound. In practice, however, program funding is limited, and states are required to "target" services to those elders with the greatest social and economic need. These terms are defined in the act as physical and mental disabilities; language barriers; cultural, social, or geographical isolation, including isolation caused by racial or ethnic status that restricts the ability of an individual to perform normal daily tasks or threatens the capacity of an individual to live independently; and income at or below the poverty line.

State agencies are charged with being "effective and visible advocate[s] for older individuals." Through their planning efforts in conjunction with the area agencies, the OAA strives to establish a comprehensive and coordinated system of services and senior centers throughout the nation. While the area agencies have considerable latitude in selecting the amounts and types of services they will make available, they are required to designate an "adequate" portion of their funds for the following service categories: access (transportation, outreach, information and assistance, and case management); in-home services; and legal assistance. Moreover, area agencies must specify how they will meet the needs of low-income minority individuals and older individuals residing in rural areas.

While some individuals use more than one OAA service, overall the unduplicated number of individuals served under Title III in 2000 was 7 million. Supportive services were provided to approximately 4.3 million older individuals. Some 116 million meals were served to 1.7 million individuals at congregate meal sites, and nearly 144 million home-delivered meals were served to 955,000 homebound elders in fiscal year 2000.

Percentages vary considerably from state to state, but nationally 30% of Title III participants were poor, 19% were minorities, and 33% were rural residents in 2000.

The 2000 reauthorization of the OAA enacted new provisions regarding participant contributions and cost sharing. Voluntary contributions from participants may now be solicited for all services provided under the act. Previously, the statute explicitly authorized voluntary contributions only for nutrition services. In addition, states may now require beneficiaries to pay a cost-sharing fee for the OAA services they receive, except for the following services: information and assistance, outreach, benefits counseling, case management, ombudsman services, elder abuse prevention, legal assistance, other consumer protection services, congregate and home-delivered meals, and any services delivered through tribal organizations. States may not subject individuals whose incomes are below the federal poverty line to cost sharing, and they may also exempt other low-income individuals from cost-sharing provisions.

A new National Family Caregiver Support Program was also enacted in 2000. This program was designed to respond to research that has documented the extensive role family members play in providing care to relatives with disabilities. Under this program, each state receives funds to provide services that include information to caregivers about available services, assistance in gaining access to services, caregiver training, respite care, and a limited amount of supplemental services. A portion of these funds is specifically allocated to help older individuals who provide care and support to people with mental and developmental disabilities. Funds for this program are allocated to states based on their share of the U.S. population age 70 and older.

### Title V—Community Service Employment

Unlike the other titles of the OAA, which are administered by the Administration on Aging in the U.S. Department of Health and Human Services, the Senior Community Service Employment Program is administered by the U.S. Department of Labor. The purpose of Title V is to provide subsidized employment opportunities to low-income older individuals with poor employment prospects. The goals of the program are both to increase employees' income and job skills and to expand community services. Program grantees also are directed to place at least 20% of their positions in unsubsidized employment in the private sector.

### Long-Term Care Ombudsman Program

A central component of the OAA's elder rights provisions is the long-term care ombudsman program. Each state that receives OAA funds is required to administer this program, which is designed to identify, investigate, and resolve complaints made by residents of nursing homes, board and care homes, assisted living facilities, and similar adult care facilities. The ombudsmen also work to bring about changes at the local, state, and national levels to improve care.

In 2000, almost 1,000 paid ombudsmen and 8,000 volunteers investigated about 232,000 complaints and provided information on long-term care to 245,000 individuals. The most frequent complaints involved lack of resident care due to inadequate staffing. (See also OLD-AGE PROVISIONS AND ECONOMIC STATUS.)

**Organizations**

AARP
National Association of Area Agencies on Aging
National Association of State Units on Aging
National Council on the Aging
National Long-Term Care Ombudsman Resource Center

**References**

AARP. 2003. *The Policy Book: AARP Public Policies 2003*. Washington, DC: Author.

Administration on Aging. 2002. *2000 State Program Reports*. Washington, DC: Author. Available online at http://www.aoa.gov/napis/2000spr/default.htm.

Administration on Aging. 2003a. "Legislation and Budget: Current Budget Information." Available online at http://www.aoa.gov/about/legbudg/current_budg/legbudg_current_budg.asp.

Administration on Aging. 2003b. "Older Americans Act Appropriation Information." Washington, DC: Author. Available online at http://www.aoa.gov/Oaa/oaaapp.html.

O'Shaughnessy, Carol V. 2001. *Older Americans Act: 2000 Reauthorization Legislation*. Washington, DC: Congressional Research Service.

Subcommittee on Human Services. 1992. *Older Americans Act: A Staff Summary (Comm. Pub. No. 102–911)*. Washington, DC: Select Committee on Aging, House of Representatives.

*Enid Kassner*

**OLDER WORKERS.** See Age Discrimination in Employment Act (ADEA); Working Retirees.

**OLDEST OLD,** a construct used in gerontology, demography, and public policy to describe the population aged 85 and older.

By the early 1980s, it had become clear that differences within the rapidly growing older population were so dramatic that it was no longer analytically or programmatically useful to treat "the elderly"—those aged 65 and older—as a single category. Those who have more recently passed into official old age, the so-called "young old," aged 65 to 74 years, and the "old," aged 75 to 84, are dissimilar to the more senior "oldest old." Condensing 25 or more years of remaining life into a single descriptor of "elderly" can only prejudice the documentation and understanding of emerging facts about old people in American society and their health and functioning, use of services, living arrangements, and financial security.

Those 85 and older are more likely than younger people to be women, to be afflicted with several chronic illnesses, and to experience significantly higher levels of disability. They are more likely to have outlived their social and familial supports, to live alone in the community, or to be housed in an institutional setting. They consume higher amounts of health and social services and receive benefits and transfer payments out of proportion to their numbers in the population.

Even more unrecognized about the oldest old, however, is their heterogeneity in sociodemographic and health characteristics. All very old people are not alike; they are as different as their accumulated life experiences. Nor is their decline into frailty, disability, dependency, and institutionalization inevitable and irreversible. The degree to which members of this cohort exhibit robustness and mental and physical plasticity will depend, of course, on their own unique endowment of social and biological attributes. But it will also be influenced—as will each subsequent birth cohort—by the shared experiences of the march through "its own slice of historical time" together (Suzman, Willis, and Manton 1992).

## Demographic Portrait

*Size and Growth.* Between 1900 and 2000, the proportion of the population that is older has increased tenfold, from 3 million in 1900 (4% of the population) to 35 million in the year 2000 (13%). But this rapid rate of increase—comparable to that seen in other developed countries—masked an even more dramatic and unique shift in America's population structure. The older population is itself becoming older, and people even at age 85 can anticipate another 6 years of life. At ages 65 to 74 the population had increased sevenfold, from 2.2 million in 1900 to 18.4 million in 2000; it had increased sixfold at ages 75 to 84; and the number of oldest old (85+) had increased 33 times to 4.2 million. Nearly 1 million of this latter group reported their age as 90 or older. Historically, high fertility levels of the past and the prior immigration of children and young adults set upper limits to the number of persons who could survive to age 85. But the more recent "aging of the aged" reflects a new population dynamic: disproportionate improvements in survival at very old ages (Taeuber 1993), which is expected to continue well into the next century, even before factoring in the aging of the baby boom.

By the year 2010, according to the consistently conservative "middle series" estimates produced by the U.S. Census Bureau, the number of persons aged 85 and older is projected to double to about 6.1 million. Alternative projections to 2050 are even more expansive; the Census Bureau's "middle series" projects 19.4 million oldest old. If significant behavioral risk factors for premature death (e.g., smoking, obesity, high blood pressure) were to be controlled among the cohorts now in their early middle years, the ranks of the oldest old could swell to over 41 million by 2050.

Average life expectancy at older ages will continue to increase differentially for men and women. By 2000, 65-year-old men could expect to live an additional 16.2 years and women 19.3 more years. Men who survived to age 85 had an additional life expectancy of 5.6 years; 6.8 years for women. The rate of gain in life expectancy for aged persons has been most dramatic since 1980. Greater numbers and percentages of the population will be beneficiaries of Medicare, Social Security, and private pensions over longer periods of time. Much of the industrialized world can anticipate comparable growth. Historical vital statistics for Sweden, for example, which are arguably the world's most complete and accurate, show that death rates have fallen substantially for octogenarians, nonagenarians, and even centenarians since the 1940s. In fact, while there were 65,000 centenarians alive in 2000, by 2030, the number will rise to 381,000; by 2050, estimates suggest the number will exceed 1 million centenarians.

*Sex Composition.* The increasing "feminization" of the oldest old is perhaps the most striking demographic imbalance. At every age, mortality among men exceeds that of women; with advancing age, the differential becomes wider. In 1900, there were 101 men for every female between the ages of 65 and 84; by midcentury, the ratio of males to females was 7 to 10. By the year 2000, between age 65 and 84, the age ratio was 4 to 5; at ages 85 and above it was 2 to 5. By 2050, under the middle series of Census Bureau projections, there will be 62 men per 100 women aged 85 and older, a considerable gain from the current 43 men per 100 women (U.S. Census Bureau 2003). Despite such relative change, however, the women will outnumber men at very old age by 4.5 million.

Among analysts and advocates, the well-being of the oldest old is justifiably characterized as a women's issue for reasons beyond sheer numbers. Women at this advanced age are more likely to be unmarried (86% compared with 46% of the men); widowhood is almost twice as common a current status among women, and remarriage after divorce is an infrequent option for older women. At any age, the loss of a spouse can be traumatic; for very old women, the consequences, whether through widowhood or divorce, are more extreme. This signal event is likely to mark the loss of considerable social support and household help in daily living, to trigger a sudden diminution of income and accumulated assets, and to accelerate the loss of independence. Few women in the current group of the oldest old had been in the labor force long enough, or at high enough levels of wages and salary, to have earned significant pension and retirement benefits in their own name. For many whose husbands had retired before the modest spousal protection of the Employee Retirement Income Security Act (ERISA) had been enacted, subsequent widowhood often led to poverty. Future cohorts of women are likely to reach age 85 with more financial assets having been protected by the spousal impoverishment rules under Medicaid that protect against the costs of a husband's terminal illness. Nevertheless, unlike younger-old married women, who are quite affluent by international standards, oldest-old women living alone in the community are likely to be very poor (Holtz-Eaton and Smeeding 1994).

*Racial and Ethnic Diversity.* Increasing racial and ethnic diversity also characterize the oldest-old population. In 2000, 8.6 persons in 10 above age 85 were identified as non-Hispanic Whites, and a high percentage had emigrated from western Europe in the earlier 1900s. African Americans constituted 7.5% of the oldest old; Asians were just about 2%, and Hispanics (of any race, but mainly from Mexico and South and Central America) were about 5% of the total. But changing immigration and fertility patterns, along with selective gains in survival, all point to a markedly different composition of the oldest old in future decades. By 2050, according to census "middle series" projections, the proportion of non-Hispanic Whites will decline to about 70% and will be almost entirely native-born. In 50 years, then, one-third (31%) of the oldest old will be members of racial and ethnic minorities.

The racial and ethnic composition of the oldest-old population may suggest differential needs for, and utilization of, public and private service programs. Precise determinations for very old ages, however, cannot be inferred from existing data on the still relatively small numbers of minorities; the data also lack a necessary historical perspective.

Indirect measures commonly associated with racial and ethnic differences, however, may indicate trends for the future. Education, for example, is almost universally accepted as positively correlated with social status and an ability to optimize personal use of preventive, treatment, and restorative services. Better-educated persons remain healthier longer, are less likely to be irreversibly disabled, and are more stable economically, even at age 85 and older. The substantial differences in educational level seen among the current oldest old are less pronounced among younger cohorts. The oldest old in 2001 are considerably better educated than earlier-born cohorts: 70% of Whites had completed high school, compared to 38% of African Americans. Among Hispanics at all ages, however, wider educational gaps persist, especially at the elementary and high school levels. In 2001, approximately 45% have only an elementary school education, compared to 23% of Asians, 20% of African Americans, and 4% of non-Hispanic Whites. A further 26% of Hispanics have from seven years of education to less than a high school diploma. Asians exhibit the largest proportional and absolute gains: in 2000, more than 60% have at least a high school education. They are expected to surpass Whites in the number of years of high school and college completed by 2010.

*Geographic Distribution.* Not surprisingly, the oldest-old population is distributed across all sections of the country in concentrations approximate to those of the younger old. Immigration by sun-seeking retirees is not the major factor contributing to concentrations of the very old. Rather, it is the nonmigration of aging persons who, through choice or circumstance, remain in their communities and "age in place." Actual postretirement relocation occurs well before age 85, most often at ages 65 to 74; such migrants subsequently age in place.

Persons aged 85 and older are found in every city, but their distribution is characterized by significant clustering of racial and ethnic subgroups. The populations of Baltimore, Maryland, and San Francisco, California, for example, although of comparable size, and each exceeding the average among cities in percentage at very old age, are otherwise dissimilar. One-third of the oldest old in Baltimore are Black; San Francisco has few very old African Americans, but one-fourth of its oldest old are Asian. In fact, four cities (Honolulu, Los Angeles, San Francisco, and New York) contain 40% of the nation's oldest-old Asians. Hispanics are somewhat more dispersed.

### Living Arrangements

*Community.* Despite considerable differences by age, sex, marital status, ethnicity, and region of the country, more than 82% of all persons age 85 and older live in the community. About two-thirds of those aged 90 to 94, and more than half of those 95 and older, continue living outside of nursing homes. This relative independence is closely associated with higher income, greater physical robustness, good cognitive functioning, and perhaps above all, presence of spousal or family supports. Among the oldest old living in the community in 1990, differences between men and women were most striking. Almost one-third of men, and over one-half of women, lived alone (most of them near family members); this represents a 10% increase since 1980. (Over the past several decades it has become less common at all ages to live with relatives.) In 2000, more than one-half of men (53%)—and 12% of women, the rare nonwidow—lived with a spouse. Adult children remain the largest source of nonspousal housing. An apparent cultural bias against institutional care of older family members may account for the significantly higher rates of oldest-old Hispanics and Asians being cared for in the community. In addition, other reasons such as lack of geographical access to skilled nursing facilities and lesser knowledge of available benefits may also play a factor in the lower utilization of institutional care by minorities.

*Nursing Homes.* Nursing home services have not been a central theme in public policy discussions since the repeal of the Medicare Catastrophic Coverage Act of 1988. Yet they are of ever-increasing importance in the lives of the oldest old and their families. In 1960, before the enactment of Medicaid, which has since become the primary source of payment for this care, only 14% of persons 85 and older lived in a nursing home; by 1997 the proportion had grown to 19%, down from a peak in 1994. The oldest old were almost 20 times more likely to reside in nursing homes than were persons aged 65 to 74. At ages 95 and older, the proportion institutionalized doubled again. However, this seemingly explosive increase in the use of nursing homes by the oldest old masks a number of significant underlying changes. A greater increase occurred between 1980 and 1985. At that time, changes in availability and coverage of skilled nursing facilities, along with the initiation of a national program of earlier hospital discharges ("quicker and sicker," it was alleged), stimulated a demand for nursing home care. The pattern established in that period—more nursing home admissions of the oldest old for short-term posthospital care—persists today.

An absolute increase in the numbers surviving to oldest-old age—an age at which one's caregiving adult children are themselves young old or even old—will continue to exert upward pressure on nursing home use. At any given level of physical and mental functioning, however, institutionalization can be deferred, shortened, or even avoided if home- and community-based services are available to complement family supportive care.

## Health and Functioning

Recent data from 13 countries of western Europe, Japan, and the United States offer clear evidence that mortality, illness, and disability do not increase exponentially at very old ages (Kannisto et al. 1994). In fact, the pace of improvement in mortality has accelerated over the past four decades. Sweden's highly reliable historical vital statistics for the oldest old are illustrative. Death rates for 85-year-old Swedish women are today less than one-half their level in the early 1900s and less than two-thirds their 1950 level. Nevertheless, poor health and impaired functioning, and the likelihood of a terminal illness, are increasingly concentrated at very old ages. The associated increase in use of expensive medical care services prompts intense discussion among medical, economic, ethical, social, and legal experts about the appropriateness of such resource allocation. Systematic data to inform such inquiry are not readily available. (See also AGING AMERICA; ECONOMIC STATUS OF OLDER MEN AND WOMEN; HEALTH AND LONGEVITY; MEDICAID; MEDICARE; MINORITY OLDER ADULTS; NURSING HOMES; RETIREMENT MIGRATION; SOCIAL SECURITY PROGRAM OF THE UNITED STATES; WIDOWHOOD.)

### References

Binstock, Robert H. 1992. "The Oldest Old and Intergenerational Equity." In *The Oldest Old*, ed. R.M. Suzman, D.P. Willis, and K.G. Manton. New York: Oxford University Press.

Holtz-Eaton, Douglas, and Timothy M. Smeeding. 1994. "Income, Wealth, and Intergenerational Economic Relations of the Aged." In *Demography of Aging*, ed. L. Martin and S.H. Preston. Washington, DC: National Academy Press.

Kannisto, V., J. Lauritsen, A.R. Thatcher, and J.W. Vaupel. 1994. "Reductions in Mortality at Advanced Ages: Several Decades of Evidence from 27 Countries." *Population and Development Review* 20(4): 793–810.

Manton, Kenneth G., Larry Corder, and Eric Stallard. 1993. "Changes in the Use of Personal Assistance and Special Equipment from 1982 to 1989: Results from the NLTCS." *The Gerontologist* 11: 168–76.

Suzman, Richard M., David P. Willis, and Kenneth G. Manton, eds. 1992. *The Oldest Old*. New York: Oxford University Press.

Taeuber, Cynthia M. 1993. "Sixty-Five Plus in America." *Current Population Reports*. Special Study P23-178RV. Washington, DC: U.S. Bureau of the Census.
U.S. Census Bureau. 2003. "Projections of the Total U.S. Resident Population." Reports # NP-T3-A, NP-T3-G, NP-T3-H, NP-T4-A, and NP-T4-G. Available online at http://www.census.gov/population/projections/summary/np-t3-a, and so on.

*David P. Willis*
*Updated by Sandra L. Reynolds*

**OMBUDSMAN,** a public official appointed to investigate citizens' complaints against local or national government agencies that may be infringing on the rights of individuals. The concept of the ombudsman, and the name, date from the mid-nineteenth century. The idea was developed in Scandinavian countries in order to give citizens a means of cutting through bureaucratic red tape to resolve personal difficulties with the political and administrative system (Gwyn 1980). The function of an independent advocate proved effective as a means of intervening in governmental processes on behalf of individuals.

## Background

The ombudsman concept provided citizens a chance to address difficulties that previously were hard to resolve because the proper authorities could not be approached or accessed. Governmental regulations may cause hardships when applied to a specific personal situation, but often there is no way to discuss or cope with the difficulty. The individual may not know where to begin. This kind of challenge is what gives the ombudsman function its unique effectiveness. The ombudsman is accessible, and independent, serving as an outside-the-system but knowledgeable figure, appointed to represent the interests of those subject to institutional regulation. Sometimes an ombudsman is created by the very institution with which it intercedes, but the ombudsman's position must have integrity and autonomy in order to achieve its purpose.

When the ombudsman was first created, it was an empowering idea in representative democracies where sheer numbers generated anonymity and powerlessness for the average citizen. In the 1950s, the idea became more widespread in the Western world, and ombudsmen served in a variety of positions in the Commonwealth nations, in France, and in the United States. Their function as intercessors was extended to many more situations: federal, state, and local governments; newspapers; hospitals; and industries. The adaptive power of the concept is further illustrated by the use that the U.S. military makes of the idea. The U.S. Navy, for example, uses an active volunteer ombudsman program to represent the concerns of the families of its military members in the command structure (Howe 1988).

Ombudsmen go by a variety of names, from public relations representative (in a corporate context) or reader advocate (for newspapers) to patient representative or patient advocate (in hospitals). To qualify as an ombudsman position, its function must be independent and include advocacy, policy explanation, and grievance presentation on behalf of the individual user vis-à-vis the institution or system.

## Long-Term Care Ombudsman Programs for Older Adults

The ombudsman concept has proven particularly useful to residents of nursing homes and board and care homes. The 1978 amendments to the Older Americans Act (OAA) authorized Long-Term Care (LTC) Ombudsman Programs to resolve complaints by nursing home residents, inform residents of their legal rights, provide information on resident needs and concerns of the community, and advocate on behalf of residents for changes in laws and regulations to improve long-term care services. As defined by OAA, the ombudsman function includes complaint settlement and consumer advocacy as well. This means that the ombudsman complements, but does not duplicate, the contributions of regulatory agencies, families, community-based organizations, and providers (Institute of Medicine [IOM] 1995).

State Agencies on Aging were required to establish and operate either directly, through contract, or by other arrangement an Office of the State Ombudsman. Subsequent amendments have strengthened the role of the program, extending the reach of ombudsmen to residents of board and care facilities and other group residential homes. Functions now include public education and outreach, training and technical assistance, referral of unlicensed homes, and the coordination of services. The coordination between ombudsman services, legal assistance, and protection and advocacy programs has become particularly important. Federal law allows each state to design a reporting system to meet the needs of its various constituencies and to collect data relevant to their needs. Today the LTC Ombudsman Program operates in all 50 states, the District of Columbia, and Puerto Rico. Paid staff number about 865 and volunteer ombudsmen about 6,750 (IOM 1995).

In considering the record of ombudsman programs for older adults, reports demonstrate great variation from state to state. Overall, access via the ombudsman program has improved because representatives have found it easier to contact residents and the homes themselves and to gain access to resident records. Access to administrative records maintained by facilities still constitutes a problem in many states (General Accounting Office 1992). As of 1990, the distribution of major complaints ranged from resident care matters (38.1%) to the administration of facilities (21.5%), resident rights (18.7%), and nutrition (14.4%) (Netting, Paton, and Huber 1992). A measure of success is documented by the research finding that the existence of ombudsman programs is often associated with better nursing care, whereas mere volunteer programs are not effective enough to have an impact on quality (Cherry 1993). Earlier, it had been found that nursing home ombudsmen called attention to aspects of quality of care that were not currently assured by other protective mechanisms.

### Outlook

The ombudsman role could also be utilized to include advocacy and explanation of financial issues in a variety of other situations affecting older adults. Since the size of the older population is growing rapidly and its specialized financial needs are increasing, the concept of a dedicated financial ombudsman for senior citizens is timely. While financial complaints constitute a relatively small part of the actions dealt with by nursing home ombudsmen, financial questions are of great concern for older persons living at home. The banking system, for instance, might utilize an ombudsman to explain policies, savings strategies, or money management to older adults and intercede/mediate with bank officials.

A useful model of ombudsman-type intervention is the financial ombudsman service offered in the United Kingdom. The job of the financial ombudsman is to settle disputes between individual consumers and all types of financial institutions. The service is free, impartial, and expert. An individual must complain directly to the firm or institution first, and then, if not satisfied with the response, the complaint can be referred to the financial ombudsman for investigation and resolution. The decision of the ombudsman, whose position is established by law, is binding on the firm or institution but not on the complainant. The complainer may resort to the court system if not satisfied. The financial ombudsman service is available online for UK residents. Canada offers a similar type of financial ombudsman service. Additional information is available at http://www.financial-ombudsman.org.uk/about/key-facts.htm.

Ombudsman-type representation to serve the needs of the older population may be considered by the institutions themselves and/or advocated by those who are concerned about the often complex financial needs of older adults. Geriatric social workers with financial experience have an ideal background for this advocacy function. Ombudsman positions could be set up at the community level with local financial institutions or financial planners who are knowledgeable regarding older person issues on a consultative or as-needed basis. Local accountants, banking executives, and others who understand the community's financial institutions and services and have cross-cutting contacts could volunteer to work on an on-call basis as ombudsmen when seniors need advice, assistance, or advocacy.

At this time the ombudsman model remains a valuable advocacy mechanism with an impressive record, waiting to be activated more extensively on behalf of those who need intervention with complicated institutions, including those of the financial world. (See also ASSISTED LIVING; BOARD AND CARE HOMES; CONSUMER PROTECTION FOR OLDER ADULTS; NURSING HOMES; OLDER AMERICANS ACT; TAXPAYER ISSUES OF OLDER ADULTS; VETERANS' BENEFITS.)

### Organizations

National Citizens Coalition for Nursing Home Reform
National Eldercare Institute on Elder Abuse and State Long-Term Care Ombudsman Services
National Society for Patient Representation

### Suggested Reading

Hunt, Sara, and Sarah Burger. 1992. *Using Resident Assessment and Care Planning as Advocacy Tools: A Guide for Ombudsmen and Other Advocates*. Washington, DC: National Citizens' Coalition for Nursing Home Reform.

### References

Cherry, Ralph L. 1993. "Community Presence and Nursing Home Quality of Care: The Ombudsman as a Complementary Role." *Journal of Health and Social Behavior* 34: 336–45.

General Accounting Office. 1992. *Older Americans Act: Access to and Utilization of the Ombudsman Program*. Washington, DC: Author.

Gwyn, William B. 1980. "The Discovery of the Scandinavian Ombudsman in English-Speaking Countries." *Western European Politics* 3: 317–38.

Howe, Harriet M. 1988. *Navy Ombudsman Training Manual*. Washington, DC: Department of the Navy.

Institute of Medicine (IOM). 1995. *Real People, Real Problems: An Evaluation of the Long-Term Care Ombudsman Programs of the Older Americans Act*. Washington, DC: National Academy of Sciences.

Netting, F. Ellen, Ruth Nelson Paton, and Ruth Huber. 1992. "Long-Term Care Ombudsman Program: What Does the Complaint Reporting System Tell Us?" *The Gerontologist* 32: 843–48.

*Harriet Howe*

# P

**PENSION PLANS,** benefits provided through employers that pay primarily monthly amounts to retirees after they leave their employment. Not all employers provide pension plans to their employees, but if one is provided, it can take a number of forms today: traditional pension plan, cash balance, 401(k), 403(b), 457, or one of several self-employed plans, such as Keogh or profit sharing plan. Also, on one's own, an employee can contribute to an Individual Retirement Account (IRA) or Roth IRA. But 50 years ago there was essentially only one type of pension plan, a final-pay plan, which is now called a traditional pension plan.

Although there were some pension plans as early as the late 1800s, there were only 10,644 people receiving industrial pensions in 1929. Pension plans only came to the fore after World War II. Employers wanted to provide an incentive to workers as the economy converted from a war effort back to a regular one. Workers, returning from the war, were looking for work and were willing to commit themselves to an employer for a full career.

## Traditional Pension Plans

The formulation of pension plans just after the war recognized the role of Social Security, which was signed into law in 1935 and was also designed to pay a monthly benefit to workers once they retired. The design of pension plans then both took into account benefits and tried to determine what replacement ratio, or percentage of final pay, after a full career, would provide a sufficient amount so retirees would have enough income on which to retire. A typical formula that emerged was:

$$(\text{Average Final Pay} \times \text{Years of Service} \times 1.5\%) - \text{Social Security Benefit} \times 0.5$$

This type of formula became popular with employers because it provided an approximately equal percentage of benefits, relative to final pay, for all levels of workers' pay, when both benefits were considered. An underlying fact of Social Security's benefit formula was that a lower-paid worker received a higher percentage of their final pay than higher-paid workers. By including the Social Security benefit in the pension formula, through a subtraction or "offset," a pension benefit in combination with Social Security resulted in about the same percentage of final pay for lower- or higher-paid workers. Although this formula was mathematically sound, it was difficult to explain the subtraction of Social Security to workers. In fact, if the subtraction was not included, then the percentage in the pension formula would have been much lower, perhaps about only 1%, versus the 1.5% shown above. This would give workers about the same result, but without counteracting the skewing of the Social Security benefit.

Pension plans of unions avoided this argument and presented a more forthright formula. Typically a union pension pays what is called a "flat-dollar" benefit. For instance, if a plan has a flat-dollar benefit of $20, then the monthly pension benefit would be $20 multiplied by years of service. As an example, if a worker had 30 years of service and the flat-dollar benefit was $20, then the pension plan benefit would be $7,200 per year ($20 times 30 equals a monthly benefit of $600; $600 times 12 equals $7,200 a year).

In time, some employers installed savings plans to augment pensions. In the 1980s, 401(k)s became popular because the contributions were made on a pretax basis, and employees could direct how their money was invested from a menu of funds selected by the employer as plan sponsor. With the stock market making sizable gains in the 1980s, these plans shifted employee focus from the traditional pension plan to these newer retirement savings vehicles. Their counterpart in plans for employees of nonprofit employers, 403(b) plans, and more recently plans for employees of state and local governments, 457 plans, have likewise seen a rise in popularity. But these plans are unlike pensions, since these plans do not promise a specific benefit at retirement. Instead, they only promise a certain contribution to the plan while working. Thus, broadly, retirement plans are separated into defined benefit plans and defined contribution plans. The traditional pension plan is a defined benefit plan, while the 401(k) plan is a defined contribution plan.

However, the popularity of traditional pension plans among employers has significantly decreased in recent years. There are at least three reasons for this development. First, they are a costly benefit from the employer's standpoint. Second, they require adherence to complicated regulations and require hiring of actuaries and consultants to provide technical calculations and guidance. Third, and finally, these plans were intended as a reward for long-term employees. In today's employment environment, however, employees typically do not stay at the same organization for very long, either because they want to leave for better positions or because the organization itself has eliminated jobs during layoffs or organizational restructurings.

### Cash Balance Plans

With the waning of interest in traditional pension plans, many employers are either eliminating the plans altogether, substituting 401(k)s or other savings or profit sharing plans, or in some cases converting the pensions into a newer type of plan called a cash balance plan. In cash balance plans, employers still contribute most, if not all, of the money to the plans, but employees are given "balances"—specific dollar figures each year that are presented as the employees' own accounts and can be taken whenever the employees leave the organization. Cash balance plans are essentially defined benefit plans with defined contribution plan features. Employers don't promise specific benefits—only specific contributions—which are typically based on a combination of wage credits and interest credits. Cash balance plans fall under the defined benefit plan regulations, which have important regulatory safeguards including the critical guarantee of the Pension Benefit Guaranty Corporation (PBGC). Like traditional pensions, employers not only contribute the money to these plans, but they also are in control of the investments in the plans, whereas in 401(k) plans employees make most of the contributions and all of the investment selections.

These plans are particularly popular with younger employees because they see an account balance that is theirs, just like 401(k) plans, even if they do not control how the money is invested. Traditional plans seem less desirable because of their complexity, which can be difficult to understand, and because they do not provide significant benefits until later in employees' careers. For older employees, especially long-service employees, however, these newer plans are not particularly welcome. The amount of steady retirement income provided is generally greater from a traditional pension plan than from a cash balance plan or 401(k) plan. These newer plans almost always provide lump sums, which can seem like large payouts, but in times of decreasing stock market returns can mean lower pension incomes along with the obvious year-to-year uncertainties. Some employers have had significant employee relations problems when they have converted existing traditional final-pay plans to cash balance plans. Other employers give current employees who meet certain criteria a choice between the types of plans.

### Self-Employed Plans

There are a number of plans available for the self-employed. These plans are generally called Keogh plans but are of a variety of plans: SEPs, or Simplified Employee Pensions; SIMPLEs, or Savings Incentive Match Plan for Employees; Money Purchase plans; or Defined Benefit plans. Each offers different limits as to contributions, benefits, and who must be included in the plan if there are employees besides the owner. Some plans, such as SEP plans, offer simplicity, so little paperwork is necessary or outside help required. For defined benefit Keogh plans, which are the most complicated, outside help is required, usually with actuaries specializing in these types of plans.

### Plan Payouts

Although some of these plans pay lump sums, notably cash balance, Keogh plans, and all defined contribution plans, most of the traditional pension plans pay only monthly benefits. The common form of payout in these plans is typically a single-life payout, or a joint-and-survivor payout for married employees.

Also, typically, an employee's benefit is reduced if taken before age 65. Some plans, however, only reduce the payouts before age 60 or 62, when an employee is eligible for Social Security. A benefit is usually not paid before age 55, before which it is assumed that retirement would not normally begin. If an employee leaves the organization before then, the employee is generally not entitled to an immediate pension benefit and in fact may have to wait to age 65 for any pension. However, if the plan does allow for early retirement, it usually applies an actuarial reduction, because an employee would expect to collect it for a longer period of time. The full actuarial reduction is normally 6.7% per year. Thus, the full reduction at age 55 may result in a pension of only 30% of what would be received at 65.

### Regulations

The most important legislation pertaining to pensions is ERISA, or the Employee Retirement Income Security Act of 1974. This federal law regulates participation rules, or who must be included in the plan; reporting and disclosure rules, or the various documents required to be filed by employers; and the fiduciary standards, or the responsibilities the employer has to plan beneficiaries.

One of the most important regulations from an employee's standpoint is that of vesting. If there is a pension plan, the employee generally must be entitled to a benefit after only five years of service. Another is that a married employee must select a joint and survivor payout, unless the spouse elects to opt out of that required benefit. Also, if requested, employees must be given any projected pension payouts when they leave the employer prior to retirement. (See also CASH BALANCE PENSION PLANS; DEFINED BENEFIT PENSION PLAN; DEFINED CONTRIBUTION PLAN; EMPLOYEE RETIREMENT INCOME SECURITY ACT (ERISA); RETIREMENT PLANS—401(k); RETIREMENT PLANS—403(b).)

**References**

Arnone, William, et al. 1994. *The Columbia Retirement Handbook.* New York: Columbia University Press.

Arnone, William, et al. 2002. *Ernst & Young's Retirement Planning Guide.* New York: John Wiley & Sons.

Westbrook, Paul. 2001. *J.K. Lasser's New Rules for Retirement and Tax.* New York: John Wiley & Sons.

*Paul Westbrook and William Arnone*

**PENSION PLANS FOR THE SELF-EMPLOYED,** tax-sheltered savings plans for owners (and employees) of unincorporated businesses. A self-employed individual is a sole proprietor or partner who works in his or her own unincorporated business. The most well-known pension plans for the self-employed are Keogh plans and Individual Retirement Accounts (IRAs). However, the self-employed can also take advantage of recent changes in the law to save for retirement using other options. Self-employed individuals can take advantage of Keogh plans, SEPs (Simplified Employee Pensions), SIMPLE plans (Savings Incentive Match Plan for Employees), Solo 401(k)s, deductible (traditional) IRAs, and Roth IRAs—sometimes in combination.

*Keogh Plans.* When originally enacted in the early 1960s, Keogh plans, also known as HR-10 plans, were limited but at least offered self-employed people an opportunity to save for retirement on a tax-favored basis similar to that enjoyed by corporate owners and employees. Over the years the distinctions between Keoghs and plans for regular corporations have been eroded. Now although some Internal Revenue Service (IRS) forms, such as the Form 5500 for pension reporting, still refer to Keogh plans, most financial and investment firms simply refer to the specific type of plan: defined benefit or defined contribution.

A Keogh plan is a qualified retirement plan that covers one or more self-employed individuals. For example, a typical Keogh plan might cover the self-employed person, the spouse of the self-employed person, and a few employees. If a self-employed person, such as a sole proprietor, has employees, they must be included in the plan.

Keogh plan contributions are deducted from gross income, and tax is deferred until funds are withdrawn from the plan at a later date. Income generated by the investments in a Keogh plan is also tax-deferred until it is withdrawn from the plan.

An advantage of Keogh plans is that the limits on contributions are significantly more liberal than those applied to IRAs. In 2003, the maximum contribution to a defined *contribution* Keogh plan is the lesser of $40,000 and 100% of net earnings from the business. The maximum contribution to a self-employed defined *benefit* pension plan depends on actuarial calculations for what is required to fund a benefit that, in 2003, may not be greater than $160,000 per year. The calculation depends on the self-employed individual's income, the target benefit, years until normal retirement age, and anticipated investment returns. The defined benefit plan will usually provide the greatest deductible contribution for high earners over age 50 or thereabouts, but it is also the most complicated to set up and the most expensive to maintain. Generally, benefit payments from a Keogh plan to a self-employed individual must begin by April 1 of the year after he or she reaches age 70½. Beginning in 2002, the owner-employee (a self-employed person or a partner owning more than 10% of the business) is able to take a loan from the Keogh plan (generally up to the lesser of $50,000, or half of the vested benefit). Prior to 2002, such loans were "prohibited transactions" subject to penalty.

An individual who works for a regular employer and is covered under that employer's qualified plan can establish a separate Keogh plan for an additional business carried on separately as a self-employed individual.

*SEPs (Simplified Employee Pensions).* SEPs, sometimes known as SEP IRAs, are traditional IRAs that can take expanded contributions from one or more employees, including a self-employed person. The contribution limits are significantly higher than a traditional IRA: in 2003, the lesser of $40,000 or 100% of net earnings. SEPs are very simple to set up, very flexible in terms of contributions year to year, and a great benefit to procrastinators because they can be opened as late as the due date of the tax return on which the deduction is being claimed, including extensions. For self-employed persons with employees, there are stringent rules about treating all employees (including owner-employees) in a nondiscriminatory manner with regard to employer contributions.

*SIMPLE Plans.* SIMPLE plans may be thought of as the middle ground of pension plans for the self-employed. Employers with no more than 100 employees (anyone earning at least $5,000 per year) may set up a SIMPLE plan for employees, but it must be the only plan in the enterprise. SIMPLE plans have been available since the 1996 Small Business Job Protection Act and were enhanced in the Economic Growth and Tax Relief Reconciliation Act of 2001 (EGTRRA 2001). In exchange for very simple administration—no annual reporting—self-employed people, partners, and small companies accept lower (but perhaps more realistic) annual contribution limits than are available in some other forms of retirement plans.

The funding mechanism can be either an individual account for each participant (SIMPLE IRA) or a single pool of money in which everyone participates (SIMPLE 401(k)). Employee contributions are limited to $8,000 annually in 2003, except that those who will be 50 or older at the end of the year can contribute an additional $1,000. Each participating employee's contribution must be matched up to 3% of the employee's pay (with some limited flexibility year to year to allow for a bad year), or the employer must make a nonelective contribution of 2% of compensation for all eligible employees, regardless of their contribution.

SIMPLE plans are more democratic than some other plans. In SIMPLE IRAs the "top-heavy" and nondiscrimination rules that apply to Keogh and SEP plans to assure that benefits are not weighted toward the owners and highly compensated individuals do not

**Table 1**
**Important Features of Traditional and Roth Individual Retirement Accounts**

| Feature | Traditional IRA | Roth IRA |
|---|---|---|
| Contributions must be made from earned income | Yes | Yes |
| Annual dollar limit | Yes (before tax) | Yes (after tax) |
| Restrictions on deduction or contribution if active participation in tax-favored employer plan | Yes, deduction limited based on adjusted gross income | No |
| 10% penalty on early withdrawals | Yes | Yes |
| Required minimum distributions | Yes, beginning at earlier of age 70½ or death | Yes, beginning at death |

*Source*: Leimberg and McFadden 2001.

apply. In a SIMPLE 401(k), the special nondiscrimination rules and top-heavy rules do not apply, but regular nondiscrimination and coverage rules do.

*Solo 401(k) Plans.* Solo 401(k) plans are newly attractive since the passage of EGTRRA 2001 but, as a practical matter, are only attractive to self-employed people with no employees except a spouse. If incorporated, the maximum contribution between employer and employee is the lesser of $40,000 or 100% of compensation, plus an over-age-50 catch-up amount twice that available in SIMPLE plans ($2,000 in 2003). They also offer great flexibility in terms of stopping and starting; there doesn't have to be a contribution to the plan in any given year. Should business falter badly, loans are available from the plan up to $50,000 without taxes or penalty.

*Individual Retirement Accounts.* IRAs were originally developed as a tax-deferred savings plan for workers without access to an employer pension. Over the years IRAs have been modified several times. Now there are two primary types of IRAs: traditional and Roth IRAs. Under the traditional IRA, contributions (up to certain limits) are deductible and investment earnings are tax-deferred. Contributions to a Roth IRA are made with after-tax earned income. Because traditional and Roth IRAs have some restrictions, a potential participant is advised to investigate the restrictions carefully (see http://www.irs.gov/). Table 1 provides a comparison of some of the features of traditional and Roth IRAs.

*Other Options for Saving for Retirement.* Many self-employed individuals depend on a spouse's employment for access to health care benefits and pension plan coverage. Doing this allows the self-employed person to reinvest earnings and profits or to invest in other savings options. A study of women business owners (DeVaney et al. 1997) showed that the owners saved the most by investing in stocks. The amount saved in other retirement savings options was (in order from second largest amount to the smallest amount): equity in their own business; savings accounts, bonds or certificates of deposit; mutual funds; IRAs; 401(k) or 403(b) tax-deferred accounts; Employee Stock Option Plans; Simplified Employee Pensions; and Keogh plans. At the time the study was conducted, loans to the employer from a Keogh plan were a "prohibited transaction."

However, the results could be taken as an indication that the self-employed prefer to save in options that are more readily accessible (such as stocks, mutual funds, savings accounts, etc.) than tax-deferred retirement accounts.

In a study comparing retirement plan participation by the self-employed and wage-and-salary earners, DeVaney and Chien (2000) found that an advanced degree, high income, and Caucasian heritage were the major factors that predicted participation by the self-employed in formal retirement plans. In contrast, wage-and-salary workers tended to be participants in formal retirement plans if they were older, if they had some college education or a degree, and if they worked full time and for a larger firm. Another study showed that the self-employed tend to retire later than wage-and-salary workers; this may influence their participation in retirement savings plans and the options used for retirement savings (DeVaney and Kim 2003). (See also DEFINED BENEFIT PENSION PLAN; DEFINED CONTRIBUTION PLAN; FINANCIAL ADVISORS; INDIVIDUAL RETIREMENT ACCOUNT [IRA]; KEOGH PLANS; RETIREMENT PLANS—401(k); SOCIAL SECURITY PROGRAM OF THE UNITED STATES.)

### Organizations

Business Owner's Toolkit
Quicken Turbotax
SmartMoney

### References

Carter, Gary W. 2002. *J.K. Lasser's Taxes Made Easy for Your Home Based Business*. 5th ed. New York: John Wiley & Sons.

Daily, Frederick W. 1998. *Tax Savvy for Small Business: Year-Round Tax Strategies to Save You Money*. 3rd ed. Berkeley, CA: Nolo Press.

DeVaney, S.A., and Y. Chien. 2000. "Participation in Retirement Plans: A Comparison of the Self-Employed and Wage and Salary Workers." *Compensation and Working Conditions* 5(4): 31–36.

DeVaney, S.A., and H. Kim. 2003. "Older Self-employed Workers and Planning for the Future." *Journal of Consumer Affairs* 37(1): 101–20.

DeVaney, S.A., Y. Su, C.Y. Kratzer, and D.L. Sharpe. 1997. "Retirement Savings of Non-Farm Self-employed Workers." *Consumer Interests Annual* 43: 58–63.

*Individual Retirement Arrangements (IRAs)*. n.d. IRS Publication 590. Available online at http://www.irs.gov/.

Internal Revenue Service. 2003. *The Digital Daily*. Available online at http://www.irs.gov/.

Leimberg, Stephan R., and John J. McFadden. 2001. *The Tools and Techniques of Employee Benefit and Retirement Planning*. Cincinnati, OH: National Underwriter Company.

*Retirement Plans for Small Business*. n.d. IRS Publication 560. Available online at http://www.irs.gov/.

Salisbury, Dallas, and Marc Robinson. 2003. *Essential Finance: IRA and 401(k) Investing*. New York: Dorling Kindersley Publishing.

Slesnick, Twila, John C. Suttle, and Amy Delpo. 1998. *Creating Your Own Retirement Plan: A Guide to Keoghs & IRAs for the Self-Employed*. 2nd ed. Berkeley, CA: Nolo Press.

*Sharon A. DeVaney*

**PENSIONS.** See Employee Retirement Income Security Act (ERISA); Employee Stock Ownership Plans (ESOPs); Individual Retirement Account (IRA); Keogh Plans; Trusts.

**PERSONAL SERVICES.** See Financial Counseling for Mid- to Later Life; Geriatric Care Managers (GCMs); Gerontological Nurse Practitioners (GNPs); Gerontological Social Work; Home Care Services for Older Adults.

**PHARMACISTS,** trained professionals who are licensed to dispense medications. Pharmacists have primary responsibility for dispensing medications and educating patients about their proper use, adverse effects, and drug interactions. Although pharmacists interact directly with people most often in community settings, they practice in most health care environments.

Pharmacists are easily accessible drug therapy experts. When filling a prescription, the pharmacist reviews patient characteristics (e.g., age, gender, medical conditions, allergies) and other medications being taken, all included in the pharmacy patient profile, to ensure that the dose is correct and that there are no incompatibilities or contraindications to its use. If problems or questions exist, the pharmacist can contact the prescriber(s) to resolve them before the patient receives the medication. The pharmacist also is required to counsel the patient regarding the proper use of any new prescription, as well as when there is a change in the prescription or if the patient requests counseling. This makes the pharmacist an ideal professional for patients to ask about the use of nonprescription medications and other remedies, as well.

Several factors should be considered when choosing a pharmacist. While the cost of medications is a major concern, it is not the only one. In addition to easily accessible location, convenient hours, and competitive prices, the level of service provided is a very important factor. Computerized patient medication profiles are an essential component of a good pharmacy practice. The profiles allow the pharmacist to immediately review all medications that a person is taking, including nonprescription remedies, to make sure that no drug interactions exist. Availability of after-hours service is a benefit that is welcomed by many older adults, even though it may rarely be required. Prescription services should be comprehensive. The pharmacist should make the patient aware of lower-priced generic alternatives, take the time to fully explain the use of the prescription and its possible side effects, and provide this service in a quiet, confidential area of the pharmacy. Questions should be encouraged and thoughtfully answered. The pharmacist should keep the patient informed about the status of pending refill medications and be familiar with the most common medical and insurance plans that have prescription drug benefits. The pharmacist also should be familiar with the unique medication-related needs of older adults.

Although most people see a pharmacist only when having a prescription filled, pharmacists are active in most areas of health care. Hospital pharmacists frequently work closely with physicians to monitor drug therapy and to determine the most appropriate dose of a medication for critically ill patients. Because age, body size, other diseases, and other medications can all affect how medicines work, doses frequently need to be individualized for patients in hospitals. A large portion of hospitals take advantage of the pharmacist's extensive knowledge in this area to help ensure accurate dosing to maximize benefits and reduce the risk of adverse reactions.

Pharmacists in health maintenance organizations often have direct interactions with patients. They may work with patients to improve adherence to complex medication regimens or may monitor and adjust medication doses for patients with diseases such as high cholesterol, diabetes mellitus, or high blood pressure, or who require warfarin or other medications to reduce the chance of blood clots.

Another important area of pharmacy services is in long-term care, such as nursing facilities, assisted living facilities, and other retirement living areas. Pharmacists are required to review the medication regimen of every resident of a nursing facility on a monthly basis. This review includes evaluating the appropriateness of any prescribed medication(s), checking for adverse effects or interactions, and ensuring that meds are administered to the resident in a prompt and timely manner. Although not required for assisted living or retirement facilities, many pharmacists provide similar services in these environments, as well. In addition, some pharmacists offer education programs to residents, families, and staff members of the facilities.

Most pharmacists can help older adults with their basic information and service needs. Because many retirees take many medications, have specific needs, and want in-depth information about their health care, pharmacists with training in geriatric pharmacy are the most helpful. Many opportunities exist for pharmacists to receive this training, both during pharmacy school and after graduation and licensure. Retirees should seek out such pharmacists whenever possible. One indicator of expertise in this area is the "Certified Geriatric Pharmacist (CGP)" credential. The CGP designation indicates that the pharmacist has passed a rigorous practice-based examination in geriatric pharmacy practice. CGP pharmacists are well prepared to meet the unique medication-related needs of older adults. A listing of certified geriatric pharmacists is available at the Commission for Certification in Geriatric Pharmacy Web site, listed at the end of this section.

Medications play an important role in maintaining the health of retirees, but they also can cause harm when not used appropriately. Choosing a pharmacist who is well qualified to serve retirees is an important consideration that must be evaluated carefully. (See also DRUGS AND SENIOR CITIZENS; GERONTOLOGICAL NURSE PRACTITIONERS [GNPs]; HEALTH MAINTENANCE ORGANIZATIONS AND MANAGED HEALTH CARE FOR OLDER ADULTS; MEDICARE; PHYSICIAN–OLDER PATIENT RELATIONSHIPS.)

### Organizations

American Society of Consultant Pharmacists
Commission for Certification in Geriatric Pharmacy

### Suggested Readings

National Council on Patient Information and Education. 1999. *Medicines: Before You Take It, Talk About It*. Available online at http://www.talkaboutrx.org/.

National Institute on Aging. 1999. *Medicines: Use Them Safely*. Available online at http://www.nia.nih.gov/health/agepages/medicine.htm.

National Institute on Aging. 1999. *Talking with Your Doctor: A Guide for Older People*. Available online at http://www.nia.nih.gov/health/pubs/talking/.

### References

Berger, Bruce. 2002. *Communication Skills for Pharmacists: Building Relationships, Improving Patient Care*. San Francisco, CA: Jossey-Bass Publishers.

Blumenthal, Dale. 1991. *Pharmacists Help Solve Medication Mysteries*. Rockville, MD: Department of Health and Human Services, Public Health Service.

*Bradley R. Williams*

**PHASED RETIREMENT AND RETIREE SKILLS BANKS,** restructured employment arrangements for an aging workforce that can accommodate today's realities for both employers and employees.

### Background

During the 1980s and early 1990s, many managers responded to potentially difficult situations, such as lower-than-expected profit reports or the need to quell shareholders' concerns about the value of company stock by "downsizing" or "rightsizing" the company. No matter how companies packaged the initiatives, employers typically had one essential goal: to reduce the number of employees. Among the packages, early retirement incentive plans (ERIPs) were often targeted to the most expensive (the most senior) employees, and they became the cornerstone of many workforce reduction efforts.

Although ERIPs, and downsizing generally, produced immediate savings, managers noted that sustained savings rarely occurred. In some cases, longer-term costs ultimately overshadowed short-term savings. While theoretically a reduced headcount should increase productivity, three reasons for decreased productivity among nonterminated employees were frequently cited:

1. The actual downsizing demoralized remaining staff, who experienced what has been described as "survivor syndrome."
2. With fewer staff, individual workloads increased—often without extra pay—which tended to degrade morale and to further decrease productivity.
3. Employees became or remained distrustful of management (e.g., expected to be fired), even when they had been assured of job security.

As a result, voluntary resignations increased, especially among the most talented and marketable employees, which resulted in additional workloads for those who remain. Total bench strength, measured by the quality and volume of work produced, continued to decline. Morale and productivity were further depressed when headcount reductions resulted in a disproportionate percentage of staff reduction. Highly paid senior staff was retained, while low paid line employees were terminated. Cost savings identified by reduction of lower-level workers with more seniority were offset by retention of higher-level workers.

This experience can serve as the foundation for a business case to reconfigure future employment and retirement arrangements of older adults. In essence, it may be in corporate America's best interests, since both older workers and government (e.g., through taxes) will look to fund solutions that ensure economic security and that constitute new ways to structure employment that meet both parties' needs.

### Phased Retirement and Retiree Skill Banks

Phased retirement and retiree skills banks, as company-sponsored investments in older workers and retirees, can produce measurable and sustainable outcomes to the company and its workforce. The two initiatives are complementary: one focuses on the period leading up to retirement, while skills banks reemploy retirees. In general terms, phased retirement, during the development, may present some complexities (e.g., administrative, communication) to the organization. These are generally not evident with retiree skills banks. However, the potential return on investment (ROI) offered by phased retirement far surpasses what might be achieved via a skills bank. A retiree skills bank will afford an employer a labor pool with skills to meet specific needs for a given time period, but phasing can facilitate corporate succession plans, training efforts, and knowledge transfer. Essentially, phasing provides the employer with greater opportunities to achieve business goals through its human capital.

With its origins in western Europe, phased retirement evolved as a natural part of a three-way partnership: employees, employers, and the government. Phased retirement offers significant potential but is less successful in the United States than in Europe. Retiree skills banks, primarily an American invention, are a spin-off of the temporary services industry.

### Phased Retirement

Phased retirement is also known as gradual retirement, gliding, and transitioning. Transitioning targets employees in the years prior to retirement. Prior to full-time retirement, phased retirement provides employees the opportunity to reduce the number of hours worked. In contrast, the most common current practice occurs at close of business on some predetermined date, when a full-time employee changes to a full-time retiree. Implicit are other symbolic changes including the change from active contributor to retired noncontributor. In a phased retirement, accountabilities during the transition and impact upon salary and benefits are identified in advance. Phased retirement emphasizes continued contributions and productivity. Successful phased retirement programs require focused communications resulting in an agreement between employer and employee. The agreement identifies a start and targeted full-retirement date.

### The Phase-in Period

The transition period is generally closed-ended and usually spans 12 to 24 months. However, the gliding period can be as short as 6 months or as long as 36 or 48 months. While phasing out, an employee works on a reduced schedule. Depending upon the arrangement, employees may keep the same schedule for the duration or incrementally increase the time not worked. Employees seldom increase the total hours worked since it contradicts the spirit of the agreement. Typically, when employees do not work full-time, benefits such as company vacation, health care, and other benefits are affected by agreement. Employees and managers agree to a structure that best meets or balances the interests of both groups. In some corporations, coworkers may need to be included in the process. Three of the most commonly altered structures are:

- *Reduced workweek.* Working four days a week for a total of 32 hours, instead of the regular 40-hour week.
- *Reduced workday.* Working 30 hours per week but only 6 hours each day instead of the traditional 8-hour day.
- *Block or extended leave.* Working full-time for several weeks or months followed by a block of time where the phasing employee has no work responsibilities.

Experience with phased retirement has been most successful within academia. Retiring faculty offer their tenure as the quid pro quo for phasing out. Phasing has also proved feasible within state governments, and both may be seen as potential models for expanding a phased retirement approach within corporate America.

### Retiree Skills Banks

Whereas phased retirement targets late-career employees, retiree skills banks provide part-time employment opportunities to retirees. In essence, skills banks are company-sponsored "temp pools." Generally composed of the company's retirees, skills banks can be structured inclusively (e.g., all exempt and nonexempt employees), or they can be restrictive (e.g., only nonunion, certain technically skilled, exclusively nonexempt employees, or those earning less than a given salary level). Companies usually adopt one of three approaches when structuring their skills banks:

- *Ad hoc assignments*. Retirees are called when needed. While some assignments can be anticipated, such as replacing an employee on vacation, retirees used for ad hoc assignments are generally called on short notice. Most ad hoc assignments require nonexempt staff, such as customer service, data entry, production, or operations. Retirees are paid on an hourly basis.
- *Contractual or temporary arrangements*. Retirees can be hired contractually for the duration of a temporary assignment. Frequently, contractual arrangements are project focused and can be structured for both executive and line employees. Frequent assignments include project management, marketing planning through rollout, internal audits, internal communications (newsletters), information technology installations, and rollouts. Temporary assignments are readily adaptable for both exempt and nonexempt employees at all salary levels within the organization. Retirees can be paid either by the project or on an hourly basis.
- *Retainer arrangements*. Generally targeted to more senior managers, retainers allow the company to access a retiree's expertise. Frequently acting like a consultant, assignments are usually highly focused and/or technical. The retiree may be asked to provide management oversight, assist in project design, coach an individual or team, or review documents. When on retainer, retirees receive regular payments for an average number of hours or months worked.

### Considerations When Developing a Skills Bank

Retiree skills banks generally present fewer complications than phased retirement programs. Essentially, the retiree is no longer actively employed by the company, so the implications for vacation, training, shift differentials, and so on, are less complex than setting up a phased retirement agreement. Companies need to look at their retirement plans (especially defined benefit plans) and potential life and health benefit designs. In addition, employers may want to try to structure the plan to ensure compliance with the Fair Labor Standards Act and other federal and state labor laws.

### Meeting Today's Workplace Realities

Multiple forces—economic, demographic, health, and attitudinal—threaten America's future role as a business and economic leader. To retain and secure its standing, the country's employers, whether local, regional, national, or global, need to define pockets of talent that ensure it both achieves and surpasses its goals. Intellectual talent is especially critical, given that the country's origins in agriculture and manufacturing have become historical foundations to its development of information-driven and knowledge-based services.

**Table 1**
**Perceived Benefits: Employees' Perspective**

| Phased Retirement | Retiree Skills Banks |
|---|---|
| Regular income for the duration of the transition period (i.e., the phasing period) | Can elect a given assignment or decide not to accept the job |
| More likely to receive benefits and other job-related perquisites | As an independent contractor, can work at different organizations |
| Stays within the same department, providing a sense of stability | Possibility of greater assignment diversity (e.g., may be able to change departments) |
| Can be a mentor to or train other employees | Greater flexibility in negotiating an hourly, weekly, or project rate |
| Allows the phasing employee the opportunity to explore postemployment options—without making a full commitment | Eliminates the job search |
| | Can provide meaningful employment |

The most resourceful corporate leaders will explore those employment/retirement options that attract the most talented of baby boomers. To retain that talent, corporations will need to adapt or introduce work/retirement initiatives that are consonant with business goals and culture and leverage the group's knowledge and skill sets.

Current late-career employees represent the best-educated generation to date, and they will likely outlive all previous generations of retirees. This group is also aware of and sensitive to the economic vagaries that can threaten their retirement. Cognizant of how working during retirement can help economically, they also recognize other dimensions offered by employment that is socially and intellectually challenging.

Phased retirement and retiree skills banks represent two complementary initiatives. These practices, when correctly configured, can create a synergy between employers and late-career employees and retirees. Phased retirement targets active employees in the years prior to the actual retirement; retiree skills banks focus upon those retirees (or other former employees) whose skills can add value to the company. Each program has its own benefits and drawbacks.

Generally, phased retirement introduces greater complexity to the processes of administration and communication. It does, however, afford a potentially greater ROI. For example, the company experiences greater stability through improved management and workforce/succession planning, training, and knowledge transfer. Through retiree skills banks, companies capture former employees' skills on a temporary or per-project basis.

Tables 1 and 2 identify, from the employee's perspective, some of the benefits and drawbacks of phased retirement and retiree skills banks. In contrast, Tables 3 and 4 assess benefits and drawbacks of these same programs from management's vantage point. Tables 5 and 6 provide human resource checklists for phased retirement and skills banks. (See also BABY BOOMERS AND RETIREMENT; BUSINESS SUCCESSION PLANNING; CONSULTING IN RETIREMENT; EARLY RETIREMENT INCENTIVE PLANS [ERIPs]; FINANCIAL SECURITY IN RETIREMENT; HEALTH BENEFITS; JOB LOCK; RETIREMENT PREPAREDNESS; WEALTH SPAN.)

**Table 2**
**Perceived Drawbacks: Employees' Perspective**

| Phased Retirement | Retiree Skills Banks |
|---|---|
| Compression of full-time work into a less than full-time position | Adequate training is not provided |
| Get the most undesirable assignments | Receive the least desirable assignments |
| Insecurity about meeting living expenses on a reduced level of income | May not receive enough assignments to generate adequate income |
| Belief that the job "requires" a full-time employee | Lack of benefits, especially health care |
| Potential long-term impact on the retiree's Social Security, pension, etc. | |
| Perception of noncommitment by phasing employees (e.g., "Since I am not there all the time, I am perceived as not committed") | |

**Table 3**
**Perceived Benefits: Employers' Perspective**

| Phased Retirement | Retiree Skills Banks |
|---|---|
| Can plan projects and other assignments knowing that specific staff and/or skill sets are available | Can select employees for specific assignments or who add the greatest value to the organization (i.e., not required to use specific employees) |
| Can capitalize on organization's knowledge and skills: retirees phasing out can train, mentor, or coach less senior employees | Can recruit employees from multiple organizations: not restricted to retirees from one company |
| Ensures a managed transition within the company | Can muster requisite forces for special projects from several sources: not restricted to current employees |
| | Employees are familiar with the company's culture and procedures |
| | Can lower temporary employee costs |
| | Applicants are motivated and self-selected |
| | Not required to offer benefits (if retirees' total time does not exceed ERISA regulations) |

References

Latulippe, Denis, and John Turner. 2000. "Partial Retirement and Pension Policy in Industrialized Countries." *International Labour Review* 139(2): 179–95.

Penner, Rudolph G., Pamela Perun, and C. Eugene Steurie. 2002. "Legal and Institutional Impediments to Partial Retirement and Part-Time Work by Older Workers." Available online at http://www.urban.org/urlprint.cfm?ID=7991.

Swank, Constance. 1982. *Phased Retirement: The European Experience*. N.p.: New Ways to Work Publishing Co.

*Victor S. Barocas*

**Table 4**
**Perceived Drawbacks: Employers' Perspective**

| Phased Retirement | Retiree Skills Banks |
|---|---|
| More people to manage, including the equitable assignment of work | Workforce availability is not guaranteed |
| Increased cost to department and organization budgets | Limited ability to screen for technical capability |
| Administrative ramifications for other rewards programs (especially retirement and Social Security) | Temporary employees have little commitment to the company |
| Need to educate phasing and nonphasing employees about how the program works | Since potential strengths or weaknesses are unknown, delegating important tasks can be difficult |
| Union response to the gradual elimination of jobs | Managing temporary employees is time and labor-intensive |

**Table 5**
**Human Resource and Management Checklist for Company-Sponsored Phased Retirement Initiative**

| Human Resource Program | Consideration/Issue |
|---|---|
| Eligibility | Which employees will be eligible?<br>What criteria for participation? |
| Approval Process | Who needs to approve/sign off? |
| Duration of the Phasing Period | How long a phasing period?<br>How will workweek be restructured (e.g., reduced workday, reduced workweek, sabbatical)? |
| Compensation | Pay will likely be reduced to reflect the non-full-time status |
| Overtime and Pay Differentials, etc. | How will eligibility be defined? |
| Incentives (e.g., bonus) | Will phasing employees remain eligible?<br>Will payouts be prorated?<br>What criteria to calculate incentive? |
| Health Care | Will phasing employees remain eligible? |
| Other Voluntary Benefits (e.g., disability, life insurance) | Will phasing employees remain eligible?<br>Will benefits be reduced? |
| Defined Benefit Pension Plan | Will phasing employees remain eligible?<br>Will the calculation of benefits be affected? |
| Defined Contribution Savings Plans | Will phasing employees remain eligible?<br>Will employer contributions or match be reduced? |

**Table 5** *(continued)*

| Human Resource Program | Consideration/Issue |
|---|---|
| Other Capital Accumulation Plans | Will phasing employees remain eligible? |
| Social Security | Ramifications for employer and employee contributions<br>Ramifications for calculation of monthly Social Security benefit |
| Other Federal and State-Mandated Programs (e.g., Workers' Compensation, Unemployment Insurance) | Ramifications for employer and employee contributions<br>Ramifications for accessing and benefit levels |
| Vacation and Holiday Benefits | Will phasing employees remain eligible?<br>Will benefits be reduced? |

**Table 6**
**Human Resource and Management Checklist for Company-Sponsored Retiree Skill Banks**

| Human Resource Program | Consideration/Issue |
|---|---|
| Eligibility | Which employees will be eligible?<br>What criteria for participation? |
| Approval Process | Who needs to approve or sign off? |
| Work Requirements | Minimum number of hours?<br>Maximum number of hours? |
| Compensation | How will pay be computed? |
| Overtime and Pay Differentials, etc. | Are retirees eligible for differentials? |
| Health Care | Will skills bank participation affect benefit eligibility? |
| Other Voluntary Benefits (e.g., disability, life insurance) | Will retirees' benefits be affected?<br>Will benefits be reduced? |
| Defined Benefit Pension Plan | How will defined benefits be affected?<br>Will benefit recalculations occur? |
| Defined Contribution Savings Plans | Will phasing employees remain eligible to re-enroll?<br>Will an employer contribution or match occur? |
| Other Capital Accumulation Plans | Will phasing employees remain eligible? |
| Social Security | Ramifications for employer and employee contributions<br>Ramifications for calculation of monthly Social Security benefit |
| Other Federal and State-Mandated Programs (e.g., Workers' Compensation, Unemployment Insurance) | Ramifications for employer and employee contributions<br>Ramifications for accessing and level of benefits |

**PHYSICIAN–OLDER PATIENT RELATIONSHIPS,** the interpersonal expectations, interactions, experiences, and emotional reactions that patients 65 years and older and physicians rely upon to understand each other's behavior and bring about the patient's present or future health care. Such a relationship is established when an older patient is receiving health care by a physician in a medical encounter. Depending on the purpose and context of the encounter, the relationship may be short term, if the patient is hospitalized temporarily for an acute condition or is just seeking a second opinion, or it may be long term, if the older patient has maintained the same physician of primary or specialty care for a long period. When the relationship has been a long-term arrangement, it encompasses the cumulative information and emotional feelings that older patients and their physicians have developed for each other throughout years. Research on physician–older patient relationships involves medicine, gerontology and geriatrics, communication, bioethics, psychology, social and behavioral sciences, economics, and policy.

## Features of the Physician–Older Patient Relationship

Older people tend to be heavy users of health care services. According to the 1999 National Hospital Discharge Survey, there were 12.7 million hospital discharges with an average hospital stay of 6.2 days among persons aged 65 and older, accounting for almost 40% of all discharges (Popovic and Hall 2001). The discharge rate among persons 65 years of age and over increased 11% from 1990 to 1999, compared with a decrease of 17% in the 15 to 44 age group and 14% in the 45 to 64 age group. The number of physician visits by persons aged 65 and over is eight on average per year, compared to five by the general population. It is estimated that the physician visits by persons aged 65 to 74 will nearly double from 100 million in 1980 to 186 million in 2040 and will quadruple by those aged 75 and older, from 66 million in 1980 to 241 million in 2040 (Manton and Suzman 1992).

Health care needs of older patients typically differ from, and are potentially more complicated than, those of younger patients. Although older people see physicians to resolve acute medical problems, visits frequently result from the need to manage more chronic yet often debilitating conditions such as arthritis, diabetes, hypertension, cardiovascular diseases, dementia, Parkinson's disease, or cancer. The nature of the illness determines the treatment goal—whether to cure the disease, to control the progression, or to offer palliative care (care that treats or soothes the symptoms of a condition but does not attempt to effect a cure). The coexistence of multiple medical problems is not uncommon in older patients, which can further complicate treatment planning. Therefore, the focus of their relationship with the physicians is on how to develop and carry out optimal treatment plans that take into account comorbid conditions and meet their special needs.

Compared with younger patients, communication with older patients is more likely to be complicated by ageist attitudes, sensory deficits, cognitive impairment, functional limitations, and the frequent presence of an accompanying relative or caregiver in the medical visit. In particular, age bias has been suggested in differential medical treatment older adults receive in the form of inadequate utilization of screening procedures, prescription of preventive regimens, and aggressive management of medical or mental health problems. Some physicians may consider older patients more "difficult" to deal with than their younger counterparts and be less attentive to their needs. They are less likely to be egalitarian, patient, engaged, and respectful and demonstrate therapeutic optimism with older patients than with younger patients. Hearing loss and visual difficulty can affect efficient communication between physician and older patient, while cognitive decline in an older adult requires special communication skills and sensitive care. Functional deficits such as inability to move around or lack of transportation can make the logistics of a medical office visit difficult.

In addition to these communication barriers, insufficient time during a visit is also a concern of an older patient. Despite greater health needs, older patients may refrain from asking questions or bringing up a topic if either party is in a hurry or senses that the other is rushed. They may also need more time to process and respond to information given by physicians during an encounter. Since older persons often visit physicians for management of chronic conditions, repeat visits are frequent. However, physicians tend to devote the same or less time with their older patients than with younger patients, especially for some types of follow-up care (Radecki et al. 1988). This may in turn prompt higher visit rates in older patients. As a result, even though each visit may be shorter than that of younger adults, older patients may actually interact with a physician for more time during the course of a year. Recent evidence also suggests that there may be a gender difference: interview length remains the same for women of all ages but actually increases significantly with age for men (Mann et al. 2001).

One major characteristic that distinguishes the geriatric medical visit from many other encounters is that the older patient is often accompanied by a third person (e.g., spouse, adult child, or hired professional caregiver). Family members are frequently involved in the care of older patients by initiating contact with the physician, coordinating treatment plans, and ensuring compliance with medical recommendations. The additional interests a companion brings may either facilitate or inhibit the development and maintenance of a trusting physician-patient relationship. When an older patient is accompanied by a companion, the same person usually serves as companion during later doctor visits (Prohaska and Glasser 1996). The continuity of the companion across medical visits thus provides an opportunity for physicians to emphasize health education directed to the companion. The role played by a caregiver may vary according to the patient's health needs and extend beyond a visit to the physician. An older patient with Alzheimer's disease, which impairs cognition, may require more direct interaction between physician and family members; whereas in a geriatric oncology patient, family caregivers usually assist physicians in managing symptoms and monitoring treatment (Weitzner, Haley, and Chen 2000).

Older patients are more likely to assume traditional, less-participatory, and passive roles than younger patients in making treatment decisions. They often have a lower desire for health-related information and control than other age groups and feel they have less of a right to challenge a physician's authority. They tend to give more socially desirable responses and show more gratitude and are more fearful of expressing complaints. The presence of a companion at the doctor's appointment, however, may further exclude or marginalize older patients from the conversation. They may raise fewer topics, be less responsive to topics they do raise, and be less assertive and expressive in three-party medical visits. They are more ready to rely upon their physicians or family members to make decisions than other segments of the population.

The content of a medical encounter with older patients is mostly biomedical. Physicians initiate more communication than their patients, raising two-thirds of the topics discussed in the visit (Beisecker 1996). Even though treatment for an older patient may be influenced very much by nonmedical factors, the psychosocial context in which illness occurs is usually not part of the consultation. Doctors' interactional responsiveness to these issues was better when younger patients raised them than when the older ones did. Rost and Frankel (1993) found that 56% of older patients failed to raise important medical problems, and 60% neglected to discuss with their physicians psychosocial problems that they considered important. While older patients are less likely to actively seek information from their physicians, they may actually receive more information, more total communication, more questions about medications, and fewer comments indicating tension release than do younger patients.

The physician–older patient relationship has significant impact on patient satisfaction and compliance, as well as patient health status. The ultimate fulfillment of patients' expectations depends on the effectiveness of communication between the older patient and the physician, the appropriateness of expectations, and the ability of the two parties to achieve an agreement. Even though older patients sometimes experience unmet expectations because many of their chronic conditions are not curable, they usually express a high level of satisfaction with medical encounters, and they are more satisfied than younger adults. Patient satisfaction with medical encounters is higher than physician satisfaction. Furthermore, when the quality of communication with the physician is rated highly, patients are more likely to be satisfied with their medical care.

The key elements of physician–older patient communication that influence satisfaction have been shown to be a caring, understanding manner on the part of the physician and the continuity of relationship between the two parties involved. Physicians' interpersonal, affective style may be more important with older patients in determining satisfaction than the actual subjects discussed during a visit. Not surprisingly, higher physician satisfaction has been associated with positive attitudes toward patients, positive assessment of the patient's health status, positive expectations of the benefits of health education, and higher patient educational level. Patients are less satisfied when physicians dominate the interview and more satisfied if they perceive that the physician treats the relationship as a partnership. Continuous care also has a positive influence on patient attitudes about the quality of care they receive.

Other important factors in predicting patient satisfaction include patient characteristics, the amount of information given to patients, and patients' perceptions that their needs are addressed. Older White women and patients with a lower level of education exhibit the greatest satisfaction, whereas sicker patients tend to be less satisfied. Although older patients tend to be satisfied with a physician's behaviors, their family caregivers are far less satisfied with the amount of information received, emotional support offered, and assistance in referrals to needed services. This may reflect the disparate needs and expectations of patients and caregivers that physicians are facing.

Older patients frequently have difficulty recalling instructions and information provided during the patient-physician encounter. Older patients' compliance is closely related to patient-physician communication. As the amount of information a physician gives increases, the percentage of information recalled by the patient decreases, and potential confusion or misunderstanding may arise that needs clarification and reassurance from the physician. Higher number and dosing of medications has been found to be a major stumbling block of adherence to treatment. Also, less time spent with the patient discussing these issues was one of the strongest predictors of lower compliance. Adherence varies with the nature of the physician recommendations, with better adherence to medication regimens and lower compliance to diet, exercise, and lifestyle changes. Patient satisfaction has been shown to influence patient compliance. The more satisfied the patient, the better chance the older patient will adhere to treatment regimens. For older patients, especially those requiring formal caregiving, compliance with the treatment regimen often relies on the caregiver.

Patient health status has been viewed both as a determinant and an outcome of physician-patient interaction. Comorbidity status of an older patient appears to affect treatment decision making. Since survival benefits may decline and the risks of treatment progressively increase with age, one major but unique goal of geriatric care is the preservation and improvement of quality of life. It has been suggested that the emotional health of the older patient can be influenced by the attitude of the physician. For instance, if a physician portrays a hopeless attitude while communicating with a patient, especially if the patient has a life-threatening illness, then depression and a sense of isolation ensue. When the patient observes that the physician adopts a negative manner, the conclusion is drawn that his or her health must be in decline, resulting in a decrease in self-esteem and effort and a consequent withdrawal from activities. Discussion of end-of-life issues is likely to become a major topic toward the end stage of a disease and may affect the emotional health of the older patient. However, there is no evidence of adverse emotional or attitudinal reaction to the discussion of advance directives in older patients.

It should be pointed out that, contrary to some conventional thoughts, the older patient population is just as heterogeneous as the younger patient population. Physicians should be aware of the individual variability in this group of patients and adjust their practice in a patient-centered way. Physician–older patient relationship is a continuing dynamic process that can be relatively stable yet evolving, as both parties know each other better through frequent medical contacts.

### Financial Implications

Features of the physician–older patient relationship have some financial implications. Older persons require access to a greater number of health care services than do younger persons, and an aging population will require more services in the foreseeable future. Costs of these services have an impact on the Medicare system, since most older Americans receive at least some of their health care benefits through Medicare. Since the total number of physician visits by older persons is expected to rise accordingly, the implication of increased medical utilization needs to be examined in an effort to improve the medical and economic consequences for both individual patients and society as a whole.

Conceptualized as a limited resource, health care has been looked at from both economic and ethical perspectives. Owing to economic constraints, health care has been viewed as an "either-or" situation where expensive technological treatment might be withheld from those near the natural term of life (i.e., older adults) so that younger people might benefit instead. It is argued that age is an ethical, objective, and cost-effective criterion for rationing health care since older people have enjoyed more life and have less life left to enjoy—an argument that has an almost seductive logic to it. However, health care rationing is essentially discriminatory. Since age *per se* is not an absolute determinant of certain treatment benefit, age-based rationing of care is both ethically unacceptable and clinically inapplicable. Rather, in light of the current interest in reforming the American health care delivery system, the goal of health care reform should not just focus on high-cost technological care but should also include inefficient aspects of care, especially in underserved older populations.

Although there is little evidence of systematic negative bias against older patients in medical visits, the degree of utilization of diagnostic tools and preventive methods in this population is not desirable. One possible way to contain expensive medical costs is for physicians to provide health risk assessment and necessary screening for older patients and emphasize preventive services. Physicians can assist older patients in maintaining their health by discussing with them the health effects of their habits and behaviors. Such habits include tobacco and alcohol use, maintaining a healthy balanced diet, use of supplements, and exercise. Behaviors include social contact, driving, and using seat belts. Lifestyle issues need to be addressed in physician-patient encounters, although changes may not be easy or immediate. However, long-term benefits to patients and health costs are obvious.

There is no doubt that medical decisions that result from physician–older patient interactions carry considerable financial implications. Choice of a specific medical therapy is affected by the patient's ability to afford the care based on health insurance coverage and out-of-pocket costs, among other things. Persistent medication therapy has become one of the major health care concerns in older patients, as well as a matter for policy debate. Prescription drug costs are currently not covered by Medicare so that many older patients are either unable or unwilling to fill all their medication prescriptions because of costs—another reason for noncompliance in this group. Physicians are becoming more sensitive to these economic issues that could influence treatment decisions and beginning to address patients' concerns during the encounter. A frank discussion with a patient regarding the cost of alternate medications may cause a physician to prescribe an alternative, cheaper regimen or to refer the patient to a social worker for possible free or low-cost prescription arrangements. This can lead to a better health outcome than would be possible if the patient neglected to fill a more expensive prescription.

In addition, decisions associated with long-term care arrangements and end-of-life care are of particular importance to older patients. About 1.6 million older persons were residing in nursing homes in 1999, and the costs of long-term care will only increase steadily. Physicians in these settings often deal with frail, older patients with multiple medical problems. Again, risk assessment and preventive measures are desirable in this population to prevent further deterioration and hospitalization for conditions common in nursing home residents, such as pressure ulcers, falls, influenza, and pneumonia. Home- and community-based long-term care services are cost-effective alternatives that physicians may present to an older patient who is at risk of institutionalization.

A large share of older people's health care expenditures are incurred in the last year or even months, if not weeks, of their lives. Although hospice provides quality end-of-life palliative care, only one out of four people who died in America in 2000 was under hospice care. Timely discussion and referral of patients to receive hospice care is a humane approach. An increasingly popular way among older patients is to designate a durable power of attorney or sign advance directives that instruct physicians about when to use or withhold extraordinary life-extending treatment. Two factors should be taken into account when making decisions regarding long-term and end-of-life care. One is patient preference of such care, and the other is the availability of a caregiver. It has been shown that the availability of a family caregiver is an important determinant of not being institutionalized or receiving home-based hospice care in older patients.

The financial implications of medical decisions for older patients are further complicated by the potential competing interests of patients' companions or third-party payers. Sometimes the final financial decision-making authority may rest with neither the patient nor the physician. Medicare, for example, establishes the physician's reimbursement schedule. The growing importance of Medicare managed care may also affect financial decision authority. When older patients use personal assets to finance their health care choices, family members or legal guardians may intervene, thus leaving older patients feeling powerless over their own health care wishes. One result of the declining payments to physicians by Medicare and other third-party payers may be restriction of the time physicians spend with older patients. By promoting shorter visits, Medicare reimbursements decrease the likelihood that physicians will spend enough time with their older patients.

Three current changes in demographics, the health care delivery system, and technology are likely to have a significant impact on shaping the physician-older patient relationship. The first change is the aging and retirement of baby boomers, who may bring a very different perspective into their relationship with health care providers. Their educational background, experience with health care, health status, and medical insurance situation may be quite dissimilar from the previous cohorts. This will likely affect the medical encounter with also the younger generation of physicians, who have been trained just recently to pay more attention to both biomedical and psychosocial aspects of health care. Individualized care plans that encourage healthy lifestyle and disease prevention may be a major topic during a medical visit of these young older patients. Their personal and medical resources coupled with health attitudes and beliefs may allow them to pursue a more active role in control of their own health care and participation in decision making.

The second change is the emergence of a health care team approach in geriatric care, which provides comprehensive assessment and coordinates care in various acute or long-term care settings. The creation of the geriatric team approach is a direct result of research evidence indicating its cost-effectiveness in providing quality health care to older patients. The team usually includes a geriatrician, nurse or nurse practitioner, social worker, and other health care professionals. Each member of the team may interact with the patient individually or in small groups and assist both physician and patient to make an informed decision. The efficiency and functioning of the multidisciplinary team depends on the communication among team members as well as the communication of the team as a whole with the older patient and family caregivers. On some occasions, older patients interact more frequently with "physician extenders" (i.e., physician assistants or nurse practitioners) during routine visits. Their conditions can be adequately monitored by less expensive medical personnel, with more time available for counseling and advice on health promotion. Other members of the team can also give professional opinions of medication usage (by a pharmacist), diet and supplements (by a dietician), or psychosocial issues (by a social worker). This is especially helpful given the multiple medical and health-related issues faced by older patients. By assessing potential risks in an older patient, the team can thus prescribe an integrated treatment plan, much of which is preventive in nature, to preserve function and quality of life.

In addition to person-to-person contact between a physician and an older patient, another excellent opportunity for the development of a robust relationship is frequent telephone communication. Informing a patient of a laboratory result or making a follow-up call to determine a patient's response to a particular medication can not only establish positive bonding and continuity of medical care but also detect patient compliance and potential problems that need to be addressed more efficiently. The increasing use of computer technology is the third change that may enhance communication between patients and their physicians, including e-mail, telemedicine, and the Internet. Communication via e-mail allows unlimited and instant correspondence between physicians and older patients without the physical barriers of an office visit or the time constraints of each individual's different schedule. Telemedicine, which uses telecommunications and computer technology to provide medical information and medical care services, enables patients to interact with specialists over long distances while retaining visual and verbal contact. It is like an electronic house call that is particularly attractive to homebound individuals or patients in remote areas. The expansion of telemedicine will depend on the rapidly decreasing costs of establishing a telemedicine system locally and the ability of physicians to be adequately reimbursed for services delivered via such a system. Finally, access to the Internet is also likely to change physician–older patient communication in terms of information inquiry, digestion, and consultation. Misinformation of health care issues over the Internet is not uncommon, so physicians need to correct any misunderstanding or confusion arising in older patients and give accurate professional advice. Online purchase of vitamin and mineral supplements and refilling of prescription drugs are becoming a trend and can be a way for patients to save money. Still, access to computers and the Internet is not universal and varies by income, education, and age. The influence of these technology advances on physician–older patient relationships should be investigated carefully.

Both physicians and their older patients should recognize the financial implications of their interactions and the decisions made regarding a patient's treatment options. Only when the financial ramifications are understood by both parties can they make fully informed and appropriate decisions. A strong physician–older patient relationship is based in part on the physician's knowledge of the patient's financial situation and a patient's understanding of the costs required by a proposed treatment regimen. Quality geriatric care should be both patient centered and cost-effective. (See also DRUGS AND SENIOR CITIZENS; HEALTH AND LONGEVITY; HEALTH MAINTENANCE ORGANIZATIONS AND MANAGED HEALTH CARE FOR OLDER ADULTS; MEDICARE; MEDICARE + CHOICE.)

### Suggested Readings

Beisecker, Analee, and Thomas Beisecker. 1996. *Research on Aging (Special Issue: Research Issues Related to Physician–Elderly Patient Interactions)* 18(1).

National Institute on Aging. 1994. *Talking with Your Doctor: A Guide for Older People*. Bethesda, MD: Author.

### References

Adelman, Ronald, Michele Greene, and Marcia Ory. 2000. "Communication between Older Patients and Their Physicians." *Clinics in Geriatric Medicine* 16: 1–24.

Beisecker, Analee. 1996. "Older Persons' Medical Encounters and Their Outcomes." *Research on Aging* 18: 9–31.

Mann, Sandeep, Karunaker Sripathy, Eugenia Siegler, Amy Davidow, Mack Lipkin, and Debra Roter. 2001. "The Medical Interview: Differences between Adult and Geriatric Outpatients." *Journal of the American Geriatrics Society* 49: 65–71.

Manton, Kenneth, and R. Suzman. 1992. "Forecasting Health and Functioning in Aging Societies: Implication for Health Care and Staffing Needs." In *Aging, Health and Behavior*, ed. M. Ory, R. Abeles, and P. Lipman. Newbury Park, CA: Sage Publications.

Popovic, Jennifer, and Margaret Hall. 2001. "1999 National Hospital Discharge Survey." Advance data from *Vital and Health Statistics* No. 319. Hyattsville, MD: National Center for Health Statistics.

Prohaska, Thomas, and Michael Glasser. 1996. "Patients' Views of Family Involvement in Medical Care Decisions and Encounters." *Research on Aging* 18: 52–69.

Radecki, Stephen, Robert Kane, David Solomon, Robert Mendenhall, and John Beck. 1988. "Do Physicians Spend Less Time with Older Patients?" *Journal of the American Geriatrics Society* 36: 713–18.

Robb, Claire, Hong-bin Chen, and William Haley. 2002. "Ageism in Mental Health and Health Care: A Critical Review." *Journal of Clinical Geropsychology* 8: 1–12.

Rost, Kathryn, and Richard Frankel. 1993. "The Introduction of the Older Patient's Problem in the Medical Visit." *Journal of Aging and Health* 5: 387–401.

Weitzner, Michael, William Haley, and Hong-bin Chen. 2000. "The Family Caregiver of the Older Cancer Patient." *Hematology/Oncology Clinics of North America* 14: 269–81.

*Hong-Bin Chen*

**PLANNING FOR SURVIVING SPECIAL NEEDS CHILDREN,** the process of assuring the financial support of disabled or marginally functioning surviving dependents at the death of caregivers or parents. Forty percent (40%) of all individuals receiving long-term care are under age 65. With advances in medicine and caregiving, many disabled or marginally functioning children can expect to live a normal life expectancy. However, the cost of care and maintenance, frequently combined with an inability to earn substantial income, means that government benefits—especially funding for medical care—is a critical component of their well-being. Most special needs children, regardless of age, are dependent on receiving government benefits to supplement their income and provide them with medical coverage. Much of the focus of planning for surviving special needs children is placed on doing everything possible to provide financially for their care and well-being while doing nothing that would disqualify them for Supplemental Security Income (SSI) and Medicaid.

People with disabilities, developmental or otherwise, need income and medical care. Of the two, it is often the medical coverage that is the most important benefit they receive. Unable to obtain private health insurance, all but the extraordinarily wealthy of these individuals have no alternative but to rely on Medicaid to pay for medical services. Though many have loving families who would give their last dime to ensure medical care, very few families could afford to pay for the intensive and regular care these disabled children need for any length of time. To understand some of the planning tools that are used in these situations, it is useful to understand how one qualifies for government assistance and how easy it is to lose qualification. There are separate government benefit programs that provide disabled individuals with income and health insurance. An individual can receive Supplemental Security Income (SSI)—which pays a stipend of up to $552 per month (in 2003, $829 for an eligible couple; amounts are adjusted annually in January) for items such as food, clothing, and shelter—and Medicaid, which is a health insurance program. If an individual qualifies for SSI, they automatically qualify for Medicaid in 32 states and the District of Columbia. In these jurisdictions, the SSI application is also the Medicaid application. An additional seven states and the Northern Mariana Islands use the same rules to determine eligibility for SSI and Medicaid but require filing of separate applications. Connecticut, Hawaii, Illinois, Indiana, Minnesota, Missouri, New Hampshire, North Dakota, Ohio, Oklahoma, and Virginia use their own eligibility rules for Medicaid, which are different from the Social Security Administration's rules for SSI. It is possible to continue to receive Medicaid if a beneficiary has enough income to disqualify a recipient from receiving an SSI payment but not without strings (see http://www.cms.hhs.gov/medicaid/).

The basic qualification for SSI is that a person must be 65 or older or disabled or blind and have limited resources and income. There are other requirements, as well (see http://www.ssa.gov/pubs/11015.html). The resource limit is $2,000 in *countable* assets for an individual and $3,000 for a couple. This is the limit even if only one member of a couple is eligible for SSI. Countable assets are cash and cash equivalents, such as stocks, bonds, and certificates of deposit. Some assets do not count toward the $2,000 limit. These assets, termed "noncountable assets" or "exempt assets," include items such as a house, a car with a value no greater than $4,500, and personal goods with a value no greater than $2,000.

There are also income restrictions, which are divided into several categories. Income, for purposes of SSI, can come in many different forms: earned income, unearned income, direct income, "not income," in-kind income, and in-kind support and maintenance. It is important to monitor the type and amount of income that an SSI/Medicaid recipient earns/receives, because the type and amount of income could cause a reduction or elimination of SSI benefits if it exceeds permitted levels. A person who receives too much income in a given month will lose his or her SSI and, possibly, Medicaid benefits for that month.

### Earned Income

When an individual earns income, the first $65 of earned income is disregarded, then half of the remaining income is disregarded. The remaining 50% of earned income reduces the SSI benefit on a dollar-for-dollar basis.

### Unearned Income

The first $20 of unearned income received in a given month is disregarded.

### Direct Income

If an individual is given a dollar, they have a dollar of unearned income, and their SSI benefit is reduced on a dollar-for-dollar basis.

### "Not Income"

If a third party pays for a service that the disabled child receives, such as certain medical services, the child has neither received cash nor an item of food, clothing, or shelter, so the payment is "not income" to the SSI recipient. A "not income" payment does not reduce SSI benefits.

### In-Kind Income

In-kind income exists when a third party provides an SSI recipient with an item other than money, food, clothing, or shelter, such as a television, for example. In-kind income does not reduce SSI benefits.

### In-Kind Support or Maintenance (ISM)

ISM exists when a third party provides an SSI recipient with an item of food, clothing, or shelter. ISM reduces SSI benefits in different ways, depending upon the living arrangements of the recipient; at most, the benefit is reduced by one-third plus $20, which is referred to as the presumed maximum value, or PMV.

The following example demonstrates how the provision of different forms of income affect an SSI recipient's benefits: if, in November of 2002, a third party gives an SSI recipient $1,000 in cash with the intention that the SSI recipient will use the cash to pay his rent, the recipient will be disqualified for SSI and Medicaid benefits for November; this is true even if the cash were given to the recipient to buy an item other than a food, clothing, or shelter item. However, if the third party pays the SSI recipient's landlord $1,000 as payment of the recipient's November rent, the recipient's SSI benefits are merely reduced by one-third ($184) plus $20, or $204. The $552 SSI monthly benefit is reduced to $348 ($552 − $204 = $348), and Medicaid is preserved.

*Done correctly*, in-kind support maintenance can be advantageous. After all, few people could afford to provide for their food, clothing, and shelter needs with $552 a month. Yet most SSI/Medicaid recipients cannot afford to lose all of their SSI or, more important, the health insurance provided through the Medicaid program. *Done incorrectly*, ISM can be costly.

### The Role of Special Needs Trusts

Because many disabled children could never afford to pay for the costs associated with the medical services they receive and because many depend upon their SSI benefits to supplement their incomes and bolster their living standards, preserving these benefits is of vital importance. Several common occurrences could disqualify a disabled child from receiving government benefits, if the disabled child—or his or her guardian—fails to address the situation properly.

Because an SSI/Medicaid recipient can have no more than $2,000 in countable assets, such events as the death of a family member or the receipt of a worker's compensation or personal injury award can easily displace the disabled child from SSI/Medicaid. Two types of special needs or supplemental needs trusts (SNTs)—third-party SNTs and self-settled SNTs—prevent this outcome and leave an award or inheritance to benefit the child rather than relieve the taxpayers. This entry is designed to provide only a thumbnail sketch of a very complex area of the law, and consultation with an attorney very knowledgeable in elder law issues is required. The rewards can be great when done correctly, but the planning must be done correctly.

### Third-Party SNTs

One hurdle to a disabled child's eligibility arises when the parents (or other family member) of the disabled child die and leave an inheritance to all of their children, including the disabled child. Most people wish to leave a part of their estate to all of their children. It is their legacy, and people tend to feel strongly about this issue, no matter what the value of their estate. For them, a disabled child is no exception, and they believe that the child should not be excluded from their will.

Some parents, in order to prevent the disabled child's displacement from SSI and Medicaid, leave that child's share of their estate to another child and instruct that child to provide for the disabled child's needs. While this technique does accomplish the goal of maintaining the disabled child's government benefits, it has several significant drawbacks.

When money is left to one individual under a will with an informal side agreement that the money will be used for the benefit of another individual, there is no enforceable legal obligation on the part of the person to whom the money was left to use the money for the benefit of the disabled child. Even if the family is very close and very dutiful, there are still problems that could prevent the money from being used for its designated purpose. The caretaker sibling might face marital problems, lawsuits, or bankruptcies—just to name a few of the issues many people encounter and all of which could cause that money to be tied up or dissipated for other uses. Furthermore, when the child to whom the money was left under the will gifts the money to the disabled child, gift tax consequences may arise—depending upon the amount and frequency of the gifts, which may cause tax consequences for the nondisabled child.

The best way to ensure that the money is used for the disabled child's benefit is to leave the money to the child. But it is the manner in which the money is left to the child that is the key to solving all of the issues involved.

If the inheritance is left outright to the disabled child, many issues arise. Most significantly, almost any inheritance will disqualify the individual from government benefits. Without SSI/Medicaid, the disabled child will have to pay for medical care privately, and having to do that means that the inheritance will be expended very rapidly. Once expended, the child would requalify for Medicaid benefits, but the inheritance will have been wasted.

There are other issues that could arise when leaving an inheritance to a disabled child. If the inheritance consists of real property and the child is incapacitated, the child could not execute a deed selling the property because of his or her minority and/or incapacity. If the inheritance consists of a business interest, the child could not participate in business decisions, and the enterprise may suffer as a result of its inability to enter transactions.

The solution to all of these issues is a properly drafted SNT. This may be in the will of the parent or separately as an irrevocable living trust for the benefit of the disabled child while the parent is still alive. These special needs trusts are referred to as third-party SNTs because the assets with which the trust is funded are not the assets of the disabled child, as they are when the SNT is self-settled (discussed below).

Whether the SNT is found in the will of the parent or contained in a trust that the parent establishes during his or her life for the child's benefit, the SNT should clearly identify its role to *supplement* but not to supplant government benefits. The trust should clearly indicate that it is designed to provide items that the SSI/Medicaid program is not designed to provide, that is, items other than food, clothing, or shelter.

If income is to be disbursed from the trust for the benefit of the child, the trustee should be directed to use the income to provide either "not income" items or "in-kind" income items to the child; if the trustee does have discretion to provide ISM to the child—reducing the SSI benefits by no more than the presumed maximum value—the trust should clearly direct that the ISM should never reach a point where the child is displaced from SSI/Medicaid. The trustee, through the trust instrument, should be directed to refrain from making direct income disbursements to the disabled child, which would reduce SSI benefits on a dollar-for-dollar basis and quickly displace the child from SSI and Medicaid.

In addition, the SNT should contain what is commonly known as a "spendthrift clause," which prevents the assets of the trust from being reached by the creditors of the disabled child. Finally, and perhaps most important, the beneficiary must have no control over the trust property and must have no right to revoke the trust. If the beneficiary does have such control, the assets of the trust will be deemed available to the child and displace him or her from SSI and Medicaid.

### Self-Settled SNTs

Some children are not born with disabilities but develop a disability suddenly as the result of a traumatic injury, for example, an injury sustained in an automobile accident. The cause of the injury may give rise to a lawsuit, which may result in an award of damages in favor of the now-disabled child.

Because of the significant injuries sustained, the award may be substantial; yet because of the dollar amount of medical bills the child incurs in the treatment of the injury, and the prospective medical bills that the child will incur as a result of procedures and services that are likely to be needed in the future, most any award of damages will be inadequate to cover medical expenses. Self-funded medical care is probably not possible, and the child is now, as a result of the accident or injury, unable to function in the workforce or obtain medical coverage. If the child were forced to simply private-pay for the necessary medical services, the award of damages would be squandered and the child would eventually qualify for SSI/Medicaid.

Recognizing a need to preserve some of the benefits of a personal injury award (or worker's compensation award or equitable distribution award, in the context of a divorce proceeding) for the benefit of the disabled child, Congress passed a law that provides for the establishment of a self-settled SNT (commonly called a d(4)(a) trust after the section of the Social Security code that contains the trust provision) to shelter some of the personal injury award and allow the disabled child to qualify for SSI/Medicaid.

Unlike a third-party SNT, a self-settled trust is funded with the assets of the disabled child, for example, the personal injury award. These trusts have strict requirements with which they must comply, requirements of both the federal and state government. The basic requirements of these trusts are as follows:

1. The trust must be funded with assets of the disabled child.
2. The disabled child must be under 65 years of age when the trust is funded.
3. The child must be disabled.
4. The trust must be established by a parent, grandparent, or legal guardian of the disabled child or by a court.

5. The trust must provide for reimbursement of Medicaid benefits that the state paid upon the death of the disabled child if any assets remain in the trust at the time of the child's death.

Note that a d(4)(a) trust can only be established for a disabled child who is under age 65. If a disabled child is age 65 or older, a d(4)(a) trust cannot be established, but another trust, commonly known as a d(4)(c) trust, or pooled trust, can be. Also, note that the disabled child cannot establish the d(4)(a) trust—only a parent, grandparent, guardian, or court can establish such a trust.

Because the trust must be funded with the assets of the disabled child, the best method of establishing the trust is to have a court sign off on the trust document. Some states have passed legislation to specifically authorizing courts to do so. At the child's death, the trust must provide for the reimbursement of the state Medicaid program for any benefits paid on behalf of the child. There is clearly a benefit to ensuring that the trust assets are used for the disabled child during his or her life and that the trust contains little or no assets at the time of death.

Like a third-party SNT, a self-settled SNT must be irrevocable and the assets must be unavailable to the disabled child, meaning that the disabled child cannot simply command that the assets be used for any purpose she or he desires. The trustee, not the disabled child, must have sole and absolute control over the use of the trust income and principal. Also, like a third-party SNT, a d(4)(a) trust should specifically address income disbursements from the trust. The trustee should be instructed to provide "not income" or "in-kind" income items whenever possible; if ISM is to be provided, it should never be provided in an amount that will displace government benefits, only reduce such benefits.

Once the trust is established and funded, the administration of the trust must also be handled in an appropriate manner. Care must be taken that distributions not be made that would displace the disabled child from SSI and Medicaid. Proper administration begins with the selection of an appropriate trustee. Typically, the trustee selected falls into one of the following categories: a sibling of the disabled child, a financial institution, or a nonprofit organization.

While a sibling may best understand the needs of the child, a financial institution or a nonprofit organization with experience in the administration of such trust devices brings expertise as far as the proper administration of the trust is concerned. It is often advisable that cotrustees are selected, perhaps a sibling and a financial institution. The two can then work together to ensure that the trust assets and income are used in the best possible manner to fulfill the needs of the disabled child and that the trust is administered in such a way that the child maintains her or his benefits.

There are many issues concerning self-settled and third-party SNTs that are not addressed here. Done properly, an SNT can preserve substantial sums of money for the benefit of individuals who desperately need the services and items that money can provide. Again, language is critically important to accomplish what these trusts are established to do, and specialized expert advice is required. (See also DISABILITY PROGRAMS, FEDERAL AND STATE; MEDICAID; SUPPLEMENTAL SECURITY INCOME (SSI); TRUSTS.)

**Organizations**

Federation for Children with Special Needs
Special Needs Alliance

**Suggested Readings**

Begley, Thomas D., Jr., and Jo-Anne Herina Jeffreys. 2002. *Representing the Elderly Client: Law and Practice*. New York: Panel Publishers.

Stengle, Linda J. 1996. *Laying Community Foundations: For Your Child with a Disability: How to Establish Relationships That Will Support Your Child After You're Gone*. Bethesda, MD: Woodbine House.

**References**

Begley, Thomas D., Jr., and Jo-Anne Herina Jeffreys. 2000. *Representing the Elderly Client*. New York: Aspen Press.

Kruse, Clifton B., Jr. 2002. *Third-Party and Self-Created Trusts*. 2nd ed. Chicago: American Bar Association.

*John W. Callinan*

**POSTRETIREMENT HEALTH COVERAGE (PRHC),** health care coverage provided to retired workers and their dependents by the retirees' former employers. For retirees not yet eligible for Medicare, postretirement health insurance is a primary source of health care coverage. Among persons aged 55 to 64, approximately one out of six (4.0 million persons) are retired, and just over half of these retirees (57%) now receive retiree health insurance (EBRI 2001). Among persons receiving Medicare, which begins at age 65 except in special circumstances, 34% also have PRHC, coverage that supplements their Medicare insurance (McArdle et al. 1999). For persons on Medicare, PRHC often helps cover beneficiary copayments required under the federal program and provides valuable insurance for several categories of care not covered by Medicare—particularly for prescription drugs.

PRHC benefits were the subject of a major change in the U.S. Accounting and Reporting Rules that became effective in 1993. The new rules, created by issuance of Statement of Financial Accounting Standards (FAS) No. 106, "Employers' Accounting for Postretirement Benefits Other Than Pensions," required that the future costs of all PRHC benefits be calculated and accrued in advance as annual charges to expense during the years that employees were working and earned those benefits (Financial Accounting Standards Board 1990). These new rules resulted in major changes to balance sheet expense—for some individual companies in the multibillions—and altered the financial profiles of companies with PRHC plans.

As a result of the increased focus on the costs of PRHC programs, there has been a clear trend over the last decade among employers to reduce or eliminate this postretirement benefit, a development likely to have major effects on future retirees and their dependents. Under law, employers have been under no obligation to provide PRHC, except to their current retirees to whom they previously promised such benefits. Companies can and have changed their promises of PRHC to currently active workers. The trend is most evident in the benefit packages offered to full-time workers in medium and large private establishments in the United States. In 1997, 32% of employees in these firms who had active worker health insurance were also promised employer-paid PRHC upon early retirement (i.e., prior to age 65), and 31% were promised employer-paid PRHC upon normal retirement (i.e., at age 65 or older) (Bureau of Labor Statistics 1999). In 1991, however, these promise rates for PRHC were 43% and 41%, respectively (Bureau of Labor Statistics 1993). Thus, access to this benefit has declined among active workers.

While fewer active workers overall are now promised PRHC, recent data on trends in health insurance among older adults suggest that many employers apparently continued to offer PRHC benefits for their workers who were near retirement and who had already met established eligibility criteria for the benefit. Most likely, these workers were "grandfathered in" under the prior benefit package. Between 1994 and 1999 among retirees ages 55 to 64, the receipt of PRHC remained fairly constant at 36% to 37% (EBRI 2001). Thus, the changes that employers have made in response to FAS 106 have had less impact on recent retirees.

Where PRHC continues to be offered, eligibility criteria have been tightened over the last decade. Among large employers, the percentage using a relatively strict age/service requirement, for example, age 55 or older with 10 to 15 years of service, increased from 30% in 1991 to 49% in 1998. Likewise, the percentage using a generous age/service requirement, for example, age 55 or older with 5 years of service, decreased from 12% to 9% over this period (McArdle et al. 1999).

Unlike pensions, survivor's benefits are uncommon for PRHC. Only three of every ten recipients receive benefits that continue indefinitely for the individual's dependent survivors. Sometimes, survivor's benefits are provided for a limited period (Jensen and Morrisey 1992).

Retirees with PRHC are increasingly being offered a choice of plans by their former employer, ones that often include a health maintenance organization (HMO) option. Among early retirees, 38% were offered a choice of plans in 1998, which is up from 30% in 1994 (Morrisey and Jensen 2001). Comparable data for normal retirees with PRHC is unavailable.

In most respects, the specific benefit provisions of PRHC are normally the same as those for active worker plans; that is, the plans cover the same categories of care and stipulate the same cost-sharing provisions for services. The employer's premium sharing provisions may differ for retirees, however. It has recently become more common for retirees to help pay the cost of PRHC. Between 1994 and 1998 the percentage of early retirees required to contribute toward their plan's premium more than doubled, increasing from 27% to 58% (Morrisey and Jensen 2001). A parallel increase in premium sharing is likely occurring for Medicare-eligible retirees with PRHC as well.

### Coordination with Medicare

Benefit levels alone do not describe the actual value of retiree coverage to persons who are also covered by Medicare. How such plans coordinate with Medicare is also important. The large majority of PRHC plans use a "carve-out" method to determine their payments as "second-payers" after Medicare (Jensen and Morrisey 1992). When expenses are incurred, the firm assesses reimbursements due the retiree, based solely on the provisions in its plan. This amount is then reduced by what Medicare pays toward the expenses. For example, a retiree may have $600 in bills for physician office visits in one year that are considered reasonable under the Medicare definition. Medicare would pay 80% of the amount over $100 (its annual Part B deductible in 2001), or $400. Suppose that the PRHC plan has a $150 deductible, an 80/20 coinsurance arrangement, and uses carve-out coordination. In this case the retiree's PRHC plan would pay $360 minus Medicare (80% of $600 − $150). However, subtracting the Medicare payment ($400) from this amount leaves an actual employer liability of $0. The retiree is left with a $200 bill ($100 deductible plus 20% of $500), the same out-of-pocket liability he or she would have had with only Medicare coverage. Under this method of coordinating with Medicare, retirees will typically face out-of-pocket cost-sharing provisions that equal those of the more generous of their two plans, that is, Medicare and their PRHC plan.

Under the less common coordination-of-benefits (COB) method, which applies to fewer than one in six PRHC recipients, the firm again first calculates its payment minus Medicare, but then applies Medicare's payment to satisfy the retiree's copayments under the employer plan. Consider the earlier example of a $150 supplement deductible, 80/20 coinsurance, and $600 in physician bills. Medicare continues to pay $400. In the absence of Medicare, the firm would pay $360 once the insured's copayments of $240 ($150 deductible plus 20% of $450) were satisfied. The firm, using COB, treats Medicare's payment as available to meet this $240 enrollee copayment. Thus, the retiree would pay nothing out of pocket. The firm's liability, however, would be $200. Thus, the COB method results in near-complete coverage for those services dually covered by Medicare and the PRHC supplement.

A third method, exclusion, is relatively rare. With exclusion, the firm applies its plan's deductible and coinsurance schedule to the expenses uncovered by Medicare. In the above example, the retiree has an out-of-pocket obligation of $200. After subtracting the firm's $150 deductible and then applying its 80% coinsurance, the employer plan pays $40. The exclusion method typically yields an employer liability between that implied by either the carve-out or COB methods.

### Benefits

The benefits under PRHC plans are nearly always identical to those provided under active worker plans. Coverage for hospital care, physician visits, and outpatient prescription drugs is routine. Extended care facility (ECF) coverage is common in retiree plans and is usually more generous than Medicare. Prior hospital stay rules are absent from most plans, and where present, usually only one or two days are required. Special day limits often apply—usually 100 days per year or 60 days per illness or confinement. But this coverage is not a substitute for long-term care insurance, since it excludes custodial care or intermediate nursing care.

Home health care benefits are also often covered in retiree plans. Hospice benefits are also increasingly available to those with retiree coverage.

For physician care, most retiree plans apply an annual deductible and coinsurance. Very few plans have a deductible lower than Medicare's ($100 per year). In employers' conventional plans the average annual deductible was $239 per individual and $545 per family in 2000, whereas in preferred provider organization (PPO) plans it was $187 per individual and $361 per family (HRET 2000). Like active worker plans, most PRHC plans entail 20% subscriber coinsurance above their deductible. Thus, under the common carve-out coordination method, most dually covered beneficiaries typically are liable for the full Medicare physician deductible.

Nearly all PRHC plans limit retirees' out-of-pocket expenses either by capping them directly or by limiting the claims on which coinsurance is paid. With the latter, when covered expenses reach a certain threshold, the plan covers additional care in full. Among those with a ceiling on out-of-pocket outlays, about half have annual limits of $1,500 or less, and fewer than 10% have a limit of $3,000 or higher (HRET 2000).

Most plans also cover several important services not covered by Medicare such as nonhospital prescription drug expenses, which are substantial for many older adults. The vast majority (86%) of policyholders have drug coverage in their PRHC plan (Davis et al. 1999). In large-employer plans, PRHC coverage often entails a $300 annual deductible, with 80% coinsurance above that amount. These are the most common provisions if the drug benefit is part of the medical plan. Another approach, becoming increasingly common, is to enroll retirees in a drug card program that requires no deductible but instead applies a copay per prescription—often $5 for a generic drug and $10 to $15 for a brand name drug (McArdle et al. 1999). Private duty nursing care, when ordered by a physician, is also covered for most retirees. Chemical dependency coverage and chiropractic coverage are also now routine in PRHC plans.

Increasingly, retirees are being offered the option of enrolling in an HMO, and many are taking it. Among early retirees with PRHC, 29% were enrolled in an HMO in 1998, up from only 17% four years earlier (Morrisey and Jensen 2001). In an HMO, the retiree typically pays a flat copay per physician visit, and there is no deductible and coinsurance as there is with conventional and PPO plans. The most common copay in 2000 was $10 per physician visit (HRET 2000). In these plans, hospital care is typically covered in full, and prescription drugs entail a tiered copay arrangement as described earlier.

### Summary

Postretirement health coverage remains an important source of insurance protection for early retirees and persons on Medicare. The prevalence of this benefit is declining, however, and future retirees are less likely to receive it. During the 1990s, in response to Financial Accounting Statement No. 106 (FAS 106), some employers eliminated this postretirement benefit, while others tightened their eligibility rules and increased premium-sharing requirements for such coverage. Employers who made these changes, however, appear to have "grandfathered in" (under their old plans) workers who were near retirement and who had already met vesting criteria. Thus, the full effects of recent employer PRHC cutbacks have yet to be seen in data on the prevalence of PRHC benefits among retirees.

For persons on Medicare, PRHC acts as a supplement to Medicare benefits. Coverage under PRHC is generally more extensive than privately purchased Medicare supplemental insurance (Medigap policies). PRHC often covers expenses and areas left uninsured by Medicare, while Medigap policies focus on covering gaps in Medicare such as copayments and deductibles.

For persons on Medicare, the value of PRHC depends on the methods used to coordinate the dual coverage. Under carve-out coordination, the most common method used by employers, the extra benefits that PRHC coverage affords Medicare beneficiaries come in seven areas:

1. Elimination of most hospital cost sharing
2. Lower overall out-of-pocket expense limits
3. More relaxed eligibility standards for extended care facility and home care benefits
4. Partial coverage for most Part B balance bills
5. More generous prescription drug coverage
6. Chemical dependency treatment coverage for care in substance abuse facilities
7. Chiropractic coverage

Employers that continue to offer PRHC benefits are increasingly offering retirees the option of enrolling in HMOs, and more PRHC recipients are choosing this option. (See also EMPLOYER-SPONSORED LONG-TERM CARE INSURANCE; JOB LOCK; LIFE PLANNING IN THE WORKPLACE; MEDICARE; MEDICARE + CHOICE; PHASED RETIREMENT AND RETIREE SKILLS BANKS; WORKFORCE PATTERNS, CHANGES IN; WORKING RETIREES; WORKPLACE FINANCIAL EDUCATION.)

**References**

Bureau of Labor Statistics. 1993. *Employee Benefits in Medium and Large Firms, 1991*. BLS Bulletin #2422. Washington, DC: GPO.

Bureau of Labor Statistics. 1999. *Employee Benefits in Medium and Large Firms, 1997*. BLS Bulletin #2517. Washington, DC: GPO.

Davis, M., J. Poisal, G. Chulis, C. Zarabozo, and B. Cooper. 1999. "Prescription Drug Coverage, Utilization, and Spending among Medicare Beneficiaries." *Health Affairs* 18(1): 231–43.

Employee Benefit Research Institute (EBRI). 2001. "Retiree Health Benefits: Trends and Outlook." *EBRI Issue Brief* No. 236. Washington, DC: Author.

Financial Accounting Standards Board of the Financial Accounting Foundation. 1990. *Statement of Financial Accounting Standards No. 106: Employers' Accounting for Postretirement Benefits Other Than Pensions*. Norwalk, CT: Author, December.

Hospital Research and Educational Trust (HRET). 2000. *Employer Health Benefits: 2000 Annual Survey*. Washington, DC: Author.

Jensen, G., and M. Morrisey. 1992. "Employer-Sponsored Post-Retirement Health Benefits: Not Your Mother's Medigap Plan." *The Gerontologist* 32: 693–703.

McArdle, F., S. Coppock, D. Yamamoto, and A. Zebrak. 1999. "Retiree Coverage: Recent Trends and Employer Perspectives on Future Benefits." The Henry J. Kaiser Family Foundation, Menlo Park, CA.

Morrisey, M., and G. Jensen. 2001. "The Near Elderly, Early Retirees, and Managed Care." *Health Affairs* 20(6).

Morrisey, M., G. Jensen, and S. Henderlite. 1990. "Employer Sponsored Health Insurance for Retired Americans." *Health Affairs* 9: 57–73.

*Gail A. Jensen*

**POVERTY.** See Economic Hardship Measures in the Older Population; Economic Status of Older Men and Women; Homelessness among Older Adults; Medicaid; Nutrition Programs; Supplemental Security Income (SSI).

**POWER OF ATTORNEY.** See Advance Directives; Agents and Brokers; Durable Power of Attorney; Living Will; Trusts; Wills.

**PREDATORY LENDING,** lending practices that carry higher-than-appropriate fees and/or rates of interest or unaffordable repayment terms. Predatory lending is targeted at unsuspecting, vulnerable, or defenseless prospective borrowers who may, for example, have fallen behind in their property taxes, face large medical expenses, or need home repairs. Low-income older persons are often prey because they may be frightened by or ashamed of the situation in which they find themselves, confused or easily intimidated, and have property—their home—to secure the loan. While predatory lending abuses can occur in many commercial and financial venues and situations, one of the most prevalent arenas in which it takes place is in mortgage and/or housing situations.

### Background

The issue of predatory lending has come to the forefront with the rise of "subprime" lending activities in many areas of the country. *Subprime lending* generally refers to financing arrangements made by companies for borrowers who do not qualify for financing at the most desirable (lowest) rates through traditional lending institutions, such as banks and savings institutions. Subprime lenders include entities such as pawnshops, payday lenders, rent-to-own stores, and auto title lending institutions, as well as lenders offering loans at higher-than-best rates to people with lower-than-best credit. Subprime lending, also known as "B&C" lending in reference to the credit ratings of typical borrowers, is legal in all 50 states and largely unregulated. It is not, in and of itself, predatory but may be used in an abusive or predatory manner.

While subprime lenders may extend credit access to individuals who are otherwise shut out of traditional lending venues, unethical lenders may take advantage of consumers in the weakest bargaining position. These practices are referred to as "predatory." Subprime lenders are expected to charge higher rates and fees for the risk they assume when originating loans to people without "A" credit, but many consumer advocacy groups have complained for years that interest rates and fees charged by some subprime lenders are much higher than necessary to cover the increased risks involved, particularly since the loans are usually secured by the value of a borrower's personal property, most often the value of one's home (Federal Trade Commission 2001).

### Contrasts with Traditional Banking Institutions

The B&C lending industry is today considered a growth industry. Table 1 details the rise in subprime lending volume since 1996. This is partially due to the fact that traditional banking institutions have been slow to lend to some distressed regions of the country, and B&C lenders have easily filled the void in what has become an increasingly profitable industry. As a testament to the increasing profitability and legitimacy of the industry, Wall Street has become increasingly more willing to raise funds for subprime loans over the last few years. In 1995, $18.5 billion in subprime loans were securitized, whereas in 2000 that figure reached almost $56 billion (Federal Trade Commission 2001). According to Fannie Mae, subprime lending services engage in at least 280 million transactions each year for gross revenues exceeding $168 billion (Carr and Schuetz 2000). Other research has focused on the exponential growth of the industry as well (D'Amours

**Table 1**
**Growth of the Subprime Lending Industry**

| Year | Loans Originated ($ Billion) |
|---|---|
| 1996 | $90 |
| 1997 | $125 |
| 1998 | $150 |
| 1999 | $160 |
| 2000 | $138 |
| 2001 | $173 |

*Source*: Inside Mortgage Finance 2002.

2000; Dove Consulting 2000; Stegman 1999). Nevertheless, while the subprime lending industry grew sevenfold from 1993 to 1998, the growth in prime lending transactions has been much smaller over the same time frame (Carr and Schuetz 2000).

It is useful to understand the dynamics of why the subprime lending industry has taken rise in certain communities instead of the traditional lending institutions. Today, as many as 12 million U.S. households either have no relationship with a traditional financial institution or depend on subprime lenders for financial services (Carr and Schuetz 2000). In many cases, the reason for this nonparticipation is due to geography, but there are other systemic reasons for this trend. To illustrate the lack of physical proximity that some communities have to mainstream banking options, a 1999 *Harvard Business Review* article highlighted the disparity of financial service options in two Los Angeles neighborhoods. In wealthy Pacific Palisades, there was one mainstream financial institution for every 1,250 people, whereas in South Central the ratio is one depository institution per 36,000 people (Foundation, Rufano, and Walker 1999). As consolidation of the traditional banking industry continues and banks remove branches from distressed communities in order to increase profitability, this disparity could become even wider. Some theories suggest that banking deregulation and pressure for increased profits have led banks to charge for previously free services and to get rid of money-losing operations.

Aside from geographical constraints, however, there are other reasons for nonparticipation in traditional banking services. In many communities (especially those consisting predominantly of immigrants), there is a severe mistrust of banks. This mistrust is only exacerbated by the complexity of many lending transactions, especially mortgage loan transactions, which many individuals have trouble interpreting. By contrast, subprime lenders make a more concerted effort to be noticed within the community, emphasizing personal attention spent on customers and encouraging small weekly payments to be made in person, thus allowing the lender to market additional products to existing customers (Carr and Schuetz 2000). One other attraction for consumers of nontraditional financial services is that these alternative institutions provide a wide range of services and flexible hours of operation that are more tailored to meet their unique needs (Financial Service Centers of America 1998)—services and options that traditional banks and credit unions do not offer.

Still, there are many powerful reasons that suggest people would benefit from avoiding these alternative financial institutions and embracing traditional banking institutions. One of the most common facets of the subprime lending industry is its lack of wealth-building characteristics. While traditional banks offer their clients a variety of opportunities for creating financial assets and accumulating wealth through long-term deposits, subprime lenders offer no such services. Thus, households that rely exclusively on them to meet their financial services have neither the incentive nor the opportunity to amass savings over time. In many cases, a borrower does not even know that he or she has legitimate banking opportunities outside the realm of the subprime industry. A recent Fannie Mae report documents that as many as 35% to 50% of the borrowers using the subprime market could have qualified for lower-cost prime loans in a traditional market. Fannie Mae goes on to say that in many cases, these households are steered to the subprime market. This is important because each additional interest point that a subprime lender charges on its loans can ultimately cost the borrower tens of thousands of extra dollars on his or her loan (Carr and Schuetz 2000).

### Examples of Predatory Lending Abuses

While predatory lending is the umbrella term given to a whole range of unscrupulous lending practices, each type of predatory practice has its own unique characteristics. The common thread for nearly all predatory lending practices is that they involve situations in which lenders hide essential information from borrowers that they need in order to make wise borrowing decisions. Predatory lending situations also seem to occur during times of borrower hardship, which is normally when borrowers are most susceptible to unscrupulous practices and high-pressure tactics (Federal Trade Commission 2001). There is not universal agreement within the lending community as to what constitutes "predatory lending practices," partially because many consumer advocacy groups tend not to distinguish between normal subprime lenders and those who engage in predatory lending practices. Nevertheless, an attempt was made on March 16, 1998, to catalog the various types and forms of predatory lending abuses. William J. Brennan of the Atlanta Legal Aid Society, in testimony before the U.S. Senate Special Committee on Aging, divided specific predatory abuses as occurring during three stages of the loan process: (1) origination; (2) servicing of the loan; and (3) collection of the loan (Brennan 1998).

A majority of predatory lending abuses occur during the origination of the loan. Often, the unwitting victim will receive a phone call or an inviting mail packet inviting the household to borrow money against their homes. These abuses then escalate from providing misleading solicitations to falsifying loan applications, to padding closing costs, to making loans in excess of 100% of loan-to-value. Table 2 provides a detailed list of some of the most popular forms of predatory lending abuse during the origination phase.

Even after the loan is originated, the borrower is not free from becoming a victim of predatory lending practices. During the servicing phase of the loan, homeowners may be required by the lender to provide force-placed insurance. This type of insurance usually requires an exorbitant premium to be sent to an insurance carrier that is often affiliated with the lender. The cost of this type of insurance is frequently padded to cover the lender for risks or losses in excess of what the lender usually requires (Brennan 1998). Also, predatory lenders are known to require daily interest charges on a loan when payments are made after the stated due date. This differs substantially from normal

**Table 2**
**Types of Predatory Lending Abuses during Origination**

| Specific Abuse | Description of Abuse |
|---|---|
| Solicitations | Usually occurs in targeted neighborhoods through various forms of media and mail campaigns. In some cases, mail solicitations resemble Social Security or U.S. government checks to ensure interest. |
| Home Improvement Scams | Most common types of scams involve steering borrower to predatory lender; overpriced repairs; and failure to secure the necessary building permits. |
| Mortgage Broker Kickbacks | Usually involves brokers who pretend to work on behalf of the borrower but who instead work for the predatory lender. Kickbacks for these referral fees generally are called "yield-spread premiums" and "servicing release fees." |
| Steering to High-Rate Lenders | Usually involves a creditworthy borrower being wrongfully denied a loan and being subsequently referred to a high-rate lender, often an affiliate of the original bank or mortgage company. |
| Lending to Unqualified Borrowers | Includes structuring the loan to intentionally trigger default, thus causing more refinancing opportunities for lender and higher fees to be paid. |
| Falsifying Loan Applications | Usually done to ensure that the noncreditworthy loan could be sent to the secondary loan market. |
| Adding Cosignors | Done to create the false impression that borrower is sufficiently creditworthy to pay off the loan. |
| Lending to Incapacitated Homeowners | Taking advantage of mentally incapacitated homeowners through coerced contract signing. |
| Forgeries | Lenders signing mortgage documents, which are then used against unwitting victims that never agreed to loan obligation in the first place. |
| High Interest Rates and Points | Interest rates normally are higher than in traditional banking situations, but increase is not commensurate with heightened risk; payment of points does not automatically translate into lower interest rate situation. |
| Balloon Payments | Usually structured so that the borrower cannot make huge lump-sum payment at the end of the mortgage term, thus triggering default. |
| Negative Amortization | Situation in which borrower's loan does not amortize over the life of the loan, and thus he or she cannot pay off accrued interest. Borrower usually owes more than the amount originally borrowed at conclusion of loan term. |
| Padded Closing Costs | Charges such as "document preparation and recording" and "credit report fees" are usually much higher than they are in traditional bank transactions. |
| Inflated Appraisal Costs | Usually only includes a "drive-by" appraisal, which is consistently charged the same rate as a full appraisal. |
| Bogus Broker Fees | Many times this occurs without borrower having known of any broker relationship. |
| Unbundling | Breaking out and itemizing of charges that are duplicative and probably should be included under other charges. |

**Table 2** *(continued)*

| Specific Abuse | Description of Abuse |
|---|---|
| Credit Insurance | Usually sold to borrower as an attachment to the loan provision. Premiums are high and often cover the total of payments made over the life of the loan, rather than simply principal of loan amount. Benefits to borrower rarely approach costs incurred. |
| Prepayment Penalties | Done in an effort to lock in the borrower for as long as possible, with no risk of exit on the part of the borrower. |
| Mandatory Arbitration Clauses | Bypasses the normal remedy of the court system if the borrower decides to sue over the predatory practice. |
| Flipping | Involves the successive, repeated refinancing of the loan by rolling the balance of existing loan instead of simply making a separate loan for the new amount. |
| Spurious Open-End Mortgages | Lender advances full amount of loan to the borrower at the outset. Borrower is unwittingly stuck with interest-only mortgage, in which loan balance is never reduced. |
| Paying Off Low-Interest Mortgages | In second purchase situations, a lender insists that borrower pay off existing low-cost mortgage. By paying off the current mortgage, lender saddles borrower with high-interest mortgage of unnecessarily high principal amount. |
| Shifting Unsecured Debt into Mortgages | By "consolidating," borrowers unknowingly increase their debt amounts, interest payments, closing costs, and the risks that they might lose their home. |
| Loan-to-Value Ratios Exceeding 100% | Borrower takes out too high of a loan. In likely event of foreclosure, borrower may even be subject to a deficiency claim made by the lender. |

*Source*: Brennan 1998.

lending situations, in which borrowers are given a small grace period after the due date to make good on their payments without fear of penalties being incurred.

The collection phase usually signifies the end of the borrower's predatory lending experience, although it is usually the most painful phase for many involved. Many predatory lenders are notorious for implementing complex loan structures that are responsible for triggering a default or subsequent refinancing of the mortgage loan, which are different loan structures from those used in the traditional lending industry. When these triggers are activated, predatory lenders have been known to institute a variety of aggressive collection tactics, such as harassing phone calls at odd hours of the day, mailed "urgent" telegrams, and visits by collection agents. Once a predatory lender has exhausted further opportunities of collecting the high prepayment penalties and extending opportunities to provide repeated refinancing of the loan, the borrower is usually faced with the prospect of foreclosure. One tool of the predatory lender is the deed in lieu of foreclosure. Once the borrower signs this document, he or she has essentially given up his or her rights to cure any defaults, and the home is eventually sold at a price below market value, usually by the lender, who will try to avoid being outbid in a competitive foreclosure situation even if it means avoiding a public foreclosure sale if at all possible.

### Implications for Older Adults

The implications of predatory lending could be devastating for those who are entering their twilight years. A survey sponsored by AARP and released in November 2000 confirmed that nearly 75% of homeowners age 50 and over receive some form of offer from a potentially predatory lender (Barry 2001). Older homeowners are frequent targets for predatory lending activities, primarily because they often have substantial equity in their homes, yet have fixed incomes with declining purchasing power (Federal Trade Commission 2001). In some cases, lenders have played on the emotional ties that older homeowners have developed with their place of residence, threatening evictions of long-time residents if certain payments are not made in a timely fashion (Brennan 1998). One of the most disturbing practices of predatory lenders is targeting their services to older homeowners who may be cognitively impaired. These lenders can take advantage of the fact that the homeowner does not understand the nature or the documentation papers of the transaction. The unwitting victim is then saddled with a mortgage loan that he or she never intended to have, payments that he or she cannot meet, and looming foreclosure or eviction (Brennan 1998). The introduction of new mortgage products and services targeted specifically for older adults, such as reverse annuity mortgages, have created even more opportunities for predatory fraud and abuse.

Because of these situations that affect older households, AARP has devoted considerable time and effort toward educating its membership about the dangers and implications of predatory lending. An entire chapter in the AARP Policy Handbook (chapter 12) is devoted to the issue of these types of abusive, unethical, and in some cases illegal behavior by lenders and their subsidiaries (AARP 2001). The organization's education effort does not stop with its membership, however, as it has provided outreach and case study examples to state and federal governments on the effects of predatory lending in older communities.

### Methods of Addressing Predatory Lending

For a variety of reasons, the issue of predatory lending has not yet gotten much attention. With the nascent status of the subprime lending industry, reports of abuses have been slow to reach lawmakers. Indeed, many politicians within urban and distressed communities have likely been reluctant to address problems of predatory lending simply because subprime and B&C lenders represent one of the few credit options for constituents within their respective communities. For some in these communities, the availability of credit extension of any sort represents progress after many years of neglect by the mainstream banking community, not to mention the implementation of redlining by the insurance and mortgage lending industries. Also, victims of predatory lending are sometimes prone to remaining silent about specific abuses either for reasons of fear of retribution or personal shame for their predicament.

Whatever the reason may be for the lack of attention given to the subject recently, the issue came to the attention of policymakers and consumer advocacy organizations consistently by the late 1990s. These organizations are now intent on curbing the abusive practices of predatory lenders within the subprime lending industry.

In the federal venue, many predatory loan practices may be illegal under various already existing federal laws. Under the Federal Trade Commission Act, many predatory lending practices may qualify as "deceptive or unfair practices" under Section 5. In other cases, provisions of the federal Truth in Lending Act may have been violated. The Home Owners' Equity Protection Act provides some protection for victims of predatory lending involving high-rate and high-fee loans. If a lender charges similarly qualified borrowers higher prices due to age, race, and/or sex, price discrimination may be evident in violation of the Equal Credit Opportunity Act. If the predatory transgression involves a home mortgage loan, the victim may be covered under some provisions of the Real Estate Settlements Procedures Act (Federal Trade Commission 2001).

Nevertheless, fraud and abuse that have occurred in the relatively new subprime lending industry have caused many federal agencies and regulators to take a fresh new look at the industry. The U.S. House Special Committee on Aging determined that the problem of predatory lending abuses among the nation's older persons had gotten so overwhelming that it held hearings on predatory lending on March 16, 1998. Under pressure from many consumer organizations, the Federal Reserve Board also addressed the problem by inviting concerned individuals and organizations to attend a series of public hearings on home loan equity abuses in the summer of 2000. The Department of Housing and Urban Development and the U.S. Treasury released a joint statement condemning the practice of predatory lending and providing possible solutions for curbing the abuses. The U.S. Senate and House of Representatives have also been busy crafting legislation on addressing the issue of predatory lending as well.

State governments and consumer organizations have also been active in drafting legislation and enacting regulations intended to curb the overall incidence and deleterious effects of predatory lending activities. Some states, such as North Carolina, have even formed active coalitions to help combat the problem. Table 3 provides a list of the various predatory lending laws that have recently been passed within the 50 states through the active participation of these types of coalitions.

Industry members have also entered the fray in trying to curb the incidence of predatory lending as well. In April 2000, Fannie Mae and Freddie Mac, two of the largest housing-related organizations and financial institutions in the world, released separate statements on efforts each will make in the future to try and combat predatory lending practices. Fannie Mae's efforts are geared at such practices as steering, excessive fees, single-premium credit insurance, prepayment penalties, and various servicing improprieties. Freddie Mac's efforts are more concentrated toward consumer education and outreach of low- and moderate-income households, based on the belief that such outreach efforts will persuade creditworthy borrowers to choose traditional lending options in the future.

In a recent position paper, the Fannie Mae Foundation even suggests a variety of policy recommendations and future actions to improve the banking options of those who presently live in communities prone to predatory lending. First, it suggests that data collection on financial services transactions needs to be improved dramatically. This would not only allow the academic and policymaking community to determine the breadth and scope of a predatory lending problem within a community, but it would also allow for increased enforcement of fair lending laws, equal credit opportunity provisions, and consumer protection regulations. Second, the foundation recommends the creation of greater competition for financial services in distressed communities by improving the range of available financial products and services. The foundation believes that government should be

**Table 3**
**States Taking Legislative Action against Predatory Lending**

| State | Bill No. | Year Enacted |
|---|---|---|
| California | A.B. 489 | 2001 |
| Colorado | H.B. 1259 | 2002 |
| Connecticut | H.B. 6131; H.B. 5073 | 2001; 2002 |
| D.C. | B 13-800; B 14-515; B 14-555; PR-546; PR-576 | 2000; 2002 |
| Florida | S.B. 2262 | 2002 |
| Georgia | H.B. 1361 | 2002 |
| Maryland | H.B. 399; S.B. 377 | 2001 |
| Minnesota | S.F. 2988 | 2002 |
| North Carolina | S.B. 1149 | 1999 |
| Ohio | S.B. 76 | 2001 |
| Oklahoma | S.B. 1481 | 2000 |
| Pennsylvania | S.B. 377 | 2001 |
| South Carolina | S.R. 1431 | 2000 |
| Texas | S.B. 317; S.B. 322; S.B. 1581 | 2001 |
| Utah | H.J.R. 2708 | 2001 |
| Virginia | H.B. 2708; H.B. 2787 | 2001 |
| West Virginia | H.B. 4379 | 2002 |

*Source*: National Conference of State Legislatures 2003.

the one that plays a large role in the innovation of financial services. Third, the foundation suggests a much more aggressive campaign to increase consumer education about the topic of predatory lending and to extol the virtues of the banking options that are available to them in traditional banking relationships (Carr and Schuetz 2000). (See also BANKING SERVICES FOR THE MATURE MARKET; CONSUMER PROTECTION FOR OLDER ADULTS; CREDIT SCORES; FINANCIAL COUNSELING FOR MID- TO LATER LIFE; FINANCIAL EDUCATION FOR SENIORS; FINANCIAL LITERACY; FINANCIAL RECOVERY IN LATER LIFE; MARKETING TO MATURE ADULTS; STATE AND AREA AGENCIES ON AGING.)

## References

AARP. 2001. *The Policy Book: AARP Public Policies*. Washington, DC: Author.

Barry, Patricia. 2001. "Beware: Predatory Lenders at Work." *AARP Bulletin* (June).

Brennan, William J. 1998. Testimony before U.S. Senate Special Committee on Aging, March 16.

Carr, James H., and Jenny Schuetz. 2000. *Financial Services in Distressed Communities: Framing the Issue, Finding Solutions*. Washington, DC: Fannie Mae Foundation.

D'Amours, Norman. 2000. "The Battle to Increase Access and Ensure Fair Pricing." *The Neighbor Works Journal* (Winter).

Dove Consulting. 2000. *Survey of Non-Bank Financial Institutions for the U.S. Department of the Treasury*. Washington, DC: U.S. Department of the Treasury.

Federal Trade Commission. 2001. Testimony before the California State Assembly Committee on Banking and Finance, February 21.

Financial Service Centers of America. 1998. *The Consumer's Choice: The Role of Deferred Deposit Services in Meeting Short-Term Financial Needs*. Washington, DC: National Check Cashers Association.

Foundation, Larry, Peter Rufano, and Patricia Walker. 1999. "Collaborating with Congregations: Opportunities for Financial Services in Inner Cities." *Harvard Business Review* (July–August): 57–68.

Inside Mortgage Finance. 2002. *Inside B&C Lending*. Bethesda, MD: Author.

Kim, Anne. 2001. "The Unbanked and the Alternative Financial Sector: Discussant Comments." Presented at the U.S. Federal Reserve System Conference on Changing Financial Markets and Community Development, April 5–6.

National Conference of State Legislatures. 2003. Available online at http://www.ncsl.org/.

Stegman, Michael A. 1999. *Savings for the Poor*. Washington, DC: Brookings Institution Press, Progressive Policy Institute.

Zimmerman, Ken, Elvyn Wyly, and Hilary Botein. 2002. *Predatory Lending in New Jersey: The Rising Threat to Low-Income Homeowners*. Newark, NJ: New Jersey Institute for Social Justice.

*Andrew Carswell*

**PROBATE,** a court procedure by which a will is determined to be valid and that involves the orderly distribution of assets in an estate by a probate court, whether or not the decedent left a will. The Latin root of probate, *probare*, means "to prove." Probate involves having the court *ap*prove how a decedent's assets are distributed, whether there is a valid will or not. *Probate* is commonly used to refer to both (1) the court process through which a will is validated and its terms are carried out and (2) the branch of the local or state court wherein this process is handled. In addition to overseeing the estates of those who die (decedents), the probate court in most states also has jurisdiction over trusts as well as guardianships and conservatorships for incapacitated persons and minors. In a few states, the probate court is called the "Orphans' " or "Surrogate's" court.

Probate may or may not be required to distribute a decedent's property. Most states provide some form of probate waiver or simple process for "small estates," though the definition of "small" varies widely from state to state. If the decedent's assets are not "small" and are titled in his/her name only and are outside of a trust with no beneficiary designations or joint tenants, probate is necessary. However, if the decedent made proper beneficiary designations for life insurance policies, IRAs (Individual Retirement Accounts), or other retirement plans, made "payable on death" designations on bank accounts, and held other property in joint tenancy or in trust, probate may be avoided. Often even the most careful planners overlook some piece of property that may make probate necessary.

The probate court oversees the administration of a decedent's estate only when it is asked to do so. While in some states the local clerk of the court may file and thus maintain a record of wills, no action regarding a decedent's will happens automatically. A probate is initiated by the filing of documents with the probate clerk in the county where the decedent lived. If the decedent owned property subject to probate in more than one state, ancillary actions are likely required in the other states.

Each state has its own *de facto* will for those who died without executing a valid will document. Without a valid will, the decedent's property will be distributed by terms dictated by the law of *intestate succession* in the decedent's home state. Although there is increasing uniformity in the probate process from state to state, each probate estate, with or without a will, is handled in accordance with the laws of the state wherein the decedent maintained his or her primary residence.

When a will is admitted to probate an executor or executrix—in some states called a personal representative or an administrator—is appointed by the court. The executor or personal representative must (1) identify the state of domicile if the decedent lived or held assets in more than one state; (2) hire an attorney and other professionals as needed; (3) ensure that beneficiaries and creditors are formally notified; (4) open an account for the decedent's estate; (5) inventory and collect the decedent's assets; (6) safeguard all assets, including investments, real estate, and businesses; (7) determine the value of the decedent's assets; (8) pay the decedent's debts; (9) communicate with the Internal Revenue Service (IRS); and (10) make distributions to beneficiaries.

Many people find probate difficult because of sadness due to a loved one's death and/or general confusion about the legal process accompanying death. The expense of probate is uniformly dreaded, though often overestimated. The executor or personal representative is entitled to charge a fee for administering the estate, and when the executor has an attorney, there are additional fees. The actual probate fees likely to be incurred are typically in the range of 1% to 2% of the estate's total value. Sometimes the fees may be as high as 5% of the estate's value. Even where an estate is very complicated, one should carefully scrutinize fees of more than 5% of an estate's value.

The legal issues involved in probate are usually well defined. However, legal fees may be driven up by emotionally charged personal disputes between beneficiaries or those who think they should be beneficiaries of estates. Before investing heavily in attorney fees to address family issues, family members are well advised to seek the input of counselors, spiritual advisors, or mediators. Feuding family members or friends often realize too late they have spent most or all of their inheritance in legal fees to fight emotional battles, as is illustrated famously through the case of *Jarndyce v. Jarndyce* in Charles Dickens's 800-page Victorian novel *Bleak House*.

In *Bleak House*, several generations of Jarndyces see their inheritance consumed entirely by legal fees as the will is churned through the English Chancery Court (or Court of Equity). In the first chapter, Dickens's narrator warns the reader about the court system:

> This is the Court of Chancery, which has its decaying houses and its blighted lands in every shire, which has its worn-out lunatic in every madhouse and its dead in every churchyard, which has its ruined suitor with his slipshod heels and threadbare dress borrowing and begging through the round of every man's acquaintance, which gives to monied might the means abundantly of wearying out the right, which so exhausts finances, patience, courage, hope, so overthrows the brain and breaks the heart, that there is not an honourable man among its practitioners who would not give—who does not often give—the warning, "Suffer any wrong that can be done you rather than come here!" (Dickens [1853] 1977)

Modern probate attorneys give clients a subtler version of the narrator's view by urging out-of-court dispute resolution whenever possible. (See also ATTORNEYS; TRUSTS; WILLS.)

**References**

Dickens, Charles [1853] 1977. *Bleak House*. Reprint, New York: Norton.

Fleming, Robert. 2000. *The Elder-Law Answer Book*. New York: Panel Publishers.

*Leigh Bernstein*

**PROFIT SHARING PLANS,** the practice whereby companies pay employees from company profits in addition to their regular salary and wages. In the United States profit sharing distributions can be paid in cash or deposited into a defined contribution plan trust (deferred profit sharing), or the employee may elect to have all or some paid in cash or deposited into a defined contribution plan trust (CODAs—cash or deferred arrangements). 401(k) plans, a form of deferred profit sharing, are arrangements in which employees may save on a pretax basis a predetermined percentage of salary or wages in a defined contribution plan trust. The employee savings may or may not be matched by employer contributions, or they may be part of a deferred profit sharing program in which matching contributions are based on profits or where employer profit sharing contributions are made regardless of elective employee savings. U.S. law also permits employee contributions to such plans on an after-tax basis as well (thrift savings arrangements).

## History: From Albert Gallatin to 401(k)

The first American profit sharing plan was introduced into the workplace over 200 years ago. Albert Gallatin, secretary of treasury under Presidents Thomas Jefferson and James Madison, initiated the first profit sharing plan in 1797 at his glass factory in New Geneva, Pennsylvania. The second profit sharing plan was not begun until 1867, 70 years later, at the Bay State & Shoe Leather Company in Massachusetts. Profit sharing took root slowly in the United States, and it is estimated that there were 34 profit sharing plans operating in 1896. One person who helped to promote profit sharing plans in their early period was Nicholas Paine Gilman. A number of Protestant clergy believed that profit sharing could address the problems accompanying the rapid industrialization of the late 1800s. Gilman, a leading member of this group, wrote two books on profit sharing (*Profit Sharing between Employer and Employee* and *A Dividend to Labor: A Study of Employee's Welfare Institutions*) and in 1892 helped to form the Association for the Promotion of Profit Sharing. Another early supporter of profit sharing plans was William Cooper Procter.

In the 1880s the Procter & Gamble Company found that it, like many other companies of the time, had labor unrest spreading through its factories. William Cooper Procter, a grandson of one of the founders, suggested that profit sharing could revolutionize a worker's relationship with production. He believed that profit sharing would empower workers and give the company a competitive edge. Procter's proposal met with strong opposition, even from some labor advocates who feared it would be difficult to call a strike if workers shared profits with a company's owners. But Procter insisted, and the plan was implemented. With the inception of the Procter & Gamble profit sharing plan in 1887, productivity and profitability at the company increased substantially, and labor strife at the company nearly vanished.

The initial Procter & Gamble profit sharing plan provided each employee with a semiannual cash dividend based on a division of net profits between the company and its employees in proportion to total cost of production and marketing. However, within a few years William Cooper Procter became dissatisfied with the original Procter & Gamble profit sharing plan. The company was issuing profit sharing bonus checks with such regularity that employees came to expect them, treating the money as an extra paycheck. In 1903 the Procter & Gamble Company altered its plan so that profit sharing distributions were made in Procter & Gamble stock rather than in cash. In order to be eligible for profit sharing, the plan also required that participants save a certain percentage of their wages. Employees who voluntarily contributed 4% of pay to purchase company stock received up to four times that amount in a matching company-stock contribution (which varied depending upon company profitability). This stock was held in trust by the company, which guaranteed that it would repurchase the stock from departing employees for no less than the original price. Procter introduced this deferred program so that profit sharing would have a more lasting effect and to encourage employees to build assets for the future.

Within a few years other major corporations began instituting profit sharing plans—including the Eastman Kodak Co. in 1912, Harris Trust & Savings Bank in 1915, and Sears, Roebuck & Company in 1916. Kodak's wage dividend plan was established in recognition of the company's faith in its employees. The Sears plan was introduced at the suggestion of a stockholder who believed that profit sharing would create a better feeling between the company and employee, which would benefit the company. The Harris Trust and Sears plans required employees to save voluntarily a portion of their earnings in a company-provided trust in order to receive a profit-based matching contribution from their employer (the first thrift savings arrangements).

Other early-twentieth-century profit sharers permitted employees to choose whether or not to take all or some of their profit sharing in cash or defer it. Still, the controversy surrounding profit sharing continued. Profit sharing was seen by some organizations, like the National Civic Federation, as a means of reducing labor problems. As one supporter wrote, "[B]y making the interests of employer and employee identical, profit sharing will tend to lessen antagonism and friction between owners and employed workers, and to substitute in their stead industrial harmony" (Burritt et al. 1918). But Samuel Gompers, president of the American Federation of Labor, held a different view. In 1916 he responded to profit sharing in this way:

> It has come under my observation that some employers who have inaugurated systems of so-called profit sharing have pared down the wages of their employees so that the combined sharing of profits and their wages did not equal the wages of employees in other companies in the same line of industry. What we are especially interested in, more than profit sharing is a fair living wage, reasonable hours and fair conditions of employment. (National Civic Federation 1916, 368–69)

Although steadily gaining supporters during this period, profit sharing still did not have universal support.

### Profit Sharing Becomes a Tax Advantage

The American approach to profit sharing began to change in 1913 with the passage of the sixteenth Amendment to the U.S. Constitution, permitting the government to impose a federal income tax. This led Congress in 1921 to pass the legislation permitting tax-favored treatment for profit sharing contributions paid into defined contribution plan trusts. The law stated that company contributions to profit sharing plans could be immediately taken as a deduction by the company, but the employee would not have to pay tax on the contribution or related earnings until he or she took constructive receipt of the money.

This resulted in a shift after World War I from cash profit sharing to deferred profit sharing, especially to programs where the employee's share of profits was distributed in the form of stock or credits on the purchase price of stock. Since stock prices were inflating rapidly, these plans were attractive to employees. Through such stock ownership plans, corporations sought to promote a sense of proprietorship and loyalty to the firm. An employee who was a stockholder would be less likely to strike, it was hoped, and more likely to see the viewpoint of owners and managers. With government legislation encouraging these deferred programs, profit sharing flourished.

In 1929 the stock market crash halted the growth of profit sharing plans. An estimated 70% of all profit sharing plans of the time were discontinued or made inactive during the Great Depression. Deferred plans especially were affected. Fortunately, this setback was not able to stop the idea of profit sharing from continuing to gain support. Only ten years later congressional interest led to renewed growth. In 1939 a study conducted by the Senator Arthur H. Vandenberg Subcommittee of the Senate Finance Committee concluded that "[profit sharing creates] employer-employee relations that make for peace, equity, efficiency and contentment, . . . and contributes substantially to financial security in retirement" (U.S. Congress 1939). Congress subsequently passed legislation granting additional tax advantages to qualified, deferred profit sharing plans.

During the period leading up to World War II most profit sharing plans in place before the depression returned to cash profit sharing plans, paying annual or semiannual cash bonuses to employees. But in 1942 when the Salary Stabilization Act restricted wage increases and disallowed the adoption of new cash plans, companies needed another way to attract high-quality workers. Tax rates were high enough during the war years to make the tax advantages of deferred profit sharing plans very attractive. Employers liked the plans because they were permitted to deduct, as a wage cost, profit sharing payments up to 15% of total compensation. Employees also liked the plans, but for a different reason—lump-sum payments made at retirement could be treated as long-term capital gains. Between 1940 and 1946 the IRS approved 2,471 deferred profit sharing plans, a vast increase over the 37 plans currently in existence. Between 1946 and 1955, an additional 6,000 plans were approved.

In the midst of the implementation of many new profit sharing plans, the bankruptcy of one company with a traditional defined benefit plan led to a different employee perspective. In the 1950s, the Studebaker Company bankruptcy attracted national attention when the value of the assets in its defined benefit plan, which consisted entirely of company stock, fell to zero. As the Studebaker employees lost their entire retirement benefits, other workers became concerned about their retirement security. Twenty years later this had grown into a national concern, and in 1974 Congress enacted the Employee Retirement Income Security Act (ERISA). ERISA was the first comprehensive pension reform law passed by Congress. The IRS had, in 1958, passed the Welfare and Pension Plans Disclosure Act to prevent discrimination in plans in favor of highly compensated individuals. However, the framers of this act were mainly interested in protecting federal revenues against excessive and unjustifiable tax deductions. ERISA included regulations on the actuarial soundness of plans, the protection of the rights of individual participants, and standards of fiduciary conduct for those handling the plan assets. ERISA also covered issues of reporting and disclosure, plan participation and vesting, funding, and fiduciary responsibility.

The passing of the ERISA legislation in 1974 posed more difficulties than benefits for the profit sharing community. ERISA was a massive and complex piece of legislation, and plan sponsors had difficulty understanding how to comply. For example, it was unclear whether qualified CODAs were still permitted. CODA plans had been very popular for decades in certain industries (financial institutions, in particular) and in certain geographic areas (the Midwest, for example). As a result, the passage of ERISA effectively stopped the formation of new profit sharing plans. Between 1974 and 1977, 40,000 of the existing 186,499 plans were discontinued.

Beginning in 1974, groups in support of deferred profit sharing programs urged Congress to enact legislation clarifying that the CODA practice continue to be permitted. This led to the passage in 1978 of Section 401(k) to the Internal Revenue Code. The number of employers and employees benefiting from Section 401(k) initially was minimal as employers waited for regulatory clarification of the law. In 1981 the IRS published its regulations clarifying Section 401(k). However, these regulations allowed employees to contribute regular earnings as well as profit sharing bonuses on an income tax deferred and FICA (Federal Insurance Contributions Act) tax-exempt basis. This ruling was popular, in part because the maximum contributions limit for such plans at this time was $45,000, and companies quickly added the new tax-deferred contribution arrangement to their existing thrift-savings and deferred profit sharing programs, and plan growth exploded.

As 401(k) plan usage grew, opponents of the defined contribution system began urging increased regulation. In 1983 the maximum contribution limit for all defined contribution plans was reduced to $30,000, and employee 401(k) plan contributions were made subject to the FICA tax. The biggest change for 401(k) plans came in the Taxpayer Reform Act (TRA) of 1986. This law lowered the maximum 401(k) employee contribution to $7,000 on an inflation-adjusted basis and imposed stricter discrimination testing on profit sharing contributions as well as earnings. However, 401(k) plans maintained their appeal even with these changes, and they continue today to grow at a significant rate. It is now estimated that approximately 400,000 companies have 401(k) plans.

Profit sharing has undergone many changes in its 200-year evolution. It began as a cash bonus system, which grew to include deferred profit sharing with employee stock ownership plans (ESOPs) and CODA programs. Most recently, this change includes the addition of 401(k) plans, which are increasingly a preferred choice among today's employer-provided retirement vehicles. The system continues to grow and is now the greatest source of new retirement savings in the United States. (See also DEFINED CONTRIBUTION PLAN; EMPLOYEE RETIREMENT INCOME SECURITY ACT [ERISA].)

### References

Allen, Everett T., Jr., Joseph J. Melone, Jerry S. Rosenbloom, and Dennis F. Mahoney, eds. 2002. *Pension Planning: Pensions, Profit-Sharing, and Other Deferred Compensation Plans*. 9th ed. New York: McGraw-Hill.

Burritt, Arthur W., et al. 1918. *Profit Sharing: Its Principles and Practice*. New York: Harper and Brothers.

Kruse, Douglas L. 1993. *Profit-Sharing: Does It Make a Difference? The Productivity and Stability Effects of Profit-Sharing Plans*. Kalamazoo, MI: W.E. Upjohn Institute.

The National Civic Federation. 1916. *Profit Sharing by American Employers*. New York: E.P. Dutton.

U.S. Congress. Senate Subcommittee of the Committee on Finance. 1939. "Survey of the Experience in Profit Sharing and Possibilities of Incentive Taxation." Washington, DC: GPO.

*David L. Wray*

# R

**REAL ESTATE INVESTMENTS,** one of the most popular methods for investors to invest their assets outside of the stock and bond markets in order to achieve long-term capital growth, earn income, and receive tax benefits. The total value of all real estate in America is over $15 trillion, and for many American investors, it has become the favorite form of investing, especially in light of large declines in stock prices and record-low bond yields in the early 2000s.

The health of the real estate market is subject to the influence of national trends such as interest rates and changes in tax laws, which greatly affect the forces of supply and demand. Yet real estate investment opportunities are even more subject to local influences, such as the strength or weakness of a local economy, the supply and demand for houses, apartments, and office buildings, and changes in property tax rates.

**Real Estate Investment Trusts (REITs)**

A Real Estate Investment Trust is a publicly traded company that owns real estate properties. Under American tax law, REITs are not taxed at the corporate level as long as they distribute at least 95% of their income to shareholders. All dividends are taxable to REIT shareholders who hold REIT shares in taxable accounts. (In a few cases, some of the dividends are considered return of capital and therefore are not taxed.) But the unique advantage REITs offer of single taxation of dividends makes them extremely attractive as an investment alternative.

REITs raise money from the public like any other company by issuing shares that become publicly traded on major exchanges like the New York and American Stock Exchanges. They then employ that capital by purchasing investment-grade real estate such as apartment buildings, office buildings, manufacturing facilities, hotels, shopping centers, and distribution centers. Some REITs specialize in a particular type of real estate property, such as hotels or health care facilities. Others specialize in a particular region of the country like Texas or Washington, DC. Other REITs diversify broadly by region and property type.

There are three kinds of REITs, depending on their investing style. Equity REITs invest in properties, hoping to improve them so that the value of their assets will rise in the long term while still providing a healthy dividend of 4% to 7% to shareholders. Mortgage REITs employ their capital by lending to real estate property owners. These

REITs offer much higher dividend yields to shareholders—typically 8% to 12%—but offer much more limited equity appreciation potential. Hybrid REITs combine equity ownership of properties and mortgage holdings, providing quite a high yield of 7% to 9% plus more appreciation potential.

For more information on REITs, contact the National Association of Real Estate Investment Trusts. A newsletter that tracks the REIT industry is the *Realty Stock Review*.

### Real Estate Mutual Funds

Certain mutual funds invest in REITs and other real estate-related stocks and bonds. As do all mutual funds, these funds provide diversification among a variety of REITs and also include housing stocks owned by homebuilders and suppliers to the housing industry. Some real estate funds also buy property stocks around the world, providing even more investment diversification. Most real estate mutual funds pay dividends of 2% to 4%, typically far below what REITs pay directly to their shareholders. REIT mutual funds tend to perform best when interest rates are falling and the economy is weakening because the REITs that they hold appreciate most during this part of the economic cycle. Conversely, when the economy is growing strongly, aggressive growth mutual funds become much more popular. For example, in the late 1990s amid the Internet stock boom, real estate funds dramatically lagged growth funds that were loaded with technology stocks. But as the Internet bubble burst in 2000, REITs and other real estate securities soared in popularity, causing billions of dollars to flow into real estate funds and causing their prices to soar to the top of the mutual fund performance charts.

### Real Estate Limited Partnerships (RELPs)

Real Estate Limited Partnerships, or RELPs as they are known for short, raise money from investors and invest in new or existing commercial real estate properties similar to the kinds of properties owned by REITs. Limited partnerships, however, are structured differently. Investors are partners whose liability is limited to the amount of their investment; they are not shareholders. Income and tax benefits such as depreciation or other deferred tax losses pass through directly to limited partners in proportion to their partnership interest, unlike REIT shareholders.

In theory, the RELP would buy properties, pass through net rents as distributions, sell the properties for large profits in future years, and distribute the profits to limited partners. In practice, under favorable tax laws that encouraged limited partnerships in the early 1980s, many partnerships raised huge amounts of money from investors eager to buy tax losses without understanding that such losses were merely deferred and would need to be recaptured when the properties were sold. General partners, flush with investment capital, overpaid for properties because of extreme competition among buyers of commercial properties. Many unfortunate general partners ended up passing through losses from the sale of depressed real estate and tax bills simultaneously to unhappy limited partners who sued them for fraud and mismanagement when the Tax Reform Act changed the tax laws in 1986. Since the favorable tax laws were curtailed, RELPs have become a largely discredited public investment, although private real estate limited partnerships remain a viable way for sophisticated and knowledgeable investors to participate in real estate investment.

### Rental Real Estate

For millions of Americans, the largest and most profitable investment they own is rental real estate. Being a landlord has advantages and disadvantages. The advantages: a well-run property can produce far more cash in rents than it costs to maintain, producing reliable positive cash flow. Over time, the tenant's rents pay off the landlord's mortgage, and the landlord's asset rises in value. Rental real estate also offers exclusive tax benefits, such as the ability to write off losses up to $25,000 against other income.

Being a landlord, however, is a business and comes with its share of hassles. Tenants complain if the heat is not working properly or the pipes leak. Renters are not always reliable, and it becomes the responsibility of the landlord to institute collection and even eviction procedures. In certain jurisdictions, rent controls prevent landlords from charging market rents and achieving positive cash flow.

Successful rental real estate owners buy properties in good locations that attract renters who take care of their dwelling units, pay their rents on a timely basis, and are amenable or even expect to pay reasonable rent increases over time. Some real estate entrepreneurs like to buy dilapidated buildings and renovate them, allowing them to raise rents that are set to recover the capital spent on such improvements and ultimately selling the buildings for large capital gains. Others buy buildings in good condition and are content to collect rents and to realize capital appreciation based on wise choices made with respect to location and tenants.

### Vacation Homes

For those wanting to use the real estate they own as well as to rent it out, vacation home properties are ideal. Under IRS rules, an owner can have personal use of real estate for up to 14 days a year and still enjoy all the tax benefits of rental real estate, such as depreciation and the ability to use losses to offset other income. Vacation homes tend to be located in desirable locations such as on or near oceans, lakes, ski resorts, beaches, mountains, or major tourist attractions. Usually the property cannot be rented out year-round because there is only seasonal demand for a few months of the year. But if the owner is able to charge a high enough rent during the prime season to cover all expenses, including maintenance, utilities, insurance, and property taxes, and has the opportunity to occupy the real estate for up to two weeks a year, it can be an ideal investment.

If the property is mortgaged, all interest is deductible on the owner's tax return as a mortgage interest expense. Servicing the mortgage may raise ownership costs considerably, however, and if rents are not adequate to cover such costs, an owner may experience negative cash flow. The ideal vacation home properties, therefore, are those in locations where a steady demand exists for rentals during the prime season. These properties tend to be in high demand and can provide considerable capital appreciation over time as well as steady income.

### Raw Land

The most speculative form of real estate investing is the purchase of raw land. If land stays undeveloped, however, it may be a serious cash drain to its owner because property taxes and maintenance must be paid while it lies unproductive. If the property is adjacent to developed property, however, its value may rise sharply, as most raw land is purchased from owners by developers who are assembling a site for a housing complex, shopping center, office building, or other commercial use. The land value increases once basic services such as sewers and utilities are brought to the property and roads are built.

The difficulty in investing in raw land is that it is illiquid. Unless a developer is interested, the market for raw land can be very limited, if not nonexistent. Many factors affect the price of land, including interest rates, local zoning, and building regulations. In addition, environmental laws protect many property settings, and investors must investigate raw land they are thinking of buying for wetlands and other protected designations, soil conditions, toxic waste, and other conditions that will impact future development and market potential of the land.

Obtaining financing to purchase raw land may also be difficult. Lenders incur a higher level of loan risk on unproductive property and typically require a higher equity investment in raw land than in developed property. For those with the necessary capital and knowledge of development patterns, however, raw land can be a profitable investment.

Investing in real estate for retirees can be quite profitable, particularly if it is some form of passive investment such as a REIT or real estate mutual fund that can produce a steady return on investment without the necessity for managing the real estate itself. Rental real estate, vacation homes, and raw land are more management intensive and may be suitable for retirees seeking regular income and the small business characteristics of real estate management. As an alternative to the volatile performance of the stock and bond markets, real estate offers either active or passive investment appeal for many Americans. (See also AGENTS AND BROKERS; CONDOMINIUMS; COOPERATIVE OWNERSHIP IN HOUSING; HOME MODIFICATIONS FINANCING; INFLUENCES ON RETIREMENT INVESTMENT DECISIONS; INVESTOR EDUCATION; MORTGAGE INSTRUMENTS; SENIORS HOUSING FINANCE; TITLING ASSETS; VACATION HOMES AND RECREATIONAL PROPERTY; ZONING.)

**Organizations**

A.D. Kessler's *Creative Real Estate Magazine*
National Association of Real Estate Investment Trusts
Realty Stock Review

**References**

Brueggeman, William B., and Jeffrey D. Fisher. 2002. *Real Estate Finance and Investments*. 11th ed. New York: McGraw-Hill.

Kennedy, Diane, Garrett Sutton, and Robert T. Kiyosaki. 2003. *Real Estate Loopholes: Secrets of Successful Real Estate Investing*. Victoria, Australia: Warner Books.

McLean, Andrew, Gary W. Eldred, and Andrew J. McLean. 2003. *Investing in Real Estate*. 4th ed. New York: John Wiley & Sons.

*Jordan E. Goodman*

**RELIGIOUS GIVING BY OLDER ADULTS,** giving practices of older persons based on theological teachings of Judaism, Christianity, and Islam. Theocentric economic theory suggests that the giving practices of persons who identify with one of these monotheistic traditions will follow one of two distinct patterns outlined in Scripture.

From an economic perspective, the earliest documents of Western theism may be examined as "economic contracts." When God called Abraham the founding patriarch of

Judaism, Christianity, and Islam, He required him to make certain religious and ethical commitments in exchange for the promise of economic prosperity. Abraham agreed that he would acknowledge that God was the only god, that he and his descendants would worship God alone, and that they would obey all the commandments of God—many of which had specific economic implications. In return, God promised that He would use His omnipotent power over all economic variables in the world He had created to assure that Abraham and all of his descendants, biological and religious, would experience economic security.

According to Scripture, God said to Abraham, "I will make of you a great nation, and I will bless you, and make your name great, so that you will be a blessing. I will bless those who bless you, and him who curses you, I will curse; and by you all the families of the earth will bless themselves" (Genesis 12:2-3). Abraham responded by building an altar, making sacrifices to God, and promising God that he and his descendants would serve God in every aspect of their lives. The economic conditions of this contract are clear. As long as Abraham and his descendants obeyed the commandments of God, He would guarantee their ultimate economic success. However, if they broke one of God's commandments in the pursuit of economic gain, their project would eventually fail. The terms of this agreement are restated throughout the sacred documents of Judaism, Christianity, and Islam and continue to form the basis of economic instruction for all who identify themselves with one of these monotheistic traditions.

Given the fact that the Scriptures, and subsequent religious instruction, are clear on this matter, one would expect religious persons in American society, most of whom say they participate in one of the monotheistic traditions, to abide by the terms of this theocentric economic theory. One would expect them to act on the conviction that one's economic success or failure is directly related to obedience or disobedience of God's commandments. Specifically, one would expect that the budget of every religious household would include a portion for charity. (Many Christians agree that this portion should be 10% of one's annual income; many Muslims agree that it should be 1% to 3% of one's total assets annually.) Of course, all religious people do not follow God's instructions in this matter. One might also expect religious elders to follow this "ordinary pattern of religious charity." Some do, while others, because of their economic and personal circumstances, may not. The Scriptures contain stories that offer economic instruction to the poor, the displaced, the outcast, and the disaffected. These stories usually contain economic instruction that is relevant to older adults.

To better understand theocentric economics in relationship to those who experience a loss or significant decrease of economic power—those who appear not to be blessed by God—other stories need to be consulted. The story of "the Widow of Zarephath," found in I Kings 17:8-24, is a good example. A prolonged drought has caused all crops to fail, and the widow of Zarephath has only enough grain and oil to prepare a cake for herself and her son. She goes to the edge of the city to gather wood to cook what she believes will be their final meal. There she meets Elijah, a prophet of God. The prophet asks her to draw water for him. This she does, because she is a believer in the God of Israel and honors God's prophet. Then Elijah tells her to feed him. When she explains that she has only enough meal for one small cake for herself and her starving son, the prophet insists that she prepare a cake first for him and then cook for her family. Without dispute, she follows the instruction of the prophet, and to her delight, there is not only enough grain for that day but enough for every day as long as the drought continues. According to I Kings 17:16: "The jar of grain was not spent, neither did the cruse of oil fail, according to the word of the Lord, which he spoke by Elijah." Thus, by obeying the prophet of God and giving everything she had to the cause of God, the economic future of her family was secured.

Some contextual factors need to be clarified before the full economic implications of this story may be understood. Without knowledge of context, one might conclude that God had failed in His economic obligations to the widow. The context of the story makes it clear that the widow and her family are not suffering the consequences of their own sin; rather, they, and all the people of Israel, are suffering because of the disobedience of King Ahab. Ahab, against the specific instructions of God, had formed alliances, political and economic, with some of the nations around Israel and, hence by implication, had made contracts with the gods of these nations. In response to this royal apostasy, God caused a drought to afflict Israel and her neighbors and He sent His prophet, Elijah, to tell the King and the people that the drought would continue until the apostasy had ceased. In ancient times, and even today in the understanding of many theists, the activities of leaders determine God's judgments on a nation. The widow was experiencing desperate economic circumstances because of the King's actions.

Without full knowledge of the context of the story, one might also conclude that the prophet was unreasonably selfish when he demanded that he be fed before the widow and her son. However, the opposite was true. According to theocentric economics, the prophet was doing the widow a special favor; for by allowing her to serve him, he was enabling her to indirectly serve God. Under the direction of God, he was calling the people of God to religious (and economic) reform. According to the promises of God, those who responded to His call would be blessed; those who failed to respond to the call would be cursed. The widow and her son were the first to join with Elijah in this divine warfare. Hence the widow, in contrast to the infamous Jezebel, wife of Ahab and the other Sidonite woman in the story, secured for herself a place of honor in the history of her people and secured the continuation of her progeny forever. From the perspective of secular economic theory, the widow made an irrational and foolish decision, but from the perspective of theistic faith, she made a wise choice. It would not be surprising that some economically disadvantaged devout persons would take instruction from the widow's example.

In summary, two models for religious giving are prescribed by Scripture. Those blessed by God financially believe these blessings are directly related to obedience to God in all things including charity. Some theists believe, or are expected to believe, that future success is contingent on continued obedience. In contrast, some who feel they are not receiving God's economic blessings may attribute their misfortune to the religious apostasy of the nation's leaders or their own unfaithfulness. These believers, however, are also obligated to give a portion of their (sometimes meager) resources to the cause of God. But following the implications of Scripture, these people would be more likely than the affluent to give their support to some "prophet of God" who is calling for a reform of national policy that would be in compliance with God's commandments.

If there is validity in these conclusions, it would be reasonable to assume that religious older persons would follow these models for religious giving. It would also be reasonable to expect that those who remain attached to their religious communities and who, either because they are cared for by their communities as the Scripture requires, or because they have sufficient personal economic resources to meet their needs, would be content with their economic circumstances and would follow the ordinary pattern of giving. To most this would mean continuing to give a portion of their economic resources to charity. Further, religious elders who experience displacement or disaffection from their religious community, for whatever reason, and who feel they are being treated unjustly in economic matters, would follow the pattern of giving prescribed by the story of the widow of Zarephath. To many of these "separated elders," this instruction would lead them to give to ministries that are clearly and aggressively prophetic. In our society, these "prophets of God" are most likely to be found in evangelical churches and in almost all popular "media ministries."

Data to test the theocentric theory of giving by elders are unavailable. Future research could attempt to demonstrate that most older people, especially those who remain in contact with a religious community, continue the same patterns of charitable giving as they practiced in middle age, and to show that a significant portion of our older population, especially those who experience some sort of disaffection with society, change these patterns and follow the economic instructions in the story of the widow.

In the search for relevant data, several churches and religious charitable organizations were consulted. None kept specific data by which giving patterns could be correlated with the age of the donor. Some media ministries keep giving statistics that are age correlated (as one would expect from the theory outlined above), but the records of media ministries are not open to researchers. So while giving patterns of religious elders appear to be predictable in theory, it is unclear just what those patterns are. (See also ASSET ALLOCATION AFTER RETIREMENT; CHARITABLE CONTRIBUTIONS; INHERITANCE; KING LEAR SYNDROME; LIFE PLANNING; RETIREMENT EXPENSE PLANNING.)

### Suggested Readings

Dayton, Howard. 1997. *Your Money Counts: The Biblical Guide to Earning, Spending, Saving, Investing, Giving, and Getting Out of Debt*. Carol Stream, IL: Tyndale House.

Lucado, Max. 2002. *A Love Worth Giving: Living in the Overflow of God's Love*. Nashville, TN: W Publishing Group.

Rodin, R. Scott. 2000. *Stewards in the Kingdom: A Theology of Life in All Its Fullness*. Downers Grove, IL: Intervarsity Press.

### References

Fischer, Kathleen. 1985. *Winter Grace: Spirituality for the Later Years*. New York: Paulist Press.

National Opinion Research Center (NORC). 1991. *Emerging Trends*. Princeton, NJ: Princeton Religious Research Center.

Peters, F.E. 1982. *Children of Abraham: Judaism, Christianity, Islam*. Princeton, NJ: Princeton University Press.

Roschen, John F. 1991. *Baby Boomers Face Midlife: Implications for the Faith Communities in the 1990s and Beyond*. Minneapolis, MN: Adult Faith Resources.

Seeber, E. 1992. *Spiritual Maturity in the Later Years*. New York: Haworth Press.

*John Collins*

**Figure 1**
**Primary Insurance Amount Calculation in 2003**

| |
|---|
| 90% of the first $606 of average indexed monthly earnings (AIME) |
| Plus (+) 32% of AIME over $606 and through $3,653 |
| Plus (+) 15% of AIME over $3,653 |

*Source*: SSA 2003.

**RETIREMENT EXPENSE PLANNING,** the process of estimating the amount of money required for a chosen lifestyle in retirement. There is no single or absolute answer to the question, "How much money will a person need for retirement?" For example, people who die before or shortly after retirement will have saved in vain. On the other hand, those who experience catastrophic uninsured medical bills or disastrous investment performance combined with high inflation will probably not be able to adequately prepare to support their chosen lifestyle without working. The fact remains, however, that the "How much?" question lingers as arguably the most important issue in retirement planning.

With the understanding that there is no single (or simple) solution for any individual situation, and certainly no "one size fits all" answer to the "How much?" question, there are nonetheless preliminary concerns that are common to all situations, assumptions that are required for any analysis, and a process that can be applied to arrive at the answer for any individual. Given these tools, planning can be done with a greater appreciation for the factors that affect the amount needed to answer the "How much?" question.

## Preliminary Concerns

### *Social Security*

One common misconception people have about their retirement income needs is that they will be able to get by solely on their pension and Social Security benefits. For the vast majority of Americans, this is not so. For many years now financial advisors have emphasized that financial security in retirement requires private savings and/or other resources to meet the need. Social Security is set up only to replace enough income to keep a person out of poverty. In 2003, the maximum annual Social Security benefit is $20,892 (Social Security Administration, [SSA] n.d.) Many people receive substantially less than this amount because their earnings record does not warrant the maximum. The estimated average annual benefit from Social Security for all retired workers is $10,740 ($895 monthly) in 2003 (SSA n.d.). As a person's salary increases, the percentage of his or her working salary that is replaced (called the replacement ratio) shrinks because the Social Security formula used to determine the primary insurance amount (PIA) favors low-income workers and discriminates against high-income workers (see Figure 1).

### *Pension Plan*

If it is clear that Social Security alone will not provide enough income for retirement, then it may be logical to ask, "What about Social Security combined with an employer pension program?" Once again, the answer is not good news. Pensions provided by employers, even combined with Social Security, will not be enough. The majority of people do not have access to the best type of private pension—a defined benefit pension plan, which provides a monthly check throughout retirement based on salary and service with the employer. Even those who do may not have a large enough benefit to sustain them. Additionally, the private pension system is set up with the assumption that employees will need to have personal savings to continue their lifestyle during retirement. Simply put, the responsibility for a comfortable retirement rests not solely with the government or the employer but also with the individual.

### *Personal Savings and Investments*

There are a variety of ways that individuals can save the supplemental amount needed for their retirement that will complement what their employer provides and what is provided under Social Security. These include:

1. *401(k) Plans and 403(b) Plans*. These are employer-sponsored plans that allow employees to make salary deferral-type contributions on a pretax basis. In 2003, the employee may be eligible to contribute $12,000 ($14,000 if 50 or older) of his or her salary toward retirement. For employees who pay taxes at the 33% marginal federal state and local rate, this can mean a $4,620 tax savings (.33 × 14,000 = $4,620)! In addition, some employers match part or all of their employees' contributions.

2. *Roth IRAs*. These are vehicles that provide a way for individuals who have adjusted gross incomes below $150,000 (married filing jointly) and $95,000 (single) to contribute $3,000 in 2003 ($3,500 if 50 or older) to an account that grows tax free. If certain requirements are met, the earnings on the Roth contribution will never be taxed. So, for example, if someone earns $10,000 on their investment and they are in the 33% marginal tax bracket (federal, state, and local), they will not have to pay $3,333.33 in taxes during retirement when they use the money. Also, note that partial contributions are allowed to a Roth IRA if your adjusted gross income is $160,000 or below (married filing jointly) or $110,000 or below (single).

3. *Regular IRAs*. Tax deductible contributions up to $3,000 ($3,500 if 50 or older) can be made to an IRA (Individual Retirement Account) if a person's adjusted gross income in 2003 is below $60,000 (married) or $40,000 (single). Also, note that partial contributions are allowed to a regular IRA if your adjusted gross income in 2003 is $70,000 or below (married filing jointly) or $50,000 or below (single).

4. *Keogh Plans*. Those people who have earnings from self-employment can start their own pension plan and contribute to it on a tax-advantaged basis. Being able to take advantage of these programs is like getting an interest-free loan from the government. By foregoing immediate taxation on amounts put into and earned by a Keogh plan, the Internal Revenue Service is, in effect, making an interest-free loan to the plan participants to help them accumulate retirement savings. The amount of this "loan" for an individual in the 38% federal, state, and local tax bracket is 38 cents for every dollar saved and for every dollar of interest earned (in other words, the amount of the tax). To put it another way, if participants had to use after-tax dollars to save for retirement, they would have only 62 cents to save for every dollar they save pretax and would earn only 62 cents for every dollar they earn without taxation. The duration of this "interest-free loan" lasts

until retirement distributions are received. For distributions paid out under a life annuity, this means that the "interest-free loan" lasts, in part, until the individual's death.

### *Homeownership*

One of the most important assets people own is their home. Those individuals who choose to downsize—that is, to sell their home in retirement and buy a smaller, less expensive one—can reap a significant amount of assets for retirement.

### *Other Savings Mechanisms*

There are a variety of other savings opportunities for individuals. People should seek the counsel of a financial advisor who can assist them with investing wisely.

## Making Proper Assumptions

In order to best understand the amount needed for retirement, one should understand the variables involved. The first and most crucial of these is inflation.

### *Inflation*

Inflation erodes purchasing power over time, making it difficult to maintain economic self-sufficiency during retirement. The effects of this erosion are dramatically illustrated when different inflation assumptions are plugged into retirement planning worksheets or computer models. Consider that in one model, by changing the inflation assumption from 4% to 6%, the amount of money the program indicated the individual would need to retire increased 20%.

To gain an appreciation for the impact of inflation, consider the plight of someone who retired in 1970. When they retired:

- Bread cost 24 cents a loaf
- Gas cost 39 cents a gallon
- Postage stamps were 4 cents
- Cars cost $3,000
- Houses cost $30,000

Most financial planners are comfortable using an inflation assumption of 3% to 4% as a proxy for long-term inflation.

### *Retirement Age*

In America, the average age for retirement is 62. More important, however, 40% of people retire prior to the time they had planned to retire. Retirement age is affected by many factors (see Figure 2).

It is important to understand that early retirement may not be possible from a financial planning standpoint. In other words, one function of the ballpark estimate calculator (discussed later) is to determine if you will have enough for retirement.

**Figure 2**
**Ten Reasons Early Retirement Is Popular**

1. *Financial goals that have been met.* The individual can continue his or her standard of living through retirement.
2. *Financial goals that have been compromised.* The individual has a personal desire to trade a lower standard of living for freedom from employment.
3. *Perceived health issues.* Individuals in good health may want to retire early while they can enjoy life. They fear poor health later will limit their activity and don't want to ruin the opportunity of an active retirement.
4. *Actual health issues.* Individuals may retire early because they have bad health and working compounds their problems.
5. *Caregiving health issues.* Some individuals retire early because they have caregiving responsibilities for a parent or a spouse.
6. *Corporate downsizing with incentives.* Called "golden handshakes" these incentive offers encourage an early retirement age.
7. *Corporate downsizing.* When a business contracts in size, some people who are near retirement age are forced into early retirement.
8. *Health and pension incentives.* The structure of the employer's health and pension plan may encourage early retirement. For example, a person with retiree health coverage at age 62 and a pension that provides 60% of salary may perceive that he or she is working for 40 cents on a dollar (while paying taxes on 100).
9. *Nonfinancial factors.* In some instances, the death of a spouse may encourage early retirement. In others, such as the two-wage-earner family, there may be a desire to retire together even though one spouse is younger than the other (the younger spouse would take early retirement).
10. *Problems in the workplace.* Some people retire because their jobs have grown intolerable. For example, recent changes may make the job environment difficult.

### *Longevity*

It is important to remember that the longer one lives, the greater the strain on financial resources. Estimating longevity is a highly speculative task, and thus it makes the estimated income needed a suspect number. Nevertheless, one should be realistic in answering whether they will outlive the averages. Look at ages at which parents and grandparents died, consider your personal medical history, and assess your current state of health behaviors. Today, 28% of people who turn 65 live to the age of 90.

### *Rate of Return*

The money earned on investments will directly impact the ability to retire financially secure. Working with a planner to assess risk tolerance level (how comfortable one is investing) and the proper asset allocation distribution model (how much of a portfolio to invest in stocks, bonds, etc.) will help to maximize results. Please note that even a 1% to 2% increase in investment returns can make a huge difference in the amount needed for retirement.

## Proxy for Required Retirement Income

In order for any computer model to work, it must first "know" the amount a person will need in the first year of retirement. There are two methods to calculate this: the

**Figure 3**
**Justification of Less Than 100% Replacement Ratio**

Cindy and Ken X. Ample (both aged 64) have a combined salary of $100,000 ($50,000 each) and would like to maintain their current purchasing power when they retire next year. If their anticipated reduced nonwork expenses are offset by increased living expenses (see below), they can maintain their purchasing power by having a retirement income of 80% of their salary as illustrated below:

Working salary $100,000

Less FICA taxes[1] $7,650

Less increase in standard deduction[2] 0

Less tax savings on tax-free part of Social Security[3] 840

Less state and local tax reduction[4] 1,400

Less deductible medical expenses[5] 0

Less reduced living expenses[6] 0

Less retirement savings[7] 10,000

Reductions subtotal 19,890

Total purchasing power needed $80,110

Percentage of final salary needed (approximate) 80%

1. Since each earns $50,000, they both pay $3,825 in FICA taxes.
2. No increase in standard deduction will occur because they itemize using Schedule A.
3. Estimated amount.
4. The Amples will get a sliding scale rebate on their property taxes equal to $1,400 (not true in all jurisdictions).
5. They will not take a medical deduction.
6. The Amples figure any reduced living expenses in retirement from work will be offset by increased retirement expenses (see below).
7. The Amples have been saving 10% of their salary in a combination of 401(k) plans where they work and IRAs.

replacement ratio approach, and the expense method. Experts have traditionally placed the initial replacement ratio needed between 70% and 80% of final salary. Justification for less than 100% of salary rests on the fact that the retiree is no longer saving for retirement and that there are several tax advantages unique to retirement (see Figure 3).

The expense method focuses on using the client's retirement budget to set the appropriate proxy for the numbers needed in the first year of retirement. Remarkably, planners have found the budget numbers come out to about 70% to 80% of a person's final salary. Still, the expense method is the preferred method of calculating need in the first year and should be done in conjunction with a financial planner or other financial advisor.

Finally, some researchers have suggested that no matter what method is used, an adjustment to account for lower spending in the later years needs to be made. For this reason, if a long life is anticipated, a reduction from the prior example—from 80% to 70% of final salary, or 75% to 68% of final salary—may be warranted.

### How Retirement Calculators Work: A Heuristic Model

To better understand the retirement calculator, it is first necessary to appreciate the methodology behind it. For many software packages and worksheets, it is essentially a five-step process. The first step is to take stock of the existing resources available for retirement (Social Security benefits, defined benefit pension, 401(k)s, IRAs, and the like). The second step is to compare what the person currently has to what the person will need at retirement. This is done by taking a *replacement ratio* or *expense method assumption* and subtracting out the income projected from existing resources. The resulting shortfall is one component of the retirement target.

*Example 1.* Cindy, aged 60, has a $100,000 salary. After using the replacement ratio approach, she and her financial advisor feel that an $80,000 (80%) target will meet her desired living standards. (Note that the $80,000 figure will have to be increased after her first year of retirement to account for inflation.) In addition, Cindy and her advisor determine that her Social Security, pension, and current savings will provide $60,000 of income per year. Cindy therefore has a shortfall of $20,000 ($80,000 need minus $60,000 provided by existing resources). The computer software will effectively calculate the amount of assets necessary at retirement to produce this $20,000 stream of income over her projected lifetime. That amount becomes a target for which Cindy must save.

Another component of the retirement calculator is the need to include inflation protection for income that is not "indexed"—automatically adjusted for inflation. To this end, the next step is to account for the declining purchasing power of income.

*Example 2.* The $15,000 that Cindy will receive from Social Security is already adjusted for inflation and need not be considered in this part of the calculation. However, Cindy's projected pension at retirement is $35,000 annually, and her other savings were assumed to be converted to a $10,000-a-year fixed annuity. Neither of these income streams will increase over time. So, due to the effects of inflation, the purchasing power of her pension and annuity will erode every year and must be bolstered to maintain a level purchasing power. In effect, Cindy must maintain her own cost-of-living adjustment (COLA) fund for these amounts. The same is true of the $20,000 shortfall. It will not continue to be enough to support Cindy's lifestyle if it is not adjusted annually for inflation.

The third step is to compute the sum needed at retirement to replace the income shortfall. Most programs will calculate a single sum representing the amount needed to provide the stream of income over the expected lifetime of the retiree, but it is not as simple as monthly income deficit times number of months to live. To reflect the impact of inflation, the program will actually calculate the amount needed to provide an increasing stream of income so as not to lose ground against inflation. Technically speaking, the number calculated is the present value (at retirement) of the inflation-protected or inflation-adjusted stream of income over the projected lifetime or payment period. Note that with this method the amount calculated will be exhausted at the end of the expected lifetime, which means that the longevity assumption is critically important.

The fourth step produces a fund for the decline in purchasing power of the fixed pension and annuity benefits. In the previous calculation the impact of inflation was actually taken into account to determine the amount needed to fund the income shortfall. Now, a similar adjustment needs to take place to, in effect, inflate the value of the pension and annuity payouts. An additional amount of assets is needed from which to make increasing payments to supplement the fixed payment stream. The number calculated represents the sum of the present values (at retirement) of all the inflation adjustments needed for all existing-resource income that will not automatically adjust for inflation.

*Example 3.* To protect against a 4% inflation rate, the $45,000 first-year retirement income from existing non-inflation-adjusted resources (pension and annuity) must grow to $46,800 in the second year ($45,000 × 1.04), to $48,672 in the third year ($45,000 × $1.04^2$), and to $50,619 in the fourth year ($45,000 × $1.04^3$) and must continue to grow at 4% a year. Thus the inflation adjustments above the $45,000 first-year retirement income are $1,800 in the second year, $3,672 in the third year, $5,619 in the fourth year, and so on, for the projected life of the client. It is these inflation adjustments that are discounted back to the retirement year and added together to calculate the fund to cover the decline in purchasing power of fixed income streams.

The fifth and final step is to determine the required annual savings amount. This is the amount of annual savings needed to meet the target. This can be a level stream or a stepped-up or graded stream, maybe a constant percentage or an increasing earned income. This is accomplished by discounting the target back to the present time and determining the annual savings needed to reach the target at an assumed net (after-tax) rate of return.

### *The Ballpark Estimate*

The final step in answering the "How much?" question is to calculate individual need. This can either be done on the Internet or on paper. A good online calculator can be found at the Web site of the American Savings Education Council (http://www.asec.org/), an independent, noncommercial source. There are also many to be found by entering "retirement planning" in any search engine, such as Google. In order to make the "Ballpark Estimate" calculation online, follow these steps:

- Go to http://www.asec.org/.
- Click on "Ballpark Estimate" or "Savings Tools" (which links to "Ballpark Estimate").
- Follow the instructions.

The Web site has an easy-to-use interactive version, which does all the math. The form can also be printed out and filled out manually.

## Conclusion

Once it is determined how much is needed for retirement expenses, one should start a savings plan to meet that goal. Remember, the numbers are not absolute. This is not an exact science. Any savings achieved will improve the outlook for meeting retirement expenses. (See also CONSUMER PROTECTION FOR OLDER ADULTS; FINANCIAL SECURITY IN RETIREMENT; FRAILTY PLANNING; RETIREMENT PLANNING; RETIREMENT PLANNING SOFTWARE; SENIOR DISCOUNTS; VACATION HOMES AND RECREATIONAL PROPERTY; WEALTH SPAN.)

### Organizations

American Savings Education Council (ASEC)
National Endowment for Financial Education
Social Security Administration

### Suggested Readings

Morris, Virginia B., and Kenneth M. Morris. 2002. *The Wall Street Journal Guide to Planning Your Financial Future: The Easy-to-Read Guide to Planning for Retirement (Wall Street Journal Guide to Planning Your Financial Future)*. 3rd ed. New York: Wall Street Journal.

Warner, Ralph E. 2002. *Get a Life: You Don't Need a Million to Retire Well.* 4th ed. Berkeley, CA: Nolo Press.

### References

Littell, David A., David M. Cordell, and Kenn B. Tacchino. 2002. *Financial Decision Making at Retirement.* 6th ed. Bryn Mawr, PA: American College.

Social Security Administration (SSA). 2003. "Social Security Benefits." Available online at http://www.ssa.gov/OACT/ProgData/retirebenefit2.html.

Social Security Administration (SSA). n.d. *Social Security Online.* Available at http://www.ssa.gov/.

*Kenn Tacchino*

**RETIREMENT MIGRATION,** change of residence to new geographic locations offering more attractive living environments for older Americans. Geographic locations that attract retirees generally develop in areas with a high level of tourism. Towns, counties, and states in the Sunbelt and the Northwest welcome, and are beginning to recruit, older interstate migrants. Rural communities that are favorably located are in a position to attract retirees as effective strategies for economic development. Some governmental units finance the marketing of their communities and provide technical assistance to their retiree attraction committees.

Older migrants in the United States have steady incomes less vulnerable to the normal down cycles in the national economy. Although income derived from interest or stocks can fluctuate with business cycles, government transfers and pension benefits are relatively stable. Only one-fourth of the income for the older Americans in metro and nonmetro areas is produced by assets (Hoppe 1991). Most of this asset income comes from interest, with the largest source of interest coming from banks, savings and loan associations, and credit unions that are insured by federal agencies. Older migrants tend to have sizable amounts of discretionary income to spend locally, which leads to economic development and job creation in the community of relocation. As a group they also have better health, better education, and earlier retirements than retirees who are aging in place.

Only about 5% of the retirement-age population move across state lines in any five-year period, but the advantages gained from recruiting retirees are many (Longino 2001). They include increases in the tax base, no need for large investments in the infrastructure or tax abatements by governments, the addition of residents who are unlikely to pollute or destroy the environment, a growth in the number of volunteers and contributors in local philanthropic and service organizations, and benefits to religious organizations. Since jobs tend to follow people with money to spend, retirement income can lead to job growth in the same way that industrial payrolls generate jobs. Although many of the jobs created are low-paying service jobs, there are also opportunities created for higher-income professionals.

A study by the Federal Reserve Bank of Kansas City found that rural counties whose incomes are based on retirees have outpaced all others in per capita income growth. Counties designated as retirement sites witnessed the largest increase in personal income and employment among all nonmetropolitan counties, although it should be noted that per capita income in nonmetropolitan retirement counties is still below average for all nonmetropolitan counties (Glasgow and Reeder 1990; Reeder and Glasgow 1990).

Older migrants add to the existing mature market, increasing the importance of this market segment. The consumption potential of older households is seen in their incomes and in their accumulated assets, a resource that can be drawn on for large purchases. The balances in their savings accounts are also larger than average households, and their homes are worth 20% more than the U.S. average (Menchin 1989). Consumption studies have shown that older consumers purchase houses and other durable goods, as well as nondurable goods and services, including food, travel, recreation, entertainment, and medical care.

Longino (1995) examined the 1989 incomes of all people aged 60 or older who reported in 1990 that they lived in a different state in 1985, estimating from 1990 census microdata (5% sample). These data do not include information on assets or on the multiplier effect of the income transfers into each state. In this examination, Florida topped the list of states benefiting from retirement migration, according to these estimates. It had a net gain of over $8.3 billion annually. After the 1989 incomes of persons age 60+ who *left* Florida during that period were netted out, the gain was $6.5 billion. Arizona netted $1.7 billion. Ten other states—North Carolina, Nevada, South Carolina, Oregon, Georgia, Washington, Arkansas, Texas, Tennessee, and Alabama—posted net gains of $100 million or more annually from their senior migrants. These estimates further suggest that most of the states in the South and West benefited economically from retirement migration. The annual income transfer between states due to retirement migration, as demonstrated, can be substantial. States with serious tourism industries outside the Sunbelt are starting to realize that retiree recruitment is an effective economic development strategy. Deller (1995) used a regional economic model to simulate the impact of a policy of retiree recruitment on the state of Maine. He argued that the short-run beneficial economic impact of retiree recruitment is significant and warrants serious consideration.

State-level analyses, however, cloak the major economic impact of older migrants on local communities. Convincing evidence of local economic impact has been turned up by several investigators. Guntersville, in the mountain lakes region of Alabama, for example, has a large river reservoir along with other recreational amenities appropriate for retirees. Fagan's (1990) data on 185 older in-migrants into this community suggest that these migrants had a positive influence on the local economy. Sometimes strong migration streams connect two specific locations. Such is the case with a stream of retired migrants from the Panama Canal Zone to Dothan, located in the southeastern corner of Alabama. Eighty-four retired households, all members of the Dothan Panama Canal Society, were surveyed in 1991 to estimate their local economic impact. The data suggest that current economic impact underestimates total or eventual impact because in-migrant retirees may encourage friends to follow them, thereby extending the economic benefits from retirees over time.

The Appalachian Regional Commission funded a study of retirees who had moved into western North Carolina. In this telephone survey of 814 retirees in 1989, which represents one of the most thorough surveys of in-migrants, Haas and Serow (1990) found that over three-quarters settled in nonmetro counties; the average household bank deposits were over $40,000; the average investment portfolios were nearly $200,000; and reported mean home values were $108,000. The 630 households who kept spending records showed that they had collectively spent an annualized $22.6 million, not counting houses and cars, with a multiplier effect totaling $45 million annually. The researchers estimated that these retirees had the following measurable impacts on the economy: the creation of 943 jobs with an average annual salary of nearly $15,000; substantial local revenues in property and sales tax; and state revenues in income tax, intangible tax, and sales tax. Further, 77% of the retirees volunteered an average of 7.4 hours a week of community service, and 55% held positions of leadership in community churches and/or faith-based organizations. Over two-fifths (41%) had an opportunity to vote on a school bond issue, and 82% supported the increase. From the perspective of direct public sector receipts and expenditures, the retirees demonstrated that they were self-supportive through the indirect economic effects of their consumption expenditures. Migrant retirees represent an addition to the fiscal status of local governments.

Homeownership for migrant retirees can also have an impact on their newly chosen communities. Eighty percent (80%) of persons in the mature market own their homes, and 80% of those are mortgage-free. When retirees come into a community, most immediately purchase a home. They then invest the proceeds from the sale of their prior home into the host community's financial institutions.

Attracting retirees is a low-risk strategy for communities. Even if few retirees relocate to a community, promoting the community should increase interest and tourism and enhance its image. Also, community promotion creates quality-of-life features that industries considering plant relocation may find attractive (Glasgow 1990). (See also CONTINUING CARE RETIREMENT COMMUNITIES [CCRCs]; HOMEOWNERSHIP; LEISURE; SENIORS HOUSING FINANCE; SNOWBIRD CHECKLIST AND TRANSBORDER ISSUES; VACATION HOMES AND RECREATIONAL PROPERTY.)

### References

Deller, S.C. 1995. "Economic Impact of Retirement Migration." *Economic Development Quarterly* 9: 25–38.

Fagan, Mark. 1990. "Economic Impact of Retirees on a Community." *Social Science Perspectives* 4(3): 72–81.

Glasgow, Nina. 1990. "Attracting Retirees as a Community Development Option." *Journal of the Community Development Society* 21: 102–14.

Glasgow, Nina, and Richard J. Reeder. 1990. "Economic and Fiscal Implications of Non-Metropolitan Retirement Migration." *Journal of Applied Gerontology* 9: 433–51.

Haas, William H., III, and William J. Serow. 1990. "The Influence of Retirement In-Migration on Local Economic Development." Unpublished Final Report to the Appalachian Regional Commission, UNC, Asheville.

Hoppe, R. 1991. "The Elderly Income and Rural Development: Some Cautions." *Rural Development Perspectives* 7: 27–32.

Longino, Charles F., Jr. 1995. *Retirement Migration in America.* Houston, TX: Vacation Publications.

Longino, Charles F., Jr. 2001. "Geographical Distribution and Migration." In *Handbook of Aging and the Social Sciences*, ed. Robert H. Binstock and Linda K. George. New York: Academic Press.

Menchin, R. 1989. *The Mature Market.* Chicago: Probus Publishing.

Reeder, Richard J., and Nina Glasgow. 1990. "Nonmetro Retirement Counties' Strengths and Weaknesses." *Rural Development Perspectives* 6: 12–18.

*Charles F. Longino, Jr., and Mark Fagan*

**RETIREMENT PLANNING,** a subset of financial planning that focuses on creating financial independence from working.

Achieving a financially independent retirement is the objective of much of the financial planning that takes place during an individual's working years. It is never too early or too late to begin financial planning for retirement. While retirement planning is, to a large extent, all encompassing, the financial aspect is a key component. Unlike most aspects of general financial planning, retirement planning is not a finite goal. Saving for a child's education or a vacation has a beginning, middle, and end to the objective, whereas retirement planning is fraught with variables, assumptions, and indefinites. Another fundamental consideration for a successful retirement is continued satisfaction with one's lifestyle and activities. Does the individual want to keep working on a part-time basis, or are there other meaningful things he or she wants to do, such as volunteer work, political activity, or increased involvement in community or religious activities? Many times, when there is a stay-at-home spouse, there are also territorial disputes when the working spouse is home full-time, another reason to plan for postretirement activity or purpose.

While people may know when they would like to retire and how much they would like to spend annually, the planning necessitates making certain assumptions as to life expectancy and unforeseen costs such as medical and long-term care needs. These contingencies are difficult to forecast. Issues that require thought and planning include when long-term care may be needed and for how long. For a couple, they must also consider how the healthy spouse would be affected and whether he or she may need long-term care as well. The effects of taxes and inflation also are very important factors to consider in retirement planning, and again, certain assumptions apply to these future projections.

Retirement planning can be difficult emotionally. People generally spend the majority of their adult lives accumulating assets for retirement. When that time actually arrives, they often find it difficult to begin spending those assets when they no longer have a regular paycheck coming in. Many people find that when they begin the retirement planning process, they are faced with more and more questions, which can result in "planning paralysis." It is essential to begin planning with well-thought-out objectives and a checklist to help move the process along.

Retirement planning begins with determining how much one anticipates spending and the sources for any fixed income such as pensions or Social Security. Once this has been determined, it also helps to know how long these income sources will be needed. Life expectancy is an extremely important factor to consider, although it is hard to project. Considering mortality tables exclusively in projecting a client's life expectancy is a commonly made mistake. This technique sets up a 50% chance of failure, as life tables are based on the average individual. Family history and the individual's health should also be considered in establishing a basis for projection. Even then, there are many unknowns, such as the very real possibility of what they would do if they live that long, or longer. Many older people would prefer to have funds left over at the time of their death, instead of outliving their financial independence.

Retirement planning, done with the appropriate care and attention, can help workers and their families plan adequately for the future. Although there are never any guarantees, by planning ahead older workers can enhance their own financial security in retirement and prevent their needs from becoming a burden to their children—two oft-expressed concerns of older adults. (See also CASH FLOW PLANNING FOR RETIREES; FINANCIAL ADVISORS; FINANCIAL EDUCATION FOR SENIORS; FINANCIAL LITERACY; FINANCIAL PLANNING PROCESS; FRAILTY PLANNING; INVESTMENT ADVICE; LIFE PLANNING; RETIREMENT EXPENSE PLANNING.)

**References**

Orman, Suze, with Linda Mead. 1997. *You've Earned It, Don't Lose It: Mistakes You Can't Afford to Make When You Retire*. New York: Newmarket Press.

O'Shaughnessy, Lynn. 2001. *Retirement Bible*. Hoboken, NJ: John Wiley & Sons.

Smith, Mary Helen, and Shuford Smith. 2000. *Secrets for a Great Retirement: Practical, Inspirational, & Fun Ideas for the Best Years of Your Life!* New York: McGraw-Hill Contemporary Books.

*Laura Addington*

**RETIREMENT PLANNING SOFTWARE,** computer programs designed to assist Certified Financial Planners™ and other financial advisors and their clients to more easily plan for the future by building a variety of assumptions and options into the planning process.

There is a wide array of choice when it comes to software for retirement planning, both professionally and for home/consumer use. In general, most consumers use retirement planning software to obtain a basic idea of their success probability for retirement. They may be attempting to estimate the amount of funds required at a given point (age) to retire successfully. Thus, most retirement planning software should have flexibility in its assumptions—that is, the ability to alter various calculations.

A few features that tend to top most professionals' wish lists include: life-cycle consumption models, probability analysis, and visual presentation capabilities. Many professionals end up using multiple programs in order to have all the components they want. Features to look for in retirement planning software include:

- Ability to change inflation rates before and after retirement
- Ability to change rates of return before and after retirement
- Ability to change expenses on a monthly or annual basis before and after retirement
- Ability to choose the order and amount of distributions from investment and qualified plan assets
- Flexible life expectancies
- Ability to produce "what if" scenarios, in other words, the software should be able to demonstrate

the impact to the plan by changing a single or multiple assumptions and show the results in a side-by-side (or similar) format

- Ability to adjust tax rates before and after retirement
- Ability to put data output in layperson's terms

The following examples give a simplistic but fairly clear view of the kind of guidance that retirement planning software can give a mature worker. In this case, assume a 53-year-old person named Jane Doe expects to retire when she is 65; her life expectancy is 89, so she will need postretirement income for at least 24 years. She has assets that will provide income in retirement, currently valued at:

| | |
|---|---|
| • Equity in house | $35,000 |
| • 401(k) | 70,000 |
| • Rollover Individual Retirement Account (IRA) | 35,000 |

As she is not sure how easy it will be for her to access the equity in her home, she decides to plan conservatively based on $105,000 in assets. Initially, she plans for an 8.0% return on her investments and an inflation adjustment of her retirement income of 3.0%. She estimates that $25,000 would suffice for her postretirement income, in today's money.

After providing her financial advisor with all of the necessary information, she receives information that looks similar to this:

Using this scenario, based on a complete set of information already shared with the financial advisor, this plan appears to give Ms. Doe good news regarding her future financial state. This plan tells her that, all things being equal, the current money she puts away for retirement is more than sufficient (39% more) to meet her goals; in fact, she could cut down her contributions to $412 per month and make her goals (Table 1).

However, her financial advisor advises her that counting on an 8.0% yield over the next 30 years may be overly optimistic; the advisor suggests that Ms. Doe plan instead on an average of 5.0%. With nothing else changed, the plan now becomes as shown in Table 2.

Clearly, this news is less favorable, but probably more realistic. By counting on a more conservative return on investments, the amount she currently puts away means that her plan will fall 20% short of meeting her goal for the future; in fact, she should be putting away $1,500 per month.

Ms. Doe feels that she can afford to put $1,500 away each month, but she also is worried about the projected life expectancy. Calculating the population's life expectancy is fairly easy, but an individual life expectancy depends on many more factors other than average death rates, including genetic disposition, lifestyle, and other health behaviors and individual medical history. The advisor and Ms. Doe decide to include one other scenario, one in which she exceeds her life expectancy by just 3 years, to age 92, requiring 27 years of postretirement income. Her plan now looks like this: what happens if she lives past age 89? What if, instead, she lives to age 92? With the life expectancy adjusted by 3 years, her plan, with these assumptions, is shown in Table 3.

Again, it appears that Ms. Doe's $1,500 contribution each month will fall 13% short

**Table 1**
**Retirement Income Estimator**

| **Prepared for Jane Doe** | | |
|---|---|---|
| Current Age | 53 | |
| Desired Retirement Age | 65 | |
| # of Years Income Required | 24 | |
| Existing Assets That Will Provide Income | 105,000.00 | |
| Monthly Savings—Target | 1,000.00 | |
| Annual Rate of Return on Investments | 8.000% | |
| Retirement Inflation Rate (Indexing) | 3.000% | |
| Annual Income Required at Retirement | 25,000.00 | |
| RESULTS | | Percent of Goal |
| Funds Accumulated by Retirement Age | 501,885.47 | 139% |
| Income Available for Retirement Period (Indexed) | 34,640.09 | |
| | | |
| SOLUTION | | |
| Funds Required for Retirement | 362,214.35 | |
| Monthly Savings Required to Reach Your Goal | 411.86 | |

*Source*: Money Minders Software, Inc. (http://www.money-software.com).

of her goal. Finally, the advisor points out that by the time she retires, her mortgage will be paid off, and the equity in her home will be $125,000 in today's dollars. By obtaining a reverse annuity mortgage, she can generate another $6,000 of annual income, bringing her even closer to the monthly sum that the current plan anticipates.

Her advisor reminds her that the plan is only as good as the accuracy of the information provided in terms of her income and asset goals, her estimate of how much income she will need in postretirement, and how well she has thought out such contingencies as long-term care needs, house maintenance, and other potential high-ticket items. As such, this plan is a guideline, and she must work with the advisor to decide which way she wants to go.

Choosing the best software package begins similarly to most objectives, with defining what the client wants. Unfortunately, planners and consumers alike find it hard to identify the perfect software program, so there is a certain amount of give and take when making the decision to purchase. After you have identified what aspects are most important to you, evaluate what each package does, what features are important, and if it will be comprehensive enough to meet current demands as well as anticipated changes. The strength of the software comes from its ability to analyze complex sets of rules, expectations, and assumptions. Does the program go into sufficient detail and cover contingencies pertaining to financial planning as well as covering uncertainties? Is the software mired in details, churning out useless or little-used information that makes the relevant information hard to identify or interpret?

**Table 2**
**Retirement Income Estimator**

| Prepared for Jane Doe | | |
|---|---|---|
| Current Age | 53 | |
| Desired Retirement Age | 65 | |
| # of Years Income Required | 24 | |
| Existing Assets That Will Provide Income | 105,000.00 | |
| Monthly Savings—Target | 1,000.00 | |
| Annual Rate of Return on Investments | 5.000% | |
| Retirement Inflation Rate (Indexing) | 3.000% | |
| Annual Income Required at Retirement | 25,000.00 | |
| RESULTS | | Percent of Goal |
| Funds Accumulated by Retirement Age | 384,704.94 | 80% |
| Income Available for Retirement Period (Indexed) | 19,940.95 | |
| | | |
| SOLUTION | | |
| Funds Required for Retirement | 482,305.10 | |
| Monthly Savings Required to Reach Your Goal | 1,497.60 | |

*Source*: Money Minders Software, Inc. (http://www.money-software.com).

Most vendors provide demonstration opportunities to allow buyers to "test-drive" the product. Since some software packages can cost thousands of dollars, this is a very important factor. For the financial advisor, an important piece of the decision is whether or not the software will integrate with other software packages that are currently used such as client databases or investment software. Minimizing the number of times data must be entered manually into multiple programs saves time and reduces the possibility of error. An import/export feature may be a great benefit.

Not to be underestimated is the fundamental look and feel of the software. It is important that the software be easily navigable with information being readily accessible and reports being easy to read. Many programs do not come with a manual, and a few do not provide online help; this should also be factored into the decision-making process.

Retirement planning software can be an extremely useful tool as well as a hazardous trap if used inappropriately, whether intentionally or unwittingly. A thorough knowledge and understanding of inflation, budgeting challenges, investment risks and returns, asset allocation, impact of taxes, and qualified retirement plan distribution rules are important prior to implementing the output of the software. While a good software package can add considerable value to an individual projecting their retirement or a professional helping multiple clients retire successfully, it is still only as good as the information going in as well as the ability of the user to interpret and evaluate the results. (See also CASH FLOW PLANNING FOR RETIREES; RETIREMENT EXPENSE PLANNING; RETIREMENT PLANNING; TAXPAYER ISSUES OF OLDER ADULTS.)

**Table 3**
**Retirement Income Estimator**

| Prepared for Jane Doe | | |
|---|---|---|
| Current Age | 53 | |
| Desired Retirement Age | 65 | |
| # of Years Income Required | 27 | |
| Existing Assets That Will Provide Income | 105,000.00 | |
| Monthly Savings—Target | 1,500.00 | |
| Annual Rate of Return on Investments | 5.000% | |
| Retirement Inflation Rate (Indexing) | 3.000% | |
| Annual Income Required at Retirement | 25,000.00 | |
| RESULTS | | Percent of Goal |
| Funds Accumulated by Retirement Age | 482,774.95 | 87% |
| Income Available for Retirement Period (Indexed) | 22,857.54 | |
| | | |
| SOLUTION | | |
| Funds Required for Retirement | 528,025.89 | |
| Monthly Savings Required to Reach Your Goal | 1,730.71 | |

*Source*: Money Minders Software, Inc. (http://www.money-software.com).

References

Donner, Eric. 2000. *2000 Planning for Retirement Distributions: Tax, Financial and Personal Aspects*. Orlando, FL: Harcourt Brace.

Robinson, Gerald R. 1999. *The Professional's Guide to Retirement Financial Management 2000.* Orlando, FL: Harcourt Brace.

*Laura Addington and Sandra L. Reynolds*

**RETIREMENT PLANS—401(k),** private employer-sponsored defined contribution plans that allow employees to make pretax contributions. Private employer-sponsored retirement plans are generally bifurcated into defined benefit and defined contribution plans. The former category typically provides a default benefit in which a nominal amount is guaranteed for the life of the worker and his or her spouse starting at some specified age. The amount of the benefit is often a function of the worker's salary and/or years of participation in the plan. In contrast, a defined contribution plan will often provide a method of determining the amount of employer contribution (if any) that will be provided to the employee's individual account. This amount may be supplemented by employee contributions in some types of defined contribution plans, such as 401(k), and the balances will be invested in one or more funds. One or both sources of contributions will often be subjected to participant direction, although there are some obvious exceptions to this generalization, such as employee stock ownership plans. Perhaps the most important distinction between defined benefit and defined contribution plans is that the latter provides no guarantee with respect to the amount of retirement income that will be available for the employee, whereas the former does. In other words, the employee bears the investment risk and rewards from participating in a defined contribution plan.

Recently a third category, often referred to as a hybrid plan, has been gaining increased acceptance among private employers. Perhaps the best-known example of this type of plan is a cash balance plan, where employers provide employees with a notional account that resembles a defined contribution plan; however, all investment risk is typically borne by the employer. The 401(k) plans are a type of defined contribution plan under which the employee typically has the option of contributing on a before-tax basis, often with some type of employer match up to a specified percentage of compensation. During the past two decades, 401(k) plans have been the primary source of the growth in the private pension system. The overall number of private retirement plans increased from 489,000 in 1980 to 730,000 in 1998, the latest year for which data from the Department of Labor are available (U.S. Department of Labor 2002). During the same period, the number of 401(k) plans, which were authorized in legislation passed by Congress in 1978, increased from virtually 0 to 300,000. Similarly, 401(k) plans accounted principally for the growth in the number of participants and assets in private sector plans. By 1998, the portion of active participants in 401(k) plans had increased to 51% of the total for all plans, while the 401(k) portion of total plan assets had grown to 38%. Contributions into 401(k) plans rose sharply, accounting for nearly 67% of all new contributions in 1998.

The average 401(k) plan account balance for nearly 12 million participants in the Employee Benefit Research Institute/Investment Company Institute (EBRI/ICI) 401(k) database was $49,024 at the end of 2000 (Holden and VanDerhei 2001b). This figure varies by both age and tenure with the employer and results in average values as high as $177,289 for participants in their sixties with more than 30 years of tenure.

## 401(k) Plan Design

The salary deferral election by the employee is normally an affirmative one, but it may be automatic under the plan unless the employee elects not to make a deferral. This is known as a "negative election" and was given regulatory blessing in 1998 (Rev. Rul. 98-30). Salary reduction arrangements must be included in an employer's profit-sharing, stock bonus, pre-ERISA (Employee Retirement Income Security Act) money purchase, or rural electric cooperative plan.

## Vesting

All employee contributions to 401(k) plans and certain employer contributions used to satisfy the ADP (actual deferral percentage) and/or ACP (actual contribution percentage) tests (described below) are immediately vested. Until 2002, all other employer contributions were subjected to normal vesting requirements (i.e., at least as liberal as 100% vested after five years of service or 20% after three years with a 20% increment each of the next four years). As a result of the Economic Growth and Tax Relief Reconciliation Act of 2001 (EGTRRA), however, employer matching contributions must now meet the vesting requirements for top-heavy plans (i.e., at least 100% vested after three years of service or 20% after two years, with a 20% increment each of the next four years).

### Contributions

There are several types of contributions that are paid into a 401(k) plan:

*Elective employee contributions* are amounts an employee authorizes the employer to contribute to a 401(k) plan on a pretax basis either by way of a salary reduction or through an election to defer an amount of cash into a profit sharing plan. Eighty-five percent (85%) of participants in the 1999 EBRI/ICI sample only made before-tax contributions to their plans, and 97% of all dollars contributed by employees were contributed on a before-tax basis. On average, participants contributed 6.8% of their salaries on a before-tax basis. Before-tax contribution activity varied among participants. About 61% of participants contributed more than 5% of their salaries on a before-tax basis, and about 21% set aside more than 10% of their salaries on a before-tax basis (Holden and VanDerhei 2001a).

*After-tax employee contributions* are employee contributions not made through a salary reduction arrangement.

*Matching employer contributions* are employer contributions made when an employee authorizes an elective deferral that matches employee contributions, although the employer does not typically provide a full dollar-for-dollar match. Less typically, the matching contribution can also be made on an employee's after-tax contribution.

*Nonelective employer contributions* are employer contributions other than matching made by the employer on behalf of eligible employees regardless of whether they have made elective deferrals. For information on qualified nonelective contributions and qualified matching contributions and their purpose in compliance with the nondiscrimination rules, see VanDerhei and Olsen (2001).

*Safe harbor employer contributions* are employer contributions made to allow a plan to meet safe harbor requirements and avoid the need for ADP testing. They must be fully vested and are subject to discrimination restrictions.

### Individual Limitations

Employer deduction limits had been a considerable constraint in plan design for some 401(k) plans prior to EGTRRA. Prior to 1987, there was no limit on the amount of elective contributions that an employee could make to the plan other than the limits on annual contributions imposed by Internal Revenue Code (IRC) Section 415. The 1986 Tax Reform Act had imposed a $7,000 annual limitation under Section 402(g) of the IRC on elective deferrals that had been indexed annually up to $10,500 in 2001. Beginning in 2002, EGTRRA increased to $11,000 the dollar limitation that an employee could elect to defer to a plan with $1,000 increments per year until it reaches $15,000 in 2006. After 2006, the dollar cap on elective deferrals will be adjusted periodically in increments of $500 to reflect cost-of-living increases.

EGTRRA also added a "catch-up" provision for participants who have attained age 50 by the end of the year and are unable to make additional deferrals because of a legal or a plan restriction. Beginning in 2002, the maximum catch-up contribution is $1,000 with $1,000 increments per year until it reaches $5,000 in 2006. After 2006, the amount of catch-up contributions will be adjusted periodically in increments of $500 to reflect cost-of-living increases.

## Nondiscrimination Requirements

### *ADP and ACP Tests for Non–Safe Harbor Plans*

A special test for 401(k)s that limits elective contributions of highly compensated employees (HCEs), defined in IRC Section 414(q) and known as the actual deferral percentage test (ADP), must be run annually. For purposes of the ADP test, all employees who are eligible to participate in the plan for the year in question are either HCEs or non–highly compensated employees (NHCEs).

The first step in applying the ADP test is to determine the actual deferral percentage for each eligible employee—that is, the percentage of each eligible employee's salary that is deferred into the plan. The percentage of each eligible employee's salary that is deferred into the plan is computed by dividing the amount of an employee's elective deferrals (contributions) by the amount of the employee's compensation. This percentage is determined individually for all employees eligible for employer contributions under the plan for that year, whether or not they actually participate.

The eligible group of employees is next divided into the HCEs and the NHCEs. Then, within each group, the percentage of compensation that is contributed on behalf of each employee is determined. The percentages for the employees are totaled and averaged to get an actual deferral percentage for the group. The ADP for the highly compensated group is then compared with the ADP for the NHCEs. The ADP test may be satisfied in one of two ways:

*Test 1.* The ADP for the eligible HCEs may not be more than the ADP of the other eligible employees multiplied by 1.25 (the basic test).

*Test 2.* The excess of the ADP for the HCEs over the NHCEs may not be more than 2 percentage points, and the ADP for the HCEs may not be more than the ADP of the NHCEs multiplied by 2 (the alternative test).

Employee after-tax and employer matching contributions in 401(k) arrangements and any other qualified retirement plan are subject to a parallel rule called the actual contribution percentage (ACP) test, or 401(m) nondiscrimination test, under IRC Section 401(m). The actual contribution percentage for each group of employees is the average of the contribution percentages of all employees in that group. The contribution percentage of each individual is determined by dividing the sum of the employee's own after-tax contributions (both basic and voluntary) and the employer's matching contributions made on his or her behalf during the year by the amount of compensation that he or she received during the year. The test is essentially the same as the ADP test applied to elective contributions.

## Safe Harbor 401(k) Plans

As part of the pension simplification provisions of the Small Business Job Protection Act (SBJPA) of 1996, the Internal Revenue Service (IRS) released Notice 98-52, which provided guidance on "alternative" or safe harbor methods of satisfying the 401(k) nondiscrimination requirements. Beginning in 1999, employers providing 401(k) plans no longer have to comply with the ADP/ACP tests if employers make sufficiently generous contributions and employees are notified in advance of these contributions.

To be eligible for the safe harbor, employers may use either of two methods. The *nonelective contribution* method requires employers to contribute at least 3% of pay to all eligible employees. The *matching contribution* method requires employers to match 100% of the first 3% of pay that employees choose to contribute and 50% of the next 2% of pay (or an enhanced matching formula at least as generous). Under either method, the employer contributions must be vested immediately and can be withdrawn only under conditions similar to those for employees' pretax deferrals. To use the safe harbor, employers must notify their employees before the start of the plan year.

### In-Service Distributions

The ability to withdraw funds before separation from service is more restricted in a 401(k) arrangement than in other types of pension plans. In general, in-service distributions of employee elective contributions (and any nonelective or matching contributions used to satisfy the ADP test) may not be distributed sooner than the earlier of reaching age 59½ or the occurrence of a financial hardship. Voluntary employee after-tax contributions, matching employer contributions, and applicable earnings are not subject to these rules.

In 1988, the IRS issued final regulations in which it retained the earlier two-part definition of hardship—the participant must (1) have an "immediate and heavy" financial need and (2) have no other resources "reasonably" available—but clarified the conditions under which each of these would be met. Each part may be satisfied through either a "facts and circumstances" test or safe harbor rules. The safe harbors provide a set of events that may be deemed automatically to cause an "immediate and heavy financial need" and that would satisfy the "other resources" provision. Furthermore, the amount available for a hardship distribution consists only of employee elective contributions and investment earnings that have accrued through December 31, 1988. Most hardship withdrawals are subject to the early distribution penalty tax.

Under prior IRS regulations, the safe harbor approach that set forth the procedures to justify that a participant had an immediate and heavy financial need for a plan distribution required the suspension of elective deferrals and all other types of employee contributions for 12 months following the hardship distribution. In addition, under certain circumstances, hardship distributions were permitted to be rolled into another tax-favored plan. Under EGTRRA, effective for plan years beginning on January 1, 2002, the safe harbor period for suspension of elective deferrals and employee contributions following a hardship distribution are reduced to six months. Hardship distributions are not permitted to be rolled over to other tax-favored plans.

### Loans

Participant loans provide a means for employees to access their 401(k) accounts without incurring tax liability. Many plan sponsors include this option in their 401(k) plans to encourage a higher rate of participation and/or contribution by lower-paid employees. Giving employees the option of borrowing from their 401(k) accounts increases participant contribution rates. On average, a participant in a plan offering loans appeared to contribute 0.6 percentage point more of his or her salary to the plan than a participant in a plan with no loan provision (Holden and VanDerhei 2001a). There are two sets of rules that must be complied with when designing a participant loan program. The Department of Labor (DoL) has jurisdiction over certain provisions of ERISA that dictate how loans must be structured in order to avoid treatment as a *prohibited transaction*, while the IRC dictates how loans must be structured in order to avoid treatment as a *taxable distribution*. The following three conditions must all be met in order to avoid taxation of a participant loan at the time the loan is made:

1. The loan must be repaid in full within five years, unless the loan is used to acquire a principal residence of the participant.
2. The loan must require substantially level amortization of principle and interest, with payments at least quarterly.
3. The loan is limited to a dollar limit equal to the lesser of (a) $50,000 or (b) the greater of one-half of a participant's vested accrued benefit or $10,000.

In December 2002, the IRS released final regulations on loans from qualified employer plans to plan participants and beneficiaries; the new regulations do not include any limitation on the number of loans that can be made under Section 72(p)(2). Treasury and the IRS recognize that because the final regulations do not include any limitation on the number of loans that can be made, there will be no Section 72(p) barrier to credit card loans that otherwise meet the requirements of that section.

### Investment of 401(k) Assets

Given their longer investment horizon, it is not surprising that younger participants tend to favor equity funds when compared with older participants who have an increased demand for fixed income securities. At year's end 2000, participants in their twenties had 61% of their account balances invested in equity funds, while participants in their sixties invested only about 40% in equity funds. Overall at year's end, 51% of plan balances were invested in equity funds, 19% in company stock, 8% in balanced funds, 5% in bond funds, and 15% in stable-value investments such as money funds or guaranteed investment contracts (Holden and VanDerhei 2001b).

Recently, the Enron and WorldCom situations have caused the retirement income policy community to focus increased attention on the current law and practices regarding company stock in 401(k) plans. Several proposals have been advanced to limit the exposure of 401(k) participants to company stock. At year's end 2000, a total of 48% of the 401(k) participants under age 40 in plans with company stock had more than 20% of their account balances invested in company stock. The percentage decreases to 47% for participants in their forties, 45% for participants in their fifties, and 41% for participants in their sixties (VanDerhei 2002). (See also ANNUITIES; DEFINED CONTRIBUTION PLAN; EMPLOYEE RETIREMENT INCOME SECURITY ACT [ERISA]; INFLUENCES ON RETIREMENT INVESTMENT DECISIONS; INVESTOR EDUCATION; PENSION PLANS FOR THE SELF-EMPLOYED.)

#### Suggested Readings

Gnabasik, Matthew. 2002. *Smart Choices: Selecting and Administering a Safe 401(k) Plan*. Chicago: Blue Prairie Group LLC.

Salisbury, Dallas, and Marc Robinson. 2003. *Essential Finance: IRA and 401(k) Investing*. New York: Dorling Kinderlsey.

### References

Holden, Sarah, and Jack VanDerhei. 2001a. "Contribution Behavior of 401(k) Plan Participants." *EBRI Issue Brief/Special Report* 238 (October).

Holden, Sarah, and Jack VanDerhei. 2001b. "401(k) Plan Asset Allocation, Account Balances, and Loan Activity in 2000." *EBRI Issue Brief* 239 (November).

U.S. Department of Labor. 2002. "Private Pension Plan Bulletin. Abstract of 1998 Form 5500 Annual Reports." Washington, DC: Pension and Welfare Benefits Administration.

VanDerhei, Jack. 2002. "The Role of Company Stock in 401(k) Plans." *Risk Management and Insurance Review* 5(1): 1–20.

VanDerhei, Jack, and Craig Copeland. 2001. "A Behavioral Model for Predicting Employee Contributions to 401(k) Plans." *North American Actuarial Journal* (1st Q).

VanDerhei, Jack L., and Kelly A. Olsen. 2001. "Section 401(k) Plans (Cash or Deferred Arrangements) and Thrift Plans." In *Handbook of Employee Benefits*, ed. Jerry S. Rosenbloom. 4th ed. Homewood, IL: Dow Jones–Irwin.

*Jack L. VanDerhei*

**RETIREMENT PLANS—403(b),** also referred to as tax-sheltered annuity (TSA) plans or tax-deferred annuity (TDA) plans, a type of pension plan available only to employees of tax-exempt organizations such as colleges, universities, research organizations, hospitals, churches, charitable organizations, independent schools, and public teaching institutions (e.g., state universities, community colleges, and K–12 public school systems). A 403(b) plan is a defined contribution pension plan that offers employees of tax-exempt organizations the same tax advantages that employees of commercial businesses enjoy. Employer contributions and earnings on those contributions, as well as employee elective pretax deferrals or contributions (known as salary reduction contributions) and earnings on those deferrals or contributions, are generally excluded from taxable income until the employee receives a distribution from the plan.

### Legislative Basis for 403(b) Plans

In 1958, Congress passed the Technical Amendments Act of 1958 that added Section 403(b) to the Internal Revenue Code (IRC). Section 403(b) stipulated that an employee of a tax-exempt organization was entitled to enter into a salary reduction agreement and make contributions to his or her Section 403(b) contract on a tax-deferred basis. In 1961, legislation extended eligibility to faculty and staff of public schools, colleges, and universities.

### Eligible Employers

Two types of employers may offer a 403(b) plan: (1) an organization exempt under Section 501(c)(3) of the IRC (see below) and (2) a public educational organization under Section 170(b)(1)(A)(ii) of the IRC. In addition, a duly ordained, commissioned, or licensed minister of a church who is either self-employed or part of an organization that, although not exempt under Section 501(c)(3), shares a common religious bond with such a minister whom it employs may also be covered under a 403(b) plan.

A Section 501(c)(3) organization is defined as a nonprofit organization organized and operated exclusively for religious, charitable, scientific, public safety testing, literary, or educational purposes. It also includes tax-exempt organizations that are organized and operated exclusively to encourage national or international amateur sports competition (but only if no part of its activities involve the provision of athletic facilities or equipment) or for the prevention of cruelty to children or animals. The organization can be a corporation, community chest, fund, or foundation. A public educational organization is one that normally maintains a regular faculty and curriculum and normally has a regularly enrolled body of students in attendance at the place where it regularly carries on educational activities, such as public primary and secondary schools, state colleges and universities, and public junior colleges.

### Eligible Employees

Individuals at eligible employers may participate in a 403(b) plan if they are present, former, or retired common-law employees. These individuals must meet criteria similar to those applied for determining employee status for the Federal Insurance Contributions Act (FICA, for Social Security and Medicare), for Federal Unemployment Tax (FUTA) purposes, and for federal income tax withholding. Individuals considered independent contractors are not eligible to participate in a 403(b) plan.

### Plan Design Options

*Voluntary Plan.* Tax-exempt organizations may offer a 403(b) plan that is funded purely by salary reduction (employee elective pretax deferrals or contributions). This type of plan can be the sole retirement plan offered by the organization or serve as a supplemental plan.

*Employer Contributory or Noncontributory Plan.* Many tax-exempt organizations, especially colleges and universities, offer a 403(b) plan as their core retirement plan for their faculty and some or all of their staff. This type of plan can be funded either as a contributory or noncontributory plan, or as a combination of both. In a contributory plan, the employer's nonelective contribution (matching contribution) is contingent upon an employee contribution. Both are usually a specified percentage of compensation and may also be based on the employee's age or length of service with the employer. In a noncontributory plan, the plan is entirely funded by the organization. In other words, the plan does not require the employee to contribute in order to receive the nonelective employer contribution. The nonelective amount contributed by the employer is usually a percentage of the employee's compensation. In some plans, the percentage of the compensation that is contributed by the employer is also based on the employee's age or length of service or is integrated with Social Security.

Assuming the 403(b) rules are followed, employer contributions and salary reduction contributions (employee elective pretax deferrals or contributions) and all earnings on both of these types of contributions are exempted from federal income tax until the employee begins to receive distributions from the plan. However, salary reduction contributions are treated as wages and are therefore subject to FICA and FUTA, and some states impose a state income tax on salary reduction amounts. Earnings on employee after-tax contributions, if any, are not subject to federal income tax until the employee begins to receive distributions from the plan.

### Annual Individual Limits on Contributions

When determining the maximum amount that can be contributed to a 403(b) plan, it is important to determine if the contributions to the 403(b) plan are elective, nonelective, or after-tax. All amounts contributed to a 403(b) plan are considered to be made by the employer on behalf of the employee. There are two major categories of contributions to a 403(b) plan: (1) elective and (2) employer or nonelective contributions. Elective deferrals or contributions are those made as a result of a salary reduction agreement whereby the employee elects to have compensation that would otherwise have been paid to the employee as cash deferred or contributed on a pretax basis to the 403(b) plan. Nonelective, or employer contributions, are contributions made to the plan by the employer. Some plans also allow an employee to make salary deduction contributions. These are voluntary employee contributions made on an after-tax basis.

### Section 401(a)(17)—The Recognizable Pay Limit

Section 401(a)(17) imposes a limit on the amount of compensation that can be taken into account to determine the allowable employer contributions to a 403(b) plan. In 2003, this amount is $200,000. That will be indexed for changes in the Consumer Price Index (CPI) in future years. This limit does not apply when determining the amount of salary reduction contributions to a 403(b) plan.

### Section 415(c)(1) Contribution Limit—Limit on Annual Additions

Section 415(c)(1) imposes a limit on the maximum amount that may be contributed to all defined contribution plans. The term *annual additions* means (1) employer contributions (including salary reduction amounts); (2) employee after-tax contributions; and (3) forfeitures. All contributions fall under this limit regardless of whether the contributions are fully vested (nonforfeitable). When completing this calculation, the employee's *compensation* must be taken into account. For these purposes, compensation is defined as taxable compensation plus certain salary reduction contributions. They are (1) elective deferrals to a 403(b) plan under a salary reduction agreement; (2) elective deferrals to a 401(k) plan; (3) elective deferrals or contributions to a Section 125 plan (see Flexible Benefit Plans); (4) deferrals made under a Section 457 plan (defined contribution plans for public sector employees); and (5) elective deferrals to a Section 132(f) Transportation Spending Account.

In the year 2003, the limit on *annual additions* to a 403(b) plan by an employer on behalf of an employee cannot exceed the *lesser of* $40,000 (this amount will be indexed for changes in the CPI in future years) or 100% of the employee's *compensation.*

### Section 402(g) Contribution Limit—Limit on Salary Reduction Contributions

This section of the Code imposes a limit on the amount that an employee can contribute on an elective or voluntary (salary reduction) basis to all plans (e.g., 403(b) and 401(k)) in a calendar year, regardless of whether the plans are maintained by different employers. For calendar year 2003, the limit is $12,000. Under the Economic Growth and Tax Relief Reconciliation Act (EGTRRA) of 2001, this amount will increase in future years to

$13,000 in 2004, $14,000 in 2005, and $15,000 in 2006. Beginning in 2007, the 402(g) limit will be adjusted for inflation in $500 increments.

### Section 402(g)(8) Contribution Limit—Alternative Contribution or the "15-Year Rule"

Section 402(g)(8), which was made available under the Tax Reform Act of 1986 (TRA 1986), provides special alternative limits that are available to employees who have completed at least 15 years of service with the current eligible employer (tax-exempt educational institutions, hospitals, home health service agencies, certain churches, and health and welfare organizations) to exceed the limit on contributions made under a salary reduction agreement. (The years of service do not have to be consecutive, but they must all have been with the current employer.) The alternative limits are not available to employees of associations, research foundations, museums, and libraries.

There is a $15,000 lifetime limit on the amount of additional contributions above the 402(g) limit that may be contributed under the Section 402(g)(8) contribution limit. This limit applies to service with all employers.

Section 402(g)(8) permits an employee to contribute the *lesser of*:

- An additional $3,000 per taxable year above the 402(g) limit ($12,000 in calendar year 2003)
- $15,000 reduced by prior contributions excluded under the 402(g)(8) election
- $5,000 times the number of years of service with the present employer minus total elective deferrals made by the employer on the employee's behalf in previous years

### Section 414(v) Contribution Limit—Age 50 Catch-up Elective Deferrals

To the extent a plan permits these contributions (plans are not required to offer this provision), participants are eligible to make catch-up contributions beginning in the year in which they attain age 50. For 2003, the limit is $2,000. This amount will increase $1,000 per year to $5,000 in 2006. Beginning in 2007, this amount will be adjusted for inflation in increments of $500. If offered, the plan must allow all plan-eligible employees age 50 and older to participate in the same manner. Plans may require individuals to elect the maximum deferral amount under Section 402(g) ($12,000 in 2003) in order to be eligible to make an additional age 50+ contributions. These contributions are not subject to either the Section 415 or 402(g) dollar limits. However, contributions cannot exceed the 100% of compensation limit under Section 415.

### Funding Vehicles

Generally, contributions to a 403(b) plan may be invested in individual or group annuity contracts issued by an insurance company, or mutual funds. When ERISA (Employee Retirement Income Security Act) was passed in 1974, it permitted contributions to a 403(b) plan to be invested in mutual funds held in a custodial account known as 403(b)(7) accounts. Most 403(b) plans permit the employees to direct the investment of the amounts allocated to their account among the investment options offered by the plan.

Most 403(b) contracts, like the tax-sheltered annuity or tax-deferred annuity contracts used before 1958, are owned by the participant and fully portable.

## Application of ERISA

Any 403(b) plan other than those maintained by a church or government entity (including public schools and colleges and universities) in which the employer's involvement goes beyond the narrow limitations found in the Department of Labor (DoL) regulations would be subject to ERISA. In that case, the plan would need to meet ERISA's participation, vesting, joint and survivor annuity, disclosure and reporting, and fiduciary requirements. In addition, many of the same rules applicable to qualified plans, such as maintaining a written plan document, issuing a Summary Plan Description (SPD), submitting a Form 5500 to the DoL—Pension and Welfare Benefits Administration (PWBA), and issuing a Summary Annual Report (SAR) to plan participants, would apply.

Under the applicable DoL regulation, 403(b) plans are exempt from ERISA where participation by the employees is completely voluntary, all rights under the annuity contract or custodial account are enforceable solely by the employee or beneficiary, and the employer has minimal involvement with the plan, such as making information available as to funding vehicles, withholding employee pretax elective (salary reduction) contributions, and forwarding those contributions to the 403(b) providers.

## Distributions and Tax

### *Distributions of Elective (Voluntary) Deferrals*

Employee elective deferrals and earnings may be distributed only if one or more of the following "triggering events" occurs: attainment of age 59½, separation from service, death, disability, or—if permitted by the employer's plans—incurring a hardship. A cash withdrawal while still working is permitted only if the employee is at least age 59½, disabled, or experiences a hardship. Distribution of benefits prior to attainment of age 59½ is usually subject to a 10% tax in addition to ordinary income tax. The distribution is exempt from the additional 10% tax only if any of the following are met:

- The distribution is made in substantially equal periodic payments (not less frequently than annually) for the life or life expectancy of the employee or the joint lives or joint life expectancies of the employee and his or her beneficiary and beginning after the employee separates from the service of the employer;
- The employee separates from service in or after the calendar year in which he or she attains age 55;
- The employee dies;
- The employee is disabled;
- The distribution is made in accordance with a Qualified Domestic Relations Order (QDRO) issued as part of a divorce settlement; or
- The distribution is to pay for unreimbursed medical expenses in excess of 7.5% of the employee's adjusted gross income.

### *Minimum Distribution Requirements*

Federal law requires participants to begin receiving benefits (e.g., annuity payments) or begin making withdrawals by a specific date. For most participants, this date is April 1 following the year one attains age 70½. Participants who continue working after age

70½ do not have to withdraw accumulations until April 1 of the year after they retire. Under a 403(b) plan, accumulations—contributions and earnings—credited before 1987 need not be withdrawn until the end of the year the participant attains age 75 or April 1 of the year after he or she retires, if later.

## Comparing 401(k) Plans with 403(b) Plans

Many individuals are more familiar with 401(k) plans than they are with 403(b) plans. The 403(b) plans are the counterpart of 401(k) plans for tax-exempt organizations, such as educational institutions. The two plans are alike in many ways as illustrated by the comparison chart shown in Table 1.

**Table 1**
**Comparison of 401(k) and 403(b) Plans**

| Feature | 401(k) Plan | 403(b) Plan |
|---|---|---|
| 1. Employee Contributions | Yes | Yes |
| 2. Employee Salary Reduction | Yes | Yes |
| 3. Employee Salary Deduction | Yes | Yes |
| 4. Determination Letter | Not required but strongly recommended | Not applicable |
| 5. IRS Form 5500 Filing (private institutions only) | Yes, more complicated than 403(b) | Yes, easy to complete |
| 6. Employee Salary Reduction Contribution Limit | $12,000 or less in 2003; governed by Sections 402(g) and 415 | Generally $12,000 or less in 2003; governed by Sections 402(g) and 415; some employees may be able to contribute more than $12,000 through the "15-Year Rule" |
| 7. Total Contribution Limit (employer + employee) | Cannot exceed lesser of $40,000[1] or 100% of compensation in 2003; governed by Section 415 | Cannot exceed lesser of $40,000[1] or 100% of compensation; governed by Section 415 |
| 8. Minimum Distribution Requirements | Applicable to entire accumulation at age 70½ or retirement, if later | Applicable to post-1986 accumulation at age 70½ or retirement, if later; on pre-1987 accumulation at age 75 or retirement, if later |
| 9. Salary Reduction Agreements | No limit on number of agreements each year | No limit on number of agreements each year |
| 10. Average Deferral Percentage Test (nondiscrimination test applicable to employee elective deferrals) | Yes | Not applicable, subject to nondiscrimination availability test |

**Table 1** *(continued)*

| Feature | 401(k) Plan | 403(b) Plan |
|---|---|---|
| 11. Catch-up Contributions (for participants age 50 and over) | Yes, $2,000 in 2003 | Yes, $2,000 in 2003 |

[1]Under the Internal Revenue Code, these amounts are indexed and are periodically increased to keep pace with cost-of-living adjustments.

(See also ANNUITIES; DEFINED CONTRIBUTION PLANS; EMPLOYEE RETIREMENT INCOME SECURITY ACT [ERISA].)

### References

Horowitz, Pam. 2001. *J.K. Lasser's Winning with Your 403(b)*. New York: John Wiley & Sons.

Rosenbloom, Jerry S., ed. 2001. *The Handbook of Employee Benefits*. 5th ed. New York: McGraw-Hill.

*Michele F. Davis*

**RETIREMENT PREPAREDNESS,** individual responsibility to prepare financially for a lengthy period of nonwork in older age, is a relatively new phenomenon. Prior to World War II, most people worked as long as they could. Being "retired" then often meant either being cared for by family or being poor. Even in 1959, after the maturation of the Social Security and private pension systems, 35% of the population age 65 and over lived in poverty.

Starting with the enactment of Social Security in 1935, and following the expansion of the private pension system during and after World War II, a new concept for providing financial security in retirement was developed. Called the "three-legged stool," this concept combined Social Security, employer pensions, and individual retirement savings to create a solid support system for retirement.

During the past quarter century there have been two important shifts affecting the three-legged stool and the need for individual financial preparation for retirement.

## The Shift from Employer to Employee Pension Funding

The first shift relates to efforts by government to encourage individuals to set aside more money for retirement. The Technical Amendments Act of 1958 added Section 403(b) to the Internal Revenue Code and permitted a deferral on taxes for employer and employee contributions to retirement plans for those who worked in religious, charitable, educational, research, or cultural organizations. This was a precursor to the Revenue Act of 1978, which allowed employers and employees to make pretax contributions to retirement plans (Section 401(k)) and allowed state and local government workers to defer taxes on the part of their salary going into a retirement plan. In 1962, Keogh plans were authorized allowing the self-employed to defer taxes on money put into retirement plans, and in 1974 Individual Retirement Accounts (IRAs) were authorized.

After 401(k) plans were authorized, the number of workers covered by defined benefit plans (which employers generally fund) contracted, and the number covered by defined contribution plans (which employees generally provide most funding for) soared. In 1975, 27.2 million workers were covered by defined benefit plans; the number dropped to 23.0 million by 1998. During this same time period the number of workers covered by defined contribution plans grew from 11.2 million to 50.3 million (Purcell 2002).

Thus, with the passage of these several laws and the resulting shift in the types of pension and retirement plans companies offered their employees, one of the legs of the three-legged stool changed character. Employers are proportionately responsible for setting aside an adequate amount of money to fund an employee's pension. With most defined contribution plans, if the employee does not adequately fund the plan, the amount available at retirement will be inadequate, and if investment performance is poor, it is the employee, not the employer, who feels the burden.

### The Increased Cost of Retirement

The second shift provides an important context for considering financial preparedness for retirement: the increased cost of the retirement period. The cost of retirement is not fixed but depends on a variety of factors including lifestyle needs and expectations, the length of the retirement period, and health and the cost of health care. Most people wish to maintain their preretirement lifestyle throughout their retirement years. As preretirement lifestyles have improved, so have financial needs during retirement.

The length of the retirement period is another factor to be considered. The median age of retirement for men fell until 1983, leveling off at age 63 (Burtless and Quinn 2002). At the same time, life expectancy at age 65 has risen consistently. It was 15.2 years in 1970 and rose to 17.9 years in 2000 (NCHS 2003). Many demographers feel this rate of increase will at least continue and probably accelerate. These trends lead to a longer and more expensive retirement period.

There is a strong likelihood that health care and long-term care will create additional expenses for the next generation to retire. There have been major advances in medical and pharmaceutical care for the maladies that occur more frequently in older persons, and many more (costly) advances are expected. The ability of Medicare to pay for all of these advances is highly questionable.

Most long-term care is provided at no direct cost by family members. However, it appears very likely that the next generation to retire will have a lower level of unpaid care and thus will increasingly have to pay for the care they require. One reason for this is a change in fertility. The fertility rate per family was 3.09 in 1950 and 3.65 in 1960, providing the old old of today with many children and thus potential caregivers (NCHS 1999). However, the fertility rate fell to 1.84 per family in 1980. After the 1960s, record numbers of women did not have any children at all, due in part to enhanced birth control technology. Also, divorce rates have increased. The rate per 1,000 population was 2.2 in 1960 and 3.5 in 1970 but rose to 5.2 in 1980 and 4.7 in 1990. (NCHS 2003). Divorce often tends to weaken the bond between child and parent and make future caregiving less likely. Also, increased geographic mobility makes it likely that the next generation of old old will be more geographically separate from their adult children and thus less likely to receive care from them.

In all, financial needs for retirement will clearly be higher for the next generation than they are for the current generation of retirees.

### Retirement Preparedness of the Baby Boom Generation: The Difficulty of Adaptation

The baby boom generation (born from 1946 to 1964) is now 39 to 57 years old. They are the next generation to fully retire, and their financial preparation for retirement should be advanced—especially the older portion. This generation has witnessed numerous changes affecting retirement since they entered the workforce.

When boomers began working, 401(k) plans and workplace education about retirement preparation had not yet been introduced. Most people entering retirement then had not accumulated much individually for retirement. Yet boomers were able to observe most of them seeming to meet their financial goals in retirement. Part of the lack of financial preparation for retirement exhibited by most baby boomers might be traced to a failure to fully realize and adapt to the implications of the shifts affecting retirement that occurred during their work lives.

### The State of Retirement Preparedness

There is a clear shortfall in baby boomers' financial preparation for retirement. Almost all workers want to retire, and most expect to retire at or before age 65. While most do not want to reduce their lifestyle after they stop working, they are not setting aside enough money to reach their retirement goals. Among workers ages 55 to 64, 50% owned at least one retirement account, such as an IRA, Keogh or 401(k) type plan, but the median value of all the retirement accounts in these workers' households was $56,000 in 2000 (Purcell 2002). For workers ages 45 to 54, 48% had a retirement account, but the median value of all retirement accounts in the households was only $48,000. For workers ages 35 to 44, 42% had a retirement account, but the median value of all accounts was only $31,000.

There are other sources of money to be used for income in retirement beyond money in retirement plans. Data from the Census Bureau's Survey of Income and Program Participation provide a measure of household wealth that the Congressional Research Service has supplemented to make it almost complete. This combined data provides a figure for wealth that includes household

> home equity, net equity in vehicles, business equity, interest-earning assets held in banking institutions, interest earning assets held in other institutions, equity in stocks and mutual fund shares, equity in real estate other than the home, equity in other assets and equity in IRA and Keogh accounts . . . all 401(k) plans and other thrift plans. (Purcell 2002)

Not included is the present value of future Social Security benefits and the future value of benefits from defined benefit plans. But only about 30% of workers are covered by defined benefit plans where they work. In 2000 the median household wealth of workers ages 55 to 64 who own a retirement plan was $273,760, and it was $85,900 for workers who did not own a retirement plan (Purcell 2002). For workers ages 45 to 54 the median wealth was $201,690 for those who owned a retirement plan, and $61,050 for those who did not. Younger boomers have less wealth.

Wealth is not the only aspect of a household's net worth. Most households are also encumbered by debt. For those ages 55 to 64, median household debt was $36,400 for those with retirement plans and $19,900 for those without retirement plans. For those ages 45 to 54, the amounts were $63,200 for those with retirement plans and $28,000 for those without. These data clearly portray a picture of inadequate financial preparation for a period that will average approximately 20 years.

One of the causes of the inadequacy of retirement preparedness is the considerable drop-off in the personal savings rate. In 1960, the savings rate (the percentage of disposable personal income that was not consumed) was 7.2%. It rose to 9.4% in 1970 and 10.2% in 1980. Even by 1990 it was as high as 7.8%. But the savings rate dropped to 5.6% in 1995, 4.2% in 1998, 2.6% in 1999, 2.8% in 2000, 2.3% in 2001, and 3.9% in 2002 (U.S. Department of Commerce 2003).

It is clear that the low savings rate is not caused by people's inability to save more. In the several nationwide Retirement Confidence Surveys, a majority of workers have asserted that they can save an additional $20 a week for retirement. Asked what they would have to give up to set aside the additional $20 a week, almost all cite such nonnecessities as entertainment, eating out, buying less expensive food. To save an additional $20 per week (in the 2003 Retirement Confidence Survey) 30% said they would give up dining out, 24% said they would spend less on entertainment and leisure activities, and 15% said they would not have to give up anything.

Clearly, almost all households above the poverty line are spending considerable amounts of money on nonessential items while foregoing financial preparation for retirement. (The population near poverty and below will be able to maintain their preretirement lifestyle through Social Security and other government programs.)

### Causes of the Lack of Retirement Preparedness

Most persons within 15 years of their expected retirement date hope for an enjoyable, meaningful, fulfilling, and lengthy period. They want to travel after they stop working, pursue a broad range of interests, visit children, and enjoy and give presents to grandchildren. This leads to questions about why these working people are not making the financial preparation necessary to achieve these goals.

A series of surveys by the research firm Mathew Greenwald & Associates, Inc., provide insight into the lack of financial preparedness. There are two main components: a lack of focus on retirement planning and misconceptions about how much retirement can cost. First, most people do not have a good sense of how much must be accumulated to be financially prepared for retirement because they have not taken the time to try to figure this out. In a 2002 national survey of people ages 45 and over who had incomes of at least $50,000 and did not own annuities, only 23% said they calculated how much they needed to save by the time they retired to be able to live comfortably in retirement (National Association for Variable Annuities 2002). Of the group that made a calculation, many clearly did not spend enough time on the calculation and did an inadequate job. Those who are younger or less affluent are less likely to have tried to make a calculation.

The 2003 Retirement Confidence Survey revealed that boomers estimated that they spent more time last year planning for holidays than planning for retirement.

When asked what proportion of their preretirement income they would need to live comfortably in retirement, 49% of workers (in the 2003 Retirement Confidence Survey) said they would need less than 70% of their preretirement income. However, almost all professional financial planners feel that 70% or more of preretirement income is necessary.

Another factor is an underestimation of life expectancy. The Retirement Risk Survey conducted by Greenwald & Associates for the Society of Actuaries surveyed 600 people ages 45 and over. It found that most underestimated how long the average 65-year-old lives. Results of in-depth interviews conducted by Greenwald & Associates confirm that most people underestimate their own life expectancy.

Most people underestimate their exposure to the potential costs of long-term care and equally tend to overestimate the extent to which Medicare will cover long-term care costs. Further, the Retirement Risk Survey exposes a certain degree of denial in the area of long-term care. While 69% of working people ages 45 and over feel it is at least somewhat likely that the average older person will have to spend at least some time in a nursing home, only 43% feel it is at least somewhat likely that they will have to do so.

### Work after Retirement

One expectation appears to contribute to the sense of well-being many workers have about their financial prospects after retirement: the expectation of earning money after they retire. The 2003 Retirement Confidence Survey found that 70% of workers expected to work for pay after they retire. However, in the same Retirement Confidence Survey, only 26% of the retired population reported that they have worked for pay since they retired. Indeed, in the 2003 Retirement Confidence Survey, 39% of retirees said that they retired earlier than they had planned. Most who retired earlier than planned did so because of ill health, disability, or layoffs. Additionally, some retirees who seek work find that the only work available to them is unappealing.

Continued participation in the labor force will be key to maintaining financial stability in retirement for the next generation of retirees. The evidence suggests that the age of retirement will rise somewhat and that more will work after retirement. But this strategy will not wholly make up for the clear deficiencies in retirement preparedness.

### Generation X: Outlook for Retirement Preparedness the Generation after the Baby Boom

The baby boom generation is the next generation to retire. Their retirement preparation should be advanced, especially the older part of the boom who are now in their fifties, because they are so close to retirement. Generation X (born 1965 to 1978) is still more than a quarter century away from retirement. What can be discerned about their retirement preparedness? There are some hopeful signs.

One of the problems that appears to have afflicted the baby boom generation is a failure to adapt to a fairly quickly evolving retirement system, a system that puts more responsibility on them to accumulate, and accumulate much more, for retirement.

Generation X has a significantly different view of the retirement system. They feel that they have the responsibility to fund their retirement and are getting the planning tools to do the funding as they enter the workforce. Most Generation Xers have little faith in Social Security; most are not depending upon it to provide much retirement income. They have entered the workplace with 401(k) plans in place and entrenched. They have received the education about retirement planning that comes with 401(k) plans at the start of their careers. Theirs is a generation that has taken a great deal of individual responsibility. They have high rates of homeownership and have exhibited higher levels of financial sophistication and savings behavior than previous generations. If, as is likely, the baby boom generation struggles financially in retirement, Generation X will observe this and increase their financial preparation to avoid this fate.

Generation X has one more advantage: government programs provide a level of support to those in financial need. The baby boom generation is a very large generation followed by a smaller generation. It will be very hard for government to provide much assistance to baby boomers, due to their big numbers. Indeed, the baby boom will make it very hard, probably impossible, for the Social Security system and Medicare to meet their current level of benefits. But Generation X (sometimes called the Baby Bust or Birth Dearth Generation) is a small generation followed by a larger one. While Generation X is in retirement, it will be much easier for the relatively larger working population of that time to expand government programs to provide needed support to those who require it. (See also ATTITUDES ABOUT RETIREMENT; BUSINESS SUCCESSION PLANNING; CASH FLOW PLANNING FOR RETIREES; ECONOMIC HISTORY OF RETIREMENT; FINANCIAL SECURITY IN RETIREMENT; FRAILTY PLANNING; RETIREMENT EXPENSE PLANNNG; RETIREMENT PLANNING.)

### References

Burtless, Gary, and Joseph F. Quinn. 2002. "Is Working Longer the Answer for an Aging Workforce?" Center for Retirement Research at Boston College, Issue in Brief, December Number II.

Mathew Greenwald & Associates. 2003. *2003 Retirement Confidence Survey*. Employee Benefit Research Institute and American Savings Education Council. Washington, DC: EBRI.

National Association for Variable Annuities. 2002. "Survey of Non-Annuity Owners." National Association for Variable Annuities, Reston, VA.

National Center for Health Statistics (NCHS). 1999. *Vital Statistics of the U.S. 1999*, Part 1: *Natality*. Hyattsville, MD: Author, table 1–7.

National Center for Health Statistics (NCHS). 2001. *Monthly Vital Statistics Report*. 43: 9.

National Center for Health Statistics (NCHS). 2003. Available online at http://www.cdc.gov/nchs/data/hus/tables/2002/02hus028.pdf.

Purcell, Patrick. 2002. *Retirement Savings and Household Wealth in 2000: Analysis of Census Bureau Data*. Washington, DC: Congressional Research Service, Library of Congress.

Society of Actuaries. 2001. "Retirement Risk Survey." Available online at http://www.soa.org/sections/rrs_report.pdf.

United States Census. 2001. *Statistical Abstract of the United States*. Washington, DC: Author.

U.S. Department of Commerce. Bureau of Economic Analysis. 2003. Available online at http://www.bea.gov/bea/dn/nipaweb/TableViewFixed.asp.

*Mathew Greenwald*

**REVERSE MORTGAGES,** loans for homeowners, age 62 and older, that are based on converting a percentage of the net home equity into a lump-sum payment, monthly payments, or a credit line to be drawn against as needed. Reverse mortgages have alternatively been called *home equity conversion mortgages*, *reverse equity mortgages*, and *reverse annuity mortgages*.

Older homeowners who want to remain in their homes as they age and who desire additional income are the primary prospective market for reverse mortgages. Their objectives typically are to supplement other, often inadequate, income sources or to meet large cash requirements caused by events such as an illness, major home repairs, unpaid taxes, long-term care needs, or other unexpected expenses. Unlike traditional home mortgage loans, there is no need to qualify based upon ability to repay a reverse mortgage. No repayment is required until the borrower dies, sells the home, or moves permanently out of the home, at which time the loan must be paid in full. A reverse mortgage loan also may become due and payable if the mortgaged property is allowed to deteriorate and is not repaired, if it is abandoned for more than a specified period, or if the borrower fails to pay property taxes or hazard insurance or violates other borrower obligations.

The potential need among older adults is sizable (Opdyke 2002; Trent 1994). While approximately 80% of older Americans are homeowners and 77% of older homeowners have paid off their mortgage debt, a significant percentage of them live on low fixed incomes. According to the American Housing Survey for the United States in 2001, the median value of homes owned by older persons was $107,398, but the median family income of older homeowners was just $23,256.

The conceptual foundation of home equity conversion should be understood in the context of the retirement income system, which frequently has been characterized as a three-legged stool: Social Security is designed to provide basic income protection, with occupational pensions and individual savings providing supplements to Social Security. The role of individual savings is modest, however, because of the typically small value of liquid assets accumulated by older adults. In 2000, 38% of the aggregate income of the older population came from Social Security benefits, 18% from occupational pensions, and another 18% from assets. Most of the remaining income consisted of current earnings of 23% (Social Security Administration 2000). The financial situation of many older adults undoubtedly would improve if their home equity were to be converted into additional income over their remaining life span.

The need for spendable cash among retirees is likely to increase as more and more individuals in the baby boom generation face the risk of long-term care in the next several decades. Converting home equity would seem a means that can satisfy several desires. It can augment the income needed for health and long-term care or other needs or desires in later life, and it can enable older adults to stay in their own homes, providing substance to the often-repeated ideal of "aging in place." It elevates the role of personal savings as part of retirement security, and it gives meaning to the principle of self-reliance.

Despite this logic, converting one's home equity remains a novel notion for many. Some older people do not like the idea of going into debt in later life. Others are concerned about reducing the size of their estate for their heirs. There appears some evidence, however, that future cohorts of older adults may not be as concerned about either of these issues.

### Brief History of Reverse Mortgage Products

Reverse mortgages were referred to as "relatively little-known loans" in a recent *Wall Street Journal* article (Opdyke 2002). This is a noteworthy observation about a type of mortgage transaction conceptualized some 40 years ago (Chen 1963, 1967). Introduced to the marketplace in the mid- to late 1980s, reverse mortgages got off to a very slow start and for many years only a few pioneering institutional lenders actually made them.

**Figure 1**
**Reverse Mortgage Originations**

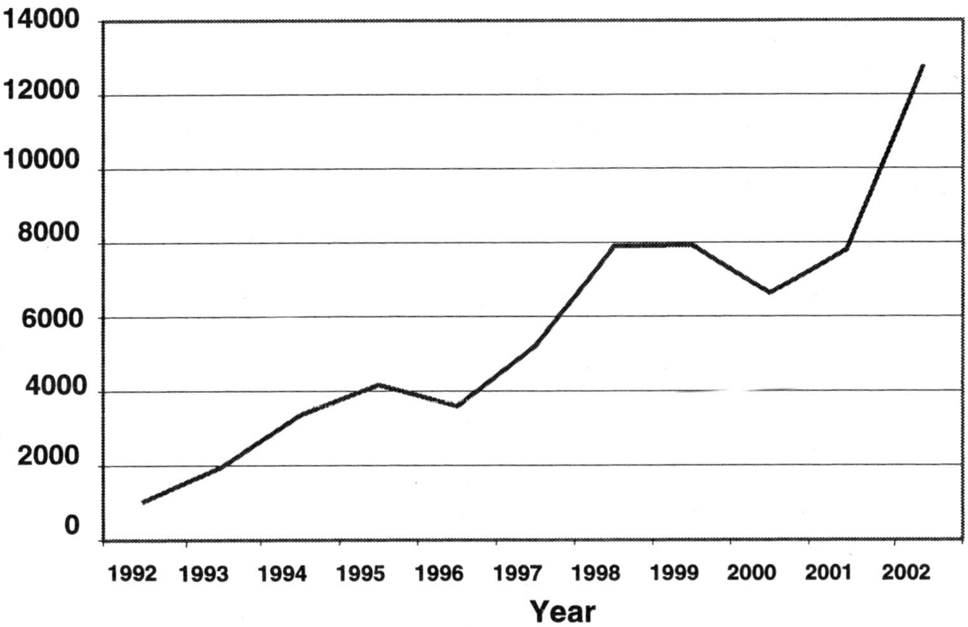


*Source*: National Reverse Mortgage Lenders Association (NRMLA), http://www.reversemortgage.org/newsitem51.htm.

While the number of reverse mortgage lenders has grown steadily over the years, loan volume still remains relatively low.

Until recently, mainstream mortgage lenders viewed reverse mortgages with a "wait and see" attitude. To most lenders, even those who were motivated to extend them to older homeowners in need, reverse mortgages were risky, untested, and costly to originate (Bailey 2000; Mayer and Simons 1994). Further barriers included lack of liquidity and diversification for lenders, unfavorable required accounting treatment, regulatory and legal uncertainties, and concerns over consumer protection (Mayer and Simons 1994).

Increasingly, mortgage lenders are becoming more comfortable with reverse mortgages, and more older homeowners are seeking them as a way—often the only way—to bolster their income security in later life. The present reverse mortgage industry numbers about 150 lenders, and the National Reverse Mortgage Lenders Association (NRMLA) reports that nearly 14,000 loans were made in 2002 (see Figure 1). Members of the reverse mortgage industry, as well as prospective borrowers, have reason to be pleased with this large increase in lending experience and volume. But the current volume of reverse mortgage originations is still only a small fraction of the number of seniors potentially needing to tap into home equity to meet living expenses and long-term care requirements. This market is estimated by Fannie Mae to become 16 million households annually by 2010 (Opdyke 2002).

**Figure 2**
**"I'd Like to Stay in My Home and Never Move"**

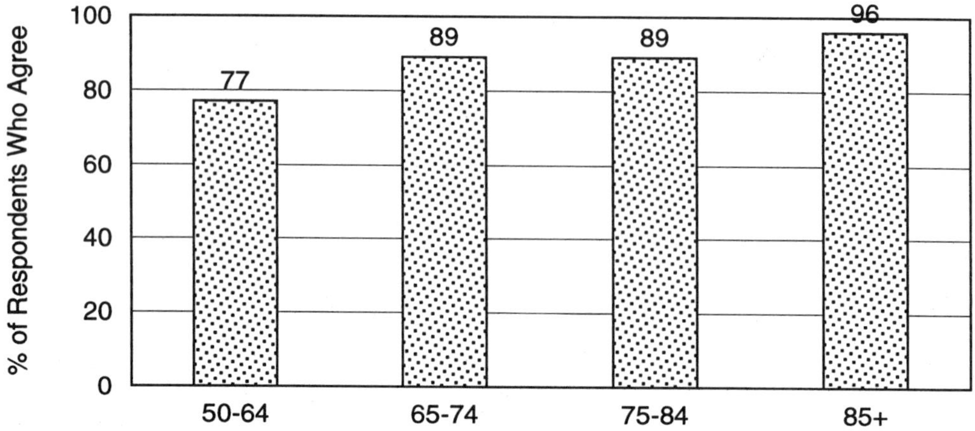


*Source*: AARP 1996.

## What Older Adults Want

AARP sponsors periodic surveys that monitor the housing needs and preferences of older Americans. The 1996 Senior Housing Survey is the fourth in a series of surveys AARP has sponsored. The strong theme that emerges in analyzing trends over the four waves of the study is continuity—both in the responses to the questions and, more important, in the desire for continuity in living arrangements. This is best shown by responses to the statement, "What I'd really like to do is stay in my own home and never move." The vast majority of older persons (83%) agreed with that statement in 1996. This was consistent with responses in earlier waves of the survey: 84% in 1992 and 1989. More significant, this desire grew stronger with the age of respondents: 89% for persons aged 75 to 84 and 96% for persons aged 85 and older (see Figure 2) (AARP 1996).

Eighty-four percent (84%) of respondents age 65 and older were more likely to believe that their current residence is where they will "*always live*." Those who are widowed (89%), those who own their homes outright (90%), and those who have difficulty getting around (89%) are also more likely than others to indicate that they want to stay in their current home "*forever*."

## Characteristics of Reverse Mortgages

All reverse mortgages entail a buildup of debt, which is the sum of the periodic principal amounts borrowed plus accumulated interest. Since no payments are made to reduce indebtedness during the life of the mortgage, interest accrues on both interest and principal, which means the amount owed increases at an escalating rate through time.

Dominant in the U.S. market for reverse mortgages in recent years has been the Home Equity Conversion Mortgage (HECM), which was introduced by the U.S. Department of Housing and Urban Development (HUD) in 1989. The HECM program allows borrowers to choose among many payment options. Cash may be received from the proceeds of the reverse mortgage as:

1. A lump sum received at the time of the loan;
2. Monthly payments for as long as the borrower resides in the house (tenure payments);
3. Higher monthly payments for a fixed period of time (term payments), after which borrowers may continue to reside in the house and defer repayment;
4. A line of credit with which borrowers may vary the amounts and timing of payments up to a maximum; and
5. Some combination of all of the above.

Recently, the HECM program has been expanded and mortgage loan limits have been increased. Any approved Federal Housing Administration (FHA) lender may initiate a mortgage according to guidelines administered by HUD. Borrowers under the HECM program must be at least age 62, own their home free (or nearly free) of debt, and reside in their home. Payments to borrowers are based on the age of the youngest member in a married household, the interest rate on the mortgage, and an adjusted property value, which is defined as the lesser of the property's appraised value and the maximum mortgage on a one-unit residence as defined by FHA criteria. In 2002, these mortgage limits ranged from $144,336 in most nonmetropolitan areas to $261,609 in many urban areas (except Honolulu, where it was $291,650). The limits are based on estimated median home value, and they are subject to change at least annually, although HUD is studying the feasibility of a single national limit.

Borrowers may choose fixed or adjustable rate loans, and they must purchase mortgage insurance to protect the lender against the possibility that proceeds from the sale of the home will be insufficient to retire the accumulated debt. This insurance premium is paid in two parts: (1) 2% of the adjusted property value at closing and (2) a monthly premium equal to .05% of the outstanding principal owed. Both of these costs may be financed.

Proprietary (or conventional) reverse mortgages are offered by financial institutions and mortgage companies that own the rights to these financial products. If a home is worth substantially more than the value limits imposed under HECM reverse mortgage loan terms, a proprietary loan may offer greater lump-sum, credit line, or monthly loan advances. Proprietary loans, however, can be quite expensive, and terms must be carefully examined and understood by prospective borrower(s) and their financial advisors before entering them.

### Cautions and Alternatives to Reverse Mortgages

In essence, reverse mortgages or home equity conversion plans in general are a financial instrument that enable homowners to change the form of an illiquid asset (home equity) into a liquid form of asset (a stream of cash). But people perceive of this exchange as incurring a debt. To assist with this and other considerations, all HECM applicants are required to obtain counseling services from a HUD-approved independent third party prior to loan closing. The requirement tries to ensure that older borrowers understand the full implications of their decision. HUD-approved reverse mortgage counselors are required to disclose to consumers that these loans "may have tax consequences, affect eligibility for assistance under Federal and State programs, and have an impact on the estate and heirs of the homeowner."

Reverse mortgages can be expensive. A borrower must pay all normal loan origination costs, such as application and appraisal fees, loan interest points, mortgage insurance premiums, and closing costs. Although the income received through a reverse mortgage is considered a loan and is not taxed, there is no tax benefit to the accruing amount of interest owed since interest is not a deductible item until the year in which it is actually paid.

Generally, a reverse mortgage should be used only if it will help the homeowner remain economically independent or will materially add to the older person's quality of life. Less costly housing options may exist, such as a less costly home, renting an apartment, or moving into assisted living or other alternative housing. Another alternative to reverse mortgage is a sale-and-leaseback agreement, by which the homeowner sells the home and then leases it back from the buyer. Most sale-leaseback arrangements involve family members; for example, the sale by a parent to an adult child. The proceeds from the sale can be invested to generate an income stream for the parent or parents. Since the sale generates tax-deductible depreciation, it may be possible to charge a modest rent and produce a break-even cash flow. Appreciation potential also exists for the buyer, who may wish to purchase the property from a parent or parents both to help them and to preserve the equity in the family home.

Another alternative is a life estate agreement, which transfers ownership of the home but gives the occupants the right to remain in the home for the remainder of their lives. The agreement can be between family members, or the beneficiary or "remainderman," which may be a charity or educational institution. The owner will usually receive no cash but will receive a gift tax deduction based on the value of the charitable contribution, usually the appraised value of the home. Generally, such agreements are limited to those who have sufficient wealth to take advantage of the gift deduction or who have a philanthropic motive. Both sale-and-leaseback and life estate agreements should not be entered into without the advice of legal counsel (Higgins 1996).

### Public Sector Applications of the Reverse Mortgage Concept

There have been certain types of home equity conversion programs available through the public sector that assist older homeowners with the payment of property taxes or the repair or improvement of homes they wish to continue to occupy. These types of single-purpose public sector home equity conversion provide a one-time lump-sum advance, and no repayment is required for as long as the borrower continues to occupy the home. These loans are not available in every community, and eligibility criteria vary. Information on single-purpose programs, usually limited to lower-income homeowners, may be obtained through local Area Agency on Aging offices.

Public policies that support such programs, however, pose a quandary. For example, if property taxes are excused or exempted for some older homeowners, other taxpayers in the community will be paying increased taxes to offset the revenue loss, unless government expenditures are reduced commensurately. A practical, if unintended, consequence of this otherwise generous gesture toward older homeowners is that younger homeowners may be making it possible for the exempt older homeowners to preserve the inheritance for their heirs. Essentially, the same issue exists for current taxpayers if property taxes are deferred for some older homeowners even though tax deferments would be repaid later.

In summary, a reverse mortgage is a voluntary financial arrangement whereby older homeowners typically convert the net equity in their house into a flow of income, coupled with assured occupancy in the home for as long as they live or remain in the home. The logical structure of this gradual process of asset liquidation may be conceptualized thusly: when young persons build up their home equity, they mortgage their future income to acquire a house; when older people dispose of their home equity, they mortgage their house to acquire a steady stream of income for later life. (See also FRAILTY PLANNING; HEALTH AND LONGEVITY; HOMEOWNERSHIP; HOUSING COUNSELING FOR OLDER AMERICANS; LIFE ESTATES; LONG-TERM CARE INSURANCE [LTCI]—A CONSUMER'S PERSPECTIVE.)

**Organizations**

AARP
American Bar Association's Commission on Legal Problems of the Elderly
National Reverse Mortgage Lenders Association (NRMLA)

**References**

AARP. 1996. *Understanding Senior Housing: Into the Next Century, Survey of Consumer Preferences, Concerns, and Needs*. Washington, DC: Author.

Bailey, Dawn. 2000. "Few Lenders Make HUD-Insured Reverse Mortgages." Thompson Publishing Corporation *National Mortgage News* 24(3): 27.

Chen, Yung-Ping. 1963. "Property Tax Burden on Aged Homeowners and Income Potential of Their Homes." Paper presented at a joint seminar of the Department of Economics and the Social Systems Research Institute, University of Wisconsin, Madison, December.

Chen, Yung-Ping. 1967. "Potential Income from Homeownership: An Actuarial Mortgage Plan." *A Compendium of Papers, Part II: The Aged Population and Retirement Income Program*. Subcommittee on Fiscal Policy, Joint Economic Committee, 90th Cong., 1st Sess. Washington, DC: GPO.

Higgins, David P. 1996. "Reverse Mortgages." In *Encyclopedia of Financial Gerontology*, ed. Lois A. Vitt and Jurg K. Siegenthaler. Westport, CT: Greenwood Press.

Mayer, Christopher, and Katerina Simons. 1994. "A New Look at Reverse Mortgages: Potential Market and Institutional Constraints." *New England Economic Review* (March–April): 15–26.

Opdyke, Jeff D. 2002. "Congress Mulls a Relaxing of Reverse-Mortgage Rules: Creation of a National Loan Limit Would Let Seniors Tap More Money." *Wall Street Journal*, April 22.

Social Security Administration. 2000. *Income of the Population 55 or Older, Office of Research, Evaluation and Statistics*. Publication No. 13-11871. Washington, DC: Author.

Trent, Tina R. 1994. "Elderly Demographics and Preferences Indicate Need for Reverse Mortgages." *Housing Research News* 2(3): 4.

U.S. Census Bureau. 2002. "American Housing Survey for the United States: 2001." *Current Housing Reports*. Series H150/01. Washington, DC: GPO.

*Yung-Ping Chen and Lois A. Vitt*

**RISK TOLERANCE,** a person's capacity to bear significant and rapid changes in the value of their investments, generally in pursuit of higher returns.

Individuals have both a perception of risks (subjective risk tolerance) and a capacity to bear risks (objective risk tolerance). An individual's investment choices may depend on both subjective and objective risk tolerance. For young individuals, it is clear that avoiding relatively high-risk/high-return investments, such as stocks, because of low risk tolerance will make it more difficult to accumulate sufficient wealth for retirement, because the alternative—investments with low volatility—historically have had very low rates of return after inflation.

### Objective Risk Tolerance

Objective risk tolerance is a person's ability to afford to take a risk or to recover from a loss of investment value. A person who doesn't "need" the money for a number of years can ride out a downturn in investment value while it has a chance to recover. Similarly, a person with $100,000 of investments is better able to afford losing $5,000 than a person with $10,000.

A key element of objective risk tolerance is the individual's time horizon—how many years until the investment funds need to be withdrawn. Generally speaking, the longer the horizon, the higher the objective risk tolerance because of the time available to recover from a loss. A younger person, who presumably will not need to withdraw from retirement funds for 20 or 40 years or even more, may be said to have a long horizon. On the other hand, someone who wants to retire in a year has a very short horizon, and a retired person may need investment income for current expenses. Malkiel (1996) suggested that a 25-year-old should have a portfolio with 70% stocks and the remainder in less volatile financial assets, and a 70-year-old should have 30% in stocks. The reason why Malkiel and other experts suggest that even older people should hold stocks is that the remaining life expectancies at age 65 have been steadily increasing and are very high for the most educated households. If someone avoids stocks because of low risk tolerance, and then lives 30 years in retirement, the purchasing power of investment income will decrease substantially over that period.

Another aspect of an individual's objective risk tolerance is the amount of risk that an individual is able to take, which can be analyzed by carefully examining the financial situation.

One factor discussed by Malkiel and by Hanna and Chen (1997) is the size of the investment portfolio relative to total wealth, including human wealth (the present value of noninvestment income such as wages, Social Security, and defined benefit pensions or the amount of money today that could provide a stream of income in the future to replace noninvestment income). Consider a 25-year-old worker holding a $1,000 portfolio consisting of the stock of one company. If the company went bankrupt, the worker might have regrets but would have 40 years of employment income during which to recover. In contrast, a retired person relying on a stock portfolio to cover normal expenses might have difficulty if investment values decreased significantly.

Consideration of the value of human wealth in relation to other wealth, including the value of investments, can add further insight into appropriate investments. Gutter (2000) found that even though the proportion of total wealth represented by investment portfolios increased with age, even among those 65 and over, for over 75% of households the investment portfolio represented less than 30% of total wealth.

Hanna and Chen (1997) suggest that even individuals with a one-year investment horizon should have stocks, with the optimal proportion depending on subjective risk tolerance and the ratio of the portfolio to total wealth. If the portfolio represents no more than 50% of total wealth, those with average subjective risk tolerance should have about 50% stocks in their portfolio, and those with low subjective risk tolerance should have about 31% stocks. Using a different approach, Vora and McGinnis (2000) concluded that an all-stock portfolio offered advantages for postretirement portfolios despite the volatility. Jagannathan and Kocherlakota (1996) offered theoretical reasons why the proportion of the portfolio devoted to stocks should not necessarily decrease with age, although they observe that it might be reasonable to decrease the stock proportion for people whose labor income is uncorrelated with the stock market.

### Subjective Risk Tolerance

There are quite a number of ways to measure subjective risk tolerance, among which Hanna, Gutter, and Fan (2001) mentioned the following:

- Asking about investment choices
- Asking a combination of investment and subjective questions
- Asking hypothetical questions with carefully specified scenarios
- Assessing actual behavior

The Federal Reserve Board has included the following investment risk tolerance question since 1983 in its Surveys of Consumer Finances (SCFs). Which of the following statements on this page comes closest to the amount of financial risk that you are willing to take when you save or make investments?

1. Take substantial financial risk expecting to earn substantial returns.
2. Take above-average financial risks expecting to earn above-average returns.
3. Take average financial risks expecting to earn average returns.
4. Not willing to take any financial risks.

By this measure, risk tolerance in the United States did not change much between 1983 and 1992, then increased between 1992 and 1998. Average risk tolerance by this measure increases with age until age 50, then decreases, with the mean for those 75 and over being about 26% of the level for those age 50 to 54 (Yao and Hanna 2003). Controlling for other variables such as gender, education, and household type, means risk tolerance steadily decreases with age, with the highest level being for those under age 30. Yao and Hanna also show that race/ethnicity, household composition/gender, and education have effects on households' risk tolerance levels. Controlling for other factors, non-Hispanic Whites were more risk tolerant than other race/ethnicity groups—Hispanics, Blacks, and those in any other race category, mostly Asians and Pacific Islanders. Single males were over twice as risk tolerant as single females, with married couples having risk tolerance levels in between. Given that the gender and race/ethnic status effects were significant after controlling for a number of other variables, it is probable that households' risk tolerance levels, which are their attitudes toward financial risk, affect their investment behavior. Thus, households' risk attitudes have effects on their likelihood of achieving long-term financial goals (e.g., an adequate retirement).

### Inferring Risk Tolerance from Behavior

Wang and Hanna (1997) found that the proportion of risky assets (broadly defined to include long-term bonds as well as stocks and other investment assets) to total wealth (including human wealth), and hence risk tolerance, increases with age up to retirement, after which it declines somewhat. This measure of risk tolerance based on actual behavior has a basis in economic theory, so it is not clear how to reconcile the effect of age on this measure of risk tolerance with the effect of age on the measure of risk tolerance found in the Survey of Consumer Finance.

In addition to inferring risk tolerance from the ratio of risky assets to wealth, other measures of risk tolerance based on behavior include variance/standard of the portfolio return and the beta (a comparative measure of how stock performs compared to the market as a whole) of the portfolio (Schooley and Worden 1996). In addition, holding stocks directly or indirectly through mutual funds can be considered a measure of financial risk tolerance. By this last measure, the risk tolerance of Americans has increased, because only 32% of households held stocks or funds with stocks in 1989 (Kennickell, Starr-McCluer, and Surette 2000), but in 2001, 52% held stocks (Aizcorbe, Kennickell, and Moore 2003). The Surveys of Consumer Finances before 1989 did not allow direct estimation of the proportion of households holding stocks directly or indirectly, but according to one estimate, the proportion was roughly the same in 1983 as in 1989 (Bertaut and Starr-McCluer 2000).

### Discussion

Subjective risk tolerance varies by age, gender, education, and other factors. However, financial advisors should not assume that any unique individual shares the average characteristics of his or her group. Within each group—for instance, among older Americans—there is a wide variation of subjective and objective risk tolerance. Some older people have high subjective risk tolerance, and some do not depend on the returns on their investment portfolios for regular expenses. It is true, however, that as a group, older people have much lower risk tolerance than people who are 50 to 54 years old, and single females are less risk tolerant than married couples, who are, in turn, less risk tolerant than single males. A financial advisor should attempt to carefully assess both the subjective risk tolerance of a client by using one or more measures (Hanna, Gutter, and Fan 2001) and the objective risk tolerance such as the importance of investment income for covering usual expenses. For a household consisting of a couple, the risk tolerance of both the partners should be measured. (See also ASSET ALLOCATION AFTER RETIREMENT; FINANCIAL EDUCATION FOR SENIORS; FINANCIAL LITERACY; FINANCIAL PLANNING; FINANCIAL RECOVERY IN LATER LIFE; INFLUENCES ON RETIREMENT INVESTMENT DECISIONS; INVESTMENT ADVICE; INVESTMENT CLUBS; INVESTOR EDUCATION.)

#### References

Aizcorbe, Ana M., Arthur B. Kennickell, and Kevin B. Moore. 2003. "Recent Changes in U.S. Family Finances: Evidence from the 1998 and 2001 Survey of Consumer Finances." *Federal Reserve Bulletin* 89: 1–32. Available online at http://www.federalreserve.gov/pubs/bulletin/2003/0103lead.pdf.

Bertaut, Carol, and Martha Starr-McCluer. 2000. "Household Portfolios in the United States."

Working Paper. Federal Reserve Board, April. Available online at http://www.federalreserve.gov/pubs/feds/2000/200026/200026pap.pdf.

Gutter, Michael S. 2000. "Human Wealth and Financial Asset Ownership." *Financial Counseling and Planning* 11(2): 9–19. Available online at http://www.hec.ohio-state.edu/hanna/gutter2000.htm.

Hanna, Sherman D., and Peng Chen. 1997. "Subjective and Objective Risk Tolerance: Implications for Optimal Portfolios." *Financial Counseling and Planning* 8(2): 17–26. Available online at http://www.hec.ohio-state.edu/hanna/chen97.htm.

Hanna, Sherman D., Michael S. Gutter, and Jessie X. Fan. 2001. "A Measure of Risk Tolerance Based on Economic Theory." *Financial Counseling and Planning* 12(2): 53–60. Available online at http://www.hec.ohio-state.edu/hanna/hanna012.htm.

Jagannathan, Ravi, and Narayana R. Kocherlakota. 1996. "Why Should Older People Invest Less in Stocks Than Younger People?" *Quarterly Review of the Federal Reserve Bank of Minneapolis* 20(3): 11–23. Available online at http://www.minneapolisfed.org/research/qr/qr2032.pdf.

Kennickell, Arthur B., Martha Starr-McCluer, and Brian J. Surette. 2000. "Recent Changes in U.S. Family Finances: Results from the 1998 Survey of Consumer Finances." *Federal Reserve Bulletin* 86: 1–29. Available online at http://www.federalreserve.gov/pubs/bulletin/2000/0100lead.pdf.

Malkiel, Burton G. 1996. *A Random Walk Down Wall Street*. New York: W.W. Norton.

Schooley, Diane K., and Debra D. Worden. 1996. "Risk Aversion Measures: Comparing Attitudes and Asset Allocation." *Financial Services Review* 5(2): 87–99.

Vora, Premal P., and John D. McGinnis. 2000. "The Asset Allocation Decision in Retirement: Lessons from Dollar Cost Averaging." *Financial Services Review* 9(1): 47–63.

Wang, Hui, and Sherman D. Hanna. 1997. "Does Risk Tolerance Decrease with Age?" *Financial Counseling and Planning* 8(2): 27–31. Available online at http://www.hec.ohio-state.edu/hanna/wang.pdf.

Yao, Rui, and Sherman D. Hanna. 2003. "Has Financial Risk Tolerance Changed since 1983?" *Consumer Interests Annual* 49 (February 11).

*Sherman D. Hanna and Rui Yao*

# S

**SAFETY.** See Assisted Living; Crime Protection; Disaster Preparedness and Older Adults; Elder Law Practice; Ethics in Financial Planning; Liability Insurance.

**SAVINGS ACCOUNT TRUSTS,** also known as "Totten trusts" and "tentative trusts," savings accounts with a testamentary feature. They operate like ordinary savings accounts during the depositor's lifetime. The depositor may add funds, make withdrawals, and close the account at any time. Upon the depositor's death, the proceeds in the account (less some possible deductions, which will be discussed below) pass directly to the named beneficiary rather than to the depositor's estate. Because of local variations, state law must be consulted to determine the validity and operation of savings account trusts in each state.

Savings account trusts are an estate planning tool available to persons of modest means who cannot afford the services of an attorney to prepare a will. They are an appropriate way to dispose of small sums of money, although their use is not limited to persons of modest means or to small sums of money. They are simple to create. At a bank or savings and loan association when a savings account is opened (or later), a notation is added to the signature card stating that the depositor holds the account "in trust for" or "as trustee for" a named beneficiary. The beneficiary designation is freely revocable; the depositor may eliminate it or change it at any time. It is also possible in some states to revoke the designation by a provision mentioning the account in the depositor's will.

If the beneficiary dies before the depositor, the trust designation is automatically canceled. The account becomes an ordinary savings account whose balance will be transferred at the depositor's death to his or her estate. However, some financial institutions provide on their forms that if the beneficiary dies before the depositor, the account becomes payable on the depositor's death to the beneficiary's estate. Generally, the provisions printed on the account form will govern. It is therefore essential to read and understand them before signing.

Savings account trusts have a number of features that make them attractive to older persons. They are easy to create and affordable compared to hiring an attorney to draft a will. Banks impose no special fees for opening these accounts or collecting the proceeds, unless payment involves closing a certificate of deposit before maturity. In that case, the bank may assess penalties for early withdrawal. The convenience offered by these accounts is another attractive feature. The accounts are available at close-by financial institutions where bank officers with whom older adults are familiar can assist them. It is not uncommon for older persons to have multiple savings account trusts at a variety of financial institutions. Often they will have accounts with roughly equivalent sums that name their children and grandchildren or nieces and nephews as the beneficiaries.

Some older persons hesitate to hire attorneys because they are reluctant to discuss their financial affairs with strangers, uncomfortable with the formality of a lawyer's office, or fear the possibility of fraud or overcharging. Others attempt to deny their own mortality by deferring estate planning, refusing to consider or talk about the financial consequences of death. As a result, many Americans die without a will, and their estates are unplanned, devolving to heirs according to state statutes of intestate succession. From this perspective, savings account trusts constitute a simple, useful, and nonthreatening estate planning device.

There are disadvantages to engaging in estate planning without the supervision of an attorney or other qualified professional. The planning decisions involved in opening savings account trusts may be piecemeal, lacking the considered advice of a professional who is knowledgeable about the individual's family situation and finances. Also, seniors may not be aware of estate planning alternatives. Bank employees may not be well trained regarding estate planning in general or about their own products, and they may not have the ability or time to explain them fully to customers. Further, as members of a retail sales force for their bank, their recommendations may not always constitute disinterested advice.

The opening of a savings account trust will not, in most cases, entirely negate the need for a will. Most individuals own assets in addition to the cash in their savings account and require a will to dispose of them. Probably the best use of savings account trusts is as one component of a comprehensive estate plan that includes other appropriate devices, such as a will and insurance, and is reviewed in its entirety by an attorney or other estate planning professional.

Savings account trusts are "testamentary substitutes" because they function like wills, channeling funds to a beneficiary at the depositor's death, just as if the depositor had left the beneficiary a legacy for that amount in his or her will. Usually, a savings account trust will perform this function more efficiently than a will. The account is a nonprobate asset that bypasses the depositor's estate and is deemed to pass directly to the beneficiary at the depositor's death. The beneficiary is often able to obtain the proceeds sooner than a legacy under a will since there is no need to wait for probate of the will nor to rely on the executor for payment. Instead, the beneficiary obtains payment directly from the bank soon after the depositor's death by presenting the passbook, a copy of the death certificate, and in some cases, a waiver from state tax authorities.

When the depositor's other assets are not sufficient at death to pay debts, taxes, and funeral and administration expenses, the depositor's executor may have a claim to part or all of the proceeds in a savings account trust that is superior to the beneficiary's. In some states the proceeds are also reachable by a surviving spouse, even if disinherited under the depositor's will, if the proceeds are determined by court order to be needed for the elective or forced share of the estate to which the surviving spouse is entitled by state law.

For purposes of administration by the executor, the proceeds in the account bypass the depositor's estate, but they are considered part of the estate for estate tax purposes. Thus, depending on the size of the depositor's overall estate, the proceeds in a savings account trust may generate federal and state death taxes. If, however, the beneficiary is the depositor's spouse, the account will pass tax free under the estate tax marital deduction. Under most state statutes, death taxes generated by the account will be a charge against the proceeds, reducing the amount the beneficiary receives. To prevent this reduction, the depositor may direct in a will that all death taxes, including any arising from nonprobate assets such as savings account trusts, shall be paid from the general assets of the estate. Whether it is advisable to make such a direction and what the impact will be on the beneficiaries of the general estate are questions one should address with an attorney or tax advisor in connection with the preparation of a will.

It must be noted that the terms "trust" and "trustee" in some respects are misnomers in this context. The opening of a savings account trust does not create a trust in the formal legal sense. No fiduciary relationship is established, no equitable rights are immediately conveyed to the beneficiary, and the depositor remains sole owner of the deposited funds until death. If any trust is created, it is only at the depositor's death when the account becomes payable to the beneficiary.

The use of the trust label in connection with savings accounts has caused confusion among the public, some lawyers, and judges. It is possible that depositors who open such accounts believe they have created "trusts" for their beneficiaries. This belief may be harmless, but after the depositor's death, courts may be required to interpret provisions printed on signature cards that confirm the trust designation. The result in numerous states is a line of sometimes inconsistent judicial decisions regarding the nature and operation of savings account trusts. These decisions do not provide clear instructions for the general public and for the bank officers, estate planners, and attorneys who attempt to advise the public on estate planning matters.

With this background, the influential Uniform Probate Code (UPC) replaced savings account trusts with "payable on death" (POD) accounts. When opening a POD account, the depositor specifies on the signature card the names of one or more beneficiaries to whom the proceeds in the account are to be paid at the depositor's death. There is no mention of "trust" or "trustee" on the documents. According to the UPC, POD accounts serve the same function as savings account trusts more directly, without the potential for confusion caused by the trust label. The UPC, therefore, seeks to discourage the creation of savings account trusts in the future. In states where these UPC provisions are enacted into state law, financial institutions will offer depositors forms for creating POD accounts rather than savings account trusts.

It is not uncommon for a depositor to name a minor as the beneficiary of a savings account trust. If, when the depositor dies, the child has attained majority, there will be no problem collecting the proceeds. If, however, the beneficiary is still a minor, problems may arise. The financial institution may be reluctant to release funds directly to a minor. State law may require that the account remain on deposit until the minor reaches majority, preventing ready access to the funds for many years except under court order in an emergency. State law may also prevent a parent from collecting the proceeds on behalf of the minor unless the father or mother is first appointed the minor's legal guardian. This requires a court order and imposes annual accounting obligations on the parent. The UPC allows the account to be paid to a legal custodian for the child under the Uniform

Transfers to Minors Act. A parent may serve as custodian and is required to pay the funds to the child upon attaining majority.

Older clients who wish to name minors such as grandchildren as beneficiaries of savings account trusts or POD accounts should be aware of the potential problem. These arrangements may not be suitable for sums of money, especially large ones, that the depositor believes should be withheld from the beneficiary for a period after attaining majority. In such cases, engaging an attorney to draft a formal trust tailored to the client's exact wishes may be preferable. If one decides to employ a savings account trust, then any trust agreement printed on the back of the bank's signature card must be scrutinized carefully. The purpose of the review is to ensure the fund will not be tied up at the financial institution under a successor trustee who is powerless to access the funds for years after the depositor's death. There should be a provision authorizing the bank to pay the funds to the minor's parent, custodian, or guardian without a court order.

As part of a comprehensive estate plan, savings account trusts remain in many jurisdictions a simple, inexpensive, and efficient estate planning device that older persons are able to access conveniently and without the services of an attorney. (See also ATTORNEYS; BANKING SERVICES FOR THE MATURE MARKET; ELDER LAW PRACTICE; ESTATE PLANNING; GUARDIANSHIP; INHERITANCE; TRUSTS; WILLS.)

#### References

American Law Institute. 1999. "Restatement of the Law, Trusts." Tentative Draft 2(26): 1–19. Philadelphia, PA: Author.

McCouch, Grayson M.P. 1993. "Will Substitutes under the Revised Uniform Probate Code." *Brooklyn Law Review* 58: 1123–94.

National Conference of Commissioners on Uniform State Laws. 1998. *Uniform Probate Code*. Sections 6-201–6-227. In *Uniform Laws Annotated*. Vol. 8, Pt. 2. St. Paul, MN: West Group, 433–48.

Roth, Jeffrey I. 1993. "Successor Trustees of Tentative Trusts: Trust Law Phantoms." *St. Louis University Law Journal* 38: 407–67.

*Jeffrey I. Roth*

**SAVINGS INVESTMENTS,** funds placed in investment instruments that involve virtually no risk of loss to principal or interest. The major investment alternatives for savings include accounts at banks, savings and loan associations, credit unions, money market funds, and U.S. savings bonds.

#### Objectives

Typical objectives for the use of these savings opportunities include the following:

*To Ensure Safety of the Monies Involved.* Federally regulated depository institutions provide insurance of accounts up to a maximum of $100,000. Institutions are required to display the FDIC (Federal Deposit Insurance Corporation) or other agency logo to inform depositors of coverage of accounts.

*To Provide Income.* Most savings accounts pay a fixed rate of interest that will vary among institutions, type of account, and amount of money involved. Some savings investments pay variable interest rates as described below.

*To Provide Liquidity.* Most savings alternatives allow immediate withdrawals. Most financial plans recommend that individuals retain some funds that are available on short notice to meet unexpected contingencies.

*To Provide Convenience.* The many branch office and automatic teller machines (ATMs) locations of financial institutions provide convenient access for most individuals.

*To Build Savings Balances.* Funds can be accumulated gradually (and earn interest income) to meet future objectives that require larger amounts of money.

### Types of Savings Investments

The most frequently used savings investments or alternatives (and the major advantages and disadvantages associated with each) are described below:

*Savings Accounts.* In the old days, savings accounts—or passbook accounts as they're sometimes known at banks, savings and loan association accounts, and share accounts at credit unions—were the most popular vehicle for short-term savings. Low minimum balances are usually required in these federally insured arrangements, and funds can be withdrawn easily. The principal disadvantage of this type of account is a relatively low rate of interest, which in the range of 1% to 2% often isn't even enough to keep pace with inflation.

*Money Market Deposit Accounts.* Money market deposit accounts offered at insured institutions provide a return that changes with the general interest rate in the economy. Although these accounts provide higher returns than savings accounts, they usually require a minimum balance and permit only a limited number of transactions (six transfers, three of which can be checks written on the account). If the account balance falls below the minimum required balance, or if the allowed number of transactions is exceeded, a penalty is levied. They are very liquid, and most institutions allow for easy access through checks, transfers, and even ATMs.

*Money Market Funds.* Money market funds are offered by brokerages and mutual fund families. The fund manager invests the savings deposited in money market funds in highly liquid, safe securities such as certificates of deposit, government securities, and commercial paper (i.e., short-term obligations issued by corporations). The returns from investing in money market funds, which vary with the asset value of the fund, are usually a little higher than money market deposit accounts. However, these funds are not federally insured, and there is no guarantee that the principal will be conserved, although fund managers go to great lengths to keep the net asset value of the fund (the price of each share of the fund) at $1 to ensure safety of principal.

*Certificates of Deposit* (CDs). CDs offered by federally insured financial institutions are debt instruments with a specific maturity, which can be anywhere from 3 months to 60 months (i.e., five years). Depending on the length to maturity, CDs may pay more than money markets. The principal disadvantage offsetting the higher returns on the investment is that the money is off-limits until the CD matures. CDs can be redeemed prior to maturity upon the payment of a penalty.

*U.S. Government Bills or Notes.* "Treasuries," as they are popularly called, are backed by the full faith and credit of the U.S. government. Treasury bills mature in less than a year; treasury notes mature between 2 and 10 years. They can be bought directly, commission-free, at the U.S. government's Web site (http://www.treasurydirect.gov/). They are exempt from state and local taxes. They are highly liquid and, held to maturity, return the specified interest and principal at maturity. Selling treasuries prior to maturity, however, may result in a loss of principal. Although returns may be better in money markets, CDs, or corporate bonds, treasuries are probably the safest instruments available.

*Inflation Indexed Bonds*. "I Bonds," as they are popularly called, are inflation-indexed savings bonds issued by the U.S. government. The amount an I Bond pays is adjusted semiannually so as to keep up with inflation and protect the purchasing power of your money. They are sold in manageable denominations ranging from $50 to $10,000 at most financial institutions. Like treasuries, they can also be bought directly from the U.S. Treasury. The earnings are exempt from state and local taxes and can be tax-free if used for postsecondary education expenses. Federal taxes on earnings can be deferred for up to 30 years. I Bonds must be held for a period of at least six months, and if redeemed before owning them for 5 years, they incur a penalty of three months' earnings.

*Municipal Bonds*. "Munis," as they are popularly known, are issued by state and local governments in order to build schools, highways, and other projects for the public good. Municipal bonds are most attractive to high-income investors looking for tax-friendly income. The earnings are exempt from federal taxes and might even be exempt from state and local taxes if the purchaser lives in the municipality that issued the bond. Munis are just a step down from U.S. securities in terms of safety. Interest from munis is relatively low, and unless tax implications suggest otherwise, better returns are obtained elsewhere. Purchase of munis usually involves the payment of a commission. If the muni is sold prior to maturity, there is the risk of loss in the original investment. (See also ANNUITIES; BANKING SERVICES FOR THE MATURE MARKET; FEDERAL AGENCY SECURITIES; FINANCIAL COUNSELING FOR MID- TO LATER LIFE; RISK TOLERANCE; SAVINGS ACCOUNT TRUSTS; U.S. PERSONAL SAVING RATE; U.S. SAVINGS BONDS.)

**References**

Burton, Maureen, Reynolds Nesiba, and Ray Lumbra. 2003. *Financial Markets and Institutions*. Cincinnati, OH: South-Western.

Cohn, R.A., W.G. Lewellen, R.C. Lease, and G.G. Schlarbaum. 1975. "Individual Investor Risk Aversion and Investment Portfolio Composition." *Journal of Finance* 30: 605–20.

Gitman, Lawrence J. and Michael D. Joehnk. 2002. *Personal Financial Planning*. 9th ed. Cincinnati, OH: South-Western.

Keown, Arthur J. 2001. *Personal Finance: Building and Protecting Your Wealth*. 2nd ed. Upper Saddle River, NJ: Prentice Hall.

Sciortino, J.J., J.H. Huston, and R.W. Spencer 1988. "Risk and Income Distribution." *Journal of Economic Psychology* 9: 399–408.

Snelbecker, G.E., M.J. Roszkowski, and N.E. Cutler. 1990. "Investors' Risk Tolerance and Return Aspirations, and Financial Advisors' Interpretations: A Conceptual Model and Exploratory Data." *Journal of Behavioural Economics* 19: 377–93.

Winger, B.J., and N.K. Mohan. 1988. "Investment Risk and Time Diversification." *Journal of Financial Planning* 1(1): 45–48.

*Ganas K. Rakes and Rajesh Narayanan*

**SENIOR DISCOUNTS,** direct price breaks for taking a specific action—buying at a certain time, a certain amount, or in a certain way—offered to older customers. Following World War II, discounts were promoted as a gesture of respect to those who had served their country. More discounts appeared after Medicare was enacted in 1964. In the 1960s and early 1970s, available data portrayed older adults as being a relatively small population group of predominantly low income or in poor health. Senior discount programs were seen as a way to relieve the burden of inflation on the older customer. The image of the senior consumer altered when the 1980 U.S. Census showed that many seniors did have discretionary funds. Sellers of nearly every product and service instituted discounts to help them spend it. In the 1990s, seniors as a group were seen to be better off financially, controlling a greater percentage of the nation's discretionary income (50%) and owning a large percentage of all financial assets (77%) (Spiller and Hamilton 1993). Discount practices that may have had their origins in cost relief measures for older adults now abound as marketing tools to access a growing and lucrative senior market. Marketers offer senior citizen discounts on a wide variety of products and services.

Discount programs for older consumers vary in application and structure. The minimum age for participation in most senior discount programs ranges from 50 to 65. Programs can be highly structured, often requiring the individual to acquire a membership, as in the discount programs offered through AARP. By negotiating as a large membership group, AARP and other organizations representing seniors' interests can influence providers of goods and services in a variety of industries to offer discounts for their members. With an AARP membership, for example, a senior has access to special group rates and discounts on travel, lodging, tours and entertainment, insurance, and prescription drug purchases. Catholic Golden Age (CGA) sponsors charitable work and helps older people meet their social, physical, economic, intellectual, and spiritual needs. They offer members various group insurance plans, discounts on eyeglasses, prescription drugs, and travel. SeniorNet, a nonprofit, educational organization that provides information and services to help older people become computer literate, offers teaching sites with introductory computer classes on various topics and discounts on computer hardware, software, and publications.

Some discount programs are sponsored by government agencies. Many states have developed statewide networks of community-based discount programs for persons 60 years of age or older. The primary goal is to extend the purchasing power of older consumers by enhancing existing discount programs. In Ohio, the state Commission of Aging sponsors the "Golden Buckeye Card" program whereby seniors receive discounts from cooperating merchants. The U.S. Administration on Aging and local Area Agencies on Aging can often direct seniors with low or limited incomes to special discounted services and programs. Beginning in the fall of 2001, Medicare beneficiaries were able to choose among Medicare-endorsed Rx (prescription) discount cards, offered by competing private drug discount card programs. Using these cards, older Americans on Medicare get discounts of 10% to 25% off retail prices on prescription drugs.

Other programs may involve special discounts on merchandise or services for seniors on certain days of the week, such as a 10% off "Senior Wednesday" from a retailer, or on specific types of merchandise, for example, discounts on pharmaceuticals, health aids, and optical products at certain discount or grocery stores.

With better health and increased discretionary income, seniors are being offered discounts on services ranging from dining and entertainment to banking and investing. Nearly 80% of banks now offer packages of senior services, many of which include services-fee free checking and financial planning (Spiller and Hamilton 1993). Amtrak advertises senior discounts of 15% or more. Many movie theater chains offer special senior rates.

Seniors who take advantage of discount programs can be divided into two categories—those who use them for "necessities" (groceries, prescription drugs, and restaurants) and those who take advantage of these programs for "luxuries" (entertainment and travel) (Spiller and Hamilton 1993). Recent research has indicated that from the viewpoint of the retailer blanket senior discounts are not particularly effective in attracting new consumers (Oates, Shufeldt, and Vaught 1996). Many feel, however, that the system of senior discounts will continue because older consumers now have a sense of entitlement to these special programs. Even relatively well-to-do consumers now expect to get a discount at the movies or when they travel. Others have criticized the senior discount system as "affirmative action for the wealthy" (Rueter 1997). (See also CONSUMER PROTECTION FOR OLDER ADULTS; HISTORY OF RETIREMENT; LEISURE; MARKETING TO MATURE ADULTS; TRANSPORTATION.)

### References

McKuen, Pamela D. 2001. "Stores Offer Discounts But Not Everybody Bites." *Chicago Tribune*, Prime Time Special Section, October 24.

Oates, Barbara, Lois Shufeldt, and Bobby Vaught. 1996. "A Psychographic Study of the Elderly and Retail Store Attributes." *Journal of Consumer Marketing* 13(6): 14–27.

Rueter, Ted. 1997. "Senior Citizen Discounts Are Affirmative Action for the Wealthy." *Christian Science Monitor*, September 2.

Spiller, Lisa D., and Richard A. Hamilton. 1993. "Senior Citizen Discount Programs: Which Senior to Target and Why." *Journal of Consumer Marketing* 10(1): 42–49.

*Jamie Losikoff-Kent*

**SENIORS HOUSING FINANCE,** the system for providing equity and debt capital to acquire, develop, or maintain seniors housing. As used here, *seniors housing* refers to multiunit residences that are intended and designed primarily for the use of older persons. Seniors housing includes a diverse range of facility types, such as independent living apartment properties that have no formal services but that are age restricted or age targeted; congregate care facilities, which offer hospitality services (such as housekeeping and meals); and assisted living facilities, which offer a host of personal care services (such as dispensing medication and assistance with bathing).

The market for service-oriented seniors housing rapidly expanded during the 1990s and in fact became overbuilt in most major markets. Nonetheless, there are indications that seniors housing has a strong future. The U.S. Census Bureau estimates that between the years 2000 and 2020, the number of age 75 and older will grow from 16.6 to 22.3 million (a 34% increase). While there is still some uncertainty about the relative demand for independent living apartments and various types of housing with supportive services, the seniors housing sector as a whole will probably benefit from this demographic pattern.

### Recent History of Seniors Housing Finance

Prior to the late 1980s, private financing came from a variety of sources, but most large loans were originated by banks, life insurance companies, and in particular, savings and loans and mutual savings banks ("thrifts"). Much seniors housing, particularly those that included supportive services, was associated with nonprofit housing sponsors, particularly those receiving federal assistance to develop housing. In the early 1980s, the savings and loan crisis led to a substantial decline in the share of lending conducted by thrifts; the share of total outstanding multifamily mortgage debt for thrifts fell from 44% to 16% between 1985 and 2000 (Schnare 2001). The share held by banks, government-sponsored enterprises (such as Fannie Mae), and state and local entities increased during that time.

The savings and loan crisis also led to deregulation and highly favorable tax incentives during the early 1980s. The effect was a speculative real estate boom that spilled over into seniors housing production. Highly favorable tax incentives enacted in 1981 fed a rapid inflation in real estate values. Many developers new to seniors housing sought to capitalize on powerful demographic trends by providing upscale "retirement housing." Eager lenders, including newly aggressive savings and loans, made debt financing readily available on very favorable terms—often with "bullet loans" that had to be refinanced in fewer than ten years.

The speculative bubble burst in the late 1980s, and real estate lenders suffered devastating losses from foreclosures. Seniors housing, a relatively small part of the total market, shared in the problem. Anticipated demand for retirement housing never materialized, vacancy rates soared, expensive projects failed, and high-leverage loans went into default. In reaction, virtually all sources of capital for seniors housing dried up for several years.

By the mid-1990s, inexperienced firms had left the seniors housing industry, and property values and financial structures had adjusted to harsh market realities. Rent revenues were increasing, and occupancy rates had increased to over 90% on average. Construction returned to high levels on the optimistic expectations of lenders and developers.

Nonetheless, despite increasing information and financial experience, the demand for seniors housing was overestimated in many sectors. By the late 1990s, it became clear that many markets had become overbuilt, and the industry again went into contraction. Occupancy rates again began to fall, and a 2002 survey by the National Investment Center indicated that the number of loan providers to the seniors housing market decreased by a third from the late 1990s. According to the American Seniors Housing Association (2002), the number of seniors housing units under construction fell by 18% in 2001, and another 26% in 2002, to reach the lowest level since data collection began in 1997. Much of the decline was in assisted living, but independent living seniors housing also showed a decline (though it continued to represent around half of all seniors housing construction). While there are probably several contributing factors for the decline in activity, one of the reasons many markets were overbuilt was the higher-than-expected turnover rate among residents (in assisted living, the average length of residency is approximately two years). Partly due to consolidation and more conservative lending activities, occupancy rates stabilized by 2002 but remain under 90% for most types of seniors housing (National Investment Center 2002).

### Underwriting Requirements

All forms of seniors housing have shared experiences with the major multifamily lending patterns of past decades, particularly those forms of seniors housing designed primarily for independent older persons. Seniors housing with services, however, has a number of unique characteristics that separate it from the rest of the multifamily industry.

Key among these are the need for professional staff to provide services, the need for sufficient common areas to deliver various services (particularly group meals), and the regulatory environment for those facilities that offer personal care. It is virtually impossible for a lender to force an unwilling or incompetent manager to control costs of labor and materials, to be known for friendly treatment of residents, to provide good meals, and to offer a variety of high-quality health care and social services. Taken together, such considerations increase the complexity of underwriting and add to the perception of risk from an investor's standpoint.

According to a recent survey by the National Investment Center, a typical loan for assisted living would have an average payment term of 13 years, an amortization of 25 years, and a current yield of around 9%. The maximum loan-to-value was around 79%, and the required debt service ratio was around 1.3 to 1 (National Investment Center 1999). However, loan characteristics are obviously subject to underlying market conditions and can change rapidly from one year to the next.

### Securitization

One of the most important developments for the seniors housing industry was the growth of a strong secondary market in multifamily mortgage-backed securities in the aftermath of the thrift crisis of the late 1980s. As a result, new sources of mortgage financing were opened for multifamily housing. Between 1985 and 2000, the share of multifamily mortgage debt outstanding held by government-sponsored enterprises, which provide a secondary market for mortgages, rose from 5% to 17% (Schnare 2001). Private conduits also play a major role in securitization.

In essence, securitization converts a group of mortgage loans into securities tailored to the financial risk and income preferences of various investors. The process gives the seniors housing sponsor access to the immense resources of the international capital markets and gives investors a relatively good investment tailored to their risk and income preferences.

Mortgage-backed securities transactions take many forms, but it can be helpful, if overly simplified, to think of the securitization of seniors housing loans as a four-step process (Anthony 1994). First, a lender originates a mortgage loan so that a borrower can acquire or refinance a seniors housing facility. This creates a financial asset that will generate a specified series of payments of principal and interest, secured by the seniors housing property.

Second, that mortgage loan, either alone or in a pool of similar loans, is used to back a "pass-through" security. The borrowers' periodic payments on mortgage loans backing the security will be passed through periodically to holders of the security.

Third, one or more nationally recognized rating agencies evaluate the creditworthiness of the pass-through security. On the basis of that evaluation, the pass-through security is divided into several classes, or "tranches," with the holders of different classes having different rights to the stream of mortgage payments into the pool—some classes offer an investor higher risks and potential returns than other classes. The size and rating of each class is determined by the rating agency's analysis. The total face value of the pass-through securities is often smaller than the aggregate value of the mortgages in the pool. This "overcollateralization" or creation of residual collateral serves to increase the creditworthiness of the securities.

Fourth, the pass-through securities are sold, generally to institutional investors, who often are the only purchasers able to handle the complexity of mortgage-backed securities. Different classes of the security are marketed to different investors on the basis of the investor's risk and return preferences.

Despite its advantages, securitization also tends to increase pressures for standardization of product and resistance to lending for new construction, which may create special problems for seniors housing finance.

### Government Impact on Seniors Housing Finance

At the federal level, there are several major programs to promote affordable seniors housing finance. For instance, the Section 232 mortgage insurance program was amended in 1994 to permit insurance of assisted living facilities. Formerly, this program was limited to nursing homes, intermediate care facilities, and board and care homes. Through this program, the Department of Housing and Urban Development (HUD) insures loans up to 85% of the value of new construction and up to 90% in the case of nonprofit developers. As part of program requirements, assisted living facilities must provide separate dwelling units for residents; this helps to promote the residential character of the setting.

In addition, the Section 202 Supportive Housing for the Elderly program is designed specifically to promote low-income seniors rental housing. Originally, the Section 202 program provided a development subsidy to nonprofit housing providers through a below-market rate direct mortgage, but in the early 1990s, Congress amended the program to become a capital grant. The program was again amended in 2000 to allow for-profit limited partners when the property would include non–Section 202 mixed-use units. Though the housing is largely geared toward the independent older person, many facilities offer a variety of architectural features and services to promote aging in place. Further, congressional acts of 1990 and 1992 authorized service coordinators, and by 1999, 37% of Section 202 facilities for older persons reported having a service coordinator on staff (Heumann, Winter-Nelson, and Anderson 2001). Service coordinators arrange for supportive services and monitor the quality and quantity of services to fit the needs of residents. Congress has also recently appropriated funds to convert a small number of Section 202 facilities to assisted living.

Another major development subsidy has been the Low-Income Housing Tax Credit. Though not a debt instrument, the tax credit may be "sold" to an investor in order to generate equity. This, in turn, makes the remaining development costs easier to finance. Between 1987 and 1998, the Low-Income Tax Credit was used in nearly 15,000 multifamily rental properties, of which nearly a quarter were intended primarily for older persons. Approximately 2% of properties were licensed, registered, or certified as assisted living or residential care facilities (Kochera 2002).

Other sources of financing for low- and moderate-income seniors housing may be generated through federal block grants to states and communities (such as the HOME and Community Development Block Grant program). In addition, many states and local governments have housing trust funds and other mechanisms to promote the development of affordable housing, including seniors housing.

### Emerging Concerns

Seniors housing finance can be expected to undergo continued rapid change. Whatever direction those changes take, the most difficult challenges for seniors housing are likely to be:

1. To provide the quality of performance data that future lenders and investors are likely to demand;
2. To accurately anticipate the needs of an aging population, whose health and supportive services needs may differ from previous generations;
3. To attract adequate financing for seniors housing that is affordable to low-income frail older persons;
4. To attract and retain qualified staff for supportive services;
5. To anticipate a changing regulatory environment for services-oriented housing; and
6. To respond to consumer preferences for quality of care in a residential setting.

(See also ASSISTED LIVING; COMMUNITY-BASED CARE; CONTINUING CARE RETIREMENT COMMUNITIES [CCRCs]; FEDERAL AGENCY SECURITIES; HOME CARE SERVICES FOR OLDER ADULTS; HUD-ASSISTED RENTAL HOUSING; MORTGAGE INSTRUMENTS; NURSING HOMES.)

### References

American Seniors Housing Association. 2002. *2002 Seniors Housing Construction Report.* Washington, DC: Author.

Anthony, Raymond. 1994. *Financing Techniques for Skilled Nursing Facilities, Assisted Living Facilities and Congregate Care Retirement Residences.* Washington, DC: National Investment Conference.

Colton, Kent, and Kate Collignon. 2001. *Multifamily Rental Housing in the 21st Century.* Boston, MA: Joint Center for Housing Studies.

Heumann, Leonard, Karen Winter-Nelson, and James Anderson. 2001. *The 1999 National Survey of Section 202 Elderly Housing.* Washington, DC: AARP.

Kochera, Andrew. 2002. *Serving the Affordable Housing Needs of Older Low-Income Renters: A Survey of Low-Income Housing Tax Credit Properties.* Washington, DC: AARP.

National Investment Center. 2002. *Key Financial Indicators Quarter Ending 09.30.02.* Annapolis, MD: Author (formerly National Investment Conference).

National Investment Center. Various years. *Lender and Investor Survey Results.* Annapolis, MD: Author (formerly National Investment Conference).

Population Projections Program. 2001. *Population Projections of the United States by Age, Sex, Race, Hispanic Origin, and Nativity: 1999 to 2100.* Washington, DC: U.S. Census Bureau.

Schnare, Anne. 2001. *The Impact of Changes in Multifamily Housing Finance on Older Urban Areas.* Washington, DC: The Brookings Institution.

Wright, Bernadette. 2001. *Assisted Living in the United States.* Washington, DC: AARP Public Policy Institute.

*W. Donald Campbell*
*Updated by Andrew S. Kochera*

**SNOWBIRD CHECKLIST AND TRANSBORDER ISSUES,** medical and legal preparedness for seniors who migrate seasonally. Every winter, thousands of older Canadians and Americans migrate to the warmth of the southern United States. On the face of it, such changes in location might not seem to present problems. However, because of different laws in different countries and even in different states within the United States or provinces in Canada, medical and legal issues may arise in the event of an emergency. Legal documents, such as advanced medical directives and unlimited powers of attorney, that are valid in one state or province may not be recognized in another state, province, or country. In some cases, depending upon the length of stay away from "home," and in the event of an unexpected death, there may be estate issues involved, not to mention the problems that may be encountered in returning the deceased's body across provincial, state, or national borders.

In normal situations, medical coverage can become a major issue. If an individual is a member of a health maintenance organization (HMO), it may not recognize costs incurred for medical services rendered to the individual by non-HMO doctors or by physicians other than his or her primary care physician when he or she is on an extended stay at another location. Some insurance companies may provide limited benefits, or no benefits, for emergency medical transportation to return an ailing person from a vacation locale back to his or her home. Similarly, medical insurance coverage is an issue for snowbirds leaving Canada for an extended stay outside of the country.

Other matters need to be taken into consideration when individuals plan to spend time away from home. Such issues as protection of their home while they are away, payment of bills, and reporting may have to be considered. If extensive travel is contemplated, either intermittently or for extended stays, all of these issues should be considered. Ownership of property in another state, province, or country can have tax ramifications and estate planning ramifications.

When you have snowbird issues and are working with a professional advisor, like a certified public accountant, chartered accountant, or an attorney, it is important to make sure that they are considering cross-border issues. Here are some items to consider when you are intending to spend a significant period of time away from your primary residence.

## Snowbird Checklist

1. Review and list sources of income, ensuring that funds will be deposited directly into your bank accounts or that alternative arrangements are made in advance for the funds.
2. Arrange to have bank statements, investment information, and other financial statements forwarded to the snowbird address or to a responsible third party.
3. Review investments and record maturity dates of interest-bearing investments so that renewal arrangements can be made.
4. Make sure your snowbird address and telephone number are given to one's professional advisors, family members, and neighbors.
5. Preview in advance what bills have to be paid during the time away and make sure appropriate arrangements have been made for handling them.
6. Determine cash needs of stay at snowbird address and ensure bank account balances, credit card lines, traveler's cheques, and other necessary funds are available to pay for snowbird disbursements.
7. Take your private telephone directory list, including toll-free and reduced direct telephone company long-distance connection numbers.

8. Cancel newspapers and make arrangements for handling and/or forwarding mail.
9. Make sure custom duties, import restrictions, and related exemptions are understood.
10. Take birth certificates—and as required, passports—and driver's licenses.
11. Make sure an extended traveler's medical plan, if required, is purchased.
12. Wills should be updated and a copy made accessible to responsible third parties.
13. Retain emergency contacts and health insurance card while out of the country.
14. Photocopy important papers and place a copy with the will and another copy to take along.
15. Have an "emergency medical kit," including any personal medications and prescription medications to cover the length of stay out of the country.
16. Review security precautions for the home and consider storing valuables off site. Arrange for periodic visits by a responsible third party to the residence, who should pick up mail and newspapers that could not be stopped or were delivered in error. Arrange for snow removal.
17. If absent from one's primary residence past December 31, ensure that all tax planning for the calendar year has been arranged and is in place prior to departure.

(See also CONDOMINIUMS; LEISURE; RETIREMENT MIGRATION; VACATION HOMES AND RECREATIONAL PROPERTY.)

**Organizations**

Canadian Association of Retired Persons
Canadian Snowbird Association

**References**

McHugh, Kevin E., and Robert C. Mings. 1996. "The Circle of Migration: Attachment to Place in Aging." *Annals of the Association of American Geographers* 85(3): 530–50.

Mings, Robert C., and Kevin E. McHugh. 1995. "Wintering in the American Sunbelt: Linking Place and Behavior." *Journal of Tourism Studies* 6(2).

Rous, Melba M., et al., eds. 2000. *Anyone Can Travel: The Essential Guide for Seniors, People with Disabilities, Health Problems, and All Travelers*. Victoria, BC: Trafford Publishing.

Sullivan, Donald L. 1994. A *Senior's Guide to Health Travel*. Franklin Lakes, NJ: Carver Press.

*Karen Duggan*

**SOCIAL ASSISTANCE.** See Medicaid; Nutrition Programs; Supplemental Security Income (SSI).

**SOCIAL SECURITY PRIVATIZATION,** the whole or partial replacement of the Social Security system by alternative accounts and/or investments. The debate over "privatizing" Social Security, in one form or another, has been raging for at least 30 years, since Martin Feldstein's theories on the effects of Social Security on the national savings rate first began to garner attention. A number of versions of the privatization case have been made over the last several years, all based on the same general proposition: Social Security should be replaced in whole or in part by a system of individual accounts managed by each individual and invested in equities, usually assumed to be stocks, and possibly long-term bonds.

Arguments for privatization can be generally divided into two categories. The first category emphasizes the positive benefits flowing from a system of private accounts that would take all or part of the money now paid into Social Security in payroll taxes and allow individuals to invest that money in the stock market or other equities or securities. The second category focuses on the problems with the current Social Security system, which, in the view of privatization advocates, necessitate a drastic change in the way Americans must secure their retirements.

Proposals to substitute private savings plans for Social Security did not begin to gain much popular attention or support until the early 1980s, during the well-publicized series of financing crises in the Social Security system that prompted congressional action in 1983 to restore short-term financial viability and to reduce long-term spending on Social Security by raising the retirement age. However, it was the long bull market that began sometime in 1982 that gave more substantial support to the idea that individuals could better secure their retirement income by managing individual investment of their payroll tax amounts in the stock market than they could by relying on the promises of the federal government to pay their Social Security benefits in the future.

The recent long downturn in the stock market that began in the year 2000 with the collapse of the dot.com bubble, and has continued for several years in the wake of Wall Street and financial scandals of various proportions, has dampened some of the enthusiasm of both the public and some policymakers for the privatization option. Nonetheless, many in Congress and in the White House remain convinced of the weakness of Social Security and continue to advocate privatization.

### The Arguments for Privatization

The major substantive arguments in support of privatization can generally be summarized as follows. First, supporters argue that an individual account system would provide a vastly improved rate of return from investment in equities, or even from straight interest compounding, for all or almost all participants, compared with the benefits they would receive from Social Security. Second, they argue that individual choice is in itself a goal—each individual would be able to take control of his or her own retirement planning and tailor savings and investment plans to individual needs and visions of retirement, which would in itself promote self-reliance, individual responsibility, and involvement in the economy and money management. Each of these arguments, however, is subject to strong critiques.

### Rate of Return

The rate of return argument is usually the most compelling one for the average worker—at least during the long stock market upturn, it seemed obvious that an astute investor could do better investing his payroll tax money than he could expect in Social Security benefits in retirement. However, the same risks of loss and failure of private equity that overwhelmed private resources in 1929 and the Great Depression years that followed will continue to apply to a private account system. The crash, and sustained lack of recovery, in the market that began in 2000 and continued at least well into 2003, in which at least 30% of the market's peak value was lost, has greatly undermined the appeal of rate of return arguments.

Moreover, while the stock market in aggregate provides positive long-term growth under most scenarios, the *real* rate of return (that is, increase in stock prices minus increase in consumer prices) is not as easy to predict. In addition, while the stock market can affect the distribution of wealth between winners and losers, it does not, over the long run, itself create real economic wealth. In general the market can be expected to keep pace with economic growth generally, just as indexed Social Security benefits do, keeping pace with wage increases before retirement and price increases after retirement Thus, the results of investing in private accounts instead of paying taxes into Social Security are likely to be some differences in the distribution of wealth between winners and losers—but there is no reason to expect a higher level of income for *everyone* when compared with payments under Social Security.

This is particularly true when two more technical issues raised by the prospect of privatization are considered—the cost of a transition from the current system to a privatized system and the ongoing administrative costs of a personal account system. The transition to a private account system involves moving from a pay-as-you-go system in which current taxes pay current benefits to in effect an advance funded system in which each individual is responsible for saving enough to finance his or her own retirement. The problem is that the benefits in current pay status would still have to be paid—thus, the working generation, at whatever point privatization were to be enacted, would be required to pay for the current benefits of the retired generations while also advance funding its own retirement.

The other specific cost hurdle, and one that casts considerable doubt on the "rate of return" argument made by privatization advocates, is the seemingly trivial issue of administrative costs of maintaining and investing private accounts. Whatever the shortcomings of a large government bureaucracy, the costs of administering the Social Security system are extremely low—about one-half of 1% of the total outlay in benefits each year, a figure that covers salaries of Social Security Administration employees, maintenance of hundreds of district offices all over the country, computers, and so on—in other words, all the costs of providing the structure for calculation and payment of benefits.

In contrast, the administrative costs of personal accounts could amount to as much as 10% to 25% of the amounts deposited, primarily in fees paid to investment advisors, stock brokers, and various types of investment and transaction fees. The experiences of the Chilean and other government pension programs that have gone private confirm that the costs of operating private accounts can seriously damage the return on individual investments.

### Individual Investment Choice

The involvement and responsibility of individuals in managing their own retirement in an individual account system are presented as a signal advantage in itself of a private account system. However, such responsibility would clearly be at best a mixed blessing, based on the enormous losses experienced over the last three years by most Americans invested in the stock market through their 401(k) plans. In fact, one prominent economist, Robert Shiller of Yale, writing just before the market collapsed, characterized the previous several years of increases in the stock market this way:

> The market level does not, as so many imagine, represent the consensus judgment of experts who have carefully weighed the long-term evidence. The market is high because of the combined effect of indifferent thinking by millions of people, very few of whom feel the need to perform careful research on the long-term investment value of the aggregate stock market, and who are motivated

substantially by their own emotions, random attentions, and perceptions of conventional wisdom. (Shiller 2000)

A system of private accounts was essentially in place as what passed for a national retirement system before the enactment of Social Security; while most women were not in the paid workforce, and most men worked long past age 65, those who did retire had to rely on private resources, at least once the generation entitled to Civil War veterans' benefits had died out. There seems to be little or no evidence that conditions today, or the proposed private account system itself, are so different from those of the last 200 years that the purely private voluntary savings and rudimentary pension plans that failed the vast majority of working Americans so profoundly during the 1930s would somehow prove adequate for current and future generations of retirees.

### The Privatizers' Arguments against Social Security

The critics' analyses of the inadequacies of the social insurance system focus both on internal design flaws that they feel make the system inadequate to meet the retirement needs of the twenty-first century and on the apparent effects of the program on the economy and society as a whole. The most frequently cited criticisms of the current system fall into two general categories: first, the coming demographic "disaster" of the baby boom generation's retirement—complaints involving comparisons of fewer workers to more retirees, and the looming burden of providing income and medical care for larger numbers of older retirees who can be expected to live longer; and second, "rate of return" issues (that is, comparison of taxes paid to benefits paid out to each individual). The demographic complaint generally comes down to a concern about how to pay for the coming baby boom retirement wave, while the rate of return complaint is essentially concerned with "equity versus adequacy," a long-standing debate about the redistributive Social Security benefit structure.

### Baby Boom Retirement Disaster

For many who advocate private accounts as a viable substitute for Social Security, the system's problems largely originate with the aging of the baby boom generation—the demographic basketball in the python. The generation born roughly from 1946 through 1960 in the industrialized world greatly outnumbers the generations born in the 1920s and 1930s and during the war years of the 1940s; as a result, the ratio of workers supporting nonworking older adults will drop from the three workers for each retiree during the period from about 1960 to 2010 to two workers, or fewer, for each retiree, by 2030.

Since, in a pay-as-you-go system, payroll taxes pay for current consumption of goods and services by the beneficiary population, those taxes would probably have to increase to provide for a larger and longer-lived generation, unless productivity so greatly increased average wages that equivalent additional revenue would be raised by the same tax rate. While the payroll tax is regressive, higher-wage workers nonetheless pay higher levels of FICA (Federal Insurance Contribution Act) taxes—and if additional revenue has to be raised within the payroll tax structure, likely measures would include increasing the taxable wage base without a concomitant increase in benefits or using some portion of general tax revenue raised by the progressive income tax, which of course imposes a higher burden on high-income than on low-income taxpayers.

There seems to be no real argument that the nation as a whole will have the capacity to produce sufficient goods and services to satisfy at least the basic needs of all its working and nonworking members throughout their lives. Thus, the adequate care of older baby boomers in the aggregate should be perfectly possible; the question is how the benefits, that is, the share of consumable goods and services, will be *distributed among* older Americans. Financing the retirement of the baby boom is clearly a question of political choices, not of demographics. The solutions to almost all of the problems potentially arising from an increasing aging population, in fact, are political and philosophical, since the demographics are simply phenomena with which our political and social systems must cope. The increase in payroll tax rates that may be necessary to sustain the current Social Security system past 2030, essentially until the baby boom generation passes from the scene, seems inherently distasteful to many critics, even apart from any ancillary economic effects such increased taxes might create.

Moreover, it is unclear exactly what a private account system in place of Social Security would do to solve the demographic issue. If the issue is presented as a question of too many retirees for too few workers, eliminating the burden-sharing system of social insurance and placing responsibility for retirement savings on each individual would change the distribution of the burden but not its overall size. Privatization of Social Security cannot be presented as a solution to the issue of too many retirees; that problem can only be addressed directly by encouraging the baby boom generation to work longer, perhaps through elimination or severe reductions of benefits at age 68 or 70.

In summary, demography may not be destiny, but fertility and longevity patterns will clearly affect retirement patterns and how twenty-first century societies will support their older adults. However, upon closer examination, the disasters seen by advocates of privatization seem to be less demographic and more political in nature. In both historic and economic terms, the working generation must *always* bear (and, as a matter of historical fact, has always borne) the burden of providing goods and services to satisfy the claims (expressed either as private savings or public entitlements) of the nonworking, both the older and the young. Private account proposals (as well as less extreme proposals to invest part of the Social Security trust funds in stock market equities) in many ways hold out a false hope that in some way the burdens of aging can be paid for in advance and shifted away from the generation who will be working at the time the baby boom retires.

### Rate of Return

For many critics, the most intractable problem inherent in the design of Social Security, and the one for which establishment of private accounts is generally offered as a direct solution, is the "rate of return" issue, discussed above in the context of the positive arguments made for privatization. The rate of return calculation depends a great deal on the economic and cost assumptions used—the rate of inflation over the worker's lifetime, the value attached to cost of living increases in benefits after retirement, the value of survivors, disability, and dependents benefits that might or might not be paid, the steadiness of the worker's earnings history, and so on. As a result, different analysts produce different estimates of the actual cost-benefit ratio for individual Social Security beneficiaries and workers covered by the system. However, it is unclear why the debate has centered primarily on the comparison between taxes paid and benefits received.

Social Security's benefit and financing structure has frequently been compared to that of a defined benefit employer pension with required employee contributions. The payroll taxes paid by each worker and his or her employer are usually thought of as being paid in exchange for the lifetime annuity due the worker beginning at age 65 (later for those retiring in 2000 and later). While the Social Security program also provides for survivor benefits in the event of the worker's death and for disability insurance coverage until the worker reaches retirement age, most workers, as well as the commentators criticizing the system's rate of return, generally assess the system's value to them as a retirement system.

However, payroll taxes are merely a method of financing the system, not the basis for benefits earned and paid out by Social Security. Benefit calculations are made based on earnings recorded in the Social Security system, not on the amount of taxes paid. In fact, benefits cannot be reduced in the event of a failure to pay such taxes by the employer who is responsible for withholding FICA taxes from workers' paychecks. Thus, Social Security could be financed through income tax revenues, like other government expenditures, without any impact on the earnings-based benefit structure.

The tax-benefit comparison routinely and unquestioningly raised as a disadvantage of Social Security may be properly applied to a private annuity or insurance policy, which the individual purchases and from which the individual expects to receive income in retirement. It is almost completely irrelevant in a direct transfer program under which the worker will receive benefits based on his or her earnings record, regardless of the amount of taxes actually paid into the system.

### Conclusion

In summary, it appears that the real differences between publicly financed retirement programs and privately controlled investment funds preserved for retirement are the ancillary consequences of the status of the latter as private equity. Equity can be individually controlled, used as a source of capital accumulation for the economy generally, inherited by the next generation if not wholly consumed in retirement, and perhaps most important, distributed among members of the working and nonworking population through the mechanics of the market and the good or bad fortune of each individual.

Social Security, on the other hand, as a public entitlement program, is controlled by the public as a whole through elected representatives, directly recycles tax revenues collected by the federal government out to beneficiaries largely for immediate spending, provides no opportunity for inheritance by heirs, and most important, redistributes income according to public policy decisions. The major complaints about Social Security from those who would make the public's retirement rights private center on the ways in which Social Security is most unlike private equity, the failure of which to prevent widespread old-age poverty in the face of economic depression in the 1930s was the point of establishing the program in the first place. (See also AGING AMERICA; FINANCIAL SECURITY IN RETIREMENT; INDIVIDUAL RETIREMENT ACCOUNT [IRAs]; STATE AND AREA AGENCIES ON AGING; WEALTH SPAN.)

#### Organizations

Institute for America's Future, Social Security Information Project

**References**

Arnold, R. Douglas, et al. 1998. *Framing the Social Security Debate: Values, Politics, and Economics*. Washington, DC: National Academy of Social Insurance.

Dilley, Patricia E. 2000. "Taking Public Rights Private: The Rhetoric and Reality of Social Security Privatization." *Boston College Law Review* 41: 975–1058.

Medill, Colleen. 2001. "Stock Market Volatility and 401(k) Plans." *University of Michigan Journal of Law Reform* 34: 469–545.

Shiller, Robert. 2000. *Irrational Exuberance*. Princeton, NJ: Princeton University Press.

Solomon, Lewis D., and Geoffrey A. Barrow. 1995. "National Issues: Privatization of Social Security: A Legal and Policy Analysis." *Kansas Journal of Law Policy* 5: 23.

Stein, Norman P., and Patricia E. Dilley. 2001. "Leverage, Linkage and Leakage: Problems with the Private Pension System and How They Should Inform the Social Security Reform Debate." *Washington and Lee Law Review* 58(4): 1369.

*Patricia E. Dilley*

**SOCIAL SECURITY PROGRAM OF THE UNITED STATES,** the social insurance program officially designated as Old-Age, Survivors, and Disability Insurance (OASDI). The program covers most workers in paid employment and provides monthly cash benefits to retirees and their dependents, to disabled workers and their dependents, and to surviving dependents of deceased workers and retirees. Internationally, Social Security has a broader meaning, including pensions, medical care benefits, unemployment insurance, workers' compensation, and family allowances. Such programs can be of a social insurance nature or of a public assistance or minimum-benefit nature. Sometimes the Medicare program is seen as part of Social Security because both OASDI and Medicare have the Social Security Act as their legislative base. Also, part of Medicare (the Hospital Insurance portion) is financed by the same payroll tax as is OASDI.

The Social Security program significantly affects the lives of a majority of Americans. About 46 million persons received monthly benefits under the program in December 2001, and about 153 million persons paid contributions (or taxes) in 2001. Millions of others are also affected by the program because they are potential beneficiaries in the event of the retirement, death, or disability of covered workers.

The financial impact of the program can be seen from the fact that total benefit disbursement in 2001 amounted to \$432 billion, while total contribution income (including \$13 billion from the income taxation of benefits) was \$602 billion. The administrative expenses involved in collecting the contributions, maintaining the earnings records, and paying the benefits were \$3.7 billion, or 0.6% of the contribution income. The assets of the trust funds of the OASDI system amounted to \$1.21 trillion at the end of 2002 and earned interest income of \$73 billion that year. In December 2000, the average monthly benefit payable to retired workers was \$830, while that for disabled workers was \$786. The maximum benefit payable to a worker who retired at age 65 in 2000 (and who never received disability benefits) was \$1,660; some who worked beyond age 65 in the past received larger amounts. The average benefit in December 2000 for widows aged 60 or over at the time of initial claim was \$810, while the average benefit for a widowed mother and two children was \$1,680.

OASDI has several basic principles: (1) benefits are based on presumptive need, (2) benefits provide a floor of protection, (3) benefits are related to earnings, (4) a balance between social adequacy and individual equity is present, and (5) the financing is on a self-supporting contributory basis.

### Benefits Based on Presumptive Need

Certain categories of social risk are established by the law, and benefits are paid accordingly. For example, old-age benefits are not payable automatically upon attainment of a given "normal" retirement age, such as 62 or 65, but only upon actual retirement (although they are payable at age 65 and older, regardless of retirement). Likewise, benefits for surviving widows are not payable for their lifetime but only while they have eligible children present or are aged 60 or over (or aged 50 or over and disabled) and only so long as they are not remarried (except that remarriage after age 60 is not disqualifying) and are not employed with earnings above those permitted under the earnings test.

The retirement requirement is frequently misunderstood as being a means or needs test (i.e., a test of the individual's situation to make certain that he or she needs the income to meet subsistence-level economic requirements). From that viewpoint, some critics believe that the earnings test is unfair. This procedure, however, is essential if there is to be a system paying retirement benefits and not a charity program based on individual needs. Furthermore, the elimination of the earnings test would be costly (about $15 billion annually at the present time) because of higher payments coming due longer-working beneficiaries later on.

### Floor-of-Protection Concept

It is generally agreed that OASDI benefits should provide only a minimum floor of protection against various risks. However, many opinions exist on how far apart the floor and the ceiling should be. Some believe that the floor should be very low, or even that there should be no OASDI program at all. Still others believe that the floor should be high enough to provide a comfortable standard of living by itself, disregarding any economic security that individual or group methods might provide. A middle group believes that OASDI benefits should, along with other income and assets, be sufficient to yield a satisfactory minimum standard of living for the majority of individuals. Then, any residual needy population should be aided by supplementary public assistance.

### Earnings-Related Benefits

As a consequence of the floor-of-protection concept, it seems desirable from a social standpoint that, compared with contributions, benefits should be relatively larger for those with low earnings than for those with high earnings. The benefit formula under the OASDI system has always been heavily weighted accordingly. A higher benefit rate applies to lower portions of earnings than to higher portions. Higher-income groups do receive larger benefits, but there is weighting in favor of low-income groups.

### Individual Equity and Social Adequacy

Whenever a social insurance system involves contributions from potential beneficiaries, the question of individual equity versus social adequacy arises. Individual equity means the contributors receive benefit protection directly related to the amount of their contributions. Social adequacy means the benefits will provide, for all contributors, a certain standard of living. The two concepts are usually in direct conflict, and social insurance systems tend to have a benefit basis falling somewhere between complete individual equity and complete social adequacy. The tendency is generally more toward social adequacy than individual equity, and this is the case with the OASDI system. If individual equity prevailed when a system started, the benefits paid would be relatively small for many years, because they would be related solely to contributions paid, or to services rendered, after the effective date. Thus, many years would elapse before the system would meet the purposes for which it was established.

### Self-Supporting Contributory Financing

The principle of self-supporting contributory financing means that no appropriations from general revenues will be needed to pay the benefits. Available for self-supporting financing under OASDI are the contributions (taxes) from workers and employers, a portion of the income taxes on benefits, and the interest earned on the trust funds that have resulted from the accumulated excess of income over outgo of the system (which, by law, must be invested only in U.S. government securities). Such interest does not represent "contributions" or "financial support" from either the Treasury or the general taxpayer, because the interest on this type of investments must be paid, regardless of whether they are held by the trust funds or by private investors.

The employer and the employee share the cost of OASDI equally. Legislation in 1983 provided that the self-employed should pay the combined employer-employee rate (but with an allowance for one-half of the tax as a business expense for income tax purposes, just as employers receive).

The principle of self-supporting contributory financing was breached in 1983 through the introduction of indirect general revenue financing in two respects. First, up to 50% of OASDI benefits received were subjected to income tax for persons with high incomes, and the proceeds are put in the OASDI trust funds. Second, the 1984 tax rate was increased for employers, but not for employees, and the OASDI trust funds received from general revenues what would have resulted if the employee rate had been increased.

### Coverage Provisions

The majority of employed persons are covered under the OASDI program (or could be covered by election). The major exceptions are federal government employees under the Civil Service Retirement System (who were employed before 1984), low-income self-employed persons, and farm and domestic workers with irregular employment. Railroad workers have a separate system (the Railroad Retirement Act) but are, in essence, covered under OASDI because of close coordination.

*Nonfarm Self-Employed.* All nonfarm, self-employed persons are covered—both nonprofessionals, such as store owners, and professionals, such as lawyers, physicians, and dentists, provided their net annual earnings are at least $400. Farm operators are covered on the same general basis as other self-employed persons, but with a special simplified reporting option based on gross income, for those with low net income. Ministers are covered on a compulsory basis, unless they object for conscience or religious reasons, by public insurance that provides death, disability, or retirement benefits.

*Employees of Nonfarm Private Employers.* All employees in private industry and commerce are compulsorily covered, with no minimum restrictions on amount of earnings or length of employment. Coverage for employees of certain nonprofit organizations such as churches, private hospitals, and private schools is compulsory; before 1984 it was optional on the part of the organization.

*Employees of State and Local Government.* As a result of legislation in 1990, all employees of state and local governments who do not have a retirement system are compulsorily covered. Formerly this was on a voluntary elective group basis. Employees of state and local governments who are covered by a retirement system can be covered at the option of the state and the employing unit. About 80% of all state and local government employees are covered under these procedures.

*Employees of Federal Government.* Most federal civilian employees not under an existing retirement system who were hired before 1984, all civilian employees hired after 1983, all members of the uniformed services, and all employees hired before 1984 who were under the Civil Service Retirement System but who shifted to the new supplementary retirement system established for new hires after 1983 are covered on a regular contributory basis.

*Other Employees.* Farm employment is covered if yearly cash wages from an employer amount to at least $150, or if the employer has a total payroll of $2,500 or more in the year. Domestic workers are covered if cash wages are $1,300 or more in a year in 2000 from a single employer. (The $1,300 figure is indexed to changes in the general wage level after 2002.) Tips of $20 or more per month received by employees are included as wages and are reported through the employer. However, restaurant owners do not pay the employer tax on tips.

*Employment Abroad.* The preceding discussion relates to employment in the United States (including possessions) and on U.S. vessels and airplanes and applies to U.S. citizens and alien residents working abroad for U.S. employers. Totalization agreements have been reached with several countries so that

1. U.S. citizens and residents temporarily employed there by a U.S. company or affiliate are not subject to the Social Security taxes of the other country (and vice versa); and
2. Covered employment in one country can be used to meet the eligibility requirements of the other country's program.

*OASDI Insured Status Conditions.* There are three kinds of insured status: fully, currently, and disability. Fully insured status provides eligibility for all types of old-age and survivor benefits. Currently insured status, in the absence of fully insured status, gives eligibility for certain young survivor benefits. Disability insured status is a partial requirement for the disability "freeze" and for disability monthly benefits. Insured status is defined in terms of quarters of coverage (QCs). Since 1978, a QC is given for a certain amount of annual earnings ($870 in 2002), with a maximum of four QCs annually; the required amount is changed each year according to national wage increases. Fully insured status is achieved if the individual has at least as many QCs (acquired at any time) as the number of years elapsed after 1950 (or at age 21, if later) and before age 62. Thus, the maximum requirement is 40 QCs.

Currently insured status is achieved by having six QCs in the 13-quarter period ending with the quarter of death, attainment of age 62, or actual retirement if after age 62. Disability insured status is generally achieved by having 20 QCs in the 40-quarter period ending with the quarter of disablement, with a lower requirement for persons becoming disabled before age 30. Periods of qualifying total disability for individuals who have both fully insured and disability insured status are excluded in measuring the elapsed period at any later time for any of the insured status categories (the "disability freeze" provision).

### OASDI Beneficiary Categories

*Old-Age Beneficiaries.* Fully insured individuals are eligible for a full old-age benefit if they claim benefits at the normal retirement age (NRA). The NRA is 65 for persons who attain that age before 2003, and it gradually increases to 66 for persons who attain that age in 2009 to 2020 and 67 for persons who attain that age in 2027 and after. The amount of this benefit is 100% of the primary insurance amount (PIA) (see explanation below). The old-age benefit can be claimed between age 62 and the NRA, with a reduction of 5/9% for each of the first 36 months below the NRA at the time of retirement and of 5/12% for months in excess of 36. Thus, a person retiring at exact age 62 before 2000 faces a 20% lifetime reduction, which closely approximates an "actuarial equivalent" basis. A person retiring at age 62 who has an NRA of 66 will have a 25% reduction; when the NRA is 67, the reduction will be 30%.

Persons retiring after the NRA receive increases in the form of delayed-retirement credits. These are at the rate of 3% for each year of deferment for persons who attained age 65 in 1982 to 1989 and increase gradually according to year of attainment of age 65, until being 8% for those attaining the NRA in 2009 and after.

*Disability Benefits.* An individual is eligible for a disability benefit of 100% of the PIA if he or she is permanently and totally disabled and has been so disabled for at least five months and has both fully and disability insured statuses.

*Auxiliary Benefits.* If the retired or disabled individual has a spouse at the NRA or over (or, regardless of age, has a child under age 16 or of any age who has been totally disabled since before age 22), an additional benefit of 50% of the PIA is payable. There is a similar benefit for each eligible child (subject to the family maximum provisions, when several persons in the family are eligible for benefits).

*Survivor Benefits.* Widow's benefits are payable at age 60 (or at ages 50 to 59 if the widow is disabled) if the deceased person was fully insured. This benefit is 100% of the PIA if first claimed at the NRA; the amount is 71.5% at ages 60 or under. Any delayed-retirement credits applicable to the worker are also applicable to the widow.

When a fully insured worker dies, parent's benefits are payable (upon attainment of age 62) to parents who had been dependent upon such individuals. When a fully or currently insured individual dies leaving an eligible child, benefits are payable to the children and the widowed parent in the same manner as for the children and spouse of a retired worker.

*General Benefit Provisions.* No individual can receive the full amount of more than one type of monthly benefit. Payments are made only after an individual files a claim, with retroactive payments of monthly benefits for as long as six months before filing. In May 2002, the House passed a bill that would make some additional divorced spouses and surviving spouses eligible for benefits, but it is not at all certain that this will be enacted.

### OASDI Benefit Amounts

The PIA, from which all benefits are determined, is based on the average earnings of the insured individual. This section will describe the method of calculating the PIA that is applicable over the long run (several other methods are applicable for certain closed groups, such as those who attained age 62 before 1979).

*Average Indexed Monthly Earnings.* The average indexed monthly earnings (AIME) is based on the indexed earnings record (which, for any year, does not include earnings in excess of the maximum earnings base) over the entire potential period of coverage, but with certain periods of low earnings disregarded. Generally, the average is computed from the beginning of 1951 (or at age 22, if later) to the beginning of the year of death, attainment of age 62, or disability, whichever is first applicable. In computing this average, five calendar years are dropped from consideration (for those disabled before age 47, fewer than five dropout years are allowed). Further, years with high earnings beginning with the year of attainment of age 62 (or before age 22) may be substituted for years at ages 22 to 61 with lower earnings.

The past earnings record is indexed (i.e., brought up to date, to alleviate the effects of inflation). Such indexing is done up to age 60 (or to 2 years before the year of disability or death, if prior to 62). The indexing is based on nationwide average wages.

*Benefits Formula.* After the AIME is determined, it is entered into the PIA benefit formula applicable to the particular "cohort" to which the individual belongs. A cohort relates to persons attaining age 62 in a particular year (or becoming disabled or dying before age 62 in that year). The formula for the 2002 cohort is: 90% of the first $592 of AIME, plus 32% of the next $3,567 of AIME, plus 15% of AIME in excess of $4,159.

The PIA formula for cohorts of subsequent years is derived from the 2002 formula. The percentage factors remain the same, but the "dollar bands" are increased on the basis of the relative changes in nationwide average wages from year to year. Individuals who do not receive retirement benefits for months after the NRA (primarily because of the earnings test, described hereafter) receive an increase in the PIA, termed "delayed-retirement credits," as described earlier. A special minimum benefit is provided for persons with long periods of coverage at low earnings.

The PIA is automatically adjusted for changes in prices, as measured by the Consumer Price Index (CPI) for All Urban Wage Earners and Clerical Workers. Such adjustment is made for benefits for each December (paid at the beginning of the following month). The adjustment is determined from the percentage increase in the CPI from the third quarter of the previous year to the third quarter of the current year; such adjustment was 2.6% for 2001.

*Income Taxation of Benefits.* Beginning in 1984, OASDI benefits have, for high-income persons, become subject to income tax. The proceeds are transferred to the trust fund that paid the benefits on which income taxes were levied. If the sum of (1) adjusted gross income (AGI) (as customarily determined for income tax purposes), (2) interest on tax-exempt bonds, (3) certain foreign-source income, and (4) 50% of OASDI benefits exceeds the basic threshold amount ($25,000 for single persons, $32,000 for married persons filing a joint return, and $0 for married persons filing separate returns who lived together at some time in the year), then 50% of the "excess"—but not more than 50%

of the OASDI benefits—is added to the AGI in computing income tax liability. Note that the threshold amounts are not indexed for future years.

Beginning in 1994, a second threshold ($34,000 for single persons and $44,000 for married persons filing a joint return) is in place; when the foregoing "excess" carries beyond the second threshold, then 85% of the "excess" beyond such threshold (as well as 50% of the difference between the thresholds) is added to the AGI in computing income tax liability—but not more than 85% of the OASDI benefits can be so added (with equitable transition provisions for those who are just above the second threshold). The additional tax proceeds are transferred to the Hospital Insurance Trust Fund.

*Earnings Test.* Benefits for retired workers and their eligible spouses and children, for eligible spouses and children of disability beneficiaries, and for survivors are usually not paid when the beneficiary is engaged in substantial employment, nor are benefits paid to the eligible spouse and children of a retired worker who is engaged in substantial employment. In 2002, benefits are payable for persons who have attained the NRA for all months in a year if the annual earnings from all types of employment (regardless of coverage) are $30,000 or less. For beneficiaries under the NRA, the annual exempt amount in 2002 is $11,280, with $1 of benefits withheld for each $2 of earnings above such amount. In the first year of benefit receipt, benefits are never withheld for a month in which the individual had wages of one-twelfth of the annual exempt amount or less and does not render substantial self-employment services. The earned-income restriction is not applicable at all after the individual reaches age 70. The annual and monthly exempt amounts for persons under the NRA are adjusted annually in the same manner as the earnings base.

*Elimination of Windfall Benefits for Retired and Disabled Workers.* A different method of computing the PIA is applicable generally for persons with less than 30 years of coverage who receive pensions based wholly or partially on earnings from noncovered employment. The percentage factor in the PIA formula applicable to the lowest band of earnings is 40% (instead of 90%), but this procedure will not reduce the PIA by more than 50% of the pension based on noncovered employment. This provision is phased in for those with 21 to 29 years of coverage (defined as the special-minimum benefit).

*Offset of Governmental Pensions for Spouses and Widow(er)s.* Two-thirds of the amount of any pension received by individuals for their service under a public employee retirement system under which the members are not also covered under OASDI as of the last day of the individual's service is offset against any OASDI spouse or widow(er) benefit.

*Coordination with Workers' Compensation and Other Governmental Disability Benefits.* OASDI benefits are reduced when they and Workers' Compensation and other government disability benefits exceed 80% of average recent earnings.

*Payment of OASDI Benefits Abroad.* Benefits are not payable in the case of deported persons whose rights are terminated until they are subsequently lawfully admitted. In the case of persons residing in certain countries where there is no reasonable assurance that checks can be delivered or cashed at full value, the benefits are withheld but can subsequently be paid if conditions change. For aliens residing outside the United States who came on the roll after 1954, benefits are payable only if the insured worker has 40 or more quarters of coverage or has resided in the United States for ten or more years, or if the country of which they are citizens has a reciprocity treaty with the United States or has a general social insurance or pension system that will continue full benefits to U.S. citizens while outside the foreign country.

### OASDI Financing Provision

The benefits and administrative expenses are paid out of two separate trust funds. The old-age and survivor benefits come from the Old-Age and Survivors Insurance Trust Fund, while the monthly benefits for disabled workers and their auxiliary beneficiaries come from the Disability Insurance Trust Fund.

In considering the financial impact and burden of the OASDI program, it is necessary to consider also the payroll taxes that support the Hospital Insurance (HI) portion of the Medicare program. The combined employer-employee tax rate is scheduled to be level at 15.3% (1990 and after), of which 2.9% is for HI. The employer-employee tax rate began at 2% for 1937 to 1949 and then increased in most subsequent years—for example, to 3% for 1950 to 1953, 7.25% for 1963 to 1965, 8.4% for 1966 (when HI first went into effect), 11.7% for 1973 to 1977, and 13.4% for 1982 to 1983.

The trust funds are invested in interest-bearing debt obligations of the United States. These can be either marketable issues or special issues bearing an interest rate approximating the average market yield on all government obligations having at least four years to run until earliest maturity as of the issuance date of the special issue. In actual practice, most of the assets have been in special issues.

The tax rates are levied only on earnings up to the applicable maximum taxable and creditable earnings base. This base is automatically adjusted upward, in accordance with changes in average wages in nationwide employment. The base was $80,400 in 2001 and $84,900 in 2002. The maximum base for the HI program was always the same as for the OASDI during 1966 to 1990, but in 1991 it was made significantly higher, and in 1994 it was eliminated.

The latest official cost estimates indicate that the OASDI program should be self-supporting from the contributions of covered workers and their employers until 2043, according to the intermediate-cost estimate. The intermediate-cost estimate in the 1994 *Trustees Report* shows a negative actuarial balance for OASDI (i.e., the financing provided is less than sufficient to meet obligations during the full 75-year valuation period—an average amount of 1.9% of taxable payroll).

This discussion of the financial status of the OASDI program indicates that some changes in the benefit structure and/or the financing are necessary. However, from a cash flow standpoint, no problems exist for the next 10 to 15 years. The HI program, however, will probably have severe problems in 5 to 10 years.

### Possible Changes in the OASDI Program

Currently, some people advocate reducing OASDI benefits to alleviate the national budget deficit crisis, now and in the future. They propose such changes as reducing the cost-of-living adjustments (COLAs) and means-testing the benefits (so that high-income people will receive much smaller benefits, or even none at all). But changes in OASDI for budget purposes may be ill-advised, because that program has not been the cause of the deficits. Reduction of COLAs is not desirable because it would affect mostly the oldest beneficiaries. Also, means-testing would encourage income manipulation, as well as destroy confidence in the program.

It is suggested that changes in the Social Security system should include an increase in financing and a reduction in benefit outflow, beginning in 2005, using a phasing procedure. The additional financing could come from a small increase in the contribution rates; the benefits reduction could best come from an increase in the normal retirement age, such as from 67 to 70 years.

If this procedure is followed, Social Security will continue to serve as the basic floor of economic protection against the risks of old-age retirement, permanent and total disability, and death of the primary wage earner. This is not to say that other changes in the Social Security program are not necessary. It is a flexible program that can, should, and will be altered occasionally to meet changing demographic, economic, and social conditions. Therefore, confidence in Social Security's future may be justified. (See also COST-OF-LIVING ADJUSTMENTS [COLAs]; DISABILITY PROGRAMS, FEDERAL AND STATE; FRAILTY PLANNING; RETIREMENT PLANNING; SOCIAL SECURITY PRIVATIZATION; SUPPLEMENTAL SECURITY INCOME [SSI].)

**References**

Beedon, Laurel. 1994. *Administering Social Security*. Washington, DC: AARP Public Policy Institute.

Board of Trustees. Federal Old-Age and Survivors Insurance and Disability Insurance Trust Funds. 2002. *Annual Report*. Washington, DC: GPO.

Myers, Robert J. 1992a. *Social Security*. Philadelphia: University of Pennsylvania Press.

Myers, Robert J. 1992b. *Within the System: My Half Century in Social Security*. Winstead, CT: ACTEX Publications.

Myers, Robert J. 1994. "The Role of Social Security in the Smoke-and-Mirrors Budget Deficit." *Benefits Quarterly* (1st Quarter): 17–21.

Rejda, George E. 1991. *Social Insurance and Economic Security*. Englewood Cliffs, NJ: Prentice-Hall.

Steuerle, C. Eugene, and Jon M. Bakija. 1994. *Retooling Social Security for the 21st Century: Right and Wrong Approaches to Reform*. Washington, DC: Urban Institute Press.

Treanor, J. Robert, Robert J. Myers, and Dale R. Detlefs. 2002. *Mercer Guide to Social Security and Medicare*. Louisville, KY: William M. Mercer. (Updated annually)

*Robert J. Myers*

**SOCIAL WORK.** See Gerontological Social Work.

**STATE AND AREA AGENCIES ON AGING,** local agencies responsible for the daily provision of Older Americans Act (OAA) services to senior citizens, either directly or by contract with a host of service providers. The services of the OAA, designed to promote the independence and dignity of persons aged 65 and older, include the National Older Americans Volunteer Program; the Nutrition Program for the Elderly; information and referral services on home health care services; Medicare, Medicaid, Social Security, and Supplemental Security Income (SSI) benefits; and transportation services. These State and Area Agencies are also conduits for connecting older persons with home modifications financing, housing programs, disaster relief programs, senior employment opportunities, and nursing home ombudsman programs and are the source of community education opportunities for older persons.

### Funding

The Administration on Aging (AoA), one of the service departments of the Department of Health and Human Services (HHS), provides funding for OAA services and programs, including for State and Area Agencies. Funds are distributed within states based on an intrastate funding formula that is reflected in the state plan for delivering OAA services. The intrastate funding formula is a critical aspect of delivering OAA services by determining the apportionment of OAA funds to various geographic areas. It is based on the number of persons 60 and older in the state, the distribution of persons in rural and urban areas, and special factors and weights for older persons who are frail, isolated, low income, or members of minority groups.

The OAA requires states to designate a unit of state government to serve as the State Unit on Aging (SUA) for purposes of the administration of OAA services. States must also create Planning and Service Areas (PSAs) that serve as geographic groupings within states (depending on the size of the state) for planning and administering OAA services. Within PSAs, the SUA is to designate one or more Area Agencies on Aging (AAAs or Triple As).

State Units on Aging and Area Agencies on Aging serve as advocates, commenting on state, local, and national legislative and administrative proposals that affect older Americans. They create advisory councils that comment on state and area plans, with a particular emphasis on assuring that state and local policy developments and administrative actions promote the interests of older adults.

Unfortunately, State and Area Agencies on Aging face decreasing fiscal resources. In an effort to extend the reach of the services of the OAA, many states use state Medicaid funds, federal community block grant funds, federal funds for transportation services for older adults, and state public assistance funds in conjunction with OAA funds. A state may, for example, use some of its transportation funds to extend OAA-funded transportation services (trips to day health centers, doctors visits, shopping, etc.), or some of its Medicaid funds to supplement its efforts to provide home health care services, community-based adult day health care, or respite care services.

### Provision of Services

In most instances, Area Agencies on Aging contract with other service providers for the delivery of services. An Area Agency on Aging may, for example, contract with a catering company to provide "meals-on-wheels" as part of the nutrition services it funds. Similarly, it may contract with a publicly funded legal services entity, a private attorney, or a law school clinic for the provision of legal services. The Area Agency on Aging is also charged with assuring that the providers of services adhere to the requirements of the OAA. Information and referral services and assessments for Medicaid qualification or in-home supportive services are often done by Area Agency on Aging staff itself.

OAA community services or in-home services are usually initiated through a telephone call to an Area Agency on Aging or senior services agency. The phone number of the local Area Agency on Aging can be found in the local telephone directory. The Eldercare Locator, a service of the AoA, is a national toll-free number available to help families and friends locate information on community services and organizations for older persons. Often, a referral to an appropriate social services agency is sufficient. Sometimes, though, the Area Agency on Aging will want to send a social worker or intake worker to the caller's home to make an assessment of the social and supportive services that are needed.

The services of the OAA are available without regard to income, although income-related questions may be requested as part of an assessment to determine whether a potential OAA services recipient might qualify for Medicaid or public financial assistance such as state general relief funds or the federal Supplemental Security Income program. Similar questions might be asked in determining whether an older person might qualify for public housing or a related federally assisted housing program.

### Financial Services

While local Area Agencies on Aging do not offer specific financial services, they can refer older persons to attorneys, planners, and public benefits counselors who are able to address financial and health care planning concerns. In many states, Area Agencies on Aging, often through their legal assistance provider networks, have lists of attorneys who will prepare wills, durable powers of attorney, and other planning documents on a reduced fee or pro bono basis.

Area Agencies on Aging can also put older persons in touch with other OAA services that have an impact on finances. These services include health insurance counseling, particularly Medicare supplemental insurance (Medigap) counseling and assistance in obtaining Medicaid (health care coverage for persons with low incomes), and Medicare. Area Agency on Aging resource persons can also refer older persons to organizations that provide assistance in obtaining Supplemental Security Income assistance, food and nutrition services, and housing.

### Diversity Participation

Over the years, Congress has been concerned with assuring ethnic and minority participation in the services and programs of the OAA. This has led to a greater emphasis on targeting services to low-income minority persons and to exploring better coordination of the activities of Area Agencies on Aging with programs that serve older Native Americans. In many instances, targeting activities have focused on how to extend assistance to more people as resources remain stagnant or decline. A related task has been one of identifying organizations and focal points among minority populations for targeting and outreach efforts. Critical issues are the location of services, access to transportation, the availability of written resources in languages other than English, and the availability of oral translation services or staff fluent in languages relevant to targeted communities. (See also LONG-TERM CARE INSURANCE, PRIVATE; NURSING HOMES; OLDER AMERICANS ACT; OMBUDSMAN.)

#### Organizations

AARP
American Bar Association, Commission on Legal Problems of the Elderly
Association on Aging: Regional Support Centers
Center for Social Gerontology

Eldercare Locator
National Asian/Pacific Center on Aging
National Association of Area Agencies on Aging
National Association of State Units on Aging
National Caucus and Center on the Black Aged, Inc.
National Citizens Coalition for Nursing Home Reform (Ombudsman Program)
National Consumer Law Center
National Council of Senior Citizens
National Council on the Aging
National Hispanic Council on Aging
National Indian Council on Aging
National Senior Citizens Law Center
Pension Rights Center

### References

Atchley, Robert C. 1985. *Social Forces and Aging*. 4th ed. Belmont, CA: Wadsworth.

Estes, Carroll. 1979. *The Aging Enterprise*. San Francisco, CA: Jossey-Bass.

Ficke, Susan Coombs. 1985. *An Orientation to the Older Americans Act*. Washington, DC: National Association of State Units on Aging.

Gelfand, Donald E. 1988. *The Aging Network: Programs and Services*. 3rd ed. New York: Springer.

O'Shaughnessy, Carol. 1991. "Older Americans Act: 1991 Reauthorization and FY 1992 Budget Issues." *Congressional Research Service Order Code 1391002*. Washington, DC: Library of Congress, November 27.

U.S. General Accounting Office. 1994. *Older Americans Act: The National Eldercare Campaign: Report to the Chairman, Subcommittee on Human Resources, Committee on Education and Labor, House of Representatives*. Washington, DC: Author.

*Alfred J. Chiplin*

**SUPPLEMENTAL SECURITY INCOME (SSI),** a means-tested, federally administered income assistance program. Established by the 1972 amendments to the Social Security Act and begun in 1974, SSI provides monthly cash payments in accordance with uniform national eligibility requirements to needy aged, blind, and disabled persons. At the outset, it was envisaged that the SSI program would "provide a positive assurance that the nation's aged, blind and disabled people would no longer have to subsist on below-poverty level incomes" (Social Security Administration [SSA] 1992). The number of recipients on SSI has increased from nearly 4 million in 1974 to 6.6 million in December 1999. Total annual benefits paid under the SSI program increased from about $5.2 billion in 1974 to $31.3 billion in 1999. The monthly federal benefit for individuals rose from $140 ($210 for couples) in 1974 to $545 ($817 for couples) in 2002.

### Eligibility

To qualify for SSI payments, a person must satisfy the program criteria for age, blindness, or other disability. The aged are defined as persons 65 years and older. A person also must be needy, that is, have limited income and resources, to be eligible for SSI. Additionally, to qualify for SSI, a person must (1) be a U.S. citizen, a refugee or asylee in the country for less than 7 years, or a "qualified alien" who was receiving SSI as of August 1996; and (2) be a resident of the United States. Since SSI payments are reduced by other income, applicants and recipients must apply for any other money benefits due them. The Social Security Administration works with recipients and helps them receive other benefits for which they are eligible. People who receive SSI checks also may receive Social Security checks if they are eligible. In 1999, 60% of aged SSI recipients also received Social Security benefits. Social Security benefits are the highest source of income for SSI recipients. Since its inception, SSI has been viewed as the "program of last resort"—that is, after evaluating all other income, SSI pays what is necessary to bring an individual to the statutorily prescribed income floor.

Under the program, $20 of monthly income from most sources is excluded from countable income. The first $65 of monthly earned income plus one-half of remaining earnings are excluded. The value of any in-kind assistance is counted as income unless such in-kind assistance is specifically excluded by statute (for example, nutrition, food stamps, housing, or social services). If an SSI applicant or recipient is living in the household of another and receiving in-kind support and maintenance from them, the SSI benefit standard for such an individual will be reduced by one-third of the federal SSI benefit standard. Living in a publicly operated community residence that serves no more than 16 people, living in a public institution mainly to attend approved educational or job training, or living in a public emergency shelter for the homeless may allow low-income persons to receive SSI. As countable income increases, a recipient's SSI benefit amount decreases. Ineligibility for SSI occurs when countable income equals the federal benefit standard plus the amount of applicable state supplementation.

SSI eligibility is restricted to qualified persons who have countable resources (assets) not exceeding $2,000 (or $3,000 for couples). In determining countable resources, a number of items are not included, such as the individual's home and household goods, personal effects, an automobile, and a burial space. The value of property that is used in a person's trade or business, or by the person as an employee, is also excluded.

Although most low-income older adults have few assets, "the asset test for SSI is so stringent that some people with inadequate incomes are denied assistance because of small amounts of savings and other resources" (Schulz 2001).

### Benefits and Costs

The regular federal SSI benefit for an individual in 2002 was $545 per month and $817 for a couple. Most states supplement the regular federal SSI benefit. For example, there is a state supplement (for individuals) of $176 in California, $84 in Wisconsin, or $2 in Oregon (1999 figures). Some states link their SSI supplement to state-only funding of aging services. It is the combined regular federal SSI/state-supplemented benefit against which countable income is compared in determining eligibility and benefit amount. The regular benefits are indexed to the Consumer Price Index (CPI).

Maximum potential SSI and food stamp benefits, combined, are of interest: they were at least $600 per month (for individuals in 2000) in most states, with a few states providing up to $100 more. Finally, it is worth comparing the combined benefits to the poverty threshold of $7,990 per year (individuals in 1999): the federal SSI benefit alone reached only about 75% of poverty in 1999 (89.3% for couples), and with Social Security benefits added, 85% (91.7% for couples). Only as food stamps were taken into account did the support exceed the poverty threshold at 101.8% (for couples). A study of the adequacy of SSI benefits in light of real costs for basic needs (shelter, food, clothing), rather than the abstract poverty threshold, made them appear even less sufficient; only about 85% of these costs could be covered by program benefits on average. "Even when food stamps and social security insurance benefits are considered, the income package fails to meet basic needs" (Meyer and Bartolomei-Hill 1994).

Federal SSI benefits and the cost of administering the program are financed from general funds from the U.S. Treasury. The Social Security Administration also administers the payment of approximately $3.3 billion of state-financed state supplementary payments. In 1991, of $30 billion in federally administered SSI benefits, almost 80% went to those who were eligible on the basis of disability, 19% to the aged, and 1% to the blind. The higher percentage of federal SSI payments for the disabled is due to the fact that only a third of the disabled have other income in the form of Social Security benefits, compared with two-thirds of the aged.

### SSI Beneficiaries

The number of SSI recipients declined from 1975 to 1983. However, in the years 1984 to 1999, the number increased from about 3.9 million to 6.6 million. About 2 million of them are older, or about 6% of Americans who are 65 or older. Still, since 1975, the number of persons receiving SSI on the basis of age alone has declined from 2.3 million to 1.3 million in 1999, primarily because of increasing incomes among seniors. But not all older adults have done well. Of those SSI recipients receiving benefits on the basis of age (i.e., age 65 or older), 37% were 80 years of age or above, that is, in the category of the oldest old. But even as needs increased for some, the rate of participation in SSI among the older poor dropped from about 75% in 1975 to 60% in 1996. It is estimated that about one-third of aged persons eligible for SSI do not participate in the program (Meyer and Bartolomei-Hill 1994).

### Administrative, Outreach, and Adequacy Issues

Overall, the administration of the SSI program is complex and expensive because even small changes in monthly income or in resources impact on eligibility and benefits. Intricate procedures determine how different types of income and resources are treated or what support a recipient may receive. According to the U.S. General Accounting Office, SSA has made only limited progress toward addressing excessively complex rules for assessing recipients' living arrangements as well (General Accounting Office 2002).

The 1983 Social Security amendments mandated that the Social Security Administration conduct two separate outreach activities aimed at the aged population. The first was a onetime notice mailed to those aged individuals and couples whose Social Security benefits were less than the SSI eligibility levels. The second outreach activity is an ongoing effort to notify two groups of Social Security beneficiaries: (1) those about to reach age 65 and (2) disabled individuals who have been receiving Social Security benefits for 21 consecutive months and will soon be eligible for Medicare.

The goal of the SSI outreach strategy is to reduce the barriers that prevent or discourage potentially SSI-eligible individuals from participating in the program. Common barriers include a lack of information or a misunderstanding about the program, a perception that program participation results in stigma, and the inherent difficulties of the application process for persons who are older or disabled. Obstacles within the application process include complex forms, the absence of "one-stop shopping," transportation difficulties, long waiting times, and poor attitudes of intake workers (Kassner 1992). Duplication of other SSA procedures, lack of publicizing the program, and insufficient referral to and complicated application modalities for food stamps at the state level were criticized independently (General Accounting Office 1992).

The Social Security Administration seeks to overcome barriers by providing better information, alleviating stigma surrounding the program, and making the process of applying for benefits easier. It tries to accomplish this through direct action and cooperative efforts with other government agencies and private sector organizations that have links with individuals whom SSA is trying to reach.

In 1990, the Social Security Administration established the SSI Modernization Project, composed of 21 experts on SSI and related policy areas, to determine the effectiveness of the SSI program. The project experts urged priority for the following four recommendations:

1. Increase benefit guarantees
2. Increase resource limits
3. Eliminate in-kind support and maintenance from consideration as income
4. Increase the number of SSA staff

A reform, according to this opinion, would bring the benefit level to 120% of the poverty guideline, lower the eligibility age from 65 to 62, eliminate income verification in situations when such verification would not be cost-effective, and personalize and individualize contact and service by SSA staff (SSA 1992).

Program costs associated with these recommendations were estimated at $3.5 billion in fiscal year 1993 and were to increase to $32.5 billion by 1997 as the improvements would gradually be implemented. Bills dealing with these issues were introduced in the 102nd Congress, but none were passed. Because of the budget deficit, many policymakers viewed the legislation as too costly and expansive, and some were concerned that it provided preference to one group of needy persons (aged, blind, and disabled individuals) over another (families with children) with generally higher rates of poverty.

In 2000, an SSA report, *The Supplemental Security Income Program at the Millennium*, once more took stock of accomplishments and problems. For beneficiaries, the SSI program has been both more generous and more consistent than the state-administered programs that it replaced. In terms of benefit adequacy, however, 58% of beneficiaries who are age 65 or older remain below the federal poverty line. The report also proposed various smaller or larger improvements in benefit adequacy that entailed increasing and indexing of benefits and higher income/resources thresholds.

Short of actual reform, the outlook for older persons in need is thus not very bright. Another suggestion that would bring an improvement was to combine the benefits reviewed here with federal housing assistance (not an entitlement), a "kind of program linkage [that] could vastly improve the economic well-being of many lower-income older people without the need to create or alter existing programs" (Meyer and Bartolomei-Hill 1994). (See also DISABILITY PROGRAMS, FEDERAL AND STATE; MEANS-TESTING IN PUBLIC PROGRAMS; MEDICAID; NUTRITION PROGRAMS; OLD-AGE PROVISIONS AND ECONOMIC STATUS.)

### Organization

Social Security Administration, Office of External Affairs

### Suggested Reading

Social Security Administration. 2002. *Supplemental Security Income (SSI).* Washington, DC: Author. Available online at http://www.ssa.gov/notices/supplemental-security-income/.

### References

General Accounting Office (GAO). 1992. *Social Security: Need for Better Coordination of Food Stamp Services for Social Security Clients.* Washington, DC: Author.

General Accounting Office (GAO). 2002. *Supplemental Security Income: Status of Efforts to Improve Overpayment Detection and Recovery.* Washington, DC: Author.

Kassner, Enid. 1992. *Falling through the Safety Net: Missed Opportunities for America's Elderly Poor.* Washington, DC: AARP.

Meyer, Daniel R., and Steve Bartolomei-Hill. 1994. "The Adequacy of Supplemental Security Income Benefits for Aged Individuals and Couples." *The Gerontologist* 34: 161–72.

Schulz, James H. 2001. *The Economics of Aging.* 7th ed. Westport, CT: Auburn House.

Social Security Administration (SSA). 1992. "SSI Modernization Project: Final Report of the Experts." *Social Security Bulletin* 55: 22–35.

Social Security Administration (SSA). 2000. *The Supplemental Security Income Program at the Millennium.* Washington, DC: Author.

U.S. House of Representatives. Committee on Ways and Means. 2000. *Overview of Entitlement Programs.* 2000 Green Book. Washington, DC: GPO.

*Jurg K. Siegenthaler*

# T

**TAX PLANNING.** See Capital Gain; Charitable Contributions; Estate Planning; Homeownership; Taxpayer Issues of Older Adults.

**TAX SHELTER.** See Condominiums; Cooperative Ownership in Housing; Employee Stock Ownership Plans (ESOPs); Homeownership; Individual Retirement Account (IRA); Keogh Plans; Reverse Mortgages.

**TAXPAYER ISSUES OF OLDER ADULTS,** tax counseling services and tax preparation assistance for older persons; federal policies that affect older taxpayers; and the age factor in audits, collection, and enforcement practices of the Internal Revenue Service (IRS). Government at all levels, federal, state, and local, is financed through a variety of taxes administered through a complex web of regulations that change frequently and usually require interpretation by tax professionals. While effective personal financial management requires familiarity with the U.S. (and local) tax environment, certain issues are of particular concern to older persons.

## Tax Planning

Tax law has become so complex that tax counseling constitutes a large, if not the largest, component of financial and estate planning. Selecting the right tax professional is crucial, and choosing a tax professional is like choosing any expert: ask for recommendations from friends, colleagues, community members, bankers, attorneys, and other financial advisors; investigate the credentials of candidates; and interview several candidates before choosing. Tax advisors should be in business all year, not just during tax season, since tax planning should be conducted on an ongoing basis.

A successful relationship with a tax counselor will be built upon a compatible financial philosophy, mutual comfort in setting and achieving clear goals, and the confidence that the advisor will provide competent representation before the IRS, should an audit occur. It is important to determine—*before selecting a tax advisor*—that he or she will not be intimidated by an aggressive revenue agent, since some representatives are more nervous about a confrontation with the IRS than their clients are.

### Income Tax Filing Assistance for Older Adults

Free help is available *from the IRS* and from many other seniors' organizations for those who need tax filing assistance. The IRS provides training and technical assistance to prepare volunteers of private and public nonprofit agencies and organizations to assist persons who are 60 and older with their federal income tax returns. Reimbursement for transportation, meals, and other expenses incurred by volunteers during training and while providing tax counseling assistance may be paid by the IRS.

Through the Tax Counseling for the Elderly (TCE) program, IRS-trained volunteers assist individuals who are 60 and older, and taxpayers who are disabled or have special needs, with their tax returns at many neighborhood locations. Also, certain Volunteer Income Tax Assistance (VITA) preparers are trained to help older Americans and others who cannot afford professional tax help with their tax returns. Volunteers who provide tax counseling frequently are retired individuals associated with nonprofit organizations that receive grants from the IRS. The grants help pay out-of-pocket expenses for volunteers for travel to older people's homes, to retirement or nursing homes, or to special TCE sites. One such organization is AARP, responding to concerns that older taxpayers were overestimating and overpaying their taxes.

Under a cooperative agreement with the IRS as part of its TCE program, AARP began its Tax-Aide program in 1968 to provide free income tax assistance to older people. Each year, AARP volunteers, trained to understand the provisions of the tax code that affect older people, help more than 1 million taxpayers nationwide. Tax-Aide volunteers are available from February 1 through April 15 each year and can be located through the local IRS information office.

In addition to these counseling services, the IRS provides toll-free telephone assistance, tax information publications, tax assistance and educational programs, and audiovisual instructional materials that are available for individuals and groups. While the IRS position is that most tax questions can be answered by reading the tax forms and reviewing the instructions, many taxpayers of all ages and older taxpayers in particular find the forms and the instructions burdensome and difficult to understand. Professional tax advisors, including income tax service companies, accountants, and other qualified tax preparers such as *enrolled agents* (often former IRS employees who have passed a comprehensive series of tests), are available as paid private tax return preparers.

The law requires a paid preparer to sign the return and to complete the "Paid Preparers Use Only" section at the bottom of the form, just below the taxpayer's signature. The taxpayer, however, remains responsible for the accuracy of every item entered on his or her return. If a mistake occurs, the IRS will require the taxpayer, not the preparer, to pay any additional required taxes, penalties, and interest. Obtaining qualified tax preparation assistance is an important consideration. The ability to locate the preparer, should the IRS have a question about the return, is also important. Since tax laws change frequently, one should never rely on information booklets, pamphlets, or taxpayer instructions that are not current.

### Audits and Collections

Breakdowns of the numbers of audits conducted by the IRS are published in the annual Report of the Commissioner by income and geographic location, but not by demographics, and it is generally unknown whether age is a factor in audits. In IRS collections procedures, it is presumed that actions are based on ability to pay. Since the IRS assumes that younger people have a longer working life, and the potential to earn more money than older persons, age is considered only indirectly (Carlson 1994).

Older persons who can afford to hire a representative should never speak directly to an IRS employee about either an audit or a collection matter. Unfortunately, while free advice from IRS and IRS-trained volunteers provides needy older taxpayers information about preparing and filing tax forms, no special help is available to them in the face of audit and collection procedures. Although hundreds of reputable books are published each year about taxes, audits, and how to deal with the IRS, many older taxpayers who cannot afford to hire competent tax advisors experience anxiety, fear, and even abuse by aggressive revenue agents. Ironically, the only assistance available for troubled older taxpayers without resources may be the IRS itself.

Congressional hearings in recent years on the subject of IRS abuses led to legislation to protect taxpayer rights, and guidelines have been issued by the IRS for collection personnel to follow. Older taxpayers who believe they have been treated discourteously or unfairly should write to the chief of the examination or collection division at their local IRS district office. If a problem persists, contact the IRS's Problem Resolution Office (PRO) and ask to have a PRO officer assigned to resolve the case. When all else fails, an older person or representative should seek help through the local office of his or her member of Congress.

The IRS's own investigations into compliance with income tax laws, according to Martin Kaplan and Naomi Weiss, authors of *What the IRS Doesn't Want You to Know*, have revealed what tax professionals have known all along: "[T]axpayers want to file their taxes correctly, but complex laws, badly designed forms, indecipherable instructions, and an adversarial relationship . . . stand in their way." Efforts are made periodically within the IRS to improve both its image and its collection practices. The size of the IRS, however, and the difficulties inherent in bringing national policy changes down to grassroots levels are unlikely to bring relief to many deserving older taxpayers without outside intervention or organized advocacy. (See also ACCOUNTANTS; ATTORNEYS; CAPITAL GAIN; CASH FLOW PLANNING FOR RETIREES; CHARITABLE CONTRIBUTIONS; FINANCIAL ADVISORS.)

### Organizations

AARP
National Taxpayers Union

### References

AARP. 1988. *Tax Aide: A Program of People Helping People*. Washington, DC: Author. Available online at http://www.aarp.org/taxaide/.

Boardroom Classics. 1992. *The Book of Tax Knowledge*. New York: Author.

Boardroom Classics. 1994. *Tax Loopholes: Everything the Law Allows*. Springfield, NJ: Author.

Carlson, Robert C. 1994. Letter to author, December 5.

Carlson, Robert C., ed. 1995. *Tax Wise Money Strategies: Protect Yourself from the Highest Taxes in History*. New York: Carroll & Graf.

Daily, Frederick W. 2001. *Stand Up to the IRS*. 6th ed. Berkeley, CA: Nolo Press.

Internal Revenue Service. 2001. *Guide to Free Tax Services*. Washington, DC: Department of the Treasury, IRS.

Kaplan, Marty, and Naomi Weiss. 1997. *What the IRS Doesn't Want You to Know: A CPA Reveals the Tricks of the Trade*. 4th ed. New York: Villard Books.

U.S. Library of Congress. 1992. "Federal Income Tax Treatment of the Elderly." *CRS Report for Congress*. Washington, DC: Congressional Research Service.

U.S. Senate. Special Committee on Aging. 2000. *Protecting Older Americans against Overpayment of Income Taxes*. Washington, DC: GPO.

*Lois A. Vitt*

**TITLING ASSETS,** the means whereby the owner of property has the just possession of the property under the law. The *title* is the evidence of ownership of the property. There are a number of different ways to hold title to property whether real (such as houses, land, buildings) or personal (such as stocks, cash, furniture, etc.).

In *tenancy in common*, each owner, whether two or more, holds title to an undivided interest in the property. The interests may or may not be equal, depending on how the owners acquired the property. In most jurisdictions, title to real property inherited by children will be held as tenants in common, with each child owning an equal undivided interest. The distinctive characteristic of tenancy in common is that each owner's interest can be severed from the others and sold or bequeathed under a will. As a practical matter, there may not be a big market for partial ownership interests, but an individual owner may force the sale of the property by filing a court action. The other tenants in common do not become owners of another's tenancy in common interest upon that owner's death.

*Joint tenancy*, another way to hold title, means that the last surviving joint tenant (i.e., joint owner) will own the entire property. This is known as the *right of survivorship.* Although the use of the word *joint* automatically includes the concept of right of survivorship in many states, this is not always the case. In Virginia, for example, the words "with common law right of survivorship" must be included in the instrument of conveyance, or a so-called joint tenancy will actually have the effect of a tenancy in common. Joint tenancies can be of equal or unequal interests, depending on how the joint owners took title. For married couples, joint tenancy automatically assumes equal ownership by each spouse. An ordinary joint tenancy with right of survivorship can usually be severed by the unilateral act of one joint tenant, by filing a court action or taking any other action inconsistent with right of survivorship.

A third way to hold title is *tenancy by the entirety*, which is joint tenancy with a common-law right of survivorship for married couples only. Generally, property owned by married couples as tenants by the entirety enjoys protection against creditors if only one of the two spouses is the debtor. For example, the husband may be a physician with a large malpractice judgment; his insurance does not cover the entire liability. If he owns his home with his spouse, as tenants by the entirety the judgment creditor cannot take the house.

Holding title by means of a *life estate/remainder interest* is best explained by understanding the two concepts that make it up. A life estate is ownership for the lifetime of the life estate title holder. What is left upon that person's death is the entire property—that is, the *remainder*. The *remainderman* becomes the sole owner of the property automatically upon the death of the life estate holder. For federal estate tax purposes, life estates are generally not counted as "resources." The life estate holder is liable for all taxes and expenses on the property and is also entitled to any income produced by the property. When the life estate holder dies, the remainderman automatically owns the property with a "step-up" in tax basis. Thus, if the property had originally been purchased for a low price, for example, $20,000, and is worth $100,000 when the life estate holder dies, the remainderman can sell the property for the $100,000 and not pay any capital gains tax.

A final way to hold title is by *community property*. Community property is property owned by married couples in community property states. Community property presupposes equal ownership by each spouse of property acquired during the marriage by means other than an inheritance or a gift to one spouse. Only nine states have community property systems: Arizona, California, Idaho, Louisiana, Nevada, New Mexico, Texas, Washington, and Wisconsin. People residing in community property states should consult with local counsel with respect to both their ownership interests and their ability to leave such property under their wills. The law is not the same in every jurisdiction.

Every jurisdiction has variations on each of the above methods of holding title to property. It is imperative that readers check with an attorney in their own jurisdiction to determine precisely what their rights are as owners. (See also ESTATE PLANNING; FINANCIAL ADVISORS; FINANCIAL LITERACY; HOMEOWNERSHIP; INHERITANCE; LIFE ESTATES; MEDICAID PLANNING; PROBATE; TRUSTS; WILLS.)

**References**

Dukeminier, Jesse. 1993. *Property*. 3rd ed. Boston, MA: Little, Brown.

Harvey, David C.B. 1966. *Harvey Law of Real Property and Title Closing*. New York: C. Boardman Co.

Maisel, Sherman J. 1992. *Real Estate Finance*. 2nd ed. Orlando, FL: Harcourt Brace Jovanovich.

Savage, Terry. 1993. *New Money Strategies for the '90s*. New York: Harper Business.

*Janet L. Kuhn*

**TRANSPORTATION,** the link to society's rich array of discrete and spatially dispersed activities. Access to friends, families, employment, shopping and commerce, personal care, social interaction, education and cultural enrichment, and religious expression—nearly all of the benefits of modern society—depends on one's ability to transport oneself from one location to another. High levels of mobility mean high levels of access, choice, and opportunity, which can lead to self-fulfillment and enrichment. Low levels of mobility can lead to isolation and cultural impoverishment.

Today's society has come to depend on cars as the means to achieve the mobility required for personal access to various opportunities. People with cars have a broad range of choices regarding where they live, work, shop, and interact with others. People who don't drive, including about 8.4 million senior citizens 65 years and older without driver's licenses, need to find what are often second-best alternatives to bridge the distances and reach the destinations that drivers take for granted as within their reach.

Many communities see rapidly growing numbers and proportions of elders with increasingly higher mobility expectations. In the face of growing travel demands and limited transportation choices, older persons face special challenges obtaining the transportation they need to maintain their independence and quality of life. To address these challenges, current trends in transportation and aging must be considered.

## Key Trends in Transportation and Aging

Personal transportation is projected to become an issue of growing importance for older persons in all parts of the United States. The big changes expected over the next several decades include the following:

*The Number of Older Persons Will Increase.* The number of people 65 years old and older can be expected to increase substantially. Compared to today's older adults, tomorrow's older adults are projected to be more highly educated, healthier, more active, and enjoying higher incomes (Burkhardt et al. 1998; OECD 2001). Tomorrow's elders will likely represent a more diverse set of backgrounds and cultures, and a wide spectrum of needs and desires, with no "typical older traveler." Increases in the older population are expected to be greatest in the West and South and lowest in the Northeast and Midwest (Rogers 1999). The areas where older population growth is projected to be highest are precisely those areas—suburban and rural communities—that at present often lack any significant mobility choices other than driving.

*More Senior Drivers Will Be Driving More.* Automotive travel currently accounts for about 90% of all trips made by older persons. The number and percentage of older drivers will likely increase significantly in the near future. The number of drivers 65 years old and older will at least double over the next 30 years. The proportion of older drivers on our streets will also increase significantly, and older drivers will be driving more (taking more trips and driving more miles). In 30 years, travel by older drivers will increase from 400% to 500%. Even by conservative estimates, the proportion of all driving done by older drivers will nearly triple by 2030 (Burkhardt et al. 1998).

*Safety and Mobility Issues Will Become More Important.* The aging process can include an increase in functional disabilities and a reduction in the skills and abilities needed to drive an automobile. Along with an increase in older drivers, driving more frequently and greater distances, the number of older persons who are unable to safely operate motor vehicles will also grow. More than 600,000 people age 70 or older stop driving each year and become dependent on others to meet their transportation needs, according to Foley et al. (2002). If there are no changes to current crash-related fatality trends, the number of fatalities involving older drivers by 2030 could be three to four times greater than in 1995 (Burkhardt et al. 1998). Based on this expected increase, the number of traffic fatalities for older adults in 2030 will be 35% to 71% greater than the total number of alcohol-related traffic fatalities in 1995—a number currently viewed by policymakers and the public as cause for serious concern.

*Expanded Travel Options Will Become More Important.* For both safety and mobility reasons, more travel choices are needed. In 2000, almost three-fourths of Americans over the age of 65 lived in suburban or rural areas, where alternatives to the automobile are often scarce or nonexistent (Rosenbloom 1996). Public transit services are now used by about 11% of older persons (Burkhardt et al. 2002). Fifty-four percent (54%) of the older population have access to, but do not use, public transit, and 34% report that no public transit service is available to them. (In nonmetro areas, 73% report that no public transit service is available to them.) Transit trips represent about 3% of all trips made by older persons. Transit usage is closely related to residential location, with older, center-city residents using transit much more frequently than elders residing elsewhere. Transit currently has problems serving older persons who are in the oldest age groups, have alternative travel options, live outside of central cities, or have multiple impairments.

As the aging of society creates more older drivers, we can expect larger numbers of older persons who are unable to safely operate motor vehicles. When people with diminished capabilities continue to drive, an increased safety risk is created for all members of society. However, older drivers facing the prospect of reducing or terminating their driving expect substantially reduced mobility with undesirable consequences. These include a loss of personal independence, social isolation, and a reduction or lack of access to essential services.

The vast majority of Americans have grown up in a culture that strongly depends on automotive transportation for mobility, and driving occupies a central role in the lives of many older adults. Thus, it is not surprising that the point at which older people voluntarily give up, or are forced to relinquish, their driving privileges is viewed by elders and those around them as a watershed event, with significant implications regarding independence, self-sufficiency, and social responsibilities. The mobility dilemma for many older persons is, "Do I continue to drive even when driving begins to pose real safety risks for myself and others?" Common consequences for older persons whose mobility has declined include fewer trips, shorter travel distances, and no trips to certain destinations or at particular times. They become less able to maintain independent lifestyles, more dependent on others, and forced into more arduous planning for even simple trips. Not responding to the mobility needs of elders could create serious consequences including increased isolation of the oldest citizens, loss of their potential contributions to society, unnecessary institutionalization, and a large number of avoidable traffic injuries and fatalities (because elders without viable travel options often continue to drive even when doing so endangers themselves and others). Enhanced transportation services can address these needs, and transportation services that better serve older persons will serve all travelers.

### Options for Addressing Mobility Issues

What can be done about the safety and mobility challenges posed by an aging society? There are good solutions available in education and counseling, additional travel options, enhancements to auto driving, and changing the structure of communities and trip patterns.

### Education and Counseling

Education and counseling is an attractive, immediate, and relatively inexpensive approach that is sorely needed—for seniors, for those who will be seniors in the near future, and for policymakers.

Just as many people now plan for retiring from work, they must also plan for retiring from driving. Many of the oldest individuals in focus groups took the "avoid it as long as possible" approach to dealing with facing the prospect of not driving. These attitudes need to change. Some advance planning for major life changes is one of the best ways to deal successfully with difficult issues. Advance planning for "retiring from driving" needs to be promoted at many levels within society, not just among the eldest citizens.

Elders and their families need more information on transportation services and choices.

Factual, nonemotional information on issues regarding the reduction or cessation of driving is difficult to find, however, making discussion of these important issues difficult. Harper and Schatz (1998) found that

> when faced with this difficult transition [from driving to not driving], most families struggle alone. Most families reported that they had never discussed this with anyone. Most could not think of any place to obtain information or advice, except perhaps from Senior Centers. There is a widespread interest in such resources.

Exemplary existing programs can offer important lessons. Driving Decisions for Seniors (DDS) in Eugene, Oregon, is one example. DDS's director established the program according to the precept, "It's far better for us to face these decisions ourselves than to lose our dignity by having someone else make them for us" (Heckman and Duke 1997). The Senior Transportation Program of the Central Plains Area Agency on Aging, headquartered in Wichita, Kansas, is another exemplary program (Central Plains AAA 1995). Their approach is based on evidence that seniors can usefully be encouraged to grow into new roles and the idea that "graduating from driving" has a much more positive connotation than "giving up your driver's license." AARP's "55 ALIVE/Mature Driving Program" is one of the oldest counseling and training programs in this field. This program helps elders recognize signs of driving problems and suggests practical defensive driving strategies for safer driving (such as avoiding left-hand turns except at signaled intersections). In a number of states, insurance companies offer discounts for seniors who have completed the 55 ALIVE program. The Maryland State Highway Administration is developing a "Safe Mobility for Life" program to identify high-risk older persons and help those who need it improve their driving skills, change their habits, or find good alternatives to driving. Other programs, such as those in Michigan, Florida, and New York, also provide sound advice and assistance for older travelers and their families.

### Alternatives to Driving

As Bly (1993) has noted, "If . . . only the car offers the flexibility required to get to the most attractive, but very dispersed, destinations, there will be considerable pressure for people to continue driving beyond the point at which they feel able to drive safely." There are indeed other ways of obtaining mobility than by driving, even though few communities in this country have paid much attention to them.

Successful interventions should provide not only mobility but also a sense of security, independence, and dignity, addressing the need to replace satisfactions that seniors previously derived from driving.

Education emphasizing the true cost of car ownership can help make nondriving alternatives attractive. For those people who continue to own cars that they seldom drive, auto travel costs can be quite high. Car ownership is expensive. An understanding of the true cost of owning a car (as described in Burkhardt et al. 1998) can make other travel alternatives look more cost-effective.

Innovative transportation options that enable older people to get around without feeling dependent or "beholden" to others are important. Seniors are reluctant to ask for rides from others, especially when they are uncertain regarding the length of time the trip may require, as when waiting for doctors' or others' services. These new transit options can range from public to private and from highly structured to very informal services.

Public mass transit services are more limited than auto travel in both space and time (otherwise described as "routing" and "scheduling"). Individuals who are accustomed to the high level of mobility and the psychological rewards of driving may find it more difficult to adapt to life without a car than those who have never been drivers. The ways in which mass transit systems are presently configured do not meet many of the travel needs of older citizens. Public transportation services must adopt a greater customer focus and a more user-friendly attitude in order to attract riders who ride by choice, not because they have no other choice. If transit agencies want to attract more older riders, they will need to do more than just wait for elders to become too old or infirm to drive: the physical problems associated with aging that make driving difficult also make using our current forms of public transportation very difficult. Transit agencies wishing to respond to the changing needs and demands of tomorrow's elders will need to make fundamental changes in five areas:

- Following the lead of consumer-oriented industries like package delivery services, personal transportation services will need to focus on tailoring travel options to the wishes of individual customers. The primary focus thus shifts to the trip instead of the travel mode.
- As is already happening in Europe, many agencies that now provide transportation should shift their focus to mobility management, organizing but not operating public transit services. Contracts for various types of services with multiple kinds of service providers could provide different kinds and levels of service for differing travel needs.
- Older travelers will demand many more travel options in the future. Multiple service types at varying prices will be needed. The current heavy emphasis on one or two modes of travel will be replaced by more travel options within an overall family of services.
- Using electronic fare payments, future transportation operators should focus on full-cost recovery for the trips that they provide; nonoperating agencies could assume responsibility for providing subsidies for those riders deemed to need subsidized trips.
- Consumer-oriented technologies can provide real-time information about when vehicles will arrive to pick someone up and how long trips may take. Low-floor vehicles should be emphasized, as should noncash financial transactions.

Public and private human services agencies operate nearly 4,000 transportation services that use at least some federal funds for vehicle purchase or operations. These services are crucial for many who use them, but they are seen in some communities as targeted to low-income persons and welfare recipients. Eisenhandler (1992) noted "an aura of neediness" associated with the use of such services, which diminishes their attractiveness to a broad range of potential users. Kihl, Goudy, and Mahayni (1990) noted that human service transportation systems were meeting the needs of the frail older persons in rural Iowa but not the needs of the more mobile older persons who could still drive but were reluctant to do so.

Privately operated services can offer a high level of mobility—with correspondingly high levels of security and dignity—for those able to afford the fares. Using significant levels of volunteers (especially for their drivers, the largest expense of any transportation service) will enable them to provide low-cost services. To make the costs low enough to apply to the majority of elders, innovative payment schemes will also be required.

Informal transportation systems—families, friends, neighbors—provide the majority of trips for older adults (Kerschner and Aizenberg 2001). Volunteer groups, faith-based organizations, and others also provide trips. Often, it is the young old providing transportation for the older old. The quality of driving capabilities of the young-old drivers and other potential volunteers should be carefully addressed. There is a role in the future for all of today's familiar transportation services and for new innovative designs. Large vehicles operating on fixed routes and schedules can still serve high-volume routes and destinations. Neighborhood routes and feeder services, with multiple stops in small areas, will grow in number and demand. A strong role for taxis and paratransit services will develop as they change to meet increased demands for quality service and flexible responsiveness and pricing. Special services operated by human resource agencies will continue to address special client needs. Volunteer services will assume an even larger role in responding to unique needs of travelers for whom other services are not cost-effective. To the extent that all of these components can be managed and coordinated by one central office, the chances for high-quality cost-effective services rises dramatically.

Innovative transportation services are beginning to appear in some communities. Many current sources of inspiration and operating experiences can guide the development of future transportation options for older persons.

### Enhancing Auto Driver Capabilities

Another approach to improving mobility for older drivers could include improvements both to older drivers (their health and abilities) and to their driving environments. The possibilities include improving the health of seniors to reduce the possible reductions in driving skills, retraining older drivers, re-engineering automobiles, re-engineering the driving environment, and changing communities in ways that simplify certain trip patterns.

### Identifying Problem Drivers

Better systems are needed for identifying drivers who are unable to drive safely. More accurate and more universal testing systems would make it easier to determine potentially unsafe drivers. These new systems would also make family members and society in general feel that it was more acceptable to identify and then act as needed to assist or restrict drivers who exhibit safety problems.

### Retraining Older Drivers

Substantial efforts are being placed on retraining older drivers or updating their driving skills. Older drivers with back pain, perceptual difficulties, or orthopedic difficulties; stroke patients; and most accident victims—these are examples of candidates for retraining. Individuals with dementia would be poor candidates for retraining as drivers. Whether or not retraining actually helps an older person improve driving skills depends on some combination of the condition and type of impairment, a willingness to learn new skills, and most important, recognition by the older driver that he or she is no longer able to drive safely using current skills.

### Reengineering Autos and Roadways

Two aspects of "reengineering the auto" should be examined. The first is actually restructuring automobiles in general in order to construct a safer vehicle for all occupants. The other is to reengineer or adapt a particular auto to meet the needs of a particular person or persons, such as frail older individuals.

Our highway transportation system was not designed with large numbers of older drivers in mind. The large increases in crashes-per-mile driven by older drivers, beginning at age 55 and increasing at ever faster rates beginning at age 80, is strong testimony to the need for planning and design focusing on older drivers. Improved signage and highway markings and safer on/off ramps and traffic patterns, especially in merging lanes, could help facilitate safer driving for older drivers.

### Changing the Structure of Communities and Their Trip Patterns

The suburban neighborhoods of the United States were built around the automobile. In older, densely settled urban environments, residents walk to the grocery or pharmacy. In the suburbs, the automobile is practically the mandatory (as well as the preferred) mode of transportation due to the need to travel long distances to reach desired destinations. Some communities have changed their zoning laws to create neighborhoods that incorporate a mixture of residential, office/small business, and retail uses. The proximity of the different types of uses in these developments allows residents to walk to meet many of their needs.

In addition to developing new communities, current living environments should be reevaluated to create changes that positively contribute to serving rapidly growing numbers and proportions of older adults. Transportation plans should be evaluated on the extent to which they create communities that enhance older-sensitive transportation.

### Summary

The vast majority of older Americans have grown up in a culture that strongly depends on automotive transportation for mobility, and driving occupies a central role in the lives of many older persons. In the near future, there may be many more older persons who are unable to drive. No longer driving is seen as a major loss for many older individuals. It has even been called "a major life crisis." The loss of autonomy and independence, two values considered central to most Americans, makes it difficult for older people to relinquish their driving privileges. Most seniors expect their lives to be more difficult and less enjoyable after they stop driving. Decisions by older drivers about driving also have consequences for their families and friends, who are often faced with providing transportation for a senior citizen and bearing the associated costs, including their own loss of time and, perhaps, income.

Today's society is not yet prepared for the imminent changes of an aging population. Additional public and private sector responses will be necessary to provide for the safe mobility of all our citizens, including new kinds of vehicles, new designs for roadways, and new forms of transportation services. The costs of not responding to these challenges include the increasing isolation of our oldest citizens and the loss of their potential contributions to our society and potential increases in avoidable traffic injuries and fatalities. (See also COMMUNITY-BASED CARE; CONTINUING CARE RETIRE-

MENT COMMUNITIES [CCRCs]; HOME CARE SERVICES FOR OLDER ADULTS; LEISURE.)

**References**

Bly, P.H. 1993. "Growing Older, Wish to Travel: An Overview of the Demography and Travel Needs of the Older Road User." In *Proceedings of a Conference on Older Road Users—The Role of Government and the Professions*, ed. A.B. Clayton. Basingstoke, United Kingdom: Road Safety Research.

Burkhardt, E., A.M. Berger, M.A. Creedon, and A.T. McGavock. 1998. *Mobility and Independence: Changes and Challenges for Older Drivers*. Bethesda, MD: Ecosometrics, Inc. for the U.S. Department of Health and Human Services and the National Highway Traffic Safety Administration.

Burkhardt, J.E., et al. 2002. *Improving Transit Options for Older Persons*. Prepared for the Transit Cooperative Research Program, Transportation Research Board. Rockville; MD: Westat.

Central Plains Area Agency on Aging (AAA). 1995. "A Positive Approach to Retirement from Driving: Senior Transportation Project." Central Plains Area Agency on Aging, Wichita, KS.

Eisenhandler, S.A. 1992. "The Asphalt Identikit: Old Age and the Driver's License." *International Journal of Aging and Human Development* 30(1): 1–14.

Foley, D.J., H.K. Heimovitz, J.J. Guralnik, and D.B. Brock. 2002. "Driving Life Expectancy of Persons Aged 70 Years and Older in the United States." *American Journal of Public Health* 92(8): 1284–89.

Harper, J., and S. Schatz. 1998. *The Premature Reduction or Cessation of Driving*. Chapel Hill, NC: FGI, Inc. for the University of North Carolina Highway Safety Research Center.

Heckman, T., and L.F. Duke. 1997. *Driving Decisions for Seniors: A Practical Model of Elders Assisting One Another to Manage Their Own Mobility Choices*. Warren, MI: General Motors Corporation Research and Development Center.

Kerschner, H., and R. Aizenberg. 2001. *Supplemental Transportation Programs for Seniors*. Washington, DC: Prepared by the Beverly Foundation for the AAA Foundation for Traffic Safety.

Kihl, M., W. Goudy, and R. Mahayni. 1990. *The Need for Transportation Alternatives for the Rural Elderly: First Year Progress Report*. Department of Community and Regional Planning, University of Iowa.

Organization for Economic Cooperation and Development (OECD). 2001. *Ageing and Transport: Mobility Needs and Safety Issues*. Paris, France: Author.

Rogers, C.C. 1999. *Changes in the Older Population and Implications for Rural Areas*. Rural Economic Development Research Report Number 90. Washington, DC: Economic Research Service, U.S. Department of Agriculture.

Rosenbloom, S. 1996. "Understanding the Influence of Older Driver Disability on Mobility and Quality of Life." Presented to the Expert Panel Conference on Safety and Mobility Issues of Older Drivers, Leesburg, VA, 1999.

*Jon E. Burkhardt*

**TRUSTS,** legal arrangements by which the legal ownership and the beneficial ownership of assets are separated. A trust is normally created by a grantor (who may also be referred to as the settlor) who enters into a written agreement with the trustee and transfers property (the corpus) to the trustee; the trustee then administers the property according to that agreement. Although a trust may be established orally, for estate planning purposes, a properly written trust agreement should be used.

To illustrate, assume that John Brown, the grantor, conveys securities to Tom Smith, the trustee, with instructions that the securities should be invested and managed for the benefit of the grantor (John Brown). Tom Smith is perceived as the owner of the securities and would have the right to manage them in any manner he deemed appropriate. However, by virtue of the trust arrangement between the grantor and the trustee, Tom Smith is legally obligated to administer the securities pursuant to the terms of the trust. The parties are largely free to provide whatever terms they may agree upon for the administration of the trust.

### General Planning Issues

While numerous types of trusts target particular objectives, tax considerations under the federal income tax, estate tax, gift tax, and/or generation skipping tax often play major roles in the design of trusts. (The state tax treatment of trusts varies from state to state and is therefore beyond the scope of this discussion.) For income tax purposes, a trust may or may not be treated as a separate taxable entity, depending upon the extent of the grantor's reserved powers. Trusts that are revocable by the grantor are generally not recognized as separate taxpaying entities. The income and deductions generated in revocable trusts are reported directly on the income tax return of the grantor. Irrevocable trusts, however, are generally treated as separate taxpayers. Thus, transfer of an income-producing asset to an irrevocable trust moves the income from the grantor's tax return to the tax return of the trust. If the trust is in a lower marginal tax bracket than the grantor, the aggregate tax liability of the grantor and the trust will be lower than if the grantor had retained the asset and continued to report its income on his or her return. Changes in federal income tax rate brackets, however, may severely limit the ability of a family to reduce its overall tax liability by using trusts. For example, a trust now enters the top marginal income tax rate (38.6% for 2003, as this goes to press) once its income exceeds $7,500. By contrast, a married couple would not enter the top bracket until their taxable income exceeded $250,000.

Trusts are often indispensable components of financial plans designed to reduce federal gift and estate taxes. Under current law, individuals have an estate tax credit (the unified credit), which effectively exempts a stated amount from tax. As this goes to press, the exemption amounts are scheduled to increase gradually according to the schedule below, culminating in repeal of the estate tax in 2010 and revival of the tax in 2011. The U.S. Congress is considering accelerating these increases and the eventual repeal of the estate tax, and the reader is advised to check the current status of the law.

| Year | Exempt Amount |
|---|---|
| 2002 and 2003 | $1 million |
| 2004 and 2005 | $1.5 million |
| 2006, 2007, and 2008 | $2 million |
| 2009 | $3 million |
| 2010 | Estate Tax Repealed |

In addition, the comparable gift tax exemption is set to remain constant at $1 million. Thus, using 2003 as an example, every individual may give away, during lifetime or at death, or in any combination, as much as $1 million before incurring any gift or estate tax liability. Additionally, individuals may make annual gifts of up to $11,000 per year to as many individuals as they wish, which is not included in the $1 million exemption. This $11,000 annual gift tax exemption was originally set at $10,000 and is indexed for inflation; here again, the reader is advised to check a dependable tax source for the current amount.

Effective tax planning for a married couple requires that each take full advantage of the exemption amount as set forth above and the marital deduction. Because the marital deduction totally eliminates gift or estate tax on transfers between spouses (provided the recipient spouse is a U.S. citizen), there may be a temptation for each spouse to leave his or her entire estate to the survivor. No tax would be levied on that transfer, but it would have the effect of accumulating the entire joint estate in the estate of the survivor. Upon the survivor's death, only one exemption would be available to shelter the joint estate from taxation. A more tax effective plan would be for the first-to-die spouse to direct the exempt amount ($1 million for 2003, or the other tax-exempt amount for the year in question) into a trust for the benefit of the surviving spouse. If the surviving spouse's access to the assets of that trust is properly limited, the trust will not be considered part of the estate of the surviving spouse at his or her death and will therefore pass free of estate tax to children or other beneficiaries.

Trusts can also be employed to take advantage of the $1 million exemption currently available for generation skipping transfers. (Note: That exemption is also scheduled to change according to the table above.) Under the law as it stands for 2003, for example, an individual may leave as much as $1 million to a grandchild or more remote descendant without imposition of a generation skipping tax. Thus, as much as $1 million could be left to a grandchild without imposition of an estate tax in the generation of the child or the imposition of a generation skipping tax. The grantor may want his child to enjoy lifetime income of the trust for the lifetime of the child, while at the same time obtaining the benefits of the $1 million generation-skipping tax exemption for his grandchild; if this result is to be achieved, a trust must be employed. In addition to the tax considerations involved, trusts can serve many other purposes.

Situations frequently arise where the grantor wishes to provide income to a person for life, or a period of years, but thereafter wants the property to revert to other individuals. A typical example is a second marriage where each spouse has children from a prior marriage. Each spouse might want the surviving spouse to enjoy income from his or her estate for the spouse's lifetime. Upon the death of the surviving spouse, the first-to-die spouse might want an estate to revert back to his or her own children, not to children of their spouse. This can easily be accomplished through the use of a trust. In another situation, the grantor of the trust may want to provide for an individual who does not have the skill and business judgment necessary to manage the gift or bequest. The grantor can transfer assets to a trust for the benefit of that individual, naming a bank or trust company or other professional to manage the estate. Similarly, the intended beneficiary may be a spendthrift. If that person were to inherit property outright, it might soon be dissipated through improvident expenditures. Rather than giving property outright to such an individual, a trust can be created with appropriate limitations and controls on the beneficiary's access to the funds.

## Selection of a Trustee

Regardless of the type of trust, careful selection of a trustee is very important. First, the trustee must be a person whom the grantor trusts and who also possesses the skills and experience to administer the trust. A trustee must be able to discharge these responsibilities competently and efficiently. Although there are methods by which grantors and beneficiaries can enforce the proper administration of a trust by a trustee, those remedies are poor substitutes for a trust that is properly administered in the first place. A dishonest trustee will have ample opportunity to misappropriate funds from the trust. Even though the trustee may ultimately be held accountable for the misappropriation, unless assets are available for a dishonest trustee to make restitution to the trust, the trust and its beneficiaries are essentially without remedy.

A trustee may be one or more individuals, a bank or trust company, or a combination of an individual(s) and a bank or trust company. Institutional trustees may have certain advantages. They are professionals in the business of administering trusts and can do so in-house, while an individual may have to hire professional advisors to assist him or her in the administration of the trust. The relative costs of trustee selection must be carefully weighed in either case. Most institutional trustees have the advantage of longevity, although after recent bank failures, this cannot be said with the same certainty as in the past. However, if a bank or trust company fails, assets that it holds and administers as trustee are not subject to the claims of creditors or shareholders. An institutional trustee should also have greater neutrality and impartiality than close family members. If it is possible that the administration of the trust will create hard feelings among members of the family, a grantor may prefer that the anger be directed outside the family. It is often desirable, particularly in irrevocable trusts, to authorize a third person to remove the incumbent trustee and designate a successor. That power should not be included, however, without careful consideration of the potential tax consequences. Since the possibility exists that an individual trustee could die or become incapacitated prior to the termination of a trust, an alternative or successor trustee should be named.

## Revocable Living Trusts

A popular form of trust is the revocable living trust. While much has been written about their advantages, these advantages have been exaggerated. Revocable living trusts offer no tax advantages that cannot be obtained through other types of planning. A will, for example, can be prepared to realize the same estate tax savings as a living trust. Some nontax advantages, however, are unique to living trusts. Perhaps the most important is protection against incapacity or incompetence. Although other means can provide for the management of one's estate in the event of incapacity (most notably, durable powers of attorney), none works as well as a revocable living trust.

A revocable living trust is an arrangement whereby the grantor transfers ownership of assets to a trustee and reserves the right to revoke the trust at any time, withdraw assets from the trust, and otherwise direct the trustee regarding the administration of the trust. When the grantor no longer wishes or is unable to exercise any of those rights, the trustee assumes more complete management responsibilities. Thus, if the grantor becomes incapacitated, the trustee assumes a more active role, managing trust assets for the grantor's benefit, paying bills, and otherwise attending to the grantor's business affairs. A second advantage of a revocable living trust is avoidance of probate to the extent that assets have actually been transferred to the trust during the grantor's lifetime.

It therefore becomes important to go beyond merely creating the shell of the revocable living trust and to actually transfer ownership of assets to the trustee in order to avoid the time, expense, and other possible burdens of probate. A will must be probated to become operative and becomes a public record open to anyone wishing to inspect it. A trust generally remains a private document available only to the grantor, the trustee, and the beneficiaries of the trust. Many argue that an estate plan embodied in a living trust is better protected from contest than a plan embodied in a will. This is a debatable proposition, but at least implementation of the plan through a living trust may shorten the time period in which a contest may be launched. The time period for contesting a will begins on the date of probate, whereas the time period for contesting a living trust typically begins upon creation of the trust, or at the latest upon transfer of a particular asset to the living trust.

Living trusts have some disadvantages. The implementation of an estate plan through a living trust normally will be more expensive than implementation of a plan by a will. Additional legal documents (trust agreements) must be prepared, which will make the legal fees higher. Another disadvantage of a living trust is that assets must be transferred to the trust during one's lifetime in order to accomplish the intended benefits. This entails paperwork and administrative work. On the other hand, it is easier for the grantor to effect the change in ownership during his or her lifetime than it would be for an executor to administer those assets through the probate system after the grantor's death. In a sense, the creation and funding of a revocable living trust moves forward in time (i.e., makes earlier) the transfer of title that would otherwise occur after death.

### Bank Account Trusts

Most banks offer trust-type accounts. In this instance, the terms of the trust are established by the signature card for the account. Those terms are typically drawn in very broad fashion and should be reviewed carefully before opening such an account. Bank account trusts are to be distinguished from a true trust account, which might be opened by a trustee under a trust agreement. In the latter case, the terms of the deposit account would probably be identical to an individual deposit account except that the owner of the account would be designated as "John Smith, Trustee" rather than simply "John Smith."

### Totten Trusts

Individuals sometimes create a joint account in a bank or other financial institution rather than leaving property under their wills or using one of the other forms of trust discussed here. For example, John Smith may place funds in a bank account designated "John Smith and Robert Jones, Payable on Death to the Survivor."

If Robert Jones is still alive when John Smith dies, the funds in the account at that time will be payable to Jones. Smith, however, retains full control of the funds during his lifetime and is free to withdraw them if desired. Such an arrangement is sometimes referred to as a Totten trust, after an early case involving such a situation. Although called a trust, such an arrangement is *not* a trust and is really only a revocable gift payable at death.

### Uniform Custodial Trust Act

Many states have adopted the Uniform Custodial Trust Act. This act creates a form of statutory trust that individual grantors may adopt. By utilizing the uniform act in appropriate circumstances, one may avoid the expense of having a trust document especially tailored to his or her particular circumstances.

### Irrevocable Living Trusts

As the name suggests, an irrevocable living trust is a trust created during lifetime that cannot be amended or revoked. Lawyers sometimes refer to these as irrevocable inter vivos trusts. The fact that the document is irrevocable is a significant disadvantage, made acceptable only by other advantages gained. These advantages are usually tax related. Most often, the tax benefit that is sought is removal of property from the taxable estate of the grantor. This would only be a consideration if the grantor otherwise would have a taxable estate in excess of the prevailing estate tax exemption equivalent of $1 million for 2003 and increasing over time as described above. If the estate exceeds that threshold, ultimate tax liability can be reduced by taking advantage of the $11,000 per year gift tax exclusion. Gifts of $11,000 each year can be made to as many individuals as one wishes, and a married couple can make gifts of $22,000 per year to as many individuals as they wish. If, however, the individuals to whom they wish to make the gift are either too young to properly manage the property or lack the judgment and maturity to administer the property for some other reason, the gift can be to a trust for the benefit of that individual.

Irrevocable trusts can be used effectively in conjunction with life insurance. If an individual retains ownership of life insurance on his life until death, the full amount of the death proceeds will be subject to estate tax in his estate. However, if, before death, the insured transfers ownership of the policy to an irrevocable trust, and if the insured survives the transfer by at least three years, the policy proceeds will be exempt from estate tax, leading to very substantial reductions in estate tax.

### Testamentary Trusts

Testamentary trusts are trusts created by will. The same estate tax savings that can be realized through proper use of revocable living trusts can likewise be realized through proper use of testamentary trusts. The major difference between the two is that a living trust can be created and funded without having to deal with the probate system. A testamentary trust, because it is created by will, takes effect once the will is probated, and funding of the trust is normally delayed until the probate process is completed. Further, in some states, a testamentary trust is required to report on an ongoing basis to the probate court. It remains under the supervision of the probate court throughout its term.

### Charitable Trusts

Charitable trusts may be created during one's lifetime or by will. In order to obtain the tax benefits of charitable contributions, a trust created during one's lifetime must be an irrevocable trust. A purely charitable trust is a trust exclusively for the benefit of one or more charities. Contributions to a purely charitable trust are fully deductible for estate and gift tax purposes. For income tax purposes the deduction is subject to certain limitations based on the income of the grantor. A charitable trust is appropriate where the grantor wishes to benefit certain charities, yet does not want to entrust the investment and management of the gift to those charities. The grantor, in that case, may transfer the gift to a trustee directed to distribute trust income periodically to designated charities. Trusts also allow a hybrid form of charitable giving. In "split-interest" trusts, both charities and noncharities have some beneficial rights. In effect, these trusts combine a charitable gift with a transfer to a family member or other noncharitable beneficiary, and if the trust is arranged properly, the donor will be entitled to a charitable deduction for the value of the charitable interest in the trust.

In a charitable lead trust, the grantor directs that an income stream be distributed to a particular charity or charities for a specific term of years. Then, the capital, or corpus, of the trust is distributed to a family member or other noncharitable beneficiary. If drawn in compliance with the complex technical requirements of the Internal Revenue Code, the charitable lead interest reduces the value of the gift to the family member, thereby enabling the grantor to make a substantial gift at minimal tax cost. More common is the charitable remainder trust, which is the reverse of a charitable lead trust. In the case of a charitable remainder trust, the grantor may direct the distribution of an income interest to himself or to a family member or other noncharitable beneficiary for a period of up to 20 years or perhaps for the lifetime of that beneficiary. At the conclusion of the term, or upon the death of the beneficiary, the capital of the trust is distributed to one or more charities. In this case, the grantor is entitled to a charitable deduction for the value of the interest passing to the charity, which is calculated at the inception of the trust.

Pooled income funds and charitable gift annuities are two other ways a gift can be made to charity with a reserved income interest for the grantor or family member. Pooled income funds are similar to charitable remainder trusts except that the grantor does not have the burden of establishing a private trust agreement. He or she simply buys into an existing pooled arrangement previously established by the particular charity. In the case of a charitable gift annuity, there is no trust created, but rather the grantor (called a donor in this context) enters into an agreement with a charity. The donor transfers property to the charity and the charity agrees to pay an annuity for life to the donor and/or his or her spouse or another beneficiary. The value of the annuity stream, computed actuarially, is always less than the value of the property transferred, and the donor is entitled to a charitable deduction for the amount of that difference. (See also ATTORNEYS; CHARITABLE CONTRIBUTIONS; ESTATE PLANNING; FINANCIAL ADVISORS; KING LEAR SYNDROME; MEDICAID PLANNING; PROBATE; SAVINGS ACCOUNT TRUSTS; WILLS.)

### References

Berg, Adriane G. 1992. *Warning. Dying May be Hazardous to Your Wealth: How to Protect Your Life Savings for Yourself and Those You Love*. Hawthorne, NJ: Career Press.

Clifford, Denis. 1992. *Plan Your Estate with a Living Trust*. Berkeley, CA: Nolo Press.

Esperti, Robert, David A. Cahoone, and Renno L. Peterson. 2001. *The Living Trust Workbook:*

*How You and Your Legal Advisors Can Design, Fund, and Maintain Your Living Trust Plan, and Secure Your Family's Future*. New York: Penguin.

Irving, J., ed. 1992. *Wills and Trusts: How to Make a Will and How to Use Trusts*. Dobbs Ferry, NY: Oceana.

Olson, Russell L. 2003. *Investing in Pension Funds and Endowments: Tools and Guidelines for the New Independent Fiduciary*. New York: McGraw-Hill Trade.

Reutlinger, Mark. 1993. *Wills, Trusts, and Estates: Essential Terms and Concepts*. Boston, MA: Little, Brown.

Shenkman, Martin M. 1993. *The Complete Book of Trusts*. New York: John Wiley & Sons.

*C.L. (Tim) Dimos*
*Updated by Jerry J. McCoy*

# U

**U.S. PERSONAL SAVING RATE.** Despite the economic prosperity of the late 1990s, the personal saving rate has declined steadily in recent years in the United States and is now very low compared to historical levels and to the saving rates of most industrial economies. Given the importance of saving for economic growth and the retirement security of American households, this trend is cause for concern among many economists and policymakers.

## The Importance of Saving

Economists and policymakers alike have long stressed the importance of saving for national economic performance. An adequate supply of savings is important for two critical reasons. First, saving is the principal source of funding for the productivity-enhancing investments that fuel our economic growth. According to the latest data, the United States had the lowest personal saving rate among the major OECD (Organization for Economic Cooperation and Development) countries—just 2.3% of disposable income in 2001. As shown in Figure 1, this figure is substantially lower than the saving rates of Italy (15.4%), Belgium (13%), France (11.5%), and Germany (10.1%). Such low levels of saving have raised concerns about the long-run competitive strength of our economy and our ability to finance domestic investment without excessive reliance on foreign funding. In fact, it is widely believed that the low saving rate has played a major role in the large current account deficits and growing international indebtedness of the United States over the last decade.

Second, savings is a vital component of the financial security of American households during their retirement years. Many public finance experts agree that the U.S. saving rate is not great enough for households to maintain their current standard of living beyond retirement. For example, Stanford University professor Douglas Bernheim (1997) has found that a typical American household would need to triple its rate of asset accumulation to finance its retirement at its current standard of living. Using a variety of different approaches, a number of other economists all have reached the same conclusion. The current personal saving rate is simply not sufficient to fund a comfortable retirement for the typical baby boomer household. The importance of increasing retirement saving is further underscored by the fact that the number of retirement-aged persons (those 60 years of age or older) in the United States is expected to reach 18.8% of the total

**Figure 1**
**Household Saving Rates: Percentage of Disposable Household Income in 2001**

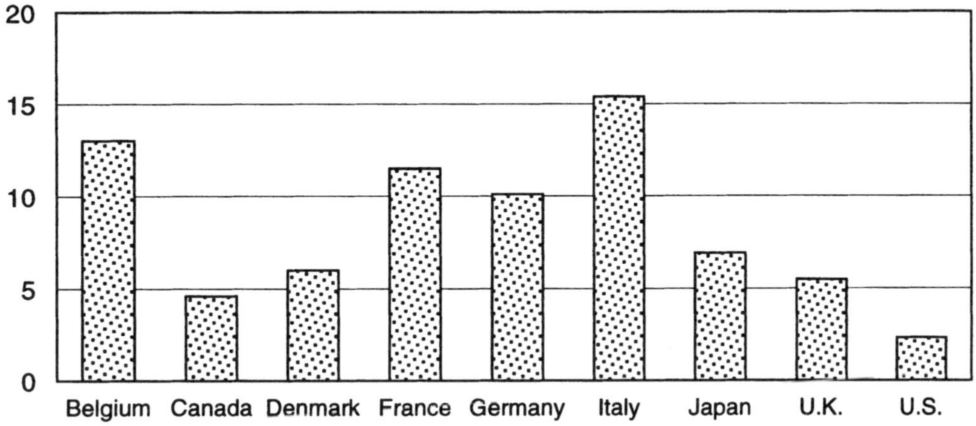


*Source*: OECD, Annex Table 24, Household Saving Rates, available at http://www.oecd.org/dataoecd/5/48/2483858.xls.

population by the year 2010 (Palacios and Pallares-Miralles 2000). In fact, the ratio of working-age population to the population over 60 years of age is estimated to decrease to 2.9 in year 2010 and to 1.7 by year 2040. These demographic changes will affect the ability of the Social Security System to meet its obligations. This is particularly alarming given that for many Americans Social Security remains the only source of funding for their retirement.

## Alternative Measures of the Saving Rate

The two most common methodologies used to measure personal saving in the United States are the National Income and Products Accounts (NIPA) approach, prepared by the Department of Commerce's Bureau of Economic Analysis, and the Flow of Funds Accounts (FoFA) approach, prepared by the Board of Governors of the Federal Reserve System.

In the NIPA approach, personal saving is measured as the residual of disposable personal income after subtracting personal consumption. The first step in this approach is to calculate personal income, which is the sum of wages and other labor income, returns to unincorporated business, other household income (such as rents, interests, and dividends), and government pension benefits. Disposable personal income is then defined to be personal income minus taxes (and certain other nontax payments). Personal saving is then defined to be the difference between disposable personal income and personal consumption expenditures, and the personal saving *rate* is the ratio of personal saving to disposable personal income. Whereas NIPA measures personal saving as a residual, the FoFA personal saving rate is a direct measure of the net addition to wealth. In other words, it is the difference between households' net acquisition of assets (financial assets such as cash, bank deposits, stocks, bonds, life insurance, pensions, and net investment in tangible assets such as residential structures, fixed assets, and consumer durables) and its net accumulation of liabilities.

**Figure 2**
**Personal Saving Rate, 1991–2001**

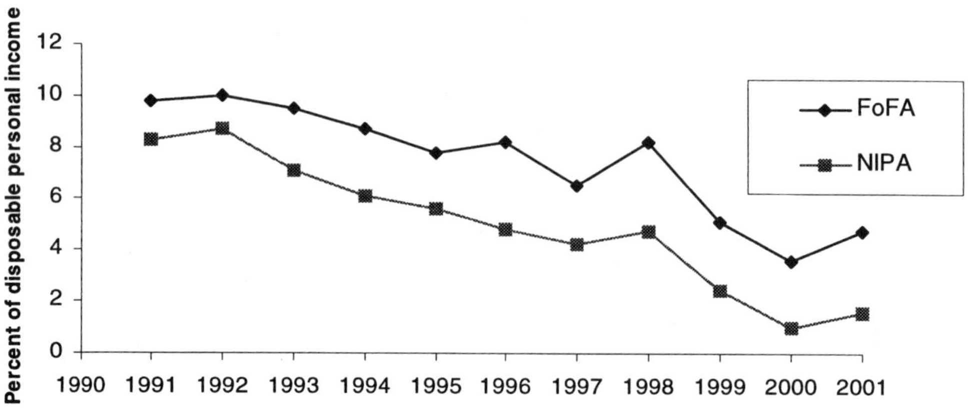


*Source*: Flow of Funds Accounts of the United States, Annual Flows and Outstandings, Board of Governors of the Federal Reserve System, available online at http://www.federalreserve.gov/releases/zl/current/data .htm.

While conceptually measuring the same macroeconomic aggregate, the NIPA and FoFA methodologies differ in two important ways: in the treatment of consumer durables and in the definition of personal income. First, while the NIPA measure treats the acquisition of consumer durables as consumption, the FoFA measure includes them in saving. Second, FoFA includes *realized* capital gains distributions (capital gains where profits have been made by the actual sale of an asset), whereas NIPA does not. Neither measure includes *unrealized* capital gains (capital gains that have not yet been obtained because an asset has not yet been sold). Because of this exclusion, some public finance experts believe that official estimates of the personal saving rate do not accurately reflect the situation in the United States. Critics, however, argue that although capital gains may increase household income, they do not directly provide new funds for firms to make investments. Furthermore, the recent sharp decline in the stock market has shown that there is no guarantee of continuous "gains."

Ultimately, the appropriateness of the NIPA and FoFA measures depends on the particular set of questions being considered. For the purposes of macroeconomic analysis and to answer questions about economic growth, the NIPA definition is usually considered to be the most useful because it measures the annual flow of funds available for saving and investment. When considering questions of household wealth and retirement saving, the FoFA measure may be more appropriate.

Although measured differently, the long-term trends in NIPA and FoFA saving rates are surprisingly similar. As shown in Figure 2, both measures have declined significantly since 1990. Although personal saving rebounded a bit in 2001, it remains very low relative to its historical levels. The FoFA personal saving rate declined from 9.8% in 1991 to 4.7% in 2001. Similarly, the NIPA saving rate fell from 8.3% to just 1.6% over the same period.

### Why Has the Saving Rate Declined?

According to a recent study by Satyendra Verma and Jules Lichtenstein (2000), the decline in personal saving rates over the last decade has for the most part been caused by four main factors: rising consumption, the wealth effect, increased transfer payments, and rising consumer credit card debt.

Many recent studies of the decline in the personal saving rate focus on the increase in personal consumption expenditures as a percentage of disposable personal income in recent years. Verma and Lichtenstein, for example, argue that increased consumption of services, and in particular medical services, has been a major source of the decline in saving. Between 1990 and 2001, real personal consumption of medical care increased from $710.9 billion to $938.3 billion, approximately 32% of personal income (Department of Commerce 2000a).

The "wealth effect" provides a second possible explanation for the recent decline in the U.S personal saving rate. The wealth effect implies that households will increase their level of spending in response to an increase in the value of their assets (regardless of whether the increase is realized or not). In fact, traditional macroeconometric models estimate that a dollar increase in household wealth boosts consumer spending by three to seven cents per year (Starr-McCluer 1998). The strong performance of the U.S. stock market in the late 1990s resulted in an enormous increase in household wealth, resulting in further increases in consumption due to the wealth effect. Over the past two years this effect has probably disappeared due to the decline in equity prices that began in late 2000.

The third factor that contributed to the decline in the saving rate is the increase in government transfer payments, which has reduced the perceived necessity of saving for many households. Government net transfer payments to individuals increased from $583.1 billion (or 10% of gross domestic product [GDP] in 1990 to $1,146.6 billion (or 14% of GDP) in 2001 (Department of Commerce 2003b). Aaron and Reischauer (1999) have argued that this increase in transfer payments has contributed to the decline in personal saving.

The fourth and final reason for the decline in the personal saving rate is the dramatic rise in consumer credit card debt. In many households, credit cards are being substituted for cash and checks as the preferred method of payment, and credit card advances are replacing other types of loans as a financing mechanism. Consumer credit, excluding mortgages, increased from $3.9 billion in 1992 to $69.5 billion in 1998, and the amount owned on consumer credit card debt soared to more that $1,289 billion during the same period. This rapid rise in the level of consumer debt has constrained households' ability to save.

### Retirement Saving: A Closer Look

As the baby boomer generation approaches retirement and demographic changes continue to put pressure on Social Security and Medicare, the extent to which households are adequately saving for retirement has attracted considerable attention in recent years. Unfortunately, many American households remain unaware of the need for further retirement saving. While financial experts believe that retirees will need 70% to 80% of their preretirement income to maintain their current living standards, many households expect to get by on much less. According to the "2002 Retirement Confidence Survey" conducted by the Employee Benefit Research Institute and the American Saving Education Council (2003), 17% of workers who participated in the study expect that they will need less than half of their preretirement income. In fact, only 32% of those surveyed have even tried to calculate how much they will need to save for retirement. According to the survey, 47% of workers have saved less than $50,000, and 15% state that they have saved nothing for retirement. A number of researchers have concluded that this is simply not enough. Bernheim (1993, 1997), for example, has shown that baby boomers on average save only about one-third as much as they will need to maintain their preretirement standard of living. A more recent study commissioned by the Consumer Federation of America found that only 44% of American households will accumulate a level of retirement savings sufficient to fund preretirement living standards throughout their retirement years (Montalto 2000). The report finds that income is the variable most closely associated with the ability to accumulate adequate retirement saving. Just 23% of households with annual income between $10,000 and $25,000 will have adequate retirement saving, whereas more than 69% of those with annual incomes in excess of $100,000 will have sufficient savings at retirement.

### How to Encourage Saving

Many experts believe that current tax law is biased against saving and that, in order to ensure continued prosperity and financial security, the United States must reform its current retirement system. To this end, a number of policy options have been suggested to help encourage saving, including the following:

1. *Increase the Limits on Contributions to 401(k)s and Individual Retirement Accounts (IRAs).* In a series of recent papers, a number of economists such as Poterba, Venti, and Wise (2001) and Pence (2001) have found a positive net effect on saving from IRAs and 401(k)s. As a result, many scholars argue that increasing the limits on contributions to 401(k)s and IRAs will have a strong positive impact on personal saving and retirement security.

2. *Improve Financial Literacy and Tax Incentives for Financial Education.* Given the facts cited above, educating America's workers about the importance of saving for retirement is a crucial part of any policy alternative. Many workers simply do not have enough financial knowledge to plan for retirement. Workplace financial education provides a useful medium for reaching these people. As such, tax incentives provided for employers who offer personal finance courses in the workplace provide one possible solution. Besides educating the worker on saving for retirement, this policy may stimulate conversation between coworkers and lead to competition among contributors—individuals may want to maintain the same standard of living as their social group. This "peer group" effect has been proven to have an important impact on saving decisions (Duflo and Saez 2000).

3. *Simplify and Stabilize the Tax Code.* The U.S. tax code is highly complicated and unpredictable. In the case of private retirement accounts, this difficulty can be an obstacle for the savers. Simplifying the tax code to make saving vehicles less complicated and easier to understand would have a positive impact on saving.

4. *Provide Tax Incentives for Savers.* Last but not least is the provision of tax incentives for savers such as tax-free rollover for reinvested mutual funds, interest, dividends,

and capital gains. Some policymakers oppose this idea, claiming that it would result in large revenue losses. However, such incentives are not really tax losses but tax deferrals. While tax receipts are lower today, tax-deferred saving vehicles result in an increase in tax receipts when the saver withdraws the funds at retirement. Furthermore, since new saving leads to new investment and presumably higher growth, the future tax base will be higher.

## Conclusions

Despite arguments to the contrary, it appears that the current level of personal saving in the United States is too low to support strong future growth of the economy and to ensure the financial security of the baby boom generation during their retirement. Furthermore, official government statistics indicate that personal saving continues to decline. Financial illiteracy, a lack of awareness about retirement needs, and the complexity of the U.S. tax code are all major factors contributing to this decline. In the current unstable economic environment, personal saving gains even more importance. As such, major steps need to be taken in order to address this alarming trend. (See also AGING INTO DEBT; ECONOMIC STATUS OF OLDER MEN AND WOMEN; FINANCIAL EDUCATION FOR SENIORS; FINANCIAL LITERACY; FINANCIAL PLANNING; INVESTMENT ADVICE; LIFE PLANNING; WEALTH SPAN.)

### References

Aaron, Henry J., and Robert D. Reischauer. 1999. *Countdown to Reform: The Great Social Security Debate*. Washington, DC: Brookings Institution Press.

Bernheim, B. Douglas. 1993. *Is the Baby Boom Generation Preparing Adequately for Retirement?* New York: Merrill Lynch.

Bernheim, B. Douglas. 1997. "The Adequacy of Personal Retirement Saving: Issues and Options." In *Facing the Age Wave*, ed. David Wise. Stanford, CA: Hoover Institute Press.

Department of Commerce. Bureau of Economic Analysis. 2003a. National Income and Product Account Tables, table 2.3: "Real Personal Consumption Expenditures by Major Type of Product, 1990–2001 Annual." Available online at http://www.bea.doc.gov/bea/dn/nipaweb/TableViewFixed.asp#Mid.

Department of Commerce. Bureau of Economic Analysis. 2003b. National Income and Product Account Tables, table 3.1: "Government Current Receipts and Expenditures." Available online at http://www.bea.doc.gov/bea/dn/nipaweb/TableViewFixed.asp#Mid.

Duflo, Esther, and Emmanuel Saez. 2000. "Participation and Investment Decisions in a Retirement Plan: The Influence of Colleagues' Choices." *NBER Working Paper* 7735.

Employee Benefit Research Institute (EBRI) and American Savings Education Council (ASEC). 2003. "2002 Retirement Confidence Survey." Available online at http://www.ebri.org/rcs/2002/.

Feldstein, Martin, ed. 1998. *Privatizing Social Security*. National Bureau of Economic Research. London: University of Chicago Press.

Mitchell, Olivia S., Brett Hammond, and Anna Rappaport, eds. 2000. *Forecasting Retirement Needs and Retirement Wealth*. Philadelphia: University of Pennsylvania Press.

Montalto, Catherine P. 2000. "Retirement Savings of American Households: Asset Levels and Adequacy." Report to the Consumer Federation of America and DirectAdvice.com, May 2.

Palacios, Robert, and Montserrat Pallares-Miralles. 2000. *International Patterns of Pension Provision*. Washington, DC: World Bank Press.

Pence, Karen M. 2001. "401(k)s and Household Saving: New Evidence from the Survey of Consumer Finances." Federal Reserve Board of Governors, mimeo.

Perozek, Maria G., and Marshall B. Reinsdorf. 2002. "Alternative Measures of Personal Saving." *Survey of Current Business* (April).

Poterba, James M., Steven F. Venti, and David Wise. 2001. "The Transition to Personal Accounts and Increasing Retirement Wealth: Macro and Micro Evidence." *NBER Working Paper* 8610.

Starr-McCluer, Martha. 1998. "Stock Market Wealth and Consumer Spending." Federal Reserve Board of Governors, mimeo.

Summers, Lawrence H. 2000. "Helping America to Save More." Remarks at the Choose to Save Forum, April 4–6, Washington, DC.

Verma, Satyendra, and Jules Lichtenstein. 2000. "The Declining Personal Saving Rate: Is There Cause for Alarm?" Washington, DC: AARP Public Policy Institute.

Warshawsky, Mark J., and John Ameriks. 2000. "How Prepared Are Americans for Retirement?" In *Forecasting Retirement Needs and Wealth*, ed. Olivia S. Mitchell, Brett Hammond, and Anna Rappaport. Philadelphia: University of Pennsylvania Press.

*Pinar Cebi, Margo Thorning, and Steven Wilber*

**U.S. SAVINGS BONDS** financial contracts that evidence loans made to and backed by the full faith and credit of the United States. Residents of the United States, its territories, and possessions, residents of Puerto Rico, U.S. citizens residing abroad, and civilian employees of and members of the armed services who have a Social Security number (regardless of citizenship) can all purchase savings bonds. Residents of Canada and Mexico who work in the United States may also purchase savings bonds, but only through payroll savings plans.

Historically attractive to smaller, conservative investors, the early and regular purchase of U.S. savings bonds offers a way to save for retirement and a method for supplementing 401(k)-type plans and other investments. Savings bonds are subject to federal tax but not state and local taxes. The payment of federal taxes is deferred until the bonds are cashed, and there are no penalties or restrictions for early liquidation. If needed, they can be used before retirement to protect other retirement investments. After retirement, bonds may be cashed to supplement other retirement income at a time when the bond owner may be in a lower income tax bracket. Savings bonds are issued by the U.S. Treasury Department. Unlike other bonds or other federal agency securities, they are not traded on the market, so holders cannot lose the redemption value of these investments despite fluctuations in the capital markets.

There are three types of savings bonds being issued today:

1. *Series EE Savings Bonds*. Accrual securities purchased at one-half face value (a $50 Series EE Savings Bond costs $25).
2. *Series I Bonds*. Inflation-indexed accrual securities that can be bought at full face value (a $50 Series I Savings Bond costs $50).
3. *Series HH Bonds*. Current income securities that can be purchased only in exchange for eligible Series E Savings Bonds, Series EE Savings Bonds, savings notes, or matured Series H Savings Bonds.

The minimum holding period for Series EE Savings Bonds and I Bonds is 12 months from the date of issue for those bonds issued February 2003 and later. Bonds issued prior to February 2003 will retain their minimum 6-month holding period.

### The Series EE Savings Bond

Series EE Savings Bonds are accrual securities issued by the Treasury Department in eight denominations—$50, $75, $100, $200, $500, $1,000, $5,000, and $10,000—for terms totaling 30 years. They are purchased at one-half face value and accumulate monthly interest that is compounded on the semiannual anniversary of the bond issue date. Its value increases as interest is added to the principal, and both principal and interest are paid in a lump sum when the bond is redeemed. Series EE Savings Bonds earn 90% of the average yields on five-year Treasury securities for the six months preceding the announcement of new rates each May and November.

### The I Bond

I Bonds are inflation-indexed accrual securities issued by the Treasury Department at full face value in the same eight denominations as Series EE Bonds. The interest rate for inflation-protected savings bonds is composed of two parts: a fixed base rate and an inflation adjustment. The fixed rate remains the same for the life of an I Bond. The inflation adjustment is updated every six months to track the inflation rate as computed using the Consumer Price Index. Each May and November, the fixed rate that will be in effect for all I Bonds issued during the following six months is announced by the Treasury Department. Also published at these times is the inflation rate and the composite rate that will be in effect for all I Bonds as they enter the new semiannual interest period during the new six-month period. While the traditional Series EE Bond is better known, in most cases the I Bond is a wiser investment because it protects the holder's earnings from inflation.

### The Series HH Savings Bond

Series HH Savings Bonds are current income securities issued by the Treasury Department for full face value in denominations of $500, $1,000, $5,000, and $10,000, *in exchange* for eligible Series E Savings Bonds, Series EE Savings Bonds, and savings notes, or upon reinvestment of the proceeds of matured Series H Savings Bonds. They cannot be purchased for cash. However, if the value of the securities being exchanged does not total the full face value of the new Series HH Savings Bond, the difference may be made up with cash. The interest rate is set when they are purchased and again at ten years from the issue date.

Unlike Series EE Savings Bonds and I Bonds, the Series HH Bond does not increase in value. Instead, every six months an interest payment is paid, and upon redemption, the face value of the bond is returned to the investor. Series HH Bonds reach final maturity, stop earning interest, and require payment of deferred income taxes 20 years from their issue date.

### Purchasing Savings Bonds

Series EE Savings Bonds and I Bonds may be purchased through any local financial institution, which serves as a savings bonds agent for the Treasury Department. Agents accept applications and payment for bonds and forward them to a Federal Reserve Bank, where the bonds are issued and mailed to the owner within 15 business days. Savings bonds may also be purchased online 24 hours a day, seven days a week, directly from the U.S. Treasury at http://www.savingsbonds.gov/. In addition, more than 40,000 employers help their employees save by offering the Payroll Savings Plan for U.S. savings bonds. (See also ASSET ALLOCATION AFTER RETIREMENT; FEDERAL AGENCY SECURITIES; INFLUENCES ON RETIREMENT INVESMENT DECISIONS; SAVINGS ACCOUNT TRUSTS.)

### Organizations

American Savings Education Council
U.S. Treasury Department

### Reference

Garner, Robert J., Robert B. Coplan, Martin Nissenbaum, Barbara J. Raasch, and Charles L. Ratner. 2000. *Ernst & Young's Personal Financial Planning Guide*. 3rd ed. New York: John Wiley & Sons.

*Lois A. Vitt*

# V

**VACATION HOMES AND RECREATIONAL PROPERTY,** any of a number of types of property used primarily for recreational purposes, vacation accommodations, or seasonal living, rather than for primary housing or investment purposes. The term *recreational properties* encompasses a variety of property types, such as vacation homes, cabins, and condominiums; lots used for camping or held for future construction of a second home; timeshare condominiums and certain types of vacation clubs; and campground memberships.

Little nonproprietary research of national or international scope is available for the recreational properties industry, when compared with other industries of similar size. However, due to the many developers, builders, realtors, marketers, and consultants involved in recreational properties, the dynamics of the market are well understood. The following discussion applies specifically to the United States, with other Westernized industrial countries displaying trends that are in some ways similar and in others significantly different.

Recent estimates indicate that about 8.6% of U.S. households, more than 9 million in total, own some form of recreational property. The number of recreational property owners is increasing by about 2.4% annually, with about 60% of this growth representing buyers of resort timeshares and related products, and the balance representing purchases of more traditional whole-ownership properties (Miner 1999). It has been estimated that about 3.1 million housing units (homes, condominiums, timeshares) are held for recreational purposes, with nearly 200,000 units changing ownership annually, not including timeshare purchases (National Association of Realtors 2000).

Ownership patterns regarding recreational property are most closely related to asset accumulation and therefore closely tied to the aging cycle. Because only the most affluent of households typically can afford recreational property or second homes when young, just 4.2% of households with a head under 40 years of age own any type of recreational property (Miner 1999). This proportion increases significantly with age, as income grows, assets accumulate, and children begin to appreciate outdoor recreation. Thus, the rate of recreational property and second-home ownership jumps to 10.6% among households headed by a 40- to 54-year-old.

By late middle age a further increase in household assets often occurs as the home mortgage matures, savings grow, and children cease being dependents. At this age, many people also begin planning for retirement. This may take the form of a recreational property or vacation home purchase, with the idea of converting the acquisition to a primary or seasonal home upon retirement. The rate of recreational property and second-home ownership jumps again among the 55 and older age group, to 15.2% (Miner 1999).

That recreational property ownership peaks among those 55 and older represents a phenomenon new to the 1990s. Prior studies showed recreational property ownership peaking among the 45 to 54 age group and declining precipitously thereafter (Miner 1990). Qualitative evidence and a variety of proprietary studies indicate that this change is due to a combination of factors: (1) greater health and longevity among those 55 and older; (2) recognition of health issues and changing cultural patterns resulting in increased physical activity among older Americans; and (3) recreational property purchase opportunities such as resort timesharing that are relatively affordable and require no personal upkeep by the owners. However, this same evidence indicates that recreational property ownership continues to decline after about age 70 or 75, when health issues that limit travel and activity levels, spousal deaths, and affordability issues become more significant. Studies have shown that about one in eight recreational property owners inherited their interest (Miner 1990).

Although these are the main trends in ownership of recreational property and vacation homes, there is marked variation depending on the specific form of recreational property. For the four main categories of recreational property, the specific trends relating to the aging cycle are as follows:

*Unimproved Land.* A recent survey found that only 14% of households aged 55 or older are interested in purchasing unimproved recreational land, as compared with 45% who are under 40 (Miner 1999). Land without a building typically is of greatest interest to younger households because of the low price and the romance of someday building a home. Proprietary studies show that older shoppers for recreational property often do not care for the added work of overseeing home construction, particularly in a location remote from where they reside. Seniors who purchase unimproved land are usually near-retirees or retirees contemplating construction of a home for retirement or semiretirement.

*Vacation Homes, Cabins, and Condominiums.* For these products, the primary difference between units purchased by the older adults and their younger counterparts is in design and location. Younger buyers may settle for a smaller unit with minimal storage or garage space to keep the price down, because they will be staying in the unit only for brief periods. Older buyers want more storage room, usually including a garage, to facilitate residential or seasonal living. Many prefer a minimum of stairs due to current or anticipated disabilities. Younger buyers purchase where they like to vacation, which may include exotic foreign locales and ski areas. Older buyers tend to prefer high-amenity areas near their primary home, or warmer Sunbelt locations. By state, the most desirable purchase locations among those 55 and older are Florida, Colorado, and California (Miner 1999).

*Timeshares and Other Shared-Ownership Accommodations.* Since the mid-1970s, the fastest-growing segment of the recreational property market has been timeshares and related types of shared-ownership vacation accommodations, if measured in terms of number of households owning such an interest (Miner 1999). Some 48% of those who own timeshares in the United States are 55 or older, and 25% are 65 or older (Miner 2000). Timeshares represent an affordable type of second home that many of today's active retirees can enjoy. Lawrence Welk Resort Villas in northern San Diego County is one of several timeshare resorts that cater specifically to senior citizens. During the past several years one of the fastest-growing subsegments within this category has been fractional ownership, which allows the purchase of three or more weeks of annual use at a time, a product ideally suited to retirees who desire multiweek vacation stays, often in off-peak periods when schools are in session.

*RV-Oriented Facilities.* Almost 7 million households own recreational vehicles (RVs), and sales run about $9 billion annually. RV ownership rates peak at about 10% among households aged 55 and over (Recreational Vehicle Industry Association 2002). Although rental sites are by far most widely used, other options include purchasing shared ownership in a private outdoor resort catering to RV owners or purchasing a lot located in a subdivision developed specifically for recreational vehicles. The latter facilities range from basic to quite luxurious: some lots are priced in excess of $100,000 and provide access to full resort amenities including golf courses, swimming pools, and recreational programs. The vast majority who purchase in such facilities are retirees.

Understanding the relationship between recreational property ownership and the aging process is increasingly important, because the number of Americans purchasing such property in anticipation of retirement or after retirement is expected to expand significantly over the next 20 to 30 years. This is due to such trends as (1) the long-term increase in affluence among the older population that facilitates ownership of this discretionary good; (2) the increased health and longevity of the population that generates more interest in maintaining quality of life and access to recreational opportunities during the senior years; and (3) the anticipated increase of the older adult population as the baby boom generation ages in coming years, potentially increasing demand for all types of goods and services desired by the older populations (Miner 1984). In anticipation of this trend, several major U.S. community developers have announced, or are investigating, initiatives to develop high-amenity vacation/seasonal/retirement communities in areas they perceive as desirable to the baby boom generation. Del Webb Corporation, developer of Sun Cities communities, has taken the step of registering the term *Zoomer* to denote the anticipated consumer of a new retirement community concept focused on highly active retirement.

The best industry sources of additional information on recreational properties and second homes are the American Resort Development Association, the Urban Land Institute, the National Association of Homebuilders, and the National Association of Realtors. All of these are located in Washington, DC. Some specialty consulting firms also conduct research regarding the recreational properties industry. Much information about recreational property also can be found on the Web, with listed organizations maintaining sites. (See also CASH FLOW PLANNING FOR RETIREES; CONDOMINIUMS; HEALTH AND LONGEVITY; HOMEOWNERSHIP; KING LEAR SYNDROME; LEISURE; MORTGAGE INSTRUMENTS; REAL ESTATE INVESTMENTS; RETIREMENT MIGRATION; SAVINGS INVESTMENTS; SENIORS HOUSING FINANCE.)

**Organizations**

American Resort Development Association
Recreation Vehicle Industry Association

Resort Condominiums International
Timeshare Users Group

### References

Miner, Steven S. 1984. "Get Ready for the Baby Boom Generation." *Resort Timesharing Today* 8: 4.

Miner, Steven S. 1990. *The American Recreational Property Survey 1990.* Washington, DC: National Association of Realtors, American Resort & Residential Development Association, National Foundation for Timesharing.

Miner, Steven S. 1999. *The American Recreational Property Survey: 1999.* Washington, DC: American Resort Development Association.

Miner, Steven S. 2000. *Timeshare Purchases: A Profile of Recent Activity, 2000 Edition, United States.* Parsippany, NJ: RCI.

National Association of Realtors. 2000. "Extrapolated Data on Second Homes/Recreational Properties." Press release, May 31.

Recreation Vehicle Industry Association. 2002. "Fast Facts." Available online at http://www.RVIA.org/.

Rezak, Sarah B. 2002. *A Competitive Analysis of the High-End Fractional Interest/Private Residence Club Market.* Parsippany, NJ: RCI.

*Steven S. Miner*

**VETERANS' BENEFITS,** payments and services provided by the U.S. government to former or current members of the armed forces or their dependents. Eligibility for Veterans Administration (VA) benefits is based on discharge from full-time active service under any circumstances other than dishonorable conditions, for a minimum period of 179 days during peacetime or 90 days during wartime. Active service generally means full-time service as a member of the army, navy, air force, marines, or Coast Guard or as a commissioned officer of the Public Health Service, the Environmental Service Administration, or the National Oceanic and Atmospheric Administration. Completion of at least six years of honorable service in the selected reserves also entitles veterans to some benefits. In addition, Veterans Administration benefits are provided for the Women's Air Force Service Pilots (WASPs), U.S. merchant seamen who served on blockships in support of Operation Mulberry, honorably discharged members of the American Volunteer Group (Flying Tigers), and American merchant marines in oceangoing service between December 7, 1941, and August 15, 1945, as well as other specifically designated groups who made a wartime contribution to our national security. Men and women veterans with similar service are entitled to the same benefits.

### Disability

Disability compensation is money paid directly to veterans disabled by injury or disease incurred or aggravated during active military service in the line of duty. The amount of the benefit depends on the degree of the disability. Veterans whose service-connected disabilities are rated 30% or more are entitled to additional allowances for dependents. Disabled veterans evaluated as 30% or more are entitled to receive a special allowance for spouses who are in need of the aid and attendance of another person. Disabled veterans may also be entitled to a grant from the VA for home modifications and may qualify for up to $5,500 toward the purchase of adaptive equipment for automobiles.

Veterans with a limited income may be eligible for support if they have 90 days or more of active military service, with at least one day during a period of war. These veterans must be permanently and totally disabled for reasons traceable neither to military service nor to willful misconduct. Payments are made to these veterans to bring the total income, including other retirement or Social Security income, to an established support level. The level of support is set by law and varies depending on number of dependents and if regular aid and attendance are needed. Pensions are not payable to those who have assets that can be used to provide adequate maintenance. Veterans aged 65 or older, or those who are blind or otherwise disabled, may be eligible for Supplemental Security Income (SSI).

### Education, Housing, and Life Insurance

The VA administers a number of educational programs. If a senior has not already used his or her educational benefits and would still like to receive education assistance from the VA, the only service still available is vocational rehabilitation. Those eligible for vocational rehabilitation are veterans and service members who served in the armed forces on or after September 16, 1940, if three conditions are met:

1. Service-connected disabilities or disabilities in active service were suffered.
2. Discharge or release occurred under other than dishonorable conditions or hospitalization occurred while awaiting separation for disability.
3. The VA determines that vocational rehabilitation is necessary to overcome employment impairments.

Enrollment in the program qualifies veterans for many other benefits programs, including some medical benefits for which they might not otherwise qualify.

Eligible veterans and surviving spouses who have not remarried may obtain VA-guaranteed loans for the purchase and refinancing of homes, condominiums, and manufactured homes. The VA guarantees part of the total loan so veterans may obtain mortgages on homes or condominiums with competitive interest rates. With VA guarantees, lenders are protected against losses up to the amount of the guarantee. To be eligible for a loan guarantee, applicants must have a good credit rating and have income sufficient to support the new mortgage payments. Applicants must also agree to occupy the property as a home. The amount of the VA guarantee is called the entitlement. The basic entitlement available to veterans is $36,000 or up to $60,000 for certain loans over $144,000.

The VA also provides certain homeowner's safeguards to veterans. Homes that were completed less than one year before purchase with VA financing, and inspected during construction by the VA or the Department of Housing and Urban Development (HUD), must meet or exceed VA minimum property requirements for construction and general acceptability. HUD administers the Federal Housing Administration (FHA) Home Mortgage Insurance Program for Veterans. These home loans require less down payment than other FHA programs.

Depending on the date of service and the date of issuance of the policy, veterans are entitled to a variety of life insurance policies. Veterans' life insurance is a complicated issue generally requiring the aid of professionals.

Most of the VA life insurance policies for seniors have closed. Generally, seniors must be enrolled in existing programs to be insured. These policies must be kept current, and collections on the policy should be made. For veterans who have life insurance under an existing plan and become totally disabled before age 65, the VA will pay the life insurance premiums. In order to qualify, veterans must be totally disabled and unable to work for at least six consecutive months.

### Dependents' Benefits

The U.S. government provides some special benefits to surviving spouses and minor children of veterans. Eligibility usually requires that the deceased veteran be discharged from active service under other than dishonorable conditions.

Dependency and indemnity compensation (DIC) benefits are paid to surviving dependents of veterans in certain circumstances. Benefits are paid for deaths due to service-connected disabilities and non-service-connected causes. Those eligible to receive DIC benefits for a death due to service-connected disabilities are surviving spouses, unmarried children under 18, helpless children, those between 18 and 23 if attending a VA-approved school, and low-income parents of service personnel or veterans who died from (1) diseases or injuries incurred or aggravated in the line of duty while on active duty or active duty training; (2) injuries incurred or aggravated in the line of duty while on inactive duty training; or (3) disabilities compensable by the VA. DIC payments are not available if death resulted from willful misconduct.

Those dependents eligible for service-connected disability DIC payments may receive them for non-service-connected deaths if (1) they were the dependents of veterans who suffered from totally service-connected disabilities at the time of death whose death was not the result of the service-connected disability and (2) either (a) the veteran was continuously rated totally disabled for a period of ten or more years immediately preceding death or (b) the rating was for a period of not less than five years from the date of discharge from military service. Payments for non-service-connected deaths are offset by any amount received from judicial proceedings. When death occurs after service, the veteran's discharge must have been under conditions other than dishonorable.

All surviving spouses of veterans who died after January 1, 1993, receive $935 a month. For deaths occurring before January 1, 1993, the amount paid is $935 or an amount based on the veteran's rank at the time of death.

A non-service-connected death pension, or "widow's pension," is available to surviving spouses of deceased veterans with wartime service and to their unmarried children under 18 or to age 23 if attending a VA-approved school. Pensions are not provided to those survivors whose estates are large enough to provide maintenance. The pension program provides monthly payments to bring survivors' incomes to a support level established by law.

Educational assistance benefits are available to spouses and children of deceased veterans under the following circumstances: (1) if the deceased veteran was totally disabled as the result of disabilities arising from active service; (2) if the veteran died from any cause while rated permanently and totally disabled from service-connected disabilities; or (3) the veteran was listed as missing in action or as a prisoner of war.

### Burial Benefits

Every honorably discharged veteran is entitled to some burial benefit provided that the veteran has not been convicted of a capital crime or of subversive activities. The benefit may include burial in a national cemetery, a headstone or marker, a Presidential Memorial Certificate, a burial flag, or even reimbursement of burial expenses. Qualified survivors may also be entitled to a one-time payment of $225 under Social Security. Burial benefits in VA national cemeteries include the gravesite, opening and closing of the grave, and perpetual care.

*National Cemeteries.* The National Cemetery Administration is authorized to bury eligible individuals in any VA national cemetery with available grave space. Many VA national cemeteries that have exhausted space for full-casket burials can still inter cremated remains. Many national cemeteries have columbaria for the interment of cremated remains or special gravesites for the burial of cremated remains. Headstones, markers, and their placement are provided at the government's expense. There is no charge for burial in a national cemetery. Deceased veterans may be buried in one of 120 national cemeteries in 39 states and Puerto Rico. Eligibility for burial in national cemeteries is limited to (1) armed forces members who die on active duty; (2) veterans who have been discharged or separated from active duty under conditions other than dishonorable and have completed the required period of service; and (3) any citizen of the United States who, during any war in which the United States has been or may hereafter be engaged, served in the armed forces of any government allied with the United States during that war, whose last active service was terminated honorably by death or otherwise, and who was a citizen of the United States at the time of entry into such service and at the time of death. For an enlisted person, service must have begun after September 7, 1980, and for an officer, service must have begun after October 16, 1981. The service must have been for a minimum of 24 months or the full period for which the person was called to active duty. There are certain exceptions, including veterans of the first Gulf War and reservists federalized by Presidential Act.

Spouses, dependents, and minor children of eligible veterans may be buried in national cemeteries, also under certain restrictions. These include (1) the spouse or not-remarried surviving spouse of an eligible person, even if that person is not buried or memorialized in a national cemetery; (2) the spouse of a member of the armed forces of the United States lost or buried at sea or officially determined to be permanently absent in a status of missing or missing in action or whose remains have been donated to science or cremated and the ashes scattered; or (3) the surviving spouse of an eligible decedent who remarries an ineligible individual and whose remarriage is void, terminated by the ineligible individual's death, or dissolved by annulment or divorce. The surviving spouse of an eligible decedent who remarries an eligible person retains his or her eligibility for burial in a national cemetery. Children of eligible service persons may also be eligible for burial in a national cemetery, provided they are unmarried and (1) under 21 years of age; (2) under 23 years of age but attending an approved educational institution; or (3) physically or mentally disabled and incapable of self-support before reaching 21 years of age.

Gravesites in national cemeteries can no longer be reserved; however, those who made reservations under previous programs will have their agreements honored. Generally, funeral directors or others making burial arrangements must apply at the time of death. There are special eligibility requirements for Arlington National Cemetery, such as service members who have died while on active duty, former POWs, and those listed as MIA, among others.

*Headstone.* The VA provides headstones and markers for the graves of veterans anywhere in the world, as well as headstones and markers for eligible dependents of veterans buried in national, state veteran, or federal cemeteries. Eligibility for a VA headstone or marker is generally the same as for burial in a national cemetery; however, the VA will not issue headstones or markers for spouses or dependents buried in private cemeteries. Pursuant to a law enacted on December 27, 2001, the VA will now furnish an appropriate marker for the graves of eligible veterans buried in private cemeteries, whose death occurred after the law's enactment, regardless of whether the grave is already marked with a nongovernment marker.

*Presidential Memorial Certificates.* Presidential Memorial Certificates, expressing the nation's grateful recognition of the veteran's service, may be obtained through the VA. The certificate is an engraved paper certificate, signed by the current president, to honor the memory of honorably discharged deceased veterans.

*American Flag.* The VA provides an American flag to drape the casket of all honorably discharged veterans and to persons entitled to retired military pay, including reservists. After the funeral service, the flag may be given to the next of kin or to a close associate of the deceased. The VA will also issue a flag on behalf of service members who were missing in action and later presumed dead. Flags may later be donated to a national cemetery to be flown on appropriate days if the cemetery has an Avenue of Flags program. By law, only one flag may be presented per veteran, and the flag cannot be replaced. Flags can be obtained at VA Regional offices, national cemeteries, and most local post offices.

*Burial at Sea.* The United States Navy Mortuary Affairs runs a burial at sea program. All active-duty members of the uniformed services, retirees, and veterans who were honorably discharged as well as civilian marine personnel of the Military Sealift Command, and dependent family members of active-duty personnel, retirees, and veterans of the uniformed services are eligible for the program. The burial at sea is a means of final disposition of remains that is performed on U.S. Navy vessels. The committal ceremony is performed while the ship is deployed. Therefore, family members are not allowed to be present. The commanding officer of the ship assigned to perform the ceremony will notify the family of the date, time, longitude, and latitude once the committal service has been completed.

*Burial Expenses.* In certain cases, the VA will reimburse some burial expenses. The VA will also pay a $300 burial and funeral allowance for veterans who, at the time of death, were entitled to receive pension or compensation or would have been entitled to compensation but for receipt of military retirement pay. Eligibility is also established when death occurs in a VA facility or a nursing home with which the VA contracted.

*Military Honors.* The Department of Defense (DoD), through the "Honoring Those Who Served" program, is responsible for providing military funeral services. The DoD, upon the family's request or at the behest of the respective funeral home on behalf of the veteran's family, gives each eligible veteran a military funeral honors ceremony to include the folding and the presentation of the U.S. burial flag and the playing of taps.

Moreover, the ceremony consists of two or more uniformed military persons with at least one member from the veteran's parent service of the armed forces.

### Health

The VA provides many health care benefits to veterans who qualify. Benefits include hospital and nursing home care, mental health care, domiciliary care, outpatient medical treatment, outpatient pharmacy services, dental treatment, counseling services, substance abuse treatment, and prosthetic and blind aids services.

Eligibility for VA health care depends on a number of factors. Generally, all veterans must be enrolled with the VA and may apply for enrollment at any time. However, they do not have to enroll if they (1) have a service-connected disability of 50% or more; (2) were discharged less than one year prior for a compensable disability; or (3) are receiving care for a service-connected disability. To permit better planning of health resources, however, these three categories of veterans are encouraged to enroll.

Veterans will be enrolled to the extent congressional appropriations allow. If appropriations are limited, enrollment will occur based on the following priorities:

1. *Priority Group One.* Veterans with service-connected conditions who are rated 50% or more disabled.
2. *Priority Group Two.* Veterans with service-connected conditions who are rated 30% or 40% disabled.
3. *Priority Group Three.* Veterans who are former prisoners of war (POWs), veterans with disabilities rated 10% to 20%, and veterans awarded special eligibility for disabilities incurred in treatment.
4. *Priority Group Four.* Veterans who are receiving aid and attendance or house-bound benefits and veterans who have been determined by the VA to be catastrophically disabled.
5. *Priority Group Five.* Non-service-connected veterans and service-connected veterans rated 0%, noncompensable disabled, who are determined to be unable to defray the expenses of needed care.
6. *Priority Group Six.* All other eligible veterans who are not required to make copayments for their treatment. This includes World War I and Mexican Border War veterans, veterans receiving care for disorders associated with exposure to toxic substances or environmental hazards while in service, and compensable 0% service-connected veterans.
7. *Priority Group Seven.* Non-service-connected veterans and noncompensable 0% service-connected veterans who agree to pay copayments.

Outpatient medical treatment for those who qualify includes medical examinations and related medical services, drugs and medicines, rehabilitation services, mental health services, and counseling. Also, as part of outpatient medical treatment, veterans may be eligible for hospital-based home health services and hospice care. Eligibility for outpatient medical treatment is limited. The VA must, however, furnish outpatient care without limitation to veterans for their service-connected disabilities and for any disability to veterans with a service-connected disability of 50% or more. Further, the VA must provide unlimited care for any injury or condition resulting from VA hospitalization. A recent Supreme Court ruling found that the VA must pay disability benefits to veterans for injuries caused by VA hospitals even when the hospitals were not negligent.

Outpatient care without limitation is also available to veterans in a VA-approved vocational rehabilitation program, former prisoners of war, World War I or Mexican Border Period veterans, and veterans who receive increased pension or compensation based on the need for regular aid and attendance of another person, or who are permanently housebound. The VA may provide outpatient medical treatment for any condition to prevent the need for hospitalization, to prepare for hospitalization, or to complete treatment after hospitalization care to veterans with service-connected disabilities of 40% or less, and veterans whose annual income is not less than the maximum annual pension rate. Veterans exposed to a toxic substance during service in Vietnam, veterans exposed to ionizing radiation following the detonation of a nuclear device, and veterans exposed to environmental contaminants in the Persian Gulf may receive outpatient medical treatment for conditions related to their exposure to these substances.

Veterans receiving medication for treatment of service-connected conditions, veterans rated with 50% or more service-connected disability, and veterans whose annual income does not exceed the maximum VA pension are not charged for pharmacy services. Veterans with a service-connected condition rated less than 50% receiving medication on an outpatient basis from a VA facility for treatment of non-service-connected disabilities or ailments are charged $2 for each 30-day supply of medication.

A full range of diagnostic, surgical, restorative, and preventative dental treatment is available to qualified veterans. Those eligible for full coverage include veterans whose dental condition or disabilities are service connected, veterans who have a dental condition upon discharge from the military and seek dental treatment within the requisite amount of time (up to one year), veterans who were prisoners of war for more than 90 days, veterans with 100% service-connected conditions, disabled veterans participating in a vocational rehabilitation program, veterans who have been admitted for inpatient medical treatment, and veterans whose dental condition can be shown to complicate a medical condition being treated by the VA. Other veterans may be eligible for some limited forms of dental treatment.

Veterans may apply for prosthetic services to treat any condition when receiving hospital, domiciliary, or nursing home care in a VA facility. Veterans who meet the basic requirements for outpatient medical treatment may be provided needed prosthetic services for a service-connected disability or adjunct condition.

Veterans whose blindness is a result of a service-connected disability, who are entitled to compensation from the VA for any service-connected disability, or who are eligible for VA medical services are also eligible to receive VA aid for the blind. Blind veterans need not be receiving compensation or a VA pension to be eligible for admission to a VA blind rehabilitation center or clinic or to receive services at a VA medical center.

The VA provides skilled or intermediate nursing care and related medical care in VA or private nursing homes for convalescents or persons who are not acutely ill and not in need of hospital care. Admission or transfer to VA nursing home care is the same as for hospital care. Direct admission to VA nursing homes is limited to (1) veterans who require nursing care for a service-connected disability; (2) any person who will require nursing care upon discharge from active service; and (3) veterans who have been discharged from a VA medical center and are receiving home health services from a VA medical center.

The VA Civilian Health and Medical Program, known as CHAMPVA, shares the cost of medical services and supplies obtained by dependents and survivors of certain veterans. The following are eligible for CHAMPVA benefits, provided they are not eligible for medical care under CHAMPUS (Civilian Health and Medical Program of the Uniformed Services) or Medicare Part A, as a result of reaching age 65:

1. Spouses or children of veterans who have a permanent and total service-connected disability;
2. Surviving spouses or children of veterans who died as a result of a service-connected condition, or who, at the time of death, were permanently and totally disabled from a service-connected condition; and
3. Surviving spouses or children of a person who died while on active military service in the line of duty, not due to misconduct, within 30 days of entry into active service.

Beneficiaries aged 65 or older who lose eligibility for CHAMPVA by becoming potentially eligible for Medicare Part A, or who qualify for Medicare Part A benefits on the basis of a disability, may reestablish CHAMPVA eligibility by submitting documents from the Social Security Administration certifying their nonentitlement to or exhaustion of Medicare Part A benefits. Persons under age 65 who are enrolled in both Medicare Parts A and B may become eligible for CHAMPVA as a secondary payer to Medicare.

Monthly retirement, disability, and survivors benefits are payable under Social Security to veterans and dependents if the veteran has earned enough work credits under the program. A one-time payment of $225 also is made upon the veteran's death and can be paid only to the veteran's eligible spouse or child who is entitled to benefits. Veterans may also qualify at age 65 for Medicare's hospital insurance and medical insurance. Medicare protection also is available to people who have received Social Security disability benefits for 24 months and insured people and their dependents who need dialysis or kidney transplants.

Active military service or active military service for training in the U.S. uniformed services has counted toward Social Security since January 1957, when taxes were first withheld from a service person's basic pay. Service personnel and veterans receive an additional $300 credit for each quarter in which they receive any basic pay for active duty or active duty for training after 1956 and before 1978. Retired veterans may be eligible for other credits, depending on the time and type of service.

Veterans and their spouses should be aware of the location of their discharge and separation papers. Because most benefits programs require honorable discharge, these papers are very important. If these documents have been lost, duplicate copies may be obtained by contacting the National Personnel Records Center. Military records that are incorrect may be corrected to redress injustices. Applications for the correction of military records, including review of discharges issued by court-martial, may be considered by a correction board.

The Defense Department issues veterans a military discharge form, identifying their condition of discharge: honorable, general, other than honorable, dishonorable, or bad conduct. Honorable and general discharges qualify veterans for most benefits, while other than honorable (dishonorable and bad conduct) generally disqualify veterans for most benefits programs. Veterans with disabilities incurred or aggravated during active military service may qualify for medical or related benefits regardless of separation and characterization of service. Because of the importance of the type of discharge, each of the military services maintains a Discharge Review Board with authority to change, correct, or modify discharges or dismissals that are not issued by a sentence of a general court-martial. (See also DEATH BENEFITS; ECONOMIC STATUS OF OLDER MEN AND WOMEN; OLD-AGE PROVISIONS AND ECONOMIC STATUS.)

### Organizations

CHAMPVA Center
Department of Veterans Affairs—Insurance Center
Department of Veterans Affairs—Office of Public Affairs
National Personnel Records Center
U.S. Soldiers' and Airmen's Home and U.S. Naval Home

### References

Department of Veterans Affairs. 1996. *Guaranteed Home Loans for Veterans.* VA Pamphlet 26-4. Washington, DC: GPO.

Department of Veterans Affairs. 2000. *Veterans Benefits for Older Americans.* VA Pamphlet 27-80-2. Washington, DC: GPO.

Department of Veterans Affairs. 2001. *A Summary of Department of Veterans Affairs Benefits.* VA Pamphlet 27-82-2. Washington, DC: GPO.

Department of Veterans Affairs. 2002. *Federal Benefits for Veterans and Dependents.* VA Pamphlet 80D. Washington, DC: GPO.

*Christopher R. McDowell*

**VOLUNTEERING,** donating time to an organization or assisting an individual or a group on an informal but regular basis. In the last four decades, older people have become an important part of the unpaid workforce in the United States. There are three major components to this change. The first and most significant is that a much larger proportion of older persons volunteer. While comparisons over time are difficult because of measurement differences, the trend is quite clear. In 1965, one in ten people over the age of 65 reported that they had volunteered at some point in the previous year. By 1990, this increased to 41% of those who were 60 and older (*Marriott Senior Volunteerism Study* 1991), and by 2000, it was 48% for people 55 and over (Independent Sector 2001).

A second trend is that people continue volunteering until much later in their lives. Approximately one in three people (33%) over the age of 75 volunteered in 1990 as compared to 43% ten years later. Given the higher incidence of serious illnesses past age 75 and the fact that poor health is a major reason why older people stop volunteering, the level of involvement by this age group compares favorably with that of teenagers and young adults.

A third development is that today's older population is better educated than in the past, and they have had lifelong patterns of community involvement. Consequently, they have a higher level of skills and a greater amount of past experience than previous generations.

### Cultural, Demographic, and Programmatic Factors

A broad array of social changes has contributed to the sharp rise in volunteerism by older adults. Perhaps the most important are cultural changes. Older people have been encouraged to become involved in volunteer work as a way to stay productive and contribute to their communities, especially during retirement. For several decades, the media has underscored the positive aspects of volunteering, describing it as a way to "make a difference" and "be a hero." More recently, there has been an emphasis on the importance of older adults as a source of wisdom, knowledge, and experience that can "give back" to their communities and to society and in some cases make a contribution to citizens in other societies.

In addition, there have been important changes in cultural conceptions about aging and the ways that older generations ought to construct their lives. In 1950, Robert Havighurst pointed out, "Few old people have the vigor, or the money, or the skill to do in their later years what they have always wanted to do but somehow have not got around to doing in their earlier life." These views began to change during the 1960s, reflecting a paradigm shift in the conceptualization of the aging process. A broad array of programs began to offer opportunities for older people to be contributors, rather than recipients of services. Older adults were no longer viewed as a problematic group in declining health and with limited social contacts who required help; instead, they were seen as a diverse population, most of whom could be active contributors to society.

The increase in older adults' involvement in volunteer work is also a reflection of demographic and economic changes. Older people are better educated and financially more secure today. There are also more opportunities to volunteer. Just as the supply of volunteers has increased—as a result of them being economically more secure, better educated, healthier, and more interested in volunteering—so too has the demand for their time and their talents.

In the past, some organizations like the Red Cross had a "retirement" age for volunteers. For the past four decades, a number of government and private sector initiatives have recruited and placed older persons in volunteer jobs, provided them with incentives to participate, and reduced financial barriers to participation.

Many public and private programs have been established to recruit and place older people in volunteer jobs. Quite a number of them were initiated or supported by the federal government. From 16 local programs for older volunteers in the United States in the mid-1960s, the number of national and local programs now defies estimation. These efforts have expanded the supply of older volunteers by making volunteerism attractive, by recruiting people and helping them find appropriate jobs, and sometimes, with programs like RSVP (Retired and Senior Volunteer Program), Senior Companion and Foster Grandparents, by reducing economic barriers through the granting of stipends, car fare, or a free lunch. Regardless of what caused it, there has been a noticeable shift in the attitudes about volunteerism. In 1974, only 10% of nonvolunteers over the age of 65 said they were interested in volunteer work (National Council on Aging 1975), compared to 25% to 37% in surveys conducted in the early 1900s (*Marriott Senior Volunteerism Study* 1991; Princeton Survey Research Associates 1991).

Four such programs are sponsored by the federal government. The Service Corps of Retired Executives (SCORE), with over 12,000 members, provides management expertise to prospective or current small business owners. Three other programs comprise the Corporation for National Service's Senior Corps. The Foster Grandparent Program, with 30,200 members, provides social and emotional support to children with special or exceptional needs, including autistic and physically handicapped, abused, and neglected children, teenage parents, and adolescents with substance abuse problems. The RSVP, with 480,000 members, sponsors volunteer placements in a broad range of nonprofit organizations. The Senior Companion Program (with 15,500 members) provides a stipend to volunteers who provide social support and visit frail and homebound people. Although these programs were originally sponsored by the federal government and continue to receive federal funding, some local RSVP, Senior Companion, and Foster Grandparent programs are public-private partnerships. They are sponsored by nongovernmental organizations and combine federal, state, and local funds, individual donations, and support from foundations and corporations.

Three kinds of jobs are especially prominent in programs under the auspices of nonprofit organizations: social support, mentoring, and business consulting. Family Friends, founded in 1986 by the National Council on Aging, receives funding from the Federal Administration on Aging. The program matches older volunteers with families experiencing stress because of homelessness or the responsibility of caring for a disabled or chronically ill child. The Experience Corps, which was founded in 1995, placed 800 retirees in 70 schools nationwide. The International Executive Service Corps (IESC) provides consulting services—in person or via the Internet—to companies throughout the world, particularly those who are developing capitalist economies. IESC works closely with the U.S. Agency for International Development doing on a global basis what SCORE volunteers do domestically. Similar work is also done in the United States by affiliates of the Executive Service Corps.

A far broader choice of jobs has been developed by AARP, the largest membership organization of older people. AARP relies on volunteers for a number of its programs including the Public Benefits Outreach Program, its lobbying work, and its voter education program. AARP's widely disseminated publications, *Modern Maturity* and *50 Plus*, have played a crucial role in shaping people's perceptions about community service.

These organizations have been an important catalyst in expanding volunteerism by older people but have directly involved a minority of them. The most recent survey on this issue was done in 1988. It revealed that 4% of older volunteers worked for RSVP, 2% for Foster Grandparents, 4% for Senior Companion, and 8% in AARP-sponsored programs (Hamilton and Schneider 1988). In fact, the largest concentration of older volunteers, 26% in 2000, is working in religious institutions. Close to 7% of Peace Corps volunteers in 1999 were over the age of 50.

### Continuity of Participation

Many of the programs designed to foster volunteerism by older persons assume that participation in volunteer activities is a way to keep active, particularly in the face of retirement and widowhood. There is, however, limited empirical support for this idea. The evidence shows that there is a great degree of continuity in volunteer patterns over the life cycle. Past involvement in volunteer work is a significant predictor of current activity, and a large proportion of older volunteers are simply continuing lifelong patterns. Older people who volunteer are generally more active: they are involved in a broader range of social activities and have stronger levels of connectedness to other people and to social institutions in general. A great deal of research on volunteerism and social involvement over the life cycle supports the proposition that people do not volunteer to become active but rather as part of a broader pattern of higher levels of activity. Two aspects of older people's lives that are important indicators in determining a willingness to volunteer—having free time and seeking companionship—were far less important than other factors. Rather than being people who have lost their main social roles and volunteer in order to keep active, older people are more often involved in volunteer work if they are married or if they are employed, irrespective of their age or health. Many older people combine paid and unpaid work, especially if they work part-time (Chambré 1987).

While involvement in community work is often an extension of people's work and family obligations, this is much less important for seniors. For example, older adults report that they are less often asked to volunteer than younger people. In 2000, 40% of people over 65 reported that they had been asked to volunteer in the past year as compared to 50% of those between 55 and 64 (Independent Sector 2001).

These findings should not be interpreted to mean that it is unrealistic to encourage older people to begin to become volunteers. Even though volunteer participation tends to be higher among elders with histories of community involvement, it is possible to attract new volunteers. Recruitment of retirees, in particular, is a cost-effective strategy because when they do volunteer, they devote more time than do other groups: 69% of retirees, 55% of working people, and 54% of homemakers devote ten or more hours a month to volunteer work (Princeton Survey Research Associates 1991).

### Social Factors Associated with Participation

The strongest predictor of volunteering is a person's educational achievement. Older people who have graduated from college are twice as likely to volunteer as those who have graduated from high school; two-thirds of college graduates over the age of 60 volunteer compared with one-third of high school graduates (*Marriott Senior Volunteerism Study* 1991). At present, racial differences in participation are not pronounced: 47% of all African Americans and 41% of Hispanics in the United States volunteer (Independent Sector 2001). Although most older volunteers are women, which is consistent with the composition of the older population, men's and women's participation have changed considerably in the last few decades. In 1965, 8% of men over age 65 volunteered, compared with 10% of women. By 1991, this pattern had reversed, and volunteering was more common for older men (46%) than for older women (38%) (*Marriott Senior Volunteerism Study* 1991).

Older volunteers are healthier and express higher levels of life satisfaction than people who do not volunteer. Although this may be due to the fact that healthier and happier people tend to be the ones who volunteer (Chambré 1987), there is a good deal of support for the idea that volunteering does in fact have a positive impact on people's well-being, particularly on their health (Midlarsky 1994; Musick, Herzog, and House 1999).

### What Will the Older Volunteer Workforce Be Like in the Future?

Several trends will alter the numbers of older volunteers in the future as well as their motives and expectations, the kinds of jobs that will interest them, and when and how much time they will be able to spend on volunteer activities. With the aging of the baby boomers, the size and the proportion of the older population will increase, which in turn will mean more older volunteers in the future. Older people are being encouraged to continue to work, often on a part-time basis, and growing numbers of people over 65 are remaining in the labor force. Older workers, particularly those who work on a part-time basis, are more likely to volunteer than those who are completely retired (Chambré 1987). One negative by-product is that this would reduce the number of older volunteers available during the 9-to-5 workday and the amount of time they work.

The average education of future generations of older people will be relatively high. In 1999, 13% of people who were 75 and older were college graduates as compared to 16% of those between 70 and 74, 20% of people in their sixties, and 25% of people between 55 and 59. This steep rise in the levels of education will not continue in the future since about 30% of all age groups under 50 are college graduates.

A better-educated older population means that there will be a larger number of people with specialized skills and past experience in community work. These qualities suggest, however, that there might be fewer people interested in clerical and unskilled tasks. This presents a challenge to volunteer directors since there are critical tasks that might not be fulfilling to a well-educated volunteer force but that nevertheless need to be done. It is the job of a volunteer director to provide creative and interesting volunteer positions but also to make critical yet mundane support tasks gratifying.

Transportation will also be a critical factor in attracting older volunteers. A larger number of elders now live in suburban areas than in central cities. This change suggests a need to arrange for transportation of older volunteers, not just to reimburse costs. In light of the suburbanization of the older population, a second strategy may be needed to create more jobs that can be done at home or close to home, such as neighborhood-based friendly visiting.

Continuing cultural changes also promise to expand the pool of older people interested in spending time volunteering. Organizations serving older persons and the mass media stress that old age is a stage in life when an older person can experience new challenges. In fact, two-thirds of adults see retirement as a time when they can start a "new chapter in life by being active, starting new activities and setting new goals." This is a far more common view than the traditional thinking of retirement as a time to take it easy, enjoy leisure time, and take a "much-deserved rest from work and responsibilities" (Peter D. Hart Research Associates 1999).

## Summary

Changes in the number of older persons who volunteer and the types of activities in which they are involved are a result of shifts in the educational and income profile of the older population as well as of new images and perceptions of later life. Due to their skills and their workday availability, older persons are currently the mainstay of many organizations. There is little evidence, however, that volunteering is a substitute for paid employment or for a decline in family responsibilities. Rather, volunteering is a way for seniors to continue and sometimes to expand their commitment to their communities, as well as a way of dealing with changes in their lives. Volunteering by older persons is conditioned by a desire to contribute to the solution of various social problems and a response to a broad range of social forces, just as it is for people in all other age groups. (See also GERONTOLOGICAL SOCIAL WORK; HEALTH AND LONGEVITY; LEISURE; LIFE PLANNING; STATE AND AREA AGENCIES ON AGING.)

### Organizations

AARP
Executive Service Corps
Experience Corps
Family Friends
Foster Grandparent Program
International Executive Service Corps
Retired and Senior Volunteer Program (RSVP)
Senior Companion Program
Service Corps of Retired Executives (SCORE)

### References

Chambré, Susan M. 1987. *Good Deeds in Old Age: Volunteerism by the New Leisure Class*. Lexington, MA: Lexington Books.

Hamilton, Frederick, and S. Schneider. 1988. *Attitudes of Americans over 45 Years of Age on Volunteerism*. Washington, DC: AARP.

Havighurst, Robert J. 1950. "Public Attitudes toward Various Activities of Older People." In *Planning the Older Years*, ed. Wilma Donahue and Clark Tibbits. Ann Arbor: University of Michigan Press.

Independent Sector. 2001. *America's Senior Volunteers*. Washington, DC: Author.

*Marriott Senior Volunteerism Study*. 1991. Commissioned by Marriott Senior Living Services and U.S. Administration on Aging. Washington, DC: U.S. Administration on Aging.

Midlarsky, Elizabeth. 1994. *Altruism in Later Life*. Thousand Oaks, CA: Sage.

Musick, Mark, A. Regula Herzog, and James S. House. 1999. "Volunteering and Mortality among Older Adults: Findings from a National Sample." *Journal of Gerontology: Social Sciences* 54B(3): S173–S80.

National Council on Aging. 1975. *The Myth and Reality of Aging in America*. Washington, DC: Author.

Peter D. Hart Research Associates. 1999. *The New Face of Retirement: Older Americans, Civic Engagement and the Longevity Revolution*. San Francisco, CA: Civic Ventures.

Princeton Survey Research Associates. 1991. *AARP's 12th Annual Survey of Middle-Aged and Older Americans*. Princeton, NJ: Author.

U.S. Department of Commerce. Bureau of the Census. 1991. *Statistical Abstract of the United States*. Washington, DC: GPO.

*Susan M. Chambré*

# W

**WEALTH SPAN,** a model introduced in 1987 by Davis W. Gregg for illustrating financial changes during stages of the human life cycle. Gregg ([1987] 1992) noted that although biologists, psychologists, and sociologists have examined human life from a developmental perspective, for much of the past hundred years "development" more often than not referred to children. Although the internationally renowned Human Development Program at the University of Chicago began to include maturation and change at the older end of the life cycle around 1941 (Havighurst 1993), the more contemporary origins of the wealth span model are found in the work of geriatrician John Rowe and psychologist Robert Kahn.

In outlining their concept of "successful aging," Rowe and Kahn (1987, 1998) argued that the *health span* can be seen as a set of developmental life-span stages through which an individual's health can be examined and then improved. Building on the same principles, the *wealth span* model (Cutler and Gregg 1991) suggests that successful aging includes a wealth dimension as well as a health dimension.

Two fundamental principles of Rowe and Kahn's health span are directly adaptable to the wealth span: first, as in health, there are identifiable stages in the wealth span. Since what happens earlier in life affects what happens later, the attributes of the earlier and later stages are fundamental building blocks of financial gerontology. Second, although for both health and wealth it is better to establish good habits earlier in life, it is never too late to start, and starting later is better than not starting good health and wealth habits at all.

The basic developmental model of the wealth span has two stages: the *accumulation stage* and the *expenditure stage*. Clearly real-life financial behavior is more complicated than this. The dichotomy of "accumulating when young" versus "spending when old" is a simplification of the complex world of individual and family financial behavior—as illustrated in the econometric controversies surrounding Modigliani's (1986) life-cycle theories of saving and dissaving. Rather, the purpose of a simplified heuristic model is not to be descriptively accurate but rather to focus attention on how the stages interact and, as noted below, how recent changes within each stage directly affect the financial behavior of middle-aged and older individuals. More generally, the wealth span model serves to introduce a number of key ideas of financial gerontology and offers a lens through which we can view several issues of both theoretical and applied importance.

**Figure 1**
**The Human Wealth Span: A Heuristic Model**

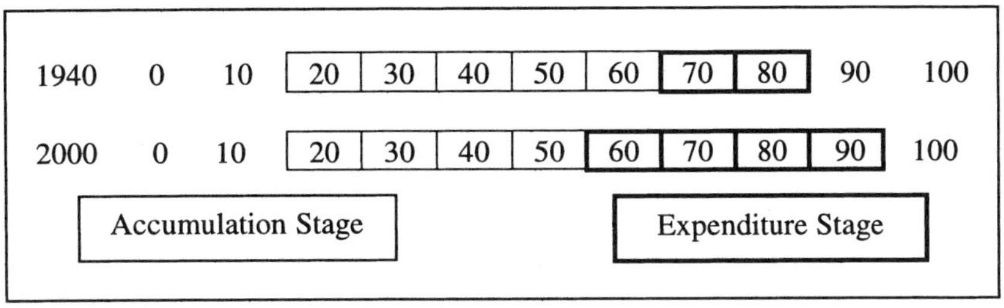


As an introduction to the wealth span model, this discussion reviews four main elements:

1. Recent historical changes in the relative size (i.e., number of years) or balance between the accumulation and expenditure stages.
2. Increasing complexities during the accumulation stage.
3. Increasing complexities during the expenditure stage.
4. The wealth span model as a lens for focusing on proactive, positive changes in financial behavior in middle age and older age. As described in greater detail elsewhere (Cutler 2002), the new complexities of the accumulation and expenditure stages, and the concomitant decisions that aging individuals and families are increasingly called upon to make because of these complexities, make the wealth span model an especially valuable tool for both researchers and financial practitioners.

## Historical Changes in the Human Wealth Span

Figure 1 displays the wealth span at two symbolic points in time: 1940 and 2000. This pair of years, illustrating the changing nature of the beginning and end of the accumulation and expenditure stages, is meant to be suggestive of "back then" versus "nowadays" and is not intended to be scientifically precise. In the 1940s, people entered the labor force at a young age, around age 17 or earlier, and could begin the accumulation process relatively early. Beginning in 1935 the Social Security system defined retirement at age 65, so the formal accumulation stage ended at about that age. Old-age life expectancy was comparatively low, suggesting that the expenditure stage in this heuristic wealth span model was fairly short, with people living on average until age 75 or 80.

By contrast, the relative size of these two stages in recent years is notably different. Currently, young people stay in school longer, including graduate and professional education, so that full-time labor force entry into the accumulation stage does not begin until the mid- to late twenties. What used to be called "early retirement" is now the norm, and many private pensions build on the fact that Social Security offers (reduced) pension benefits as early as age 62, and federal tax regulations allow withdrawals from defined contribution pension plans at age 59½. In Figure 1 retirement in 2000 is shown around age 60. These historical changes shorten the accumulation stage.

Although we fully recognize that for many families some accumulation continues during the retirement years, with retirement available around age 60, along with gains in longevity, the expenditure stage is now substantially longer than it was in 1940 (Cutler 1994).

Taken together, these demographic, social, and financial trends tend to *shorten the accumulation stage* of the wealth span and, simultaneously, *lengthen the expenditure stage* due to earlier retirement and greater old-age longevity. The pattern is clear: on average, people now accumulate for a smaller number of years, and what is thereby accumulated must last for a larger number of expenditure years. Consequently, the accumulation of personal, public, and employment-related financial resources must be planned in a more informed and systematic way than in years past.

### The Accumulation Stage Is Not Only Shorter But More Complex

The increased personal responsibility for informed accumulation strategies, that is, financial literacy, is prompted not only by the shorter accumulation stage of the wealth span but by its greater complexity. In the past (what some might now describe as "the good old days") financial security in old age often was seen as a simple function of the "three-legged stool"—Social Security as a basic retirement income pension, a guaranteed union- or employer-provided pension whose dollar benefit to the employee was defined in advance, and personal savings.

Social Security rules have changed many times in recent years, including the taxation of benefits. Accumulating personal savings as a source of income in old age has dramatically changed from the 14% interest rates of the 1970s to the 4% or lower rates of 1990–2000; and the dissolution of the 1985–2000 bull market has eroded confidence in equities as a safe haven for retirement investments. The most dramatic change in the accumulation stage of the wealth span, however, is in the financial structure of the American pension system. The trend from defined benefit pensions to defined contribution pensions puts much greater financial responsibility on the shoulders of individual citizens.

Where a defined benefit pension tells an employee and his or her family how much money they will get upon retirement, defined contribution pension plans define only what the employer and employee together put into the investment process. What those invested funds financially produce 20 to 40 years later is the responsibility of the employee (including knowledge, skill, temperament, and luck) and not the employer or the union. In turn, this requires substantial financial literacy on the part of the individual to answer such questions as what investments to choose, what kinds of risk to accept, how to manage risk and return, and how to balance inflation risk and capital loss risk. The accumulation stage of the wealth span, therefore, is not only shorter than it used to be but demands a much fuller and more literate understanding of financial dynamics and choices.

### The Expenditure Stage: Additional Complexities

The changing balance between a shorter accumulation stage and a longer expenditure stage seems like a plentiful financial challenge to today's middle-aged and older workers, but the situation is even more complex. Research points to two additional clusters of complexity related to the changing connections among families, finance, and aging. One of the basic principles of financial gerontology is that financial decisions are family decisions, and in this context the financial decisions made in middle age and later life have become much more intricate than they used to be.

*Who Are the DIPPIES?* "DIPPIES" is an acronym for Double Income (DI)–Plural Pensions (PP) and describes families in which both husband and wife are employed. During their working years, they not only earn current double income but also are accumulating two sets of future retirement income, that is, plural pensions. While having more money is not usually seen as a serious problem, from the perspective of the dynamics of the wealth span the key characteristic of DIPPIES is the *complexity* of their current and future income profile.

DIPPIES are not necessarily wealthy. In many working-class and middle-class families both husband and wife work just to make ends meet. The issue here is not riches but complexity. DIPPIES have complex financial situations during their working years but face additional planning challenges as they anticipate their future retirement income profile. They should anticipate two Social Security benefits, two employer pensions (which is made even more complex if either or both pensions are defined contribution pensions), two sets of savings and investments, home equity, and perhaps supplemental retirement accounts.

From the perspective of the wealth span model, the primary implication for DIPPIES is the challenge of financial planning for the future. As the family anticipates these multiple sources of future retirement income, decisions and choices must be made in advance. Issues of taxation, of investment strategies, and of allocation of financial resources to different categories of risk and return all focus attention on the changing dynamics of the contemporary wealth span.

*Financially Complex Intergenerational Relations.* Discussions of increasing life expectancy typically focus either on "individual aging," the implications of longevity for older men and women (such as problems of health and illness, including the cost of health care) or on "population aging," the implications for society as a whole (such as the impact of larger numbers of older persons on Social Security and Medicare). Often overlooked is "family aging," the impact of increasing longevity on the age structure of the family unit. Because financial decisions are so often family decisions, family aging plays a central role in responding to the changes taking place in the twenty-first-century wealth span.

The impact of family aging on intergenerational financial planning takes on greater significance as important decisions are confronted concerning health care, long-term care for self and for older parents, residential changes, intergenerational transfers, and estate planning. A recent study of the impact of greater life expectancy on American families provides dramatic evidence of the linkages among aging, families, and finance, with clear implications for the general principle that financial decisions are family decisions. Looking at changes in longevity over a hundred years, Uhlenberg (1996) traced the age structure of American families from 1900 to 2000 (see Table 1).

In years past, middle-aged couples might look forward to a period of dependent-free, "empty-nest" income-accumulation years in which funds could be set aside for later-life income security. By contrast, nowadays a majority of middle-agers have at least one parent alive. As Table 1 documents, between 1960 and 2000 the number of 50-year-olds with both parents alive increased from 14% to 27%, and the number of *60-year-old children* with at least one parent alive almost doubled, from 24% to 44%. In the context of the pressures on the accumulation and expenditure stages of the wealth span, the

**Table 1**
**Family Aging: The Impact of Longevity on Parent-Child Relationships**

| | 1900 | 1940 | 1960 | 2000 |
|---|---|---|---|---|
| At Age 50 | | | | |
| At least one parent alive | 39% | 52% | 67% | 80% |
| Both parents alive | 4% | 8% | 14% | 27% |
| At Age 60 | | | | |
| At least one parent alive | 7% | 13% | 24% | 44% |

*Source*: Uhlenberg 1996.

magnitude of the responsibility for aging parents is indicated by the mathematical observation that the mother of a "60-year-old child" is not 75 years old.

## The Good News: It's Never Too Late to Start Planning

Despite these several concerns, the wealth span model is not about "bad news." Rather, the intellectual origins of the model suggest an optimistic message. Recall that the origins of the wealth span concept are Rowe and Kahn's health span model with its two important principles: (1) what happens earlier in life affects what happens later; and (2) changes initiated even later in the health span life will have positive effects on the rest of life. Among other examples, Rowe and Kahn point to cigarette smoking. The bad news is that even a person who smokes half a pack a day is twice as likely to have heart disease compared to a nonsmoker. But the good news is that as soon as a person stops smoking, the risk of coronary heart disease declines, no matter how long the person has smoked:

> Within a few months, smokers who have managed to quit begin to reap the benefits. In five years, an ex-smoker is not much more likely to have heart disease than a person who has never smoked . . . [and] the good effects of quitting smoking hold regardless of age. (Rowe and Kahn 1998)

The same logic applies to financial behavior. It is best when individuals and families develop good financial habits early in life. But teaching young people good financial habits can be difficult; saving for "retirement" involves seeing oneself as old, which is difficult for most young adults. As in the health span, starting good habits later is better than not starting them at all. Learning the principles of compound interest, of tax-free accumulations in retirement accounts, of the differences between inflation risk and capital erosion risk, of the current and changing public and private pension rules and eligibilities—these are all central elements of financial literacy to acquire "now" even if they will not be implemented until later. Even starting at age 50 or later, implementing new or revised financial planning strategies can have a substantial positive impact on later life financial security.

### Summary

The wealth span model identifies three basic principles for understanding and anticipating financial planning across the life span. First, a combination of demographic, cultural, and economic trends has evolved to create a new balance (or imbalance) between the relative amounts of time available for accumulation compared with expenditure. Compared to "back then" there are now fewer years to accumulate the resources needed for a longer time spent in older age.

Second, within this shorter accumulation stage, financial life has become more complex, demanding a higher level of financial literacy. Individuals (and families) now have more personal responsibility for decisions concerning pensions, investments, and savings strategies. At the same time, the linkages among financial issues and family (and health) issues have become more complex due to such trends as an increasing number of DIPPIES—couples with dual incomes now and plural pensions in the future—and the consequences of "family aging," with an increasing number and percentage of middle-age children with surviving older parents.

Third, the wealth span, like the health span, suggests that "better late than never" has validity for financial behavior as it does for health habits. It is better to be financially literate and to begin good financial habits earlier in life. But if circumstances do not allow an early start, even later implementation of good wealth habits can have a positive influence on financial well-being in later life. (See also ASSET ALLOCATION AFTER RETIREMENT; FINANCIAL ADVISORS; FINANCIAL EDUCATION FOR SENIORS; FINANCIAL GERONTOLOGY, HISTORY OF; FINANCIAL SECURITY IN RETIREMENT; LIFE PLANNING.)

#### References

Cutler, Neal E. 1994. "Live Long (90+ Years) and Prosper: The Personal Financial Implications of Demographic Trends." *Journal of the American Society of CLU and ChFC* 48 (November): 35–37.

Cutler, Neal E. 1997. "The False Alarms and Blaring Sirens of Financial Literacy: Middle-Agers' Knowledge of Retirement Income, Health Finance, and Long-Term Care." *Generations* 21(Summer): 34–40.

Cutler, Neal E. 2002. *Advising Mature Clients: The New Science of Wealth Span Planning*. New York: John Wiley and Sons.

Cutler, Neal E., and D.W. Gregg. 1991. "The Human Wealth Span and Financial Well-Being in Old Age." *Generations* 15: 45–48.

Gregg, D.W. [1987] 1992. "The Wealth Span: A Promising Dimension for Gerontological Research." Invitational Symposium, Bryn Mawr, PA. Reprinted as: "Human Wealth Span: The Financial Dimensions of Successful Aging." In *Aging, Money, and Life Satisfaction: Aspects of Financial Gerontology*, ed. N.E. Cutler, D.W. Gregg, and M.P. Lawton. New York: Springer.

Havighurst, R.J. 1993. "History of Developmental Psychology: Socialization and Personality Development through the Life Span." In *Life-Span Developmental Psychology*, ed. P.B. Baltes and K.W. Schaie. New York: Academic Press.

Modigliani, F. 1986. "Life Cycle, Individual Thrift, and the Wealth of Nations." *Science* 234: 704–12.

Rowe, J.W., and R.L. Kahn. 1987. "Human Aging: Usual and Successful." *Science* 237: 143–49.

Rowe, J.W., and R.L. Kahn. 1998. *Successful Aging*. New York: Pantheon Books.

Salisbury, D.L. 1993. "Policy Implications of Changes in Employer Pension Protection." In *Pensions in a Changing Economy*, ed. R.V. Burkhauser and D.L. Salisbury. Washington, DC: Employee Benefit Research Institute.

Uhlenberg, P.I. 1996. "Mortality Decline in the Twentieth Century and Supply of Kin over the Life Course." *The Gerontologist* 20: 682–85.

*Neal E. Cutler*

**WIDOWHOOD,** marital status and phase in the life cycle prompted by separation from one's husband by death. The term refers to the survival of a wife. Widowerhood is used to define the status of a man when his wife dies. The financial concern associated with a spouse's death is due to the loss of economic resources, either of income that had been received or of assets that had been owned by the deceased spouse. To the extent that the reduction in economic resources is equal to the reduction in consumption of the now-smaller (by one) household, the surviving spouse may be no worse off financially than prior to widow(er)hood. However, widowhood is more likely than is widowerhood to be accompanied by a greater decline in income than in consumption needs. Indeed, data indicate that widowers are on average no worse off economically than they were when married; a wife's death reduces household income and assets by far less on average than when it is the husband who dies. This difference is due to men tending to be the larger income earner in married couple households and, therefore, the recipient of the larger share of a couple's retirement income and holder of the larger share of the couple's assets.

Income that is paid directly to one spouse is likely to cease or be reduced upon death unless some explicit arrangement is made for that income to continue to the surviving spouse. Declines in income upon a spouse's death that exceed consumption declines suggest insufficient preparation against that contingency. This may be because widowhood occurs unexpectedly early, because couples fail to correctly estimate the mortality risk and its financial consequences, because insufficient insurance is available against the loss of income upon widow(er)hood, or because couples choose against allocating resources from their joint lifetime to the period when only one survives. Each of these reasons plays some role in explaining the decline in incomes when husbands die.

### Measuring Change in the Economic Status of Widows

*Measures of Change.* Economic status indicators attempt to measure the ability of individuals and families to consume the goods and services that provide for their economic well-being and satisfaction. While some argue that a measure of consumption is the best measure of economic well-being, income and wealth are more commonly used measures of consumption potential because of their availability over time and across countries. These "economic resource" measures of economic status incorporate decisions about the income, assets, and in-kind benefits that should be included as "resources" and the consumption needs or standards with which these are to be compared. It is this comparison that allows an assessment of the adequacy of available resources or of the change in status when both income and household size change. The consequent ratio—most often labeled an "income-to-needs" measure—can then be used to compare the economic status of individuals as well as to compare an individual over different periods of time (e.g., when married and when widowed).

Income measures are the most widely available measure of resources, as these are regularly collected in monthly economic surveys and censuses. More complete resource measures would include "in-kind" benefits, on the argument that individuals who have, for example, employer-provided health insurance or Medicare coverage are better off than is someone without such coverage and who must pay out of pocket for health insurance. Because assets can be drawn on for consumption purposes, these should also be included to fully assess potential consumption and economic status. These include the assets that an individual holds and controls, such as bank savings, stocks and bonds, and retirement accounts. Deferred forms of income, such as employer-provided pension and Social Security, should also be included. The argument for the inclusion of these is that when savings can take many forms, one should not count someone who must save for retirement through his or her own purchase of mutual funds or bank savings as being better off than someone who saves for retirement through an employer-provided pension fund from which benefits will be received some years hence. Likewise, individuals covered by Social Security and those expecting higher benefits are better off than those not covered or with expected lower benefits. The "wealth value" of these deferred benefits is increasingly included in estimates of household economic status.

The poverty status of individuals is a measure that indicates whether a person's income falls below a specified income threshold. The U.S. official poverty threshold is an "absolute" threshold that in 2003 was $8,990 for a single individual and $12,120 for a two-person household. The threshold increases with family size and is adjusted each year by the Consumer Price Index (see http://aspe.os.dhhs.gov/poverty). This implies that two people can live as well as one with only a 26% increase in income. A "relative poverty scale" may also be used; cross national comparisons typically select a threshold that is some percentage (typically 40% or 50%) of median national household income. However, these measures as well require an estimate of the "economies of scale" of shared living (e.g., the U.S. poverty scale's 1.26 for a two versus one-person household). There are several other widely used scales (Buhmann et al. 1988), the use of each having an effect on the changes in "income to need" measured when one spouse of a couple dies (and the household is required to meet the consumption needs of the smaller household).

Using the U.S. official (absolute) poverty threshold, 21.8% of older unmarried women were poor in 2000 compared to the 10.2% poverty rate for all persons 65 and older (Social Security Administration 2002). A 40% of median household income standard gives similar results: in 1997, 25.5% of older unmarried women 65 and older fell below this threshold, compared to 12.0% of all older unmarried women (Holden and Brand 2003). The inclusion of wealth reduces poverty rates since the assumption that couples and individuals could draw on (e.g., by annuitizing) their wealth leads to higher potential income available to meet assumed consumption requirements. A study by Haveman, Holden, and Wolf (2003) that looks only at Social Security retired workers estimates "annuitized wealth" poverty of the single women sample at 8.9% compared to "income poverty" of 11.5%. The income-to-needs measure of this group was 2.11 compared to an annuitized wealth-to-needs measure of 2.63.

Regardless of the resource definition and of the consumption needs measure, U.S. widows are worse off on average compared to their married peers and, most important, compared to their status when married. Holden and Brand (2003) have shown that this is not the case in Germany and Britain, owing, they conclude, to the more uniform provisions of a broad public retirement system in those two countries compared to the more varied provisions of the private-public mixed retirement system in the United States.

*Data.* It is important to understand the best data resources for understanding the economic consequences of widowhood. Data collected in a single survey or census provide information only on the economic status of widows and married women at the time of the survey (or during the relevant income reference period) but in fact give little information on how financial status changes when husbands die. Widows identified at any point in time are an aggregate of women with different histories of marriage and widowhood. This and other factors may lead to biases of unknown magnitude and direction.

Only when women are followed from marriage into widowhood—as they can be with longitudinal panel studies—can the consequence of the widowhood event itself be observed and separated from other influences that may confound the measure of its economic effects. The availability of several major panel studies has advanced our understanding of the financial effects of widowhood. These include the Health and Retirement Study (see http://hrsonline.isr.umich.edu/), the Panel Survey of Income Dynamics (see http://hrsonline.isr.umich.edu/), and the Survey of Income and Program Participation (see http://www.sipp.census.gov/sipp/). This does not exhaust the list of appropriate panel surveys, including some focused on select populations but with rich income and asset data.

Yet even panel studies must take care to accurately assess the impact of widowhood itself on economic status. Examining financial changes only of couples in which the husband dies without comparison to other marital status groups implies that widowhood is the primary variable explaining changes in income in the years before and after the husband's death. Yet, over the same period, other women of the same age—those who remain married and those who were never married—may be experiencing similar changes. For example, job market conditions may lead to earlier retirements or layoffs among all women, inflation rates may increase, or the stock market or housing prices may fall; these factors will erode the real value of income and income-producing assets of all individuals. The effect of widowhood on women widowed during these periods will be exaggerated. To capture these societywide influences, comparisons should be made with women who remained married during the same period.

*Changes in Economic Status.* The higher poverty rate of unmarried women in their later years is a consequence of three general phenomena: the economic disadvantages faced by women alone at any age, the association between mortality and economic status, and the loss of resources when husbands die. The first implies that for women who were widowed or divorced early in life or who never married, poverty may be a continuation of lifelong economic vulnerability. Long-term gains in education, occupational attainment, and earnings of women will reduce the vulnerability of this group. The second suggests that, for some women, poverty when widowed is a consequence of less healthy husbands' lower earnings and higher risk of mortality. The selection of poorer couples into widowhood accounts for some of the higher poverty rates for them than for couples. Work by Holden and Brand (2003) and Zick and Holden (2000) documents the lower income and assets when married of women who later become widowed. Thus for some share of older women, their lower economic status is a continuation of economic disadvantages faced throughout their lives—of marriage to low-income and less-healthy men and of gender-based labor market hiring and work decisions. This appears to account for an important but minority share of observed changes in economic resources when spouses die. The larger difference is due to the direct economic consequences of a husband's death.

As described, changes in economic status upon widowhood may be measured in a variety of ways, with changes in poverty rates and changes in income (or resources) relative to a needs measure the most often used. Income-to-needs ratios adjust household income for the consumption needs of households of different sizes. Changes in poverty status identify widows whose income crosses a specific threshold (even with a small income change) but do not identify income changes that may be large for those remaining above or below that threshold. Large changes in income are more prevalent at widowhood than declines into poverty and distinguish a different group of women at risk.

While greater income as a couple reduces the chances of a widow entering poverty, it increases the chances of her suffering a major decline in income to needs. Women who were relatively better off when married experience larger average percentage income-to-needs changes when their husbands die than do widows from couples with lower incomes. In part, this occurs because a lower percentage of the income of better-off couples comes from sources (e.g., Social Security) that continue automatically to the widow. There is also some evidence that higher-income couples are more likely to underinsure against income loss.

Studies using panel data document an important role for prewidowhood differences and postwidowhood changes in income in explaining observed cross-sectional differences between married and widowed women. Nevertheless, these studies also show that widowhood itself exacts a large economic loss (Holden and Brand 2003; Holden and Smock 1991). These changes appear to be especially large for women widowed at younger ages, in part because of age-related eligibility rules in Social Security and private pensions but also because younger couples may underestimate the risk of widowhood and, although they have had less time to self-insure through their own accumulated savings, purchase far less insurance than is optimal against the loss of the husband's earnings. Zick and Smith (1991) report that average income-to-needs ratios five years after widowhood are more than 60% below the ratios for intact couples. For younger widows (under age 60), the drop in income at their husbands' death fully accounted for the difference between them and the comparable group of intact couples. For older widows (age 60 and above), lower prewidowhood income-to-needs ratios explained a larger share of the difference between them and intact couples, in part because husbands were already retired. However, for those widows whose husbands had worked just prior to death, the income decline was large. For them the income consequences of the husband's "retirement" and his death coincided. This different situation for older than younger widows is due to older couples having had more years to accumulate savings and to the greater dependence of the older couples on Social Security and pensions, some of which continues to be paid to the widow.

## Protection against the Loss of Financial Resources

Widowhood presents a financial issue because both partners in a marriage will not usually survive for exactly the same number of years and because the timing of death and duration of widowhood are uncertain for an individual. Even if on average male and female life expectancies were equal, variations in individuals' death and survival mean that most women and men could expect to lose their partners and live some years alone. As cohorts aged, they would be increasingly composed of widows (and widowers). Higher mortality among men than women and the average younger ages of wives make outliving one's spouse a far more likely event for women than for men. Women are more likely to lose their spouses through death at younger ages than men, are far less likely to remarry after their spouses die, are far more likely to remarry older partners, and are more likely to survive alone for a far longer period of time following their husbands' deaths. Although issues of survivorship are equally applicable to men and women, it is for women that protection against the loss of financial resources when their spouse dies is most important and most inadequate.

The greater dependence of wives on husbands' income than vice versa makes the economic hazards of a spouse's death greater for women than men. The greater work participation of women will reduce this risk over time but will not eliminate it. And changes in Social Security rules and the greater dependence on defined contribution pension plans and personal savings may in fact offset some of the impact of lengthening work lives.

*Pension Protection.* Both Social Security and federal pension regulations aim to reduce the economic vulnerability of women to their husbands' deaths. The 1974 Employee Retirement Income Security Act (ERISA) established minimum fiduciary, coverage, and vesting requirements for private pension plans. It mandated that pension plans' default payment option for married workers be a joint and survivor pension (a pension that continues to pay benefits to a survivor), payable to the worker's spouse, and paying an amount equal at least to 50% of the worker's benefit under this option. Because payment is over a longer period of time under this option, the worker's benefit will be reduced from the single-life benefit (a benefit payable only until the worker's death). Under ERISA the worker could unilaterally opt out of the joint-and-survivor option; the 1984 Retirement Equity Act (REA) amendments to ERISA require that the spouse sign a notarized form permitting this opt-out. The effect of ERISA and REA are limited by their coverage only of private employer–provided pensions, excluding the 22% of pension participants in public plans from its protection. In addition, private retirement plans that are not "employee welfare benefit plans" are not regulated by ERISA pension plan provisions (e.g., Individual Retirement Accounts and annuities purchased from life insurance companies). Consequently, when an individual takes a lump-sum pension distribution at retirement and rolls it over into another savings vehicle, the annuities are not subject to ERISA survivorship payout rules. Further, ERISA requires benefit payments only to the current spouse of a retiring worker, although support obligations or the division at divorce of pensions earned during marriage may protect former spouses.

Pensions can reduce economic vulnerability for the widows only of the 50% to 60% of men who are eligible for a pension when they retire. Even among this group, a survivor pension is more likely to be selected (in both the pre- and post-ERISA years) by couples with higher income and more assets and whose pension wealth is a higher proportion of all wealth. These relationships are consistent with the expectation that couples who can afford to forego current income while both are alive in return for survivor benefits will purchase insurance against the consequences of widowhood. While couples without pension coverage may use other forms of insurance, including life insurance, data on life insurance holdings and the decline in income observed even among high-income widows are evidence of inadequate life insurance coverage among couples in general.

*Social Security Protection.* Old-Age Income and Survivors Insurance (OASI), also known in the U.S. as "Social Security," provides an assured benefit to surviving spouses (including divorced surviving spouses) who meet eligibility requirements. Benefits are equal to the benefit for which the deceased worker would have been eligible. Benefits are payable to surviving spouses of Social Security, fully insured workers at age 60, or at age 55 if disabled. However, benefits are reduced (but to no less than 82.5% of the deceased worker's benefit) when received at ages below the full retirement age (65 for individuals turning age 62 prior to 1999, gradually rising to age 67 for those turning age 62 in 2020). Younger survivors are eligible if caring for a child under age 16 or the adult disabled child of the deceased worker. Survivor benefits are offset by any retired worker benefit for which the survivor is eligible, which is equivalent to paying the higher of any benefit for which the beneficiary is eligible (the so-called dual entitlement provision). Benefits may also be offset by earnings of beneficiaries under the age of 65, the age above which there is no limit on earnings. Divorced survivor benefits are payable when a marriage lasted 10 years or more. Survivor benefits are not payable when the survivor remarries or has remarried before reaching age 60 (age 55 for disabled widows). However, the death of or divorce from a subsequent spouse reinstates eligibility for benefits based on the prior spouse's record (see http://www.ssa.gov/ for detailed benefit descriptions).

The age distinction in Social Security appears to matter to the magnitude of change in economic status when husbands die (Holden, Burkhauser, and Feaster 1988). Wives younger than 60 when widowed are more likely to enter poverty after widowhood, which is evidence of the protection from age-conditioned insurance and, perhaps, of the short-term difficulties faced by younger women in adjusting their employment to the loss of a husband's income.

The offset of the survivor's benefit by an individual's own benefits (the so-called dual entitlement provisions) means that though some benefit level is guaranteed, for some survivors that level may be no greater than the benefit received prior to widow(er)hood. Consider a couple in which covered earnings were identical and therefore whose retired worker benefits were equal. The death of either one entitles the survivor to a benefit equal to 100% of the deceased spouse's. But because benefits are identical, the survivor benefit, while guaranteeing that amount, pays no more. Thus, the death of one spouse in an equal-earner couple will leave the survivor with only his or her benefit—an amount equal to only one-half of the combined Social Security benefit received when both were alive. The death of one spouse in a single-earner couple results in a payment equal to two-thirds of the combined benefits since a nonworking spouse is paid a benefit equal to 50% of the worker's.

For low-income two-earner couples, who are likely to be more dependent on Social Security in retirement, the loss of one-half the couple's combined income may cause financial hardship. A decline in income by 50%, when the decline in consumption needs implied by the U.S. poverty threshold is only 20%, will alone result in a measured decline in economic status upon widowhood using either poverty- or income-to-needs-based measures. Legislative proposals to change survivor benefits to equal some higher percentage of the combined couple's benefits would both raise incomes of widows and reduce the implicit cost to widows of greater sharing of earnings efforts between spouses (Burkhauser and Smeeding 1994).

### Insuring against the Costs of Widowhood

The evidence indicates that widowhood continues to exact an economic cost on women at the time of their husband's death. Even when one takes account of the negative association between economic status and mortality (i.e., that widows tend to come from couples with lower economic resources) and adjusting for the decline in consumption needs, women who were widowed during the 1990s in the United States experienced a decline in income and assets. The exact magnitude of this decline depends critically on the "equivalence scale" that is used in adjusting for consumption changes. Using the U.S. poverty threshold, that decline is by about 27%. This contrasts with the experience of men when wives die; while loss of wives' Social Security benefits is observed, the needs-adjusted income of husbands remains stable for widowers.

The chances of widows entering poverty will diminish as wives' ownership of assets and eligibility for employer-provided pensions and Social Security retired worker benefits provide a protective floor. However, as equality of earnings between spouses increases, the share of the couple's combined Social Security benefits continuing to the widow will decline from two-thirds for single-earner couples to 50%. As wives become eligible for their own employer pensions, husbands may be less likely to provide for a survivor benefit, thereby offsetting the protective effects of the wife's own greater retirement income. For some couples, lower levels of protection from pensions may be offset by other forms of insurance. But evidence suggests severe underinsurance by couples against widowhood. For these reasons and because of higher rates of marital disruption and longer postdivorce lives, there is some concern that the economic status of older women may not improve greatly in the future (Smeeding, Estes, and Glasse 1999).

The existing body of literature does not satisfactorily explain what factors couples consider when choosing how to allocate resources over their remaining lifetimes, including the period when only one survives. The changes in income observed among widows are large and clearly compound the emotional difficulties associated with a husband's death. In contrast to divorce, where reluctance of a husband to protect his ex-wife against the loss of his own income is expected, the decline in economic well-being upon widowhood is more difficult to explain. Until we know more about the decisions couples make about protecting the wife as a widow, it will be difficult to predict the future well-being of widows. (See also ACCELERATED DEATH BENEFITS; DEATH BENEFITS; PENSION PLANS; SOCIAL SECURITY PROGRAM OF THE UNITED STATES; VETERANS' BENEFITS.)

#### Organization

Older Women's League

#### References

Auerbach, Alan J., and Laurence J. Kotlikoff. 1987. "Life Insurance of the Elderly: Its Adequacy and Determinants." In *Work, Health and Income among the Elderly*, ed. G. Burtless. Washington, DC: Brookings Institution.

Buhmann, B., L. Rainwater, G. Schmaus, and T.M. Smeeding. 1988. "Equivalence Scales, Well-being, Inequality, and Poverty: Sensitivity of Estimates across Ten Countries Using the Luxembourg Income Study (LIS) Database." *Review of Income and Wealth* 34(2): 115–42.

Burkhauser, Richard V., J.S. Butler, and Karen C. Holden. 1991. "How the Death of a Spouse Affects Economic Well-being after Retirement: A Hazard Model Approach." *Social Science Quarterly* 72: 504–19.

Burkhauser, Richard V., and Timothy M. Smeeding. 1994. "Social Security Reform: A Budget Neutral Approach to Reducing Older Women's Disproportionate Risk of Poverty." Policy Brief No. 2. Syracuse, NY: Syracuse University Center for Policy Research.

Haveman, R., K. Holden, and B. Wolfe. 2003. "Have Newly Retired Workers Saved Enough to Maintain Well-being through Retirement Years?" *Discussion Paper*. Institute for Research on Poverty, Madison, WI.

Holden, Karen C., and J. Brand. 2003. "Income Change and Distribution upon Widowhood: Comparison of Britain, U.S., and Germany." In *Pensions: Challenges and Reform*, ed. Einar Overbye and Peter Kemp. Aldershot: Ashgate.

Holden, Karen C., Richard V. Burkhauser, and Daniel Feaster. 1988. "The Timing of Falls into Poverty after Retirement and Widowhood." *Demography* 25: 405–14.

Holden, Karen C., and Pamela J. Smock. 1991. "The Economic Costs of Marital Dissolution: Why Do Women Bear a Disproportionate Cost?" *Annual Review of Sociology* 17: 51–78.

Smeeding, Timothy M., Carroll L. Estes, and Lou Glasse. 1999. *Social Security Reform and Older Women: Improving the System*. Washington, DC: Gerontological Society of America.

Social Security Administration. 2002. "Annual Statistical Supplement, 2002, to the Social Security Bulletin." Washington, DC: GPO.

Social Security Advisory Board. 1999. *The 1999 Technical Panel on Assumptions and Methods*. Washington, DC: Author.

Zick, Cathleen D., and Karen C. Holden. 2000. "An Assessment of the Wealth Holdings of Recent Widows." *Journal of Gerontology: Social Sciences* 55(2): S90–S97.

Zick, Cathleen D., and Ken R. Smith. 1991. "Patterns of Economic Change Surrounding the Death of a Spouse." *Journal of Gerontology* 46: 310–20.

*Karen C. Holden*

**WILLS,** legal documents by which persons may direct the disposition of property upon death. The right to a will has not been common to all societies throughout history. In countries and legal systems that recognize and accord the right, it is not absolute. Strict technical formalities must be observed to create a valid will, and certain property rights cannot be altered or defeated by will. Many of the technical requirements that surround the preparation, execution, and administration of a will are because the testator (the person executing the will) is no longer available to interpret the document or supervise its administration. Thus, in the United States, the law requires that formalities be observed in the execution of a will to ensure the authenticity of documents that are admitted to probate. In most states, the will must be executed in the presence of at least two witnesses, who in turn must subscribe their names to the document. In many states, a self-proving affidavit may also be attached as part of the will. The latter is a sworn (notarized) statement of the testator and the witnesses in which they confirm that the required formalities were observed. Typically, those formalities include the testator declaring to the witnesses that he or she intends the document to become a will, the testator signing the document in the presence of the witnesses, requesting the witnesses to sign the document, and the witnesses signing the document in the presence of the testator.

In order to make a valid will, the testator must be competent and not under undue influence from any source. The competency required to make a will is generally defined as follows: the testator must be aware of the "natural objects of his or her bounty" (i.e., the members of his family); the testator must be aware of the property that he or she owns; and the testator must understand the nature of the will and its legal effect when he or she signs it.

In most states, the surviving spouse of the decedent is entitled to a minimum portion of the estate. If less than that amount is left to the spouse by will, he or she may have the right to "renounce" the will in favor of the larger statutory entitlement. Marital property rights may be modified by contract between the parties. A contract executed prior to the marriage (a premarital agreement) is generally more easily enforced than a contract entered into after the marriage.

A further restriction on the right to dispose of property by will is the federal estate tax (and in most states, a state inheritance or estate tax). The federal government is often one of the largest beneficiaries of an estate.

### Probate

A will does not acquire legal force or effect until it is "probated." In its narrowest sense, probate is a process by which a purported will is offered to and accepted by a court and declared to be the true last will and testament of a decedent. If no one contests the validity of the offered document, probate, in its narrow sense, can be accomplished informally and quickly. If the offered will is contested, a trial may be required to determine its validity.

### Naming an Executor

A necessary component of a will is the nomination of a person or institution as executor or personal representative. The executor is the person responsible for probating the will and carrying out the testator's instructions. It is a position that should be filled carefully. Generally, the choice is between one or more individuals or a bank or trust company, or a combination of the two. For example, a family member and a bank could be named to serve together as coexecutors. Banks and trust companies may offer certain advantages over individuals, but the relative expenses in connection with estate administration should be explored and weighed carefully. First, bank trust departments and trust companies are in the business of administering estates and trusts, but bank charges for these services can be sizable. An individual, on the other hand, may not have previously administered an estate and may require the services of professionals, which can also be costly.

A bank trust department may also have the advantage of neutrality and objectivity. Choosing an executor from among family members could leave those not chosen feeling slighted and prone to believe that the chosen executor will be biased. In many instances, the executor is required to make decisions in the administration of the estate that are likely to upset one or more beneficiaries. Normally, one would prefer that the anger be directed outside the family (at a bank executor) rather than at a family member. As an institution, a bank or trust company also enjoys a longevity and permanence that an individual does not. An individual who is named as executor may predecease the testator, or become ill, incapacitated, or move out of the state or country and be unavailable to administer the estate. That is unlikely to happen with a sound bank. The principal disadvantage in naming an institution is that the testator does not know with certainty who in the bank will be making the critical decisions. If an individual is named, and assuming that individual survives the testator and is available to serve, the testator knows exactly who the decision maker will be.

### Bequests and Trusts

There are several types of bequests that may be made in a will. A specific bequest is a gift of a specific item to a specific person. For example, "I give my engagement ring to my daughter, Sally." A general or pecuniary gift is a gift of a specific sum of money. For example, "I give Sally the sum of $1,000." A residuary bequest is a gift of the estate that remains after payment of debts and costs of administration and all specific or pecuniary gifts in the will.

The different types of bequests have unique advantages and disadvantages. Specific bequests may be appropriate for certain important and unique assets where it is important that they be distributed in a precise fashion. The disadvantage of specific bequests is that circumstances may frequently change, which will require the revision of the will. For example, the particular item might be given during lifetime to the intended recipient, the testator may sell or otherwise dispose of the property before his or her death, or the intended recipient may decide that he or she does not want that particular item.

A pecuniary gift is appropriate when the testator wants to recognize a friend or a charity with a fixed amount that will not fluctuate with changes in value of the overall estate. A pecuniary gift should normally be small in relation to the total value of the estate. Residuary gifts are appropriate for the principal beneficiaries. For example, if a testator wants to leave his or her entire estate to his or her two children, the statement: "After payment of my debts and the expenses of administering my estate, I give my remaining estate in equal shares to my children" may suffice. The will need not allocate assets between the two children; that can be left for the executor in consultation with the children after the testator's death.

Because a will speaks only at death and because circumstances constantly change, the testator should always direct alternate gifts if certain contingencies arise. For example, the testator may want to leave his or her estate equally to children, but an alternate disposition of each child's share should be addressed in the event that one or more of the children dies before she or he does. The gift may, for example, be left to the children of the deceased child (grandchildren of the testator) or to the other surviving children of the testator.

Trusts may be created by will. A trust is appropriate for bequests to minors and young adults who have not matured sufficiently to prudently hold and manage the intended bequest. Similarly, a trust would be appropriate for a disabled beneficiary. However, care must be taken in the case of an individual who is receiving financial assistance through a government program that is based on need, for example, the Supplemental Security Income (SSI) program.

Charitable gifts may also be made by will. For example, a specific sum of money may be left to a church, school, or other charity, or a portion of the residuary estate may be given to charity. Outright charitable gifts are fully deductible for federal estate tax purposes.

### Additional Contents of a Will

While the essential components of a will are (1) directions regarding the distribution of property and (2) naming an executor, many other provisions may also be properly included, such as funeral instructions, anatomical gifts, and tax planning provisions.

It is generally preferable to communicate preferences or instructions regarding funeral and burial outside the will, since the will may not be found or read until after burial. However, if it is anticipated that one or more members of the family may resist the requested funeral arrangements, it is helpful to have them established in the will. Because a will is a formal legal document, inclusion of funeral instructions in the document tends to lend additional weight to those instructions and gives greater assurance that they will be followed.

If one wishes to make gifts of body organs for research, education, or transplantation (i.e., going beyond organ donation noted on a driver's license), his or her wish should be included in the will. As in the case of funeral instructions, anatomical gifts should also be recorded in a separate document since the will may not be immediately accessible and speed is necessary to effect gifts of organs. Family physicians and hospitals should be able to provide preprinted forms for making anatomical gifts.

Additionally, effective planning to reduce estate taxes may be incorporated into a will. A will is as effective as a revocable living trust for that purpose. (Irrevocable living trusts, on the other hand, offer tax planning options that cannot be duplicated by a will.) Proper tax planning is especially advisable for married couples whose combined estate exceeds the prevailing federal estate tax exemption equivalent, currently $600,000. A couple with a combined estate of $1.2 million can reduce estate taxes by $240,000 or more through proper tax planning.

### Contest

Unlike the protection given to surviving spouses, there are virtually no similar inheritance protections for children or other descendants. A child or other descendant who is disinherited by his or her parent has no recourse except to contest the probate of the will. In order to bring such a suit, the contestant must have "standing"; for example, the contestant must stand to benefit if he prevails in the suit. If an offered will is set aside, one of two results ensues. If there is a previously executed will still in existence, it will "move up" in line and may then be offered for probate as the last will and testament of the decedent. If there is no previous will, the decedent will be deemed to have died intestate, that is, without a will, in which case the estate will pass to those individuals designated by state law as the intestate heirs. Standing to contest a will may be established by demonstrating that the contestant is a beneficiary under a previous will that will move up in line, or by establishing that the contestant is one of the intestate heirs who would inherit in the absence of a will.

A will contest may be based on any of several grounds. The contestant may allege that the signing of the will was technically deficient in some respect. For example, wills have been denied probate when the required witnesses were not present throughout the execution of the document. The contestant may allege that the testator, who is the person executing the will, lacked "testamentary capacity" (i.e., the minimum level of competence necessary to execute a valid will). The contestant may allege that a third party brought undue influence to bear on the testator with the result that the offered will does not represent the true volitional intent of the testator but rather represents the wishes of the third party.

Will contests may be discouraged in some cases by including a "no-contest" clause in the will. A no-contest clause typically provides that if a beneficiary under the will takes any action to contest the validity of the will, the beneficiary will automatically forfeit his or her gift under the will. A no-contest clause is only effective if the would-be contestant receives some benefit under the will. If no benefit is received under the will, he or she risks nothing by pursuing the contest.

### Will Preparation and Review

A will should be prepared by a competent attorney who has expertise specific to the task. The process of selecting an attorney should include consulting with friends and neighbors to obtain word-of-mouth references. Published references are also generally available in public libraries. Word-of-mouth references might also be obtained through the trust departments of local banks. Finally, the attorney tentatively chosen should be asked directly to confirm that he or she has particular experience in the trust and estate area.

The attorney will need information about the client's family and assets. Before the first meeting, the client should compile a list of all significant assets, the approximate fair market value of the assets, and the exact form of titling. The list should include life insurance, pension plans, and joint property, all of which will be part of the estate for federal estate tax purposes.

A list of the members of the family and others whom the client may wish to provide for under the will is also needed. The will should address a reasonable number of alternate contingencies. For example, the client may wish to leave the estate equally to his or her two children but must make an alternative plan, should one or both of those children die before the client. The client should be prepared to answer those questions as early as possible in the engagement to expedite the preparation of the will. Since estate planning engagements are frequently accepted on an hourly billing basis, less time means lower cost.

Periodic review of one's will is as important as creating it. Although a will should anticipate and address a reasonable number of foreseeable contingencies, it is impossible to anticipate and address every possible event. To attempt to do so would yield a document of unmanageable length and complexity. The only alternative is to address a more modest range of possibilities and then periodically review and revise the will as circumstances change and as contingencies unfold. A will should be reviewed annually by the client and reviewed professionally at least every five years. Circumstances that might require a revision of the will include maturing of children, births, deaths, marriages, divorces, significant changes in net worth, and changes in the law. Changes in the federal estate tax law in 1976 and 1981, for example, required broad changes in many wills.

Minor changes in a will may be made by codicil (amendment or modification of a will) rather than completely rewriting the will. However, unless the change is minor (e.g., changing the executor), it is often no less expensive to redo the entire will, especially if the lawyer preparing the codicil is not the lawyer who prepared the will. (See also

ATTORNEYS; ELDER LAW PRACTICE; ESTATE PLANNING; GUARDIANSHIP; PROBATE; TRUSTS.)

**References**

Belin, David W. 1992. *Leaving Money Wisely: Creative Estate Planning for Middle and Upper Income Americans for the 1990s*. New York: Collier Books.

Berg, Adriane G. 1995. *Warning. Dying May Be Hazardous to Your Wealth: How to Protect Your Life Savings for Yourself and Those You Love*. 2nd ed. Hawthorne, NJ: Career Press.

Daly, Eugene J. 1990. *Thy Will Be Done: A Guide to Wills, Taxation, and Estate Planning for Older Persons*. Buffalo, NY: Prometheus Books.

Manning, Jerome A. 1992. *Estate Planning: How to Preserve Your Wealth for Your Loved Ones*. New York: Practicing Law Institute.

Runde, Robert H., and J. Barry Zischang. 1993. *The Commonsense Guide to Estate Planning*. Burr Ridge, IL: Irwin Professional Publications.

*C.L. (Tim) Dimos*
*Updated by Jerry J. McCoy*

**WORKFORCE PATTERNS, CHANGES IN,** changing retirement behaviors and the impact of an older population on the workforce at the beginning of the twenty-first century. The relationship between aging and workforce participation is complex. In the first place, the aging of the population has resulted in the slow, but growing, acknowledgment that older workers will be needed in the future workforce, due to the increasing number of retirees during the baby boom retirement years. In the second place, the racial/ethnic composition of the population will be significantly changing in the twenty-first century, raising issues of the type of workforce that will be needed and how, adequately, to educate and train it.

The essence of the first factor, the changing age composition of the population, has enormous impact on the changing patterns in the workforce since it requires a shift in the conventional wisdom of pension and social welfare policies, originally intended to create incentives for older workers to exit the workforce. Many individual and societal factors go into an individual worker's decision to retire. These factors include eligibility for and adequacy of pension benefits, underlying personal financial status, health of the worker and spouse/family, social support, attitudes toward retirement, and occupation. Researchers note that many of these factors interact, and no single factor is paramount (McMahan and Phillips 2000). However, human resource professionals often note that the retirement decision is made a number of years before the actual retirement date. If employers are to change the culture of early retirement and to encourage their workers to stay longer, establishment of (and education in) such policies and incentives must take place earlier rather than later in the retirement decision process (McEvoy and Blahna 2001).

### Changing Retirement Behavior

Since the creation of Social Security and the institutionalization of private pensions, incentives have always been in favor of early retirement. These incentives have resulted, generally, in men choosing to retire earlier and earlier throughout the latter part of the twentieth century. Examination of U.S. Social Security retirement records indicates that in the late 1980s and 1990s there has begun a reversal in the early exit of men aged 65

**Figure 1**
**Labor Force Participation of Men by Age Group, 1965 to 2000**

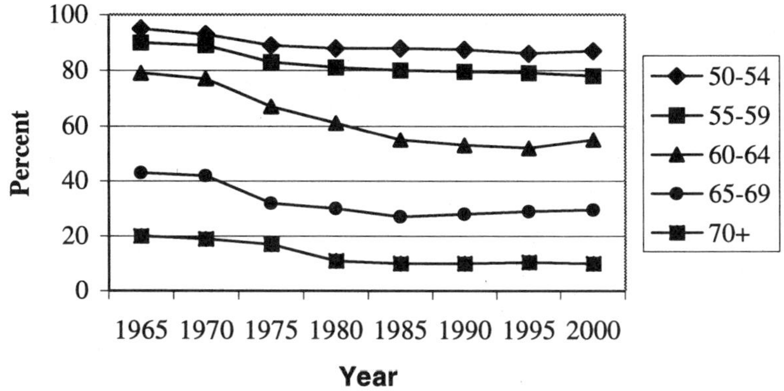


*Source*: U.S. Bureau of Labor Statistics, 2000 data.

and older from the workforce. For example, the 2000 workforce participation rates for men aged 65 to 69 and 70 to 74 exceeded the 1985 rates by 10% (Figure 1). Interestingly, women of all ages, including women aged 60 and older, have had increasing labor force participation since the 1970s (Gendell 2001) (see Figure 2). A *New York Times* story on the phenomenon in 1999 quoted economist Joseph Quinn, known for his studies of retirement behavior, who said, "We have entered a new era . . . where earlier and earlier retirement has come to an end." Often cited as reasons for this reversal are the change from defined benefit pension plans to defined contribution plans, leading to declines in real value of pensions (Herz 1995), relaxation of Social Security earnings tests, and reductions in health benefits for retirees. The United States is not alone in this phenomenon, as studies of European economies indicate that growing pension coverage for workers has resulted in later retirement in a number of other advanced industrialized nations (OECD 1995).

In addition to the aging of the workforce, a growing labor shortage and economic expansion since the 1990s have begun to signal the need for retention of older workers (Herz 1995). Currently 12% to 16% of retirees work, depending on which age range determines the definition of retirees. With the aging of the baby boom cohort, a major demographic event, the notions of retirement and work will change into at least the middle of the twenty-first century. At present, 80% of the baby boom cohort expects to work after retirement (Fandray 2000). Half that number will be forced to work due to inadequate pensions or assets; the other half may continue working but will not need to do so for economic reasons (Fandray 2000).

It is estimated that between 2005 and 2010 employers will come to realize that there are not enough skilled younger workers entering the labor force to replace those older employees leaving for retirement. When that happens, employers will embrace the question of what they can do to recruit, retain, encourage, and retool older workers (McEvoy and Blahna 2001). By the year 2016, the number of annual retirees will double to approximately 4 million (Cyr 1996). These older workers have a vision of semiretirement

**Figure 2**
**Labor Force Participation of Women by Age Group, 1965 to 2000**

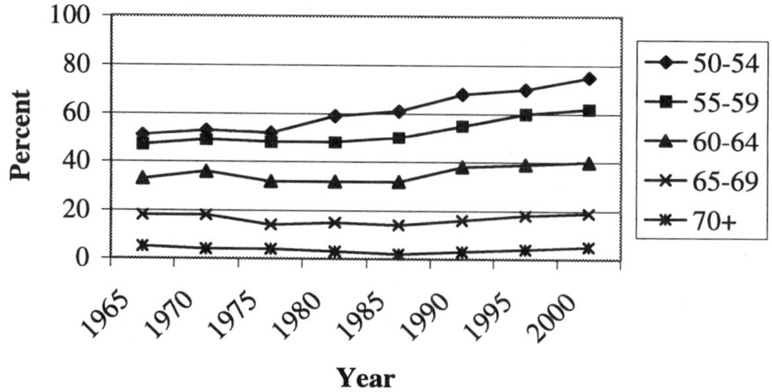


*Source*: U.S. Bureau of Labor Statistics, 2000 data.

somewhere between full-time work and complete withdrawal from the work world, in addition to fulfilling personal goals and contributing to society.

In an example of moving incentives away from early retirement, the Senior Citizen's Freedom to Work Act (2000) eliminated the Social Security earnings test on additional income earned by the retired person in and after the month in which they turn normal retirement age—currently age 65 plus 2 months (Baum and Ford 2001). This paves the way for workers to continue on their jobs, start new jobs, establish their own businesses, and work full-time or part-time without loss of part of their Social Security earnings. Retiree work programs will grow in abundance as demographic trends merge with employer and employee needs (Cyr 1996).

In addition, phased retirement, allowing some workers to work at reduced schedules, may be some employers' answer to the demographic demands of an aging workforce. Bridge employment, after retiring from the first career, usually with a new employer, is becoming an option for a significant number of Americans (Feldman 2000; Latulippe and Turner 2000). Currently, however, few employers are actively courting older workers, although many try to retain their own older employees with gradually reduced hours of work (Greenwald 2001). Corporations and some government agencies are recruiting their retirees in the forms of emeritus positions, consultant positions, contract workers, part-time workers, and volunteers to augment their workforce during temporary work needs, for special projects, for civic responsibilities in the community, and to maintain an able and willing pool of workers (Gerbman 1999). Examples of companies employing this strategy are Hewlett-Packard, Heinz, Amoco Corp., American Express Financial Services, a number of insurance companies, and several hotel chains (Cyr 1996; Gerbman 1999). This large resource pool of experienced retiree workers with immediately useable skills and intimate knowledge of the corporate structure and history allows a company more flexibility in the borderless economy (Cyr 1996).

### Impact of Changes in the Older Population on the Workforce

Given the imperatives of the demographic shift in older workers, improvements in the health of older persons in recent years, and a dearth of younger workers, older workers

**Table 1**
**Increasing Diversity of the Future Workforce: Changes in Diversity of "Retirees"**

| | 2000 | 2040 | 2050 | % Change (2050–2000) |
|---|---|---|---|---|
| Whites | 84 | 74 | 64 | –31.3 |
| African Americans | 8 | 10 | 12 | 33.3 |
| Others | 8 | 16 | 24 | 66.7 |

*Source*: Hattiangadi 1998.

should find it easier to remain in the workforce for the next several decades. Those in the baby boom cohort born between 1946 and 1954 should be able to continue to find employment opportunities in retirement, should they choose to do so. This cohort, nearly 76 million strong, is better educated than its parents' generation, and more of them work in skilled occupations (Best and Balkrishna 1996). With increased retirement age for full Social Security benefits (from 65 to 67), baby boom workers will remain somewhat longer in the labor force. But there are additional financial incentives for this group to continue working past retirement age, since Social Security and pensions replace a smaller percentage of income for workers in skilled occupations (Best and Balkrishna 1996).

## Gender and Race Differences in the Workforce

The most dramatic change in the workforce in the past 30 years has been the growing presence of women. In the future, the share of Whites and males in the workforce will continue to fall, while the share of female employees and both males and females from diverse ethnic and racial backgrounds (particularly Hispanics and Asians) will continue to grow (see Table 1). Immigration will also play a greater role in the workforce of the twenty-first century, and language skills will play a bigger issue in managing this workforce (Hattiangadi 1998). In this older and more diverse workforce of tomorrow, diversity will mean more than just race and ethnicity. There will be a corresponding diversity of skills, culture, religion, and sexual orientation. There is an approaching critical mass of a diversity of options to continued limited participation in the workforce for older workers.

Between the increasing diversity of the older workforce, the increasing numbers of baby boom retirees, and the development of our economy from a domestic manufacturing base to a global services and information economy, it is fairly clear that we need to make sure that we are going to need older workers in the future. In fact, older workers often do well in service jobs, as they are generally more experienced in life and more empathetic than younger workers. In any case, the employers who have the foresight to begin planning their human resource needs around an older workforce will be the ones who have best prepared for the foreseeable changes in workforce patterns. (See also AGING AMERICA; BABY BOOMERS AND RETIREMENT; ECONOMIC HISTORY OF RE-

TIREMENT; HEALTH AND LONGEVITY; HISTORY OF RETIREMENT; PENSION PLANS.)

**References**

Baum, C.L., and W.F. Ford. 2001. "The Effect of the Senior Citizens' Freedom to Work Act of 2000 on Delayed Retirement Incentives." *Labor Law Journal* 52(1): 3–9.

Best, J.R., and D.K. Balkrishna. 1996. "Older Workers in the 21st Century: Active and Educated, a Case Study." *Monthly Labor Review* 120(6): 18–29.

Cyr, D. 1996. "Lost and Found—Retired Employees." *Personnel Journal* 75 (November): 40–41.

Fandray, D. 2000. "Gray Matters." *Workforce* 79(7): 26–32.

Feldman, D.C. 2000. "Bridge Employment during Retirement: A Field Study of Individual and Organizational Experiences with Post-Retirement Employment." *Human Resource Planning* 23(1): 14–25.

Gendell, M. 2001. "Retirement Age Declines Again in 1990s." *Labor Review* 124(10): 12–21.

Gerbman, R. 1999. "Reach Out with Retirees: Companies and Their Retirees Extend Their Reach by Partnering for Volunteer Work." *HR Magazine* 44(7): 74–78.

Greenwald, J. 2001. "Phased Retirement Begins to Catch On." *Business Insurance* 35(22): 10–12.

Hattiangadi, A.V. 1998. *The Changing of the 21st Century Workforce: Trends in Ethnicity, Race, Age and Gender.* Washington, DC: Employment Policy Foundation.

Herz, D.E. 1995. "Work after Early Retirement: An Increasing Trend among Men." *Monthly Labor Review* 118 (April): 13–20.

Latulippe, D., and J. Turner. 2000. "Partial Retirement and Pension Policy in Industrialized Countries." *International Labour Review* 139(2): 179–95.

McEvoy, G.M., and M.J. Blahna. 2001. "Engagement or Disengagement? Older Workers and the Looming Labor Shortage." *Business Horizons* 44(5): 46–52.

McMahan, S., and K. Phillips. 2000. "Aging and Employment." *Journal of Education for Business* 76(1): 11–14.

OECD. 1995. "The Labour Market and Older Workers." *Social Policy Studies* (Paris) (17).

*Suzanne Reynolds-Scanlon*

**WORKING RETIREES,** older adults who have retired but remain in the labor force either part-time or full-time. Being retired today does not necessarily translate into being unemployed. Many older adults are retiring and finding that they need to continue to work. Some need to work for financial reasons—their retirement income is insufficient for survival. Others choose to work to avoid loneliness or to maintain the feeling of contributing to society. Retirement affects men and women differently. In a study of how postretirement affects quality of life, Cornell University researchers Jungeen E. Kim and Phyllis Moen (APA 1999) found that men typically return to work by choice—for feelings of staying involved and for self-satisfaction. Men who work part-time or consult with former employers are more satisfied with their lives and marriages than men who retire permanently. Returning to work, however, did not make a significant impact on women's feelings of well-being. Retired women were happiest if their marriages were running smoothly after retirement (APA 1999).

As in many countries, Americans are living longer, healthier lives. In addition, people retire earlier than they did at the turn of the last century. In 1910, men retired at the average age of 74; today the average man retires at age 63. For women, just 30 years ago, the retirement age was 65; today it is age 63 (C. May 2000). As a result, older adults are spending more time in retirement than ever before. In 1965, a male worker could typically expect to spend 13 years in retirement; today, he will spend 18 years. Retirement today, therefore, can mean many more years of life out of the workforce than in the past, and troubling uncertainties can arise from this eventuality. As the baby boomer generation nears retirement age, these issues will become central to vastly increasing numbers of people.

### Retirees Seeking Work

Since 2000, there has been a reduction of an aggregate $678 billion in the personal financial portfolios of older adults, according to a recent study by the Institute of Social Research at the University of Michigan (Ligos 2002). About 20 million older Americans rely on investment income during retirement years, and the reduction in income from shrinking investments has caused some alarm among the older population. Some retirees are seeking jobs as a result. The Bureau of Labor Statistics reported that the number of people age 55 and older who returned to the workforce rose by 7% in 2002, while the number of workers in all other age groups declined (Ligos 2002).

Career experts report a built-in bias by some against retirees returning to work. Some younger employees feel retirees do not need the job, and are depriving younger workers, while some employers view retirees as "washed up." Although discrimination is illegal in the workplace, career consultants agree that retirees can and will face age discrimination when seeking employment. They suggest that retirees accentuate experience and those attributes they have that young employees may not, that is, a willingness to work part-time and a lower salary. They advise older retirees to tell interviewers they do not enjoy retirement and feel a need to contribute and not to reveal they need the money (Ligos 2002). Since stamina may be a concern, it is important for retirees to convince prospective employers that they are healthy and can handle the job. Although age discrimination certainly exists, the unemployment rate among the elderly is deceiving, since current statistics do not show whether older people are not working due to choice or inability to obtain employment. Also, a concern exists among many older people about losing benefits if they accept work.

Retirees must above all consider the effect employment will have on their retirement benefits before they seek a job. This will vary not only from state to state but from company to company.

### Retirees and Social Security Benefits

In 2000, federal laws relating to Social Security removed the penalty that reduced benefits for those employed at 65 and older and earning a salary above the permitted level (May 2000). This encouraged some older workers to stay in the workforce and helped others decide to work full-time rather than part-time, as in the past. Workers no longer lose any Social Security benefits if they continue to work after their full-retirement age (now 65 to 67, depending on date of birth.) Electing to receive Social Security benefits before full-retirement age substantially reduces benefits (see Table 1) (Lankford 2003).

### Retirees with 401(k) and 403(b) Plans

It is possible to delay payment of an employer-sponsored 401(k) or 403(b) plan in addition to Social Security benefits until the decision is made to quit work completely.

**Table 1**
**Full-Retirement Age**

| Year of Birth | Full-Retirement Age | Age 62 Reduction Months | Monthly % Reduction | Total % Reduction |
|---|---|---|---|---|
| 1937 or Earlier | 65 | 36 | .555 | 20.00 |
| 1938 | 65 and 2 months | 38 | .548 | 20.83 |
| 1939 | 65 and 4 months | 40 | .541 | 21.67 |
| 1940 | 65 and 6 months | 42 | .535 | 22.50 |
| 1941 | 65 and 8 months | 44 | .530 | 23.33 |
| 1942 | 66 | 46 | .525 | 24.17 |
| 1943–1954 | 66 and 2 months | 48 | .520 | 25.00 |
| 1955 | 66 and 6 months | 50 | .516 | 25.84 |
| 1956 | 66 and 4 months | 52 | .512 | 26.66 |
| 1957 | 66 and 6 months | 54 | .509 | 27.50 |
| 1958 | 66 and 8 months | 56 | .505 | 28.33 |
| 1959 | 66 and 20 months | 58 | .502 | 29.17 |
| 1960 and Later | 67 | 60 | .500 | 30.00 |

*Source*: Social Security Administration 2003.

It is also possible to draw payments from a private plan but not take Social Security benefits, which eliminates the concern of lowered Social Security payments. While working, a retiree may continue to make payments into Social Security, which would insure a higher payment when fully retired. However, if a retiree has a 403(b) plan and is age 70 or older, minimum distributions must be taken from the plan. Once begun, distributions from these plans may be stopped only if a retiree returns to the same employer. If, however, the retiree is hired by a new employer, distributions must continue (Jayasanker 2001).

In a 401(k) plan, under certain circumstances, that is, returning to the same industry, trade, and same geographical area covered by the benefit plan, payments may be suspended. The plan must notify you of any suspension during the first calendar month in which the plan withholds payments.

Many variables exist, and it is vitally important for a retiree to check private pension or retirement plan rules and to research and understand state and federal rules about retirement benefits before returning to work. When making the decision to return to work after retirement, there is a need to strike a balance between financial need and emotional need, and with careful planning, it is possible to accomplish both. (See also BABY BOOMERS AND RETIREMENT; CONSULTING IN RETIREMENT; ENTREPRENEURSHIP; FINANCIAL RECOVERY IN LATER LIFE; HISTORY OF RETIREMENT; LIFE PLANNING; RETIREMENT PREPAREDNESS; SOCIAL SECURITY PROGRAM OF THE UNITED STATES; WORKFORCE PATTERNS, CHANGES IN.)

### References

American Psychological Association (APA). 1999. "Post-Retirement Bliss Is Different for Men and Women, Say Researchers." *APA Monitor Online*. Available online at http://www.apa.org/monitor/oct99/nb10.html.

Jayasanker, Laresh. 2001. "403(b) Planning for Working 'Retirees.' " *mPower Café*. Available online at http://www.mpowercafe.com/retirement/features/features.1.3.2_03152001.html.

Lankford, Kim. 2003. "Post-Retirement Jobs Could Cut Your Benefits." *Kiplinger Online*, February 21. Available online at http://www.kiplinger.com/.

Ligos, Melinda. 2002. "As Portfolios Shrink, Retirees Warily Seek Work." *New York Times*, September 8.

May, Bess Ritter. 1993. *Starting and Operating a Business after You Retire: What You Need to Know to Succeed*. New York: Avery Penguin Putnam.

May, Catherine R. 2000. "Young Retirees, Older Workers." *Berkshire Senior Online*. Available online at http://www.esbci.org/BSO2000/August/frmdir.html.

Sedlar, Jeri, Rick Miners, and Howard Fillit. 2002. *Don't Retire, REWIRE!* New York: Alpha Books.

Social Security Administration. 2003. "Full Retirement Age Is Increasing." Available online at http://www.ssa.gov/retirechartred.htm.

*V. Karen McMahon*

**WORKPLACE FINANCIAL EDUCATION,** the array of financial education programs, including those that address financial literacy, preretirement, retirement, health finances, and investment education, that is sponsored by employers and taught to employees in the workplace. Such education has been shown to be of benefit both to employers and to employees.

## The Need

The number of employer-provided financial education programs is declining at a time when the need has never been greater. Personal finances play a significant factor in the level of stress that Americans experience. They have been taught how to "make money" but not how to effectively manage the income they earn. Spending patterns and high levels of consumer debt derail financial goals of many U.S. workers today, who lack the knowledge and confidence to evaluate even their own insurance needs. Not only are they ill-equipped to make day-to-day financial decisions, but they are critically unprepared to manage the 401(k) investments that will have a dramatic impact on their long-term financial security.

Research has shown that American workers are concerned about not having sufficient financial resources in their retirement years. For example, the 2000 Retirement Confidence Survey, conducted by the Employee Benefit Research Institute (EBRI 2000) indicated that only 26% of the employees surveyed were "very confident" of having enough money to live comfortably throughout their retirement years. Confirming these concerns, the EBRI researchers also found that the amounts accumulated for retirement were surprisingly low. On the low end of the savings continuum, 10% of those surveyed had saved nothing. Equally disturbing was the finding that on the high end of the savings continuum only 21% had saved $100,000 or more.

Today's workers need to understand early in their careers the importance of developing and monitoring a personal financial plan. Increased life span, complexity of financial and benefit choices, as well as changing patterns of employment necessitate more and earlier worker education. In addition, workers have indicated a strong desire to have such issues addressed in the workplace. A recent survey of benefits specialists identified retirement and investment issues as three of the top five benefits issues for employees in 2003:

1. Evaluating current investment options (64%)
2. Evaluating current levels of retirement savings (61%)
3. Identifying additional ways to save for retirement (44%)

### Roles of Financial Education

Traditionally, workplace financial education has been restricted to providing information specific to the employer's benefit programs. Philosophically, the core employer benefits protect employees from catastrophic health care costs, provide some income replacement in the form of insurance programs, and allow the employee to accumulate wealth for retirement. More recently, the main objective of most financial education programs offered in workplace settings is directed to increasing 401(k) participation. Not surprisingly, several studies have confirmed the effectiveness of financial education in this realm. For example, research conducted by KPMG found that 77% of lower-paid employees participated in 401(k) plans in companies that offered educational seminars as compared to 33% in companies where no education was offered (Infante 2000).

Employers also want to help employees to better understand investment risks, comply with Section 404(c) of the Employee Retirement Income Security Act (ERISA), and avoid litigation (Quinn 2000). To manage these risks, employers have accelerated investment education efforts. Hewitt Associates found that 86% of surveyed employers either have programs to educate employees in 401(k) investing or are planning to implement such a program in the coming year (Kronson 2000).

### A New HR/Benefits Perspective

In addition to traditional benefits education and fostering 401(k) success, financial education could have and should have a much broader application in the human resources (HR)/benefits arena. In reflecting on employer practices over the last century, it is obvious that the principles of supply and demand have had the greatest influence on workplace practices. Simply put, when employers do not have to compete to attract and retain labor, the workplace environment, including benefits, wages, and education, reduces to a level at par with the industry and business sector.

The business case for benefits is for the employer to maintain or enhance its competitive position via an appropriately skilled workforce. In addition, enlightened management understands the relationship of its workforce to the competitiveness and profitability of the company. In the last century, competition for capital was the constraint on business. Going forward, skilled labor will be the constraining force, and employers will be increasingly challenged to find ways to make themselves stand out as an employer of choice.

Because comprehensive financial education is highly valued by employees, it can be positioned as an effective tool for retaining employees and reducing the direct and indirect costs of employee turnover. According to David Wray, president of the Profit Sharing/401(k) Council of America, "there is an emerging awareness" in corporate America that—in light of the extremely tight labor market where employers are competing for quality employees—comprehensive financial education can be a cost-effective way for employers to differentiate themselves in the workplace (Wray, quoted in Quinn 2000).

Employers can help to build employee loyalty by providing the financial education the employee did not receive at home or at school. Venita Van Caspel (1988), a well-known financial advisor and author, wrote that "there is an educational void in our nation" because students are not being taught "the one subject they will need to live well in our free enterprise system—how to manage their money." She also lamented that "this vacuum is so great that the average couple cannot begin to confront the financial uncertainties and the multitude of choices they face in our complex society."

David Wray agrees with this perspective and makes the following recommendation to employers:

> American workers need to be lifetime investors. They need to be responsible for their personal financial lives and build a lifetime financial plan, which would include planning for retirement. It's critical that employees have the tools necessary to implement that lifetime plan, monitor and maintain it. And one of those tools that companies are increasingly investigating offering is not simply 401(k) advice, but full service financial planning. (Wray, quoted in Quinn 2000)

(See also ECONOMIC HISTORY OF RETIREMENT; FINANCIAL ADVISORS; FINANCIAL EDUCATION FOR SENIORS; FINANCIAL LITERACY; LIFE PLANNING; LIFE PLANNING IN THE WORKPLACE; RETIREMENT PREPAREDNESS.)

**References**

Employee Benefit Research Institute (EBRI). 2000. *The 2000 Retirement Confidence Survey Summary of Findings*. Washington, DC: Author. Available online at http://www.ebri.org/.

Infante, Victor E. 2000. "Retirement Plan Trends." *Workforce* 79(11) (November).

International Society of Certified Employee Benefit Specialists. 2002. *Top 5 Benefit Priorities for 2003*. International Society of Certified Employee Benefit Specialists and Deloitte and Touche LPP. Available online at http://www.iscebs.org/.

Kronson, Marc. 2000. "Employee Costs and Risks in 401(k) Plans." *Compensation and Working Conditions* (Summer).

Quinn, Jacqueline M. 2000. "Mainstreaming Financial Education as an Employee Benefit." *Journal of Financial Planning* (May).

Van Caspel, Venita. 1988. *Money Dynamics for the 1990s*. New York: Simon & Schuster.

*Sally Hass*

# Z

**ZONING,** a legal vehicle for a city government, or alternatively, the legislature, to implement land use and/or planning regulations. It is a tool for land use allocation or to reshape areas that need redevelopment. Zoning can be differentiated from other rules and regulations as a "police power." Police power is a state legislature's authority to enforce conditions of land use and planning regulations that are created to promote the public good and to protect the public health, safety, and welfare. The power of a legislature to pass zoning laws in most states is only available to the extent that those zoning laws do not conflict with the minimum standards established in constitutional state zoning law. Zoning is used to change a region's land use when such use is no longer feasible or to preserve an existing land use. Its use as a tool for land allocation increases as a region's population, wants, and needs grow. Zoning allocates the types of land uses that comply with state planning and more specific plans of local communities. Zoning ordinances dictate consistent, appropriate, and planned land use patterns for a particular area. A familiarity with zoning issues is helpful when planning to develop retirement communities, nursing homes, or adult day centers.

As a tool for land use allocation, zoning significantly impacts the expansion, shrinkage, and status quo of land use patterns in states, large cities, small communities, and rural areas. As the land allocation of regions evolves into specific land use patterns, the public (i.e., local governments) continues to create and enforce land use guidelines through the police powers of zoning. However, before realizing the role, impact, and limitations of zoning as an allocative tool, an examination of land planning and land use controls related to zoning is necessary.

## Implementation of Land Use Allocation

There is a certain framework within which the legislature must stay to implement land use policies. A number of groups, commissions, and consultants have been created for the specific purpose of aiding the legislature in its land use decisions. For example, the planning commission and the port commission exist to aid in the allocation of land and coastline, respectively. A number of broadly interpreted laws also exist to provide guidelines for the legislature and the groups created to aid in the allocation process. The specific purposes of these groups and laws are contained in the state government code. Of the advisory committees and laws created to aid the city council in its land use decisions, the planning commission, the city attorney's office, and the public works department play the most significant roles. These groups assist with the city council's decisions on newly created or challenged land use policies and help ensure that the proposal review procedure is correct. These departments are the experts in land use policy and are cognizant of the likely effects of a proposed addition or change in policy. When a land use policy, zoning ordinance, or proposal for the redevelopment of land is submitted to the city council, the proposal is given to the planning commission for a recommendation. After the planning commission, the city attorney and/or public works department review the proposal. The planning commission then makes a recommendation to the council for accepting, rejecting, or revising the proposal. The council then considers the recommendation of the planning commission and has several options. The council can follow the recommendations of the planning commission by approving or denying the proposal, or it can disregard the planning commission and resubmit the proposal for further consideration. However, before any recommendations are made by the planning commission, a thorough review of the city's general plan must be made.

When a city approves a land use change, compliance with certain established legal guidelines is required. These guidelines, which are based in state planning law, are established in the area's general plan. The plan consists of a statement of development policies that include a diagram or diagrams and a text setting forth objectives, principles, standards, and plan proposals. According to state planning, the general plan is required to examine a land use element, a circulation element, a housing element, a conservation element, an open space element, a noise element, a safety element, and any other optional elements that are specific to a proposal. According to the required elements of the general plan, the policies of zoning (e.g., public good, health, and safety) closely resemble the objectives of the general plan. In addition to the general plan, a specific plan is adopted to outline zoning, subdivisions, and public works projects. Development agreements are also a part of a city's implementation of the general plan, except that they may be amended to reflect changing land uses. As the focus of land use narrows, our attention is directed to zoning. Zoning divides a city into districts and assigns different regulations to each according to the general and specific plans.

### Limitations of and Exceptions to Zoning Regulations

Exceptions exist to the general plan, the specific plan, and zoning ordinances. These are categorized as (1) nonconforming uses, (2) conditional uses, and (3) variances. A nonconforming use is a land use that existed before a conflicting zoning ordinance was implemented. A conditional use is a land use that is allowed to exist even though it is inconsistent with current zoning and plan policies in order to provide flexibility to the community district. A variance is a land use that is in direct conflict with the zoning and planning of a district, but the legislature allows the use since compliance with the current zoning would cause undue hardship on the owner. Compliance under a variance usually deals with aspects of the parcel's size, topography, shape, or location. These exceptions are not automatic; each case is reviewed by the legislature on an individual basis, and permits are required.

### Other Land Use Allocation Tools

In addition to the aforementioned exceptions, other significant allocative aspects of land use allocation include the subdivision and environmental quality regulations. Subdivision regulations are a statewide legislative tool that allows local government agencies to control the types of subdivisions to be planned in each community. They also dictate the physical improvements to the land and require that final maps of the proposed projects be filed and approved before development begins. Before approving the final map, a tentative map of the project undergoes a rigid legislative approval process. After the final map has been approved, it is then recorded and construction may begin. State environmental regulations allow local governments to require an environmental impact report on any potential project they feel may strongly affect the area surrounding the project. These subdivision and environmental quality regulations attempt to accomplish land use allocation on more of a macrolevel, while zoning ordinances tend to be site specific.

### What Zoning Attempts to Accomplish

Most, if not all, zoning goals can be found in the form of municipal code ordinances. In addition to the purpose of general police power goals of zoning—to promote the public good and protect the public health, safety, and welfare—in recent years, this definition has been expanded to include the promotion and advancement of order, convenience, prosperity, and general welfare. The specific guidelines of zoning regulations encompass most of a region's land uses. The specific land uses that have been traditionally regulated by zoning ordinances include:

1. The use of buildings, structures, land, and businesses;
2. The size, shape, and color of signs and billboards;
3. The location, size, and height of structures in the path of airport approach runways;
4. The size and use of lots;
5. The percentage of a lot occupied by a structure;
6. The intensity of land use;
7. Set-back requirements for buildings;
8. Requirements for off-street parking; and
9. The creation of civic districts around parks, public buildings, and other public grounds.

Residential zoning is based in the theory of zoning itself by providing land uses conducive to the overall public health, safety, morale, and welfare of land users. Residential zoning can include provisions for single-family dwellings, multiple-family dwellings, and housing operations for income purposes such as hotels, apartments, private clubs, and boarding houses, while excluding more or less intensive land uses. When a zoning ordinance excludes a certain use designation such as a commercial use in a residentially zoned district, it must bear some reasonable relation to the overall public interest; adaptability and suitability are not valid reasons for allocating a particular type of land use. Commercial and industrial zoned areas, due to their potential for hazardous conditions, may be subjected to special regulations and are delineated as such. Commercial and industrial zoned districts, depending on the nature of operation, are subdivided into their respective uses, including general commercial districts, light commercial districts permitting retail, general industrial districts, light industrial districts, and heavy industrial districts. The creation of set-back requirements, off-street parking, and civic districts around parks, public buildings, and other public grounds can all be traced back to the original theories of zoning and why they exist.

### Zoning and Housing Needs of Older Adults

Zoning regulations have often prevented or restricted the locations of four principal types of residential options specifically relevant to older Americans: (1) accessory apartments (in-law suites) or ECHO housing (elder cottage housing opportunities, also called granny flats); (2) shared living residences (unrelated occupants in the same dwelling); (3) board and care, assisted living, and related group housing facilities designed for the occupancy of more functionally dependent older persons; and (4) manufactured (mobile) housing offering an affordable shelter option.

Opposition to these alternatives has most often occurred in neighborhoods zoned for single-family use. Three types of zoning provisions have most frequently been used to protect the "single-family" status of the neighborhood. One type restricts dwelling uses to the land use category designated for a district or locality. This effectively restricts accessory apartments, ECHO units, and group homes from many neighborhoods that allow only one dwelling unit per lot. A second type restricts household arrangements to family occupancy. Many communities have restrictive definitions of what constitutes a "family" for zoning purposes, with the result that various categories of household or group shelter arrangements composed of unrelated persons would be in violation. This has effectively prohibited older persons in some communities from renting their house to a boarder or from sharing their accommodations with other unrelated older persons. A third type of zoning provision imposes excessive construction and site development standards on their residential districts. These zoning ordinances have successfully been used to exclude manufactured housing from many residential districts and to keep them confined to mobile home parks. Attempts to appeal local rulings to the state courts have had mixed success. State courts have differed, for example, in their appraisals of whether a certain group of people would constitute a family under the terms of the zoning ordinance and their willingness to view particular groups of unrelated persons as functional equivalents of families. As Pollak (1994) emphasizes, however:

> To date, there has been no wholesale trend for communities to change family definitions that have not been legally challenged, to make them conform to the standards in [other] court decisions; as legislation, zoning is legal until successfully challenged.

Municipalities and their residents have not consistently opposed housing options. Some communities allow accessory apartments in single-family neighborhoods, for example, if they meet certain quality and appearance standards. Other states and communities have created a zoning class of "senior citizens," whereupon a residential district can restrict occupancy to persons of an older age. Some states and courts have allowed the creation of special zoning provisions specifically for older adults. Many state courts are viewing highly restrictive family definitions as discriminatory and violations of an individual's right to privacy that are contrary to their own state constitutions. Some states have revoked or curtailed the exclusionary zoning controls exercised by municipalities. Some municipalities have used zoning devices (e.g., conditional use permits) to encourage the development of specialized housing options.

The Fair Housing Amendments Act of 1988 (FHAA) has resulted in yet another judicial influence on zoning decisions relevant to older Americans. Among its various provisions, FHAA prohibits zoning and land use regulations from discriminating against persons with disabilities. The broad definition of *disability* would include most older persons usually defined as physically or mentally disabled. Recent case law suggests that some municipal zoning laws that prevent the siting of group homes in certain residential districts are in conflict with the protections given by FHAA to disabled persons, namely, their right to live in neighborhoods of their choice.

## Conclusion

As a tool for land use allocation, zoning ordinances empower a community's exercise of land use control through its police power. The guidelines that zoning ordinances create for such uses must be followed in order to preserve the safety and comfort of its inhabitants and to protect them from conditions that arise from land uses that may be reasonably anticipated from a particular activity or business. Through zoning, a pattern is developed that meets the goals of what the inhabitants expect from their land and the planned goals of state and local governments. (See also ATTORNEYS; BOARD AND CARE HOMES; COMMUNITY-BASED CARE; COOPERATIVE OWNERSHIP IN HOUSING; HUD-ASSISTED RENTAL HOUSING; REAL ESTATE INVESTMENTS; SENIORS HOUSING FINANCE.)

### References

Curtin, Daniel J. 1990. *California Land-Use and Planning Law*. 10th ed. Solano, CA: Solano Press Books.

Pollak, Patricia B. 1994. "Rethinking Zoning to Accommodate the Elderly in Single Family Housing." *Journal of the American Planning Association* 60: 521–31.

Pollak, Patricia B., and Alice N. Gorman. 1989. *Community-Based Housing for the Elderly*. Planning Advisory Service Report Number 420. Washington, DC: American Planning Association.

*Andrew Quang Do*

# Appendix A

# Chronological Summary of Post-ERISA Benefit Legislation

### *Employee Retirement Income Security Act (ERISA)—1974*

- Establishes participation, vesting, and funding standards for defined benefit and defined contribution retirement plans. Sets limits on pension plan benefits and profit sharing contributions.
- Guarantees certain levels of benefits in the event of pension plan termination. Establishes the Pension Benefit Guaranty Corporation to administer plan termination insurance programs.
- Sets guidelines governing fiduciary conduct and reporting responsibilities.

### *Tax Reduction Act—1975*

- Increases allowable investment tax credit if contributions are made to an ESOP (employee stock ownership plan).

### *Tax Reform Act—1976*

- Removes favorable tax treatment for qualified stock options.
- Allows entire lump-sum distribution to be taxed at ordinary rates using ten-year forward averaging.
- Prepaid legal plans approved as a tax-free benefit.

### *Social Security Amendments—1977*

- Provides significant increases in Social Security tax rates and taxable wage base.
- Adjusts Social Security benefit formula to produce a decline in the percentage of pay replaced by Social Security. Repeals "double indexing."

### *Revenue Act—1978*

- Reinstates favorable tax treatment for cash or deferred profit sharing arrangements and sets nondiscrimination requirements for such plans.
- Reduces taxes on long-term capital gains for individual taxpayers.
- Reemphasizes that deferred compensation is eligible for taxation only when paid or otherwise made available.
- Requires uninsured health plans to meet nondiscrimination rules.

- Excludes nontaxable cafeteria plan benefits from employee's income. Sets coverage, eligibility, and benefit tests for cafeteria plans.
- Section 127 education assistance approved as a tax-free benefit.

### *Age Discrimination in Employment Act (ADEA)—1978*

- Extends protection against discriminatory treatment based on age to individuals less than age 70.
- Permits employer to reduce benefits (within limits) for employees age 65 to 69, provided the reduction can be cost-justified.

### *Pregnancy Discrimination Act—1978*

- Prohibits employers from discriminating in employee benefits or employment practices on the basis of pregnancy, childbirth, or related medical conditions. Pregnant women must be offered the same sick leave benefits as any disabled employee.
- Rules that an employer must cover costs of pregnancy, childbirth, and related medical conditions under the same terms of coverage as other medical conditions.

### *Multiemployer Pension Plan Amendments Act—1980*

- Restructures PBGC (Pension Benefit Guaranty Corporation) coverage of multiemployer pension plans.
- Requires all employers withdrawing from a multiemployer pension plan to continue funding their share of the plan's unfunded vested benefits through payment of a withdrawal liability.
- Establishes guidelines for identifying plans experiencing financial difficulties and requires these plans to enter reorganization status for corrective action.

### *Revenue Act—1980*

- Allows employers to add a deferred compensation choice to a cafeteria program.

### *Economic Recovery Tax Act (ERTA)—1981*

- Permits employees covered by qualified employer-provided retirement plans to make tax-deductible IRA (Individual Retirement Account) contributions.
- Establishes incentive stock options.
- Reemphasizes that distributions from qualified retirement plans are taxed only when actually received.
- Dependent care assistance programs approved as a tax-free benefit.

### *Tax Equity and Fiscal Responsibility Act (TEFRA)—1982*

- Reduces the Section 415 limits for defined benefit and defined contribution retirement plans.
- Subjects "top-heavy" plans to stricter qualification rules.
- Sets limits and repayment rules for loans from qualified retirement plans.
- Reduces the allowable amount of Social Security integration in a defined contribution plan.
- Removes exclusion for first $50,000 of life insurance for "key employees" in a discriminatory plan.
- Rules that employers must offer active employees and their dependents age 65 to 69 the same

health plan benefits offered younger employees. Establishes the employer's health care plan as primary to Medicare for active employees age 65 to 69.

### *Social Security Amendments—1983*

- Extends Social Security coverage to new federal, state, and local government employees, as well as employees of nonprofit organizations.
- Accelerates FICA (Federal Insurance Contribution Act) payroll tax, and Social Security tax for self-employed.
- Reduces dependent and survivor Social Security benefits for public pension recipients.
- Subjects Section 401(k) deferrals and nonqualified deferred taxation to FICA and FUTA (Federal Unemployment Tax) taxation.
- Extends the Social Security normal retirement age to 67 while reducing early retirement benefits.
- Increases Social Security late retirement benefit.
- Fixes payment for Medicare reimbursement to hospitals based on national averages for established categories of hospital treatment.

### *Retirement Equity Act (REA)—1984*

- Reduces the minimum age for qualified retirement plan participation to age 21.
- Sets new break-in-service rules for crediting service in qualified retirement plans for vesting and benefit purposes.
- Rules that qualified retirement plans must provide automatic survivor benefits in the form of qualified preretirement survivor annuities to the spouse of a vested participant who has died prior to annuity start date.
- Recognizes the assignment of participant benefits to alternate payees under qualified domestic relations orders (divorce proceedings).

### *Deficit Reduction Act (DEFRA)—1984*

- Freezes the Section 415 limits for defined benefit and defined contribution plans until 1988.
- Permits tax-free rollovers to IRAs if the distribution is at least 50% of the employee's plan value.
- Limits tax-deductible benefits and reserve accumulation in funded welfare benefit plans.
- Rules that dividends paid on stock held by PAYSOPs (payroll deduction stock ownership plans)/ ESOPs are deductible only if distributed directly to plan participants.
- Limits the types of benefits available under cafeteria plans and restricts the percentage of cafeteria plan benefits that can be paid to key employees.
- Establishes rules for income tax exclusions for miscellaneous fringe benefits.
- Limits depreciation on company cars and adds more restrictive recordkeeping requirements.
- Sets limits on "golden parachute" payments.

### *Consolidated Omnibus Reconciliation Act (COBRA)—1986*

- Rules that employers must offer continuation of group health plan coverage to beneficiaries who no longer qualify for coverage, to terminated employees, and to employees with reduced hours.
- Increases PBGC premiums for single-employer defined benefit pension plans.
- Increases employer liability when a single-employer defined benefit pension plan is terminated due to insufficient assets.

### *Tax Reform Act (TRA)—1986*

- Requires all qualified retirement plans to satisfy new nondiscrimination standards, minimum vesting standards, and integration rules.
- Reduces maximum early retirement benefits for defined benefit pension plans.
- Requires after-tax employee contributions to be included in calculating limits for defined contribution plans.
- Limits employee 401(k) deferrals to $7,000 per calendar year.
- Repeals ten-year averaging tax treatment for lump-sum retirement plan distributions. Replaces with one-time choice of five-year forward averaging.
- Imposes additional taxes on retirement distributions taken before age 59½ and annual benefits exceeding $150,000.
- Establishes new requirements that health, group life, and dependent care plans must meet to avoid resulting in imputed income for high-paid employees.
- Reduces maximum corporate and individual tax rates.
- Repeals preferential tax treatment for long-term capital gains.
- Phases out interest deductions on consumer loans.

### *Omnibus Budget Reconciliation Act (OBRA)—1986*

- Prohibits qualified retirement plans from reducing or freezing the rate of benefit accruals or contributions because of age.
- Prohibits qualified retirement plans from excluding employees hired within five years of plan's normal retirement age.
- Establishes employer's health plan as primary to Medicare for disabled employees and their family members eligible for Medicare.

### *Age Discrimination in Employment Act Amendments—1986*

- Prohibits cessation of retirement plan accruals or contributions because of age.

### *Pension Protection Act (PPA)—1987*

- Increases PBGC premium from $8.50 to $16.00 per participant, plus variable rate premium for underfunded plans.
- Increases minimum funding requirements.
- Prohibits deductions for plan contributions in excess of 150% of current liability.
- Requires FICA withholding for key employees for imputed income on group term life insurance above $50,000.

### *Family Support Act—1988*

- Reduces maximum expenses for calculation of dependent care credit by amount of expenses in the income exclusion.
- Lowers maximum age for eligible dependents from age 15 to age 13, except for disabled dependents.
- Requires employees to provide taxpayer identification (ID) of dependent care provider to claim the dependent care credit or exclusion.

### *Medicare Catastrophic Coverage Act—1988*

- Expands Medicare Part A and Part B. Expansion paid for by increased Part B premiums and a supplemental premium based on income.
- Requires employers that offer coverage duplicative of expanded benefits to either refund one year's actuarial value of duplicated benefits or increase benefits by a like amount.

### *Health Maintenance Organization (HMO) Act Amendments—1988*

- Requires that contributions to a federally qualified HMO may not financially discriminate against an employee enrolled in the HMO. Additional rate-setting method allowed for HMOs.
- Repeals dual-choice requirement as of October 24, 1995.

### *Technical and Miscellaneous Revenue Act (TAMRA)—1988*

- Changes penalty for COBRA violations to an employer excise tax.
- Makes numerous technical changes to TRA 86 including allowing the minimum participation test to be passed on a separate line of business basis and providing an alternative definition of highly compensated employee.
- Restricts favorable tax treatment of life insurance products that are primarily for investment purposes.

### *Omnibus Budget Reconciliation Act (OBRA)—1989*

- Increases Social Security wage base for 1990.
- Revises physician reimbursement under Medicare using the resource-based relative value system (RBRVS).
- Lengthens COBRA period for certain disabled employees.
- Makes technical corrections to pension plan rules.
- Restricts exclusion of 50% of interest on ESOP loans to ESOPs that own at least 50% of the corporation. Deductibility of dividends limited to dividends from securities acquired by the same ESOP loan.

### *Repeal of Medicare Catastrophic Coverage Act—1989*

- Repeals Medicare Catastrophic Act. Employers still required to make "maintenance of effort" payment for 1989.

### *Americans with Disabilities Act (ADA)—1990*

- Mandates that employers may not discriminate against disabled individuals in any aspect of employment and must make "reasonable accommodations" to enable the disabled to work.

### *Older Workers Benefit Protection Act—1990*

- Restores the "equal benefit or equal cost" requirement for age-based differences in employee benefits.
- Allows a retirement plan to continue to have minimum age for eligibility for normal or early retirement benefits and have subsidized early retirement benefits.
- Requires that early retirement incentives be voluntary and "consistent with the relevant purpose or purposes of the Act."

- Requires that waivers of rights under the Age Discrimination in Employment Act (ADEA) be made on a "knowing and voluntary" basis.

### *Omnibus Budget Reconciliation Act (OBRA)—1990*

- Increases both the flat and variable rate PBGC premiums to $19 and a maximum of $53.
- Allows employers to transfer a certain portion of excess plan assets to a retiree medical account.
- Increases tax for pension reversions from 15% to 20% or 50%.
- Prohibits a health care spending account from reimbursing for cosmetic surgery.
- Increases the Medicare wage base to $125,000.
- Removes requirement that employers withhold FICA on imputed income for retiree group term life.

### *Civil Rights Act—1991*

- Overturns several Supreme Court cases that had made it more difficult for employees to prevail in employment discrimination cases.
- Adds punitive and compensatory damages in the case of intentional discrimination and adds the opportunity for jury trials.

### *Unemployment Compensation Amendments (UCA)—1992*

- Extends unemployment benefits.
- Expands types of distributions eligible for rollover.
- Allows employees to elect direct transfers into IRA or another qualified plan.
- Mandates 20% withholding for nonperiodic distributions not directly transferred to another qualified plan or IRA.

### *Family and Medical Leave Act (FMLA)—1993*

- Requires employers to grant up to 12 weeks of unpaid leave to care for newborn or newly adopted children, to care for a seriously ill family member, or for the employee's own serious illness.
- Requires continuation of health coverage to employees on FMLA leave on same basis as coverage for active employees.

### *Omnibus Budget Reconciliation Act (OBRA)—1993*

- Adds 36% and 39.6% income tax brackets.
- Reduces recognizable pay cap to $150,000.
- Eliminates corporate deduction for chief executive officer (CEO) and top executive pay over $1 million.
- Uncaps wage base for 1.45% Medicare portion of FICA tax.
- Retroactively extends Section 127 income tax exclusion for employer-provided education reimbursement.
- Mandates various provisions and reporting requirements for group health plans, including recognition of "qualified medical child support orders."

### *Defense Appropriations—1994*

- Limits executive pay that can be charged to federal defense contracts.

### *Defense Appropriations—1995*

- Further limits executive pay that can be charged to federal defense contracts.

### *Personal Responsibility and Work Opportunity Reconciliation Act—1996*

- Requires employer-sponsored medical plans to comply with medical child support orders issued by state agencies if equivalent to court order under state law.
- Requires each state to establish an automated State Directory of New Hires containing information supplied by employers on each newly hired employee.

### *Contract with America Advancement Act—1996*

- Increases the Social Security earnings test for age 65 to 69 retirees.

### *Taxpayer Bill of Rights 2—1996*

- Creates new penalty tax for "excess benefits" in tax-exempt organizations.

### *Small Business Job Protection Act—1996*

- Increases the minimum wage.
- Simplifies 401(k) testing by permitting use of prior year nonhighly compensated deferrals.
- Simplifies definition of "highly compensated employee."
- Repeals five-year income averaging for lump-sum distributions.
- Permits postponement of mandatory distributions until retirement.
- Allows tax-exempt nongovernmental employers to offer 401(k) plans.
- Modifies the rules for determining whether a worker is an employee or independent contractor for employment tax purposes.

### *Health Insurance Portability and Accountability Act (HIPAA)—1996*

- Tightens allowable preexisting condition limits.
- Provides tax-favored treatment for long-term care insurance and accelerated death benefits.
- Creates pilot project for medical savings accounts.

### *Newborns' and Mothers' Health Protection Act—1996*

- Prohibits employer-sponsored health plans from restricting hospital stays for childbirth to less than 48 hours (96 hours in the case of a caesarian section).

### *Mental Health Parity Act—1996*

- Requires employer-sponsored health plans to treat mental health coverage the same as medical coverage for purposes of determining the amount, scope, or duration of mental health benefits.

### *Medicare and Medicaid Coverage Data Bank Repeal Act—1996*

- Repeals requirement from Omnibus Budget Reconciliation Act of 1993 that required employers to provide the Health Care Financing Administration (HCFA) the names of all individuals covered by the employer's group health plans.

### *Savings Are Vital to Everyone's Retirement Act (SAVER)—1997*

- Authorizes national summit to raise public awareness of the importance of retirement savings.

### *Defense of Marriage Act—1997*

- Stipulates that no other state would have to recognize the validity of a marriage between same-sex domestic partners authorized in another state and defines marriage under federal law as the union of a man and a woman, thus preventing same-sex domestic partners from sharing benefits such as Social Security.

### *Taxpayer Relief Act—1997*

- Increases small cashout amounts for qualified retirement plans.
- Reduces top capital gains rates.
- Reinstates the tax exclusion for employer-provided educational assistance.
- Increases pension plan full funding limit.
- Directs the Internal Revenue Service (IRS) and the Department of Labor (DoL) to issue paperless administration guidance for benefit plans.
- Permits employers to offer choice between cash and nontaxable parking benefits.

### *Balanced Budget Act—1997*

- Expands health plan choices for Medicare recipients through Medicare Part C (Medicare + Choice), providing health plan choices, including traditional fee-for-service Medicare, HMOs, PPOs, provider-sponsored organizations (also known as PSOs), private fee-for-service plans, and a pilot program of Medicare Medical Savings Accounts (MSAs) (limited to 390,000 beneficiaries).
- Makes Medicare secondary payer rules permanent for the disabled and for data match program.
- Makes employer plan primary for 30 months for end-stage renal disease.
- Allows Medicare to recover overpayments if requested within three years of the date of the service and overpayments from third-party administrators under certain circumstances.
- Expands Medicare coverage to include certain preventive benefits (with some limitations), including, for example, mammography, diabetes self-management, Pap smear and pelvic exams, screening for prostate and colorectal cancer, and bone-mass measurements.
- Applies new formulas to Medicare payments for hospital services and physicians.

### *Higher Education Amendments Act—1998*

- Allows colleges and universities to offer tenured faculty certain voluntary supplemental early retirement incentive plans that are reduced or eliminated based on age.

### *Omnibus Consolidated and Emergency Supplemental Appropriations Act—1998*

- Requires group health plans that provide coverage for mastectomy to also provide coverage for reconstructive surgery and to notify each participant and beneficiary of the new coverage, in writing (also known as the Women's Health and Cancer Rights Act of 1998).
- Increases amounts Medicare must pay to providers of home health care services.
- Accelerates the full deduction of health insurance expenses by the self-employed for years beginning in 2003.

- Allows the child credit, adoption credit, HOPE and lifetime learning credits, and other nonrefundable personal credits to offset the individual's regular tax (as opposed to only the amount by which the regular tax exceeds the alternative minimum tax, as under prior rules).

### *Ticket to Work and Work Incentives Improvement Act—1999*

- Provides Social Security Disability Insurance (SSDI) and disabled Supplemental Security Income (SSI) beneficiaries with a "ticket" to obtain employment services, vocational rehabilitation (VR) services, and other support services from a provider of their choice to enable them to enter the workforce.
- Provides payments to employment networks that develop an individual employment plan for each beneficiary to select an employment goal and specific services to achieve that goal.
- Establishes a Work Incentives Advisory Panel to advise the president, Congress, and the Commission of Social Security on issues related to work incentives programs, planning, and assistance for individuals with disabilities.
- Expands state options under the Medicaid program for workers with disabilities.
- Extends Medicare coverage for Old-Age, Survivors, and Disability Insurance (OASDI) disability benefit recipients.

### *Victims of Terrorism Tax Relief Act—2001*

- Waives income tax liability for both 2001 and 2002 for those killed in the September terrorist attacks or in the subsequent anthrax terrorism, as well as 1994 and 1995 Oklahoma casualties.
- Provides tax-free treatment of employer-provided death benefits to families of victims.
- Allows employers to establish private foundations to provide tax-free assistance to victims' families.

### *Economic Growth and Tax Relief Reconciliation Act—2001*

- Marginal Rate Reduction Provisions (Sunset 12/31/10).
- Tax Benefits Relating to Children (Sunset 12/31/10).
- Marriage Penalty Relief Provisions (Sunset 12/31/10).
- Affordable Education Provisions (Sunset 12/31/10).
- Estate, Gift, and Generation Skipping Transfer Tax Provisions (Sunset 12/31/10).
- Pension and IRA Provisions (Generally Sunset 12/31/10).

### *Job Creation and Worker Assistance Act—2002*

- Special Depreciation Allowance for Certain Property.
- 5-Year Carryback of Net Operating Losses.
- Tax Benefits for Area of New York City Damaged in Terrorist Attacks on September 11, 2001.
- Extended the Work Opportunity Tax Credit (Sunset 12/31/03).
- Extended the Welfare to Work Credit (Sunset 12/31/03).
- Extended the Archer Medical Savings Accounts (MSAs) (Sunset 12/31/03).
- Provided unemployment benefits for certain unemployed workers up to 13 weeks, extending unemployment benefits to 39 weeks for most states.

### *Sarbanes-Oxley Act—2002*

- Establishes an accounting oversight board of five members, appointed for five-year terms. Two of the members must be or have been certified public accountants (CPAs), and the remaining three must not be and cannot have been CPAs. The chair may be held by one of the CPA members, provided he or she has not been engaged as a practicing CPA for five years.
- Requires executives to certify the contents of the company's most recent financial statements filed with the Securities and Exchange Commission (SEC).
- Prohibition of most loans to directors and executive officers.
- Accelerated reporting of insider trading transactions.

Appendix B

# Major Post-ERISA Benefit Legislation

1974 ERISA

1975 Tax Reduction Act

1976 Tax Reform Act

1977 Social Security Amendments

1978 Revenue Act

1978 Age Discrimination in Employment Act

1978 Pregnancy Discrimination Act

1980 Multiemployer Pension Plan Amendments Act

1980 Revenue Act

1981 ERTA

1982 TEFRA

1983 Social Security Amendments

1984 REA

1984 DEFRA

1986 COBRA

1986 Tax Reform Act

1986 OBRA-86

1986 ADEA Amendments

1987 Pension Protection Act

1988 Family Support Act

1988 Medicare Catastrophic Coverage Act

1988 HMO Act Amendments

1988 TAMRA

1989 OBRA-89

1989 Medicare Catastrophic Coverage Act Repeal

1990 Americans with Disabilities Act

1990 Older Workers Benefit Protection Act

1990 OBRA-90

1991 Civil Rights Act

1992 Unemployment Compensation Amendments

1993 Family and Medical Leave Act

1993 OBRA-93

1994 Defense Appropriations

1995 Defense Appropriations

1996 Personal Responsibility and Work Opportunity Reconciliation Act

1996 Contract with America Advancement Act (SS earnings test)

1996 Taxpayer Bill of Rights 2

1996 Small Business Job Protection Act

1996 HIPAA

1996 Newborns' and Mothers' Health Protection Act

1996 Mental Health Parity Act

1996 Medicare and Medicaid Coverage Data Bank Repeal Act

1997 Savings Are Vital to Everyone's Retirement Act (SAVER Act)

1997 Defense of Marriage Act

1997 Taxpayer Relief Act

1997 Balanced Budget Act

1998 Higher Education Amendments Act

1998 Omnibus Consolidated and Emergency Supplemental Appropriations Act

1999 Ticket to Work and Work Incentives Improvement Act

2001 Victims of Terrorism Tax Relief Act

2001 Economic Growth and Tax Relief Reconciliation Act

2002 Job Creation and Worker Assistance Act

2002 Sarbanes-Oxley Act

*Sources*: Adapted from various issues of "A Special Report," Hewitt Associates LLC, Washington, DC. Revenue laws also regularly affect the scope, types, and levels of retirement income. A useful review of deficit-reduction measures (several Omnibus Budget Reconciliation Acts, Deficit Reduction Acts, etc.) is contained in David Koitz, "Major Deficit-Reduction Measures Enacted in Recent Years," *CRS Report for Congress* (Washington, DC: Congressional Research Service. Report 94-719 EPW, 1994). In addition, appendices in volumes on "General Explanation of Tax Legislation" enacted in various Congresses, published by the Joint Tax Committee, U.S. Congress, contain detailed information helpful in preparing this list.

Appendix C

# Organizations and Resources

AARP
601 E Street, NW
Washington, DC 20049
Phone: (202) 434-2277; (800) 424-3410
http://www.aarp.org/

About, Inc.
249 West 17th Street
New York, NY 10011
Phone: (212) 745-0634

A.D. Kessler's Creative Real Estate Magazine
Drawer L
Rancho Santa Fe, CA 92067
Phone: (858) 756-1441
http://www.adkessler.net/

Administration on Aging
330 Independence Avenue, SW
Washington, DC 20201
Phone: (202) 619-7501
http://www.aoa.gov/

American Academy of Estate Planning Attorneys
9360 Town Centre Drive, #300
San Diego, CA 92121
Phone: (800) 846-1555
http://www.estateplanforyou.com/home/html

American Academy of Family Physicians
11400 Tomahawk Creek Parkway
Leawood, KS 66211-2672
Phone: (800) 274-2237
http://www.familydoctor.org/

American Academy of Nurse Practitioners
P.O. Box 12846
Austin, TX 78711
Phone: (512) 442-4262
http://www.aanp.org/

American Association of Daily Money Managers
P.O. Box 8857
Gaithersburg, MD 20898
Phone: (301) 593-5462
http://www.aadmm.com/

American Association of Health Plans
1129 20th Street, NW, Suite 600
Washington, DC 20036
Phone: (202) 778-3200
http://www.aahp.org/

American Association of Homes and Services for the Aging (AAHSA)
2519 Connecticut Avenue, NW
Washington, DC 20008-1520
Phone: (202) 783-2242
http://www.aahsa.org/

American Association of Individual Investors
625 North Michigan Avenue
Chicago, IL 60611
Phone: (800) 428-2244
http://www.aaii.com/

American Bar Association
Commission on Legal Problems of the Elderly
740 15th Street, NW

Washington, DC 20005-1019
Phone: (202) 662-1000
http://www.abanet.org/aging/

American Benefits Council
1212 New York Avenue, NW, Suite 1250
Washington, DC 20005
Phone: (202) 289-6700
http://www.americanbenefitscouncil.org/

American College of Nurse Practitioners
1111 19th Street, NW, Suite 404
Washington, DC 20036
Phone: (202) 659-2190
http://www.nurse.org/acnp/

American Council of Life Insurers
101 Constitution Avenue, NW
Washington, DC 20001-2133
Phone: (202) 624-2000
http://www.acli.org/

American Federation of Government Employees
80 F Street, NW
Washington, DC 20001
Phone: (202) 737-8700
http://www.afge.org/

American Federation of State, County, and Municipal Employees
1625 L Street, NW
Washington, DC 20036
Phone: (202) 429-1000
http://www.afscme.org/

The American Institute for Chartered Property Casualty Underwriters (AICPCU)
720 Providence Road
P.O. Box 3016
Malvern, PA 19355-0716
Phone: (800) 644-2101
http://www.aicpcu.org/

American Institute of Certified Public Accountants
1010 North Fairfax Street
Alexandria, VA 22314
Phone: (703) 549-6400; (800) 966-6679
http://www.aicpa.org/

American Institute of Financial Gerontology (AIFG)
1525 NW 3rd Street, Suite 8
Deerfield Beach, FL 33442
Phone: (888) 367-8470
http://www.aifg.org/

American Nurses Association
600 MD Avenue, SW, Suite 100 West
Washington, DC 20024
Phone: (800) 274-4ANA
http://www.nursingworld.org/

American Resort Development Association (ARDA)
1201 15th Street NW, Suite 400
Washington, DC 20005
Phone: (202) 371-6700
http://www.arda.org/

American Savings Education Council (ASEC)
2121 K Street, NW, Suite 600
Washington, DC 20037
Phone: (202) 659-0670
http://www.asec.org/

American Seniors Housing Association
5100 Wisconsin Avenue, NW, Suite 307
Washington, DC 20016
Phone: (202) 237-0900
http://www.seniorshousing.org/

American Society of Consultant Pharmacists
1321 Duke Street
Alexandria, VA 22314
Phone: (703) 739-1300; (800) 355-2727
http://www.ascp.com/

ASEC Savings Education Brochures
American Savings Education Council
2121 K Street NW, Suite 600
Washington, DC 20037
Phone: (202) 775-6360
http://www.asec.org/

Assisted Living Federation of America
11200 Waples Mill Road, Suite 150
Fairfax, VA 22030
Phone: (703) 691-8100
http://www.alfa.org/

Association for Financial Counseling and Planning Education (AFCFE)
2121 Arlington Avenue, Suite 5

Upper Arlington, OH 43221
Phone: (614) 485-9650
http://www.afcpe.org/

Association on Aging: Regional Support Centers
Administration on Aging
200 Independence Avenue
Washington, DC 20201
Phone: (202) 619-0724
http://www.aoa.gov/about/org/regional_support_center/org_regional_support_centers.asp

The Ballpark Estimate
American Savings Education Council (ASEC)
2121 K Street, NW, Suite 600
Washington, DC 20037
Phone: (202) 659-0670
http://www.asec.org/

Bank Rate, Inc.
11811 U.S. Highway 1
North Palm Beach, FL 33408
Phone: (561) 630-2400
http://www.bankrate.com/

BenefitsCheckup
NCOA
300 D Street, SW, Suite 801
Washington, DC 20024
Phone: (202) 479-1200
http://www.benefitscheckup.org/

Blue Cross Blue Shield Association
1310 G Street, NW
Washington, DC 20005
Phone: (202) 626-8624
http://www.babs.com/

Brookdale National Group Respite Program
The Brookdale Foundation
950 Third Avenue, 19th floor
New York, NY 10022
Phone: (212) 308-7355
http://www.brookdalefoundation.org/

The Bureau of National Affairs
1231 25th Street, NW
Washington, DC 20037
Phone: (800) 372-1033
http://www.bna.com/

Canadian Association of Retired Persons
27 Queen Street, East, Suite 1301
Toronto, Ontario, MSC 2M6, Canada
Phone: (416) 363-8748; (800) 363-9736
http://www.fifty-plus.net/

Canadian Snowbird Association
180 Lesmill Road
Toronto, Ontario, M3B 2T5 Canada
Phone: (416) 391-9000; (800) 265-3200
http://www.snowbirds.org/

CardWeb
450 Prospect Boulevard
Frederick, MD 21701
Phone: (301) 631-9100
http://www.cardweb.com/

Center for Long-Term Care Financing (CLTC)
2212 Queen Anne Avenue, North, #110
Seattle, WA 98109
Phone: (206) 283-7036
http://www.centerltc.org/

Center for Mental Health Services
P.O. Box 42490
Washington, DC 20015
Phone: (800) 789-2647
http://www.mentalhealth.org/

Center for Social Gerontology
2307 Shelby Avenue
Ann Arbor, MI 48103
Phone: (734) 665-1126
http://www.tcsg.org/

Center for Studying Health System Change (HSC)
600 MD Avenue, SW, Suite 550
Washington, DC 20024
Phone: (202) 484-5261
http://www.hschange.org/

Centers for Medicare & Medicaid Services
7500 Security Boulevard
Baltimore, MD 21244
Phone: 1-800-MEDICARE (1-800-633-4227)
TTY 1-877-486-2048
http://www.medicare.gov/

Certified Financial Planner Board of Standards, Inc.

1700 Broadway, Suite 2100
Denver, CO 80290
Phone: (303) 830-7500
http://www.cfp.net/

CHAMPVA Center
VA Health Administration Center
P.O. Box 65023
Denver, CO 80206-9023
Phone: (800) 733-8387
http://www.va.gov/hac/champva/champva.html

Children of Aging Parents
1609 Woodbourne Road, Suite 302A
Levittown, PA 19057
Phone: (800) 227-7294
http://www.caps4caregivers.org/

Choice in Dying, Inc.
1620 Eye Street, NW, Suite 202
Washington, DC 20006
Phone: (202) 296-8071; Hotline: (800) 989-9455
http://www.partnershipforcaring.org/

Coalition for Responsible Lending
P.O. Box 3619
Durham, NC 27702
Phone: (919) 956-4485
http://www.responsiblelending.org/

Commission for Certification in Geriatric Pharmacy
1321 Duke Street
Alexandria, VA 22314
Phone: (703) 535-3038
http://www.ccgp.org/

Commission on Legal Problems of the Elderly
740 15th Street, NW
Washington, DC 20005
Phone: (202) 662-8694
http://www.abanet.org/

Commodity Futures Trading Commission (CFTC)
1155 21st Street, NW
Washington, DC 20581
Phone: (202) 418-5446
http://www.cftc.gov/

The Conference Board
845 Third Avenue
New York, NY 10022
Phone: (212) 339-0345
http://www.conference-board.org/

Consumer Consortium on Assisted Living (CCAL)
2342 Oak Street
Falls Church, VA 22046
Phone: (703) 533-8121
http://www.ccal.org/

Consumer Counseling Centers of America, Inc.
#900, South Building
601 Pennsylvania Avenue, NW
Washington, DC 20004
Phone: (202) 637-4851
http://www.consumercounseling.org/

Consumer Direction
National Council on the Aging
409 Third Street, SW, Suite 200
Washington, DC 20024
Phone: (202) 479-6666
http://www.consumerdirection.org/

Consumer Federation of America
1424 16th Street, NW, #604
Washington, DC 20036
Phone: (202) 387-6121
http://www.consumerfed.org/

Consumer Information Center
P.O. Box 7062
Cave Creek, AZ 85327
Phone: (480) 575-8353
http://www.zmfact.com/cic/

Consumers Union
1666 Connecticut Avenue, NW, #310
Washington, DC 20036
Phone: (202) 462-6262
http://www.consumersunion.org/

Continuing Care Accreditation Commission
2519 Connecticut Avenue, NW
Washington, DC 20008
Phone: (202) 783-7286
http://www.ccaconline.org/

The Cooperative State Research, Education, and Extension Service
U.S. Department of Agriculture
1400 Independence Avenue, SW, Stop 2201
Washington, DC 20250-2201
Phone: (202) 720-7441
http://www.reeusda.gov/1700/about/about_csrees.htm

Council of Better Business Bureaus
4200 Wilson Boulevard, #800
Arlington, VA 22203
Phone: (703) 276-0100
http://www.bbb.org/

Council of State Governments
2760 Research Park Drive
P.O. Box 11910
Lexington, KY 40578
Phone: (859) 244-8000
http://www.csg.org/

CPAdirectory
CPAdirect Marketing, Inc.
2001 Grove Street
Wantagh, NY 11793
Phone: (516) 409-8357
http://www.cpadirectory.com/

Debtors Anonymous
P.O. Box 920888
Needham, MA 02492
Phone: (781) 453-2743
http://www.debtorsanonymous.org/

Department of Veterans Affairs
Office of Public Affairs
Washington, DC 20011
Phone: (800) 827-1000
http://www.va.gov/

Duff & Phelps
280 Park Avenue
East Building, 23rd Floor
New York, NY 10017
Phone: (212) 450-2800
http://www.duffllc.com/

Eldercare Locator
U.S. Administration on Aging
927 15th Street, NW, 6th Floor
Washington, DC 20005
Phone: (800) 677-1116
http://www.eldercare.gov/

Employee Benefit Research Institute (EBRI)
2121 K Street, NW
Suite 600
Washington, DC 20037
Phone: (202) 659-0670
http://www.ebri.org/

Equifax
P.O. Box 740241
Atlanta, GA 30374
Phone: (888) 202-4025
http://www.equifax.com/

Equity Analytics, Ltd.
504 Stonegate Way
Middle Island, NY 11953
Phone: (631) 696-9784
http://www.e-analytics.com/

ERISA Industry Committee
1400 L Street, NW, Suite 350
Washington, DC 20005
Phone: (202) 789-1400
http://www.eric.org/

The ESOP Association
1726 M Street, NW, Suite 501
Washington, DC 20036
Phone: (202) 293-2971
http://www.esopassociation.org/

Executive Service Corps of Southern California
520 South Lafayette Park Place, Suite 210
Los Angeles, CA 90057
Phone: (213) 381-2891
http://www.escsc.org/

Experian (formerly TRW)
P.O. Box 949
Allen, TX 75013
Phone: (888) 397-3742
http://www.experian.com/

Experience Corps
Metropolitan Family Service
1808 SE Belmont Street
Portland, OR 97214
Phone: (503) 232-0007 ext. 203
http://www.metfamily.org/pages/excorps.html

Family Friends
The National Council on the Aging
409 Third Street, SW
Washington, DC 20024
Phone: (202) 479-0735
http://www.family-friends.org/index.htm

Federal Emergency Management Agency (FEMA)
500 C Street, SW
Washington, DC 20472
Phone: (202) 566-1600; (800) 629-3362
http://www.fema.gov/

Federal Trade Commission Response Center
600 Pennsylvania Avenue, NW
Washington, DC 20580
Phone: 1-877-IDTHEFT
http://www.consumer.gov/idtheft/

Federation for Children with Special Needs
135 Tremont Street, Suite 420
Boston, MA 02120
Phone: (617) 236-7210; (800) 331-0688
http://www.fcsn.org/

Financial Engines, Inc.
1804 Embarcadero Road
Palo Alto, CA 94303
Phone: (650) 565-4900
http://www.financialengines.com/

Financial Planning Association (FPA)
5775 Glenridge Drive, NE
Suite B-300
Atlanta, GA 30328
Phone: (800) 322-4237; (404) 845-0011
http://www.fpanet.org/

FoolMart
123 North Pitt Street
Alexandria, VA 22314
Phone: (888) 665-FOOL (3665)
http://www.foolmart.com/

Foster Grandparent Program
1201 New York Avenue, NW
Washington, DC 20525
Phone: (202) 606-5000
http://www.seniorcorps.org/

The Gerontological Society of America
1303 15th Street, NW, Suite 250
Washington, DC 20005
Phone: (202) 842-1275
http://www.geron.org/

Government Finance Officers Association
203 North LaSalle Street, Suite 2700
Chicago, IL 60601-1210
Phone: (312) 977-9700
http://www.gfoa.org/

Green Path Debt Solutions
38505 Country Club Drive, #120
Farmington Hills, MI 48331
Phone: (800) 550-1961
http://www.debthelpnow.org/

Habitat for Humanity International
121 Habitat Street
Americus, GA 31709
Phone: (229) 924-6935
http://www.habitat.org/

Health Insurance Association of America
1201 F Street, NW, #500
Washington, DC 20004
Phone: (202) 824-1600
http://www.hiaa.org/

Hemlock Society
P.O. Box 101810
Denver, CO 80250
Phone: (800) 247-7421
http://www.hemlock.org/

Hospice Association of America
228 Seventh Street, SE
Washington, DC 20003
Phone: (202) 546-4759
http://www.hospice-america.org/

Identity Theft Resource Center (ITRC)
P.O. Box 26833
San Diego, CA 92196
Phone: (858) 693-7935
http://www.idtheftcenter.org/

Institute for America's Future
Campaign for America's Future
1025 Connecticut Avenue, NW, Suite 205
Washington, DC 20036
Phone: (202) 955-5606
http://www.ourfuture.org/

Institute of Certified Financial Planners
The Financial Planning Association
5775 Glenridge Drive, NE, Room B300
Atlanta, GA 30328
Phone: (888) 806-7526
http://www.fpanet.org/

Insurance Information Institute
110 Williams Street
New York, NY 10038
Phone: (212) 346-5500
http://www.iii.org/

International Association of Financial Planners
The Financial Building, P.O. Box 42506
Middletown, OH 45042
Phone: (800) 532-9060
http://www.iarfc.org/

International Board of Standards and Practices for Certified Financial Planners
1700 Broadway, Suite 2100
Denver, CO 80290
Phone: (303) 830-7500
http://www.cfp.net/

International Executive Service Corps
333 Ludlow Street
P.O. Box 10005
Stamford, CT 06904
Phone: (203) 967-6000
http://www.iesc.org/

International Personnel Management Association
1617 Duke Street
Alexandria, VA 22314
Phone: (703) 549-7100
http://www.ipma-hr.org/

Intersections, Inc.
P.O. Box 222455
Chantilly, VA 20153
Phone: (800) 777-9700
http://www.intersections.com/

Investment Company Institute
1401 H Street, NW, Suite 1200
Washington, DC 20005
Phone: (202) 326-5800
http://www.ici.org/

The Kauffman Center for Entrepreneurial Leadership
4801 Rockhill Road
Kansas City, MO 64110
Phone: (816) 932-1000
http://www.entreworld.org/

The Legacy Center
1629 West 25th Street
Minneapolis, MN 55405
Phone: (612) 333-2833
http://www.thelegacycenter.net/

LIMRA
300 Day Hill Road
Windsor, CT 06095
Phone: (860) 688-3358
http://www.limra.com/

Medicare Rights Center
1460 Broadway, 17th Floor
New York, NY 10036
Phone: (212) 869-3850
http://www.medicarerights.org/

Mental Health Policy Resource Center
1201 North Beauregard Street, 12th Floor
Alexandria, VA 22311
Phone: (800) 969-6642
http://www.nmha.org/

Moody's Corporation
99 Church Street
New York, NY 10007
Phone: (212) 553-7194
http://www.moodys.com/

Morningstar, Inc.
225 West Wacker Drive
Chicago, IL 60606
Phone: (312) 696-6000
http://www.morningstar.com/

mPower
1355 Sansome Street
San Francisco, CA 94111
Phone: (415) 875-2000
http://www.mpower.com/
http://www.mpowercafe.com/

National Academy of Elder Law Attorneys, Inc.
1604 North Country Club Road

Tucson, AZ 85716
Phone: (520) 881-4005
http://www.naela.org/

National Adult Day Services Association, Inc.
8201 Greensboro Drive, Suite 300
McLean, VA 22102
Phone: (866) 890-7357; (703) 610-9035
http://www.nadsa.org/

The National Aging Information Center
330 Independence Avenue, SW, Room 4656
Washington, DC 20201
Phone: (202) 619-7501
http://www.aoa.dhhs.gov/naic/

National Alliance for the Mentally Ill
Colonial Place Three
2107 Wilson Boulevard, Suite 300
Arlington, VA 22201
Phone: (703) 524-7600; NAMI HelpLine: 1-800-950-NAMI [6264]
http://www.nami.org/

The National Alliance of Caregiving
4720 Montgomery Lane, 5th Floor
Bethesda, MD 20814
Phone: (301) 718-8444
http://www.caregiving.org/

National Alzheimer's Association
919 North Michigan Avenue, Suite 1100
Chicago, IL 60611-1676
Phone: (800) 272-3900; (312) 335-8700
http://www.alz.org/

National Asian Pacific Center on Aging (NAPCA)
1511 3rd Avenue, Suite 914
Seattle, WA 98101
Phone: (206) 624-1221
http://www.aoa.gov/directory/136.html

National Association for Home Care
228 7th Street, SE
Washington, DC 20003
Phone: (202) 547-7424
http://www.nahc.org/

National Association for Variable Annuities
11710 Plaza America Drive, Suite 100
Reston, VA 20190
Phone: (703) 707-8830
http://www.navanet.org/

National Association of Area Agencies on Aging
927 15th Street NW, 6th Floor
Washington, DC 20005
Phone: (202) 296-8130
http://www.n4a.org/

National Association of Financial and Estate Planning (NAFEP)
525 East 4500 South, #F-100
Salt Lake City, UT 84107
Phone: (801) 266-9900
http://www.nafep.com/

National Association of Housing Co-operatives
1614 King Street
Alexandria, VA 22314
Phone: (703) 549-5201
http://www.coophousing.org/

National Association of Insurance and Financial Advisors (NAIFA)
P.O. Box 12012
Falls Church, VA 22042
Phone: (877) TO-NAIFA
http://www.naifa.org/

National Association of Insurance Commissioners
2301 McGee Street, Suite 800
Kansas City, MO 64108-2604
Phone: (816) 842-3600
http://www.naic.org/

National Association of Investors Corporation
711 West Thirteen Mile Road
Madison Heights, MI 48071
Phone: (877) 275-6242
http://www.better-investing.org/

National Association of Personal Financial Advisors (NAPFA)
3250 North Arlington Heights Road, Suite 109
Arlington Heights, IL 60004
Phone: (800) 366-2732
http://www.napfa.org/

National Association of Professional
Geriatric Care Managers
1604 North Country Club Road
Tucson, AZ 85716
Phone: (520) 881-8008
http://www.caremanager.org/

National Association of Real Estate
Investment Trusts
1875 Eye Street, NW
Washington, DC 20006
Phone: (202) 739-9400; (800) 362-7348
http://www.nareit.com/

National Association of State Units on
Aging
1201 15th Street NW, Suite 350
Washington, DC 20005
Phone: (202) 898-2578
http://www.ncoa.org/

National Caucus and Center on Black Aged,
Inc. (NCBA)
1220 L Street, NW, Suite 800
Washington, DC 20005
Phone: (202) 637-8400
http://www.aoa.gov/directory/154.html

The National Center for Employee
Ownership
1736 Franklin Street, 8th Floor
Oakland, CA 04612
Phone: (512) 208-1300
http://www.nceo.org/

National Center for Health Statistics
Division of Data Services
Hyattsville, MD 20782-2003
Phone: (301) 458-4636
http://www.cdc.gov/nchs/

National Center of Assisted Living
(NCAL)
1201 "L" Street, NW
Washington, DC 20005
Phone: (202) 842-4444
http://www.ncal.org/

National Citizens' Coalition for Nursing
Home Reform
1424 16th Street, NW, Suite 202
Washington, DC 20036
Phone: (202) 332-2275
http://www.nccnhr.org/

National Conference of Gerontological Nurse
Practitioners
P.O. Box 232230
Centreville, VA 20120
Phone: (703) 802-0088
http://www.ncgnp.org/

National Consumer Law Center
18 Tremont Street, #400
Boston, MA 02108
Phone: (617) 523-8010
http://www.consumerlaw.org/

National Council of Senior Citizens
8403 Colesville Road, Suite 1200
Silver Spring, MD 20910
Phone: (301) 578-8800
http://www.elderweb.com/

National Council on the Aging
409 Third Street, SW, Suite 200
Washington, DC 20024
Phone: (202) 479-1200
http://www.ncoa.org/

National Eldercare Institute on Elder Abuse
and State Long-Term Care Ombudsman
Services
2033 K Street, NW, Suite 304
Washington, DC 20006
Phone: (202) 898-2578
http://www.seniorcitizensguide.com/listings/

National Family Caregivers Association
10400 Connecticut Avenue, #500
Kensington, MD 20895
Phone: (800) 896-3650
http://www.nfcacares.org/

National Foundation for Credit Counseling
801 Roeder Road, Suite 900
Silver Spring, MD 20910
Phone: (301) 589-5600
http://www.nfcc.org/

National Guardianship Association
1604 North Country Club Road
Tucson, AZ 85716
Phone: (520) 881-6561
http://www.guardianship.org/

National Hispanic Council on Aging
2713 Ontario Road, NW
Washington, DC 20009
Phone: (202) 265-1288
http://www.nhcoa.org/

National Hospice and Palliative Care Organization
1700 Diagonal Road, Suite 625
Alexandria, VA 22314
Phone: (703) 837-1500; (800) 646-6460
http://www.nhpco.org/

National Hospice Foundation
1700 Diagonal Road, Suite 625
Alexandria, VA 22314
Phone: (703) 516-4928
http://www.hospiceinfo.org/

National Indian Council on Aging
10501 Montgomery Boulvard, NE, Suite 210
Albuquerque, NM 87111
Phone: (505) 292-2001
http://www.nicoa.org/index1.html

National Insurance Consumer Organization
121 North Payne Street
Alexandria, VA 22314
Phone: (703) 549-8050
http://www.P.O.werinvestor.com/Primer/Insurance-and-Annuities/

National Institute of Mental Health
Mental Disorders of the Aging Branch
6001 Executive Boulevard
Bethesda, MD 20892
Phone: (301) 443-4513
http://www.nimh.nih.gov/

National Institute of Mental Health
Public Inquiries Office
6001 Executive Boulevard, Room 8184, MSC 9663
Bethesda, MD 20892
Phone: (301) 443-4513
http://www.nimh.nih.gov/publicat/index.cfm

National Institute on Aging
Alzheimer's Disease Education and Referral Center (ADEAR)
P.O. Box 8250
Silver Spring, MD 20907-8250
Phone: (301) 496-4000
http://www.alzheimers.org/

National Institute on Aging—NIA Information
P.O. Box 8057
Gaithersburg, MD 20898
Phone: (800) 222-2225
http://www.nia.nih.gov/

National Long-Term Care Ombudsman Resource Center
1424 16th Street, NW, Suite 202
Washington, DC 20036
Phone: (202) 332-2275
http://www.ltcombudsman.org/

National Organization of Nurse Practitioner Faculties
1522 K Street, NW, Suite 702
Washington, DC 20005
Phone: (202) 289-8044
http://www.nonpf.org/

National Personnel Records Center
Military Personnel Records
9700 Page Avenue
St. Louis, MO 63132
Phone: (866) 272-6272
http://www.archives.gov/facilities/mo/st_louis/military_personnel_records.html

National Reverse Mortgage Lenders Association (NRMLA)
1625 Massachusetts Avenue, NW, Suite 601
Washington, DC 20036
Phone: (202) 939-1760
http://www.reversemortgage.org/

National Senior Citizens Law Center
1101 14th Street, NW, Suite 400
Washington, DC 20005
Phone: (202) 289-6976
http://www.nsclc.org/

National Society of Accountants
1010 North Fairfax Street
Alexandria, VA 22314
Phone: (703) 549-2984
http://www.nsacct.org/

NCB Coming Home Project
1725 Eye Street, NW, Suite 600
Washington, DC 20006
Phone: (202) 336-7680
http://www.ncbdc.org/

Office of Workers' Compensation Programs
U.S. Department of Labor
200 Constitution Avenue, NW
Washington, DC 20210
Phone: (866) 4-USA-DOL
http://www.dol.gov/esa/owcp_org.htm

Older Women's League
1750 New York Avenue, NW, #350
Washington, DC 20006
Phone: (202) 783-6686; (800) 825-3695
http://www.owl-national.org/

Outcome and Assessment Information Set (OASIS)
Centers for Medicare & Medicaid Services
7500 Security Boulevard
Baltimore, MD 21244-1850
Phone: (877) 267-2323
http://www.cms.hhs.gov/oasis/

Partners in Caregiving: The Dementia Services Program
A Project of the Robert Wood Johnson Foundation
P.O. Box 2316
Princeton, NJ 08543
Phone: (888) 631-9989
http://www.rwjf.org/

Partnership for Caring
1620 Eye Street, NW, Suite 202
Washington, DC 20006
Phone: (202) 296-8071
http://www.partnershipforcaring.com/

Pension Rights Center (PRC)
1140 19th Street, NW, Suite 602
Washington, DC 20036
Phone: (202) 296-3776
http://www.pensionrights.org/

Profit Sharing/401(k) Council of America
10 South Riverside Plaza, Suite 1610
Chicago, IL 60606
Phone: (312) 441-8550
http://www.psca.org/

Realty Stock Review
802 West Park Avenue, Suite 222
Ocean, NJ 07712
Phone: (732) 493-1999
http://www.realtystockreview.com/

Rebuilding Together
1536 Sixteenth Street, NW
Washington, DC 20036
Phone: (202) 483-9083
http://www.rebuildingtogether.org/

Recreation Vehicle Industry Association
1896 Preston White Drive, P.O. Box 2999
Reston, VA 20195
http://www.rvia.org/

Referrals for Financial Planners
Society of Financial Service Professionals
270 South Bryn Mawr Avenue
Bryn Mawr, PA 19010
Phone: (888) 243-2258
http://www.financialpro.org/ [click on "Consumers"]

Resort Condominiums International
6 Sylvan Way
Parsippany, NJ 07054
Phone: (877) 724-4500
http://www.rci.com/

Retired and Senior Volunteer Program (RSVP)
1201 New York Avenue, NW
Washington, DC 20525
Phone: (202) 606-5000
http://www.nationalservice.org/

Senior Companion Program
1201 New York Avenue, NW
Washington, DC 20525
Phone: (202) 606-5000
http://www.seniorcorps.org/

Seniors-site.com
5443 Stag Mt. Rd.
Weed, CA 96094
Phone: (530) 938-3163
http://www.seniors-site.com/

Small Business Administration
409 3rd Street, NW
Washington, DC 20416
Phone: (800) U-ASK-SBA
http://www.sba.gov/

Social Security Administration
Office of Public Inquiries
Windsor Park Building

6401 Security Boulvard
Baltimore, MD 21235
Phone: (800) 325-0778; (800) 772-1213
http://www.ssa.gov/

Society for Human Resources Management
606 North Washington Street
Alexandria, VA 22314
Phone: (703) 548-3440
http://www.shrm.org/

Society of Certified Senior Advisors
1777 South Bellaire Street, #230
Denver, CO 80222
Phone: (800) 658-1785
http://www.society-csa.com/

Society of Financial Services Professionals
The American College
270 South Bryn Mawr Drive
Bryn Mawr, PA 19010
Phone: (610) 526-2500
http://www.financialpro.org/

Society of Healthcare Consumer Advocacy
American Hospital Association
One North Franklin
Chicago, IL 60606
Phone: (800) 242-2626
http://www.shca-aha.org/

Special Needs Alliance
509 S. Lenola Road, Building 7
Moorestown, NJ 08057
Phone: (877) 572-8472
http://www.specialneedsalliance.com/

Springboard, Consumer Credit Counseling Service
6370 Magnolia Avenue, #200
Riverside, CA 92506
Phone: (888) 462-2227
http://www.credit.org/

Standard and Poor's
55 Water Street
New York, NY 10041
Phone: (212) 438-1006
http://www.standardandpoors.com/

State Health Insurance Assistance Programs
1460 Broadway, 11th Floor
New York, NY 10036
Phone: (212) 333-5511; (800) 333-4114
http://www.hiicap.state.ny.us/home/link08.htm

Three Arrows Capital
7517 Westfield Drive, Suite A
Bethesda, MD 20817
Phone: (301) 229-6240
http://www.threearrowscapital.com/

Timeshare Users Group
P.O. Box 1442
Orange Park, FL 32067
Phone: (904) 298-3185
http://www.timeshare-users-group.com/

Trans Union
760 West Sproul Road
P.O. Box 390
Springfield, PA 19064
Phone: (800) 916-8800
http://www.transunion.com/

Truth about Credit
A Program of U.S. PIRG
218 D Street, SE
Washington, DC 20003
Phone: (202) 546-9707
http://www.truthaboutcredit.org/

U.S. Attorney General's Office
Department of Justice
950 Pennsylvania Avenue, NW
Washington, DC 20530-0001
Phone: (202) 353-1555
http://www.usdoj.gov/ag/

U.S. Bureau of Labor Statistics
Postal Square Building
2 Massachusetts Avenue, NE
Washington, DC 20212-0001
Phone: (202) 691-5200
http://www.bls.gov/

U.S. Census Bureau
4700 Silver Hill Road
Washington, DC 20233-0001
Phone: (301) 763-INFO (4636)
http://www.census.gov/

U.S. Department of Agriculture
1400 Independence Avenue, SW
Washington, DC 20250

Phone: (202) 320-2791
http://www.usda.gov/da/comments/htm.

U.S. Department of Housing and Urban Development
451 7th Street, SW
Washington, DC 20410
Phone: (202) 708-1112
http://www.hud.gov/

U.S. Department of Veterans Affairs
810 Vermont Avenue, NW
Washington, DC 20420
Phone: (202) 273-5400
http://www.va.gov/

U.S. Federal Reserve System
20 Street & Constitution Avenue, NW
Washington, DC 20551
Phone: (202) 452-3000
http://www.federalreserve.gov/

U.S. Federal Trade Commission
600 Pennsylvania Avenue, NW
Washington, DC 20580
Phone: (877) 382-4357
http://www.ftc.gov/

U.S. House of Representatives
Committee on Financial Services
B-301C Rayburn Building
Washington, DC 20510
Phone: (202) 225-7141
http://www.house.gov/banking_democrats/

U.S. Office of Personnel Management
1900 E Street, NW
Washington, DC 20415
Phone: (202) 606-2400
http://www.opm.gov/

U.S. Public Interest Research Group
218 D Street, SE
Washington, DC 20003
Phone: (202) 546-9707
http://www.pirg.org/

U.S. Senate, Committee on Banking, Housing, and Urban Affairs
534 Dirksen Senate Office Building
Washington, DC 20510
Phone: (202) 224-7391
http://banking.senate.gov/

U.S. Soldiers' and Airmen's Home and U.S. Naval Home
Public Affairs Office, USSAH
Washington, DC 20317
Phone: (800) 422-9988
http://www.afrh.com/sol-airm.htm

U.S. Treasury, Office of the Comptroller of the Currency
1500 Pennsylvania Avenue, NW
Washington, DC 20220
Phone: (202) 622-2000
http://www.treas.gov/org.htm

Viatical Life Settlement Association
800 Mayfair Circle
Orlando, FL 32803
Phone: (800) 842-9811
http://www.viatical.org/

Women's Institute for a Secure Retirement (WISER)
1920 N Street, NW, Suite 300
Washington, DC 20036
Phone: (202) 393-5452
http://www.wiser.heinz.org/

### *Web Sites Only*

CCH Business Owners Toolkit
http://www.toolkit.cch.com/

CyberSmart Safety Coalition
http://www.fda.gov/

e-analytics
http://www.e-analytics.com/

FICO
http://www.myfico.com/

Helpguide/Board & Care Homes
http://www.helpguide.org/elder/board_care_homes.htm

Inc. Magazine
http://www.inc.com/

Medicare Personal Plan Finder
http://www.medicare.gov/MPPF/Home.asp

Medigap Compare
http://www.medicare.gov/MGCompare/Home.asp

Service Corps of Retired Executives (SCORE)
http://www.score.org/

SmartMoney
http://www.smartmoney.com/

State Health Insurance Assistance Programs (SHIPs)
http://www.medicare.gov/contacts/related/ships.asp

Quicken Turbotax
http://www.turbotax.com/

SeniorJournal.com
http://www.seniorjournal.com/

# Appendix D

# Types of Benefits by Tax Treatment and by Function

## SELECTED BENEFITS

### Types of Benefits by Tax Treatment

#### *Mandatory*

- Social Security retirement (OASI)
- Social Security disability (DI)
- Medicare Part A (Social Security HI)
- Workers' compensation
- Unemployment insurance
- Medicaid[a]
- Supplemental Security Income (SSI)[a]
- Public assistance[a]

#### *Voluntary*

- Fully taxable
- Vacations
- Paid lunch
- Rest periods
- Severance pay
- Cash bonuses and awards

#### *Tax Exempt*[b]

- Employee and dependent health insurance
- Retiree health insurance
- Dental insurance
- Vision insurance
- Medicare Part B (Social Security SMI)
- Educational assistance

- Legal assistance
- Child care
- Discounts
- Flexible spending accounts
- Parking
- Cafeteria facility
- Meals

### *Tax Deferred*[b]

- Keogh plans
- Defined benefit pension plans
- Defined contribution pension plans
    - money purchase pension plans
    - deferred profit sharing plans
    - savings and thrift plans
    - employee stock ownership plans
    - stock bonus plans
    - simplified employee pension plans
    - individual retirement account plans
    - cash or deferred arrangements
      —401(k)
      —403(b)

### *Other Tax Preferred*[b, c]

- Life insurance
- Long-term disability insurance
- Sick leave or sickness and accident insurance
- Other leave (maternity, funeral, jury, etc.)

## Types of Benefits by Function

### *Retirement Income Benefits*

- Social Security retirement (OASI)
- Supplemental Security Income (SSI)[a]
- Keogh plans
- Defined benefit pension plans
- Defined contribution pension plans
    - money purchase pension plans
    - deferred profit sharing plans
    - savings and thrift plans
    - employee stock ownership plans
    - stock bonus plans
    - simplified employee pension plans

- individual retirement account plans
- cash or deferred arrangements
  —401(k)
  —403(b)

### *Health Care*

- Employee and dependent health insurance
- Retiree health insurance
- Dental insurance
- Vision insurance
- Medicare (Social Security HI, SMI)
- Medicaid[a]

### *Other Benefits*

- Social Security disability (DI)
- Long-term disability insurance
- Life insurance
- Workers' compensation
- Unemployment insurance
- Public assistance[a]
- Severance pay
- Child care
- Vacations
- Sick leave or sickness and accident insurance
- Other leave (maternity, funeral, jury, etc.)
- Paid lunch
- Rest periods
- Legal assistance
- Education
- Flexible spending accounts
- Bonuses and awards
- Parking
- Cafeteria facility
- Meals
- Discounts

[a]Eligibility based on need; financed from general government revenues.
[b]Subject to conditions and limitations.
[c]Value of insurance and leave availability are not taxed; insurance benefits and leave pay generally are taxed when paid.
*Source*: Employee Benefit Research Institute.

# Index